Corporations and Other Business Organizations

Corporations and Other Business Organizations

Cases, Materials, Problems

NINTH EDITION

Lawrence A. Cunningham
HENRY ST. GEORGE TUCKER III RESEARCH PROFESSOR OF LAW
THE GEORGE WASHINGTON UNIVERSITY LAW SCHOOL

CAROLINA ACADEMIC PRESS
Durham, North Carolina

ISBN 978-1-5310-0019-6
LCCN 2016950657

Carolina Academic Press, LLC
700 Kent Street
Durham, North Carolina 27701
Telephone (919) 489-7486
Fax (919) 493-5668
www.cap-press.com

Printed in the United States of America

*To Stephanie Cuba and
Rebecca and Sarah Cunningham,
with love and thanks, always and forever.*

Summary of Contents

Contents

Preface

Most chapters of this book begin with a situation involving one or more hypothetical clients, with later situations building on earlier ones. Classroom work can involve the situations as much or as little as the teacher wishes, or it can exclude the situations entirely. For example, the situations can simply be used, as part of assigned readings, to place the cases and other materials in an understandable context. The inclusion of these situations, then, is not meant to dictate the agenda for the class.

The book is designed to be used in a three- or four-semester-hour corporation law or business associations course. Chapters 1 and 2 deal with unincorporated business organizations. The remaining chapters focus on corporations. Some of the securities related materials have been included simply to give students a first acquaintance with a few of the more common securities law questions likely to arise in a corporate practice.

Teachers who wish to deal only selectively with these questions, or to save them for another course, will find no difficulty in doing so. An introduction to the reading of financial statements is included in an appendix. The materials on reading financial statements were designed to be understandable to students with little or no help.

Citations of authority and references of various sorts have been omitted, as have footnotes, except where inclusion or partial inclusion has served a specific purpose. These deletions generally have not been indicated. Other deletions and revisions usually have been, except for the correction of typographical errors and the deletion of paragraphs and longer portions of text appearing before or after excerpts from non-case materials, and except for a few miscellaneous deletions and revisions of a minor nature. Where footnotes have been retained, the original footnote numbers have been indicated with brackets.

I want to honor my late co-editors who created the earliest editions of this book decades ago and maintained them over many years: Larry D. Soderquist and A.A. Sommer, Jr., two towering figures in corporate legal history. I am also grateful to my other co-editors on more recent editions, including especially Linda Smiddy, who added so much to the book but has now retired. Many others helped in the preparation of the book, including Benjamin Field, George Washington University Law School class of 2017, and two of its adopters, Professors Anna Han and Jennifer Taub, who offered insightful comments on previous versions. Thanks to my thousands of students who have read this book over the years and shared their feedback to make it better.

Lawrence A. Cunningham

Introduction

Approaching Corporate Law

This book is about the law of business organizations, the legal rules defining the rights, responsibilities, and obligations of the individuals who own, manage, and invest in businesses. The text is also about corporate lawyers. At their best, corporate lawyers are skilled practitioners with a broad understanding of business and business law and the social and ethical implications of the tasks at hand. Without this broad understanding, lawyers risk becoming little more than technicians whose limited view of their professional role diminishes the quality of their service and may even cause them to make mistakes on seemingly simple tasks. This book will help students begin to develop some of the broader perspectives that are an important component of the practice of corporate law.

Section I
Putting Business Organizations in Context

A. Business Organizations Generally

The study of the law of business organizations is about the men and women who own, invest in, and manage businesses of all sizes. It is about the corner grocer, the owner of the local plumbing supply company, the directors, officers and shareholders of a multinational enterprise, the partner in a law firm, the founder of an environmental consulting firm, the movie mogul, and the art dealer. It is about individuals whose abilities to manage a company's employees and assets and make difficult financial decisions determine the fate of a business venture.

People become business owners for many reasons. They may need to make a living or want to earn a return on an investment. Other motivating factors are the desire to provide particular services or products, retain control over their lives, or to spend their working lifetimes in activities of particular interest to them.

A business organization consists of people who work together for a common business purpose and who share the risks and rewards of their efforts. People go into business with others to obtain talent, skills, or money that they cannot provide themselves. They may also want the companionship that comes with working with others.

Members of a business organization may be owners, employees, or investors or hold positions that combine these roles. They may actively manage the business or become passive investors who leave the management of the company to others. Their numbers may range from a very few persons to participants counted in the millions. Whatever the nature of their relationships or the extent of their numbers, the results of their combined efforts comprise the work of the enterprise.

In many respects, other organizations, such as labor unions, charities, and private colleges and universities, have much in common with business organizations. They often have similar governance structures. They hire employees, are operated by professional managers, own property, open bank accounts, incur debt and make money (have revenues that exceed their expenses). The distinguishing features of business organizations are that they are formed for a business purpose, are intended to be profitable and are financed by investors who expect to make money by sharing in the company's profits. In contrast, although many non-profit organizations engage in commercial activities (such as operating a museum store, owning rental property and the like), revenues that are not needed to pay expenses are reinvested in the enterprise rather than paid out to investors.

B. The Business Landscape

Before we comment on specific types of business organizations, we will make a few observations about the general business landscape. For the purposes of this discussion, companies will be grouped by size according to revenues earned, number of employees, or value of assets owned. We will ignore, for the time being, categories based on particular types of legal entities.

1. The Large Enterprise

When one imagines a business organization, often the type that first comes to mind is a large, multinational enterprise. The economic power of companies such as these sometimes borders on the incomprehensible. The largest have revenues in the hundreds of billions of dollars, an amount exceeding the total revenues of some small countries. Some companies employ more people than the total population of several small New England states.

Individually and collectively, these companies have significant economic and social power. They also wield significant influence in our lives. In the United States, large companies typically provide their employees with a range of health care and pension benefits that are governmental responsibilities in other countries. The pervasive influence of these vast enterprises was anticipated by Berle and Means in their classic work on the modern corporation first published in 1932. They posited that the concentration of economic power in the largest corporations would enable these organizations to compete as equals with or even supersede the power of the nation state. In their view, the corporation could become the pre-eminent form of "social organization [with] the law of corporations … considered as a potential constitutional law for the new economic state…."[1]

---

1. Adolf A. Berle & Gardiner C. Means, The Modern Corporation and Private Property 313 (Harcourt Brace & World 1968 rev. ed).

In the 1950s, approximately 90% of investors in public companies were individuals. Today, institutional investors predominate. CalPERS, the California Public Employees' Retirement System, and other institutional investors have actively pressed for improved corporate governance and greater management responsiveness to shareholder demands.

Socially responsible investing has also grown significantly. Stocks are selected for "socially responsible" portfolios based on a number of factors including corporate environmental and social responsibility and responsiveness to shareholder resolutions attempting to influence corporate behavior. Over recent decades, the number of such shareholder resolutions has increased dramatically.

2. The Small and Medium Sized Business

Mega-companies are only part of the story of U.S. business. Based on numbers alone, most U.S. companies are small, whether measured by revenues, assets, or employees. For example, more than 80% of all corporations have business revenues under a million dollars a year. Collectively, however, small and medium sized companies play an important role in the U.S. economy. In some industries, these companies, rather than large multinationals, collectively produce the greatest percentage of revenues. In the construction, agriculture, forestry and fishing industries, the smallest companies, as measured by value of assets, collectively produced approximately 70% of total industry revenues. This same category of companies also produced 58% of service industry revenues.

Small companies also employ most U.S. workers. For example, recent data suggest that, of the total number of persons employed in the private sector, almost one-fourth work for businesses with fewer than 20 employees, over half work for businesses with fewer than 100 employees and four-fifths for companies with fewer than 500 employees. Only 13% worked for companies with 1,000 or more employees. These trends are likely to continue, with the smaller companies employing most of the work force. The economic power of small and mid-sized companies is evident in other ways, as well. They reportedly produce nearly half of all U.S. exports.

3. The Changing Demographics of the Work Force

During the last several decades, the demographics of the work force have changed in two important ways. One is the shift in the structure of the employment market. The other is the change in the roles played by women and minorities.

The traditional predominance of manufacturing companies has yielded to service oriented businesses. The services industry now employs more than three-fourths of the U.S. workforce, far outstripping manufacturing. Minorities comprise approximately one third of the labor force and women comprise almost half.

Women now hold almost 30% of senior level and management positions in Fortune 500 companies and account for roughly 17% of members of corporate boards, but their numbers in these areas have been increasing only incrementally. They have had greater success in other areas. Women-owned businesses generate approximately $2 trillion in sales and tend to be one of the leading areas of growth in local economies. Further, the number of new women-owned businesses has grown at double the national rate, with businesses owned by minority women increasing by as much as five times the national average. Minorities hold slightly less than 17% of executive or senior level positions and about 15% of corporate board positions. Minority owned businesses produce approximately $660 billion in gross receipts. Many are likely to be financed with short term debt and are thus more vulnerable in times of recession than are other businesses generally.

Section II
Other Perspectives on Business

Members of many different disciplines study business organizations: accountants, lawyers, economists, and moral philosophers, to name a few. Understanding the law of business organizations is aided by some familiarity with the perspectives of accountants and economists. Legal rules governing businesses may be based on principles originating in these disciplines. For example, correct application of the rules governing payment of corporate dividends requires an understanding of the underlying accounting principles.

Accountants perform several functions for businesses. They design and implement control systems that help companies avoid waste and detect wrongdoing. Accountants are also a company's financial historians. They develop systems to record business transactions as they occur and summarize the results in reports known as financial statements. Independent accountants are used to audit a company's books and records to verify that the company's financial representations are correct.

In contrast to accountants, business organization lawyers are mainly concerned with the legal status of a business entity and the legal rules that govern it. These rules apply to the company's formation, structure, ability to raise capital and distribute earnings, and the relationships among the company, its owners, its managerial employees and its creditors. (Issues concerning non-managerial employees are primarily covered in other areas of the law.)

Economists focus on the economic functions of the business enterprise or firm. Often taking a broader view of the business organization than either lawyers or accountants, economists consider the economic interrelationships of owners, creditors, and employees within a firm, and the position of the firm within markets. Some economists and lawyers view a business organization as an association of contractual relationships, whereas other lawyers have traditionally focused on the company's legal status as an entity created by the state.

The view that a corporation is an entity created by the state is based on the idea that corporate formation requires state approval. Corporate existence begins when the articles of incorporation are filed with the Secretary of State. Under this view, the state has the authority to regulate corporate activity directly. In contrast, proponents of the contractual theory of the corporation view:

> the corporation as founded in private contract, where the role of the state is limited to enforcing contracts. In this regard, a state charter merely recognizes the existence of a "nexus of contracts" called a corporation. Each contract in the "nexus of contracts" warrants the same legal and constitutional protections as other legally enforceable contracts. Moreover, freedom of contract requires that parties to the "nexus of contracts" must be able to structure their relations as they desire.[2]

Other commentators are concerned with the questions of whose interests the corporation must serve. One view holds that shareholders own the corporation and that the goal of corporate governance is to advance the interests of the shareholders. Proponents of this view advocate for corporate governance reforms that increase management responsiveness to shareholder interests. A contrasting view is that managers' decisions are already influenced too much by the interests of shareholders, who probably are focused on short term gains and may not understand what would be best for them in the long-term. Proponents of this view argue for corporate reform that either shields management from the pressure of having to achieve short term gains or encourages shareholders to invest for the long-term. Yet a third view is that shareholders in fact do understand their own short-term and long-term interests, but corporate policies benefitting shareholders may not also advance broader social interests. In this case, reformers pursue policies producing the greatest social benefit.

Finally, some ethicists and moral philosophers view the business organization as a moral agent, accountable to groups extending beyond the enterprise constituents. Proponents of this view reject the idea that a company is only the property of its owners. They focus, instead, on the company as a social institution:

> [C]orporate decision makers should recognize that their firms are responsible to a broader constituency than shareholders alone; a constituency including employees, customers, local communities, and the public at large. This recognition reinforces social expectations which encourage corporate decision makers to act more as public trustees, and not merely as agents for the shareholders, in the performance of their corporate roles.[3]

Section III
Distinguishing Features of Business Law Practice

What does it take to be a business lawyer? The following comments provide a brief introduction to some of the skills that are most important for an effective business

---

2. Henry N. Butler, *The Contractual Theory of the Corporation*, 11 Geo. Mason U. L. Rev. 99, 100 (1989).

3. Jeffrey Nesteruk & David T. Risser, *Conceptions of the Corporation and Ethical Decision Making in Business*, 12 Bus. & Prof. Ethics J., 87–88 (1993).

lawyer to have. Some skills are common to all areas of law practice; others, unique to the business law attorney.

A. Prospective Viewpoint

Business lawyers work as planners, viewing transactions prospectively. They take the law as a given and the basis for structuring transactions. Litigators, on the other hand, view transactions retrospectively. They take the facts as a given and attempt to portray the law, by analysis and argument, as fitting the facts in a manner favorable to the client. This prospective/retrospective dichotomy leads business lawyers and litigators to approach law quite differently. For example, whether a particular statement by a court is dictum may be important to the litigator but virtually irrelevant to the business lawyer. The litigator does not mind working in the vanguard, and sometimes that is the only place from which a case can be won. The business lawyer, on the other hand, wishes to take no avoidable chance of running afoul of the law, and so if a court has interpreted a statutory provision to say a particular act may not be done, that usually is enough to dissuade the business lawyer, whether the court's interpretation was in dicta or holding.

B. Skill as a Drafter

In much the same way as a dexterous use of the hands distinguishes the surgeon, skill as a drafter distinguishes the business lawyer. The prototypical business lawyer is a consummate drafter. Care and precision, along with elegant use of the language, are points of the business lawyer's pride. That being true, business lawyers heavily judge other business lawyers on their drafting skill.

One often hears about the predilection of surgeons to solve patients' problems by an operation. And perhaps litigators see lawsuits as the solution to clients' problems more frequently than do other lawyers. Along these same lines, business lawyers think first about drafting to solve a client's problem. If in structuring a transaction a business lawyer comes across a legal ambiguity, his or her inclination is not to do research with the hopes of resolving the ambiguity; it is rather to avoid the ambiguity by drafting around it.

C. Special Issues in Counseling Clients

The mind set of the business lawyer is to find a way to accomplish what the client basically wants. Good business lawyers not only listen to the specific questions clients ask them, but they try to discern what at base the client wants to accomplish. Business lawyers might have to say no to the specific question or the client's original proposal for accomplishing the objective, but if at all possible they will present a permissible alternative designed to accomplish the real, often unspoken, goal. A president of a client might say, for example, that the corporation wants to pay a dividend of one dollar on its common stock. Realizing that the corporation has not enough surplus available for dividends under the governing statute, the lawyer may have to say that that cannot be done. The good lawyer would not leave the matter there, however. Understanding that what the client really wants is to take one dollar per share out of the corporation and give it to its shareholders, the good lawyer would look for a legally permissible way to do so. The point is that a creative business lawyer will try to find legally permissible ways to accomplish the client's objectives.

When considering this notion that business lawyers try to find legally permissible ways to accomplish the client's objectives, it is important to recognize the limits of this frame of mind. It is not a license to accomplish those objectives using any means possible, even if the means is entirely lawful. Ethical and moral considerations and a sense of the public interest also play a role. One of the authors of previous editions of this book, the eminent securities lawyer A. A. Sommer, then an SEC Commissioner, gave a famous and recently quoted address in the mid-1970s admonishing lawyers on the limitations of creative lawyering. He stated:

> I would suggest that in securities matters (other than those where advocacy is clearly proper), the attorney will have to function in a manner more akin to that of auditor than to that of the attorney. This means several things. It means that he will have to exercise a measure of independence that is perhaps uncomfortable if he is also the close counselor of management in other matters, often including business decisions. It means he will have to be acutely cognizant of [a] responsibility to the public who engage in securities transactions that would never have come about were it not for his professional presence. It means that [the attorney] will have to adopt the healthy skepticism toward the representation of management which a good auditor must adopt. It means that he will have to do the same thing the auditor does when confronted with an intransigent client—resign.

The scope of a business lawyer's obligation is a matter of contextual imperatives. For securities lawyers, moreover, special duties apply. The Sarbanes-Oxley Act requires the SEC to establish minimum standards of professional conduct for securities lawyers practicing before it.[4] The SEC's rules impose on those lawyers obligations to report violations of law of which they become aware to designated authorities within the enterprise they represent.[5] Debate accompanying adoption of those rules also considered whether lawyers should also have a duty to withdraw publicly from representation if such violations are not satisfactorily resolved (referred to as the "noisy withdrawal" proposal). Such impositions assign the securities lawyer the role of what is sometimes called a "gatekeeper." This designates participants in transactions who serve as a guardian for the public interest when assisting clients in gaining access to the public capital markets.[6] Not all corporate lawyers participate in such transactions, but many do.

---

4. Sarbanes-Oxley Act of 2002 § 304.

5. SEC Rules, part 205.

6. *See* John C. Coffee, Jr., *The Attorney as Gatekeeper: An Agenda for the SEC*, 103 Colum. L. Rev. 1293 (2003).

D. Involvement in Clients' Affairs

Business lawyers do not merely give clients advice. Usually, business lawyers are intimately involved in the accomplishment of business transactions about which they give advice, and very often these transactions are accomplished almost solely by the effect of documents drafted by the lawyer. One consequence of this involvement in clients' affairs is that if anyone raises a problem about the legality or propriety of a business transaction, it is likely that the company's lawyer will be in the middle of the controversy.

E. Main Client Contact

The business lawyer typically is a law firm's main contact with a business client, even if most of the firm's work for the client is done by other specialists. Here the business lawyer's role is reminiscent of that of the internist in medical practice, who tends to be the intake physician in a group practice. Another way of describing this role of the business lawyer is that it is the role of a traffic cop. One thing this means is that the business lawyer has to know enough about other specialties to decide (1) whether the client has a legal problem and (2) if the client does have a legal problem, what other lawyer to get involved.

F. Conservatism

Business lawyers are generally conservative in their risk-taking. In everything they do for clients they ask themselves where problems might lie and what they can do to avoid them. Business lawyers often are willing to go to or have others go to whatever trouble it takes to avoid even the extremely remote possibility of a problem.

One can question the application of the conservative approach to a specific situation, but that approach in general is exactly the correct one. The business lawyer works prospectively, but he or she continually tries to look at a transaction being planned through the eyes of a court viewing the transaction retrospectively. The skillful lawyer knows that what appears at the time of the transaction to be objective truth, if it exists at all, may not be nearly so important as how an opposing lawyer subsequently characterizes the facts. And finally, the skillful lawyer knows that it is impossible to tell when planning a transaction how a judge or jury might someday view the transaction. The lawyer's only course is to button up both the facts (by documentation) and the legalities (usually by precisely drawn contractual provisions) of a transaction so tightly that a court will have no basis for finding against the business lawyer's client.

G. Collegial Approach

Business lawyers working on a transaction typically find business lawyers working on the other side. The relationship between these lawyers almost invariably is collegial rather than adversarial. Negotiations on documents, for example, are characterized by good-natured civility. So much is this the case that to an outside observer it might often appear that the lawyers are working for the same client. This illusion may come partially from the fact that each client does want basically the same thing: the transaction done smoothly and quickly. It comes also from the fact that the two lawyers share approaches and values, and so they understand each other. The borrower's lawyer, for example, does not argue when the bank's lawyer requests a specific borrowing resolution from the borrower's board of directors.

H. Involvement of Securities Law

Business practice is intertwined with the practice of securities law to such an extent that they are virtually two parts of the same whole. Much of this intertwining arises from the fact that some federal securities law serves to fill gaps in state corporation law and is, in reality, federal corporation law. But some of the intertwining also comes from the fact that a corporation cannot avoid some involvement in pure securities law. All corporations need to sell stock, for example, and anytime the corporation— or one of its shareholders—sells stock, the sale involves securities law questions. This does not mean, of course, that all business lawyers need to be full-blown securities lawyers. What it does mean is that every business lawyer needs to be expert in some areas of securities law.

I. Special Ethical Problem

Business lawyers face a special ethical problem that arises from the fact that their business clients do not exist in a form that can be dealt with directly. Everything a company does must be done through agents. The special ethical problem arises when the interest of an agent with whom the lawyer deals differs from the company's interest. The first problem of the lawyer is to see the conflict. That is not always as easy as it might seem, partly because the lawyer often does not know enough facts to discern, for example, that a proposed action is good for the company's president but bad for the enterprise. The second problem is to handle the conflict without violating the lawyer's ethical obligations and without damaging the lawyer's relationship with people in the company. That typically can be done if the lawyer exercises enough skill.

Perhaps the clearest example of this conflict arises when the president of a corporation asks the corporation's lawyer to draft the president's employment contract. Initially, the lawyer must determine whether further action is consistent with an attorney's ethical responsibilities. If it is, the lawyer would then determine whether there is an acceptable way the lawyer might handle this situation. A good and practical way would be to have the president secure the agreement of the board of directors that the lawyer will draft the contract as he or she believes the contract likely would come out if negotiated by two good business lawyers, and further that the corporation will pay for the legal work. (Essentially this would mean that the contract would include a full array of protective provisions for each party and no overreaching provisions favoring either.) This and other ethical issues that the business lawyer faces will be addressed in the following chapters.

J. Public Service

One of the hallmarks of the legal profession is the opportunity to serve the public good. Business lawyers are no exception. Business lawyers of all types have the skills and talent to provide public service in many ways. For example, the American Bar Association Section of Business Law has joined with the National Legal Aid and Defender Association to match business lawyers with legal service organizations and public service community programs lacking the finances to hire an attorney. Some of the projects undertaken by business lawyers working pro bono with members of these organizations include assistance in securing financing for low income housing, obtaining insurance proceeds for terminal patients, and structuring loans granted by community development corporations. Other business lawyers have helped low income families form trailer park co-operatives and have provided struggling start-up companies with business formation advice. Business lawyers have also helped emerging democracies throughout the world develop constitutions, legal systems, and bar associations.

Corporations and Other Business Organizations

Chapter 1

Business Organizations and Agency Principles

Situation
(This situation applies to Chapters 1 and 2)

A business client of yours recommends your law firm to William Anderson and Letoya Baker, who want to start a business. An appointment is arranged, and at the designated hour Baker and Anderson enter your office. They explain that their associate, James Phillips, will be a little late. He is tied up at a directors' meeting but should be arriving soon. Phillips, they say, is a person of significant personal means who made his money investing in established companies. He owns a private equity firm and is particularly interested in minority-owned businesses.

Baker tells you about their business plan. Baker is a molecular biologist who has worked in a university research laboratory for several years. She developed a rapid, efficient process for synthesizing DNA. She is well known for this process and is often asked for advice by other laboratories around the country. Because of the considerable start-up costs required to set up a laboratory capable of performing DNA synthesis, Baker is convinced that many researchers would be interested in having this process done for them on a contract basis. Therefore, the first stage in Anderson's and Baker's plan is to set up and operate a laboratory to do this work. The second stage, which they will develop as time and money allow, is to conduct the necessary research to perfect a patentable process for using DNA manipulation to make plants disease resistant. Baker has done preliminary work in this area, but has not wanted to proceed further, as any resulting patent would be the property of her present employer.

Anderson then addresses the business details. Anderson is the vice president for finance and administration of a small chemical supply company. He manages the company's finances and is in charge of an office staff. He expects to handle the business end of the new enterprise. Since Baker will need to spend her time in the laboratory, Anderson plans to handle most contacts with prospective customers, except when Baker's involvement is absolutely necessary. This will be like old times, he says, since his first job with his present company involved calling on customers.

Anderson explains that he and Baker will not be able to contribute all of the required capital to the new business. Together they can raise only about $80,000 in cash. However, Anderson searched for a prospective investor and found Phillips. Phillips is willing to contribute, or guarantee loans for, $500,000 to $700,000 if the terms are

3

satisfactory. Baker also believes that her mother-in-law, Roberta Arriz, may be persuaded to invest $200,000 to $300,000. Arriz owns and operates a successful property management company, Arriz Corp. Arriz's funding may be either a source of start-up capital or may provide additional capital resources once the company is established. The parties have not developed a long-term strategy for raising additional capital.

In the ensuing general discussion, Anderson and Baker also give you the following information:

1. Neither Anderson nor Baker expect to have any substantial source of income other than what they can earn from their new business. Each requires about $60,000 per year to survive financially.

2. Estimated expenses, for the first year of operation, include:

Estimated Annual Expenses
(amounts in dollars)

Equipment and supplies		400,000
Salaries:		
Anderson and Baker	120,000	
Laboratory Technician	50,000	
Clerical	30,000	
Total Salaries		200,000
Rent		30,000
Miscellaneous		20,000
TOTAL		650,000

3. It is difficult to estimate first year revenues, but Anderson and Baker believe they can generate enough business to keep at least one laboratory technician busy. It will take a few months before the company can deliver and be paid for its first products. After that the two entrepreneurs should at least be able to cover expenses out of revenues.

Anderson and Baker ask you to advise them as to what kind of business entity they should form and what they should do next. As the meeting is about to break up, Phillips arrives. He apologizes for being late, but explains that, although he is involved in more business ventures than he has time for, he cannot resist making his presence known when his money is involved. He tells you that he has always invested in established companies rather than new businesses, but has confidence in Baker and Anderson and sees a big future for biotechnology ventures. Phillips also says he looks forward to having your advice on a legal structure for the new business.

The three partners ask you about your fees are and whether you would consider being paid with an interest in the new company. And finally, they would like to hear your opinion on the business venture itself. They know that you have many years experience in representing business clients and would like to have the benefit of that experience. In responding to their questions, you should also address applicable professional responsibility issues.

Section I
Introduction to Forms of Business Organizations

Persons forming a business may choose from among over a dozen business organization forms. These forms overlap in some aspects, are inexplicably different in others and, taken together, may seem to lack a coherent rationale. The selection process may seem daunting to someone unfamiliar with the array of possibilities. Lawyers advising entrepreneurs should be able to help their clients select which organization form best suits the client's needs.

A company may be formed as a sole proprietorship, a general partnership, a limited liability partnership, a limited partnership, a partnership association, a general corporation, a closely held corporation, a limited liability company, a business trust, an unincorporated association such as a joint stock company or, if certain requirements are met, a professional corporation, or numerous variations. These forms extend along a continuum of simplicity and scale, from the modest sole proprietorship at one end to the large, multinational corporation at the other. Each type of business organization except the sole proprietorship is governed by state statute. These statutes define the management and investment structure of the enterprise. They also control the company's internal affairs (the rights, obligations, and authority of the company's investors and managers) and some of the consequences of the company's interactions with third parties.

Not all forms are widely used. Partnership associations and joint stock companies are two forms with limited appeal. Nor are all forms suitable for all types of businesses. Publicly held companies with shares traded on a securities exchange, like the New York Stock Exchange, are commonly general corporations, although some are limited partnerships.

The drama of forming a business arises from the interactions of a stock set of characters—the company's owners/investors and its high level managers. The characters' roles vary according to the nature of their investment in the business and their expectations concerning their participation in the management of the enterprise. Some investors use real, personal, or intellectual property to acquire an interest in a company, while others contribute human capital in the form of services. Some entrepreneurs plan to be active managers of the firm's day to day business operations while others have no interest in management and seek only a satisfactory return on their investments. The latter are called passive investors. Although they are not active in the business, they are nevertheless counted among the owners of the enterprise because they hold an equity interest in the company. Their opportunities for a return on their investments are thus directly tied to the fortunes of the company, and they share the risk of the venture.

Owners' relationships with their company contrast with those who lend money to the company. Lenders have a contractual right to be repaid the principal of the loan with interest according to a specified payment schedule, whether or not the company is flourishing. The lender's rights and obligations are defined in a contract with the borrower. In contrast, state business organization law defines the basic relationship between a company and its owners. In some situations, the statutory rule is mandatory; in others, the statute provides a default rule that applies unless the parties choose a different approach.

While all members of these groups have a common purpose—forming a successful enterprise—sometimes their individual priorities vary and may even conflict. These competing interests create challenging legal and ethical dilemmas for the lawyer advising upon the appropriate organization form. In deciding what business form is best for a particular enterprise, lawyers and their clients should consider the following questions.

What is required to form and operate the business?

The formation of certain types of businesses, such as a general partnership, is relatively simple. Owners of the company are not required to file documents with state authorities or pay franchise taxes for the privilege of forming the business. Owners do not even need to have a written business agreement, although one is certainly recommended. The operation and oversight of the business may be conducted with as little or as much formality as the parties wish. In contrast, business forms offering limited liability to investors, like the general corporation, require filings with a state office (usually dubbed the secretary of state, despite how such terminology may be confused with the senior federal cabinet official, the Secretary of State) and the payment of an annual franchise tax. Investors in corporations must also hold annual meetings and follow specified procedures for making certain types of decisions.

Who will manage the business and how will business decisions be made?

When one person owns and operates a company, a formal governance structure is unnecessary. However, when a business is owned by multiple individuals, the above question must be addressed. It can be answered in several ways. Owners may manage the company themselves (participatory management) or they may hire professional managers to act on their behalf (centralized management). Participatory management is characteristic of general partnerships in which partners typically play an active role in managing the business. Centralized management is characteristic of general corporations, in which the board of directors manages the company for the benefit of the owners (the shareholders). The number of owners is one factor used to determine what type of management structure is preferred. A few owners can easily vote on all matters, but this approach becomes cumbersome as the number of owners increases. In this case, efficiency and cost concerns may make centralized management preferable.

Joint ownership also requires the parties to determine what type of collective action will be needed to decide the many issues that inevitably arise in the operation of a business. The owners need to determine who is eligible to vote on a particular matter, how votes are allocated, and what vote is required to approve a particular action. Votes can be allocated on a per capita basis or by the amount of an owner's investment in the company. Making a decision may require a unanimous, super majority, majority, or plurality vote. Deciding what vote is required has important implications for the allocation of power between majority and minority owners. The higher the required vote, the greater the opportunity for minority veto. The lower the required vote, the greater the power of the majority.

To what extent will the investors be personally liable for the company's obligations?

In some business forms, like the sole proprietorship and the general partnership, the owners are personally liable for the company's financial obligations. If the company cannot meet its obligations, company creditors may seize the owners' personal assets to payback the company's debts. In a jointly owned business, each owner may be jointly and severally liable for company obligations. The extent of an owner's liability may be based on a per capita allocation, the amount of the individual's ownership interest, or some other agreed upon allocation.

Owners can protect themselves from liability for company debts in several ways. One is to select a business form that provides limited liability. Limited liability means that owners will not be personally liable for the company's obligations beyond the amount of their original investment. They may lose the value of their investment if the business fails, but they will not be required to use their personal assets to satisfy the company's creditors. But this approach is not always possible. A bank lending money to a business may require shareholders of a corporation to be personally responsible for the company's debts even though shareholders have limited liability under the applicable corporate statute.

Owners with unlimited liability can protect themselves in other ways. They can purchase insurance to cover tort liability. They may use contracts to limit their liability. Contracting parties may agree that creditors' claims will be satisfied only from security interests in the company's personal property or in mortgages on real property. The success of this approach will depend on the sophistication and relative bargaining power of the parties to the agreement.

How will the business be financed?

The question of how the business will be financed has two parts: (1) how will the capital needed to start the company business be raised, and (2) will additional needed capital be raised once the business is underway. The founding entrepreneurs usually provide some of the initial funding for a new business, and often provide additional capital once the business has taken off.

Often, however, a company's owners are unable to provide enough capital to cover all the start-up costs or satisfy additional requirements of the business once it is underway. Consequently, the owners must look elsewhere for funding. They may want to bring in additional owners. These owners may be individuals or businesses, such as venture capital firms formed for the purpose of investing in new and ongoing businesses. To raise capital from a significant number of investors, the company may sell ownership interests or shares to the general public. The owners may also borrow money from banks, insurance companies and other financial institutions who will be lenders but not co-owners of the business.

How do investors receive a return on their investments?

Owners make money on their investments in a company in two ways. They may receive a portion of the company's profits or they may sell their interest in the company and thereby realize any appreciated value in their ownership interest. Shares in the profits of an ongoing venture may, like voting rights, be allocated on a per capita basis or according to the amount of each owner's investment. Some state statutes impose restrictions on the distribution of company earnings to company owners. Shareholders in a corporation may be paid a share of the profits only if the company can satisfy higher priority claims, such as those of lenders. In contrast, partners are not restricted in the distribution of company profits so long as the company is solvent.

The issue of investment liquidity becomes important when one or more owners want to leave the company and be paid the value of their ownership interests. The departure may be caused by friction among the owners, a desire to invest elsewhere, a change in the company fortunes, or the death of one of the principals. In these situations, investors in companies traded on a securities exchange need only sell their shares to exit the company and receive the market value of their investment.

Withdrawing from a privately held company that lacks a ready market for the ownership interests may be problematic, particularly when the law does not provide an exit procedure. Careful planning is a must when the investment is not liquid. Just as the voting requirements for approval of company action have important implications for the allocation of power between majority and minority interests, so do the procedures for departure from a privately held company. Permitting investors to withdraw at any time and compel payment of the value of their interests may impair the company's financial stability and jeopardize the reasonable expectations of the remaining owners. Conversely, unduly restricting individuals' opportunities to withdraw may leave minority interests at the mercy of an oppressive majority.

What are the tax consequences of forming a business?

Two of the most important considerations when choosing a business form are the quests to limit liability and minimize taxes. Although corporations and general partnerships are both aggregates of people engaged in a common business enterprise, the two forms may be treated very differently for tax purposes. Corporations are dealt with as legal taxpaying entities separate and distinct from the individuals who own and manage the business. Corporations pay income tax at the corporate tax rate on the money they earn. If corporate earnings are subsequently distributed to shareholders, the shareholders are taxed at the individual tax rate on the earnings they receive. Thus, corporate earnings are taxed twice: once when received by the corporation and a second time when distributed to shareholders. This arrangement is often referred to as a double taxation scheme. In addition, corporations are subject to state franchise taxes in all states where they are qualified to do business.

Under the Internal Revenue Code, a business taxed as a partnership is not treated as a separate, taxpaying entity. Although an informational return must be filed with the I.R.S., the business, itself, does not pay taxes. Instead, the owners are taxed at individual tax rates on their proportionate share of the business income, as though they had earned it themselves. This is referred to as pass through taxation. Tax liability is passed through the business organization directly to the owners. Today the federal tax treatment of most unincorporated business forms depends on whether the enterprise elects to be treated like a corporation or a partnership.[1]

Changes in corporate and individual tax rates affect the choice of business form. When corporate tax rates are low, the corporate form is appealing. Conversely, when corporate tax rates are high, businesses eligible for pass-through taxation acquire a certain cachet.

Chapters 1 and 2 focus primarily on the predominant forms of business organizations: sole proprietorships, limited liability partnerships, limited liability companies, and corporations. You will also be introduced to other business organization forms combining attributes of both partnerships and corporations. As tax considerations and the quest for limited liability increasingly affect the choice of business entity, these variant business organization forms are gaining popularity.

Section II
Sole Proprietorships

The sole proprietorship is the most popular business organization form in the United States, particularly for small start-up ventures. It is simple and easy to operate. Sometimes the form is chosen because the sole proprietorship is the best option for a particular business. Often, however, business owners choose this form without legal advice, sometimes to their regret.

A sole proprietorship is a business owned by one person who has sole decision-making authority, an exclusive claim to business's profits, and direct ownership of all the business's assets. A sole proprietorship having employees is a business organization. Although there is only one owner, the organization is comprised of more than one person. Sole proprietorship might operate businesses such as beauty salons, car washes, restaurants, and retail shops.

Since the legal identity of the sole proprietorship and its owner are one and the same, there is no business entity to form. Equally important, no formalities are re-

---

1. Before January 1, 1997, the application of what are called the Kinter Regulations (Treas. Reg. §§ 301.7701 *et seq.*) determined whether an unincorporated business would be taxed like a corporation. An unincorporated company would be taxed like a corporation if it had three of the four following attributes: centralized management, continuity of life, free transferability of interests, and limited liability. Effective January 1, 1997, regulations §§ 301.7701-1 through 301.7701-3 were amended to permit most unincorporated business associations to elect whether to be treated as a corporation or a partnership for federal tax purposes.

quired to operate the business.[2] The absence of formation and operational formalities translates to a direct cost-saving for the business owner. The absence of legal requirements also gives the owner maximum flexibility in structuring and operating the business.

The sole proprietorship suffers from serious disadvantages, however. For one thing, its single owner management structure is suitable only for small businesses with a few employees. As the company grows in scope of operations and number of employees, it will necessarily develop a number of different departments to take care of the company's internal affairs. The owner can make up a management structure, with the heads of each division or department given whatever responsibilities and titles the owner wishes, but that structure will not exist until the owner devises it, and unless the owner uses traditional business titles, the titles the owner chooses may not carry a widely understood meaning.

The primary drawback of sole proprietorships is the owner's unlimited liability for the company's obligations. The attribute of unlimited liability and the problem of management structure are related. In a business in which the owner is the sole decision-maker and worker, unlimited liability is not much of a detriment if the owner's main fear is tort liability, because tortfeasors can always be sued in their individual capacity. As the operation of the business becomes complex, with a broad array of managers and workers, the sole proprietor becomes subject to vicarious liability for the acts of others. In some circumstances, the risk of financial responsibility for the acts of others can be significantly reduced through contracts or by purchasing insurance. Without these precautions, the sole proprietorship may be an unacceptable organization form because the owner is exposed to significant risks of vicarious liability.

Section III
Agency Law

A. Forming an Agency Relationship

Business organizations consist of groups of individuals—owners, managers, and employees—who are participants in a common enterprise. The work of every business must be accomplished through the efforts of the people who are a part of it. The business, itself, is incapable of acting on its own behalf.

Agency law provides the fundamental legal underpinnings of many business relationships. It creates a standard form contract that applies to the members of business associations inter se and to their interactions with third parties. When a company employs another person to act on the its behalf, the common law of agency applies to the relationship. The company is the principal, on whose behalf action is taken. The employee acting on behalf of the principal is the agent. For example, when an

---

2. If the company is doing business under a trade name, the state may require a filing under its fictitious name statute.

employer hires a purchasing employee, the employee acts as an agent on behalf of the company when dealing with company suppliers. Both principals and agents may be individuals or legal entities.

Employers and employees may enter into a principal/agent relationship. An agency relationship may be created expressly by an agreement between the parties or may arise as a matter of law when the parties enter into an association that has the legal attributes of an agency relationship.

The appointment of one or more agents to work on behalf of the principal enables the principal to accomplish more than would be possible if the principal were acting alone. However, the creation of an agency relationship is not cost-free. The principal will have to supervise or monitor the activities of the agent, because the agent may not always act in the principal's best interests. The principal must bear the cost when the agent's performance diverges from that which would be most beneficial to the principal.

As you read the cases that follow, consider the different ways in which the agency relationships are created.

A. Gay Jenson Farms Co. v. Cargill, Inc.

Minnesota Supreme Court
309 N.W.2d 285 (1981)

Peterson, Justice.

Plaintiffs, 86 individual, partnership or corporate farmers, brought this action against defendant Cargill, Inc. (Cargill) and defendant Warren Grain & Seed Co. (Warren) to recover losses sustained when Warren defaulted on the contracts made with plaintiffs for the sale of grain. After a trial by jury, judgment was entered in favor of plaintiffs, and Cargill brought this appeal. We affirm.

This case arose out of the financial collapse of defendant Warren Seed & Grain Co., and its failure to satisfy its indebtedness to plaintiffs. Warren, which was located in Warren, Minnesota, was operated by Lloyd Hill and his son, Gary Hill. Warren operated a grain elevator and as a result was involved in the purchase of cash or market grain from local farmers. The cash grain would be resold through the Minneapolis Grain Exchange or to the terminal grain companies directly. Warren also stored grain for farmers and sold chemicals, fertilizer and steel storage bins. In addition, it operated a seed business which involved buying seed grain from farmers, processing it and reselling it for seed to farmers and local elevators.

Lloyd Hill decided in 1964 to apply for financing from Cargill.[3] Cargill's officials from the Moorhead regional office investigated Warren's operations and recommended that Cargill finance Warren.

---

3. [1] Prior to this time, Atwood Larson had provided working capital for Warren, and Warren had used Atwood Larson as its commission agent for the sale of market grain on the grain exchange.

Warren and Cargill thereafter entered into a security agreement which provided that Cargill would loan money for working capital to Warren on "open account" financing up to a stated limit, which was originally set as $175,000.[4] Under this contract, Warren would receive funds and pay its expenses by issuing drafts drawn on Cargill through Minneapolis banks. The drafts were imprinted with both Warren's and Cargill's names. Proceeds from Warren's sales would be deposited with Cargill and credited to its account. In return for this financing, Warren appointed Cargill as its grain agent for transactions with the Commodity Credit Corporation. Cargill was also given a right of first refusal to purchase market grain sold by Warren to the terminal market.

A new contract was negotiated in 1967, extending Warren's credit line to $300,000 and incorporating the provisions of the original contract. It was also stated in the contract that Warren would provide Cargill with annual financial statements and that either Cargill would keep the books for Warren or an audit would be conducted by an independent firm. Cargill was given the right of access to Warren's books for inspection.

In addition, the agreement provided that Warren was not to make capital improvements or repairs in excess of $5,000 without Cargill's prior consent. Further, it was not to become liable as guarantor on another's indebtedness, or encumber its assets except with Cargill's permission. Consent by Cargill was required before Warren would be allowed to declare a dividend or sell and purchase stock.

Officials from Cargill's regional office made a brief visit to Warren shortly after the agreement was executed. They examined the annual statement and the accounts receivable, expenses, inventory, seed, machinery and other financial matters. Warren was informed that it would be reminded periodically to make the improvements recommended by Cargill.[5] At approximately this time, a memo was given to the Cargill official in charge of the Warren account, Erhart Becker, which stated in part: "This organization (Warren) needs very strong paternal guidance." ...

During this period, Cargill continued to review Warren's operations and expenses and recommend that certain actions should be taken.[6] Warren purchased from Cargill

---

4. [2] Loans were secured by a second mortgage on Warren's real estate and a first chattel mortgage on its inventories of grain and merchandise in the sum of $175,000 with 7% interest. Warren was to use the $175,000 to pay off the debt that it owed to Atwood Larson.

5. [3] Cargill headquarters suggested that the regional office check Warren monthly. Also, it was requested that [Cargill] be given an explanation for the relatively large withdrawals from undistributed earnings made by the Hills, since Cargill hoped that Warren's profits would be used to decrease its debt balance. Cargill asked for written requests for withdrawals from undistributed earnings in the future.

6. [4] Between 1967 and 1973, Cargill suggested that Warren take a number of steps, including: (1) a reduction of seed grain and cash grain inventories; (2) improved collection of accounts receivable; (3) reduction or elimination of its wholesale seed business and its speciality grain operation; (4) marketing fertilizer and steel bins on consignment; (5) a reduction in withdrawals made by officers; (6) a suggestion that Warren's bookkeeper not issue her own salary checks; and (7) cooperation with Cargill in implementing the recommendations. These ideas were apparently never implemented, however.

various business forms printed by Cargill and received sample forms from Cargill which Warren used to develop its own business forms.

Cargill wrote to its regional office in 1970 expressing its concern that the pattern of increased use of funds allowed to develop at Warren was similar to that involved in two other cases in which Cargill experienced severe losses. Cargill did not refuse to honor drafts or call the loan, however. A new security agreement which increased the credit line to $750,000 was executed in 1972, and a subsequent agreement which raised the limit to $1,250,000 was entered into in 1976.

Warren was at that time shipping Cargill 90% of its cash grain. When Cargill's facilities were full, Warren shipped its grain to other companies. Approximately 25% of Warren's total sales was seed grain which was sold directly by Warren to its customers.

As Warren's indebtedness continued to be in excess of its credit line, Cargill began to contact Warren daily regarding its financial affairs. Cargill headquarters informed its regional office in 1973 that, since Cargill money was being used, Warren should realize that Cargill had the right to make some critical decisions regarding the use of the funds. Cargill headquarters also told Warren that a regional manager would be working with Warren on a day-to-day basis as well as in monthly planning meetings. In 1975, Cargill's regional office began to keep a daily debit position on Warren. A bank account was opened in Warren's name on which Warren could draw checks in 1976. The account was to be funded by drafts drawn on Cargill by the local bank.

In early 1977, it became evident that Warren had serious financial problems. Several farmers, who had heard that Warren's checks were not being paid, inquired or had their agents inquire at Cargill regarding Warren's status and were initially told that there would be no problem with payment. In April 1977, an audit of Warren revealed that Warren was $4 million in debt. After Cargill was informed that Warren's financial statements had been deliberately falsified, Warren's request for additional financing was refused. In the final days of Warren's operation, Cargill sent an official to supervise the elevator, including disbursement of funds and income generated by the elevator.

After Warren ceased operations, it was found to be indebted to Cargill in the amount of $3.6 million. Warren was also determined to be indebted to plaintiffs in the amount of $2 million, and plaintiffs brought this action in 1977 to seek recovery of that sum. Plaintiffs alleged that Cargill was jointly liable for Warren's indebtedness as it had acted as principal for the grain elevator....

The jury found that Cargill's conduct between 1973 and 1977 had made it Warren's principal.[7] Warren was found to be the agent of Cargill with regard to contracts for:

1. The purchase and sale of grain for market.
2. The purchase and sale of seed grain.
3. The storage of grain.

---

7. [6] At trial, plaintiffs sought to establish actual agency by Cargill's course of dealing between 1973 and 1977 rather than "apparent" agency or agency by estoppel, so that the only issue in this case is one of actual agency.

The court determined that Cargill was the disclosed principal of Warren. It was concluded that Cargill was jointly liable with Warren for plaintiffs' losses, and judgment was entered for plaintiffs.[8]

Cargill seeks a reversal of the jury's findings or, if the jury findings are upheld, a reversal of the trial court's determination that Cargill was a disclosed principal....

Issue

The major issue in this case is whether Cargill, by its course of dealing with Warren, became liable as a principal on contracts made by Warren with plaintiffs. Cargill contends that no agency relationship was established with Warren, notwithstanding its financing of Warren's operation and its purchase of the majority of Warren's grain. However, we conclude that Cargill, by its control and influence over Warren, became a principal with liability for the transactions entered into by its agent Warren.

Holding

Rule

Agency is the fiduciary relationship that results from the manifestation of consent by one person to another that the other shall act on his behalf and subject to his control, and consent by the other so to act. In order to create an agency there must be an agreement, but not necessarily a contract between the parties.... An agreement may result in the creation of an agency relationship although the parties did not call it an agency and did not intend the legal consequences of the relation to follow. The existence of the agency may be proved by circumstantial evidence which shows a course of dealing between the two parties. When an agency relationship is to be proven by circumstantial evidence, the principal must be shown to have consented to the agency since one cannot be the agent of another except by consent of the latter.

Cargill contends that the prerequisites of an agency relationship did not exist because Cargill never consented to the agency, Warren did not act on behalf of Cargill, and Cargill did not exercise control over Warren. We hold that all three elements of agency could be found in the particular circumstances of this case. By directing Warren to implement its recommendations, Cargill manifested its consent that Warren would be its agent. Warren acted on Cargill's behalf in procuring grain for Cargill as the part of its normal operations which were totally financed by Cargill.[9] Further, an agency relationship was established by Cargill's interference with the internal affairs of Warren, which constituted de facto control of the elevator.

A creditor who assumes control of his debtor's business may become liable as principal for the acts of the debtor in connection with the business. Restatement (Second) of Agency § 14 O (1958). It is noted in comment a to § 14 O that:

---

8. [Eds.] Read the materials in Chapter 1, Section III. E., *infra*, on an agent's liability when the principal is disclosed or unidentified. Then reread the court's statement about Cargill's joint liability with Warren. Is the court's statement correct as applied to: a disclosed principal; an unidentified principal; an undisclosed principal? Why or why not?

9. [7] Although the contracts with the farmers were executed by Warren, Warren paid for the grain with drafts drawn on Cargill. While this is not in itself significant ... it is one factor to be taken into account in analyzing the relationship between Warren and Cargill.

A security holder who merely exercises a veto power over the business acts of his debtor by preventing purchases or sales above specified amounts does not thereby become a principal. However, if he takes over the management of the debtor's business either in person or through an agent, and directs what contracts may or may not be made, he becomes a principal, liable as a principal for the obligations incurred thereafter in the normal course of business by the debtor who has now become his general agent. The point at which the creditor becomes a principal is that at which he assumes de facto control over the conduct of his debtor, whatever the terms of the formal contract with his debtor may be.

A number of factors indicate Cargill's control over Warren, including the following:

(1) Cargill's constant recommendations to Warren by telephone;

(2) Cargill's right of first refusal on grain;

(3) Warren's inability to enter into mortgages, to purchase stock or to pay dividends without Cargill's approval;

(4) Cargill's right of entry onto Warren's premises to carry on periodic checks and audits;

(5) Cargill's correspondence and criticism regarding Warren's finances, officers['] salaries and inventory;

(6) Cargill's determination that Warren needed "strong paternal guidance";

(7) Provision of drafts and forms to Warren upon which Cargill's name was imprinted;

(8) Financing of all Warren's purchases of grain and operating expenses; and

(9) Cargill's power to discontinue the financing of Warren's operations.

We recognize that some of these elements, as Cargill contends, are found in an ordinary debtor-creditor relationship. However, these factors cannot be considered in isolation, but, rather, they must be viewed in light of all the circumstances surrounding Cargill's aggressive financing of Warren.

It is also Cargill's position that the relationship between Cargill and Warren was that of buyer-supplier rather than principal-agent. Restatement (Second) of Agency § 14 K (1958) compares an agent with a supplier as follows:

> One who contracts to acquire property from a third person and convey it to another is the agent of the other only if it is agreed that he is to act primarily for the benefit of the other and not for himself.

Factors indicating that one is a supplier, rather than an agent, are: (1) That he is to receive a fixed price for the property irrespective of price paid by him. This is the most important. (2) That he acts in his own name and receives the title to the property which he thereafter is to transfer. (3) That he has an independent business in buying and selling similar property. Restatement (Second) of Agency § 14 K, Comment a (1958).

Under the Restatement approach, it must be shown that the supplier has an independent business before it can be concluded that he is not an agent. The record establishes that all portions of Warren's operation were financed by Cargill and that Warren sold almost all of its market grain to Cargill. Thus, the relationship which existed between the parties was not merely that of buyer and supplier....

Further, we are not persuaded by the fact that Warren was not one of the "line" elevators that Cargill operated in its own name. The Warren operation, like the line elevator, was financially dependent on Cargill's continual infusion of capital. The arrangement with Warren presented a convenient alternative to the establishment of a line elevator. Cargill became, in essence, the owner of the operation without the accompanying legal indicia.

The amici curiae assert that, if the jury verdict is upheld, firms and banks which have provided business loans to county elevators will decline to make further loans. The decision in this case should give no cause for such concern. We deal here with a business enterprise markedly different from an ordinary bank financing, since Cargill was an active participant in Warren's operations rather than simply a financier. Cargill's course of dealing with Warren was, by its own admission, a paternalistic relationship in which Cargill made the key economic decisions and kept Warren in existence.

Although considerable interest was paid by Warren on the loan, the reason for Cargill's financing of Warren was not to make money as a lender but, rather, to establish a source of market grain for its business. As one Cargill manager noted, "We were staying in there because we wanted the grain." For this reason, Cargill was willing to extend the credit line far beyond the amount originally allocated to Warren. It is noteworthy that Cargill was receiving significant amounts of grain and that, notwithstanding the risk that was recognized by Cargill, the operation was considered profitable.

On the whole, there was a unique fabric in the relationship between Cargill and Warren which varies from that found in normal debtor-creditor situations. We conclude that, on the facts of this case, there was sufficient evidence from which the jury could find that Cargill was the principal of Warren within the definitions of agency set forth in Restatement (Second) of Agency §§ 1 and 14 O....

Notes and Questions

1. Although the *Cargill* decision is based on the Restatement of the Law (Second) of Agency (1958) (hereinafter Restatement (Second) of Agency), the outcome of the case would be the same if it was decided under the Restatement of the Law (Third) of Agency (2006) (hereinafter Restatement (Third) of Agency) § 1.01.

In addressing the defendant's contention that the Warren/Cargill relationship was only that of a debtor/creditor or supplier/buyer, the Cargill court referred to §§ 14K and 14O of the Restatement (Second) of Agency, both of which have been eliminated in the Restatement (Third) of Agency. However, the general point made by the omitted sections is continued in § 1.02 of the Restatement (Third) of Agency § 1.02.

The Comment to § 1.02 elaborates as follows:

Many common legal relationships do not by themselves create relationships of agency as defined in § 1.01. These include relationships between suppliers and resellers of goods or property, franchisors and franchisees, lenders and borrowers, and parent corporations and their subsidiaries.... Relationships like these are also relationships of agency when the elements stated in § 1.01 are present.[10]

2. The court used *Cargill* and other classic cases as a point of contrast in *Coppola v. Bear Stearns & Co.*, 499 F.3d 144, 150 (2d Cir. 2007):

Under [traditional] principles [of lender liability], a creditor that has not assumed the formal indicia of ownership may become liable for the debts of its borrower if the lender's conduct is such as to cause it to become the debtor's agent, partner, or alter ego. See generally A. Gay Jenson Farms Co. v. Cargill, Inc., 309 N.W.2d 285 (Minn.1981) (agency); Martin v. Peyton, 246 N.Y. 213, 158 N.E. 77 (1927) (partnership), Krivo Indus. Supply Co. v. Nat'l Distillers & Chem. Corp., 483 F.2d 1098 (5th Cir. 1973) (alter ego). On each of these theories, an essential part of the inquiry is whether the creditor has joined in or assumed control of the borrower's business as a going concern rather than as a means to protect its security for repayment.

For example, in Cargill, the court affirmed a jury verdict holding a lender, Cargill, liable for transactions entered into by its borrower, Warren. 309 N.W.2d at 290. The court emphasized that "Cargill was an active participant in Warren's operations [for some ten years] rather than simply a financier," id. at 292, and that "the reason for Cargill's financing of Warren was not to make money as a lender but, rather, to establish a source of market grain for its [seed] business," id. at 293. In Martin, the New York Court of Appeals affirmed judgment in favor of lender defendants and described the question as "whether in fact [the lender defendants] agree[d] to so associate themselves with the firm as to 'carry on as co-owners a business for profit.'" 158 N.E. at 79–80. The court found that no partnership had been created, even though the lenders had imposed a complex of arrangements giving them substantial control over the firm and its principals.

[T]he dispositive question is whether a creditor is exercising control over the debtor beyond that necessary to recoup some or all of what is owed, and is operating the debtor as a de facto owner of an ongoing business.

[In *Cargill*, the lender] purchased all or nearly all of the debtor's output and the debtor's operations were financially dependent on the lender's infusions of capital. 309 N.W.2d at 292.... [T]he lender in *Cargill* did so for ten years in order to get a steady supply of grain, id. at 288–89 ... [This contrasted

---

10. Restatement Third of Agency § 1.02 Comment. Copyright © 2006 by the American Law Institute. Reproduced with permission. All rights reserved. (Hereinafter Restatement (Third) of Agency.)

with the *Coppola* case, where the lender] took no long-term interest in the operation of [the borrower] as a business. Rather, ... [the lender's] conduct was prompted solely by a short-term interest in facilitating the sale of NFC as a means of salvaging some of the debt it had extended.

B. The Principal's Liability for Authorized Acts of the Agent

A principal is liable for the authorized acts of the agent. Thus, to prevail in a claim against a principal, a plaintiff must establish that the agent was authorized to engage in the conduct in question. A principal will be liable if the agent had actual or apparent authority. The creation of both types of authority originates with the principal. Actual authority is created by the principal's manifestations to the agent. Apparent authority is created by the principal's manifestations to a third party.

1. Actual Authority

As the *Cargill* court indicated in the court's footnote [6], at trial the plaintiffs based Cargill's liability on actual agency authority. The applicable section in the Restatement (Third) of Agency provides:

§ 2.01 Actual Authority

An agent acts with actual authority when, at the time of taking action that has legal consequences for the principal, the agent reasonably believes, in accordance with the principal's manifestations to the agent, that the principal wishes the agent so to act.

In determining whether actual authority exists, both the Restatement (Second) and the Restatement (Third) of Agency focus on the principal's communications to the agent and the agent's reasonable understanding of those communications. How was actual authority created in the *Cargill* case?

2. Determining the Scope of Actual Authority

The terms "express authority," "implied authority," and "incidental authority" refer to the manner in which the agent's authority is created. Express authority refers to authority created by the principal's oral or written communications to the agent concerning the scope of the agent's authority. "Implied authority" refers to the scope of the agent's authority as determined by the principal's conduct, acquiescence, or other related circumstances. "Incidental authority" commonly means that the agent has the authority to do whatever is required and appropriate in the usual course to accomplish the agent's responsibilities. Comment d of § 2.02 of the Restatement (Third) of Agency provides the following elaboration with respect to incidental authority:

d. Acts necessary or incidental to achieving [a] principal's objectives. If a principal's manifestation to an agent expresses the principal's wish that something be done, it is natural to assume that the principal wishes, as an incidental matter, that the agent take the steps necessary and that the agent proceed in the usual and ordinary way....

Koval & Koval v. Simon Telelect, Inc.

Indiana Supreme Court
693 N.E.2d 1299 (1998)

[In *Koval* the issue was whether, in the context of an ADR proceeding, an attorney's settlement of a claim without the client's consent was binding on the client. In the following passage, the court addresses the extent of an attorney's implied authority to settle the claim. The court reasoned:]

A. An attorney's implied authority

... Authority can be express or implied and may be conferred by words or other conduct, including acquiescence. Implied authority can arise from words used, from customs, or from the relations of the parties. The agent is authorized if the agent is reasonable in drawing an inference from the principal's actions that the principal intended to confer authority. It is well settled that an attorney, by virtue of the representation, becomes a powerful agent with a great deal of authority. Retention confers on an attorney the general implied authority to do on behalf of the client all acts in or out of court necessary or incidental to the prosecution or management of the suit or the accomplishment of the purpose for which the attorney was retained. Decisions relating to trial tactics for example—when to object, what motions to file, which arguments to present—or how to negotiate are left to the attorney. See, e.g., *Hoffman v. Hoffman*, 115 Ind. App. 277, 57 N.E.2d 591 (1944) (attorneys could agree to change of venue without client's consent).[11]

As a general proposition an attorney's implied authority does not extend to settling the very business that is committed to the attorney's care without the client's consent. The vast majority of United States jurisdictions hold that the retention of an attorney to pursue a claim does not, without more, give the attorney the implied authority to settle or compromise the claim. The rationale for this rule is that an attorney's role as agent by definition does not entitle the attorney to relinquish the client's rights to the subject matter that the attorney was employed to pursue to the client's satisfaction.

Some of these cases explicitly focused on the distinction between the implied authority to conduct litigation and the authority to settle a claim.... [P]arties do not normally assume that an attorney in informal negotiations has authority to bind the client. It is not too much to ask that other parties dealing with an attorney verify the

---

11. [2] An attorney not only has the authority to conduct and control a lawsuit and make tactical decisions, but also to stipulate to binding admissions of fact. An attorney can bind a client to a default judgment entered due to an attorney's neglect. See, e.g., *International Vacuum, Inc. v. Owens*, 439 N.E.2d 188 (Ind. Ct. App. 1982) (no abuse of discretion in refusing to vacate default judgment against the client where attorney's failure to keep apprised of court proceedings resulted in the attorney's absence at pre-trial hearing, hearing on a motion for a default judgment, and hearing on damages). In these respects, a client is bound by the skill, bad luck, or incompetence of the agent it chooses. In the absence of fraud by the attorney, the client is bound by the action of the attorney, even though the attorney is guilty of gross negligence.

authority to settle before they may expect the negotiation with the attorney to bind the client. Accordingly, the general rule in Indiana is that retention of an attorney does not without more carry implied authority to the attorney to settle.

––––––––––

1. A power of attorney is a document appointing an agent to act on behalf of a principal. Powers of attorney may be used in any situation involving the appointment of an agent. Persons involved in a real estate transaction who do not wish to attend the closing may use a power of attorney to authorize their lawyers to sign documents for them. Often the power of attorney for land transactions must be created with the same formalities as are required for the conveyance of land: it must be in writing, signed and acknowledged by the grantor, and witnessed. This rule is often referred to as the equal dignities rule. Why is it common to apply the equal dignities rule to transactions involving real estate?

2. Ordinarily the appointment of an agent terminates if the principal dies or becomes mentally incapacitated or incompetent. A durable power of attorney is an appointment designed to survive the principal's mental incapacity or incompetence. Durable powers of attorney may be used for a variety of purposes, such as to appoint someone to manage the affairs of or to make health care decisions on behalf of an infirm person. Statutes controlling the creation of a durable power of attorney often provide that the power of attorney must be in writing, signed by the principal, and executed and witnessed in the same manner as required for wills. In addition, the writing must contain words such as "this power of attorney shall not be affected by the subsequent disability or incompetence of the principal." Conn. Gen. Stat. Ann. §45a-562. Why are these formalities required?

3. Apparent Authority

As a general rule, if an agency relationship exists and the agent's acts were authorized by the principal, third parties who have dealt with the agent may hold the principal liable for the agent's acts. The principal may establish the agent's authority by communicating with the agent directly (actual authority), by communicating with the third party dealing with the agent (apparent authority) or both.

The following cases explore the doctrine of apparent authority in the context of the attorney/client relationship. The application of the doctrine in the attorney/client context can be particularly difficult because of the competing policy issues involved.

Fennell v. TLB Kent Co.

United States Court of Appeals, Second Circuit
865 F.2d 498 (1989)

MAHONEY, CIRCUIT JUDGE.

This is an appeal from a final judgment of the United States District Court for the Southern District of New York, Louis L. Stanton, Judge, entered on June 16, 1987, which dismissed plaintiff's action and approved a $10,000 settlement agreement.... The attorneys for the parties negotiated a settlement and reported it to the court by telephone. Based on this conference call, the district court entered an order on January 20, 1987 which dismissed the action with prejudice, but provided that "within sixty days of the date of this order any party may apply by letter for restoration of the action to the calendar of the undersigned." Plaintiff's counsel requested that the action be restored to the calendar on March 20, 1987. After a hearing on June 16, 1987, the district court dismissed the action and approved the settlement, finding that plaintiff's attorney had had apparent authority to settle the case and plaintiff was accordingly bound by the settlement agreement.

We reverse and remand.

Background

Plaintiff-appellant Louis Fennell commenced this action in the United States District Court for the Southern District of New York on January 7, 1985 against his employer, ... alleging wrongful discharge because of his race and age in violation of 42 U.S.C. § 1981. Fennell was represented by C. Vernon Mason and several of his associates, including Fred K. Brewington.

The case was on Judge Stanton's ready calendar on January 6, 1987. On January 16, 1987, however, Brewington and Eugene Frink, defendants' attorney, agreed to settle the case for $10,000 during a telephone conversation. The settlement was reported to the court by both attorneys in a telephone conference call on January 20, 1987. The district court issued an order of dismissal on the same day which provided that either party could apply to the court by letter to restore the case to the court's calendar within sixty days of the order. The settlement was conditioned upon Fennell signing a general release and a stipulation of discontinuance being filed with the court, which never occurred.

Fennell expressed his dissatisfaction with the settlement in a letter to the district court dated March 28, 1987. Fennell there contended that he had told Brewington on January 16, 1987 that he would not approve a $10,000 settlement, but he was willing to settle the case out of court "with the intentions of getting it out of the way and behind me." He also claimed that he had told Mason on January 20, 1987 that $10,000 was not a satisfactory settlement, and that he had tried several times in early February, 1987 to contact Mason's office by telephone about the case, but elicited no response. Fennell further stated that he had gone to Mason's office on February 20, 1987, at which time Mason informed him that the case had been settled for $10,000, whereupon Fennell reiterated his dissatisfaction with that settlement.

On February 27, 1987, Fennell wrote Mason expressing his dissatisfaction with the settlement agreement and indicating that he had "no further use of [Mason's] services." A copy of this letter was sent to the district court and received there on March 3, 1987. On March 20, 1987, Brewington wrote to the district court requesting that the "matter be restored to the calendar as the settlement which was authorized and accepted by our client is no longer acceptable to him," and that Mason and his associates be released by the court as counsel to Fennell.

Following a status conference on June 5, 1987, the district court held a hearing on June 16, 1987 to determine whether Fennell's case should be restored to the calendar. At the conclusion of the hearing, the district court dismissed the action and approved the settlement. This ruling was based upon a finding that Fennell's attorney had been clothed with "apparent authority" when he settled the case, and the court's expressed view that "[t]o allow a client to reject a settlement which has been agreed upon by his attorney with apparent authority is to open the door to a mild form of chaos."

On appeal, Fennell asserts that it was an abuse of discretion for the district court not to have vacated its order of dismissal pursuant to Fed.R.Civ.P. 60(b)(1). Appellees contend that since Fennell's attorney was clothed with apparent authority to settle the case, Fennell is bound by that settlement.

Discussion

... We turn now to the district court's determination that Fennell's attorney was clothed with apparent authority to settle the case, resulting in denial of the motion to vacate the prior order of dismissal.

We begin with the undisputed proposition that the decision to settle is the client's to make, not the attorney's.... Model Code of Professional Responsibility EC 7-7 (1980) ("in civil cases, it is for the client to decide whether he will accept a settlement offer"). On the other hand, if an attorney has apparent authority to settle a case, and the opposing counsel has no reason to doubt that authority, the settlement will be upheld....

The district court made the following findings concerning the issue of apparent authority: 1) that Mason and his associates represented Fennell "in dealing with the other side," 2) that they were authorized to appear at conferences for him, 3) that Fennell knew that settlement was being discussed, 4) that Fennell did not tell his counsel not to continue discussing settlement, 5) that Fennell would have accepted a higher settlement figure ($50,000–75,000), and 6) that Fennell did not tell defendants' counsel that the authority of plaintiff's counsel was limited in any way. The district court concluded that Fennell's counsel "had every appearance of being authorized to make a binding agreement with [defendants' counsel]." The district court then applied the common law principle that an agent clothed with apparent authority binds the principal as to actions taken within the scope of that authority, together with the principle favoring settlement agreements, to conclude that Fennell was bound by the settlement agreement.

Apparent authority is "the power to affect the legal relations of another person by transactions with third persons, professedly as agent for the other, arising from and in accordance with the other's manifestations to such third persons." Restatement (Second) of Agency § 8 (1958).... Further, in order to create apparent authority, the principal must manifest to the third party that he "consents to have the act done on his behalf by the person purporting to act for him." Id. § 27. Second Circuit case law supports the view that apparent authority is created only by the representations of the principal to the third party, and explicitly rejects the notion that an agent can create apparent authority by his own actions or representations.

In this case, taking the facts as the district court found them, Fennell made no manifestations to defendants' counsel that Mason and his associates were authorized to settle the case. Fennell's attorneys accordingly had no apparent authority to settle the case for $10,000 without Fennell's consent. The district court's findings that Mason and his associates represented Fennell, and that they were authorized to appear at conferences for him, do not prove otherwise. A client does not create apparent authority for his attorney to settle a case merely by retaining the attorney.

Further, the court's findings that Fennell knew settlement was being discussed, did not ask his attorneys not to discuss settlement, would have accepted a higher settlement figure, and did not tell defendant's counsel that the authority of plaintiff's counsel was limited in any way, do not lead to a different outcome. These findings involve only discussions between Fennell and his attorneys or things that Fennell did not say to opposing counsel. None of these findings relates to positive actions or manifestations by Fennell to defendants' counsel that would reasonably lead that counsel to believe that Fennell's attorneys were clothed with apparent authority to agree to a definitive settlement of the litigation....

We realize that the rule we announce here has the potential to burden, at least occasionally, district courts which must deal with constantly burgeoning calendars. A contrary rule, however, would have even more deleterious consequences. Clients should not be faced with a Hobson's choice of denying their counsel all authority to explore settlement or being bound by any settlement to which their counsel might agree, having resort only to an action against their counsel for malpractice. In any event, even if we were to consider such a rule advisable, the applicable precedents and settled principles of agency law would preclude its adoption....

Apparent Authority and Inherent Agency

The Restatement (Second) of Agency § 8A incorporated a doctrine called inherent agency power that applied when a third party harmed by an agent's act was unable to establish actual or apparent authority or to apply the doctrine of estoppel. The doctrine of inherent agency power was developed in some jurisdictions to allocate fairly losses resulting from an agent's unauthorized conduct. That doctrine, which was not well received by the courts, provided part of the basis for the *Koval* decision.

The Restatement (Third) of Agency has eliminated the doctrine of inherent authority. Instead, the Restatement (Third) has added in § 1.03 a broad definition of "manifestation" to cover situations originally dealt with through the doctrine of inherent agency power. The change expands the potential reach of the use of apparent authority to provide relief to an aggrieved third party. The Reporter's notes to § 1.03 explain:

> The definition of manifestation in this section is intended to be broader than that assumed to be operative at points in the Restatement (Second) of Agency. One consequence of this breadth is to eliminate the rationale for a distinct doctrine of inherent-agency power applicable to disclosed principals when an agent disregards instructions or oversteps actual authority. See Re-

statement Second, Agency § 8 A, Comment *b* (noting that in some situations to which the doctrine of inherent agency power is applicable, "the courts have rested liability upon the ground of 'apparent authority'.... If the meaning of the term [apparent authority] is restricted, as is done in Section 8, to those situations in which the principal has manifested the existence of authority to third persons, the term does not apply to the above situations"). In this Restatement, conduct may constitute a manifestation sufficient to create apparent authority even though it does not use the word "authority" and even though it does not consist of words targeted specifically to a third party.[12]

1. The *Koval* and *Fennell* cases address the issue of the enforcement of unauthorized settlement agreements entered into by attorneys on behalf of their clients. Which approach do you prefer? What should a client be required to do, if anything, and when, in order to bring a successful challenge to an unauthorized agreement?

2. What role does Model Rules of Professional Conduct Rule 1.2(a) play in establishing a lawyer's authority with respect to representation of a client?

Rule 1.2 (a) provides:

(a) Subject to paragraphs (c) and (d), a lawyer shall abide by a client's decisions concerning the objectives of representation and, as required by Rule 1.4, shall consult with the client as to the means by which they are to be pursued. A lawyer may take such action on behalf of the client as is impliedly authorized to carry out the representation. A lawyer shall abide by a client's decision whether to settle a matter....[13]

3. A corporation registering to do business in a state other than the one of incorporation is required to appoint an agent for service of process. The agent may be an individual or another company. The document creating the appointment usually must be signed by the corporation (through a representative) and by the agent and filed with the Secretary of State's office. What kind(s) of authority does the document create?

4. Review the facts of the *Cargill* case. Could the plaintiffs have successfully based Cargill's liability on apparent authority?

C. Principal's Liability for Agent's Unauthorized Acts

Agency law has developed doctrines that apply when a third party has been harmed by an agent's unauthorized acts. Depending on the circumstances, an aggrieved person may base recovery on theories of ratification or estoppel. Plaintiffs in jurisdictions whose agency law is based on the Restatement (Second) may potentially use inherent agency power, described above. The doctrine of inherent agency power has been eliminated from the Restatement (Third).

---

12. Restatement (Third) of Agency § 1.03, Reporter's Notes.
13. Model Rules of Professional Conduct Rule 1.2 (American Bar Association Center for Professional Responsibility 2009) (hereinafter "ABA Model Rules of Professional Conduct").

1. Ratification

Daynard v. Ness, Motley

United States Court of Appeals, First Circuit

290 F.3d 42 (2002)

LYNCH, CIRCUIT JUDGE.

[Richard Daynard, a law professor at Northeastern University, sued two Mississippi law firms for breach of an oral agreement to compensate him based on a percentage of fees for work performed in connection with litigation against tobacco companies. The issue on appeal was whether the Massachusetts federal district court could assert personal jurisdiction over the Scruggs Millette law firm and one of its partners (the Scruggs defendants). Daynard claimed that the Ness, Motley law firm acted as the agent of the Scruggs defendants in hiring him. Daynard further alleged that the Ness, Motley law firm's contacts with Massachusetts should be imputed to the Scruggs defendants to establish the court's personal jurisdiction over the Scruggs defendants. The district court ruled in favor of the Scruggs defendants. The Court of Appeals concluded that personal jurisdiction could be established based on contacts established by the Ness, Motley law firm, which acted as agent of the Scruggs defendants.]

The defendant law firms in this case have been responsible for instituting, litigating, and settling litigation against the tobacco industry on behalf of forty-six different states. This settlement was accomplished, in part, in what is known as the Master Settlement Agreement. Daynard says this settlement will result in a distribution of billions of dollars to the two firms.... Daynard says that his efforts were central to many of these titanic recoveries....

The parties agree that Charles Patrick, then a partner at Ness Motley, came to Boston, Massachusetts in the fall of 1993 to meet with Daynard. Daynard says that, at the time Patrick traveled to Boston to retain his services, Ness Motley and Scruggs Millette were engaged in a tobacco litigation joint venture.... Daynard insists that Patrick was acting on behalf of both firms and that Patrick retained him to advance the objectives of the firms' joint venture....

As a result of Ness Motley's retention of him, purportedly on behalf of both firms, Daynard ... began "communicat[ing] regularly" with the Mississippi law firm Scruggs Millette and providing the firm with "advice and assistance." Beginning in the fall of 1993, members of both firms came to Boston to meet with and receive advice from Daynard, in furtherance of his engagement by them. According to his affidavit, Daynard "had many conversations, meetings and written communications in Boston with members of the defendant firms, in which [he] provided advice and undertook specific projects for their use in the tobacco litigation." ...

Initially, Ness Motley compensated Daynard based on hourly fees for his services rendered. As Daynard's relationship with the two firms progressed, he had "several conversations" with "both Mr. Motley and Mr. Scruggs in which they stated that they would appropriately compensate [Daynard] ... and that the final form of compensation would be" in the form of a share of the fees the firms obtained from handling the states' tobacco litigation. Ronald Motley advised Daynard that he would be compensated for his assistance as a member of the Ness Motley "team." After this communication, Daynard says that he received no further compensation from Ness Motley. As to payment by Scruggs Millette, the parties agree that Scruggs Millette never compensated Daynard....

Daynard says that, at a meeting in late August of 1996, Scruggs Millette and Ness Motley "confirmed" their agreement to compensate him in the form of a share of the fees. On August 25 through August 27, 1996, Daynard, Motley, and Scruggs were in Chicago, Illinois, participating in meetings related to the state tobacco litigation. Scruggs and Motley scheduled a meeting with Daynard during that period to discuss Daynard's specific share of any fee award. Although Motley was ultimately not able to attend the meeting, Daynard met with Scruggs. Daynard says he asked Scruggs "whether he was speaking for both himself and Mr. Motley" and Scruggs stated that he was, that Daynard could rely on this, and that he was acting with at least "apparent authority" for Motley. Scruggs promised Daynard 5% of any fees ultimately recovered, in any state tobacco litigation in which any of the defendants were counsel, as compensation for Daynard's past and continuing assistance. Daynard says he accepted the 5% agreement and that he and Scruggs shook hands on it. Based on the conduct of the Scruggs and Motley defendants during the course of the tobacco litigation, Daynard says that he reasonably believed Scruggs to be acting with apparent authority for both firms.

Relying on this 5% figure, and "ongoing assurances and representations," Daynard continued to work for the two firms. For example, Scruggs requested that Daynard be available during the trial in the Mississippi litigation and agreed to compensate Daynard for the cost of paying a substitute teacher to cover his Northeastern University teaching obligations. Daynard agreed by committing $15,000 of his own personal funds to buy himself out of his teaching obligations so that he could be present full-time during the trial.

Almost a year after the alleged handshake on the 5% compensation figure, and after the Mississippi state litigation had reached a tentative settlement, Daynard wrote a letter to Scruggs confirming the fee arrangement and identifying certain expenses that Daynard had incurred associated with the Mississippi litigation. Scruggs never responded. A few months later, Daynard wrote another letter, this time to both Scruggs and Motley, referring to the 5% fee arrangement. At this point, both firms were expecting to reap significant attorney's fees from the Mississippi settlement and also from the Florida settlement. Joseph Rice of Ness Motley and Richard Scruggs both responded to this second letter and both disavowed the 5% fee arrangement. Neither firm has paid Daynard any of the legal fees it has received to date. Daynard alleges that the firms based their refusal to pay him the 5% on his failure to support certain national tobacco liability legislation, a requirement he says the defendants never mentioned in any previous communication....

[The Motley defendants conceded the issue of personal jurisdiction but denied owing Daynard any money, claiming that they had already paid any money due.]

The Scruggs defendants pursued a different legal strategy. On April 20, 2001, they moved to dismiss Daynard's complaint for lack of personal jurisdiction....

Daynard alleges that the relationship between the Motley defendants and the Scruggs defendants is such that some of the Motley defendants' contacts with Massachusetts should be imputed to the Scruggs defendants [for the purposes of establishing personal jurisdiction.]....

For purposes of personal jurisdiction, the actions of an agent may be attributed to the principal. Whether or not an agent is initially authorized to act on behalf of a principal, the agent's actions may be attributed to the principal, for purposes of personal jurisdiction, if the principal later ratifies the agent's conduct....

The facts as alleged by Daynard are sufficient to make the jurisdictional showing that, in Boston, Patrick of Ness Motley hired Daynard, that Daynard reasonably understood Patrick to be acting on behalf of a joint venture or other agency relationship between Ness Motley and Scruggs Millette, and that Daynard relied on this understanding by providing his services to both defendants.

Many of these same facts support the conclusion that the Scruggs defendants subsequently ratified the Motley defendants' conduct. Even if Patrick, when he hired Daynard, was acting without actual authority from the Scruggs defendants, Daynard says Patrick purported to act as an agent for both firms when Patrick retained Daynard, and that Scruggs effectively ratified that representation.

"A person may ratify a prior act done by another without actual or apparent authority ... by ... conduct that is justifiable only on the assumption that the person so consents." Restatement (Third) of Agency § 4.01 (Tentative Draft No. 2, 2001).[14] "The sole requirement for ratification is a manifestation of assent or other conduct indicative of consent by the principal." Restatement (Third) of Agency, *supra*, § 4.01, cmt. b; see also *Inn Foods, Inc. v. Equitable Coop. Bank*, 45 F.3d 594, 597 (1st Cir. 1995) (stating that "[u]nder Massachusetts law, ratification of an agent's acts may be express or implied"). The Scruggs defendants, on the facts alleged, engaged in such conduct.

After Ness Motley retained Daynard, and as a result of this employment, Daynard asserts that he began providing information directly to the Scruggs defendants. Daynard says that he "communicated regularly" with the Scruggs defendants, that they came to Boston to receive his advice, and that he "had many conversations, meetings and written communications in Boston with members of the defendant firms, in which [he] provided advice and undertook specific projects for their use in the tobacco litigation." Even if the Scruggs defendants did not come to Boston, we think there is adequate other evidence of ratification, accepting Daynard's allegations.

Daynard says that he had "several conversations" with "both Mr. Motley and Mr. Scruggs in which they stated that they would appropriately compensate [Daynard] ...

---

14. [9] As described in the Restatement (Second), "Ratification is the affirmance by a person of a prior act which did not bind him but which was done or professedly done on his account, whereby the act, as to some or all persons, is given effect as if originally authorized by him." Restatement (Second) of Agency, *supra*, § 82.

and that the final form of compensation would be" in the form of a share of the fees the firms obtained from handling the state tobacco litigation. Daynard says Ronald Motley advised him that he would be compensated for his assistance as a member of the Ness Motley "team." Further evidence of ratification comes from Daynard's version of the Chicago meeting, where Scruggs said he acted with at least apparent authority for both firms and reached an agreement. Daynard says that Scruggs shook hands on a deal to pay him 5% of these fees. These assurances and reassurances that Daynard would be paid a portion of the recovered fees were an integral part of the ongoing relationship existing between Daynard, the Motley defendants, and the Scruggs defendants.

Finally, Daynard asserts that in reliance on his arrangements with the Scruggs defendants and at their request, he had to commit out-of-pocket expenses of $15,000 to retain someone to meet his teaching obligations. Again, there is no evidence that Scruggs disavowed any contractual relationship as he accepted Daynard's assistance. To be sure, Scruggs says Daynard was a volunteer, but reasonable inferences support Daynard's version.

The Scruggs defendants had many opportunities to disavow a relationship with Daynard or to clarify the relationship. For example, they could have rejected his assistance or accepted it only on certain conditions. Instead, according to Daynard, they repeatedly encouraged and accepted his assistance and during several conversations agreed to pay him in the form of a share of the fees generated. When Daynard wrote his first letter to Scruggs in July 1997 confirming the fee arrangement, Scruggs remained silent.[15]

By knowingly accepting the benefits of the transaction initiated in Massachusetts, the Scruggs defendants ratified Patrick's act of hiring and retaining Daynard on behalf of both firms, which ultimately gave rise to this law suit. *See Inn Foods*, 45 F.3d at 597 n. 7 (noting that "benefits received are certainly strong evidence that the principal acquiesced in the agent's transaction"); Restatement (Third) of Agency, *supra*, § 4.01, cmt. d. In addition, by repeatedly agreeing to compensate Daynard for ongoing work conducted in Massachusetts, agreeing to pay Daynard a share of the fees and later shaking hands on the 5% figure, and accepting his coming from Boston to Mississippi to assist at trial, Scruggs, acting on behalf of his firm and, according to Daynard, the Ness Motley firm as well, ratified the arrangement in which the Motley defendants agreed to pay Daynard for his ongoing services as a member of the team. . . .

We conclude that the Scruggs defendants' contacts properly imputed from the Motley defendants, against the backdrop of the Scruggs defendants' direct contacts with Massachusetts, constitute "minimum contacts" with Massachusetts "such that the maintenance of the suit does not offend 'traditional notions of fair play and sub-

---

15. [10] It was not until November 1997, after Daynard had provided years of services and the firms were expecting to reap significant financial rewards from at least the Mississippi and Florida litigation, that Scruggs responded to Daynard's second letter, after he ignored the first letter, and disavowed the 5% fee arrangement. Daynard asserts that, even at this point, Scruggs disputed only the extent of Daynard's compliance with the agreement, not the existence of the agreement.

stantial justice.'" *Int'l Shoe*, 326 U.S. at 316, 66 S.Ct. 154 (quoting *Milliken*, 311 U.S. at 463, 61 S.Ct. 339).... Nothing in the opinion precludes the Scruggs defendants, in the prospective district court proceedings, from challenging these facts, if they wish, and renewing their jurisdictional challenge, if appropriate....

For these reasons, we *reverse* the dismissal of the Scruggs defendants for lack of personal jurisdiction and *remand* to the district court for further proceedings consistent with this opinion.

The Restatement (Third) of Agency § 4.01 defines ratification and the process by which it is created.

According to Restatement (Third) of Agency § 4.06, in order for ratification to be effective, at the time of ratification the principal must have knowledge of all material facts respecting the act being ratified.

2. Estoppel

Estoppel is a second doctrine that may be used to impose liability on a principal based on an agent's unauthorized acts. The Restatement (Third) of Agency § 2.05 bases estoppel on the principal's inducement of a third party's detrimental reliance. Thus, a principal may be estopped from denying the existence of an agency relationship if the principal caused a third party to believe that (1) an unauthorized act was done on behalf of the principal and (2) the third party detrimentally relied on that belief.

Estoppel differs from apparent authority in both purpose and application. The doctrine of apparent authority is used to impose liability on a principal by establishing that an agent's act was authorized. Apparent authority arises from the principal's manifestations to the third party. In contrast, the doctrine of estoppel is used when the agent's act was unauthorized. Estoppel liability is imposed on the principal because the principal was responsible for inducing the third party's detrimental reliance based on the third party's incorrect understanding that the act in question was done on behalf of the principal.

D. Principal's Liability for Agent's Torts

When liability issues arise in tort rather than contract, the inquiry changes. In contract, the principal is liable for the agent's actually or apparently authorized acts. The agent is also liable only if the principal is unidentified or undisclosed. In tort, however, the primary focus of the analysis is on the principal's liability rather than the liability of the agent. Agents are, whether individuals or entities, personally liable for their own tortious acts.[16]

According to § 7.03 of the Restatement (Third) of Agency, a principal may be liable for an agent's tortious conduct in several ways. First, the principal will be held liable

---

16. Restatement (Third) of Agency § 7.02.

if the agent acts with actual or apparent authority or the principal ratifies the agent's act. Further, liability may be imposed on the principal if the principal is negligent in choosing or supervising the agent or if the agent fails to perform a duty to act carefully that has been delegated to the agent by the principal. And finally, a principal will be liable for the acts of an employee acting within the scope of employment.[17]

The factual inquiry as to whether or not an agent is an employee focuses on the extent to which the principal has the right to control the manner and means of the performance of the agent's work.[18] A determination of whether an agent's acts were within the "scope of employment" is based on § 7.07(2) of Restatement (Third), which is discussed in the case below.

The Restatement (Third) of Agency has eliminated some of the terminology found in the Restatement (Second) of Agency. The later Restatement uses the term "employee" in lieu of the word "servant" to denote someone who acts within an employer's control and may subject the employer to liability for tortious acts. Further, the Restatement (Second) distinguishes between agents who are servants (employees) and those who are independent contractors. Under the Restatement (Second) a principal may be liable for the torts of a servant but is not usually liable for the torts of an independent contractor unless the activity involved is inherently dangerous or the principal was negligent in selecting the independent contractor. The text of the Restatement (Third) eliminates this distinction and focuses instead on whether an agency relationship has been formed between the parties in question.

Papa John's International, Inc. v. McCoy

Kentucky Supreme Court
244 S.W.3d 44 (2008)

MINTON, JUSTICE.

… [This case arose] in the context of a malicious prosecution and defamation lawsuit filed by a customer as a result of a Papa John's pizza delivery gone wrong. [The plaintiff was the customer, Gary McCoy, who ordered two pizzas from RWT, Inc. a franchisee doing business as Papa John's Pizza. McCoy sued both RWT, Inc. [RWT] and Papa John's International, Inc., the franchisor. [Papa John's] The circuit court granted summary judgment in favor of the defendants. The Court of Appeals concluded that genuine issues of material fact precluded summary judgment.]

As is well-settled in our case law, the driver's employer, RWT, is subject to vicarious liability for a tort committed by its employee acting within the scope of employment. We conclude that the acts complained of here occurred within an independent course of conduct that could not have been intended by the driver to serve any purpose of the employer. So, although for different reasons that we will discuss below, we conclude that the circuit court properly granted summary judgment dismissing the malicious

17. *Id.* § 2.04.
18. *Id.* § 7.07(3)(a).

prosecution claim against RWT. Accordingly, we reverse the Court of Appeals as to RWT....

Gary McCoy is a resident of Prestonsburg, Kentucky.... On the evening of February 18, 2000, [he] ordered the pizzas from a Papa John's store ... [a]nd he asked if the delivery driver could stop off at his business for payment....

The delivery driver that night was Wendell Burke. Burke delivered the two pizzas and then stopped at McCoy's business for payment. Burke and McCoy tell two stories of what occurred next, although their versions are not entirely different.

According to McCoy, after McCoy paid him, Burke remained at McCoy's business in McCoy's office and inquired about employment. McCoy was preoccupied with other matters, and it became obvious to him that Burke had no intention of leaving. So McCoy placed a hunting video in his VCR and told Burke to watch it. McCoy admitted that he had a beer can on his desk while Burke was in his office and a rifle in one corner of his office. The tape lasted about fifteen minutes. When the tape concluded, Burke left. After Burke left, McCoy received a call from the Papa John's store during which they inquired as to Burke's whereabouts.

According to Burke, when he arrived at McCoy's business, McCoy asked him to come in, which Burke did. McCoy took Burke back to his office where he paid him for the two pizzas. McCoy asked Burke to sit and talk awhile. McCoy expressed to Burke that he had been having suicidal and homicidal thoughts and had visions. While talking to him, Burke alleges that McCoy was drinking liquor and chasing it with beer. And at one point when Burke attempted to leave, McCoy stood up, picked up a rifle, showed it to Burke, and then laid it on his desk. While Burke was there, McCoy took several phone calls. After hanging up from one of the phone calls, McCoy informed Burke that that call had been from the Papa John's store; and they were inquiring as to Burke's whereabouts. Eventually, the subject of deer hunting came up; and McCoy asked Burke to watch a videotape of one of his deer hunting trips with him. When the tape ended, McCoy got up to take the tape out; and Burke slipped out. He returned to Papa John's about an hour and a half to two hours after he first left the store to deliver the pizzas.

Upon hearing Burke's version of the story and observing that Burke was quite upset, another employee of the Papa John's store felt that he should tell the police what had occurred and contacted them for him.... A few hours later, the officers obtained a warrant and arrested McCoy at his home on the charge of unlawful imprisonment in the first degree. The local newspaper ran a story about the arrest a few days later.

A little over two months after the arrest, the district court, on McCoy's motion and with no opposition by the county attorney, dismissed the charge against McCoy.... The amended final judgment reflected that the district court dismissed the charges against Gary McCoy with prejudice and with no stipulations. [After the charges were dismissed, McCoy brought suit against RWT and Papa John's, alleging malicious prosecution and defamation.]

McCoy sued RWT, Burke's employer, under a vicarious liability/respondeat superior theory. Under the doctrine of respondeat superior, RWT can be held vicariously liable for Burke's actions if he committed the tortious acts in the scope of his employment.

[T]he concept of scope of employment is complex. And it is even more complex when the alleged tort in question is intentional, as is malicious prosecution, as opposed to the result of employee negligence. In the area of intentional torts, however, the focus is consistently on the purpose or motive of the employee in determining whether he or she was acting within the scope of employment. For example, our predecessor court has held that an employee bus driver did not act within his scope of employment when he stopped the employer's bus in the middle of the street, left the bus, and assaulted another driver in a fit of road rage. In that case, the employee's motive was to settle a personal controversy; there being no issue of fact, the case stood dismissed for failure to state a cause of action. But an employee store clerk acted within the scope of his employment when he shot and killed a person in a grocery store during what he believed was a robbery. In that case, the employee's purpose was to protect the premises; scope of employment was not a jury question. And this Court has held that an automobile dealership employee acted within the scope of his employment when he sought to repossess a vehicle by intercepting a person at a stoplight, demanding that he get out of the car, and shooting the tires out on the vehicle when the person refused to get out. In that case, the trial court was correct in allowing the jury to impute liability to the employer for the employee's actions because he was acting at all times within the scope of his employment.

... [T]he American Law Institute has written the **Restatement (Third) of Agency** § 7.07 (2006) [Now § 7.03], entitled "Employee Acting Within Scope of Employment." It is as follows:

(1) An employer is subject to vicarious liability for a tort committed by its employee acting within the scope of employment.

(2) An employee acts within the scope of employment when performing work assigned by the employer or engaging in a course of conduct subject to the employer's control. An employee's act is not within the scope of employment when it occurs within an independent course of conduct not intended by the employee to serve any purpose of the employer.

(3) For purposes of this section,

(a) an employee is an agent whose principal controls or has the right to control the manner and means of the agent's performance of work, and

(b) the fact that work is performed gratuitously does not relieve a principal of liability.

This general rule is consistent with the standard advanced by Prosser and Keeton ... in their treatise on tort law: "[I]n general, ... the master is held liable for any intentional tort committed by the servant where its purpose, however misguided, is wholly or in part to further the master's business."[19] Thus, if the servant "acts from purely personal motives ... which [are] in no way connected with the employer's interests, he is considered in the ordinary case to have departed from his employment, and the

---

19. [16] W. Page Keeton, et al., Prosser and Keeton on the Law of Torts 505 (5th ed. 1984).

master is not liable."[20] This approach "conforms to the economic theory of vicarious liability ... because when the employee acts for solely personal reasons, the employer's ability to prevent the tort is limited."[21]

Turning to the facts of this case, RWT's business was pizza and pizza delivery. Burke was supposed to deliver the two pizzas, collect payment, and return to the store to pick up more pizzas for delivery. Making a false statement to the police about a customer is no way connected to RWT's business. Indeed, there seems no more certain way to send customers to another pizza place than to accuse them falsely of imprisoning delivery drivers when they are delivering pizza. The motive alleged by McCoy is that Burke was trying to account for the inordinate amount of time that he loitered at McCoy's business. Another theory of McCoy's is that Burke's purpose was to accuse McCoy falsely of committing a crime so that he could later sue him in a civil lawsuit and obtain a judgment against him, a man who owned two businesses. But under either theory, Burke's actions did not serve any purpose of RWT; the motives advanced for Burke's conduct are purely personal. His actions, as alleged, are totally independent of RWT's purpose of pizza delivery.

If, for whatever reason, Burke did not intentionally make a false statement to the officers—either he was simply confused about what had occurred or told the truth about what had occurred—then there is no tort; and no one is liable. But if he did lie, ... then he was acting outside the scope of his employment; and RWT is not subject to vicarious liability for a tort committed by its employee acting outside the scope of employment.... [W]e conclude, nonetheless, that there being no genuine issue of material fact, summary judgment in favor of RWT was appropriate.

McCoy argues that RWT is liable for Burke's conduct under two different theories: (1) he was acting within the scope of his employment at the time, which theory we rejected in the preceding discussion; and (2) RWT ratified the act. However, McCoy cannot demonstrate ratification in this case. So we reject this argument, as well.

In order to have ratified Burke's alleged malicious prosecution of McCoy, RWT had to have both (1) knowledge that Burke's statement was false and (2) the intention to ratify it. But McCoy can point to no facts that support his contention that RWT had knowledge that Burke's statement was false. The only two persons who know what happened that night between Burke and McCoy are Burke and McCoy. Burke has never renounced his allegation against McCoy. McCoy's malicious prosecution claim against Burke will not be resolved until a jury decides the case. And for that reason, McCoy's vicarious liability claim against RWT under a ratification theory fails as a matter of law....

Under the doctrine of respondeat superior, an employer can be held vicariously liable for an employee's tortious actions if committed in the scope of his or her em-

---

20. [17] Id. at 506.
21. [18] Patterson, 172 S.W.3d at 369 (*citing* William M. Landes & Richard A. Posner, The Economic Structure of Tort Law, 208–09 (1987)).

ployment. In the area of intentional torts, the focus is consistently on the purpose or motive of the employee in determining whether he or she was acting within the scope of employment. Here, we conclude that the acts complained of occurred within an independent course of conduct that could not have been intended by the employee to serve any purpose of the employer.... We reverse the opinion of the Court of Appeals and reinstate the judgment of the trial court for RWT ... on all claims.

Opinion by JUSTICE SCOTT Concurring in Part and Dissenting in Part.

... [T]he majority goes too far in insulating employers from liability for intentional torts committed by their employees. Thus, I write separately to address the malicious prosecution claim against RWT, Inc. In my view, summary judgment on that claim was improper because there is a genuine issue of material fact as to whether Wendell Burke, the delivery driver, was acting within the scope of his employment with RWT at the time of the reporting of the matter. Remember it was the false reporting of the incident that McCoy alleges caused the injury....

In this matter, there is evidence that Burke was acting within the scope of his employment at the time the unlawful imprisonment charge, which was based on events that allegedly occurred on the job, was filed. After stating that he had been held captive against his will at McCoy's office, Burke told his coworkers that he did not want to call the police, nor press charges. Despite this, Burke's supervisors recommended that the police be called and actually made the call. RWT management even provided a written statement to the police. It was primarily those managers, not Burke, who wanted the charge brought against McCoy. Burke only did so at the advice and direction of RWT, his employer. These facts, which tend to show that RWT was not just a mere bystander to the tort, are sufficient to preclude summary judgment.

While I believe without a doubt that the scope of employment issue should be for the jury to decide, I do not mean to suggest that McCoy will necessarily prevail against RWT on his malicious prosecution claim. I do, however, believe that the present case should proceed on the merits, regardless of the anticipated outcome, because RWT entangled itself in the controversy between Burke and McCoy by making its reporting an employment-related matter. I therefore dissent.

Notes and Questions

1. Questions of the principal's liability for an agent's tortious acts have arisen in numerous contexts. Many of the following examples are based on the Restatement (Second), but they are equally apposite to situations arising under the Restatement (Third). In *Burlington Industries, Inc. v. Ellerth*, 524 U.S. 742 (1998), the United States Supreme Court held that a plaintiff in a Title VII sexual harassment suit could base recovery on any one of three theories based on agency law. The Court stated that "[a]n employer is subject to vicarious liability to a victimized employee for an actionable hostile environment created by a supervisor with immediate (or successively higher) authority over the employee." Alternatively, an employer may be liable for the torts of employees committed within the scope of employment. Employers may also be liable for conduct outside the scope of employment if the employer knew or

should have known about the sexual harassment and failed to stop it. And finally, liability may also be based upon the apparent authority of a harassing employee.

2. For an employer, the question whether or not a worker is determined to be an employee has significance beyond the issue of the employer's liability for the worker's tortious acts. The issue is central to the application of federal and state employment laws, to an employer's obligations to make specified deductions under federal employment tax laws, and to the determination of eligibility for employment benefit plans. For example, an employer is subject to withholding and/or payment of payroll (FICA) and unemployment (FUTA) taxes if a worker is an employee. In these situations, the test most frequently used is the "common law" test involving consideration of many factors. Workers qualifying as employees under the common law agency rules will be classified as employees for federal tax purposes. The cost of these taxes may be significant.

3. Congress and the courts have struggled with the difficulties of defining the boundaries separating individuals who are classified as employees from those who are not. For example, in *Vizcaino v. Microsoft Corporation*, 120 F.3d 1006 (9th Cir. 1997), Microsoft entered into contracts with several workers to perform various types of production services. The workers' contracts classified them as independent contractors. As a result of an IRS audit, the workers were determined to be employees. After that determination was made, the workers claimed eligibility for benefits under the employer's savings and stock purchase plans. After rehearing en banc, the Court of Appeals, Fernandez, Circuit Judge, held that the classification by the IRS of the workers as employees, rather than independent contractors, made them eligible for employee benefits, even though they had been labeled as independent contractors in the employment agreements. Although the workers in the *Microsoft* case sought employee benefits after the IRS had reclassified them as employees, in other cases the workers themselves have sought the reclassification from independent contractor to employee status. *See Trombetta v. Cragin Federal Bank for Savings Employees Stock Ownership Plan*, 102 F.3d 1435 (7th Cir. 1996).

4. Attorneys are agents of their clients. They may, however, have different types of agency relationships with their clients. Consider the following: Duane Margolis is Vice President and General Counsel of Invent Co. and Susan Harris is Invent Co.'s outside counsel. Compare each attorney's relationship with Invent Co.

5. Comment [1] of the ABA Model Rules of Professional Conduct Rule 1.3 states, "A lawyer has professional discretion in determining the means by which a matter should be pursued." What type of agent is envisioned in this comment?

E. Agent's Liability — Disclosed, Unidentified, and Undisclosed Principals

In some situations in which the agent enters into a contract on behalf of the principal, only the principal is liable on the contract. In others, both the principal and the agent are liable for the agent's acts. When the third party knows both the identity of the principal and that the agent is acting on the principal's behalf, the principal is considered to be disclosed and only the principal is liable on the contract. When the third party knows only of the agency relationship, but not the identity of the principal, the principal is unidentified. In this situation both the agent and the principal are liable on the contract. And finally, if the third party knows neither that an agency relationship exists nor the identity of the principal, the principal is undisclosed. Again, both the agent and the principal are liable.

Situations concerning disclosed, unidentified and undisclosed principals arise in a variety of contexts. One involves the purchase of property, where a buyer may want to conceal his or her identity from the seller during the negotiation process to avoid the risk of an inflated price. A convenient way to accomplish this result is to have an agent purchase the property on the buyer's behalf without disclosing the buyer's true identity. These issues may also arise because a contract did not accurately identify the parties or was not signed properly (or both).

You recall that the court in the *Cargill* case (Section III. A. of this chapter), imposed liability on both Cargill and Warren despite the court's conclusion that Cargill was a disclosed principal. As the preceding paragraphs indicate, the general rule is that agents are not liable on contracts in which principals are disclosed. Agents are only personally liable for contracts in which the principals are unidentified or undisclosed. Although the plaintiffs claimed only actual authority, they may have also been able to base their claim on apparent authority (Cargill told the plaintiffs that they would be paid) or estoppel.

African Bio-Botanica v. Leiner

New Jersey Superior Court, Appellate Division
624 A.2d 1003 (1993)

BROCHIN, J.A.D.

Plaintiff African Bio-Botanica, Inc. sued defendant "Sally Leiner, individually and t/a Ecco Bella," in the Special Civil Part to recover $1530 as the unpaid purchase price of merchandise that it had sold and delivered to her. Ms. Leiner is the sole stockholder, director, and president of Ecco Bella Incorporated, a New Jersey corporation that was formed October 28, 1987, and that continued in existence during all times pertinent to the law suit. Ms. Leiner defended against plaintiff's claim solely on the ground that the merchandise had been ordered by and delivered to Ecco Bella Incorporated, and that the liability was solely that of the corporation.

The case was tried to the court. The evidence showed that plaintiff began selling merchandise to Ms. Leiner or to her corporation in December 1987. African Bio-Botanica, Inc. did not conduct any credit investigation. It did not inquire or, insofar as appears from the evidence, think about, whether its customer was an individual or a corporation. It sold the first six or seven orders for cash on delivery. Plaintiff's sales manager delivered two of the early shipments to Ms. Leiner's home, where she repackaged the merchandise for resale to retail customers. Later orders were directed to "Ecco Bella" at Ms. Leiner's address and shipped on fifteen days' credit. Initially, plaintiff's records listed Sally Leiner as the customer; subsequently, Ms. Leiner's name was whited out and the name, Ecco Bella, was substituted, without any indication that it was a corporation.

The order for the merchandise that is the subject matter of this law suit was placed either by Ms. Leiner herself or by others at her direction. Plaintiff addressed its bill for the purchase price to "Ecco Bella." That bill admittedly remains unpaid. Plaintiff received payment for prior orders by checks imprinted with the name "Ecco Bella." Ms. Leiner's company's letterhead also read "Ecco Bella." Neither the checks nor the letterhead carried the name "Ecco Bella Incorporated" or otherwise indicated that Ecco Bella was a corporation. Plaintiff's sales manager testified, without contradiction, that no one had told him Ecco Bella was a corporation and he did not know that it was.

The trial judge held that Ms. Leiner's failure to affirmatively disclose the corporate status of her company led the plaintiff to believe that it was a sole proprietorship and that, since it had not filed a trade name certificate, N.J.S.A. 14A:2-2(1)(d) required it to indicate its corporate status on its letterhead, presumably by using its full corporate name, Ecco Bella Incorporated. For those reasons, the judge ruled that Ms. Leiner was personally liable for plaintiff's unpaid bill, and he entered judgment for $1530, but he did not award prejudgment interest.

Ms. Leiner has appealed from the judgment. African Bio-Botanica, Inc. has cross-appealed, challenging the court's denial of pre-judgment interest. For the following reasons, we modify the judgment to award interest from the date the complaint was filed, and we otherwise affirm.

We agree with the trial judge that for Ms. Leiner to be shielded from personal liability, she was required to affirmatively disclose to plaintiff that she was acting as agent for Ecco Bella Incorporated. She failed to make her representative capacity clear. We therefore affirm, but we prefer to offer a somewhat different rationale for our decision from that adopted by the trial court....

A corporation acts only through its agents. In the present case, Ms. Leiner claims that when she entered into contracts with plaintiff for the purchase of its products, she did so only on behalf of her corporate principal, Ecco Bella Incorporated. Whether or not she is personally liable on those contracts must therefore be determined in accordance with the law of principal and agent.

Unless the parties agree otherwise, an agent who enters into a contract for an undisclosed or for a partly disclosed [unidentified] principal is personally liable on the contract; an agent who contracts on behalf of a fully disclosed principal is not personally liable on the contract. The Restatement (Second) of Agency § 4 (1958) defines "disclosed principal," "partially disclosed principal," and "undisclosed principal" as follows:

> (1) If, at the time of a transaction conducted by an agent, the other party thereto has notice that the agent is acting for a principal and of the principal's identity, the principal is a disclosed principal.

(2) If the other party has notice that the agent is or may be acting for a principal but has no notice of the principal's identity, the principal for whom the agent is acting is a partially disclosed [unidentified] principal.

(3) If the other party has no notice that the agent is acting for a principal, the one for whom he acts is an undisclosed principal.

"Notice" is defined as follows: (1) A person has notice of a fact if he knows the fact, has reason to know it, should know it, or has been given notification of it. (2) A person is given notification of a fact by another if the latter (a) informs him of the fact by adequate or specified means or of other facts from which he has reason to know or should know the facts; ... Restatement (Second) of Agency § 9 (1958).

In the present case, the court found as a fact, with adequate support in the record, that African Bio-Botanica, Inc. was not informed and did not know that Ecco Bella was a corporation. The record gives no indication that African Bio-Botanica, Inc. was "inform[ed] of other facts from which [it had] reason to know or should [have known]" that Ecco Bella was a corporation. Consequently, according to the Restatement definition, it did not have "notice" that Ecco Bella was a corporation unless the law is that it should have asked and, therefore, had "reason to know" or "should [have known]" of its customer's corporate status even if it did not ask.

Fairness and expediency dictate a contrary rule. The agent who seeks protection from his status as agent has the means and the motive to communicate that status to the person with whom he is dealing. If the person with whom the agent is dealing does not know of the agency and has no reasonable way to know except by asking, the agent has the burden of disclosing his agency and the identity of his principal in order to avoid liability on contracts which he makes. In that situation the person with whom the agent is dealing has no duty to inquire. [3A William M. Fletcher, Fletcher Encyclopedia of the Law of Private Corporations (perm. Ed. Rev. vol. 1986)] § 279, states:

> A corporate agent is required to disclose his or her agency status in order to avoid personal liability. This is in keeping with the general agency principle that if an agent fails to reveal his or her true status as [an] agent, he or she is bound as [a] principal. *The duty of disclosure clearly lies with the agent alone, so that a third party with whom the agent deals has no duty to discover the existence of the agency or to discover the identity of the principal.* Accordingly, the agent is not relieved from personal liability on the contract involving an undisclosed or partially disclosed principal merely because the party with whom he or she deals had the theoretical means of discovering that the agent was acting only in a representative capacity....

If an agent conducts business candidly as an agent for a disclosed principal, he should be readily able to prove that he disclosed his agency. The allocation of the burdens of proof between the purported agent and the third party with whom he deals reflects this reality. One bringing an action upon a contract has the burden of showing that the other is a party to it. This initial burden is satisfied if the plaintiff proves that the defendant has made a promise, the form of which does not indicate that it was given as agent. The defendant then has the burden of going forward if he wishes to show that his promise was made only as an agent and that this should have been so understood. Restatement (Second) of Agency, supra, § 320 Comment b.

In the present case, the evidence shows that Ms. Leiner entered into an oral purchase contract, either directly or through a subagent acting at her direction. She therefore has the burden of proving that she disclosed that she was buying merchandise solely as an agent on behalf of Ecco Bella Incorporated, a corporation. The trial court found that she did not sustain that burden. The fact that African Bio-Botanica, Inc. had the opportunity to inquire did not put it on notice that its customer was a corporation. If Ms. Leiner was acting as an agent for her corporation, she was an agent for an undisclosed or partially disclosed principal and she was therefore personally liable on its purchase contracts.... [Affirmed.]

F. Fiduciary Duties of Agents and Principals

1. Fiduciary Duties of Agents

Agents occupy positions of trust. They deal with their principals' property, make representations on their principals' behalf, and engaging in acts that may impose legal liability on their principals. Agents often engage in these activities when their principals are absent. Thus, principals are not always able to monitor their agents' conduct to make sure that the agents are acting in the principals' best interests rather than serving the interests of third parties or the agents themselves. To address this situation, the law implies fiduciary obligations into every agency relationship. These obligations provide general guidelines for agents' conduct and require agents to act in their principals' best interests. The penalties for breaching these duties can be severe.

a. The Fiduciary Duty of Loyalty

Section 8.01 of the Restatement of the Law (Third) of Agency establishes the agent's duty of loyalty.

The comment to Section 8.01 elaborates:

... Although an agent's interests are often concurrent with those of the principal, the general fiduciary principle requires that the agent subordinate the agent's interests to those of the principal and place the principal's interests first as to matters connected with the agency relationship....

The fiduciary principle supplements manifestations that a principal makes to an agent, making it unnecessary for the principal to graft explicit qualifications and prohibitions onto the principal's statements of authorization to the agent.[22]

In fulfilling the obligations of the duty of loyalty to the principal, the agent must not acquire an improper personal, material benefit,[23] act on behalf of an adverse

22. Restatement (Third) of Agency § 8.01, Comment b.
23. *Id.* § 8.02.

party,[24] compete with the principal,[25] or improperly use the principal's property or disclose the principal's confidential information.[26] In certain situations, however, an agent will not be liable for a breach of the duty of loyalty if, with knowledge of all material facts, the principal consents to the act in question.[27] The following case explores these issues in the context of the sale of a business.

Huong Que, Inc. v. Luu

California Court of Appeals, Sixth District
58 Cal. Rptr. 3d 527 (2007)

RUSHING P.J.

Appellants Mui Luu and Cu Tu Nguyen challenge an order temporarily enjoining them from engaging in certain activities found by the trial court to constitute, among other things, tortious disloyalty to, and interference with the business of, plaintiffs Huong Que, Inc., and Con Tu. Appellants contend that the trial court erred in finding that plaintiffs were likely to succeed on the merits in several of their claims. We find no error, and affirm.

Plaintiff Con is the president and sole owner of plaintiff Huong Que, Inc., a California corporation (Huong Que). According to the complaint Huong Que is a "Vietnamese calendar distribution corporation" founded by appellants Nguyen and Luu, under whom it became, over 20 years, "the most well known, recognized and trusted brand name for traditional style Vietnamese calendars" known as " 'Bloc calendars.' " At the beginning of 2003, appellants-who are apparently husband and wife-sold the corporation to plaintiff Con under a written contract. In a portion of the contract entitled "Purchase and Sale," plaintiffs agreed to pay appellants $205,000 in three annual installments. In a section [of the contract] entitled "Compensation Agreement," plaintiffs agreed to pay bonus and "pension amount[s]" of $100,700 to appellant Nguyen and $161,750 to appellant Luu. In a section entitled "Management Agreement," appellants agreed to "act as Buyer's Managing Agents for a minimum period of four (4) years from January 1, 2003," during which time they would "provide Buyer with business dealings, bookkeeping activities, and design of publishing samples." Plaintiffs undertook to pay appellants' expenses in rendering these services, including "air fares, transportation, lodging, and meals." They further agreed to pay $3,000 monthly to Luu, plus $1,150.74 monthly "to continue the current lease" of Nguyen's Mercedes Benz.

The "Purchase and Sale" section of the agreement included a paragraph entitled "Covenant not to Compete," which provided in its entirety, "Shareholders [i.e., appellants] shall not directly or indirectly, carry on or engage in, as an owner, the business of publishing services except for publishing Buddhist bible and book." ...

---

24. *Id.* § 8.03.
25. *Id.* § 8.04.
26. *Id.* § 8.05.
27. *Id.* § 8.06.

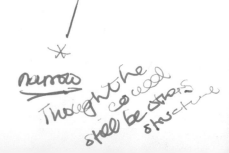

It is asserted by plaintiffs, and not disputed by appellants, that on May 23, 2005, plaintiffs discovered an e-mail message entitled "address list" in the electronic mailbox of appellant Luu.[28] The message constituted an apparent response by one Huan Nguyen to an earlier message from Luu in which she had written, "Please remember to email address list to me." His reply stated, "Attached are customers' addresses and meeting's report on 5/22/05. Please forward to other procalendar's members." Attached to the e-mail was a text file in Vietnamese, which plaintiffs later translated into English. Entitled "Minutes of meeting regard [*sic*] creation of PROCALENDAR," it called for the formation of a company using capitalization of $100,000 in five equal shares, of which two ($40,000) would be distributed to one Amy Khuu "c/o Mr. & Mrs. Nguyen Tu Cu,[29] Mr. Phan Don." The minutes set forth, among other things, the "responsibilities of each partner...." As relevant here, they stated, "Mrs. Luu Mui will be responsible for bookkeeping, tax, contact with Taiwan for calendar/book printing for customer, and distributing calendar for customer-no direct contact with customer, and no salary.... Mr. Cu[30] will be responsible for direct sales with Mr. Xanh, no salary."

Also attached to the e-mail, according to a declaration by plaintiff ... was a document entitled "2001address.xls." This consisted of a list, as he declared, of "approximately 1000 names and addresses," of which he said "approximately ninety percent ... are names and address on Huong Que's customer list."

On July 26, 2005, plaintiffs Con and Huong Que filed a complaint naming as defendants Nguyen and Luu, as well as one Don Phan, and two business entities: Pro Enterprise, LLC, described as a limited liability company, and Pro Calendar, "a business entity, form unknown." In later filings, appellants stated that Pro Enterprise, LLC, did business under the name of Pro Calendar....

In their complaint plaintiffs alleged, among other things, that in 2004, appellants "began to neglect their duties" as managing agents; that in March 2005, they stopped performing those duties entirely; and that they misappropriated Huong Que's customer list and used it to solicit business for Pro Calendar. They asserted causes of action for breach of contract, breach of the implied covenant of good faith and fair dealing,

---

28. [2] A Huong Que employee, Binh Tu, declared that when he first worked there the enterprise had no e-mail accounts for its employees, who therefore used their own accounts to conduct company business, including contacts with customers. Because appellant Luu "had limited knowledge of the internet and e-mail," she would often ask Tu to "help her log onto the Internet and log onto her e-mail account and help her check and send e-mail messages." Toward that end she gave him her user name and password. Beginning in 2004, he declared, appellants stopped actively attending to Huong Que business. He then began logging in to Luu's email account using the user name and password she had given him, "to check for emails having to do with Huong Que business." This is how he discovered the message at issue.

29. [3] We infer that this was a reference to appellants. "Nguyen Tu Cu" is presumably the Vietnamese rendering of "Cu Tu Nguyen." Vietnamese naming conventions reverse the European order, with family name followed by middle and then given name. (See Vietnamese Names, Things Asian <http://www.thingsasian.com/stories-photos/1044> (as of Apr. 30, 2007)).

30. [4] In Vietnamese the ordinary form of address, or at least formal address, is title followed by given name. Thus "Mr. Cu" presumably refers to appellant Cu Tu Nguyen. (See Vietnamese Names, Things Asian <http://www.thingsasian.com/stories-photos/1044> (as of Apr. 30, 2007)).

breach of the duty of trust and loyalty arising from appellants' positions as managing agents, misappropriation of a trade secret, i.e., Huong Que's customer list, and tortious interference with Huong Que's relations with its existing customers. Plaintiffs prayed for compensatory and punitive damages, and temporary and permanent injunctive relief. [Plaintiffs also filed for a preliminary injunction, which the trial court issued.]

I. *Rule of Decision and Standard of Review*

The ultimate questions on a motion for a preliminary injunction are (1) whether the plaintiff is "likely to suffer greater injury from a denial of the injunction than the defendants are likely to suffer from its grant," and (2) whether there is "a reasonable probability that the plaintiffs will prevail on the merits." *Robbins v. Superior Court* (1985) 38 Cal.3d 199, 206, 211 Cal.Rptr. 398, 695 P.2d 695....

II. *Breach of Duty of Loyalty*

A. *Introduction*

Plaintiffs alleged in their complaint that defendants Nguyen and Luu, while employed by plaintiffs "in a position of trust and confidence" as managing agents, owed a duty of loyalty to plaintiffs, which they breached by, in essence, using their positions at Huong Que, and information acquired in those positions, to compete with it. The elements of a cause of action for breach of a duty of loyalty, by analogy to a claim for breach of fiduciary duty, are as follows: (1) the existence of a relationship giving rise to a duty of loyalty; (2) one or more breaches of that duty; and (3) damage proximately caused by that breach. The trial court's ruling necessarily implies that plaintiffs were likely to establish each of these elements to the satisfaction of a fact finder at trial.... Appellants raise a host of points in derogation of that finding, which we will analyze under the elements to which they relate.

B. *Duty of Loyalty*

Appellants' main challenge appears to be that no duty of loyalty can be imposed upon them without running afoul of the rights the parties voluntarily created in their contract [with plaintiffs]. The argument is rather nebulous, but centers on the propositions that appellants had "limited duties" under the contract, the terms of which "should control the obligations between the parties." To fully evaluate this contention it is necessary to review the law of agency with respect to the duty of loyalty on which the present cause of action rests.

The duty of loyalty arises not from a contract but from a relationship — here, the relationship of principal and agent. Agency is "the fiduciary relationship that arises when one person (a 'principal') manifests assent to another person (an 'agent') that the agent shall act on the principal's behalf and subject to the principal's control, and the agent manifests assent or otherwise consents so to act." (Rest.3d, Agency, § 1.01.) Where such a relationship arises, the agent assumes "a fiduciary duty to act loyally for the principal's benefit in all matters connected with the agency relationship." (*Id.* § 8.01.)

While the creation of an agency relationship requires the assent of both parties, it does not require or depend on the law of contracts. "The consensual aspect of agency does not mean that an enforceable contract underlies or accompanies each relation of agency. Many agents act or promise to act gratuitously. While *either acting as an agent or promising to do so creates an agency relation*, neither the promise to act gratuitously nor an act in response to the principal's request for gratuitous service creates an enforceable contract." (Rest.3d, Agency, § 1.01, com. d, p. 21, italics added.)

Here there is ample evidence that appellants assented to act as agents for plaintiffs; after all, their agreement explicitly characterized them as such. They seem to suggest, however, that notwithstanding this agreement, to find them bound by a duty of loyalty, and particularly a duty not to compete, would conflict with the purchase contract's non-competition clause, which only prohibited appellants from competing with plaintiffs "as an owner." There is no logical conflict between this prohibition and a recognition of a distinct, additional duty of loyalty arising from the parties' relationship.[31] Appellants imply, however, that the effect of the contractual provision was to *limit* any restriction on their right to compete, so that they were only forbidden to compete "as an owner." They thus appear to invoke, albeit tacitly, the maxim *expressio unius exclusio alterius est*, i.e., "mention of one matter implies the exclusion of all others." But that rule can only be invoked if a contract is ambiguous, in which case "other legal techniques for the resolution of ambiguities … also come into play," including the admission of extrinsic evidence "to prove the intent of the parties."

We are directed to nothing on the face of the contract, and certainly to no extrinsic evidence, that would support the supposition that the parties intended to excuse appellants from the duty of loyalty otherwise flowing from their agency relationship. On the contrary, the non-competition clause appeared in a part of the contract concerning the provisions outlining the sale of the entity, under the heading "Purchase and Sale." This was followed by a section entitled "Compensation Agreement," reciting the sum due to each appellant as "bonus" and "pension amount." Appellants' undertaking to act for four years as "managing agents" appeared under the separate heading "Management Agreement." The non-competition clause could readily be understood as intended not to affect appellants' duties as agents or employees, but only to obligate them as sellers. We cannot say that the trial court erred in failing to find that appellants' interpretation of the agreement was the one likely to prevail at trial. …

… In the absence of an agreement to the contrary, appellants, as agents, owed a duty of undivided loyalty, including a duty not to compete, to plaintiffs, their principals. Viewed through the lens of contract law, plaintiffs were entitled to consider this duty of loyalty an integral part of the relationship, just as a buyer expects an automobile to come with tires. If appellants wished to modify or delimit the duties imposed on them by law — to deliver a car without tires — it was incumbent upon them to make

---

31. [5] The two duties would not be wholly duplicative of one another in any event. As agents or employees, appellants would presumably not be barred from owning part or all of a competing concern, so long as they refrained from acting disloyally toward plaintiffs. Working for Ford does not disable one from buying stock in General Motors. The contract provision, however, did have this effect. Also, the duty of loyalty flowing from the agency relationship would tend to exist only for the duration of the relationship, which was agreed to be four years. The contractual prohibition included no termination date and would therefore presumably persist for a reasonable time.

that modification or delimitation an express subject of the contract. They could not rely on the contract's silence to excuse them from the legal consequences of disloyalty to their principals.

Appellants assert that their employment agreement was "essentially ... a consulting contract" and that they should not be burdened with a duty of loyalty merely because, in selling their business, they agreed to perform "simple post-sale consulting duties." ... An agent may be distinguished in this respect from a "service provider [who] simply furnishes advice and does not interact with third parties as the representative of the recipient of the advice...." (Rest.3d, Agency, § 1.01, com. c., p. 19.) The absence of a representative capacity, however, does not necessarily excuse such a provider from any duty of loyalty; an "adviser may be subject to a fiduciary duty of loyalty even when the adviser is not acting as an agent." (*Id.*)

Moreover *employees* are deemed agents for present purposes even if they are employed in a wholly non-representative capacity. (Rest.3d, Agency, § 1.01, com. c, pp. 19–20 ["The common law of agency ... encompasses the employment relation, even as to employees whom an employer has not designated to contract on its behalf or otherwise to interact with parties external to the employer's organization"].) Thus an employee, while employed, owes undivided loyalty to his employer.... The duty of loyalty is breached, and the breach "may give rise to a cause of action in the employer, when the employee takes action which is inimical to the best interests of the employer." *Stokes v. Dole Nut Co.*, (1995) 41 Cal.App.4th 285, 295, 48 Cal.Rptr.2d 673. Indeed, by statute, "[a]n employee who has any business to transact on his own account, similar to that intrusted to him by his employer, shall always give the preference to the business of the employer."

Here the trial court may have been entitled to find that appellants would probably be found to have been hired as employees for purposes of these principles. Even if it was not, it could certainly find that they assented to and did act as agents in the core, representative sense of the term. They expressly agreed not only "to act as Buyer's *Managing Agents*," but in doing so to "provide Buyer with *business dealings*, bookkeeping activities, and design of publishing samples." (Italics added.) There was ample evidence that the "business dealings" thus undertaken included representing Huong Que in its interactions with customers and service providers. Thus plaintiff ... declared that appellant Nguyen participated in "sales trips" on Huong Que's behalf. Huong Que employee Binh Tu declared that when he accompanied Nguyen on a 2002 sales trip, Nguyen "introduced me to the customers" and "taught me about his sales techniques and taking calendar orders from customers." In 2003, after the sale of Huong Que, the declarant again accompanied Nguyen on the "yearly interstate sales trip." ... Meanwhile, Binh Tu declared, it was appellant Luu's duty "to deal directly with the printer and the printing company." By the end of 2004, he said, appellants were "refus[ing] to cooperate in contacting the printer and photographers and dealing with customers and conducting sales." The court thus found that appellants not only assented to be described as but actually represented (and then refused to represent) plaintiffs in dealings with third persons.

Appellants suggest that the "compensation level" they received as managing agents militates against a finding that they were burdened with a duty of loyalty to plaintiffs. No authority is cited for this proposition. As previously noted, one becomes an agent, and thereby assumes a duty of loyalty, by acting or assenting to act for another— even if *no* consideration is furnished and no contract is formed. (See Rest.3d, Agency, § 1.01, com. d.)....

Appellants imply that their status as "prior owners" distinguishes them from the agents and employees held subject to a duty of loyalty in other cases. If that were their only relationship to plaintiffs they would surely have a point. But in addition to selling their business, they voluntarily assumed a relationship to plaintiffs as "managing agents." ...

We have no doubt that the trial court acted correctly in determining that plaintiffs were likely to succeed in establishing that appellants owed them a duty of loyalty.

C. *Breach of Duty*

The duty of loyalty embraces several subsidiary obligations, including the duty "to refrain from competing with the principal and from taking action on behalf of or otherwise assisting the principal's competitors" (Rest.3d, Agency, § 8.04), the duty "not to acquire a material benefit from a third party in connection with ... actions taken ... through the agent's use of the agent's position" (*id.*, § 8.02), and the duty "not to use or communicate confidential information of the principal for the agent's own purposes or those of a third party" (*id.*, § 8.05(2)).

Plaintiffs alleged that appellants breached one or more of these duties by "secretly organizing a competing business, utilizing confidential information acquired during the course of their employment by plaintiffs, and informing customers of Huong Que that Huong Que had changed owners and was now operating under the name Pro Calendar." The trial court ruled that plaintiffs were likely to succeed at showing that appellants "appropriate[d] Huong Que's customer list, covertly [met] with other Defendants to plan the formation of Pro Calendar ... and steer[ed] away Huong Que's customers to Pro Calendar." In connection with another cause of action the court observed that appellants "assisted in promoting Pro Calendar by doing such things as knowingly and intentionally soliciting business from plaintiffs' customers." The court expressly found "credible" the averments by plaintiffs' witnesses "that Defendant Cu Tu Nguyen, while he was still a Managing Agent of Huong Que, did in fact actively solicit Huong Que customers for Pro Calendar, a business that directly competed with Plaintiffs."

Appellants assert that they were entitled "to meet with other individuals to discuss the formation of a new business," and to "discuss creating a new business that might compete with an employer." This is true as far as it goes; "California law permit[s] an employee to seek other employment and even to make some 'preparations to compete' before resigning...." *Fowler v. Varian Associates, Inc., supra,* 196 Cal.App.3d at p. 41, 241 Cal.Rptr. 539. But assuming this might shield an agent from liability based on helping to form a competitive business, that was only one of the several breaches of loyalty that plaintiffs alleged and the trial court found likely to be established at trial. Assuming appellants were entitled to participate in the formation of Pro Calendar and to plan eventual employment with that entity, they would still breach a duty of loyalty by diverting plaintiffs' customers to Pro Calendar while ostensibly remaining plaintiffs' employees or agents.

D. *Damage*

Appellants do not separately challenge the necessary finding that plaintiffs could probably establish the third element of the tort, i.e., damage proximately caused by the breach of the duty of loyalty.... [Affirmed.]

————————

The *Huang Que* court did not address the issue of damages caused by the breach of the duty of loyalty. That issue was the subject of the following frequently cited case:

Tarnowski v. RESOP
Minnesota Supreme Court
51 N.W.2d 801 (1952)

KNUTSON, JUSTICE.

Plaintiff desired to make a business investment. He engaged defendant as his agent to investigate and negotiate for the purchase of a route of coin-operated music machines. On June 2, 1947, relying upon the advice of defendant and the investigation he had made, plaintiff purchased such a business from Phillip Loechler and Lyle Mayer of Rochester, Minnesota, who will be referred to hereinafter as the sellers. The business was located at LaCrosse, Wisconsin, and throughout the surrounding territory. Plaintiff alleges that defendant represented to him that he had made a thorough investigation of the route; that it had 75 locations in operation; that one or more machines were at each location; that the equipment at each location was not more than six months old; and that the gross income from all locations amounted to more than $3,000 per month. As a matter of fact, defendant had made only a superficial investigation and had investigated only five of the locations. Other than that, he had adopted false representations of the sellers as to the other locations and had passed them on to plaintiff as his own. Plaintiff was to pay $30,620 for the business. He paid $11,000 down. About six weeks after the purchase, plaintiff discovered that the representations made to him by defendant were false, in that there were not more than 47 locations; that at some of the locations there were no machines and at others there were machines more than six months old, some of them being seven years old; and that the gross income was far less than $3,000 per month. Upon discovering the falsity of defendant's representations and those of the sellers, plaintiff rescinded the sale. He offered to return what he had received, and he demanded the return of his money. The sellers refused to comply, and he brought suit against them in the district court of Olmsted county. The action was tried, resulting in a verdict of $10,000 for plaintiff. Thereafter, the sellers paid plaintiff $9,500, after which the action was dismissed with prejudice pursuant to a stipulation of the parties.

In this action, brought in Hennepin county, plaintiff alleges that defendant, while acting as agent for him, collected a secret commission from the sellers for consummating the sale, which plaintiff seeks to recover under his first cause of action. In his second cause of action, he seeks to recover damages for (1) losses suffered in operating the route prior to rescission; (2) loss of time devoted to operation; (3) expenses in connection with rescission of the sale and his investigation in connection therewith; (4) nontaxable expenses in connection with prosecution of the suit against the sellers; and (5) attorneys' fees in connection with the suit. The case was tried to a jury, and plaintiff recovered a verdict of $5,200. This appeal is from the judgment entered pursuant thereto.

Defendant contends that after recovery of a verdict by plaintiff in his action for rescission against the sellers he cannot maintain this action against defendant. Principally, defendant argues that recovery in the action against the sellers is a bar to this action....

1. With respect to plaintiff's first cause of action, the principle that all profits made by an agent in the course of an agency belong to the principal, whether they are the fruits of performance or the violation of an agent's duty, is firmly established and universally recognized. It matters not that the principal has suffered no damage or even that the transaction has been profitable to him. The rule and the basis therefor are well stated in *Lum v. McEwen*, 56 Minn. 278, 282, 57 N.W. 662, where, speaking through Mr. Justice Mitchell, we said:

> Actual injury is not the principle the law proceeds on, in holding such transactions void. Fidelity in the agent is what is aimed at, and, as a means of securing it, the law will not permit him to place himself in a position in which he may be tempted by his own private interests to disregard those of his principal.... It is not material that no actual injury to the company (principal) resulted, or that the policy recommended may have been for its best interest. Courts will not inquire into these matters. It is enough to know that the agent in fact placed himself in such relations that he might be tempted by his own interests to disregard those of his principal. The transaction was nothing more or less than the acceptance by the agent of a bribe to perform his duties in the manner desired by the person who gave the bribe. Such a contract is void. This doctrine rests on such plain principles of law, as well as common business honesty, that the citation of authorities is unnecessary.

The right to recover profits made by the agent in the course of the agency is not affected by the fact that the principal, upon discovering a fraud, has rescinded the contract and recovered that with which he parted. Restatement, Agency, §407(2). Comment a on Subsection (2) reads:

> If an agent has violated a duty of loyalty to the principal so that the principal is entitled to profits which the agent has thereby made, the fact that the principal has brought an action against a third person and has been made whole by such action does not prevent the principal from recovering from the agent the profits which the agent has made. Thus, if the other contracting party has given a bribe to the agent to make a contract with him on behalf of the principal, the principal can rescind the transaction, recovering from the other party anything received by him, or he can maintain an action for damages

against him; in either event the principal may recover from the agent the amount of the bribe.

It follows that, insofar as the secret commission of $2,000 received by the agent is concerned, plaintiff had an absolute right thereto, irrespective of any recovery resulting from the action against the sellers for rescission.

2. Plaintiff's second cause of action is brought to recover damages for (1) losses suffered in the operation of the business prior to rescission; (2) loss of time devoted to operation; (3) expenses in connection with rescission of the sale and investigation therewith; (4) nontaxable expenses in connection with the prosecution of the suit against the sellers; and (5) attorneys' fees in connection with the suit.

... Our inquiry is limited to a consideration of the question whether a principal may recover of an agent who has breached his trust the items of damage mentioned after a successful prosecution of an action for rescission against the third parties with whom the agent dealt for his principal.

The general rule is stated in Restatement, Agency, § 407(1), as follows:

> If an agent has received a benefit as a result of violating his duty of loyalty, the principal is entitled to recover from him what he has so received, its value, or its proceeds, and also the amount of damage thereby caused, except that if the violation consists of the wrongful disposal of the principal's property, the principal cannot recover its value and also what the agent received in exchange therefor.

In comment a on Subsection (1) we find the following:

> ... In either event, whether or not the principal elects to get back the thing improperly dealt with or to recover from the agent its value or the amount of benefit which the agent has improperly received, he is, in addition, entitled to be indemnified by the agent for any loss which has been caused to his interest by the improper transaction. Thus, if the purchasing agent for a restaurant purchases with the principal's money defective food, receiving a bonus therefor, and the use of the food in the restaurant damages the business, the principal can recover from the agent the amount of money improperly expended by him, the bonus which the agent received, and the amount which will compensate for the injury to the business.

The general rule with respect to damages for a tortious act is that "The wrongdoer is answerable for all the injurious consequences of his tortious act, which according to the usual course of events and the general experience were likely to ensue, and which, therefore, when the act was committed, he may reasonably be supposed to have foreseen and anticipated."

The general rule is given in Restatement, Torts, § 910, as follows: "A person injured by the tort of another is entitled to recover damages from him for all harm, past, present and prospective, legally caused by the tort."

... So far as the right to recover attorneys' fees is concerned, the same may be said in this case. Plaintiff sought to return what had been received and demanded a return of his down payment. The sellers refused. He thereupon sued to accomplish this purpose, as he had a right to do, and was successful. His attorneys' fees and expenses of suit were directly traceable to the harm caused by defendant's wrongful act. As such, they are recoverable.

... The general rule applicable here is stated in 15 Am. Jur., Damages, § 144, as follows: "It is generally held that where the wrongful act of the defendant has involved the plaintiff in litigation with others or placed him in such relation with others as makes it necessary to incur expense to protect his interest, such costs and expenses, including attorneys' fees, should be treated as the legal consequences of the original wrongful act and may be recovered as damages." The same is true of the other elements of damage involved.

3. Defendant contends that plaintiff had an election of remedies and, having elected to proceed against the sellers to recover what he had paid, is now barred from proceeding against defendant. It is true that upon discovery of the fraud plaintiff had an election of remedies against the sellers. It is not true, however, that, having elected to sue for recovery of that with which he had parted, he is barred from proceeding against his agent to recover damages for his tortious conduct.... Many of the elements of damage against the agent are not available to plaintiff against the sellers. For instance, he has no right to recover attorneys' fees and expenses of the litigation against the sellers. He has that right against the agent. Plaintiff may recover profits made by the agent, irrespective of his recovery against the sellers. Losses directly flowing from the agent's tortious conduct are not recoverable against the sellers in an action for rescission, but they may be recovered against the agent, whose breach of faith has caused such losses....

Settlement of the action for rescission against the sellers is not a bar to an action against the agent to recover those elements of damages not involved in the action for rescission brought against the sellers.

Affirmed.

———————

Issues of confidentiality and conflict of interest assume a particular importance in the attorney/client context. What common law Agency rules are Model Rules of Professional Conduct 1.6, 1.7, 1.8 and 1.9 based on?

In a 1997 opinion, the Delaware State Bar Association Committee on Professional Ethics addressed the following situation. A law firm initially had represented a director and several officers of a corporation in connection with the possible elimination of their jobs without cause as a result of a merger. The law firm later represented the same corporation in a for cause termination of the director. The director objected to the representation on the basis of conflict of interest. Applying Delaware Rule of Professional Conduct 1.9, the committee found that the two matters were not substantially related. The earlier representation had dealt only with the merger's effect on the termination of the director's and officers' employment, whereas the later case dealt with the "for cause" termination of the director. With respect to the initial representation, the committee found that since the firm had communicated with the director and officers as a group and had not communicated directly with the director, the individual director had no opportunity to disclose confidential information that could be used against him.

b. Other Fiduciary Duties of Agents

An agent has additional fiduciary duties to the principal. Among the most important is the agent's duty to act carefully, using "the care, competence and diligence normally exercised by agents in similar circumstances."[32] Further, the agent must "use reasonable effort to provide the principal with facts that the agent knows, has reason to know, or should know concerning the agency relationship."[33] Equally important, the agent must keep accounts regarding any money or property within the agent's control and must not co-mingle the principal's property with anyone else's property, including the agent's own.[34]

2. Fiduciary Duties of Principals

In the U. S., the duties of a principal to an agent are limited, particularly when compared with the duties agents owe to principals in the U. S. or with the duties imposed on principals in other legal systems, as, for example by 1993 European Union Regulations dealing with the duties owed by a principal to a non-employee agent. The Introductory Note to Chapter 8 of the Restatement (Third) of Agency provides the following rationale:

> The agency-law duties of principals to their agents are less numerous than the duties of agents to principals. This is because an agent's position always enables the agent to take action with consequences for the principal's legal relations, often but not necessarily situates the agent in proximity to property of the principal, and often induces the principal to repose trust in the agent.[35]

A principal must also "act in accordance with the express and implied terms of any contract between the principal and the agent."[36] The obligations arising under section 8.13 differ from those imposed by a contract. Section 8.13 imposes on the principal the obligation to deal fairly with the agent, to furnish the agent with information related to the agency relationship, and to refrain from conduct that may be harmful to the agent's business reputation.[37] The principal must also indemnify the agent for losses incurred by the agent in connection with the agency relationship.[38]

---

32. Restatement (Third) of Agency §8.08.
33. *Id.* §8.11.
34. *Id.* §8.12.
35. *Id.* Chapter 8. Duties Of Agent and Principal To Each Other, Topic 2. Principal's Duties To Agent, Introductory Note.
36. *Id.* §8.13.
37. *Id.* §8.13, Comment.
38. *Id.* §8.14.

Chapter 2

Traditional Business Forms and Their Progeny

Situation
(See Situation for Chapter 1)

Section I
Partnerships

A. Introduction

Partnership law, like agency law, developed to meet the needs of persons jointly engaged in a business enterprise. It, too, consists of rules providing the terms of a contract for the members of a partnership. Some terms can be varied by agreement of the parties. Others are mandatory. Like agency law, partnership law defines the formation process, standards of conduct for the participants in a joint enterprise and termination of the relationship. It also addresses issues of liability among the members of the venture and between the venture and third parties. In fact, many of the provisions of partnership law are based on agency principles. Because a partnership involves multiple owners, the resolution of issues is often more complex than in situations where a single person has full decision making responsibility.

Early forms of partnership developed during the Middle Ages in the form of organizations known as *Compagnia* or *Societas.* The participants pooled their monetary and human capital resources and spread the risk of the enterprise. Although joint ownership offered efficiencies of operation unavailable to multiple, independently owned sole proprietorships, it also increased exposure to liability, because partners were personally liable for the wrongful acts of other members of the enterprise.

Originally, United States partnership law was a common-law creation. In the early twentieth century, however, the National Conference of Commissioners on Uniform State Laws adopted the Uniform Partnership Act (UPA) (1914) which was passed in all states but Louisiana. In many respects, this act was a codification of the partnership provisions that had developed in the common law. In 1994, and again in 1997, the National Conference adopted revised versions of the original Uniform Partnership Act.[2] In many respects the later Acts continued the fundamental direction set by the earlier Act.

---

2. Uniform Partnership Act (1994) (hereinafter "UPA (1994)") and Uniform Partnership Act (1997) (hereinafter "UPA (1997)"). Copyright © 1994 and 1997 by the Uniform Law Commission. Selected provisions are reproduced herein with permission. All rights reserved.

Many of the assumptions about the nature of partnerships that underlie all versions of the Uniform Partnership Act reflect the development of the law during the Middle Ages. The fundamental concept is one of a firm operated by a few members having close personal relationships. The UPA's fully participatory management structure in which all partners have equal votes (unless they agree otherwise) is suitable to a small number of members, as large numbers of owners make direct participation unwieldy. Other provisions reflect the personal nature of the members' relationships. The admission of new partners requires unanimous consent and conveyance of a partner's interest confers management rights on the transferee only if the remaining partners agree. The assumption that partners know each other underlies provisions authorizing individual partners to bind the partnership. Partners' relations are essentially contractual in nature; partners can vary components of the basic partnership structure by agreement.

UPA (1997) introduced an important change to partnership law. It provides for the formation of Limited Liability Partnerships (LLP). An LLP is like a general partnership except with respect to partners' personal liability for partnership debts. In a general partnership, if the partnership's assets are not sufficient to satisfy its debts, partners are jointly and severally liable for unpaid partnership obligations. Their personal assets may be used to pay partnership creditors. In a limited liability partnership, once partners have made their capital contributions, they are not personally liable for partnership debts.

Although in most situations a partnership is treated as a legal entity separate and distinct from the partners, this is not the case when it comes to partnership taxation. The partnership itself is not required to pay either federal or state income taxation. Instead, the partnership merely files an information return, and then each partner pays tax on his or her proportionate share of the partnership's profits or takes a deduction for the partner's proper share of its losses. This approach is referred to as pass through taxation. In contrast, a corporation is treated as a separate taxable entity. Thus, the organization pays taxes on its earnings. A second tax is imposed when corporate earnings are distributed to shareholders. Since partnership earnings are taxed only to individual partners, and not also to the business entity, partnerships offer opportunities for tax savings that are not generally available to investors in corporations. When the marginal tax rates applied to individuals are lower than those imposed on corporations, the partnership pass through taxation scheme becomes increasingly attractive. When individual marginal tax rates are higher than corporate rates, the corporate tax rate may have some appeal. Today, partnerships, like most other unincorporated business organizations, may elect whether to be taxed like a corporation or a partnership.

A joint venture is a business organization similar to a partnership. In fact, the distinctions between the two are often blurred. The term "joint venture" is usually used in connection with businesses organized to complete a specific project, such as developing a particular piece of real estate, rather than to engage in an ongoing enterprise.

B. Partnership Formation

1. General Partnerships

A general partnership, like an agency relationship, may be created through the express agreement of the parties or may arise by operation of law when the parties have entered into an arrangement having the legal attributes of a partnership.[3] No formalities are required to form a general partnership, although many states require the filing of a trade name registration, and under UPA (1997), certain filings are permitted, although not required.[4]

Persons entering into any type of partnership are well-advised to document their relationship in a partnership agreement addressing such issues as management and voting, sharing of profits and losses, the continuation of the business when a partner withdraws, retires or is expelled, and valuation of interests in the partnership. Preparing a partnership agreement will require the parties to discuss these matters in advance so that the partners will have common expectations when these events occur. (As you read the following materials, consider what additional issues should be addressed in a partnership agreement.) Having a partnership agreement prepared can be expensive. Very often, however, the initial investment in a carefully drafted document is more than recouped when problems arise. It is less costly, in time and impact on relationships, to decide difficult matters in advance, rather than when relations are strained and passions run high.

Because business relationships are flexible rather than static, persons dealing with a business may acquire the attributes of partners, even though they do not intend to be partners. One example is an employee having significant management responsibilities or the right to share in the profits of the enterprise. Another is a business creditor who has contracted for the right to approve certain business decisions in order to protect against the loss of funds lent to the venture. The case that follows provides an example of the problems that can arise when a partnership arises by operation of law.

Holmes v. Lerner
California Court of Appeals
88 Cal. Rptr. 2d 130 (1999)

MARCHIANO, J.

This case involves an **oral partnership agreement** to start a cosmetics company known as "Urban Decay." Patricia Holmes prevailed on her claim that Sandra Kruger Lerner breached her partnership agreement and that David Soward interfered with the Holmes-Lerner contract, resulting in Holmes' ouster from the business. Lerner and Soward appeal from the judgment finding them liable to Holmes for compensatory and punitive damages of over $1 million....

---

3. *Id.* §§6, 7; UPA (1997) §202.
4. UPA (1997) §§303, 304.

We affirm the judgment against Lerner, primarily because we determine that an express agreement to divide profits is not a prerequisite to prove the existence of a partnership. We also determine that the oral partnership agreement between Lerner and Holmes was sufficiently definite to allow enforcement....

BACKGROUND

... Sandra Lerner is a successful entrepreneur and an experienced business person. She and her husband were the original founders of Cisco Systems. When she sold her interest in that company, she received a substantial amount of money, which she invested, in part, in a venture capital limited partnership called "& Capital Partners." By the time of trial in this matter, Lerner was extremely wealthy. Patricia Holmes met Lerner in late 1993, when Lerner visited Holmes' horse training facility to arrange for training and boarding of two horses that Lerner was importing from England. Holmes and Lerner became friends, and after an initial six-month training contract expired, Holmes continued to train Lerner's horses without a contract and without cost.

In 1995, Lerner and Holmes traveled to England to a horse show and to make arrangements to ship the horses that Lerner had purchased. On this trip, Lerner decided that she wanted to celebrate her 40th birthday by going pub crawling in Dublin. Lerner was wearing what Holmes termed "alternative clothes" and black nail polish, and encouraged Holmes to do the same.[5] Holmes, however, did not like black nail polish, and was unable to find a suitable color in the English stores. At Lerner's mansion outside of London, Lerner gave Holmes a manicuring kit, telling her to see if she could find a color she would wear. Holmes looked through the kit, tried different colors, and eventually developed her own color by layering a raspberry color over black nail polish. This produced a purple color that Holmes liked. Holmes showed the new color to Lerner, who also liked it.

On July 31, 1995, the two women returned from England and stayed at Lerner's West Hollywood condominium while they waited for the horses to clear quarantine. While sitting at the kitchen table, they discussed nail polish, and colors. Len Bosack, Lerner's husband, was in and out of the room during the conversations. For approximately an hour and a half, Lerner and Holmes worked with the colors in a nail kit to try to recreate the purple color Holmes had made in England so they could have the color in a liquid form, rather than layering two colors. Lerner made a different shade of purple, and Holmes commented that it looked just like a bruise. Holmes then said that she wanted to call the purple color she had made "Plague." ... Lerner and Holmes discussed the fact that the names they were creating had an urban theme, and tried to think of other names to fit the theme. Starting with "Bruise" and "Plague,"

---

5. [1] There were references throughout the trial to Lerner's "alternative" look and to "alternative" culture. Lerner, who referred to herself as an "edgy cosmetics queen," described "alternative culture" as "not really mainstream," "edgy," and "fashion forward." As an example, she noted her own purple hair. She defined "edgy" as not trying to be cute, and being unconventional.

they also discussed the names "Mildew," "Smog," "Uzi," and "Oil Slick." Len Bosack walked into the kitchen at that point, heard the conversation about the urban theme, and said "What about decay?" The two women liked the idea, and decided that "Urban Decay" was a good name for their concept.

Lerner said to Holmes: "This seems like a good [thing], it's something that we both like, and isn't out there. Do you think we should start a company?" Holmes responded: "Yes, I think it's a great idea." Lerner told Holmes that they would have to do market research, determine how to have the polishes produced, and that there were many things they would have to do. Lerner said: "We will hire people to work for us. We will do everything we can to get the company going, and then we'll be creative, and other people will do the work, so we'll have time to continue riding the horses." Holmes agreed that they would do those things. They did not separate out which tasks each of them would do, but planned to do it all together.

"For profit language"

Lerner went to the telephone and called David Soward, the general partner of "& Capital," and her business consultant. Holmes heard her say "Please check for the name, Urban Decay, to see if it's available and if it is, get it for us." Holmes knew that Lerner did not joke about business, and was certain, from the tone of her voice, that Lerner was serious about the new business. The telephone call to secure the trademark for Urban Decay confirmed in Holmes' mind that they were forming a business based on the concepts they had originated in England and at the kitchen table that day. Holmes knew that she would be taking the risk of sharing in losses as well as potential success, but the two friends did not discuss the details at that time. Lerner's housekeeper heard Lerner tell Holmes: "It's going to be our baby, and we're going to work on it together." After Holmes left, the housekeeper asked what gave Lerner the idea to go into the cosmetics business, since her background was computers. Lerner replied: "It was all Pat's idea over in England, but I've got the money to make it work." Lerner told her housekeeper that she hoped to sell Urban Decay to Estee Lauder for $50 million.

Although neither of the two women had any experience in the cosmetics business, they began work on their idea immediately. Holmes and Lerner did market research by going to stores, talking with people about nail polish, seeing what nail polishes were available, and buying samples to bring back to discuss with each other. They met frequently in August and September at Lerner's home, and experimented with nail colors. They took pictures of various color mixing sessions. In early August, they met with graphic artist, Andrea Kelly and discussed putting together a logo and future advertising work for Urban Decay.

Prior to the first scheduled August meeting, Holmes told Lerner she was concerned about financing the venture. Lerner told her not to worry about it because Lerner thought they could convince Soward that the nail polish business would be a good investment. She told Holmes that Soward took care of Lerner's investment money. Holmes and Lerner discussed their plans for the company, and agreed that they would attempt to build it up and then sell it. Lerner and Holmes discussed the need to visit chemical companies and hire people to handle the daily operations of the company.

However, the creative aspect, ideas, inspiration, and impetus for the company came from Holmes and Lerner.

Lerner, Holmes, Soward, and Kelly attended the first scheduled meeting. The participants in these meetings referred to them as "board meetings," even though there was no formal organizational structure, and technically, no board. They discussed financing, and Soward reluctantly agreed to commit $500,000 towards the project. Urban Decay was financed entirely by & Capital, the venture capital partnership composed of Soward as general partner, and Lerner and her husband as the only limited partners. Neither Lerner nor Holmes invested any of their individual funds.

Lerner and Soward went to Kirker Chemical Company later in August of 1995 and learned about mixing and manufacturing nail polish colors. Lerner discouraged Holmes from accompanying them. Although Lerner returned to Kirker, she never took Holmes with her. At the second board meeting, in late August, Soward introduced Wendy Zomnir, a friend of Soward's former fiance, as an advertising and marketing specialist. After Zomnir and Kelley left the meeting, Holmes, Lerner and Soward discussed her presentation. Holmes was enthusiastic about Zomnir and they decided to hire her. At the conclusion of the September board meeting, after Holmes had left, Lerner and Soward secretly made Zomnir an offer of employment, which included a percentage ownership interest in Urban Decay. It wasn't until a couple of meetings later, when Lerner or Soward referred to Zomnir as the "Chief Operating Officer" of Urban Decay, that Holmes learned of the terms of the offer.

In early October, after Holmes learned of the secret offer to Zomnir, she asked Lerner to define her role at Urban Decay. Lerner responded: "Your role is anything you want it to be." When Holmes asked to discuss the issue in more detail, Lerner turned and walked away. Holmes believed that Lerner was nervous about an upcoming photo session, and decided to discuss it with Lerner at a later date. At their regular board meetings, Holmes participated with Soward, Lerner, Zomnir, Kelly and another person in discussing new colors, and deciding which ones they wanted to sell, and which names would be used.

In September of 1995, Soward signed an application for trademark registration as President of Urban Decay. In December of 1995, Urban Decay was incorporated. Holmes asked for a copy of the articles of incorporation, but was given only two pages showing the name and address of the company. On December 31, Holmes sent a fax to Lerner stating that it had been difficult to discuss her position in Urban Decay with Lerner. Holmes asked Lerner: "What are my responsibilities and obligations, and what are my rights or entitlements?" Holmes also asked: "What are my current and potential liabilities and assets?" She requested that Lerner provide the information in writing. At this point, Holmes wanted to memorialize the agreement she and Lerner had made on July 31.

Soward intercepted the fax and called Holmes, asking: "What's going on?" Holmes explained that she wanted a written agreement, and Soward apologized, telling her that Lerner had asked him to get "something … in writing" to Holmes. Soward told Holmes that no one in the company had a written statement of their percentage interest in the company yet. Soward asked: "What do you want, one percent, two percent?" When Holmes did not respond, he told her that five percent was high for an idea. Holmes told him: "I'm not selling an idea. I'm a founder of this company." Soward exclaimed: "Surely you don't think you have fifty percent of this company?" Holmes told him that it was a matter between herself and Lerner, and that Soward should speak to Lerner. Soward agreed to talk to Lerner.

On January 11, 1996, Lerner and Holmes met at a coffee shop to discuss the fax. Holmes explained that she wanted "something in writing" and an explanation of her interest and position in the company. Lerner responded that a start up business is "like a freight train ... you can either run and catch up, and get on, and take a piece of this company and make it your own, or get out of the way." As a result of this conversation, Holmes decided to double her efforts on behalf of Urban Decay. Because she was most comfortable working at the warehouse, she focused on that aspect of the business.[6] Holmes was reimbursed for mileage, but received no pay for her work.

During January and February, Urban Decay was launching its new nail polish product. Publicity included press releases, brochures, and newspaper interviews with Lerner. An early press release stated: "The idea for Urban Decay was born after Lerner and her horse trainer, Pat Holmes, were sitting around in the English countryside." Lerner approved the press release. In February of 1996, an article was printed in the San Francisco Examiner containing the following quotes from Lerner. "Since we couldn't find good nail polish in cool colors there must be a business opportunity here. Pat had the original idea. Urban Decay was my spin." The Examiner reporter testified at trial that the quote attributed to Lerner was accurate. Lerner was also interviewed in April by CNN. In that interview she told the story of herself and Holmes looking for unusual colors, mixing their own colors at the kitchen table, and that "we came up with the colors, and it just sort of suggested the urban thing."

Lerner had always notified Holmes whenever there was a board meeting, and she sent Holmes an agenda for the February 20, 1996 meeting. Lerner also sent a memo stating that she thought they should have an "operations meeting" with the warehouse supervisor first. Lerner's memo continued: "and then have a regular board meeting, including [Zomnir], me, David, and Pat, and no one else." Holmes understood that the regular board meeting would be for the purpose of discussing general Urban Decay business. At the operations meeting, Holmes made a presentation regarding the warehouse operations. The financial report showed $205,000 in revenues and

---

6. [4] Holmes testified that her work at the warehouse included responding to requests for brochures, developing a system for handling increased telephone inquiries, and negotiating a contract with a skills center to assist with the mail order business. She had authority to hire and fire employees and to sign checks on the Urban Decay account. Only Holmes, Soward, Lerner, Zomnir and the warehouse manager were authorized to sign on the account. Only the manager's authority was limited to $1,500. Holmes was spending four to five days a week at the warehouse. Urban Decay accountant Sharon Land testified that Holmes "contributed a great deal" to Urban Decay, and directed the retail business. Soward, Lerner and Zomnir seldom came to the office. Soward told Land that Holmes was on the board of directors.

$431,000 in expenses.[7] The "directors" thought this early sales figure was "terrific." Soward handed out an organizational chart, which showed Lerner, with the title "CEO" at the top, Soward, as "President" beneath her, and Zomnir, as "COO" beneath Soward. Holmes asked "Where am I?" Lerner responded by pointing to the top of the chart and telling Holmes that she was a director, and was at the top of the chart, above all the other names.

In March of 1996, Holmes received a document from Soward offering her a one percent ownership interest in Urban Decay. Soward explained that Urban Decay had been formed as a limited liability company, which was owned by its members.[8] For the first time, Holmes realized that Lerner and Soward had produced an organizational document that did not include her, and she was now being asked to become a minor partner. When she studied the document, she discovered that it referred to an Exhibit A, which was purported to show the distribution of ownership interests in Urban Decay. Soward had given Zomnir a copy of Exhibit A when he offered her an ownership interest in Urban Decay. However, when Holmes asked Soward for a copy of Exhibit A, he told her it did not exist.[9] By this time, Holmes was planning to consult an attorney about the document.

Despite the deterioration of her friendship with Lerner, and her strained relationship with Soward, Holmes continued to attend the scheduled board meetings, hoping that her differences with Lerner could be resolved. She also continued to work at the warehouse on various administrative projects and on direct mail order sales. As late as the April board meeting, Holmes was still actively engaged in Urban Decay business. She made a presentation on a direct mail project she had been asked to undertake. As a result of Holmes' attendance at a sales presentation when she referred to herself as a co-founder of Urban Decay, Lerner instructed Zomnir to draft a dress code and an official history of Urban Decay. Lerner told Zomnir that it was a "real error in judgment" to allow Holmes to attend the sales presentation because she did not project the appropriate image. The official history, proposed in the memo, omitted any reference to Holmes. Finally, matters deteriorated to the point that Soward told Holmes not to attend the July board meeting because she was no longer welcome at Urban Decay.

On August 27, 1996, Holmes filed a complaint against Lerner and Soward, alleging [inter alia] an oral contract.... At the trial, cosmetic industry expert Gabriella Zuck-

7. [7] Urban Decay was involved in a lawsuit with Revlon, over Revlon's use of similar colors and names for its new line of "Streetwear" nail colors. Lerner believed that Revlon's actions had potentially impacted sales.

8. [9] "A limited liability company is a hybrid business entity that combines aspects of both a partnership and a corporation. It is formed under the Corporations Code and consists of 'members' who own membership interests." (9 Witkin, Summary of Cal. Law (9th ed. 1999 Supp.) Partnership, § 120, p. 245.)

9. [10] Holmes was never given Exhibit A, and did not see it until trial. It showed & Capital Partners, L.P. with a 92 percent interest, having contributed $489,900. It also showed Lerner and her husband with contributions of $5,050 each, and 1 percent apiece. Zomnir's contribution was listed as $5,050, but she had a 5 percent interest. None of the individuals actually paid in the listed contributions.

erman testified that Urban Decay was not just a fad. In her opinion, Urban Decay had discovered and capitalized on a trend that was just beginning. She reviewed projected sales figures of $19.9 million in 1997, going up to $52 million in 2003, and found them definitely obtainable. Arthur Clark, Holmes' expert at valuing start-up businesses, valued Urban Decay under different risk scenarios. In Clark's opinion, the value of Urban Decay to a potential buyer was between $4,672,000 and $6,270,000. Lerner's expert, who had never valued a cosmetics company, testified that Urban Decay had $2.7 million in sales in 1996. He estimated the value of Urban Decay as approximately $2 million, but concluded that it was not marketable.[10]

Lerner and Soward claimed that Holmes was never a director, officer, or even an employee of Urban Decay. According to Lerner, she was just being nice to Holmes by letting her be present during Urban Decay business. Lerner denied Holmes had any role in creating the colors, names, or concepts for Urban Decay. When Holmes asked Lerner about her assets and liabilities in Urban Decay, Lerner thought she was asking for a job. She explained her statements to the press regarding Urban Decay being Holmes' idea as misquotes or the product of her stress.

The jury found in favor of Holmes on every cause of action.... Lerner and Soward moved for a judgment notwithstanding the verdict, which was denied on December 16, 1997. They appealed from the judgment and the order denying their post-verdict motion....

DISCUSSION

... Holmes testified that she and Lerner did not discuss sharing profits of the business during the July 31, "kitchen table" conversation. Throughout the case, Lerner and Soward have contended that without an agreement to share profits, there can be no partnership.

The applicable version of the UPA [1914] ... defines a partnership as: "an association of two or more persons to carry on as co-owners a business for profit." [§ 6] The UPA [located] the provision regarding profits [in] section 7, which provides that in determining whether a partnership exists, "[t]he receipt by a person of a share of the profits of a business is prima facie evidence that he is a partner...." This [location] of the element of sharing the profits indicates that the Legislature intends profit sharing to be evidence of a partnership, rather than a required element of the definition of a partnership.[11] The presence or absence of any of the various elements set forth in section [7], including sharing of profits and losses, is not necessarily dispositive. [T]he rules to establish the existence of a partnership in section [7] should be viewed in the light of the crucial factor of the intent of the parties revealed in the terms of their agreement, conduct, and the surrounding circumstances when determining whether a partnership exists.

---

10. [11] Soward testified that & Capital had invested a total of $2 million in Urban Decay by the time of trial. The investment at the time of the breach of contract was just under $800,000.

11. [14] Under the provisions of the UPA of 1994, effective, January 1, 1999, the sharing of profits is recharacterized as an evidentiary presumption, rather than prima facie evidence. (§ 16202, subd. (c)(3)).

The UPA provides for the situation in which the partners have not expressly stated an agreement regarding sharing of profits. Section [18] provides in relevant part: "The rights and duties of the partners in relation to the partnership shall be determined, subject to any agreement between them, by the following rules: (a) Each partner shall ... share equally in the profits and surplus remaining after all liabilities, including those to partners, are satisfied." This provision states, subject to an agreement between the parties, partners "shall" share equally in the profits. Lerner and Soward argue that using section [18] to supply a missing term regarding profit sharing ignores the provision of section [7], subdivision (2). That section, headed "rules for determining existence of partnership," provides that mere joint ownership of common property "does not of itself establish a partnership, whether such co-owners do or do not share any profits made by the use of the property." Lerner and Soward are mistaken. The definition in section [6] provides that the association with the intent to carry on a business for profit is the essential requirement for a partnership. Following that definition does not transform mere joint ownership into the essence of a partnership....

... The cases relied on by Lerner and Soward involved attempts to impose tort liability on alleged joint venturers. It may be a fair policy to require a defendant to have a specified share in the benefits of a venture before imposing tort liability based solely on participation in the venture. Nevertheless, the policy emphasizing sharing in the profits is not compelling in the business context of determining whether parties have orally contracted to do business as partners....

Two of the cases relied on in *People v. Park* 151 Cal. Rptr. 146 (Cal. Ct. App. 1978) were partnership cases that actually characterized the sharing of profits as evidence, rather than as a required element of a partnership.... In *Constans v. Ross*, 106 Cal. App. 2d 381, 386, 235 P.2d 113 (1951) the court ... stated: "Ordinarily the existence of a partnership is evidenced by the right of the respective parties to participate in the profits and losses and in the management of the business." Both cases refer to profit sharing as evidence. Neither case holds that profit sharing is an indispensable element of a partnership.

... The actual sharing of profits (with exceptions which do not apply here) is prima facie evidence, which is to be considered, in light of any other evidence, when determining if a partnership exists. [§ 7(4)] In this case, there were no profits to share at the time Holmes was expelled from the business, so the evidentiary provision of section [7(4)] is not applicable. According to section [6], parties who expressly agree to associate as co-owners with the intent to carry on a business for profit, have established a partnership. Once the elements of that definition are established, other provisions of the UPA and the conduct of the parties supply the details of the agreement.[12] Certainly implicit in the Holmes-Lerner agreement to operate Urban Decay together was an understanding to share in profits and losses as any business owners would. The evidence supported the jury's implicit finding that Holmes birthed an

---

12. [18] "The parties [to a partnership] need only possess the general intent to engage in the acts that constitute a partnership rather than the specific intent to be partners.... [Under the UPA] parties who act as partners in conducting their business will likely be treated as partners for legal purposes." ...

idea which was incubated jointly by Lerner and Holmes, from which they intended to profit once it was fully matured in their company.

… [Turning to the question of definiteness,] … Holmes produced substantial evidence of an agreement as well as evidence of actions of the parties in conformance with their agreement.…

The agreement between Holmes and Lerner was to take Holmes' idea and reduce it to concrete form. They decided to do it together, to form a company, to hire employees, and to engage in the entire process together. The agreement here, as presented to the jury, was that Holmes and Lerner would start a cosmetics company based on the unusual colors developed by Holmes, identified by the Urban theme and the exotic names. The agreement is evidenced by Lerner's statements: "We will do … everything," "it's going to be our baby, and we're going to work on it together." Their agreement is reflected in Lerner's words: "We will hire people to work for us." "We will do … everything we can to get the company going, and then we'll be creative, and other people will do the work, so we'll have time to continue riding the horses." The additional terms were filled in as the two women immediately began work on the multitude of details necessary to bring their idea to fruition.

The fact that Holmes worked for almost a year, without expectation of pay, is further confirmation of the agreement. Lerner and Soward never objected to her work, her participation in board meetings and decision making, or her exercise of authority over the retail warehouse operation. Even as late as the trial in this matter, when Lerner was claiming that everything Holmes said was a lie, Lerner admitted: "It was not only my intention to give Pat every opportunity to be a part of this, but I had hoped that she would." … Holmes was not seeking specific enforcement of a single vague term of the agreement. She was frozen out of the business altogether, and her agreement with Lerner was completely renounced. The agreement that was made and the subsequent acts of the parties supply sufficient certainty to determine the existence of a breach and a remedy. [Affirmed.]

Notes and Questions

1. Is there a difference between an agreement to share profits generally and an agreement delineating the specific manner and amounts of allocating shared profits?

2. The court stressed that Holmes worked a year without pay. Why is that fact so relevant?

3. In *Schlumberger Technology Corporation v. Swanson*, 959 S.W.2d 171 (Tex. 1997), plaintiffs, consultants for a diamond mining project, alleged claims of breach of fiduciary duty in connection with the sale of their interests in the business to defendant and their associated releases of certain claims against the defendant. The plaintiffs claimed the defendant owed them fiduciary obligations because the consultants and the defendant had formed a partnership. The court described the business arrangement as follows:

> In the 1970s, John Swanson and his brother George Swanson approached SEDCO, Inc. about a proposal to mine diamonds from the ocean floor in deep waters off the South African coast. SEDCO had expertise in offshore

oil and gas drilling and had mined manganese nodules off the ocean floor. The Swansons, whose family had been in the mining industry in South Africa for several decades, had contacts with the South African government. By letter dated October 17, 1978, SEDCO agreed to a three-phase project. In Phase I, SEDCO would study the feasibility of the sea-diamond project. In Phase II, a lease was to be acquired and prospecting was to begin. Phase III was to be commercial mining. The agreement provided that SEDCO had exclusive authority to determine whether to proceed with Phases II and III.

The Swansons were to use their goodwill and contacts to obtain concession rights and any licenses or permits the South African government required. They also were to provide SEDCO with information on diamond mining generally and offshore mining specifically. For their part, the Swansons would be paid a consulting fee through Phases I and II and a royalty, if any, on any diamonds mined during Phases II and III. Should the project ever become commercially productive, the Swansons had the right to purchase five percent of the shares in the company contemplated to be formed to mine the diamonds. SEDCO was to bear the expense of all phases of the project, with the exception of the Swansons' own out-of-pocket expenses. Any diamond grants or offshore concessions or leases were to be held by SEDCO, by the company to be formed, or by the Swansons, but as trustees.

In rejecting plaintiffs' claim that a partnership had been formed, the court stated:

> Under the Texas Uniform Partnership Act, a partnership or joint venture is an association of two or more persons to carry on as co-owners a business for profit. As the issue was submitted to the jury, a partnership consists of an express or implied agreement containing four required elements: (1) a community of interest in the venture, (2) an agreement to share profits, (3) an agreement to share losses, and (4) a mutual right of control or management of the enterprise. Accordingly, if there is no evidence of any one element of a partnership, we cannot sustain the jury's affirmative finding.

> We conclude that there is no evidence of an agreement to share profits. The undisputed evidence is that the Swansons were to receive a royalty on diamonds mined in Phases II and III and that their royalty was to be paid before expenses. Entitlement to a royalty based on gross receipts is not profit sharing.... Of course, the payment of consultation fees is not the sharing of profits. Such payments are compensation for services rendered and are unrelated to the venture's profits. *Gutierrez v. Yancey*, 650 S.W.2d 169, 172 (Tex. App.-San Antonio 1983) (partners must participate in profits and share them as principals of business and not as compensation)....

> Because there is no evidence of an agreement to share profits, there is no evidence of a partnership under the question submitted to the jury. This conclusion renders unnecessary any consideration of Schlumberger's other

evidentiary contentions on the remaining elements of a partnership. We conclude that the Swansons and Schlumberger were not partners.

If the *Schlumberger* court had decided the *Holmes* case, would the outcome have been different?

4. The court in *MacArthur Company v. Stein*, 934 P.2d 214 (Mont. 1997), took the following approach in determining whether a partnership had been formed. Prior to 1991, Karl Stein had operated Midland Roofing as a sole proprietorship. Stein then entered into a business arrangement with Potter, Evans and Beebe to form Midland Roofing and Gutters. Beebe arranged a line of credit from MacArthur Company, a supplier for the new Midland Company. The credit documents listed Beebe as the company principal and did not mention Stein's association with the company. Subsequently MacArthur provided supplies to Midland, which were not paid for. Beebe, Evans and Potter then left the area, and MacArthur sued Stein for the unpaid credit balance, claiming that Stein was a partner in the company. According to the court, the determination of the existence of a partnership required proof of the following:

> (1) the parties must clearly manifest their intent to associate themselves as a partnership; (2) each party must contribute something that promotes the enterprise; (3) each party must have a right of mutual control over the subject matter of the enterprise; and (4) the parties must agree to share the profits of the enterprise.

Id. at 217. The court's reasoning included the following:

> The initial test for the determination of whether a partnership exists is the intent of the parties. At trial, Stein testified that he did not intend to create a partnership through his negotiations with Beebe and Potter....

> ... [I]t is not necessary that Stein intended to be a partner in Midland Roofing and Gutters; it is only necessary that he intended his actions and that his actions created a partnership in fact.

> In this case, the District Court found that, regardless of Stein's intentions, the parties had created a partnership in fact through their actions and conduct. Specifically, the court found that the remaining three elements—contribution, joint interest and control, and the right to share profits—had been proven and were indicative of the parties' intent to establish a partnership.

> ... [I]n addition to the requirement of intent, each of the purported partners must contribute something that promotes the enterprise.... The uncontroverted evidence at trial established that Stein lent his business name, his telephone number, his business leads, his good will, his business license, and his expertise to Midland Roofing and Gutters. We hold that such contribution was promotive of the enterprise of Midland Roofing and Gutters....

> A further requirement ... is that each party to an enterprise have a joint proprietary interest in, and right of control over the subject matter of the

enterprise.... [P]ursuant to the parties' agreement, Stein had the right to exercise quality control over the work performed by Midland Roofing and Gutters and, after inspection, could have required that the work conform with his standards. In addition, the court found that Stein had agreed to perform future warranty work for Midland Roofing and Gutters and had established a joint account for the payment for that work. Finally, the court found that Stein had reserved the right to discontinue the parties' arrangement and prohibit Midland Roofing and Gutters from using his telephone number and business license. Although the court noted that Stein did not specifically hire the employees of Midland Roofing and Gutters or arrange for their work schedule or payment, the court found that "there are sufficient indices of control and proprietary interest to determine that he was in fact a partner."

In addition ... the record reflects that Stein was involved in the oversight of the day-to-day workings of Midland Roofing and Gutters. Stein testified at trial that he visited Midland Roofing and Gutter job sites and gave advice on local building code requirements. In addition, Stein testified that he was in the offices of Midland Roofing and Gutters on a daily basis and answered the phones for that entity. Moreover, the evidence presented at trial established that Stein and Midland Roofing and Gutters worked together to contact the general public. This evidence was clearly indicative of Stein's interest in and control of Midland Roofing and Gutters....

The final element ... requires that there must be an agreement to share profits in order to establish a partnership. In this case, the District Court found that Stein was entitled to receive a percentage of Midland Roofing and Gutters' profit. Specifically, the court noted that both the written agreement formalizing the parties' arrangement and its subsequent modification entitled Stein to a percentage of the gross revenue on all work done by Midland Roofing and Gutters. In addition, the court noted that, according to testimony at trial, Stein earned between $75,000 and $92,000 in both cash and materials from his agreement with Midland Roofing and Gutters. As the District Court correctly stated, "[t]he receipt by a person of a share of the profits of a business is prima facie evidence that such person is a partner in the business." Section 35-10-202(4), MCA (1991)....

Because we uphold the District Court's findings regarding the establishment of the four elements of a partnership, we hold that the court's conclusion that Stein, Beebe, Potter, and Evans had created a partnership is correct. The only remaining question, then, is whether Stein is liable, as a partner, for Midland Roofing and Gutters' debt to MacArthur Company.

Section 35-10-307(2), MCA (1991), provides that "[a]ll partners are liable ... jointly for all ... debts and obligations of the partnership." In this case, because we hold that Stein was a partner in Midland Roofing and Gutters, we further conclude he was jointly liable for the partnership's debt to MacArthur Company.... Furthermore, we reject Stein's contention that he is not liable to MacArthur because MacArthur was not aware of his relationship with Midland Roofing and Gutters when it extended credit to the company. Reliance is an element of partnership by estoppel; it is not necessary to the establishment of liability of a partner in fact. Therefore, we hold that the District Court was correct in its conclusion that, pursuant to § 35-10-307, MCA (1991), Stein was jointly liable for the partnership's debt to MacArthur Company.

Id. at 217–19.

5. Compare the tests used by the *MacArthur*, *Holmes*, and *Schlumberger* courts. In *MacArthur*, the plaintiff was a third party seeking to impose partnership liability on the defendant. In *Holmes* and *Schlumberger*, the plaintiff claimed to be one of the principals of the alleged partnership. The *Holmes* court suggested that the nature of the plaintiff may make a difference to the court's inquiry. Do you agree?

6. People starting up businesses, such as Holmes and Lerner, often take a casual approach at the outset. The formation of companies such as Facebook and Snapchat illustrate this [the former in the popular motion picture, "The Social Network," and the latter summarized, along with *Holmes v. Lerner*, in my book, *Contracts in the Real World: Stories of Popular Contracts and Why They Matter* 11–14 (2d ed. 2016)].

2. Limited Liability Partnerships

Although limited liability partnerships are a product of the 1990s, their development is reminiscent of the advent of professional corporations in the 1960s. Professional corporations developed so that licensed professionals, such as physicians, attorneys, and accountants, could take advantage of certain tax code provisions that gave favorable treatment to companies organized as corporations. Then, as now, in many states professionals could not organize as a limited liability business.

A parallel movement occurred in the 1990s, a time when individual tax rates were often lower than corporate rates, and taxation as a partnership became very attractive. The limited liability company ("LLC," which is discussed *infra*, Section III.C. of this chapter) was the first new form to respond to those changes. In many states, however, licensed professionals were prohibited from using the form because of its broad grant of limited liability to members. These professionals turned to state legislatures to provide them with protection from personal liability for damages arising from wrongful acts that became partnership obligations, such as those arising from their partners' malpractice or other similar misconduct. (In the 1980s, several large law firms and their partners declared bankruptcy as a result of their inability to pay for the misconduct of a partner responsible for an exceptionally large transaction.) The result was the limited liability partnership.

In most states, the limited liability partnership is not a separate business form but an option included in the general partnership statutes. Limited liability partnerships, like most other unincorporated businesses, may elect either the partnership or corporate form of taxation. Like other unincorporated associations, for diversity of citizenship purposes, a limited liability partnership is deemed to be a citizen of every state in which each of its partners is a citizen.

The rapidity with which states have recently passed limited liability partnership statutes is noteworthy. As of this writing, almost all states provide for this type of business organization. As the field of alternative forms of business organizations becomes increasingly crowded, one is compelled to ask whether so many types of different business organization forms can or should survive.

Limited Liability Partnerships (LLP) are created by following the procedures set out in UPA (1997) § 1001. LLPs cannot arise as a matter of law. Initially, the partners must approve the decision to organize as a limited liability partnership. Creating an LLP or converting an existing general partnership to an LLP is considered to be a significant event. Thus the vote required to become an LLP is the same as that required to amend a partnership agreement. If the partnership agreement is silent on the issue of the required vote, the default rule of unanimity will apply. The UPA voting requirement has been amended in a number of states, requiring approval by only a majority of partners.

Once the necessary approval to become an LLP has been effected, the partners must file an LLP partnership statement of qualification, usually with the Secretary of State's Office. The statement of qualification provides information about the limited liability partnership, the name of the partnership's agent for service of process if required, and a statement that the partnership has elected to be a limited liability partnership. The company's name must indicate that it is a limited liability partnership, usually through the use of LLP or a similar designation. The statement of qualification becomes effective upon filing, and the company comes into existence as an LLP. Partners who have paid in the full amount of their capital contributions will not be liable for partnership obligations, which must be satisfied from partnership assets only.

Like corporations and limited liability companies, LLPs must annually file a report with the Secretary of State's office and pay a franchise fee. The grant of limited liability will continue so long as the company is in good standing.

C. Financing

A partnership, like any other enterprise, needs money and other assets to conduct its business. The types and amount of assets a company should have depend on the nature of the venture. A fledgling software development company may need only a personal computer system and some office space to get started. A transportation company, on the other hand, may require substantial capital investment in equipment. The left hand side of a company's balance sheet describes the types and historical costs of its assets. (See the Appendix, Financial Statements.)

A business can raise capital through contributions of owners or by borrowing money, either from third party lenders or from company owners. The UPA (1997) anticipates the possibility that a partner may have a variety of financial arrangements with the business by recognizing that a partner may both provide capital to and lend money to the partnership.[13] Obligations to creditors, including those who are also partners, are recorded in the liabilities section of the company's balance sheet, whereas the value of partners' ownership interests appears in the equity section.

It is essential to establish at the outset a plan to raise additional capital. An ongoing partnership has relatively few options for raising additional capital. If the partners do not have a plan in place before the capital is needed, if the company is prospering, they may lose important business opportunities. Conversely, if the business is struggling, they may not have the time to wait if the capital is needed immediately. The company may borrow money, but doing so will increase the liability of all partners. Further, if the company is in a financial downturn, borrowing may not be an option or may be an option only if the company pays very high rates of interest.

The company may take in new partners, but this action may require a change in management structure if the number of partners becomes too large. In addition, this approach will reduce the equity interests of the current partners. The new partners may be able to drive a hard bargain if the partnership needs money badly. The result may be that the new partners will have larger profit or equity shares than they would have had if they had been among the original investors. The company may also try to obtain additional capital from the current owners. Without an agreement, however, they cannot be compelled to contribute.

If the partnership has significant financial needs, the partners contributing additional capital may, like the new partners described above, try to bargain for greater financial share or returns than they would otherwise have. If they take advantage of the circumstances and reach a bargain highly favorable to themselves, hard feelings may develop among the formerly collegial partners. If those contributing additional funds do not approach the situation in the way a new partner would, the contributing partners may resent the benefits accruing to the noncontributing partners. A partnership agreement should anticipate and address problems such as these.

Additional issues should be addressed in the partnership agreement such as the following. What happens to the interest of someone who is unable to contribute or of a partner whose primary contribution is services? Should the additional capital be contributed in the form of a loan, of an equity interest or a combination of the two?

D. Management

Partnership acts provide a structure for the ongoing management of the business by containing default rules that determine who has a right to vote, how votes are allocated, and what vote is required for approval of a proposed action. These rules may be varied by agreement of the partners. The two versions of the UPA vest in all partners the right to manage the business.[14] The right to vote is therefore tied

13. UPA (1997) §§ 401(e), 807(a).
14. UPA (1914) § 18(e); UPA (1997) § 401(f).

to one's status as a partner. This vesting of management rights in all partners is one reason partnership law requires unanimous approval for the admission of a new partner.

Both versions of the UPA allocate votes on a *per capita* basis,[15] giving every partner one vote, irrespective of the amount of the partner's capital contribution. In most situations, the vote of a majority will carry the day.[16] Extraordinary matters, such as the admission of a new partner or an act in contravention of the partnership agreement, require unanimity.[17] This requirement shifts voting power to the minority interests by creating a veto power in an individual partner who is thus able to thwart the will of the majority.

The voting structure reveals much about the assumptions upon which partnership law is based. A fully participatory management structure is workable when a firm has only a few owners who are engaged in the business and are not merely passive investors. The equal allocation of votes makes sense if one assumes that all partners will work in the business as well as contribute capital. When these assumptions do not apply, either because there are many partners, or because a significant proportion are passive investors, a management structure in which owners cede decision-making authority to a few managers becomes desirable. This deviation from the statutory default rules can be accomplished in a partnership agreement describing who has management authority, the scope of that authority, how the authority is to be exercised, and how votes are allocated.

The allocation of voting power and the vote required for approval must be given careful consideration. In a two-person partnership, all decisions must be unanimous, because a split vote will not produce the majority required for approval of ordinary matters. Some provision should, therefore, be made for breaking deadlocks. In a three- or four-person partnership, the vote of a super majority is needed to approve an ordinary proposal or action. Similarly, the decision whether voting rights should accrue on a *per capita* basis, be tied to the amount of capital contribution, or be allocated on a different basis requires careful thought. Persons who invest significantly more capital than their partners may want greater voting power to protect their investments because if the partnership business takes a downturn, the largest investors will assume the greatest financial risks.

A partnership agreement may also create different classes of partners grouped by financial and/or voting rights. Law firms often use this approach, distinguishing between partners that are essentially salaried employees and those that share in the profits.

E. Fiduciary Duties

Fiduciary obligations of partners are a central component of partnership law. They are both aspirational and practical in nature. In order for a joint enterprise to function

---

15. *Id.*
16. UPA (1914) § 18(h); UPA (1997) § 401(j).
17. UPA (1914) § 18(g), (h); UPA (1997) § 401(i), (j).

well, the members must conform their conduct according to what is in the best interests of their common venture. They must be able to trust each other to act honorably, to treat each other fairly, and to share the benefits of the enterprise. If this were not the case, then all partners would not only have to perform their own required functions, they would also have to monitor the others to make sure they were behaving appropriately, and not working solely to their own personal advantage and to the disadvantage of the enterprise and the other partners.

The following case is a frequently cited classic that has set the standard for fiduciary obligations among partners. Although the business under consideration was characterized as a joint venture, the rule and rationale of Justice Cardozo's opinion have been widely applied to all forms of privately held companies: general and limited liability partnerships, limited liability companies and closely held corporations.

Meinhard v. Salmon

New York Court of Appeals
164 N.E. 545 (1928)

CARDOZO, C.J.

On April 10, 1902, Louisa M. Gerry leased to the defendant Walter J. Salmon the premises known as the Hotel Bristol at the northwest corner of Forty-Second street and Fifth avenue in the city of New York. The lease was for a term of 20 years, commencing May 1, 1902, and ending April 30, 1922. The lessee undertook to change the hotel building for use as shops and offices at a cost of $200,000. Alterations and additions were to be accretions to the land.

Salmon, while in course of treaty with the lessor as to the execution of the lease, was in course of treaty with Meinhard, the plaintiff, for the necessary funds. The result was a joint venture with terms embodied in a writing. Meinhard was to pay to Salmon half of the moneys requisite to reconstruct, alter, manage, and operate the property. Salmon was to pay to Meinhard 40 per cent of the net profits for the first five years of the lease and 50 per cent for the years thereafter. If there were losses, each party was to bear them equally. Salmon, however, was to have sole power to "manage, lease, underlet and operate" the building. There were to be certain preemptive rights for each in the contingency of death.

They were coadventures, subject to fiduciary duties akin to those of partners. As to this we are all agreed. The heavier weight of duty rested, however, upon Salmon. He was a coadventurer with Meinhard, but he was manager as well. During the early years of the enterprise, the building, reconstructed, was operated at a loss. If the relation had then ended, Meinhard as well as Salmon would have carried a heavy burden. Later the profits became large with the result that for each of the investors there came a rich return. For each the venture had its phases of fair weather and of foul. The two were in it jointly, for better or for worse.

When the lease was near its end, Elbridge T. Gerry had become the owner of the reversion. He owned much other property in the neighborhood, one lot adjoining the Bristol building on Fifth avenue and four lots on Forty-Second street. He had a plan to lease the entire tract for a long term to some one who would destroy the buildings then existing and put up another in their place. In the latter part of 1921, he submitted such a project to several capitalists and dealers. He was unable to carry it through with any of them. Then, in January, 1922, with less than four months of the lease to run, he approached the defendant Salmon.

The result was a new lease to the Midpoint Realty Company, which is owned and controlled by Salmon, a lease covering the whole tract, and involving a huge outlay. The term is to be 20 years, but successive covenants for renewal will extend it to a maximum of 80 years at the will of either party. The existing buildings may remain unchanged for seven years. They are then to be torn down, and a new building to cost $3,000,000 is to be placed upon the site. The rental, which under the Bristol lease was only $55,000, is to be from $350,000 to $475,000 for the properties so combined. Salmon personally guaranteed the performance by the lessee of the covenants of the new lease until such time as the new building had been completed and fully paid for.

The lease between Gerry and the Midpoint Realty Company was signed and delivered on January 25, 1922. Salmon had not told Meinhard anything about it. Whatever his motive may have been, he had kept the negotiations to himself. Meinhard was not informed even of the bare existence of a project. The first that he knew of it was in February, when the lease was an accomplished fact. He then made demand on the defendants that the lease be held in trust as an asset of the venture, making offer upon the trial to share the personal obligations incidental to the guaranty. The demand was followed by refusal, and later by this suit. A referee gave judgment for the plaintiff, limiting the plaintiff's interest in the lease, however, to 25 per cent. The limitation was on the theory that the plaintiff's equity was to be restricted to one-half of so much of the value of the lease as was contributed or represented by the occupation of the Bristol site. Upon cross-appeals to the Appellate Division, the judgment was modified so as to enlarge the equitable interest to one-half of the whole lease. With this enlargement of plaintiff's interest, there went, of course, a corresponding enlargement of his attendant obligations. The case is now here on an appeal by the defendants.

Joint adventurers, like copartners, owe to one another, while the enterprise continues, the duty of the finest loyalty. Many forms of conduct permissible in a workaday world for those acting at arm's length, are forbidden to those bound by fiduciary ties. A trustee is held to something stricter than the morals of the market place. Not honesty alone, but the punctilio of an honor the most sensitive, is then the standard of behavior. As to this there has developed a tradition that is unbending and inveterate. Uncompromising rigidity has been the attitude of courts of equity when petitioned to undermine the rule of undivided loyalty by the "disintegrating erosion" of particular exceptions. Only thus has the level of conduct for fiduciaries been kept at a level higher than that trodden by the crowd. It will not consciously be lowered by any judgment of this court.

The owner of the reversion, Mr. Gerry, had vainly striven to find a tenant who would favor his ambitious scheme of demolition and construction. Baffled in the search, he turned to the defendant Salmon in possession of the Bristol, the keystone of the project. He figured to himself beyond a doubt that the man in possession would prove a likely customer. To the eye of an observer, Salmon held the lease as owner in his own right, for himself and no one else. In fact he held it as a fiduciary, for himself and another, sharers in a common venture. If this fact had been proclaimed, if the lease by its terms had run in favor of a partnership, Mr. Gerry, we may fairly assume, would have laid before the partners, and not merely before one of them, his plan of reconstruction. The preemptive privilege, or, better, the preemptive opportunity, that was thus an incident of the enterprise, Salmon appropriated to himself in secrecy and silence. He might have warned Meinhard that the plan had been submitted, and that either would be free to compete for the award. If he had done this, we do not need to say whether he would have been under a duty, if successful in the competition, to hold the lease so acquired for the benefit of a venture then about to end, and thus prolong by indirection its responsibilities and duties. The trouble about his conduct is that he excluded his coadventurer from any chance to compete, from any chance to enjoy the opportunity for benefit that had come to him alone by virtue of his agency. This chance, if nothing more, he was under a duty to concede. The price of its denial is an extension of the trust at the option and for the benefit of the one whom he excluded.

No answer is it to say that the chance would have been of little value even if seasonably offered. Such a calculus of probabilities is beyond the science of the chancery. Salmon, the real estate operator, might have been preferred to Meinhard, the woolen merchant. On the other hand, Meinhard might have offered better terms, or reinforced his offer by alliance with the wealth of others. Perhaps he might even have persuaded the lessor to renew the Bristol lease alone, postponing for a time, in return for higher rentals, the improvement of adjoining lots. We know that even under the lease as made the time for the enlargement of the building was delayed for seven years. All these opportunities were cut away from him through another's intervention. He knew that Salmon was the manager. As the time drew near for the expiration of the lease, he would naturally assume from silence, if from nothing else, that the lessor was willing to extend it for a term of years, or at least to let it stand as a lease from year to year. Not impossibly the lessor would have done so, whatever his protestations of unwillingness, if Salmon had not given assent to a project more attractive.

At all events, notice of termination, even if not necessary, might seem, not unreasonably, to be something to be looked for, if the business was over and another tenant was to enter. In the absence of such notice, the matter of an extension was one that would naturally be attended to by the manager of the enterprise, and not neglected altogether. At least, there was nothing in the situation to give warning to any one that while the lease was still in being, there had come to the manager an offer of extension which he had locked within his breast to be utilized by himself alone. The very fact that Salmon was in control with exclusive powers of direction charged him the more obviously with the duty of disclosure, since only through disclosure could opportunity be equalized. If he might cut off renewal by a purchase for his own benefit when four months ere to pass before the lease would have an end, he might do so with equal right while there remained as many years. He might steal a march on his comrade under cover of the darkness, and then hold the captured ground. Loyalty and comradeship are not so easily abjured.

Little profit will come from a dissection of the precedents. None precisely similar is cited in the briefs of counsel. What is similar in many, or so it seems to us, is the animating principle. Authority is, of course, abundant that one partner may not appropriate to his own use a renewal of a lease, though its term is to begin at the expiration of the partnership.... Equity refuses to confine within the bounds of classified transactions its precept of a loyalty that is undivided and unselfish. Certain at least it is that a "man obtaining his locus standi, and his opportunity for making such arrangements, by the position he occupies as a partner, is bound by his obligation to his copartners in such dealings not to separate his interest from theirs, but, if he acquires any benefit, to communicate it to them."... A constructive trust is, then, the remedial device through which preference of self is made subordinate to loyalty to others.

We have no thought to hold that Salmon was guilty of a conscious purpose to defraud. Very likely he assumed in all good faith that with the approaching end of the venture he might ignore his coadventurer and take the extension for himself. He had given to the enterprise time and labor as well as money. He had made it a success. Meinhard, who had given money, but neither time nor labor, had already been richly paid. There might seem to be something grasping in his insistence upon more. Such recriminations are not unusual when coadventurers fall out. They are not without their force if conduct is to be judged by the common standards of competitors. That is not to say that they have pertinency here. Salmon had put himself in a position in which thought of self was to be renounced, however hard the abnegation. He was much more than a coadventurer. He was a managing coadventurer. For him and for those like him the rule of undivided loyalty is relentless and supreme.

A different question would be here if there were lacking any nexus of relation between the business conducted by the manager and the opportunity brought to him as an incident of management. For this problem, as for most, there are distinctions of degree. If Salmon had received from Gerry a proposition to lease a building at a location far removed, he might have held for himself the privilege thus acquired, or so we shall assume. Here the subject-matter of the new lease was an extension and enlargement of the subject-matter of the old one. A managing coadventurer appropriating the benefit of such a lease without warning to his partner might fairly expect to be reproached with conduct that was underhand, or lacking, to say the least, in reasonable candor, if the partner were to surprise him in the act of signing the new instrument. Conduct subject to that reproach does not receive from equity a healing benediction.

A question remains as to the form and extent of the equitable interest to be allotted to the plaintiff. The trust as declared has been held to attach to the lease which was in the name of the defendant corporation. We think it ought to attach at the option of the defendant Salmon to the shares of stock which were owned by him or were under his control. The difference may be important if the lessee shall wish to execute an assignment of the lease, as it ought to be free to do with the consent of the lessor. On the other hand, an equal division of the shares might lead to other hardships. It might take away from Salmon the power of control and management which under the plan of the joint venture he was to have from first to last. The number of shares to be allotted to the plaintiff should, therefore, be reduced to such an extent as may be necessary to preserve to the defendant Salmon the expected measure of dominion. To that end an extra share should be added to his half.

Subject to this adjustment, we agree with the Appellate Division that the plaintiff's equitable interest is to be measured by the value of half of the entire lease, and not merely by half of some undivided part. A single building covers the whole area. Physical division is impracticable along the lines of the Bristol site, the keystone of the whole. Division of interests and burdens is equally impracticable....

The judgment should be modified by providing that at the option of the defendant Salmon there may be substituted for a trust attaching to the lease a trust attaching to the shares of stock, with the result that one-half of such shares together with one additional share will in that event be allotted to the defendant Salmon and the other shares to the plaintiff, and as so modified the judgment should be affirmed with costs.

ANDREWS, J. (dissenting).

Where the trustee, or the partner or the tenant in common, takes no new lease but buys the reversion in good faith a somewhat different question arises. Here is no direct appropriation of the expectancy of renewal. Here is no offshoot of the original lease. The issue, then, is whether actual fraud, dishonesty, or unfairness is present in the transaction. If so, the purchaser may well be held as a trustee.

With this view of the law I am of the opinion that the issue here is simple. Was the transaction, in view of all the circumstances surrounding it, unfair and inequitable? I reach this conclusion for two reasons. There was no general partnership, merely a joint venture for a limited object, to end at a fixed time. The new lease, covering additional property, containing many new and unusual terms and conditions, with a possible duration of 80 years, was more nearly the purchase of the reversion than the ordinary renewal with which the authorities are concerned....

The one complaint made is that Mr. Salmon obtained the new lease without informing Mr. Meinhard of his intention. Nothing else. There is no claim of actual fraud. No claim of misrepresentation to any one. Here was no movable property to be acquired by a new tenant at a sacrifice to its owners. No good will, largely dependent on location, built up by the joint efforts of two men. Here was a refusal of the landlord to renew the Bristol lease on any terms; a proposal made by him, not sought by Mr. Salmon, and a choice by him and by the original lessor of the person with whom they wished to deal shown by the covenants against assignment or under-letting, and by their ignorance of the arrangement with Mr. Meinhard.

What then was the scope of the adventure into which the two men entered? It is to be remembered that before their contract was signed Mr. Salmon had obtained the lease of the Bristol property. Very likely the matter had been earlier discussed between them. The $5,000 advance by Mr. Meinhard indicates that fact. But it has been held that the written contract defines their rights and duties. Having the lease, Mr. Salmon assigns no interest in it to Mr. Meinhard. He is to manage the property. It is for him to decide what alterations shall be made and to fix the rents. But for 20 years from May 1, 1902, Salmon is to make all advances from his own funds and Meinhard is to pay him personally on demand one-half of all expenses incurred and all losses sustained "during the full term of said lease," and during the same period Salmon is to pay him a part of the net profits. There was no joint capital provided.

It seems to me that the venture so inaugurated had in view a limited object and was to end at a limited time. There was no intent to expand it into a far greater undertaking lasting for many years. The design was to exploit a particular lease. Doubtless in it Mr. Meinhard had an equitable interest, but in it alone. This interest terminated when the joint adventure terminated. There was no intent that for the benefit of both any advantage should be taken of the chance of renewal — that the adventure should be continued beyond that date. Mr. Salmon has done all he promised to do in return for Mr. Meinhard's undertaking when he distributed profits up to May 1, 1922.

Suppose this lease, nonassignable without the consent of the lessor, had contained a renewal option. Could Mr. Meinhard have exercised it? Could he have insisted that Mr. Salmon do so? Had Mr. Salmon done so could he insist that the agreement to share losses still existed, or could Mr. Meinhard have claimed that the joint adventure was still to continue for 20 or 80 years? I do not think so. The adventure by its express terms ended on May 1, 1922. The contract by its language and by its whole import excluded the idea that the tenant's expectancy was to subsist for the benefit of the plaintiff. On that date whatever there was left of value in the lease reverted to Mr. Salmon, as it would had the lease been for thirty years instead of twenty. Any equity which Mr. Meinhard possessed was in the particular lease itself, not in any possibility of renewal. There was nothing unfair in Mr. Salmon's conduct....

––––––––––––

Neither the majority nor the dissenting opinion characterizes Meinhard and Salmon, the co-adventurers, as "partners." There is little question, however, that the terms of their relationship could meet the traditional and contemporary definitions of partnership (an association of two or more persons to carry on as co-owners a business for profit). (Consider how each side would argue that the Meinhard/Salmon business organization was or was not a partnership.) A technical issue not discussed in the opinions may explain why the court chose not to characterize the business as a partnership.

Apparently, in 1917 Meinhard had assigned his interest in the arrangement to his wife for tax planning purposes (the latter would be taxed at lower rates on related income) and his tax lawyer had separately given him an opinion that, also for tax purposes, the arrangement would not be treated as a partnership. Salmon sought to use the latter opinion to argue against imposition of fiduciary duties in the case. It seems that the opinions did not characterize the arrangement in any specific way to avoid getting into these somewhat technical issues. *See* Geoffrey P. Miller, *A Glimpse of Society via a Case and Cardozo:* Meinhard v. Salmon, *in* THE ICONIC CASES IN CORPORATE LAW 21 (Jonathan R. Macey, ed. 2008).

F. Partners' Liability for Partnership Obligations

At one time it was customary for owners of businesses to have unlimited liability for company debts. Business owners were personally responsible for company obligations. If business assets were insufficient to satisfy creditors' claims, owners' personal assets could be used to pay company debts. Today, much has changed. Limited liability has become the norm. Limited liability means that company assets alone will be used to meet company obligations. Owners' personal assets will not be used to pay business debts. Owners of corporations, limited liability companies and limited liability partnerships enjoy the protection of limited liability, as do limited partners of limited partnerships. Only sole proprietors and partners in a general partnership may be held personally liable for a company's debts.

1. General Partnerships

UPA (1997) makes several changes to the UPA (1914) rules governing a partner's liability for the obligations of a general partnership. One is that partners are jointly and severally liable for all partnership obligations.[22] Creditors must, however, exhaust partnership assets before partners' personal assets may be used to satisfy creditors' claims. A second change eliminates an ambiguity in the statement in UPA (1914) § 9(1) that "the act of every partner ... for apparently carrying on in the usual way the business of the partnership of which he is a member binds the partnership." That formulation was unclear as to whether the act must be of the type conducted in the business of the particular partnership in question or in the business of partnerships of the kind under consideration. UPA (1997) § 301(1) has resolved the question in favor of the latter approach.

UPA (1997) § 303 permits a partnership to file a statement of authority either to grant or to limit the authority of an individual partner. Although the purpose of the section is to facilitate the transfer of real property held in the partnership name by identifying which partners have the authority to make a particular transfer, it may also be used to specify the extent of a partner's authority for conducting ordinary business transactions. When properly filed and recorded in the land records, a statement of a grant or limitation of authority to transfer real estate is conclusive against third parties. UPA (1997) also avoids some procedural hurdles that third parties enforcing claims against the partnership had to contend with under the old act. The

---

22. UPA (1997) § 306(a).

imposition of joint and several liability for all partnership obligations and the treatment of a partnership as an entity that may sue and be sued in the partnership name eliminate the need to join individual partners. The following case provides an example of the roles played by UPA provisions and the common law of Agency in establishing liability for partnership obligations.

Kansallis Finance Ltd v. Fern

Massachusetts Supreme Judicial Court

659 N.E.2d 731 (1995)

FRIED, JUSTICE.

The United States Court of Appeals for the First Circuit has certified to this court, the following two questions of State law:

1. Under Massachusetts law, to find that a certain act is within the scope of a partnership for the purpose of applying the doctrine of vicarious liability, must a plaintiff show, inter alia, that the act was taken at least in part with the intent to serve or benefit the partnership?

In order that we may give the guidance that the Court of Appeals seeks, we offer the more extensive "discussion of relevant Massachusetts law" that the Court of Appeals invites in its certification order....

The questions arise out of an appeal by Kansallis Finance Ltd. (plaintiff) from a trial in the United States District Court for the District of Massachusetts. The Court of Appeals stated that the first question concerns an issue on which an apparent conflict exists in Massachusetts precedent, and that the second question concerns a separate issue on which there is no controlling Massachusetts precedent.

I

We summarize the facts relevant to the questions certified. Stephen Jones and the four defendants were law partners in Massachusetts when, in connection with a loan and lease financing transaction, the plaintiff sought and obtained an opinion letter from Jones. In the order of certification, the Court of Appeals states that the letter, executed in Massachusetts and issued on "Fern, Anderson, Donahue, Jones & Sabatt, P.A." letterhead, "contained several intentional misrepresentations concerning the transaction and was part of a conspiracy by Jones and others (though not any of the defendants here) to defraud Kansallis." Although Jones did not personally sign the letter, he arranged for a third party to do so, and both the District Court judge and the jury found that Jones adopted or ratified the issuance of the letter. Jones was later convicted on criminal charges for his part in the fraud, but the plaintiff was unable to collect its $880,000 loss from Jones or his co-conspirators.

In an effort to recover its loss, the plaintiff brought suit in the United States District Court for the District of Massachusetts seeking compensation from Jones's law partners on the theory that the partners were liable for the damage caused by the fraudulent letter.... Both the judge and jury, for different reasons, decided that defendants were not liable for Jones's conduct. The Court of Appeals affirmed both the judge's and the jury's factual findings and certified two questions to this court in order to resolve the legal issues.

On plaintiff's common law claims, the jury based their verdict on their findings that (1) Jones did not have apparent authority to issue the opinion letter[23] and (2) that his action in issuing the opinion letter was outside the scope of the partnership. On appeal to the Court of Appeals, the plaintiff contended that the jury based their second finding on an erroneous instruction directing that, to find Jones's actions within the scope of the partnership, the issuance of the letter must satisfy a three-prong test. It must have: (1) been "the kind of thing a law partner would do"; (2) "occurred substantially within the authorized time and geographic limits of the partnership; and" (3) been "motivated at least in part by a purpose to serve the partnership." Although the jury did not indicate which prong the plaintiff failed to satisfy, the plaintiff objected to the addition of the third prong, and it is on the correctness of including this third prong in the test that the Court of Appeals now seeks guidance. The Court of Appeals found our law on this issue unclear because it found that two decisions appeared to pull in opposite directions. The Court of Appeals therefore certified this first question to us....

II
A

The parties have cited to us cases from this and other jurisdictions, as well as general principles set out in the Restatement (Second) of Agency and in the Uniform Partnership Act. Whatever difficulties this array of authorities presents may in part be attributed to the fact that the issue of vicarious liability has engendered somewhat divergent formulations in the several different contexts in which it has arisen. The genus here is agency, and two of its species, for which there are special rules for determining vicarious liability, are partnership and master-servant. In the context of a partnership, the person acting and the persons who might be held liable for his actions usually stand on an equal footing and may be thought of as equally implicated in a joint enterprise. By contrast, the law of the vicarious liability of a master for the acts of his servant grew up in circumstances where the actor was often in a subordinate position and had a limited interest in the enterprise which he assists. *See* Restatement (Second) of Agency § 218 (1957). Yet both servants and partners are categorized as agents of their principals....

In the partnership context, while each partner is the agent of the partnership, he also stands in the role of a principal—a reciprocity that is lacking in the master-servant relation. Finally, there is an important practical distinction between determining vicarious liability for harms that come about through the victim's voluntary interactions with the purported agent—as in the case of contracts, of fraud and of misrepresentation—and those that are inflicted on a victim who has made no choice to deal with the agent, as in the case of an accident, an assault or a trespass. Only in the former instance is the inquiry into apparent authority particularly apt, since where the victim transacts business with the agent, the victim's ability to assess the agent's authority will bear on whether and in what ways he chooses to deal with him. By contrast, where

---

23. [2] The judge instructed the jury that "[t]here is no contention here that Jones had actual authority from the defendants to issue this Opinion Letter."

the victim has not chosen to deal with the agent by whose act he suffers harm—as in an automobile accident—the scope of employment seems the natural determinant of vicarious liability, and that is where the concept has had its most usual application.

Standing behind these diverse concepts of vicarious liability is a principle that helps to rationalize them. This is the principle that as between two innocent parties—the principal-master and the third party—the principal-master who for his own purposes places another in a position to do harm to a third party should bear the loss. A principal who requires an agent to transact his business, and can only get that business done if third parties deal with the agent as if with the principal, cannot complain if the innocent third party suffers loss by reason of the agent's act. Similarly, the master who must put an instrument into his servant's hands in order to get his business done, must also bear the loss if the servant causes harm to a stranger in the use of that instrument as the business is transacted.

This overarching principle measures the imposition of vicarious liability in particular contexts and suggests its own limitations. Where there is actual authority to transact the very business or to do the very act that causes the harm, the agent acts as the extension of the will of his principal and the case for vicarious liability is clear. Where the authority is only apparent, vicarious liability recognizes that it is the principal who for his own purposes found it useful to create the impression that the agent acts with his authority, and therefore it is the principal who must bear the burden of the misuse to which that appearance has been put. Restatement (Second) of Agency § 8 (1957). But there is little fairness in saddling the principal with liability for acts that a reasonable third party would not have supposed were taken on the principal's behalf. Similarly, where the servant acts beyond the scope of his employment he is more like a thief who causes harm with an instrumentality he had no right to use.

Where the wrongdoer transacts business with the victim, the authority—actual or apparent—of the agent to act on the principal's behalf may be conceptualized as the dangerous instrumentality the principal has put in the agent's hands, enabling him to do harm with it. And this creates the temptation to use the concepts of apparent authority and scope of employment interchangeably. But they are not equivalent concepts. A servant or agent may sometimes act within the scope of his master's employment and yet lack apparent authority. The clearest instances are in accident cases where the victim neither knew nor cared what the wrongdoer's relation to his employer might be. Another rarer divergence may be illustrated by the present case.

The scope of employment test asks the question: is this the kind of thing that in a general way employees of this kind do in employment of this kind. It does not ask the different question: whether a reasonable person in the victim's circumstances in the particular case would have taken the agent to be acting with the principal's authority. And so there arises the possibility of vicarious liability where the victim transacted business or otherwise dealt with an agent who lacked even apparent authority in the particular matter. In the case before us here, the jury instructions required the jury to consider both routes to vicarious liability. The jury found that Jones acted without actual or apparent authority, presumably because the form and circumstances of the letter were such that they concluded that no reasonable person in the plaintiff's position would have believed that the letter was issued with the partnership's authority. But then they were asked in the alternative whether Jones "acted in the scope of the partnership." This further question was taken to ask whether writing this opinion letter was the kind of thing that the partnership did—even if there was no apparent authority for this particular letter.

This is the alternative theory, which the District Court labeled "vicarious liability," and under this alternative the defendants might yet be liable if the jury found all three of the conditions set out above in its charge on that issue. The rationale for this possibly more extended liability recognizes an authority in each partner to take the initiative to enlarge the partnership enterprise even without the authority—actual or apparent— of his partners, so long as what he does is within the generic description of the type of partnership involved. Whatever the harshness may be of such a rule extending vicarious liability past apparent authority, it is mitigated by the third factor, requiring that the unauthorized but law partner-like act be intended at least in part to serve the partnership. Since there is then some possibility that the partnership will benefit from the errant partner's act, then as between two innocent parties it is not unfair that the one whom the wrongful act may have and was meant to benefit must bear the burden of the harm.

B

Our cases and statutes can readily be rationalized against the background of these principles. The Uniform Partnership Act provides as general principles that: the law of agency shall apply under that chapter, [UPA (1914)] § 4(3); the act of every partner apparently carrying on in the usual way the business of the partnership binds it, [UPA (1914)] § 9(1); and an act of the partner which is not apparently for the carrying on of the business of the partnership in the usual way does not bind it unless authorized, *id.* [UPA (1914)] § 9(2). Where, however, by any wrongful act of a partner acting in the ordinary course of the business of the partnership, or with the authority of the copartners, loss or injury is caused to a third person, or a penalty is incurred, the partnership is liable therefore, [UPA (1914)] § 13.

Because the Uniform Partnership Act [(1914)] at § 4(3) specifically provides that the law of agency applies, it is appropriate to refer, as did the District Court in formulating its jury instructions, to the Restatement (Second) of Agency (1957). The District Court derived the second theory of liability, which it labeled vicarious liability and on which it instructed the jury regarding the scope of the partnership business, from § 228(1) of the Restatement (Second) of Agency. Section 228(1) provides in relevant part that conduct of a servant is within the scope of his employment, if but only if the conduct is (a) of the kind he is employed to perform, (b) within the partnership's authorized time and space limits, and (c) actuated, at least in part, by a purpose to serve the master. Subsection (2) states the complementary proposition that conduct is not within the scope of employment if it is different in kind from that authorized or too little actuated by a purpose to serve the master. Section 261 states the alternative ground of vicarious liability based on apparent authority: that a principal who puts an agent in a position which enables the agent, while apparently acting within his authority, to commit a fraud on a third party is subject to liability to the third party. And §262 states the complementary proposition that a person who otherwise would be liable to another for the misrepresentations of one acting for him is not relieved from liability by the fact that the agent acts entirely for his own purposes, unless the other has notice of that. Thus, under §262, if an agent has actual or apparent authority, the principal is not relieved of liability for that agent's misrepresentation even though the requirements of §228(1)(c) have not been met.

The two cases which concerned the Court of Appeals may be understood in this light. *Wang Labs., Inc. v. Business Incentives, Inc.*, 398 Mass. 854, 501 N.E.2d 1163 (1986), a [consumer protection] case, did indeed require and find an intention to benefit the corporate principal as a condition of vicarious liability, but in that case we did not address and so did not negate the possibility of vicarious liability by the route of apparent authority. Moreover, the harm complained of in *Wang*, which was akin to the tort of intentional interference with contractual relations, did not require for its accomplishment that the victim rely on the agent's authority, and so an analysis in terms of apparent authority would have been beside the point—every bit as much as it would be in an automobile accident or an assault. By contrast, in *New England Acceptance Corp. v. American Mfrs. Mut. Ins. Corp.*, 368 N.E.2d 1385 (1977), a contract or tort case, the fraud that was worked on the plaintiff depended for its accomplishment on the plaintiff's believing that the agent was acting with his principal's authority. It is for that reason that we adopted our Appeals Court's conclusion in that case that there could be vicarious liability even though "the agents were acting entirely for their own purposes." Indeed, as we have pointed out, that will usually be the case where a dishonest agent misuses his apparent authority to work a fraud upon both his principal and a third party.

C

Accordingly, if we take the first certified question to ask whether a partner must necessarily at least in part act for the benefit of the partnership if the partnership is to be liable for his actions, the answer is "no." But the answer is "no" only because under our law—and the law of partnership and agency generally—there are two routes by which vicarious liability may be found. If the partner has apparent authority to do the act, that will be sufficient to ground vicarious liability, whether or not he acted to benefit the partnership. It is only where there is no apparent authority, which is what the jury found on the common law counts here, that there may yet be vicarious liability on the alternative ground requiring such an intent to benefit the partnership. Since there is no evidence that Jones was acting to benefit the partnership, the District Court's judgment for the defendants on the common law counts accords with our statutes and precedents. The jury instructions on the common law claims were correct....

IV

To summarize, we hold that under the law of the Commonwealth a partnership may be liable by one of two routes for the unauthorized acts of a partner: if there is apparent authority, or if the partner acts within the scope of the partnership at least in part to benefit the partnership. Where there is neither apparent authority nor action intended at least in part to benefit the partnership, there cannot be vicarious liability. Accordingly, we answer the first question "no," but only because even if a partner acts with no purpose to benefit the partnership, vicarious liability may yet be appropriate, if he is clothed with apparent authority. In this case, however, the jury found that there was no apparent authority. . . .

2. Limited Liability Partnerships

As previously discussed in Section I.B.2., *supra*, limited liability partnerships must be created following the procedures set out in UPA (1997) § 1001. The partners must elect to create a limited liability partnership and file a statement of qualification with the Secretary of State's Office. Upon a proper filing, UPA § 306 (c) applies, and only the company's assets may be used to satisfy creditors' claims. LLP partners do not have joint and several liability for company obligations, and partners' personal assets will not be applied to pay company debts. Partner status no longer carries with it an obligation to pay partnership creditors' claims that cannot be satisfied from company assets.

The two cases that follow address the issues of: (1) the consequences of failing to satisfy the required LLP formation procedures; and (2) the scope of limited liability protection.

Apcar Investment Partners VI, Ltd. v. Gaus

Texas Court of Appeals
161 S.W.3d 137 (2005)

McCall, Justice.

Apcar Investment Partners VI, Ltd. [Apcar] brought suit for breach of a lease agreement against Smith & West, L.L.P. [Smith & West] Apcar also sought to recover for the alleged breach of the lease against Smith & West's partners, Michael L. Gaus and John C. West, in their individual capacities. The trial court granted summary judgment to Gaus and West. The trial court severed Apcar's claims against Gaus and West from the remainder of the suit. Thus, the judgment in favor of Gaus and West became final and appealable. We reverse the judgment of the trial court and remand this cause for further proceedings consistent with this opinion.

Background Facts

On March 6, 1995, Smith & West registered as a domestic limited liability partnership under Article 6132b-3.08 of the Texas Revised Partnership Act. . . . On August 11, 1999, MF Partners I, Ltd. [MF] and Smith & West entered into the lease in question. Under the lease, Smith & West leased office space from MF for a term of 60 months. In connection with the lease, Gaus and West signed a guaranty personally guaranteeing Smith & West's performance during the first 24 months of the lease.

MF assigned its interest in the lease to Apcar. Apcar claimed that, on October 31, 2002, Smith & West stopped paying rent under the lease and abandoned the leased premises. Apcar filed suit for breach of lease against: Smith & West, [and] Gaus and West. Gaus and West moved for summary judgment on two grounds: (1) that, as partners in a registered limited liability partnership, they were not individually liable for the partnership's obligations under the lease and (2) that the guaranty they signed in connection with the lease limited their personal liability to the first two years of the lease term. Apcar moved for partial summary judgment, asserting that Gaus and West were individually liable for Smith & West's obligations under the lease because Smith & West was not a registered limited liability partnership when it entered into the lease in question. The trial court granted Gaus and West's motion for summary judgment and denied Apcar's motion for partial summary judgment.

Issues Presented

Apcar presents four points of error for review. In its first point of error, Apcar argues that the trial court erred in granting Gaus and West's motion for summary judgment and in denying its motion for partial summary judgment. Because our holding in the first issue is dispositive of this appeal, we need not address Apcar's other issues.

Standard of Review

Gaus and West's Motion for Summary Judgment

This appeal involves the review of a traditional motion for summary judgment.... The trial court's order granting summary judgment does not specify the grounds upon which it was based. When a trial court's order granting summary judgment does not specify the ground or grounds relied upon for its ruling, summary judgment will be affirmed on appeal if any of the summary judgment grounds advanced by the movant are meritorious....

Registered Limited Liability Partnership Statute

As one ground for summary judgment, Gaus and West argued that they were protected from individual liability under Article 6132b-3.08(a)(1) of the Texas Revised Partnership Act. The determination of this issue involves the interpretation of Article 6132b-3.08. No Texas case has addressed the issue before this court.

Article 6132b-3.08 is entitled "Liability in and Registration of Registered Limited Liability Partnership." Article 6132b-3.08(a)(1) provides that "a partner in a registered limited liability partnership is not individually liable ... for debts and obligations ... incurred while the partnership is a registered limited liability partnership." Apcar contends that the lease obligations were not incurred while Smith & West was a registered limited liability partnership because Smith & West's status as a registered limited liability partnership expired in 1996—three years before the lease was executed. Therefore, Apcar asserts that Gaus and West are personally liable for the lease obligations. Gaus and West contend that Smith & West's initial registration as a registered limited liability partnership in 1995 protects them from individual liability in this case. To support their argument, Gaus and West rely on cases involving the statutory filing requirements for limited partnerships. They assert that, based on the reasoning of the limited partnership cases, Smith & West did not need to comply with statutory renewal requirements for maintaining its status as a registered limited liability partnership in order to protect them from individual liability under the lease....

Smith & West filed its initial application registering as a registered limited liability partnership on March 6, 1995. Article 6132b-3.08(b)(5) provided that the initial registration would expire one year after the date of registration (on March 6, 1996) unless renewed in accordance with Subdivision (7). Smith & West did not file a renewal application before the expiration date. Therefore, its status as a registered limited liability partnership expired on March 6, 1996.

Smith & West entered into the lease three years after its status as a registered limited liability partnership expired. Article 6132b-3.08(a)(1) protects partners from individual liability for debts and obligations that are incurred while the partnership is a registered limited liability partnership. Smith & West was not a registered limited liability partnership when it incurred the lease obligations. Thus, the clear language of Article 6132b-3.08(a)(1) supports Apcar's position that Gaus and West are not protected from individual liability for the lease obligations.

Gaus and West argue that a limited liability partnership is not required to strictly comply with the registration requirements in Article 6132b-3.08(b) for its partners to be protected from individual liability under 6132b-3.08(a)(1). In the context of limited partnerships,[24] courts have held that it is not necessary for limited partnerships to strictly comply with statutory filing requirements for its limited partners to receive limited liability protection....

The limited partnership cases are distinguishable from registered limited liability partnership cases for two reasons. First, the clear language of Article 6132b-3.08(a)(1) provides that partners are protected from individual liability only for debts and obligations that are incurred while the partnership is a registered limited liability partnership. Article 6132b-3.08(b)(5) and (b)(7) provides that registration expires in one year unless it is renewed prior to the expiration date. To apply the reasoning of the limited partnership cases would conflict with the clear language of Article 6132b-3.08. Second, the Texas Revised Limited Partnership Act Article 6132a-1 contains a provision that is not present in Article 6132b-3.08 Article 6132a-1, section 2.01(b) provides in part as follows:

> [A] limited partnership is formed at the time of the filing of the initial certificate of limited partnership with the secretary of state or at a later date or time specified in the certificate if there has been substantial compliance with the requirements of this section.

Article 6132b-3.08 does not contain a "substantial compliance" section, nor does it contain a grace period for filing a renewal application. We hold that a [limited li-

---

24. [A limited partnership has one or more general partners with unlimited liability and one or more limited partners with limited liability. For a discussion of limited partnerships, see Chapter 2, Section III.B.—Eds.]

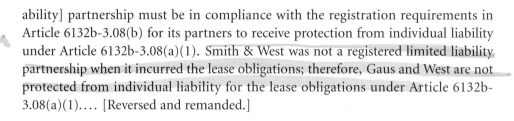

ability] partnership must be in compliance with the registration requirements in Article 6132b-3.08(b) for its partners to receive protection from individual liability under Article 6132b-3.08(a)(1). Smith & West was not a registered limited liability partnership when it incurred the lease obligations; therefore, Gaus and West are not protected from individual liability for the lease obligations under Article 6132b-3.08(a)(1).... [Reversed and remanded.]

The limited liability partnership statutes vary in the scope of their grant of limited liability. At a minimum, partners are shielded from liability for other partners' torts. In some statutes, partners may be liable for specified types of partnership obligations. In other statutes, like UPA (1997) the extent of protection is much broader, approximating the broad grant of limited liability afforded shareholders and members of limited liability companies [LLC].[25]

According to UPA (1997) Prefatory Note, UPA (1997) § 306(c) changes the liability of partners for partnership obligations. As a result of their status as partners, partners in a general partnership have joint and several liability for partnership obligations. When partnership assets are insufficient to pay creditors' claims, partners are obligated to use personal assets to meet the partnership obligations. In contrast, partners in a limited liability partnership do not have joint and several liability for partnership debts. Under UPA (1997) § 306(c), partners in a limited liability partnership are granted a broad limited liability shield similar to that found in corporations and LLCs. LLP partners are protected from personal liability for all partnership obligations incurred while a partnership is a limited liability partnership. This broad grant represents the trend among the states. Under the UPA (1997), only partnership assets may be used to satisfy creditors' claims. Partners' personal assets will not be used to meet partnership obligations, and partners who have made their full capital contributions are not required to pay in additional funds when partnership assets are insufficient to satisfy creditors' claims. Like corporate shareholders and LLC members, however, partners remain personally liable for their own torts and other personal misconduct. Thus, it is important to distinguish between the scope of liability imposed as a result of one's status as a partner in a limited liability partnership and liability resulting from the partner's own personal misconduct.

Notably, unlike statutes governing limited liability companies and corporations, many LLP statutes do not restrict partnership distributions to partners. To protect creditors, a few states do, however, require a minimum amount of liability insurance.

The following case explores the relationship between an LLP's grant of limited liability and claims made by one partner against another for breach of fiduciary duty. The case is based on the New York counterpart of UPA (1997) § 306(c).

---

25. Limited liability companies are discussed in Chapter 2, Section III.C.

Ederer v. Gursky

New York Court of Appeals
881 N.E.2d 204 (2007)

READ, J.

This appeal calls upon us to explore the nature and scope of Partnership Law § 26(b). We hold that this provision does not shield a general partner in a registered limited liability partnership from personal liability for breaches of the partnership's or partners' obligations to each other....

The relationship that deteriorated into this acrimonious dispute began promisingly enough in 1998 when plaintiff Louis Ederer affiliated with the law firm of Gursky & Associates, P.C.,[26] which promptly changed its name to Gursky & Ederer, P.C. (the PC). Ederer joined the PC as a salaried, nonequity contract partner, but he had an understanding with defendant Steven R. Gursky, the PC's sole shareholder, that if their practice developed as anticipated, he would become a full equity partner in about two years' time.

Right on schedule, in May 2000 Gursky orally agreed to increase Ederer's annual compensation by about 17% and to make him a 30% shareholder in the PC as of July 1, the beginning of the PC's fiscal year....

In February 2001, the PC became a registered limited liability partnership known as Gursky & Ederer, LLP (the LLP). Significantly, there was no written partnership agreement. The LLP began billing all new legal services, while the PC billed and collected work-in-process and preexisting accounts receivable, and loaned money to the LLP to fund its start-up. In July 2001, the LLP admitted three new partners, defendants Mitchell B. Stern, Martin Feinberg and Michael A. Levine....

In July 2002, the LLP increased Ederer's annual compensation by about 28%. Gursky also agreed to forgive the remaining $300,000 owed by Ederer for the purchase of his 30% equity interest. Ederer characterizes this gesture as an acknowledgment of his major contributions to the firm's revenue growth; Gursky, as a concession made solely upon Ederer's assurances that he was committed to remaining with the LLP to assure its long-term success.

In June 2003, Ederer advised Gursky that he was withdrawing as a partner in the LLP.... Ederer chalks up his decision to a severe falling out with Gursky in early 2003 over the representation of a firm client. Gursky retorts that Ederer left because the LLP was cash-strapped and unprofitable, and blames him in no small part for this purported state of affairs.

On June 26, 2003, Ederer entered into a withdrawal agreement with ... the LLP, which Gursky signed as president of the PC and a partner in the LLP. Under this

---

26. [A PC is a professional corporation, which is discussed in Chapter 2, Section III.A, *infra.*— Eds.]

agreement, Ederer agreed to remain a partner in the LLP so as to serve as lead counsel for a trial scheduled to commence in Georgia on June 30, 2003, although he was not obligated to delay his withdrawal from the LLP beyond July 8. In exchange, the LLP agreed to "continue to pay Ederer his [regular draw and other compensation through the date of his withdrawal from the LLP]"; to have files on which he was working transferred to his new firm upon the client's request; to give him the opportunity to review his clients' bills before the LLP asked for payment; and to allow him and/or his representatives (including accountants) access to the LLP's ... books and records after his withdrawal from the LLP.

... Ederer withdrew from the LLP on or about July 4, 2003 after having helped secure a $2 million verdict in the Georgia trial, which generated a $600,000 contingency fee for the LLP After Ederer's departure, the LLP continued in business under the name Gursky & Partners, LLP until March 1, 2005, when it ceased operations.

In December 2003, Ederer commenced this action against ... Gursky & Partners, LLP and Gursky, Stern, Feinberg and Levine.... In his amended verified complaint dated November 1, 2005, Ederer sought an accounting of his interest in ... the LLP (the second cause of action)....

... On November 7, 2005, defendants moved to dismiss the complaint as to defendants Gursky, Stern, Feinberg and Levine.... As relevant to this appeal, defendants argued that Ederer's complaint set forth no cognizable causes of action upon which relief could be granted against the individual defendants because Partnership Law § 26(b) shielded them from any personal liability....

Supreme Court determined that Ederer was entitled to an accounting against all defendants because Partnership Law § 26, which places limits on the personal liability of partners in an LLP applies "to debts of the partnership or the partners to third parties" and "has nothing to do with a partner's fiduciary obligation to account to his partners for the assets of the partnership...."

... Defendants appealed. The Appellate Division affirmed Supreme Court's order on December 5, 2006.... Defendants subsequently moved in the Appellate Division for leave to appeal to this Court. On March 20, 2007, the Appellate Division granted defendants' motion and certified the following question to us: "Was the order of Supreme Court, as affirmed by this Court, properly made?" ... To the extent appealed from, as limited by defendants' brief, we now affirm, answering the certified question in the affirmative....

This appeal comes down to a dispute over the effect of the Legislature's 1994 amendments to section 26 of the Partnership Law (L. 1994, ch. 576, § 8). As originally adopted by the Legislature in 1919 (L. 1919, ch. 408), section 26 was identical to section 15 of the Uniform Partnership Act (UPA), which was drafted by the National Conference of Commissioners on Uniform State Laws and approved by the Conference in 1914.[27] ...

---

27. [2] The UPA (1914), which governed general partnerships and limited partnerships except where the limited partnership statute was inconsistent, was adopted in every state except Louisiana, and was "the subject of remarkably few amendments in those states" (see Prefatory Note to Uniform

Partnership Law § 26, as originally enacted, and its prototype, section 15 of the UPA, have always been understood to mean what they plainly say: general partners are jointly and severally liable to nonpartner creditors for all wrongful acts and breaches of trust committed by their partners in carrying out the partnership's business. . . .

The nationwide initiative to create a new business entity combining the flexibility of a partnership without the onus of this traditional vicarious liability originated with a law adopted [in Texas in 1991]. . . .

In New York, the Legislature enacted limited liability partnership legislation [that] . . . eliminated the vicarious liability of a general partner in a registered limited liability partnership by amending section 26 of the Partnership Law. . . . Specifically, new section 26(b) creates an exception to the vicarious liability otherwise applicable by virtue of section 26(a) . . . by providing that:

> "[e]xcept as provided by subdivisions (c) and (d) of this section, no partner of a partnership which is a registered limited liability partnership is liable or accountable, directly or indirectly (including by way of indemnification, contribution or otherwise), for any debts, obligations or liabilities of, or chargeable to, the registered limited liability partnership or each other, whether arising in tort, contract or otherwise, which are incurred, created or assumed by such partnership while such partnership is a registered limited liability partnership, solely by reason of being such a partner."

Section 26(c) excludes from section 26(b)'s liability shield "any negligent or wrongful act or misconduct committed by a partner or by any person under his or her direct supervision and control while rendering professional services on behalf of the] registered limited liability partnership." Section 26(d) allows partners to opt out from or reduce the reach of section 26(b)'s protection from vicarious liability. . . .

Defendants point out that section 26(b) eliminates the liability of a partner in a limited liability partnership for "any debts" without distinguishing between debts owed to a third party or to the partnership or each other. As a result, they contend, the Legislature did not "leave open to conjecture whether § 26(b) was intended to cover debts which may be owed by the limited liability partnership] (or one partner) to other partners." This argument ignores, however, that the phrase "any debts" is part of a provision (section 26) that has always governed only a partner's liability to third parties, and, in fact, is part of article 3 of the Partnership Law ("Relations of Partners to Persons Dealing with the Partnership"), not article 4 ("Relations of Partners

---

Partnership Act 1997]). The Conference did not set out to revise the UPA until the 1980s, resulting in a Revised Uniform Partnership Act (RUPA), adopted in 1992, which was amended and restyled the Uniform Partnership Act (1993). Subsequently, another round of changes was incorporated, and the Conference adopted the Uniform Partnership Act (1994). Finally, the Conference added provisions "authorizing the creation of a new form of general partnership called a limited liability partnership (LLP)," which became part of the Uniform Partnership Act (1997) (also referred to as RUPA) (Prefatory Note Addendum). By that time, more than 40 states, including New York, had already amended their general partnership statutes to add limited liability partnership provisions (*id.*).

to One Another"). The logical inference, therefore, is that "any debts" refers to any debts owed a third party, absent very clear legislative direction to the contrary.

Defendants also note that chapter 576's legislative history illustrates the desire to enact liability protection for partners in limited liability partnerships that is "the same as that accorded to shareholders of a professional corporation organized under the Business Corporation Law and as that accorded to members of a professional LLC" (Senate Introducer Mem in Support, Bill Jacket, L. 1994, ch. 576). They point out that "the legislative history of the LLP Act plainly indicates that the Legislature intended to provide an *even greater shield* of individual liability to partners in LLPs than that enacted by other states as of the date of the legislation."

These observations are correct, but do not advance defendants' cause. Chapter 576 does, in fact, afford limited liability partners the same protection from third-party claims as New York law provides shareholders in professional corporations or professional limited liability companies. And unlike New York, most states "have adopted a partial liability shield protecting the partners only from vicarious personal liability for all partnership obligations arising from negligence, wrongful acts or misconduct, whether characterized as tort, contract or otherwise, committed while the partnership is an LLP" (*see* Prefatory Note Addendum to Uniform Partnership Act 1997 explaining that RUPA, by contrast, "provid(es) for a corporate-styled liability shield which protects partners from vicarious personal liability for all partnership obligations incurred while a partnership is a limited liability partnership"; *see also* Walker § 14:5, at 346 "The type of LLP generally permitted by the states (other than Minnesota and New York) ... offers less insulation against personal liability than many other types of organization"). Nowhere in the voluminous commentary on limited liability partnerships has anyone suggested that New York (or any other state) has adopted a statute expanding the concept of limited liability in the way asserted by defendants.

Next, defendants make two arguments in their attempt to reconcile their interpretation of section 26(b) with Partnership Law § 74, which gives a partner "[t]he right to an account of his interest ... as against the winding up partners or the surviving partners or the person or partnership continuing the business, at the date of dissolution, in the absence of agreement to the contrary" ... First, they argue that their fiduciary duty as partners to account to one another "is not the same as personal liability for the debts disclosed by the accounting." ... Second, defendants claim that a partner is only personally liable for debts disclosed in an accounting which are attributable to that partner's own torts or wrongful conduct or supervisory lapses, as excluded by Partnership Law § 26(c) from the protection of section 26(b). If the Legislature had intended to qualify section 74 in this manner, however, it surely would have explicitly made section 74 subject to sections 26(b) and/or 26(c). It did not do so for the same reason that defendants arguments fail generally: section 26(b) only addresses a partner's vicarious liability for partnership obligations.... [Affirmed.]

SMITH, J. (dissenting).

The text of Partnership Law § 26(b) seems clear to me: "no partner of a partnership which is a registered limited liability partnership is liable ... for any debts, obligations or liabilities of ... the registered limited liability partnership ... whether arising in tort, contract or otherwise." The statute contains two specific exceptions, applicable when a partner acts wrongfully or when partners agree to vary the liability scheme (Partnership Law § 26 c, d), but there is no exception for liabilities to former partners claiming a share of the partnership's net assets. We should not create an exception that the Legislature did not. The majority draws a distinction between liability to "third parties" and liabilities to former partners—but a *former* partner is a third party where the partnership is concerned, and there is no good reason to treat him more favorably than any other third party.

No one suggests that section 26(b) exempts partners from any of their fiduciary duties; if a partner has diverted partnership funds to himself, or otherwise received more than his fair share, he will not escape liability and his former partners, as well as his existing partners, will be made whole. The issue is whether a former partner claiming his partnership share may reach the personal assets of partners who are no more blameworthy, and have no more been unjustly enriched, than he has.

I can think of two situations in which this issue may be important. First, without any fault by any partner, the business of the partnership may go badly after a partner withdraws from the firm but before he is paid his share, leaving the firm without enough assets to satisfy his claim. (This is apparently what happened here.) Secondly, the partnership's insolvency may result from the fault of a partner who is himself insolvent; in that case, the question is whether the former partner can proceed against the innocent remaining partners.

In the first case, there is no apparent reason why a former partner should be allowed to collect his debt when other third-party creditors may not; in fact, the Partnership Law provides in another context that debts to nonpartners have a preferred status (Partnership Law § 71b). In the second case, the rule adopted by the majority can produce even more clearly perverse results. Take an extreme example: Suppose there are three partners, two with a 49% interest each and one with a 2% interest. One of the 49% partners withdraws, and is entitled to 49% of the firm's assets. Before he can be paid, however, it is found that the other 49% partner has stolen all of those assets, lost them at a casino and gone bankrupt. Why should the innocent 2% partner have to make good the former partner's large loss?

If the Gursky & Ederer firm had remained a professional corporation, instead of turning itself into a limited liability partnership, the result in this case would not be in question: the individual shareholders of the corporation would not be liable for its obligation to Ederer. I do not see why the partners of an LLP should have an obligation that the shareholders of a PC do not, and I therefore dissent.

G. Partnership Property

The 1997 UPA brought a long needed overhaul of the 1914 Act's treatment of partnership property. The earlier Act's approach reveals a statute at war with itself. To understand why that is true, we need only revisit the issue of whether a partnership should be dealt with as an aggregate of individual partners or an entity separate and distinct from its owners. The theoretical treatment of the business affects such issues as whether the business will be taxed as a separate legal entity, whether the enterprise can sue and be sued in its own name rather than in the name of the individual partners, and whether the business, itself, or the individual partners own the company property. Although UPA (1914) primarily adopts an aggregate approach, it in fact mixes the two, in wanton disregard of the muses of clarity and simplicity. The mixed approach is the product of a conflict between the views of the original drafter of the Act, Dean James Barr Ames of Harvard Law School, who adopted an entity approach, and his successor, Dean William Draper Lewis of the University of Pennsylvania Law School, who was an advocate for the aggregate approach. The provisions relating to partnership property are the battleground for the clash of those two approaches.

Section 24 of UPA (1914) groups partnership property into three categories: partners' management rights (previously described); partners' financial interests in the partnership; and the assets of the business. Partners' financial interests include partners' rights to share in the profits of the business and to be paid upon partnership dissolution, the value of their equity (their residual interest in the enterprise). A partner's financial interest is characterized as personal property. It may be transferred to a third party by the partner and levied against by a creditor of the individual partner. This type of property is discussed more fully in the following section. The most troubling component of partnership property is the last of the three, the ownership of the business assets. It is here that the uneasy mix of the entity and aggregate approaches becomes apparent.

The distinction between property belonging to the partnership and that owned by individual partners is important in determining what property can be used by the partners in the conduct of partnership business and is available to satisfy the claims of business creditors. Fortunately, the UPA (1997) clearly establishes that a partnership is an entity[28] and that the partnership, not individual partners, owns partnership property.

H. Partners' Return on Investment

In a successful going concern, partners earn a return on their investments by receiving their respective shares of the profits. If the company is sold for a profit to a third party, partners receive the appreciated value of their residual shares of the business. The value of a partner's investment will also be realized if the partnership or other partners buy out a partner's interest or a partner transfers the partner's individual interest to a third party.

1. Allocation of Profits and Losses

In partnership accounting, the balance sheet equity capital account reflects the total value of partners' equity, the partners' residual claim to partnership assets. This

---

28. UPA (1997) §201.

account thus represents the collective value of individual partners' accounts as recorded in the company books. UPA § 401 (a) provides that accounts also be kept for individual partners. An individual partner's account is increased by the value of the applicable partner's capital contributions and share of the profits, and decreased by the partner's share of the losses and the amounts of any draws.[29] Thus, the value in an individual partner's account represents the book value of that partner's equity interest in the partnership.

A partner's capital contribution is the money or property the partner transfers to the partnership in exchange for a share of the business. Capital contributions may be made when the company begins and, if required, later on, when it is operating as a going concern. A partner's share of the profits is the partner's share of the earnings produced by the company's ongoing operations during a given time period. UPA (1997) § 401 (a) provides that partners share profits equally in the absence of an agreement. Further, according to comment 3 of § 401 (b),

> each partner's share of the profits is credited to his account under subsection (a) (1). Absent an agreement to the contrary, however, a partner does not have a right to receive a current distribution of the profits credited to his account, the interim distribution of profits being a matter arising in the ordinary course of business to be decided by a majority vote of the partners.

The term "draw" refers to cash distributions to partners. Whether partners receive draws and, if so, their respective amounts are determined either by a partnership agreement or by a vote of the partners. UPA (1997) does not restrict distributions to partners, even when the company is losing money. Protection of creditors depends on fraudulent conveyance statutes.

A partner's share of partnership losses is the partner's share of company obligations that cannot be satisfied from partnership assets. The amount of each partner's share of losses is determined either by the partnership agreement or by the provisions of the partnership act. Partnership losses are charged to each partner's account as provided in § 401 (a)(2). Partners of a general partnership have unlimited liability for partnership obligations. Consequently, a negative value in a partner's individual account represents a debt owed by the partner to the partnership, unless the partners agree otherwise. A partner must pay the amount of the negative value to the partnership so that it can be used to satisfy partnership obligations. A partner's obligation to contribute to partnership losses arises when the partner withdraws from the partnership or the partnership is liquidated. In contrast, partners in limited liability partnerships are not required to contribute to partnership losses under either circumstance. The claims of LLP creditors may be satisfied only from partnership assets. Thus, a negative value in an LLP partner's individual account does not create a debt owed by the partner to the partnership and does not impose on the partner an obligation to contribute additional funds when the partner withdraws or when the partnership terminates.

---

29. *Id.* § 401(a).

In both general partnerships and limited liability partnerships, partners share profits equally in the absence of an agreement.[30] Losses are shared in proportion to a partner's share of the profits,[31] which means that losses are also shared equally if the default rules apply to sharing of profits. These rules make sense when capital contributions to the business have parity. All partners have equal opportunities for gain and equal exposure to the financial risks of the business.

The rules are less acceptable when there is a disparity in the value of the capital contributions to the partnership. Applying a *per capita* profit-sharing rule to a situation where some partners contribute significantly more capital than the others reduces the proportional return of the investors who have made the greatest contributions, while an equal share of the profits may give a windfall to investors who have made lesser contributions. Ordinarily, in situations like this, the partnership agreement will link profit share to share of contribution. The converse is true when a *per capita* allocation applies to losses. In this case, the advantage is shifted to large contributors whose proportionate risks are reduced; smaller contributors assume a financial exposure greater than their proportionate contributions.

Assume, for purposes of illustration, that A contributes $80,000 to a partnership and B contributes $20,000. If the partnership profits for a particular year total $10,000, under the *per capita* rule A and B will each receive $5,000, a 6.25% return for A and a 25% return for B. If the profits were distributed according to capital contribution, A would receive $8,000 and B would receive $2,000, a 10% return for each. If, instead, the business lost $10,000 the same allocations would apply to *per capita* and proportional distributions of losses. Thus, *per capita* allocation of profits is an advantage to B and a disadvantage to A, while an equal allocation of losses advantages A and disadvantages B.

A related and somewhat more complicated problem arises when one partner contributes money or property to the partnership and the other contributes services, typically in the form of special skills or know-how. This problem is caused by the interplay among the UPA's rules regarding capital contributions, compensation for services, and distributions on termination of the business. Under the default rules of both versions of the UPA, contribution of capital means contribution of money or property and does not include services. Thus, when a partner contributes only services to a partnership, the capital contribution portion of that partner's account will be zero and will not reflect the value of the services rendered. If a partnership agreement does not address this issue, the services partner may be disadvantaged by the application of the rules requiring profits and losses to be shared equally. The particular outcome will depend on the proportional relationship between the actual value of the services rendered and the value of the other partners' capital contributions. If the value of the services is disproportionately higher than the other partners' capital contributions, the result will be the same as for partner A described above. If the

---

30. *Id.* § 401(b).
31. *Id.*

actual value is lower, then the result will track the impact on partner B. The services partner is doubly disadvantaged because the default rules also provide that a partner may not be compensated for services performed on behalf of the business.

The problem has another dimension that emerges when the partnership is ended. When the partnership is winding up, the assets of the business are liquidated to pay partnership obligations. Creditors are paid first. Any amounts remaining are used to satisfy the residual claims of the partners based on the value in their capital accounts. Partners with positive values in their accounts will receive distributions if surplus funds are available. This approach works against services partners in the following two ways. First, the services partner's account will be undervalued because the original capital contribution component will be zero. This, in itself, diminishes the services partner's opportunity to recoup the value of the original investment. Second, in a general partnership if after the allocation of partnership losses, the services partner's account has a negative value and another partner's account has a positive value, the services partner will have to contribute to the partnership additional funds equal to the amount of the negative value. These funds may be used to repay to other partners the value of their capital contributions. The result is that in this situation, the services partner will not be reimbursed for the original contribution to the partnership and will have to contribute additional funds as well.

Some courts have attempted to remedy this situation. One example may be found in *Kovacik v. Reed*,[32] which concerned a general partnership in which one partner had made an initial capital contribution in cash and the other had contributed services only. When the partnership was terminated, Kovacik, the partner contributing cash, sought to recover one half of the partnership's losses from Reed, the services-only partner. The court held in favor of Reed, stating:

> The rationale of this rule ... is that where one party contributes money and the other contributes services, then in the event of a loss each would lose his own capital the one his money and the other his labor. Another view would be that in such a situation the parties have, by their agreement to share equally in profits, agreed that the value of their contributions the money on the one hand and the labor on the other were likewise equal; it would follow that upon the loss, as here, of both money and labor, the parties have shared equally in the losses.

The rationale has generally been applied only to cases in which one or more partners contribute only services and not to situations in which a partner contributes a combination of capital and services.

Not all courts agree with the approach taken in *Kovacik*. For example, the court in *Richert v. Handly*[33] held that the provisions of the UPA applied when the parties had not agreed how losses would be shared. The services-only partner was thus required to contribute toward the partnership losses. (Although the *Richert* court did

---

32. 315 P.2d 314 (CA 1957).
33. 330 P.2d 1079 (WA 1958).

not address this particular point, it may have made a difference that the services-only partner had received compensation for the services rendered to the partnership.)

A partnership agreement that defines how profits and losses are to be allocated is essential when partners make contributions to the partnership that differ significantly in either amount or type of consideration. The options available to the parties are many. The agreement may provide that partners contributing services will be paid a salary or will have the value of their services included in their capital accounts.

Designing a compensation scheme is one of the thorniest challenges facing attorneys forming a law practice partnership. Attorneys in a large law firm may have a variety of types of relationships with the firm: partner-track associates, permanent associates, profit-sharing partners, salaried partners, contract attorneys who are paid for working on particular projects or are hired for a term, and of counsel attorneys who may be retired partners or lawyers with another type of special relationship with the firm. Some firms compensate attorneys based on their number of years at the firm. Others apply a formula based on a variety of factors including hours billed and fees collected, business generated, and capital contributed.

2. Transfer of Partnership Interest

Shareholders in a publicly traded corporation may easily realize the current value of their investment. They have an unrestricted right to sell their shares, representing their full complement of ownership rights, at any time and to anyone they wish. In addition, established securities exchanges provide a ready market for their shares. Investors in privately held companies typically do not have these opportunities. Partners are no exception.

Under partnership law default rules, partners may freely assign to third parties only their financial interests in the partnership: the partners' share of the profits and their right to receive distributions. Transferring a partner's management rights requires the permission of all of the remaining partners, because these interests are inextricably linked to one's status as a partner. Although the legal restrictions on transferability can be cured in a partnership agreement, unrestricted transferability may not be suitable for a business with only a few owners having a close working relationship. The absence of an available market for the interests also makes it difficult to transfer a partnership interest, as a buyer may not be found easily. The combination of the restrictions on transfer and the absence of a market make it difficult to leave an ongoing partnership.

A partnership buyout of a partner's interest provides an alternative to a sale to a third party. By statute, the partnership must compensate resigning or retiring partners for the value of their partnership interests.[34] This rule also applies to the estate of a partner who dies.[35] If, however, a partner's resignation violates the terms of the partnership agreement, the amount owed to the partner may be offset by the remaining

---

34. UPA (1997) § 701(a).
35. UPA (1997) §§ 601(7), 701(a).

partners' claim for damages for breach of contract.[36] The practical difficulties that emerge in this situation are common to all privately held companies: the valuation of the interest being bought and the timing of the payments by the partnership. A partnership may not have ready cash to settle the withdrawing partner's account.

Because of the difficulties of withdrawing from a partnership, careful planning is essential. At a minimum, the agreement should identify those situations in which withdrawal is permitted, whether transfer to a third party is permitted, and, in the case of a buyout by the partnership, how the financial interest will be valued and how payments will be made. The following case addresses problems arising from the transfer of a partnership interest.

Casey v. Chapman
Washington Court of Appeals
98 P.3d 1246 (2004)

Cox, C.J.

The primary issue that we decide is the nature of the interest that a successful bidder at a UCC foreclosure sale of a partnership interest acquires at the sale. Governing law generally restricts the rights of an assignee of a partnership interest to profits, not management or voting rights. Here, there is no agreement by all the partners of the partnership that either the original assignee of the partnership interest or the successful bidder at a UCC foreclosure sale selling that pledged collateral was entitled to anything more than profits. Accordingly, we hold that the successful bidder at the foreclosure sale in this case acquired only the right to receive profits allocable to the partnership interest sold at sale, not voting or management rights....

By partnership agreement dated October 28, 1985, Daniel Casey, James Chapman and others formed a general partnership known as the South 320th Federal Way Partnership. They formed it for the purpose of acquiring, developing, and managing commercial real property.

By early 1993, South 320th had five partners. Their names and percentages of interest in the partnership were then: Casey (40 percent), Chapman (20 percent), Charles Binford (10 percent), Charles Eggener (20 percent), and QCI, Inc. (10 percent).

By a purchase agreement dated February 10, 1993, Casey purchased Chapman's "entire Partnership Interest" for $200,000. All of the then partners signed the purchase agreement and expressly acknowledged that Chapman would withdraw from the partnership as of the closing date specified in the agreement.

As part of the same transaction, Casey made a down payment of $15,000 and delivered a non-recourse promissory note to Chapman for $185,000, the deferred balance of the $200,000 purchase price. The parties concurrently executed a security agreement in which Casey pledged to Chapman the partnership interest that was the subject of the purchase as collateral for his obligation to pay the note. The se-

---

36. UPA (1997) §§ 602(c), 701(c).

curity agreement contained an acceleration clause under which the entire unpaid balance would become immediately due and payable if Casey remained in default after 30 days written notice and further provided for foreclosure and sale of the collateral.

By January 1995, Casey ceased paying the obligation evidenced by the note. Chapman commenced foreclosure proceedings by giving notice of default. Casey commenced this action and obtained a temporary restraining order and preliminary injunction prohibiting the sale from going forward. While this litigation was pending, the parties entered into a settlement agreement. In brief, it required Casey to pay Chapman $400,000 in exchange for additional time to make payments on the original note. If he failed to make the required payment, a foreclosure sale of the collateral under the UCC was to occur on October 15, 1999.

Casey failed to make the required payment, and Chapman conducted the sale on the date scheduled. Bruno Investments, LLC was the successful bidder at the sale, purchasing for $200,000 the partnership interest that Casey pledged as collateral.

After the sale, Chapman moved for entry of a declaratory judgment regarding the effect and validity of the UCC sale. Specifically, he sought a judgment determining that the sale was valid and that the purchaser acquired the partnership interest Casey pledged, including "all voting rights, equity interests and economic interests." [The court granted Chapman's motion and Casey appeals.]

THE PARTNERSHIP INTEREST

Casey contends that the trial court erroneously entered its declaratory judgment in favor of Chapman. Specifically, he argues that Bruno Investments, the successful bidder at the foreclosure sale, acquired only the rights to profits, not voting and management rights, at the sale. We agree.

We reverse a superior court's order confirming a sale only for a manifest abuse of discretion. We may affirm an order granting summary judgment if there are no genuine issues of material fact and the moving party is entitled to judgment as a matter of law. When there are no factual disputes and an appellant seeks reversal of the trial court's legal conclusions, we review the trial court's decision on declaratory relief de novo.

Nature of the Interest Purchased

Casey argues that the purchaser of the partnership interest at the UCC sale acquired the right to receive a pro rata share of the profits of the partnership, nothing more. Specifically, he claims that the collateral sold at sale did not include voting and management rights in South 320th.

We first note there are no genuine issues of material fact in this case. Rather, we are confronted with issues of law: the nature of the interest that Casey purchased in 1993 and that was sold in the 1999 UCC foreclosure sale. Nothing in the record suggests that the nature of the partnership interest changed between the time it was purchased and later sold at the foreclosure sale.

To determine the nature of the partnership interest that Casey purchased from Chapman in the February 10, 1993 transaction, we turn to the Washington Partnership Statute that was then in effect. Former RCW 25.04.270 [UPA (1914) § 27] states:

(1) A conveyance by a partner of his interest in the partnership does not of itself dissolve the partnership, *nor, as against the other partners in the absence of agreement, entitle the assignees,* during the continuance of the partnership, *to interfere in the management or administration of the partnership business or affairs,* or to require any information or account of partnership transactions, or to inspect the partnership books; *but it merely entitles the assignee to receive in accordance with his contract the profits to which the assigning partner would otherwise be entitled.*

The plain language of the above statute makes two things clear. First, a partner may assign his or her interest without dissolving the partnership. Second, to the extent that the assignment involves management, administration, and other partnership issues, all partners must agree that such rights follow the assignment.

Here, we look to the purchase agreement and its attached assignment of the partnership interest. Neither document states that all partners agree that management, administration, or voting rights go with the sale of Chapman's partnership interest to Casey. In the absence of a clear statement that management, administration, or voting rights were included in the sale, we must conclude that such rights were not part of the transaction. The statute then in effect required such agreement by the partners. Thus, Chapman sold only the right to participate pro rata in profits when he sold the partnership interest to Casey and withdrew from the partnership in 1993.

Nature of the Collateral Pledged

It is axiomatic that if Casey only purchased the right to profits, not voting and management rights, in his 1993 transaction with Chapman, Casey could not pledge any greater rights to Chapman, who withdrew from the partnership at the closing of the transaction. While the language of the security agreement is broad and the enforcement mechanisms contained therein are elaborate, the simple fact of the matter is that the collateral consisted solely of the right to receive profits, nothing more. Chapman argues that the phrase "entire partnership interest," as stated in the purchase agreement, shows that the property sold and pledged in 1993 and sold at the UCC foreclosure sale to Bruno in 1999 was the same. We agree. But that begs the question of what the law requires for a partner to transfer more than a right to receive profits of a partnership. The former statute, which we have quoted and discussed in a prior portion of this opinion, shows what is required. And the record before us shows that the parties did not comply with that statute. In short, only the right to receive profits was sold, nothing more.

Chapman also points to RCW 25.05.005(9) [UPA (1997) § 101 (9)[37]] for support that "the partnership interest" is something more than we hold. That statute states:

---

37. [Compare UPA (1997) § 101(9), which is quoted in the case, and § 502, which states:
   The only transferable interest of a partner in the partnership is the partner's share of the

"partnership interest" or "partner's interest in the partnership" means all of a partner's interests in the partnership, including the partner's transferable interest *and* all management and other rights.[38]

The chief problem with this argument is that the quoted statute became effective in Washington on January 1, 1999. The transaction before us predated the statute by six years. We see no basis for retroactively applying this statute to a 1993 transaction.

Chapman also claims that if he sold only the right to profits in 1993, this appeal is moot. He claims that he must have retained his management and voting rights even though he sold the former to Casey, which were then pledged as collateral for the note. We do not agree.

It is difficult to see how a partner who has withdrawn from the partnership as of the sale of his interest retains management rights or anything else in the partnership. But more importantly, this argument fails to deal with the former statute and fails to show anything in the record to show compliance with it.

Chapman also argues that Casey and all the other partners gave their consent to the successful purchaser at a possible foreclosure sale becoming a partner by consenting to the sale of the partnership interest and the use of that interest as collateral for the note. A careful review of the record shows that this argument is unsupported by the sale and security agreement documentation.

All partners signed the security agreement. The default provisions of the agreement allow the secured party to "proceed against the Partnership Interest." But that does not inform us that the partners agreed that a foreclosing creditor would have voting and management rights. This is especially true since there is no evidence of any agreement by the partners that such rights were sold in the first place. [Affirmed] in all respects except that we reverse the provision stating Bruno was entitled to all voting rights, equity interests and economic interest in the partnership in the purchaser.

I. Dissociation and Dissolution

As with so many situations in life, forming a partnership is easy, but leaving the partnership is another matter. One reason is that it may be difficult for a partner to sell his or her interest as a member in a partnership. In addition, there is not a market for the financial interests that may be assigned to third parties. Thus, a partner who wants to withdraw from an ongoing partnership has few options. Fur-

---

profits and losses of the partnership and the partner's right to receive distributions. The interest is personal property.

with UPA (1914) §26, which states,

a partner's interest in the partnership is his share of the profits and surplus, and the same is personal property.

and with §27, which is quoted in the case. Would the result have been different had the later act been applied?—Eds.]

38. [12] (Emphasis added.)

ther, there are issues that must be addressed when the partners decide to close down the business.

The partnership rules for dissociating from and/or dissolving the business serve two purposes. They function as buyout provisions enabling departing partners to recoup their investments when the business is ongoing. They also provide for an ordered closing down of the venture, when that is the desired result.

As discussed previously, partnership default rules severely restrict partners' ability to transfer their full partnership interests to third parties. Transfer of management rights is prohibited unless all of the remaining partners agree. Even when transfer is permitted, finding a purchaser can be difficult because of the unavailability of a market for trading partnership interests. Withdrawing from a professional partnership may be even more difficult because other restrictions apply. The difficulty of withdrawal exacerbates struggles between minority and majority interests and the reluctance of third parties to invest in the business.

Thus, when individual partners want to recoup their investments or leave the firm for other reasons, they will turn to the procedures for concluding the business. Understanding the process of concluding a partnership requires a mastery of four terms: dissociation; dissolution; winding up; termination. Dissociation refers to the withdrawal of a partner. The remaining partners have the option of continuing the business, and the withdrawing partner has the right to be paid the value of his or her partnership interest. Dissolution occurs when the partners decide to or are required to close down the business entirely. Once dissolution begins, the partnership continues only for the purpose of concluding the business. Winding up refers to the process of closing down the business. During this time, the partnership completes work in progress and then proceeds to sell the company assets, to pay creditors, and to distribute the net balance, if any, to the partners according to their respective partnership interests. When winding up is complete, the partnership entity terminates.

UPA (1997) specifies conditions and events under which a partner's dissociation is permitted or required.[39] A partner in an at will partnership may dissociate at any time without penalty. A partner in a partnership for a specified term may also dissociate at any time, but if the dissociation is in violation of the partnership agreement, the dissociating partner may have to pay damages for breach of the partnership agreement. A partnership agreement may specify an event or circumstance in which partners are permitted or required to dissociate. Further, a partner may be expelled according to the terms of the partnership agreement or as a result of a court order. Additional events triggering dissociation for individual partners include death of the partner, the appointment of a guardian or conservator for the partner or a judicial determination that the partner no longer has the capacity to fulfill the partner's obligation under the partnership agreement. If the remaining partners elect to continue

39. §§ 601, 602.

the business, the withdrawing partner must be paid his or her share of the firm, less any damages caused by a wrongful dissociation.[40]

Dissociation terminates one's status as a partner. Depending on the circumstances, it may lead either to a continuation of the business by the remaining partners, with a mandatory buyout of the dissociating partner's interest, or to dissolution and winding up of the partnership business. Thus, the threat of liquidation is a constant cloud over an at-will partnership. A partnership for a term may, however, be continued at the option of the remaining partners. A dissociation followed by a continuation of the partnership does not affect the rights of creditors against the continuing partnership and its partners. Unless released by the firm's creditors, the dissociating partner remains liable for partnership obligations incurred during the time he or she was a partner. Pursuant to UPA (1997) § 704, a dissociated partner or the partnership may file a statement of dissociation with the designated state office. The purpose of the statement is to put third parties on notice of the dissociation and to make it clear that the dissociating partner is not liable for partnership obligations arising after the dissociation.

Dissolution marks the beginning of the process of closing down the business. According to UPA (1997) § 801, many of the same events triggering a dissociation of a partner may also trigger a dissolution of the business, as, for example, when a partner decides to dissociate and the remaining partners decide not to continue the business. The triggering event may be specified in the partnership agreement or may arise by operation of law, such as the death or incapacity of a partner. The partnership agreement, itself, may require dissolution upon the occurrence of a particular event and the partners may simply decide to dissolve the business. Circumstances making it illegal to continue the business or a court order may also require dissolution.

Winding up refers to the process of closing down the business. This is the time either to sell the company as a going concern or to liquidate its assets. The proceeds of the sale are used to settle company debts, and if there are excess funds, to compensate the partners in cash for their respective interests in the firm. Payments to a partner who has wrongfully dissolved the partnership may be offset by the amount of damages caused by the breach of the partnership agreement. If the funds resulting from the sale are insufficient to pay off all company debts, including those to partners, then partners in a general partnership with negative values in their partnership accounts must contribute additional amounts from their personal assets. Partnership termination occurs when the winding up process is complete and the partnership stops conducting business.

The dissolution provisions of UPA (1997) continue the disadvantages to the partner who contributes only services. The official comment to UPA (1997) § 401(b) expressly rejects the holding of the *Kovacik* case (previously discussed in Section I.H.1. of this

---

40. § 701.

chapter) and of a later case, *Becker v. Killarney*, 532 N.E. 2d 931 (Ill. App. 3 Dist. 1988), which followed *Kovacik*. According to UPA (1997) §401, Official Comment 3:

> The default rules apply … where one or more of the partners contribute no capital, although there is case law to the contrary. It may seem unfair that the contributor of services, who contributes little or no capital, should be obligated to contribute toward the capital loss of the large contributor who contributed no services. In entering a partnership with such a capital structure, the partners should foresee that application of the default rule may bring about unusual results and take advantage of their power to vary by agreement the allocation of capital losses.

The fundamental partnership structure common to both statutes has important implications for business law attorneys and their clients. An at-will partnership, the default form provided in the statutes, is an unstable form of business. The dissociation or dissolution provisions of the respective acts can be used by an individual to compel a buyout at any time. The limitations on transferring partnership interests and the absence of a ready market for these interests increase the likelihood that a forced buyout will occur. Thus, when a partner wants to leave the partnership, either because the partners are not getting along or because the partner wants to invest elsewhere, compulsory buyout may be inevitable. Depending on the firm's financial position, the business may be forced to liquidate.

An individual partner's opportunities for unilateral withdrawal and compulsory buyout shift bargaining power with respect to the continuation of the business to a minority of the partners. The compelled buyout may come at a time when the company does not have ready cash to pay the departing partner or when liquidation disadvantages everyone because the company's assets are more valuable to the partnership as a going concern than to third-party purchasers. In addition, valuation of the firm may be difficult. These problems should be addressed in a partnership agreement controlling the circumstances of withdrawal, the opportunities for continuing the business, and the terms of the buyout.

The cases that follow raise additional issues associated with dissolution or dissociation. An important question is whether an at-will partnership has been formed or whether the partnership is one for a particular undertaking or a specified term.

Girard Bank v. Haley

Pennsylvania Supreme Court
332 A.2d 443 (1975)

Predates Partnership law

Pomeroy, Justice.

This suit in equity was brought by appellants' decedent, Anna Reid, who averred in her complaint that she had dissolved a partnership between herself and the defendants, and prayed that the business of the firm be wound-up and its assets distributed. During the course of the proceedings Mrs. Reid died and the executors of her estate were substituted as parties plaintiff. The principal question for decision is whether the partnership was dissolved during Mrs. Reid's lifetime, as she averred and her personal representatives urge, or upon her death, as the trial court found.

The following facts are not in dispute. On September 28, 1958, Mrs. Reid and the three defendants, appellees here, entered into a written partnership agreement for the purpose of leasing for profit certain real property located in Montgomery County, Pennsylvania. Mrs. Reid was to manage the property, and the defendants were to perform the physical labor necessary to maintain the premises in good condition. The initial partnership assets consisted of real estate valued at $50,000 and $10,000 in cash, both contributed by Mrs. Reid, and an additional sum of $10,000 in cash contributed in equal shares by the three other partners. By letter addressed to her partners, the defendants, Mrs. Reid notified them that she was dissolving the partnership and requested that the partnership assets be liquidated as soon as possible.[41] Meetings between the partners following receipt of this letter failed to produce agreement for a plan for liquidation or as to the respective rights of the parties in the assets of the partnership. This suit praying for a winding up of the affairs of the partnership and a liquidation of its assets was then brought.

The chancellor found that the partnership had been dissolved, not by Mrs. Reid's letter, but rather by her death, and concluded that the defendants, as surviving partners, were entitled to exercise their option under the partnership agreement to purchase the interest of the deceased partner.[42] Having determined that the defendants

---

41. [1] The letter was undated, but the record establishes that it was sent on February 10, 1971. The text of the letter was as follows:

"Gentlemen:

I hereby notify you that I am terminating the partnership which the four of us entered into on the 28th day of September, 1958, and request that steps be taken to liquidate the assets of the Partnership as soon as possible. I hereby authorize you to deal with my attorney, J. William Wetter, Jr., in the matter of negotiating the steps necessary to bring this matter to a speedy and satisfactory conclusion.

"I trust that our friendship will continue and that you will recognize that terminating this partnership has been necessitated by my need to clarify the status of my various assets at this particular time.

Very truly yours,

Anna Reid."

42. [2] The pertinent provisions of the partnership agreement are as follows:

"11. Upon the death of any partner, the surviving partners or any of them shall have the right to purchase the interest of the decedent in the partnership. If the surviving partners or any of them elect to purchase the interest of the decedent, they or he or she shall serve notice in writing of such election within three months after the death of the decedent, upon the executor or administrator of the decedent, or, if at the time of such election no legal representative shall have been appointed, then upon any one of the known legal heirs of the decedent at the last known address of such heir.

"12. If the surviving partners or any of them elect to purchase the interest of the decedent in the partnership, the purchase price shall be equal to the decedent's capital account on the date of his death adjusted as herein provided. The decedent's capital account on the date of his or her death shall be increased by his or her share of partnership profits, for the period from the beginning of the year in which his death occurred until the date of his death. Losses shall be treated conversely in the same manner. The real estate shall be taken at a value equivalent to the assessed value fixed by the local authorities for real estate tax

had in fact exercised their option to purchase Mrs. Reid's interest, the chancellor entered a decree nisi ordering the defendants to pay the estate in discharge of the purchase price the sum of $29,165.48 plus seventy per cent of the income of the partnership for the calendar year 1971. Exceptions filed by the executors to the adjudication were dismissed and the decree nisi was adopted as the final decree. This appeal followed.

None of the parties disputes the chancellor's conclusion that the partnership has been dissolved; the dispute, as indicated at the outset, is when that event occurred. Dissolution of a partnership is statutorily defined as "the change in the relation of the partners caused by any partner ceasing to be associated in the carrying on, as distinguished from the winding up, of the business." Uniform Partnership Act (1914) §29 ("the Act"). There is no doubt that dissolution of a partnership will be caused by the death of any partner, §31(4) of the Act, and if Mrs. Reid's death was the cause of the dissolution here involved, the chancellor was quite correct in looking to the provisions of paragraphs 11 and 12 of the agreement ... as defining the rights and obligations of the surviving partners on the one hand and the estate of the deceased partner on the other. If, however, dissolution occurred during the lifetime of Mrs. Reid, those portions of the agreement, which are concerned solely with the effect of the death of a partner, are not germane. The agreement being otherwise silent as to winding up and liquidation, the provisions of the Act will control.

The chancellor was impressed with the fact that the decedent "was a strong willed person" who dominated the partnership enterprise, that the defendant partners had each contributed many thousands of hours of hard work and planning to the "joint venture", and that neither Mrs. Reid (who testified at the first hearing, but who then, according to the adjudication, "appeared confused and feeble") nor her personal representatives had offered "evidence to justify a termination." In supposing that justification was necessary the learned court below fell into error. Dissolution of a partnership is caused, under §31 of the Act, "by the express will of any partner." The expression of that will need not be supported by any justification. If no "definite term or particular undertaking [is] specified in the partnership agreement," such an at-will dissolution does not violate the agreement between the partners; indeed, an expression of a will to dissolve is effective as a dissolution even if in contravention of the agreement. Ibid. We have recognized the generality of a dissolution at will. If the dissolution results in breach of contract, the aggrieved partners may recover damages for the breach and, if they meet certain conditions, may continue the firm business for the duration of the agreed term or until the particular undertaking is completed. See §38 of the Act.

There is no doubt in our minds that Mrs. Reid's letter ... effectively dissolved the partnership between her and her three partners. It was definite and unequivocal: "I

_____

purposes for the year in which such death occurs, and the decedent's capital account shall be adjusted to reflect this valuation. As thus adjusted the decedent's capital account shall be taken as shown on the books of the partnership, without any allowance for good will, trade name, or other intangible assets. In the event of the death of Anna Reid, her interest, subject to the limitations and conditions aforementioned shall be liquidated over a period of ten years following her death."

am terminating the partnership which the four of us entered into on the 28th day of September, 1958." The effective termination date is therefore February 10, 1971, and Mrs. Reid's subsequent death after this litigation was in progress is an irrelevant factor in determining the rights of the parties.

The remaining question is whether or not the unilateral dissolution made by Mrs. Reid violated the partnership agreement. The agreement contains no provision fixing a definite term, and the sole "undertaking" to which it refers is that of maintaining and leasing real property. This statement is merely one of general purpose, however, and cannot be said to set forth a "particular undertaking" within the meaning of that phrase as it is used in the Act. A "particular undertaking" under the statute must be capable of accomplishment at some time, although the exact time may be unknown and unascertainable at the date of the agreement. Leasing property, like many other trades or businesses, involves entering into a business relationship which may continue indefinitely; there is nothing "particular" about it. We thus conclude, on the record before us, that the dissolution of the partnership was not in contravention of the agreement.

In light of our conclusion that an inter-vivos dissolution took place, the provisions of the Act rather than the post-mortem provisions of the agreement, will govern the winding-up of the partnership affairs and the distribution of its assets. Because compliance with the Act requires findings and conclusions which were not made by the chancellor in view of his disposition of the case, we must remand for further proceedings....

Notes and Questions

1. The court in *Fischer v. Fischer*, 197 S.W.3d 98 (Ky. 2006), also addressed the issue of whether a partnership formed for the purpose of developing, leasing and selling real estate is at-will or one for a particular undertaking or a term. Like *Girard*, the *Fischer* decision was based on 1914 UPA § 31. The *Fischer* court distinguished *Girard* and concluded that a partnership formed "for the purpose of developing and selling a particular tract of land would be one for a particular undertaking and hence not rightfully terminable at will until the purpose was accomplished."

2. UPA (1997) § 801, like its predecessor UPA (1914) § 31, distinguishes between dissolution of a partnership at will and of one for a term or particular undertaking. Under both acts, a partner wrongfully causing dissolution may be liable for damages caused by the wrongful dissolution. Thus the issue whether a partnership is at will or for a term is significant under the dissolution provisions of both acts.

3. Assume that you are the lawyer who completed the legal work necessary to form the business referred to in the preceding case and you have represented it ever since. Before Mrs. Reid sent her letter, the partners had been discussing whether or not to continue the business. Disagreement among the partners on this subject ultimately led Mrs. Reid to write the letter. What role(s) may you potentially play? *See* Model Rules of Professional Conduct 1.7, 1.9, 1.13, and 2.2. What is your role if the matter, as here, results in litigation?

4. What do you think were the expectations of the parties at the time the partnership was formed with respect to termination of the venture? Was the litigation the result of a drafting error on the part of the attorney who prepared the partnership agreement?

The following cases address the issue of whether the dissolution of a partnership requires a liquidation of the partnership assets in order to settle partners' claims. UPA (1997) § 807 continues the rule established in UPA (1914) § 38 that partners have the right to be compensated in cash for the value their partnership interests. Further, UPA (1997) § 402 also makes clear that a partner "has no right to receive and may not be required to accept, a distribution in kind." These judicial opinions explore alternative forms of determining and distributing the value of partnership interests in the context of partnership dissolution.

McCormick v. Brevig
Montana Supreme Court
96 P.3d 697 (2004)

Rice, Justice.

This case involves a protracted dispute between a brother and sister concerning their respective interests in a ranching partnership that is before the Court a second time. The litigation began in 1995 when Joan McCormick ("Joan") brought this action against her brother, Clark Brevig ("Clark"), and their partnership, Brevig Land Live and Lumber (hereinafter, "the Partnership"), seeking a Partnership accounting and dissolution. . . .

On December 27, 2001, the District Court concluded that the parties' Partnership agreement did not apply, and that a judicial dissolution of the Partnership was warranted[.] The court further recognized that § 35-10-629, MCA, explicitly required any surplus assets after paying creditors to be paid to the partners in cash in accordance with their right to distribution. Nonetheless, the court found that it would be inequitable to order the liquidation of the Partnership assets in order to satisfy Joan's interest in the Partnership. Therefore, in keeping with its desire to preserve the family farm, the court ordered Joan to sell her interest in the Partnership to her brother following an appraisal and determination of the value of her share. With the assistance of a special master, and following an accounting of Partnership assets, the District Court eventually fixed a price of $1,107,672 on Joan's 50 percent interest in the Partnership. Joan appeals from the District Court's accounting and order requiring her to sell her interest in the Partnership to her brother. . . . We affirm in part, reverse in part, and remand for further proceedings.

The following issues are presented on appeal:

6 1. After ordering dissolution of the Partnership, did the District Court err by failing to order liquidation of the Partnership assets, and instead granting Clark the right to purchase Joan's Partnership interest at a price determined by the court?

. . .

7 2. Did the District Court err by failing to grant Joan's petition for an accounting of the Partnership's business affairs?

FACTUAL AND PROCEDURAL BACKGROUND

Joan and Clark are the children of Charles and Helen Brevig (hereinafter, "Charles" and "Helen"). In 1960 Charles purchased the Brevig Ranch outside of Lewistown from his parents. In 1971, Charles transferred his sole interest in the ranch by warranty deed to himself and Helen as joint tenants. . . .

When Charles and Helen divorced in 1977, Helen conveyed her interest in the ranch to Charles in the property settlement agreement. Thereafter, Clark and his father owned the ranch in equal shares, and began operating the ranch as Brevig Land, Live & Lumber, a partnership, pursuant to a written agreement.

Although she was not a partner in the ranch operation, Joan lived on the ranch and assisted in ranch operations from 1975 until 1981. In 1981, with the ranch facing severe financial hardship, Joan left the ranch to work as an oil and gas "landman," in order to generate outside income to enable the ranch to meet its financial obligations. . . .

In 1982, Charles and Clark sought to refinance the farm debt in the amount of $422,000 with the Federal Land Bank. Because the ranch operation did not generate sufficient cash flow to meet the projected debt payment, the bank required Joan to sign the mortgage which was secured by the ranch real estate. Joan's income as a landman became committed to assist in repayment of the ranch debt.

During the time of Joan's employment as a landman from 1981 through 1986, it was Joan's practice to contribute all of her income, less expenses, to the support of the ranch operation. In 1983, Joan closed her personal bank account and began to deposit all of her income into the partnership bank account. From this account, Joan would pay her personal expenses and the balance would be applied to the obligations of Charles and Clark's partnership. After she married in 1986, Joan made payments directly to the banks for the ranch obligations rather than to deposit the money in the ranch operating account. Joan also made direct payments for taxes and insurance.

On October 28, 1982, Charles died unexpectedly after a short illness. . . . Clark and Joan each received one-half of Charles' estate, which principally consisted of his 50 percent interest in the ranch and Partnership. As a result of the distributions, Clark then owned 75 percent of the ranch assets, and Joan 25 percent. A written partnership agreement was thereafter executed by Clark and Joan reflecting their respective 75/25 percent interests in the Partnership. Except for these ownership percentages, the written agreement was identical to the one executed between Charles and Clark in 1978.

After Charles' death, Joan continued her work as a landman, and made financial contributions to the new Partnership. She also maintained the Partnership's books and records. Meanwhile, Clark assumed responsibility for the day-to-day affairs of the ranch. Clark and Joan made management decisions together.

In 1984, Joan obtained an additional 25 percent in the Partnership, fully paying for this interest by the following year. For his share of the sale, Clark received a capital credit of approximately $60,000. From 1984 to 1993, Joan was listed as a 50/50 partner on all the tax returns for the Partnership.

Around November 1986, at the recommendation of the Partnership's principle [sic] accountant, Clark and Joan executed an addendum to the Partnership agreement, reflecting their agreement to make adjustments in the Partnership interests based on varying capital contributions. The addendum was needed to account for the excess capital contributions made by Joan, and to conform that part of the agreement to the tax returns which showed Clark and Joan as equal partners. The parties had agreed, however, that Joan's interest in the Partnership would not exceed 50 percent, regardless of the amount of her excess capital contributions.

Disagreements concerning management of the ranch, and particularly, management of the debt load on the ranch, caused Clark and Joan's relationship to deteriorate. By the early 1990s, cooperation between Clark and Joan regarding the operation of the ranch and securing of loans necessary to fund the ranch had essentially ceased, and they began looking for ways to dissolve the Partnership.

In 1995, Joan brought suit against Clark and the Partnership, alleging that Clark had converted Partnership assets to his own personal use, and sought an accounting of the Partnership's affairs. She also requested a determination that Clark had engaged in conduct warranting a decree of expulsion. Alternatively, Joan sought an order dissolving and winding up the Partnership. [Clark alleged that he personally owned the property and that it was not a Partnership asset. Clark lost on appeal and the case was remanded to the trial court for resolution of Joan's claims.]

... On April 3, 2000, the District Court issued findings of fact and conclusions of law, finding that neither Clark nor Joan had dissociated from the Partnership, that Joan was a 50 percent partner and should be credited for any excess capital contributions she made to the Partnership, and that Clark was not entitled to receive compensation as a partner. The court further concluded that the Partnership should be dissolved and its business wound up ...

... On December 27, 2001, the District Court ordered the value of Joan's interest in the Partnership to be determined following an appraisal conducted and paid for by the Partnership. Following such determination, Clark would have sixty days in which to purchase Joan's interest, or the Partnership assets would be liquidated and the net assets distributed to the partners.... On January 29, 2003, the District Court entered findings of fact and conclusions of law, ... valuing Joan's interest in the Partnership at $1,107,672. Clark thereafter tendered this amount to Joan for the purchase of her interest, which Joan rejected. This appeal followed....

DISCUSSION

After ordering dissolution of the Partnership, did the District Court err by failing to order liquidation of the Partnership assets, and instead granting Clark the right to purchase Joan's Partnership interest at a price determined by the court?

Joan contends that when a partnership is dissolved by judicial decree, Montana's Revised Uniform Partnership Act, § 35-10-101 et seq., MCA (2001), requires liquidation by sale of partnership assets and distribution in cash of any surplus to the partners. In response, Clark asserts that there are other judicially acceptable methods of distributing partnership assets upon dissolution besides liquidating assets through a forced sale. For the reasons set forth below, we conclude that the Revised Uniform Partnership Act requires liquidation of partnership assets and distribution of the net surplus in cash to the partners upon dissolution entered by judicial decree when it is no longer reasonably practicable to carry on the business of the partnership.

We begin our analysis by reviewing the law of partnerships as it pertains to the issues in this case. A partnership is an association of two or more persons to carry on as co-owners a business for profit. See § 35-10-102(5)(a), MCA; see also § 35-10-201(1), MCA (1991). An informal or oral agreement will usually suffice to create a partnership, and where a partnership agreement exists, it will generally govern relations among partners. Thus, statutory rules are merely default rules, which apply only in the absence of a partnership agreement to the contrary. See § 35-10-106, MCA. In the present case, the parties do not dispute that the partnership agreement did not apply to situations involving a court ordered dissolution of a partnership....

In 1993, our legislature significantly amended the UPA by adopting the Revised Uniform Partnership Act, or RUPA. Unlike the UPA, RUPA now provides two separate tracks for the exiting partner. The first track applies to the dissociating partner, and does not result in a dissolution, but in a buy-out of the dissociating partner's interest in the partnership. See § 35-10-616, MCA. The term "dissociation" is new to the act, and occurs upon the happening of any one of ten events specified in § 35-10-616, MCA. Examples of events leading to dissociation include bankruptcy of a partner and death, see § 35-10-616(6)(a) and (7)(a), MCA, but does not include a judicially ordered dissolution of the partnership.

The second track for the exiting partner does involve dissolution and winding up of the partnership's affairs. Section 35-10-624, MCA, sets forth the events causing dissolution and winding up of a partnership, and includes the following:

> (5) a judicial decree, issued upon application by a partner, that:
>
> (a) the economic purpose of the partnership is likely to be unreasonably frustrated;
>
> (b) another partner has engaged in conduct relating to the partnership business that makes it not reasonably practicable to carry on the business in partnership with that partner; or
>
> (c) it is not otherwise reasonably practicable to carry on the partnership business in conformity with the partnership agreement[.]

In this case, the District Court dissolved the Partnership pursuant to § 35-10-624 (5), MCA. In so doing, it recognized that, in the absence of a partnership agreement to the contrary, the only possible result under RUPA was for the partnership assets to be liquidated and the proceeds distributed between the partners proportionately.

The court reasoned, however, that the term "liquidate" had a variety of possible meanings, one of which was "to assemble and mobilize the assets, settle with the creditors and debtors and apportion the remaining assets, if any, among the stockholders or owners." Applying this definition, which the court had obtained from Black's Law Dictionary, the court concluded that a judicially ordered buy-out of Joan's interest in the Partnership by Clark was an acceptable alternative to liquidation of the partnership assets through a compelled sale.

It is well established that "the role of courts in applying a statute has always been to 'ascertain and declare what is in terms or in substance contained therein, not to insert what has been omitted or to omit what has been inserted.'" *State v. Goebel*, 2001 305 Mont. 53, 31 P.3d 335 ... "[T]he intent of the Legislature is controlling when construing a statute. The intention of the Legislature must first be determined from the plain meaning of the words used, and if interpretation of the statute can be so determined, the courts may not go further and apply any other means of interpretation."

It is true that this Court has previously utilized dictionaries when seeking to define the common use and meaning of terms. However, in this case, we conclude that it was not necessary for the District Court to resort to such devices. Section 35-10-629(1), MCA, clearly provides that "[i]n winding up a partnership's business, the assets of the partnership must be applied to discharge its obligations to creditors, including partners who are creditors. Any surplus must be applied to pay in cash the net amount distributable to partners in accordance with their right to distributions pursuant to subsection (2)." Furthermore, subsection (2) of the statute provides:

> Each partner is entitled to a settlement of all partnership accounts upon winding up the partnership business. In settling accounts among the partners, the profits and losses that result from the liquidation of the partnership assets must be credited and charged to the partners' accounts. The partnership shall make a distribution to a partner in an amount equal to that partner's positive account balance.

Thus, the common purpose and plain meaning of the term "liquidation," as it is used in § 35-10-629(2), MCA, is to reduce the partnership assets to cash, pay creditors, and distribute to partners the value of their respective interest. This is all part of the process of "winding up" the business of a partnership and terminating its affairs.

Clark invites this Court to take a liberal reading of § 35-10-629, MCA, and cites *Creel v. Lilly* (1999), 354 Md. 77, 729 A.2d 385 in support of the proposition that judicially acceptable alternatives exist to compelled liquidation in a dissolution situation. At issue in *Creel* was whether the surviving partners of a partnership had a duty to liquidate all partnership assets because there was no provision in the partnership agreement providing for the continuation of the partnership upon a partner's death, and the estate had not consented to the continuation of business. After examining cases in which other courts had elected to order an in-kind distribution rather than a compelled liquidation, or had allowed the remaining partners to purchase the withdrawing partner's interest in the partnership, the court concluded that the UPA did not mandate a forced sale of all partnership assets in order to ascertain the true value of the business, and that "winding up" was not always synonymous with liquidation. The court further noted that it would have reached the same conclusion regardless of whether the UPA or RUPA governed since, under RUPA, the remaining partners could have elected to continue business following the death of one of the partners.

However, of critical distinction between the facts in *Creel* and the case sub judice is the manner in which the partners exited the entity. In *Creel* one of the partners had died. Here, Joan sought a court ordered dissolution of the Partnership. Under RUPA, the death of a partner triggers the provisions of § 35-10-619, MCA, which allows for the purchase of the dissociated partner's interest in the partnership, much like what was ordered in *Creel*. Conversely, a court ordered dissolution pursuant to § 35-10-624(5), MCA, as in this case, results in the dissolution and winding up of the partnership. Thus, *Creel* is both legally and factually distinguishable....

Accordingly, we conclude that when a partnership's dissolution is court ordered pursuant to § 35-10-624(5), MCA, the partnership assets necessarily must be reduced to cash in order to satisfy the obligations of the partnership and distribute any net surplus in cash to the remaining partners in accordance with their respective interests. By adopting a judicially created alternative to this statutorily mandated requirement, the District Court erred....

Horne v. Aune

Washington Court of Appeals
121 P.3d 1227 (2005)

HOUGHTON, J.

In this appeal, we are asked to decide whether in winding up a partnership, the Revised Uniform Partnership Act (RUPA), chapter 25.05 RCW, requires a public sale of partnership property; or whether the court may instead allow a partner to purchase the property for its agreed value with cash payment to the other partner of his partnership interest?

Steven Aune appeals a court order requiring him to sell his one-half partnership interest in real property to Cecilia Horne. He demands a public sale of the property, with cash distribution of the proceeds.

Because RUPA's winding-up provision, RCW 25.05.330, does not mandate a public sale of partnership property as the only means of liquidating partnership assets, we affirm. And given the facts of this case, we hold the trial court did not abuse its discretion by allowing Horne to purchase the property instead of listing her home with a real estate agent....

FACTS

In July 2002, when Horne and Aune intended to pursue a family life together, they purchased property in Gig Harbor as tenants in common. As experienced real estate investors, they viewed the $303,500 purchase as an investment opportunity. Each contributed equally toward the down payment and obtained joint financing for the balance.

Horne, Aune, and Horne's son, William (then 12 years old), moved into the house in August 2002. Horne and Aune experienced relationship troubles almost immediately. Aune refused to pay half the utilities because he believed Horne and her son consumed more than half. In October, Aune and Horne argued during a road trip, and Aune left Horne and her son by the side of the road in Port Angeles.

On November 4, they signed a written agreement describing their respective rights and obligations for the property. Horne drafted the agreement. It opens with, "This will serve as the legal jargon to indicate that this is a legal and binding agreement which supersedes any other legal and binding agreements, obligations, encumbrances or matters of inheritance involving [the property]." The agreement states that Horne and Aune "are equal partners in said property sharing equally in ownership, care, upkeep and title and mortgage obligations including property taxes and property insurance costs." The agreement provides that both parties would deposit sufficient funds in a joint bank account to pay property expenses. Both parties agreed to maintain life insurance policies to cover their mortgage obligation and to submit any disputes to mediation.

Finally, the agreement has the following provision:

> If either party is lawfully, but unwillingly removed from the property by law enforcement or invoking a restraining order or any other method, the party remaining in residence will be solely financially responsible for upholding all expense obligations pertaining to the mortgage, taxes, insurance and care and upkeep of the property until the removed party returns and peaceable co-habitation resumes. Upon return, both parties will resume the equally shared obligations of this real estate agreement as stated herein.

The parties dispute which of them formulated this language, but they do not dispute that Horne drafted the document and both of them signed it in the presence of a notary. Horne understood that Aune wanted this provision because his ex-wife had obtained a protection order against him during their marital dissolution, forcing him out of the home that he had built and lived in. He believed that he had been treated unfairly and wanted to ensure that the same thing would not happen to him again.

On December 8, an altercation occurred at the home. During an argument, Aune pushed Horne aside and assaulted her son, William. Both William and Horne called 911. Aune left. A deputy sheriff took a report and referred it to the prosecutor's office. Aune returned and, at Horne's urging, left on a trip five days later for a "cooling off period" to visit his brother in the Midwest. While he was gone, Horne obtained a protection order against him. The prosecutor charged Aune with two counts of fourth degree assault.

… He entered [a] plea and received a deferred sentence.… Horne has remained in possession of the home and has paid all expenses, including the mortgage, since January 2003. Horne asked Aune to continue to pay half of the home expenses but he refused, invoking paragraph 6 of the partnership agreement.

Horne and Aune unsuccessfully sought to mediate in spring 2003. In April 2003, Horne sent Aune a letter purporting to nullify the partnership agreement. Aune did not respond.

Horne sued Aune in September 2003.... She alleged [*inter alia*] that the partnership could no longer function, necessitating a winding up and dissolution. She requested that the real property be sold and that she be permitted to purchase Aune's interest in the property at a reasonable sum to be determined by the court.

In his answer, Aune admitted that the partnership should be dissolved and wound up.... He requested a formal accounting, followed by a judgment for his share of the partnership property.

Horne and Aune attempted to mediate the lawsuit issues in March 2004. Both parties agreed that it would be better for one or the other to buy the house rather than publicly sell it in order to avoid the transaction costs of a public sale. But they were unable to agree on who would buy out whom, or at what price.... Horne also resisted efforts to have the house appraised, but an appraiser eventually valued the house at $335,000. Both parties agreed to the appraisal's accuracy....

The court found the written partnership agreement valid and enforceable, including paragraph 6.... The court valued the property at $335,000, with a mortgage balance of $235,000. The court concluded that the partnership had $100,000 equity in the home and each party would receive 50 percent of the gross equity and/or net proceeds on its sale....

Following the hearing, the court determined that the property would not be sold to wind up the partnership. Instead, the court ordered Horne to buy Aune's partnership interest for $50,000. The court ordered Aune to quitclaim his interest to Horne in exchange for the cash payment and a release from his mortgage obligation.

Aune appeals and Horne cross-appeals.

ANALYSIS

Aune first contends that the court impermissibly ordered a distribution in kind by requiring him to quitclaim his interest in the property to Horne in exchange for a cash payment. He asserts that, in the absence of agreement, a court must order a public sale of partnership property to wind up a partnership.

The question raised is whether RUPA requires a public sale of partnership property to wind up a partnership. This question involves statutory interpretation that we engage de novo....

Partnership law in Washington originally derived from common law and courts had broad equitable powers to resolve partnership disputes. But in 1945, Washington adopted the Uniform Partnership Act (UPA). Since then, the court's equitable discretion has been subject to partnership statutes. *Guntle v. Barnett*, 73 Wash. App. 825, 837, 871 P.2d 627 (1994).

Under UPA, the departure of any partner resulted in dissolution and winding up, absent agreement to the contrary. It had been unclear under the common law whether, on winding up, partners were entitled to cash distribution of their partnership interest, as opposed to physical partition of the surplus property. UPA resolved the ambiguity by providing that each partner was entitled to cash distribution.

In 1998, Washington adopted RUPA. RUPA limits the circumstances under which a partnership must dissolve and be wound up following the departure of a partner. When a partner dissociates from a partnership, remaining partners generally may elect to either buy out the exiting partner's interest and continue the partnership business, or else dissolve and wind up the partnership. RCW 25.05.235. But when partners choose the path of dissolution and winding up, the procedures are substantially the same under RUPA as they were under UPA.

> 33 RCW 25.05.330 governs winding up of partnership business. It provides in part:
>
> (1) In winding up a partnership's business, the assets of the partnership, including the contributions of the partners required by this section, must be applied to discharge its obligations to creditors, including, to the extent permitted by law, partners who are creditors. Any surplus must be applied to pay in cash the net amount distributable to partners in accordance with their right to distributions under subsection (2) of this section.
>
> (2) Each partner is entitled to a settlement of all partnership accounts on winding up the partnership business. In settling accounts among the partners, profits and losses that result from the liquidation of the partnership assets must be credited and charged to the partners' accounts. The partnership shall make a distribution to a partner in an amount equal to any excess of the credits over the charges in the partner's account.

No Washington court has construed this statute. But in *Guntle*, we considered UPA's analogous winding-up statute, former RCW 25.04.320 (1997) (Each partner is entitled to have "the partnership property applied to discharge its liabilities, and the surplus applied to pay in cash the net amount owing to the respective partners.")....

... *Guntle* does not hold that the phrase have "the partnership property applied to discharge its liabilities" means that the court must order a public sale of partnership property. It merely holds that, in winding up a partnership, the court cannot distribute partnership assets and debts in kind, as it would in a marital dissolution, but must have "the partnership property applied to discharge its liabilities, and the surplus applied to pay in cash the net amount owing to the respective partners."

Guntle did not resolve the central issue here: whether the winding-up statute necessarily requires a forced sale of partnership assets, as opposed to permitting a partner to purchase the property, with cash payment to the other partner of his interest. This issue is one of first impression. Other jurisdictions are split.

Aune urges us to follow Montana's Supreme Court where it held that RUPA's winding-up provision requires liquidation of partnership assets through a forced sale. *McCormick v. Brevig*, 322 Mont. 112, 96 P.3d 697 (2004)....

... [T]he Montana Supreme Court rejected the trial court's resort to the dictionary, reasoning that the plain meaning of "liquidation of the partnership assets" is to reduce the partnership assets to cash, pay creditors, and distribute the cash surplus to partners. *McCormick*, 96 P.3d at 703–04. The court suggests that, because RUPA provides one track for buy out and another for dissolution and winding up, the legislature did not intend to permit a buy out where partners opt for dissolution.

Horne urges us to follow Alaska, Maryland, Oregon, and other states that have permitted a broader interpretation of the winding-up provision.

These jurisdictions hold that, while winding up generally has been equated with the forced sale of partnership assets, the statute does not strictly require such a result. Historically, the purpose of forced sale was to accurately determine the value of partnership assets. In reality, forced sale often results in economic waste. Thus, courts have accepted alternatives to forced sale as a means of winding up partnership business. Some courts have permitted distribution in kind. *Logoluso v. Logoluso*, 233 Cal.App.2d 523, 43 Cal.Rptr. 678, 682 (1965) (distribution in kind permissible absent great prejudice to the parties); *Kelley v. Shay*, 206 Pa. 208, 55 A. 925 (1903) (distribution in kind ordered where one party would have unfair advantage over the other in liquidation sale). Others have permitted a buyout. *Nicholes v. Hunt*, 273 Or. 255, 541 P.2d 820 (1975) (buy out permissible means of winding up, under UPA, where compelled liquidation would result in economic waste).

In *Disotell v. Stiltner*, 100 P.3d 890 (Alaska 2004) [the Alaska Supreme Court held that UPA (1997)] does not absolutely compel liquidation and forbid a buy out.[43] "Under appropriate, although perhaps limited, circumstances, a buyout [sic] seems a justifiable way of winding up a partnership." Disotell, 100 P.3d at 894. A buy-out option reduced economic waste by avoiding the transaction costs of a forced sale; it also guaranteed Disotell a fair value for his partnership interest. Moreover, the property was also Stiltner's residence: the court deemed it inequitable to force him out.

In *Creel v. Lilly*, 354 Md. 77, 729 A.2d 385 (1999), the Maryland Supreme Court held that neither UPA nor RUPA absolutely requires, on winding up, a forced sale of partnership assets.[44] Creel involved a partnership that dissolved because of a partner's death. The deceased's estate demanded forced sale of the partnership, invoking UPA's winding-up provision. After finding that there was no dispute concerning the value of the partnership assets, the trial court permitted the surviving partners to continue the business on cash payment of the deceased partner's interest.

The Maryland Supreme Court affirmed, siding with the line of cases holding that winding up does not equal forced sale. The court construed UPA's winding-up provision, while expressly noting that the result would be same under RUPA. The court noted that RUPA's reforms primarily target the economic waste of compelled liquidation. In the court's view, where partnership assets can accurately be valued by means other than forced sale, judicial alternatives to forced sale, including buy out, may be an acceptable means of winding up the partnership.

---

43. [3] Although *Disotell* involves UPA, as we note above, the winding-up statute is substantially the same as under RUPA.

44. [4] The case involved both statutes because RUPA was being phased in by the legislature.

We decline Aune's invitation to follow the Montana Supreme Court's reasoning in *McCormick*. Instead, we adopt Maryland's approach in *Creel*. Contrary to McCormick, the winding-up statute does not plainly mean forced sale. Thus, in our view, the trial court's resort to the dictionary in *McCormick* was appropriate. According to Black's Law Dictionary, "liquidate" means:

> 1. To settle (an obligation) by payment or other adjustment; to extinguish (a debt). 2. To ascertain the precise amount of (debt, damages, etc.) by litigation or agreement. 3. To determine the liabilities and distribute the assets of (an entity), esp. in bankruptcy or dissolution. 4. To convert (a non-liquid asset) into cash. 5. To wind up the affairs of (a corporation, business, etc.).

As used in RCW 25.05.330, the phrase "liquidation of the partnership assets," guarantees partners the right to receive, in cash, the fair value of their property interest upon winding up and dissolution of the partnership. But that result may be achieved by means other than forced sale. Historically, liquidation equaled forced sale because that was deemed the most accurate method of valuing partnership assets. But where, as here, the parties stipulate to the partnership assets' value, there is no reason to equate liquidation with forced sale.

A key factual distinction between *Guntle* and this case is that Aune is not being forced to accept property in lieu of cash; he is receiving the full cash value of his partnership interest. Absent a valid dispute concerning the value of the partnership property, he has no legal right, under the winding-up statute, to force the public sale of partnership assets.

Although the court's equitable discretion is subject to partnership statutes, RUPA does not do away altogether with equitable considerations. "Unless displaced by particular provisions of this chapter, the principles of law and equity supplement this chapter." RCW 25.05.020(1). The court's exercise of equitable discretion to grant Horne the right to purchase the property is not inconsistent with the winding-up statute. [Affirmed.]

----

1. In the preceding cases, the assets being divided were real property. The important assets of a law firm are the income streams produced by the clients. If you decide to leave your law firm, may you take your clients with you?

2. What if the assets of the firm include contingent fees or fees on matters for which work has not been fully completed? How should these fees be allocated? What is the relationship between the provisions of the UPA and Model Rule 1.5?

Section II
Corporations

Since the remaining chapters of this book will deal with corporations, we would get ahead of ourselves if we attempted to discuss the corporation completely at this point. Nevertheless, in order for you to appreciate the ways that new forms of business organizations combine general partnership and corporate attributes, it will be helpful to examine briefly the attributes of a corporation and the advantages and disadvantages of operating a business as a corporation.

At the outset, however, you should distinguish between two types of corporations: those whose shares are publicly traded on a securities exchange, and those that are privately or closely held. Publicly traded corporations are organized under general corporation codes. The general corporate structure was developed to help entrepreneurs raise significant amounts of capital from a large number of investors having little or no interest in managing the day-to-day operations of the business. Privately or closely held companies may be organized either under the general corporation codes or under close corporation statutes, which were developed expressly for privately held companies. Corporations taking the latter approach are referred to as statutory close corporations. Most corporations, large and small alike, are incorporated under general corporation statutes. Relatively few have made the statutory close corporation election.

A. Advantages of the Corporate Form

The key advantages of operating a business in the form of a corporation are:

1. Flexible capital structure
2. Centralized management structure
3. Perpetual life of company
4. Scope of limited liability for shareholders
5. Well-established form for all types of businesses

1. Flexible Capital Structure

The corporate capital structure combines a basic and relatively simple form that serves the needs of most corporations, coupled with the flexibility to vary the traditional structure almost at will. This combination of simplicity and flexibility makes the corporation's capital structure adaptable to almost any business requirement for raising money. In the simplest capital structure, a corporation has one class of stock, typically called common stock, which represents the sole ownership interest in the corporation. That is all the capital structure the average corporation needs when it begins its existence.

The first move away from this simple structure typically is the issuance of a promissory note to evidence a loan taken by the corporation, thus leaving the corporation with one type of equity interest, the common stock, and one type of debt interest, the note. From here the permutations in capital structure are almost endless. A corporation might have two classes of common stock, with the rights of ownership in the corporation split between the classes in any way those controlling the corporation wish. For example, the classes might be equal in every way except that one class carries the right to vote and the other does not. A corporation might have one or more classes of preferred stock[45] in addition to common stock.

Debt interests can vary as much as equity interests. A corporation might issue several different promissory notes having varying provisions with respect to interest payable and the terms of payment. The corporation might also issue a number of different bonds and debentures.[46]

One type of interest in the corporation may also be convertible into another type of interest. For example, a bond might be convertible into common or preferred stock at the option of the bondholder, or preferred stock might be convertible into common stock. Or, for that matter, preferred stock or a class of common stock might be convertible into bonds or debentures.

In short, those controlling a corporation have virtual carte blanche to create any capital structure they wish. That being true, those wanting to exercise financial creativity have the full chance to do so. What is more important in the usual situation is that a full range of permutations in capital structure is already in existence and well known to corporate lawyers, so that the need for the creation of a unique structure is rare. What most clients want in a capital structure is available "off the shelf."

2. Centralized Management Structure

As we will discuss below, the attribute of limited liability makes the corporation an extraordinarily effective device for amassing capital. The management structure of the general corporation makes it an equally effective device for managing capital, particularly capital raised from large numbers of people. The strengths of the corporate form in this regard flow from two factors. First, the traditional management structure created in corporation statutes works very well for most businesses. This should not be surprising, since the gradual evolution of this structure has been driven by the desire of businesses to find the most usable management structure. Second, modern corporation statutes, which provide a default management structure, give corporations broad authority to vary the structure as their owners wish, so that any unusual needs are easily served.

The traditional management structure provided by corporate law default rules is three-tiered. It consists of shareholders, directors, and officers. In this structure, shareholders, typically passive investors of capital, elect directors and approve certain extraordinary corporate actions. As votes usually are allocated on a per-share rather than *per capita* basis, voting power is directly tied to the amount of capital contribution. Directors, acting as a board, set policy and either manage or direct the management of the corporation. The authority of the board is restricted only by the

---

45. Preferred stock is simply stock that is preferred, in one or more respects, to the common stock. For example, the holders of the preferred stock might have the right to receive a certain dollar amount of dividends before any dividends are paid to the holders of the common stock. For further information on preferred and common stock, see Chapter 4, Section I.A.

46. The differences between notes, bonds, and debentures are discussed in Chapter 4, Section I.B.

shareholders' limited powers. Directors elect officers, who manage the day-to-day operations of the corporation in whatever ways the directors authorize. This traditional structure provides substantial flexibility as directors can decide how much authority to retain and how much to delegate to officers.

Flexibility can be introduced in another way. The traditional management structure is suitable for a company with a large number of shareholders who do not want to be involved in the day-to-day operations of the company and are willing to relinquish their management authority and responsibility to a group of managers (the directors), who will serve on their behalf. In other situations, however, the traditional structure may be cumbersome because of the layers of formality. That occurs when the corporation has a few shareholders who also serve as the company managers. In this situation, the shareholders may want to take advantage of options provided in the Model Act or in close corporation statutes and either restrict the powers of the board of directors or eliminate the board altogether.

Unlike the partnership form, management rights are not tied to shareholder status. Shareholders have residual financial claims to the equity of the corporation and a limited right to vote on significant corporate matters. These attributes are associated with the shares, which are freely transferable. The fact that the shares are freely transferable means that investors generally can exit the business easily, except as limited by contract.

3. Perpetual Life

The term "perpetual life" is associated with the corporation's status as a legal entity separate and distinct from its investors. Although other business forms are also accorded entity status, the scope of a corporation's entity status creates advantages in at least two ways. First, the death or bankruptcy of an owner, which may require the dissolution of a partnership, has no institutional effect on the corporation. When a shareholder dies, for example, his or her shares are distributed to the shareholder's heirs as personal property. Second, in Model Act jurisdictions, a shareholder may not seek judicial dissolution of a publicly traded corporation or of one that is privately held and has at least 300 shareholders and a market value of $20 million or more. Thus the corporate form may offer a level of stability not found in other business forms.

4. Limited Liability for Shareholders

The attribute of limited liability makes the corporation an extraordinarily effective device for amassing capital, and, as we have seen, the management structure of a general corporation makes the company equally effective at managing the capital that is raised. Although today all new business organization forms offer limited liability, not all provide the scope of limited liability available in the corporate form. For example, in most jurisdictions, Limited Liability Partnerships may not shield investors from liability for all partnership obligations. Thus, the corporation's broad grant of limited liability to shareholders continues to be an advantage for most businesses operating in the corporate form.

Limited liability means that the corporation is solely responsible for its obligations and that the personal assets of the shareholders will not be used to satisfy corporate liabilities, whether in the form of corporate debt or other third-party claims against the corporation. The few exceptions are: lending institutions may require owners of small companies personally to guarantee loans to the business; shareholders are required to satisfy any unpaid amounts of capital contributions they are obligated to pay; and, in certain circumstances, the corporate veil of limited liability may be pierced in situations where the corporation is a sham.

5. Well-Established Form

The corporation is the usual form for the operation of large, jointly-owned businesses, and it continues to be a popular form for smaller companies, as well. The advantages of operating in a well-established and frequently used form should not be underestimated. In the business world, things work more smoothly if one operates in the usual way. Take, for example, something as simple as opening a business bank account. When a corporation wishes to open an account, any customer service employee in the bank can provide the standard forms. This might also be true for a partnership, or a limited liability company, but it would not be true for a business trust or any other less common form of business. The same sort of experience will be encountered when a business wants to sign a lease or buy expensive equipment. Those on the other side of the transaction are used to dealing with corporations and are familiar with how documents are signed on behalf of corporations. With other forms of business, save the partnership and the limited liability company, that may not be the case.

B. Disadvantages of the Corporate Form

There are three clear disadvantages of operating a business in the corporate form:

1. Expense and trouble of formation and maintenance
2. Required initial and continuing formalities
3. Tax treatment

1. Expense and Trouble of Formation and Maintenance

To form a corporation, a charter (articles of incorporation) must be drafted in accordance with the statutory requirements and then filed in one or more offices in the state of incorporation. After incorporation, bylaws need to be drafted for adoption, as do minutes for the company's first organizational meeting. All this work should be done by a knowledgeable lawyer, with attendant fees that may be costly. The state's fees will generally not be substantial for a closely held (or privately held) corporation, but they will add to the total costs. If the corporation is to operate in any state other than the one in which it is incorporated, it will have to qualify to do business in that state. Qualification will entail drafting and filing other forms and paying additional fees.

In addition to these one-time costs of incorporation and qualification to do business, the filing of an annual report and the payment of an annual fee will be required in the state of incorporation and in most states in which the corporation is qualified to do business. In addition to the legal fees corporations pay initially and each year in connection with the filing of annual reports, a corporation almost certainly will incur legal fees on a continuing basis for advice on corporation law, for drafting charter and bylaw amendments, for drafting minutes of meetings, and for other work relating to the corporation's internal affairs.

All such corporate expenses could be avoided in a sole proprietorship, and all could also be avoided in a partnership if the partners choose to operate without a partnership agreement. Operating without a partnership agreement is usually unwise, however, and drafting a proper partnership agreement often gives rise to higher legal fees than does the drafting of a corporation's charter and bylaws, because a partnership agreement frequently involves more custom drafting than do a corporation's charter and bylaws. Still, the total legal expenses and fees to states typically will be more in a corporation than in a partnership, particularly if the corporation has a complex capital structure.

2. Required Initial and Continuing Formality

Sole proprietorships, partnerships, limited liability companies, and, to a degree, limited partnerships, can be operated without formalities and without records of decisions that are made. The rules are quite different in a corporation. Both the shareholders and the directors must have meetings, or take action by formal written consent in lieu of meetings, and proper records must be kept of shareholders' and directors' actions. Further, the funds of the corporation must be kept separate from those of its owner or owners, and proper financial records must be maintained.

None of these requirements typically seems onerous to lawyers, but clients often view them as needless bothers. Unless their lawyers convince them otherwise, managers of closely held corporations tend to ignore some or all of these formalities. As will be seen in the chapters that follow, the cost of ignoring formalities might be that a court will disregard the corporate form and allow creditors to collect from a corporation's shareholders.

3. Tax Treatment

The tax disadvantage of operating in the corporate form is double taxation. A partnership as a legal entity is not subject to federal income taxation unless it elects to be taxed like a corporation, because federal tax law, tracking UPA (1914) state partnership law, treats a partnership as an aggregate of partners rather than as an entity separate from its owners. In contrast, a corporation is subject to federal income taxation precisely because, under both federal and state law, it is treated as a separate entity. Unlike a partnership, a corporation pays income taxes on its earnings. When a corporation distributes its after-tax profits to its shareholders as dividends, those dividends are subject to taxation as the ordinary income of the shareholders. Thus corporate income that is distributed to shareholders is twice subjected to taxation, once when it is earned by the corporation and again when it is distributed to shareholders.

Double taxation can be avoided in some circumstances, however, and once it is avoided, the corporate form may provide tax advantages. Congress has provided certain closely held corporations with the most straightforward way of avoiding double taxation. A corporation meeting specified requirements of the Internal Revenue Code can choose to be treated for federal tax purposes as if it were a partnership. In that case, the corporation will file merely an information return, and any corporate profits or losses will flow through to its shareholders for inclusion in their individual income tax returns. Such corporations now are called type S corporations, with that designation coming from the fact that the provisions in the Code dealing with such corporations were originally contained in subchapter S of the Internal Revenue Code of 1954. Here are the requirements for type S treatment:

1. No more than seventy-five shareholders.
2. Incorporation in the United States.
3. Only one class of stock.
4. Shareholders must be individuals, estates, or specified types of trusts.
5. No shareholder may be a nonresident alien.
6. The corporation may not be a life insurance company or certain other excluded types of businesses.
7. All shareholders must agree to the type S election.

In some corporations that have not elected type S treatment, double taxation can be avoided to an extent, or at least deferred, if the company does not pay dividends. The shareholders do not necessarily see this as a hardship, because they usually want their corporation to keep available cash invested in the corporation, rather than pay it out in dividends, so that the corporation will grow and the shareholders' shares will become more valuable. This is especially true in a closely held corporation that is owned and managed by the same group of people, since the group can take money out of the corporation as salaries and directors' fees, which are deductible expenses for the corporation, and thus not subject to double taxation.

Corporations may avoid double taxation by reinvesting available cash and paying salaries to their owner-managers; they may also minimize or at least defer even single taxation by the same means. Good managers often are able shrewdly to expand the business by using cash that otherwise would end up as a taxable profit. If the managers successfully use this approach, the corporation can become larger and more successful each year, while paying substantially minimized income taxes.

In many situations, the opportunities for using this approach may be limited and the company will look for other ways to minimize taxes. For example, some expenditures for officer and employee benefits are deductible to the corporation and not taxable to the recipients. Generally, these expenditures relate to medical payment and disability plans, group term life insurance and death benefits up to specified limits, and certain deferred compensation plans. The availability of this tax-free treatment can be especially valuable to owner-managers, because as officers or employees they themselves can receive these tax-free benefits.

Even though the impact of double taxation often can be substantially reduced, the fact that it exists as a possibility and that corporate managers must devote efforts to avoiding it makes double taxation a clear disadvantage of operating in the corporate form.

Section III
Synthesis — Other Forms of Business Organizations

The current growth industry in developing or significantly revising business organization forms is the product of the very human desire to have it all. Having it all refers to business owners' desire for advantageous tax treatment, limited liability, and the flexibility to structure the company as they wish. The quest for limited liability and flexible structure was evident in the late nineteenth century with the emergence of the partnership association, a form that never really took hold in the United States, although similar forms flourished in Europe. Considerations of tax consequences became important in the latter half of the twentieth century with the development of different tax treatments for corporations and partnerships. With the exception of the limited partnership, which was an early nineteenth century import from French law, the statutory forms discussed below have emerged during the past forty years, as business owners and their lawyers sought to combine the best of partnership and corporate forms.

The rapid development and abundance of business organizations having both partnership and corporate attributes have presented special problems for courts resolving disputes among company members or between the company and third parties. For example, what analytical model should a court apply to a business having a partnership management structure and limited liability? Should the court use a corporate model, a partnership model, or apply corporate theory to those elements of the company that are corporate in nature (such as issues related to limited liability) and partnership theory to attributes that resemble a partnership, such as the management structure? How should the court approach issues of diversity jurisdiction? These issues arise in connection with all types of business organization forms having both corporate and partnership attributes.

A. Statutory Close and Professional Corporations

The development of close corporation statutes began in the late 1950's, a time when Congress developed a pass through taxation scheme for corporations with few owners, so that these businesses could be taxed like partnerships. At that time, corporate tax rates were lower than those imposed on individuals, and corporations could take advantage of retirement plan options then unavailable to unincorporated businesses. Small business owners also wanted a more flexible management structure than that offered by general corporation statutes. State legislatures responded by passing elective close corporation statutes that provided structural flexibility.

Statutory close corporations typically shed many attributes characteristic of general corporations and substitute those of partnerships. Their management structure can be informal. Shareholders may dispense with the Board of Directors and run the company themselves. They also may dissolve the corporation at will or on the occurrence of a particular event. In addition, share transfer restrictions are common. Although many statutory close corporations possess more non-corporate than corporate characteristics, the fact that they are organized as a corporation under state law means that, without Subchapter S, they will very likely receive corporate tax treatment. Companies making both statutory close corporation and subchapter S elections can have a pass-through taxation scheme, limited liability, flexible management structure, and corporate advantages regarding retirement plans. Today, closely held corporations not making a statutory close corporation election can achieve many of the same results by preparing shareholder agreements and taking advantage of special statutory provisions included in many general corporation statutes. Closely held corporations are discussed more fully in later chapters.

Professional Corporations developed during approximately the same period and for many of the same reasons. Licensed professionals wanted to be able to take advantage of the tax and retirement plan options available only to a corporation, a business organization form forbidden to them under state law and applicable codes of ethics, because corporate shareholders have limited liability. Ultimately, states developed the professional corporation, a form like other corporations except that it makes shareholders personally liable to their clients or patients.

B. Limited Partnerships

The limited partnership developed during the Middle Ages, concurrently with the general partnership. Limited partnerships were used to finance speculative enterprises, primarily maritime trade. Small merchants and shippers needed to obtain credit and spread the risk of their venture. Investors who were owners of, rather than lenders to, an enterprise were able to increase their return on capital without violating usury laws. By the end of the Middle Ages, partnerships affording investors limited liability and freely alienable shares had begun to develop.

By the sixteenth century, the key characteristics of limited partnerships as we know them today were well established. The business organization had two classes of members. The commendators (limited partners) were passive investors whose liability was limited to the amount of their capital contribution. Tractators (general partners) had full responsibility for the conduct of the business and had unlimited liability for its obligations. Generally, the business was conducted in the tractators' names, and parties trading with the business did not know the identity of the passive investors.

In 1822, borrowing from the French, the New York legislature passed the first limited partnership statute in this country, thus introducing this form of business organization into the United States. Other states soon followed New York's lead. Limited partnerships proved to be popular in the United States as investors sought to avoid an early court decision imposing liability on lenders to a general partnership who took a share of the profits in lieu of interest. Limited partners were protected from such a result. The limited partnership form was also attractive because corporate charters providing limited liability were difficult to obtain at that time. General corporation acts did not become common for many more years. In addition, the limited partnership form avoided technical limitations then associated with incorporation.

Today, all states except Louisiana have passed one of the modern versions of the Uniform Limited Partnership Act. The original Uniform Limited Partnership Act (ULPA 1916)[47] dates from 1916. That act was superseded by the 1976 Uniform Limited Partnership in all but one state other than Louisiana. The new act was in turn amended in 1985[48] and again in 2001.[49] Both of these amendments are discussed in the text that follows.

As compared with the 1916 Act, the 1976 Act creates no revolution. In large measure, it can be viewed as a cleaning up and streamlining of limited partnership law. The 1976 Act is, nevertheless, a helpful improvement for those involved in limited partnerships, especially those serving as limited partners, and for limited partnerships conducting business in multiple jurisdictions.

Both the 1916 and the 1976 Acts retain many of the attributes developed during the Middle Ages and considered essential to advance investment in speculative enterprises. These forms have two classes of partners: general and limited partners. General partners in a limited partnership have the same relationships to each other and to third parties as do members of a general partnership. General partners manage the business of the limited partnership, have unlimited liability for the company's debts, and cannot transfer their interests in the limited partnership without the others' consent. Their withdrawal, death, or bankruptcy will cause the dissolution of the limited partnership. General partners may be individuals, corporations, limited liability companies, or other legal entities. Thus, a general partner may, itself, be a limited liability entity.

Limited partners are prohibited from managing the business and the extent of their liability is limited to the amount of their investments. Their interests in the partnership may be transferred to a third party only if the other partners agree. As with the general partnership, the relationship among members of a limited partnership is essentially consensual and may be varied by agreement. An important difference between general and limited partnerships is that a limited partnership cannot be created informally. In all states, forming a limited partnership requires that a certificate of limited partnership be filed in one or more state offices. The certificate contains such information as the partnership's name, information about the agent for service of process, the name and business address of each general partner, the term of the business, and any other information the general partners wish to include. The business entity is created at the time of the required filing. Although the statute does not

---

47. Uniform Limited Partnership Act (1916) (hereinafter ULPA (1916)) (U.L.A.).

48. Uniform Limited Partnership Act (1976) (with 1985 amendments) (hereinafter ULPA 1976) (U.L.A.).

49. Uniform Limited Partnership Act (2001) (hereinafter ULPA (2001)) (U.L.A.).

require one, partnership agreements are an essential component of forming a limited partnership. The agreements define the rights and obligations of the members of the business, and their provisions are also used in determining tax consequences.

In limited partnerships, as in corporations, the passive investors often supply substantially all, if not all, of the capital. However, any partner's capital contribution may consist of cash, property, services rendered, an obligation to perform services, or a promissory note to contribute cash or property.

Partners in a limited partnership may transfer their right to receive distributions, but not other rights of the partner making the assignment. Transferring all the rights of a limited partner requires the consent of the other partners unless the partnership agreement specifies otherwise. Such a transfer does not dissolve the limited partnership. Limited partners may also withdraw with prior written notice and be paid the value of their partnership interests.

A change in the identity of the limited partners does not interrupt the continuation of the partnership. In contrast, the business will generally end if the general partner withdraws for any reason. The partnership agreement may, however, provide for the continuation of the business when such an event occurs.

Under the 1916 and the 1976 Acts, the main features that distinguish limited partners from general partners are the differences in their liability and the placement of management power solely in the hands of the general partners. It is perhaps in their treatment of the liability and management rules that the differences between the 1916 and 1976 Limited Partnership Acts are most important. The 1916 Act's provision on limited partners' liability and involvement in management is very simple: a limited partner has no liability to creditors unless the limited partner "takes part in the control of the business."[50] Limited partners who take part in the control of the business lose their limited liability. There can be, however, a good deal of argument about what constitutes taking part in the control of a business.

The drafters of the 1976 Uniform Limited Partnership Act started with the same concept for determining a limited partner's liability as did the drafters of the 1916 Act. Although they used essentially equivalent operative words (substituting "participates in" for "takes part in" the control of the business), they added substantial elaboration in an attempt to reduce the area of uncertainty. This elaboration takes the form of an eight-item "safe harbor" list of actions that do not constitute participation in the control of the business.[51] Examples are: (1) consulting with a general partner with respect to the business of the partnership, (2) requesting or attending a meeting of partners, and (3) voting on any matter relating to the business of the partnership that under the partnership agreement is subject to the approval or disapproval of the limited partners.

The 1976 Act also made a more fundamental change with respect to limited partners' liability. Under the 1976 Act, a limited partner who does participate in the control of the business is liable "only to persons who transact business with the limited

50. ULPA (1916) §7.
51. ULPA (1976) §303(b).

partnership reasonably believing, based upon the limited partner's conduct, that the limited partner is a general partner."[52] In a large percentage of cases involving conduct by a limited partner that arguably constitutes participation in the control of the business, this provision may prove to be the Act's most effective liability shield.

There is one more change from the 1916 Act to the 1976 Act that deserves attention. The old Act makes no mention of the possibility that a limited partnership may operate across state lines. This presents a substantial problem for a business operating in more than one state, because it is not clear how a particular state may treat a foreign limited partnership, with the risk being that a state will treat it as a general partnership. This uncertainty often has led careful lawyers to form separate limited partnerships in each state in which a business will operate. The 1976 Act, on the other hand, devotes an entire article to the question of foreign limited partnerships and provides that limited partnerships formed in other states may register under the Act as foreign limited partnerships.

The limited partnership acts do not expressly address the issue of fiduciary obligations. Section 403 of the 1976 Act, however, imposes on the general partners the same liabilities that partners in a general partnership have to the partnership and to the other partners. This would include fiduciary obligations. The limited partnership acts also provide that the provisions of the general partnership acts apply to matters not covered by the respective limited partnership acts.

Limited partnerships formed under the 1916 or 1976 Act tend to be used in several types of business situations. A business operating as a general partnership sometimes finds it convenient to recast itself as a limited partnership for the purpose of attracting new capital from investors who will share in the profits of the business, but who have no desire to participate in its management. In addition, a general partnership is sometimes reorganized as a limited partnership upon the retirement of a partner who wishes to leave capital invested in the partnership, and thus share in its profits, but who does not wish to be subjected to the unlimited liability of a general partner in a business that he or she no longer manages. Family limited partnerships have also become popular planning tools in which parents give limited partnership equity interests in the business to their children without enabling the children to participate in the control of the business. These uses of the limited partnership are obviously closely related. Limited partnerships are also used for many other types of businesses. Oil exploration companies often use this form, as do shareholder servicing companies which, among other things, maintain records of shareholders in publicly traded companies.

Limited partnerships are also used as vehicles for tax-shelter investments, designed to take advantage of the fact that most limited partnerships are taxed like general partnerships. Until January 1, 1997, limited partnerships were generally taxed like general partnerships, whereas today, they may elect to be taxed either like a partnership or like a corporation. Limited partnerships are used for investments in real estate, venture capital, sports teams, and movies, to name a few. Until the 1980s, a limited

---

52. *Id.* § 303(a).

partnership formed to build and operate a real estate venture, such as an apartment complex or a shopping center, offered many tax advantages. In those types of ventures, promoters looked for investors anxious to make an investment that (1) would generate losses while the project was under construction, so that the investors could write these losses off against their other income and (2) would later make profits that could be passed through to the investors without taxation at the partnership level (in each case with these tax consequences flowing from the fact that partnerships are exempt from federal and most state income taxation). The Tax Reform Act of 1986 substantially reduced the tax benefits available from the use of such tax shelters, including investors' ability to apply these losses against other income.

The master limited partnership is an exception to the rule that limited partnerships are usually taxed like general partnerships. Master limited partnerships are publicly traded limited partnerships. They were originally developed to provide public markets for limited partners' interests in oil and gas tax shelters, while retaining pass through taxation and limited liability. Using the limited partnership form avoided the restrictions of Subchapter S and the impact of the corporate taxation scheme. Since 1988, however, master limited partnerships have been taxed as corporations when certain criteria are met.

In 2001, the Limited Partnership Act was again revised, largely in response to the recent appearance in the 1990s of two new business forms: the limited liability partnership (based on general partnership law) and the limited liability company. Today, the limited liability partnership and the limited liability company are used to accommodate needs formerly met by limited partnerships. Consequently, the 2001 Limited Partnership Act has been drafted for a narrower range of business activities than were its predecessors. According to its Prefatory Note, the 2001 Act is intended to be used for "(i) sophisticated, manager-entrenched commercial deals whose participants commit for the long term, and (ii) estate planning arrangements (family limited partnerships)."[53] The Act is based on the assumption that persons forming these types of partnerships will want to have "strong centralized management, strongly entrenched, and ... passive investors with little control over or right to exit the entity."[54]

The structure of the 2001 Limited Partnership Act is a significant departure from earlier limited partnership law. Unlike its predecessors, the 2001 Act is a stand alone act and is not linked to either of the general partnership statutes: the original Uniform Partnership Act (1914) or the revised Uniform Partnership Act (1997). The 2001 Act, however, incorporates provisions based on general partnership acts and limited liability company acts. This borrowing is reflected in the length and complexity of the 2001 Limited Partnership Act.

The 2001 Act continues the distinction between general and limited partners, with certain modifications. Section 404(a) of the Act also continues the usual rule that the

---

53. ULPA (2001), Prefatory Note.
54. ULPA (2001), Prefatory Note.

general partners have joint and several liability for all partnership obligations. The 2001 Act, however, permits a limited partnership to be organized as a limited liability limited partnership (LLLP), a form that provides protection from liability for all partners, whether general or limited. According to Section 404(c) of the 2001 Act, obligations of LLLPs are solely the obligation of the partnership. LLLP obligations thus do not accrue to the general partners.

The 2001 Act has also made important changes that apply to limited partners. The Act rejects the approach of the earlier limited partnership acts, which provided that a limited partner would not be liable for partnership debts unless the limited partner participated in the control of the business. According to Section 303 of the 2001 Act, a limited partner has limited liability even if the limited partner participates in the management and control of the business. The grant of limited liability is thus based on the partner's status as a limited partner and not on the partner's activities.

With respect to a limited partner's withdrawal from the partnership, the 2001 Act distinguishes between the partner's right to dissociate and the partner's power to do so. Section 601 of the 2001 Act expressly provides that a limited partner does not have the right to dissociate from the limited partnership before its termination. Should a limited partner exercise the partner's power to dissociate, even though wrongful, the partnership is not obligated to purchase the departing partner's interest. According to Section 602(3), "any transferable interest owned by the [dissociating] person in the person's capacity as a limited partner immediately before dissociation is owned by the person as a mere transferee." In sum, the departing partner continues to hold the partner's own transferable interest. The difference is that the person holding the interest is no longer a limited partner. This approach contrasts with the approach taken by the earlier acts in which dissociating partners are paid their value of the partnership interests, with an offset for any damages caused by the wrongful dissociation.

C. Limited Liability Companies[55]

Limited liability companies are among the latest efforts to achieve favorable tax treatment while combining the best of the partnership and corporate forms. The limited liability company offers several advantages: it usually qualifies for partnership pass through taxation while avoiding the restrictions imposed by Subchapter S and it resembles a partnership in which all members have limited liability. All states have passed limited liability company acts. Most acts have been passed since a 1988 Revenue Ruling[56] provided that limited liability companies with certain attributes qualified for

---

55. The discussion that follows is primarily based on the Uniform Limited Liability Company Act (1995), approved by the Uniform Law Commission in 1995 (hereinafter "ULLCA (1995)").
56. Rev. Rul. 88-76, 1988-2 C.B. 360.

partnership taxation. Today, limited liability companies, like most other unincorporated business organizations, may elect either partnership or corporate tax treatment.

The limited liability company is an extremely popular form in which to do business. As expected, small, emerging companies are attracted to this form. But large companies are using the form to organize subsidiaries and to form joint ventures with other companies by uniting two independently owned businesses under common control: the independently owned businesses become the members of the limited liability company.

One or more persons may form a limited liability company by filing articles of organization in the office of the secretary of state. Although an operating agreement is not required for formation, most acts are based on the assumption that an agreement will be prepared to address issues of company governance and operations not covered by the statute or to make elections where the statute provides options. As with other privately held firms, a well drafted operating agreement is essential for the successful operation of the company.

All LLC members have unrestricted limited liability so long as the company was properly formed, members have paid their promised capital contributions in full, and the company is not operating in a fraudulent manner. The business may be managed either by its members or by a designated group of managers, who may or may not be members of the company. The member-managed firm is very much like a partnership in the relations of the members to each other and in their ability to bind the firm through their individual acts. Each is an agent of the firm. Similarly, each manager in a manager-managed firm may also bind the firm, but individual members who are not also managers may not.

Members' capital contributions may consist of property, money, promissory notes, services performed, or agreements to contribute property, money or services. Members are liable for the full amount of their promised contributions. Distributions to members during the conduct of the company's business may be made in equal shares or according to capital contribution. A limited liability company may not make distributions to its members that would render the company insolvent. This approach is similar to that found in corporate statutes. Liability is imposed for unlawful distributions. As in partnerships, members may transfer their financial interests in the company, but the transferee does not become a member unless the other members consent or the operating agreement so provides. The transferee is entitled to receive only the distributions that the transferor had a right to receive. Members have the right to access company records and are subject to fiduciary obligations of due care and loyalty. The scope of these obligations depends on whether the company is managed by members or by managers.

A limited liability company may be at will or be organized for a term. All members have the right to dissociate from the company at any time and to be paid the value of their interests. Dissociation does not ordinarily cause dissolution. Wrongful dissociation may, however, result in a dissolution of the firm.

The introduction of a new business form often creates a range of problems. The LLC is not an exception. Of primary concern are issues associated with interpreting the LLC operating agreement. LLC statutes are generally permissive, giving the members great latitude in designing the structure and operation of the company. This permissiveness in turn increases the need to have a well-drafted operating agreement, so that subsequent interpretation by a court will not produce unintended outcomes. The flexibility afforded by the LLC form also gives the organizers the option of picking and choosing among attributes drawn from other business forms.

For example, as stated previously an LLC may have either a participatory management structure, like a partnership, or a centralized management structure, like a corporation. This flexibility requires courts to resolve disputes by reference to either partnership or corporate statutes if the LLC statute does not provide direction on a particular point. In addition, problems may arise when existing statutes predating the LLC are not modified to accommodate the LLC. For example, a merger statute may be silent on the issue of whether pre-existing business forms may be merged with an LLC. Another variation of this problem arises when other business forms are included in a statutory definition, such as the definition of "person," and the LLC form is not mentioned.

The limited liability company has become, in a few short years, one of the most popular business organization forms. With this increased popularity has come a burgeoning number of lawsuits involving LLCs. The courts' work in resolving disputes involving LLCs is complicated by the fact that this new form of business organization combines attributes of partnerships and corporations. In *Anderson v. Wilder*,[57] the court described its methodology as follows:

> … The typical LLC act is usually a hybrid of provisions culled from the individual state's partnership statutes and business corporation law.…
>
> [W]hen a court is interpreting an LLC act or agreement, the court will focus on the particular aspect of the LLC that gives rise to the problem, with emphasis on the foundational business form from which that characteristic originated. Usually, the particular aspect can be traced to either the corporate components or the partnership components of the LLC act or agreement. In such cases where the characteristic originated from the partnership aspects of the LLC, the court will use the established princip[le]s and precedent of the partnership law to resolve the issue … In such cases where the characteristic originated from the corporate aspects of the LLC, the court will utilize the established princip[le]s and precedent of corporate law to resolve the issue. [Citing Annotation, Construction and Application of Limited Liability Company Acts, 79 A.L.R.5th 689.]

The cases that follow introduce some of the problems courts address. As you read, consider the extent to which each court's analysis is based on traditional contract principles, LLC statutory provisions or reference to the law of other business forms such as partnerships or corporations.

---

57. 2003 Tenn. App. LEXIS 819.

1. The Operating Agreement

The following case discusses the historical development of the LLC form in Delaware and the policies underlying this business form.

Elf Atochem North America, Inc. v. Jaffari and Malek LLC

Delaware Supreme Court
727 A.2d 286 (1999)

VEASEY, CHIEF JUSTICE:

This is a case of first impression before this Court involving the Delaware Limited Liability Company Act (the "Act"). The limited liability company ("LLC") is a relatively new entity that has emerged in recent years as an attractive vehicle to facilitate business relationships and transactions. The wording and architecture of the Act is somewhat complicated, but it is designed to achieve what is seemingly a simple concept—to permit persons or entities ("members") to join together in an environment of private ordering to form and operate the enterprise under an LLC agreement with tax benefits akin to a partnership and limited liability akin to the corporate form.

This is a purported derivative suit brought on behalf of a Delaware LLC calling into question whether: (1) the LLC, which did not itself execute the LLC agreement in this case ("the Agreement") defining its governance and operation, is nevertheless bound by the Agreement; and (2) contractual provisions directing that all disputes be resolved exclusively by arbitration or court proceedings in California are valid under the Act. Resolution of these issues requires us to examine the applicability and scope of certain provisions of the Act in light of the Agreement.

We hold that: (1) the Agreement is binding on the LLC as well as the members; and (2) since the Act does not prohibit the members of an LLC from vesting exclusive subject matter jurisdiction in arbitration proceedings (or court enforcement of arbitration) in California to resolve disputes, the contractual forum selection provisions must govern.

Accordingly, we affirm the judgment of the Court of Chancery dismissing the action brought in that court on the ground that the Agreement validly predetermined the fora in which disputes would be resolved, thus stripping the Court of Chancery of subject matter jurisdiction.

Facts

Plaintiff below-appellant Elf Atochem North America, Inc., a Pennsylvania Corporation ("Elf"), manufactures and distributes solvent-based maskants to the aerospace and aviation industries throughout the world. Defendant below-appellee Cyrus A. Jaffari is the president of Malek, Inc., a California Corporation. Jaffari had developed an innovative, environmentally-friendly alternative to the solvent-based maskants that presently dominate the market.

For decades, the aerospace and aviation industries have used solvent-based maskants in the chemical milling process. Recently, however, the Environmental Protection Agency ("EPA") classified solvent-based maskants as hazardous chemicals and air contaminants. To avoid conflict with EPA regulations, Elf considered developing or distributing a maskant less harmful to the environment.

In the mid-nineties, Elf approached Jaffari and proposed investing in his product and assisting in its marketing. Jaffari found the proposal attractive since his company, Malek, Inc., possessed limited resources and little international sales expertise. Elf and Jaffari agreed to undertake a joint venture that was to be carried out using a limited liability company as the vehicle.

On October 29, 1996, Malek, Inc. caused to be filed a Certificate of Formation with the Delaware Secretary of State, thus forming Malek LLC, a Delaware limited liability company under the Act. The certificate of formation is a relatively brief and formal document that is the first statutory step in creating the LLC as a separate legal entity. The certificate does not contain a comprehensive agreement among the parties, and the statute contemplates that the certificate of formation is to be complemented by the terms of the Agreement.[58]

Next, Elf, Jaffari and Malek, Inc. entered into a series of agreements providing for the governance and operation of the joint venture. Of particular importance to this litigation, Elf, Malek, Inc., and Jaffari entered into the Agreement, a comprehensive and integrated document[59] of 38 single-spaced pages setting forth detailed provisions for the governance of Malek LLC, which is not itself a signatory to the Agreement.

The Agreement is the operative document for purposes of this Opinion, however. Under the Agreement, Elf contributed $1 million in exchange for a 30 percent interest in Malek LLC. Malek, Inc. contributed its rights to the water-based maskant in exchange for a 70 percent interest in Malek LLC.

The Agreement contains an arbitration clause covering all disputes. The clause, Section 13.8, provides that "any controversy or dispute arising out of this Agreement, the interpretation of any of the provisions hereof, or the action or inaction of any Member or Manager hereunder shall be submitted to arbitration in San Francisco, California...." Section 13.8 further provides:

> No action ... based upon any claim arising out of or related to this Agreement shall be instituted in any court by any Member except (a) an action to compel arbitration ... or (b) an action to enforce an award obtained in an arbitration proceeding....

---

58. [5] See 6 Del.C. § 18-201(d), which provides:
   A limited liability company agreement may be entered into either before, after or at the time of the filing of a certificate of formation and, whether entered into before, after or at the time of such filing, may be made effective as of the formation of the limited liability company or at such other time or date as provided in the limited liability company agreement.

59. [6] See the definition section of the statute, 6 Del.C. § 18-101(7), defining the term "limited liability company agreement" as "any agreement ... of the ... members as to the affairs of a limited liability company and the conduct of its business," and setting forth a nonexclusive list of what it may provide.

The Agreement also contains a forum selection clause, Section 13.7, providing that all members consent to:

> exclusive jurisdiction of the state and federal courts sitting in California in any action on a claim arising out of, under or in connection with this Agreement or the transactions contemplated by this Agreement, provided such claim is not required to be arbitrated pursuant to Section 13.8;

and personal jurisdiction in California. . . .

Elf's Suit in the Court of Chancery

On April 27, 1998, Elf sued Jaffari and Malek LLC, individually and derivatively on behalf of Malek LLC, in the Delaware Court of Chancery, seeking equitable remedies. Among other claims, Elf alleged that Jaffari breached his fiduciary duty to Malek LLC, pushed Malek LLC to the brink of insolvency by withdrawing funds for personal use, interfered with business opportunities, failed to make disclosures to Elf, and threatened to make poor quality maskant and to violate environmental regulations. Elf also alleged breach of contract, tortious interference with prospective business relations, and (solely as to Jaffari) fraud.

The Court of Chancery granted defendants' motion to dismiss based on lack of subject matter jurisdiction. The court held that Elf's claims arose under the Agreement, or the transactions contemplated by the agreement, and were directly related to Jaffari's actions as manager of Malek LLC. Therefore, the court found that the Agreement governed the question of jurisdiction and that only a court of law or arbitrator in California is empowered to decide these claims. Elf now appeals the order of the Court of Chancery dismissing the complaint.

Contentions of the Parties

Elf claims that the Court of Chancery erred in holding that the arbitration and forum selection clauses in the Agreement governed, and thus deprived that court of jurisdiction to adjudicate all of Elf's claims, including its derivative claims made on behalf of Malek LLC. Elf contends that, since Malek LLC is not a party to the Agreement, it is not bound by the forum selection provisions. . . . Finally, Elf argues that the dispute resolution clauses of the Agreement are invalid under Section 109(d) of the Act, which, it alleges, prohibits the parties from vesting exclusive jurisdiction in a forum outside of Delaware.[60]

Defendants claim that Elf contracted with Malek, Inc. and Jaffari that all disputes that arise out of, under, or in connection with the Agreement must be resolved exclusively in California by arbitration or court proceedings. Defendants allege that ... the Agree-

---

60. [10] See 6 Del.C. § 18-109(d), which provides:

> In a written limited liability company agreement or other writing, a manager or member may consent to be subject to the nonexclusive jurisdiction of the courts of, or arbitration in, a specified jurisdiction, or the exclusive jurisdiction of the courts of the State of Delaware, or the exclusivity of arbitration in a specified jurisdiction or the State of Delaware ...

ment provides that the members would not institute "any" action at law or equity except one to compel arbitration, and that any such action must be brought in California....

 With regard to the validity of Section 13.7, defendants argue that Section 18-109(d) of the Act is a permissive statute and does not prohibit the parties from vesting exclusive jurisdiction outside of Delaware. Thus, defendants assert that the Court of Chancery correctly held that the dispute resolution provisions of the Agreement are valid and apply to bar Elf from seeking relief in Delaware.

General Summary of Background of the Act

The phenomenon of business arrangements using "alternative entities" has been developing rapidly over the past several years. Long gone are the days when business planners were confined to corporate or partnership structures.

Limited partnerships date back to the 19th Century. They became an important and popular vehicle with the adoption of the Uniform Limited Partnership Act in 1916. Sixty years later, in 1976, the National Conference of Commissioners on Uniform State Laws approved and recommended to the states a Revised Uniform Limited Partnership Act ("RULPA"), many provisions of which were modeled after the innovative 1973 Delaware Limited Partnership (LP) Act. Difficulties with the workability of the 1976 RULPA prompted the Commissioners to amend RULPA in 1985.

To date, 48 states and the District of Columbia have adopted the RULPA in either its 1976 or 1985 form. Delaware adopted the RULPA with innovations designed to improve upon the Commissioners' product. Since 1983, the General Assembly has amended the LP Act eleven times, with a view to continuing Delaware's status as an innovative leader in the field of limited partnerships.

The Delaware Act [Limited Liability Company Act] was adopted in October 1992. The Act is codified in Chapter 18 of Title 6 of the Delaware Code. To date, the Act has been amended six times with a view to modernization. The LLC is an attractive form of business entity because it combines corporate-type limited liability with partnership-type flexibility and tax advantages. The Act can be characterized as a "flexible statute" because it generally permits members to engage in private ordering with substantial freedom of contract to govern their relationship, provided they do not contravene any mandatory provisions of the Act. Indeed, the LLC has been characterized as the "best of both worlds."

The Delaware Act has been modeled on the popular Delaware LP Act. In fact, its architecture and much of its wording is almost identical to that of the Delaware LP Act. Under the Act, a member of an LLC is treated much like a limited partner under the LP Act. The policy of freedom of contract underlies both the Act and the LP Act.

...

Policy of the Delaware Act

The basic approach of the Delaware Act is to provide members with broad discretion in drafting the Agreement and to furnish default provisions when the members' agreement is silent.[61] The Act is replete with fundamental provisions made subject to modification in the Agreement (e.g. "unless otherwise provided in a limited liability company agreement....").[62]

Although business planners may find comfort in working with the Act in structuring transactions and relationships, it is a somewhat awkward document for this Court to construe and apply in this case. To understand the overall structure and thrust of the Act, one must wade through provisions that are prolix, sometimes oddly organized, and do not always flow evenly. Be that as it may as a problem in mastering the Act as a whole, one returns to the narrow and discrete issues presented in this case.

Freedom of Contract

Section 18-1101(b) of the Act, like the essentially identical Section 17-1101(c) of the LP Act, provides that "[i]t is the policy of [the Act] to give the maximum effect to the principle of freedom of contract and to the enforceability of limited liability company agreements." Accordingly, the following observation relating to limited partnerships applies as well to limited liability companies:

> The Act's basic approach is to permit partners to have the broadest possible discretion in drafting their partnership agreements and to furnish answers only in situations where the partners have not expressly made provisions in their partnership agreement. Truly, the partnership agreement is the cornerstone of a Delaware limited partnership, and effectively constitutes the entire agreement among the partners with respect to the admission of partners to, and the creation, operation and termination of, the limited partnership. Once partners exercise their contractual freedom in their partnership agreement, the partners have a great deal of certainty that their partnership agreement will be enforced in accordance with its terms.[63]

In general, the commentators observe that only where the agreement is inconsistent with mandatory statutory provisions will the members' agreement be invalidated. Such statutory provisions are likely to be those intended to protect third parties, not necessarily the contracting members. As a framework for decision, we

---

61. [25] According to Lubaroff & Altman, "the Act gives members virtually unfettered discretion to define contractually their business understanding, and then provides assurance that their understanding will be enforced in accordance with the terms of their limited liability company agreement." Id.

62. [26] For example, members are free to contract among themselves concerning management of the LLC, including who is to manage the LLC, the establishment of classes of members, voting, procedures for holding meetings of members, or considering matters without a meeting.

63. [27] Martin I. Lubaroff & Paul Altman, Delaware Limited Partnerships § 1.2 (1999) (footnote omitted). In their article on Delaware limited liability companies, Lubaroff and Altman use virtually identical language in describing the basic approach of the LLC Act. Clearly, both the LP Act and the LLC Act are uniform in their commitment to "maximum flexibility." See Lubaroff & Altman, supra note 14, at § 20.4.

apply that principle to the issues before us, without expressing any views more broadly.

The Arbitration and Forum Selection Clauses in the Agreement are a Bar to Jurisdiction in the Court of Chancery

In vesting the Court of Chancery with jurisdiction, the Act accomplished at least three purposes: (1) it assured that the Court of Chancery has jurisdiction it might not otherwise have because it is a court of limited jurisdiction that requires traditional equitable relief or specific legislation to act; (2) it established the Court of Chancery as the default forum in the event the members did not provide another choice of forum or dispute resolution mechanism; and (3) it tends to center interpretive litigation in Delaware courts with the expectation of uniformity. Nevertheless, the arbitration provision of the Agreement in this case fosters the Delaware policy favoring alternate dispute resolution mechanisms, including arbitration. Such mechanisms are an important goal of Delaware legislation, court rules, and jurisprudence.

Malek LLC's Failure to Sign the Agreement Does Not Affect the Members' Agreement Governing Dispute Resolution

Elf argues that because Malek LLC, on whose behalf Elf allegedly brings these claims, is not a party to the Agreement, the derivative claims it brought on behalf of Malek LLC are not governed by the arbitration and forum selection clauses of the Agreement.

Elf argues that Malek LLC came into existence on October 29, 1996, when the parties filed its Certificate of Formation with the Delaware Secretary of State. The parties did not sign the Agreement until November 4, 1996. Elf contends that Malek LLC existed as an LLC as of October 29, 1996, but never agreed to the Agreement because it did not sign it. Because Malek LLC never expressly assented to the arbitration and forum selection clauses within the Agreement, Elf argues it can sue derivatively on behalf of Malek LLC pursuant to 6 Del.C. § 18-1001.[64]

We are not persuaded by this argument. Section 18-101(7) defines the limited liability company agreement as "any agreement, written or oral, of the member or members as to the affairs of a limited liability company and the conduct of its business." Here, Malek, Inc. and Elf, the members of Malek LLC, executed the Agreement to carry out the affairs and business of Malek LLC and to provide for arbitration and forum selection.

Notwithstanding Malek LLC's failure to sign the Agreement, Elf's claims are subject to the arbitration and forum selection clauses of the Agreement. The Act is a statute designed to permit members maximum flexibility in entering into an agreement to govern their relationship. It is the members who are the real parties in interest. The

---

64. [35] 6 Del. C. § 18-1001 provides: "Right to bring action. A member may ... bring an action in the Court of Chancery in the right of a limited liability company to recover a judgment in its favor if managers or members with authority to do so have refused to bring the action or if an effort to cause those managers or members to bring the action is not likely to succeed."

LLC is simply their joint business vehicle. This is the contemplation of the statute in prescribing the outlines of a limited liability company agreement....

The Court of Chancery was correct in holding that Elf's claims bear directly on Jaffari's duties and obligations under the Agreement. Thus, we decline to disturb its holding....

Validity of Section 13.7 of the Agreement under 6 Del. C. § 18-109(d)

Elf argues that Section 13.7 of the Agreement, which provides that each member of Malek LLC "consents to the exclusive jurisdiction of the state and federal courts sitting in California in any action on a claim arising out of, under or in connection with this Agreement or the transactions contemplated by this Agreement..." is invalid under Delaware law. Elf argues that Section 13.7 is invalid because it violates 6 Del.C. § 18-109(d).

Subsection 18-109(d) is part of Section 18-109 relating to "Service of process on managers and liquidating trustee." It provides:

> In a written limited liability company agreement or other writing, a manager or member may consent to be subject to the nonexclusive jurisdiction of the courts of, or arbitration in, a specified jurisdiction, or the exclusive jurisdiction of the courts of the State of Delaware, or the exclusivity of arbitration in a specified jurisdiction or the State of Delaware....

Section 18-109(d) does not expressly state that the parties are prohibited from agreeing to the exclusive subject matter jurisdiction of the courts or arbitration fora of a foreign jurisdiction. Thus, Elf contends that Section 18-109(d) prohibits vesting exclusive jurisdiction in a court outside of Delaware, which the parties have done in Section 13.7.

We decline to adopt such a strict reading of the statute. Assuming, without deciding, that Section 109(d) relates to subject matter jurisdiction and not merely in personam jurisdiction, it is permissive in that it provides that the parties "may" agree to the non-exclusive jurisdiction of the courts of a foreign jurisdiction or to submit to the exclusive jurisdiction of Delaware. In general, the legislature's use of "may" connotes the voluntary, not mandatory or exclusive, set of options. The permissive nature of Section 18-109(d) complements the overall policy of the Act to give maximum effect to the parties' freedom of contract. Although Section 18-109(d) fails to mention that the parties may agree to the exclusive jurisdiction of a foreign jurisdiction, the Act clearly does not state that the parties must agree to either one of the delineated options for subject matter jurisdiction. Had the General Assembly intended to prohibit the parties from vesting exclusive jurisdiction in arbitration or court proceedings in another state, it could have proscribed such an option. The Court of Chancery did not err in declining to strike down the validity of Section 13.7 or Section 13.8 of the Agreement.

Conclusion

We affirm the judgment of the Court of Chancery dismissing Elf Atochem's amended complaint for lack of subject matter jurisdiction.

1. In 2015, the Delaware legislature amended the Delaware General Corporation Law, but not the Delaware LLC statute, to prohibit corporate charters or bylaws from stripping Delaware courts of jurisdiction over disputes amongst shareholders and managers. Consistent with the law governing LLCs and the holding and reasoning of *Elf Atochem*, the statute does not prohibit such ouster through separately formed contracts executed by shareholders involved in the related disputes.

2. LLC Management

A limited liability company may be either a member-managed company or a manager-managed company. A member-managed company is based on the partnership model. All members have equal rights to participate in the management of the business. Each member is an agent of the limited liability company, and the acts of a member may impose liability on the company.

The control structure of a manager-managed company is based on the corporate model. The members of an LLC choose the managers, who may or may not also be members. Only managers are agents of the firm. Their individual acts may bind the firm. Members who are not also managers are not agents of the firm solely because they are members. These members do, however, have the authority to participate in control to a limited extent. They may vote on designated matters including: changes to the articles of organization or the operating agreement; the admission of new members; and the merger or dissolution of the company.

Resolving issues concerning the management of an LLC may be determined by reference to the company's articles of organization or its operating agreement, to common law principles, to the provisions of the LLC statute, by analogy to partnership or corporation statutes and theory, or a combination of the foregoing.

The following case concerns the removal and subsequent appointment of managers of a limited liability company.

In re DeLuca

United States Bankruptcy Court, Eastern District of Virginia
194 B.R. 65 (1996)

MITCHELL, BANKRUPTCY JUDGE:

In this action, the plaintiffs, Joel T. Broyhill and Northern Virginia Realty, Inc. Profit Sharing Trust seek a declaration that the defendants, Robert and Marilyn DeLuca, were properly removed as the managers of D & B Countryside, L.L.C., and that Joel T. Broyhill was properly appointed as the successor manager. A trial of the issues was held on September 15 and 18, 1995....

Findings of Fact

D & B Countryside, L.L.C., ("D & B Countryside") is a Virginia limited liability company that was formed on April 12, 1994 to develop a shopping center and office development in Sterling, Virginia, known as Parc City Centre. The project originally consisted of approximately 12 acres, but at the present time there remain 3.766 acres which are intended to be subdivided into four retail "pad sites."[66] The original members of the company were Joel T. Broyhill ("Broyhill") and Robert and Marilyn DeLuca ("the DeLucas"). The organization of the company was set forth in an Operating Agreement dated April 12, 1994 ("the operating agreement"), signed by Broyhill and the DeLucas. Under the terms of the operating agreement, Broyhill and the DeLucas were each 50% members,[67] and the DeLucas were named as joint managing members. The operating agreement stated that the manager of the company must be appointed by unanimous vote[68] but was silent on removal of a manager. The operating agreement further required written consent of the other members for the assignment or pledge of a member's interest. Finally, the agreement provided ... for the dissolution of the company on December 31, 2024 or the earlier occurrence of certain specified events, including:

> (c) the death, resignation, expulsion, bankruptcy or dissolution of a Member ... unless the business of the Company is continued by the unanimous consent of the remaining Members.

... With respect to termination occurring because of the death, resignation, expulsion, bankruptcy or dissolution of a member the agreement further provided:

> The business of the Company shall be continued on the terms and conditions of this Agreement if, within ninety (90) days after such event, the remaining Members elect in writing that the business of the Company should be continued and, if the Affected Member was also the only Manager, elect a new Manager....

Under the terms of the operating agreement, Broyhill and the DeLucas were each to make $1,000,000 capital contributions; any further contributions were to be made *pro rata*. This would have resulted in $2,000,000 of paid-in capital, but from the testimony it appears that significantly less was actually paid in. The source of the capital funds for both Broyhill and the DeLucas was a $1,500,000 loan from NationsBank. Broyhill testified his understanding was that the entire loan proceeds were to be paid to D & B Countryside. In fact, as it turns out, only $200,000 of the loan proceeds were actually deposited in D & B Countryside's bank account.

---

66. [3] The fair market value of the property is listed on D & B Countryside's schedules at $3,625,000.

67. [4] Contributions and Membership Interests. Simultaneously with the full execution of this Agreement, Broyhill shall make an initial cash contribution to the Company in an amount equal to $1,000,000 and R. DeLuca and M. DeLuca shall each make an initial cash contribution to the company in an amount equal to $1,000,000 for a total of $2,000,000. Thereupon, each Member shall have an interest in the Company expressed as a percentage of the whole ("Membership Interest"). The Membership Interest of R. DeLuca and M. DeLuca jointly shall be fifty percent (50%) and the Membership Interest of Broyhill shall be fifty percent (50%)."

68. [5] Appointment of Manager. The management of the affairs of the Company shall be vested in one or more managers (the "Manager") elected by the unanimous vote of the "Members."

In July 1994, the DeLucas solicited Theodore Boinis ("Boinis"), the president of Northern Virginia Realty, Inc. ("NVRI") and trustee of its profit sharing plan, to become a member and offered him a 15% interest in the company in exchange for a $600,000 investment. Additionally, the DeLucas offered to personally guarantee a 10% minimum rate of return on NVRI's investment. NVRI agreed to the proposal and wire-transferred the $600,000 to D & B Countryside's bank account on July 22, 1994. Within a week, $594,300 of those funds had been transferred to other DeLuca-related entities or Robert DeLuca personally. Sometime later (apparently in September), Boinis and the DeLucas signed an Amended and Restated Operating Agreement dated "as of July 22, 1994" ("the amended operating agreement"), which assigned to the NVRI Profit Sharing Trust [NVRI] a 7.5% portion of the Deluca's interest in the company and a 7.5% portion of Broyhill's interest. Although the DeLucas told Boinis that the amended operating agreement would be sent to Broyhill for signature, it never was, and was never signed by Broyhill. Broyhill testified at trial that, although he had not seen the amended operating agreement until approximately mid-January, 1995, he had no objection to any of its provisions except for language in one paragraph acknowledging his having "received all amounts and other consideration due ... on account of this membership assignment." ... Indeed, in a memorandum to the DeLucas dated September 27, 1994, Broyhill acknowledged the existence of NVRI's 15% interest and registered no protest.

Beginning in September or October 1994, the relationship between the DeLucas and Broyhill soured, largely because the DeLucas did not respond to a number of requests by Broyhill for information concerning his investment. After Broyhill learned that almost all of the $600,000.00 invested by Boinis had been immediately transferred out of D & B Countryside and that the DeLucas had placed a $3,000,000.00 deed of trust against D & B Countryside's property without his knowledge,[69] Broyhill and NVRI Profit Sharing Trust executed a document on April 14, 1995, purporting to remove the DeLucas as D & B Countryside's managers and electing Broyhill as manager. No notice was given to the DeLucas of the meeting of Broyhill and Boinis at which the document was signed. Written notice was sent to the DeLucas that same date, however, that the action had been taken. In addition, notice was also sent that same date to the attorney who was representing the DeLucas, and who subsequently filed the chapter 11 petition on behalf of D & B Countryside, advising him that the DeLucas had been removed as managers and that he had no authority to represent D & B Countryside or to make any filings for D & B Countryside in the United States Bankruptcy Court. On May 5, 1995, the DeLucas filed a voluntary chapter 11 petition in this court, and on May 9, 1995, they caused D & B Countryside to file a voluntary

---

69. [11] The deed of trust secured a promissory note in favor of S.P. "Chip" Newell that consolidated four prior promissory notes that had been personal liabilities of the DeLucas.... At the time the deed of trust was placed on the property, the DeLucas executed a borrowing authorization on behalf of D & B Countryside in which they certified that they "are, or have the authority of, all Members" of the limited liability company. In fact, neither Broyhill nor NVRI knew of or consented to the deed of trust.

chapter 11 petition. Subsequent to the DeLucas' petition, Broyhill and NVRI Profit Sharing Trust executed a document in which they elected to continue the business and confirmed the election of Broyhill as the new manager.

Conclusions of Law

There are two major issues raised by the complaint and the evidence. The first is whether the April 28, 1995 action by Broyhill and NVRI was effective to remove the DeLucas as the managers of D & B Countryside and to appoint Broyhill as the successor manager. If not, the second issue is whether the chapter 11 filing by the DeLucas terminated their right to act as manager and permitted Broyhill and NVRI Profit Sharing Trust to elect to continue the business with Broyhill as the manager. Each of these issues will be discussed in turn.

A. Whether the April 28, 1995 action was effective to remove the DeLucas as managers.

As noted above, D & B Countryside is a limited liability company. Limited liability companies, although a relatively recent innovation, have become an increasingly popular form of business organization. As explained by one commentator:

> In response to favorable tax rulings, most states recently have followed the lead of Wyoming and Florida and enacted legislation for the formation and recognition of the limited liability company (LLC). The LLC is a form of legal entity that has attributes of both a corporation and a partnership but is not formally characterized as either one. Generally, an LLC offers all of its members, including any member-manager, limited liability as if they were shareholders of a corporation but treats the entity and its members as a partnership for tax purposes.

In Virginia, limited liability companies are governed by the Virginia Limited Liability Company Act, enacted in 1991. A Virginia limited liability company may engage in any lawful business that a corporation, partnership or other business entity may conduct under Virginia law. A limited liability company in Virginia is formed by filing articles of organization with the State Corporation Commission. A person that owns an interest in the company is called a "member." The members may (and in practice invariably do) also enter into an operating agreement which regulates and establishes the conduct of the company's business and the relationship of its members. Management of the company is vested in the members in proportion to their capital contributions, as adjusted for additional contributions and distributions, unless the articles of organization or the operating agreement provide that the company will be managed by one or more managers. Managers, if provided for in the articles of organization or operating agreement, are elected by the members. In a manager-managed limited liability company, only managers can contract for the company's debts or execute documents for the acquisition, mortgage or disposition of the company's property.

In order to determine whether the April 28, 1995 action by Broyhill and NVRI was effective to remove the DeLucas as managers, it is necessary first to resolve just who the members of D & B Countryside were. The DeLucas, in their pleadings and through counsel, have denied that NVRI became a member of the company because the operating agreement required unanimous consent to assign a membership interest or to admit a new member and Broyhill never signed the amended operating agreement which assigned a portion of Broyhill's and the DeLucas' membership interest to NVRI and recognized NVRI as a member. In addition, counsel for the DeLucas point out that in correspondence, counsel for NVRI referred to his client's investment in the company as a "loan."

The DeLucas themselves in testimony (as distinguished from their attorneys in argument) candidly admitted on the witness stand that they always regarded NVRI, following its $600,000 investment, as owning a 15% interest in the company. This is consistent with their conduct, in connection with the Regal Cinema sale, in remitting to NVRI a "15% distribution" of the net sales proceeds ($68,105.75 of $454,038.34). Additionally, D & B Countryside's schedules, signed by Robert DeLuca under penalty of perjury, reflect NVRI (although erroneously called "Virginia Realty Trust") as the holder of a 15% equity interest in the company. The DeLucas, by signing the Amended and Restated Operating Agreement, effectively (1) assigned a 7.5% portion of their own membership interest to NVRI and (2) consented to an assignment of a 7.5% portion of Broyhill's interest to NVRI. Although Broyhill never executed a writing explicitly assigning the 7.5% portion of his interest or consenting to the assignment of a similar portion of the DeLuca's interest, he testified at trial that he consented in fact to both actions, that he had never been sent the amended operating agreement to sign, and that the only reason he would not now sign the amended operating agreement was because of the language acknowledging that he had received all amounts to which he was due on account of the assignment. The requirement in the original operating agreement that any assignment and consent to assignment be in writing is clearly for the protection and benefit of the party whose interest would be adversely affected by the assignment, and that party is free to waive, as Broyhill has done in this case, the requirement of a writing. Accordingly, the court concludes that Broyhill's failure to sign the amended operating agreement did not, under the facts of this case, prevent NVRI from becoming a 15% member of D & B Countryside and that NVRI is in fact the holder of a 15% membership interest.

As discussed above, the original operating agreement required that the manager of the company be elected by unanimous vote of the members but was silent on removal of an existing manager. The plaintiffs argue, and the court concurs, that where the operating agreement is silent, resort must be had to the statute. In this connection, § 13.1-1024(F), Va. Code Ann. provides:

> All managers or any lesser number may be removed in the manner provided in the articles of organization or an operating agreement. If the articles of organization or an operating agreement does not provide for the removal of managers, then all managers or any lesser number may be removed with or without cause by a majority vote of the members....

Since Broyhill's 42.5% interest and NVRI's 15% interest clearly constituted a majority of the membership interest, their joint action removing the DeLucas as managers was, under the plain language of the statute, effective to accomplish its stated purpose. The court rejects the DeLucas' argument that, because the operating agreement required election of a manager to be unanimous, removal likewise necessarily had to be unanimous. That result simply does not follow. The obvious purpose of the operating agreement was to prevent a manager from being elected who did not enjoy the unanimous support of the members. By April 28, 1995, the DeLucas not only no longer had the unanimous support of the members, their continued retention in office was actively opposed by the majority of the members. Thus, their removal from office by the majority, pursuant to the statute, was not at all inconsistent with the requirement of the operating agreement that a manager had to be elected by unanimous vote.

At the same time, the requirement in the operating agreement for a unanimous vote in order to elect a manager presents an obvious practical difficulty. Since the manager may be removed by a majority, but less than unanimous, vote, the company could well find itself in the difficult and untenable position of having removed a manager but being unable to elect a new one, thereby leaving the company essentially paralyzed. If that were to occur, the only apparent remedy would be a judicial winding up.[70] That potentially is the situation that exists in the present case. Although the April 28, 1995 action was effective to remove the DeLucas as the managers of D & B Countryside, since the plain language of the operating agreement requires a unanimous vote to elect a manager, NVRI and Broyhill could not, by their sole act, elect Broyhill as the new manager, unless, as argued by NVRI and Broyhill, the DeLucas' subsequent chapter 11 filing in effect terminated their membership and gave NVRI and Broyhill the right under the operating agreement to elect to continue the business of the company and select a new manager. It is to that question that we must now turn.

B. The effect of the DeLucas' chapter 11 filing on their management rights.

As noted above, the operating agreement explicitly provided that the bankruptcy of a member would trigger the dissolution of the company,[71] but that within 90 days of the bankruptcy "event," the remaining members could elect in writing to continue the business of the company and, if the bankrupt member were also the only manager, could elect a new manager. Since Broyhill and NVRI have done precisely that, the

---

70. [16] On application by or for a member, the circuit court of the locality in which the registered office of the limited liability company is located may decree dissolution of a limited liability company if it is not reasonably practicable to carry on the business in conformity with the articles of organization and any operating agreement.

71. [17] This provision of the operating agreement is consistent with § 13.1-1046, Va. Code Ann., which at the time the DeLucas filed their chapter 7 petition, provided as follows:

> A limited liability company ... is dissolved and its affairs shall be wound up upon the happening of the first to occur of the following events:
>
> ...

3. Upon the death, resignation, retirement, expulsion, bankruptcy, or dissolution of a member or occurrence of any other event that terminates the continued membership of a member in the limited liability company, unless within six months after the event the limited liability company is continued by the consent of all or such lesser percentage or number (but not less than a majority in interest) of the remaining members as may be provided in writing in the articles or organization or operating agreement of the limited liability company.

question is whether the provisions of the operating agreement are enforceable in bankruptcy or whether, as argued by the DeLucas, they constitute an impermissible "ipso facto" clause[72] which is unenforceable in bankruptcy.

Limited liability companies are a recent innovation. It is not surprising, therefore, that counsel have been unable to cite the court to any cases specifically dealing with this issue in the context of a limited liability company, nor has the court's own research found any such case. As discussed above, limited liability companies are a conceptual hybrid, sharing some of the characteristics of partnerships and some of corporations. "In general, the purpose of forming a limited liability company is to create an entity that offers investors the protections of limited liability and the flow-through tax status of partnerships." In order to achieve the desired goal of pass-through tax treatment, it is necessary under applicable U.S. Treasury Regulations that the company have more of the attributes of a partnership than of a corporation. Treas.Reg. § 301.7701-2(a)(1).

In particular, a limited liability company will be treated as a partnership for tax purposes as long as the company does not possess the corporate characteristics of (1) continuity of life and (2) free transferability of interests. Rev.Rul. 88-76, 1988-2 C.B. 360, 361. On the other hand, simply because a limited liability company is most closely analogous to a partnership (or limited partnership) for tax purposes, does not mean that it might not be considered a corporation for other purposes. For example, the Bankruptcy Code defines a "corporation" as including, among other entities, a "partnership association organized under a law that makes only the capital subscribed responsible for the debts of such association." Under § 13.1-1019, Va. Code Ann., the members of a Virginia limited liability company are not, solely by reason of their membership interest, personally liable for the company's debts, obligations, and liabilities. Nevertheless, for the purpose of analyzing the effect of a member's bankruptcy filing upon the continued exercise of membership rights, it seems most appropriate to treat the relationship among member of a limited liability company as analogous to that of that among the partners of a partnership.

In particular, the fact that membership interests in a limited liability company, unlike shares of stock in a corporation, are not freely transferable mirrors the restriction on entry of new members into a partnership, which ordinarily cannot occur without the agreement of all existing members. (Although membership interest may be assigned unless assignment is restricted by the operating agreement or articles of organization, the assignee becomes a member only if the members unanimously consent to the assignee's admission; otherwise assignment only entitles the assignees to receive the distributions to which the assignor would be entitled, and does not permit participation in the company's management or affairs.) Whether the provision in D & B Countryside's operating agreement for dissolution of the company upon the bankruptcy of a member is enforceable depends on the interplay of several sections of the bankruptcy code....

---

72. [An "ipso facto" clause provides that an agreement will terminate on bankruptcy.—Eds.]

As an initial matter, the court is required to determine the nature of the DeLucas' interest in D & B Countryside. In the partnership context, it has been held that the interest of a debtor general partner is comprised of three components: the right to participate in profits, losses, distributions and proceeds of the partnership ("Economic Interest"); the right to participate in the management of the partnership ("Management Interest"); and the ownership share in partnership property as a tenant-in-partnership. In a limited liability company, members have no direct interest in the company's property,[73] but members have an economic interest, referred to in the statute as a "membership interest,"[74] and, in addition, both the managing member and, where the manager cannot or is not authorized to act, all members, have a management interest.

… With respect specifically to real estate partnerships, [one may distinguish] between "development" projects on the one hand "in which the general partner must administer the planning, construction and leasing of the building," and "matured" projects on the other "that require only routine management and leasing functions." In the former, "the identity of a general partner will be critical to the limited partners and to the prospect of a successful investment," while in the latter, "the identity of a general partner is less significant." D & B Countryside is a paradigm example of a development project where the identity of the managers is material to very existence of the company. Since the court has concluded that the DeLucas were properly removed as the managers of the company prior to the filing of their chapter 11 petition, the issue of their assuming the management functions specified in the operating agreement is not implicated, but upon their removal they would have had the right and duty to participate in the election of a successor manager, acceptable to all the members, to carry on the management function.

Additionally, they would have had the right and duty to vote on any matter with respect to which a manager could not act unilaterally. Particularly in view of the highly questionable conduct of the DeLucas in having allowed a deed of trust to be recorded against the company's property to secure a personal loan and in having siphoned out of the company essentially all of NVRI's $600,000 investment within a week of its having been paid in, and given that the Parc City Centre project is still very much in the development phase, with important decisions to be made with respect to the sale or lease of parcels and possible further financing (which, as with the

---

73. [20] See § 13.1-1021, Va. Code Ann. ("Any estate or interest in property may be acquired in the name of the limited liability company, and title to any estate or interest so acquired vests in the limited liability company."); § 13.1-1034 ("Except as provided in writing in the articles of organization or an operating agreement, a member, regardless of the nature of his or its contribution, has no right to demand and receive any distribution from a limited liability company in any form other than cash."); § 13.1-1038 ("A membership interest in a limited liability company is personal property."); § 13.1-1041 (judgment creditor has right to obtain a charging order against member's interest but "has only the rights of an assignee of the interest in the limited liability company.").

74. [21] "'Membership interest' or 'interest' means a member's share of the profits and the losses of the limited liability company and the right to receive distributions of the limited liability company's assets." …

current financing, could very well require the personal guarantees of members), there is no way the identity of the DeLucas would not be material to the other members and to the success of the project. [The court concluded that the provisions of the operating agreement were not invalid under the Bankruptcy Code.]

It therefore follows that the action taken by Broyhill and NVRI following the DeLucas' bankruptcy "confirming" the prepetition election of Broyhill as the new manager was effective under … the operating agreement to accomplish the election of Broyhill as the new manager, effective at least as of the date the document was signed. Such action, of course, does not deprive the DeLucas' bankruptcy estate of the economic interest— the right to share in profits, losses, and distributions—the DeLucas have as a result of their 42.5% membership interest…. Section 13.1-1041, a. Code Ann., gives … a creditor the right to obtain a charging order against the member's interest in the company. Such an order confers on the creditor the rights of an assignee of the member's interest, which includes, the right "to receive … any share of profits and distributions to which the assignor would be entitled." Thus, the DeLucas' bankruptcy estate will be entitled to any distributions due on account of the DeLucas' membership interest….

For the foregoing reasons … the court determines (1) that the DeLucas were properly removed as the managers of D & B Countryside prior to the filing of their chapter 11 petition and (2) that Broyhill was, subsequent to the DeLucas' chapter 11 filing, properly elected as the successor manager. A separate judgment will be entered consistent with this opinion.[75]

––––––––––

The following three cases explore the interplay among (1) statutory or operating agreement provisions and (2) common law or statutory fiduciary standards. In the first of these cases, *McConnell v. Hunt Sports Enterprises*,[76] referred to earlier, the court addresses the extent to which provisions of an operating agreement may limit the scope of members' fiduciary duties to each other.

––––––––––

75. [The lives of real estate developers Marilyn and Bob DeLuca have been colorful, to say the least. Before the problems referred to in this case arose, they were well respected citizens of the State of Virginia. In 1994, the Virginia legislature passed a joint resolution recognizing their "long history of high-quality, environmentally sensitive, and people-friendly … [real estate] development, throughout the Middle Atlantic region.…" Only a short time later, everything changed. When the problems with Countryside Development (the development mentioned in the case) emerged, they filed for bankruptcy with total personal liabilities of about $52 million. (Ironically, the street address for Countryside Development, which was associated with many of their fraudulent activities, was Pidgeon Hill Drive.) In 1998, they pled guilty to various fraud-based crimes and were sentenced to time in federal prison. (She received an 18 month sentence. He was sentenced for 60 months.) It is not known how Marilyn DeLuca weathered her time in prison. Robert DeLuca's experience is another story. He reportedly is proud to have turned a difficult situation into a positive experience. He saved the life of a 35 year old inmate suffering from heat exhaustion and organized and taught classes in construction and business organization and management. He reportedly planned to continue in business on his release from prison. — Eds.]

76. 725 N. E. 2d 1193 (C.A. Ohio 1999).

McConnell v. Hunt Sports Enterprises

Ohio Court of Appeals
725 N.E. 2d 1193 (1999)

Tyack, Judge:

On June 17, 1997, John H. McConnell and Wolfe Enterprises, Inc. filed a complaint for declaratory judgment in the Franklin County Court of Common Pleas against Hunt Sports Enterprises, Hunt Sports Enterprises, L.L.C., Hunt Sports Group, L.L.C. ("Hunt Sports Group"), and Columbus Hockey Limited ("CHL"). CHL was a limited liability company formed under R.C. Chapter 1705....

In 1996, the National Hockey League ("NHL") determined it would be accepting applications for new hockey franchises. In April 1996, Gregory S. Lashutka, the mayor of Columbus, received a phone call from an NHL representative inquiring as to Columbus's interest in a hockey team. As a result, Mayor Lashutka asked certain community leaders who had been involved in exploring professional sports in Columbus to pursue the possibility of applying for an NHL hockey franchise. Two of these persons were Ronald A. Pizzuti and McConnell.

Pizzuti began efforts to recruit investors in a possible franchise. Pizzuti approached Lamar Hunt, principal of Hunt Sports Group, as to Hunt's interest in investing in such a franchise for Columbus. Hunt was already the operating member of the Columbus Crew, a professional soccer team whose investors included Hunt Sports Group, Pizzuti, McConnell, and Wolfe Enterprises, Inc. Hunt expressed an interest in participating in a possible franchise. The deadline for applying for an NHL expansion franchise was November 1, 1996.

On October 31, 1996, CHL was formed when its articles of organization were filed with the secretary of state pursuant to R.C. 1705.04. The members of CHL were McConnell, Wolfe Enterprises, Inc., Hunt Sports Group, Pizzuti Sports Limited, and Buckeye Hockey, L.L.C. Each member made an initial capital contribution of $25,000. CHL was subject to an operating agreement that set forth the terms between the members. Pursuant to section 2.1 of CHL's operating agreement, the general character of the business of CHL was to invest in and operate a franchise in the NHL.

On or about November 1, 1996, an application was filed with the NHL on behalf of the city of Columbus. In the application, the ownership group was identified as CHL, and the individuals in such group were listed as Pizzuti Sports Limited, McConnell, Wolfe Enterprises, Inc., and Hunt Sports Group. Also included within the application package was Columbus's plan for an arena to house the hockey games. There was no facility at the time, and the proposal was to build a facility that would be financed, in large part, by a three-year countywide one-half percent sales tax. The sales tax issue would be on the May 1997 ballot.

On May 6, 1997, the sales tax issue failed. The day after, Mayor Lashutka met with Hunt, and other opportunities were discussed. The mayor also spoke with Gary

Bettman, commissioner of the NHL, and they discussed whether an alternate plan for an arena was possible. Also on May 7, 1997, Dimon McPherson, chairman and chief executive officer of Nationwide Insurance Enterprise ("Nationwide"), met with Hunt, and they discussed the possibility of building the arena despite the failure of the sales tax issue.... Hunt was interested, and Nationwide began working on an arena plan. On or about May 9, 1997, the mayor spoke with Bettman and let him know that alternate plans would be pursued, and Mr. Bettman gave Columbus until June 4, 1997 to come up with a plan.

By May 28, 1997, Nationwide had come up with a plan to finance an arena privately and on such date, Nationwide representatives met with representatives of Hunt Sports Group. Hunt Sports Group did not accept Nationwide's lease proposal. Nationwide informed Hunt Sports Group that it needed an answer by Friday, May 30, 1997 as to whether, in general terms, the lease proposal was acceptable. Hunt Sports Group stated that it would continue to evaluate the proposal, and it wanted the weekend to do so. Nationwide informed appellant that it needed an answer by close of business Friday, May 30.

On May 30, 1997, McPherson called McConnell and requested that they meet and discuss "where [they] were on the arena." ... McPherson told McConnell about appellant's rejection of the lease proposal and discussed the NHL's June 4 deadline. McConnell stated that if Hunt would not step up and lease the arena and, therefore, get the franchise, McConnell would. Hunt Sports Group did not contact Nationwide on May 30, 1997.

On Saturday, May 31, McPherson told Nationwide's board of directors that there was not yet a lease commitment but that if Hunt Sports Group did not lease the arena, McConnell would. On Monday, June 2, 1997, City Council passed the resolution that set forth the terms for Nationwide to build an arena downtown. On or about Tuesday, June 3, McConnell was informed that appellant had not yet accepted the lease proposal. On June 3, Hunt [asked for] ... a copy of the ordinance passed by City Council. On that same date, Hunt Sports Group told Nationwide that it still found the terms of the lease to be unacceptable. On June 3 or June 4, McConnell, in a conversation with the NHL, orally agreed to apply for a hockey franchise for Columbus. On June 4, ... Hunt informed McPherson that he was still interested in pursuing an agreement with Nationwide.

On June 4, 1997, the NHL franchise expansion committee met. Bettman informed the committee that Nationwide would build an arena, and McConnell was prepared to go forward with the franchise even if he had to do it himself. The committee was told that Hunt Sports Group's involvement was an open issue, but McConnell as an owner was more than adequate. The expansion committee recommended Columbus to the NHL board of governors as one of four cities to be granted a franchise.

On June 5, 1997, the NHL sent Hunt a letter requesting that he let the NHL know by Monday, June 9, 1997 whether he was going forward with his franchise application. In a June 6, 1997 letter to the NHL, Hunt responded that CHL intended to pursue the franchise application. Hunt informed the NHL that he had arranged a meeting with the members of CHL to be held on June 9, 1997. Hunt indicated that the application was contingent upon entering into an appropriate lease for a hockey facility.

On June 9, 1997, a meeting took place at Pizzuti's office. Those present at the meeting included McConnell, Hunt, Pizzuti, John F. Wolfe, chairman of Wolfe Enterprises, Inc., and representatives of Buckeye Hockey, L.L.C. and Ameritech. The NHL required that the ownership group be identified and that such ownership group sign a lease term sheet by June 9, 1997. Brian Ellis, president and chief operating officer of Nationwide, presented the lease term sheet to those present at the meeting....

Hunt indicated the lease was unacceptable.... Pizzuti and Wolfe agreed to participate along with McConnell. John Christie ... informed Ellis that McConnell had accepted the term sheet and was signing it in his individual capacity. The term sheet contained a signature line for "Columbus Hockey Limited" as the franchise owner. Ellis phoned his secretary and had her omit the name "Columbus Hockey Limited" on her computer from under the signature line and fax the change to Ellis at Pizzuti's office. McConnell then signed the term sheet as the owner of the franchise. Christie faxed the signed lease term sheet to Bettman that day along with a cover letter and a description of the ownership group. Such ownership group was identified as John H. McConnell, majority owner, Pizzuti Sports, L.L.C., John F. Wolfe, and "[u]p to seven (7) other members." The cover letter indicated that the attached material signified an amendment to the November 1, 1996 application from the city.

On June 17, 1997, the NHL expansion committee recommended to the NHL board of governors that Columbus be awarded a franchise with McConnell's group as owner of the franchise. On the same date, the complaint in the case at bar was filed. On or about June 25, 1997, the NHL board of governors awarded Columbus a franchise with McConnell's group as owner. Hunt Sports Group, Buckeye Hockey, L.L.C. and Ameritech have no ownership interest in the hockey franchise.

On July 3, 1997, after the complaint had been filed, Hunt Sports Group, on behalf of CHL, filed a verified complaint in the Supreme Court of New York, County of New York, against the NHL, Nationwide, McConnell and his son, John P. McConnell, Wolfe Enterprises, Inc., and Pizzuti Sports Limited. Hunt Sports Group set forth various claims for relief arising out of the events set forth above and requested, in part, that the NHL be enjoined from granting a franchise for Columbus to McConnell/COLHOC or from allowing any person other than CHL to obtain or maintain such a franchise. In such complaint, Hunt Sports Group admitted that the franchise had already been awarded to McConnell/COLHOC.

In their complaint, McConnell and Wolfe Enterprises, Inc. requested a declaration that section 3.3 of the CHL operating agreement allowed members of CHL to compete with CHL. Specifically, McConnell and Wolfe Enterprises, Inc. sought a declaration that under the operating agreement, they were permitted to participate in COLHOC and obtain the franchise....

On June 23, 1997, Hunt Sports Group filed an answer and counterclaim on its behalf and on behalf on CHL. The counterclaim was asserted against McConnell and alleged breach of contract, breach of fiduciary duty, and interference with prospective business relationships.

On July 3, 1997, McConnell and Wolfe Enterprises, Inc. filed a motion for summary judgment as to count one of the first amended complaint (declaratory judgment as to section 3.3 of the operating agreement) and as to counts one through five of the counterclaim (breach of contract and breach of fiduciary duty). On October 31, 1997, the trial court rendered a decision, granting summary judgment in favor of McConnell and Wolfe Enterprises.... Specifically, the trial court found that section 3.3 of the operating agreement was clear and unambiguous and allowed McConnell and Wolfe Enterprises, Inc. to compete against CHL and obtain the NHL franchise. In addition, the trial court found McConnell did not breach the operating agreement by competing against CHL....

[A] second amended complaint added two claims for relief. Count three sought a declaration that McConnell, Wolfe Enterprises, Inc., and other members of COL-HOC had not violated any fiduciary duties or committed any other tortious or wrongful acts in connection with the hockey franchise and arena lease....

A jury trial was held in May 1998 on counts three and four of the second amended complaint. On May 15, 1998, the trial court rendered a decision, denying Hunt Sports Group's motion and granting McConnell and Wolfe Enterprises, Inc.'s motion for directed verdicts on counts three and four of the second amended complaint....

On October 15, 1998, the trial court filed a final judgment entry as to all claims. Hunt Sports Group filed a notice of appeal on October 29, 1998....

As indicated above, count one of the first amended complaint sought a declaration that section 3.3 of CHL's operating agreement allowed members to compete against CHL to obtain an NHL franchise. Appellees contend section 3.3 is plain and unambiguous and allows what occurred here—COLHOC competing for and obtaining the NHL franchise. Appellant asserts, in part, that the trial court's interpretation of section 3.3 was incorrect and that section 3.3 is ambiguous and subject to different interpretations. Therefore, appellant contends extrinsic evidence should have been considered, and such evidence would have shown the parties did not intend section 3.3 to mean members could compete against CHL and take away CHL's only purpose.

The construction of written contracts is a matter of law. The purpose of contract construction is to discover and effectuate the intent of the parties, and the intent of the parties is presumed to reside in the language they chose to use in the agreement. If a contract is clear and unambiguous, there is no issue of fact to be determined, and the court cannot create a new contract by finding an intent not expressed in the clear language employed by the parties. Only where the language of a contract is unclear or ambiguous or when the circumstances surrounding the agreement invest the language of the contract with a special meaning, will extrinsic evidence be considered in an effort to give effect to the parties' intentions.

The test for determining whether a term is ambiguous is that common words in a written contract will be given their ordinary meaning unless manifest absurdity results or unless some other meaning is clearly evidenced from the face or overall content of the contract. A writing will be read as a whole, and the intent of each part will be gathered from a consideration of the whole. For the reasons that follow, we conclude that section 3.3 is plain and unambiguous and allowed members of CHL to compete against CHL for an NHL franchise.

Section 3.3 of the operating agreement states:

> "Members May Compete. Members shall not in any way be prohibited from or restricted in engaging or owning an interest in any other business venture of any nature, including any venture which might be competitive with the business of the Company."

Appellant emphasizes the word "other" in the above language and states, in essence, that it means any business venture that is different from the business of the company. Appellant points out that under section 2.1 of the operating agreement, the general character of the business is "to invest in and operate a franchise in the National Hockey League." Hence, appellant contends that members may only engage in or own an interest in a venture that is not in the business of investing in and operating a franchise with the NHL.

Appellant's interpretation of section 3.3 goes beyond the plain language of the agreement and adds words or meanings not stated in the provision. Section 3.3, for example, does not state "[m]embers shall not be prohibited from or restricted in engaging or owning an interest in any other business venture that is different from the business of the company." Rather, section 3.3 states: "any other business venture of any nature." ... It then adds to this statement: "including any venture which might be competitive with the business of the Company." The words "any nature" could not be broader, and the inclusion of the words "any venture which might be competitive with the business of the Company" makes it clear that members were not prohibited from engaging in a venture that was competitive with CHL's investing in and operating an NHL franchise. Contrary to appellant's contention, the word "other" simply means a business venture other than CHL. The word "other" does not limit the type of business venture in which members may engage.

Hence, section 3.3 did not prohibit appellees from engaging in activities that may have been competitive with CHL, including appellees' participation in COLHOC. Accordingly, summary judgment in favor of appellees was appropriate, and appellees were entitled to a declaration that section 3.3 of the operating agreement permitted appellees to request and obtain an NHL hockey franchise to the exclusion of CHL. ...

A motion for a directed verdict may be granted when the trial court, construing the evidence most strongly in favor of the nonmoving party, finds that upon any determinative issue, reasonable minds can come to but one conclusion upon the evidence submitted and that conclusion is adverse to the nonmoving party. ... Our review of the trial court's ruling on a motion for a directed verdict is de novo.

Before we can review the propriety of the directed verdict in this case, the law on fiduciary duty ... must be addressed. The term "fiduciary relationship" has been defined as a relationship in which special confidence and trust is reposed in the integrity and fidelity of another, and there is a resulting position of superiority or influence acquired by virtue of this special trust. In the case at bar, a limited liability company is involved which, like a partnership, involves a fiduciary relationship. Normally, the presence of such a relationship would preclude direct competition between members of the company. However, here we have an operating agreement that by its very terms allows members to compete with the business of the company. Hence, the question we are presented with is whether an operating agreement of a limited liability company may, in essence, limit or define the scope of the fiduciary duties imposed upon its members. We answer this question in the affirmative.

A fiduciary has been defined as a person having a duty, created by his or her undertaking, to act primarily for the benefit of another in matters connected with such undertaking. A claim of breach of fiduciary duty is basically a claim for negligence that involves a higher standard of care. In order to recover, one must show the existence of a duty on the part of the alleged wrongdoer not to subject such person to the injury complained of, a failure to observe such duty, and an injury proximately resulting therefrom. These principles support our conclusion that a contract may define the scope of fiduciary duties between parties to the contract.

Here, the injury complained of by appellant was, essentially, appellees' competing with CHL and obtaining the NHL franchise. The operating agreement constitutes the undertaking of the parties herein. In becoming members of CHL, appellant and appellees agreed to abide by the terms of the operating agreement, and such agreement specifically allowed competition with the company by its members. As such, the duties created pursuant to such undertaking did not include a duty not to compete. Therefore, there was no duty on the part of appellees to refrain from subjecting appellant to the injury complained of herein.

We find further support for our conclusion in case law concerning close corporations and partnerships. In *Cruz v. S. Dayton Urological Assoc., Inc.* (1997), 121 Ohio App.3d 655, 700 N.E.2d 675, the plaintiff filed suit against his former shareholders in a close corporation, alleging, in part, breach of fiduciary duty. The plaintiff had been a shareholder in a professional corporation organized for the practice of medicine. The plaintiff was employed by the corporation pursuant to a written agreement. Such agreement provided that the corporation or employee could terminate the employment contract unilaterally and without specification of cause upon ninety days' written notice. The plaintiff was terminated after the other shareholders voted to terminate him.

The Cruz case stands for the proposition that close corporation employment agreements may limit the scope of fiduciary duties that otherwise would apply absent certain provisions in such agreements. The same principle has been applied in situations involving partnerships that are subject to partnership agreements (the respective rights of partnership members depend primarily on the specific provisions contained within the partnership contract as recognized in R.C. 1775.17, which states that the rights and duties of partners are subject to any agreement between the partners).

"Operating agreement" is defined in R.C. 1705.01(J) as "all of the valid written or oral agreements of the members as to the affairs of a limited liability company and the conduct of its business." R.C. 1705.03(C) sets forth various activities limited liability companies may engage in and indicates such are subject to the company's articles of organization or operating agreement. Indeed, many of the statutory provisions in R.C. Chapter 1705 governing limited liability companies indicate they are, in various ways, subject to and/or dependent upon related provisions in an operating agreement. Here, the operating agreement states in its opening paragraph that it evidences the mutual agreement of the members in consideration of their contributions and promises to each other. Such agreement specifically allowed its members to compete with the company.

Given the above, we conclude as a matter of law that it was not a breach of fiduciary duty for appellees to form, COLHOC and obtain an NHL franchise to the exclusion of CHL. In so concluding, we are not stating that no act related to such obtainment could be considered a breach of fiduciary duty. In general terms, members of limited liability companies owe one another the duty of utmost trust and loyalty. However, such general duty in this case must be considered in the context of members' ability, pursuant to operating agreement, to compete with the company.

VGS, Inc. v. Castiel

Delaware Court of Chancery
2004 Del. Ch. LEXIS 48 (Apr. 22, 2004)

STEELE, VICE CHANCELLOR:

I. Facts

David Castiel formed Virtual Geosatellite LLC (the "LLC") on January 6, 1999 in order to pursue a Federal Communications Commission ("FCC") license to build and operate a satellite system which its proponents claim could dramatically increase the "real estate" in outer space capable of transmitting high speed internet traffic and other communications. When originally formed, it had only one Member—Virtual Geosatellite Holdings, Inc. ("Holdings"). On January 8, 1999, Ellipso, Inc. ("Ellipso") joined the LLC as its second Member. Several weeks later, on January 29, 1999, Sahagen Satellite Technology Group LLC ("Sahagen Satellite") became the third Member of the LLC.

David Castiel controls both Holdings and Ellipso. Peter Sahagen, an aggressive and apparently successful venture capitalist, controls Sahagen Satellite.

Pursuant to the LLC Agreement, Holdings received 660 units (representing 63.46% of the total equity in the LLC), Sahagen Satellite received 260 units (representing 25%), and Ellipso received 120 units (representing 11.54%). The founders vested management of the LLC in a Board of Managers. As the majority unit holder, Castiel had the power to appoint, remove, and replace two of the three members of the Board of Managers. Castiel, therefore, had the power to prevent any Board decision with which he disagreed. Castiel named himself and Tom Quinn to the Board of Managers. Sahagen named himself as the third member of the Board.

Not long after the formation of the LLC, Castiel and Sahagen were at odds. Castiel contends that Sahagen [had] wanted to control the LLC ever since he became involved, and that Sahagen repeatedly offered, unsuccessfully, to buy control of the LLC. Sahagen maintains that Castiel ran the LLC so poorly that its mission had become untracked, additional necessary capital could not be raised, and competent managers could not be attracted to join the enterprise. Further, Sahagen claims that Castiel directed LLC assets to Ellipso in order to prop up a failing, cash-strapped Ellipso. At trial, these issues and other similar accusations from both sides were explored in great detail. For our purposes here, all that need be concluded is the unarguable fact that Castiel and Sahagen had very different ideas about how the LLC should be managed and operated.

Sahagen ultimately convinced Quinn that Castiel must be ousted from leadership in order for the LLC to prosper. As a result, Quinn (Castiel's nominee) covertly "defected" to Sahagen's camp, and he and Sahagen decided to wrest control of the LLC from Castiel. Many LLC employees and even some of Castiel's lieutenants testified that they believed it to be in the LLC's best interest to take control from Castiel.

On April 14, 2000, without notice to Castiel, Quinn and Sahagen acted by written consent to merge the LLC under Delaware law into VGS, Inc. ("VGS"), a Delaware corporation. Accordingly, the LLC ceased to exist, its assets and liabilities passed to VGS, and VGS became the LLC's legal successor-in-interest. VGS's Board of Directors is comprised of Sahagen, Quinn, and Neel Howard. Of course, the incorporators did not name Castiel to VGS's Board.

On the day of the merger, Sahagen executed a promissory note to VGS in the amount of $10 million plus interest. In return, he received two million shares of VGS Series A Preferred Stock. VGS also issued 1,269,200 shares of common stock to Holdings, 230,800 shares of common stock to Ellipso, and 500,000 shares of common stock to Sahagen Satellite. Once one does the math, it is apparent that Holdings and Ellipso went from having a 75% controlling combined ownership interest in the LLC to having only a 37.5% interest in VGS. On the other hand, Sahagen and Sahagen Satellite went from owning 25% of the LLC to owning 62.5% of VGS.

There can be no doubt why Sahagen and Quinn, acting as a majority of the LLC's board of managers did not notify Castiel of the merger plan. Notice to Castiel would have immediately resulted in Quinn's removal from the board and a newly constituted majority which would thwart the effort to strip Castiel of control. Had he known in advance, Castiel surely would have attempted to replace Quinn with someone loyal to Castiel who would agree with his views. Clandestine machinations were, therefore, essential to the success of Quinn and Sahagen's plan.

II. Analysis

A. The Board of Managers did have authority to act by majority vote.

The LLC Agreement does not expressly state whether the Board of Managers must act unanimously or by majority vote. Sahagen and Quinn contend that because a number of provisions would be rendered meaningless if a unanimous vote was required, a majority vote is implied. Castiel, however, maintains that a unanimous vote must be implied when the majority owner has blocking power.

Section 8.01(b)(i) of the LLC Agreement states that, "[t]he Board of Managers shall initially be composed of three (3) Managers." Sahagen Satellite has the right to designate one member of the initial board, and if the Board of Managers increased in number, Sahagen Satellite could "designate a number of representatives on the Board of Managers that is less than Sahagen's then current Percentage Interest." If unanimity were required, the number of managers would be irrelevant—Sahagen, and his minority interest, would have veto power in any event. The existence of language in the LLC Agreement discussing expansion of the Board is therefore quite telling.

Also persuasive is the fact that Section 8.01(c) of the LLC Agreement, entitled "Matters Requiring Consent of Sahagen," provides that Sahagen's approval is needed for a merger, consolidation, or reorganization of the LLC. If a unanimity requirement indeed existed, there would have been no need to expressly list matters on which Sahagen's minority interest had veto power.

Section 12.01(a)(i) of the LLC Agreement also supports Sahagen's argument. This section provides that the LLC may be dissolved by written consent by either the Board of Managers or by Members holding two-thirds of the Common Units. The effect of this Section is to allow any combination of Holdings and Sahagen Satellite, or Holdings and Ellipso, as Members, to dissolve the LLC. It seems unlikely that the Members designed the LLC Agreement to permit Members holding two-thirds of the Common Units to dissolve the LLC but denied their appointed Managers the power to reach the same result unless the minority manager agreed.

Castiel takes the position that while the Members can act by majority vote, the Board of Managers can act only by unanimous vote. He maintains that if the Board fails to agree unanimously on an issue the issue should be put to an LLC Members' vote with the majority controlling. The practical effect of Castiel's interpretation would be that whenever Castiel and Sahagen disagreed, Castiel would prevail because the issue would be submitted to the Members where Castiel's controlling interest would carry the vote. If that were the case, both Sahagen's Board position and Quinn's Board position would be superfluous. I am confident that the parties never intended that result, or if they had so intended, that they would have included plain and simple language in the agreement spelling it out clearly.

B. By failing to give notice of their proposed action, Sahagen and Quinn failed to discharge their duty of loyalty to Castiel in good faith.

Section 18-404(d) of the LLC Act states in pertinent part:

> Unless otherwise provided in a limited liability company agreement, on any matter that is to be voted on by managers, the managers may take such action without a meeting, without prior notice and without a vote if a consent or consents in writing, setting forth the action so taken, shall be signed by the managers having not less than the minimum number of votes that would be necessary to authorize such action at a meeting....

Therefore, the LLC Act, read literally, does not require notice to Castiel before Sahagen and Quinn could act by written consent. The LLC Agreement does not purport to modify the statute in this regard.

Those observations can not complete the analysis of Sahagen and Quinn's actions, however. Sahagen and Quinn knew what would happen if they notified Castiel of their intention to act by written consent to merge the LLC into VGS, Inc. Castiel would have attempted to remove Quinn, and block the planned action. Regardless of his motivation in doing so, removal of Quinn in that circumstance would have been within Castiel's rights as the LLC's controlling owner under the Agreement.

Section 18-404(d) has yet to be interpreted by this Court or the Supreme Court. Nonetheless, it seems clear that the purpose of permitting action by written consent without notice is to enable LLC managers to take quick, efficient action in situations where a minority of managers could not block or adversely affect the course set by the majority even if they were notified of the proposed action and objected to it. The General Assembly never intended, I am quite confident, to enable two managers to deprive, clandestinely and surreptitiously, a third manager representing the majority interest in the LLC of an opportunity to protect that interest by taking an action that the third manager's member would surely have opposed if he had knowledge of it. My reading of Section 18-404(d) is grounded in a classic maxim of equity — "Equity looks to the intent rather than to the form." In this hopefully unique situation, this application of the maxim requires construction of the statute to allow action without notice only by a constant or fixed majority. It can not apply to an illusory, will-of-the wisp majority which would implode should notice be given. Nothing in the statute suggests that this court of equity should blind its eyes to a shallow, too clever by half, manipulative attempt to restructure an enterprise through an action taken by a "majority" that existed only so long as it could act in secrecy.

Sahagen and Quinn each owed a duty of loyalty to the LLC, its investors and Castiel, their fellow manager. Castiel or his entities owned a majority interest in the LLC and he sat as a member of the board representing entities and interests empowered by the Agreement to control the majority membership of the board. The majority investor protected his equity interest in the LLC through the mechanism of appointment to the board rather than by the statutorily sanctioned mechanism of approval by members owning a majority of the LLC's equity interests. It may seem somewhat incongruous, but this Agreement allows the action to merge, dissolve or change to corporate status to be taken by a simple majority vote of the board of managers rather than rely upon the default position of the statute which requires a majority vote of the equity interest. Instead the drafters made the critical assumption, known to all the players here, that the holder of the majority equity interest has the right to appoint and remove two managers, ostensibly guaranteeing control over a three member board. When Sahagen and Quinn, fully recognizing that this was Castiel's protection against actions adverse to his majority interest, acted in secret, without notice, they failed to discharge their duty of loyalty to him in good faith. They owed Castiel a duty to give him prior notice even if he would have interfered with a plan that they conscientiously believed to be in the best interest of the LLC.[79] Instead, they launched a preemptive strike that furtively converted Castiel's controlling interest in the LLC to a minority interest in VGS without affording Castiel a level playing field on which to defend his interest. "[Another] traditional maxim of equity holds that equity regards and treats that as done which in good conscience ought to be done." In good conscience, under these circumstances, Sahagen and Quinn should have given Castiel prior notice.

Many hours were spent at trial focusing on contentions that Castiel has proved to be an ineffective leader in whom employees and investors have lost confidence. I listened to testimony regarding delayed FCC licensing, a suggested new management team for the LLC, and the alleged unlocked value of the LLC. A substantial record exists fully flushing out the rancorous relationships of the members and their wildly disparate views on the existing state of affairs as well as the LLC's prospects for the future. But the issue of who is best suited to run the LLC should not be resolved here but in board meetings where all managers are present and all members appropriately represented, and/or in future litigation, if it unfortunately becomes necessary.

Likewise, the parties spent much time and effort arguing over the standard to be applied to the actions taken by Sahagen and Quinn.... It should be clear that the actions of Sahagen and Quinn, in their capacity as managers constituted a breach of their duty of loyalty and that those actions do not, therefore, entitle them to the benefit or protection of the business judgment rule. They intentionally used a flawed process to merge the LLC into VGS, Inc., in an attempt to prevent the member with majority equity interest in the LLC from protecting his interests in the manner contemplated by the very LLC Agreement under which they purported to act. Analysis beyond a look at the process is clearly unnecessary. Perhaps, had notice been given and an attempt then made to block Castiel's anticipated action to replace Quinn, the allegedly disinterested and independent member that Castiel himself had appointed, the analysis might be different. However, this, as all cases must be reviewed as it is presented, not as it might have been.

III. Conclusion

For the reasons stated above, I find that a majority vote of the LLC's Board of Managers could properly effect a merger. But, I also find that Sahagen and Quinn failed to discharge their duty of loyalty to Castiel in good faith by failing to give him advance notice of their merger plans under the unique circumstances of this case and the structure of this LLC Agreement. Accordingly, I declare that the acts taken to merge the LLC into VGS, Inc. to be invalid and the merger is ordered rescinded.

Notes and Questions

In 2013, § 18-1104 of the DLLCA was amended to read as follows: "In any case not provided for in this chapter, the rules of law and equity, including the rules of

---

79. I make no ruling here as to whether I believe the merger and the resulting recapitalization of the LLC was in the LLC's best interests, nor do I rule here regarding the wisdom of Castiel's actions had he in fact been able to remove Quinn before the merger.

law and equity relating to fiduciary duties and the law merchant, shall govern." The accompanying legislative materials explain the rationale: "to confirm that in some circumstances fiduciary duties not explicitly provided for in the limited liability company agreement apply. For example, a manager of a manager-managed limited liability company would ordinarily have fiduciary duties even in the absence of a provision in the limited liability company agreement establishing such duties...."

Anderson v. Wilder

Tennessee Court of Appeals
2003 Tenn. App. LEXIS 819 (Nov. 21, 2003)

GODDARD, P. J.:

This case involves a dispute between members of a limited liability company ("LLC") entitled FuturePoint Administrative Services, LLC. The Plaintiffs were expelled from the LLC by a vote of the Defendants, who together owned 53% of FuturePoint. The Plaintiffs received a buyout price of $150.00 per ownership unit in FuturePoint after they were expelled, pursuant to the operating agreement of the LLC. Shortly after the expulsion, the Defendants sold 499 ownership units, amounting to a 49.9% interest in the LLC, to a third party at a price of $250.00 per ownership unit. Plaintiffs filed this action, alleging, among other things, that the Defendants' actions violated their fiduciary duty and duty of good faith to Plaintiffs. Defendants moved for summary judgment, arguing that their actions were authorized by the operating agreement and that they acted in good faith in expelling the Plaintiffs. The Trial Court granted summary judgment in Defendants' favor. We vacate the order of summary judgment and remand....

The Plaintiffs brought this action on December 17, 2001, alleging breach of fiduciary duty and breach of the statutory and common law duty of good faith and fair dealing. Defendants moved for summary judgment, arguing that their actions were expressly permitted under the operating agreement, and that they acted in good faith in expelling the Plaintiffs. Specifically, Defendants relied upon the following provision of the operating agreement:

> 13.6 Expulsion of a Member. The Company may expel a Member, with or without cause, from the Company upon a vote or written consent of the Members who hold a majority of Units. In the event of a Member's expulsion, the remaining Members shall be obligated to purchase the expelled Member's Financial Rights at the Agreed Price and on the Agreed Terms within thirty (30) days of such expulsion. The remaining Members shall purchase the expelled Member's Financial Rights in proportion to their Financial Rights (excluding the Offered Financial Rights), or in such other proportion as they may agree.

The Trial Court granted the Defendants summary judgment, finding only that "no genuine issues of material fact exist for adjudication and the Defendants are entitled to summary judgment as a matter of law." Plaintiffs have appealed this ruling, raising the issue, which we restate, of whether the Trial Court erred in granting summary judgment....

We begin with the Plaintiffs' assertion that the majority shareholders in a member-managed, closely-held LLC stand in a fiduciary relationship to the minority shareholders, such as Plaintiffs in this case....

It is well-recognized that a fiduciary relationship exists between members of either a partnership or a closely-held corporation under established principles of both partnership law and corporate law. In *Lightfoot v. Hardaway*, 751 S.W.2d 844 (Tenn.App. 1988), the court stated as follows regarding business partnerships:

> The fundamental rule that the relationship of partners is fiduciary and imposes on them the obligation of the utmost good faith and integrity in their dealings with one another with respect to partnership affairs is universally recognized in the modern cases and is reinforced by the Uniform Partnership Act.... Also well established is the applicability of this fiduciary duty on the sale of one partner's interest to another partner, the courts often characterizing the duty as being "particularly" or "especially" applicable to this situation. Although it is no longer disputed, at least in theory, that such a sale will be sustained only when it is made in good faith, for a fair consideration, and on a full and complete disclosure of all important information as to value, the rule's application is by no means as clear and simple as its statement; and the specific content of such terms as "good", "fair", "full", and "important" can be known only by relating the particular conduct and circumstances of the parties to the results reached in the cases.

The General Assembly has clarified the duties owed by partners by passage in 2001 of T.C.A. 61-1-404 [1997 UPA § 404].

The Supreme Court has provided the following guidance as regards members of corporate associations:

> This Court has stated that majority shareholders owe a fiduciary duty to minority shareholders....

> In *Intertherm v. Olympic Homes Systems*, 569 S.W.2d 467 (Tenn.App. 1978), the court noted that the transactions of majority or dominant shareholders will be closely scrutinized for good faith and fairness if challenged. The court stated that it would "apply the rule of close scrutiny and place the burden on the shareholder to justify a transaction with his corporation only when the shareholder owns a majority of stock, or is shown to dominate or control the corporation to a significant degree in some other way." *Id.* at 472....

> The Court has not addressed specifically the issues presented in this case, the relationship between shareholders in a close corporation where there is no majority or dominant shareholder and the dispute relates to the shareholders' interests as shareholders. The Court of Appeals relied upon the decision in *Wilkes v. Springside Nursing Home, Inc.*, 370 Mass. 842, 353 N.E.2d 657 (1976), in which the Massachusetts court held there is a fiduciary relationship between shareholders of a close corporation. In *Wilkes*, the Court stated that "stockholders in the close corporation owe one another substantially the same fiduciary duty in the operation of the enterprise that partners

owe to one another." Id. 353 N.E.2d at 661 (quoting *Donahue v. Rodd Electrotype Co.*, 367 Mass. 578, 328 N.E.2d 505, 515 (1975)).[80] That standard of duty is one of "utmost good faith and loyalty." ...

Defendants in the present case argue that an LLC is a "creature of statute" and because the LLC Act, found at T.C.A. 48-201-101 et seq., does not specifically prescribe a fiduciary duty of majority shareholders to a minority, this Court should not recognize such a duty. ...

The statute at issue here is T.C.A. 48-240-102, and it provides in pertinent part as follows:

(a) FIDUCIARY DUTY OF MEMBERS OF MEMBER-MANAGED LLC. Except as provided in the articles or operating agreement, every member of a member-managed LLC must account to the LLC for any benefit, and hold as trustee for it any profits derived by the member without the consent of the other members from any transaction connected with the formation, conduct, or liquidation of the LLC or from any use by the member of its property including, but not limited to, confidential or proprietary information of the LLC or other matters entrusted to the member as a result of such person's status as a member.

(b) STANDARD OF CONDUCT. A member of a member-managed LLC shall discharge such member's duties as a member, including all duties as a member of a committee:

(1) In good faith;

(2) With the care an ordinarily prudent person in a like position would exercise under similar circumstances; and

(3) In a manner the member reasonably believes to be in the best interest of the LLC.

Pursuant to the above analysis, we are of the opinion that finding a majority shareholder of an LLC stands in a fiduciary relationship to the minority, similar to the Supreme Court's teaching in Nelson regarding a corporation, is warranted in this case. Such a holding does not conflict with the statute, and is in keeping with the statutory requirement that each LLC member discharge all of his or her duties in good faith.

We now turn to the question of whether Defendants' actions, viewed in the light most favorable to Plaintiffs under our summary judgment standard, could reasonably be said to have violated their fiduciary duty of dealing fairly and honestly with the minority Plaintiffs, and acting in good faith toward them. ...

The basis for Defendants' argument that they expelled the Plaintiffs in good faith is their assertion that "the Plaintiff members of the management committee were planning to vote to distribute the remaining cash of the company, approximately $60,000, to the members, including themselves." FuturePoint's management committee had the authority and responsibility to distribute the net cash flow of the company

---

80. [*Donahue v. Rodd Electrotype Co. of New England, Inc.*, 328 N.E.2d 505 (Mass. 1975) appears in Chapter 7, Section IV.B. — Eds.]

to the members. Up until this point, it appears that no cash distributions had been made to any member of the company. The record reflects that after Plaintiffs were expelled, the company made cash distributions to the remaining members in amounts of $13,405.20 on March 27, 2002 and $40,000.00 on April 4, 2002. In their affidavits, Plaintiffs Mr. Quade and Mr. Atkins deny Defendants' allegation that they intended to distribute the remaining cash among the members.

Plaintiffs further argue that Defendants' assertion is false and pretextual for at least two reasons. First, several of the expelled members, Ms. Anderson, Mr. and Mrs. Zimmerman, and Mr. Martin, were not on the management committee and thus had no role in any alleged decision to make a cash distribution. Mr. Quade offered another reason in somewhat colorful fashion in his affidavit:

> The Defendants claim in their affidavits that myself, Mike Atkins, and Bill Thompson, as members of the management committee, were planning to vote to distribute all the remaining cash of the company so as to cause the company to not meet its payroll and other financial obligations. This is just not true. For one thing, I WAS ONE SUCH PAYROLL OBLIGATION. That is, I worked at FuturePoint. The notion that I would vote to ruin my investment and put myself out of a job is nuts!

We find that there exists a genuine issue of material fact regarding whether the Defendants' actions in expelling the minority Plaintiffs were taken in good faith, as required by the LLC Act, or whether they expelled Plaintiffs solely in order to force the acquisition of their membership units at a price of $150.00 in order to sell them at $250.00 per unit, in violation of their fiduciary duty....

For the foregoing reasons, we find there are questions of material fact regarding whether the Defendants' actions in expelling the minority Plaintiffs were taken in good faith and in accordance with their fiduciary duty to them. The Trial Court's grant of summary judgment is vacated, and the cause remanded for proceedings consistent with this opinion ...

3. Dissociation and Dissolution

The following cases address two key issues related to dissociation and dissolution: (1) to what extent does an expelled or withdrawing member (a dissociated member) have a right to payment of the value of the member's equity interest? and (2) when does the dissociation of a member require the company to be dissolved? The *Lieberman* court discusses the first of these two issues.

<h2 style="text-align:center">Lieberman v. Wyoming.com LLC</h2>

Wyoming Supreme Court
82 P.3d 274 (2004)

GOLDEN, JUSTICE:

Wyoming.com LLC (hereinafter "Wyoming.com") is a Wyoming limited liability company of which E. Michael Lieberman was a member. In 1998, Lieberman filed a notice of withdrawal of member with Wyoming.com, and the remaining members of Wyoming.com accepted Lieberman's withdrawal as tendered. The parties subsequently could not agree on the financial consequences of Lieberman's withdrawal and filed a petition for declaratory judgment on the issue. Ultimately, the district court, by way of summary judgment, ordered liquidation of Lieberman's equity interest at its capital account value as of the date of his withdrawal as a member. Lieberman appeals.

The Wyoming LLC Act contains no provision relating to the fate of a member's equity interest upon the member's dissociation. Thus, it was entirely up to the members of Wyoming.com to contractually provide for terms of dissociation. Upon careful review of all the agreements entered into by the parties regarding Wyoming.com, we determine that the agreements contain no provision regarding the equity interest of a dissociating member. Since we can find no provision mandating a different result, Lieberman retains his equity interest. Lieberman is under no obligation to sell his equity interest, and Wyoming.com is under no obligation to buy Lieberman's equity interest. The question of valuation is moot. The decision of the district court liquidating Lieberman's equity interest is reversed, and we remand to the district court for a declaration of the parties' rights consistent with this opinion....

FACTS

This is the second time this case has been before this Court on appeal. The facts as stated in *Lieberman v. Wyoming.com LLC*, 11 P.3d 353 (Wyo. 2000) (*Lieberman I*), are as follows:

On September 30, 1994, Steven Mossbrook, Sandra Mossbrook, and Lieberman created Wyoming.com LLC by filing Articles of Organization with the Wyoming Secretary of State. The initial capital contributions to Wyoming.com were valued at $50,000. Lieberman was vested with an initial capital contribution of $20,000, to consist of services rendered and to be rendered. According to the Articles of Organization, Lieberman's contribution represented a 40% ownership interest in the LLC. The Mossbrooks were vested with the remaining $30,000 capital contribution and 60% ownership interest. In August of 1995, the Articles of Organization of Wyoming.com were amended to reflect an increase in capitalization to $100,000. The increase in capitalization was the result of the addition of two members, each of whom was vested with a capital contribution of $25,000, representing a 2.5% ownership interest for each new member. Despite the increase in capitalization, Lieberman's ownership interest, as well as his stated capital contribution, remained the same.

On February 27, 1998, Lieberman was terminated as vice-president of Wyoming.com and required to leave the business premises. The other members of Wyoming.com met the same day and approved and ratified the termination. On March 13, 1998, Lieberman served Wyoming.com and its members with a document titled "Notice of Withdrawal of Member Upon Expulsion: Demand for Return of Contributions to Capit[a]l." In addition to giving notice of his withdrawal from the company, Lieberman's notice demanded the immediate return of "his share of the current value of the company," estimating the value of his share at $400,000, "based on a recent offer from the Majority Shareholder."

In response to Lieberman's notice of withdrawal, the members of Wyoming.com held a special meeting on March 17, 1998, and accepted Lieberman's withdrawal. The members also elected to continue, rather than dissolve, Wyoming.com. Additionally, they approved the return of Lieberman's $20,000 capital contribution. However, Lieberman refused to accept the $20,000 when it was offered.

Wyoming.com filed suit in June of 1998 asking for a declaration of its rights against Lieberman. Lieberman filed suit the same month requesting dissolution of Wyoming.com, and the actions were consolidated. After a hearing on cross motions for summary judgment, the district court granted Wyoming.com's motion for summary judgment and denied Lieberman's motion for partial summary judgment. The district court ruled that, because the remaining members of Wyoming.com LLC agreed to continue the business under a right to do so in the Articles of Organization, the company was not in a state of dissolution. The district court further ruled that Lieberman had the right to demand return of only his stated capital contribution, $20,000, which the district court ordered to be paid in cash. Lieberman appealed.

In *Lieberman I*, this Court agreed that Wyoming.com was not in a state of dissolution. With regard to Lieberman's demand for the return of his capital contribution we stated:

> Lieberman claims the term "contribution to capital" found in Wyo. Stat. Ann. § 17-15-120 should be interpreted to encompass the fair market value of his interest in the LLC and that his return should not be limited to the amount of his initial capital contribution. At this juncture, a distinction must be drawn between withdrawal of a member's capital contribution and the withdrawal from membership in an LLC, often termed dissociation. After a thorough review of § 17-15-120, we conclude nothing in that provision contemplates a member's rights upon dissociation. Besides the fact that § 17-15-120 speaks only to withdrawal of capital contributions, other provisions in the LLC act support our conclusion that § 17-15-120 does not govern dissociation. The following passage from § 17-15-119, which controls division of profits, envisions withdrawal of capital contribution without dissociation: "If the operating agreement does not so provide, distributions shall be made on the basis of the value of the contributions made by each member to the extent they have been received by the limited liability company and have not been returned." This quoted material clearly contemplates a situation where a member has withdrawn some (or even all) of his capital contribution but has not dissociated as a member. We conclude a withdrawal of capital contributions pursuant to § 17-15-120 does not also govern a member's rights upon dissociation.

This Court thus held that, pursuant to statute, Lieberman was entitled to the return of his capital contribution, regardless of his status as a member of Wyoming.com. Since Lieberman expected more, however, we remanded the case "because it is unclear what became of Lieberman's ownership or equity interest (as represented by a membership certificate)" requiring further proceedings "for a full declaration of the parties' rights."

Upon remand, no new evidence was introduced. Wyoming.com filed a motion for partial summary judgment requesting the district court to make two determinations: at what time should Lieberman's equity interest be valued and how should it be valued. Obviously, the parties proceeded under the assumptions that: Lieberman had withdrawn as a member and an equity owner; that he was entitled to his equity interest; and a valuation and buyout was necessary.

Wyoming.com relied upon language in the Operating Agreement to argue that Lieberman's equity interest should be limited to the value of his capital account. The district court agreed with Wyoming.com that the Operating Agreement provided the appropriate method to fully value Lieberman's equity interest. The district court also determined that Lieberman's equity interest should be valued as of the date of his withdrawal as a member. The district court therefore granted Wyoming.com's motion for partial summary judgment on these two issues, holding that "[t]he defendant is entitled to the balance of his capitol [sic] account as of the date of defendant's withdrawal from the LLC." Since it appears that the value of Lieberman's capital account at the date of his withdrawal was negative, Lieberman appeals.

STANDARD OF REVIEW

This appeal comes to this Court from the grant of a summary judgment. Summary judgments are appropriate when there are no genuine issues as to any material fact and the moving party is entitled to a judgment as a matter of law. As there are no issues of material fact in dispute, in this appeal we are called upon to review issues of law. We review issues of law de novo.

DISCUSSION

The district court determined that, as a matter of law, Lieberman "is entitled to the balance of his capitol [sic] account as of the date of [his] withdrawal from the LLC." In reaching this conclusion, the district court misinterpreted the operative documents. The provision defining a member's capital account is found in the Operating Agreement:

ARTICLE VI CAPITAL ACCOUNTS DISTRIBUTION OF PROFITS AND LOSSES

6.1 The Company shall maintain accurate records of the Capital Accounts of the Members. Each Member's capital account shall be credited with:

a. The amount of money the Member has contributed to the Company.

b. The fair market value of property the partner has contributed to the Company.

c. The Member's distributive share of Company income and gain.

Each Member's capital account shall be debited with:

a. The amount of money distributed to the Member by the Company.

b. The fair market value of property distributed to the Member by the Company.

c. The Member's distributive share of Company loss and deduction.

6.2 Upon liquidation of the Company (or any Member's interest in the Company), liquidating distributions shall in all cases be made in accordance with the positive capital account balances of the Members. If any Member has a deficit balance in his capital account following the liquidation of his interest in the Company, as determined after taking into account all capital account adjustments for the Company taxable year during which such liquidation occurs, he is unconditionally obligated to restore the amount of such deficit balance to the Company by the end of such taxable year (or, if later, within 90 days after the date of such liquidation)....

 In granting summary judgment, the district court relied upon paragraph 6.2. However, paragraph 6.2 contains no provision addressing the rights and obligations of the members with regard to a member who has withdrawn. Paragraph 6.2 provides a method for distributing capital upon liquidation. It contains no indication of when liquidation can or must occur. It does not mandate a buyout or a liquidation of a member's equity interest. As such, it has no application to the immediate issue and the district court's reliance upon it was misplaced.

Although we could end our discussion here, this appeal involves solely issues of law. In the interest of judicial economy, we deem it prudent to resolve the present issues. Returning then to our question upon remand, what has become of Lieberman's equity interest? This Court began the process of attempting to determine the fate of Lieberman's equity interest in *Lieberman I*:

Having determined that § 17-15-120 does not control a member's rights upon dissociation, we must determine what became of Lieberman's interest, other than his capital contribution, in Wyoming.com. Unfortunately, it is unclear from the district court's decision letter precisely what became of Lieberman's ownership interest. The Articles of Organization of Wyoming.com credited Lieberman with a 40% ownership interest in Wyoming.com, and he now argues he is entitled to payment for this interest at fair market value. In the alternative, he contends he retains that 40% interest because the district court has not resolved that portion of the parties' dispute. Wyoming.com disagrees.

We begin by examining Lieberman's notice of withdrawal. Lieberman strongly disputes any contention that he has simply forfeited his interest, other than his capital contribution, in the LLC. After examining the notice of withdrawal, we cannot say, as a matter of law, that Lieberman forfeited his interest upon his withdrawal because nothing in his withdrawal indicates his intent to do so. Indeed, Lieberman's demand for "his share of the current value of the company," whose value he estimated at $400,000, "based on a recent offer from the Majority Shareholder," indicates he would not easily part with, much less forfeit, his interest. Because we cannot say that, as a matter of law, Lieberman's withdrawal amounted to forfeiture of his interest, and because there is no statutory provision governing dissociation, we look to Wyoming.com's Operating Agreement to determine Lieberman's remedy.

Under the Wyoming.com's Operating Agreement, a member's equity interest was to be represented by a membership certificate. The Operating Agreement provides:

ARTICLE IV Membership Certificates and their Transfer

...

4.3 Transfers of Shares. Any Member proposing a transfer or assignment of his Certificate must first notify the Company, in writing, of all the details and consideration for the proposed transfer or assignment. The Company, for the benefit of the remaining Members, will have the first right to acquire the equity by cancellation of the Certificate under the same terms and conditions as provided in the formal Articles of Organization as filed with the Wyoming Secretary of State for Members who are deceased, retired, resigned, expelled, or dissolved....

Under these provisions, it is clear that a member's interest in Wyoming.com was to be represented by membership certificates. There is nothing in the record indicating what became of Lieberman's membership certificate; there is no indication it has been canceled or forfeited....

Since Lieberman has not voluntarily forfeited his equity interest, this Court must look to the agreements entered into by the members of Wyoming.com to determine the rights and obligations of the members with regards to a member who has dissociated.[81] The rights and obligations of the members of Wyoming.com are determined pursuant to the operating agreements of Wyoming.com. The record reveals that the parties entered into "Articles of Organization of Wyoming.com LLC" (the "Articles") and an "Operating Agreement of Wyoming.com LLC" (the "Operating Agreement"). These agreements establish Wyoming.com, provide for Wyoming.com's operation, and set forth the mutual obligations between each of Wyoming.com's members. At all times the members have been free to contract any provision they desired, so long as the provision did not conflict with the limited requirements of the Wyoming LLC Act. Determining the fate of Lieberman's equity interest requires this Court to construe these agreements....

The operating agreements of Wyoming.com vest Lieberman with an ownership interest. Lieberman can only be divested of this ownership interest if the members of Wyoming.com contracted for such divestment. Wyoming.com argues that Lieberman's withdrawal as a member mandates his withdrawal as an equity owner, thus triggering a liquidation of his equity interest. In *Lieberman I*, this Court clarified that "[u]nder the Wyoming LLC act, a member's interest in an LLC consists of economic and non-economic interests." These interests are distinct. It is clear from Lieberman's

81. [2] Our review is limited to the agreements between the parties because, as stated previously, there is no statutory provision regarding the rights and obligations of members upon the dissociation of a member.

notice of withdrawal that he had no intention of forfeiting his economic, or equity, interest in the company. Lieberman's withdrawal regarded his non-economic membership interest only.

The operating agreements clearly anticipate a situation where a person could be an equity owner in Wyoming.com but not a member. Provision 4.3 of the Operating Agreement, quoted above, provides that, if a transferee of an ownership interest is not unanimously approved by the remaining members, the transferee maintains the rights of equity ownership but will not be a member.[82] Logically, given the absence of any contractual provision to the contrary, there is no reason to treat a withdrawing member any differently from someone who buys into Wyoming.com without becoming a member. Thus, Lieberman is not a member of Wyoming.com, but he maintains his equity interest and all rights and obligations attendant thereto.

The parties essentially admit this in their respective briefs. Lieberman argues that there is nothing in the agreements allowing Wyoming.com to acquire his ownership interest at less than fair market value, while Wyoming.com argues that there is nothing in the agreements requiring Wyoming.com to pay fair market value for Lieberman's ownership interest. Both arguments are correct. There simply is no contractual agreement that any party must buy or sell an ownership interest for any amount.

Having failed to contractually provide for mandatory liquidation or a buyout, the parties are left in status quo. We have long held that it is the duty of this Court to construe contracts made between parties, not to make a contract for them.... We must abide by the terms of their contract. This is especially so since the parties are asking us to create terms and conditions which do not exist in their contract.[83] We decline to alter the contract as written and accepted by these parties in the name of contract interpretation. We will enforce the contract as written and accepted by the parties.[84] Lieberman maintains his equity interest in Wyoming.com.

---

82. [3] Wyo. Stat. Ann. § 17-15-122 contains a similar provision regarding the transferability of interest. The transferee does not become a member without unanimous approval of all members.

83. [4] This Court would be required to supply a liquidation or buy-out provision, including a valuation method, with no evidence as to what these parties intended when they formed Wyoming.com.

84. [5] In *Roussalis v. Wyoming Medical Center, Inc.*, 4 P.3d 209, 245 (Wyo. 2000), this Court said: Our reluctance to redraw or nullify the provisions of a contract made by competent parties draws strength from the eloquent statement from the United States Supreme Court which we favorably quoted in *Sinclair Oil Corp.* [*v. Columbia Cas Co.*, 682 P.2d 975 (Wyo. 1984)]:

> The right of private contract is no small part of the liberty of the citizen, and that the usual and most important function of courts of justice is rather to maintain and enforce contracts, than to enable parties thereto to escape from their obligation on the pretext of public policy, unless it clearly appears that they contravene public right or the public welfare. It was well said by Sir George Jessel, M.R., in *Printing & Co. v. Sampson, L.R.* 19 Eq. 465: 'It must not be forgotten that you are not to extend arbitrarily those rules which say that a given contract is void as being against public policy, because if there is one thing which more than another public policy requires it is that men of full age and competent understanding shall have the utmost liberty of contracting, and that their contracts, when entered into freely and voluntarily, shall be held sacred, and shall be enforced by courts of justice. Therefore, you have this paramount public policy to consider—that you are not lightly to interfere with this freedom of contract.'

CONCLUSION

Lieberman has withdrawn as a member of Wyoming.com and all remaining members unanimously accepted his withdrawal as a member. Lieberman thus is no longer a member of Wyoming.com. Lieberman does, however, maintain his equity interest in Wyoming.com. There is no contractual provision for a buy-out of his equity interest. Therefore Lieberman cannot force Wyoming.com to buy his interest, and Wyoming.com cannot force Lieberman to sell his interest. Because the members of Wyoming.com failed to contractually provide for a buy-out, Lieberman remains an equity holder in Wyoming.com. There are no further rights or obligations of the parties for this court to construe with regards to this situation. The grant of summary judgment is reversed and the matter remanded to the district court for a declaration of the parties' rights consistent with this opinion.

Lehman, Justice, dissenting, with whom Kite, Justice, joins:

I respectfully dissent. I agree that paragraph 6.2 of the Operating Agreement only provides a method for distributing capital upon liquidation and that the district court erred in relying on that subsection to find that Lieberman was entitled to only his capital contribution upon withdrawal. I also agree with the majority that a thorough review of the Operating Agreement discloses no express provision for dealing with a dissociated member's equity interest.

However, I must disagree with the majority's determination of the consequence for the failure to provide such a provision. As the majority noted, we must review the contract of the parties as a whole with the goal of determining the intent of the contracting parties. The right of a member to withdraw from membership in the LLC is evidenced in the provisions of the operating agreement. Also clearly expressed is the right of the remaining members to continue the business after such a withdrawal. The provision addressing this right states:

> 9. Continuity. The remaining members of the LLC, providing they are two or more in number, will have the right to continue the business on the death, retirement, resignation, expulsion, bankruptcy or dissolution of a member or occurrence of any other event which terminates the continued membership of a member in this LLC, in accordance with the voting provisions of the Operating Agreement of the Company.

This provision allows any member to terminate his membership in Wyoming.com by taking any of the listed actions and provides the remaining members the right to continue the business. This provision evidences the parties' intent to allow a member to completely terminate his membership in the LLC without also terminating the LLC. Hand in hand with these rights is the implication that should the remaining members elect to continue, they will have to compensate the withdrawing member for his interest in some manner. It seems intuitive that if the parties allowed for withdrawal and continuation, they must have had some intent to deal with those events.

Id. at 978–79 (quoting *Baltimore & Ohio Southwestern Railway Co. v. Voigt*, 176 U.S. 498, 505, 20 S.Ct. 385, 387, 44 L.Ed. 560, 565 (1900)).

Because the provision mentions nothing of forfeiting the interest or simply becoming a non-member equity owner, the agreement to continue thus implies that there must be some sort of buyout.

Furthermore, the LLC statutory scheme implies that, absent other agreement, a member has a right to terminate his continued membership in the LLC and be compensated for this interest. As we stated in Lieberman I, at 357, an LLC is a hybrid organization including characteristics of both a partnership and a corporation. At the time the legislature enacted the original LLC statutes, an important consideration was the tax ramifications of the newly created entity. At that time, in order to obtain taxation as a partnership, an LLC could have no more than two of four corporate characteristics: limited liability, central management, free transferability of interests, and continuity of life. The LLC entity provided for limited liability and central management. Therefore, to avoid corporate taxation, the typical LLC statutes choose to utilize partnership principles, rather than corporate principles, for exiting members in order to avoid the LLC having continuity of life.

Partnership exit rules ordinarily allow for any partner to dissolve the firm at any time and demand liquidation and accordingly be paid for his equity interest. The legislature clearly recognized this as the normal partnership rule and impliedly endorsed such a rule by providing for an exception to this rule if the members agreed otherwise in their operating agreement. Wyo. Stat. Ann. § 17-15-123. In a sense, carrying on the business following a terminating event became the exception to the general rule that the business would cease when a member left for any reason. Thus, the resulting implication is a member may terminate his membership in an LLC and must be paid for this interest unless otherwise provided.

Therefore, I reach the conclusion that under the terms of the LLC as provided by the Articles of Organization and Operating Agreement, and under the statute, Lieberman could withdraw as a member of Wyoming.com resulting in a forced buyout of his entire interest. The majority concludes, "Lieberman's withdrawal regarded his non-economic membership interest only." I cannot agree with this conclusion. While a member's interest does in fact consist of an economic and non-economic interest, a withdrawing member does not envision that his withdrawal will result in this split in his interest. As we noted in *Lieberman I*, at 355–56, Lieberman demanded "his share of the current value of the company," which value he estimated at $400,000, "based on a recent offer from the Majority Shareholder." Clearly Lieberman intended to withdraw his entire interest from the LLC. As such, Lieberman essentially declared his intention to no longer be associated with the LLC. Having accepted this withdrawal, the remaining members were now required and expected to compensate Lieberman for his interest.

The majority has recognized this and stated, "the parties proceeded under the assumptions that: Lieberman had withdrawn as a member and an equity owner; that he was entitled to his equity interest; and a valuation and buyout was necessary." However, they now refuse to provide relief for this situation. In fact, the majority's resolution has created a situation where the remaining members are in a position of power to dictate the terms of any negotiations for a buyout. The remaining members are now conceivably in a position to retain earnings and avoid distributions, but as an equity owner Lieberman would still be required to pay taxes on those earnings. Additionally, Lieberman is no longer a member. He will not be drawing the salary of the member or controlling his equity interest in any manner. While it could be said that this situation arose because of Lieberman's withdrawal, it should be noted that under the majority's analysis the result would apply equally to an expelled member. In such an instance, some of the members could expel a member and then refuse to negotiate for a buyout. Such a result begs for the oppression of one party. While I agree with the majority that it is not our duty to write contract provisions for parties that have failed to do so, I believe it would be much worse to fail to provide a remedy.

Therefore, I would provide such a remedy. Because the Operating Agreement does not provide for a valuation method, I look to the statutes to see if the legislature provided a default valuation method. As we said in *Lieberman I*, express provisions for valuing a member's share when that member terminates his membership in the LLC do not exist. However, I do not believe this requires us to unilaterally create a valuation method. The statute expressly provides for the distribution of assets on dissolution. Wyo. Stat. Ann. § 17-15-126. Granted, as we stated in *Lieberman I*, Lieberman is not entitled to a distribution of assets upon dissolution under this section because there was no dissolution. *Lieberman I*, at 358. However, this statute would be a proper valuation tool. This conclusion logically flows from the fact that the general rule is that an LLC must be dissolved upon the termination of a member's membership in the LLC, and the exception to this rule is when the operating agreement contains a provision for carrying on the business. If such a carrying on provision is not placed in the operating agreement, the members receive a distribution in conformance with the provisions of Wyo. Stat. Ann § 17-15-126. The legislature has established this as the proper method of discharging members' equity interests. I see no reason to value the departing member's share differently when the business carries on and only one member departs.

Therefore, absent a provision in the operating agreement, a member's equity interest should be valued at what he would have received had the business been dissolved on the day he terminated his membership in the LLC. I recognize that, because the business is not actually dissolving, this valuation may be difficult and will have to be based to some extent on estimates and appraisals. However, a similar valuation method is used upon the dissociation of a partner from a partnership when the partnership agreement has failed to provide for a valuation method. See Wyo. Stat. Ann. §§ 17-21-603(a), 17- 21-701(a), (b). Presumably, then, such estimates and appraisals are attainable.

Additionally, Wyo. Stat. Ann. § 17-15-126 provides that upon dissolution the proceeds are to be applied first to pay the creditors and then the remainder is to go to the members "in respect of their share of the profits and other compensation by way of income on their contributions" and then lastly to the members "in respect of their contributions to capital." As can be seen by that statute's wording, the proceeds upon dissolution are used to extinguish debt and then are used not only to return a member's capital contribution but also to provide for the member's share of profits and other compensation by way of income on that contribution. Such a provision can encompass many things including the increase in value of any assets, any retained profits, and the goodwill of the company. Therefore, fair market value, which generally accounts for these relevant factors, would be a reasonable alternative estimate of the departing member's share.[85]

Lastly, in instances where a departing member's share is to be valued as detailed above, the remaining members have elected to continue the company. Therefore, some consideration must be given to the duties and hardship the company may encounter as a result of paying the departing member's equity interest. The whole of the LLC statutes evidences the legislature's overall concern for the protection of the LLC's creditors. It is evident that the legislature wanted to assure that the LLC's creditors were provided for before the LLC members. Wyo. Stat. Ann. §§ 17-15-120, -126. These observations lead me to conclude that the payment of the departing member's equity interest may take place over a reasonable period of time to avoid the liquidation of essential assets and the possible undercapitalization of the LLC. To be entitled to prolong the payment over a reasonable time, the LLC must show that immediate payment in full would jeopardize the company's ability to carry on its ordinary business and provide for its creditors. Should payment over time be required, such payment should be secured by a promissory note that provides for reasonable interest. Furthermore, until the member is paid in full, that member should still receive any distributions to which his interest is entitled much like a transferee without the right to participate in the management of the business would under Wyo. Stat. Ann. § 17-15-122 (LexisNexis 2003).

The *Dunbar* case addresses the second issue raised above: When does the dissociation of a member require an LLC to be dissolved?

The Dunbar Group, LLC v. Tignor

Virginia Supreme Court
593 S.E.2d 216 (2004)

Keenan, Justice:

In this appeal from a judgment ordering the dissolution of a limited liability company, the dispositive issue is whether the evidence was sufficient to support the chancellor's judgment.

XpertCTI, LLC (Xpert), is a limited liability company that provides "computer telephony integration" (CTI) software to dealers and manufacturers for installation in certain telephone systems and equipment. CTI software enables the use of computers to "interface" with and control telephone systems.

---

85. [6] Fair market value is generally defined as the amount at which property would change hands between a willing buyer and a willing seller, neither being under any compulsion to buy or sell and both having reasonable knowledge of the relevant facts. Black's Law Dictionary, 597 (6th ed. 1990).

Xpert was formed in March 2000, by The Dunbar Group, LLC (Dunbar), and Archie F. Tignor, who each owned a membership interest of 50 percent in Xpert. Edward D. Robertson, Jr., a computer software developer and consultant, was the sole member and manager of Dunbar.

Tignor, a commercial telephone and telecommunications equipment dealer and installer, owned 50 percent of the stock of X-tel, Inc. (X-tel), a telecommunications sales firm. Tignor served as the president of X-tel, which was a dealer in equipment for Samsung Telecommunications America, Inc. (Samsung), a manufacturer, distributor, and seller of telecommunications equipment.

Dunbar and Tignor executed an "Operating Agreement" for Xpert under which they were the sole managers of Xpert. Dunbar created Xpert's proprietary software, or "source code," and conducted the daily operations of the company. Tignor's main function was to provide Xpert with access to his business contacts in the telecommunications industry, including Samsung.

Xpert's operating agreement provided a procedure for a company member to assert a breach of the agreement by another company member. The agreement specified that if the breach was not timely cured by the defaulting member, the complaining member had the "right to petition a court of competent jurisdiction for dissolution of the Company." The agreement also stated that the "dissolution of a [m]ember or occurrence of any other event that terminates the continued membership of a [m]ember in the Company shall not cause the dissolution of the Company."

In December 2000, Xpert entered into a contract with Samsung to supply Samsung with software-driven security devices called "dongles," which were to be included in all telecommunications systems sold by Samsung. Xpert received about $20,000 per month from the Samsung contract. The Samsung contract contained a provision specifying the contract's duration:

> This Agreement shall come into force and effect on the date written above [December 5, 2000] and shall remain in full force and effect for consecutive periods of thirty-six (36) months thereafter.... After this time the contract will continue on an annual basis unless terminated by either party giving 90 days notice before the anniversary of the contract date.

Certain disputes arose between Robertson and Tignor over matters primarily related to the management and disbursement of Xpert's assets. In May 2002, Dunbar's counsel sent a letter to Tignor's counsel stating that it was apparent to Robertson that "his continued working relationship with Mr. Tignor [was] no longer possible." Dunbar's counsel further stated that "Mr. Robertson is of the opinion that it is in the parties' best interest to sever their ties as fully and quickly as possible."

In September 2002, Dunbar, Xpert, and Robertson, in his capacity as a manager of Xpert, (collectively, Dunbar) filed an amended bill of complaint against Tignor and X-tel requesting, among other things, entry of an order "expelling and dissociating Tignor as a member of Xpert pursuant to Virginia Code § 13.1-1040.1(5)." Dunbar alleged that Tignor engaged in "numerous acts of misconduct as a member and manager of Xpert," including the commingling of Xpert's funds with the funds of Tignor and "his corporate alter ego, X-tel."

Code § 13.1-1040.1, which provides for a court-ordered expulsion of a member of a limited liability company, states in relevant part:

> [A] member is dissociated from a limited liability company upon the occurrence of any of the following events:
>
> 5. On application by the limited liability company or another member, the member's expulsion by judicial determination because:
>
>> a. The member engaged in wrongful conduct that adversely and materially affected the business of the limited liability company;
>>
>> b. The member willfully or persistently committed a material breach of the articles of organization or an operating agreement; or
>>
>> c. The member engaged in conduct relating to the business of the limited liability company which makes it not reasonably practicable to carry on the business with the member.

Tignor filed a separate "Application for Judicial Dissolution" against Dunbar and Xpert. Tignor requested, among other things, the dissolution of Xpert under Code § 13.1-1047 on the ground that "it is not reasonably practicable to carry on the business of [Xpert] in conformity with the Articles of Organization and [the] Operating Agreement." Tignor alleged that "serious differences of opinion as to company management have arisen between the members and managers" of Xpert, and that the company was "deadlocked" in its ability to conduct its business affairs, including contracting with customers for goods and services and the "receipt and disbursement of [Xpert's] assets and company funds."

The chancellor consolidated for trial Dunbar's amended bill of complaint and Tignor's application for judicial dissolution. At a hearing, the chancellor received evidence relating to both pleadings.

The evidence showed that Tignor commingled Xpert's funds with X-tel's funds by placing several checks, which were made payable to Xpert, into X-tel's bank account. Tignor provided inaccurate information to Robertson concerning one of those checks, which was made payable to Xpert in the amount of about $47,000. Tignor used the proceeds from that check to pay some of X-tel's expenses and to meet X-tel's payroll, including the payment of Tignor's own salary.

Without informing Robertson, Tignor also authorized a change in the status of Xpert's checking account that prevented checks from being written on the account. When Robertson, who was unaware of the change, wrote a check payable to one of Xpert's vendors, the check "bounced."

Although Dunbar had been renting office space from X-tel, Tignor evicted Robertson from X-tel's premises. Tignor also restricted Robertson's access to various testing equipment located in X-tel's offices, reducing Robertson's ability to test

Xpert's products. Robertson needed access to this equipment to ensure the quality of Xpert's products before they were delivered to Xpert's customers. Due to Robertson's restricted ability to test Xpert's products, Xpert's customers did not receive their orders in a timely manner and products were sent to customers "in less than quality condition."

Tignor also terminated Robertson's e-mail account with Xpert without giving him prior notice. This sudden termination of Robertson's e-mail account created "a lot of confusion" among Xpert's customers, giving the appearance that Xpert had "gone out of business."

In December 2002, the chancellor entered an order in which he found that Tignor commingled Xpert's funds with his own funds and the funds of X-tel. The chancellor also concluded that Tignor's actions had been contrary to Xpert's best interests and had "adversely affected Xpert's ability to carry on its business." The chancellor further determined that Tignor had acted "in violation of" subparagraph five of Code § 13.1-1040.1.

The chancellor ordered that Tignor be "immediately expelled as an active member of Xpert" and that Robertson "shall continue to operate Xpert" and provide to Tignor a monthly accounting of Xpert's finances. The chancellor also ordered:

> Xpert ... shall continue the arrangement pursuant to this order until its contract with [Samsung] expires or otherwise terminates, including any extensions. Following the fulfillment or non-renewal of the [Samsung] contract, the court orders that Xpert ... be dissolved and its assets distributed pursuant to the Virginia Code and the operating agreement of Xpert.

Dunbar appeals.

Dunbar does not challenge that part of the chancellor's order expelling Tignor as a member of Xpert, but attacks only the portion of the order providing for the dissolution of Xpert. Dunbar argues that the evidence is insufficient to support the dissolution of Xpert because the evidence did not satisfy the standard required by Code § 13.1-1047 for the judicial dissolution of a limited liability company. In support of this argument, Dunbar primarily asserts that the record fails to show that after the expulsion of Tignor as a member of Xpert, it would not be reasonably practicable to carry on Xpert's business.

In resolving Dunbar's claim, we first observe that an established standard of review governs our inquiry. Because the chancellor heard the evidence *ore tenus*, his decree is entitled to the same weight as a jury verdict. Therefore, on appeal, we will not set aside the chancellor's findings unless they are plainly wrong or without evidence to support them.

The chancellor resolved the dissolution issue in Tignor's favor. Thus, we consider the evidence relating to the dissolution determination in the light most favorable to Tignor.

This appeal presents our first opportunity to consider the statutory standard provided in Code § 13.1-1047 for the judicial dissolution of a limited liability company. The statute states that

> [o]n application by or for a member, the circuit court of the locality in which the registered office of the limited liability company is located may decree dissolution of a limited liability company if it is not reasonably practicable to carry on the business in conformity with the articles of organization and any operating agreement.

Id.

Because this statutory language is plain and unambiguous, we apply the plain meaning of that language. The statutory standard set by the General Assembly for dissolution of a limited liability company is a strict one, reflecting legislative deference to the parties' contractual agreement to form and operate a limited liability company. Only when a circuit court concludes that present circumstances show that it is not reasonably practicable to carry on the company's business in accord with its articles of organization and any operating agreement, may the court order a dissolution of the company.

The record here, however, does not show that the chancellor evaluated the evidence in light of the fact that Tignor was being expelled as a member and manager of Xpert. Although Tignor's actions in those capacities had created numerous problems in the operation of Xpert, his expulsion as a member changed his role from one of an active participant in the management of Xpert to the more passive role of an investor in the company. The record fails to show that after this change in the daily management of Xpert, it would not be reasonably practicable for Xpert to carry on its business pursuant to its operating authority.

Moreover, we observe that the terms of the chancellor's dissolution order refute a conclusion that dissolution was appropriate under the statutory standard of Code § 13.1-1047. While the chancellor concluded that judicial dissolution of Xpert was warranted, he nevertheless ordered that Xpert continue operating as a limited liability company for as long as the Samsung contract remained in effect. This provision in the chancellor's order indicates that he concluded that Tignor's expulsion from Xpert would make it reasonably practicable for Xpert to continue to operate for an extended period of time.

Accordingly, we hold that the evidence does not support that part of the chancellor's order providing for the dissolution of Xpert. Further, because the evidence is insufficient to support such a judicial dissolution, we do not reach Dunbar's additional argument that the chancellor erred under Code § 13.1-1047 in ordering that Xpert be dissolved at an uncertain, future date.

For these reasons, we will affirm that part of the chancellor's judgment expelling Tignor as a member of Xpert, reverse that part of the judgment ordering the dissolution of Xpert, and enter final judgment.

Affirmed in part, reversed in part, and final judgment.

———————

For an elaboration of the legal standard applicable to dissolution, we return one last time to *McConnell v. Hunt Sports Enterprises*,[86] the case concerning the NHL Hockey franchise. The *McConnell* court considered the relevance of a member's wrongful conduct to the order of dissolution. In *McConnell*, the court stated the following:

> In its sixth assignment of error, ... appellant asserts that the trial court erred in finding appellant wrongfully caused the dissolution of CHL....
>
> The trial court found that appellant unlawfully usurped control of CHL by unilaterally rejecting the Nationwide lease proposal, by failing to disclose the proposal to CHL, and by commencing litigation in the trial court, in the Supreme Court of New York, and in the Supreme Court of Ohio. The trial court found that such actions made it no longer feasible, profitable, advantageous, and reasonably practicable to operate the business of CHL. Based on these findings of fact, the trial court concluded that as a result of appellant's wrongful conduct, CHL should be judicially dissolved. Further, the trial court cited section 9.2(a) of the operating agreement that stated that members who have not wrongfully caused the dissolution of CHL or the liquidating trustee shall proceed with CHL's liquidation. Therefore, the trial court concluded that all members of CHL except for appellant shall be responsible for and have the legal authority and power to undertake the winding up, or liquidation, of CHL. Lastly, the trial court granted judgment in favor of appellees on count two of the second amended complaint and ordered appellant to bear all costs.
>
> R.C. 1705.47 states that upon application by a member of a limited liability company, a court of common pleas may decree the dissolution of that company if it is not reasonably practicable to carry on the business of the company in conformity with its articles of organization and operating agreement.... As a matter of law, neither R.C. 1705.47 nor any other provision of the Revised Code requires a determination of wrongful conduct prior to making a finding that it is not reasonably practicable to carry on the business of the company and, therefore, decreeing the dissolution of such company. Rather, all that is required is a determination that it is not reasonably practicable to carry on the business in conformity with the articles of incorporation and operating agreement....
>
> Hence, it is only as to who may participate in the liquidation of CHL that a determination of wrongful conduct is necessary. For the reasons that follow, we determine that the trial court erred in finding appellant wrongfully caused the dissolution of CHL. However, the evidence does support the trial court's conclusion that it was no longer practicable to carry on the business of CHL.
>
> We note first that while it is not necessary under R.C. 1705.47 to determine that wrongful conduct caused the dissolution of a company, it is possible that wrongful conduct is the underlying reason for it no longer being practicable to carry on the business of a company. This is essentially what the trial court

---

86. 725 N.E. 2d 1193 (C.A. Ohio 1999).

found below—that appellant's wrongful conduct made it no longer practicable to carry on the business of CHL. Related to this was the trial court's determination that appellant could not participate in the winding up of CHL's affairs since it wrongfully caused the dissolution. The trial court's determinations in this regard were erroneous because, while appellant did act wrongfully and breached the operating agreement in usurping control of CHL, such was not the reason it became no longer practicable to carry on the business of CHL....

The above evidence shows that the cause of it being no longer practicable to carry on the business of CHL was the fact that CHL was not the ownership group awarded the NHL franchise. While appellant did breach the CHL operating agreement by unilaterally rejecting the lease proposal, such was not the reason CHL did not become the ownership group. In addition, appellant's actions in unilaterally filing the lawsuits in the name of CHL did not cause the dissolution of CHL. June 9, 1997 was the deadline for the ownership group to be identified. This ownership group was not CHL. Hence, as of June 9, 1997, the reason for CHL's existence was gone. Hence, anything appellant did in breach of the operating agreement after June 9, 1997 was not a cause of it being no longer practicable to carry on the business of CHL.

The preceding cases present only a few of the many issues courts must address in matters involving LLCs. The work of the courts is complicated because limited liability statutes generally provide considerable flexibility in organizing and operating the company and provisions of each company's individual operating agreement usually assume an important role in the resolution of disputes.

D. Digital Organizations

Electronic communications via the Internet, cell phone text messaging, and other emerging technologies are reshaping many aspects of life. In a few, short years, the relatively simple medium of email has become a primary mode of text-based communication. In the commercial world, individuals use the internet to complete many types of personal transactions, including banking, shopping, investing, making travel arrangements, and conducting research, to name just a few. In general, all of these activities, even those requiring high levels of security, work extremely well when effected using electronic communications.

Electronic communications have also affected how people organize and operate businesses. Many employees now "telecommute" to work. People who are physically located in different geographic areas use technology to work on joint projects without having to be in physical proximity. During the technology boom of the 1990s, when highly skilled labor was in short supply, U. S. based companies often contracted with businesses around the world to provide the needed skilled labor pool. In these situations, contracts were formed, products were developed and shipped and business was conducted online successfully without requiring people to relocate to a common geographical location in order to work together. In addition, online dispute resolution systems, such as arbitration, have been developed to resolve conflicts among actors located in different parts of the world.

Not surprisingly, it is now possible to create what have come to be called digital organizations. These companies are usually formed by people located in different geographical locations. Digital organizations may exist only in cyberspace. They may not have a physical presence in a particular geographic location, such as an office in a building. Digital companies use the internet and other forms of electronic communication to organize and conduct business, produce products and services, and engage in all matter of commercial activities.

Although countries such as Bermuda have passed legislation making it possible to form a digital organization, U. S. business organization law has been slow to catch up with the digital age. Recently, however, several states have begun to work on legislation enabling the formation of digital organizations. Vermont is among the first states to pass a digital corporation act. Although a digital company could be based on almost any type of organization, as it happens, the proposals currently under consideration are primarily focused on creating digital corporations and digital limited liability companies.

A digital organization is typically based on one of the established business organization forms, such as a corporation or a limited liability company. It differs from traditional business forms in that a digital company exists and operates in cyberspace through the use of electronic technology. It makes all required filings electronically and uses electronic signatures for documents that must be signed; it uses electronic communications technology to conduct meetings, to vote on company matters and to communicate among company investors and management. Although a digital company does not have a physical presence in any particular geographic location, it is governed by the laws of the place of incorporation, particularly the business organization and tax laws. Several jurisdictions currently permit some or all of the following to be accomplished electronically: filing corporate documents; convening shareholders' and directors' meetings; voting through the use of "written" consents or by proxy. Some of the thorniest issues associated with the operation of digital organizations are taxation issues, particularly determining the extent to which a company's revenues should be taxed in the state of incorporation.

E. Social Enterprises

1. Introduction

Social enterprises or mission-driven companies combine attributes of both nonprofit and business corporations. Social enterprises use market-based strategies to finance the achievement of social goals. Unlike nonprofit companies, social enterprises can distribute company profits to equity investors. In contrast with business organizations, social enterprises engage in profit-making activities to accomplish social objectives. Thus, being organized to engage in profit-making activities distinguishes these companies from nonprofit organizations, and their formation for the express purpose of using business profits to accomplish social goals distinguishes them from the usual business enterprise.

In one sense, combining business and social objectives is nothing new. The concept of corporate social responsibility has been around for years. In addition, from the outset, U.S. business corporations have often engaged in profit-making activities while advancing broader social goals. During the early years of this country's post-revolutionary period, for example, entrepreneurs formed private corporations to engage in activities that in modern times would be considered public works, such as building bridges and turnpikes. Today one can readily name business corporations that have adopted corporate policies or codes of conduct expressing a commitment to corporate social responsibility and that act upon those commitments. It is equally easy to name nonprofit corporations engaging in what would generally be considered commercial activities to produce revenues to support the nonprofit objectives. These commercial activities — the sales of goods and services that must be related to the company's social purpose — reportedly provide as much as 70% of these entities' revenues.

Social enterprises are different in that, from the outset, they give equal weight to both profit-making and social objectives. For example, Alaska Native tribes have formed business corporations whose corporate charters formally express the dual purposes of engaging in profit making activities and advancing the social welfare of the tribes of which the shareholders are members. (Generally not all members of a tribe are shareholders. Thus, the companies' recognition and advancement of the educational and social welfare of a tribe serves a constituency including people who are not also shareholders.) The formal acknowledgment from the time of incorporation of dual economic and social purposes, given equal weight in both the corporate charter and in directors' decision-making processes, distinguishes these companies from business enterprises that engage in some social activities.

Social enterprises may be formed using traditional legal structures or they may take advantage of new legislation created especially for companies of this type. Today, business organization lawyers may be asked to counsel companies that in many respects are hybrid organizations combining attributes of both for profit and nonprofit companies. L3C's and Benefit Corporations are two such organizational forms.

2. The Low Profit Limited Liability Company (L3C)

Although most hybrid organizations have been formed using modified versions of standard for profit or nonprofit organization forms, some are organizing as a low-profit limited liability company ("L3C"), a form especially designed to suit the needs of the social enterprise. As of this writing nine states, the Ogala Sioux Tribe and the Crow Indian Nation of Montana have enacted L3C legislation. More than 20 additional states have L3C legislation under consideration. Proposals for L3C legislation have also been made at the federal level.

The L3C form was originally created to enable foundations and other nonprofits to provide financial support to small business organizations formed primarily for charitable or educational purposes. For example, a U. S. foundation could donate money to an L3C business organization providing micro-financing to impoverished individuals living in developing countries. If the L3C proved to be profitable, the tax status of the donor foundation would not be jeopardized. Companies wishing to qualify for tax-exempt status would still organize as a foundation or a nonprofit organization, rather than as an L3C.

An L3C must meet the following criteria:

(1) The company must be organized for a business purpose;

(2) The company must be formed to accomplish charitable or educational purposes as defined by the IRS code applicable to organizations.[91]

(3) The production of income or the appreciation of property may not be a significant company purpose, although the company may produce income.

The company must also meet other IRS requirements applicable to charitable organizations, such as those restricting political and legislative activities. A company failing to meet any one of the criteria would revert to being an ordinary, for profit LLC.

The L3C business form has not been met with enthusiasm in all quarters. For example, the American Bar Association Limited Liability Company Committee passed a resolution recommending that states not enact L3C legislation at this time, in large part because of unresolved tax issues concerning the use of the L3C. Other opponents of L3C legislation believe that established business forms can be adapted to accomplish the same result.

3. Benefit Corporations

The impulse to combine mission-driven objectives with the business organization form is also evident in what are commonly referred to as "Benefit" Corporations. Like other forms of social enterprises, Benefit Corporations use business models to solve problems benefiting society at large. The Benefit Corporation is not really a new type of business organization, although it is often advertised as such. Instead, it is a corporation whose company documents have been amended to formalize its commitment to social responsibility and to the welfare of its stakeholders, including employees and the members of communities where the companies conduct business.

In order to be classified as a Benefit Corporation, a company must undergo an independent audit using a social responsibility rating system to assess a company's social and environmental performance. An independent, nonprofit organization called "B Lab" conducts the audit. A company earning a satisfactory score may use the Benefit Corporation designation to communicate to the public its commitment to social responsibility. Thus, a Benefit Corporation designation is intended to help the public distinguish between "good companies" and "good marketing." To maintain the Benefit Corporation designation, a company must be re-certified every two years and also be subject to random, unannounced audits. A majority of states rapidly enacted benefit corporation statutes, including California, Connecticut, Delaware, Florida, Illinois, Maryland, Massachusetts, Minnesota, Nebraska, Nevada, New Hampshire, New Jersey, New York, Pennsylvania, Vermont, Virginia — as well as the nation's capital, Washington DC.

---

91. The organization must significantly further the accomplishment of one or more charitable or educational purposes as determined by 26 U.S.C. § 170 (c)(2)(B).

Chapter 3

Incorporation

Situation

a. One week after your last meeting with your clients, and before you have been able to proceed further than helping them decide on incorporation, you receive an agitated phone call from Anderson. He tells you that two weeks ago, after reaching a "solid" agreement with Baker that they should go into business together, he entered into a one-year lease with Southhold Properties, Inc. He signed in the name of "Biologistics Corporation" and purported to commit that corporation to pay $20,000 annual rent, for space in a building recently erected in an industrial park. He does not recall informing Baker of the details of the signing, but says, "She knows I did something about getting a place to set up shop, and it's O.K. by her." He is certain that Phillips knows nothing about the transaction. He said that at the time he entered into the lease, he guessed they would want to form a corporation and felt he needed to finalize the lease since someone else was interested in the space.

His call has been prompted by a recent confrontation with Southhold's rental manager, who accidentally learned of the non-existence of Biologistics Corporation. Anderson is not sure what Southhold's position ultimately is going to be, but he is concerned about the legality of the lease, which he says the enterprise needs, and also about his own possible liability.

b. After you resolve the problems relating to the Southhold lease, your clients want you to proceed as quickly as possible to form their corporation. Discussion has revealed the following:

1. If possible, your clients would like to have their organization called Biologistics, Inc.

2. They have definitely decided that Anderson, Baker, and Phillips should be on the board of directors. Baker thinks it would be a good idea to add one additional director. She proposes Professor Herbert Li, a nationally known expert on DNA who teaches at the local university. Anderson thinks the selection would be good from the point of view of publicity, but fears dilution of his share of control over the enterprise.

3. At least in the next several years, your clients expect their corporation to have an office or laboratory only in the state where your firm has its offices. They are hoping, however, to develop a nationwide reputation and have definite plans to sell out of state.

4. Your clients want to insure that their corporation will be fully authorized to synthesize and sell DNA and to develop and exploit the DNA manipulation process on which they expect to work. Baker has also pointed out that, as time goes by, they may wish to branch into related areas.

5. Anderson has heard that there might be benefits from incorporating in Delaware.

c. If your clients decide they want to incorporate in Delaware or another state where you are not licensed, may you represent them? May/should an attorney act as the incorporator? The secretary of the corporation? A member of the board of directors? (*See* Model Rule 1.7)

Section I
The Corporation

The history of American business organization law is a compelling story. During the nineteenth century, the energy of the fledgling U.S. economy encouraged experimentation with different business forms. The following pages tell the story of the rise of the modern business corporation and the influences that shaped its development.

A. What a Corporation Is

One of the oldest and most interesting questions in corporation law is the question of what a corporation is. A corporation, or at least its legal form,[1] is a creation of the state. Individuals have never had the power by themselves to create business corporations or, put another way, never have individuals had the power to create enterprises as corporations. In the United States, business corporations have been formed by the special act of a state legislature or of Congress[2] or, more usually in modern times, by a state official acting under the authority of a general corporation statute.

If a corporation, or at least its legal form, is a creation of the state, just what kind of creation is it? In American law, our earliest authoritative answer was by Chief

---

1. This parenthetical is necessary because there is a body of scholarship developed by the corporate "realists" during the seventy-five-year period ending in the late 1940s that views the corporation essentially as the corporate enterprise. Adolph Berle, for example, wrote that "the entity commonly known as 'corporate entity' takes its being from the reality of the underlying enterprise." Berle, *The Theory of Enterprise Entity*, 47 Colum. L. Rev. 343 (1947).

Unlike corporations, individuals do not need state authorization to form sole proprietorships and general partnerships. Partnerships are, however, governed by state business organization law. There are no separate state business codes establishing sole proprietorships as a form of business.

2. Probably the most famous private corporation formed by a special Act of Congress was the Second Bank of the United States, which was the subject of *McCulloch v. Maryland*, 17 U.S. 316 (1819).

Justice Marshall in the *Dartmouth College* case: "A corporation is an artificial being, invisible, intangible, and existing only in contemplation of law."[3]

American judicial comment has tended to follow the Marshall conception, but there are some exceptions, the most notable being from *Farmers' Loan & Trust Co. v. Pierson*:

> [A] corporation is more nearly a method than a thing, and ... the law in dealing with a corporation has no need of defining it as a person or an entity, or even as an embodiment of functions, rights and duties, but may treat it as a name for a useful and usual collection of jural relations, each one of which must in every instance be ascertained, analyzed and assigned to its appropriate place according to the circumstances of the particular case, having due regard to the purposes to be achieved.[4]

Along this same line is *Scandia Down Corp. v. Euroquilt, Inc.*,[5] in which the Seventh Circuit said that "[t]he corporation is just a convenient name for a complex web of contracts among managers, workers, and suppliers of equity and debt capital." Cases like *Farmers' Loan* and *Scandia Down* are not so much rejections of Marshall's conception as they are reminders that reference to that conception does not answer specific legal questions about the rights and obligations of a particular corporation and the persons involved with it.

The most useful conception of the corporation begins with a view of the corporation as an entity having a legal status separate and distinct from the people who comprise it and consisting of a structure within which the corporate enterprise (basically its assets and its personnel taken together as a going concern) is contained.

Taking this into consideration, we can now say that: A corporation is an entity that consists of an intangible structure for the conduct of the entity's affairs and operations, the essence of which is created by the state, and that possesses the rights and obligations given or allowed it by the state.[6]

As to both rights and obligations, drafters of statutes of general applicability typically wish to include corporations along with natural persons, and they usually accomplish this by including corporations within the definition of "person." For example, Congress has provided at 1 U.S.C. § 1 that "[i]n determining the meaning of any Act of Congress, unless the context indicates otherwise ... the [word] 'person'... [includes] corporations." State codes often provide likewise.

The common law has also long considered a corporation to possess the same rights and obligations as a natural person when that seems appropriate. Criminal law offers the most interesting example, with courts having a history, going back at least to the

---

3. *Trustees of Dartmouth College v. Woodward*, 17 U.S. 518, 636 (1819).

4. 222 N.Y.S. 532, 544–45 (1927).

5. 772 F.2d 1423 (7th Cir. 1985).

6. The Model Business Corporation Act (1984, as amended through 2008), hereinafter the Model Act, was drafted by the Committee on Corporate Laws of the American Bar Association's Section of Business Law. It has been adopted in whole or in significant part by more than half of the states.

mid-seventeenth century, of treating corporations as they would natural persons in the context of some common law crimes.

With respect to federal constitutional rights, the picture changes only slightly. All questions relating to the constitutional rights of corporations as persons have not been answered, but the most important have been. Corporations have the first amendment right of free speech and enjoy the due process and equal protection rights granted to persons by the fifth and fourteenth amendments. Corporations have fourth amendment protection against unreasonable searches and seizures, although the Supreme Court has indicated that this protection is not necessarily as extensive as that enjoyed by natural persons. Finally, the Supreme Court has held that corporations do not enjoy the fifth amendment's protection against self-incrimination.

In sum, it may be said that corporations have largely the same rights and obligations as do natural persons, although the parallel is not exact. This conclusion allows us to complete our statement of what a corporation is: A corporation is an entity that consists of an intangible structure for the conduct of the entity's affairs and operations, the essence of which is created by the state, and that possesses the rights and obligations given or allowed it by the state, which rights and obligations more or less parallel those of natural persons.

B. Development of American Business Corporation Law

The law in America relating to business corporations underwent extensive development during the nineteenth century, and that development has continued, along somewhat different lines, to the present time. It will be helpful if we examine those developments one century at a time.

1. Nineteenth Century

At the beginning of the nineteenth century, American entrepreneurs could choose to form either a common law general partnership or a statutory corporation. Both were British imports. At that time, investors in both types had unlimited liability. The key differences between the two lay in their governance structures. The general partnership had a participatory form of governance; the corporation had centralized management. In the 1820s, the U.S. imported the limited partnership form from France. The form offered limited liability to partners who did not participate in management. It also avoided some of the technical requirements then characteristic of corporate formation. Over time, the corporate form shed many attributes that had originally limited its popularity. The transformation to the modern corporation resulted from three separate movements in the development of American business corporation law during the nineteenth century:

> 1. The movement from incorporation by special legislative acts to incorporation under the provisions of a general corporation statute.
>
> 2. The movement from restrictive toward enabling corporation statutes.
>
> 3. The movement from unlimited to limited liability of shareholders.

Each movement formed an essential step in creating the modern American business corporation and the ascendancy of the popularity of the corporate form.

a. From Special Acts to General Corporation Statutes

At the beginning of the nineteenth century, corporations were formed only by the special acts of state legislatures or, occasionally, Congress. That began to change in 1811, when New York passed what might be called the first general corporation statute, although "general" is a bit strained in this context, since the statute provided only for the incorporation of businesses engaged in the manufacture of a few specified products. Other states began following New York's lead, and in 1837 Connecticut adopted a general corporation statute that allowed the incorporation of any lawful business. This process of moving to truly general corporation statutes continued state by state throughout the rest of the nineteenth century and was complete by the century's end.

b. From Restrictive to Enabling Statutes

At the beginning of the nineteenth century, all the corporate charters granted by special legislative acts were restrictive, and that restrictiveness carried over into the general corporation statutes that states passed with increasing frequency as the century progressed. The statutory restrictions on corporations took many forms, all relating to the widely held fear of the evils that might befall society from the existence of powerful corporations. One restriction was a limit on the amount of capital a corporation could amass. As Brandeis described the reason behind that restriction, "[t]here was a sense of some insidious menace inherent in large aggregations of capital, particularly when held by corporations."[7]

A nineteenth century restriction that went hand in hand with the limitation on capital was a limitation on the amount of indebtedness a corporation could maintain. Another typical provision in the restrictive statutes of the nineteenth century was a limitation on the duration of corporations, with the usual limits ranging from twenty to fifty years. Also among these limitations was a prohibition on a corporation's owning stock in another corporation.

The corporate trust came into prominence in the 1870s as a way to minimize the effect of these restrictions, with the Standard Oil Trust the most famous. The nineteenth century trust was the forerunner of the modern holding company, and it operated in much the same way. Shareholders in a group of related corporations, each with a restrictive charter, deeded their shares to trustees who managed the corporate group as a single enterprise.

The nineteenth century corporate trust was short-lived, however, as a device for avoiding restrictive corporation statutes. The reason was simple: Restrictive statutes began to disappear. In 1896, New Jersey passed a full-blown enabling (non-restrictive)

---

7. *Louis K. Liggett Co. v. Lee*, 288 U.S. 517, 549 (1933) (Brandeis, J., dissenting).

statute. The New Jersey corporation rather than the trust became the vehicle of choice for large businesses. (The Standard Oil Trust was an early convert, incorporating in New Jersey in 1882.) During the last quarter of the nineteenth century, other states began following New Jersey's lead. As Justice Brandeis put it, "the great industrial states yielded in order not to lose wholly the prospect of revenue and the control incident to domestic incorporation."[8] The enabling concept continues to be fine-tuned to the present time. Most of the recent examples of fine-tuning have concerned internal matters of corporate decision making.

c. From Unlimited to Limited Liability

Perhaps the most important nineteenth century development in corporation law was the movement from unlimited to limited liability of shareholders. When the century opened, unlimited shareholder liability was the norm for American corporations. That rule eroded as the century progressed, and by 1900 limited liability was virtually universal. In 1911, when Nicholas Murray Butler was president of Columbia University, he put the importance of these developments this way:

> I weigh my words when I say that in my judgment the limited liability corporation is the greatest single discovery of modern times.... Even steam and electricity are far less important than the limited liability corporation, and they would be reduced to comparative impotence without it.[9]

A 2015 publication of *Popular Science* celebrates the limited liability feature of the corporation as among the "100 inventions that changed the world"—along with rockets, satellites and other accomplishments. Corporate separateness is valuable because it enables entrepreneurs and financiers to take risks knowing precisely what their financial exposure is.

Business people put heavy and valuable reliance on the practice of using separate entities to do business, whether entities that are entirely independent of one another or mutually dependent and whether operated autonomously or subject to stringent oversight. Recognizing the legitimacy and genuineness of these important business practices and attitudes, it is difficult to justify disregarding the separate existence of duly organized corporate entities, whether traditional corporations or modern limited liability companies. There is a presumption in favor of respecting corporate separateness to protect the reasonable reliance of entrepreneurs and financiers alike.

On the other hand, limited liability is not free from a social standpoint. The cost is incurred every time a company goes bankrupt leaving creditors unpaid. The net social gain is huge but the costs should not be ignored entirely. To repeat, the gains are mainly: (1) an increased amount of capital invested for the provision of goods and services and (2) an increased tolerance for risk taking with the capital that is invested.

---

8. *Id.* 559–60.
9. *Quoted in* 1 William Meade Fletcher, Cyclopedia of the Law of Private Corporations § 21 (1917).

2. Twentieth Century

During the twentieth century, American business corporation law continued to develop. Delaware emerged as the leading corporate state, accompanied by a trend toward congruence with Delaware in other states' laws and approaches to corporations. Further, there was the movement from corporate regulation by the states to increasing co-regulation by the federal government.

a. Delaware and Congruence

When the twentieth century began, New Jersey was the premier corporate state. That soon changed. When Woodrow Wilson became governor in 1911, he immediately mounted an effort to return to a restrictive approach to corporations. The legislature agreed and in 1913 gutted the enabling provisions from New Jersey's corporation statute. Consequences followed quickly. Corporations flocked to Delaware, which had a statute very much like the old New Jersey statute. And under the commerce clause of the federal Constitution, these corporations had the right to operate in New Jersey and in any other state so long as they were engaged in interstate commerce. From New Jersey's viewpoint the net results were these: salutary effect from corporate reforms, zero; loss of revenues from corporations, substantial. New Jersey stood that for only four years. In 1917, with Woodrow Wilson in the White House, the New Jersey legislature again amended its corporation statute, this time to undo the Wilson-era reforms.

By 1917, however, large corporations had come to like their home in Delaware, and they had no interest in moving back to New Jersey. Delaware ever since has continued to be hospitable to corporations. Its legislature has moved quickly in response to corporate desires for changes in its corporation statute. Its approach to corporate taxation has always been a gentle milking, with care being taken not to squeeze enough to hurt. Its secretary of state's office has been run like a good service business. And its courts, which like those of all states have the power to hear cases involving domestic corporations no matter where a controversy arises, have had judges who are knowledgeable in corporation law. As a result, most of America's largest corporations have been incorporated in Delaware.

During the twentieth century, however, there has developed a great congruence in corporation statutes and to a lesser degree in the ways in which the states approach corporations. All states have and have had for decades an enabling corporation statute. This has resulted from two forces. First, each state knows that having a restrictive corporation statute will cost it revenues and will have no real effect, as New Jersey learned to its great cost. Second, the Model Business Corporation Act (1969), hereinafter Model Act (1969), and its successor, the Model Act (1984), have been available for easy adoption, as a majority of the states have done.

b. State and Federal Oversight

At the turn of the twentieth century, the regulation of corporations was virtually the sole concern of the states, and that was especially true with respect to regulation of the internal affairs of corporations. The New Deal securities legislation, especially the Securities Exchange Act of 1934 (the Exchange Act), changed this substantially. Most of this legislation relates directly to the issuance or trading of securities and is properly considered securities regulation rather than corporate regulation. Some of this legislation, however, serves almost purely to fill gaps that Congress saw in the state scheme for the regulation of the affairs of corporations.

c. Alternatives to the Corporate Form

A final notable phenomenon in the development of business law in the latter 20th and early 21st centuries was the proliferation of alternative forms of business organization. The rise of the limited liability partnership and the limited liability company are the most prominent examples. These trace their origins to the limited partnership and the corporation, respectively, and are defined by the high degree to which investors in them may enjoy the benefits of limited liability along with other advantages. At one time, entrepreneurs had to accept trade-offs among alternative forms of business organization, such as between the limited shareholder liability of the corporate form that was subject to two levels of taxation or the single taxation of the partnership that exposed partners to unlimited liability. The rise of these alternative forms has eliminated such trade-offs, thanks to statutory and contractual innovations that combine the appealing attributes of historical forms of business organization into modern hybrids. Governance features in these new forms of business organization are extensively tailored by contract and therefore even more variable than the traditional partnership and corporation.

C. Types of American Corporations

There are four types of corporations in America: public, government, nonprofit, and business.

1. Public Corporations

Public corporations are corporations that function as governments. The most common examples are municipalities such as cities, towns, and villages. Also common are governmental authorities of various sorts that serve some special purpose, airport authorities being a common example. Public corporations are sometimes formed by a special legislative act. In most situations, however, incorporation is by the secretary of state or another state official acting under the authority of a general incorporation statute. As in the case of all corporations, the rights and obligations of public corporations are spelled out by statute, and typically these rights and obligations are in general similar to the rights and obligations of business corporations.

2. Government Corporations

Government corporations are corporations that are wholly or partly owned by a government and that were formed by that government to perform some special purpose. Examples are Amtrak and the Tennessee Valley Authority, the first of which is partly owned and the second of which is wholly owned by the federal government.

These corporations and twenty-two others were formed by special Acts of Congress and are subject to a common set of laws relating, in the main, to their finances. The reason Congress formed these government corporations was to take their organization, their operations, and their finances out of the governmental sphere and place them in a more businesslike structure. The best-known government corporation is the United States Postal Service.

3. Nonprofit Corporations

There is a great deal of confusion in the public's mind about what it means to be a nonprofit corporation. What distinguishes nonprofit from business corporations is the fact that nonprofit corporations do not have shareholders or owners of any kind. They may or may not have members. If they do, the members may function very much like shareholders. In a nonprofit corporation, however, profits may not be paid to the members as dividends. This does not mean that the corporation may not or should not make profits. Many hospitals, for example, are operated by nonprofit corporations, and their managers try hard to earn profits. The difference in this respect between nonprofit and business corporations simply is in what may be done with the profits.

Nonprofit corporations are of two types: charitable and mutual-benefit. The distinguishing characteristic is whether the purpose of the corporation is to benefit its members or to benefit some other group or groups. Hospitals, private universities, and charities of all descriptions are typically organized in the form of charitable nonprofit corporations, while social clubs offer a common example of mutual-benefit nonprofit corporations.

The tax treatment of nonprofit corporations varies depending upon whether the corporation is eleemosynary or mutual-benefit. Basically, a charitable eleemosynary corporation does not pay taxes on its profits, and contributions to the corporation are deductible by the donors. As in the case of a charitable corporation, a mutual-benefit nonprofit corporation escapes taxes on its profits, but contributions to the mutual-benefit corporation are not deductible by the contributors. Profits of nonprofit corporations that arise from essentially commercial activities are taxable in a manner comparable to profits of business corporations.

4. Business Corporations

Business corporations are of two types: publicly held and closely held. We believe the best way to define the closely held corporation is by reference to whether there is a ready market for the corporation's stock. The presence or absence of a ready market for a corporation's stock is the major determinant in how a shareholder views his or her relationship to the corporation. In a corporation whose stock cannot easily be traded, a shareholder is likely to take a personal, long-term interest in the corporation. This shareholder is likely to view himself or herself as an owner of the corporation in a direct sense, and one can view this kind of shareholder relationship as a secondary characteristic of a closely held corporation. In a corporation having stock with a ready market, however, a shareholder is much more likely to view himself or herself primarily as the owner of a corporation's shares rather than as an owner of the corporation itself in any real sense. The owner of a small percentage of the stock of a local business may say, "I own a piece of that business." If he or she owns a small percentage of the shares of Microsoft Corporation, the statement is more likely to be, "I own some Microsoft stock."

Finally, of course, the opposite of "closely held" is "publicly held," and when one looks at the publicly held corporation, one almost necessarily focuses on the ease with which shares of the corporation trade in the public markets, which is another way of saying that there is a ready market for the corporation's stock. A well-known and easy-to-apply test exists, one that nearly fits the requirements for distinguishing between closely held and publicly held corporations. The test is whether the corporation is required to file the reports called for by § 13 of the Securities Exchange Act of 1934 (the Exchange Act). This filing requirement arises in one of three ways: (1) the corporation has securities registered under § 12(b) of the Exchange Act because these securities trade on a securities exchange, (2) the corporation has securities registered under § 12(g) of the Exchange Act because it has assets exceeding $10 million and a class of equity security held of record by 500 or more persons, or (3) the corporation is required, under the provisions of Exchange Act § 15(d), to file § 13 reports because it has in the past registered securities for public sale under the Securities Act of 1933. If a corporation meets any one of these requirements, it becomes what corporation lawyers call a "reporting company." The reporting company/nonreporting company dichotomy almost exactly duplicates the publicly held/closely held corporation dichotomy insofar as corporations go, because this duplication is exactly what the Exchange Act is designed to accomplish with its reporting requirements. If a corporation's stock is traded in the public markets, Congress wanted to ensure that the corporation would make public the information that is contained in the reports required to be filed by Exchange Act § 13.

There are consequences of the determination as to whether a corporation is closely held or publicly held. First, closely held corporations sometimes are allowed greater latitude than publicly held corporations in their internal management. The second consequence of being classified as a closely held corporation can be more important. In a series of decisions going back over several three decades, courts have developed the doctrine that shareholders in closely held corporations stand in a fiduciary relationship to each other. Finally, and what may be most important, publicly held corporations having securities registered under Exchange Act § 12 are subject to a whole range of special requirements and constraints.

These differing treatments of closely held and publicly held corporations are important. More interesting is the fact that in a significant part of corporation law, closely held and publicly held corporations are treated exactly the same, because corporate statutes have flexibility built into the statutory provisions. With this flexibility, the statute can serve the needs of the large publicly held corporation and the desires of the sole shareholder of a one person corporation. The Model Act also contains some provisions applicable only to privately held companies. Further, some states, like Delaware, have passed statutes or statutory supplements relating only to closely held corporations.

Section II
Promoters' Contracts

The term "promoter" is a term of art applied to persons who organize a business. They are the entrepreneurs responsible for bringing together all of the components required to transform a business opportunity into a business operation. To accomplish this result, they coordinate and complete several types of activities. They organize the business aspects of the company, such as finding investors, arranging for office space, hiring employees, purchasing capital equipment and the like, many of which involve entering into contracts. At the same time, they plan the business organization's legal structure, and have the necessary documents prepared and filed. When the company being formed is a limited liability firm, like a corporation, the interrelationships among these activities are more complicated than is the case with the formation of a sole proprietorship or general partnership. The reasons are that limited liability businesses do not legally exist until all statutory formalities have been completed, and the persons organizing the business do not expect to be personally liable for the company's obligations. Consequently, contractual obligations are often undertaken on behalf of the company to be formed, rather than by the promoters themselves.

There are many ways these contracts can be handled, some of which may have results that are not intended or desired by those who make the contracts. The rules relating to these contracts are part of the common-law doctrine of promoters' contracts, and questions relating to them can most helpfully be divided into two categories. The first category is the rights and liabilities of corporations on promoters' contracts, and the second is the rights and liabilities of promoters on promoters' contracts. These two categories will be taken up in separate sections of this chapter.

A. Liabilities of Corporations on Promoters' Contracts

The legal difficulties surrounding promoters' contracts stem from two circumstances. One is that although the promoter enters into the contract, all parties expect that the corporation to be formed will be responsible for contract performance. Thus, at the time of contracting, the promoter acts on behalf of a nonexistent principal. The second is that once formed, the corporation may accept or reject the contract. Consequently, no matter what a contract by its terms provides about the liabilities of a corporation that is not yet formed, the corporation is not bound by the contract unless after it is formed it takes some action to make the contract its own or takes some action that will cause a court to estop the corporation from denying that it is bound by the contract.

Ratification

The doctrine of ratification is so generally useful in the corporate context that when faced with the problem of how to make a promoter's contract a corporation's own, lawyers often think first of having the corporation ratify the acts of a promoter in making the contract. Ratification is accomplished formally when the board of directors adopts a resolution saying that the acts of the promoter in executing and delivering the contract are ratified. The problem with ratification, however, is that it relates back to the point in time when the action that is being ratified occurred. That is, the effect of ratification is retroactively to authorize whatever act is being ratified, as of the time of the act. Since, in the case of a promoter's contract, no corporation was in existence at the time the promoter executed and delivered the contract, ratification is a logical impossibility.

Adoption

In the case of promoters' contracts, the way for a corporation to bind itself to the contract is by adoption, which works in much the same way as ratification, except that adoption does not have retroactive effect. A corporation may adopt a contract in one of two ways, formally or informally. For a formal adoption, the board of directors passes a resolution stating that it adopts the contract. This is the safest course if a corporation has any question about the desire of the party on the other side of the contract to go through with the contract. Usually, however, adoption is informal, with the typical adoption scenario seeing the newly formed corporation performing obligations under the contract with knowledge of the contract's terms.

McArthur v. Times Printing Co.

Minnesota Supreme Court
51 N.W. 216 (1892)

MITCHELL, J.

The complaint alleges that about October 1, 1889, the defendant contracted with plaintiff for his services as advertising solicitor for one year; that in April, 1890, it discharged him, in violation of the contract. The action is to recover damages for the breach of the contract. The answer sets up two defenses: (1) That plaintiff's employment was not for any stated time, but only from week to week; (2) that he was discharged for good cause. Upon the trial there was evidence reasonably tending to prove that in September, 1889, one C. A. Nimocks and others were engaged as promoters in procuring the organization of the defendant company to publish a newspaper; that, about September 12th, Nimocks, as such promoter, made a contract with plaintiff, in behalf of the contemplated company, for his services as advertising solicitor for the period of one year from and after October 1st, — the date at which it was expected that the company would be organized; that the corporation was not, in fact, organized until October 16th, but that the publication of the paper was commenced by the promoters October 1st, at which date plaintiff, in pursuance of his arrangement with Nimocks, entered upon the discharge of his duties as advertising solicitor for the paper; that after the organization of the company he continued in its employment in the same capacity until discharged the following April; that defendant's board of directors never took any formal action with reference to the contract made in its behalf by Nimocks, but all of the stockholders, directors, and officers of the corporation knew of this contract at the time of its organization, or were informed of it soon afterwards, and none of them objected to or repudiated it, but, on the contrary, retained plaintiff in the employment of the company without any other or new contract as to his services.

There is a line of cases which hold that where a contract is made in behalf of, and for the benefit of, a projected corporation, the corporation, after its organization, cannot become a party to the contract, either by adoption or ratification of it. This, however, seems to be more a question of name than of substance; that is, whether the liability of the corporation, in such cases, is to be placed on the grounds of its adoption of the contract of its promoters, or upon some other ground, such as equitable estoppel. This court, in accordance with what we deem sound reason, as well as the weight of authority, has held that, while a corporation is not bound by engagements made on its behalf by its promoters before its organization, it may, after its organization, make such engagements its own contracts. And this it may do precisely as it might make similar original contracts; formal action of its board of directors being necessary only where it would be necessary in the case of a similar original contract. That it is not requisite that such adoption or acceptance be expressed, but it may be inferred from acts or acquiescence on part of the corporation, or its authorized agents, as any similar original contract might be shown. The right of the corporate agents to adopt an agreement originally made by promoters depends upon the purposes of the corporation and the nature of the agreement. Of course, the agreement must be one which the corporation itself could make, and one which the usual agents of the company have express or implied authority to make. That the contract in this case was of that kind is very clear; and the acts and acquiescence of the corporate officers, after the organization of the company, fully justified the jury in finding that it had adopted it as its own.

The defendant, however, claims that the contract was void under the statute of frauds, because, "by its terms, not to be performed within one year from the making thereof," which counsel assumes to be September 12th, — the date of the agreement between plaintiff and the promoter. This proceeds upon the erroneous theory that the act of the corporation, in such cases, is a ratification, which relates back to the date of the contract with the promoter, under the familiar maxim that "a subsequent ratification has a retroactive effect, and is equivalent to a prior command." But the liability of the corporation, under such circumstances, does not rest upon any principle of the law of agency, but upon the immediate and voluntary act of the company. Although the acts of a corporation with reference to the contracts made by promoters in its behalf before its organization are frequently loosely termed "ratification," yet a "ratification," properly so called, implies an existing person, on whose behalf the contract might have been made at the time. There cannot, in law, be a ratification of a contract which could not have been made binding on the ratifier at the time it was made, because the ratifier was not then in existence. What is called "adoption," in such cases, is, in legal effect, the making of a contract of the date of the adoption, and not as of some former date. The contract in this case was, therefore, not within the statute of frauds. The trial court fairly submitted to the jury all the issues of fact in this case, accompanied by instructions as to the law which were exactly in the line of the views we have expressed; and the evidence justified the verdict. [**Affirmed.**]

B. Rights and Liabilities of Promoters on Promoters' Contracts

Promoters generally are personally liable under promoters' contracts, largely because, to be enforceable, a contract has to have at least one party on each side, and as we have just seen, a corporation cannot be bound to a contract when it is not yet in existence. In the garden-variety promoters' contract, where the promoter simply signs on behalf of the to-be-formed corporation, if the promoter were not bound by the contract, there would not be a contract. In terms of agency principles, this result is explained by the rule that if an agent purports to act for a nonexistent principal, the agent is personally bound. The general rule of promoters' liability does not always hold true, however, and whether or not a promoter is bound by a promoters' contract often turns on (1) what the parties seem to have intended and (2) how the contract is drafted.

Promoter's Liability After a Corporation's Adoption

Assume that a promoter enters into a standard promoters' contract under which he or she is bound, and assume further that the corporation that is to have the benefit of the contract is formed and adopts the contract. Is the promoter thereby released from personal liability? The promoter probably will assume so, but that is not the case. Absent a novation whereby the other contracting party releases the promoter from liability upon accepting a substituted party, the promoter will remain liable along with the now formed corporation. To guard against promoters' liability, then, either (1) language contemplating an automatic novation upon adoption of the contract by the to-be-formed corporation must be included in the contract or (2) a novation (either formal or one that can be inferred from words or actions of the other contracting party) must be effected after the to-be-formed corporation has adopted the contract.

Intent of the Parties

Care is needed in dealing with the question of intent of the parties in the context of promoters' contracts, because the question of what the parties intended needs to be approached in a special way. Suppose, as is often the case, a promoter negotiates a contract on behalf of a nonexistent corporation without telling the other party that the corporation has not yet been formed and then the promoter signs in the name of the corporation. In such a situation, the parties clearly intended that the corporation and not the promoter be bound. This situation, however, is an example of the classic, garden-variety promoters' contract that is covered by the general rule that the promoter is liable and the corporation is not. So looking for "what the parties intended" cannot be taken literally.

How a Contract Is Drafted

How a contract is drafted also significantly affects a promoter's possible liability. Any language that a court can interpret as indicating an intent that the promoter is not to be personally liable may be used by the court to relieve the promoter of liability. But unless the language is clear beyond argument, a court can be expected to be guided in its contract interpretation, subconsciously at least, by how it perceives the equities of the situation. That being the case, the only safe course for a promoter who wishes to escape personal liability on a standard promoters' contract is to include clear language in the contract saying explicitly that the other contracting party will look only to the to-be-formed corporation for performance. A pitfall to be avoided here, of course, is lack of consideration, so the promoter should ensure that the other party receives something in the bargain that will provide the necessary consideration.

Another possibility for a promoter is to secure a written option from the other contracting party by which the other party grants to the promoter, for the benefit of the to-be-formed corporation, an option to enter into a specified contract. This is often the most artful way to ensure that the promoter escapes personal liability while also assuring the right of the to-be-formed corporation to enter into a desired contract. As in the case of the standard promoters' contract, of course, the promoter needs to be sure that the option is supported by sufficient consideration.

Section III
Where and How to Incorporate

A. State Chartering Business

Key considerations. The decision where to incorporate involves consideration of three factors: the substantive provisions of state incorporation law; the cost of incorporating in a state other than the one where the company does business; and whether the company will be closely or publicly-held. Substantive provisions of state corporate laws are a factor because the law of the state of incorporation governs the corporation's internal affairs. It also determines what options are available for the corporate governance and financial structures. Today, however, there is widespread congruence of corporation law among the various states. This congruence usually makes it easy to choose the state of incorporation.

For the typical corporation, the clear choice is the state where the corporation is principally to operate. Virtually without exception, the corporation law of that state will be based on a modern enabling statute that offers any options needed for the efficient operation of a start-up corporation. Some desirable options admittedly may not be available in the home state's corporation statute, but for the start-up corporation, usually it is preferable to forgo such options rather than to incorporate in another state. This is not to say, of course, that home state incorporation is always desirable. Suppose, for example, that the proposed directors of a particular corporation live in different states, so that getting together for board meetings is impractical. In such a corporation, it is necessary to incorporate in a state that allows either telephone board meetings or written consents in lieu of board meetings.

The second consideration relates to the expense and trouble of incorporating in a state other than the one where the company does business. If a firm is incorporated in a state other than its home state, it will be treated as a corporation of the other state, and must therefore qualify to do business in its home state as a foreign corporation. It will also have to file reports and pay fees each year not only in its state of incorporation but in its home state as well. These additional costs may be strong negatives for the closely-held corporation that does business in only one state.

For some corporations there will be tax savings to be had by incorporating other than in the home state. For the typical start-up corporation, the tax rates of the various states are irrelevant, since in almost all cases the corporation will pay the state's minimum tax, typically $100 or so. The rates become relevant, however, for corporations that expect to have their shares publicly held by a large number of shareholders, since taxes often are based on the number of shares that the corporation is authorized to issue.

Companies planning to operate in multiple states or to be publicly held usually give serious consideration to incorporating in Delaware. Delaware's corporation statute has a full range of options a particular corporation may find necessary or desirable. For example, it allows board meetings to be conducted by telephone and written consents in lieu of board meetings. It also contains a chapter addressing issues of closely held corporations. And when it comes to tax savings for corporations that are to have a large number of public shareholders, Delaware often wins out as the state of incorporation, since its corporate tax structure has been carefully designed to beat the competition.

For the corporation that does business in many states, Delaware also is often the state of choice for incorporation because of its judiciary, which is highly competent in corporation law, and its large and well developed body of existing corporate case law, which sometimes adds a legal certainty that may be lacking in other states. For such corporations, which already have to stand the expense and trouble of qualifying to do business in many states, the possible extra expense of qualifying in the corporation's home state is too small to worry about. Also, the fast and efficient service available from the Delaware Secretary of State's office adds a benefit to Delaware incorporation. In addition, the appeal to lawyers or clients of Delaware's law on one or more particular matters, such as directors' liability, may be enough to make them settle on Delaware incorporation.

Note on the "Race" Debtate

Why is Delaware the leading state of incorporation among large publicly-traded corporations? As a small state in both geographic area and population, its sources of revenues are somewhat limited. Corporation franchise taxes contribute a substantial percentage of the state's total budget—a source of revenue that is trivial in large commercial states such as California and New York or Texas and Florida. For nearly a century, therefore, Delaware's leadership, has put a high premium on corporate law preeminence.

All branches of Delaware government manifest the state's commitment to corporate law preeminence: the state's executive branch processes corporate forms and provides related services efficiently; its legislative branch promptly passes legislation in response to changing business conditions; and its judiciary handles cases swiftly and proficiently and maintains a separate court of equity to hear corporate disputes (the Court of Chancery). Associated professional and civic organizations reinforce the states culture of corporate professionalism: the state bar association's corporate lawyers help draft legislation and many take turns serving tenures on the state's courts.

For all that, debate has long existed about whether Delaware's leadership serves the national interest or might that interest be better served by a national corporation law enacted by Congress in preemption of state corporation law. The terms of that debate, whose tenor varies with the country's economic and business fortunes, are summarized in the following passage from a book by Roberta Romano, *The Genius of American Corporation Law* (1993).

> The extraordinary success of tiny Delaware in the corporate charter market due to its responsiveness to changing corporate demands is the source, then, of a recurrent corporate law debate on the efficacy of federalism. Who benefits from the laws produced in a federal system, and, in particular, from Delaware's corporation code: managers, who select the state of incorporation, or shareholders, who ratify that selection? Does state competition produce corporation codes that mitigate the agency problem or exacerbate it? If state codes favor managers over shareholders, then from the objective of corporate law itself, the output of state competition is undesirable. Whether the current allocation of authority between the state governments and the national government should be maintained under such circumstances depends on whether the outcome would differ under a national corporation code....
>
> The classic positions in the modern debate on whether state corporation codes benefit shareholders were formulated in the 1970s by William Cary, professor at Columbia Law School and former commissioner of the Securities and Exchange Commission, and Ralph Winter, professor at Yale Law School (currently a federal appeals court judge). Cary contended that Delaware's heavy reliance on incorporation fees for revenue led it to engage in a "race for the bottom" with other states to adopt laws that favor managers over shareholders. He therefore advocated national corporate law standards to end state competition. Cary's position was, for many years, the consensus view of commentators on corporate law, and his agenda still attracts support....
>
> Winter identified a crucial flaw in Cary's analysis, which, when corrected, suggested that the race was more to the top than the bottom: Cary had overlooked the many markets in which firms operate — the capital, product, and corporate control markets — and that constrain managers from choosing a legal regime detrimental to the shareholders' interest. While agreeing with Cary's characterization of the power of competition in producing laws that firms demand, Winter's important point was that firms operating under a legal regime that did not maximize firm value would be outperformed by

firms operating under a legal regime that did and the former would therefore have lower stock prices.

A lower stock price could subject a firm's managers to either employment termination, as the firm is driven out of business because of a higher cost of capital than that of competitors operating under a value-maximizing regime, or replacement by a successful takeover bidder that could increase a firm's value by reincorporating (the term of art for a change in statutory domicile). Winter concluded that this threat of job displacement would lead managers to demand a value-maximizing regime for their shareholders and that states would provide it, as such a strategy maintains, if not enhances, a state's incorporation business. Winter's critique forced adherents of the Cary position to amend it. The contention became that markets are imperfect constraints on managers and, hence, there is sufficient slack in the system to produce non-value-maximizing state laws.

In both the Cary and the Winter positions, the goal of maximizing revenues functions as an invisible hand guiding the decentralized system of state corporation laws to codify the arrangements that firms desire. The crux of their disagreement concerns [whether managers or shareholders are] driving the system. Cary and the proponents of a national corporation code consider [corporate law] to be derived from managers' preferences. They view the state legislative process as a political market failure in which managers are better organized than the more numerous but dispersed shareholders, and they characterize managers' preferences for codes as diametrically opposed to those of shareholders'.

Winter and advocates of state chartering conclude that shareholders' preferences [control] because of the constraining influence on managers of the many markets in which firms operate, which reduces or eliminates the agency problem. They further maintain that even if there is slack in the system, ... it does not follow that national legislation would do a better job than state competition at mitigating the agency problem. Of course, in the absence of conflict between shareholder and manager preferences, the debate is moot, since the substantive content of state laws would be invariant with whoever, managers or shareholders, makes the incorporation decision or lobbies state legislators. The choice of incorporation state would therefore automatically enhance the value of the firm and, accordingly, shareholder wealth.

In somewhat simpler terms, the debate over Delaware's leadership in corporate law may be posed as whether the state tends to be pro-management or pro-shareholder. As you study the materials in this book, both those from Delaware and elsewhere, consider whether you can establish any such preference. Consider further whether such a bias would in fact be sustainable over the near-century of Delaware's dominance. Thus consider another possibility, which is that Delaware caters to neither group as a whole but instead offers, better than rival states, a practical, responsive, sophisticated, and fair administration of corporate law.

B. Preincorporation Agreements

Attorneys often have their clients enter into preincorporation agreements spelling out the important terms and arrangements the parties have agreed to. Section 7.32 of the Model Act authorizes these agreements and gives the parties wide latitude concerning the content of these agreements. Pre-incorporation agreements may also include matters other those related to financing the corporation. For example, if a closely held corporation is being formed, the agreement may contain provisions covering any or all of the matters listed in Model Act § 7.32 or any other matters that the parties wish to finalize before the company is formed.

A well-drafted preincorporation agreement is advisable for several reasons. At the very least it will impose a discipline on the corporate formation process and require the initial investors to clarify their understanding of the business relationship. Further, after time has passed and memories dim, the preincorporation contract will provide evidence of what the parties agreed to at the outset. If the incorporation process is expected to take a long time, the agreement will assure the continued commitment of the early investors during the time it takes to raise additional capital. And finally, it will document aspects of the business bargain not otherwise addressed in the company's articles of incorporation or bylaws.

C. How to Incorporate

The actual process of incorporating a business is not difficult, provided it is preceded by careful planning and attention to detail. One temptation attorneys should resist is the unexamined use of pre-printed, standardized documents. If used, these documents should be carefully reviewed and modified to fit the needs of the particular corporation in question. Corporate attorneys should also develop checklists of the matters that need to be completed for a successful incorporation.

The following are some of the key activities in the corporate creation process, most of which proceed concurrently. Relevant state and federal statutes should be checked for every step. In addition, it is useful for the corporate attorney to obtain forms that have been used successfully in the state of incorporation and, if relevant, for qualification to do business in other states.

- Select a corporate name and, if necessary, reserve it.
- Establish the company's capital structure and, if necessary, prepare stock subscription agreements in compliance with state and federal securities laws.
- Determine statutory requirements, if any, for incorporators, officers and directors.
- Prepare articles of incorporation and bylaws.

- File articles with Secretary of State and, if appropriate, with other governmental authorities, together with any required fees.
- Prepare initial draft of minutes of organization meeting or prepare written consents to accomplish without a meeting the actions to be taken at the organization meeting.

State corporation statutes determine what must be included in the corporate articles of incorporation, or certificate of incorporation—the corporate charter as it is commonly called. Typically, the articles include such information as:

1. The name of the corporation.
2. The number and types of shares that the corporation is authorized to issue.
3. The name and address of the company's registered office and its registered agent for service of process.
4. The name and address of the incorporators.
5. The corporate purposes.
6. The number and names and addresses of the initial board of directors.
7. Optional provisions concerning the management of the business and the regulation of the company's affairs.

Model Act §§ 2.01 through 2.03 define the necessary steps for preparing and filing the articles of incorporation, and the substantive requirements for the contents of the articles. These sections are supplemented by §§ 1.20 and 1.21, which prescribe the standards for the form of the documents, such as that the documents must be typewritten or printed. According to § 2.02, the articles of incorporation at a minimum must include the corporate name, the number of authorized shares, the name and address of the registered office and agent, and the name and address of each incorporator. Corporations formed under the Act automatically have perpetual duration, the purpose of engaging in any lawful business as provided in § 3.01(a), and a grant of limited liability to shareholders. These attributes may be modified in the articles of incorporation. The articles may also contain, among other things, optional provisions concerning management structure, limitations on director liability, and indemnification of directors. Corporate existence begins when the articles of incorporation are filed with the Secretary of State.

D. The Purposes and Powers Clauses

The purposes clause of the corporate charter designates the type(s) of business which the company may conduct. At one time, the purposes clause of corporate charters included information about the type of business conducted by the company, such as the computer software business. Today, a stated purpose of engaging in any lawful business will satisfy the charter requirements in most states. The Model Act does not require a purposes statement in the charter. Section 3.01 provides a default purposes clause by stating that: "Every corporation incorporated under this Act has the purpose of engaging in any lawful business unless a more limited purpose is set forth in the articles of incorporation."

Charter requirements concerning corporate powers have developed in a similar fashion. At one time, corporate charters were required to include a statement of powers, the types of acts a corporation could engage in to achieve its purpose. Today, statements of corporate powers are typically not required. Section 3.02 of the Model Act provides that every corporation organized under the Act "has the same powers as an individual to do all things necessary or convenient to carry out its business and affairs...." It includes a nonexclusive list of powers such as to sue and be sued in the corporate name, to acquire and convey real and personal property, to enter into contracts, to lend and borrow money, and the like.

At one time, corporate operations were limited to the confines established in the purposes clause of its charter. Anything else was *ultra vires*, or beyond the power conferred upon the corporation by the state, and could potentially be set aside as a result of successful challenges by persons conducting business with the corporation. Today, little remains of the *ultra vires* doctrine. Corporate charter purposes clauses are broad and generic; powers clauses afford corporations powers like those of natural persons. Section 3.04 of the Model Act limits challenges to corporate action based on lack of power to proceedings brought by shareholders of the corporation, by the corporation itself, or by the Attorney General.

Section IV
Issues Related to Successful Incorporation

A. The Internal Affairs Doctrine

VantagePoint Venture Partners 1996 v. Examen, Inc.

Delaware Supreme Court
871 A.2d 1108 (2005)

HOLLAND, JUSTICE:

... On March 3, 2005, the plaintiff-appellant, Examen, Inc. ("Examen"), filed a Complaint in the Court of Chancery against VantagePoint Venture Partners, Inc. ("VantagePoint"), a Delaware Limited Partnership and an Examen Series A Preferred shareholder, seeking a judicial declaration that pursuant to the controlling Delaware law and under the Company's Certificate of Designations of Series A Preferred Stock ("Certificate of Designations"), VantagePoint was not entitled to a class vote of the Series A Preferred Stock on the proposed merger between Examen and a Delaware subsidiary of Reed Elsevier Inc.

California Action

On March 8, 2005, VantagePoint filed an action in the California Superior Court seeking: (1) a declaration that Examen was required to identify whether it was a "quasi-California corporation" under section 2115 of the California Corporations

Code;[16] [and] (2) a declaration that Examen was a quasi-California corporation pursuant to California Corporations Code section 2115 and therefore subject to California Corporations Code section 1201(a), and that, as a Series A Preferred shareholder, VantagePoint was entitled to vote its shares as a separate class in connection with the proposed merger....

Delaware Action Decided

On March 10, 2005, the Court of Chancery granted Examen's request for an expedited hearing on its motion for judgment on the pleadings. On March 21, 2005, the California Superior Court stayed its action pending the ruling of the Court of Chancery. On March 29, 2005, the Court of Chancery ruled that the case was governed by the internal affairs doctrine as explicated by this Court in *McDermott v. Lewis*.[17] In applying that doctrine, the Court of Chancery held that Delaware law governed the vote that was required to approve a merger between two Delaware corporate entities.

On April 1, 2005, VantagePoint filed a notice of appeal with this Court. On April 4, 2005, VantagePoint sought to enjoin the merger from closing pending its appeal. On April 5, 2005, this Court denied VantagePoint's request to enjoin the merger from closing, but granted its request for an expedited appeal.

[The merger was consummated that same day. The court nevertheless opted to decide the issues raised in the case on the grounds that it was not moot.]

Facts

Examen was a Delaware corporation engaged in the business of providing web-based legal expense management solutions to a growing list of Fortune 1000 customers throughout the United States. Following consummation of the merger on April 5, 2005, LexisNexis Examen, also a Delaware corporation, became the surviving entity. VantagePoint is a Delaware Limited Partnership organized and existing under the laws of Delaware. VantagePoint, a major venture capital firm that purchased Examen Series A Preferred Stock in a negotiated transaction, owned eighty-three percent of Examen's outstanding Series A Preferred Stock ... and no shares of Common Stock.

On February 17, 2005, Examen and Reed Elsevier executed the Merger Agreement, which was set to expire on April 15, 2005, if the merger had not closed by that date. Under the Delaware General Corporation Law and Examen's Certificate of Incorporation, ... adoption of the Merger Agreement required the affirmative vote of the holders of a majority of the issued and outstanding shares of the Common Stock and

---

16. [1] Section 2115 of the California Corporations Code purportedly applies to corporations that have contacts with the State of California, but are incorporated in other states. *See* Cal. Corp. Code §§ 171 (defining "foreign corporation"); and Cal. Corp. Code §§ 2115(a), (b). Section 2115 ... provides that, irrespective of the state of incorporation, foreign corporations' articles of incorporation are deemed amended to comply with California law and are subject to the laws of California if certain criteria are met [relating to significant portions of property or payroll in California and large numbers of California stockholders].... Included among the California corporate law provisions that would govern is California Corporations Code section 1201, which states that the principal terms of a reorganization shall be approved by the outstanding shares of each class of each corporation the approval of whose board is required. *See* Cal. Corp. Code §§ 2115, 1201.

17. [2] *McDermott Inc. v. Lewis*, 531 A.2d 206 (Del. 1987).

Series A Preferred Stock, voting together as a single class. Holders of Series A Preferred Stock had the number of votes equal to the number of shares of Common Stock they would have held if their Preferred Stock was converted. [For VantagePoint, this translated into 1.4 million shares of voting stock out of a total of 8.6 million. Accordingly, whereas it could block any proposal on which the Preferred Stock voting alone was required it could not block any proposal on which the two classes of stock voted together.] VantagePoint acknowledges that, if Delaware law applied, it would not have a class vote....

Internal Affairs Doctrine

In *CTS Corp. v. Dynamics Corp. of Am.*, the United States Supreme Court stated that it is "an accepted part of the business landscape in this country for States to create corporations, to prescribe their powers, and to define the rights that are acquired by purchasing their shares."[18] In *CTS*, it was also recognized that "[a] State has an interest in promoting stable relationships among parties involved in the corporations it charters, as well as in ensuring that investors in such corporations have an effective voice in corporate affairs." The internal affairs doctrine is a long-standing choice of law principle which recognizes that only one state should have the authority to regulate a corporation's internal affairs — the state of incorporation.

The internal affairs doctrine developed on the premise that, in order to prevent corporations from being subjected to inconsistent legal standards, the authority to regulate a corporation's internal affairs should not rest with multiple jurisdictions. It is now well established that only the law of the state of incorporation governs and determines issues relating to a corporation's internal affairs. By providing certainty and predictability, the internal affairs doctrine protects the justified expectations of the parties with interests in the corporation.

The internal affairs doctrine applies to those matters that pertain to the relationships among or between the corporation and its officers, directors, and shareholders. The Restatement (Second) of Conflict of Laws § 301 provides: "application of the local law of the state of incorporation will usually be supported by those choice-of-law factors favoring the need of the interstate and international systems, certainty, predictability and uniformity of result, protection of the justified expectations of the parties and ease in the application of the law to be applied." Accordingly, the conflicts practice of both state and federal courts has consistently been to apply the law of the state of incorporation to "the entire gamut of internal corporate affairs."

The internal affairs doctrine is not, however, only a conflicts of law principle. Pursuant to the Fourteenth Amendment Due Process Clause, directors and officers of corporations "have a significant right ... to know what law will be applied to their actions" and "stockholders ... have a right to know by what standards of accountability they may hold those managing the corporation's business and affairs." [*McDermott, supra.*] Under the Commerce Clause, a state "has no interest in regulating the internal

---

18. [6] *CTS Corp. v. Dynamics Corp. of Am.*, 481 U.S. 69, 91, 107 S. Ct. 1637, 95 L. Ed. 2d 67 (1987). [*CTS* is reproduced in Chapter 18. Eds.]

affairs of foreign corporations." [*Id.*] Therefore, this Court has held that an "application of the internal affairs doctrine is mandated by constitutional principles, except in the 'rarest situations,'" *e.g.*, when "the law of the state of incorporation is inconsistent with a national policy on foreign or interstate commerce." [*Id.*]

California Section 2115

VantagePoint contends that section 2115 of the California Corporations Code is a limited exception to the internal affairs doctrine. Section 2115 is characterized as an outreach statute because it requires certain foreign corporations to conform to a broad range of internal affairs provisions. Section 2115 defines the foreign corporations for which the California statute has an outreach effect as those foreign corporations, half of whose voting securities are held of record by persons with California addresses, that also conduct half of their business in California as measured by a formula weighing assets, sales and payroll factors.

VantagePoint argues that section 2115 "mandates application of certain enumerated provisions of California's corporation law to the internal affairs of 'foreign' corporations if certain narrow factual prerequisites [set forth in section 2115] are met." Under the California statute, if more than one half of a foreign corporation's outstanding voting securities are held of record by persons having addresses in California (as disclosed on the books of the corporation) on the record date, and the property, payroll and sales factor tests are satisfied, then on the first day of the income year, one hundred and thirty five days after the above tests are satisfied, the foreign corporation's articles of incorporation are deemed amended to the exclusion of the law of the state of incorporation. If the factual conditions precedent for triggering section 2115 are established, many aspects of a corporation's internal affairs are purportedly governed by California corporate law to the exclusion of the law of the state of incorporation.

...

Internal Affairs Require Uniformity

In *McDermott*, this Court noted that application of local internal affairs law (here California's section 2115) to a foreign corporation (here Delaware) is "apt to produce inequalities, intolerable confusion, and uncertainty, and intrude into the domain of other states that have a superior claim to regulate the same subject matter...." [I]t is imperative that only the law of the state of incorporation regulate the relationships among a corporation and its officers, directors, and shareholders. To require a factual determination to decide which of two conflicting state laws governs the internal affairs of a corporation at any point in time, completely contravenes the importance of stability within inter-corporate relationships that the United States Supreme Court recognized in *CTS*....

State Law of Incorporation Governs Internal Affairs

In *McDermott*, this Court held that the "internal affairs doctrine is a major tenet of Delaware corporation law having important federal constitutional underpinnings." Applying Delaware's well-established choice-of-law rule—the internal affairs doctrine—the Court of Chancery recognized that Delaware courts must apply the law of the state of incorporation to issues involving corporate internal affairs, and that disputes concerning a shareholder's right to vote fall squarely within the purview of the internal affairs doctrine.

Examen is a Delaware corporation. The legal issue in this case—whether a preferred shareholder of a Delaware corporation had the right, under the corporation's Certificate of Designations, to a Series A Preferred Stock class vote on a merger—clearly involves the relationship among a corporation and its shareholders. As the United States Supreme Court held in *CTS*, "no principle of corporation law and practice is more firmly established than a State's authority to regulate domestic corporations, including the authority to define the voting rights of shareholders."

In *CTS*, the Supreme Court held that the Commerce Clause "prohibits States from regulating subjects that 'are in their nature national, or admit only of one uniform system, or plan of regulation,'" and acknowledged that the internal affairs of a corporation are subjects that require one uniform system of regulation. In *CTS*, the Supreme Court concluded that "so long as each State regulates voting rights only in the corporations it has created, each corporation will be subject to the law of only one State." Accordingly, we hold Delaware's well-established choice of law rules and the federal constitution mandated that Examen's internal affairs, and in particular, VantagePoint's voting rights, be adjudicated exclusively in accordance with the law of its state of incorporation, in this case, the law of Delaware.

Notes and Questions

1. The discussion in Section I.B. of this chapter of major twentieth-century developments in corporation law noted widespread congruence of corporation law among the various states. This congruence may facilitate choosing the state of incorporation and foreseeing the likely consequences of that choice with respect to application of the internal affairs doctrine. In most cases, the internal affairs doctrine is regarded as a choice of law rule that is clear, easy to apply, and predictable.

A clear understanding of the application of the internal affairs doctrine is particularly important to companies regularly doing business in multiple states. Although there is substantial congruence among state corporation laws, they are not identical. As seen in the *VantagePoint* case, a difference in law can mean the difference between a transaction's success or failure.

Knowing in advance what state corporation law will apply to a company's internal affairs becomes important for several reasons. One is that some states, like California, have enacted "outreach statutes" that apply to foreign corporations conducting a substantial amount of business within these states' borders. [In this context, a foreign corporation is one incorporated in another jurisdiction.] Not surprisingly, courts in the states of incorporation, like the *VantagePoint* court, have used the internal affairs doctrine to apply their own law rather than apply the outreach statutes of other jurisdictions.

The internal affairs doctrine has broad application with respect to matters of corporate governance. For example, the doctrine has taken precedence over contractual choice-of-law provisions naming a jurisdiction other than the state of incorporation.[20] The internal affairs doctrine is not, however, without limits. Its application has yielded to the doctrines of full faith and credit and collateral estoppel and to the public policy of foreign jurisdictions, as, for example, when California law was applied to an alleged wrongful termination of the CEO of a Delaware corporation conducting business in California.[21]

While the internal affairs doctrine determines applicable law, it does not address the forum. Many disputes involving Delaware corporate law are resolved by federal courts and courts in other states as well as by arbitrators. Although the substantive content of Delaware law reflects a high level of sophistication, not all judges command the corporate law expertise of the Delaware Court of Chancery or its Supreme Court justices. As litigation outside Delaware proliferated, many corporations began to experiment with ways to channel disputes to Delaware. A series of innovations followed. They were soon the subject first of litigation in Delaware and then of legislative responses in Delaware.

The resulting materials are rich because they illuminate several themes. For one, they offer important substantive lessons in the current content of Delaware corporate dispute resolution law. Moreover, they provide good illustrations of corporate governance devices such as the bylaws and charter, as well as the allocation of power between boards of directors and shareholders. Finally, the interaction of the Delaware judiciary and legislature is instructive on the process of law production—at least insofar as it relates to that of Delaware corporate law but consider broadly the different perspectives and roles of courts versus legislative bodies.

Boilermakers Local 154 Ret. Fund v. Chevron Corp.

73 A.3d 934 (2013)
Delaware Court of Chancery

STRINE, CHANCELLOR:

[Each board of two large corporations, Chevron, the oil company, and FedEx, the shipping company] adopted a bylaw providing that litigation relating to [the corporation's] internal affairs should be conducted in Delaware, the state where [each] is incorporated and whose substantive law [each company's] stockholders know governs the corporation's internal affairs. The boards of both companies have been empowered in their certificates of incorporation to adopt bylaws under 8 Del. C. § 109(a).

The plaintiffs, stockholders in Chevron and FedEx, have sued the boards for adopting these "forum selection bylaws." The plaintiffs' complaints are nearly identical and were filed only a few days apart by clients of the same law firm. In Count I, the plaintiffs claim that the bylaws are statutorily invalid because they are beyond the board's authority under the Delaware General Corporation Law ("DGCL"). In Count IV, the plaintiffs allege that the bylaws are contractually invalid, and therefore cannot be en-

---

20. *See, e.g.*, Heine v. Streamline Foods Inc., 805 F. Supp. 2d 383 (N.D. Ohio 2011).
21. Lidow v. Superior Court, 206 Cal. App. 4th 351 (2012).

forced like other contractual forum selection clauses under the test adopted by the Supreme Court of the United States in *The Bremen v. Zapata Off-Shore Co.,* [407 U.S. 1 (1972)] because they were unilaterally adopted by the Chevron and FedEx boards using their power to make bylaws. The plaintiffs have attempted to prove their point by presenting to this court a number of hypothetical situations in which, they claim, the bylaws might operate inconsistently with law or unreasonably. The plaintiffs have also claimed that the boards of Chevron and FedEx breached their fiduciary duties in adopting the bylaws....

[T]he bylaws are valid under our statutory law. [DGCL] 109(b) provides that the bylaws of a corporation "may contain any provision, not inconsistent with law or with the certificate of incorporation, relating to the business of the corporation, the conduct of its affairs, and its rights or powers or the rights or powers of its stockholders, directors, officers or employees." The forum selection bylaws, which govern disputes related to the "internal affairs" of the corporations, easily meet these requirements. The bylaws regulate the forum in which stockholders may bring suit, either directly or on behalf of the corporation in a derivative suit, to obtain redress for breaches of fiduciary duty by the board of directors and officers

The bylaws also regulate the forum in which stockholders may bring claims arising under the DGCL or other internal affairs claims. In other words, the bylaws only regulate suits brought by stockholders as stockholders in cases governed by the internal affairs doctrine. Thus, the bylaws, by establishing these procedural rules for the operation of the corporation, plainly relate to the "business of the corporation[s]," the "conduct of [their] affairs," and regulate the "rights or powers of [their] stockholders." Because Delaware law, like federal law, respects and enforces forum selection clauses, the forum selection bylaws are also not inconsistent with the law. For these reasons, the forum selection bylaws are not facially invalid as a matter of statutory law.

As to Count IV of the complaints, the court finds that the bylaws are valid and enforceable contractual forum selection clauses. As our Supreme Court has made clear, the bylaws of a Delaware corporation constitute part of a binding broader contract among the directors, officers, and stockholders formed within the statutory framework of the DGCL. This contract is, by design, flexible and subject to change in the manner that the DGCL spells out and that investors know about when they purchase stock in a Delaware corporation. The DGCL allows the corporation, through the certificate of incorporation, to grant the directors the power to adopt and amend the bylaws unilaterally.

The certificates of incorporation of Chevron and FedEx authorize their boards to amend the bylaws. Thus, when investors bought stock in Chevron and FedEx, they knew (i) that consistent with [DGCL] 109(a), the certificates of incorporation gave the boards the power to adopt and amend bylaws unilaterally; (ii) [DGCL] 109(b) allows bylaws to regulate the business of the corporation, the conduct of its affairs, and the rights or powers of its stockholders; and (iii) that board-adopted bylaws are binding on the stockholders. In other words, an essential part of the contract stockholders assent to when they buy stock in Chevron and FedEx is one that presupposes the board's authority to adopt binding bylaws consistent with [DGCL] 109. For that reason, our Supreme Court has long noted that bylaws, together with the certificate of incorporation and the broader DGCL, form part of a flexible contract between corporations and stockholders, in the sense that the certificate of incorporation may authorize the board to amend the bylaws' terms and that stockholders who invest in such corporations assent to be bound by board-adopted bylaws when they buy stock in those corporations.

The plaintiffs' argument to the contrary—that stockholders' rights may not be regulated by board-adopted bylaws—misunderstands the relationship between the corporation and stockholders established by the DGCL, and attempts to revive the outdated "vested rights" doctrine. [A] forum selection clause adopted by a board with the authority to adopt bylaws is valid and enforceable under Delaware law to the same extent as other contractual forum selection clauses. Therefore, this court will enforce the forum selection bylaws in the same way it enforces any other forum selection clause, in accordance with the principles set down by the United States Supreme Court in *Bremen* …

In an attempt to defeat the defendants' motion, the plaintiffs have conjured up an array of purely hypothetical situations in which they say that the bylaws of Chevron and FedEx might operate unreasonably. [But] it would be imprudent and inappropriate to address these hypotheticals in the absence of a genuine controversy with concrete facts. Delaware courts "typically decline to decide issues that may not have to be decided or that create hypothetical harm." [T]here is a presumption that bylaws are valid. By challenging the facial statutory and contractual validity of the forum selection bylaws, the plaintiffs took on the stringent task of showing that the bylaws cannot operate validly in any conceivable circumstance. The plaintiffs cannot evade this burden by conjuring up imagined future situations where the bylaws might operate unreasonably, especially when they acknowledge that in most internal affairs cases the bylaws will not operate in an unreasonable manner.

Nor does the adherence to the accepted standard of review in addressing facial invalidity claims work any unfairness. [A]s-applied challenges to the reasonableness of a forum selection clause should be made by a real plaintiff whose real case is affected by the operation of the forum selection clause. If a plaintiff faces a motion to dismiss because it filed outside the forum identified in the forum selection clause, the plaintiff can argue under *Bremen* that enforcing the clause in the circumstances of that case would be unreasonable. In addition, if a plaintiff-stockholder believes that a board is breaching its fiduciary duties by applying a forum selection clause to obtain dismissal of an actual case filed outside the forum designated by the bylaws, it may sue at that time. But the plaintiffs here, who have no separate claims pending that are affected by the bylaws, may not avoid their obligation to show that the bylaws are invalid in all circumstances by imagining circumstances in which the bylaws might not operate in a situationally reasonable manner. Such circumstantial challenges are required to be made based on real-world circumstances by real parties, and are not a proper basis for the survival of the plaintiffs' claims that the bylaws are facially invalid under the DGCL.

Therefore, the defendants' motion for judgment on the pleadings on Counts I and IV is granted.

.... The Chevron and FedEx boards say that they have adopted forum selection by-laws in response to corporations being subject to litigation over a single transaction or a board decision in more than one forum simultaneously, so-called "multiforum litigation." The defendants' opening brief argues that the boards adopted the forum selection bylaws to address what they perceive to be the inefficient costs of defending against the same claim in multiple courts at one time. The brief describes how, for jurisdictional purposes, a corporation is a citizen both of the state where it is incorporated and of the state where it has its principal place of business. Because a corporation need not be, and frequently is not, headquartered in the state where it is incorporated, a corporation may be subject to personal jurisdiction as a defendant in a suit involving corporate governance matters in two states. Therefore, any act that the corporation or its directors undertake is potentially subject to litigation in at least two states. Furthermore, both state and federal courts may have jurisdiction over the claims against the corporation. The result is that any act that the corporation or its directors undertake may be challenged in various forums within those states simultaneously. The boards of Chevron and FedEx argue that multiforum litigation, when it is brought by dispersed stockholders in different forums, directly or derivatively, to challenge a single corporate action, imposes high costs on the corporations and hurts investors by causing needless costs that are ultimately born by stockholders, and that these costs are not justified by rational benefits for stockholders from multiforum filings.

Thus, the boards of Chevron and FedEx claim to have tried to minimize or eliminate the risk of what they view as wasteful duplicative litigation by adopting the forum selection bylaws. Chevron and FedEx are not the only boards to have recently unilaterally adopted these clauses: in the last three years, over 250 publicly traded corporations have adopted such provisions....

Within the course of three weeks in February 2012, a dozen complaints were filed in this court against Delaware corporations, including Chevron and FedEx, whose boards had adopted forum selection bylaws without stockholder votes. As a threshold issue, these complaints, which were all substantively identical and filed by clients of the same accomplished law firm, alleged that the boards of the defendant corporations had no authority to adopt the bylaws, and sought a declaration that the bylaws were invalid and a breach of fiduciary duty. The complaints also brought a salmagundi of other claims, alleging hypothetical ways in which the forum selection bylaws could potentially be enforced in an unreasonable and unfair manner, and accusing the directors of breaching their fiduciary duties by adopting them.

Ten of the twelve defendant corporations repealed their bylaws, and the complaints against them were dismissed. Chevron and FedEx did not repeal their bylaws and answered the plaintiffs' complaints. The defendants then asked the court to hear a consolidated action on the facial validity of the forum selection bylaws, not only because the plaintiffs' lawsuits were chilling the adoption of such bylaws under the DGCL, but, most importantly, because the "fundamental question[s]" of statutory validity and contractual enforceability were "ripe for adjudication now[.]" The plaintiffs wrote in response that they objected to the defendants' "attempt to truncate discovery and abruptly seek an advisory opinion on the theoretical permissibility of the director-adopted exclusive forum bylaws." ...

[Legal Analysis]

[T]he plaintiffs have to confront the broad subjects that § 109(b) permits bylaws to address. The DGCL provides that bylaws may address any subject, "not inconsistent with law or with the certificate of incorporation, relating to the business of the corporation, the conduct of its affairs, and its rights or powers or the rights or powers of its stockholders, directors, officers or employees." The most important consideration for a court in interpreting a statute is the words the General Assembly used in writing it. As a matter of easy linguistics, the forum selection bylaws address the "rights" of the stockholders, because they regulate where stockholders can exercise their right to bring certain internal affairs claims against the corporation and its directors and officers. They also plainly relate to the conduct of the corporation by channeling internal affairs cases into the courts of the state of incorporation, providing for the opportunity to have internal affairs cases resolved authoritatively by our Supreme Court if any party wishes to take an appeal. That is, because the forum selection bylaws address internal affairs claims, the subject matter of the actions the bylaws govern relates quintessentially to "the corporation's business, the conduct of its affairs, and the rights of its stockholders [qua stockholders]." ...

By contrast, the bylaws would be regulating external matters if the board adopted a bylaw that purported to bind a plaintiff, even a stockholder plaintiff, who sought to bring a tort claim against the company based on a personal injury she suffered that occurred on the company's premises or a contract claim based on a commercial contract with the corporation. The reason why those kinds of bylaws would be beyond the statutory language of [DGCL] 109(b) is obvious: the bylaws would not deal with the rights and powers of the plaintiff-stockholder as a stockholder. As noted earlier, the defendants themselves read the forum selection bylaws in a natural way to cover only internal affairs claims brought by stockholders qua stockholders....

Despite the contractual nature of the stockholders' relationship with the corporation under our law, the plaintiffs argue, in Count IV of their complaints, that the forum selection bylaws by their nature are different and cannot be adopted by the board unilaterally. The plaintiffs' argument is grounded in the contention that a board-adopted forum selection bylaw cannot be a contractual forum selection clause because the stockholders do not vote in advance of its adoption to approve it. The plaintiffs acknowledge that contractual forum selection clauses are "prima facie valid" under *The Bremen v. Zapata Off-Shore Co.* ... But, the plaintiffs say, the forum selection bylaws are contractually invalid in this case, because they were adopted by a board, rather than by Chevron's and FedEx's dispersed stockholders. The plaintiffs argue that this method of adopting a forum selection clause is invalid as a matter of contract law, because it does not require the assent of the stockholders who will be affected by it. Thus, in the plaintiffs' view, there are two types of bylaws: (i) contractually binding bylaws that are adopted by stockholders; (ii) non-contractually binding bylaws that are adopted by boards using their statutory authority conferred by the certificate of incorporation.

By this artificial bifurcation, the plaintiffs misapprehend fundamental principles of Delaware corporate law. Our corporate law has long rejected the so-called "vested rights" doctrine. That vested rights view, which the plaintiffs have adopted as their own, "asserts that boards cannot modify bylaws in a manner that arguably diminishes or divests pre-existing shareholder rights absent stockholder consent." ...

In an unbroken line of decisions dating back several generations, our Supreme Court has made clear that the bylaws constitute a binding part of the contract between a Delaware corporation and its stockholders. Stockholders are on notice that, as to those subjects that are subject of regulation by bylaw under [DGCL] 109(b), the board itself may act unilaterally to adopt bylaws addressing those subjects. Such a change by the board is not extra-contractual simply because the board acts unilaterally; rather it is the kind of change that the overarching statutory and contractual regime the stockholders buy into explicitly allows the board to make on its own.... The plaintiffs' argument that stockholders must approve a forum selection bylaw for it to be contractually binding is an interpretation that contradicts the plain terms of the contractual framework chosen by stockholders who buy stock in Chevron and FedEx....

Even so, the statutory regime provides protections for the stockholders, through the indefeasible right of the stockholders to adopt and amend bylaws themselves. "[B]y its terms Section 109(a) vests in the shareholders a power to adopt, amend or repeal bylaws that is legally sacrosanct, i.e., the power cannot be non-consensually eliminated or limited by anyone other than the legislature itself." Thus, even though a board may, as is the case here, be granted authority to adopt bylaws, stockholders can check that authority by repealing board-adopted bylaws. And, of course, because the DGCL gives stockholders an annual opportunity to elect directors, stockholders have a potent tool to discipline boards who refuse to accede to a stockholder vote repealing a forum selection clause. Thus, a corporation's bylaws are part of an inherently flexible contract between the stockholders and the corporation under which the stockholders have powerful rights they can use to protect themselves if they do not want board-adopted forum selection bylaws to be part of the contract between themselves and the corporation.

... U.S. Supreme Court precedent reinforces the conclusion that forum selection bylaws are, as a facial matter of law, contractually binding. *In Carnival Cruise Lines v. Shute,* [499 U.S. 585 (1991)], the respondent, a cruise ship passenger from Washington State, was injured during the ship's travel between Los Angeles and Mexico. Mrs. Shute tried suing the company in Washington. But the fine print on the ticket contained a forum selection clause designating the courts of Florida as an exclusive forum for disputes. The Supreme Court held that the forum selection provision, although it was not subject to negotiation and was printed on the ticket she received after she purchased the passage, was reasonable, and thus enforceable.

Unlike cruise ship passengers, who have no mechanism by which to change their tickets' terms and conditions, stockholders retain the right to modify the corporation's bylaws. That plaintiffs did not vote on the bylaws at the time of their adoption is not relevant to the question of whether the bylaws are valid or contractually binding under Delaware law. Like any other bylaw, which may be unilaterally adopted by the board and subsequently modified by stockholders, these bylaws are enforced according to their terms. Thus, they will be enforced just like any other forum selection clause....

Notes

1. In 2015, the Delaware legislature amended the DGCL to add § 115:

> The certificate of incorporation or the bylaws may require, consistent with applicable jurisdictional requirements, that any or all intracorporate claims shall be brought solely and exclusively in any or all of the courts in this State, and no provision of the certificate of incorporation or the bylaws may prohibit bringing such claims in the courts of this State. "Intracorporate claims" means claims, including claims in the right of the corporation, (i) that are based upon a violation of a duty by a current or former director or officer or stock-holder in such capacity, or (ii) as to which this title confers jurisdiction upon the Court of Chancery.

The accompanying legislative history explained:

> ... Section 115 confirms, as held in *Boilermakers Local 154 Retirement Fund v. Chevron Corporation*, 73 A.2d 934 (Del. Ch. 2013), that the certificate of incorporation and bylaws of the corporation may effectively specify, consistent with applicable jurisdictional requirements, that claims arising under the DGCL, including claims of breach of fiduciary duty by current or former directors or officers or controlling stockholders of the corporation, or persons who aid and abet such a breach, must be brought only in the courts (including the federal court) in this State. Section 115 does not address the validity of a provision of the certificate of incorporation or bylaws that selects a forum other than the Delaware courts as an additional forum in which intracorporate claims may be brought, but it invalidates such a provision selecting the courts in a different State, or an arbitral forum, if it would preclude litigating such claims in the Delaware courts.

> Section 115 is not intended, however, to prevent the application of any such provision in a stockholders' agreement or other writing signed by the stockholder against whom the provision is to be enforced. Section 115 is not intended to foreclose evaluation of whether the specific terms and manner of adoption of a particular provision authorized by Section 115 comport with any relevant fiduciary obligation or operate reasonably in the circumstances presented. For example, such a provision may not be enforceable if the Delaware courts lack jurisdiction over indispensable parties or core elements of the subject matter of the litigation. Section 115 is also not intended to authorize a provision that purports to foreclose suit in a federal court based on federal jurisdiction, nor is Section 115 intended to limit or expand the jurisdiction of the Court of Chancery or the Superior Court.

Roberts v. TriQuint Semiconductor, Inc.

364 P.3d 328 (Ore. 2015)

KISTLER, JUSTICE (FOR THE COURT EN BANC):

TriQuint Semiconductor, Inc.... is a Delaware corporation headquartered in Hillsboro, Oregon. TriQuint designs and manufactures radio frequency products used in a number of high-technology industries. Late in February 2014, TriQuint's board of directors amended the company's bylaws to designate the Delaware Court of Chancery as the exclusive forum for resolving internal corporate disputes, including shareholder derivative suits. The board adopted the bylaw pursuant to TriQuint's certificate of incorporation, which allows the board of directors to "adopt, amend, or repeal" the company's bylaws unilaterally....

Two days after the board adopted the forum-selection bylaw, TriQuint announced plans to merge with RF Micro Devices, Inc. Each corporation's board of directors unanimously approved the merger. Some of TriQuint's shareholders objected to the merger, however. They filed two shareholder derivative suits in Oregon and three similar suits in Delaware.... [The] complaint alleged that TriQuint's directors had breached their fiduciary duties to the corporation by approving the merger....

TriQuint moved to dismiss ... TriQuint argued that its bylaws designate the Delaware Court of Chancery as the exclusive forum in which shareholder derivative suits can be filed. The trial court denied TriQuint's motion. The trial court recognized that Delaware law authorized TriQuint's board to unilaterally adopt a binding forum-selection bylaw. The court noted, however, that Delaware law also authorized TriQuint's shareholders to modify or repeal the company's bylaws. The trial court reasoned that adopting the forum-selection bylaw contemporaneously with the merger effectively deprived TriQuint's shareholders of their statutory right to repeal the forum-selection bylaw. The court explained that "[f]orcing the plaintiffs to proceed in Delaware would force them to accept the [forum-selection] bylaw" in contravention of their rights under Delaware corporate law to modify or repeal the bylaws adopted by the board. The trial court accordingly declined to enforce the bylaw....

The Delaware courts have held that a corporation's board of directors can unilaterally adopt a forum-selection bylaw, which will bind shareholders contractually. Specifically, a Delaware corporation may "confer the power to adopt, amend or repeal bylaws upon the directors." 8 Del. C. § 109(a). Those bylaws are a contract between the corporation and its shareholders. *See Airgas, Inc. v. Air Prod. & Chem., Inc.,* 8 A.3d 1182, 1188 (Del.2010) (explaining that "[c]orporate charters and bylaws are contracts among a corporation's shareholders"). Although a corporation's bylaws may address only certain statutorily prescribed subjects, *see* 8 Del. C. § 109(b), forum-selection bylaws regarding internal corporate governance — such as shareholder derivative suits — come within the subjects that a corporation's bylaws may address....

The Delaware Chancery Court accordingly held in [*Boilermakers Local 154 Ret. Fund v. Chevron Corp.,* 73 A.3d 934 (2013)] that a board-adopted forum-selection bylaw was a facially valid contract that bound the corporations' shareholders. *Id.*

Having recognized that the bylaw was facially valid, the court also recognized that it was possible that a forum-selection bylaw could be invalid as applied. The court explained that a shareholder could argue that, "under *Schnell [v. Chris-Craft Indus., Inc.,* 285 A.2d 437 (Del.1971)]*, the forum-selection clause should not be enforced because the bylaw was being used for improper purposes inconsistent with the directors' fiduciary duties." *Chevron,* 73 A.3d at 958; *see Black v. Hollinger Int'l, Inc.,* 872 A.2d 559, 564 (Del.2005) (explaining that facially valid bylaws were nevertheless "invalid in equity and of no force and effect, because they had been adopted for an inequitable purpose and had an inequitable effect").... Having noted the possibility that a forum-selection bylaw could be invalid as applied, the court limited its holding to the conclusion that forum-selection bylaws were facially valid under Delaware law....

Given *Chevron,* plaintiffs do not dispute that TriQuint's forum-selection bylaw is facially valid. They argue, however, that the bylaw is invalid as applied in this case because it "[i]s being used for improper purposes inconsistent with the directors' fiduciary duties."... Alternatively, they argue that the bylaw is unenforceable or unfair under *Bremen* or *Reeves* primarily because giving effect to the bylaw would deprive TriQuint's shareholders of their statutory right to amend the bylaws....

Whether TriQuint's board adopted the forum-selection bylaw in violation of its fiduciary duties is a question of Delaware law. Two Delaware cases bear on that issue: *Schnell* and *City of Providence v. First Citizens BancShares, Inc.,* 99 A.3d 229 (Del.Ch.2014). *Schnell* did not involve a forum-selection bylaw. Rather, in *Schnell,* a group of dissident shareholders notified the Securities and Exchange Commission that they intended to wage a proxy contest against the defendant corporation's current management.... In response, the corporation's board withheld critical information from the dissident shareholders; it also amended the corporation's bylaws to advance the date of the annual shareholders' meeting and to designate a relatively remote location for the shareholders' meeting....

Although the board's actions in amending the bylaws were technically permissible under Delaware law, the Delaware Supreme Court concluded that the board improperly had used the "corporate machinery and the Delaware Law for the purpose of perpetuating itself in office[.]"... Specifically, the dissident shareholders needed time to rally support to have a realistic chance of prevailing in their proxy contest, and the court determined that the board had "advance[d] the date [of the shareholder meeting] in order to obtain an inequitable advantage in the contest." *Id.* That inequitable conduct rendered what otherwise would have been a valid bylaw inequitable and unenforceable ...

[In contrast, in] *First Citizens,* the board of a North Carolina bank incorporated in Delaware unilaterally adopted a forum-selection bylaw designating North Carolina as the exclusive forum for resolving internal corporate disputes, including shareholder derivative suits. The same day that the board adopted the bylaw, it announced that it had agreed to a merger with a bank holding company.... A shareholder filed a derivative suit in the Delaware courts challenging both the forum-selection bylaw and the merger. The shareholder alleged that the board had breached its fiduciary duty to the shareholders in adopting the forum-selection bylaw because the board had been " 'motivated by a desire to protect the interests of the individual members' " and " 'to insulate itself from the jurisdiction of Delaware courts.' " ...

The Chancery Court rejected the plaintiff's breach of fiduciary duty claim. It reasoned that designating North Carolina as the exclusive forum for shareholder derivative suits "d[id] not insulate the Board's approval of the proposed merger from judicial review." ... The court previously had rejected the idea that only Delaware had the expertise to adjudicate matters of Delaware corporate law, and it noted the absence of any "well-pled facts to call into question the integrity of the * * * courts of North Carolina or to explain how the defendants are advancing their 'self-interests' by having claims [challenging the merger] adjudicated in those courts as opposed to the courts of Delaware." Applying Delaware law, the court granted the defendant's motion to dismiss, reasoning that the plaintiff had failed to rebut the board's exercise of its business judgment in adopting the forum-selection bylaw or to show that the board's "selection of North Carolina as the exclusive forum was irrational."

Although plaintiffs argue that *Schnell* governs their claim in this case, we think that *First Citizens* is the more applicable precedent. In *Schnell*, the board refused to give the plaintiffs access to shareholder lists, unilaterally accelerated the date of the annual shareholder meeting, and moved the meeting to a remote location in upstate New York. Given those facts, the court found that the board had acted with the purpose and effect of frustrating the plaintiffs' attempts to wage an effective proxy context. This case, by contrast, is far closer to *First Citizens*. It is true that the TriQuint board adopted the forum-selection bylaw making Delaware the exclusive forum for resolving disputes contemporaneously with its approval of the merger. But that was true in *First Citizens* as well. To paraphrase the court's reasoning in *First Citizens*, TriQuint's forum-selection bylaw does not prevent its shareholders from challenging the merger. It only provides where they may do so.... Guided by *First Citizens* and *Chevron*, we conclude that TriQuint's forum-selection bylaw is not invalid or unenforceable under Delaware law as a breach of the board's fiduciary duty.

The remaining question is whether the trial court erred in not giving effect to TriQuint's forum-selection bylaw. As noted, the trial court reasoned that applying the bylaw in these circumstances would effectively deprive TriQuint's shareholders of their statutory right to modify or repeal the bylaw.... *First Citizens* did not consider the specific issue presented here. The shareholders in that case did not argue that the forum-selection bylaw should not be given effect because the shareholders did not have time to modify or repeal the bylaw. The court's reasoning, however, provides persuasive guidance on that issue. As a matter of Delaware law, the court in *First Citizens* gave effect to a board-adopted bylaw even though it was not "realistically possible that stockholders may repeal it." *Id.* at 241. Put differently, the fact that shareholders lacked either the votes or, by inference, the time to override a board-adopted bylaw did not mean that the bylaw should not be given effect. Rather, as a matter of Delaware law, a board-adopted bylaw will be given effect until the shareholders modify or repeal it, unless the board lacked authority to adopt it or the board breached its fiduciary duty in adopting it. To hold otherwise would effectively read out of Delaware law a corporate board's authority to adopt bylaws unilaterally because there always will be a gap between the time that a board adopts a bylaw and the time that shareholders have an opportunity to modify or repeal it....

... When purchasing stock in a Delaware corporation, shareholders buy into a legal framework that allows corporate directors to unilaterally amend the corporation's bylaws and gives the shareholders the right to repeal those bylaws. Comity and respect for Delaware's corporate law lead us to conclude that, in the absence of compelling public policies to the contrary, we should not interfere with that framework or attempt to regulate the relationship between TriQuint's directors and its shareholders. *See* ORS 60.714(3) (providing that Oregon should not attempt to regulate the internal affairs of foreign corporations); *Tripp v. Pay 'N Pak Stores, Inc.,* 268 Or. 1, 518 P.2d 1298 (1974) (explaining that an Oregon statute regulating the issuance of stock options did not apply to Washington corporation). We discern no public policy sufficient to overcome that consideration or that would warrant our subjecting the internal relationship between TriQuint and its shareholders to the possibility of inconsistent regulation in different forums. *Cf. CTS Corp. v. Dynamics Corp. of America,* 481 U.S. 69, 88, 107 S.Ct. 1637, 95 L.Ed.2d 67 (1987) (recognizing constitutional limitations on state laws that adversely affect interstate commerce by subjecting corporate activities to inconsistent regulations); *Edgar v. MITE Corp.,* 457 U.S. 624, 645–46, 102 S.Ct. 2629, 73 L.Ed.2d 269 (1982) (same).

We also note that proceeding in the Delaware courts will not be "seriously inconvenient" for the parties. *See Reeves,* 262 Or. at 98, 495 P.2d 729. Plaintiffs have not argued that they lack the financial resources to litigate their derivative claims in the Delaware Court of Chancery, nor have they identified any basis for saying that it would be seriously inconvenient for them to do so. Moreover, the Delaware courts are well-equipped to resolve intra-corporate disputes involving Delaware corporations. Finally, no evidence in the record demonstrates that requiring plaintiffs to pursue their claims in Delaware will infringe their substantive rights, only that they will lose the ability to select the forum in which to exercise those rights.

TriQuint, on the other hand, has the authority to "protect against" the "potential for duplicative law suits in multiple jurisdictions over single events" by channeling those suits to a single forum. *Chevron,* 73 A.3d at 953. To that end, TriQuint has chosen to direct such suits to its state of incorporation, the "most obviously reasonable forum" in which to litigate intra-corporate disputes. *Id.* Plaintiffs have not been deprived of their right to challenge the merger, only the ability to challenge the merger in a forum other than Delaware....

In the United States, the longstanding default rule provides that each litigant bears their own lawyers' fees and other costs of litigation. A variety of specialized statutes alter that rule to provide that the loser pays. Some American corporations opted for such tailoring through board-adopted bylaws providing that shareholders who lose suits against directors were obliged to pay the directors' fees and costs. Howls erupted. The following case and ensuing statutes resulted.

ATP Tour, Inc. v. Deutscher Tennis Bund

91 A.3d 554 (Del. 2014)

BERGER, JUSTICE (FOR THE COURT EN BANC):

This Opinion constitutes the Court's response to four certified questions of law concerning the validity of a fee-shifting provision in a Delaware … corporation's by-laws. The provision, which the directors adopted pursuant to their charter-delegated power to unilaterally amend the bylaws, shifts attorneys' fees and costs to unsuccessful plaintiffs in intra-corporate litigation. The United States District Court for the District of Delaware found that the bylaw provision's validity was an open question under Delaware law and certified [several] questions to this Court, asking it to decide whether, and under what circumstances, such a provision is valid and enforceable. Although we cannot directly address the bylaw at issue, we hold that fee-shifting provisions in a … corporation's bylaws can be valid and enforceable under Delaware law.…

The following undisputed facts are drawn from the District Court's Certification of Questions of Law. ATP Tour, Inc. (ATP) is a Delaware membership corporation that operates a global professional men's tennis tour (the Tour). Its members include professional men's tennis players and entities that own and operate professional men's tennis tournaments. Two of those entities are Deutscher Tennis Bund (DTB) and Qatar Tennis Federation (QTF, and collectively, the Federations). ATP is governed by a seven-member board of directors, of which three are elected by the tournament owners, three are elected by the player members, and the seventh directorship is held by ATP's chairman and president. Upon joining ATP in the early 1990s, the Federations "agreed to be bound by ATP's Bylaws, as amended from time to time." In 2006, the board amended ATP's bylaws to add an Article 23, which provides, in relevant part:

> (a) In the event that (i) any [current or prior member or Owner or anyone on their behalf ("Claiming Party")] initiates or asserts any [claim or counterclaim ("Claim")] or joins, offers substantial assistance to or has a direct financial interest in any Claim against the League or any member or Owner (including any Claim purportedly filed on behalf of the League or any member), and (ii) the Claiming Party (or the third party that received substantial assistance from the Claiming Party or in whose Claim the Claiming Party had a direct financial interest) does not obtain a judgment on the merits that substantially achieves, in substance and amount, the full remedy sought, then each Claiming Party shall be obligated jointly and severally to reimburse the League and any such member or Owners for all fees, costs and expenses of every kind and description (including, but not limited to, all reasonable attorneys' fees and other litigation expenses) (collectively, "Litigation Costs") that the parties may incur in connection with such Claim.

In 2007, ATP's board voted to change the Tour schedule and format. Under the board's "Brave New World" plan, the Hamburg tournament, which the Federations own and operate, was downgraded from the highest tier of tournaments to the second highest tier, and was moved from the spring season to the summer season. Displeased by these changes, the Federations sued ATP and six of its board members in the United States District Court for the District of Delaware, alleging both federal antitrust claims and Delaware fiduciary duty claims.

After a ten-day jury trial, the District Court granted ATP's and the director defendants' motion for judgment as a matter of law on all of the fiduciary duty claims, and also on the antitrust claims brought against the director defendants. The jury then found in favor of ATP on the remaining antitrust claims. Thus, the Federations did not prevail on any claim. ATP then moved to recover its legal fees, costs, and expenses under Rule 54 of the Federal Rules of Civil Procedure. ATP grounded its motion on Article 23.3(a) of ATP's bylaws. The District Court denied ATP's Rule 54 motion because it found Article 23.3(a) to be contrary to the policy underlying the federal antitrust laws. The District Court effectively ruled that "federal law preempts the enforcement of fee-shifting agreements when antitrust claims are involved." *Deutscher Tennis Bund v. ATP Tour Inc.*, 480 Fed.Appx. 124, 126 (3d Cir.2012).

ATP appealed, and the United States Court of Appeals for the Third Circuit vacated the District Court's order. The Third Circuit found that the District Court should have decided whether Article 23.3(a) was enforceable as a matter of Delaware law before reaching the federal preemption question. On remand, the District Court reasoned that the question of Article 23.3(a)'s enforceability was a novel question of Delaware law that should be addressed in the first instance by this Court. The District Court certified ... questions of law ... and [this opinion] will address each question in turn.

1. Fee-shifting bylaws are permissible under Delaware Law. The first certified question asks whether the board of a Delaware ... corporation may lawfully adopt a bylaw that shifts all litigation expenses to a plaintiff in intra-corporate litigation who "does not obtain a judgment on the merits that substantially achieves, in substance and amount, the full remedy sought." Under Delaware law, a corporation's bylaws are "presumed to be valid, and the courts will construe the bylaws in a manner consistent with the law rather than strike down the bylaws." *See Frantz Mfg. Co. v. EAC Indus.*, 501 A.2d 401, 407 (Del.1985). To be facially valid, a bylaw must be authorized by the Delaware General Corporation Law (DGCL), consistent with the corporation's certificate of incorporation, and its enactment must not be otherwise prohibited. That, under some circumstances, a bylaw might conflict with a statute, or operate unlawfully, is not a ground for finding it facially invalid.

A fee-shifting bylaw, like the one described in the first certified question, is facially valid. Neither the DGCL nor any other Delaware statute forbids the enactment of fee-shifting bylaws. A bylaw that allocates risk among parties in intra-corporate litigation would also appear to satisfy the DGCL's requirement that bylaws must "relat[e] to the business of the corporation, the conduct of its affairs, and its rights or powers or the rights or powers of its stockholders, directors, officers or employees." The corporate charter could permit fee-shifting provisions, either explicitly or implicitly by silence. Moreover, no principle of common law prohibits directors from enacting fee-shifting bylaws.

Delaware follows the American Rule, under which parties to litigation generally must pay their own attorneys' fees and costs. *Mahani v. Edix Media Grp., Inc.*, 935 A.2d 242, 245 (Del.2007) ("Under the American Rule and Delaware law, litigants are normally responsible for paying their own litigation costs."). But it is settled that contracting parties may agree to modify the American Rule and obligate the losing party to pay the prevailing party's fees. *See Sternberg v. Nanticoke Mem'l Hosp., Inc.*, 62 A.3d 1212, 1218 (Del.2013) ("'An exception to [the American R]ule is found in contract litigation that involves a fee shifting provision.'") (citation omitted). Because corporate bylaws are "contracts among a corporation's shareholders," *Airgas, Inc. v. Air Prods. & Chems., Inc.*, 8 A.3d 1182, 1188 (Del.2010), a fee-shifting provision contained in a ... corporation's validly-enacted bylaw would fall within the contractual exception to the American Rule. Therefore, a fee-shifting bylaw would not be prohibited under Delaware common law.

Whether the specific ATP fee-shifting bylaw is enforceable, however, depends on the manner in which it was adopted and the circumstances under which it was invoked. Bylaws that may otherwise be facially valid will not be enforced if adopted or used for an inequitable purpose. In the landmark *Schnell v. Chris-Craft Industries* [285 A.2d 437 (Del.1971)] decision, for example, this Court set aside a board-adopted bylaw amendment that moved up the date of an annual stockholder meeting to a month earlier than the date originally scheduled. The Court found that the board's purpose in adopting the bylaw and moving the meeting was to "perpetuat[e] itself in office" and to "obstruct [ ] the legitimate efforts of dissident stockholders in the exercise of their rights to undertake a proxy contest against management." The *Schnell* Court famously stated that "inequitable action does not become permissible simply because it is legally possible."

More recently, in *Hollinger International, Inc. v. Black*, [844 A.2d 1022 (Del.Ch.2004), *aff'd sub. nom.*, Black v. Hollinger Int'l Inc., 872 A.2d 559 (Del.2005)] the Court of Chancery addressed bylaw amendments, enacted by a controlling shareholder, that prevented the board "from acting on any matter of significance except by unanimous vote" and "set the board's quorum requirement at 80%," among other changes. The Court of Chancery found, and this Court agreed, that the bylaw amendments were ineffective because they "were clearly adopted for an inequitable purpose and have an inequitable effect." That finding was based on an extensive review of the facts surrounding the controller's decision to amend the bylaws.

Conversely, this Court has upheld similarly restrictive bylaws that were enacted for proper purposes. In *Frantz Manufacturing Co. v. EAC Industries*, [*supra*] a majority stockholder amended the corporation's bylaws by written consent in order to "limit the [ ] board's anti-takeover maneuvering after [the stockholder] had gained control of the corporation." The amended bylaws, like those invalidated in *Hollinger*, increased the board quorum requirement and mandated that all board actions be unanimous. The Court found that the bylaw amendments were "a permissible part of [the stockholder's] attempt to avoid its disenfranchisement as a majority shareholder" and, thus, were "not inequitable under the circumstances."

In sum, the enforceability of a facially valid bylaw may turn on the circumstances surrounding its adoption and use. *See, e.g., Stroud v. Grace*, 606 A.2d 75, 83 (Del.1992) (upholding bylaw amendments against claims of entrenchment because "there [was] no evidence that the board adopted the Amendments as defensive measures," and the "record clearly indicate[d]" that "there was no threat to the board's control"); *Datapoint Corp. v. Plaza Sec. Co.*, 496 A.2d 1031, 1036 (Del.1985) (invalidating board-adopted bylaw amendments because the "underlying intent" behind them was "to give management an opportunity distribute 'opposing solicitation material'" to challenge written stockholder consents) ...

The Certification does not provide the stipulated facts necessary to determine whether the ATP bylaw was enacted for a proper purpose or properly applied. Moreover, because certifications by their nature only address questions of law, we are able to say only that a bylaw of the type at issue here is facially valid, in the sense that it is permissible under the DGCL, and that it may be enforceable if adopted by the appropriate corporate procedures and for a proper corporate purpose.

2. The bylaw, if valid and enforceable, could shift fees if a plaintiff obtained no relief in the litigation. The second certified question essentially asks whether a more limited version of the ATP bylaw would be valid. Article 23.3(a) states that it can be invoked against any plaintiff who does not obtain a judgment "that substantially achieves, in substance and amount, the full remedy sought." Since there might be difficulty applying the "substantially achieves" standard, the District Court asks whether the bylaw would be enforceable, at least, where plaintiff obtains "no relief at all against the corporation." Subject to the limitations set forth in our answer to the first certified question, we answer the second question in the affirmative.

3. The bylaw would be unenforceable if adopted for an improper purpose. The third certified question asks whether the bylaw is "rendered unenforceable as a matter of law if one or more Board members subjectively intended the adoption of the bylaw to deter legal challenges by members to other potential corporate action then under consideration." Again, we are unable to respond fully. Legally permissible bylaws adopted for an improper purpose are unenforceable in equity. The intent to deter litigation, however, is not invariably an improper purpose. Fee-shifting provisions, by their nature, deter litigation. Because fee-shifting provisions are not *per se* invalid, an intent to deter litigation would not necessarily render the bylaw unenforceable in equity....

Notes

1. The opinion in *ATP Tour* ran merely 2,800 words. Characteristic of Justice Berger's opinions, it was to the point and clear without digressions or extraneous citations typical of the opinions of many other Delaware judges.

2. After *ATP Tour*, scores of corporations, in Delaware and other states, adopted fee shifting bylaws. The DGCL was updated in 2015:

> § 102(f): The certificate of incorporation may not contain any provision that would impose liability on a stockholder for the attorneys' fees or expenses of the corporation or any other party in connection with an intracorporate claim, as defined in § 115 of this title.

§ 109(b): The bylaws may not contain any provision that would impose liability on a stockholder for the attorneys' fees or expenses of the corporation or any other party in connection with an intracorporate claim, as defined in § 115 of this title.

These sections invalidate charters or bylaws "that purport[] to impose liability upon a stockholder for the attorneys' fees or expenses of the corporation or any other party in connection with an intracorporate claim...." The sections address only disputes concerning internal affairs among shareholders, directors, and officers, per DGCL 115, not suits by consumers under antitrust laws, employees under labor laws, or shareholders and other securities law claimants under securities laws.

B. Qualifying to Do Business in Another State

Once a corporation is formed, it will become a domestic corporation of the state where it is incorporated. It will be deemed to be a foreign corporation to states other than the state of incorporation. In this context, the term "foreign corporation" includes corporations formed under another state's laws as well as corporations formed under the laws of another country.

A foreign corporation must obtain a certificate of authority from the secretary of state of each jurisdiction where it plans to conduct business, other than its state of incorporation. Companies conducting business without a certificate of authority are generally barred from initiating proceedings in the state's courts until a certificate is obtained. A company may also be fined by each state in which it transacts business without a certificate of authority. If the corporation wants to stop doing business in a state, it must obtain a certificate of withdrawal from the secretary of state.

A foreign corporation must be in good standing in order to conduct business in a state. If it fails to file its annual report, neglects to pay annual registration fees, or is without a registered office or a registered agent for more than sixty days, the secretary of state may initiate proceedings to revoke the company's certificate of authority. A foreign corporation has the right to appeal the secretary of state's decision.

C. Domestication

The term "domestication" refers to the process used to change a corporation's state of incorporation. The domestication process permits a domestic corporation of a particular state to reincorporate in another state. The result of this change is that the corporation becomes a foreign corporation of its original home state and a domestic corporation of another state. Today, this change can be accomplished directly if it is permitted by the laws of both jurisdictions. Previously, reincorporations could be accomplished by merging a parent company with a wholly owned subsidiary incorporated in the destination state.

Changing the jurisdiction of incorporation usually involves several steps. A plan of domestication must be adopted by the board of directors and approved by the shareholders. If shareholders approve the plan, articles of domestication will be filed with the secretary of state's office in the state of domestication and articles of charter surrender will be filed with the secretary of state in the original state of incorporation. The corporation acquires the same status, rights, powers, and privileges as if it had been incorporated in the jurisdiction of domestication from the beginning. If the corporation wishes to continue to conduct business in its original jurisdiction of incorporation, it must qualify to do business there as a foreign corporation.

Section V
Defective Incorporation

A. *De Facto* Corporation and Corporation by Estoppel

In their early development, corporation laws set up technical multi-step procedures for establishing a corporation. For example, an incorporator might have to publish notice of intent to incorporate, file properly executed papers with the secretary of state and with one or more county officers, publish notice of those filings, and then capitalize the corporation at a certain level, all before a court would recognize the existence of what is called a *de jure* corporation, or a corporation "of right." To stumble over one of those procedures, and to operate a business that only appeared to be a corporation, was to risk being held personally liable for the business's debts. To alleviate the perceived inequities of personal liability in some of those circumstances, courts established two doctrines, the *de facto* corporation doctrine and the corporation by estoppel doctrine.

In order to establish the existence of a *de facto* corporation, one must prove three things:

1. There is a law under which the purported corporation could have been incorporated;
2. There was a good faith attempt to incorporate under that law; and
3. There was a use of corporate power in the honest belief that a corporation existed.

For all of this century, the first requirement has been met in each American jurisdiction, and in situations involving real-world questions about the existence of a *de facto* corporation, the third requirement also tends to be met without much question. The real issue usually is whether there has been a good faith attempt to incorporate.

One of the more interesting modern *de facto* corporation doctrine cases is *Cantor v. Sunshine Greenery, Inc.*, 398 A.2d 571 (N.J. Super. Ct. App. Div. 1979). That case nicely illustrates how the question of whether a good faith attempt has been made to incorporate can arise. In *Cantor*, the incorporators signed a corporate charter on December 3 and on that same day mailed the charter to the office of the Secretary of State. Evidently believing that the charter had been received by that office and filed, one of the incorporators signed a lease in the corporation's name on December 16. In fact, the charter was not filed by the Secretary of State until two days later. Those facts were enough to allow a New Jersey court to find a bona fide attempt to incorporate and, with the other elements of the *de facto* corporation doctrine met, also to find the existence of a *de facto* corporation. "To deny such existence because of a mere technicality caused by administrative delay in filing runs counter to the purpose of the *de facto* concept," the court said, "and would accomplish an unjust and inequitable result in favor of plaintiffs contrary to their own contractual expectations." The most important learning from *Cantor* is probably found in that quoted explanation by the court of its decision, *i.e.*, that to reach another result would be inequitable. The theme of equity in the judicial resolution of liability questions is one that runs through this chapter.

The corporation by estoppel doctrine is a misnomer. The effect of applying that doctrine is not to create a corporation. Instead, a court applying the doctrine will estop a plaintiff from arguing the nonexistence of a corporation that patently does not exist as a *de jure* corporation. As might be expected, the occasion for a court to invoke the doctrine relates to its appraisal of the equities of the situation before it in litigation, with the basic question for the court being, "Is it equitable to allow the plaintiff to collect from persons who thought they were officers, directors, or shareholders of a corporation?"

Although some courts get confused on the subject, the corporation by estoppel doctrine and the *de facto* corporation doctrine are two distinct doctrines, and the elements of a *de facto* corporation do not have to be found before a court can find a corporation by estoppel. Some of the confusion is understandable, however, because each doctrine ultimately is underpinned by concepts of equity, and the facts that support one doctrine often also support the other. For example, a typical fact situation finds a defendant facing personal liability for a contract that both the defendant and the plaintiff believed was a corporate debt, thus leading to questions about the equity of allowing the plaintiff to collect from an individual defendant because of a technical problem in the incorporation of the defendant's corporation. A further look at the facts may indicate that they fit the required elements of the *de facto* corporation doctrine, and so the overlap between the two doctrines may be fairly extensive. Perhaps it can most helpfully be said that the usual effect of the corporation by estoppel doctrine is to backstop the *de facto* corporation doctrine by allowing courts to excuse defendants from liability, where doing so would work equity, in situations where one or more elements of the *de facto* corporation doctrine are not met.

State court decisions testify to the continued vitality of the *de facto* corporation and corporation by estoppel doctrines and to courts' apparently greater willingness to sound the death knell for the *de facto* corporation doctrine than for the corporation by estoppel doctrine. In a 1994 decision, the court in *American Vending Services, Inc. v. Morse*, 881 P.2d 917 (Utah 1994), interpreted Model Act (1969) §§ 56 and 146 as expressly abolishing the *de facto* corporation doctrine. The court concluded that since a *de jure* corporation is created when the certificate of incorporation is issued, anything less than obtaining a certificate would not constitute sufficient compliance with the Act. In a footnote, the court observed that the rationale for abolishing the *de facto* corporation doctrine was based on the need for a bright line rule to avoid inconsistent and conflicting results.

In its discussion of the corporation by estoppel doctrine the *American Vending* Court stated the following:

> The doctrine developed in the courts of equity to prevent unfairness. As one court has stated, "Corporation by estoppel is a difficult concept to grasp and courts and writers have 'gone all over the lot' in attempting to define and apply the doctrine." *Timberline Equipment Co. v. Davenport*, 267 Or. 64, 514 P.2d 1109, 1111 (1973)....

> Generally, courts apply this doctrine according to who is being charged with estoppel. Usually the courts are willing to apply corporation by estoppel when the case involves a defendant seeking to escape liability to a [corporate plaintiff] by complaining that the corporation's existence is flawed. On the other hand, courts are typically more reluctant to apply the doctrine when individuals, usually incorporators, seek to escape liability by contending that the debtor is a corporation rather than the individuals who purported to act as a corporation.

> ....

> I agree with this reasoning and would hold that the doctrine of corporation by estoppel ... can be invoked only where both parties reasonably believe they are dealing with a corporation and neither party has actual or constructive knowledge that the corporation does not exist.

B. Statutory Developments

Over the last few decades, questions of defective incorporation have been answered to an increased degree by reference to corporation statutes. Those statutes, typified by the Model Act, now universally make establishing a corporation a simple one-step process, thus arguably lessening the need for the *de facto* corporation doctrine and, perhaps to a lesser extent, for the corporation by estoppel doctrine as well. Some of those statutes also include language speaking directly to the question of liability for those who assume to act as a corporation without authority to do so. Here are the two relevant Model Act sections:

Section 2.03 Incorporation

> (a) Unless a delayed effective date is specified, the corporate existence begins when the articles of incorporation are filed.

> (b) The secretary of state's filing of the articles of incorporation is conclusive proof that the incorporators satisfied all conditions precedent to incorporation except in a proceeding by the state to cancel or revoke the incorporation or involuntarily dissolve the corporation.

Section 2.04 Liability for Preincorporation Transactions

All persons purporting to act as or on behalf of a corporation, knowing there was no incorporation under this Act, are jointly and severally liable for all liabilities created while so acting.

When the drafters of the Model Act addressed the question of personal liability for the obligations of a defectively incorporated enterprise, they found that the doctrines of *de facto* corporations, *de jure* corporations and corporations by estoppel retained a certain vitality.

The Official Comment to § 2.04 summarizes the current state of the law:

Earlier versions of the Model Act, and the statutes of many states, have long provided that corporate existence begins only with the acceptance of articles of incorporation by the secretary of state. Many states also have statutes that provide expressly that those who prematurely act as or on behalf of a corporation are personally liable on all transactions entered into or liabilities incurred before incorporation. A review of recent case law indicates, however, that even in states with such statutes courts have continued to rely on common law concepts of de facto corporations, de jure corporations, and corporations by estoppel that provide uncertain protection against liability for preincorporation transactions. These cases caused a review of the underlying policies represented in earlier versions of the Model Act and the adoption of a slightly more flexible or relaxed standard.

Incorporation under modern statutes is so simple and inexpensive that a strong argument may be made that nothing short of filing articles of incorporation should create the privilege of limited liability. A number of situations have arisen, however, in which the protection of limited liability arguably should be recognized even though the simple incorporation process established by modern statutes has not been completed.

(1) The strongest factual pattern for immunizing participants from personal liability occurs in cases in which the participant honestly and reasonably but erroneously believed the articles had been filed....

(2) Another class of cases, which is less compelling but in which the participants sometimes have escaped personal liability, involves the defendant who mails in articles of incorporation and then enters into a transaction in the corporate name; the letter is either delayed or the secretary of state's office refuses to file the articles after receiving them or returns them for correction....

(3) A third class of cases in which the participants sometimes have escaped personal liability involves situations where the third person has urged immediate execution of the contract in the corporate name even though he knows that the other party has not taken any steps toward incorporating....

(4) In another class of cases the defendant has represented that a corporation exists and entered into a contract in the corporate name when he knows that

no corporation has been formed, either because no attempt has been made to file articles of incorporation or because he has already received rejected articles of incorporation from the filing agency. In these cases, the third person has dealt solely with the "corporation" and has not relied on the personal assets of the defendant....

(5) A final class of cases involves inactive investors who provide funds to a promoter with the instruction, "Don't start doing business until you incorporate." After the promoter does start business without incorporating, attempts have been made, sometimes unsuccessfully, to hold the investors liable as partners....

After a review of these situations, it seemed appropriate to impose liability only on persons who act as or on behalf of corporations "knowing" that no corporation exists. Analogous protection has long been accorded under the uniform limited partnership acts to limited partners who contribute capital to a partnership in the erroneous belief that a limited partnership certificate has been filed....

While no special provision is made in section 2.04, the section does not foreclose the possibility that persons who urge defendants to execute contracts in the corporate name knowing that no steps to incorporate have been taken may be estopped to impose personal liability on individual defendants. This estoppel may be based on the inequity perceived when persons, unwilling or reluctant to enter into a commitment under their own name, are persuaded to use the name of a nonexistent corporation, and then are sought to be held personally liable under section 2.04 by the party advocating that form of execution. By contrast, persons who knowingly participate in a business under a corporate name are jointly and severally liable on "corporate" obligations under section 2.04 and may not argue that plaintiffs are "estopped" from holding them personally liable because all transactions were conducted on a corporate basis.

Although the Model Act attempts to limit the doctrine of corporations by estoppel, the question remains whether courts in states adopting the Model Act will pay attention to § 2.04, or will apply the case law that precedes it.

Chapter 4

Capitalization

Situation

You have been asked to work out the details of the capitalization of Biologistics, Inc. Anderson, Baker and Phillips are to share equally in the corporation's long-term profits, and are to have equal power as shareholders in corporate decision-making. Baker has agreed to contribute $30,000 and a fairly extensive list of prospective customers. Anderson has agreed to contribute $45,000, and it is understood that he has already performed valuable promotional services. Phillips has agreed to contribute $75,000 and to guarantee bank loans of up to $200,000, so long as Anderson and Baker also sign any guaranty. Baker's mother-in law has decided not to invest in the business. The probable need to raise additional money to support research and development has been noted by each of your clients, and they have asked you to take this into account when advising them on how to capitalize.

Anderson and Baker are well aware that their financial resources are more limited than those of Phillips. They would like to take whatever steps are possible to insure that if the corporation wishes to sell additional stock in the future, they will have an opportunity to buy a *pro rata* share, and that if they do not have the funds to do so, neither Phillips nor anyone else will be able to do so either without their consent.

Section I
Basics

Students without any business background often have initial problems with capitalization. There seem to be two reasons for this. First, many of the terms are new. Although the concepts to which they relate are quite simple, the concepts obviously cannot be understood by a student who has not been given the necessary vocabulary. Second, students sometimes expect more complexity than in fact exists. That is, they may in fact understand a concept but feel a sense of unease because they do not realize how well they understand it. Some of the matters discussed in this Chapter are introduced in the Appendix (Reading Financial Statements). The Appendix should be read or reviewed at this point. For students without a business background, the Appendix will provide all the help that is needed. Beyond this, the following discussion should help provide the necessary familiarity with terms and concepts. Perhaps it also will dispel ideas about the amount or depth of complexity involved here.

Basically, a corporation's capitalization (which we can take roughly to mean the cash or other assets put into the corporation on a long-term basis) consists of equity and, if desired, debt. With respect to the initial capitalization of a new corporation, the equity capitalization will be the cash or other assets contributed by shareholders in exchange for stock. "Equity," then, is an ownership interest in the corporation. Equity owners have a residual interest in the assets of the corporation. Their claims are paid on liquidation only after all superior claims are satisfied. "Debt," of course, is cash or other assets that are borrowed. Nothing prevents a person from contributing some capital as equity and some as debt, making the person both a shareholder and a creditor. In fact, for reasons that will be discussed below, that is often done.

A. Equity

1. Types of Equity Securities

Common Stock: Equity is represented by some form of security, typically stock of one type or another. Modern corporation statutes allow great flexibility in devising forms of stock, but in most cases corporations will start out simply with common stock. In that situation, the holders of the common stock will be the only owners of the corporation, and they generally will share among themselves, in proportion to the number of shares they own, all the rights shareholders have in a corporation. Chief among those are a right to vote on certain matters, a right to the corporation's profits, and a right to the corporation's assets if the corporation is liquidated. Sometimes corporations establish more than one class of common stock, so as to distribute the traditional rights of common shareholders in some way other than equally to all common shareholders. For example, a corporation might have two classes of common stock, one of which carries the right to vote for directors and the other of which does not.

Preferred Stock: Some corporations have preferred stock in addition to common stock. Preferred stock virtually always will be preferred (have priority) over the common stock as to the shareholders' right to receive assets if the corporation is dissolved. Almost as often it will carry with it the preferred shareholders' right to receive a portion of the corporation's profits, in the form of a dividend, before the common shareholders receive a dividend. Almost always, however, the preferred shareholders' call on the corporation's profits will be limited to stated amounts. That is, preferred shareholders do not typically share in the corporation's successes beyond an agreed level. A particular preferred stock, for example, may have a per share preference as to dividends of ten dollars per year. No matter how successful the corporation becomes, an annual payment of ten dollars per share is all the dividend a holder of that stock will ever receive.

Preferred stock dividends usually are made cumulative, which means that no dividends may be paid to the common shareholders until all dividends that should have been paid to the preferred shareholders have been paid. Typically, preferred shareholders do not have a right to vote on most matters that are submitted for a share-holders' vote.[1] If, however, preferred stock dividends are not paid for a stated period, often twelve months, many corporations give their preferred shareholders the right to elect some or all of the corporation's directors until all dividends in arrears are paid. Unlike the typical common stock, preferred stock usually is callable or redeemable at the option of the corporation. That is, the board of directors usually is able to require the preferred shareholders to sell their shares to the corporation upon the payment to them of an amount of cash that is stated in the charter. In the usual case, that amount is equal to the original purchase price of the stock plus one year's dividends. As may be apparent from this discussion, although preferred stock is technically an equity security, in practical terms it usually seems closer to debt than it does to common stock. In order to give preferred shareholders the best features of both equity and debt, however, preferred stock sometimes is made convertible into common stock upon terms specified in the charter.

Model Act: The Model Business Corporation Act does not use the terms "common" and "preferred" to describe types of shares, although §§ 6.01(a) and (c) expressly permit a corporation to have classes of shares that differ based on preferences, limitations and relative rights. Section 6.01(b), however, requires the articles of incorporation to authorize "(1) one or more classes of shares that together have unlimited voting rights, and (2) one or more classes of shares (which may be the same class or classes as those with voting rights) that together are entitled to receive the net assets of the corporation upon dissolution." Section 6.01(c) (2) authorizes the issuance of shares that may be redeemed at the option of either the corporation, the shareholder or a third person (such as the holder of another class of security in the same corporation) or upon the occurrence of a predetermined event.

2. Issuance

a. Par Value

Under many modern corporation statutes, any form of stock may have a "par value" stated in the corporation's charter, or the charter may state that the stock is without par value. The concept of par value often is baffling to the uninitiated. A common problem is the belief that there must be more substance to the concept than there is. In fact, there is very little to the concept of par value. The best way to view par value is as a dollar figure specified in the charter, from which certain well-defined consequences flow. Once one understands those consequences, one understands par value. We would be getting ahead of ourselves if we go too deeply into that, but here is a short introduction to the three main consequences. The consequences apply in jurisdictions whose corporate statutes are based on the concept of par.

---

1. *See, e.g,.* Benihana of Tokyo, Inc v. Benihana, Inc, 906 A. 2d 114 (Del. 2006) in Chapter 11, *infra.*

First, stock typically cannot be issued by the corporation for less than par value. Second, when par value shares are issued by the corporation, a dollar figure equal to the par value is shown on the corporation's books as stated capital and in many states there are limitations, spelled out in the corporation statute, about what can be done with stated capital. No dividends, for example, may be paid out of it. Third, fees and taxes payable to the state of incorporation often are based on par value. A typical arrangement sets fees or taxes as a percentage of a number that is derived by multiplying par value by the number of shares authorized in the corporation's charter.

Here an interesting twist is that stock without par value typically is taxed as if it had relatively high par value, such as $100 per share, thus making stock without par value an unpopular choice in states, such as Delaware, that follow that practice. As a result of one or more of these consequences of par value, in the case of common stock, corporations typically either choose no par value stock (in situations where there are no unfavorable tax consequences) or they choose to set par at a small fraction of the proposed selling price of the stock. One dollar par value is perhaps most usual. Largely for reasons of tradition, corporations typically set the par value of preferred stock at or near its selling price, which often is $100 per share.

Model Act § 6.21 significantly changed the financial provisions of corporate codes by adopting a legal capital structure that is not based on the concepts of par value and stated capital. The Official Comment to the section explains the nature of the changes and the reasons for them:

> The financial provisions of the Model Act reflect a modernization of the concepts underlying the capital structure and limitations on distributions of corporations. This process of modernization began with amendments in 1980 to the 1969 Model Act that eliminated the concepts of "par value" and "stated capital," and further modernization occurred in connection with the development of the revised Act in 1984. Practitioners and legal scholars have long recognized that the statutory structure embodying "par value" and "legal capital" concepts is not only complex and confusing, but also fails to serve the original purpose of protecting creditor and senior security holders from payments to junior security holders. Indeed, to the extent security holders are led to believe that it provides this protection, these provisions may be affirmatively misleading. The Model Act has therefore eliminated these concepts entirely and substituted a simpler and more flexible structure that provides more realistic protection to these interests....

A company may, however, continue to use the par and no par stock designations if it wishes. Section 2.02(b)(2)(iv) of the Model Act permits the articles of incorporation to include "a par value for authorized shares or classes of shares."

The Comment to § 6.21 also distinguishes between corporate law mandates and principles of accounting. It further provides that:

> [B]ookkeeping details are not the statutory responsibility of the board of directors. The statute also does not require the board of directors to determine

the corresponding entry on the right-hand side of the balance sheet under owner's equity to be designated as 'stated capital' or be allocated among 'stated capital' and other surplus accounts. The corporation, however, may determine that the shareholders' equity account should be divided into these traditional categories if it wishes.

The Model Act does not make clear what consequences will follow if a corporation elects to assign par value to the shares it issues. Section 6.40 controls whether a corporation may make distributions to its shareholders. The Official Comment to §6.40 indicates that the board may also use the traditional designations of stated capital and capital surplus if it wishes. It is unclear the extent to which these designations may be used to restrict the board's ability to make distributions to shareholders if the distributions were otherwise permissible under §6.40.

b. Mechanics

The best way to learn more about capitalization is to go through the mechanics involved in a corporation's equity capitalization. The starting point is a corporation statute, and here we shall use both the Delaware General Corporation Law and the Model Business Corporation Act as representative examples of two approaches to capitalization.

Section 102(a)(4) of the DGCL provides that a corporation has authority to issue the number of shares that are stated in its charter, and that those shares may be divided into classes if the corporation so desires. That section also provides that the corporation must state in its charter the par value of its shares, or state that the shares are without par value.

As would be expected, §153 of the DGCL provides two separate rules for the consideration that a corporation must charge for its shares upon their original sale (called an "issuance") by the corporation, one rule for par value shares and the other for shares without par value. In each case, the consideration is typically to be that set by the board of directors. For par value shares, the board may not set the consideration at less than par value. For shares without par value, the stock may be issued for such consideration "as is determined" by the board of directors.

Section 152 needs to be read along with §153, because §152 specifies what kind of consideration is allowable in payment for the issuance of shares. Basically, under §152 the consideration must be in the form of cash, tangible or intangible property, any benefit to the corporation, or any combination of the foregoing.[7] If the stock is to be issued for an amount greater than its par value, and if an amount equal to par value has been paid in one of the forms of consideration just described, the corporation may accept a binding obligation of the purchaser to pay the remaining amount.

---

7. The predecessor to §152 provided that the consideration must be paid in money, in property or in labor or services rendered to the corporation. This approach is still followed in some jurisdictions.

No matter what form of consideration is accepted by the board, § 154 says that the board of directors must express the consideration in dollars. That allows the consideration to be entered properly in the corporation's books, which are kept in terms of dollars.

At this point it will be helpful to look at how a Delaware corporation accounts on its books for the consideration it receives upon the issuance of shares, using both par value and no par value shares as examples, and then to look at the legal consequences of that accounting. The accounting involved in our discussion will be very simple.

Section 154 of the DGCL provides that when a company issues shares having a par value, the amount determined to be capital must be at least equal to the aggregate par value of the outstanding shares. Thus, if a corporation issues 1,000 shares of $2 par value stock, capital must equal $2,000 ($2 par × 1,000 shares of stock). A corporation may issue shares for an amount greater than their par value. For example, $2 par stock may be issued for $5. In this case, the excess of the amount paid for the stock over the par value, or $3, may be designated as surplus. If it wishes to do so, however, the board of directors may include some or all of the excess in the capital account. For no par stock, § 154 provides that all consideration received for the issuance of shares constitutes stated capital unless the board determines that only a part of the consideration is to be stated capital. In that case, any amount the board wishes, short of all the consideration, can be designated as surplus.

It may be useful to digress briefly to review the statutory terminology and describe how the same concepts are used differently by lawyers and accountants. The Delaware statute uses the term "capital" for par stock and "stated capital" for no par stock. Lawyers often use the term "stated capital" to refer collectively to both capital and stated capital. Under the Delaware statute, the term "surplus" includes all accounts in the equity section of the balance sheet except capital or stated capital. Lawyers and accountants distinguish among different types of surplus according to the source of the funds. The terms "earned surplus" (lawyers) and "retained earnings" (accountants) refer to company earnings that have not been distributed to shareholders as dividends. The terms "capital surplus" (lawyers) and "paid in capital in excess of par" (accountants) refer to the amount of consideration received for shares in excess of the amount of capital or stated capital.

Looking at examples using lawyers' terminology will help the student understand how all of this works.

Suppose that a corporation issues 1,000 shares of $1 par value stock for $10 per share. After the issuance, the corporation's balance sheet will probably look like this:

Sample Balance Sheet
(amounts in dollars)

Assets		Liabilities	
Cash	10,000	None	0
		Owners' Equity	
		Stated Capital	1,000
		Capital Surplus	9,000
		Total Owners' Equity	10,000
Total Assets	10,000	**Total Liabilities and**	10,000
		Owners' Equity	

In the case of no par value stock, the balance sheet would show $10,000 in stated capital unless the board decided to place some portion of the consideration in capital surplus.

Suppose the corporation then invested its $10,000 in some venture that returned $15,000 on the investment, thereby producing earnings of $5,000. The $5,000 earnings would be recorded as earned surplus. Taking into account the results of that investment, the corporation's balance sheet will look like this in the case of one dollar par value stock:

Sample Balance Sheet
(amounts in dollars)

Assets		Liabilities	
Cash	15,000	None	0
		Owners' Equity	
		Stated Capital	1,000
		Capital Surplus	9,000
		Earned Surplus	5,000
		Total Owners' Equity	15,000
Total Assets	15,000	**Total Liabilities and**	15,000
		Owners' Equity	

To this point we have not said anything about what difference it makes whether a particular amount appears in stated capital, capital surplus, or earned surplus. Understanding that requires a brief discussion of cash dividends. (Stock dividends are discussed in a later chapter.) In modern parlance, a cash dividend is a payment to shareholders constituting a return *on* their investment. According to DGCL § 170, dividends may be paid from surplus or from current profits, but not from a capital account. The account a particular amount appears in, therefore, determines whether that amount is available for paying dividends.

In Delaware, dividends may be paid from either the earned surplus or capital surplus accounts. These accounts indicate the source of funds used for dividends. Dividends from earned surplus constitute a payout to the shareholders of the corporation's earnings, a return *on* shareholders' investments. Distributions from capital surplus (also called dividends in Delaware) generally represent a return *of* shareholders' capital rather than a payment of corporate earnings, as the usual source of capital surplus is the amount paid for shares in excess of par. Thus, distributions from capital surplus typically constitute a payback to shareholders of amounts previously invested by them in the corporation.

From the standpoint of the typical shareholder, a dividend and a distribution look alike. In each, the shareholder receives a check in the amount of the per share dividend or distribution, multiplied by the number of shares owned by the shareholder. But while a dividend typically is a payout to the shareholders of a corporation's earnings, a distribution usually is a payback to shareholders of amounts previously invested by them in the corporation. (There is no provision in the DGCL or in other corporation statutes using this approach for a payback to shareholders of a corporation's stated capital.)

That is not the end of the DGCL's story about the capital and surplus accounts, however, because the statute, like most others, allows certain transfers between those accounts. Under § 154, the board can transfer capital surplus to stated capital, thus restricting the company's ability to make distributions. That is understandable, since the drafters of the statute had no reason to prevent a board from restricting a corporation's ability to pay dividends if the board wants to do so. However, under § 244, the directors may also transfer amounts from stated capital to capital surplus as long as the amount left in stated capital is at least equal to the total par value of the corporation's issued stock, plus some amount representing no par shares, if any. What that often comes down to with par value stock is that if the board transfers an amount of capital surplus to stated capital, in the usual case the board later can transfer out of stated capital what the board had transferred in.

Here the question may arise what happens if a corporation has a deficit in earned surplus. Suppose, in our example above, that from the corporation's investment of $10,000 it received only $5,000 in return, thus losing $5,000. After that loss, the corporation's balance sheet would look like this, with parentheses indicating a negative number:

Sample Balance Sheet
(amounts in dollars)

Assets		Liabilities	
Cash	5,000	None	0
		Owners' Equity	
		Stated Capital	1,000
		Capital Surplus	9,000
		Earned Surplus	(5,000)
		Total Owners' Equity	5,000
Total Assets	5,000	**Total Liabilities and Owners' Equity**	5,000

If the board wishes to eliminate that earned surplus deficit, it may do so by a transfer from capital surplus. It may not, however, transfer from capital surplus any greater amount than that necessary to eliminate the deficit. If such a transfer were made, earned surplus would have a value of $0 and capital surplus a value of $4,000.

As discussed in the preceding section, the Model Act has eliminated the use of par value and the legal requirement to distinguish among capital and surplus accounts, although a company may continue with the practice if it wishes. Model Act changes to the rules governing dividends and distributions are discussed in a later chapter.

The case that follows provides one example of the kinds of controversies that can arise in connection with the application of the legal capital provisions.

Toms v. Cooperative Management Corp.

Louisiana Court of Appeals
741 So. 2d 164 (1999)

PEATROSS, J.

Defendant-in-Intervention, Janet Evans Toms ("Mrs. Toms"), appeals the judgment of the trial court granting Plaintiffs'-in-Intervention, the minority stockholders of Cooperative Management Corporation ("CMC"), Motion for Writ of Mandamus to prevent the issuance of stock to Mrs. Toms in violation of its by-laws. For the reasons stated herein, we affirm.

FACTS AND PROCEDURAL HISTORY

Mrs. Toms has sued CMC, a closely held family corporation, to rescind a 1988 transaction in which 150 shares of stock in CMC were redeemed by CMC for $22,500. It is the assertion of Mrs. Toms that she learned from a subsequent appraisal of CMC's immovable assets that she received significantly less for her stock than it was actually worth. After filing of suit by Mrs. Toms, a majority of CMC's Board of Directors ("the Board") decided, in an attempt to settle this litigation, to issue 150 new shares of CMC stock to be sold to Mrs. Toms for $22,500. A group of minority shareholders of CMC did not approve of the Board's decision and have intervened seeking to prevent the proposed sale on the basis that the transaction will necessarily result in an increase of CMC's stated capital account, an action that requires approval of the shareholders owning 85 percent of the stock in CMC under Article VII(2) of its by-laws. No such approval has been sought by, or granted to, the Board.

The parties have stipulated to the following facts:

1) CMC was formed in 1971 with its shareholders being Mr. and Mrs. J. O. Evans, their children, J. Bruce Evans, Barbara Evans Rogers, Janis Evans Leach and Janet Evans Toms, and their respective spouses. The capital contributions of the original shareholders included land owned or donated by Mr. and Mrs. J. O. Evans. The assets of CMC consist of approximately 1700 acres of timber land with long-term timber leases on 974 acres. All of the CMC stock is no par stock.

2) The Articles of Incorporation and the by-laws were offered as joint exhibits. The pertinent section to this case is Article VII(2) of the by-laws, which reads as follows:

The affirmative vote or written consent of 85% of the holders of each class or series of stock as may be issued and outstanding shall be necessary for any of the following voluntary corporate actions: ...

(2) Reduction or increase in the stated capital of the corporation....

3) Mrs. Toms owned 150 shares of stock in CMC prior to November 1988.

4) On November 24, 1988, the Board of CMC, by unanimous vote, authorized the redemption and cancellation of Mrs. Toms' 150 shares of stock for a total redemption price of $22,500, or $190 per share. The directors who authorized the action owned more than 85 percent of the stock of CMC. The minutes of the November 24, 1988 meeting were also entered as a joint exhibit.

5) On April 1, 1997, Mrs. Toms sued CMC for rescission of the 1988 stock redemption transaction alleging that a 1993 independent appraisal of CMC immovable property revealed that there was an error in the valuation of her CMC stock resulting in a payment to her of less than fair market value for her stock.

6) The CMC Board, by majority vote, approved a resolution on October 19, 1997, authorizing an increase of its stock by 150 shares, the entirety of which were to be sold to Mrs. Toms at a price of $22,500 ($190 per share). The di-

Rather than paying her what they owe they instead want just the cash. → redemption (see older of corp.) of facts

rectors who voted in favor of the resolution owned less than 85 percent of the stock of CMC. Mrs. Toms agreed to dismiss her suit upon receipt of the shares.

7) On that same date, the Board, by majority vote, approved a resolution providing that any consideration paid to CMC by a person for shares of stock be allocated to the capital surplus account of CMC rather than to stated capital. The directors voting in favor of the resolution owned less than 85 percent of the stock of CMC. The Board intends to allocate the sums paid by Mrs. Toms for the 150 shares of stock to the capital surplus account of CMC and allocate $0.00 to the stated capital account.

8) ... Evan Rogers, a director and shareholder, objected to the resolution [arguing] that "this was simply an attempt to circumvent the 85% requirement." Evan Rogers also passed out copies of several statutes concerning fiduciary duty (La. R.S. 12:61, 91 and 92) to all members of the Board and explained the duty to only issue stock for fair market value and that the amount offered in the proposal was not fair market value. A motion was then made to increase CMC's shares by 150 to be sold to Mrs. Toms for $22,500. The motion was passed with some opposition.

DISCUSSION

... The Defendants-in-Intervention, CMC and Mrs. Toms, take the position that they are able to engage in the proposed transaction for two reasons. First, they assert that La. R.S. 12:61(A), which states, in pertinent part:

> Upon the initial issuance of shares without par value, the board of directors shall state an amount to be allocated to stated capital and the remainder of any consideration [received] shall be allocated to capital surplus...,

allows a board of directors, in its discretion, to allocate all of the consideration paid for no par value stock to the capital surplus account without having any effect on stated capital. It is their intention to allocate $0 to stated capital, which they [argue] is a stated amount in accordance with La. R.S. 12:61(2). We disagree. The trial court succinctly addressed this issue, stating:

> The Court is of the opinion that a clear reading of [La. R.S. 12:61(A)] requires at least a portion of the sales price of the new stock be allocated to stated capital. The words of the statute are clear: The board of directors shall state an amount to be allocated to stated capital. Clearly the law requires some portion of the [consideration] from the new stock be allocated to stated capital. To hold otherwise would render this portion of the statute meaningless.

The trial court also relied on Fletcher's Cyclopedia of Law of Private Corporations, Volume II, Section 5128, which states:

5128. Increase of shares and capital—in general

To increase its number of authorized shares, a corporation must amend its articles or certificate of incorporation to reflect the increase. For corporations adhering to legal capital rules, the amendment may include an adjustment to the authorized capital representing the aggregate par value, if any, of the newly authorized shares.

In states that adhere to legal capital requirements, an increase in issued shares may require an adjustment of the corporation's stated capital account. The stated capital account includes the aggregate par value of all issued shares, plus at least a portion of the consideration received on the issuance of no-par shares.

We find no error with the trial court's interpretation of La. R.S. 12:61. Any other reading would render the statute meaningless. Zero is not an amount. Zero is no amount.

Second, the Defendants-in-Intervention, CMC and Mrs. Toms, argue that the 150 shares of stock originally redeemed by Mrs. Toms constitute treasury stock[8] which the Board simply ordered to be reissued again to Mrs. Toms, in accordance with La. R.S. 12:55, with no effect on stated capital. We find no merit to this argument. As the trial court pointed out, the evidence clearly shows that the shares redeemed from Mrs. Toms were canceled and the stated capital was proportionately reduced. The minutes of the October 19, 1997 Board meeting show that a motion was made to "increase [CMC's] shares by 150." Further, the minutes of the November 24, 1988 meeting note an official authorization to remove from the CMC books and treasury those shares redeemed by Mrs. Toms on November 10, 1988, reducing the "total shares of outstanding stock in [CMC] from 1200 (original issue) to currently 850."[9]

We find, therefore, that the trial court was correct in its finding that the record does not support Mrs. Toms' position that the reissuance of existing treasury stock would not result in an increase in the stated capital of the corporation. Moreover, the trial court was correct in issuing a Writ of Mandamus, as prayed for by the intervening shareholders, directing CMC to adhere to its own by-laws, specifically Article VII(2), in obtaining approval of the shareholders owning 85 percent of the stock in CMC to increase [stated] capital … prior to the issuance of any new stock. [Affirmed.]

Note

Making some inferences from the given facts, including those in the penultimate paragraphs, the initial capitalization in 1971 was likely 1,200 shares, with 600 shares held by Mr. and Mrs. J. O. Evans and 150 shares held by each of their children and that child's spouse. Who knows why, 17 years later, in 1988, Janet Evans decided to sell. Perhaps she had other investment opportunities or simply wanted the money to travel. In any event, when she sought her shares back a decade after that, in 1997, it was apparently her nephew, Evan Rogers, grandson of Mr. and Mrs. J. O. Evans,

---

8. The term "treasury shares" refers to shares that a corporation has issued and subsequently repurchased and that have been neither cancelled nor designated as authorized but unissued shares. Treasury shares are considered to be issued shares that are not outstanding. [Eds.]

9. [1] The secretary-treasurer was authorized to remove those stocks redeemed from Mrs. Toms, as well as 100 shares acquired by donation from J. O. Evans and 100 shares acquired by donation from Constance C. Evans, from the books of CMC, reducing the total outstanding stock by 350.

who led the opposition. Who seems to have been acting in a fairer manner, daughter Janet or grandson Evan?

B. Debt

1. Types of Debt

Debt capitalization involves corporate borrowing. The lender may be an independent third party or a shareholder of the corporation. In all cases, the corporation promises to repay to the lender at designated times the amount borrowed (the principal) plus interest. The obligation to repay is memorialized in an agreement that contains additional terms and conditions applicable to the obligation. The most common forms of debt capitalization are short-term and long-term (one to ten years) loans from banks, private investors, or shareholders to the corporation. Such loans typically are represented by notes, which may be secured or unsecured. A note holder may be protected by contractual provisions contained in a loan agreement between the corporation and the lender.

Bonds and debentures are often encountered in larger corporations. The term "bond" is used in two different ways. It may refer generally to long-term debt instruments of five to ten years or more. "Bond" is also used to describe a long-term debt instrument secured by a mortgage or deed of trust on corporate property, while an unsecured long-term debt instrument usually is called a "debenture." A bond or a debenture differs from a note in that bond and debenture holders are protected by contractual provisions contained in an indenture covering a multitude of corporate financial matters. (Today, notes may also be issued subject to an indenture.) An indenture is a contract between the corporation and an indenture trustee, usually a bank, that acts for the benefit of the bond or debenture holders.

There can be many advantages to a corporation and to its shareholders in having the corporation include debt in its capital structure. From the point of view of the corporation, an important advantage of debt is that interest payments on debt are tax deductible, while payments of dividends on stock are not. If, therefore, the corporation is considering issuing either long-term notes or preferred stock, issuing notes likely will be much less expensive, largely because of the tax advantage inherent in the notes. Often shareholders wish to put into a corporation some of their total contribution as equity and some as debt, and often a prospective investor wishes to be a creditor rather than a shareholder — usually a creditor having the right to convert his or her debt into common stock if all goes well for the corporation.

Of major interest to debt holders is that (1) debt may be repaid without any tax consequences, but if stock is redeemed when the corporation has had profits, the redemption may be taxed as a dividend; (2) if the corporation goes bankrupt, debt holders have prior preference, that is, the right to be repaid before any payments are made to preferred or common shareholders; and (3) if debt holders are not repaid, they can qualify for a current income tax deduction in the amount of their loss more readily than can a holder of equity who has suffered an investment loss. Largely for those reasons, owners of a corporation often wish to split their own contribution to the corporation between equity and debt, hoping to avoid some taxes if all goes well, and hoping also to salvage at least some of their investment if the corporation goes bankrupt.

During the 1980s, high-yield bonds became a popular form of security for raising new capital. High yield bonds are more popularly known as "junk bonds," which are bonds with below investment grade ratings.

> Junk bonds are issued by companies without long track records of sales and earnings, or by those with questionable credit strength. They are a popular means of financing takeovers. Since they are more volatile and pay higher yields than investment grade bonds, many risk-oriented investors specialize in trading them.[10]

Typically, junk bonds are below investment grade when they are issued. They may, however, also be what are often referred to as "fallen angels," that is bonds that were investment grade when originally issued but which subsequently lost their investment grade rating.

2. Leverage

Investors often try to achieve the competing goals of maximum safety and maximum return on their investment. Persons designing the capital structure of a corporation have similar objectives as they decide how much money to raise through equity and how much through debt. The results of their decisions determine how highly leveraged the company will be.

> The word "*leverage*" is used to describe the financial consequences of the use of debt and equity. The use of debt ("other people's money") creates financial leverage for the equity. The greater the debt the greater the leverage. The greater the leverage the greater the potential gains and losses for the equity and the greater the risk of loss for the debt. The effects of leverage result from the facts that (a) the debt holder (the lender) has a *fixed claim* (that is, a claim for a fixed amount of interest and for repayment of the amount of the loan); (b) the return on the investment or business financed by the debt is uncertain; and (c) the equity holder (the borrower) has a *residual claim* (that is, the right to whatever is left after the debt holder's claim is satisfied).[13]

By having their corporation borrow some of its capital from others, shareholders get the benefit of leverage. The benefits of leverage exist for the shareholders any time the corporation can make a return on borrowed money that is greater than the cost of the borrowed money. The easiest example of leverage for most people is the leverage enjoyed by homeowners during periods of rising real estate prices.

---

10. Dictionary of Financial Terms at 284.
13. William A. Klein & John C. Coffee, Jr., Business Organization and Finance 8 (11th ed. Foundation Press 2010).

Assume, for example, that a young lawyer buys a condominium for $100,000, paying $10,000 down and borrowing $90,000. If the lawyer later sells the condominium for $110,000 after expenses, the gain has been $10,000. If the lawyer had paid $100,000 cash for the house, the lawyer's gain on the invested funds would have been 10%. Since the lawyer's investment was instead highly leveraged, the gain on the $10,000 of invested funds was 100%. If the condominium had sold for $90,000 after expenses, in the leveraged transaction, the lawyer's loss would have been 100%, whereas if the lawyer had paid cash for the condominium, the loss would have been 10%.

As the preceding example demonstrates, leverage can be a disadvantage as well as an advantage, because it increases the amount of risk in a particular transaction. Thus, the higher the ratio of debt to equity, the greater the impact of leverage. (Notice that the preceding example did not include interest and other costs associated with borrowing. They would have to be considered as well.)

Shareholders can use leverage in the same way as can a homeowner, by causing their corporation to borrow money at a lower rate of interest than it can earn by using the money it borrowed. If, for example, a corporation borrows from a bank $50,000 at 10% interest and its shareholders contribute an additional $50,000 in exchange for all the corporation's common stock, and then the corporation makes a 15% return on its $100,000 total capital, the shareholders' return on their $50,000 investment is $10,000, or 20% on the funds they had invested. That is calculated as follows: $15,000 profit, minus $5,000 interest paid on the debt, equals $10,000, which is 20% of the $50,000 that the shareholders had invested.

Since, as indicated above, preferred stock is in financial terms more like debt than it is like common stock, the common shareholders can leverage their investment by causing their corporation to issue preferred stock just as easily as they can by having the corporation issue debt. In that case, for leveraging to be beneficial, the hoped-for return on the money obtained from the preferred shareholders must be greater than the dividends payable on the preferred stock.

The corporation can, of course, issue both preferred stock and debt, thus maximizing the common shareholders' leverage. Public utility corporations, for example, typically do just that, with a usual capitalization of one of those corporations being 30% common stock, 15% preferred stock, and 55% debt. One might ask why the entire leveraging amount of such a corporation is not made up of debt, since dividends on preferred stock are not tax deductible. A major reason is that public utility commissions have to approve the capital structures of public utilities, and those commissions will not allow public utilities to obligate themselves to make interest payments on more than about 55% debt. But those commissions usually will allow public utilities further to leverage their common shareholders by the issuance of perhaps 15% preferred stock. (Since preferred shareholders are not promised dividend payments, dividends are not a corporate obligation in the way that interest payments are.)

The use of leverage played an important role in the recent financial crisis. Leverage is particularly attractive when two factors combine: low interest rates and rising values of investment assets, such as real estate and equity securities. Low interest rates encourage investors to borrow money to finance investment. Rising values in investment assets reduce the perceived level of risk. Both factors—low interest rates and rising asset values—were present during the late 1990s and the early years of the 21st century.

During this same period, banks began conducting their business with increased amounts of leverage. Deregulation of chartered banks and the lack of regulation in the shadow banking system led to greater competition in the banking industry. Increased competition caused a decline in banks' profit margins. In an effort to restore profit margins to previous levels, banks became more highly leveraged. Greater use of leverage, however, also increased the banks' risks. When housing prices plunged, banks did not have sufficient assets to cover all of their outstanding obligations.

C. Introduction to Other Forms of Financing

The meaning of the words "capital" and "capitalization" can vary with context. We began this chapter by suggesting that a corporation's capitalization roughly amounts to its long-term resources and identified main components of equity and debt securities that provide it. Three more advanced points of corporate finance are worth noting. First, a corporation's short-term resource needs can be met in other ways, including through bank loans, trade credit, and commercial paper. Second, the long-term capital resources that can be represented by equity and debt instruments can also be supplemented by a variety of other devices like leases, convertible securities, and asset-backed securities. Third, corporate financial matters can be managed using various instruments collectively called "derivatives." The following attempts thumbnail sketches of these arrangements, but note that many are complex and space in this volume does not permit treating that complexity.

Short-Term Resources

Bank Loans

Corporations, especially smaller ones, may obtain short-term resources by taking loans from commercial banks. Payment terms can be payable "on demand" or within a year or less, though of course commercial banks often make loans on longer terms too. Short-term loans can be renewed, but continual renewal suggests that a corporation may be better off obtaining long-term financing of the form of debt capital discussed previously. Short-term loans tend to involve less extensive documentation and complexity compared to conventional debt arrangements.

Trade Credit

A common source of corporate finance is the simple extension of credit from suppliers of raw materials, inventory or other inputs into a corporation's operations. As examples, car manufacturers obtain tires or seats from suppliers, and computer hardware makers obtain plastic materials and software from vendors. Payment terms vary, but typically require a buyer to pay the supplier within thirty to ninety days. Buyers thus enjoy credit for that period. This form of credit is referred to as "trade credit." It generally is short-term, unsecured, and, in ongoing relationships, means there is invariably some amount due, referred to as trade credit on "open account." Arrangements are usually documented using standard and relatively simple forms of master agreement, with periodic bills of lading and invoices documenting exchanges.

Commercial Paper

A corporation's need for cash resources and generation of cash resources fluctuate daily. On some days, a corporation will have more cash than it needs for daily operations, and on other days it will need more cash than it has for that purpose. Facilitating balancing these changing and offsetting aggregate corporate needs is an active market, called the "commercial paper market." In it, large corporations needing cash issue promissory notes, called "commercial paper," in large amounts, at least $100,000, payable within short time periods, usually ninety days. Buyers of commercial paper include other large corporations enjoying cash surpluses, as well as banks and other financial institutions. Commercial paper generally is considered low-risk debt, compared to long term corporate debt, though not seen as riskless as government bonds. Individual corporations sometimes become unable to meet these short-term obligations, and credit nervousness about widespread inability to repay short-term debts can even freeze-up economic activity, as occurred in the early phases of the global financial crisis of 2008.

Beyond Equity and Debt

Leases

Leases are a substantial source of corporate finance. Leases are an alternative to buying real property, equipment, and other resources. When funds are borrowed on a long-term basis, it is reasonable to describe the debt commitment as contributing to and constituting part of the corporation's capital and capitalization. A corporation's decision to lease property or equipment on a long-term basis, under a contractual commitment to pay periodic rent, is similar in economic effect, combining command of resources with financial commitment. Yet, in several substantive contexts the two arrangements may receive different treatment, including for purposes of taxation, financial accounting, and bankruptcy. Even so, long-term lease arrangements do present similar consequences as long-term debt concerning a corporation's leverage and related risk.

Convertibles

Discussion in this chapter highlighted the concepts of equity securities and debt securities and distinguished these two categories. Though the differences are sharp conceptually in many practical applications, it is also possible for a particular security to have features of both equity and debt. Preferred stock provides a preliminary example, containing features of both debt and equity. Another example of such "hybrid securities" is a debt or preferred stock issuance that gives the investor the right to convert it into common stock. The parties would agree by contract on how the conversion right can be exercised, including during what time period, in what ratio of exchange, and at what price. The conversion feature becomes a form of option whose economic value will be a function of those terms. From the corporation's perspective, that additional economic value can improve the other terms of the debt or preferred stock arrangement, as by lowering the interest rate required to be paid on a debt instrument. In that sense, it is a sweetener in much the way that warrants can be sweeteners, as discussed earlier in this chapter.

Asset-Backed Securities

"Asset-backed securities" are instruments whose pay-out of interest and principal to investors comes from cash flows on particular assets set aside for that purpose. A common example is a bank that has accumulated a large amount of credit card receivables in the ordinary operation of its business. It transfers a portion of these to a special-purpose entity that, in turn, issues securities backed by the cash flows from those receivables. Investors buy the securities from the special-purpose entity and receive periodic payments, much as lenders on debt instruments receive periodic payments. For the bank, it has turned its receivables into instant cash from the transfer to the special-purpose entity funded by the investors' investment. It is akin to generating capital by borrowing it, secured by the receivables, but has the added advantage of transferring the receivables for cash, meaning a sale of those has occurred, rather than a lending. That means the bank's total debt, and therefore leverage, is lower than if it had obtained a conventional loan.

Derivatives

Corporate financial transactions present a bewildering variety of risks and trade-offs, and there are a nearly infinite variety of devices that can be designed to address or alter them. Many of these advanced devices are referred to as "derivative instruments," so called because their economic value is not determined solely by reference to some direct reference like a corporation's value but according to the changes in value of some other instrument or benchmark. Under this view, instruments like options are characterized as derivatives, as are an even broader class of contracts under which parties agree to swap cash payments according to external references like a designated interest rate, foreign currency exchange ratio, or commodity price index (collectively called "forward contracts" or, if traded on an organized market exchange, called "futures contracts").

All derivative arrangements are private-party contracts consummated using a relatively standardized set of legal form contracts initially developed by a trade association established in 1985, the International Swaps and Derivatives Association, Inc. (ISDA, pronounced *iz-dah*). It developed the products and, with the assistance and leadership of a group of business lawyers, the documentation to facilitate the rapid and dramatic expansion of the types, scope, and dollar amounts of derivatives in existence—measured in the trillions of dollars. ISDA boasts hundreds of member organizations, chiefly financial institutions and corporations, as well as professional services firms, including major law firms and public accounting firms.

Interest, Currency, and Commodity Swaps

For corporations, it is customary to use derivatives to manage certain kinds of business risk. For example, a corporation may borrow funds at an interest rate that is to vary over the life of the loan according to prevailing market conditions. But suppose the corporation would prefer to lock in today's prevailing rate, say, because it deems it very favorable compared to probable future rates or simply for the assurance of a fixed financial commitment. It can enter into a contract with another party, usually a financial intermediary, under which it swaps obligations with the counterparty, so it pays the other side the fixed rate and the counterparty pays the floating rate, with the two positions netted out at each payment date. That kind of derivative instrument, whose value is derived from the level of prevailing interest rates, is called an "interest rate swap" agreement. The corporation is hedged against adverse changes in interest rates.

Similar devices are available to hedge against adverse changes in other benchmarks or indices that define a corporation's financial obligations. These include hedges against adverse changes in foreign currency values that pose risks, especially for large multi-national corporations that borrow and deploy resources in many countries in multiple currencies. The resulting instruments are called "foreign currency swaps." Likewise, corporations that know they must fund acquisition of raw materials for their business can address the risk of skyrocketing prices in those materials by entering into contracts that essentially lock in today's price. Thus, an airline knows it will need a certain minimum quantity of jet fuel in coming years and faces risk of adverse price fluctuations. It can lock in the prevailing price by entering into a contract with a financial intermediary that pays it the excess if the future price is higher and on which it must pay the shortfall if the future price is lower. These devices, called "commodities forwards" (or "commodities futures" if traded on an organized exchange) are staples of contemporary risk management.

Equity Total Return, Credit Default Swaps, and CDOs

Another class of derivative instruments has developed to alter the risks and rewards of equity share ownership in corporations. In this arrangement, an existing corporate shareholder contractually commits to sell shares to another party for a stated price to be exchanged at a set future date. One effect of this arrangement, called an "equity swap" or sometimes an "equity total return swap," is to transfer the equity risk from the existing to the future shareholder: The existing shareholder is now entitled solely to the contractually agreed sum, and the future shareholder is now entitled to enjoy the upside potential and face the downside risk of corporate equity ownership. Note, however, that the existing shareholder would continue to be treated as the shareholder for corporation law purposes, including as to voting and other matters discussed in this book. In effect, the parties sever the economic features of the stock from the legal features.

Yet another class of derivative instruments addresses risk of defaults on debt. In this arrangement, an existing holder of corporate bonds contractually commits with another to make periodic insurance-like payments to the other in exchange for the other party paying a lump sum to the holder in the event that the corporate borrower defaults in its obligations under the bonds. It is called a "credit default swap," the person making the periodic payments is called the "buyer of protection" and the other party the "seller of protection." These arrangements resemble insurance in form, although there is no requirement that the buyer of protection actually own bonds on which it buys protection. That contrasts with insurance law and practice, which require that a buyer of insurance have an insurable interest to protect — you can buy insurance on your life or your home but not on your neighbor's life or home.

A related product innovation in the derivatives markets concerned "collateralized debt obligations" (CDOs). In their simplest form, this term referenced new ways to package combinations of asset-backed securities, principally those involving banks' mortgage loan assets. In general, instead of pooling a single batch of such assets into a single issuance of asset-backed securities, the pool of assets is split into multiple slices (called "tranches"), with different risk attributes, for sale to different kinds of investors who have different risk appetites. (The theory is that the value of the whole would be greater than merely the sum of its parts when split this way.) A more exotic variation on this theme involved "synthetic CDOs," meaning pure side bets on the referenced tranche or pool rather than ownership of the securities or the assets backing them. In that aspect, they are akin to credit default swaps involving buyers of protection who do not own the related bonds.

Regulation of Financial Derivatives

During the first few decades of their widespread use, derivative financial instruments were not subject to systematic regulatory oversight. In fact, the 2000 Commodity Futures Modernization Act (CFMA) put most derivatives beyond the regulatory reach of the Securities and Exchange Commission (SEC) and the Commodity Futures Trading Commission (CFTC). Instead, over-the-counter derivatives between sophisticated parties were treated as most contracts are, with parties free to negotiate, set terms, and either perform or breach and pay damages as they wished. The growth of the derivatives markets and the resulting concentration of risk that was manifest during the 2008–10 financial crisis induced Congress to regulate derivatives by passing the Dodd-Frank Act of 2010. The Act is designed to create transparency and accountability in the derivatives market.

Numerous provisions of the Dodd-Frank Act establish federal oversight of financial derivatives markets and contracts. In general, through dozens of particularized provisions, the Act establishes a comprehensive framework for the regulation of derivative financial markets. As a result, many derivative securities are no longer regarded as mere private contracts. Instead, they are listed for trading in organized trading and clearing exchanges much as common stocks have long been listed and traded on exchanges. Certain market professionals, such as those specializing in dealing in derivatives, must register with regulatory authorities and are subject to related oversight. Financial regulators such as the CFTC and SEC enjoy expanded authority to establish regulations across a wide range of matters, such as establishing capital and margin requirements on market participants and setting limits on acceptable positions.

Section II
Duly Authorized, Validly Issued, Fully Paid, and Nonassessable Stock

Corporate lawyers often are asked to give an opinion that certain shares of a corporation's stock are duly authorized, validly issued, fully paid, and nonassessable. That typically occurs when a corporation sells shares to the public or to private investors. "Duly authorized" simply means that when the shares were issued, the corporation had sufficient shares authorized in its charter to cover the issuance. For example, if the opinion relates to 100 shares issued on May 1, the lawyer would check to be sure that, when the 100 shares were issued, the corporation's charter had authorized at least 100 shares in excess of the shares that were already outstanding on that date.

"Validly issued" indicates that the issuance of shares was in accordance with corporation law. "Validly issued" raises two questions: (1) Did the proper corporate body authorize and implement the issuance of the shares? (2) Were the shares issued for the proper type and amount of consideration?

In answer to the first question, all corporation statutes give the board the power to approve the issuance of stock.[15] Model Act § 7.32 also permits shareholders of closely held corporations to enter into shareholder agreements transferring the power to authorize and issue stock to the shareholders. The discussion that follows will describe the usual procedures based on board authorization. The reader should keep in mind, however, that under certain circumstances the shareholders may be the proper authority to approve the issuance of shares. In the usual case, a lawyer will first determine whether the board approved the issue and, if so, whether the officers took the proper steps to issue the shares according to board's specifications. To answer that question, the lawyer will examine the applicable corporate documents to determine that the issuance was properly authorized and implemented.

Answering the second question regarding the proper type and amount of consideration reveals some overlap between "validly issued," "fully paid" and "nonassessable." At the time the board approves the issuance of stock, it will specify the type and amount of consideration for which the shares will be issued. Both the type and amount specified must comply with the applicable corporate statutes, as more fully described below. Thus, at this stage, the lawyer determines whether the specific provisions of the board resolution concerning the issuance of the shares complies with applicable law.

"Fully paid" means that, the appropriate type and amount of consideration that was to have been paid upon issuance has been paid. In almost all cases if stock is fully paid, it is nonassessable or, put another way, if stock is fully paid, the owner cannot

---

15. That power typically is covered in the section of the statute giving the board of directors general management power. In the Model Act, that power is granted by § 8.01(b), which says: "All corporate powers shall be exercised by or under the authority of, and the business and affairs of the corporation managed by or under the direction of, its board of directors...." Model Act § 801(b).

be assessed for further payments. There are two ways that stock could be assessable. Once in a great while a corporation's charter authorizes "assessable stock," which simply means that in certain specified circumstances the corporation has the right to demand future payments from the holders of that stock. Stock also can be assessable if the proper type and amount of consideration that was to have been paid upon its issuance was not paid.

Under a statute like the Model Act, it usually is easy to determine if the statutory requirements as to type of consideration have been met, since those requirements are clearly spelled out. Model Act § 6.21(b) provides that: "[t]he board of directors may authorize shares to be issued for consideration consisting of any tangible or intangible property or benefit to the corporation, including cash, promissory notes, services performed, contracts for services to be performed, or other securities of the corporation." Other states have adopted a more restrictive approach than the Model Act by not including contracts for future services in the list of valid types of consideration.

The Comment to the Model Act explains that:

> Section 6.21(b) specifically validates contracts for future services (including promoters' services), promissory notes or "any tangible or intangible property or benefit to the corporation," as consideration for the present issue of shares. The term "benefit" should be broadly construed to include, for example, a reduction of a liability, a release of a claim, or benefits obtained by a corporation by contribution of its shares to a charitable organization or as a prize in a promotion. In the realities of commercial life, there is sometimes a need for the issuance of shares for contract rights to such intangible property or benefits. And, as a matter of business economics, contracts for future services, promissory notes, and intangible property or benefits often have value that is as real as the value of tangible property or past services, the only types of property that many older statutes permit as consideration for shares. Thus, only business judgment should determine what kind of property should be obtained for shares....[16]

Determining whether the required amount of consideration has been paid involves the following issues. In jurisdictions retaining the concept of par value, the lawyer must determine whether the consideration was at least equal to par value if the shares had par value or at least equal to the specified stated value applicable to no-par shares. If cash is received as consideration for the issuance of stock, it is of course easy to tell if the required amount has been received. This is not so easy to do when the consideration is property or services. The Model Act offers some assistance by vesting in the board of directors responsibility for determining that the consideration received for shares is adequate. According to Model Act § 6.21(c):

> Before the corporation issues shares, the board of directors must determine that the consideration received or to be received for shares is adequate. That determination by the board of directors is conclusive insofar the adequacy

---

16. Model Act § 6.21 Official Comment.

of consideration for the issuance of shares relates to whether the shares are validly issued, fully paid and nonassessable.

Model Act §6.21(e) permits the corporation to hold in escrow shares issued for a contract for future services, a promissory note or other benefit until the corporation has received the full amount of the consideration.

Model Act §6.21(d) further states that: "[W]hen the corporation receives the consideration for which the board of directors authorized the issuance of shares, the shares issued therefor are fully paid and nonassessable." Sections 6.21(c) and (d) leave little doubt as to what it takes to have stock that is fully paid and nonassessable. Shareholders who have not paid the full amount of consideration for their shares remain liable for any unpaid amounts outstanding. Thus, in a Model Act jurisdiction, the only additional requirement the lawyer usually has to worry about is whether the consideration set by the board actually has been paid. In preparing a legal opinion as to whether shares are nonassessable and fully paid, the lawyer would first determine that the consideration set by the board met the statutory requirements, for example, that the transfer of a piece of real estate appraised at $10,000 is an acceptable type of consideration for 1,000 shares of stock. The lawyer would then check to see if title to the real estate actually passed to the corporation in exchange for the stock.

Shares issued for less than the full amount of permissible consideration set by the board are often referred to as "watered stock." So long as it is outstanding and not fully paid, watered stock dilutes the value of other issued shares because the corporation has not received full value for watered stock.

Historically, the concept of watered stock was tied to the concept of par value. It was also based on the assumption that corporate creditors relied on a corporation's balance sheet values when deciding whether or not to extend credit to the company. Stock could be "watered" in one of two ways. One is that the shareholder to whom shares were issued did not pay to the corporation the amount that was legally to have been paid. Thus, if the corporation did not receive at least $1,000 in exchange for an issue of 100 shares of $10 par value stock, the stock was considered to be watered.

A second way is that the value of the consideration used to pay for the stock was inflated. If 100 shares of $10 par value stock were issued for property actually worth only $500 at the time of the transfer, but recorded on the company books at the inflated amount of $1,000, the stock would be watered. If, therefore, the full amount of the required consideration, at least that equal to par, is not received by the corporation or its value is inflated at the time of transfer, the associated stock would be watered.

The Model Act changed the conceptual approach to the legal capital structure by eliminating the concepts of par value and stated capital. It also expanded the types of consideration for which a corporation may issue shares. Thus, under the Model Act, the central question is whether the full amount of the promised consideration has been received by the corporation issuing shares. According to the Official Comment for Model Act §6.21:

Since shares need not have a par value, under section 6.21 there is no minimum price at which specific shares must be issued and therefore there can be no "watered stock" liability for issuing shares below an arbitrarily fixed price. The price at which shares are issued is primarily a matter of concern to other shareholders whose interests may be diluted if shares are issued at unreasonably low prices or for overvalued property. This problem of equality of treatment essentially involves honest and fair judgments by directors and cannot be effectively addressed by an arbitrary doctrine establishing a minimum price for shares such as "par value" provided under older statutes.

The Model Act makes a shareholder liable for the full amount of the consideration established by the board of directors. The Delaware General Corporation Law, which retains the concept of par value, takes a similar approach.

A corporate board authorizing a share issuance often retains outside counsel to assist with all aspects of the transaction. Among the roles of such counsel is the delivery of a legal opinion attesting to the legality and validity of the issuance. A sample form of such an opinion follows. It would be the product of negotiation between outside counsel and the corporation's general counsel's office. What areas of negotiation would you foresee, if any?

[LAW FIRM LETTERHEAD]

[Date]

Board of Directors
[Name of Company]
[Address of Company]

Securities Issuance

Dear Ladies and Gentlemen:

We have acted as counsel for [Name of Company], a Delaware corporation (the "Company"), in connection with the issuance and sale of shares of common stock, at $.01 par value per share, of the Company (the "Common Stock") and shares of a series A preferred stock, at $100 par value (the "Preferred Stock"), of the Company....

1. In connection with this opinion, we have examined originals, or copies certified or otherwise identified to our satisfaction, of such corporate records as we have deemed necessary or appropriate for the purposes of this opinion, including the Company's certificate of incorporation and bylaws, certificates of corporate officers and government officials and such other documents. As to various questions of fact material to this opinion, we have relied upon representations of officers or directors of the Company and documents furnished to us by the Company without independent verification of their accuracy. We have also assumed the genuineness of all signatures, the authenticity of all documents submitted to us as originals and the conformity to authentic original documents of all documents submitted to us as copies. Based upon and subject to the foregoing, we are of the following opinions:

2. With respect to shares of the Common Stock, when (A) the Board has taken all necessary corporate action to approve the issuance of and the terms of the offering,

(B) certificates representing shares of the Common Stock have been duly executed, countersigned, registered and delivered and (C) the consideration approved by the Board (which consideration is not less than the par value of the Common Stock), then such shares of the Common Stock will be validly issued, duly authorized, fully paid and nonassessable....

3. With respect to shares of the Preferred Stock, when (A) the Board has taken all necessary corporate action to approve the issuance and terms thereof, including the adoption of a Certificate of Designations relating to such shares of the Preferred Stock and the filing of such Certificate of Designations with the Secretary of State of the State of Delaware, (B) such Certificate of Designations has been properly filed with the Secretary of State of the State of Delaware, (C) certificates representing such shares of the Preferred Stock have been duly executed, countersigned, registered and delivered and (D) the consideration approved by the Board (which consideration is not less than the par value of the Common Stock) is received by the Company, then such shares of the Preferred Stock will be validly issued, duly authorized, fully paid and nonassessable.

We are admitted to practice only in the State of New York and express no opinion as to matters governed by any laws other than the laws of the State of New York, the Delaware General Corporation Law and the Federal laws of the United States of America....

Very truly yours,

[Law Firm]

The following case demonstrates one view of the consequences that flow from a shareholder's failure to pay the amount of consideration due.

Hanewald v. Bryan's, Inc.

North Dakota Supreme Court

429 N.W.2d 414 (1988)

MESCHKE, JUSTICE.

Harold E. Hanewald appealed from that part of his judgment for $38,600 plus interest against Bryan's, Inc. which refused to impose personal liability upon Keith, Joan, and George Bryan for that insolvent corporation's debt. We reverse the ruling that Keith and Joan Bryan were not personally liable.

On July 19, 1984, Keith and Joan Bryan incorporated Bryan's, Inc. to "engage in and operate a general retail clothing, and related items, store...." The Certificate of Incorporation was issued by the Secretary of State on July 25, 1984. The first meeting of the board of directors elected Keith Bryan as president and Joan Bryan as secretary-treasurer of Bryan's, Inc. George Bryan was elected vice-president, appointed registered agent, and designated manager of the prospective business. The Articles of Incorporation authorized the corporation to issue "100 shares of common stock with a par value of $1,000 per share" with "total authorized capitalization [of] $100,000.00." Bryan's, Inc. issued 50 shares of stock to Keith Bryan and 50 shares of stock to Joan

Bryan. The trial court found that "Bryan's, Inc. did not receive any payment, either in labor, services, money, or property, for the stock which was issued."

On August 30, 1984, Hanewald sold his dry goods store in Hazen to Bryan's, Inc. Bryan's, Inc. bought the inventory, furniture, and fixtures of the business for $60,000, and leased the building for $600 per month for a period of five years. Bryan's, Inc. paid Hanewald $55,000 in cash and gave him a promissory note for $5,000, due August 30, 1985, for the remainder of the purchase price. The $55,000 payment to Hanewald was made from a loan by the Union State Bank of Hazen to the corporation, personally guaranteed by Keith and Joan Bryan.

Bryan's, Inc. began operating the retail clothing store on September 1, 1984. The business, however, lasted only four months with an operating loss of $4,840. In late December 1984, Keith and Joan Bryan decided to close the Hazen store. Thereafter, George Bryan, with the assistance of a brother and local employees, packed and removed the remaining inventory and delivered it for resale to other stores in Montana operated by the Bryan family. Bryan's, Inc. sent a "Notice of Rescission" to Hanewald on January 3, 1985, in an attempt to avoid the lease. The corporation was involuntarily dissolved by operation of law on August 1, 1986, for failure to file its annual report with the Secretary of State.

Bryan's, Inc. did not pay the $5,000 promissory note to Hanewald but paid off the rest of its creditors. Debts paid included the $55,000 loan from Union State Bank and a $10,000 loan from Keith and Joan Bryan. The Bryan loan had been, according to the trial court, "intended to be used for operating costs and expenses."

Hanewald sued the corporation and the Bryans for breach of the lease agreement and the promissory note, seeking to hold the Bryans personally liable. The defendants counterclaimed, alleging that Hanewald had fraudulently misrepresented the business's profitability in negotiating its sale. After a trial without a jury, the trial court entered judgment against Bryan's, Inc. for $38,600 plus interest on Hanewald's claims and ruled against the defendants on their counterclaim. The defendants have not cross appealed these rulings.

The trial court, however, refused to hold the individual defendants personally liable for the judgment against Bryan's, Inc., stating: "Bryan's, Inc. was formed in a classic manner, the $10,000.00 loan by Keith Bryan being more than sufficient operating capital. Bryan's Inc. paid all obligations except the obligation to Hanewald in a timely fashion, and since there was no evidence of bad faith by the Bryans, the corporate shield of Bryan's Inc. should not be pierced." Hanewald appealed from the refusal to hold the individual defendants personally liable.

Insofar as the judgment fails to impose personal liability upon Keith and Joan Bryan, the corporation's sole shareholders, we agree with Hanewald that the trial court erred. We base our decision on the Bryans' statutory duty to pay for shares that were issued to them by Bryan's, Inc.

Organizing a corporation to avoid personal liability is legitimate. Indeed, it is one of the primary advantages of doing business in the corporate form. *See generally* 1

W. Fletcher, Cyclopedia of the Law of Private Corporations §14 (1983). However, the limited personal liability of shareholders does not come free. As this court said in *Bryan v. Northwest Beverages*, 69 N.D. 274, 285 N.W. 689, 694 (1939), "[t]he mere formation of a corporation, fixing the amount of its capital stock, and receiving a certificate of incorporation, do not create anything of value upon which the company can do business." It is the shareholders' initial capital investments which protect their personal assets from further liability in the corporate enterprise. *See Cross v. Farmers' Elevator Co. of Dawson*, 31 N.D. 116, 153 N.W. 279, 282 (1915); *Jablonsky v. Klemm*, 377 N.W.2d 560, 566 (N.D.1985) (*quoting Briggs Transp. Co. v. Starr Sales Co.*, 262 N.W.2d 805, 810 (Iowa 1978)) ["shareholders should in good faith put at the risk of the business unencumbered capital reasonably adequate for its prospective liabilities."]; and J. Gillespie, *supra*, 45 N.D.L.Rev. at 388 ["Proper capitalization might be envisioned as the principal prerequisite for the insulation of limited liability."]. Thus, generally, shareholders are not liable for corporate debts beyond the capital they have contributed to the corporation. *See* 1 F. O'Neal and R. Thompson, O'Neal's Close Corporations §1.09 (3rd ed. 1987).

This protection for corporate shareholders was codified in the statute in effect when Bryan's, Inc. was incorporated and when this action was commenced, former §10-19-22, N.D.C.C.

> "Liability of subscribers and shareholders.—A holder of or subscriber to shares of a corporation shall be under no obligation to the corporation or its creditors with respect to such shares other than the obligation to pay to the corporation the full consideration for which such shares were issued or to be issued."

This statute obligated shareholders to pay for their shares as a prerequisite for their limited personal liability. The kinds of consideration paid for corporate shares may vary. Article XII, §9 of the state constitution says that "[n]o corporation shall issue stock or bonds except for money, labor done, or money or property actually received; and all fictitious increase of stock or indebtedness shall be void." Section 10-19-16, N.D.C.C., allowed "[t]he consideration for the issuance of shares [to] be paid, in whole or in part, in money, in other property, tangible or intangible, or in labor or services actually performed for the corporation.... [But] [n]either promissory notes nor future services shall constitute payment or part payment for shares of a corporation." And only "[w]hen payment of the consideration ... shall have been received by the corporation, [can] such shares ... be considered fully paid and nonassessable." *Id.* The purpose of these constitutional and statutory provisions is "to protect the public and those dealing with the corporation...." *Bryan v. Northwest Beverages, supra*, 285 N.W. at 694.

In this case, Bryan's, Inc. was authorized to issue 100 shares of stock each having a par value of $1,000. Keith Bryan and Joan Bryan, two of the original incorporators and members of the board of directors, were each issued 50 shares. The trial court determined that "Bryan's Inc. did not receive any payment, either in labor, services, money, or property, for the stock which was issued." [T]he Bryans have not challenged this finding of fact on this appeal. We hold that Bryans' failure to pay for their shares in the corporation makes them personally liable under § 10-19-22, N.D.C.C., for the corporation's debt to Hanewald.

Drafters' comments to § 25 of the Model Business Corporation Act [(1969)], upon which § 10-19-22 was based, sketched the principles: "The liability of a subscriber for the unpaid portion of his subscription and the liability of a shareholder for the unpaid balance of the full consideration for which his shares were issued are based upon contract principles. The liability of a shareholder to whom shares are issued for overvalued property or services is a breach of contract. These liabilities have not been considered to be exceptions to the absolute limited liability concept." Where statutes have been silent, courts have differed as to whether the cause of action on the liabilities of shareholders for unpaid consideration for shares issued or to be issued may be asserted by a creditor directly, by the corporation itself or its receiver, or by a creditor on behalf of the corporation. The Model Act [(1969)] is also silent on the subject for the reason that it can be better treated elsewhere. 1 Model Business Corporation Act Annotated 2d, Comment to § 25, at pp. 509–510 (1971). This court, in *Marshall-Wells Hardware Co. v. New Era Coal Co.*, 13 N.D. 396, 100 N.W. 1084 (1904), held that creditors could directly enforce shareholders' liabilities to pay for shares held by them under statutes analogous to § 10-19-22. We believe that the shareholder liability created by § 10-19-22 may likewise be enforced in a direct action by a creditor of the corporation.

Our conclusion comports with the generally recognized rule, derived from common law, that "a shareholder is liable to corporate creditors to the extent his stock has not been paid for." 18A Am. Jur. 2d Corporations § 863, at p. 739 (1985)....

We conclude that the trial court, having found that Keith and Joan Bryan had not paid for their stock, erred as a matter of law in refusing to hold them personally liable for the corporation's debt to Hanewald. The debt to Hanewald does not exceed the difference between the par value of their stock and the amount they actually paid. Therefore, we reverse in part to remand for entry of judgment holding Keith and Joan Bryan jointly and severally liable for the entire corporate debt to Hanewald. The judgment is otherwise *Affirmed*.

———

Under the most traditional view of watered stock liability, a shareholder was liable for the difference between the amount paid for a share and the share's par value. That view made good sense in the nineteenth and early twentieth centuries, when most watered stock cases were decided, because the practice then was to sell stock at its par value, which traditionally was $100 per share. If that practice is assumed, (1) not paying par value for shares and (2) not paying the consideration set by the board in accordance with statutory requirements would come down to the same thing. Put another way, the target amount for avoiding watered stock liability would be par value under both traditional and some modern formulations, such as that in Delaware.

In the traditional view, the amount of a stock's par value was thought to have great importance to a corporation's creditors because (1) if stock is sold at its par value, the entire consideration paid for the stock goes into stated capital and, (2) as seen in the *Hanewald* case, stated capital traditionally was the basis for a corporation's credit.

Even under modern statutes, stated capital arguably does provide creditors some protection in that it may be said to set a limit on what amounts can be taken out of the corporation by dividends or distributions. For example, a creditor looking at the following balance sheet could conclude rightly that at that point the corporation could take no money out of the corporation as dividends or distributions.

Notice, however, that "at that point" is an important qualifier. As discussed above in connection with Delaware's approach to these issues, if at any time stated capital exceeds the aggregate par value of a corporation's outstanding stock, the board can vote to transfer the excess stated capital to capital surplus, and all of a corporation's capital surplus may be taken out of the corporation by a distribution (called a dividend in Delaware) to shareholders.

Also, a corporation at any time can amend its charter to change the par value of its stock so as to create an excess in stated capital that may be transferred to capital surplus. In Model Act jurisdictions, the stated capital and surplus accounts may be retained for accounting purposes, but they are not intended to impose constraints on directors wishing to issue dividends or other distributions (although a court could perhaps find otherwise). All in all, the protection that stated capital gives creditors is more illusory than real. Partly for this reason, creditors in modern times focus on corporations' income and cash flow statements (described in the Appendix), rather than on stated capital, in making credit decisions.

Section III
Subordination

There are dangers for shareholders if they go too far with their use of shareholder debt or if they are not careful enough in establishing and maintaining their debtor-creditor relationship with the corporation. In each case, the problem is that there may be found to exist what is called "thin incorporation." The consequences of thin incorporation fall into two categories. First, the Internal Revenue Service may consider the debt to be equity for tax purposes, causing the interest payments on the debt to be treated as nondeductible dividends. Second, a court may subordinate the shareholders' debt to that of other creditors in the event of bankruptcy or other financial calamity.

The question of whether a company is "thinly incorporated" is usually raised when a company is financed with both debt and equity and some portion of the debt consists of loans from shareholders. The central issue is whether the debt is actually equity disguised as a loan. With careful planning of the company's financial structure, one can avoid having shareholder debt re-characterized as equity and thereby avoid suffering unwanted tax and other consequences.

First, the company should have sufficient equity to acquire needed assets and to operate the business. Second, the amount of debt should be within the company's ability to repay from business operations. Third, the debt should be bona fide debt, with the obligation to repay a sum certain, with interest, by an established date. The terms of the loan should be one that a third party lender would agree to. Fourth, the company should repay principal and interest according to a preset schedule, and the shareholder should act as a creditor ordinarily would if payments are not made as required. Fifth, there should be a bona fide business purpose served by the loan.

Although there is not a magic debt-to-equity ratio that will guarantee protection, exercising restraint is advised. What debt-to-equity ratio is reasonable depends on the specific circumstances, which vary with both different kinds of businesses and different economic environments. For instance, financial institutions customarily operate with considerably more leverage than retailing or manufacturing operations. Average debt-to-equity ratios tend to be higher in periods of economic expansion and to contract significantly during recessions or periods of stagnation. When comparing companies, moreover, care must be taken to calculate the various components of debt and equity so that calculations are done in the same manner. The following cases suggest some of the uses and limits of debt-to-equity ratios—along with other factors associated with leverage and capital structure—in the context of the distribution of assets of an insolvent corporation.

Obre v. Alban Tractor Co.

Maryland Court of Appeals

179 A.2d 861 (1962)

The single question raised by this appeal is whether the Chancellor erred in his finding that a note of a corporation to its principal stockholder represented a risk capital investment in the corporation and not a bona fide debt entitling the stockholder to share as a general creditor in distribution of the corporation's assets due to insolvency.

The Annel Corporation began its existence in January, 1959, when the appellant, Henry Obre, and F. Stevens Nelson pooled certain equipment and cash for the purpose of forming the corporation to engage in the dirt moving and road building business. As his share, Obre transferred to the corporation equipment independently appraised at $63,874.86, plus $1,673.24 cash, for a total of $65,548.10. Nelson's contribution was equipment valued at $8,495.00 and $1,505.00 in cash, totaling $10,000.00.

In return, Obre received $20,000.00 par value non-voting preferred stock and $10,000.00 par value voting common stock. In addition, he received the corporation's unsecured note for $35,548.10, dated January 2, 1959, which was the date of the incorporation. The note, which is the subject of this appeal, was made payable five years after date and carried interest at the rate of five percent per annum, though no interest was ever actually paid. Nelson received for his contribution voting common stock of $10,000.00 par value.

The corporation, with Obre as president and Nelson as vice-president, experienced financial difficulty very soon after beginning its operations, requiring Obre to pay certain creditors and meet a payroll in March, 1959, by use of his own funds. For the same reason he discontinued taking his salary of $75.00 a week in May, 1959. In April, 1959, the corporation borrowed $27,079.20 from a bank, securing the loan with a chattel mortgage. During its period of operation the corporation prepared monthly financial reports in which Obre's note was listed as a debt of the corporation.

In 1959 the corporation showed an operating loss of $14,324.67. Its continued lack of success led to the execution of a deed of trust for the benefit of creditors on October 19, 1960, and the Circuit Court for Baltimore County, sitting in equity, assumed jurisdiction of the trust.

Obre filed four separate claims in the case which were excepted to by Alban Tractor Co. and certain other trade creditors (appellees here). The Chancellor, after hearing, issued a decree sustaining the exceptions to Obre's claim on the note in question, on the ground that the note represented a contribution to the capital of the corporation and not a bona fide debt owed to Obre upon which he could share as a general creditor. The Chancellor based his decision on his finding that the corporation could not have carried on its operations without the equipment contributed by Obre. He felt that the fact that the note was given on the same day the corporation was formed, and that it was a five year note, indicated that the transaction was not a loan but was really a risk capital contribution. He held that, in view of these factors, equity required that the claim be subordinated to the claims of the general creditors. Under the circumstances of this case we are unable to agree with the conclusion of the Chancellor....

[A]ppellees contend that they have shown a "subordinating equity" in that the corporation, in which Obre was a dominant stockholder, was an undercapitalized venture, and that where such a situation exists, fraud or mismanagement need not be present in order to subordinate the claims of the principal stockholders. The test in such a case, it is argued, is whether the transaction can be justified within the bounds of reason and fairness. There is, principally in bankruptcy cases, some authority indicating support for this argument. See, for example, *Costello v. Fazio*, 256 F.2d 903 (C.A. 9, 1958). However, even if we assume, without deciding, that there may be situations in which the doctrine of subordination would be applied in a case short of fraud or estoppel, on general equitable principles, we do not believe that the facts present such a case here.

... Because of the expressed desire of Obre and Nelson that their control of the corporation be equal from the outset, and their ownership eventually equal, the corporate structure had to be planned carefully. Since Obre's contribution in the way of equipment was substantially greater than that of Nelson, the stock was issued so that each received an equal amount of common voting stock, but additional preferred stock was issued to Obre with the condition that it should have voting power if and when it became necessary to [not pay] the dividend on the preferred stock. The remaining excess of assets brought in by Obre, over and above the stock issued to him, was not to be considered a capital investment since this would have made the desired end of eventual equal ownership that much more difficult. Hence the note in question was executed for the excess of $35,548.10. The result of this planning was that a permanent equity capital of $40,000 would be invested, which, as was noted in a memorandum of the firm planning the corporate structure, "all parties consider it entirely adequate for the foreseeable needs of the corporation." The note was made payable in five years, instead of in equal annual installments, for the explicit purpose of gaining tax advantage....

... There is no showing that $40,000 was inadequate capitalization for an enterprise of this size, particularly in view of the careful planning that went into determining its capital structure. What may appear hazardous by hind-sight may not have been unreasonable at the outset. It is not unusual in corporate financing to have approximately one-half of contributions put in as risk capital and the balance as loan capital. There can be no question but that, if a third party had advanced the money represented by Obre's note, he would validly be considered a creditor of the corporation.

Our view in no way compromises the position of the corporate creditor. As this Court stated in [an earlier case]:

> So long as the corporate plan is adopted and pursued in good faith and in accordance with the ... laws of the state, those dealing with the corporation have only themselves to blame if they suffer from neglect to seek information obtainable from public records and other available sources.

It is obvious that the creditors in this case could have determined (if they actually did not do so) the financial status of the corporation by simply inspecting the stock issuance certificate filed with the State Tax Commission, or by requesting financial reports, or by obtaining credit ratings from the sources available....

In our opinion there is no basis in fact or law to justify the subordinating of appellant's claim under the note, and the decree must therefore be

Reversed.

Fett Roofing and Sheet Metal Co. v. Moore

United States District Court, Eastern District of Virginia
438 F. Supp. 726 (1977)

CLARKE, DISTRICT JUDGE.

This matter comes before the Court on the appeal by plaintiff from an order of United States Bankruptcy Judge Hal J. Bonney, Jr., which dismissed plaintiffs' complaint, subordinated the note claims of the plaintiff to the claims of all other creditors and set aside deeds of trust which purported to secure the note claims. Appellant contends that the Bankruptcy Judge's findings of fact and conclusions of law were completely erroneous and that appellant's claims against the bankrupt should be reinstated....

The Facts

The record below discloses that the bankrupt, Fett Roofing and Sheet Metal Co., Inc., was owned and run prior to 1965 by plaintiff herein, Donald M. Fett, Sr., as a sole proprietorship. During 1965, Mr. Fett incorporated his business, transferring to the new corporation assets worth $4,914.85 for which he received 25 shares of stock. The stated capital of the corporation was never increased during the course of the corporation's existence. Mr. Fett was the sole stockholder and also the president of the corporation. The roofing business continued to be run completely by Mr. Fett much as it had been prior to its incorporation.

In short, Fett Roofing was a classic "one-man" corporation. Over the years, plaintiff advanced money to his business as the need arose. Three of these transactions made in 1974, 1975 and 1976 involved the transfer to the corporation of $7,500, $40,000 and $30,000, respectively. In each instance plaintiff borrowed from the American National Bank, made the funds available to his business and took back demand promissory notes. On April 6, 1976, at a time his business had become insolvent, plaintiff recorded three deeds of trust intended to secure these notes with the realty, inventory, equipment and receivables of Fett Roofing and Sheet Metal Co., Inc. The deeds were backdated to indicate the dates on which the money had actually been borrowed. On November 8, 1976, an involuntary petition in bankruptcy was filed.

After a trial in which both sides presented considerable evidence and the plaintiff personally testified regarding his claim, Judge Bonney made the following findings of fact.

1. The bankrupt was undercapitalized at its inception in 1965, and remained undercapitalized throughout its existence. The capital necessary for the operation and continuation of its business was provided by the complainant in the form of so-called loans on an "as-needed" basis. Promissory notes, including the three involved herein, were given to the complainant in the course of such transactions.

2. The three deeds of trust which purport to secure the said notes were all backdated to create the impression that they were executed contemporaneously with the advance of funds and the giving of the notes; all three were in fact executed and recorded during the first week of April 1976, when the notes were, by their terms, past due.

3. The purpose of the deeds of trust was to delay, hinder, and defraud the creditors of the bankrupt, and to give the complainant a preference over them, in the event a liquidation of assets became necessary.

4. Complainant was in sole control of the affairs of the bankrupt, and was its sole stockholder. His interests were at all times identical to and indistinguishable from that of the bankrupt; he was the alter ego of the bankrupt.

5. At the time these three deeds of trust were executed and recorded, the bankrupt was, and for several months had been, unable to meet its obligations as they came due in the ordinary course of business. Many of the debts listed in the schedules filed by the bankrupt were incurred and delinquent prior to April 1976.

6. Complainant knew that his corporation was insolvent no later than February 1976.

Based on these findings, Judge Bonney concluded that the advances made by plaintiff to his corporation were actually contributions to capital, not loans, and that claims based on them therefore should be subordinated to those of all the other creditors of the bankrupt. The Judge further found that even if the transfers had been bona fide loans, the deeds of trust intended to secure them would have been null and void as having been given with actual intent to delay, hinder and defraud creditors in violation of §67d(2)(d) of the Bankruptcy Act, 11 U.S.C. §107(d)(2)(d). In addition, Judge Bonney determined that such loans were given in fraud of creditors under state law and therefore were voidable....

Because we have concluded that the Bankruptcy Judge was correct in his determination that the plaintiff's transfers of money to his corporation were capital contributions and not loans we do not consider the soundness of the last two legal findings.

The Law

At the outset the Court notes that a Bankruptcy Judge's findings of fact will be accepted unless "clearly erroneous." Bankruptcy Rule 810. In examining the entire record, the opinion and order of the Judge below and the briefs and oral argument of the parties, the Court is satisfied that substantial evidence supports the findings of fact of the Bankruptcy Judge and as they are not clearly in error, they will not be disturbed.

Although the Court is not bound by the Bankruptcy Judge's conclusions of law and is free to make its own legal deductions, an analysis of the particular facts of this case and the relevant authorities clearly shows that the determination that plaintiff made capital contributions to the bankrupt rather than loans is legally sound.

A director, officer, majority shareholder, relatives thereof or any other person in a fiduciary relation with a corporation can lawfully make a secured loan to the corporate beneficiary. However, when challenged in court a fiduciary's transaction with the corporation will be subjected to "rigorous scrutiny" and the burden will be on him "... not only to prove the good faith of the transaction but also to show its inherent fairness from the viewpoint of the corporation and those interested therein." *Pepper v. Litton*, 308 U.S. 295, 60 S. Ct. 238, 84 L. Ed. 281 (1939).

Where a director or majority shareholder asserts a claim against his own corporation, a bankruptcy court, sitting as a court of equity, will disregard the outward appearances of the transaction and determine its actual character and effect. Similar results have properly been reached in ordinary bankruptcy proceedings. Thus, salary claims of officers, directors and stockholders in the bankruptcy of "one-man" or family corporations have been disallowed or subordinated where the courts have been satisfied that allowance of the claims would not be fair or equitable to other creditors. And that result may be reached ... where on the facts the bankrupt has been used merely as a corporate pocket of the dominant stockholder, who, with disregard of the substance or form of corporate management, has treated its affairs as his own. And so-called loans or advances by the dominant or controlling stockholder will be subordinated to claims of other creditors and thus treated in effect as capital contributions by the stockholder not only in the foregoing types of situations but also where the paid-in capital is purely nominal, the capital necessary for the scope and magnitude of the operation of the company being furnished by the stockholder as a loan. *Pepper v. Litton*, *supra* 308 U.S. at 308–310, 60 S. Ct. at 246.

The record on this appeal reveals the bankrupt to have been a large construction contractor requiring ample amounts of capital. As indicated above, the corporation was capitalized at slightly under $5,000 when it was created in 1965. No increment to this initial amount was ever formally made. According to the schedule filed with the Bankruptcy Judge, the bankrupt's debt to secured creditors alone stood at $413,000. This is a debt-to-equity ratio of over 80 to 1. While this fact by itself will not serve to convert what is otherwise a bona fide loan into a contribution to capital, it does cast serious doubt on the advances by a person in plaintiff's special situation being considered debt rather than equity. The fact that no evidence was adduced by plaintiff to show that the "borrowings" in question were formally authorized by the corporation or that interest was ever paid on them, coupled with the undisputed day-in-and-day-out control over corporate affairs wielded by plaintiff, as president and sole stockholder leave little doubt that plaintiff, ignoring corporate formalities, was infusing new capital into his business and avoiding such necessities as charter amendment or the issuance of new stock. The record discloses that the funds transferred to the corporations were used to finance the acquisition of equipment and material necessary to the functioning of the business. Although one of the advances was used to pay a bona fide tax liability, this does not affect its character as a capital contribution under the particular circumstances of this case. The fact that plaintiff at various times characterized these advances as "recapitalization" can only reinforce a conclusion which consideration of the entire record makes inevitable.

The Courts of this circuit have had no reluctance to pierce through surface appearances in these matters and distinguish contributions to capital from genuine loans. In *Braddy v. Randolph*, 352 F.2d 80 (4th Cir. 1965), a case with some striking similarities to the present dispute, the plaintiff, president, director and a principal stockholder of a bankrupt corporation, filed four claims based on four notes secured by deeds of trust. In affirming the rejection of these claims, the Court of Appeals stated:

> To finance this volume and to keep the business going even though operating at a loss, the Bankrupt borrowed heavily and constantly from the four officers and the North Carolina National Bank (hereinafter Bank). The money which officers, Braddy, Zeliff, Craft and Foster, "loaned" the Bankrupt was normally acquired from the Bank by use of their personal credit and personal assets. Based on the volume of business and the fact that the Bankrupt began borrowing from the officers and the Bank at the outset of operations, we think the referee and court could reasonably conclude that these "loans" were necessitated by the initial insufficiency of the Bankrupt's equity capital and that the "loans" made by the officers were, in effect, contributions to capital. Rather than invest more capital the officers and stockholders, by the use of the borrowed funds, substantially shifted and evaded the ordinary financial risks connected with this type of business enterprise and, at the same time, permitted the corporation to remain in a constant state of or in imminent danger of insolvency.

Similarly in *L & M Realty Corp. v. Leo*, 249 F.2d 668 (4th Cir. 1957), the Court of Appeals subordinated the claim of a principal shareholder, noting:

> While the amounts thus advanced were treated by the stockholders as loans to the corporation and it was not contemplated that stock was to be issued in payment of them, it is clear that they were not loans in the ordinary

sense and were not intended to be paid in ordinary course, as were the claims of other creditors. The corporation was not adequately capitalized, the advancements were made shortly after it was organized and no steps were ever taken looking to their repayment. They were made in approximately equal amounts by the two stockholders owning the corporation, who actually paid other creditors in priority to themselves year after year, no interest was ever paid on them and the evidence is that the money was advanced as loans rather than as subscription to stock in the thought that this would be helpful for income tax purposes. In such situation, while the loans are not to be treated as investments in stock, it is clear that they were capital contributions to a corporation inadequately capitalized and that, having been made by the two stockholders, who completely owned and controlled the corporation, they should be subordinated to the claims of other creditors.

Although the advances contested here were made well after the corporation was created, there is evidence in the record that plaintiff had "loaned" the bankrupt money over the years and that the transfers here in issue were only the latest in a series of contributions made necessary by the corporation's grossly inadequate capitalization. Since these three transactions were "part of a plan of permanent personal financing," the fact that they did not occur at the outset of corporate existence is not crucial and the claims based on them are properly subordinated to those of other creditors.

Since the transfers made by plaintiff to the bankrupt were, in contemplation of law, capital contributions, the deeds of trust purporting to secure these advances were properly set aside since there was in fact "no debt to be secured."

As the cases make clear, no one fact will result in the determination that putative loans are actually contributions to capital. The Court is guided by equitable principles that look to the result of the transaction as well as to the formal indicia of its character. A person in the special position of the plaintiff "... cannot by the use of the corporate device avail himself of the privileges normally permitted outsiders in a race of creditors." *Pepper v. Litton, supra*, 308 U.S. at 311, 60 S. Ct. at 247. It is not necessary that fraud, deceit or calculated breach of trust be shown. Where, as here, a corporate insider, indeed the corporate alter ego has so arranged his dealings with his corporate principal that he achieves an unfair advantage over outside creditors dealing at arms length, the Court will subordinate his claim to theirs. [Affirmed.]

Section IV
Preemptive Rights

Preemptive rights enable shareholders to maintain their proportionate ownership interests in a corporation when the company sells new issues of stock. Shareholders with preemptive rights are given the opportunity to buy a proportionate share of new issues of stock so that their ownership interests will not be diluted. These rights are particularly important for shareholders in a closely held corporation who often depend on the corporation for their livelihood and who may have limited opportunities to purchase additional shares other than when they are issued. Shareholders in publicly traded companies may easily increase or decrease their holdings by trading in the open market.

Although the objective of granting preemptive rights is laudable, accomplishing that goal may be difficult. One reason is that implementation is often complicated, particularly if the corporation has multiple classes of stock with different dividend and voting rights. A second reason is that broad grants of preemptive rights may make it more difficult or more costly for the corporation to accomplish legitimate business objectives, such as a merger or acquisition. Corporate attorneys should counsel their clients on maintaining the proper balance between affording shareholders the protections they desire and not unduly limiting the company's ability to act.

Corporate statutes take three approaches to grants of preemptive rights: (1) the grant of rights is mandatory; (2) preemptive rights are granted unless the corporate charter provides to the contrary (opt-out provisions); or (3) the rights are granted only if the corporate charter elects them (opt-in provisions). The common law also provides preemptive rights.

Model Act § 6.30 adopts the opt-in approach and requires the corporate charter expressly to state the election of preemptive rights. Under § 6.30, unless the corporate charter provides otherwise, preemptive rights do not apply to: (1) shares issued as compensation or to satisfy a conversion or other right, (2) shares issued within six months of incorporation, or (3) "shares sold otherwise than for money." In addition, not all shareholders may have preemptive rights. For example, the section excludes holders of preferred shares without voting rights.

Planning for preemptive rights requires careful consideration. The following materials raise additional issues associated with the grant of preemptive rights.

Katzowitz v. Sidler

New York Court of Appeals
249 N.E.2d 359 (1969)

KEATING, JUDGE.

Isador Katzowitz is a director and stockholder of a close corporation. Two other persons, Jacob Sidler and Max Lasker, own the remaining securities and, with Katzowitz, comprise Sulburn Holding Corp.'s board of directors. Sulburn was organized in 1955 to supply propane gas to three other corporations controlled by these men. Sulburn's certificate of incorporation authorized it to issue 1,000 shares of no par value stock for which the incorporators established a $100 selling price. Katzowitz, Sidler and Lasker each invested $500 and received five shares of the corporation's stock.

The three men had been jointly engaged in several corporate ventures for more than 25 years. In this period they had always been equal partners and received identical compensation from the corporations they controlled. Though all the corporations controlled by these three men prospered, disenchantment with their inter-personal relationship flared into the open in 1956. At this time, Sidler and Lasker joined forces to oust Katzowitz from any role in managing the corporations. They first voted to replace Katzowitz as a director of Sullivan County Gas Company with the corporation's private counsel. Notice of directors' meetings was then caused to be sent out by Lasker and Sidler for Burnwell Gas Corporation. Sidler and Lasker advised Katzowitz that they intended to vote for a new board of directors. Katzowitz at this time held the position of manager of the Burnwell facility.

Katzowitz sought a temporary injunction to prevent the meeting until his rights could be judicially determined. A temporary injunction was granted to maintain the *status quo* until trial. The order was affirmed by the Appellate Division.

Before the issue could be tried, the three men entered into a stipulation in 1959 whereby Katzowitz withdrew from active participation in the day-to-day operations of the business. The agreement provided that he would remain on the boards of all the corporations, and each board would be limited to three members composed of the three stockholders or their designees. Katzowitz was to receive the same compensation and other fringe benefits which the controlled corporations paid Lasker and Sidler. The stipulation also provided that Katzowitz, Sidler and Lasker were "equal stockholders and each of said parties now owns the same number of shares of stock in each of the defendant corporations and that such shares of stock shall continue to be in full force and effect and unaffected by this stipulation, except as hereby otherwise expressly provided." The stipulation contained no other provision affecting equal stock interests.

The business relationship established by the stipulation was fully complied with. Sidler and Lasker, however, were still interested in disassociating themselves from Katzowitz and purchased his interest in one of the gas distribution corporations and approached him with regard to the purchase of his interest in another.

In December of 1961 Sulburn was indebted to each stockholder to the extent of $2,500 for fees and commissions earned up until September, 1961. Instead of paying this debt, Sidler and Lasker wanted Sulburn to loan the money to another corporation which all three men controlled. Sidler and Lasker called a meeting of the board of directors to propose that additional securities be offered at $100 per share to substitute for the money owed to the directors. The notice of meeting for October 30, 1961 had on its agenda "a proposition that the corporation issue common stock of its unissued common capital stock, The total par value which shall equal the total sum of the fees and commissions now owing by the corporation to its ... directors." Katzowitz made it quite clear at the meeting that he would not invest any additional funds in Sulburn in order for it to make a loan to this other corporation. The only resolution passed at the meeting was that the corporation would pay the sum of $2,500 to each director.

With full knowledge that Katzowitz expected to be paid his fees and commissions and that he did not want to participate in any new stock issuance, the other two directors called a special meeting of the board on December 1, 1961. The only item on the agenda for this special meeting was the issuance of 75 shares of the corporation's common stock at $100 per share. The offer was to be made to stockholders in "accordance with their respective preemptive rights for the purpose of acquiring additional working capital." The amount to be raised was the exact amount owed by the corporation to its shareholders. The offering price for the securities was 1/18 the book value of the stock. Only Sidler and Lasker attended the special board meeting. They approved the issuance of the 75 shares.

Notice was mailed to each stockholder that they had the right to purchase 25 shares of the corporation's stock at $100 a share. The offer was to expire on December 27, 1961. Failure to act by that date was stated to constitute a waiver. At about the same time Katzowitz received the notice, he received a check for $2,500 from the corporation for his fees and commissions. Katzowitz did not exercise his option to buy the additional shares. Sidler and Lasker purchased their full complement, 25 shares each. This purchase by Sidler and Lasker caused an immediate dilution of the book value of the outstanding securities.

On August 25, 1962 the principal asset of Sulburn, a tractor trailer truck, was destroyed. On August 31, 1962 the directors unanimously voted to dissolve the corporation. Upon dissolution, Sidler and Lasker each received $18,885.52 but Katzowitz only received $3,147.59.

The plaintiff instituted a declaratory judgment action to establish his right to the proportional interest in the assets of Sulburn in liquidation less the $5,000 which Sidler and Lasker used to purchase their shares in December, 1961.

Special Term (Westchester County) found the book value of the corporation's securities on the day the stock was offered at $100 to be worth $1,800. The court also found that "the individual defendants ... decided that in lieu of taking that sum in cash (the commissions and fees due the stockholders), they preferred to add to their investment by having the corporate defendant make available and offer each stockholder an additional twenty-five shares of unissued stock." The court reasoned that Katzowitz waived his right to purchase the stock or object to its sale to Lasker and Sidler by failing to exercise his preemptive right and found his protest at the time of dissolution untimely.

The Appellate Division (Second Department), two Justices, dissenting, modified the order of Special Term 29 A.D.2d 955, 289 N.Y.S.2d 324. The modification was procedural. The decretal paragraph in Special Term's order was corrected by reinstating the complaint and substituting a statement of the parties' rights. On the substantive legal issues and findings of fact, the Appellate Division was in agreement with Special Term. The majority agreed that the book value of the corporation's stock at the time of the stock offering was $1,800. The Appellate Division reasoned, however, that showing a disparity between book value and offering price was insufficient without also showing fraud or overreaching. Disparity in price by itself was not enough to prove fraud. The Appellate Division also found that the plaintiff had waived his right to object to his recovery in dissolution by failing to either exercise his pre-emptive rights or take steps to prevent the sale of the stock.

The concept of pre-emptive rights was fashioned by the judiciary to safeguard two distinct interests of stockholders—the right to protection against dilution of their equity in the corporation and protection against dilution of their proportionate voting control. (Ballantine, Corporations (rev. ed., 1946), § 209.) After early decisions (*Gray v. Portland Bank*, 3 Mass. 364; *Stokes v. Continental Trust Co.*, 186 N.Y. 285, 78 N.E. 1090, 12 L.R.A., N.S., 969), legislation fixed the right enunciated with respect to proportionate voting but left to the judiciary the role of protecting existing shareholders from the dilution of their equity.

It is clear that directors of a corporation have no discretion in the choice of those to whom the earnings and assets of the corporation should be distributed. Directors, being fiduciaries of the corporation, must, in issuing new stock, treat existing shareholders fairly. Though there is very little statutory control over the price which a corporation must receive for new shares, the power to determine price must be exercised for the benefit of the corporation and in the interest of all the stockholders.

Issuing stock for less than fair value can injure existing shareholders by diluting their interest in the corporation's surplus, in current and future earnings and in the assets upon liquidation. Normally, a stockholder is protected from the loss of his equity from dilution, even though the stock is being offered at less than fair value, because the shareholder receives rights which he may either exercise or sell. If he exercises, he has protected his interest and, if not, he can sell the rights, thereby compensating himself for the dilution of his remaining shares in the equity of the corporation.

When new shares are issued, however at prices below fair value in a close corporation or a corporation with only a limited market for its shares, existing stockholders, who do not want to invest or do not have the capacity to invest additional funds, can have their equity interest in the corporation diluted to the vanishing point.

The protection afforded by stock rights is illusory in close corporations. Even if a buyer could be found for the rights, they would have to be sold at an inadequate price because of the nature of a close corporation. Outsiders are normally discouraged from acquiring minority interests after a close corporation has been organized. Certainly a stockholder in a close corporation is at a total loss to safeguard his equity from dilution if no rights are offered and he does not want to invest additional funds.

Though it is difficult to determine fair value for a corporation's securities and courts are therefore reluctant to get into the thicket, when the issuing price is shown to be markedly below book value in a close corporation and when the remaining shareholder-directors benefit from the issuance, a case for judicial relief has been established. In that instance, the corporation's directors must show that the issuing price falls within some range which can be justified on the basis of valid business reasons. If no such showing is made by the directors, there is no reason for the judiciary to abdicate its function to a majority of the board or stockholders who have not seen fit to come forward and justify the propriety of diverting property from the corporation and allow the issuance of securities to become an oppressive device permitting the dilution of the equity of dissident stockholders.

The defendant directors here make no claim that the price set was a fair one. No business justification is offered to sustain it. Admittedly, the stock was sold at less than book value. The defendants simply contend that, as long as all stockholders were given an equal opportunity to purchase additional shares, no stockholder can complain simply because the offering dilutes his interest in the corporation.

The defendants' argument is fallacious.

The corollary of a stockholder's right to maintain his proportionate equity in a corporation by purchasing additional shares is the right not to purchase additional shares without being confronted with dilution of his existing equity if no valid business justification exists for the dilution.

A stockholder's right not to purchase is seriously undermined if the stock offered is worth substantially more than the offering price. Any purchase at this price dilutes his interest and impairs the value of his original holding. "A corporation is not permitted to sell its stock for a legally inadequate price at least where there is objection. Plaintiff has a right to insist upon compliance with the law whether or not he cares to exercise his option. He cannot block a sale for a fair price merely because he disagrees with the wisdom of the plan but he can insist that the sale price be fixed accordance with legal requirements." Judicial review in this area is limited to whether under all the circumstances — including the disparity between issuing price of the stock and its true value, the nature of the corporation, the business necessity for establishing an offering price at a certain amount to facilitate raising new capital, and the ability of stockholders to sell rights — the additional offering of securities should be condemned because the directors in establishing the sale price did not fix it with reference to financial considerations with respect to the ready disposition of securities.

Here the obvious disparity in selling price and book value was calculated to force the dissident stockholder into investing additional sums. No valid business justification was advanced for the disparity in price, and the only beneficiaries of the disparity were the two director-stockholders who were eager to have additional capital in the business.

It is no answer to Katzowitz' action that he was also given a chance to purchase additional shares at this bargain rate. The price was not so much a bargain as it was a tactic, conscious or unconscious on the part of the directors, to place Katzowitz in a compromising situation. The price was so fixed to make the failure to invest costly. However, Katzowitz at the time might not have been aware of the dilution because no notice of the effect of the issuance of the new shares on the already outstanding shares was disclosed. In addition, since the stipulation entitled Katzowitz to the same compensation as Sidler and Lasker, the disparity in equity interest caused by their purchase of additional securities in 1961 did not affect stockholder income from Sulburn and, therefore, Katzowitz possibly was not aware of the effect of the stock issuance on his interest in the corporation until dissolution.

No reason exists at this time to permit Sidler and Lasker to benefit from their course of conduct. Katzowitz' delay in commencing the action did not prejudice the defendants. By permitting the defendants to recover their additional investment in Sulburn before the remaining assets of Sulburn are distributed to the stockholders upon dissolution, all the stockholders will be treated equitably. Katzowitz, therefore, should receive his aliquot share of the assets of Sulburn less the amount invested by Sidler and Lasker for their purchase of stock on December 27, 1961.

Accordingly, the order of the Appellate Division should be reversed, with costs, and judgment granted in favor of the plaintiff against the individual defendants....

What issues does the corporate attorney face when planning for preemptive rights for a corporation with multiple classes of stock with different voting, dividend and liquidation rights? See, e.g., *Benihana of Tokyo, Inc. v. Benihana, Inc.*, 906 A. 2d 114 (Del. 2006), in Chapter 11.

Section V
Transfer Restrictions and Buyout Agreements

Agreements containing share transfer restrictions and buyout provisions are most commonly used in closely held corporations to accomplish two closely related purposes. One is to give remaining shareholders control over who will become shareholders when one or more shareholders want to liquidate ownership interest. The second purpose is to provide a mechanism for liquidating the interests of shareholders who die or want to terminate their relationship with the company.

A. Transfer Restrictions

Model Act § 6.27 authorizes agreements restricting the transfer of shares. These agreements may be between the corporation and shareholders or among shareholders or both. Restrictions may be used to: (1) maintain the corporation's tax status or status as a statutory close corporation; (2) preserve securities laws exemptions; (3) limit membership in professional corporations to qualifying personnel pursuant to state law; or (4) ensure that existing shareholders will be able to choose new shareholders.

In preparing share transfer restrictions, the corporate attorney should consider who should be a party to the agreement and what kinds of restrictions should be implemented. Generally, it is preferable for both the corporation and all current shareholders to be parties to the agreement. Having the corporation as a party can be a useful tool in enforcing the terms of the agreement, as the corporation may be authorized not to record on its books shares transferred in violation of the agreement. In addition, the agreement should provide that future shareholders should be permitted to acquire shares only if they agree to be subject to its terms.

Share transfer restrictions may be structured in several ways. Share transfers may be prohibited entirely. On the other hand, transfers may be mandatory when certain triggering events occur, such as the death of one of the shareholders. Share transfer restrictions may also be optional, giving either the corporation or other shareholders, or both, a right of first refusal to purchase the shares when a shareholder wants to exit the company. If the right of first refusal is not exercised, exiting shareholders may transfer their shares to third parties. Similarly, share transfers may be permitted, but limited to members of a certain group, such as other family members of existing shareholders.

B. Buyout Agreements

One of the key purposes of buyout agreements is to provide a market for shares when a shareholder dies or simply wants to exit the corporation. There are several ways to structure a buyout agreement. Each approach has special considerations.

When share transfers are permitted, there is considerable overlap between share transfer restrictions and buyout agreements. The purpose of share transfer restrictions is to enable existing shareholders to control whether and to whom shares may be transferred. Share transfer restrictions are implemented for the benefit of shareholders wishing to continue to be equity holders in the corporation. Buyout agreements, on the other hand, are intended to provide a market for the transfer of shares in a closely held company. These agreements enable shareholders to exit the company and be compensated for their shares at the time they depart.

Buyout agreements may be structured in several ways. They may require that the corporation or remaining shareholders purchase the departing shareholder's interest in the company. They may also give the corporation or the shareholders the right of first refusal. Careful planning is required when the corporation is the purchaser. In that case, one must consider what requirements, if any, are imposed by applicable legal capital statutes and how will the company—or other shareholders—raise the money needed to purchase the shares. In Delaware and other states using the Delaware model, the share repurchase must satisfy the legal capital statutes discussed in Chapter 9, Sections I.A., B., *infra*.

Specifically, the company must have sufficient surplus to repurchase the shares. If the company does not satisfy that requirement, the shares may not be repurchased. In this case, the purpose of the buyout agreement will be frustrated unless the remaining shareholders can find additional funding or unless exiting shareholders are permitted to sell their shares to third parties or to compel dissolution of the company. Although Model Act jurisdictions have more relaxed requirements, one must still be sure that legally permissible funds are available for the repurchase. One way to provide funds for the repurchase of a deceased shareholder's stock is for the corporation to purchase life insurance policies for its shareholders. If a shareholder dies, the proceeds from the policy can be used to fund the repurchase of the decedent's stock. Further, one should consider the tax implications when the corporation repurchases the shares.

The corporate lawyer encounters issues related to business valuation in several contexts: when a company is being sold; when an owner in a company wants to be bought out; when interests in a company are being valued for estate tax purposes or as part of divorce proceedings. Although lawyers are not expected to determine the valuation, they must understand some of the basics when addressing related legal questions.

A well-drafted shareholders' agreement will set out the method of valuation used to value a departing shareholder's interest. The valuation method must be carefully selected because it will likely be used years later, when the company's financial condition may have changed considerably—for better or for worse. Because company conditions vary, the valuation formula should be reviewed from time to time and modified as required. And finally, planners should realize that no single approach to valuation will be equally suitable for all businesses. The following parable of valuation methods suggests some of the possible approaches.

The Old Man and the Tree

Once there was a wise old man who owned an apple tree. The tree was fine and with little care it produced a crop of apples each year that he sold for $100. The man was getting old and wanted to retire to a new climate, so he decided to sell the tree. He enjoyed teaching a good lesson, so he placed an advertisement in the Business Opportunities section of *The Wall Street Journal* in which he said he wanted to sell the tree for "the best offer."

The first person to respond to the ad offered to pay the $50, which, he said, was what he could get for selling the apple tree for firewood after he had cut it down. "You don't know what you are talking about," the old man chastised. "You are offering to pay only the salvage value of this tree. That might be a good price for a pine tree or even this tree if it had stopped bearing fruit or if the price of apple wood had gotten so high that the tree was more valuable as a source of wood than as a source of fruit. But you do not understand these things so you can't see that my tree is worth far more than 50 bucks."

The next person who visited the old man offered to pay $100 for the tree. "For that," she opined, "is what I would be able to get for selling this year's crop of fruit which is about to mature."

"You are not as out of your depth as the first one," responded the old man. "At least you see that this tree has more value as a producer of apples than it would as a source of firewood. But $100 is not the right price. You are not considering the value of next year's crop of apples, nor that of the years after. Please take your $100 and go elsewhere."

The third person to come along was a young man who had just dropped out of business school. "I am going to sell apples on the Internet," he said. "I figure that the tree should live for at least another fifteen years. If I sell the apples for $100 a year, that will total $1,500. I offer you $1,500 for your tree."

"Oh, no," scoffed the old man, "you're even more ill-informed about reality than the others I've spoken with.

"Surely the $100 you would earn by selling the apples from the tree fifteen years from now cannot be worth $100 to you today. In fact, if you placed $41.73 today in a bank account paying 6% interest, compounded annually, that small sum would grow to $100 at the end of fifteen years. So the present value of $100 worth of apples fifteen years from now, assuming an interest rate of 6%, is only $41.73 not $100. Pray," pleaded the beneficent old man, "take your $1,500 and invest it safely in high-grade corporate bonds and go back to business school and learn something about finance."

Before long, there came a wealthy physician, who said, "I don't know much about apple trees, but I know what I like. I'll pay the market price for it. The last fellow was willing to pay you $1,500 for the tree, and so it must be worth that."

"Doctor," advised the old man, "you should get yourself a knowledgeable investment adviser. If there were truly a market in which apple trees were traded with some regularity, the prices at which they were sold might tell you something about their value. But not only is there no such market; even if there were, taking its price as the value is just mimicking the stupidity of that last knucklehead or the others before him. Please take your money and buy a vacation home."

The next would-be buyer was an accounting student. When the old man asked, "What price are you willing to give me?" the student first demanded to see the old man's books. The old man had kept careful records and gladly brought them out.

After examining the books, the accounting student said, "Your books show that you paid $75 for this tree ten years ago. Furthermore, you have made no deductions for depreciation. I do not know if that conforms with generally accepted accounting principles, but assuming that it does, the book value of your tree is $75. I will pay that."

"Ah, you students know so much and yet so little," chided the old man. "It is true that the book value of my tree is $75, but any fool can see that it is worth far more than that. Valuation based on assets cannot be limited to book value," he advised, "for that is an accounting concept not a valuation concept. An entity's book value equals total assets minus total liabilities. Business valuation may use such accounting concepts as starting points but not as end points."

Feeling that his profession had been somehow insulted, the accounting student replied: "Fair enough, but I could use this information to estimate what resources would be required to generate an equivalent business position. In the case of your tree, this would mean assessing what it would take to replicate: (1) the acreage on which the tree stands, (2) the tree itself, (3) equipment related to maintenance and production, and (4) the resources required to merchandise the apples."

The old man acknowledged that this is true, but opined: "While these are not impossible judgments to make, they are very difficult. They also ask the valuation question from only one perspective: what it takes to build a business. At least as important is the question from the other perspective: what the business can do for its owner." The accounting student left.

The last prospect to visit the old man was a young stockbroker who had recently graduated from business school. Eager to test her new skills she, too, asked to examine the books. After several hours she came back to the old man and said she was prepared to make an offer that valued the tree on the basis of the capitalization of its earnings. For the first time the old man's interest was piqued and he asked her to go on.

The young woman explained that while the apples were sold for $100 last year, that figure did not represent profits realized from the tree. There were expenses attendant to the tree, such as the cost of fertilizer, pruning, tools, picking apples, and carting them to town and selling them.

Somebody had to do these things, and a portion of the salaries paid to those persons ought to be charged against the revenues from the tree. Moreover, the purchase price, or cost, of the tree was an expense. A portion of the cost should be taken into account each year of the tree's useful life. Finally, there were taxes. She concluded that the profit from the tree was $50 last year.

"Wow!" the old man blushed. "I thought I made $100 off that tree."

"That's because you failed to match expenses with revenues, in accordance with generally accepted accounting principles," she explained.

"You don't actually have to write a check to be charged with what accountants consider to be your expenses. For example, you bought a station wagon some time ago and you used it part of the time to cart apples to market. The wagon will last a while and each year some of the original cost has to be matched against revenues. A portion of the amount has to be spread out over the next several years even though you expended it all at one time. Accountants call that depreciation. I'll bet you never figured that into your calculation of profits."

"I'll bet you're right," he replied. "Tell me more."

"I also went back into the books for a few years and I saw that in some years the tree produced fewer apples than in other years, the prices varied and the costs were not exactly the same each year. Taking an average of only the last three years, I came up with a figure of $45 as a fair sample of the tree's earnings. But that is only half of what we have to do to figure the value."

"What's the other half?" he asked.

"The tricky part," she told him. "We now have to figure the value to me of owning a tree that will produce average earnings of $45 a year. If I believed that the tree was a 'one year wonder', I would say 100% of its value—as a going business—was represented by one year's earnings."

"But if I believe, as both you and I do, that the tree is more like a corporation, in that it will continue to produce earnings year after year, then the key is to figure out an appropriate rate of return. In other words, I will be investing my capital in the tree, and I need to compute the value to me of an investment that will produce $45 a year in income. We can call that amount the capitalized value of the tree."

"Do you have something in mind?" he asked.

"I'm getting there. If this tree produced entirely steady and predictable earnings each year, it would be like a U.S. Treasury bond. But its earnings are not guaranteed. So we have to take into account risks and uncertainty. If the risk of its ruin was high, I would insist that a single year's earnings represent a higher percentage of the value of the tree. After all, apples could become a glut on the market one day and you would have to cut the price thus reducing the profits from selling them."

"Or," she continued, "some doctor could discover a link between eating an apple a day and heart disease. A drought could cut the yield of the tree. Or the tree could become diseased and die. These are all risks. And we don't even know whether the costs that we are sure to incur will be worth incurring."

"You are a gloomy one," reflected the old man. "There could also be a shortage of apples on the market and the price of apples could rise. If you think about it, it is even possible that I have been selling the apples at prices below what people would be willing to pay, and you could raise the price without reducing your sales. Also, there are treatments, you know, that could be applied to increase the yield of the tree. This tree could help spawn a whole orchard. Any of these things would increase earnings."

"The earnings also could be increased by lowering costs of the sort you mentioned," the old man continued. "Costs can be reduced by speeding the time from fruition to sale, by managing extensions of credit better, and minimizing losses from bad apples. All these things would boost the relationship between overall sales and net earnings or, as the financial types say, the tree's profit margin. And that in turn would boost the return on your investment."

"I know all that," she assured him. "We will include all those things in the calculus. The fact is, we are talking about risk. And investment analysis is a cold business. We don't know with certainty what's going to happen. You want your money now and I'm supposed to live with the risk. That's fine with me, but then I have to look through a cloudy crystal ball, and not with 20/20 hindsight. And my resources are limited. I have to choose between your tree and the strawberry patch down the road. I cannot do both, and the purchase of your tree will deprive me of alternative investments. That means I have to compare the opportunities and the risks."

"To determine a proper rate of return," she continued, "I looked at investment opportunities comparable to the apple tree, particularly in the agribusiness industry, where these factors have been taken into account. I then adjusted my findings based on how the things we discussed worked out with your tree. Based on those judgments, I figure that 20% is an appropriate rate of return for the tree."

"In other words," she concluded, "assuming that the average earnings from the tree over the last three years, which seems to be a representative period, are indicative of the return I will receive, I am prepared to pay a price for the tree that will give me a 20% return on my investment. I am not willing to accept any lower rate of return because I don't have to; I can always buy the strawberry patch instead. Now, to figure the price, we simply divide $45 of earnings per year by the 20% return I am insisting on."

"Long division was never my strong suit. Is there a simpler way of doing the figuring?" he asked.

"There is," she replied. "We can use an approach we Wall Street types prefer, called the price-earnings (or P/E) ratio. To compute the ratio, just divide 100 by the rate of return we are seeking. If I were willing to settle for an 8% return, that would be 100 divided by 8 which equals 12.5. So we'd use a P/E ratio of 12.5 to 1. But since I want to earn 20% on my investment, I divided 100 by 20 and came up with a P/E ratio of 5:1. In other words, I am willing to pay five times the tree's estimated annual earnings. Multiplying $45 by 5, I get a value of $225. That's my offer."

The old man sat back and said he greatly appreciated the lesson. He would have to think about her offer, and he asked if she could come by the next day.

When the young woman returned she found the old man emerging from a sea of work sheets, small print columns of numbers and a calculator. "Delighted to see you," he enthralled. "I think we can do some business.

"It's easy to see how you Wall Street smarties make so much money, buying people's property for less than its true value. I think I can get you to agree that my tree is worth more than you figured."

"I'm open minded," she assured him.

"The $45 number you came up with yesterday was something you called profits, or earnings. I'm not so sure it tells you anything that important."

"Of course it does," she protested. "Profits measure efficiency and business performance."

"Fair enough," he mused, "but it sure doesn't tell you how much money you're getting. I looked in my safe yesterday after you left and I saw some stock certificates I own that never paid a dividend to me. And I kept getting reports each year telling me how great the earnings were. Now I know that the earnings increased the value of my stocks, but without any dividends I sure couldn't spend them. It's just the opposite with the tree.

"You figured the earnings were lower because of some amounts I'll never have to spend, like depreciation on my station wagon," the old man went on. "It seems to me these earnings are an idea worked up by the accountants."

Intrigued, she asked, "What is important, then?"

"Cash," he answered. "I'm talking about dollars you can spend, save, or give to your children. This tree will go on for years yielding cash."

"Don't forget the risks," she reminded him. "And the uncertainties."

"Quite right," he observed. "I think we can deal with that. Chances are that you and I could agree on the possible range of future revenues and expenses. Given our agreement that earnings averaged around $45 the last few years, I suspect we can agree on some fair estimates of cash flow over the coming five years: How about that there is a 25% chance that cash flow will be $40; a 50% chance it will be $50; and a 25% chance it will be $60?

"That would make $50 our best guess, if you average it out," the old man figured. "Then let's just say that for ten years after that, the average will be $40. And that's it. The tree doctor tells me it can't produce any longer than that.

"Now all we have to do," he finished up, "is figure out what you pay today to get $50 a year from now, two years from now, and so on for the first five years until we figure what you would pay to get $40 a year for each of the ten years after that. Then, throw in the 50 bucks we can get for firewood at that time, and that's it."

"Simple," she confessed. "You want to discount to the present value future receipts, including salvage value. Of course you need to determine the rate at which you discount."

"Precisely," he concurred. "That's what my charts and the calculator are for." She nodded knowingly as he showed her discount tables that revealed what a dollar received at a later time is worth today, under different assumptions of the discount rate. It showed, for example, that at an 8% discount rate, a dollar delivered a year from now is worth $.93 today, simply because $.93 today, invested at 8%, will produce $1 a year from now.

"You could invest your money in US Treasury obligations and earn say 4% interest (depending on prevailing interest rates). That looks like the risk free rate of interest to me. Anywhere else you put your money deprives you of the opportunity to earn 4% risk free. Discounting by 4% will only compensate you for the time value of the money you invest in the tree rather than in Treasuries. But the cash flow from the apple tree is not risk-free, sad to say, so we need to use a higher discount rate to compensate you for the risk in your investment. For example, putting your money in a commercial bank savings account might suggest a 5% discount rate, in high-grade corporate bonds an 8% discount rate and so on.

"Our apple tree here is riskier than these. Let's agree that we discount the receipt of $50 a year from now by 15%, and so on with the other deferred receipts. That is about the rate that is applied to investments with this magnitude of risk. You can check that out with my neighbor who just sold his strawberry patch yesterday. According to my figures, the present value of the expected yearly cash flow is $267.42, and today's value of the firewood is $2.46, for a grand total of $269.88. Let's make it $270 even. You can see how much I'm allowing for risk because if I discounted the stream at 8%, it would come to $388.61."

After a few minutes of reflection, the young woman said to the old man, "It was a bit foxy of you yesterday to let me appear to be teaching you something. Where did you learn so much about finance as an apple grower?"

The old man smiled sagely: "Wisdom comes from experience in many fields."

"I enjoyed this little exercise but let me tell you something that some financial whiz kids told me," she replied. "Whether we figure value on the basis of the discounted cash flow method you like or the capitalization of earnings I proposed, so long as we apply both methods perfectly, we should come out at exactly the same point."

"Of course!" the old man exclaimed. "The wunderkinds are catching on. But the clever ones are not simply looking at old earnings, but copying managers by projecting earnings into the future. The question is which method is more likely to be misused?

"I prefer my method of using cash rather than earnings because I don't have to monkey around with costs like depreciation of my station wagon and other long-term assets. You have to make these arbitrary assumptions about the useful life of the thing and how fast you're going to depreciate it. That's where I think you went wrong in your figuring."

"Nice try, you crafty old devil," she rejoined. "You know there is plenty of room for mistakes in your calculations too. It's easy to discount cash flows when they are nice and steady, but that doesn't help you when you've got some lumpy expenses that do not recur. For example, several years from now, that tree will need serious pruning and spraying expenses that don't show up in your flow. The cost of labor and chemicals for that occasion throw off the evenness of your calculations."

"But I'll tell you what," she bellied up, "I'll offer you $250. My cold analysis tells me I'm overpaying, but I really like that tree. I think the delight of sitting in its glorious shade must be worth something."

"It's a deal," agreed the old man. "I never said I was looking for the highest offer, but only the best offer."

Lessons.

The parable of the old man and the tree introduced a number of alternative methods of valuing productive property, whether a single asset or an entire business enterprise. The original $50 bid was based on the tree's salvage value, also sometimes called its scrap value. This valuation method will virtually always be inappropriate for valuing a productive asset, business or share of stock (though many bust-up takeover artists of the 1980s popularized the opposite claim).

The $100 bid was based only on one year's earnings and ignored the earning power over future time. The $1,500 overvaluation ignored the concept of the time value of money by simply adding together the raw dollar amounts of expected earnings over future years. Neither of these approaches even qualifies as an appropriate valuation method.

The doctor's bid drew on market-based valuation techniques by considering what other willing buyers had offered. But that technique will only ever be helpful if the property under consideration or similar properties are regularly traded in reasonably well-developed markets. Even then, it is circular because it uses the question ("what's it worth?," according to others) to get the answer (what it's worth, according to others).

The deal was ultimately sealed when the buyer and the old man agreed that the two methods they used—capitalizing earnings and discounting cash flows—made the most sense (noting that these two techniques if perfectly applied give the same answer). The buyer preferred to use earnings because accounting rules regarding earnings are intended to reflect economic reality pretty well. The old man held less confidence in those rules, principally because they call for deducting from revenues accounting depreciation, which he was not sure accurately reflected economic reality.

Although reasonable people can differ, both methods show that valuation is not a fool's game. The buyer and the old man both wisely and correctly acknowledged the importance of keen judgment in business analysis. Financial records track earnings and cash flows so the histories are there for all to see, but projecting them forward and then selecting the right discount rate are Herculean exercises. As the type of investment you consider becomes more uncertain, your judgment must become proportionately more razor-sharp.

Picking an index fund or even a mutual fund requires the least amount of knowledge or judgment; picking a classic stock a bit more than these; a vintage stock much more; and a rookie stock the greatest. In terms of apples, the apple tree our old man just sold is much like a classic business: an IBM or General Electric. It is mature, productive, and has an extensive track record.

At the other extreme might be a high-tech start-up business whose only record is on paper—a business plan that is the apple tree equivalent of a bag of seeds. Even if the ingredients are there, the execution is entirely in front of you. You may still have a basis for gauging the probable future—the quality of seeds, soil, fertilizer and farmer—but you are leaving more to judgment than in the case of the mature tree.

A few additional morals. Methods are useful as tools, but good judgment comes not from methods alone, but from experience. And experience comes from bad judgment. Listen closely to the experts, and hear those things they don't tell you. Behind all the sweet sounds of their confident notes, there is a great deal of discordant uncertainty. One wrong assumption can carry you pretty far from the truth.

The parable examined valuation of a business. Analogous techniques apply to determine the value of any productive asset held for financial gain (farms, patents, stocks, bonds, and so on). The value of any asset is the net cash flows (discounted at an appropriate rate), that an investor can reasonably expect the asset to generate during its remaining life.

Bond values are usually the easiest to measure. Standard bonds bear a designated interest rate and a set maturity date. The combination defines expected cash flows and the appropriate discount rate (subject to adjustment as discussed in Chapter 10).

Common stock values are usually the most difficult to measure. They have no such interest rate and there is no maturity date. An analyst thus must estimate both components in the valuation exercise.

People generally agree that the value of any productive asset held for financial gain is equal to the present value of the cash that it generates for its owner. But, bonds

278 4 · CAPITALIZATION

aside, disagreement arises concerning the factors used to estimate cash flows and the relevant discount rate.

Debate focuses on what data most reliably indicates this value. Cash flows are pictures of the future and gauging the future can only be done by drawing on the past. Which historical indicators are the best gauges of future performance? Candidates include historical cash flows themselves, relevant earnings history, and existing asset and liability levels.

Chapter 5

Organizing the Corporation

Situation

a. A few days ago you delivered Biologistics, Inc.'s ["Biologistics"] Articles of Incorporation to a corporation service company for filing with the Secretary of State, and this morning the service company called and said the articles have been filed by the Secretary of State. Your clients want to begin business as soon as possible and want to know what has to be done before they can do so. They know they need to elect officers, and they have discussed bylaws with you to some extent. Anderson and Baker say that Phillips is so busy he may not be able to make all board meetings. They want you to provide in the bylaws some way that Phillips can vote on important matters without being at a meeting, perhaps by giving one of them power to vote for him. Phillips has suggested that you provide in the bylaws that neither the Articles of Incorporation nor the bylaws may be amended without the unanimous vote of the board.

b. Some weeks ago a written consent in lieu of the organization meeting of Biologistics was executed by which bylaws were adopted, officers were elected and other actions were taken by the board of directors. The corporation commenced business almost immediately and has entered into a number of contracts, both for the purchase of equipment and supplies and for DNA synthesis. Yesterday you noticed that the corporation service company to whom you gave Biologistics' Articles of Incorporation for filing had not sent you a copy of the document showing its filing. You called and asked them to check on it. A company representative just called back and said there has been a mistake. Biologistics' Articles, it turned out, were not filed until this morning. They were mislaid and not found until your call prompted the service company to search for them. The message you received saying they had been filed was meant for another lawyer in your office and related to the articles of another corporation. As you determine what action to take, you should also consider the professional responsibility issues that arise in connection with an improperly formed corporation.

Section I
Procedures

The terms "incorporation" and "organization" of a corporation often are confused. Not infrequently, lawyers use them interchangeably. Actually, incorporation and organization are two separate events in the life of a corporation. Incorporation occurs when the state issues the corporate charter. At that point only the barest corporate skeleton exists, one consisting basically of the few items covered in the charter, such as the corporation's name and the type of business in which it may engage. It is during the process of organization that the corporation is given bylaws, shareholders, officers, and often its first directors. It is only at the completion of that process that enough meat has been added to the corporate bones to establish the corporation as a legal entity ready to do business.

Organization Meeting

Corporation statutes provide for the holding of an organization meeting after the issuance of a corporation's charter, to accomplish the organization of a corporation. Model Act § 2.05(a)(1) requires a meeting to be held "to complete the organization of the corporation by appointing officers, adopting bylaws, and carrying on any other business brought before the meeting...." Whether the meeting is to be held by the incorporator or by the directors depends on whether the directors are named in the charter, as required by some corporation statutes. If directors are named in the articles of incorporation, then they hold the organization meeting. If directors are not named in the charter, then one of the most important items on the agenda of the organization meeting is the election of the corporation's first directors.

Consent in Lieu of Meeting

Modern corporation statutes typically provide a convenient alternative to holding an organization meeting: written consent in lieu of meeting. Under statutes that allow that procedure, the incorporator or incorporators or the directors may forgo the organization meeting and act by written consent in lieu of meeting. Usually, the consent must be unanimous, but that rule is not without exception.

There is much to be said for organizing a corporation by written consent. For one thing, in cases where directors are not named in the charter and thus not available to hold an organization meeting, there typically is only one incorporator. While it is possible for a sole incorporator to hold an organization meeting, doing so is either cumbersome or strange. The cleanest way for a sole incorporator to conduct an organization meeting is to ask another person to preside as chair and then to interact with the chair. The organization meeting can also be held with only the incorporator present, with the only requirement being that the incorporator actually accomplish the necessary tasks, such as the adoption of bylaws and the election of directors and officers. The incorporator could go through the agenda out loud ("I hereby elect Mary Smith as the sole director of the corporation"), but presumably the incorporator's actions would be equally valid if done in the incorporator's head. Either way, holding a meeting with oneself is outside the norms of ordinary conduct.

Even if there is more than one person who has power to act at an organization meeting, it usually is better to organize the corporation by written consent in lieu of meeting, as provided in § 2.05(b) of the Model Act. As will be seen in the course of this chapter, there are a number of technical items to handle in connection with a corporation's organization, but at that point in a corporation's life there usually is not much that needs to be discussed at a meeting. Even critical decisions, such as who the officers are to be, typically will have been decided informally before the organization of the corporation. As a result, an organization meeting tends to be merely tedious rather than productive in terms of decisionmaking.

Finally, the kind of technical matters involved in organizing a corporation can be handled most reliably and at the least cost in a written consent drafted by the corporation's lawyer. In resolving the issue of whether to operate by written consent, an important question to consider is whether those who would conduct the meeting can be relied upon to take all the proper actions that need to be taken, and even if they can, whether they will draft proper minutes showing those actions. Considering the importance of starting the corporation's life without defects in its organization, and the expense of having a lawyer supervise the organization meeting and the preparation of accurate minutes in an attempt to ensure correctness, it turns out to be rare that holding an organization meeting makes more sense than operating by written consent.

Bylaws

The adoption of bylaws for the regulation of the corporation's affairs is the first step in organizing a corporation. Since there are many issues relating to bylaws, we will not discuss them here but rather will return to them in a subsequent section of this chapter, which is directed entirely to bylaws.

Election of Directors

If directors are not named in the charter, the incorporator typically adopts bylaws, which usually contain a provision on the number of directors, and then elects the corporation's first directors. Depending on the corporation statute involved and sometimes on the preference of the lawyer handling the organization of the corporation, the incorporator may continue with the organization or the new directors may take up the job at that point. The latter is preferable, if for no other reason than that one item that needs to be handled immediately is the sale of stock to the first shareholders. Virtually all corporation statutes require that item to be handled by the directors. Other important items, such as fixing the compensation of officers, may also need to be done by the directors rather than the incorporators, and so it usually is best simply to have the directors finish the whole task of organization. If the organization is being accomplished by consent in lieu of meeting, that simply means having two separate consents, one of the incorporator(s) and one of the directors.

Appointment of Officers

After the adoption of bylaws and, if necessary, the election of directors, the next step in organizing a corporation is the appointment of officers. All corporation statutes have a provision on the question of required officers, although Model Act § 8.40 provides simply that the corporation shall have "the officers described in its bylaws or appointed by the board of directors in accordance with the bylaws." Many states require certain named officers, however, and then allow the board to appoint any other officers it desires. A typical provision requires that a corporation have a president and a secretary, and some statutes go further and also require a vice president and a treasurer.

Especially in small, closely held corporations, the question arises as to whether one person may hold more than one office. The answer is that a person may hold any number of offices, with the exception in many states that a person may not hold the offices of president and secretary. The reason for that prohibition, as will better be seen in a later chapter dealing with the subject of corporate authority, is that the secretary is the principal officer who certifies the correctness of corporate actions, such as the signing of documents in the corporate name, and the president is the most likely officer to take those actions. That being so, it is not surprising that the drafters of corporate statutes usually have decided that the president and the secretary should be different persons. The Model Act, however, does not require the two offices to be held by different persons.

Bylaws typically list the officers a corporation is to have, along with a brief recitation of their basic powers and duties, and then give the board of directors (and perhaps certain officers, depending on what the corporation statute provides) the power to elect or appoint additional officers. Obviously, in planning the organization of a corporation, decisions on corporate officers need to be made before the lawyer finishes drafting the bylaws.

Section II
Other Organizational Matters

Once a corporation has bylaws, directors, and officers, the basics of its organization have been completed. There are, however, other matters that should be handled at the time of organization. If they are not handled then, some will need to be handled almost immediately, probably to the annoyance of clients who thought the details of getting their corporation started were out of the way.

Sale of Stock

Without question, the most important of the additional organizational matters is the sale of stock to the first shareholders. Corporation statutes provide that the directors must authorize the sale of stock against consideration approved by them. If the consideration is other than cash, then the directors generally must put a dollar value on the consideration. Those details need either to be memorialized in the minutes of an organization meeting or handled in a written consent in lieu of meeting. In addition to covering such details, the directors typically authorize certain corporate officers to issue the agreed number of shares against the specified consideration.

Modern corporation statutes typically allow shares to be issued without certificates. Especially in corporations with only one or two owners, that option can be useful in achieving simplicity and minimizing costs. If the corporation is to issue stock certificates, the lawyer handling the organization of the corporation needs to obtain from a corporate stationer certificates that meet the requirements of the corporation statute. The board then should approve the form of those certificates at the time it authorizes the first stock issuance.

Promoters' Contracts and Expenses

Often, clients enter into promoters' contracts on behalf of a corporation before it is formed. Whether or not clients have entered into promoters' contracts, typically they have taken some actions on the corporation's behalf (such as having preliminary discussions with prospective suppliers and customers) and in so doing have incurred expenses. Usually, clients wish to have the board of directors adopt such actions that were taken before incorporation and ratify those taken between the corporation's incorporation and its organization. Also, clients often wish to be reimbursed by the corporation for costs they have incurred on behalf of the corporation. The clients' desires in those regards can all be taken care of at the time of organization by a simple resolution of the directors.

Compensation

At the time of organization, the directors should pass a resolution approving the compensation of directors, or at minimum approving the reimbursement of their costs, and also approving the compensation of at least the chief executive officer. It may be legally possible for the chief executive officer to approve his or her own salary, but no one believes that to be good practice. In the typical closely held corporation, the board approves all or most officers' salaries.

Corporate Seal

Corporation statutes do not require corporate seals, but they do authorize them. While from the standpoint of contract law seals have come to be viewed as quaint anachronisms, that is not the case for corporations. Most corporations have a seal, and the use of it often is called for in connection with the execution of corporate documents. When that is the case, it can be easier to have and use a seal than to explain that the corporation does not have one. Besides that practical benefit, the use of a corporate seal often has evidentiary effect, usually serving either as *prima facie* evidence of due authorization or due execution of the sealed document. If a corporation is to have a seal, the form of the seal should be approved in connection with the corporation's organization.

Qualification to Do Business

A domestic corporation is one that conducts business in the state where it is incorporated. A foreign corporation is one doing business in one or more states that are not the state of incorporation. Corporations doing business in a state other than their state of incorporation will have to qualify to do business as a foreign corporation in each state in which they intend to operate. At a minimum, the board should pass a general resolution authorizing and directing the officers to take all necessary steps to effect those qualifications. A better practice is promptly to obtain the documents that will be required for qualification and then determine if a specific board resolution is necessary in connection with any qualification.

Banking Relationship

The lawyer handling the organization of a corporation should ask the client where the corporation intends to open a bank account and then should obtain from that bank, or ask the client to obtain from the bank, the form of board of directors' resolutions the bank will require before opening an account. Those resolutions should then be passed in connection with the organization of the corporation. If that is not done, immediately after the organization is complete and the corporation has received checks from its shareholders in payment for their stock, a corporate officer will be confronted with the need for new board action to pass those resolutions as soon as the officer attempts to open a bank account.

Those resolutions authorize specified persons to open a corporate checking account, sell commercial paper, take out loans, and so on. In handling those resolutions, a lawyer can save the corporation future trouble by listing corporate offices, rather than the names of individuals, as those the board of directors authorizes to act for the corporation. That way, the banking resolutions will not have to be passed again and again as new persons are elected to corporate offices.

Agreements Among Shareholders

A later chapter deals with distributing control within the corporation, and so we would be getting ahead of ourselves if we went too deeply at this point into the kinds of agreements shareholders may wish to enter into with respect to their corporation. It is important to note two things about such agreements, however, in connection with the discussion of the organization of corporations. First, in closely held corporations owned by more than one person, there usually is a need for one or more agreements among shareholders on such matters as voting for each other as directors and officers and on such questions as to whom shareholders may sell their stock. Second, the best time for entering into such agreements is at the very beginning of a corporation's life.

Minutes

If the organization of a corporation is accomplished at an organization meeting, the question arises as to what record of the meeting must be prepared. Corporate minutes provide records of organization meetings, as well as of directors' and shareholders' meetings. Typically they include information such as: the time the meeting began and ended; identification of attendees; whether a quorum was properly convened; the nature of any action taken, with a record of affirmative and negative votes as well as abstentions; and information about reports given. The minutes may be brief, providing information only on subjects covered and indicating whether there was discussion, but not the content of the discussion. Or, alternatively, they may be more elaborate, depending on the situation, the topic, and the possible uses of the minutes. Corporate minutes are generally available for inspection by shareholders and directors. They may also be discoverable and admissible in litigation.

Section III
Bylaws

A. Bylaws in the Corporate Hierarchy

The adoption of bylaws is the first step in the organization of a corporation. Model Act § 2.06(b) provides a good starting point for discussing bylaws. That section provides: "The bylaws of a corporation may contain any provision for managing the business and regulating the affairs of the corporation that is not inconsistent with law or the articles of incorporation." Compare that provision with the first sentence of § 8.01(b), which is the usual statement of the power of the board of directors: "All corporate powers shall be exercised by or under authority of, and the business and affairs of the corporation managed by or under the direction of, its board of directors, subject to any limitation set forth in the articles of incorporation or in an agreement authorized under § 7.32."

Each of those provisions relates to the hierarchy of authority in a corporation, and the first important thing to understand about bylaws is their place in that hierarchy. Notice first that § 2.06 relates to the power of the bylaws over the business and affairs of a corporation, and § 8.01(b) speaks about the power of the board over both business and affairs. Remember that the affairs of a corporation consist of those actions relating to the corporation's internal workings as an entity, as opposed to those actions relating to the conduct of the corporation's business.

This being said, one might perceive a conflict between §§ 2.06 and 8.01(b), in that § 2.06 says the bylaws may contain any provision relating to the regulation of a corporation's business and affairs "that is not inconsistent with law or the articles of incorporation" and § 8.01(b) may seem to give the board plenary power to manage the business and affairs of the corporation subject to limitations established by the articles or in an agreement authorized under § 7.32. Section 7.32 requires the agreement to be set forth in the articles of incorporation, the bylaws or "in a written agreement that is signed by all persons who are shareholders at the time of the agreement and is made known to the corporation." In other words, under § 2.06, the hierarchy of corporate regulation with respect to a corporation's business and affairs has the bylaws directly after the charter, whereas under § 8.01(b) directors may seem to occupy that position.

Actually, there is no conflict between §§ 2.06 and 8.01(b). In § 2.06 the drafters did intend to set out a hierarchy of corporate regulation. In § 8.01(b), on the other hand, what the drafters intended was merely to say where one would look (in an agreement or the charter or the bylaws) to find exceptions to the general rules that all corporate powers are to be exercised by the directors and that all of a corporation's business and affairs are at least to be supervised by a board of directors. The Model Act contains a number of such exceptions to the plenary power of directors, as for example, the requirement that shareholders must vote to approve a charter amendment. And § 2.02(b)(2) of the Model Act provides that the charter may contain any provision for the regulation of the business and internal affairs of a corporation, so long as the provision is not inconsistent with law. Section 8.01(b) thus does not speak to the general position of the bylaws in the hierarchy of regulation. That being said, here is the correct corporate hierarchy, through the level of the board of directors:

1. Law
2. Charter
3. Bylaws
4. Board Resolutions

B. Bylaw Scope and Conflict

Bylaws may contain any provision relating to the business and affairs of the corporation, so long as the provision does not conflict with law or the charter. In point of fact, however, bylaws prepared by experienced corporate lawyers are highly stylized, with the subjects covered and the way those subjects are covered being marked by little variation. A brief examination will show that these bylaws are divided into articles and sections. The major articles relate to the shareholders, the directors, and the officers, and those articles are followed by others relating to such subjects as certificates for shares and the corporate seal. Within the articles, detailed sections cover a multitude of rules relating to the subjects at hand. With respect to the shareholders, for example, each of the following is covered: annual meeting, special meetings, place of meetings, notice of meetings, fixing of record date, shareholder list, shareholder quorum and voting requirements, increasing either quorum or voting requirements, proxies, voting of shares, corporation's acceptance of votes, informal action by shareholders, voting for directors, shareholders' rights to inspect corporate records, furnishing corporate financial statements to shareholders, and dissenters' rights.

More often than the uninitiated might suppose, corporate bylaws are defective. There are many reasons. Sometimes the lawyer drafting the bylaws fails to include a provision that needs to be included, or the lawyer creates ambiguities because of inartful drafting. There are, however, other common problems: bylaws that conflict either with the corporation statute or with the corporation's own charter. This type of problem typically occurs because the lawyer uses a form of bylaws as a model without carefully checking it against the statute and charter, or because the lawyer drafts a particular bylaw provision afresh without doing this checking. Also, of course, bylaws must be kept up-to-date. Bylaws that originally are free of defects may develop them when the corporation statute or charter is amended and the bylaws are left alone. The following cases discuss the consequences of different types of bylaw conflicts.

Roach v. Bynum

Alabama Supreme Court
403 So. 2d 187 (1981)

PER CURIAM.

This is an appeal from John Roach, Jr., from an order granting the dissolution of a corporation, appointing a receiver, and denying a counterclaim. We affirm in part, and reverse in part.

The Legal Center, Inc., was formed in 1968 by Roach, his wife and Hjalma Johnson, the three of whom were Legal's only shareholders and directors. In the interim between 1968 and 1975, during which time the corporation remained dormant, Roach's wife and Johnson surrendered their holdings and resigned their positions as directors, thus leaving Roach as the sole shareholder and director. On May 15, 1975, Roach held a shareholder meeting and, as Legal's sole shareholder, adopted new bylaws which provided, inter alia:

ARTICLE IV QUORUM AND VOTING OF STOCK

Section 1. The holders of 70 percent of the shares of stock issued and outstanding and entitled to vote, represented in person or by proxy, shall constitute a quorum at all meetings of the shareholders for the transaction of business....

Section 2. If a quorum is present, the affirmative vote of 70 percent of the shares of stock represented at the meetings shall be the act of the shareholders unless the vote of a greater number of shares is required by law....

(e) Any amendment, alteration, modification or repeal of any provision of the Articles of Incorporation or By-laws of this Corporation must be approved by the affirmative vote of 70 percent of all the shareholders of the corporation.

ARTICLE VI MEETINGS OF THE BOARD OF DIRECTORS

Section 6. 70 percent of the directors shall constitute a quorum for the transaction of business unless the vote of a greater number of directors is required by law. The act of 70 percent of the directors present at any meeting at which a quorum is present shall be the act of the Board of Directors, unless the act of a greater number is required by statute. If a quorum shall not be present at any meeting of directors, the directors present thereat may adjourn the meeting from time to time, without notice other than announcement at the meeting, until a quorum shall be present.

ARTICLE IX OFFICERS — THE PRESIDENT

Section 6. The President shall be the chief executive officer of the corporation, shall preside at all meetings of the shareholders and the Board of Directors, shall have general and active management of the business of the corporation and shall see that all resolutions of the Board of Directors made in accordance with these By-Laws are given due consideration.

Section 7. He shall execute bonds, notes, mortgages and other contracts requiring a seal, under the seal of the corporation, except where required or permitted by law to be otherwise signed and executed and except where the signing and execution thereof shall be expressly delegated by the Board of Directors by their affirmative vote of 70 percent to some other officer or agent of the corporation.

ARTICLE XII AMENDMENTS

Section 1. These By-Laws may be altered, amended or repealed or new By-Laws adopted at any regular or special meeting of the shareholders at which a 70 percent quorum is present or represented, by the affirmative vote of 70 percent of all the stock of this corporation entitled to vote, provided notice of the proposed alteration, amendment or repeal be contained in the notice of such meeting.

During the same shareholder meeting in which these bylaws were adopted, Roach elected himself and James Forstman to serve as Legal's directors. Upon conclusion of the shareholder meeting, a meeting of the board of directors was held during which Roach was elected to serve as President/Treasurer and Forstman was elected to serve as Vice President/Secretary. By resolution of the directors, the ownership of the corporation was then realigned so that Roach and Forstman each owned 500 shares of Legal's stock....

Both Roach and Forstman contributed $14,000.00 towards the construction costs of a building in which they intended to maintain their separate law offices. After a site was purchased and bids from local contractors were submitted, it became apparent to the parties that the cost of constructing the building as planned exceeded the funds available. In an effort to reduce those costs, Roach offered to, and did, act as the general contractor for the project.

Prior to the completion of the building, a special shareholder meeting was held on September 24, 1975, during which Frank K. Bynum, another practicing attorney, was elected to serve as Legal's third director. The directors then issued Bynum 500 shares of Legal stock and elected him to the position of Secretary. The issuance of stock to Bynum brought the total number of issued and outstanding Legal shares to 1500, with each of the stockholders owning one-third. Bynum contributed $14,000.00 toward the building fund....

Soon after the building was completed and the three moved their law practices into the building, disagreements arose over their respective financial obligations to the corporation. Approximately one month after Forstman removed his law practice from the building, all three attended a shareholder meeting where, in keeping with the shareholder agreement, each was reelected to the position of director. Forstman, however, refused to vote for Roach as President/Treasurer....

At the annual meeting in March, 1977, Roach utilized the seventy percent vote requirement to successfully block several of Forstman's and Bynum's motions[1] by casting

---

1. [1] These included proposals (1) that a court reporter or someone capable of taking shorthand be allowed to transcribe the business conducted at the meetings; (2) that the bylaws be changed; and

his vote against the proposals. Forstman's nomination of Bynum and himself as Legal's only directors as well as his nomination of Bynum as President/Treasurer and himself Vice President/Secretary also failed to receive Roach's assenting vote. Once again, the meeting adjourned with Roach remaining as the holdover President.

On May 17, 1977, Bynum and Forstman sued for dissolution under Code 1975, §10-2-204.... The trial judge, sitting without a jury, found the corporation hopelessly deadlocked ... ordered the corporation dissolved and appointed a receiver to liquidate Legal's assets....

Standard

I

Roach contends the trial judge's findings that the corporation was hopelessly deadlocked within the meaning of Code 1975, § 10-2-204 is unsupported by the evidence. Although not for those reasons advanced by Roach, we agree that Legal is not deadlocked.

All allegations of deadlock arise from the seventy percent quorum and vote requirement imposed by Articles IV, VI and XII of the bylaws. Assuming these bylaws are valid, they in effect require the presence of all the shareholders in order to constitute a quorum at shareholder meetings and, more importantly, that all shareholder action must be by unanimous consent. The same is required for director action at meetings of Legal's directors.

As a general rule, bylaws of a corporation are valid if they are reasonable, proper objects of the corporation, and are consistent with the charter and statutory law governing the corporation. The Alabama Business Corporation Act follows this rule by authorizing corporations to make and alter "all needful bylaws" "unless inconsistent with the nature, character or object of the corporation or unless such powers are expressly denied to the corporation by its charter." Roach, at the time he was the sole shareholder and director of Legal, attempted to exercise this grant of authority by passing, inter alia, Article IV of the bylaws which imposed seventy percent quorum and vote requirements for shareholder action; Article V, § 3, and IX, § 6, which vested in the President the power and authority to manage the corporation; and Article XII which imposed a seventy percent quorum and vote requirement for shareholder action to alter, amend, repeal or adopt bylaws.

Roach contends that Legal is not deadlocked because he continues to manage the affairs of the corporation under the power and authority vested in him as President by Articles V, § 3, and IX, § 6, of the bylaws. We disagree. According to the Alabama Business Corporation Act, "(e)xcept as may otherwise be provided in the certificate of incorporation, the business and affairs of a corporation shall be managed by a board of directors." Legal's Articles of Incorporation, Article Eighth, § 4, provides that the business affairs of the corporation shall be under the management and control of Legal's directors. Those bylaws which vest the authority to manage Legal's affairs in the President conflict with both the Corporation Act and Legal's Articles of Incor-

---

(3) that a restriction be placed upon the President/Treasurer's authority to borrow and lend money on behalf of the corporation.

poration and are therefore void. However, in the light of the dissension among the directors, "control" in the sense of continuing management by the directors is made illusory by the seventy percent quorum and vote requirement for director action imposed by Article VI, §6, of the bylaws. Although these circumstances appear to indicate a director deadlock, we think that the power to break this and any other deadlock is held by Legal's shareholders.

At common law, the presence of a simple majority of shareholders entitled to vote on a matter constituted a quorum, and a majority vote of that quorum was all that was necessary to validly transact shareholder business. Many states have modified this rule by enacting statutes which permit greater than majority quorum/vote requirements for shareholders and direction action.

The requirement of unanimity or high quorum/vote for shareholder and director action is one of the most effective methods of protecting the interests of the minority shareholders and preventing the majority from "squeezing out" the minority. In addition to giving the minority what is in effect a veto power over corporate decisions, unanimity or high vote requirements permit the shareholders in a close corporation to be "shareholders to the outside world but partners among themselves."

The statutory language in many state corporations acts permits high vote requirements to be set out in either the certificate of incorporation or the bylaws. Other statutory language indicates that such requirements as to shareholder action are valid only if included in the charter or articles of incorporation. On this point it has been noted:

> In some states, the part of the corporation act which lists items for inclusion in the charter is couched in language that lends some support to an argument that matters authorized for coverage in optional charter clauses cannot be covered by a bylaw provision or in a shareholder agreement. Thus, the Maryland statute provides that the articles of incorporation "shall state ... (7) The restrictions, if any, imposed upon the transferability of shares of any class." Statutory language of this kind could conceivably be interpreted to mean that share restrictions elsewhere would be ineffective.

1 F. O'Neal, Close Corporations, §3.79, at 3-114 (2d ed. 1971) (footnote and citation omitted). Several decisions supporting this interpretation have established the general rule that when the corporation's statute commands that a provision which governs shareholder rights be set out in the certificate of incorporation, but the provision is not so set out, a bylaw which purports to regulate the same subject is void.

The provisions of the Alabama Business Corporation Act in effect both at the time when Legal was formed and when this action was commenced provided:

> The certificate of incorporation ... shall set forth:

> > (11) VOTING The certificate of incorporation may contain provisions requiring for any corporate act the vote of a larger proportion of the stock or any class thereof than is required by this chapter.

We think this language is susceptible of the same interpretation other courts have given similarly worded statutes. A provision mandating a greater than majority shareholder vote is valid only if set forth in the certificate of incorporation, and a bylaw which purports to impose the same requirement is void.

Legal's certificate of incorporation is silent as to the number of votes necessary to transact shareholder business. The record is devoid of any evidence of an amendment to the certificate which addressed this issue. We therefore conclude that, at the time of its "passage," the bylaw which mandated shareholder vote of seventy percent was void and, unless the Corporation Act imposes a different requirement, a simple majority vote of the quorum present at a shareholder meeting was all that was necessary to validly transact shareholder business. This conclusion equally applies to those bylaws which require a seventy percent shareholder vote to alter, amend or repeal existing bylaws or to adopt new bylaws....

Our resolution of these issues compels us to conclude that the corporation is not deadlocked. Any one of the shareholders may call a special shareholders meeting during which they may, by a simple majority of the quorum, exercise their right under Article Eighth of the Articles of Incorporation to vote to alter, amend or repeal any existing bylaw they find oppressive or burdensome.[2] In sum, the shareholders themselves hold the power to break any deadlock which may have arisen from Legal's existing bylaws. Therefore, the trial judge's order dissolving the corporation and appointing a receiver to liquidate Legal's assets is due to be reversed....

TORBERT, CHIEF JUSTICE (concurring specially).

I agree that the by laws requiring the vote of 70% of the issued and outstanding stock to take corporate action is void under Alabama law. That is not to say that the same result would follow if such a requirement was provided in an otherwise valid agreement among all of the stockholders. The stockholders' agreement here does not provide for such a high vote requirement. Paragraph 5(a) of the stockholders' agreement only provides for certain alternatives "if any action be taken or authorized at a meeting ... by a vote of less than seventy (70%) percent," namely, rescission of the action or the purchase by the corporation of the stock owned by the dissenter....

Notes and Questions

Can you think of any explanations for why Mr. Roach made what appears to have been the big mistake of putting charter-level provisions in the bylaws? Obviously, he did not read the applicable Alabama corporate statutes, which allow corporations to adopt supermajority quorum and voting requirements but only in their charter. Compare the Delaware corporate statute, DGCL 216, which permits such provisions to be in either the charter or the bylaws. Does that suggest the source of Roach's mistake? Corporate lawyers commonly use precedent forms to draft governing documents

---

2. [6] Although the power to alter bylaws is typically vested in the board of directors, such power may be reserved to the shareholders if so provided in the certificate of incorporation. Article Eight of Legal's Articles of Incorporation reserves to the shareholders the power to make, alter, amend and repeal bylaws.

rather than reinvent the wheel. In doing so, however, care must be taken to adapt precedents to the particulars of the transaction or jurisdiction. What is effective for one deal under one state statute or corporate charter may not be effective for others.

Datapoint Corp. v. Plaza Securities Co.

Delaware Supreme Court
496 A.2d 1031 (1985)

HORSEY, JUSTICE.

This appeal by Datapoint Corporation from an order of the Court of Chancery, preliminarily enjoining its enforcement of a bylaw adopted by Datapoint's board of directors, presents an issue of first impression in Delaware: whether a bylaw designed to limit the taking of corporation action by written shareholder consent in lieu of a stockholders' meeting conflicts with 8 Del. C. §228, and thereby is invalid.[3] The Court of Chancery ruled that Datapoint's bylaw was unenforceable because its provisions were in direct conflict with the power conferred upon shareholders by 8 Del. C. §228. We agree and affirm.

II

In December of 1984, Asher B. Edelman, general partner of both plaintiffs and beneficial owner of more than 10% of Datapoint's stock, advised the latter's chairman that he was interested in acquiring control of Datapoint. However, Datapoint's board of directors was opposed to this, and on January 11, 1985, when Edelman submitted a written proposal to acquire Datapoint, the offer was rejected the same day.

On January 24, Edelman renewed his offer and stated that if it were rejected he would consider the solicitation of consents from shareholders. Datapoint's composite certificate of incorporation then (and now) lacks any provision relating to the solic-

---

3. [1] 8 Del. C. §228 reads, in pertinent part:

§228. Consent of stockholders or members in lieu of meeting.
(a) Unless otherwise provided in the certificate of incorporation, any action required by this chapter to be taken at any annual or special meeting of stockholders of a corporation, or any action which may be taken at any annual or special meeting of such stockholders, may be taken without a meeting, without prior notice and without a vote, if a consent in writing, setting forth the action so taken, shall be signed by the holders of outstanding stock having not less than the minimum number of votes that would be necessary to authorize or take such action at a meeting at which all shares entitled to vote thereon were present and voted.... (c) Prompt notice of taking of the corporate action without a meeting by less than unanimous written consent shall be given to those stockholders or members who have not consented in writing. In the event that the action which is consented to is such as would have required the filing of a certificate under any other section of this title, if such action had been voted on by stockholders or by members at a meeting thereof, the certificate filed under such other section shall state, in lieu of any statement required by such section concerning any vote of stockholders or members, that written consent has been given as provided in this section.

itation of shareholder consents under § 228. However, the next day Texas counsel to Datapoint recommended that the Datapoint board adopt a bylaw amendment to regulate consents. Counsel stated, "While the resolution will not prevent a hostile takeover, it will provide management with additional time to explore alternatives."

On January 28, Datapoint's directors, meeting telephonically, unanimously adopted bylaw amendments (the "January bylaw") which the Chancellor later found to be "designed to establish a procedure to govern any attempt to take corporate action on Datapoint's behalf by written shareholder consent."

On January 30, 1985, Edelman withdrew his offer to buy Datapoint and announced his intention to solicit shareholder consents for removal of the board and the election of his own candidates. On February 5, plaintiffs commenced this action in the Court of Chancery for preliminary and permanent injunctive relief against enforcement of Datapoint's January bylaw amendment.

... On February 12, Datapoint's board amended its January bylaw on the recommendation, among others, of Datapoint's investment advisor, Kidder Peabody.... Datapoint's February bylaw provided, in part, that:

(1) No action by shareholder consent could take place until the 45th day after the established record date;

(2) That a record date should be fixed of not more than (or less than) 15 days after receipt of a shareholder's notice of intent to solicit consents, unless requested by the shareholder; and

(3) No shareholder consent action would become effective "until the final termination of any proceeding which may have been commenced in the Court of Chancery of the State of Delaware or any other court of competent jurisdiction for an adjudication of any legal issues incident to determining the validity of the consents, unless and until such court shall have determined that such proceedings are not being pursued expeditiously and in good faith."

On February 19, Datapoint's board, in response to Edelman's notice of intent to solicit shareholder consents, set March 4 as the record date and April 18 as the "action" date for counting shareholder consents submitted under § 228. On February 28, Datapoint filed suit in the United States District Court for the Western District of Texas to invalidate any consents obtained by plaintiffs. The suit thereby triggered the litigation "hold" mechanism of the February bylaw.

On March 5, 1985, the Court of Chancery granted plaintiffs a preliminary injunction enjoining defendant Datapoint from enforcing the February bylaw. Based on the Court's construction of § 228 and the impact of Datapoint's February bylaw, the Court concluded that plaintiffs had made "a clear and reasonable showing ... of the likelihood that the Datapoint bylaw directly conflicts with the statutory grant of power to the shareholders" under § 228; and that plaintiffs had demonstrated the likelihood of immediate irreparable harm to their efforts to solicit consents under § 228 for the purpose of removing Datapoint's present board and electing a new slate of directors.

III

On appeal, defendant asserts essentially a three-step argument in support of its contention that the Chancellor committed legal error in enjoining the enforcement of Datapoint's February bylaw. First, defendant contends that the Court erred in construing § 228 as not permitting the consent solicitation procedure—as to which § 228 is silent—to be regulated by bylaw. Second, defendant argues that the Court erred in construing § 228 as requiring a consent accomplished thereunder to be put into effect immediately and without any review of its legality being permitted. Defendant then makes a derivative argument which assumes the correctness of its first two contentions. It argues that the February bylaw constitutes a reasonable regulation of a shareholder § 228 solicitation. Defendant contends that the "delay and review" features of its bylaw are designed to prevent the possibility of "midnight raids" on an uninformed electorate. However, a further objective of the February bylaw's 45-day waiting period (actually 60 days in the aggregate), defendant concedes, is to permit management to solicit its own proxies on the subject.

As to Datapoint's first contention, defendant argues that § 228's introductory language ("Unless otherwise provided in the certificate of incorporation") means that the right of shareholders to act by written consent in lieu of meeting may only be denied shareholders by a charter provision; and that the Chancellor erroneously construed the clause to mean that the regulation of shareholder consent action may not be imposed by a board of directors through the enactment of bylaws. Since bylaws are the proper means for implementing the internal regulation of corporations, defendant reasons that corporate elections, including those accomplished under § 228, are proper subjects for regulation by bylaw.

Relating its February bylaw to general Delaware law, defendant argues that Datapoint's bylaw represents reasonable internal corporate regulation which is … not inconsistent with § 228.…

IV

The issue in this case is not an abstract one. Nor is the case in its present posture as multifaceted as the parties make it. The issue is not whether § 228 tolerates any delay in effectuating a shareholder consent action taken thereunder. Nor is the issue whether § 228 permits a board of directors to regulate by bylaw solicitation procedures under § 228. These threshold disputes between the parties are more theoretical than real. The injunctive relief that is here challenged was bottomed on the Court's finding of likelihood that the Datapoint bylaw "directly conflicts" with § 228's grant of power to the shareholders and the Court's conclusion that the lengthy delay provisions of the bylaw are "totally at odds" with the statutory right given shareholders to take action by written consent under § 228.

The determinative question is whether Datapoint's February bylaw conflicts with the letter and intent of § 228. The Chancellor found a clear conflict; and we agree with the Court's construction of § 228 as it applies to the bylaw before us.

Confining our ruling to this bylaw, we find it clearly in conflict with the letter and intent of § 228. Section 228 contains no language suggesting that action accomplished by stockholders through written consent "without a meeting, without prior notice and without a vote" may be lawfully deferred or thwarted on grounds not relating to the legal sufficiency of the consents obtained. The Chancellor similarly construed § 228 in stating that it "gives shareholders the right to take immediate action by written consent provided that they have at a given point in time obtained a written expression of authority on behalf of shares representing sufficient votes to take such action."

Datapoint's bylaw is not designed simply to defer consummation of shareholder action by consent in lieu of meeting until a ministerial-type review of the sufficiency of the consents has been performed by duly qualified and objective inspectors. Instead, the bylaw imposes an arbitrary delay upon shareholder action in lieu of meeting by postponing accomplishment of such action until 60 days after the corporation's receipt of a shareholder's notice of intent to solicit consents. . . .

ministerial

This delay is not only arbitrary, it is unreasonable. For the underlying intent of the bylaw is to provide the incumbent board with *time* to seek to defeat the shareholder action by management's solicitation of its own proxies, or revocations of outstanding shareholder consents. . . . Moreover, the bylaw's further provision staying the effective date of any shareholder consent action until termination of any lawsuits challenging such action effectively places within the incumbent board the power to stultify, if not nullify, the shareholders' statutory right. Such a result can only be found to be "repugnant to the statute" which the bylaw is intended to serve, not master.

Although we find defendant's bylaw to be invalid, we do not hold that § 228 must be construed as barring a board of directors from adopting a bylaw which would impose minimal essential provisions for ministerial review of the validity of the action taken by shareholder consent. . . .

Notes and Questions

1. Concerning shareholder action by written consent in lieu of a meeting under DGCL 228: (a) the default rule is *majority* vote with (b) an *opt-out* via the charter. Under MBCA 7.04, the same topic of shareholder action by written consent in lieu of a meeting is treated differently: (a) the default rule is *unanimous* vote with (b) an *opt-in* via the charter.

2. Is there a sense in which *Roach* and *Datapoint* are analytically identical cases? In both, putative bylaws were ineffective because the statute required the given topic to be addressed, if at all, in the charter. Then again, *Datapoint* is more contestable for two reasons: (1) the board's argument that it was not eliminating shareholder action by written consent but only regulating it and (2) the court's willingness to condone genuine ministerial regulation while finding that the board's regulation was neither limited nor legitimate.

3. The Delaware Supreme Court's opinion in *ATP Tour*, considered earlier, cites *Datapoint v. Plaza Securities* as an illustration of a bylaw adopted by a board for an improper purpose.

Paulek v. Isgar

Colorado Court of Appeals
551 P.2d 213 (1976)

BERMAN, JUDGE.

Plaintiff, Victor A. Paulek, commenced this action for himself and all other similarly situated stockholders in the H.H. Ditch Co. (H.H.) to restrain the defendant officers, directors, and shareholders from proceeding to consolidate the Short Line Ditch Co. (Short Line) with H.H. From an adverse judgment in the trial court, plaintiffs appeal. We affirm.

At a special meeting of the shareholders of H.H., 56% of the shares represented at the meeting voted to consolidate the two ditch companies under the existing articles of incorporation and bylaws of H.H. At the next annual meeting of the shareholders, an amendment to the minutes of the special meeting was approved, again by majority vote. The amendment provided that as part of the consolidation Short Line was to pay a proportionate share of any indebtedness of H.H. and that all property of Short Line was to become the property of H.H.

Paulek first contends the trial court erred in its holding that series D stock of H.H. could be issued in exchange for water rights and other property of Short Line without amending its bylaws. The bylaws provide as follows:

"The capital stock of this company shall be classed in three series as follows: A series, B series, and C series, and shall be assessable for the purposes stated in the Articles of Incorporation and these Bylaws."

However, the articles of incorporation authorize the issuance of 8,000 shares of par value stock divided into four series: A, B, C, and D. Each series of stock was to be issued "in the ratio of 80 shares of stock for each cubic foot [of water] per second of time" conveyed to the company. The articles provide that series A, B, and C would be issued to the owners of rights and interests in the H.H. Ditch and subsequent enlargements, but that the D series of stock "shall be placed in the treasury of the Company to be issued at the ratio of 80 shares for each cubic foot of water per second of time … upon conveyance of such water to this Company by the owner thereof. …"

The trial court held that there was a conflict or inconsistency between the articles of incorporation and the bylaws relating to the series D stock, and concluded that the articles controlled. Paulek however contends that the series D stock could not be issued until the bylaws were amended, pursuant to the bylaw provision permitting amendment, by a two-thirds vote of the stock represented at a meeting of the shareholders held to authorize the issuance of the series D stock.

Paulek's contention ignores the fact that the articles of H.H. also provide that the board of directors, rather than shareholders, shall have the power to make the bylaws. Thus, the provision in the bylaws attempting to give this power to the shareholders is in conflict with the articles of incorporation. Where bylaws conflict with the articles of incorporation, the articles of incorporation control and the bylaws in conflict are void....

Notes and Questions

1. Consider the facts of *Paulek* under a state corporation statute that, like Delaware's, reserves the power to amend bylaws for shareholders even if the certificate of incorporation confers that power upon directors. *See* DGCL 109. Would the case come out differently?

2. The way to avoid bylaw conflicts is simple in theory: Do not draft bylaws or any bylaw provision without a careful checking against the statute and corporate charter. Actually avoiding conflicts is not so simple in practice, because most corporate law firms have office forms of bylaws that lawyers are encouraged to use without much checking. Still, use of office forms without checking, even in the best firms, results in more risks than one would imagine. That is true of do-it-yourself practitioners, such as John Roach, as well as large firms you would expect to operate better.

Meticulously check the office form bylaws in twenty good law firms, and you probably will find at least one or two problems. Not infrequently, one at least will find upon checking that the lawyer who was supposed to look after updating corporate forms has not done so frequently enough. If office form bylaws have not been updated at least as recently as the latest changes to the state's corporation statute, a lawyer should view them with more than ordinary suspicion.

C. Bylaws as a Contract

Despite colloquial talk that corporate statutes, charters, and bylaws amount to a "corporate contract," such provisions are not necessarily contracts and are not necessarily formed according to the law of contracts. Rather, the rules governing corporate internal affairs are adopted through the intricate machinery of the corporate law hierarchy (statute, charter, bylaw, board resolutions), which, in turn, reflects the specific types of participants and relationships involved: boards, officers, and shareholders. The route to enacting rules binding on corporate internal affairs is therefore entirely different from the traditional route to contract formation.

That is why it is generally a mistake to believe that if a particular bylaw provision is ineffective as a bylaw, then it might nevertheless be seen to have formed a binding contract. That only would occur, if at all, in a closely held corporation and only when the bylaw's infirmity is due to some highly technical or ministerial error rather than to a conflict with the statute or the corporation's charter (as in *Roach*, *Datapoint* or *Paulek*). The following case rejects an argument by shareholders that an ineffective bylaw could nevertheless be enforced as a contract.

Jones v. Wallace

Oregon Supreme Court
628 P.2d 388 (1981)

LINDE, JUSTICE.

Under the Oregon Business Corporation Act, a shareholders' meeting requires a quorum of a majority of the voting shares unless a different quorum is provided in the articles of incorporation. The issue before us here is whether a 100 percent quorum requirement that is adopted as a corporate bylaw but not in the articles, as the statute provides, nevertheless may be enforced as a binding agreement among the shareholders of a closely held corporation by setting aside corporate action taken without such a quorum.

In 1972, when defendant Wallace was the sole shareholder of Capital Credit & Collection Service, Inc. as well as one of its directors, the directors adopted bylaws which included the following:

> "At any meeting of stockholders all of the outstanding shares of the corporation entitled to vote, represented in person or by proxy, shall constitute a quorum at a meeting of stockholders."

In 1976 plaintiffs Jones and Gaarde each purchased 49? shares of the corporation's stock. Wallace retained 100 shares, or 50.25 percent. The three shareholders also constituted the board of directors. According to plaintiffs' complaint, although not conceded by defendants, there was a directors' meeting in June, 1979, at which a majority of the directors removed Wallace as president and elected Jones president and Gaarde secretary of the corporation. Both sides agree that the following month a shareholders' meeting occurred at which Gaarde was not present in person nor represented by proxy, and at which Wallace used his majority of the voting shares to remove both the minority shareholders as directors of the corporation and to replace them with defendants Roberts and Smith.

The minority shareholders thereupon sued for a declaratory judgment that they rather than Roberts and Smith remain directors and officers of the corporation. The circuit court allowed summary judgment for defendants on the grounds that the shareholders' meeting satisfied the statutory quorum requirement, and that this requirement could not be overridden by the bylaw. The Court of Appeals reversed, accepting plaintiffs' argument that the bylaw could be enforced as a contract among assenting shareholders. As this question has not previously been decided under the Oregon Business Corporation Act, we allowed review. We reverse the Court of Appeals and affirm the judgment of the circuit court.

The choice whether an extraordinary quorum requirement can be imposed by bylaws or only in the articles of incorporation is not an unimportant technicality. The articles are on file with the Corporation Commissioner, and thus are publicly available to the original and subsequent investors as well as others doing business with the corporation; and the pertinent classes of shareholders are entitled to vote on any amendments. Bylaws, on the other hand, are adopted and changed by the board of directors without prior notice to or participation by the shareholders, unless such shareholder rights are expressly reserved. Accordingly, the statute limits bylaws to "provisions for the regulation and management of the affairs of the corporation not inconsistent with law or the articles of incorporation."

. . .

In view of the statute, plaintiffs do not press a claim that the bylaw on which they rely effectively requires a 100 percent quorum for a shareholders' meeting. Instead they contend, and the Court of Appeals held, that a bylaw, even if invalid, can be enforced as a contract against a shareholder who has assented to the bylaw, and that this bylaw should be so enforced.

We need not here question the general proposition that a contractual agreement may be given the form of a bylaw or, conversely, that a bylaw sometimes may incorporate a binding commitment to a corporation's shareholders or members, and that such contractual obligations may bind the parties thereto apart from the bylaw as such. The broad generalization that an invalid bylaw may be enforceable as a contract has been stated in a number of cases, although the two Oregon cases cited for this proposition involved membership associations incorporated under other statutes than the business corporation act. The decisions from other states cited on either side also are distinguishable for a variety of reasons. Some involve bylaws which were ineffective as such only because they were faultily adopted; some concern the enforcement of corporate rights against a shareholder; the older cases antedate the modern corporation statutes; or the argument made here was not presented.

Moreover, the question before us is not whether an agreement among corporate shareholders not to act at a shareholders' meeting unless all are represented, if such an agreement were actually made, could give rise to a contract cause of action by one shareholder against another or whether such an agreement would be void as contrary to ORS 57.165. The question here is whether a bylaw in existence when a shareholder buys his shares can be construed into a contract in order to enforce it by setting aside corporate action taken in accordance with the statute and the corporate articles. This contract theory, whatever its merits in other contexts, cannot be used in this fashion to circumvent the statutory procedures for corporate decisions and accomplish by indirection what the bylaw could not accomplish directly. . . .

Chapter 6

Corporate Authority

Situation

Biologistics, Inc. has been in business for a little over a year. The initial earnings projections have more than been met. After salaries and expenses, the corporation had earnings of $50,000 during its first year, and its prospects continue to look good. In addition to the laboratory technician and office assistant the corporation hired originally, the company has recently hired one more laboratory technician and a molecular biologist. Baker has had little opportunity to do research and development work. With the addition of more laboratory help, however, the plan is now for her to devote substantial time to this.

Over the next several months you are asked in various situations who has power to take action on behalf of the corporation. In each case, the person asking wants the action taken at the lowest corporate level that is relatively sure to be effective.

How do you respond to each of the following:

1. Purchasing laboratory and office supplies and equipment, basically to sustain the current operation, the total cost of which would be several thousand dollars annually.

2. Purchasing equipment for the research and development work, to total $40,000.

3. Entering into a lease on space adjoining that which the corporation currently leases under an extension of its original one-year lease. The lease is to be for five years at $10,000 annually.

4. Establishing a line of credit at a local bank in the amount of $20,000 and borrowings thereunder. Amounts are to be borrowed under the line to pay current expenses when the corporation is short of cash, and paid back as soon as cash is available.

5. Taking a five-year bank loan from the same local bank in the amount of $50,000, the proceeds to be used for research and development.

6. Hiring an additional laboratory assistant.

———————

Corporate authority is an especially important subject for lawyers because questions about corporate authority arise frequently. Most of those questions involve one or both of the following aspects:

1. What person or corporate body has power to take action?

2. What formalities are required for the action to be taken?

In terms of who can take action, there are usually three choices: the shareholders, the directors, or one or more of the officers. In a general corporation, the members of the board of directors, acting collectively, have oversight responsibility for managing the corporation and making important policy decisions. The board appoints the officers, who supervise the day to day operations of the company. The shareholders elect directors and approve fundamental corporate changes, such as mergers with other companies, amendments to the articles of incorporation and the like.

In closely held corporations, the shareholders may take a more active role in company management, as will be discussed below. Shareholders of closely held corporations are typically individuals for whom the corporation is both an investment and a primary source of income. These individuals often have a close, personal identification with the company. However, shareholders of closely held corporations may also be other corporations, any type of unincorporated business entity, as well as any other form of legal entity.

Recent years have witnessed a shift in the ownership of publicly traded companies. Originally, shareholders were typically individuals. Today, stock is predominately held by institutional investors, such as mutual funds, pension funds, and hedge funds. Although the relative holdings of a single institutional investor in any one company may be only a small percentage of the whole, collectively institutional ownership is a powerful force in the ownership of publicly held companies. Large institutional investors can influence company policy by communicating directly with company management. The demographic shift from primarily individual stock ownership to institutional ownership has led to a concomitant shift in power from boards of directors and senior managers to shareholders. This power shift is reflected in numerous corporate law devices discussed in this chapter and later in the book.

Section I
Functions and Authority of Shareholders

For a lawyer to be prepared for questions about the authority of shareholders, it helps to understand the contexts in which those questions tend to arise. One occurs when a shareholders' meeting is imminent or in progress and a lawyer is asked whether the shareholders can vote on a particular matter or whether the matter has to wait for directors' action. Another arises when it is possible to assemble a quorum of the shareholders but not of the directors, or, along those same lines, where shareholders are available to sign consents in lieu of a meeting but the directors are not. When the need exists for the corporation to take action quickly, it is sometimes hard to convince shareholders that they lack the necessary power. That especially is the case where (1) the shareholders and directors are exactly the same persons, which is not an unusual situation, and (2) a quorum for a directors' meeting cannot be obtained but a quorum for a meeting of shareholders can be (e.g., because shareholder quorums are based on the number of shares owned whereas board quorums are based on the number of directors). Another difference is that shareholders can be represented at a meeting by proxy holders while directors cannot.[1]

A. Scope of Shareholders' Powers

Although it surprises many clients, the universal rule in corporation law is that shareholders have no general power to manage a corporation. Rather, shareholders have only those powers specifically given them by the corporation statute, by shareholders' agreements authorized by statute, or in some instances by common law. In a general corporation, the members of the board of directors, acting collectively, have oversight responsibility for managing the corporation and making important policy decisions. The board appoints the officers, who supervise the day-to-day operations of the company. In closely held corporations, the shareholders may take a more active role in company management and may exercise powers not permitted to shareholders of publicly traded companies.

Thus, the role of shareholders in the management of a corporation may vary according to whether the firm is a company with a large number of shareholders or one with only a few. In companies with a large number of shareholders, the functional separation between company management and company ownership is typically greater than in those companies with just a few shareholders. Management by a large number of people is unwieldy. In addition, the likelihood that the owners will be widely dispersed with individual holdings amounting only to a small percentage of the total shares outstanding discourages participation in management. It is not cost effective for a shareholder with little corporate power to devote significant time to oversight of the business. Furthermore, individual shareholders may lack the necessary expertise to govern a large corporation.

In contrast, corporation statutes such as MBCA 7.32 permit shareholders in closely held corporations to assume some or all of the powers usually accorded to the board of directors. At the same time, the shareholders may retain those powers traditionally allocated to them. In sum, shareholders of closely held corporations are free to design a management structure that suits their particular needs so long as all shareholders agree to change the traditional form of management. The substance of the agreement must either be included in the articles of incorporation or in a shareholders' agreement signed by all shareholders.

The overwhelmingly important power of shareholders, of course, is to elect directors, and it is this authority to choose directors of their liking that gives shareholders their greatest power, especially when combined with the ability to remove directors at any time with or without cause,[2] which is the modern statutory norm, and when

---

1. *See, e.g.,* MBCA §7.22 (regarding shareholders acting through proxy holders).
2. MBCA §8.08(a).

combined with the further ability to elect new directors to fill vacancies thus created.[3] Typically, all directors are elected annually, unless their terms are staggered so that not all terms will conclude at the same time.[4]

Some corporation statutes give the shareholders the power to amend the corporation's bylaws, unless the charter provides that the directors have that power. The MBCA provides that the authority to amend bylaws resides with the shareholders and the directors, unless shareholders reserve to themselves exclusive power to amend particular provisions or the bylaws as a whole.[5] All or almost all other instances of shareholders' powers relate to specific consents required for particular corporate actions. In each of those instances there is the statutory requirement that the board of directors first vote on the action and then send it on to the shareholders for their consent. Examples are charter amendments,[6] mergers and share exchanges,[7] certain dispositions of corporate assets,[8] and voluntary dissolution.[9]

Shareholders of closely held corporations tend to assume that they have broad powers, as shareholders, to make corporate decisions. This assumption may arise because of their close, personal identification with the corporation and because they often depend on the corporation for their livelihoods. Such was the case with the shareholders of the Rawhide Ranch Gold and Silver Mining Company when, in 1865, they met and voted to sell the corporation's mine and its other assets, thus setting the stage for one of the classic cases on shareholders' power, *Gashwiler v. Willis*.

Gashwiler v. Willis
California Supreme Court
33 Cal. 11 (1867)

By the Court, SAWYER, J.:

The Rawhide Ranch Gold and Silver Mining Company is a corporation duly organized under the statutes of California for the purpose of carrying on the business of mining. On the 29th of April, 1865, a special meeting of the stockholders of the corporation was held, pursuant to notice, at the office of the company, at which all the stockholders were present. At this meeting of the stockholders, all the stockholders being present and all the capital stock represented, a resolution was unanimously adopted authorizing S. S. Turner, T. N. Willis and James J. Hodges, Trustees of said corporation, for and on behalf of said corporation, to sell and convey to D. W. Barney the mine, mill, buildings, mining implements, and appurtenances belonging to said

---

3. *Id.* § 8.10(a)(1).

4. *Id.* §§ 8.05, 8.06.

5. *Id.* § 10.20.

6. *Id.* § 10.03. Section 10.05 authorizes the directors to amend the articles without shareholder action in certain limited situations, such as deleting names and addresses of initial directors, or deleting the name and address of the initial registered agent or registered office when a change is being made.

7. *Id.* §§ 11.01–11.04.

8. *Id.* § 12.02.

9. *Id.* § 14.02.

company. In pursuance of said resolution, and without any other authority shown, on the 5th of June following a conveyance was executed by said Turner, Willis, and Hodges, Trustees, the commencement and form of execution of which are as follows:

> "This indenture, made the 5th day of June, A. D. 1865, between the Rawhide Ranch Gold and Silver Mining Company, a corporation under the laws of the State of California, by S. S. Turner, T. N. Willis and James J. Hodges, Trustees of said corporation, who are duly authorized and empowered by resolution and order of said corporation to sell and convey," etc.

> "In witness whereof we, as the Trustees of and for and on behalf of said corporation, have hereunto set our hands and seal (the said corporation having no seal) the day and year first above written.

> "T. N. WILLIS. [L. S.]

> "JAMES J. HODGES. [L. S.]

> "S. S. TURNER. [L. S.]

> "Trustees of the Rawhide Ranch Gold and Silver Mining Company."

On the trial, after proving the adoption of the resolution before referred to at a meeting of the stockholders, as stated, the plaintiffs offered said deed in evidence, and defendants objected to its introduction on the three grounds — that it did not appear to be the act or deed of the corporation; that it had not the signature of the corporation, and that it was not sealed with the corporate seal but with the individual seals of the Trustees. The Court sustained the objection and excluded the deed, to which ruling plaintiffs excepted; and this ruling presents the question to be determined.

Under the view we take, it will only be necessary to consider the first ground of the objection, and the question is, does the instrument in question appear to be the act or deed of the corporation? If not, it was properly excluded, and the judgment must be affirmed. It is claimed by respondents that no authority is shown in the parties executing to execute the deed on behalf of the corporation. If the deed of a natural person, purporting to have been executed by an attorney in fact, were offered in evidence, it would, clearly, be inadmissible, without first showing the authority of the attorney. The recital of the authority in the deed itself would furnish no evidence whatever of its existence. The same is true of an artificial person — a corporation — at least, where the corporate seal is not affixed.... The authority of the Trustees to execute the instrument in question must, therefore, affirmatively appear, or it does not appear to be the act or deed of the corporation.

We are not aware of anything in the law, independent of any authority expressly conferred by the corporation, which authorizes Turner, Willis and Hodges, in their official character as Trustees, to execute the instrument in question on behalf of the corporation. No law of the kind has been called to our attention, and we do not understand that any is claimed by appellants' counsel to exist. And there is nothing in the nature of those offices, as connected with the object and business of the company, from which a general power in the Trustees, when not acting as a Board, to sell and convey the mine, mill and other property of the company, could be implied. The parties executing the instrument, then, if they had any authority in the premises, must have derived it from some corporate act; and the only act proved or relied on is the resolution adopted at the stockholders' meeting before mentioned. This was a meeting of the stockholders only. It was called as such, and the proceedings all appear to have been conducted as a stockholders' meeting. The resolution authorizing the sale and conveyance of the mine, etc., in question, was adopted by the stockholders, as such, at said meeting, and not by the Board of Trustees, or at any meeting of said Board. The Board of Trustees do not appear to have ever acted at all upon the matter in the character of a Board, but the testimony shows that they acted in pursuance of the said resolution adopted at the meeting of stockholders.

Section five of the Act authorizing the formation of corporations for mining purposes provides: "That the corporate powers of the corporation shall be exercised by a Board of not less than three Trustees, who shall be stockholders," etc. And section seven provides that: "A majority of the whole number of Trustees shall form a Board for the transaction of business, and every decision of a majority of the persons duly assembled as a Board shall be valid as a corporate act." Conferring authority to sell and convey the corporate property is the exercise of a corporate power, and under these provisions the "corporate powers of the corporation" are to be exercised by the Board of Trustees when the majority are "duly assembled as a Board." When thus assembled and acting the decision of the majority "shall be valid as a corporate act." We find nothing in the Act authorizing the stockholders, either individually or collectively in a stockholders' meeting, to perform corporate acts of the character in question. The property in question was the property of the artificial being created by the statute. The whole title was in the corporation. The stockholders were not in their individual capacities owners of the property as tenants in common, joint tenants, copartners or otherwise. This proposition is so plain that no citation of authorities is needed. Had the stockholders all executed a deed to the property, they could have conveyed no title, for the reason that it was not in them and what they could not do themselves they could not by resolution or otherwise authorize another to do for them. The corporation could only act — could only speak — through the medium prescribed by law, and that is its Board of Trustees.... It is said, however, that the Trustees were also all present and participated in the proceedings at the stockholders' meeting and assented to the resolution; that the resolution therefore was approved by all of the constituents of the corporation, and the powers of the corporation were exhaustively exercised. But they were acting in their individual characters as stockholders, and not as a Board of Trustees. In this character they were not authorized to perform a corporate act of the kind in question.... The power to sell and convey could only be conferred by the Trustees when assembled and acting as a Board. This is the mode prescribed. As a Board they could perform valid corporate acts, and confer authority within the province of their powers, upon the Trustees individually or upon any other parties to perform acts as the agents of the corporation....

By the Court, Sawyer, J., on petition for rehearing:

The consequences assumed as the only basis of the argument in the petition for rehearing do not follow from anything determined or in any way suggested in the opinion in this case. We have nowhere held, or even intimated, that the Board of Trustees of a corporation can convey all the property of the corporation necessary to enable it to carry on the business for which it was organized, or do anything else destructive of the objects of its creation without the consent of its stockholders. We have not even held that it was competent for the Trustees, acting as a Board, to authorize the conveyance of the property now in question without the consent of the stockholders. There was no such question in the case. We simply held that the stockholders themselves could not authorize the Trustees, acting as individual Trustees, or anybody else, to convey it—that nobody could convey it unless authorized by some act of the Board of Trustees, acting as a Board. It may be conceded for the purposes of this case that the Board of Trustees itself could not authorize a conveyance of the property in question without the consent of the stockholders. But it is unnecessary to consider that question, for the case does not present or even suggest it. It will be time enough to decide that question when it arises.

Rehearing denied.

B. Exercising Shareholders' Voting Rights

1. The Power to Vote

MBCA section 7.21(a) states that "Only shares are entitled to vote," thus establishing the general rule that "the power to vote cannot be granted generally to nonshare-holders."[10] However, as the Official Comment to section 7.21 provides, other means are available to accomplish the same result. For example, holders of debt may acquire the power to vote if the corporation takes any of the following actions: creates for the creditors a special class of redeemable voting shares; creates a voting trust and makes the creditors the trustees; or grants the creditors a proxy to vote some or all of the outstanding shares.

In some jurisdictions, including Delaware,[11] the holders of bonds, debentures, or other obligations of the corporation may be accorded the power to vote with respect to the company's affairs and management. The extent and manner of exercising the power must be provided for in the corporation's articles of incorporation. If the articles of incorporation so provide, holders of corporate debt can be deemed to be shareholders with respect to any matters requiring the vote of shareholders. Further, if creditors are given voting power, the articles may provide that holders of capital stock may be divested of their right to vote on any matter, except an amendment to the articles of incorporation.

2. Eligibility to Vote

For purposes of determining who is eligible to vote shares, the registered owner is usually deemed to be the owner of shares. Frequently, however, shares are held in the name of a nominee rather than in the name of the actual owner. A nominee may be

---

10. MBCA § 7.21 Official Comment 2.
11. Del. Gen. Corp. Law § 221.

a broker-dealer, a financial institution, or a securities clearing house. Registration in the name of a nominee enables trades of securities to be effected more efficiently than if the shares are held in the name of the owner. MBCA Section 7.23 permits the corporation to establish procedures to facilitate communication between the corporation and the beneficial owner of the shares. These procedures may apply to any or all of the following: giving notice of and voting at shareholders' meetings; distributing proxy statements and annual reports; and payment of dividends. For publicly traded companies, additional rules, such as those promulgated by stock exchanges, may apply regarding who may vote shares held by a nominee or in the name of an organization.

3. Shareholders' Meetings

Shareholders generally exercise their powers at annual or specially convened shareholders' meetings. Corporation statutes, as well as corporate charters, tend to contemplate or require annual meetings to occur approximately on a yearly basis, but do not otherwise direct the exact timing. These provisions, however, are usually understood to mean that annual meetings are to occur approximately every twelve months—not such shorter or longer times as four, eight or sixteen months apart. The issue can be significant in surprising contexts, especially when participants dueling for control by election of the board of directors would prefer to accelerate or delay the timing of holding an annual meeting. Bylaws passed to hasten meeting times mere months apart can conflict with charter provisions and statutes contemplating "annual" meetings and elections, with the effect of enabling removal of directors earlier than the charter or statute envisions.

In *Airgas, Inc. v. Air Prods. & Chems., Inc.*, 8 A.3d 1182, 1194 (Del. 2010), Air Products elected three director nominees to the Airgas ten-person staggered board at one annual meeting and sought to speed up electing another three at the next annual meeting by proposing a bylaw directing the next annual meeting to occur four months later. The court held the bylaw invalid because it conflicted with both the statute and the corporate charter, which contemplated directors on the staggered board serving three-year terms. To recognize the bylaw as valid would be to truncate the three-year terms unduly, rendering the bylaw in conflict with the statute and charter and therefore invalid.

Shareholders elect directors at the annual meeting, which is held at the time and place specified by or in accordance with the bylaws.[12] Shareholders also vote on other matters properly before them, including fundamental corporate changes. Special meetings may be called by the board of directors, any person(s) authorized by the charter or bylaws, or the holders of, in the usual case, at least 10% of shares entitled to vote.[13]

A notice containing the date, time and place of a meeting must be given to shareholders unless they waive the notice requirement.[14] In addition, the notice must specify the record date for determining what shares are entitled to vote if that record date differs from the record date used to determine the shareholders entitled to notice

12. *See id.* § 7.01.
13. *See id.* § 7.02.
14. *See id.* §§ 7.05, 7.06.

of the meeting. And finally, the notice must also state the means of remote communications, if any, that shareholders may use to be counted as present at the meeting and to vote. In MBCA jurisdictions, a required writing, signature, delivery, and notice, and other similar communications may be in electronic form. In contrast, in Delaware, notice of a shareholder meeting must be in writing even if shareholders may use remote communications to be counted present at the meeting and to vote. Thus, in Delaware, although the meeting notice must be in writing, shareholders may vote electronically.

4. Voting Rules

For a meeting to be properly convened, a quorum must be present. The MBCA sets quorum at a majority of shares entitled to vote on the particular matter, unless a different requirement is included in the articles of incorporation.[15] In order to vote, shareholders must own their shares as of a specified record date.[16] Shareholders may vote either in person or by proxy.[17]

Ordinary matters before the shareholders will be approved in MBCA jurisdictions if the votes cast in favor of an action exceed the votes in opposition.[18] Thus, abstentions are not counted. In contrast, some jurisdictions require for approval of ordinary matters the affirmative vote of a majority of shares entitled to vote on the matter. In this case, abstentions count as negative votes.

Extraordinary matters, such as the fundamental corporate changes referred to earlier, usually require approval by a majority of shares entitled to vote on the matter.[19] In this case, abstentions count as a vote against the proposed action. Directors are usually elected by a plurality of votes cast, which means that the directors with the most votes are elected even if they did not receive a majority of votes. The articles of incorporation may, however, include provisions requiring a majority or super-majority vote for the election of directors as well as for the approval of ordinary or extraordinary matters.

In certain situations, shares may be voted in voting groups. A voting group is comprised of one or more classes of shares authorized to vote and be counted collectively on a particular matter. Voting groups are created and authorized to vote pursuant to provisions in the articles of incorporation or the applicable corporate code.[20] When multiple voting groups are eligible to vote on a particular matter, each voting group must satisfy its own quorum and voting requirements. The matter voted on will be approved only if it has received the affirmative vote of each separate voting group.[21] When a corporation has more than one class of shares, the MBCA requires certain

15. *See id.* §7.25(a).
16. *See id.* §7.07.
17. *See id.* §7.22.
18. *See id.* §7.25(c).
19. *See, e.g., id.* §10.03 (e).
20. *See id.* §§1.40(26), 7.25, 7.26. For a discussion of the use of voting groups in the context of allocating corporate control, see Chapter 7, *infra.*
21. *See id.* §§7.25, 7.26

charter amendments to be separately approved by each class voting as a separate voting group.[22] In these situations, a class of shares will be entitled to vote even though: the shares are designated as non-voting shares in the articles of incorporation; they are not otherwise eligible to vote on the particular matter; or the charter has included them as part of another voting group. Similar voting rules apply to fundamental corporate changes.

5. Methods of Casting Shareholder Votes

Shareholders may cast their votes in several ways, including in person, by proxy, by electronic means, or by using written consents. Shareholders may vote either in person at a shareholder meeting or by proxy.[25] A shareholder's appointment of another person to act as proxy may be made in writing or by electronic means. Appointments of proxies typically expire after eleven months, but a longer period may apply if the parties agree. Generally, the appointment of a proxy is revocable. In certain cases, the appointment may be made irrevocable. Irrevocable appointments may arise when the appointment is made to: a pledgee; a purchaser of the shares associated with the appointment; a corporate creditor requiring the appointment; an employee whose contract requires the appointment; or a party to a voting agreement. Unless the terms of the appointment specify otherwise, when shares are transferred or sold, an irrevocable proxy will ordinarily apply to the acquirer of the shares associated with the appointment.

In Delaware, shareholder meetings may now be convened electronically. If the board of directors is authorized to determine the place of the shareholders meeting, the board "may, in its sole discretion, determine that the meeting shall not be held at any place, but may instead be held solely by means of remote communication...." DGCL § 211(a)(1), (2). Stockholders and proxy holders using electronic technology to "attend" the meeting will be deemed to be present at the meeting and will have their votes counted as though they were physically present.

The MBCA also permits shareholders to use electronic communications, such as the Internet and conference calls, to attend and vote at shareholder meetings to the extent authorized by the directors.[26] The option for shareholder electronic attendance and voting does not, however, eliminate the requirement of holding shareholder meetings at a physical location.[27] If the board authorizes the use of remote electronic communications for use by any group(s) of shareholders, the meeting notice to those shareholders must specify the types of remote communications that may be used. Shareholders attending the meeting electronically are considered to be present at the meeting.[28]

---

22. *See id.* § 10.04.
25. *See id.* § 7.22
26. MBCA § 7.09.
27. *Id.* Official Comment.
28. *Id.* § 7.09.

In MBCA jurisdictions and in Delaware, shareholders may also take action by using written or electronic consents instead of holding a meeting. [In this text, both written and electronic consents are referred to as "written consents."] Written consents may be used for the election of directors and for resolution of matters that shareholders could authorize or vote on at a shareholders' meeting. The MBCA default rule appears in Section 7.04(a), which requires unanimous consent of all shareholders entitled to vote on the particular action in order for a written vote to be effective. The default requirement of unanimous consent to effect shareholder action may, as a practical matter, be useful only to companies with a few shareholders and for matters that are not controversial. Unanimous written consents are always required when shareholders use cumulative voting to elect directors.[29]

Unanimous consent is not, however, required in all circumstances in which written consents are used. A company's articles of incorporation may provide that shareholder action may be effected without a meeting and without prior notice to other shareholders if the following condition is met: the action must be approved by written consents signed by the holders of outstanding shares having the required votes to approve the action at a meeting. Thus, if an action requires approval by a majority of votes, written consents by a majority of eligible votes will constitute approval of an action. By eliminating the unanimity requirement, the MBCA has made written consent procedures suitable for use by shareholders of both public corporations and closely held corporations having more than a few shareholders.

Delaware takes a somewhat different approach for shareholder consents. Unanimity is not a statutory requirement under any circumstance. Instead, the action must be approved by the "holders of outstanding stock having not less than the minimum number of votes necessary to authorize or take action at a meeting at which all shares entitled to vote thereon were present and voted...." DGCL § 228. This rule is altered slightly in the context of certain director elections. DGCL § 211(b).

C. Electing Directors

1. Voting Rules in Director Elections

Electing directors is an important shareholder power. As previously stated, directors are generally elected by a plurality of votes cast, which means that the directors with the most votes win even if they have not achieved a majority of votes cast. Alternatively, the articles of incorporation may require a majority or super-majority vote for the election of directors.

Many large institutional investors, like pension funds, find the traditional system of electing directors insufficiently responsive to shareholder desires, particularly when plurality voting is used in uncontested elections of directors. Critics believe that share-

---

29. Cumulative voting is discussed in Chapter 7, *infra.*

holders of public corporations often do not have an effective way to express disapproval of candidates for directors when only one slate of candidates is presented to the shareholders in an uncontested election. Under the default plurality vote system, shareholders may either vote for the proposed candidates or withhold their votes in protest against one or more members of the slate. Withheld votes are not counted, and shareholders do not have the option of casting negative votes against candidates. Consequently, a director in an uncontested election could theoretically be elected with only one vote cast for the director's election, with the rest of the votes withheld in protest.

To address such concerns, MBCA §§ 7.27(a) and 7.28(a) permits charter amendments to increase the plurality vote[36] otherwise required for the election of directors or to use cumulative voting to elect directors.[37] In the absence of such charter provisions, MBCA § 10.22 permits public companies to use bylaw provisions to change certain procedures used in uncontested elections for directors: the way votes are counted and the application of the holdover rule.[38] Bylaw provisions authorized by § 10.22 permit shareholders to vote for a director, against a director or abstain. In order to hold office, a director must receive a plurality of votes, with more votes cast in favor of the director's election than against it. Directors failing to meet this standard must resign within 90 days of the election. The § 10.22 option does not apply to contested elections, in which shareholders typically vote in favor of the candidates of their choice rather than vote against a candidate. Thus, in contested elections "against" votes are not counted and the candidates with the most votes win.

Section 10.22 elections may be made only by qualified public companies, those whose charter does not prohibit such a modification and does not require a higher than plurality vote or provide for cumulative voting in the election of directors. Section 10.22 elections are not available to closely held corporations. Instead, Section 7.32 of the Act grants shareholders of closely held corporations significant flexibility in modifying the traditional governance structure through the use of shareholder agreements signed by all shareholders or included in the company's charter or bylaws. Section 10.22 bylaw provisions may be adopted by the directors or the shareholders. Bylaw provisions adopted by the shareholders may be repealed only by shareholders unless the bylaws provide otherwise.

Delaware, like the MBCA, uses an opt-in approach to dealing with the issue. In Delaware, the election of directors by a plurality vote continues to be the default rule, with shareholders having the option to increase the required vote in either the company's charter or bylaws.[40] If a bylaw provision determines the required vote for directors, that provision may not be unilaterally amended by the directors, even if a

---

36. MBCA §§ 7.27(a), 7.28(a).

37. MBCA § 7.28(a).

38. MBCA § 2.02(b)(3) also permits an election to have § 10.22 apply to be included in the articles of incorporation. In this situation, both the directors and the shareholders must approve the amendment. Amendments to bylaws are usually easier to make than amendments to corporate charters.

40. Del. Gen. Corp. Law § 216.

company's charter permits the board of directors to amend bylaws.[41] Delaware applies the holdover rule to uncontested elections using an approach similar to that taken by the MBCA. Delaware permits a director's resignation to be effective at a specified date in the future or on the occurrence of a designated future event, such as the failure to receive a majority vote.

2. Shareholder Ballot Access

Shareholders increasingly seek to enhance their power over aspects of corporate governance. A leading example concerns nominations of directors for election to the board. Historically, as a matter of general practice, a corporation's incumbent board nominates directors for election and presents its nominations in annual proxy statements produced at the corporation's expense. Under that regime, shareholders wishing to nominate a different slate of directors would prepare and circulate their own proxy statement, bearing associated costs, which can be substantial—and very expensive for corporations having large numbers of shareholders.

Lately, shareholders have sought to expand access to the corporation's proxy state ment to nominate their own directors. In response, state and federal law have been adjusting. Notably, neither the DGCL nor the MBCA traditionally spoke to the matter—although both have changed, as discussed below. For public corporations, it was left to federal law and the Securities and Exchange Commission, which struggled to address the matter several times, including in 2003 and 2007, but never succeeded in doing so. Applicable SEC rules, discussed in Chapter 17 of this casebook, permit shareholders to make proposals for inclusion in a corporation's proxy statement and require corporations to include them unless one of some dozen regulatory grounds are available to exclude them. Among those grounds are proposals that are duplicative, beyond the corporation's power or, most relevant here, relate to an election of directors.

There was never much legal doubt that a shareholder proposal to elect a particular director to a particular board seat could be excluded under those federal laws. A shareholder promoting such a proposal must prepare and circulate her own proxy statement for that purpose and bear associated costs. A more difficult question had been whether a shareholder proposal to amend a corporation's bylaws to enable shareholder nomination of directors in future corporation proxy statements may be so excluded. A definitive resolution of that question had eluded both federal courts and the SEC. For a recap, see *American Federation of State, County & Municipal Employees v. American International Group, Inc.*, 462 F.3d 121 (2d Cir. 2006), reproduced in Chapter 17 of this casebook. Since then, both state and federal law have been changing to address this issue.

First, in 2009, DGCL Section 112 and MBCA Section 2.06 were amended. They permit, but do not require, corporations to adopt bylaws allowing stockholder access to a corporation's proxy materials for director elections. They also permit bylaws that make such access conditional. Examples of permissible conditions include (a) requiring

---

41. *Id.*

the nominating shareholder to have stated attributes, such as the amount or duration of stock ownership and that it provide disclosure concerning itself and nominees; (b) limitations on the number or percentage of directors eligible per shareholder and on the number of times a shareholder may nominate candidates; (c) prohibiting nomination of persons owning or intending to acquire stated percentages of the corporation's voting stock; or (d) requiring nominating shareholders to indemnify the corporation for losses arising from any false or misleading statements made in connection with the nomination.

DGCL Section 113 and MBCA Section 2.06 were also amended to permit bylaws requiring a corporation to reimburse stockholders for expenses incurred in soliciting proxies for director elections. There may likewise be various conditions on this right, including limitations on reimbursement measured according to the proportion of votes cast in favor of the shareholder's nominees. Section 113 of the DGCL codifies, in part, *CA, Inc. v. AFSCME Employees Pension Plan*, 953 A.2d 227 (Del. 2008). This advisory opinion, written for the SEC, said that it would generally be valid for a shareholder proposal to amend a corporation's bylaws to require the corporation to reimburse shareholders for proxy-related expenses. But the opinion qualified this conclusion by saying that any such by-law also provide that directors can make the reimbursement determination on a case-by-case basis in accordance with their fiduciary duties. Notably, Section 113 does not refer to such a provision.

Second, in 2009, the SEC proposed rule amendments to facilitate shareholder access to corporate proxy statement ballots. Unlike the DGCL's and MBCA's classical approach of permitting or enabling rather than requiring or mandating access, the SEC proposes a mandatory approach. Under the SEC proposal, shareholders meeting stated conditions would be entitled to nominate directors, have their nominees included in the corporation's proxy statement ballot and make shareholder proposals to amend the corporation's nomination procedures or disclosure about elections, so long as proposals do not conflict with state law or SEC rules.

The proposed rule would allow stockholders to include director nominees in the corporation's proxy solicitation materials so long as stated eligibility requirements are met. These include: (a) a minimum percentage ownership interest (which varies from 1% to 5% depending on a corporation's size); (b) ownership for at least one year before making the nomination; (c) notifying the corporation of the nomination within 120 days before the proxy statement is circulated; and (d) shareholder certification that the shareholder intends to maintain designated ownership levels through the election, that it is not seeking to change control of the corporation or obtain more than a minority position on it, and that the nominee is independent within the meaning of applicable state law and stock exchange listing requirements. The proposed rule would allow shareholders to nominate up to 25% of a board's directors.

The federal rules were subsequently struck down by the D. C. Circuit.[43] The court concluded that the rulemaking process had not complied with the Administrative

---

43. Bus. Roundtable v. SEC, 647 F.3d 1144 (D.C. Cir. 2011.)

Procedures Act. The process was deficient in that it had failed to assess properly the economic impact of the rule, to consider sufficient empirical data, and to assess the impact of the rule on election contests.

D. Shareholders' Information Rights

1. Access to Corporate Financial Statements

Companies organized in MBCA jurisdictions must provide shareholders with annual financial statements.[44] The financial statements must include a balance sheet covering the most recently completed fiscal year as well as an income statement and a statement of changes in shareholders' equity for the same accounting period. Any accountants' reports must accompany the financial statements. As appropriate, the financial statements may be combined or consolidated statements for the corporation and its subsidiaries.

To avoid unduly burdening closely held corporations, the MBCA does not require the financial statements to be prepared based on Generally Accepted Accounting Principles (GAAP). However, if any of a company's financial statements are based on GAAP, those statements must be sent to shareholders. Whether or not the statements are prepared according to GAAP principles, the company must send its financial statements to shareholders within 120 days of the close of the fiscal year. (The Securities Exchange Act of 1934 also requires certain publicly traded corporations to provide their shareholders with financial statements.)

2. Inspection of Corporate Books and Records

Shareholders have the right to inspect and make copies of certain corporate records, such as shareholders' lists, corporate accounting records, and minutes from board of directors' meetings.[45] Shareholder lists must be available for inspection for a time beginning soon after the company sends notice of a shareholder meeting and extending through the meeting itself.[46] These lists are useful to someone trying to solicit the votes of other shareholders.

Seinfeld v. Verizon Communications, Inc.

Delaware Supreme Court
909 A.2d 117 (2006)

HOLLAND, JUSTICE:

The plaintiff-appellant, Frank D. Seinfeld ("Seinfeld"), brought suit under section 220 of the Delaware General Corporation Law to compel the defendant-appellee, Verizon Communications, Inc. ("Verizon"), to produce, for his inspection, its books and records related to the compensation of Verizon's three highest corporate officers

---

44. *See id.* § 16.20.
45. *See id.* § 16.02.
46. *See id.* § 7.20.

from 2000 to 2002. Seinfeld claimed that their executive compensation, individually and collectively, was excessive and wasteful. On cross-motions for summary judgment, the Court of Chancery applied well-established Delaware law and held that Seinfeld had not met his evidentiary burden to demonstrate a proper purpose to justify the inspection of Verizon's records.

The settled law of Delaware required Seinfeld to present some evidence that established a credible basis from which the Court of Chancery could infer there were legitimate issues of possible waste, mismanagement or wrongdoing that warranted further investigation. Seinfeld argues that burden of proof "erects an insurmountable barrier for the minority shareholder of a public company." We have concluded that Seinfeld's argument is without merit.

We reaffirm the well-established law of Delaware that stockholders seeking inspection under section 220 must present "some evidence" to suggest a "credible basis" from which a court can infer that mismanagement, waste or wrongdoing may have occurred. The "credible basis" standard achieves an appropriate balance between providing stockholders who can offer some evidence of possible wrongdoing with access to corporate records and safeguarding the right of the corporation to deny requests for inspections that are based only upon suspicion or curiosity. Accordingly, the judgment of the Court of Chancery must be affirmed.

FACTS

Seinfeld asserts that he is the beneficial owner of approximately 3,884 shares of Verizon.... His stated purpose for seeking Verizon's books and records was to investigate mismanagement and corporate waste regarding the executive compensations of Ivan G. Seidenberg, Lawrence T. Babbio, Jr. and Charles R. Lee. Seinfeld alleges that the three executives were all performing in the same job and were paid amounts, including stock options, above the compensation provided for in their employment contracts. Seinfeld's section 220 claim for inspection is further premised on various computations he performed which indicate that the three executives' compensation totaled $205 million over three years and was, therefore, excessive, given their responsibilities to the corporation.

During his deposition, Seinfeld acknowledged he had no factual support for his claim that mismanagement had taken place. He admitted that the three executives did not perform any duplicative work. Seinfeld conceded he had no factual basis to allege the executives "did not earn" the amounts paid to them under their respective employment agreements. Seinfeld also admitted "there is a possibility" that the $205 million executive compensation amount he calculated was wrong.

The issue before us is quite narrow: should a stockholder seeking inspection under section 220 be entitled to relief without being required to show some evidence to suggest a credible basis for wrongdoing? We conclude that the answer must be no.

Stockholder Inspection Rights

Delaware corporate law provides for a separation of legal control and ownership. The legal responsibility to manage the business of the corporation for the benefit of the stockholder owners is conferred on the board of directors by statute. The common law imposes fiduciary duties upon the directors of Delaware corporations to constrain their conduct when discharging that statutory responsibility.

Stockholders' rights to inspect the corporation's books and records were recognized at common law because "[a]s a matter of self-protection, the stockholder was entitled to know how his agents were conducting the affairs of the corporation of which he or she was a part owner."[47] The qualified inspection rights that originated at common law are now codified in **Title 8, section 220 of the DGCL,** which provides, in part:

i.e. even 1 share

> (b) Any stockholder, in person or by attorney or other agent, shall, upon written demand under oath stating the purpose thereof, have the right during the usual hours for business to inspect for any proper purpose.

Section 220 provides stockholders of Delaware corporations with a "powerful right."[48] By properly asserting that right under section 220, stockholders are able to obtain information that can be used in a variety of contexts. Stockholders may use information about corporate mismanagement, waste or wrongdoing in several ways. For example, they may: institute derivative litigation; "seek an audience with the board [of directors] to discuss proposed reform or, failing in that, they may prepare a stockholder resolution for the next annual meeting, or mount a proxy fight to elect new directors."[49]

Inspection Litigation Increases

More than a decade ago, we noted that "[s]urprisingly, little use has been made of section 220 as an information-gathering tool in the derivative [suit] context."[50] Today, however, stockholders who have concerns about corporate governance are increasingly making a broad array of section 220 demands. The rise in books and records litigation is directly attributable to this Court's encouragement of stockholders, who can show a proper purpose, to use the "tools at hand" to obtain the necessary information before filing a derivative action. Section 220 is now recognized as "an important part of the corporate governance landscape."[51]

Seinfeld Denied Inspection

The Court of Chancery determined that Seinfeld's deposition testimony established only that he was concerned about the large amount of compensation paid to the three executives. That court concluded that Seinfeld offered "no evidence from which [it] could evaluate whether there is a reasonable ground for suspicion that the executive's compensation rises to the level of waste." It also concluded that Seinfeld did not "submit any evidence showing that the executives were not entitled to [the stock] options." The Court of Chancery properly noted that a disagreement with the business

---

47. [8] *Saito v. McKesson HBOC, Inc.,* 806 A.2d 113, 116 (Del. 2002).

48. [9] *Disney v. Walt Disney Co.,* 857 A.2d 444, 447 (Del. Ch. 2004).

49. [10] *Saito v. McKesson HBOC, Inc.,* 806 A.2d at 117.

50. [11] *Rales v. Blasband,* 634 A.2d 927, 934–35 n. 10 (Del. 1993) (quoted in *Grimes v. Donald,* 673 A.2d 1207, 1216 n. 11, (Del. 1996)).

51. [14] *Security First Corp. v. U. S. Die Casting & Dev. Co.,* 687 A.2d 563, 571 (Del. 1997).

judgment of Verizon's board of directors or its compensation committee is not evidence of wrongdoing and did not satisfy Seinfeld's burden under section 220.... [The Court announces that ensuing analysis will] review the current balance between the rights of stockholders and corporations that is established by *Thomas & Betts Corp. v. Leviton Mfg. Co.*[52] and *Security First Corp. v. U.S. Die Casting & Dev. Co.*[53] and their progeny.

Credible Basis From Some Evidence

In a section 220 action, a stockholder has the burden of proof to demonstrate a proper purpose by a preponderance of the evidence. It is well established that a stockholder's desire to investigate wrongdoing or mismanagement is a "proper purpose." Such investigations are proper, because where the allegations of mismanagement prove meritorious, investigation furthers the interest of all stockholders and should increase stockholder return.

The evolution of Delaware's jurisprudence in section 220 actions reflects judicial efforts to maintain a proper balance between the rights of shareholders to obtain information based upon credible allegations of corporation mismanagement and the rights of directors to manage the business of the corporation without undue interference from stockholders. In *Thomas & Betts*, this Court held that, to meet its "burden of proof, a stockholder must present some credible basis from which the court can infer that waste or mismanagement may have occurred." Six months later, in *Security First*, this Court held "[t]here must be some evidence of possible mismanagement as would warrant further investigation of the matter."

Our holdings in *Thomas & Betts* and *Security First* were contemporaneous with our decisions that initially encouraged stockholders to make greater use of section 220. In *Grimes v. Donald*, decided just months before *Thomas & Betts*, this Court reaffirmed the salutary use of section 220 as one of the "tools at hand" for stockholders to use to obtain information.[54] When the plaintiff in *Thomas & Betts* suggested that the burden of demonstrating a proper purpose had been attenuated by our encouragement for stockholders to use section 220, we rejected that argument:

> Contrary to plaintiff's assertion in the instant case, this Court in *Grimes* did not suggest that its reference to a Section 220 demand as one of the "tools at hand" was intended to eviscerate or modify the need for a stockholder to show a proper purpose under Section 220....

Standard Achieves Balance

Investigations of meritorious allegations of possible mismanagement, waste or wrongdoing, benefit the corporation, but investigations that are "indiscriminate fishing expeditions" do not.... Accordingly, this Court has held [in *Security First*]

---

52. [22] *Thomas & Betts Corp. v. Leviton Mfg. Co.*, 681 A.2d 1026, 1031 (Del. 1996).
53. [23] *Security First Corp. v. U. S. Die Casting & Dev. Co.*, 687 A.2d 563 (Del. 1997).
54. [29] *Grimes v. Donald*, 673 A.2d 1207, 1216 n. 11 (Del. 1996).

that an inspection to investigate possible wrongdoing where there is no "credible basis," is a license for "fishing expeditions" and thus adverse to the interests of the corporation:

> Stockholders have a right to at least a limited inquiry into books and records when they have established some credible basis to believe that there has been wrongdoing.... Yet it would invite mischief to open corporate management to indiscriminate fishing expeditions.

A stockholder is "not required to prove by a preponderance of the evidence that waste and [mis]management are actually occurring."[55] Stockholders need only show, by a preponderance of the evidence, a credible basis from which the Court of Chancery can infer there is possible mismanagement that would warrant further investigation—a showing that "may ultimately fall well short of demonstrating that anything wrong occurred." That "threshold may be satisfied by a credible showing, through documents, logic, testimony or otherwise, that there are legitimate issues of wrongdoing."[56]

Although the threshold for a stockholder in a section 220 proceeding is not insubstantial, the "credible basis" standard sets the lowest possible burden of proof. The only way to reduce the burden of proof further would be to eliminate any requirement that a stockholder show some evidence of possible wrongdoing. That would be tantamount to permitting inspection based on the "mere suspicion" standard that Seinfeld advances in this appeal. However, such a standard has been repeatedly rejected as a basis to justify the enterprise cost of an inspection.

In Delaware and elsewhere, the "credible-basis-from-some-evidence" standard is settled law.... A review of the cases that have applied the "credible basis" standard refutes Seinfeld's premise that requiring "some evidence" constitutes an insurmountable barrier for stockholders who assert inspection rights under section 220.

Requiring stockholders to establish a "credible basis" for the Court of Chancery to infer possible wrongdoing by presenting "some evidence" has not impeded stockholder inspections. Although many section 220 proceedings have been filed since we decided *Security First* and *Thomas & Betts*, Verizon points out that Seinfeld's case is only the second proceeding in which a plaintiff's demand to investigate wrongdoing was found to be entirely without a "credible basis." In contrast, there are [many] cases where stockholders have successfully presented "some evidence" to establish a "credible basis" to infer possible mismanagement and thus received some narrowly tailored right of inspection.

We remain convinced that the rights of stockholders and the interests of the corporation in a section 220 proceeding are properly balanced by requiring a stockholder to show "some evidence of possible mismanagement as would warrant further inves-

55. [30] *Thomas & Betts Corp. v. Leviton Mfg. Co.*, 681 A.2d 1026 (Del. 1996).
56. [39] *Security First Corp. v. U. S. Die Casting & Dev. Co.*, 687 A.2d 563 (Del. 1997).

tigation."[57] The "credible basis" standard maximizes stockholder value by limiting the range of permitted stockholder inspections to those that might have merit. Accordingly, our holdings in *Security First* and *Thomas & Betts* are ratified and reaffirmed....

Notes and Questions

1. In *Wal-Mart Stores, Inc. v. Indiana Electrical Workers Pension Trust Fund IBEW*, 295 A.2d 1264 (Del. 2014), a stockholder of Wal-Mart made a demand to inspect the books and records of the superstore following a *New York Times* report asserting bribery at a Mexican subsidiary. Wal-Mart furnished some 3,000 documents but plaintiff wanted more and sued. The Court of Chancery ordered Wal-Mart to produce additional documents, including some protected by the attorney-client privilege, as these were "necessary and essential" to the stockholder's "proper purposes" of investigating potential mismanagement and alleged breaches of fiduciary duty by Wal-Mart executives in connection with bribery allegations.

In affirming, the Delaware Supreme Court reiterated that the proper standard to be applied in Section 220 actions is "necessary and essential" to achieve a "proper purpose." Furthermore, the court noted that documents are "necessary and essential" if they reach the "crux of the shareholder's purpose" and if that information "is unavailable from another source." The Delaware Supreme Court also noted that Delaware courts must circumscribe orders granting inspection "with rifled precision."

Concerning privileged material, the court drew on a leading case on the subject, *Garner v. Wolfinbarger*, 430 F.2d 10993 (5th Cir. 1970), to explain that it permits stockholders of a corporation to "invade the corporation's attorney-client privilege in order to prove fiduciary breaches by those in control of the corporation upon showing good cause." In applying *Garner* to Section 220, the Delaware Supreme Court noted that "the necessary and essential inquiry must precede any privilege inquiry because the necessary and essential inquiry is dispositive of the threshold question — the scope of document production to which the plaintiff is entitled under Section 220."

2. The question of what is a proper purpose for shareholder inspection has arisen in many contexts. The court in *MMI Investments, L.L.C. v. Eastern Co.*, 701 A.2d 50 (Conn. Super. Ct. 1996), elaborated on this issue. In its opinion the court addressed the law in other jurisdictions, as well as the law of Connecticut....

> At common law, the right of inspection of the books and records of a corporation at reasonable times and for a proper purpose was a privilege incident to the ownership of shares in a corporation. That common law right was not absolute, but was "qualified by the condition, among others, that the purpose of the stockholder desiring to make the examination is germane to his interest as such stockholder, proper and lawful in its character, and not inimical to the interests of the corporation itself." [A] statute in effect

---

57. [46] *Security First Corp. v. U. S. Die Casting & Dev. Co.*, 687 A.2d at 568.

at the time changed the common law with respect to stock records by making the theretofore qualified right absolute. Nevertheless, the court[s] [will examine] the shareholder's purpose in requesting inspection, on the ground that the requisite writ of mandamus would not issue unless the request therefor were "made in good faith and not to serve an ulterior improper purpose." ...

[In] *DeRosa v. Terry Steam Turbine Co.*, 214 A.2d 684 (Conn. Super. Ct. 1965), ... [t]he plaintiffs were employees of the defendant corporation, and members of a labor union in the midst of a labor dispute with the defendant. Each plaintiff owned one share of stock, paid for by the union, which received the dividends. Their purpose for obtaining the shareholders list was to enable their union to communicate with the shareholders regarding the defendant's labor relations, and to inform the shareholders of employee dissatisfaction with the defendant's labor policies. Inspection was allowed, the court stating that it could not find that the purpose for inspection was not proper or was inimical to the interest of the corporation or its shareholders. In addition, the court held that it did not matter that the plaintiffs were acting for the union, because a registered shareholder acting for the beneficial owner is not precluded from inspecting the list of shareholders....

In some jurisdictions, a shareholder is entitled to examine the record of shareholders for any "proper purpose." [DGCL] §220(b). Under the Delaware statute, a proper purpose is defined as "a purpose reasonably related to [the stockholder's] interest as a stockholder."

The Delaware statute has been interpreted to take into account the interests of the corporation. "However, even though the purpose may be proper in the sense that it is reasonably related to the person's interest as a stockholder, it must also not be adverse to the interests of the corporation. To this extent a stockholder's right of inspection is a qualified right depending upon the facts of the particular case." ... Applying these standards, the court ... approved a request for inspection of stock ledgers and other types of records for the purpose of investigating possible mismanagement, and ruled that an ulterior motive to gain control of the corporation was not sufficient to show either overriding bad faith or a threat to the business interests of the corporation.

[When] a group of stockholders requested to examine E.L. Bruce Company's record of shareholders to "solicit support for their slate of directors at the forthcoming stockholders' meeting ... or to attempt to buy additional stock from the other stockholders, or both," [t]he court held that "[i]nspection of the stock ledger to solicit proxies at the stockholders' meeting is obviously proper; and an intention to purchase additional shares from other stockholders is likewise proper."

The court in *Mite Corp. v. Heli-Coil Corp.*, 256 A.2d 855 (Del.Ch.1969) applied the law to a corporate takeover situation. Heli-Coil Corporation was a takeover target for the Mite Corporation. The Mite Corporation desired Heli-Coil Corporation's list of stockholders "to solicit offers from other Heli-Coil's stockholders to exchange their stock for stock of Mite." ... The court ... stated that "inspection of a stock list is proper where it is sought in order to purchase additional shares of a company's stock from other stockholders." ...

[The Court contrasted the Connecticut statute under consideration with its Massachusetts counterpart.] [T]he proper purpose test did not apply under the corporation laws of Massachusetts. The relevant statute provided that a stockholder is entitled to examine the list of stockholders so long as the stockholder would not be "using the [list] for a purpose other than in the interest of the applicant, as a stockholder, relative to the affairs of the corporation." The court rejected application of the proper purpose test since the common law in Massachusetts only permitted inspection of the stockholder list if the request was "motivated by the purposes of advancing the corporation's interest." Furthermore, the court stated that although courts in other states applied the proper purpose test to their statutes, "the statutes interpreted by those courts appear to emphasize the personal interest of the stockholder and do not contain [Massachusetts'] statutory language referring to the interest of the applicant, as a stockholder, relative to the affairs of the corporation." The shareholder's purpose "was to learn the identity of Company stockholders in order to determine whether there were stockholders willing to sell their Company shares to him." He was found to be motivated solely by personal investment concerns. It is doubtful whether the request in *Shabshelowitz* would pass muster under the present Connecticut statute.

3. The inspection rights discussed above are limited to shareholders (although directors enjoy parallel information rights, as noted in the next section). The term "shareholder" includes both the registered owner of the shares as reflected in the corporation's records and the beneficial owner of the shares based on a nominee certificate filed with the corporation.[58] Persons seeking to inspect a company's books and records must establish their status as shareholders, whether registered or beneficial owners.[59] Further, even though one is a shareholder, the right to inspect is not absolute if the shareholder demanding inspection has interests adverse to the corporation.[60]

Section II
Functions and Authority of Directors

A. Source of Directors' Authority and Powers

A popular misconception about the authority of directors, which goes along with misconceptions about shareholders' power, is that the directors get their authority from

---

58. [6] MBCA § 1.40 (21).
59. [7] *See, e.g.,* Central Laborers Pension Fund v. News Corp., 45 A.3d 139 (Del. 2012).
60. Barasch v. Williams Real Estate Co., Inc., 104 A.D.3d 490, 961 N.Y.S.2d 125 (N.Y. App. 2013).

the shareholders. The issue of where directors get their power is nicely explored in *Manson v. Curtis*, an opus opinion of the New York Court of Appeals during World War I.

Manson v. Curtis
New York Court of Appeals
119 N.E. 559 (1918)

COLLIN, J.

The action is to recover the damages arising to the plaintiff by reason of the acts of the defendant. The Special Term decided ... that the complaint did not state facts sufficient to constitute a cause of action, and should be dismissed. The consequent judgment was affirmed by the Appellate Division.

[The complaint grew out of an alleged breach by the defendant of an agreement, between the plaintiff and the defendant, relating to control by the plaintiff of the Bermuda-Atlantic Steamship Company, a corporation in which each was a shareholder.]

... The fundamental and dominant purpose and intent of the parties [to the agreement] ... necessitated ... passive directors. The conditions which the parties wished to meet and their intent necessitated and contemplated the selecting of directors who should remain passive or mechanical to the will and word of the plaintiff. The management of the affairs of the corporation by its board of directors and the management of them by the plaintiff as contemplated by the agreement are irreconcilable and mutually destructive.

The prerogatives and functions of the directors of a stock corporation are sufficiently defined and established. The affairs of every corporation shall be managed by its board of directors (General Corporation Law § 34), subject, however, to the valid by-laws adopted by the stockholders (Stock Corporation Law § 30). In corporate bodies, the powers of the board of directors are, in a very important sense, original and undelegated. The stockholders do not confer, nor can they revoke, those powers. They are derivative only in the sense of being received from the state in the act of incorporation.

The directors convened as a board are the primary possessors of all the powers which the charter confers, and like private principals they may delegate to agents of their own appointment the performance of any acts which they themselves can perform. The recognition of this principle is absolutely necessary in the affairs of every corporation whose powers are vested in a board of directors. All powers directly conferred by statute, or impliedly granted, of necessity, must be exercised by the directors who are constituted by the law as the agency for the doing of corporate acts. In the management of the affairs of the corporation, they are dependent solely upon their own knowledge of its business and their own judgment as to what its interests require.

While the ordinary rules of law relating to an agent are applicable in considering the acts of a board of directors on behalf of a corporation when dealing with third persons, the individual directors making up the board are not mere employees, but a part of an elected body of officers constituting the executive agents of the corporation. They hold such office charged with the duty to act for the corporation according to their best judgment, and in so doing they cannot be controlled in the reasonable exercise and performance of such duty. As a general rule, the stockholders cannot act in relation to the ordinary business of the corporation, nor can they control the directors in the exercise of the judgment vested in them by virtue of their office.

The relation of the directors to the stockholders is essentially that of trustee and cestui que trust. The peculiar relation that they bear to the corporation and the owners of its stock grows out of the inability of the corporation to act except through such managing officers and agents. The corporation is the owner of the property, but the directors in the performance of their duty possess it, and act in every way as if they owned it. Directors are the exclusive, executive representatives of the corporation, and are charged with the administration of its internal affairs and the management and use of its assets. Clearly the law does not permit the stockholders to create a sterilized board of directors. Corporations are the creatures of the state, and must comply with the exactions and regulations it imposes. We conclude that the agreement here is illegal and void, and its violation is not a basis for a cause of action....

B. Scope of Directors' Authority and Powers

Contemporary definitions of the roles of directors can be found in the American Law Institute Principles of Corporate Governance: Analysis and Recommendations (1994) ("ALI") and the MBCA. The ALI has defined the role of the directors of publicly held corporations in the following way. Section 3.01 provides that:

> The management of the business of a publicly held corporation should be conducted by or under the supervision of such principal senior executives as are designated by the board of directors, and by those other officers and employees to whom the management function is delegated by the board or those executives, subject to the functions and powers of the board under § 3.02.

ALI § 3.02 describes the powers of the board of directors as follows:

> (a) Except as provided by statute, the board of directors of a publicly held corporation should perform the following functions: (1) Select, regularly evaluate, fix the compensation of, and where appropriate, replace the principal senior executives; (2) Oversee the conduct of the corporation's business to evaluate whether the business is being properly managed: (3) Review and, where appropriate, approve the corporation's financial objectives and major corporate plans and actions; (4) Review and, where appropriate, approve major changes in, and determinations of other major questions of choice respecting, the appropriate auditing and accounting principles and practices to be used in the preparation of the corporation's financial statements; (5) Perform such other functions as are prescribed by law, or assigned to the board under a standard of the corporation;

> (b) A board of directors also has power to: (1) Initiate and adopt corporate plans, commitments, and actions; (2) Initiate and adopt changes in account-

ing principles and practices; (3) Provide advice and counsel to the principal senior executives; (4) Instruct any committee, principal senior executive, or other officer and review the actions of any committee, principal senior executive, or other officer; (5) Make recommendations to shareholders; (6) Manage the business of the corporation; (7) Act as to all other corporate matters not requiring shareholder approval.

MBCA §8.01(b) is the prototypical modern statutory grant to directors of their general power over the management of a corporation. Its most essential provision is: all corporate powers shall be exercised by or under the authority of the board of directors of the corporation, and the business and affairs of the corporation shall be managed by or under the direction, and subject to the oversight, of its board of directors, subject to any limitation set forth in the articles of incorporation or in an agreement authorized under section 7.32. Section 7.32 permits shareholders of privately held corporations to enter into shareholder agreements modifying the traditional management structure. The language of §8.01 makes clear that directors are not required to manage a corporation directly on a day-to-day basis, but may do so through delegation and oversight.

In MBCA §8.01(b), the phrase "subject to any limitation set forth in the articles of incorporation or in an agreement authorized under §7.32" serves two purposes. First, it warns the reader that limitations on the board's power may also be imposed by provisions in the company's charter and private agreements. Second, it introduces the concept, fairly new to corporation law, that management structures other than one featuring a supremely powerful board may be established in the charter and by private agreement. That brief provision, read along with the language in MBCA §2.02(b)(2) allowing a charter to contain any provision not inconsistent with law regarding "(ii) managing the business and regulating the affairs of the corporation; (iii) defining, limiting, and regulating the powers of the corporation, its board of directors, and shareholders ..." gives corporate planners nearly carte blanche to vary the corporate management scheme. The charter could, for example, limit the board's power in specific areas or take away all the board's power and give it to the shareholders. (The Official Comment to MBCA §7.32 affirms for privately held corporations, the validity of shareholders' agreements containing provisions "inconsistent with the statutory norms.")

Management flexibility was written into the MBCA and other statutes as a result of suggestions that traditional corporation statutes did not fit the needs of closely held corporations. It has been thought by some, for example, that it is preferable in the typical small closely held corporation to simplify corporate decision-making by having only shareholders and officers. This approach is allowed under some statutes. Actually, however, in many situations, the main effect of the flexible management options of modern statutes has been to show the usefulness inherent in the traditional centralized management structure. Exceptionally few corporations operate without a board, for example, and those that do may pay a high price for apparent simplicity unless their counsel has planned carefully.

Trouble may begin as soon as an officer or shareholder of a closely held corporation operating without a board of directors attempts the early corporate act of opening a bank account. Banking procedures are set up to handle accounts that have been authorized by a corporation's board of directors. The expectation is that the bank account has been authorized by the board through the adoption of an appropriate resolution at a properly convened board meeting. At minimum, the officer attempting to open an account may encounter resistance from bank employees who are unclear how to proceed in situations where a board does not exist. At maximum, the bank's officers insist on consulting their lawyers before opening an account for a directorless corporation. The result is delay and, possibly, additional cost for both parties to the transaction. That sort of problem follows such a corporation throughout its life, coming up every time the corporation wants to enter into a transaction that traditionally is accompanied by an authorizing board resolution.

The problems arising in connection with a closely held corporation that has eliminated its board of directors also apply to other forms of limited liability business forms in which the principals have opted for a participatory rather than centralized management structure. Limited liability companies and limited liability partnerships are two such forms. As the preceding banking example demonstrates, the procedures and forms for many routine business transactions are based on practices that developed when the two common business types were general partnerships and corporations. Business persons dealing with corporations knew that decision-making authority resulted from provisions in the articles of incorporation, the bylaws or resolutions of the board of directors. Business persons dealing with general partnerships knew that the partners have individual, unlimited liability for transactions entered into on behalf of the company. It may not be clear to third parties dealing with other limited liability firms that have eliminated centralized management just who is authorized to make binding decisions on behalf of the firm.

Refer again to *Gashwiler v. Willis*, which appears at the beginning of Section I, and recall that the statute discussed in that case required a board of at least three directors, each of whom must be a shareholder. Those were the traditional statutory requirements. Most modern statutes have done away with such requirements, however. The MBCA, for example, requires only one director, and it does not require directors to be shareholders.[63] Experience taught that those traditional requirements serve no purpose. In the one- or two-shareholder corporation, the requirement of three directors typically ends up a meaningless formality, since any non-shareholder director can be replaced at will by the shareholder or shareholders. Similarly, the requirement that each director be a shareholder is an empty stricture in a corporation in which the number of real owners is fewer than the number of directors. Such a requirement merely leads to the issuance of what are referred to as directors' qualifying shares. Typically, a certificate representing one share is issued to each "extra" director, who immediately indorses the certificate for transfer and gives it back to the corporation with the understanding that the transfer will be effective as soon as the director's term is over.

The requirement in the statute in *Gashwiler* that the board act by majority decision at a meeting at which a majority of the whole number of directors is present also has

---

63. MBCA § 8.03.

been the traditional norm. There is a trick here for the uninitiated. Suppose that a corporation's charter or bylaws provide for a board of nine members, but that because of resignations or failures to fill all the positions the corporation has only five directors. How many directors are necessary for a quorum? The answer is "five," because the phrase "whole number of directors" is a term of art meaning the number of directors the corporation would have if there were no vacancies.

In modern statutes, the quorum requirement is usually stated as a majority of "whole board," "full board," "entire board" or of the "fixed number of directors." Because corporation statutes generally have been drafted and refined by practical lawyers who have tried hard to make the governance portions of the statutes easily usable by corporate managers, statutory provisions usually track the expectations of those managers. The rules on quorums are one place where that is not the case. Unless they are taught otherwise, clients almost invariably assume that quorum requirements are based on the number of directors the corporation actually has, not on the number it is authorized to have.

While the *Gashwiler* statutory quorum and voting requirements stated what was the traditional norm, modern statutes generally contain some important differences. Under the MBCA, for example, both the percentage of directors that constitutes a quorum and the percentage of the quorum whose agreement is required to take action may be increased beyond a mere majority in a corporation's charter or bylaws.[64] The quorum may also be decreased to one-third of the fixed number of directors.[65] A far more important addition in modern statutes is the opportunity given directors to act by unanimous written consents in lieu of a meeting, which is a possibility that is discussed in preceding materials. Directors may also take action by conference call or other form of technology that permits all directors simultaneously to hear each other during the meeting.

Note that under neither the traditional nor the more liberal modern statutory approaches to directors' decision-making do directors have any power as individuals. Their power is collective only. Further, individual directors are not also agents of the corporation simply because they are directors. The theory behind the traditional rule that directors may act only as a group, and only while assembled at a meeting, is that the give and take of a group discussion will help ensure the best corporate decisions. Since directors' written consents in lieu of meetings almost always must be unanimous, they fit within that theory by virtue of the idea that if all the directors are already of one mind on an issue, there would be no give and take at a meeting.

There is one final exception to the rule that directors must act together and at a meeting: under modern statutes directors may act through a committee they have established. The typical statutory provision on board committees provides that the board[66] may designate from among its members any committees it wishes, and may

---

64. *See id.* § 8.24.

65. *See id.*

66. Note that the special vote required for the establishment of committees under the MBCA is the greater of a majority of all directors in office or the number specified in the bylaws for general

delegate to a committee any of the board's powers, except for certain powers that the statute prohibits to committees. The MBCA's prohibitions are representative:

> A committee may not ... (1) authorize or approve distributions, except according to a formula or method, or within limits, prescribed by the board of directors; (2) approve or propose to shareholders action that this Act requires to be approved by shareholders; (3) fill vacancies on the board of directors or ... on any of its committees; or (4) adopt, amend, or repeal bylaws.[67]

The first committee that a board usually appoints is an executive committee, which traditionally is a committee having all the powers of the board when the board is not in session, except those powers prohibited to a committee by statute. To call a committee an executive committee and then give it substantially different powers than that is to invite trouble, since everyone dealing with the corporation will assume that its executive committee has standard authority. Often a corporation has a board made up of both inside and outside directors.[68] Because of their everyday involvement in the corporation's affairs, inside directors usually are more available for meetings on short notice than are outside directors. Partly for that reason, it is common for an executive committee's members to be all or almost all inside directors. Other committees that are common are the nominating committee, audit committee (which selects and supervises the company's auditors) and the compensation committee.

Corporate governance improvements often look to board committees, either when particular boards face a specific need such as responding to a lawsuit or when many boards are seen to need general enhancement in certain areas. After accounting scandals plagued much of corporate America in 2000–2001, for example, Congress passed the Sarbanes-Oxley Act of 2002 to enhance corporate accounting oversight. One tool was to fortify the qualifications and functions of board audit committees: they must be staffed by outside directors and must oversee the external financial auditor.

After the financial crisis of 2008 was traced in part to perverse incentives under executive pay packages, the Dodd-Frank Act of 2010 was passed to accomplish sweeping reform of the financial sector. Included were new corporate governance rules requiring that board compensation committees be comprised solely of independent directors. For this purpose, the concept of "independence" is given a specific meaning

---

director action. Unless clients are reminded of that requirement, they are inclined to consider valid board action to be taken if the ordinary voting requirements are met. What saves the situation in many cases is that votes by directors tend to be unanimous — after whatever discussion is necessary to reach consensus. (Note that many states require the vote of a majority of the full board to establish a committee.)

67. MBCA § 8.25.

68. Inside directors are directors who, as officers, work full-time for the corporation. For outside directors, their directorship is their only position in the corporation. Other common adjectives to group director types are "interested director" versus "disinterested director" or "independent director." Interested directors are either insiders or outsiders with a stake in a corporate decision while disinterested or independent directors face no such potential conflict of interest. We will consider precise legal usage of these groupings in various detailed contexts as we proceed in this book.

that considers how and by whom the board member is paid and whether the board member is affiliated with the company's subsidiaries.

Directors also have informational rights to corporate books and records. According to MBCA Section 16.05, directors may inspect and copy the company's books, records, and documents as reasonably required to fulfill their obligations as board members and as members of board committees. If a court order is required for the production of the requested information, the court may include provisions protecting the corporation from excessive burden or expense, restricting the director's use of the information and requiring the corporation to pay the reasonable expenses of production.

C. How Boards Function

So far, our discussion of directors has focused on what directors have the power to do—which is just about anything relating to the business and affairs of a corporation, save for those few things for which directors need the shareholders' consent. That is important, but it also is important to understand what directors actually do in corporations and what they tend to leave to others.

Here it is necessary to distinguish between corporations whose directors are substantial shareholders and those whose directors are not, because in the former corporations, directors can be expected to take an unusually active role in decision-making. Partially because the director who is a substantial shareholder is much more likely to be found in the closely held than in the publicly held corporation, closely held corporations more often have active directors than do publicly held ones. Beyond that, it is hard to generalize about what directors actually do in closely held corporations, because the distribution of real power in those corporations varies so greatly. In many closely held corporations, one majority shareholder dominates all corporate decisions, rendering board action a mere formality. In other closely held corporations, a board of equally powerful director-shareholders meets often to argue out all important decisions. On the continuum between those two extremes there exists a seemingly infinite variety of director involvement in corporate decision-making.

There is more consistency in the level and type of director decision-making in the publicly held corporation, once you set aside those publicly held corporations whose directors also are substantial shareholders. Myles Mace of the Harvard Business School conducted extensive research on what outside directors do and don't do in the typical large or medium-sized publicly held corporation. He reported his findings in a classic book, *Directors: Myth and Reality*, and in a not so well known, but more widely available article, *The President and the Board of Directors*.[71]

Mace found that in the kinds of corporations he studied, outside directors typically did three things: "[S]erve as a source of advice and counsel, offer some sort of dis-

---

71. Myles L. Mace, *The President and the Board of Directors*, 50 Harv. Bus. Rev. 37 (1972) (hereinafter Mace).

cipline value, and act in crisis situations."[72] Directors also elected senior management. Directors did not, he found, establish objectives, strategies, or major policies, but rather left those jobs to the corporation's officers.

During the years that Mace described, the board functioned as "an 'advisory' board, in which the CEO's trust in the board was critical, rather than as a 'monitoring' board, in which the board's trust in the CEO was the question."[73] According to Jeffrey Gordon, under the advisory model:

> The senior management team, headed by the CEO, was thus perceived as having two tasks: running the centralized planning and production-oversight structures within the firm and then allocating enterprise rents among the various potential claimants on the firm. This conception fit with the idea of an advisory board that included many insiders and outsiders with important economic relationships with the firm, such as bankers, lawyers, and suppliers. Such knowledgeable parties could serve as a useful sounding board for the CEO, a kitchen cabinet, and could provide expertise in the face of increasing complexity. In an important sense, boards were an extension of management. Similarly, the 1950s-style board could also play a useful role in finding the right balance to the corporation's mission statement. Indeed, social commentators such as Peter Drucker argued that board alignment with shareholder interests would undercut the desirable capacity of managers to manage in the public interest.

> In this view, a "monitoring board" would inject dissonance and distrust. How could the CEO trust and thus confide in directors whose ultimate mission was to hold him to account? The board selection and nomination mechanism followed upon the managerialist conception of the board's role. If the CEO was looking for trusted advisors who might widen his decisional frame, then it followed that the CEO would play a large role in director selection.[74]

Under the "advisory" board model, several aspects of board members' relationships with the corporation they served affected their willingness and ability to exercise their oversight role actively. First, the company's chief executive officer played an important role in selecting board members, even though the formal process of selection may have been accomplished by the recommendations of a board nominating committee, with approval by the full board. Board members who wished to continue in their role had to maintain a good relationship with the chief executive officer. Second, outside directors often had other business connections with the company. They may have been the company's outside counsel, a consultant, or perhaps, a supplier. These additional roles made it more difficult for an outsider to be truly independent. Third, the full board itself met only six to twelve times a year at most and then for only a

---

72. *See Id.* 38.

73. Jeffrey N. Gordon, *The Rise of Independent Directors in the United States, 1950–2005*, 59 Stan. L. Rev. 1465, 1512 (2007) (hereinafter Gordon).

74. *Id.* at 1512, 1513.

few hours at a time. The amount of information that could be presented and digested at such meetings was limited by time. Additionally, much of the board's work was done in committees, which reported back to the full board. Depending on the makeup of the committees, outside directors may or may not have played an influential role in the work of important committees. And finally, prior to the 1980s, boards were comprised primarily of inside directors.

From reading Myles Mace's and Jeffrey Gordon's observations, it would be easy to underestimate the value to the corporation of the things directors do. That is a mistake. In their advisory role, directors discuss troublesome corporate matters with the chief executive officer, almost exclusively on the telephone or in informal settings outside board meetings. When one considers that outside directors are familiar with the corporation in a way that management consultants typically cannot be, and that outside directors tend to be chief executive officers of other corporations or to have other significant management or professional experience, outside directors provide a chief executive officer with a source of help in decision making that is unavailable from anyone else.

Mace describes the discipline value of directors this way:

> Presidents and other members of top management in describing the discipline value of boards, indicated that the requirement of appearing formally before a board of directors consisting of respected, able people of stature, no matter how friendly, motivates the company managers to do a better job of thinking through their problems and of being prepared with solutions, explanations, or rationales.[75]

One also can easily see how that discipline value carries over into corporate actions generally, not just actions that are formally presented to the board. Because directors typically are given fairly broad information about their corporations, officers know that any significant decision they make may come to the directors' attention.

The role of directors in crisis situations can be a critical one. One classic crisis that Mace describes is the sudden death of the chief executive officer when succession has not been decided upon in advance. Another is when the chief executive officer's performance is so poor that a replacement must be found promptly. In situations such as those, it is only the directors who have either the statutory power or the real-world ability to act.

In the years since Mace did his research, several developments have influenced the behavior of directors. First, lawsuits against directors, alleging mismanagement, have become much more numerous. Second, there has been a widespread agreement among both scholars and corporate managers that the main function of directors should be to monitor the performance of the chief executive and other principal officers. As a result of those two developments, the first of which pushed directors toward being more active and the second of which told directors the way they should

---

75. *See* Mace at 39.

be more active, the "advisory" model of the board was replaced by the model of the "monitoring" board.

Several corporate scandals, beginning in the 1970s and extending through the present time, stimulated the change from the accepted role of directors as passive advisors to the demand for directors to play an active, monitoring role in setting corporate policy and overseeing management.[76] These scandals involved the sudden financial collapse of companies that had been considered blue chip enterprises, disclosures that corporate personnel were making illegal payments to obtain or maintain business, and problems with improper and misleading financial reporting. During investigations by the SEC and other authorities, it became clear that members of corporate boards often had little knowledge of what was going on in the companies they served. These and other scandals led many to conclude that the advisory board model with its passive directors led to management entrenchment and did not prevent corporate wrongdoing. Further, the sluggish economic performance of many major corporations also resulted in pressure for change originating with large institutional shareholders, hostile takeovers, and judicial decisions defining the scope of directors' fiduciary duties.

Concurrently, issues of corporate social responsibility came to the forefront as corporations were asked to consider their role in society as a whole. Shareholder proposals requiring corporate management to address broader social issues became common. In addition, a growth industry in hostile takeovers developed during the 1980s, in which one company acquired control of another (the target) through the purchase of the target company's stock. The justification for hostile takeovers was that poor management caused the target company's stock to be undervalued. Consequently, the realization of shareholder value, as reflected in the price of the target company's stock, became a key measurement of the board's performance.

In response to these and other compelling events, the board's structure and role changed from the "advisory" model comprised primarily of inside directors to a "monitoring" board composed predominantly of outside, independent directors. Companies have attempted to strengthen the board's independence by: having a board member, rather than the CEO, serve as chair of the board; having independent directors meet without management present to evaluate management's performance; establishing a nominating committee of independent directors to select new board members; and having an audit committee composed entirely of outside directors. It has proved to be difficult, however, to determine the extent to which active and more independent boards have produced improved corporate performance and superior value for the shareholders.

One last point should be made about outside directors' relations with the corporation they serve. Inside directors, by virtue of their positions as officers or employees, have ready access to corporate records, at least those within their sphere of operations. That may not necessarily be the case with outside directors. However, MBCA § 16.05

---

76. The ideas and information presented in the paragraphs providing the historical information are significantly drawn from Gordon, *supra*, at 1514–26.

and § 3.03 of the Principles of Corporate Governance give directors the right to inspect and copy corporate books and records.

Section III
Functions and Authority of Officers

Officers are agents of the board of directors acting collectively as the corporation, not of the shareholders. Just as the MBCA contains provisions relevant to directors' actions and obligations, corporation statutes have very similar provisions with respect to corporate officers. The structure and the substance of MBCA § 8.40 are instructive in that its provisions control what officers a corporation must have and who shall choose them. The section provides that a corporation will have "the offices described in its bylaws or designated by the board of directors in accordance with the bylaws." The MBCA thus does not prescribe either in number or position that the company have specific officers, although it does require one officer to have "responsibility for preparing minutes of the directors' and shareholders' meetings and for maintaining and authenticating the records of the corporation...." These functions are usually associated with the corporate secretary. In addition, under the MBCA, the "same individual may simultaneously hold more than one office in a corporation." This last provision is particularly suitable for small companies with only a few officers. It should also be noted that if authorized by the bylaws or the board of directors, "A duly authorized officer may appoint one or more officers...." This approach adds a measure of flexibility to the appointment of additional corporate officers. They may be chosen in any way the corporation wishes, so long as the procedure is authorized by the bylaws or the board.

The flexibility of the MBCA approach contrasts with those jurisdictions requiring specified officers, (usually at least a president and secretary, and often also a vice president and treasurer), and prohibiting the same person from acting as both president and secretary. However, even states requiring named officers typically allow corporations to have whatever other officers they wish.

So far we have discussed what officers a corporation must or may have and how they are to be chosen. The equally important question is: What are their powers? MBCA § 8.41 continues the statute's customary flexibility regarding officers' powers: "Each officer has the authority and shall perform the duties set forth in the bylaws or, to the extent consistent with the bylaws, the duties prescribed by the board of directors or by direction of an officer authorized by the board of directors to prescribe the duties of other officers."

Although a board could establish the authority of an officer either by adopting a bylaw provision containing a general statement of the officer's powers or by adopting a resolution, in fact, the board often determines the exact powers of officers by acquiescence rather than by formal action. After that, it may "give" an officer power simply by allowing the officer to continue doing what he or she has been doing, which often is something the officer has been told to do by another officer. There is no real doubt about the effectiveness of the board's grant of power by acquiescence in such a case—there being no significant chance, for example, that a court would allow the corporation to disavow a contract signed by an officer in the exercise of such authority. Thus the MBCA provision is somewhat misleading in that it seems to require an affirmative act—adoption of bylaw or act of board or another officer—to establish the authority of an officers.

The MBCA provision we have been discussing actually is misleading in a more basic way. As indicated above, the MBCA seems to say that for an officer to have authority, the authority must either be spelled out in the bylaws or the result of an affirmative act of the board or another officer. The provision leaves unsaid anything about a number of types of authority, arising under the principles of agency law, that the board grants to officers by electing them to specified offices. Those are implied authority, incidental authority, and apparent authority.[77] Simply by being elected to a particular office with generally recognized duties, the officer is automatically granted the powers that are associated with that office, save when the board specifically indicates that the officer will not have a particular power. An example is the power of the vice president to act for the president when the president is incapacitated.

Incidental authority of an officer is the authority to perform acts that are incidental to acts for which the officer has actual authority (actual authority may include implied authority and also any authority that is specifically granted to the officer, for example in the bylaws or by the board). Suppose that the board gives the treasurer the authority to invest the corporation's funds in common stocks. In that situation, the treasurer probably would have the incidental power to contract with an investment banking firm for investment advice, so long as the terms of the contract were reasonable in the circumstances.

Apparent authority of officers can be the most troublesome form of authority for a corporation, because that form of authority cannot easily be controlled. The apparent authority of an officer is coextensive with the authority that usually resides in the office held. That sounds complicated, but in this case apparent authority is quite simple. If the board of directors elects a person to the office of vice president, but indicates that the person will not have the power to act for the president if the president becomes incapacitated, the vice president obviously will not have the actual authority to act in that situation. Nevertheless, since the power to act when the president is incapacitated usually resides in the office of vice president, the vice president will have the apparent authority to act unless third parties dealing with the vice president know of the limitation. The result is that if, when the president is incapacitated, the vice president signs a contract that the president could have signed, the corporation ordinarily will be bound. Apparent authority is only defeated if a person dealing with an officer having apparent authority knows of the officer's lack of actual authority.

---

77. For a discussion of actual, implied, and apparent authority, *see* Chapter 1, *supra*.

With that background in mind, it may be helpful to examine the authority associated with the more common corporate offices: president, chair of the board, vice president, secretary, and treasurer.

A. President

Molasky Enterprises, Inc. v. Carps, Inc.

Missouri Court of Appeals, Eastern District
615 S.W.2d 83 (1981)

WEIER, JUDGE.

[Herbert and Emile Carp were members of the board of directors and president and executive vice-president, respectively, of Carps, Inc. In December 1972, the Carp brothers applied to Lindell Trust for a personal loan in the amount of $267,000. They told the bank that the loan proceeds would be used to satisfy their personal obligations to Carps, Inc. so that the corporation's annual financial statements would not reflect outstanding loans to officers. Lindell Trust would not approve the loan without a third party guaranty of the note to the Carp brothers. The note was guaranteed by one Molasky, who assigned the note to Molasky Enterprises, Inc. [Molasky]. In addition, Herbert Carp, the company president, endorsed the note so that Carps Inc. also became a guarantor of the loan. The Carp Inc. directors did not formally approve the corporation's guarantee of the loan and although Lindell Trust requested a corporate resolution authorizing it, one was never forthcoming. Following a default by Herbert and Emile, Molasky paid the money owed to Lindell Trust and then sought to enforce Carps Inc.'s obligation. The trial entered judgment in favor of Carps, Inc. Molasky appealed.]

When the original instruments were executed, the board of directors of Carps, Inc. consisted of seven persons [six of whom, including Herbert and Emile, were members of the Carp family and three of whom were Herbert and Emile's uncles. By the time of trial, the three uncles were deceased.]

... There is testimony in the record that Herbert and Emile showed the notes and agreement to their uncles who gave them their "blessing." [Two directors] Stephen Carp and Herman Willer were not informed of the transaction....

Initially, plaintiff contends that Carps, Inc., a Delaware corporation, was fully empowered to endorse the note and other papers which are the subject of this lawsuit. In support of this position plaintiff cites sections of the Delaware Corporation Act. We concede that the laws of Delaware apply as urged by the parties because the powers and existence of a corporation are derived from the state creating it. It functions under its charter which is a contract between it and the state in which it is organized. The statutory laws of the state applicable to it enter into and become a part of its articles of incorporation.

Section 143 of the Delaware Corporation Act authorizes a corporation to lend money to or guarantee any obligation of any officer or other employee of the corporation. Such action by the company, however, is conditioned by the statute upon an exercise of the judgment of the directors and a determination by them that such loan, guaranty or assistance may reasonably be expected to benefit the corporation. 8 Del.Code Ann. §143....

Considering Section 143 of the DGCL above described as it bears upon the record before us, there is no actual proof that any disinterested director of Carps, Inc. exercised his judgment after an opportunity was afforded him to consider the extension of corporate credit to the personal loan of Herbert and Emile and authorize the execution of the documents on behalf of the corporation. As is more fully demonstrated hereafter it would be impossible to sustain an inference that Herbert and Emile had authority, either formal or informal, to bind the corporation as guarantor of their personal obligations. The issue of whether Herbert and Emile Carp had the necessary authority to bind the corporation becomes, as is recognized by the plaintiff, a question of agency.

A corporation is an artificial being and it can act only through its agents. Its officers are its agents and many of the principles of law applicable to the relationship of principal and agent apply to the questions arising out of the existence and extent of the powers of corporate officers. *Joseph Greenspon's Sons Iron & Steel Co. v. Pecos Valley*, 156 A. 350, 351, 4 W.W. Harr. 567 (Del. Super.1931).

In this light we examine the contention that Herbert and Emile had both actual and apparent authority as officers to endorse and execute the instruments which are the subject of this lawsuit to secure their personal indebtedness and thus bind the corporation. As heretofore stated, the record does not support this position. It is clear that Herbert and Emile were given a free hand in the day-to-day management of the corporation. At no place, however, does it appear in the corporate minutes that Herbert and Emile were authorized to pledge the assets of the corporation or guarantee the payment of any indebtedness of officers.

Although the president of a corporation is empowered to transact without special authorization from the board of directors all acts of an ordinary nature which are incident to his office by usage or necessity which extends even to authority to bind the corporation for the execution and transfer of negotiable paper in the ordinary course of company business, such power to bind the principal by making, accepting or endorsing negotiable paper is an important power, susceptible to abuse and dangerous in its consequences to the company. It is obvious that authority of this nature is limited to the transaction of the corporation's regular business and for the benefit of the corporation. Authority to transact acts of an ordinary nature in the usual course of business does not include authority to sign accommodation paper or as security for a third person. Such authority must be specially given.

The court properly found by its judgment there was no actual authority to bind the corporation in the endorsement and execution of the instruments on which the litigation was based. No corporate resolution was passed authorizing the transaction. No other document was produced which authorized such action by the officers of the company. No minutes of the board of directors or of any committee of the corporation were produced which indicated that the authorization had been acted on.

Plaintiff contends that express authority was given orally by five of the members of
the board of directors. The evidence indicates Herbert Carp informed his three
elderly uncles that he and Emile were borrowing money to pay off a personal loan.…
One [uncle] would have had to have been approached on this subject in his home
since he was so ill he could not come to work at the time of the transaction. Herbert
showed the Lindell Trust note to his uncles. According to Herbert they gave their
"blessing," a term which he considered to mean consent. He did not tell them, however, that Carps, Inc., was going to be an accommodation party. There is no formal
convening of the board of directors. Two directors Stephen Carp and Herman Willer
were not even informed of the transaction.… There is obviously a failure to present
the matter for consideration and obtain the consent of a majority of the board of
directors.

Even as we have held on the issue of express authority, plaintiff may not rely on
implied authority. Implied authority depends on the actual relationship between
principal and agent and not what a third party may have been told or may believe as
to that relationship. It is a type of actual authority and the evidence as we have pointed
out fails to establish this kind of relationship. Past conduct of the officers and board
in connection with other matters that are not involved with the same type of transaction as this case is not proof that the president had implied authority to make the
company liable on a personal loan of the president.

The contention that Herbert and Emile Carp had apparent authority to sign on
behalf of the corporation also fails. Apparent authority is brought into existence by
the corporation's creation of an appearance of affairs which would cause a reasonable
person to believe that the officer had actual authority to do a particular act upon
which appearance a third party relies. It is the conduct of the principal not the acts
of the agent which create apparent authority.

Ratification and estoppel are also urged as an effective basis to reverse the trial court
on the grounds that the evidence was overwhelming that the board of directors of
Carps, Inc., ratified the action of Herbert and Emile by acquiescence or under the principle of estoppel. Neither estoppel nor ratification were [sic] pled by the plaintiff. Even
if this had been done, it would appear that the facts presented to the court below could
not compel a favorable determination on either theory. Two members of the board of
directors were not made aware of the December 1972 transaction. Herbert Carp testified
that his three uncles, one of whom was ill at home, saw the Lindell Trust notes.

Herbert and Emile, also members of the board of directors, cannot be counted to
make up a majority of the board of directors as previously pointed out because they
were interested in the transaction. Directors of a corporation may ratify any unauthorized act not done or entered into by themselves which they could have originally
authorized, but such action must be taken by a majority of the directors. Here there
is no indication there was a full disclosure of the facts to the other members of the
board and that they actually knew what had happened or that anything similar had
happened before. The first essential in ratification is that the principal have full knowledge of all the material facts at the time he is charged with having accepted the trans-

action as his own. [The court also concluded that the facts did not support a claim based on estoppel.]

Notes

1. *Molasky* states what continues to be the general rule for a president's implied authority: the president has the power to bind the corporation in the usual course of its business. For matters outside the usual course of business, the president's authority to act must be granted by: a state statute; the corporation's charter or bylaws; a resolution of the board of directors or after-the-fact ratification by the board. Despite the general rule, courts sometimes stretch to find that a corporation is bound by the actions of the president that were outside the usual course of a corporation's business.

2. In *Elblum Holding Corp. v. Mintz*, 1 A.2d 204 (N.J. 1938), the issue of first impression before the court was whether a corporation's president, as such, has the authority to hire an attorney and initiate a lawsuit on behalf of the corporation. The court stated:

> [O]ur courts have held that the president of a corporation, as such, may, without special authority, perform all the acts, which either because of usage or necessity, are incidental to his office, and may bind the corporation by contracts arising in the usual course of its business. And beyond this he, as president, has no more control over the corporate funds than any other director. And we have held that a president of a corporation may in pursuance of a power incidental to his office, take the necessary steps in defense of litigation prosecuted against his corporation in order to preserve the corporate assets.

> But, it is argued for defendant, the by-laws specifically limited the powers of the president, as was found by the learned justice, "to that of a moderator at meetings of directors, of temporary chairman at those of stockholders, and of a clerical nature in making reports and signing papers." *Ergo*, to permit plaintiff to employ counsel to institute a suit at law against a co-director is directly contrary to the contractual relationship created between the stockholders, and thus is an illegal exercise of power. It is further argued for defendant that a suit such as is here sought to be prosecuted will create strife and discord in the internal management of the corporation to the injury of the stockholders and creditors; and that if a president may institute such a suit ... he may also contract to pay counsel for his services out of corporate funds....

> We think that these arguments lack persuasion.... [W]e are merely concerned with a simple suit brought at law to enforce a rent claim allegedly due the corporation. It is difficult to perceive what greater strife and discord in the internal affairs of the instant corporation can be created by this suit than that which already obtains by reason of the existing deadlock....

> We are fully in accord with the views of the learned justice who observed that "what we have here is a case where the president, on the face of things,

has undertaken to institute the obvious and proper step to protect the interests of his corporation; and where the defendant, by the same token, has undertaken to prejudice those very interests in favor of his own."

If, as we have seen, a president of a corporation may take the necessary steps in defense of litigation prosecuted against his corporation in order to preserve the corporate assets, so, in reason and justice, he may employ and authorize counsel to institute necessary legal proceedings for the like purpose of preserving the interests of his corporation. We so hold. For, in each instance the power exercised by the chief executive officer of the corporation is to accomplish the same results. If the president were to fail to exercise the power to protect and defend the assets of his corporation he might well be liable to his corporation for the resultant losses. And so if the president exceeds his power the corporation may likewise look to him for any damages it may have sustained."

3. In *Bresnahan v. Lighthouse Mission, Inc.*, 496 S.E.2d 351 (Ga. Ct. App. 1998), plaintiff Bresnahan entered into an agreement with Lighthouse to purchase certain real estate. The agreement was signed by Dorothy Pinkerton, then president of Lighthouse. Pinkerton's signature did not specify whether she signed as president on behalf of Lighthouse or individually. Lighthouse later refused to sell the property. Ruling in favor of Lighthouse, the court stated:

> In this case, Lighthouse showed that Pinkerton acted outside the scope of authority that had been granted to her by Lighthouse. Lighthouse had an express provision in its by-laws requiring any sale of property to be signed by two officers acting on behalf of Lighthouse. According to the record, every document authorizing the sale or transfer of property standing in the name of Lighthouse has always included the signature of two officers of Lighthouse acting in their official capacity. Clearly, the agreement at issue was signed only by Pinkerton and did not even show that she was signing in a representative capacity. "[O]fficers appointed by the directors are clothed with only such powers and authority as are expressly conferred upon them by the charter or the by-laws, or as may be implied by usage and acquiescence." Pinkerton lacked the actual authority to bind Lighthouse.
>
> … Bresnahan contends that Pinkerton, as president of Lighthouse, had apparent authority sufficient to bind Lighthouse.... Where there were no manifestations of authority by the principal to a third party, apparent authority is not in issue.
>
> While Bresnahan offered evidence that Pinkerton informed the real estate broker at the time the purchase agreement was presented that Pinkerton had the authorization and approval of the Lighthouse Board of Directors to sign the agreement on behalf of Lighthouse and that this information was conveyed by the broker to him, Bresnahan failed to offer evidence of any conduct by Lighthouse that clothed Pinkerton with apparent authority. The evidence is undisputed that Lighthouse has never held Pinkerton out as anyone who,

on her sole signature, could bind the corporation on the sale or transfer of any property. Pinkerton did not have apparent authority to bind Lighthouse in this transaction.

While Bresnahan argues that Pinkerton, as president of Lighthouse, necessarily had apparent authority to enter into the agreement, this argument lacks merit. "A president of a corporation does not, by virtue of his office alone, have authority to contract in its behalf, although being the alter ego of the corporation he may be presumed to have power to act for it in matters within the scope of its ordinary business." In the present case, the agreement was not executed in Lighthouse's name, was not executed by Pinkerton "as president of" or "on behalf of" Lighthouse, and did not involve matters within the scope of Lighthouse's ordinary business. Lighthouse has successfully rebutted the presumption of Pinkerton's apparent authority as president of Lighthouse.

B. Chairman of the Board

Most corporations do not have a chair of the board, or as often used, a "chairman." The use of that title becomes increasingly common, however, as the size of a corporation increases, and most of the largest corporations do have a chair of the board. The person with this title may be an officer, but not always. Sometimes, especially in smaller corporations, the title is simply given to the director who is chosen to preside at meetings, without also making the director an officer. Beginning in the late 1990s, it became common among large public corporations to require that there be a board chair and further to provide that the person holding it cannot also be the chief executive officer. The policy of separating the two functions advanced the goal of minimizing the concentration of power in the boardroom and in executive suites.

It is not unusual, however, for the office of chair of the board to be largely ceremonial. Often, the office is occupied by a former chief executive officer who is serving out his or her time until retirement or until a suitable position outside the corporation becomes available. In such cases, there probably are no powers that are implied in the office, save arguably the power to preside at directors' meetings (and even that power is not the power of an officer, but rather of a director). Even so, corporations should not be surprised if courts do not allow them to avoid a contract entered into by a chair of the board, whatever the position's actual authority. One suspects that courts often will be inclined to make the chair of the board's corporation, rather than the other party to a contract, suffer from the ambiguity of the title "chair of the board" or "chairman of the board."

C. Vice President

The vice president has but one inherent power: to serve in the place of the president, most commonly in the event of the president's death, incapacity, or absence. In that connection, there are two problems. First, if there is more than one vice president, do they share those powers or is there an order of succession? Second, what constitutes "incapacity" or "absence"?

The first of those problems is the easiest to answer. In the absence of a bylaw or board action on the question, there seems to be no basis for distinguishing between vice presidents, and so each would seem to have the same power to substitute for the president. Well-drafted bylaws always speak to that question, for example, by providing that "in the event there be more than one vice president, the vice presidents in the order designated at the time of their election, or in the absence of any designation, then in the order of their appointment," shall serve in the place of the president. The usual way to set one vice president apart from others is to use a different title, such as "executive vice president" or "senior vice president." That should be enough to establish the order of succession.

Determining just when a vice president may step in for a president is more difficult. Take incapacity as an example. Is it enough that the president be home with a cold, or must the president be in a coma before he or she will be considered incapacitated? Questions such as these are particularly troubling to those on the other side of a corporate transaction, because they do not wish to run the risk that a vice president's authority later will be denied by the officer's corporation. In order to make it easier for their vice presidents to serve when needed, many corporations place in their bylaws language like the following: "The performance of any duty by a vice president shall, in respect of any other person dealing with the corporation, be conclusive evidence of the vice president's power to act."

Besides the implied power to serve in the place of the president, certain vice presidents may be given additional implied authority by virtue of their specialized titles. For example, it seems unlikely that a corporation that has elected someone to the office of vice president-purchasing could later avoid a contract for the purchase of office supplies that was signed by that vice president. Here the more interesting question relates to how far that additional authority might go. If that vice president purported to commit the corporation to purchase multimillion-dollar manufacturing equipment, for example, would the corporation be bound? Answers to those questions cannot be reached in the abstract, but will depend on how a court views the facts and, probably more important, the equities.

The following case discusses the authority of a vice president in the context of a muddled factual situation.

Anderson v. Campbell

Minnesota Supreme Court
223 N.W. 624 (1929)

WILSON, C. J.

… In 1924 the Pioneer Granite Company, having three stockholders, Great Northern Granite Company, having five stockholders, and the Campbell North Star Granite

Company, having three stockholders, corporations, were engaged separately in the business of monumental and construction work and operating granite quarries at St. Cloud. The stockholders in these corporations perfected a consolidation by organizing another corporation, the defendant North Star Granite Corporation, which took over the assets, except working capital, of the three corporations.

... The real estate of the Pioneer Granite Company was conveyed to the new corporation. A deed was prepared for the president and secretary to sign. The officers' names were apparently unknown to the scrivener, who left blank places in the acknowledgment for their insertion. When the time came for execution the president was absent and plaintiff Anderson, the vice president, executed the deed. The word "vice" was not inserted before the word president appearing below the signature nor in the acknowledgment.

The claim is now made by plaintiffs that the deed is void. It is valid on its face. It however shows Anderson to be president when he was vice president only. The president ... had the power to execute it. If the corporation had any by-laws, they did not define or limit the duties of the vice president contemplated by the articles of incorporation. His title, including the qualifying word "vice," indicates that he was to act for another, to wit, the president. This means in itself that in certain cases he may assume the duties of the president, and the most usual occasion for him so to act would be in the absence of the president. In the absence of by-laws defining or limiting his authority, he is a substitute for and when the president is absent or disqualified. Under such circumstances he is within the authority extended to the president to make the conveyance.

... When the deed was executed and delivered all the parties, including plaintiffs, intended it to be just what it purported to be. The erroneous description of Anderson as president instead of vice president was a harmless clerical inadvertence, and the plaintiffs are not in a position to take advantage thereof....

Note

In *Hufstedler v. Sides*, 165 S.W.2d 1006 (Tex. Civ. App. 1942), a case also addressing a vice-president's authority to execute a deed on a corporation's behalf, plaintiffs sued to recover land that they had purchased from a corporation. The defendant claimed the deed was invalid as it had not been signed by the appropriate corporate officer. In ruling for the plaintiffs, the court stated:

> The deed from the General American Life Insurance Company to H. H. Sides and wife is attacked by appellant for the reason that it shows to have been executed by its vice-president and attested by its secretary when the statute requires that a corporation may convey lands by deed sealed with its common seal and signed by the president or presiding member or trustee of said corporation. In considering the party named in the statute as qualified to execute a conveyance for a corporation in which the vice-president had acted, the Supreme Court in *Ballard et al. v. Carmichael*, 83 Tex. 355, 18 S.W. 734, 739 (Tex. 1892), ... says:

"We may safely assume to know judicially that a vice-president, in the common acceptation of that term, is an officer designated for the purpose of performing the functions of the president when for any reason the latter cannot act. In case of the absence of the president, or of his inability for any reason to perform the function of his place, as a very general rule, at least, the vice-president becomes invested with his powers and responsibility. In such contingencies the vice-president is in fact and in law the president in all except the name. He certainly becomes 'the presiding member' of the corporation. When, therefore, a deed is produced, signed by the vice-president of the corporation, and sealed with its seal, we think, in the absence of evidence to the contrary, it should be presumed that the contingency has arisen which authorized the vice-president to act, and that he is to be deemed pro hac vice the presiding member of the corporation."

Id. at 1009.

D. Secretary

Unlike the implied authority of the president and the vice president, the power associated with the office of secretary (or in the case of MBCA jurisdictions, the persons designated to perform the secretary's functions), relates only to the internal affairs of the corporation and not to its business. They are the powers to keep minutes of meetings and other nonfinancial corporate records, to have custody of the corporate seal, to attest the seal, to certify corporate records, and so on. The secretary's functions are ministerial in nature and do not vest the secretary to transact business on behalf of the corporation.

Insofar as dealings with those outside the corporation go, the certification of corporate records and particularly of minutes of meetings is by far the most important function of the secretary. Often, in connection with a corporate transaction, the person on the other side of the transaction will demand a certified copy of the board of directors' resolution approving the transaction. The person may also demand a certified list of the corporation's officers along with an attestation of the officers' signatures. The secretary has the implied power to deliver those certifications and attestations. The following case deals with the effect of such a certification or attestation.

In re Drive In Development Corp.

United States Court of Appeals, Seventh Circuit
371 F.2d 215 (1966)

Swygert, Circuit Judge.

The principal question in this appeal relates to the circumstances which may bind a corporation to a guaranty of the obligations of a related corporation when it is contended that the corporate officer who executed the guaranty had no authority to do so. The facts giving rise to the question underlie a claim filed by the National Boulevard

Bank of Chicago in an arrangement proceeding under chapter XI of the Bankruptcy Act, in which the Drive In Development Corporation was the debtor. National Boulevard's claim was disallowed by the referee, whose decision was confirmed by the district court.

On September 4, 1963, Tastee Freez and each of its subsidiaries, including Drive In, filed voluntary petitions under chapter XI of the Bankruptcy Act. National Boulevard filed a claim against Drive In before the referee, asserting the guaranty executed on April 11, 1962 as the basis for it.... The referee disallowed National Boulevard's claim in its entirety....

Turning to the merits of the objections to National Boulevard's claim, the referee found that Drive In's minute book did not show that a resolution authorizing Maranz to sign the guaranty was adopted by the directors and that Dick could not recall a specific directors' meeting at which such a resolution was approved. From these findings, the referee concluded that Maranz, who signed the guaranty on behalf of Drive In, had no authority, "either actual or implied or apparent," to bind Drive In. This conclusion was erroneous. Drive In was estopped to deny Maranz' express authority to sign the guaranty because of the certified copy of a resolution of Drive In's board of directors purporting to grant such authority furnished to the bank by Dick, whether or not such a resolution was in fact formally adopted. Dick was the secretary of the corporation. Generally, it is the duty of the secretary to keep the corporate records and to make proper entries of the actions and resolutions of the directors. Therefore it was within the authority of Dick to certify that a resolution such as challenged here was adopted. Statements made by an officer or agent in the course of a transaction in which the corporation is engaged and which are within the scope of his authority are binding upon the corporation. Consequently Drive In was estopped to deny the representation made by Dick in the certificate forwarded to National Boulevard, in the absence of actual or constructive knowledge on the part of the bank that the representation was untrue.

[The court allowed National Boulevard's claims to the extent that they had been guaranteed.]

First Securities Company v. Dahl

Iowa Supreme Court
560 N.W.2d 327 (1997)

SNELL, JUSTICE.

This appeal comes from First Securities Company, as plaintiff, which filed a declaratory judgment action, seeking to remove a restriction on its ownership of Lot 20, Crestview Heights, Fourth Addition to the City of Bettendorf, Scott County, Iowa. The trial court denied the relief requested. We affirm.

... First Securities Company is an Iowa corporation. The company's present shareholders and directors include John Guenther, vice president and secretary, Jerome Guenther, president, and Judith Guenther, treasurer. Evelyn Guenther, now deceased, was a fifty percent shareholder until February 10, 1994, and secretary and director until September 7, 1993....

Defendant Christine Dahl owns Lot 1 in Crestview Heights Fourth Addition and defendants Robert and Jeanne Nakamaru own Lot 2....

In 1984, the Crestview Heights Homeowners Association filed an action against, among others, the company and Evelyn and John Guenther. As part of the settlement of this lawsuit, on October 24, 1984, Evelyn Guenther signed an affidavit as the company's secretary purporting to restrict use of the 52-foot easement for access to Lot 20. The affidavit provided that the company relinquished any right to improve Outlot A and the outlot would continue to be used for recreational purposes by those living in the Crestview Heights subdivisions. The affidavit further stated, "Nor shall said lot be used as access to any other property, by First Securities Company or their heirs, successors and assigns." The affidavit was recorded on October 30, 1984.

Based on this affidavit, First Securities Company was able to settle the lawsuit and was relieved of paying any road assessment for Outlot A. Evelyn and John Guenther subsequently sold their interests in Lot 1 to Christine Dahl. The company subsequently became interested in selling Lot 20 for residential development. The company asked Dahl and Nakamaru to execute releases of any restriction to access to Lot 20 across Outlot A. They refused to do so.

The company then filed an application for declaratory judgment seeking a ruling that Evelyn Guenther's affidavit did not create a restrictive covenant preventing use of the easement across Outlot A, or, if it did, the restrictive covenant was void and unenforceable. Following a hearing, the district court entered its findings, conclusions and judgment. The court held Evelyn's affidavit is binding on the company to the extent the restriction inhibits the company's use of the road easement over Outlot A....

The company then appealed, [claiming that the trial court had erred in] concluding Evelyn Guenther had any authority, express, implied, or apparent, to bind the company in matters affecting title to real estate....

The validity of the affidavit restricting access is the critical issue in this case. The company asserts that Evelyn Guenther as secretary, acting alone, did not have authority to bind the corporation to a restrictive covenant concerning real estate owned by the corporation because both the president and secretary's signatures were needed. We note, however, that either actual or apparent authority in Evelyn is sufficient to bind the corporation. The evidence of actual authority is substantial.

Evelyn was secretary, and a fifty percent owner of the corporation. Jerome, the president, was in California. The affidavit was needed to settle litigation, the trial of which was imminent. Evelyn's affidavit was recorded which gave notice to the world, including the corporation. It had actual knowledge, and her act was not denied or repudiated for many years. The notarization of Evelyn's affidavit stated that she executed as its secretary, on behalf of the board of directors, and as the voluntary act and deed of the corporation. In fact, it was recognized by the corporation.

The homeowners' association relied on the affidavit in not making road repair or maintenance assessments on Outlot A and additional assessments on Lot 20. Dahl relied on the affidavit in purchasing Lot 1 in Crestview Heights Fourth Addition. The company abandoned the right to use the road when John and Evelyn sold their property. The affidavit was then of record. The company is estopped to deny the affidavit after all these years. These facts also show the apparent authority through which Evelyn acted as secretary. [Affirmed.]

Questions

Could the home owners have successfully claimed that Evelyn's acts had been ratified by the company? Why?

E. Treasurer

A corporation may have one or more officers with fiscal responsibilities. They are the treasurer and the comptroller (also referred to as the controller). Depending on the particular corporate structure, the treasurer and comptroller may report directly to the Board of Directors or, in a large company, may report to a Chief Financial Officer, who in turn reports to the board.

Although corporate statutes do not usually refer to the office of the comptroller,[78] the statutes often provide for the office of treasurer, the position responsible for the receipt and disbursement of company funds and for company loans and their repayment. Treasurers are also often responsible for investing a company's funds, and creating and monitoring a company's budget.

> ... [T]he ordinary duties of a treasurer are to receive, safely keep, and disburse the funds of the company, under the supervision of the directors, but he has no authority to pay debts of the company, unless by order of the directors, nor to cancel, compromise, or set off claims due from the company by those due to it. Any attempt on his part thus to control the business of the company would be to assume powers specifically conferred by the charter upon the directors, and all such acts, unless ratified by the company, would be void.

Blackwell v. Saddleback Lumber Co., 151 A. 534, 536 (Me. 1930).

With respect to the scope of implied and apparent authority arising from the position, itself, the treasurer has much in common with the corporate secretary. Both officers' powers exclusively relate to the internal affairs of the corporation. Absent a grant of authority originating with the board or the corporate bylaws, the treasurer lacks the implied or apparent authority to bind the corporation in contracts or other transactions with third parties. Appropriate authorization is also required for a treas-

---

78. The comptroller is the company's senior accounting officer, responsible for preparing corporate books of account and financial statements (balance sheets, income statements, etc.) for review by the company's board of directors, officers and shareholders. Comptrollers also oversee a company's management accounting and financial planning and its audit activities.

urer to dispose of corporate assets. Simply put, the treasurer has the power to care for the funds of the corporation. That includes depositing the funds in proper depositories and disbursing them in accordance with orders from the board of directors or an authorized senior officer, maintaining records of the funds, and rendering reports on the corporation's funds to the board of directors.

General Overseas Films, Ltd. v. Robin International, Inc.

United States District Court, Southern District of New York.
542 F. Supp. 684 (1982)

Sofaer, District Judge.

In this action, plaintiff General Overseas Films, Ltd. ("GOF") seeks to collect on a loan guarantee that it alleges was provided on behalf of The Anaconda Company ("Anaconda") by Charles H. Kraft, Anaconda's Vice President and Treasurer. Plaintiff GOF claims that Anaconda promised through Kraft to guarantee the repayment of loans made by GOF to Robin International, Inc. ("Robin"). [Robin was one of several companies owned and controlled by Nicholas Reisini.] Plaintiff also claims that Anaconda, acting through Kraft, guaranteed Robin's obligations and liabilities in connection with certain related transactions....

Anaconda asserts as its primary defense to the action that the guarantee extended by Kraft does not bind Anaconda, since Kraft lacked actual or apparent authority to engage in the transaction. Plaintiff concedes that Kraft had no actual authority to bind Anaconda to this undertaking; it relies solely on Kraft's apparent authority to do so. Since on this record it is clear that Kraft lacked apparent authority to engage in the transactions considered, Anaconda's other defenses need not be addressed.

... The doctrine of apparent authority delineates the grounds for imposing on the principal losses caused by its agent's unauthorized acts. The law recognizes that an agent, such as Kraft, may engage in a fraudulent transaction entirely without his principal's approval but nevertheless under circumstances that warrant holding his principal accountable....

The doctrine rests not upon the agent's acts or statements but upon the acts or omissions of the principal. It is invoked when the principal's own misleading conduct is responsible for the agent's ability to mislead. As defined in the Restatement a principal causes his agent to have apparent authority by written or spoken words or any other conduct of the principal which, reasonably interpreted, causes the third person to believe that the principal consents to have the act done on his behalf....

The initial question, therefore, is whether Anaconda's conduct permitted Haggiag [GOF's representative] actually and reasonably to believe that Kraft was authorized to execute this guarantee. Under the law of New York, the circumstances of the transaction known to the plaintiff must also be scrutinized to determine whether it fulfilled its primary "duty of inquiry."

GOF relies on several aspects of Anaconda's conduct in arguing that Anaconda conferred apparent authority on Kraft for the transactions in which he engaged with

GOF. Anaconda placed Kraft in a high and visible corporate position, with broad powers over financial affairs. It gave Kraft Anaconda stationery displaying his corporate titles, an office in the company's executive suite, business cards, access to the corporate seal, and put his picture in its annual report. Anaconda officers and publications announced to the financial community that Kraft was the individual at Anaconda with whom to discuss the company's "financial needs." Plaintiff argues that "Anaconda held Kraft out as having the full range of authority and responsibility for Anaconda's financial matters," and characterizes Kraft as Anaconda's "emissary to the financial community." Specifically, Anaconda adopted and made available to Kraft Article 9 of Anaconda's bylaws, conferring upon Kraft, as Treasurer, authority "to sign checks, notes, drafts, bills of exchange and other evidences of indebtedness...." Kraft showed this bylaw, as well as his picture in Anaconda's annual report, to Haggiag at their initial meeting. By these actions, plaintiff contends, Anaconda gave such convincing evidence of Kraft's authority to sign guarantees that several sophisticated banks extended some $34 million in credit to Reisini's companies, at Kraft's request, through transactions similar to GOF's with Robin....

[The transactions involving the sophisticated banks], moreover, constitute in plaintiff's view strong evidence of the reasonableness of GOF's conduct: "six sophisticated financial institutions and Kraft's own superiors did not question for more than six years the fact that Kraft's actions on behalf of Anaconda were proper, legitimate and fully authorized." Further, GOF cites as evidence of the reasonableness of its belief in Kraft's apparent authority the fact that Haggiag asked a distinguished member of the bar whether the papers Kraft presented Haggiag were in good order; the attorney allegedly told Haggiag that the papers appeared to be in proper form. Haggiag also inquired as to Anaconda's interest [in the transaction with Robin], and was told that the company had supplied or produced the walls of the Russian mission that Robin had built. Finally, GOF contends that, had Haggiag inquired further into Kraft's authority, he would not have discovered anything to cast doubt upon the transactions' propriety, since Kraft was the person at Anaconda authorized to produce evidence as to both the authority to transact business on behalf of Anaconda and any changes in that authority.

GOF's arguments would have force in a situation that fell within the range of transactions in which companies like Anaconda normally engage. But the transaction involved in this case is extraordinary, and should have alerted Haggiag to the danger of fraud. Because the circumstances surrounding the transaction were such as to put Haggiag on notice of the need to inquire further into Kraft's power and good faith, Anaconda cannot be bound.

A corporate treasurer, it is true, must be regarded as having broad authority to commit his or her company in financial dealings. Large companies such as Anaconda generally establish ongoing relations with several banks. The banks are kept informed of the financial status of these companies through regular reports. They are also advised of exactly whom to deal with at such companies in all financial matters, and are provided with evidence of the individual officer's authority. In this case, Anaconda designated Kraft as its authorized contact in financial affairs, and it widely published Article 9 of its bylaws as evidencing the scope of Kraft's authority. Anaconda thereby placed Kraft in a position that enabled him to commit the company, when he was acting within the scope of Article 9, to any transaction that appeared reasonably related to Anaconda's business. Anaconda and companies like Anaconda often need on-the-spot, informal commitments from banks, and they operate in a manner that enables them to obtain such commitments. Banks, on the other hand, need and compete for customers such as Anaconda, and they reasonably attempt to meet the needs of such customers by dealing as swiftly and informally with authorized officers as the circumstances of a particular transaction reasonably permit.

The existence of apparent authority depends in part upon "who the contracting third party is." *Lee v. Jenkins Bros.*, 268 F.2d at 370 (2d Cir. 1959). GOF is not a bank, or otherwise the type of company with whom Anaconda needed to deal swiftly and regularly in its financial affairs. It had no relationship with Anaconda before the transaction concerning Robin. It had neither the need nor the capacity to seek or compete for Anaconda's financial business by extending services or courtesies without the investigation normally made. GOF maintained no file on Anaconda; it had no idea of the company's financial condition beyond glancing at Anaconda's latest annual report. A bank with whom Anaconda (and Kraft) regularly dealt might more reasonably rely on Kraft's position as evidence of broad authority in most types of financial matters. But given GOF's lack of experience and knowledge in banking, GOF's lack of a prior relationship with Anaconda, and GOF's lack of any interest in creating an ongoing relationship with Anaconda, it cannot claim to have the same reasonable basis for such reliance. The messages Anaconda implicitly may have conveyed in its dealings with banks could not have been intended for a company in GOF's situation nor reasonably available to such a company as a basis for its reliance.

More important, the nature of the specific transaction—a guarantee by Anaconda of the debt of an unrelated corporation—was extraordinary and thus sufficient to require inquiry by GOF before it relied on Kraft's purported authority. Article 9 of Anaconda's bylaws is properly cited by plaintiff as conduct of the principal which could give rise to apparent authority. But GOF has no basis for arguing that Article 9 of Anaconda's bylaws conferred or reasonably appeared to confer authority on Kraft to sign a guarantee, let alone one to a third, unrelated company. The bylaw implicitly but clearly refutes the notion that Kraft had authority to sign guarantees. The language conferring power on him to sign evidences of indebtedness occurs in a context that pertains entirely to Anaconda's direct borrowing activities. It reads:

> The Treasurer or Assistant Treasurer shall have the custody of all the funds and securities of the Company, and shall have power on behalf of the Company to sign checks, notes, drafts, bills of exchange and other evidences of indebtedness, to borrow money for the current needs of the business of the Company and assign and deliver for money so borrowed stocks and securities and warehouse receipts or other documents representing metals in store or transit and to make short-term investments of surplus funds of the Company

and shall perform such other duties as may be assigned to him from time to time by the Board of Directors, the Chairman of the Board, the Vice Chairman of the Board or the President.

Plaintiff argues that the phrase "evidences of indebtedness" includes guarantees, citing *Shire Realty Corp. v. Schorr*, 55 A.D.2d 356, 359, 390 N.Y.S.2d 622, 624 (2d Dept. 1977), for the proposition that a guarantee is "an agreement to pay a debt owed by another." A guarantee is not, however, an "evidence of indebtedness"; it is an agreement collateral to the debt itself. The general rule is that "(e)xpress authority to execute or indorse commercial paper in the principal's name ... does not include authority to draw or indorse negotiable paper for the benefit ... of any other person; authority to sign accommodation paper or as security for a third person must be specially given." ...

Plaintiff contends that, regardless of whether a guarantee is an evidence of indebtedness, the language of Article 9, when reasonably interpreted, gives the appearance of such authority. This argument proceeds on the theory that Kraft's actual "authority in other transactions gave him apparent authority in this transaction." But the nature of a guarantee is such that "(h)owever general the character of the agency may be, a contract of guaranty or suretyship is not normally to be inferred from such an agency." 2 S. Williston, A Treatise on the Law of Contracts, s 277A, at 230 (3d Ed. 1959). The guarantee of Robin's debt to GOF, standing alone, had no apparent connection with the financial interests of Anaconda. Unlike a loan or other debt undertaken by Anaconda for its own benefit, a guarantee results in a loan by the creditor of funds to a third party, or, as in this case, in the creditor's agreement to defer collecting on a loan previously extended to a third party. Unless the transaction has other elements connecting it to the guarantor, it is not the sort of arrangement in which the guarantor company's treasurer or other financial officer normally should be expected to engage:

> (S)uch a contract is unusual and extraordinary and so not normally within the powers accruing to an agent by implication, however general the character of the agency; ordinarily the power exists only if expressly given. Consequently a manager, superintendent, or the like, of business or property cannot ordinarily bind his principal as surety for third persons.

... Had Kraft purported to borrow money for Anaconda, or in a credible manner for Anaconda's benefit, he could have bound Anaconda even if he in fact intended and managed to steal the money involved. Had Anaconda itself done anything to suggest it had an interest in Robin or in the transactions at issue, a stronger case for apparent authority would be presented. But in this case, Anaconda was neither directly nor indirectly involved in the transaction between GOF and Robin, and GOF has not pointed to any actions by Anaconda suggesting involvement. The only connection between Anaconda and Robin suggested to Haggiag was a vague statement by Reisini that Anaconda had provided "curtain walls" in the Russian mission. These remarks are of minimal significance since they can in no way be attributed to Anaconda, and therefore cannot give rise to apparent authority. Moreover, Haggiag admits that the words curtain walls "sounded strange," and that he had no real interest in the subject. Kraft made no representation about any connection between

Robin and Anaconda, and even if he had, he could not thereby have supplied any more of a basis for apparent authority than he did by his assertions to Haggiag that he had the power to execute the guarantee. The situations in which courts have bound principals on guarantees issued by their agents are those in which authority to do so is express, or clearly implied from functions assigned to and performed by the agent involved. Otherwise, such a guaranty has no apparent relationship to the principal's business, and one who receives what appears to be a guarantee is put on notice that he must inquire further before relying on it. Under these circumstances, Kraft's authority to bind Anaconda to this transaction was far from apparent.

Plaintiff relies heavily on the fact that six banks were also taken in by Kraft and Reisini in various ways. It argues that the banks' similar conduct shows that GOF's belief in Kraft's authority, and its reliance on him, was commercially reasonable; GOF also argues that Haggiag properly relied on the existence of parallel transactions as evidence of Kraft's authority. But the banks in fact treated Article 9 of Anaconda's bylaws as evidence that Kraft lacked authority to sign guarantees. Not one of them accepted a simple guarantee arrangement. Instead they designed alternative arrangements that they felt provided them security, but at the same time avoided a guarantee as such....

In fact, the only transaction involving Kraft and Reisini of which Haggiag had any detailed knowledge should have alerted him to the importance of requiring a board of directors resolution demonstrating express authority for a corporate officer to execute a guarantee of an unrelated third party's debt. Two months before Haggiag's first business contact with Kraft, Reisini asked Haggiag if he would introduce him to one of Haggiag's banks for the purpose of securing a loan to Robin with the guarantee of Anaconda. Haggiag spoke with his banker at Swiss Bank of Basle and the banker expressed interest in the transaction. Reisini then asked Haggiag to introduce Kraft to the bank, so Haggiag arranged a visit with an officer of the Swiss Bank Corporation in New York City. According to Haggiag:

> Kraft came with me downtown and I introduced him because he wanted to borrow money with the guarantee of Anaconda from the Swiss Bank Corporation.... They asked [for] a specific Board of Directors' approval and Kraft said he would do it....

... Despite Haggiag's awareness of his own bank's insistence on board-of-directors approval, Haggiag went ahead without similar documentation. He chose to rely on Kraft's representations without inquiry, rather than on the sound practice suggested by his bank's demands....

The evidence in the record fails to establish that Anaconda through its conduct misled plaintiff so as to warrant a finding that Kraft had "apparent authority" to bind Anaconda to the guarantee. Indeed, Haggiag's negligence, not Anaconda's, precipitated the loss. Accordingly, judgment shall be entered for the defendant Anaconda, with costs. The case will be closed without prejudice to reopening against Robin after the stay occasioned by Robin's involuntary bankruptcy proceedings is lifted.

Notes and Questions

1. Does a treasurer have the implied power to sign a promissory note? In concluding that a treasurer does not have this power, the court in *Jacobus v. Jamestown Mantel Co.*, 105 N. E. 210, 212 (2d Cir. 1914), stated the following:

> One who deals with the officers or agents of a corporation is bound to know their powers and the extent of their authority.... A treasurer of a manufacturing corporation has no power to make promissory notes in its name unless such power is expressly given to such officer by the bylaws of the corporation or by resolution of its board of directors. No presumption existed that the defendant's treasurer had power to make or indorse business paper. It was necessary, therefore, for the plaintiff to show that the treasurer had authority to execute promissory notes in the name of the corporation in the ordinary course of its business, or that the defendant was estopped from denying such authority.

2. One final word about the authority of officers: most vice presidents and treasurers, and many secretaries, have substantial corporate powers in addition to those generally associated with their offices. The important thing to remember is that when considering any alleged power beyond that which is generally recognized, the power must ultimately have been given by the bylaws or the board, either directly or through another officer. The board may have granted the power formally in a bylaw or a resolution or it may have acted by acquiescence or ratification, but the bylaws or the board must have granted the power in some way—or the power does not exist.

3. This chapter describes the powers corporate officers traditionally have. When the corporation in question is closely held, the powers may be modified according to the terms of applicable statutory close corporation provisions or, in a MBCA jurisdiction, by a shareholders' agreement satisfying the requirements of MBCA section 7.32. Allocation of corporate control is discussed in the next chapter.

Chapter 7

Distributing Corporate Control

Situation

Although the company continues to do well, Anderson and Baker believe that they will each be in a precarious position if, in future months or years, their percentage share of corporate stock is reduced as a result of raising additional capital by adding new shareholders. They understand that if one of them sides with the other shareholders, the other could be left without a voice in the business. They do not expect a falling out, but each wants protection if it happens.

Their concern is general, but they have voiced specific concerns about the following: (1) their future employment with Biologistics, Inc.; (2) the possibility that the size of the board will be increased, thus diminishing the power of any one director; (3) the possibility that one of them will be removed from the board; (4) the possibility that the charter or bylaws will be changed without the consent of both of them; and (5) the possibility of a deadlock on an important issue, as a result of which the company will be paralyzed.

They have asked your advice on each of these matters and, in general, have made it clear that each is interested in maintaining as much personal control over the company as possible. In responding to their questions, you should also consider what issues of professional responsibility are raised by their request.

The corporate lawyer has available a large number of diverse tools for fine-tuning the control relationships within a corporation. Theoretically, that fine-tuning may occur at any time during a corporation's life, but most of the tools require shareholder agreement for their use. That means that often those tools cannot be used in the midst of struggles for control or other corporate strife. For that reason, good corporate lawyers attempt to foresee possible control problems and to use those tools prophylactically. Typically, the best time for their use is at the beginning of a corporation's life.

Issues of allocation of control are particularly important in closely held corporations. One reason is that shareholders in closely held corporations usually also participate in management so that the lines demarcating the roles of shareholders and directors become blurred. Often the operation of the business more closely resembles a partnership than a general corporation. A second is that shareholders typically look to the company for their livelihood. Their financial security depends on continued receipt of salaries as employees or payment of dividends as shareholders. A third is that there generally is little or no market for the shares of a closely held corporation.

Consequently, owners of such an enterprise often find themselves locked in an embrace from which there is no easy exit. For these reasons, striking a balance between majority and minority interests assumes an additional importance. Allocating too much power to the majority raises the specter of oppressive action that ignores legitimate interests of the minority. Shifting too far in the opposite direction creates the possibility that a lone voice can virtually paralyze the company's operations. The sections that follow explore structural options available to effect a balanced governance structure. The options are interrelated and function like pieces on a legal chess board; one option can be used to check the advantages of another.

Section I
Cumulative Voting, Staggered Boards, and Class Voting

A. Cumulative Voting

You will recall from the previous chapter that directors are elected by a plurality of votes. The directors with the most votes win. Corporation statutes vary in the voting procedures required to elect directors. Most statutes mandate so-called straight voting, unless the corporate charter provides for cumulative voting. Some statutes, however, take the opposite approach and require cumulative voting unless the charter calls for straight voting. In straight voting, the shareholders have one vote per share, which they may cast to fill each vacant directorship. Under straight voting, shares are voted in blocks. If there are five directors to be elected, a shareholder having 100 shares could vote those 100 shares five times, once for each favored candidate. Notice that in this example, someone else owning as few as 101 shares could out-vote the shareholder with 100 shares and thereby fill each vacancy. In other words, under straight voting, a shareholder or shareholder group owning a majority of a corporation's voting stock can elect all of the directors.

When used effectively, cumulative voting increases the likelihood that shareholders owning minority interests in the corporation will be able to elect a director. The Model Act describes cumulative voting in the following way: shareholders "are entitled to multiply the number of votes they are entitled to cast by the number of directors for whom they are entitled to vote and cast the product for a single candidate or distribute the product among two or more candidates."[1] Under cumulative voting, the shareholder in the above example who holds 100 shares at a time when five directors are to be elected would have 500 votes (5 directors x 100 votes), and those votes could be cast for one candidate or could be spread among the candidates in any way the shareholder wishes.

The question immediately arises, of course, as to how shareholders can use their votes most effectively. There is a formula a shareholder can use to determine

---

1. Model Act §7.28(c). Subsection (b) of §7.28 makes straight voting mandatory unless the articles of incorporation provide for cumulative voting. *Id.* §7.28(b).

how many directors can be elected with a particular number of shares. Here is the formula:

$$\text{Achievable Slots} = \frac{(\text{Shares Held} - 1)(\text{Total Slots} + 1)}{\text{Total Shares}}$$

Achievable Slots	=	Number of directors who can be elected with the shares held
Shares Held	=	Total shares held or controlled by an individual shareholder or a shareholder group
Total Slots	=	Number of directors to be elected at the meeting
Total Shares	=	Number of shares to be voted by all shareholders

Here is how the formula would work, adapting the preceding example. Suppose 500 shares owned by one shareholder (Shares Held = 500) and five directors to be elected (Total Slots = 5), and assume that all shareholders will vote a total of 1,500 shares in the election of directors (Total Shares = 1500):

$$\text{Achievable Slots} = \frac{(500 - 1 = 499)(5 + 1 = 6)}{1500} = \frac{2994}{1500}$$

or

$$\text{Achievable Slots} = 1.996$$

Here the shareholder would be able to elect one director. Since 500 shares will get that shareholder so close to being able to elect two directors, perhaps an alliance can be formed to put together a few additional votes. With that in mind, the shareholder may wonder how many shares it would take to elect two directors. Here again, there is a formula the shareholder can use, this time one that will show the number of shares needed to elect a particular number of directors:

$$\text{Required Shares} = \frac{\text{Total Shares x Desired Slots}}{\text{Total Slots} + 1} + 1$$

Required Shares	=	Number of shares needed to elect a specified number of directors (Desired Slots)
Total Shares	=	Number of shares to be voted by all shareholders
Desired Slots	=	Number of directors a shareholder or shareholder group wishes to elect
Total Slots	=	Number of directors to be elected at the meeting

Using the numbers in the above example, here is the answer to the question of how many shares would be needed to elect two directors:

$$\text{Required Shares} \ = \ \frac{1500 \times 2}{5 + 1} \ = \ \frac{3000}{6} \ + 1$$

or

$$\text{Required Shares} \ = \ 501$$

After determining the number of directors who can be elected by a given number of votes, shareholders wishing to maximize their cumulative voting power simply need to distribute their votes as evenly as possible among their candidates. In the above example, that would mean casting 251 votes for one candidate and 250 for the other.

Director removal is also an issue when cumulative voting is used. Ordinarily, a director elected cumulatively can be removed by a majority of shareholder votes unless special provisions apply. To guard against this result, Model Act § 8.08 (c) provides that a director elected cumulatively "may not be removed if the number of votes sufficient to elect him under cumulative voting is voted against his removal."

The decision whether to use cumulative voting can be a difficult one. Cumulative voting potentially gives persons with significant minority interests the opportunity to elect one or more directors and thereby make the board more truly representative of the range of shareholder interests. If, however, directors elected cumulatively regard themselves as representing a particular interest group, rather than the corporation as a whole, they may approach their obligations in a manner inconsistent with fiduciary requirements and introduce divisiveness or factionalism into board proceedings.

B. Staggered Boards

As is obvious from the preceding discussion on cumulative voting, the fewer directors there are to be elected at a particular meeting, the less chance there is that a minority shareholder or shareholder group can elect even one director. In order to minimize the effective voting power of minority shareholders, corporate planners sometimes divide the directors into classes, with only one of the classes coming up for election each year. That scheme, which is called "classification of directors" or "staggering the board," is allowed by the MBCA and most other corporation statutes. Here is the heart of the provision as found in MBCA § 8.06:

> The articles of incorporation may provide for staggering the terms of directors by dividing the total number of directors into two or three groups, with each group containing one-half or one-third of the total, as near as may be. In that event, the terms of directors in the first group expire at the first annual shareholders' meeting after their election, the terms of the second group expire at the second annual shareholders' meeting after their election, and

the terms of the third group, if any, expire at the third annual shareholders' meeting after their election. At each annual shareholders' meeting held thereafter, directors shall be chosen for a term of two years or three years, as the case may be, to succeed those whose terms expire.

There are reasons aside from effects on cumulative voting to adopt a staggered board, of course. For one, a staggered board promotes institutional stability over multiple time periods. That may be a plus from the viewpoint of corporate directors. It may be a minus to those shareholders frustrated with incumbent directors and wishing to unseat them in elections at annual shareholders' meetings. Unseating all directors on an unclassified board can be done at a single annual meeting, whereas voting out all directors on a three-class staggered board requires three annual meetings.

If the purpose of many staggered board provisions is to prevent the ouster of the full board at a single meeting, then it is desirable to adjust related corporate rules governing shareholder removal of directors. As discussed further below, a longstanding common law rule holds that, since shareholders have the power to elect directors, they also have the inherent power to remove directors, at least for cause. Many statutes have gone further and recognize a shareholder right to remove directors even without cause.

Specifically, the MBCA provision on removal contemplates removal with or without cause unless the charter provides otherwise, and does not distinguish between classified and non-classified boards. MBCA 8.08(a). Therefore, under the MBCA, absent a contrary charter provision, directors on classified boards can be removed without cause. It is therefore usually desirable for an MBCA corporation opting to have a staggered board to also provide that directors may be only be removed with cause.

The DGCL likewise permits shareholders to remove directors either "with or without cause" but that rule is immutable—the statute does not offer alteration by charter. *See* DGCL 141(k)(1). However, the DGCL further provides that, unless the charter states otherwise, directors on classified boards may only be removed for cause. The latter provision reflects the classified board provision's rationale of curtailing the shareholders' ability to oust the full board all at once.

Some Delaware corporations adopting staggered board provisions also add charter provisions expressly stating that directors can only be removed for cause, even though these provisions are redundant under the DGCL. What happens if such a company subsequently amends its charter to revert from a classified board to a regular board but fails to amend the for cause removal provision? The for cause removal provision becomes invalid. *See VAALCO Energy Inc. Consol.*, C.A. No. 11776-VCL (Del. Ch. 2015).

C. Class and Weighted Voting

Class voting is an alternative mechanism that can be used to empower minority interests to elect directors or to make sure that all members of a small, closely held corporation have representation on the board. According to § 8.04 of the MBCA, "If the articles of incorporation authorize dividing the shares into classes, the articles may also authorize the election of all or a specified number of directors by the holders of one or more authorized classes of shares...." This approach ensures that each shareholder or group of shareholders can elect a board member.

There are many ways different classes of stock may be structured. For example, there may be two or three classes of common, Classes A, B, and C, each with the same voting, dividend and liquidation rights, the difference being that each elects one director. The classes may also differ as to voting and proprietary rights. Class A could have voting rights and no liquidation or dividend rights, while Class B could have proprietary rights but no voting rights. The possibilities are many. *Lehrman v. Cohen*, 222 A.2d 800 (Del. 1966), in Section V of this chapter, provides a well known example of the uses of classified stock in a closely held corporation.

Another way to structure voting rights is to use weighted voting, which is an exception to the general rule that each share has only one vote. With weighted voting, some stock will be given super voting power, that is, more than one vote per share. Weighted voting is used in anti-takeover devices. It is also used to maintain control within a particular group without requiring proportionate investment.

In *Providence and Worcester Co. v. Baker*, 378 A.2d 121 (Del. 1977), the Delaware Supreme Court upheld a provision in a corporation's Articles of Incorporation restricting the voting rights of investors with large share holdings. The provision limited voting rights based on the number of shares held by an individual shareholder. A shareholder was entitled to one vote for each of the first fifty shares owned, and one vote for every twenty shares in excess of fifty. No shareholder could vote in his or her own right more than one fourth of the total outstanding shares.

The plaintiff claimed the arrangement was impermissible because all shares of stock within the same class did not have uniform voting rights. The court, however, upheld the scheme, finding that it restricted the voting rights of the shareholder but did not create variations in the voting power of the stock itself.

Not all courts have agreed with the approach taken in *Providence*. In *Asarco Inc. v. Holmes A. Court*, 611 F. Supp. 468 (D.N.J. 1985), the Asarco directors planned to issue a preferred stock dividend in response to an unwelcome takeover attempted by a shareholder. The court enjoined the issuance of the preferred stock because it would have caused shares within the same class to have different voting rights.

Both class voting and weighted voting can be used to allocate voting power independently of the size of financial investment. As a result, shareholders in a closely held corporation who have made unequal capital contributions can have equal voting rights on some or all of the matters properly decided by shareholders. This, in effect, creates a partnership like structure. All of the voting options described above affect the allocation of voting power among shareholders and do not disturb the allocation of power between the directors and the shareholders. Mechanisms for accomplishing the latter result are discussed in later sections of this chapter.

Section II
Charter Provisions

Modern corporation statutes allow the drafters of corporate charters and charter amendments a virtual free hand in arranging the control of a corporation in any way that suits them. The MBCA contains representative provisions, the most important of which are §§ 8.01, 2.02, and 10.01. Section 8.01(b) gives power over the management of a corporation to the board of directors, "subject to any limitation set forth in the articles of incorporation or in an agreement" authorized by the MBCA. Section 2.02, which is the MBCA's general provision on charters, allows articles of incorporation to contain "provisions, not inconsistent with law, regarding: ... (ii) managing the business and regulating the affairs of the corporation; (iii) defining, limiting, and regulating the powers of the corporation, its board of directors, and shareholders...." And § 10.01 allows the free amendment of charters at any time.

As a result of these provisions, the power to manage a corporation can be split among its shareholders, directors, and officers in any way desirable. It is even possible to take away all of the board's powers and simply have the shareholders or one of the officers exercise those powers, although that is not generally practical. It is practical, however, to take power away from the board piecemeal. For example, a corporation's charter might provide that only a shareholders' vote is required for a merger, for the sale of all of a corporation's assets, or for dissolution, each of which usually would require the prior recommendation of the directors. Or instead of enhancing the power of shareholders, a charter could take authority away from the directors and give it to an officer. A corporation may wish to provide, for example, that all questions relating to a particular line of business will be decided by the president rather than the board.

The most common charter provision that changes the ordinary control relationships is a super-majority voting requirement. Under statutory provisions typified by MBCA §§ 7.27 and 8.24, the charter (and, in the case of directors, also the bylaws) may require a higher percentage vote of directors or shareholders than the majority vote usually specified in the statute. The super-majority requirement can be used for all actions by shareholders or directors, but usually it is limited to specified actions of particular importance. In one corporation that might be the election of directors; in another, the sale of a specified corporate asset. As a means of impeding hostile tender offers, many publicly held corporations have adopted charter provisions that require 80 to 90% majorities to approve mergers and other transactions with shareholders having a specified amount of common stock, for example, 10%. High quorum requirements are also permissible and can be used with equal effect in many situations. The danger posed by a high quorum requirement for actions by shareholders or directors is that convening a meeting will become that much more difficult and may prevent even ordinary types of business from being conducted.

When one is drafting a super-majority provision, it usually is desirable to protect the provision from being amended by a vote of the shareholders or directors that is less than the super-majority called for by the provision. That is done by specifying in the charter that a super-majority vote is required to amend the charter provision containing the super-majority requirement. The MBCA has anticipated this result by including §7.27 (b), which provides:

> An amendment to the articles of incorporation that adds, changes, or deletes a greater quorum or voting requirement must meet the same quorum requirement and be adopted by the same vote and voting groups required to take action under the quorum and voting requirements then in effect or proposed to be adopted, whichever is greater.

Section III
Removal Of Directors

In a closely held corporation, there often are two conflicting desires on the part of shareholders with respect to the removal of directors. First, the shareholders wish to have unlimited power to remove non-shareholder directors at will. Second, each shareholder who is also a director wants to have substantial protection against being removed personally as a director. Following the lead of the MBCA, some modern statutes provide that the shareholders may remove directors "with or without cause" at any meeting called for the purpose. That provision gives the shareholders the power they wish to have over nonshareholder directors, but it provides the shareholders who are also directors with little personal protection. The MBCA addresses such concerns by allowing the charter to provide for removal only for cause.

Statutory provisions like that found in the MBCA raise the question of whether, under such statutes, a corporation's charter could provide that directors who also are shareholders could be removed only for cause. The answer seems clearly to be no, since the statutory language seems unequivocally to permit shareholders to remove any or all directors without cause. One way to give such shareholders substantial protection against being removed as directors is to provide for a supermajority vote for the removal without cause of any director who also is a shareholder.

The following two cases raise interesting issues relating to the removal of directors.

Auer v. Dressel
New York Court of Appeals
118 N.E.2d 590 (1954)

DESMOND, J.

This ... proceeding was brought by class A stockholders of appellant R. Hoe & Co., Inc., for an order in the nature of mandamus to compel the president of Hoe to comply with a positive duty imposed on him by the corporation's by-laws. Section 2 of article I of those by-laws says that: "It shall be the duty of the President to call a special meeting whenever requested in writing so to do, by stockholders owning a majority of the capital stock entitled to vote at such meeting." On October 16, 1953, petitioners submitted to the president written requests for a special meeting of class

A stockholders, which writings were signed in the names of the holders of record of slightly more than 55% of the class A stock.

The president failed to call the meeting and, after waiting a week, the petitioners brought the present proceeding. The answer of the corporation and its president was not forthcoming until October 28, 1953, and it contained, in response to the petition's allegation that the demand was by more than a majority of class A stockholders, only a denial that the corporation and the president had any knowledge or information sufficient to form a belief as to the stockholdings of those who had signed the requests. Since the president, when he filed that answer, had had before him for at least ten days the signed requests themselves, his denial that he had any information sufficient for a belief as to the adequacy of the number of signatures was obviously perfunctory and raised no issue whatever.

There was no discretion in this corporate officer as to whether or not to call a meeting when a demand therefor was put before him by owners of the required number of shares. The important right of stockholders to have such meetings called will be of little practical value if corporate management can ignore the requests, force the stockholders to commence legal proceedings, and then, by purely formal denials, put the stockholders to lengthy and expensive litigation, to establish facts as to stockholdings which are peculiarly within the knowledge of the corporate officers. In such a situation, Special Term did the correct thing in disposing of the matter summarily....

The petition was opposed on the further alleged ground that none of the four purposes for which petitioners wished the meeting called was a proper one for such a class A stockholders' meeting. Those four stated purposes were these: (A) to vote upon a resolution indorsing the administration of petitioner Joseph L. Auer, who had been removed as president by the directors, and demanding that he be reinstated as such president; (B) voting upon a proposal to amend the charter and by-laws to provide that vacancies on the board of directors, arising from the removal of a director by stockholders or by resignation of a director against whom charges have been proffered, may be filled, for the unexpired term, by the stockholders only of the class theretofore represented by the director so removed or so resigned; (C) voting upon a proposal that the stockholders hear certain charges proffered, in the requests, against four of the directors, determine whether the conduct of such directors or any of them was inimical to the corporation and, if so, to vote upon their removal and vote for the election of their successors; and (D) voting upon a proposal to amend the by-laws so as to provide that half of the total number of directors in office and, in any event, not less than one third of the whole authorized number of directors constitute a quorum of the directors.

The Hoe certificate of incorporation provides for eleven directors, of whom the class A stockholders, more than a majority of whom join in this petition, elect nine and the common stockholders elect two. The obvious purpose of the meeting here sought to be called (aside from the indorsement and reinstatement of former president Auer) is to hear charges against four of the class A directors, to remove them if the charges be proven, to amend the by-laws so that the successor directors be elected by the class A stockholders, and further to amend the by-laws so that an effective quorum of directors will be made up of no fewer than half of the directors in office and no fewer than one third of the whole authorized number of directors. No reason appears why the class A stockholders should not be allowed to vote on any or all of those proposals.

The stockholders, by expressing their approval of Mr. Auer's conduct as president and their demand that he be put back in that office, will not be able, directly, to effect that change in officers, but there is nothing invalid in their so expressing themselves and thus putting on notice the directors who will stand for election at the annual meeting. As to purpose (B), that is, amending the charter and by-laws to authorize the stockholders to fill vacancies as to class A directors who have been removed on charges or who have resigned, it seems to be settled law that the stockholders who are empowered to elect directors have the inherent power to remove them for cause (*Matter of Koch*, 257 N.Y. 318, 321, 322). Of course, as the *Koch* case points out, there must be the service of specific charges, adequate notice and full opportunity of meeting the accusations, but there is no present showing of any lack of any of those in this instance. Since these particular stockholders have the right to elect nine directors and to remove them on proven charges, it is not inappropriate that they should use their further power to amend the by-laws to elect the successors of such directors as shall be removed after hearing, or who shall resign pending hearing.

Quite pertinent at this point is *Rogers v. Hill* (289 U.S. 582, 589) which made light of an argument that stockholders, by giving power to the directors to make by-laws, had lost their own power to make them; quoting a New Jersey case, the United States Supreme Court said: " 'It would be preposterous to leave the real owners of the corporate property at the mercy of their agents, and the law has not done so.' " Such a change in the by-laws, dealing with class A directors only, has no effect on the voting rights of the common stockholders, which rights have to do with the selection of the remaining two directors only. True, the certificate of incorporation authorizes the board of directors to remove any director on charges, but we do not consider that provision as an abdication by the stockholders of their own traditional, inherent power to remove their own directors. Rather, it provides an additional method. Were that not so, the stockholders might find themselves without effective remedy in a case where a majority of the directors were accused of wrongdoing and, obviously, would be unwilling to remove themselves from office.

We fail to see, in the proposal to allow class A stockholders to fill vacancies as to class A directors, any impairment or any violation of paragraph (h) of article Three of the certificate of incorporation, which says that class A stock has exclusive voting rights with respect to all matters "other than the election of directors." That negative language should not be taken to mean that class A stockholders, who have an absolute right to elect nine of these eleven directors, cannot amend their by-laws to guarantee a similar right in the class A stockholders, and to the exclusion of common stockholders, to fill vacancies in the class A group of directors.

There is urged upon us the impracticability and unfairness of constituting the numerous stockholders a tribunal to hear charges made by themselves, and the incongruity of letting the stockholders hear and pass on those charges by proxy. Such questions are really not before us at all on this appeal. The charges here are not, on their face, frivolous or inconsequential, and all that we are holding as to the charges is that a meeting may be held to deal with them. Any director illegally removed can have his remedy in the courts....

[The court did not address purpose D, concerning the by-law quorum change, with any further particularity.]

Campbell v. Loew's, Inc.

Delaware Court of Chancery
134 A.2d 852 (1957)

SEITZ, CHANCELLOR.

This is the decision on plaintiff's request for a preliminary injunction to restrain the holding of a stockholders' meeting or alternatively to prevent the meeting from considering certain matters or to prevent the voting of certain proxies. Certain other relief is also requested.

The corporate defendant appeared and resisted the motion. The four individual defendants, who are directors, were given until September 23, to appear and as of this date (September 19, 1957) have not appeared. Consequently, reference to "defendant" will embrace only the corporation unless otherwise indicated.

Some background is in order if the many difficult and novel issues are to be understood. Two factions have been fighting for control of Loew's. One faction is headed by Joseph Tomlinson (hereafter "Tomlinson faction") while the other is headed by the President of Loew's, Joseph Vogel (hereafter "Vogel faction"). At the annual meeting of stockholders last February a compromise was reached by which each nominated six directors and they in turn nominated a thirteenth or neutral director. But the battle had only begun. Passing by much of the controversy, we come to the July 17–18 period of this year when two of the six Vogel directors and the thirteenth or neutral director resigned. A quorum is seven.

On the 19th of July the Tomlinson faction asked that a directors' meeting be called for July 30 to consider, inter alia, the problem of filling director vacancies. On the eve of this meeting one of the Tomlinson directors resigned. This left five Tomlinson directors and four Vogel directors in office. Only the five Tomlinson directors attended the July 30 meeting. They purported to fill two of the director vacancies and to take other action. This Court has now ruled that for want of a quorum the two directors were not validly elected and the subsequent action taken at that meeting was invalid. *See Tomlinson v. Loew's, Inc.*, Del. Ch., 134 A.2d 518 (1957).

On July 29, the day before the noticed directors' meeting, Vogel, as president, sent out a notice calling a stockholders' meeting for September 12 for the following purposes:

1. to fill director vacancies.

2. to amend the by-laws to increase the number of the board from 13 to 19; to increase the quorum from 7 to 10 and to elect six additional directors.

3. to remove Stanley Meyer and Joseph Tomlinson as directors and to fill such vacancies.

Still later, another notice for a September 12 stockholders' meeting as well as a proxy statement went out over the signature of Joseph R. Vogel, as president. It was accompanied by a letter from Mr. Vogel dated August 9, 1957, soliciting stockholder support for the matters noticed in the call of the meeting, and particularly seeking to fill the vacancies and newly created directorships with "his" nominees. Promptly thereafter, plaintiff began this action. An order was entered requiring that the stockholders' meeting be adjourned until October 15, to give the Court more time to decide the serious and novel issues raised.

[The court first considered the authority of Vogel, the president, to call the stockholders' meeting for the purposes announced in his September 12 notice. It concluded that he did have authority to call that meeting.]

Plaintiff next argues that the stockholders have no power between annual meetings to elect directors to fill newly created directorships.

Plaintiff argues in effect that since the Loew's by-laws provide that the stockholders may fill "vacancies," and since our Courts have construed "vacancy" not to embrace "newly created directorships" (*Automatic Steel Products v. Johnston*, 31 Del. Ch. 469, 64 A.2d 416), the attempted call by the president for the purpose of filling newly created directorships was invalid.

Conceding that "vacancy" as used in the by-laws does not embrace "newly created directorships," that does not resolve this problem. I say this because in *Moon v. Moon Motor Car Co.*, 17 Del. Ch. 176, 151 A. 298, it was held that the stockholders had the inherent right between annual meetings to fill newly created directorships. There is no basis to distinguish the *Moon* case unless it be because the statute has since been amended to provide that not only vacancies but newly created directorships "may be filled by a majority of the directors then in office … unless it is otherwise provided in the certificate of incorporation or the by-laws…." 8 Del. C. §223. Obviously, the amendment to include new directors is not worded so as to make the statute exclusive. It does not prevent the stockholders from filling the new directorships.

Is there any reason to consider the absence of a reference in the by-laws to new directorships to be significant? I think not. The by-law relied upon by plaintiff was adopted long before the statutory amendment and it does not purport to be exclusive in its operation. It would take a strong by-law language to warrant the conclusion that those adopting the by-laws intended to prohibit the stockholders from filling new directorships between annual meetings. No such strong language appears here and I do not think the implication is warranted in view of the subject matter.

I therefore conclude that the stockholders of Loew's do have the right between annual meetings to elect directors to fill newly created directorships.

Plaintiff next argues that the shareholders of a Delaware corporation have no power to remove directors from office even for cause and thus the call for that purpose is invalid. The defendant naturally takes a contrary position.

While there are some cases suggesting the contrary, I believe that the stockholders have the power to remove a director for cause. See *Auer v. Dressel*, 306 N.Y. 427, 118 N.E.2d 590; compare *Bruch v. National Guarantee Credit Corp.*, 13 Del. Ch. 180, 116 A. 738. This power must be implied when we consider that otherwise a director who is guilty of the worst sort of violation of his duty could nevertheless remain on the board. It is hardly to be believed that a director who is disclosing the corporation's trade secrets to a competitor would be immune from removal by the stockholders. Other examples, such as embezzlement of corporate funds, etc., come readily to mind.

But plaintiff correctly states that there is no provision in our statutory law providing for the removal of directors by stockholder action. In contrast he calls attention to § 142 of 8 Del. C., dealing with officers, which specifically refers to the possibility of a vacancy in an office by removal. He also notes that the Loew's by-laws provide for the removal of officers and employees but not directors. From these facts he argues that it was intended that directors not be removed even for cause. I believe the statute and by-law are of course some evidence to support plaintiff's contention. But when we seek to exclude the existence of a power by implication, I think it is pertinent to consider whether the absence of the power can be said to subject the corporation to the possibility of real damage. I say this because we seek intention and such a factor would be relevant to that issue. Considering the damage a director might be able to inflict upon his corporation, I believe the doubt must be resolved by construing the statutes and by-laws as leaving untouched the question of director removal for cause. This being so, the Court is free to conclude on reason that the stockholders have such inherent power.

I therefore conclude that as a matter of Delaware corporation law the stockholders do have the power to remove directors for cause. I need not and do not decide whether the stockholders can be appropriate charter or by-law provision deprive themselves of this right.

Plaintiff next argues that the removal of Tomlinson and Meyer as directors would violate the right of minority shareholders to representation on the board and would be contrary to the policy of the Delaware law regarding cumulative voting. Plaintiff contends that where there is cumulative voting, as provided by the Loew's certificate, a director cannot be removed by the stockholders even for cause.

It is true that the Chancellor noted in the *Bruch* case that the provision for cumulative voting in the Delaware law was one reason why directors should not be considered to have the power to remove a fellow director even for cause. And it is certainly evident that if not carefully supervised the existence of a power in the stockholders to remove a director even for cause could be abused and used to defeat cumulative voting.

Does this mean that there can be no removal of a director by the stockholders for cause in any case where cumulative voting exists? The conflicting considerations involved make the answer to this question far from easy. Some states have passed statutes dealing with this problem but Delaware has not. The possibility of stockholder removal action designed to circumvent the effect of cumulative voting is evident. This is particularly true where the removal vote is, as here, by mere majority vote. On the other hand, if we assume a case where a director's presence or action is clearly damaging the corporation and its stockholders in a substantial way, it is difficult to see why that director should be free to continue such damage merely because he was elected under a cumulative voting provision.

On balance, I conclude that the stockholders have the power to remove a director for cause even where there is a provision for cumulative voting. I think adequate protection is afforded not only by the legal safeguards announced in this opinion but by the existence of a remedy to test the validity of any such action, if taken.

The foregoing points constitute all of the arguments advanced by plaintiff which go to the validity of the call of the meeting for the purposes stated. It follows from my various conclusions that the meeting was validly called by the president to consider the matters noticed.

I turn next to plaintiff's charges relating to procedural defects and to irregularities in proxy solicitation by the Vogel group.

Plaintiff's first point is that the stockholders can vote to remove a director for cause only after such director has been given adequate notice of charges of grave impropriety and afforded an opportunity to be heard....

[I]t is certainly true that when the shareholders attempt to remove a director for cause, "there must be the service of specific charges, adequate notice and full opportunity of meeting the accusation...." *See Auer v. Dressel*, above. While it involved an invalid attempt by directors to remove a fellow director for cause, nevertheless, this same general standard was recognized in *Bruch v. National Guarantee Credit Corp.*, above. The Chancellor said that the power of removal could not "be exercised in an arbitrary manner. The accused director would be entitled to be heard in his own defense."

Plaintiff asserts that no specific charges have been served upon the two directors sought to be ousted; that the notice of the special meeting fails to contain a specific statement of the charges; that the proxy statement which accompanied the notice also failed to notify the stockholders of the specific charges; and that it does not inform the stockholders that the accused must be afforded an opportunity to meet the accusations before a vote is taken.

Matters for stockholder consideration need not be conducted with the same formality as judicial proceedings. The proxy statement specifically recites that the two directors are sought to be removed for the reasons stated in the president's accompanying letter. Both directors involved received copies of the letter. Under the circumstances I think it must be said that the two directors involved were served with notice of the charges against them. It is true, as plaintiff says, that the notice and the proxy statement failed to contain a specific statement of charges. But as indicated, I believe the accompanying letter was sufficient compliance with the notice requirement.

Contrary to plaintiff's contention, I do not believe the material sent out had to advise the stockholders that the accused must be afforded an opportunity to defend the charges before the stockholders voted. Such an opportunity had to be afforded as a matter of law and the failure to so advise them did not affect the necessity for compliance with the law. Thus, no prejudice is shown.

I next consider plaintiff's contention that the charges against the two directors do not constitute "cause" as a matter of law. It would take too much space to narrate in detail the contents of the president's letter. I must therefore give my summary of its charges. First of all, it charges that the two directors (Tomlinson and Meyer) failed to cooperate with Vogel in his announced program for rebuilding the company; that their purpose has been to put themselves in control; that they made baseless accusations against him and other management personnel and attempted to divert him from his normal duties as president by bombarding him with correspondence containing unfounded charges and other similar acts; that they moved into the company's building, accompanied by lawyers and accountants, and immediately proceeded upon a planned scheme of harassment. They called for many records, some going back twenty years, and were rude to the personnel. Tomlinson sent daily letters to the directors making serious charges directly and by means of innuendos and misinterpretations.

Are the foregoing charges, if proved, legally sufficient to justify the ouster of the two directors by the stockholders? I am satisfied that a charge that the directors desired to take over control of the corporation is not a reason for their ouster. Standing alone, it is a perfectly legitimate objective which is a part of the very fabric of corporate existence. Nor is a charge of lack of cooperation a legally sufficient basis for removal for cause.

The next charge is that these directors, in effect, engaged in a calculated plan of harassment to the detriment of the corporation. Certainly a director may examine books, ask questions, etc., in the discharge of his duty, but a point can be reached when his actions exceed the call of duty and become deliberately obstructive. In such a situation, if his actions constitute a real burden on the corporation then the stockholders are entitled to relief. The charges in this area made by the Vogel letter are legally sufficient to justify the stockholders in voting to remove such directors. In so concluding I of course express no opinion as to the truth of the charges.

I therefore conclude that the charge of "a planned scheme of harassment" as detailed in the letter constitutes a justifiable legal basis for removing a director.

I next consider whether the directors sought to be removed have been given a reasonable opportunity to be heard by the stockholders on the charges made.

The corporate defendant freely admits that it has flatly refused to give the five Tomlinson directors or the plaintiff a stockholders' list. Any doubt about the matter was removed by the statement of defendant's counsel in open court at the argument that no such list would be supplied. The Vogel faction has physical control of the corporate offices and facilities. By this action the corporation through the Vogel group has deliberately refused to afford the directors in question an adequate opportunity to be heard by the stockholders on the charges made. This is contrary to the legal requirements which must be met before a director can be removed for cause....

There seems to be an absence of cases detailing the appropriate procedure for submitting a question of director removal for cause for stockholder consideration. I am satisfied, however, that to the extent the matter is to be voted upon by the use of proxies, such proxies may be solicited only after the accused directors are afforded an opportunity to present their case to the stockholders. This means, in my opinion, that an opportunity must be provided such directors to present their defense to the stockholders by a statement which must accompany or precede the initial solicitation of proxies seeking authority to vote for the removal of such director for cause. If not provided then such proxies may not be voted for removal. And the corporation has a duty to see that this opportunity is given the directors at its expense. Admittedly, no such opportunity was given the two directors involved. Indeed, the corporation admittedly refused to supply them with a stockholders' list.

To require anything less than the foregoing is to deprive the stockholders of the opportunity to consider the case made by both sides before voting and would make a mockery of the requirement that a director sought to be removed for cause is entitled to an opportunity to be heard before the stockholders vote....

Section IV
Deadlocks, Oppression, and Dissolution

When shareholders in a publicly traded company are unhappy with the management or each other, they may sever their relationship with the company simply by selling their stock. In contrast, shareholders in closely held corporations, lacking such a market, find it difficult to exit from the company. This difficulty and the fact that closely held corporation shareholders often depend on the company for their livelihood exacerbate the problems caused by conflicts among participants in the enterprise. For the corporate lawyer, conflicts are particularly troublesome when they result either in deadlock or in an attempt by one group, usually the majority shareholders, to defeat the legitimate expectations of another group, usually the minority. One reason is that conflict situations raise difficult ethical issues for the counseling attorney. (*See* Model Rule of Professional Conduct 2.2.) A second reason is that the remedy is often draconian — dissolution of an economically viable corporation. The cases that follow explore these issues.

A. Deadlocks

Deadlocks at either the shareholder or the director level can create some of a corporation's most serious problems. There are many possible unpleasant scenarios involving deadlocks. The one that usually comes to mind is a corporation whose actors are deadlocked; it is unable to act. That can be a serious problem for a corporation and its shareholders, but it is far from the worst deadlock scenario. Since the president has the power to act for the corporation on any matter that is within the corporation's usual course of business, when the board is deadlocked, the president can operate relatively unfettered. Since the president typically also is a board member, that means that he or she can put into play many of the wishes of one board faction, perhaps to the substantial detriment of some shareholders.

Probably the worst deadlock scenarios occur when the shareholders are deadlocked and cannot replace a board that is dominated by one shareholder faction. The next case offers a good example.

Hall v. Hall

Missouri Court of Appeals
506 S.W.2d 42 (1974)

Clark, Special Judge.

This action involves a dispute among shareholders in a closely held corporation. The facts are not in dispute.

Respondent Musselman and Hall Contractors, Inc. (hereafter the corporation) is a Missouri corporation, the corporate stock of which was wholly owned immediately prior to September 19, 1969 in equal proportions by Edward H. Hall and respondent Harry L. Hall. On the last mentioned date, Edward H. Hall died leaving his widow, appellant surviving him. Appellant thereafter succeeded to a fifty percent stock interest in the corporation in her representative capacity as the duly appointed and acting executrix of the estate of her deceased husband and is also interested as residuary devisee of the estate.

Prior to Edward Hall's death, he and respondent Harry Hall were the only directors of the corporation. Acting to fill the vacancy created by the death of Edward, respondent Harry Hall appointed his wife, respondent Florence E. Hall, as a director of the corporation and thereafter, acting as the then board of directors, they appointed themselves as president and vice-president of the corporation. To the date of the filing of this action, no further election of directors or officers has been held and the individual respondents have continued to serve as the only directors and officers of the corporation.

Upon the failure of the individual respondents to call or convene the required annual meeting of the corporation, appellant by written and published notice called an annual meeting for the second Tuesday in May, 1970, such being the date specified in the corporate by-laws. Appellant appeared at the registered office of the corporation to participate in the business of the meeting and to vote the shares held by her in her representative capacity, but respondent Harry Hall, the only other shareholder, failed and refused to attend. The equal division of stock requires the participation of both shareholders to achieve a quorum. Being unable to transact any business without the vote of the shares of the other stockholder, appellant has subsequently adjourned the 1970 annual meeting from week to week.

Subsequent to September 19, 1969, the individual respondents have been in practical control of the corporation. As no election of directors could be held, respondents have continued in office by reason of the failure to elect or qualify any successors. At a special meeting of directors held August 6, 1970, the individual respondents by resolution directed the offering and sale of 3000 shares of the capital stock of the corporation being the balance of authorized but unissued stock. The purchase or offering price was set at $10.00 per share. Appellant indicated her desire and ability to exercise her preemptive right to purchase one-half of the additional stock so offered but contended that the stock issue would be invalid having been approved by directors unlawfully holding office.

In her petition to the court below, appellant sought to enjoin respondent Harry Hall from refusing to attend shareholders' meetings of the corporation, to enjoin the individual respondents from establishing a terminal date for exercise of preemptive purchase rights for the new issue and from continuing to act as directors and officers of the corporation pending a meeting of shareholders. On the motion of respondents asserting failure to state a cause of action, [appellant's] petition was dismissed and this appeal has resulted....

The substance of appellant's complaint is that her fifty percent ownership interest in the corporation has been rendered impotent by the refusal of respondent Harry Hall to attend and participate in stockholders' meetings. Of course, such is an inevitable consequence where disputes between equal shareholders occur as [the Missouri corporation statute] constitutes a quorum as the majority of outstanding shares entitled to vote and conditions valid corporate acts on the decision of majority of the quorum. Recognizing then that the owners of fifty percent or more of the corporate stock may frustrate the conduct of business at stockholder's meetings, is such inaction unlawful and if not, do remaining stockholders have a remedy?

The very nature of the corporate form is the creation by statute of an entity separate and apart from the individuals who own, manage and operate it. One who acquires corporate stock obtains an interest in the corporate assets after payment of corporate debts and a right to participate in management which he may or may not exercise. The holder of shares is under no obligation whatever to the corporation other than to make full payment of the consideration for which the shares are issued. As participation by a shareholder in management of corporate affairs is voluntary, it necessarily follows that no shareholder may be compelled to attend or participate in shareholders' meetings. Any different rule would contradict the distinction which separates the corporate existence from the identity of its shareholders and which vests management responsibilities in the directors.

Conceding that the failure of respondent Harry Hall to attend stockholders' meetings has injured appellant in preventing her from participating in the management of the corporation, if respondent is under no legal duty to participate, how may a court of equity compel him by injunction to attend and vote at a stockholders' meeting? No maxim of equity may be invoked to destroy an existing legal right nor may equity create a right at law which does not exist....

No allegation was made by appellant of any contractual obligation on the part of respondent Harry Hall to attend and participate in stockholders' meetings and none exists by statute or rule of law. It therefore follows of necessity that a court of equity may not by injunction compel that for which no legal duty lies. The trial court was correct in refusing to grant the mandatory injunction requested.

Although appellant's petition alleged oppression by respondent Harry Hall in the matter of salary payments from corporate funds to the individual respondents and further alleged dilution, wasting and diversion of corporate assets, no suggestion is made as to why appellant may not move to dissolve the corporation under [the Missouri corporation statute], or, as the trial court suggested, try by quo warranto the right of the individual respondents to continue in the offices of directors and corporate officers when the statutory requirements for annual stockholders' meetings have been subverted. As is noted in Fletcher, Cyclopedia Corporations, Vol. 5, Chapter 13, p. 22, although quo warranto as a remedy to oust one from an office illegally held would not produce a judgment requiring an election of officers, it might produce a vacancy necessitating one. Alternative methods whereby appellant may obtain redress do not require ruling on this appeal....

B. Oppression and Dissension

Dissension among shareholders can arise in many different types of situations, as, for example, when the actions of one shareholder group work to the financial disadvantage of another. The cases and statutory provisions that follow present several approaches to dealing with dissension among shareholders, and, as appropriate, also with deadlock. Assess the merits of each approach.

Donahue v. Rodd Electrotype Co.
Massachusetts Supreme Judicial Court
328 N.E.2d 505 (1975)

TAURO, CHIEF JUSTICE.

The plaintiff, Euphemia Donahue, a minority stockholder in the Rodd Electrotype Company of New England, Inc. (Rodd Electrotype), a Massachusetts corporation, brings this suit against the directors of Rodd Electrotype, Charles H. Rodd, Frederick I. Rodd and Mr. Harold E. Magnuson, against Harry C. Rodd, a former director, officer, and controlling stockholder of Rodd Electrotype and against Rodd Electrotype (hereinafter called defendants). The plaintiff seeks to rescind Rodd Electrotype's purchase of Harry Rodd's shares in Rodd Electrotype and to compel Harry Rodd "to repay to the corporation the purchase price of said shares, $36,000, together with interest from the date of purchase." The plaintiff alleges that the defendants caused the corporation to purchase the shares in violation of their fiduciary duty to her, a minority stockholder of Rodd Electrotype.

The trial judge, after hearing oral testimony, dismissed the plaintiff's bill on the merits. He found that the purchase was without prejudice to the plaintiff and implicitly found that the transaction had been carried out in good faith and with inherent fairness. The Appeals Court affirmed with costs. The case is before us on the plaintiff's application for further appellate review....

The evidence may be summarized as follows: In 1935, the defendant, Harry C. Rodd, began his employment with Rodd Electrotype, then styled the Royal Electrotype

Company of New England, Inc. (Royal of New England). At that time, the company was a wholly-owned subsidiary of a Pennsylvania corporation, the Royal Electrotype Company (Royal Electrotype). Mr. Rodd's advancement within the company was rapid. The following year he was elected a director, and, in 1946, he succeeded to the position of general manager and treasurer.

In 1936, the plaintiff's husband, Joseph Donahue (now deceased), was hired by Royal of New England as a "finisher" of electrotype plates. His duties were confined to operational matters within the plant. Although he ultimately achieved the positions of plant superintendent (1946) and corporate vice president (1955), Donahue never participated in the "management" aspect of the business.

In the years preceding 1955, the parent company, Royal Electrotype, made available to Harry Rodd and Joseph Donahue shares of the common stock in its subsidiary, Royal of New England. Harry Rodd took advantage of the opportunities offered to him and acquired 200 shares for $20 a share. Joseph Donahue, at the suggestion of Harry Rodd, who hoped to interest Donahue in the business, eventually obtained fifty shares in two twenty-five share lots priced at $20 a share. The parent company at all times retained 725 of the 1,000 outstanding shares....

In June of 1955, Royal of New England purchased all 725 of its shares owned by its parent company....

The stock purchases left Harry Rodd in control of Royal of New England. Early in 1955, before the purchases, he had assumed the presidency of the company. His 200 shares gave him a dominant eighty per cent interest. Joseph Donahue, at this time, was the only minority stockholder.

Subsequent events reflected Harry Rodd's dominant influence. In June, 1960, more than a year after the last obligation to Royal Electrotype had been discharged, the company was renamed the Rodd Electrotype Company of New England, Inc. In 1962, Charles H. Rodd, Harry Rodd's son (a defendant here), who had long been a company employee working in the plant, became corporate vice president. In 1963, he joined his father on the board of directors. In 1964, another son, Frederick I. Rodd (also a defendant), replaced Joseph Donahue as plant superintendent. By 1965, Harry Rodd had evidently decided to reduce his participation in corporate management. That year Charles Rodd succeeded him as president and general manager of Rodd Electrotype.

From 1959 to 1967, Harry Rodd pursued what may fairly be termed a gift program by which he distributed the majority of his shares equally among his two sons and his daughter, Phyllis E. Mason. Each child received thirty-nine shares. Two shares were returned to the corporate treasury in 1966.

We come now to the events of 1970 which form the grounds for the plaintiff's complaint. In May of 1970, Harry Rodd was seventy-seven years old. The record indicates that for some time he had not enjoyed the best of health and that he had undergone a number of operations. His sons wished him to retire. Mr. Rodd was not averse to this suggestion. However, he insisted that some financial arrangements be made with respect to his remaining eighty-one shares of stock. A number of conferences ensued. Harry Rodd and Charles Rodd (representing the company) negotiated terms of purchase for forty-five shares which, Charles Rodd testified, would reflect the book value and liquidating value of the shares.

A special board meeting convened on July 13, 1970. As the first order of business, Harry Rodd resigned his directorship of Rodd Electrotype. The remaining incumbent directors, Charles Rodd and Mr. Harold E. Magnuson (clerk of the company and a defendant and defense attorney in the instant suit), elected Frederick Rodd to replace his father. The three directors then authorized Rodd Electrotype's president (Charles Rodd) to execute an agreement between Harry Rodd and the company in which the company would purchase forty-five shares for $800 a share ($36,000).

The stock purchase agreement was formalized between the parties on July 13, 1970. Two days later, a sale pursuant to the July 13 agreement was consummated. At approximately the same time, Harry Rodd resigned his last corporate office, that of treasurer.

Harry Rodd completed divestiture of his Rodd Electrotype stock in the following year. As was true of his previous gifts, his later divestments gave equal representation to his children. Two shares were sold to each child on July 15, 1970, for $800 a share. Each was given ten shares in March, 1971. Thus, in March, 1971, the shareholdings in Rodd Electrotype were apportioned as follows: Charles Rodd, Frederick Rodd and Phyllis Mason each held fifty-one shares; the Donahues held fifty shares.

A special meeting of the stockholders of the company was held on March 30, 1971. At the meeting, Charles Rodd, company president and general manager, reported the tentative results of an audit conducted by the company auditors and reported generally on the company events of the year. For the first time, the Donahues learned that the corporation had purchased Harry Rodd's shares. According to the minutes of the meeting, following Charles Rodd's report, the Donahues raised questions about the purchase. They then voted against a resolution, ultimately adopted by the remaining stockholders, to approve Charles Rodd's report. Although the minutes of the meeting show that the stockholders unanimously voted to accept a second resolution ratifying all acts of the company president (he executed the stock purchase agreement) in the preceding year, the trial judge found, and there was evidence to support his finding, that the Donahues did not ratify the purchase of Harry Rodd's shares.

A few weeks after the meeting, the Donahues, acting through their attorney, offered their shares to the corporation on the same terms given to Harry Rodd. Mr. Harold E. Magnuson replied by letter that the corporation would not purchase the shares and was not in a financial position to do so. This suit followed.

In her argument before this court, the plaintiff has characterized the corporate purchase of Harry Rodd's shares as an unlawful distribution of corporate assets to controlling stockholders. She urges that the distribution constitutes a breach of the fiduciary duty owed by the Rodds, as controlling stockholders, to her, a minority stockholder in the enterprise, because the Rodds failed to accord her an equal opportunity to sell her shares to the corporation. The defendants reply that the stock purchase was within the powers of the corporation and met the requirements of good faith and inherent fairness imposed on a fiduciary in his dealings with the corporation. They assert that there is no right to equal opportunity in corporate stock purchases for the corporate treasury. For the reasons hereinafter noted, we agree with the plaintiff and reverse the decree of the Superior Court. However, we limit the applicability of our holding to "closely held corporations," as hereinafter defined. Whether the holding should apply to other corporations is left for decision in another case, on a proper record.

A. *Closely Held Corporations.* In previous opinions, we have alluded to the distinctive nature of the closely held corporation, but have never defined precisely what is meant by a closely held corporation. There is no single, generally accepted definition. Some commentators emphasize an "integration of ownership and management" (Note, Statutory Assistance for Closely Held Corporations, 71 Harv. L. Rev. 1498 [1958]), in which the stockholders occupy most management positions. Others focus on the number of stockholders and the nature of the market for the stock. In this view, closely held corporations have few stockholders; there is little market for corporate stock. The Supreme Court of Illinois adopted this latter view in *Galler v. Galler*, 32 Ill.2d 16, 203 N.E.2d 577 (1965): "For our purposes, a closely held corporation is one in which the stock is held in a few hands, or in a few families, and wherein it is not at all, or only rarely, dealt in by buying or selling." *Id.* at 27, 203 N.E.2d at 583. We accept aspects of both definitions. We deem a closely held corporation to be typified by: (1) a small number of stockholders; (2) no ready market for the corporate stock; and (3) substantial majority stockholder participation in the management, direction and operations of the corporation.

As thus defined, the closely held corporation bears striking resemblance to a partnership. Commentators and courts have noted that the closely held corporation is often little more than an "incorporated" or "chartered" partnership. The stockholders "clothe" their partnership "with the benefits peculiar to a corporation, limited liability, perpetuity and the like." *In the Matter of Surchin v. Approved Bus. Mach. Co., Inc.*, 55 Misc.2d 888, 889, 286 N.Y.S.2d 580, 581 (Sup. Ct. 1967). In essence, though, the enterprise remains one in which ownership is limited to the original parties or transferees of their stock to whom the other stockholders have agreed, in which ownership and management are in the same hands, and in which the owners are quite dependent on one another for the success of the enterprise. Many closely held corporations are "really partnerships, between two or three people who contribute their capital, skills, experience and labor." *Kruger v. Gerth*, 16 N.Y.2d 802, 805, 263 N.Y.S.2d 1, 3, 210 N.E.2d 355, 356 (1965) (Desmond, C. J., dissenting). Just as in a partnership, the relationship among the stockholders must be one of trust, confidence and absolute loyalty if the enterprise is to succeed. Closely held corporations with substantial assets and with more numerous stockholders are no different from smaller closely held corporations in this regard. All participants rely on the fidelity and abilities of those stockholders who hold office. Disloyalty and self-seeking conduct on the part of any stockholder will engender bickering, corporate stalemates, and, perhaps, efforts to achieve dissolution.

In *Helms v. Duckworth*, 249 F.2d 482, 101 U.S. App. D.C. 390 (1957), the United States Court of Appeals for the District of Columbia Circuit had before it a stockholders' agreement providing for the purchase of the shares of a deceased stockholder by the surviving stockholder in a small "two-man" closely held corporation. The court held the surviving stockholder to a duty "to deal fairly, honestly, and openly with ... [his] fellow stockholders." *Id.* at 487. Judge Burger, now Chief Justice Burger, writing for the court, emphasized the resemblance of the two-man closely held corporation to a partnership: "In an intimate business venture such as this, stockholders of a closely held corporation occupy a position similar to that of joint adventurers and partners. While courts have sometimes declared stockholders 'do not bear toward each other that same relation of trust and confidence which prevails in partnerships,' this view ignores the practical realities of the organization and functioning of a small 'two-man' corporation organized to carry on a small business enterprise in which the stockholders, directors, and managers are the same persons." *Id.* at 486.

Although the corporate form provides the above-mentioned advantages for the stockholders (limited liability, perpetuity, and so forth), it also supplies an opportunity for the majority stockholders to oppress or disadvantage minority stockholders. The minority is vulnerable to a variety of oppressive devices, termed "freeze-outs," which the majority may employ. An authoritative study of such "freeze-outs" enumerates some of the possibilities: "The squeezers [those who employ the freeze-out techniques] may refuse to declare dividends; they may drain off the corporation's earnings in the form of exorbitant salaries and bonuses to the majority shareholder-officers and perhaps to their relatives, or in the form of high rent by the corporation for property leased from majority shareholders ... they may deprive minority shareholders of corporate offices and of employment by the company; they may cause the corporation to sell its assets at an inadequate price to the majority shareholders...." F.H. O'Neal and J. Derwin, Expulsion or Oppression of Business Associates, 42 (1961). In particular, the power of the board of directors, controlled by the majority, to declare or withhold dividends and to deny the minority employment is easily converted to a device to disadvantage minority stockholders.

The minority can, of course, initiate suit against the majority and their directors. Self-serving conduct by directors is proscribed by the director's fiduciary obligation to the corporation. However, in practice, the plaintiff will find difficulty in challenging dividend or employment policies. Such policies are considered to be within the judgment of the directors.... Although contractual provisions in an "agreement of association and articles of organization" or in by-laws have justified decrees in this jurisdiction ordering dividend declarations, generally, plaintiffs who seek judicial assistance against corporate dividend or employment policies do not prevail.

Thus, when these types of "freeze-outs" are attempted by the majority stockholders, the minority stockholders, cut off from all corporation-related revenues, must either suffer their losses or seek a buyer for their shares. Many minority stockholders will be unwilling or unable to wait for an alteration in majority policy. Typically, the minority stockholder in a closely held corporation has a substantial percentage of his personal assets invested in the corporation. The stockholder may have anticipated that his salary from his position with the corporation would be his livelihood. Thus, he cannot afford to wait passively. He must liquidate his investment in the closely held corporation in order to reinvest the funds in income-producing enterprises.

At this point, the true plight of the minority stockholder in a closely held corporation becomes manifest. He cannot easily reclaim his capital. In a large public corporation, the oppressed or dissident minority stockholder could sell his stock in order to extricate some of his invested capital. By definition, this market is not available for shares in the closely held corporation. In a partnership, a partner who feels abused by his fellow partners may cause dissolution by his "express will … at any time" and recover his share of partnership assets and accumulated profits. If dissolution results in a breach of the partnership articles, the culpable partner will be liable in damages.

By contrast, the stockholder in the closely held corporation or "incorporated partnership" may achieve dissolution and recovery of his share of the enterprise assets only by compliance with the rigorous terms of the applicable chapter of the General Laws. "The dissolution of a corporation which is a creature of the Legislature is primarily a legislative function, and the only authority courts have to deal with this subject is the power conferred upon them by the Legislature." *Leventhal v. Atlantic Fin. Corp.*, 316 Mass. 194, 205, 55 N.E.2d 20, 26 (1944). To secure dissolution of the ordinary closely held corporation subject to [the Massachusetts corporation statute], the stockholder, in the absence of corporate deadlock, must own at least fifty percent of the shares or have the advantage of a favorable provision in the articles of organization. The minority stockholder, by definition lacking fifty per cent of the corporate shares, can never "authorize" the corporation to file a petition for dissolution … by his own vote. He will seldom have at his disposal the requisite favorable provision in the articles of organization.

Thus, in a closely held corporation, the minority stockholders may be trapped in a disadvantageous situation. No outsider would knowingly assume the position of the disadvantaged minority. The outsider would have the same difficulties. To cut losses, the minority stockholder may be compelled to deal with the majority. This is the capstone of the majority plan. Majority "freeze-out" schemes which withhold dividends are designed to compel the minority to relinquish stock at inadequate prices. When the minority stockholder agrees to sell out at less than fair value, the majority has won.

Because of the fundamental resemblance of the closely held corporation to the partnership, the trust and confidence which are essential to this scale and manner of enterprise, and the inherent danger to minority interests in the closely held corporation, we hold that stockholders in the closely held corporation owe one another substantially the same fiduciary duty in the operation of the enterprise that partners owe to one another. In our previous decisions, we have defined the standard of duty owed by partners to one another, as the "utmost good faith and loyalty." *Cardullo v. Landau*, 329 Mass. 5, 8, 105 N.E.2d 843 (1952); *DeCotis v. D'Antona*, 350 Mass. 165, 168, 214 N.E.2d 21 (1966). Stockholders in closely held corporations must discharge their management and stockholder responsibilities in conformity with this strict good faith standard. They may not act out of avarice, expediency or self-interest in derogation of their duty of loyalty to the other stockholders and to the corporation.

We contrast this strict good faith standard with the somewhat less stringent standard of fiduciary duty to which directors and stockholders of all corporations must adhere in the discharge of their corporate responsibilities. Corporate directors are held to a good faith and inherent fairness standard of conduct and are not "permitted to serve two masters whose interests are antagonistic." *Spiegel v. Beacon Participations, Inc.*, 297 Mass. 398, 411, 8 N.E.2d 895, 904 (1937). "Their paramount duty is to the corporation, and their personal pecuniary interests are subordinate to that duty." *Durfee v. Durfee & Canning, Inc.*, 323 Mass. 187, 196, 80 N.E.2d 522, 527 (1948).

The more rigorous duty of partners and participants in a joint adventure, here extended to stockholders in a closely held corporation, was described by then Chief Judge Cardozo of the New York Court of Appeals in *Meinhard v. Salmon*, 249 N.Y. 458, 164 N.E. 545 (1928): "Joint adventurers, like copartners, owe to one another, while the enterprise continues, the duty of the finest loyalty. Many forms of conduct permissible in a workaday world for those acting at arm's length, are forbidden to those bound by fiduciary ties.... Not honesty alone, but the punctilio of an honor the most sensitive, is then the standard of behavior." *Id.* at 463–464, 164 N.E. at 546....

... In the instant case, we extend this strict duty of loyalty to all stockholders in closely held corporations. The circumstances which justified findings of relationships of trust and confidence in these particular cases exist universally in modified form in all closely held corporations....

B. *Equal Opportunity in a Closely Held Corporation.* Under settled Massachusetts law, a domestic corporation, unless forbidden by statute, has the power to purchase its own shares. An agreement to reacquire stock "[is] enforceable, subject, at least, to the limitations that the purchase must be made in good faith and without prejudice to creditors and stockholders." *Scriggins v. Thomas Dalby Co.*, [290 Mass. 414, 418, 195 N.E. 749, 752 (1939)]; *Winchell v. Plywood Corp.*, [324 Mass. 171, 174–75, 85 N.E.2d 313, 315 (1949)]. When the corporation reacquiring its own stock is a closely held corporation, the purchase is subject to the additional requirement, in the light of our holding in this opinion, that the stockholders, who, as directors or controlling stockholders, caused the corporation to enter into the stock purchase agreement, must have acted with the utmost good faith and loyalty to the other stockholders.

To meet this test, if the stockholder whose shares were purchased was a member of the controlling group, the controlling stockholders must cause the corporation to offer each stockholder an equal opportunity to sell a ratable number of his shares to the corporation at an identical price. Purchase by the corporation confers substantial benefits on the members of the controlling group whose shares were purchased. These benefits are not available to the minority stockholders if the corporation does not also offer them an opportunity to sell their shares. The controlling group may not, consistent with its strict duty to the minority, utilize its control of the corporation to obtain special advantages and disproportionate benefit from its share ownership.

The benefits conferred by the purchase are twofold: (1) provision of a market for shares; (2) access to corporate assets for personal use. By definition, there is no ready market for shares of a closely held corporation. The purchase creates a market for shares which previously had been unmarketable. It transforms a previously illiquid investment into a liquid one. If the closely held corporation purchases shares only from a member of the controlling group, the controlling stockholder can convert his shares into cash at a time when none of the other stockholders can. Consistent with its strict fiduciary duty, the controlling group may not utilize its control of the corporation to establish an exclusive market in previously unmarketable shares from which the minority stockholders are excluded.

The purchase also distributes corporate assets to the stockholder whose shares were purchased. Unless an equal opportunity is given to all stockholders, the purchase of shares from a member of the controlling group operates as a *preferential* distribution of assets. In exchange for his shares, he receives a percentage of the contributed capital and accumulated profits of the enterprise. The funds he so receives are available for his personal use. The other stockholders benefit from no such access to corporate property and cannot withdraw their shares of the corporate profits and capital in this manner unless the controlling group acquiesces. Although the purchase price for the controlling stockholder's shares may seem fair to the corporation and other stockholders under the tests established in the prior case law, the controlling stockholder whose stock has been purchased has still received a relative advantage over his fellow stockholders, inconsistent with his strict fiduciary duty—an opportunity to turn corporate funds to personal use.

The rule of equal opportunity in stock purchases by closely held corporations provides equal access to these benefits for all stockholders. We hold that, in any case in which the controlling stockholders have exercised their power over the corporation to deny the minority such equal opportunity, the minority shall be entitled to appropriate relief. To the extent that language in *Spiegel v. Beacon Participations, Inc.*, 297 Mass. 398, 431, 8 N.E.2d 895 (1937), and other cases suggests that there is no requirement of equal opportunity for minority stockholders when a closely held corporation purchases shares from a controlling stockholder, it is not to be followed.

C. *Application of the Law to This Case.* We turn now to the application of the learning set forth above to the facts of the instant case.

The strict standard of duty is plainly applicable to the stockholders in Rodd Electrotype. Rodd Electrotype is a closely held corporation. Members of the Rodd and Donahue families are the sole owners of the corporation's stock. In actual numbers, the corporation, immediately prior to the corporate purchase of Harry Rodd's shares, had six stockholders. The shares have not been traded, and no market for them seems to exist. Harry Rodd, Charles Rodd, Frederick Rodd, William G. Mason (Phyllis Mason's husband), and the plaintiff's husband all worked for the corporation. The Rodds have retained the paramount management positions.

Through their control of these management positions and of the majority of the Rodd Electrotype stock, the Rodds effectively controlled the corporation. In testing the stock purchase from Harry Rodd against the applicable strict fiduciary standard, we treat the Rodd family as a single controlling group. We reject the defendants' contention that the Rodd family cannot be treated as a unit for this purpose. From the evidence, it is clear that the Rodd family was a close-knit one with strong community of interest. Harry Rodd had hired his sons to work in the family business, Rodd Electrotype. As he aged, he transferred portions of his stock holdings to his children. Charles Rodd and Frederick Rodd were given positions of responsibility in the business as he withdrew from active management. In these circumstances, it is realistic to assume that appreciation, gratitude, and filial devotion would prevent the younger Rodds from opposing a plan which would provide funds for their father's retirement.

Moreover, a strong motive of interest requires that the Rodds be considered a controlling group. When Charles Rodd and Frederick Rodd were called on to represent the corporation in its dealings with their father, they must have known that further advancement within the corporation and benefits would follow their father's retirement and the purchase of his stock. The corporate purchase would take only forty-five of Harry Rodd's eighty-one shares. The remaining thirty-six shares were to be divided among Harry Rodd's children in equal amounts by gift and sale. Receipt of their portion of the thirty-six shares and purchase by the corporation of forty-five shares would effectively transfer full control of the corporation to Frederick Rodd and Charles Rodd, if they chose to act in concert with each other or if one of them chose to ally with his sister. Moreover, Frederick Rodd was the obvious successor to his father as director and corporate treasurer when those posts became vacant after his father's retirement. Failure to complete the corporate purchase (in other words, impeding their father's retirement plan) would have delayed, and perhaps have suspended indefinitely, the transfer of these benefits to the younger Rodds. They could not be expected to oppose their father's wishes in this matter. Although the defendants are correct when they assert that no express agreement involving a quid pro quo—subsequent stock gifts for votes from the directors—was proved, no express agreement is necessary to demonstrate the identity of interest which disciplines a controlling group acting in unison.

On its face, then, the purchase of Harry Rodd's shares by the corporation is a breach of the duty which the controlling stockholders, the Rodds, owed to the minority stockholders, the plaintiff and her son. The purchase distributed a portion of the corporate assets to Harry Rodd, a member of the controlling group, in exchange for his shares. The plaintiff and her son were not offered an equal opportunity to sell their shares to the corporation. In fact, their efforts to obtain an equal opportunity were rebuffed by the corporate representative. As the trial judge found, they did not, in any manner, ratify the transaction with Harry Rodd.

Because of the foregoing, we hold that the plaintiff is entitled to relief. Two forms of suitable relief are set out hereinafter. The judge below is to enter an appropriate judgment. The judgment may require Harry Rodd to remit $36,000 with interest at the legal rate from July 15, 1970, to Rodd Electrotype in exchange for forty-five shares of Rodd Electrotype treasury stock. This, in substance, is the specific relief requested in the plaintiff's bill of complaint. Interest is manifestly appropriate. A stockholder, who, in violation of his fiduciary duty to the other stockholders, has obtained assets from his corporation and has had those assets available for his own use, must pay for that use. In the alternative, the judgment may require Rodd Electrotype to purchase all of the plaintiff's shares for [the same per share price paid to Harry Rodd].

Notes and Questions

1. *A.W. Chesterton Company, Inc. v. Chesterton*, 128 F.3d 1 (1st Cir. 1997) extends *Donahue* fiduciary obligations to minority shareholders of a closely held corporation. In *Chesterton*, the majority shareholders of a closely held corporation ("Company") claimed that a minority shareholder had breached his fiduciary duty by proposing to transfer his shares to another corporation, thereby defeating the Company's type S tax election. The Court of Appeals enjoined the transfer of the shares and found that the attempted transfer constituted a breach of defendant's fiduciary duties to the Company.

In *Chesterton*, the Company's articles of incorporation had been amended to provide the Company with a right of first refusal if a shareholder wanted to transfer shares to a person other than a family member. If the Company declined to purchase, the shareholder could proceed with the planned sale. After the articles were amended, the Company's shareholders unanimously elected to be governed as a type S entity. When Chesterton proposed to sell his stock in a transaction that would defeat the type S election, the corporation was unable to exercise its option because of financial inability. The court of appeals concluded that in electing type S status, the shareholders had agreed not to act in a way that would jeopardize the Company's tax status, that the proposed sale would defeat shareholder expectations with respect to the election, and that the Company's refusal to purchase Chesterton's shares did not alter those expectations. In addition the court found that Chesterton's proposed transfer would not serve a corporate business purpose, but instead served only Chesterton's individual interests. And finally, the court concluded that Chesterton's compliance with the procedural requirements specified in the articles of incorporation did not relieve him of his fiduciary duties and that appraisal rights were not available to him.

2. The shareholder-to-shareholder fiduciary duty recognized in *Donahue* for closely held corporations is followed in numerous other jurisdictions. *E.g., Fought v. Morris*, 543 So. 2d 167 (Miss. 1989); *Daniels v. Thomas, Dean & Hoskins, Inc.* 804 P.2d 359 (Mont. 1990); *Crosby v. Beam*, 548 N.E.2d 217 (Ohio 1989); *A. Teixeira & Co. v. Teixeira*, 699 A.2d 1383 (R.I. 1997). However, its recognition of the equal opportunity concept is less widely followed. Indeed, even in Massachusetts, the scope of the equal opportunity concept was later narrowed to permit unequal treatment so long as the challenged action is supported by a legitimate business purpose and there is no alternative transaction that is less harmful to the minority shareholders. *See Wilkes v. Springside Nursing Home, Inc.*, 353 N.E.2d 657 (Mass. 1976). In the following case, the Massachusetts Supreme Court again addresses the issue of shareholder-to-shareholder fiduciary duty for closely held corporations.

In re Kemp & Beatley, Inc.

New York Court of Appeals
473 N.E.2d 1173 (1984)

COOKE, CHIEF JUDGE.

… The business concern of Kemp & Beatley, incorporated under the laws of New York, designs and manufactures table linens and sundry tabletop items. The company's stock consists of 1,500 outstanding shares held by eight shareholders. Petitioner Dissin had been employed by the company for 42 years when, in June 1979, he resigned. Prior to resignation, Dissin served as vice-president and a director of Kemp & Beatley. Over the course of his employment, Dissin had acquired stock in the company and currently owns 200 shares.

Petitioner Gardstein, like Dissin, had been a long-time employee of the company. Hired in 1944, Gardstein was for the next 35 years involved in various aspects of the business including material procurement, product design, and plant management. His employment was terminated by the company in December 1980. He currently owns 105 shares of Kemp & Beatley stock.

Apparent unhappiness surrounded petitioners' leaving the employ of the company. Of particular concern was that they no longer received any distribution of the company's earnings. Petitioners considered themselves to be "frozen out" of the company; whereas it had been their experience when with the company to receive a distribution of the company's earnings according to their stockholdings, in the form of either dividends or extra compensation, that distribution was no longer forthcoming.

Gardstein and Dissin, together holding 20.33% of the company's outstanding stock, commenced the instant proceeding in June 1981, seeking dissolution of Kemp & Beatley pursuant to section 1104-a of the Business Corporation Law. Their petition alleged "fraudulent and oppressive" conduct by the company's board of directors such as to render petitioners' stock "a virtually worthless asset." …

The involuntary-dissolution statute (Business Corporation Law, § 1104-a) permits dissolution when a corporation's controlling faction is found guilty of "oppressive action" toward the complaining shareholders. The referee considered oppression to arise when "those in control" of the corporation "have acted in such a manner as to defeat those expectations of the minority stockholders which formed the basis of [their] participation in the venture." The expectations of petitioners that they would not be arbitrarily excluded from gaining a return on their investment and that their stock would be purchased by the corporation upon termination of employment, were deemed defeated by prevailing corporate policies. Dissolution was recommended in the referee's report, subject to giving respondent corporation an opportunity to purchase petitioners' stock.

Supreme Court confirmed the referee's report. It, too, concluded that due to the corporation's new dividend policy petitioners had been prevented from receiving any return on their investments. Liquidation of the corporate assets was found the only means by which petitioners would receive a fair return. The court considered judicial dissolution of a corporation to be "a serious and severe remedy." Consequently, the order of dissolution was conditioned upon the corporation's being permitted to purchase petitioners' stock. The Appellate Division affirmed, without opinion.

At issue in this appeal is the scope of section 1104-a of the Business Corporation Law. Specifically, this court must determine whether the provision for involuntary dissolution when the "directors or those in control of the corporation have been guilty of ... oppressive actions toward the complaining shareholders" was properly applied in the circumstances of this case. We hold that it was, and therefore affirm....

Judicially ordered dissolution of a corporation at the behest of minority interests is a remedy of relatively recent vintage in New York. Historically, this State's courts were considered divested of equity jurisdiction to order dissolution, as statutory prescriptions were deemed exclusive. Statutes permitting judicial dissolution of corporations either limited the types of corporations under their purview or restricted the parties who could petition for dissolution to the Attorney-General, or the directors, trustees, or majority shareholders of the corporation.

Minority shareholders were granted standing in the absence of statutory authority to seek dissolution of corporations when controlling shareholders engaged in certain egregious conduct. Predicated on the majority shareholders' fiduciary obligation to treat all shareholders fairly and equally, to preserve corporate assets, and to fulfill their responsibilities of corporate management with "scrupulous good faith," the courts' equitable power can be invoked when "it appears that the directors and majority shareholders 'have so palpably breached the fiduciary duty they owe to the minority shareholders that they are disqualified from exercising the exclusive discretion and the dissolution power given to them by statute.'"....

Supplementing this principle of judicially ordered equitable dissolution of a corporation, the Legislature has shown a special solicitude toward the rights of minority shareholders of closely held corporations by enacting section 1104-a of the Business Corporation Law. That statute provides a mechanism for the holders of at least 20% of the outstanding shares of a corporation whose stock is not traded on a securities market to petition for its dissolution "under special circumstances." The circumstances that give rise to dissolution fall into two general classifications: mistreatment of complaining shareholders or misappropriation of corporate assets by controlling shareholders, directors or officers.

Section 1104-a describes three types of proscribed activity: "illegal", "fraudulent", and "oppressive" conduct. The first two terms are familiar words that are commonly understood at law. The last, however, does not enjoy the same certainty gained through long usage. As no definition is provided by the statute, it falls upon the courts to provide guidance.

The statutory concept of "oppressive actions" can, perhaps, best be understood by examining the characteristics of close corporations and the Legislature's general purpose in creating this involuntary-dissolution statute. It is widely understood that, in addition to supplying capital to a contemplated or ongoing enterprise and expecting a fair and equal return, parties comprising the ownership of a close corporation may expect to be actively involved in its management and operation. The small ownership cluster seeks to "contribute their capital, skills, experience and labor" toward the corporate enterprise.

As a leading commentator in the field has observed: "Unlike the typical shareholder in a publicly held corporation, who may be simply an investor or a speculator and cares nothing for the responsibilities of management, the shareholder in a close corporation is a co-owner of the business and wants the privileges and powers that go with ownership. His participation in that particular corporation is often his principal or sole source of income. As a matter of fact, providing employment for himself may have been the principal reason why he participated in organizing the corporation. He may or may not anticipate an ultimate profit from the sale of his interest, but he normally draws very little from the corporation as dividends. In his capacity as an officer or employee of the corporation, he looks to his salary for the principal return on his capital investment, because earnings of a close corporation, as is well known, are distributed in major part in salaries, bonuses and retirement benefits." (O'Neal, Close Corporations [2d ed.], §1.07, at pp. 21–22 [n. omitted].)

Shareholders enjoy flexibility in memorializing these expectations through agreements setting forth each party's rights and obligations in corporate governance. In the absence of such an agreement, however, ultimate decision-making power respecting corporate policy will be reposed in the holders of a majority interest in the corporation. A wielding of this power by any group controlling a corporation may serve to destroy a stockholder's vital interests and expectations.

As the stock of closely held corporations generally is not readily salable, a minority shareholder at odds with management policies may be without either a voice in protecting his or her interests or any reasonable means of withdrawing his or her investment. This predicament may fairly be considered the legislative concern underlying the provision at issue in this case; inclusion of the criteria that the corporation's stock not be traded on securities markets and that the complaining shareholder be subject to oppressive actions supports this conclusion.

Defining oppressive conduct as distinct from illegality in the present context has been considered in other forums. The question has been resolved by considering oppressive actions to refer to conduct that substantially defeats the "reasonable expectations" held by minority shareholders in committing their capital to the particular enterprise. This concept is consistent with the apparent purpose underlying the provision under review. A shareholder who reasonably expected that ownership in the corporation would entitle him or her to a job, a share of corporate earnings, a place in corporate management, or some other form of security, would be oppressed in a very real sense when others in the corporation seek to defeat those expectations and there exists no effective means of salvaging the investment.

Given the nature of close corporations and the remedial purpose of the statute, this court holds that utilizing a complaining shareholder's "reasonable expectations" as a means of identifying and measuring conduct alleged to be oppressive is appropriate. A court considering a petition alleging oppressive conduct must investigate what the majority shareholders knew, or should have known, to be the petitioner's expectations in entering the particular enterprise. Majority conduct should not be deemed oppressive simply because the petitioner's subjective hopes and desires in joining the venture are not fulfilled. Disappointment alone should not necessarily be equated with oppression.

Rather, oppression should be deemed to arise only when the majority conduct substantially defeats expectations that, objectively viewed, were both reasonable under the circumstances and were central to the petitioner's decision to join the venture. It would be inappropriate, however, for us in this case to delineate the contours of the courts' consideration in determining whether directors have been guilty of oppressive conduct. As in other areas of the law, much will depend on the circumstances in the individual case.

The appropriateness of an order of dissolution is in every case vested in the sound discretion of the court considering the application. Under the terms of this statute, courts are instructed to consider both whether "liquidation of the corporation is the only feasible means" to protect the complaining shareholder's expectation of a fair return on his or her investment and whether dissolution "is reasonably necessary" to protect "the rights or interests of any substantial number of shareholders" not limited to those complaining. Implicit in this direction is that once oppressive conduct is found, consideration must be given to the totality of circumstances surrounding the current state of corporate affairs and relations to determine whether some remedy short of or other than dissolution constitutes a feasible means of satisfying both the petitioner's expectations and the rights and interests of any other substantial group of shareholders.

By invoking the statute, a petitioner has manifested his or her belief that dissolution may be the only appropriate remedy. Assuming the petitioner has set forth a prima facie case of oppressive conduct, it should be incumbent upon the parties seeking to forestall dissolution to demonstrate to the court the existence of an adequate, alternative remedy. A court has broad latitude in fashioning alternative relief, but when fulfillment of the oppressed petitioner's expectations by these means is doubtful, such as when there has been a complete deterioration of relations between the parties, a court should not hesitate to order dissolution. Every order of dissolution, however, must be conditioned upon permitting any shareholder of the corporation to elect to purchase the complaining shareholder's stock at fair value.

One further observation is in order. The purpose of this involuntary dissolution statute is to provide protection to the minority shareholder whose reasonable expectations in undertaking the venture have been frustrated and who has no adequate means of recovering his or her investment. It would be contrary to this remedial purpose to permit its use by minority shareholders as merely a coercive tool. Therefore, the minority shareholder whose own acts, made in bad faith and undertaken with a view toward forcing an involuntary dissolution, give rise to the complained-of oppression should be given no quarter in the statutory protection....

There was sufficient evidence presented at the hearing to support the conclusion that Kemp & Beatley had a long-standing policy of awarding de facto dividends based on stock ownership in the form of "extra compensation bonuses." Petitioners, both of whom had extensive experience in the management of the company, testified to this effect. Moreover, both related that receipt of this compensation, whether as true dividends or disguised as "extra compensation", was a known incident to ownership of the company's stock understood by all of the company's principals. Finally, there was uncontroverted proof that this policy was changed either shortly before or shortly after petitioners' employment ended. Extra compensation was still awarded by the company. The only difference was that stock ownership was no longer a basis for the payments; it was asserted that the basis became services rendered to the corporation. It was not unreasonable for the fact finder to have determined that this change in policy amounted to nothing less than an attempt to exclude petitioners from gaining any return on their investment through the mere recharacterization of distributions of corporate income. Under the circumstances of this case, there was no error in determining that this conduct constituted oppressive action within the meaning of section 1104-a of the Business Corporation Law.

Nor may it be said that Supreme Court abused its discretion in ordering Kemp & Beatley's dissolution, subject to an opportunity for a buy-out of petitioners' shares. After the referee had found that the controlling faction of the company was, in effect, attempting to "squeeze-out" petitioners by offering them no return on their investment and increasing other executive compensation, respondents, in opposing the report's confirmation, attempted only to controvert the factual basis of the report. They suggested no feasible, alternative remedy to the forced dissolution. In light of an apparent deterioration in relations between petitioners and the governing shareholders of Kemp & Beatley, it was not unreasonable for the court to have determined that a forced buy-out of petitioners' shares or liquidation of the corporation's assets was the only means by which petitioners could be guaranteed a fair return on their investments.

Accordingly, the order of the Appellate Division should be modified, with costs to petitioners-respondents, by affirming the substantive determination of that court but extending the time for exercising the option to purchase petitioners-respondents' shares to 30 days following this court's determination.

Notes and Questions

1. In *Kemp*, the New York Court of Appeals upheld the remedy of court ordered dissolution subject to the corporation's being permitted to purchase the petitioners' shares. Until 2013, Section 14.34 of the MBCA provided a more elaborate approach. Section 14.34 provides that in a judicial proceeding brought by shareholders to dissolve a closely-held corporation, the corporation or one or more of its other shareholders can elect to purchase at fair value all of the shares owned by the shareholder petitioning for dissolution. Fair value is determined either by agreement of all the parties or, absent agreement, by the court. For many years, the statute also provided that if fair value was determined by the court and not by agreement, the corporation could elect to dissolve rather than proceed with the buyout. The latter provision was ultimately

perceived to be unfair to the petitioning shareholder(s) and was deleted by amendment. Additional notes concerning the MBCA's approach to shareholder petitions for judicial dissolution appear later in this chapter.

2. Two additional New York cases shed further light on the issue of judicial proceedings to dissolve a corporation.

In *Williamson v. Williamson, Picket, Gross, Inc.*, 259 A.D.2d 362, 687 N.Y.S.2d 53 (N.Y. App. Div. 1999), a shareholder brought an action to dissolve the corporation based on alleged oppressive action by the remaining shareholders. The plaintiff alleged that he had been involuntarily ousted from any involvement or ownership in the corporation of which he was a founding one-third shareholder. In upholding the lower court's decision to dissolve the corporation, the appellate court found that dissolution was in order because "there is no provision in the shareholders' buy-back agreement for involuntary discharge and that petitioner's employment was an incident of his stock ownership, cloaking him with a reasonable expectation of continued employment."

The court that decided *Williamson*, however, refused to grant dissolution in the case of *In re Application of Parveen for the Dissolution of Hina Pharmacy Health and Beauty Aids, Inc.*, 259 A.D.2d 389, 687 N.Y.S.2d 90 (N.Y. App. Div. 1999). In *Parveen*, a 50% shareholder sought dissolution of a corporation when the other shareholders refused to hold a shareholders' meeting and provide her with financial information. The court limited the dissolution remedy to situations in which the directors or shareholders were deadlocked or the complainant was the subject of oppressive conduct such as:

> the complaining shareholder's frustrated expectations in such matters as continued employment or a share in the profits and management of the corporation, such that she feels that the other shareholders have deprived her of a reasonable return on her investment. Moreover ... the court has discretion to fashion a less drastic alternative remedy. For instance, rather than dissolve a viable ongoing business, the court may order the other shareholders to buy out the petitioner's ownership interest. As this appears to be the relief petitioner is seeking, an action under Business Corporation Law s 1104-a seems most appropriate.

The subject of oppression of minority shareholders has legal implications for the corporate attorney as well as for the majority shareholders. *Granewich v. Harding*, 985 P.2d 788 (Ore. 1999), involved a motion to dismiss the complaint of a minority shareholder and director claiming that the controlling shareholders and directors had amended the corporate by-laws to exclude plaintiff from the corporation and issued new shares of stock to themselves to dilute plaintiff's ownership interest in the corporation. The complaint also named the company's lawyers as defendants, alleging that they breached their own fiduciary duties to plaintiff by assisting the majority with the alleged squeeze out. The Supreme Court overruled the lower court's dismissal of the complaint. Although there was no Oregon law directly addressing the issue whether one person can be held liable for another's breach of fiduciary duty, the court found that there was sufficient authority for the "proposition that one who knowingly aids another in the breach of a fiduciary duty is liable to the one harmed thereby. That principle readily extends to lawyers." The court concluded that the complaint stated a claim against the lawyers for joint liability, based on their alleged participation with other defendants in breaching fiduciary duties owed to plaintiff.

Nixon v. Blackwell

Delaware Supreme Court
626 A.2d 1366 (1992)

Veasey, Chief Justice (for the Court en banc) ...

I. Facts

A. The Parties

Plaintiffs are 14 minority stockholders of Class B, non-voting, stock of E.C. Barton & Co. (the "Corporation"). The individual defendants are the members of the board of directors (the "Board" or the "directors"). The Corporation is also a defendant. Plaintiffs collectively own only Class B stock, and own no Class A stock. Their total holdings comprise approximately 25 percent of all the common stock outstanding as of the end of fiscal year 1989.

At all relevant times, the Board consisted of ten individuals who either are currently employed, or were once employed, by the Corporation. At the time this suit was filed, these directors collectively owned approximately 47.5 percent of all the outstanding Class A shares. The remaining Class A shares were held by certain other present and former employees of the Corporation.

B. Mr. Barton's Testamentary Plan

The Corporation is a non-public, closely-held Delaware corporation headquartered in Arkansas. It is engaged in the business of selling wholesale and retail lumber in the Mississippi Delta. The Corporation was formed in 1928 by E.C. Barton ("Mr. Barton") and has two classes of common stock: Class A voting stock and Class B non-voting stock. Substantially all of the Corporation's stock was held by Mr. Barton at the time of his death in 1967.... Pursuant to Mr. Barton's testamentary plan, 49 percent of the Class A voting stock was bequeathed outright to eight of his loyal employees. The remaining 51 percent [of the Class A stock], along with 14 percent of the Class B non-voting stock, was placed into an independently managed 15-year trust for the same eight people. Sixty-one percent of the Class B non-voting stock was bequeathed outright to Mrs. Barton. Mr. Barton's daughter and granddaughter received 21 percent of the Class B stock in trust. The non-voting Class B shares Mr. Barton bequeathed to his family represented 75 percent of the Corporation's total equity.

Ownership interests in the Corporation began to change in the early 1970s following the distribution of Mr. Barton's estate.... These transactions left Mrs. Barton's three children collectively with 30 percent of the outstanding Class B non-voting stock. The children have no voting rights despite their substantial equity interest in the Corporation. The children are also the only non-employee Class B stockholders.

There is no public market for, or trading in, either class of the Corporation's stock. This creates problems for stockholders, particularly the Class B minority stockholders, who wish to sell or otherwise realize the value of their shares. The corporation purported to address this problem in several ways over the years.

C. The Self-Tenders

[During the 1970s] the Corporation occasionally offered to purchase the Class B stock of the non-employee stockholders through a series of self-tender offers.... The Corporation made no further repurchase offers until May 1985, [when there was a self-tender to repurchase] at a price of $25 per share. The book value of the Class A stock and the Class B stock at that time was $38.39 and $26.35, respectively. The remaining children and the other plaintiffs in the present action refused to sell.

D. The Employee Stock Ownership Plan ("ESOP")

In November 1975 the Corporation established an ESOP designed to hold Class B non-voting stock for the benefit of eligible employees of the Corporation. The ESOP is a tax-qualified profit-sharing plan whereby employees of the Corporation are allocated a share of the assets held by the plan in proportion to their annual compensation, subject to certain vesting requirements. The ESOP is funded by annual cash contributions from the Corporation. Under the plan, terminating and retiring employees are entitled to receive their interest in the ESOP by taking Class B stock or cash in lieu of stock. It appears from the record that most terminating employees and retirees elect to receive cash in lieu of stock. The Corporation commissions an annual appraisal of the Corporation to determine the value of its stock for ESOP purposes. Thus, the ESOP provides employee Class B stockholders with a substantial measure of liquidity not available to non-employee stockholders. The Corporation had the option of repurchasing Class A stock from the employees upon their retirement or death. The estates of the employee stockholders did not have a corresponding right to put the stock to the Corporation.

E. The Key Man Insurance Policies

The Corporation also purchased certain key man life insurance policies with death benefits payable to the Corporation. Several early policies insuring the lives of key executives and directors were purchased during Mr. Barton's lifetime with death benefits payable to the Corporation. In 1982, the Corporation purchased additional key man policies in connection with agreements entered into between the Corporation and nine key officers and directors. Each executive executed an agreement giving the Corporation a call option to substitute Class B non-voting stock for their Class A voting stock upon the occurrence of certain events, including death and termination of employment, so that the voting shares could be reissued to new key personnel. In return, the Board adopted a resolution creating a non-binding recommendation that a portion of the key man life insurance proceeds be used to repurchase the exchanged Class B stock from the executives' estates at a price at least equal to 80 percent of their ESOP value.... [T]he ultimate decision on the use of insurance proceeds for this purpose was left to the discretion of the Corporation's management or the Board....

II. Proceedings in the Court of Chancery

... At trial, the plaintiffs charged the defendants with (1) attempting to force the minority stockholders to sell their shares at a discount by embarking on a scheme to pay negligible dividends, (2) breaching their fiduciary duties by authorizing excessive compensation for themselves and other employees of the Corporation, and (3) breaching their fiduciary duties by pursuing a discriminatory liquidity policy that favors employee stockholders over non-employee stockholders through the ESOP and key man life insurance policies. The plaintiffs sought money damages for past dividends, a one-time liquidity dividend, and a guarantee of future dividends at a specified rate.

The Vice Chancellor held that the Corporation's low-dividend policy was within the bounds of business judgment, that the executive compensation levels were not excessive, and ruled in favor of defendants on these issues. The Vice Chancellor further held, however, that the defendant directors had breached their fiduciary duties to the minority. The basis for this ruling was that it was "inherently unfair" for the defendants to establish the ESOP and to purchase key man life insurance to provide liquidity for themselves while providing no comparable method by which the non-employee Class B stockholders may liquidate their stock at fair value. Holding that the "needs of all stockholders must be considered and addressed when providing liquidity," the court ruled that the directors breached their fiduciary duties, and granted relief to plaintiffs. The trial court ruled against the plaintiffs on all the other issues. Since plaintiffs have not appealed those rulings, they are not before this Court.

The finding for the plaintiffs and the form of the relief granted to the plaintiffs (which the defendants also contest) are set forth in paragraphs 4 and 5 of the Order and Final Judgment of March 10, 1992:

> 4. On the claim of the plaintiffs presented at trial that the individual defendants breached their fiduciary duty as directors and treated the plaintiffs unfairly as the non-employee, minority Class B stockholders of the Company by providing no method by which plaintiffs might liquidate their stock at fair value while providing a means through the ESOP and key-man life insurance whereby the stock of terminating employees could be purchased from them, judgment is entered in favor of the plaintiffs.

> 5. Pursuant to the judgment entered in paragraph 4 above, defendants shall take the following steps in order to remedy the unfair treatment of Class B stockholders:

> a. An amount equal to the total of all key man life insurance premiums paid to date, together with interest from the date of payment shall be used to re-purchase Class B stock other than shares held by the ESOP or defendants, at a price to be set by an independent appraiser. b. Hereafter, neither the ESOP[2] nor the company shall purchase or repurchase any stock without offering to purchase the same number of shares, on the same terms and conditions, from the Class B stockholders other than defendants and the ESOP.

Plaintiffs were awarded attorneys' fees and costs in a subsequent order entered on May 20, 1992....

---

2. [4] It is to be noted that the ESOP is not a party to the proceedings, so in all events this relief is void to the extent that it purports to bind the ESOP.

V. Applicable Principles of Substantive Law

Defendants contend that the trial court erred in not applying the business judgment rule. Since the defendants benefited from the ESOP and could have benefited from the key man life insurance beyond that which benefited other stockholders generally, the defendants are on both sides of the transaction. For that reason, we agree with the trial court that the entire fairness test applies to this aspect of the case. Accordingly, defendants have the burden of showing the entire fairness of those transactions....

The entire fairness analysis essentially requires "judicial scrutiny." *Weinberger*, 457 A.2d at 710. In business judgment rule cases, an essential element is the fact that there has been a business decision made by a disinterested and independent corporate decisionmaker. *Aronson v. Lewis*, Del.Supr., 473 A.2d 805, 812 (1984); *Smith v. Van Gorkom*, Del.Supr., 488 A.2d 858, 872–73 (1985). When there is no independent corporate decisionmaker, the court may become the objective arbiter.

The trial court in this case, however, appears to have adopted the novel legal principle that Class B stockholders had a right to "liquidity" equal to that which the court found to be available to the defendants. It is well established in our jurisprudence that stockholders need not always be treated equally for all purposes. *See Unocal Corp. v. Mesa Petroleum Co.*, Del.Supr., 493 A.2d 946, 957 (1985) ("Unocal") (discriminatory exchange offer held valid); and *Cheff v. Mathes*, Del.Supr., 199 A.2d 548, 554–56 (1964) (selective stock repurchase held valid). To hold that fairness necessarily requires precise equality is to beg the question: Many scholars, though few courts, conclude that one aspect of fiduciary duty is the equal treatment of investors. Their argument takes the following form: fiduciary principles require fair conduct; equal treatment is fair conduct; hence, fiduciary principles require equal treatment. The conclusion does not follow. The argument depends on an equivalence between equal and fair treatment. To say that fiduciary principles require equal treatment is to beg the question whether investors would contract for equal or even equivalent treatment. Frank H. Easterbrook and Daniel R. Fischel, The Economic Structure of Corporate Law 110 (1991). This holding of the trial court overlooks the significant facts that the minority stockholders were not: (a) employees of the Corporation; (b) entitled to share in an ESOP; (c) qualified for key man insurance; or (d) protected by specific provisions in the certificate of incorporation, by-laws, or a stockholders' agreement.

There is support in this record for the fact that the ESOP is a corporate benefit and was established, at least in part, to benefit the Corporation. Generally speaking, the creation of ESOPs is a normal corporate practice and is generally thought to benefit the corporation. The same is true generally with respect to key man insurance programs. If such corporate practices were necessarily to require equal treatment for non-employee stockholders, that would be a matter for legislative determination in Delaware. There is no such legislation to that effect. If we were to adopt such a rule, our decision would border on judicial legislation.

Accordingly, we hold that the Vice Chancellor erred as a matter of law in concluding that the liquidity afforded to the employee stockholders by the ESOP and the key man insurance required substantially equal treatment for the non-employee stockholders. Moreover, the Vice Chancellor failed to evaluate and articulate, for example, whether or not and to what extent (a) corporate benefits flowed from the ESOP and the key man insurance; (b) the ESOP and key man insurance plans are novel, extraordinary, or relatively routine business practices; (c) the dividend policy was even relevant; (d) Mr. Barton's plan for employee management and benefits should be honored; and (e) the self-tenders showed defendants' willingness to provide an exit opportunity for the plaintiffs.... We hold on this record that defendants have met their burden of establishing the entire fairness of their dealings with the non-employee Class B stockholders, and are entitled to judgment. The record is sufficient to conclude that plaintiffs' claim that the defendant directors have maintained a discriminatory policy of favoring Class A employee stockholders over Class B non-employee stockholders is without merit. The directors have followed a consistent policy originally established by Mr. Barton, the founder of the Corporation, whose intent from the formation of the Corporation was to use the Class A stock as the vehicle for the Corporation's continuity through employee management and ownership.

Mr. Barton established the Corporation in 1928 by creating two classes of stock, not one, and by holding 100 percent of the Class A stock and 82 percent of the Class B stock. Mr. Barton himself established the practice of purchasing key man life insurance with funds of the Corporation to retain in the employ of the Corporation valuable employees by assuring them that, following their retirement or death, the Corporation will have liquid assets which could be used to repurchase the shares acquired by the employee, which shares may otherwise constitute an illiquid and unsalable asset of his or her estate. Another rational purpose is to prevent the stock from passing out of the control of the employees of the Corporation into the hands of family or descendants of the employees.

The directors' actions following Mr. Barton's death are consistent with Mr. Barton's plan. An ESOP, for example, is normally established for employees. Accordingly, there is no inequity in limiting ESOP benefits to the employee stockholders. Indeed, it makes no sense to include non-employees in ESOP benefits. The fact that the Class B stock represented 75 percent of the Corporation's total equity is irrelevant to the issue of fair dealing. The Class B stock was given no voting rights because those stockholders were not intended to have a direct voice in the management and operation of the Corporation. They were simply passive investors—entitled to be treated fairly but not necessarily to be treated equally. The fortunes of the Corporation rested with the Class A employee stockholders and the Class B stockholders benefited from the multiple increases in value of their Class B stock. Moreover, the Board made continuing efforts to buy back the Class B stock.

We hold that paragraphs 4 and 5 of the March 10, 1992 order of the trial court and the order of May 20, 1992, awarding fees and costs to plaintiffs, are reversed and remanded with instructions to conform the judgment to the findings and conclusions in this opinion.

VI. No Special Rules For a "Closely-Held Corporation" Not Qualified as a "Close Corporation" Under Subchapter XIV of the Delaware General Corporation Law.

We wish to address one further matter which was raised at oral argument before this Court: Whether there should be any special, judicially-created rules to "protect" minority stockholders of closely-held Delaware corporations.

The case at bar points up the basic dilemma of minority stockholders in receiving fair value for their stock as to which there is no market and no market valuation. It is not difficult to be sympathetic, in the abstract, to a stockholder who finds himself or herself in that position. A stockholder who bargains for stock in a closely-held corporation and who pays for those shares (unlike the plaintiffs in this case who acquired their stock through gift) can make a business judgment whether to buy into such a minority position, and if so on what terms. One could bargain for definitive provisions of self-ordering permitted to a Delaware corporation through the certificate of incorporation or by-laws by reason of the provisions in 8 Del. C. §§ 102, 109, and 141(a). Moreover, in addition to such mechanisms, a stockholder intending to buy into a minority position in a Delaware corporation may enter into definitive stockholder agreements, and such agreements may provide for elaborate earnings tests, buy-out provisions, voting trusts, or other voting agreements. *See, e.g.*, 8 Del. C. § 218.

The tools of good corporate practice are designed to give a purchasing minority stockholder the opportunity to bargain for protection before parting with consideration. It would do violence to normal corporate practice and our corporation law to fashion an ad hoc ruling which would result in a court-imposed stockholder buy-out for which the parties had not contracted.

In 1967, when the Delaware General Corporation Law was significantly revised, a new Subchapter XIV entitled "Close Corporations; Special Provisions," became a part of that law for the first time. While these provisions were patterned in theory after close corporation statutes in Florida and Maryland, "the Delaware provisions were unique and influenced the development of similar legislation in a number of other states...." *See* Ernest L. Folk, III, Rodman Ward, Jr., and Edward P. Welch, 2 Folk on the Delaware General Corporation Law 404 (1988). Subchapter XIV is a narrowly constructed statute which applies only to a corporation which is designated as a "close corporation" in its certificate of incorporation, and which fulfills other requirements, including a limitation to 30 on the number of stockholders, that all classes of stock have to have at least one restriction on transfer, and that there be no "public offering." 8 Del. C. § 342. Accordingly, subchapter XIV applies only to "close corporations," as defined in section 342. "Unless a corporation elects to become a close corporation under this subchapter in the manner prescribed in this subchapter, it shall be subject in all respects to this chapter, except this subchapter." 8 Del. C. § 341. The corporation before the Court in this matter, is not a "close corporation." Therefore it is not governed by the provisions of Subchapter XIV.[4]

---

4. [19] We do not intend to imply that, if the Corporation had been a close corporation under Subchapter XIV, the result in this case would have been different. [S]tatutory close corporations have not found particular favor with practitioners. Practitioners have for the most part viewed the complex

One cannot read into the situation presented in the case at bar any special relief for the minority stockholders in this closely-held, but not statutory "close corporation" because the provisions of Subchapter XIV relating to close corporations and other statutory schemes[5] preempt the field in their respective areas. It would run counter to the spirit of the doctrine of independent legal significance, and would be inappropriate judicial legislation for this Court to fashion a special judicially- created rule for minority investors when the entity does not fall within those statutes, or when there are no negotiated special provisions in the certificate of incorporation, by-laws, or stockholder agreements. The entire fairness test, correctly applied and articulated, is the proper judicial approach.

VII. Conclusion

We hold that the Court of Chancery correctly determined that the entire fairness test is applicable in reviewing the actions of the defendants in establishing and implementing the ESOP and the key man life insurance program. The Vice Chancellor erred, however, as a matter of law in concluding on this record that the defendants had not carried their burden of showing entire fairness. The trial court erroneously undertook to create a novel theory of corporation law and erroneously failed to set forth and apply articulable standards for determining fairness. Moreover, certain findings of fact by the trial court were not the product of an orderly and deductive reasoning process.

In a case such as this where the business judgment rule is not applicable and the entire fairness test is applicable, the imposition of the latter test is not, alone, outcome-determinative. The doctrine of entire fairness does not lend itself to bright line precision or rigid doctrine. Yet it does not necessarily require equality, it cannot be a matter of total subjectivity on the part of the trial court, and it cannot result in a random pattern of ad hoc determinations which could do violence to the stability of our corporation law.

Accordingly, we REVERSE the judgment of the Court of Chancery and REMAND the matter for proceedings not inconsistent with this opinion.

---

statutory provisions underlying the purportedly simplified operational procedures for close corporations as legal quicksand of uncertain depth and have adopted the view that the objectives sought by the subchapter are achievable for their clients with considerably less uncertainty by cloaking a conventionally created corporation with the panoply of charter provisions, transfer restrictions, by-laws, stockholders' agreements, buy-sell arrangements, irrevocable proxies, voting trusts or other contractual mechanisms which were and remain the traditional method for accomplishing the goals sought by the close corporation provisions. David A. Drexler, Lewis S. Black, Jr., and A. Gilchrist Sparks, III, Delaware Corporation Law and Practice § 43.01 (1993).

5. [20] It is to be noted that Delaware statutory law provides for many forms of business enterprise: partnerships pursuant to 6 Del. C. §§ 1501–43; limited partnerships pursuant to 6 Del. C. § 17-101-1109; limited liability companies pursuant to 6 Del. C. §§ 18-101-1106; business trusts pursuant to Title 12, §§ 3801–20. Compare the Close Corporation Supplement to the Model Business Corporation Act, especially Section 20 relating to "Shareholder Agreements."

C. Statutory and Contractual Provisions

Recognizing that the issues raised above typically arise in the closely held corporation context, state corporation statutes address problems of deadlock, dissension and oppression in one of two ways. General corporation statutes may either include special provisions for closely held corporations throughout the general corporate code or they may contain a separate unit of code applicable to closely held corporations. The MBCA takes the former approach and Delaware the latter in Subchapter XIV of the Delaware General Corporation Law. The MBCA special provisions are limited to companies whose shares are not traded on a national exchange. Delaware limits the application of the separate subchapter to companies that elect to become statutory closely held corporations. In both cases, the applicable provisions are elective and enabling. The discussion that follows focuses on the MBCA provisions.

1. Judicial Dissolution of the Corporation

Chapter 14 of the MBCA establishes the procedures for both voluntary and involuntary dissolution of all types of corporations. Voluntary dissolution is governed by §§ 14.01 through 14.07. The Act requires that a proposal for dissolution must be recommended by the Board of Directors and approved by the shareholders. The corporation must then file articles of dissolution with the Secretary of State and proceed to liquidate its business by collecting its assets, disposing of its properties, discharging its liabilities and distributing any remaining property to its shareholders. Under § 14.30, a shareholder may initiate dissolution proceedings if the directors or shareholders are deadlocked and the deadlock cannot be broken, if the directors or those in control have acted in an illegal, oppressive or fraudulent manner, or if the corporation's assets are being wasted. The Secretary of State may initiate a dissolution proceeding if the corporation is delinquent in paying franchise taxes, filing its annual report, or notifying the Secretary of changes in its registered office or agent.[6] The Attorney General may initiate a proceeding against corporations obtaining their articles of incorporation through fraud or exceeding or abusing their authority.[7] Creditors of insolvent corporations may also initiate proceedings to recover judgment claims against insolvent corporations.[8]

Shareholders of closely held corporations may also enter into an agreement that mandates dissolution if one or more shareholders request it or if a specified event or contingency occurs.[9] This approach is also found in general partnership statutes and introduces a significant measure of instability into the corporate form.

2. Buyout of Shareholder Petitioning for Dissolution

We have already seen that shareholders may enter into an agreement restricting the transfer of shares and providing for corporate or shareholder buyout of an exiting

6. Model Act § 14.20.
7. *Id.* § 14.30.
8. *Id.*
9. *Id.* § 7.32 (a)(7).

owner. MBCA § 14.34 provides a buyout alternative to court ordered dissolution. The section permits a closely held corporation or its shareholders to elect to purchase at fair value all the shares owned by the shareholder petitioning for judicial dissolution. The Official Comment to § 14.34 states:

> The proceeding for judicial dissolution has become an increasingly important remedy for minority shareholders of closely-held corporations who believe that the value of their investment is threatened by reason of circumstances or conduct described in section 14.30(2). If the petitioning shareholder proves one or more grounds under section 14.30(2), he is entitled to some form of relief but many courts have hesitated to award dissolution, the only form of relief explicitly provided, because of its adverse effects on shareholders, employees, and others who may have an interest in the continuation of the business.
>
> Commentators have observed that it is rarely necessary to dissolve the corporation and liquidate its assets in order to provide relief: the rights of the petitioning shareholder are fully protected by liquidating only his interest and paying the fair value of his shares while permitting the remaining shareholders to continue the business. In fact, it appears that most dissolution proceedings result in a buyout of one or another of the disputants' shares either pursuant to a statutory buyout provision or a negotiated settlement.

The Model Statutory Closely Held Corporation Supplement provides a range of additional options to a court confronting deadlock, dissension or oppression in a closely held corporation. Under § 41, the court was authorized to:

> ... order one or more of the following types of relief: (1) the performance, prohibition, alteration or setting aside of any action of the corporation or of its shareholders, directors, or officers of or any other party to the proceeding; (2) the cancellation or alteration of any provision in the corporation's articles of incorporation or bylaws; (3) the removal from office of any director or officer; (4) the appointment of any individual as a director or officer; (5) an accounting with respect to any matter in dispute; (6) the appointment of a custodian to manage the business and affairs of the corporation; (7) the appointment of a provisional director (who has all the rights, powers, and duties of a duly elected director) to serve for the term and under the conditions prescribed by the court; (8) the payment of dividends; (9) the award of damages to any aggrieved party.

These options were in addition to the share purchase and dissolution options described above.

The Official Comment to § 40 noted that although the sections described above would probably "be invoked most frequently by minority shareholders, the ground for relief ... may be used by the holders of the majority of shares to seek relief from deadlocks created by veto rights given minority shareholders which threaten the corporation's continued existence."

3. Appointment of a Custodian or Provisional Director

DGCL § 352 permits a shareholder having the right to dissolve the corporation to petition for the appointment of a custodian to manage the company. Section 353 provides for the appointment of a provisional director when the board of directors is deadlocked. MBCA § 14.32 authorizes the appointment of one or more custodians either to wind up the company's business or to manage it.

Section V
Contractual Arrangements

Contractual arrangements are the most common tool shareholders use to tailor corporate control to suit their particular needs. Contractual arrangements take various forms, but most of them can be categorized as voting trusts, shareholders' agreements, or employment contracts.

A. Voting Trusts and Shareholder Voting Agreements

Shareholders often enter into agreements designed to control how they will vote their shares with respect to the election of directors or any other matter that is subject to shareholder approval. These agreements may be limited in scope or they may apply to all matters on which shareholders are eligible to vote. They may specify in advance how the shares are to be voted or provide a mechanism for deciding at the time that the votes are to be cast. There are two forms of agreements of this type: voting trusts and pooling agreements.

The classic voting trust is a trust formed in the ordinary way under trust law with voting stock as its corpus. The shareholders who wish to participate in the trust serve as the grantors by transferring to a trustee legal title to their shares. The trustee then votes the shares according to the terms of the trust, which may be specifically enforced, and otherwise acts for the benefit of the former shareholders, who now are the beneficiaries of the trust. Trust beneficiaries will typically continue to receive any dividends declared on the stock held in the trust and, in MBCA jurisdictions, will retain their rights to inspect corporate books and records. The voting trust is an old device, going back at least as far as the mid-nineteenth century. At first it operated strictly under common law, but now the voting trust has come under supervision in corporation statutes. Commonly, modern statutes, typified by MBCA § 7.30, require that the trust agreement be in writing, and require that a copy of the agreement, and in the case of the MBCA, a list of the beneficiaries, be given to the corporation whose shares are held in trust. Some statutes set an initial 10-year duration on voting trusts, with an option to extend. Proposed changes to the MBCA would eliminate the ten-year limit; Delaware no longer imposes a limit.

Voting trusts can be used in several situations. In a family owned business, the founders may want to give a younger generation financial interests in the company without relinquishing control. They can accomplish this by putting stock issued to the younger generation in a voting trust, with a senior family member serving as trustee. A voting trust may also be used to maintain a particular control structure or to protect a creditor lending a substantial amount of money to the company. As part of the lending arrangement, shareholders can be required to transfer their stock to a voting trust, with the creditor acting as trustee. The creditor will thus be able to control the firm until the loan is repaid.

The voting trust, however, is not a popular device for controlling a corporation, partly because of its limited duration under modern statutes, but mostly because establishing a voting trust is such a drastic measure. Few shareholders wish to divest themselves of all control over their shares just for the sake of shareholder unity. For that reason, shareholder voting or pooling agreements, in which the drafters attempt to secure that unity while at the same time allowing shareholders reasonable control of their own shares, are much more popular than are voting trusts.

There is a risk, however, that if the drafter of a shareholders' agreement is not careful, the agreement may be held to be a voting trust and, what is more important, an illegal and void voting trust because the agreement does not meet the statutory requirements for a voting trust. The following case nicely presents the issues involved.

Lehrman v. Cohen

Delaware Supreme Court
222 A.2d 800 (1966)

HERRMANN, JUSTICE.

The primary problem presented on this appeal involves the applicability of the Delaware Voting Trust Statute. Other questions involve the legality of stock having voting power but no dividend or liquidation rights except repayment of par value, and an alleged unlawful delegation of directorial duties and powers.

These are the material facts:

Giant Food Inc. (hereinafter the "Company") was incorporated in Delaware in 1935 by the defendant N. M. Cohen and Samuel Lehrman, deceased father of the plaintiff Jacob Lehrman. From its inception, the Company was controlled by the Cohen and Lehrman families, each of whom owned equal quantities of the voting stock, designated Class AC (held by the Cohen family) and Class AL (held by the Lehrman family) common stock. The two classes of stock have cumulative voting rights and each is entitled to elect two members of the Company's four-member board of directors.

Over the years, as may have been expected, there were differences of opinion between the Cohen and Lehrman families as to operating policies of the Company. Samuel Lehrman died in 1949; each of his children inherited part of his stock in the Company; but a dispute arose among the children regarding an *inter vivos* gift of certain shares made to the plaintiff by his father shortly before his death. To eliminate the Lehrman family dispute and its possible disruption of the affairs of the Company, an arrangement was made which settled the dispute and permitted the plaintiff to acquire all of the outstanding Class AL stock, thereby vesting in him voting power equal to that held by the Cohen family. The arrangement involved repurchase by the Company of the stock held by the plaintiff's brothers and sister, their relinquishment of any claim to the stock gift, and an equalizing surrender of certain stock by the Cohens to the Company for retirement. An essential part of the arrangement, upon the insistence of the Cohens, was the establishment of a fifth directorship to obviate the risk of deadlock which would have continued if the equal division of voting power between AL and AC stock were continued.

To implement the arrangement, on December 31, 1949, the Company's certificate of incorporation was amended, *inter alia*, to create a third class of voting stock, designated Class AD common stock, entitled to elect the fifth director. Article Fourth of the amendment to the certificate of incorporation provided for the issuance of one share of Class AD stock, having a par value of $10, and the following rights and powers:

> "The holder of Class AD common stock shall be entitled to all of the rights and privileges pertaining to common stock without any limitations, prohibitions, restrictions or qualifications except that the holder of said Class AD stock shall not be entitled to receive any dividends declared and paid by the corporation, shall not be entitled to share in the distribution of assets of the corporation upon liquidation or dissolution either partial or final, except to the extent of the par value of said Class AD common stock, and in the election of Directors shall have the right to vote for and elect one of the five Directors hereinafter provided for.

> "The corporation shall have the right, at any time, to redeem and call in the Class AD stock by paying to the holder thereof the par value of said stock, provided however, that such redemption or call shall be authorized and directed by the affirmative vote of four of the five Directors hereinafter provided for."

By resolution of the board of directors, the share of Class AD stock was issued forthwith to the defendant Joseph B. Danzansky, who had served as counsel to the Company since 1944. All corporate action regarding the creation and the issuance of the Class AD stock was accomplished by the unanimous vote of the AC and AL stockholders and of the board of directors. In April 1950, pursuant to the arrangement, Danzansky voted his share of AD stock to elect himself as the Company's fifth director; and he served as such until the institution of this action in 1964. During that entire period, the AC and AL stock have been voted to elect two directors each. From 1950 through 1964, Danzansky regularly attended board meetings, raised and discussed general items of business, and voted on all issues as they came before the board. He was not obliged to break any deadlock among the directors prior to October 1, 1964 because no such deadlock arose before that date.

Beginning in December 1959, 200,000 shares of non-voting common stock of the Company were sold in a public issue for over $3,000,000. Each prospectus published in connection with the public issue contained the following statement:

"Common Stock AD is not a participating stock, and the only purpose for the provision and issuance of such stock is to prevent a deadlock in case the Directors elected by the Common Stock AC and the Directors elected by the Common Stock AL cannot reach an agreement."

... From the outset and until October 1, 1964, the defendant N. M. Cohen was president of the Company. On that date, a resolution was adopted at the Company's annual stockholders' meeting to give Danzansky a fifteen year executive employment contract at an annual salary of $67,600, and options for 25,000 shares of the non-voting common stock of the Company. The AC and AD stock were voted in favor and the AL stock was voted against the resolution. At a directors meeting held the same day, Danzansky was elected president of the Company by a 3–2 vote, the two AL directors voting in opposition. On December 11, 1964, Danzansky resigned as director and voted his share of AD stock to elect as the fifth director, Millard F. West, Jr., a former AL director and investment banker whose firm was one of the under-writers of the public issue of the Company's stock. The newly constituted board ratified the election of Danzansky as president; and, on January 27, 1965, after the commencement of this action and after a review and report by a committee consisting of the new AD director and one AL director, Danzansky's employment contract was approved and adopted with certain modifications.

The plaintiff brought this action on December 11, 1964.... It charges that the creation, issuance, and voting of the one share of Class AD stock resulted in an arrangement illegal under the law of this State for the reasons hereinafter set forth.... The plaintiff and the defendants filed cross-motions for summary judgment.... The Court of Chancery, after considering the contentions now before us and discussed *infra*, granted summary judgment in favor of the defendants and denied the plaintiff's motion for summary judgment. The plaintiff appeals.

I

The plaintiff's primary contention is that the Class AD stock arrangement is, in substance and effect, a voting trust; that, as such, it is illegal because not limited to a ten year period as required by the Voting Trust Statute. The defendants deny that the AD stock arrangement constitutes a disguised voting trust; but they concede that if it is, the arrangement is illegal for violation of the Statute. Thus, issue is clearly joined on the point.

The criteria of a voting trust under our decisions have been summarized by this Court in *Abercrombie v. Davies*, 36 Del. Ch. 371, 130 A.2d 338 (1957). The tests there set forth, accepted by both sides of this cause as being applicable, are as follows: (1) the voting rights of the stock are separated from the other attributes of ownership; (2) the voting rights granted are intended to be irrevocable for a definite period of time; and (3) the principal purpose of the grant of voting rights is to acquire voting control of the corporation.

Adopting and applying these tests, the plaintiff says, as to the first element, that the AD arrangement provides for a divorcement of voting rights from beneficial ownership of the AC and AL stock; that the creation and issuance of the share of AD stock is tantamount to a pooling by the AC and AL stockholders of a portion of their voting stock and giving it to a trustee, in the person of the AD stockholder, to vote for the election of the fifth director; that after the creation of the AD stock, the AC and AL stockholders each hold but 40% of the voting power, and the AD stockholder holds the controlling balance of 20%; that the AD stock has no property rights except the right to a return of the $10 paid as the par value; and that, therefore, there has been a transfer of the voting rights devoid of any participating property rights. So runs the argument of the plaintiff in support of his contention that the first of the *Abercrombie* criteria for a voting trust is met.

The contention is unacceptable. The AD arrangement did not separate the voting rights of the AC or the AL stock from the other attributes of ownership of those classes of stock. Each AC and AL stockholder retains complete control over the voting of his stock; each can vote his stock directly; no AL or AC stockholder is divested of his right to vote his stock as he sees fit; no AL or AC stock can be voted against the shareholder's wishes; and the AL and AC stock continue to elect two directors each.

The AD stock arrangement as we view it, became a part of the capitalization of the Company. The fact that there is but a single share, or that the par value is nominal, is of no legal significance; the one share and the $10 par value might have been multiplied many times over, with the same consequence. It is true that the creation of the separate class of AD stock may have diluted the voting *power* which had previously existed in the AC and AL stock—the usual consequence when additional voting stock is created—but the creation of the new class did not divest and separate the voting *rights* which remain vested in each AC and AL shareholder, together with the other attributes of the ownership of that stock. The fallacy of the plaintiff's position lies in his premise that since the voting power of the AC and AL stock was reduced by the creation of the AD stock, the percentage of reduction became the *res* of a voting trust. In any recapitalization involving the creation of additional voting stock, the voting power of the previously existing stock is diminished; but a voting trust is not necessarily the result.

Since the holders of the Class AC and Class AL stock of the Company did not separate the voting rights from the other attributes of ownership of those classes when they created the Class AD stock, the first *Abercrombie* test of a voting trust is not met.

… Having held that the AC and AL stockholders have not divested themselves of their voting rights, although they may have diluted their voting powers, we do not reach the remaining *Abercrombie* tests, both of which assume the divestiture of voting rights.

In the final analysis, the essence of the question raised by the plaintiff in this connection is this: Is the substance and purpose of the AD stock arrangement sufficiently close to the substance and purpose of § 218 to warrant its being subjected to the restrictions and conditions imposed by that Statute? The answer is negative not only for the reasons above stated, but also because § 218 regulates trusts and pooling agreements amounting to trusts, not other and different types of arrangements and undertakings possible among stockholders. Compare *Ringling Bros.-Barnum & Bailey Combined Shows, Inc. v. Ringling*, 29 Del. Ch. 610, 53 A.2d 441 (1947); *Abercrombie v. Davies, supra.* The AD stock arrangement is neither a trust nor a pooling agreement.

We hold, therefore, that the Class AD stock arrangement is not controlled by the Voting Trust Statute.

II

The plaintiff's second point is that even if the Class AD stock arrangement is not a voting trust in substance and effect, the AD stock is illegal, nevertheless, because the creation of a class of stock having voting rights only, and lacking any substantial participating proprietary interest in the corporation, violates the public policy of this State as declared in § 218.

The fallacy of this argument is twofold: First, it is more accurate to say that what the law has disfavored, and what the public policy underlying the Voting Trust Statute means to control, is the separation of the vote from the stock — not from the stock ownership. 5 Fletcher Cyclopedia Corporations, § 2080, pp. 363–369; compare *Abercrombie v. Davies, supra.* Clearly, the AD stock arrangement is not violative of that public policy. Secondly, there is nothing in § 218, either expressed or implied, which requires that all stock of a Delaware corporation must have both voting rights and proprietary interests. Indeed, public policy to the contrary seems clearly expressed by 8 Del. C. § 151(a) which authorizes, in very broad terms, such voting powers and participating rights as may be stated in the certificate of incorporation. Non-voting stock is specifically authorized by § 151(a); and in the light thereof, consistency does not permit the conclusion, urged by the plaintiff, that the present public policy of this State condemns the separation of voting rights from beneficial stock ownership.

We conclude that the plaintiff's contention in this regard cannot withstand the force and effect of § 151(a). In our view, that Statute permits the creation of stock having voting rights only, as well as stock having property rights only. The voting powers and the participating rights of the Class AD stock being specified in the Company's certificate of incorporation, we are of the opinion that the Class AD stock is legal by virtue of § 151(a)....

We are told that if the AD stock arrangement is allowed thus to stand, our Voting Trust Statute will become a "dead letter" because it will be possible to evade and circumvent its purpose simply by issuing a class of non-participating voting stock, as was done here. We have three negative reactions to this argument:

First, it presupposes a divestiture of the voting rights of the AC and AL stock — an untenable supposition as has been stated. Secondly, it fails to take into account the main purpose of a Voting Trust Statute: to avoid secret, uncontrolled combinations of stockholders formed to acquire voting control of the corporation to the possible detriment of non-participating shareholders. It may not be said that the AD stock arrangement contravenes that purpose. Finally on this point, if we misconceive the legislative intent, and if the AD stock arrangement in this case reveals a loophole in

§ 218 which should be plugged, it is for the General Assembly to accomplish — not for us to attempt by interstitial judicial legislation. . . .

———————

The following case demonstrates how a combination of a pooling agreement and a buy/sell agreement can be used to address issues of control in a closely held corporation.

Ramos v. Estrada

California Court of Appeals
10 Cal. Rptr. 2d 833 (1992)

GILBERT, ASSOCIATE JUSTICE.

Defendants Tila and Angel Estrada appeal a judgment which states they breached a written corporate shareholder voting agreement. We hold that a corporate shareholders' voting agreement may be valid even though the corporation is not technically a close corporation. We affirm.

Facts

Plaintiffs Leopoldo Ramos et al. formed Broadcast Corporation for the purpose of obtaining a Federal Communications Commission (FCC) construction permit to build a Spanish language television station in Ventura County.

Ramos and his wife held 50 percent of Broadcast Corp. stock. The remaining 50 percent was issued in equal amounts to five other couples. The Estradas were one of the couples who purchased a 10 percent interest in Broadcast Corp. Tila Estrada became president of Broadcast Corp., sometimes known as the "Broadcast Group."

In 1986, Broadcast Corp. merged with a competing applicant group, Ventura 41 Television Associates (Ventura 41), to form Costa del Oro Television, Inc. (Television Inc.). The merger agreement authorized the issuance of 10,002 shares of Television Inc. voting stock.

Initially, Television Inc. was to issue 5,000 shares to Broadcast Corp. and 5,000 to Ventura 41. Each group would have the right to elect half of an eight member board of directors. The two remaining outstanding shares were to be issued to Broadcast Corp. after the television station had operated at full power for six months. Television Inc.'s board would then increase to nine members, five of whom would be elected by Broadcast Corp.

The merger agreement contained restrictions on the transfer of stock and required each group to adopt internal shareholder agreements to carry out the merger agreement. With FCC approval, Broadcast Corp. and Ventura 41 modified their agreement to permit stock in Television Inc. to be issued directly to the respective owners of the merged entities instead of to the entities themselves. Ventura 41 sought this change so that Television Inc. would be treated as a Subchapter S corporation for tax purposes. In part, Broadcast Group agreed to this change in exchange for approval by Ventura

41 of the agreement at issue here, which is known as the June Broadcast Agreement. Among other things, the June Broadcast Agreement provides for block voting for directors by the Broadcast Group shareholders according to their ownership.

In January 1987, Broadcast Group executed a written shareholder agreement, known as the January Broadcast Agreement, to govern the voting and transfer of Broadcast Corp. shares in Television Inc. stock. At a later date, Broadcast Group drafted a written schedule showing the valuation of shares transferred pursuant to the January Broadcast Agreement. It set the price for purchase and sale of shares as their investment cost plus 8 percent per annum.

In June 1987, the shareholders of Broadcast Group executed a Master Shareholder Agreement. This agreement was designed to implement the Merger Agreement. It permits direct shareholder ownership of stock and governs various voting and transfer provisions. It requires that shareholder votes be made in the manner voted by the majority of the shareholders.

Members of Broadcast Group subscribed for shares of Television Inc. in their respective proportion of ownership pursuant to written subscription agreements attached to the Master Shareholder Agreement. The Ventura 41 group acted similarly.

Television Inc. issued stock to these subscribers in December 1987, and they elected an eight-member board. They also elected Leopoldo Ramos president, and Tila Estrada as one of the directors.

At a special directors' meeting held on October 8, 1988, Tila Estrada voted with the Ventura 41 group block to remove Ramos as president and to replace him with Walter Ulloa, a member of Ventura 41. She also joined Ventura 41 in voting to remove Romualdo Ochoa, a Broadcast Group member, as secretary and to replace him with herself.

Under the June Broadcast Agreement and the Merger Agreement, each of the groups were required to vote for the directors upon whom a majority of each respective group had agreed. The terms of that agreement expressly state that failure to adhere to the agreement constitutes an election by the shareholder to sell his or her shares pursuant to buy/sell provisions of the agreement. The agreement also calls for specific enforcement of such buy/sell provisions.

On October 15, 1988, the Broadcast Group noticed another meeting to decide how its members would vote their shares for directors at the annual meeting. All members attended except the Estradas. The group agreed to nominate another slate of directors which did not include either of the Estradas.

The Estradas unilaterally declared the June Broadcast Agreement null and void as of October 15, 1988, in a letter dictated for them by Paul Zevnik, the attorney for Ventura 41. Tila Estrada refused to recognize the October 15 vote of the majority of the Broadcast Group to replace her as a director of Television Inc. Ramos et al. sued the Estradas for breach of the June Broadcast Agreement, among other things.

The court ruled that the Estradas materially breached the valid June Broadcast Agreement, and it ordered their shares sold in accordance with the specific enforcement provisions of the June Broadcast Agreement. The court restrained the Estradas from voting their shares other than as provided in the June Broadcast Agreement.

Discussion

The Estradas contend that the June Broadcast Agreement is void because it constitutes an expired proxy which the Estradas validly revoked.

The interpretation of statutes and contracts is a matter of law subject to independent review by this court.

Corporations Code section 178 defines a proxy to be "a written authorization signed ... by a shareholder ... giving another person or persons power to vote with respect to the shares of such shareholder."

Section 7.1 of the June Broadcast Agreement details the voting arrangement among the shareholders. It states, in pertinent part: "The Stockholders agree that they shall consult with each other prior to voting their shares in the Company. They shall attempt in good faith to reach a consensus as to the outcome of any such vote. In the case of a vote for directors, they agree that no director shall be selected who is not acceptable to at least one member (*i.e.*, spousal unit) of each of Group A and Group B. (*See* P 1.2(b)(1) above [which states that: "The Stockholders shall be divided into two groups, Group 'A' being composed of Leopoldo Ramos and Cecilia Morris, and Group 'B' being composed of all the other Stockholders."]) In the case of all votes of Stockholders they agree that, following consultation and compliance with the other provisions of this paragraph, they will all vote their stock in the manner voted by a majority of the Stockholders."

No proxies are created by this agreement. The agreement has the characteristics of a shareholders' voting agreement expressly authorized by section 706, subdivision (a) for close corporations. Although the articles of incorporation do not contain the talismanic statement that "This corporation is a close corporation," the arrangements of this corporation, and in particular this voting agreement, are strikingly similar to ones authorized by the Code for close corporations.

Section 706, subdivision (a) states, in pertinent part: "an agreement between two or more shareholders of a close corporation, if in writing and signed by the parties thereto, may provide that in exercising any voting rights the shares held by them shall be voted as provided by the agreement, or as the parties may agree or as determined in accordance with a procedure agreed upon by them...."

Here, the members of this corporation executed a written agreement providing that they shall try to reach a consensus on all votes and that they shall consult with one another and vote their own stock in accordance with the majority of the stockholders. They entered into this agreement because they "mutually desire[d]" to limit the transferability of their stock to ensure "the Company does not pass into the control of persons whose interests might be incompatible with the interests of the Company and of the Stockholders, establishing their mutual rights and obligations in the event of death, and establishing a mechanism for determining how the Stockholders' voting rights in the Company shall be exercised...."

The instant agreement is valid, enforceable and supported by consideration. It states, in pertinent part, that the stockholders entered into the agreement for the purposes of "limiting the transferability of ... stock in the Company, ensuring that the Company does not pass into the control of persons whose interests might be incompatible with the interests of the Company and of the Stockholders, establishing their mutual rights and obligations in the event of death, and establishing a mechanism for determining how the Stockholders' voting rights ... shall be exercised...."

Section 7.2 of the agreement states that "[t]he Stockholders understand and acknowledge that the purpose of the foregoing arrangement is to preserve their relative voting power in the Company.... Accordingly, in the event that a Stockholder fails to abide by this arrangement for whatever reason, that failure shall constitute on [sic] irrevocable election by the Stockholder to sell his stock in the Company, triggering the same rights of purchase provided in Article IV above."

The agreement calls for enforcement by specific performance of its terms because the stock is not readily marketable. Section 709, subdivision (c) expressly permits enforcement of shareholder voting agreements by such equitable remedies. It states, in pertinent part: "The court may determine the person entitled to the office of director or may order a new election to be held or appointment to be made, may determine the validity, effectiveness and construction of voting agreements ... and the right of persons to vote and may direct such other relief as may be just and proper."

The Estradas contend that the forced sale provision is unconscionable and oppressive. They portray themselves as naive, small-town business people who were forced to sign an adhesion agreement without reviewing its contents.

Substantial evidence supports the findings that Tila Estrada has been a licensed real estate broker. She is an astute businesswoman experienced with contracts concerning real property. The consent and signatures of the Estradas to the agreement were not procured by fraud, duress or other wrongful conduct of Ramos. The Estradas read and discussed with other members of Broadcast Group, and with their own counsel, the voting, buy/sell and other provisions of the agreement and the January Broadcast Agreement, as well as various drafts of these documents, and they freely signed these agreements.

On direct examination, under Evidence Code section 776, Tila Estrada admitted she owns and operates a real estate brokerage business; she regularly reviews a broad variety of real estate documents; she and her husband own and manage investment property; and she has considered herself "to be an astute business woman" since 1985. Tila Estrada also has been a participant and owner in another application before the FCC, for an FM radio station, before the instant suit was filed.

Ms. Estrada stated she got copies "of all the drafts and all the Shareholders Agreements." She discussed these agreements with other members of Broadcast Group and with its counsel, Mr. Howard Weiss.

The June Broadcast Agreement, including its voting and buy/sell provisions, was unanimously executed after the Estradas had a full and fair opportunity to consider it in its entirety. As the trial court found, the buy-out provisions at issue here are valid, favored by courts and enforceable by specific performance....

The Estradas breached the agreement by their written repudiation of it. Their breach constituted an election to sell their Television Inc. shares in accordance with the terms of the buy/sell provisions in the agreement. This election does not constitute a forfeiture—they violated the agreement voluntarily, aware of the consequences of their acts and they are provided full compensation, per their agreement....

MBCA §7.31 resolves two of the problems long associated with voting trusts and vote pooling agreements. The first is whether a pooling agreement will be recast as a voting trust and held to be invalid. Section 7.31 states that "(a) Two or more shareholders may provide for the manner in which they will vote their shares by signing an agreement for that purpose. A voting agreement created under this section is not subject to the provisions of §7.30 [which controls voting trusts]."

The Official Comment to §7.31(a) sheds further light on this issue. It states:

> Section 7.31(a) explicitly recognizes agreements among two or more shareholders as to the voting of shares and makes clear that these agreements are not subject to the rules relating to a voting trust. These agreements are often referred to as "pooling agreements." The only formal requirements are that they be in writing and signed by all the participating shareholders; in other respects their validity is to be judged as any other contract. They are not subject to the 10-year limitation applicable to voting trusts.

The second issue is one of enforceability. Voting trusts could be specifically enforced, whereas voting agreements could not, unless the terms of the agreement expressly provided an enforcement mechanism. Subsection (b) of §7.31 settles that issue as well. It provides that "A voting agreement created under this section is specifically enforceable." The Official Comment to subsection 7.31(b) states:

> ... A voting agreement may provide its own enforcement mechanism, as by the appointment of a proxy to vote all shares subject to the agreement; the appointment may be made irrevocable under section 7.22. If no enforcement mechanism is provided, a court may order specific enforcement of the agreement and order the votes cast as the agreement contemplates. This section recognizes that damages are not likely to be an appropriate remedy for breach of a voting agreement, and also avoids the result reached in *Ringling Bros. Barnum & Bailey Combined Shows v. Ringling*, 53 A.2d 441 (Del. 1947), where the court held that the appropriate remedy to enforce a pooling agreement was to refuse to permit any voting of the breaching party's shares.

B. Shareholders' Agreements Allocating Control

Agreements among shareholders can contain provisions governing anything the parties wish, so long as the agreement does not constitute an illegal voting trust and so long as it does not violate public policy. We have already discussed some of the issues raised by shareholder agreements concerning voting. The agreements referred to in this section typically affect the allocation of power between shareholders and directors. Questions of public policy usually arise when a shareholders' agreement intrudes into areas governed by a state's corporation statute. Considering that all corporate issues ultimately are resolvable either by the shareholders or the directors, agreements among shareholders almost always relate to matters within the bailiwick of one or the other of those two groups.

Agreements among shareholders relating to actions within the statutory province of shareholders generally do not run into problems on public policy grounds. The general rule is that shareholders may vote their shares in any way they wish. While it is true that shareholders, especially those in closely held corporations, may sometimes have fiduciary duties toward their fellow shareholders, those duties generally do not limit shareholders' ability to look out for their own interests. If, therefore, shareholders believe it is in their interest to agree on such matters as for whom they will vote as directors or to whom and under what conditions they may sell their shares, the state typically will take no interest in the matter. And, in fact, agreements among shareholders on such matters are common.

The problem arises when agreements among persons who are both shareholders and directors relate to matters over which the corporation statute gives the directors control, as, for example, the oversight management of the corporation or appointment of officers. It is the job of directors to represent all of the shareholders equally, and in so doing they exercise fiduciary responsibilities to all of the shareholders. Therefore, courts traditionally have not usually favored agreements limiting the discretion or authority of the directors, including binding directors to act in the future in agreed-upon ways.

If courts wish, however, they can allow substantial leeway to shareholders and directors in closely held corporations, and sometimes courts will uphold agreements that seem, on their face, to violate public policy as reflected in the corporation statute. A leading case on this point is *Galler v. Galler*, 203 N.E.2d 577 (Ill. 1964).

Section 7.32 of the MBCA eliminates some of the historical concerns associated with shareholder agreements restricting the discretion of the members of the board of directors of a closely held corporation. Section 7.32(a) provides in part:

> An agreement among shareholders of a corporation that complies with this section is effective among the shareholders and the corporation even though it is inconsistent with one or more other provisions of this Act in that it: (1) eliminates the board of directors or restricts the discretion or powers of the board of directors; (2) governs the authorization or making of distributions whether or not in proportion to ownership of shares, subject to the limitations in section 6.40; (3) establishes who shall be directors or officers of the corporation, or their terms of office or manner of selection or removal; (4) governs, in general or in regard to specific matters, the exercise or division of voting power by or between the shareholders and directors or by or among any of

them, including use of weighted voting rights or director proxies; ... (6) transfers to one or more shareholders or other persons all or part of the authority to exercise the corporate powers or to manage the business and affairs of the corporation, including the resolution of any issue about which there exists a deadlock among directors or shareholders; ... (8) otherwise governs the exercise of the corporate powers or the management of the business and affairs of the corporation or the relationship among the shareholders, the directors and the corporation, or among any of them, and is not contrary to public policy.

The Official Comment states:

> Shareholders of closely-held corporations, ranging from family businesses to joint ventures owned by large public corporations, frequently enter into agreements that govern the operation of the enterprise. In the past, various types of shareholder agreements were invalidated by courts for a variety of reasons, including so-called "sterilization" of the board of directors and failure to follow the statutory norms of the applicable corporation act. *See, e.g., Long Park, Inc. v. Trenton-New Brunswick Theaters Co.*, 297 N.Y. 174, 77 N.E.2d 633 (1948). The more modern decisions reflect a greater willingness to uphold shareholder agreements....

> Rather than relying on further uncertain and sporadic development of the law in the courts, section 7.32 rejects the older line of cases. It adds an important element of predictability currently absent from the MBCA and affords participants in closely-held corporations greater contractual freedom to tailor the rules of their enterprise.

> Section 7.32 is not intended to establish or legitimize an alternative form of corporation. Instead, it is intended to add, within the context of the traditional corporate structure, legal certainty to shareholder agreements that embody various aspects of the business arrangement established by the shareholders to meet their business and personal needs.... Thus, Section 7.32 validates for nonpublic corporations various types of agreements among shareholders even when the agreements are inconsistent with the statutory norms contained in the Act.[11]

C. Employment Contracts

One contractual arrangement that can be used to distribute corporate control is the employment contract. Since in a closely held corporation shareholders often wish to work full-time in their corporation, such contracts can be used along with other devices to distribute control among the shareholders. Employment agreements also can be used, of course, to place limited control in the hands of nonshareholders who will serve as officers. There are, however, significant limitations on the protections available through employment contracts, and a number of things to consider in drafting them.

---

11. Model Act § 7.32 Official Comment.

Corporation statutes universally provide that a corporation's officers are to be chosen by its directors and that the officers may be removed by the directors at will. Partially for that reason, specific performance is not a remedy that will be available to an officer if a corporation breaks the officer's employment contract, except perhaps in the most extraordinary circumstances. MBCA § 8.43(b) speaks directly to the issue by providing that "An officer may be removed at any time with or without cause by: (i) the board of directors...." Section 8.44 adds "(a) The appointment of an officer does not itself create contract rights. (b) An officer's removal does not affect the officer's contract rights, if any, with the corporation...."

To offer much protection to an officer, a salary escalator must be built into an employment contract. The simplest way to do that is to provide for minimum annual percentage increases. In financial terms, the next big choice for the drafter of an employment contract is whether to provide for liquidated damages. Although a provision for liquidated damages is not always desirable, it may make a breach of the contract too unpalatable for a board to contemplate, if breaking an employment contract is likely to cost the corporation a substantial amount of money.

In these circumstances, an officer also faces the possibility that the corporation will change the officer's job, or the duties incident to the job, in an attempt to force the officer to resign. That, in fact, often is the first thing corporate managers think of when faced with getting rid of an unwanted officer who has an employment contract. Not surprisingly, since most employment contracts are drafted by the corporation's lawyer, a usual provision in employment contracts calls for the person signing the contract to "hold such offices and perform such services as the board of directors shall provide." That obviously provides an officer with little protection.

Some protection comes from specifying the office to be held, but not so much protection as may at first seem. At the time an employment contract for the president is signed, for example, the president may be the chief executive officer. If the board of directors wants to force the president's resignation, the first thing it likely will do is elect a chair of the board and make the chair the chief executive officer. That may be followed by other actions, such as the election of a vice chair who is made chief operating officer and the removal from the president of all duties of significance. While it is true that a court may, if it wishes, interpret such corporate actions as breaches of the president's contract, there can be no assurance that that will be the case.

The best way to avoid such problems is to describe an officer's corporate role in functional terms, such as chief executive officer, chief operating officer, chief financial officer, and so on. A long-term employment contract that does that, and that has a reasonable salary escalator and perhaps a good liquidated damages clause, can give an officer substantial protection.

Many corporations have entered into so-called golden parachute contracts with their principal executives. Those contracts typically apply when there is a change of control (as defined) and an executive is either discharged without cause or is subject to a significant change of duties. Upon leaving the company, the executive is usually entitled to the continuation of any compensation, bonuses, and other benefits for a stipulated period notwithstanding any other employment the executive may secure. The Internal Revenue Code, however, by imposing confiscatory taxes, does limit the aggregate amounts that may be paid under such contracts.

Chapter 8

Piercing the Corporate Veil

Situation

As Biologistics, Inc. continues to grow, the corporation continues to assume various obligations. For instance, the corporation is responsible for ongoing payments under its lease agreement with Southland Properties, Inc. At the same time, there are other potential liabilities. For example, what if a customer is dissatisfied with the corporation's work and successfully sues the corporation for negligent and faulty DNA analysis? The corporation's operations also use various chemicals that, if improperly disposed of, could lead to environmental law problems.

Biologistics' shareholders want assurance that they will not be held personally responsible for these corporate obligations. What advice do you offer them?

Section I
Introduction

As a fundamental corporate law principle, shareholders' liability for corporate obligations is limited to the amount which they contribute to the corporation in exchange for their equity interest.[1] Thus, their financial risk is limited to the amount of their deliberate investment, and creditors of the corporation cannot access shareholders' personal assets. Shareholders' limited liability also is consistent with the notion that the corporation is a separate legal entity from its shareholders.

The courts, however, have created an exception to this fundamental principle of limited liability. As we will explore in this chapter, under certain "equitable" circumstances, courts will "pierce the corporate veil." By disregarding the corporate entity, creditors of the corporation can then hold shareholders personally liable for the corporation's obligations. This shift of the loss from the corporate creditor to the shareholders effectively alters the amount of financial risk that the shareholders had anticipated and relied upon.

It is often difficult to discern the underlying legal principles in "piercing the corporate veil" cases. In part, this results from some courts' inclination to be vague about their specific reasoning, and instead defer to metaphorical but obscure rhetoric, such as describing the corporation as the "alter ego," "instrumentality," or "dummy" of the

---

1. Model Act § 6.22(b), Del. Code Ann. tit. 8 § 102(b)(6).

shareholders. In part, courts have not definitively determined what extreme situations would prompt them to overcome the important presumption of limited liability.

The following cases explore various distinctions. In contract cases, where the plaintiff creditor and the corporation voluntarily entered into their relationship, should the corporation's adequate capitalization or its observance of corporate formalities be determinative? What if the shareholders misrepresented their roles in the corporation? Should tort cases be treated differently than contract cases, given that tort plaintiffs typically become corporate creditors involuntarily? Should the fact that the shareholder is a sole individual, one of many individuals, or another business enterprise make a difference?

Section II
Tort-Based Claims and Other Considerations

The majority and dissenting opinions in the following two tort-based cases offer contrasting views of when it is appropriate to pierce the corporate veil. Consider how the justices' perspectives on the limits of the corporate form affect their conclusions.

Baatz v. Arrow Bar, Inc.

South Dakota Supreme Court
452 N.W.2d 138 (1990)

SABERS, JUSTICE:

Kenny and Peggy Baatz (Baatz), appeal from summary judgment dismissing Edmond, LaVella, and Jacquette Neuroth, as individual defendants in this action.

Facts

Kenny and Peggy were seriously injured in 1982 when Roland McBride crossed the center line of a Sioux Falls street with his automobile and struck them while they were riding on a motorcycle. McBride was uninsured at the time of the accident and apparently is judgment proof.

Baatz alleges that Arrow Bar served alcoholic beverages to McBride prior to the accident while he was already intoxicated. Baatz commenced this action in 1984, claiming that Arrow Bar's negligence in serving alcoholic beverages to McBride contributed to the injuries they sustained in the accident. Baatz supports his claim against Arrow Bar with the affidavit of Jimmy Larson. Larson says he knew McBride and observed him being served alcoholic beverages in the Arrow Bar during the afternoon prior to the accident, while McBride was intoxicated....

Edmond and LaVella Neuroth formed the Arrow Bar, Inc. in May 1980. During the next two years they contributed $50,000 to the corporation pursuant to a stock subscription agreement. The corporation purchased the Arrow Bar business in June 1980 for $155,000 with a $5,000 down payment. Edmond and LaVella executed a promissory note personally guaranteeing payment of the $150,000 balance. In 1983 the corporation obtained bank financing in the amount of $145,000 to pay off the purchase agreement. Edmond and LaVella again personally guaranteed payment of the corporate debt. Edmond is the president of the corporation, and Jacquette Neuroth serves as the manager of the business…. [T]he corporation did not maintain dram shop liability insurance at the time of the injuries to Kenny and Peggy.

In 1987 the trial court entered summary judgment in favor of Arrow Bar and the individual defendants. Baatz appealed that judgment and we reversed and remanded to the trial court for trial. Shortly before the trial date, Edmond, LaVella, and Jacquette moved for and obtained summary judgment dismissing them as individual defendants. Baatz appeals. We affirm.

…

2. Individual liability by piercing the corporate veil

Baatz claims that … the corporate veil of Arrow Bar, Inc. should be pierced, leaving the Neuroths, as the shareholders of the corporation, individually liable. A corporation shall be considered a separate legal entity until there is *sufficient reason* to the contrary. When continued recognition of a corporation as a separate legal entity would "produce injustices and inequitable consequences," then a court has sufficient reason to pierce the corporate veil. *Farmers Feed & Seed, Inc. v. Magnum Enter., Inc.*, 344 N.W.2d 699, 701 (S.D. 1984). Factors that indicate injustices and inequitable consequences and allow a court to pierce the corporate veil are:

1) fraudulent representation by corporation directors;

2) undercapitalization;

3) failure to observe corporate formalities;

4) absence of corporate records;

5) payment by the corporation of individual obligations; or

6) use of the corporation to promote fraud, injustice, or illegalities.

Id.…

Baatz advances several arguments to support his claim that the corporate veil of Arrow Bar, Inc. should be pierced, but fails to support them with facts, or misconstrues the facts.

First, Baatz claims that since Edmond and LaVella personally guaranteed corporate obligations, they should also be personally liable to Baatz. However, the personal guarantee of a loan is a contractual agreement and cannot be enlarged to impose tort liability. Moreover, the personal guarantee creates individual liability for a corporate obligation, the opposite of factor 5, above. As such, it supports, rather than detracts from, recognition of the corporate entity.

Baatz also argues that the corporation is simply the alter ego of the Neuroths, and … the corporate veil should be pierced. Baatz' discussion of the law is adequate, but he fails to present evidence that would support a decision in his favor in accordance with that law. When an individual treats a corporation "as an instrumentality through which he [is] conducting his personal business," a court may disregard the corporate entity. *Larson v. Western Underwriters, Inc.*, 87 N.W.2d 883, 886 (S.D. 1958). Baatz fails to demonstrate how the Neuroths were transacting personal business through the corporation. In fact, the evidence indicates the Neuroths treated the corporation separately from their individual affairs.

Baatz next argues that the corporation is undercapitalized. Shareholders must equip a corporation with a reasonable amount of capital for the nature of the business involved. Baatz claims the corporation was started with only $5,000 in ... capital, but does not explain how that amount failed to equip the corporation with a reasonable amount of capital. In addition, Baatz fails to consider the personal guarantees to pay off the purchase contract in the amount of $150,000, and the $50,000 stock subscription agreement. There simply is no evidence that the corporation's capital in whatever amount was inadequate for the operation of the business.... [S]imply asserting that the corporation is undercapitalized does not make it so. Without some evidence of the inadequacy of the capital, Baatz fails to present specific facts demonstrating a genuine issue of material fact.

Finally, Baatz argues that Arrow Bar, Inc. failed to observe corporate formalities because none of the business' signs or advertising indicated that the business was a corporation. Baatz cites SDCL § 47-2-36 as requiring the name of any corporation to contain the word corporation, company, incorporated, or limited, or an abbreviation for such a word. In spite of Baatz' contentions, the corporation is in compliance with the statute because its corporate name — Arrow Bar, Inc. — includes the abbreviation of the word incorporated. Furthermore, the "mere failure upon occasion to follow all the forms prescribed by law for the conduct of corporate activities will not justify" disregarding the corporate entity. *Larson, supra*, 87 N.W.2d at 887 (*quoting P.S. & A. Realties, Inc. v. Lodge Gate Forest, Inc.*, 127 N.Y.S.2d 315, 324 (1954)). Even if the corporation is improperly using its name, that alone is not a sufficient reason to pierce the corporate veil. This is especially so where, as here, there is no relationship between the claimed defect and the resulting harm....

In summary, Baatz fails to present specific facts that would allow the trial court to find the existence of a genuine issue of material fact. There is no ... evidence indicating that the Neuroths treated the corporation in any way that would produce the injustices and inequitable consequences necessary to justify piercing the corporate veil. In fact, the only evidence offered is otherwise. Therefore, we affirm summary judgment dismissing the Neuroths as individual defendants.

Wuest, C.J., and Morgan and Miller, JJ., concur.

Henderson, Justice (dissenting):

This corporation has no separate existence. It is the instrumentality of three shareholders, officers, and employees. Here, the corporate fiction should be disregarded....

A corporate shield was here created to escape the holding of this Court relating to an individual's liability in a dram shop action....

As a result of this holding, the message is now clear: Incorporate, mortgage the assets of a liquor corporation to your friendly banker, and proceed with carefree entrepreneuring....

Peggy Baatz, a young mother, lost her left leg; she wears an artificial limb; Kenny Baatz, a young father, has had most of his left foot amputated; he has been unable to work since this tragic accident. Peggy uses a cane. Kenny uses crutches. Years have gone by since they were injured and their lives have been torn asunder.

Uninsured motorist was drunk, and had a reputation of being a habitual drunkard; Arrow Bar had a reputation of serving intoxicated persons. (Supported by depositions on file). An eyewitness saw uninsured motorist in an extremely intoxicated condition, shortly before the accident, being served by Arrow Bar....

Are the Neuroths subject to personal liability? It is undisputed, by the record, that the dismissed defendants (Neuroths) are immediate family members and stockholders of Arrow Bar. By pleadings, at settled record 197, it is expressed that the dismissed defendants are employees of Arrow Bar. Seller of the Arrow Bar would not accept Arrow Bar, Inc., as buyer. Seller insisted that the individual incorporators, in their individual capacity be equally responsible for the selling price. Thus, the individuals are the real party in interest and the corporate entity, Arrow Bar, Inc., is being used to justify any wrongs perpetrated by the incorporators in their individual capacity. Conclusion: Fraud is perpetrated upon the public. At a deposition of Edmond Neuroth (filed in this record), this "President" of "the corporation" was asked why the Neuroth family incorporated. His answer: "Upon advice of counsel, as a shield against individual liability." The corporation was undercapitalized (Neuroths borrowed $5,000 in capital)....

Clearly, it appears a question arises as to whether there is a fiction established to escape our previous holdings and the intent of our State Legislature. Truly, there are fact questions for a jury to determine: (1) negligence or no negligence of the defendants and (2) did the Neuroth family falsely establish a corporation to shield themselves from individual liability, *i.e.*, do facts in this scenario exist to pierce the corporate veil?...

Walkovszky v. Carlton

New York Court of Appeals
223 N.E.2d 6 (1966)

FULD, JUDGE:

This case involves what appears to be a rather common practice in the taxicab industry of vesting the ownership of a taxi fleet in many corporations, each owning only one or two cabs.

The complaint alleges that the plaintiff was severely injured four years ago in New York City when he was run down by a taxicab owned by the defendant Seon Cab Corporation and negligently operated at the time by the defendant Marchese. The individual defendant, Carlton, is claimed to be a stockholder of 10 corporations, including Seon, each of which has but two cabs registered in its name, and it is implied that only the minimum automobile liability insurance required by law (in the amount of $10,000) is carried on any one cab. Although seemingly independent of one another, these corporations are alleged to be "operated … as a single entity, unit and enterprise" with regard to financing, supplies, repairs, employees and garaging, and all are named as defendants. The plaintiff asserts that he is also entitled to hold their stockholders personally liable for the damages sought because the multiple corporate structure constitutes an unlawful attempt "to defraud members of the general public" who might be injured by the cabs.

The defendant Carlton has moved, pursuant to [N.Y. Civ. Prac. L.&R. (CPLR)] § 3211(a)7, to dismiss the complaint on the ground that as to him it "fails to state a cause of action." The court at Special Term granted the motion but the Appellate Division, by a divided vote, reversed, holding that a valid cause of action was sufficiently stated. The defendant Carlton appeals to us, from the nonfinal order, by leave of the Appellate Division on a certified question.

The law permits the incorporation of a business for the very purpose of enabling its proprietors to escape personal liability but, manifestly, the privilege is not without its limits. Broadly speaking, the courts will disregard the corporate form, or, to use accepted terminology, "pierce the corporate veil," whenever necessary "to prevent fraud or to achieve equity." (*International Aircraft Trading Co. v. Manufacturers Trust Co.*, 79 N.E.2d 249, 252 [(N.Y. (1948)]). In determining whether liability should be extended to reach assets beyond those belonging to the corporation, we are guided, as Judge Cardozo noted, by "general rules of agency." (*Berkey v. Third Ave. Ry. Co.*, 155 N.E. 58, 61 [(N.Y. 1926)], 50 A.L.R. 599.) In other words, whenever anyone uses control of the corporation to further his own rather than the corporation's business, he will be liable for the corporation's acts "upon the principle of *respondeat superior* applicable even where the agent is a natural person." (*Rapid Tr. Subway Constr. Co. v. City of New York*, 259 N.Y. 472, 488, 182 N.E. 145, 150.) Such liability, moreover, extends not only to the corporation's commercial dealings but to its negligent acts as well.

In [*Mangan v. Terminal Transportation System, Inc.*, 286 N.Y.S. 666 (N.Y. App. Div. 1936)], the plaintiff was injured as a result of the negligent operation of a cab owned and operated by one of four corporations affiliated with the defendant Terminal. Although the defendant was not a stockholder of any of the operating companies, both the defendant and the operating companies were owned, for the most part, by the same parties. The defendant's name (Terminal) was conspicuously displayed on the sides of all of the taxis used in the enterprise and, in point of fact, the defendant actually serviced, inspected, repaired and dispatched them. These facts were deemed to provide sufficient cause for piercing the corporate veil of the operating company—the nominal owner of the cab which injured the plaintiff—and holding the defendant liable. The operating companies were simply instrumentalities for carrying on the business of the defendant without imposing upon it financial and other liabilities incident to the actual ownership and operation of the cabs.

In the case before us, the plaintiff has explicitly alleged that none of the corporations "had a separate existence of their own" and, as indicated above, all are named as defendants. However, it is one thing to assert that a corporation is a fragment of a larger corporate combine which actually conducts the business. (See Berle, *The Theory of Enterprise Entity*, 47 Col. L. Rev. 343, 348–350.) It is quite another to claim that the corporation is a "dummy" for its individual stockholders who are in reality carrying on the business in their personal capacities for purely personal rather than corporate ends. Either circumstance would justify treating the corporation as an agent and piercing the corporate veil to reach the principal but a different result would follow in each case. In the first, only a larger *corporate* entity would be held financially responsible while, in the other, the stockholder would be personally liable. Either the stockholder is conducting the business in his individual capacity or he is not. If he is, he will be liable; if he is not, then it does not matter—insofar as his personal liability is concerned—that the enterprise is actually being carried on by a larger "enterprise entity." (See Berle, *supra*.)

At this stage in the present litigation, we are concerned only with the pleadings[.] ... Reading the complaint in this case most favorably and liberally, we do not believe that there can be gathered from its averments the allegations required to spell out a valid cause of action against the defendant Carlton.

The individual defendant is charged with having "organized, managed, dominated and controlled" a fragmented corporate entity but there are no allegations that he was conducting business in his individual capacity. Had the taxicab fleet been owned by a single corporation, it would be readily apparent that the plaintiff would face formidable barriers in attempting to establish personal liability on the part of the corporation's stockholders. The fact that the fleet ownership has been deliberately split up among many corporations does not ease the plaintiff's burden in that respect. The corporate form may not be disregarded merely because the assets of the corporation, together with the mandatory insurance coverage of the vehicle which struck the plaintiff, are insufficient to assure him the recovery sought.

If Carlton were to be held individually liable on those facts alone, the decision would apply equally to the thousands of cabs which are owned by their individual drivers who conduct their businesses through corporations organized pursuant to section 401 of the Business Corporation Law, Consol. Laws, c. 4 and carry the minimum insurance required by subdivision 1 (par. (a)) of section 370 of the Vehicle and Traffic Law, Consol. Laws, c. 71. These taxi owner-operators are entitled to form such corporations and we agree with the court at Special Term that, if the insurance coverage required by statute "is inadequate for the protection of the public, the remedy lies not with the courts but with the Legislature." It may very well be sound policy to require that certain corporations must take out liability insurance which will afford adequate compensation to their potential tort victims. However, the responsibility for imposing conditions on the privilege of incorporation has been committed by the Constitution to the Legislature (N.Y. Const., art. X, § 1) and it may not be fairly implied, from any statute, that the Legislature intended, without the slightest discussion or debate, to require of taxi corporations that they carry automobile liability insurance over and above that mandated by the Vehicle and Traffic Law.

This is not to say that it is impossible for the plaintiff to state a valid cause of action against the defendant Carlton. However, the simple fact is that the plaintiff has just not done so here. While the complaint alleges that the separate corporations were undercapitalized and that their assets have been intermingled, it is barren of any "sufficiently particular(ized) statements" (CPLR § 3013; *see* 3 Weinstein-Korn-Miller, *N.Y. Civ. Prac.*, par. 3013.01 *et seq.*, pp. 30–142 *et seq.*) that the defendant Carlton and his associates are actually doing business in their individual capacities, shuttling their personal funds in and out of the corporations "without regard to formality and to suit their immediate convenience." (*Weisser v. Mursam Shoe Corp.*, 127 F.2d 344, 345 [(2d Cir. 1942)], 145 A.L.R. 467.) Such a "perversion of the privilege to do business in a corporate form" (*Berkey*, 155 N.E. at 61, 50 A.L.R. 599, *supra*) would justify imposing personal liability on the individual stockholders. Nothing of the sort has in fact been charged, and it cannot reasonably or logically be inferred from the happenstance that the business of Seon Cab Corporation may actually be carried on by a larger corporate entity composed of many corporations which, under general principles of agency, would be liable to each other's creditors in contract and in tort.

... If it is not fraudulent for the owner-operator of a single cab corporation to take out only the minimum required liability insurance, the enterprise does not become either illicit or fraudulent merely because it consists of many such corporations. The plaintiff's injuries are the same regardless of whether the cab which strikes him is owned by a single corporation or part of a fleet with ownership fragmented among many corporations. Whatever rights he may be able to assert against parties other than the registered owner of the vehicle come into being not because he has been defrauded but because, under the principle of *respondeat superior*, he is entitled to hold the whole enterprise responsible for the acts of its agents.

In sum, then, the complaint falls short of adequately stating a cause of action against the defendant Carlton in his individual capacity.

The order of the Appellate Division should be reversed, with costs in this court and in the Appellate Division, the certified question answered in the negative and the order of the Supreme Court, Richmond County, reinstated, with leave to serve an amended complaint.

KEATING, JUDGE (dissenting):

The defendant Carlton, the shareholder here sought to be held for the negligence of the driver of a taxicab, was a principal shareholder and organizer of the defendant corporation which owned the taxicab. The corporation was one of 10 organized by the defendant, each containing two cabs and each cab having the "minimum liability" insurance coverage mandated by section 370 of the Vehicle and Traffic Law. The sole assets of these operating corporations are the vehicles themselves and they are apparently subject to mortgages.[2]

---

2. [*] It appears that the medallions, which are of considerable value, are judgment proof. (Administrative Code of City of New York, § 436-2.0.) [Municipal governments issue a set number of "medallions," typically for a fee, that function like a license for operating a taxicab.—Eds.]

From their inception these corporations were intentionally undercapitalized for the purpose of avoiding responsibility for acts which were bound to arise as a result of the operation of a large taxi fleet having cars out on the street 24 hours a day and engaged in public transportation. And during the course of the corporations' existence all income was continually drained out of the corporations for the same purpose.

The issue presented by this action is whether the policy of this State, which affords those desiring to engage in a business enterprise the privilege of limited liability through the use of the corporate device, is so strong that it will permit that privilege to continue no matter how much it is abused, no matter how irresponsibly the corporation is operated, no matter what the cost to the public. I do not believe that it is.

Under the circumstances of this case the shareholders should all be held individually liable to this plaintiff for the injuries he suffered. At least, the matter should not be disposed of on the pleadings by a dismissal of the complaint. "If a corporation is organized and carries on business without substantial capital in such a way that the corporation is likely to have no sufficient assets available to meet its debts, it is inequitable that shareholders should set up such a flimsy organization to escape personal liability. The attempt to do corporate business without providing any sufficient basis of financial responsibility to creditors is an abuse of the separate entity and will be ineffectual to exempt the shareholders from corporate debts. It is coming to be recognized as the policy of law that shareholders should in good faith put at the risk of the business unincumbered capital reasonably adequate for its prospective liabilities. If capital is illusory or trifling compared with the business to be done and the risks of loss, this is a ground for denying the separate entity privilege." (Ballantine, *Corporations* (Rev. ed., 1946), § 129, pp. 302–303.)...

The policy of this State has always been to provide and facilitate recovery for those injured through the negligence of others. The automobile, by its very nature, is capable of causing severe and costly injuries when not operated in a proper manner. The great increase in the number of automobile accidents combined with the frequent financial irresponsibility of the individual driving the car led to the adoption of section 388 of the Vehicle and Traffic Law which had the effect of imposing upon the owner of the vehicle the responsibility for its negligent operation. It is upon this very statute that the cause of action against both the corporation and the individual defendant is predicated.

In addition the Legislature, still concerned with the financial irresponsibility of those who owned and operated motor vehicles, enacted a statute requiring minimum liability coverage for all owners of automobiles. The important public policy represented by both these statutes is outlined in section 310 of the Vehicle and Traffic Law. That section provides that: "The legislature is concerned over the rising toll of motor vehicle accidents and the suffering and loss thereby inflicted. The legislature determines that it is a matter of grave concern that motorists shall be financially able to respond in damages for their negligent acts, so that innocent victims of motor vehicle accidents may be recompensed for the injury and financial loss inflicted upon them."

The defendant Carlton claims that, because the minimum amount of insurance required by the statute was obtained, the corporate veil cannot and should not be pierced despite the fact that the assets of the corporation which owned the cab were "trifling compared with the business to be done and the risks of loss" which were certain to be encountered. I do not agree.

The Legislature in requiring minimum liability insurance of $10,000, no doubt, intended to provide at least some small fund for recovery against those individuals and corporations who just did not have and were not able to raise or accumulate assets sufficient to satisfy the claims of those who were injured as a result of their negligence. It certainly could not have intended to shield those individuals who organized corporations, with the specific intent of avoiding responsibility to the public, where the operation of the corporate enterprise yielded profits sufficient to purchase additional insurance. Moreover, it is reasonable to assume that the Legislature believed that those individuals and corporations having substantial assets would take out insurance far in excess of the minimum in order to protect those assets from depletion. Given the costs of hospital care and treatment and the nature of injuries sustained in auto collisions, it would be unreasonable to assume that the Legislature believed that the minimum provided in the statute would in and of itself be sufficient to recompense "innocent victims of motor vehicle accidents ... for the injury and financial loss inflicted upon them."

The defendant, however, argues that the failure of the Legislature to increase the minimum insurance requirements indicates legislative acquiescence in this scheme to avoid liability and responsibility to the public. In the absence of a clear legislative statement, approval of a scheme having such serious consequences is not to be so lightly inferred. . . .

The defendant contends that a decision holding him personally liable would discourage people from engaging in corporate enterprise.

What I would merely hold is that a participating shareholder of a corporation vested with a public interest, organized with capital insufficient to meet liabilities which are certain to arise in the ordinary course of the corporation's business, may be held personally responsible for such liabilities. Where corporate income is not sufficient to cover the cost of insurance premiums above the statutory minimum or where initially adequate finances dwindle under the pressure of competition, bad times or extraordinary and unexpected liability, obviously the shareholder will not be held liable.

The only types of corporate enterprises that will be discouraged as a result of a decision allowing the individual shareholder to be sued will be those such as the one in question, designed solely to abuse the corporate privilege at the expense of the public interest.

For these reasons I would vote to affirm the order of the Appellate Division.

Notes

1. On remand, the plaintiff was able to amend his complaint to adequately allege that the defendant conducted the business in his individual capacity.

Walkovszky v. Carlton, 287 N.Y.S.2d 546 (N.Y. App. Div. 1968), *aff'd,* 244 N.E.2d 55 (N.Y. 1968).

2. Notice what assets the plaintiffs in veil piercing cases seek and the routes they theorize to reach them. In veil piercing cases, the creditor is generally trying to reach the assets of a corporation's shareholders. Such shareholder assets might include cash and other property, as well as shares of other corporations. In *Walkovszky v. Carlton,* the plaintiff pursued such a route to secure access to Carlton's assets, including shares in all the sibling corporations. The plaintiff also pursued a more direct route to the *assets* of those sibling corporations by asserting that the sibling corporations were themselves directly liable for the obligations of the harm-inflicting corporation. The majority opinion prescribes a roadmap for an amended complaint to pursue the former route to the defendants' shares of the sibling corporations, but the opinion demonstrates the difficulty of pursuing the latter route of seeking direct access to all the assets of the sibling corporations.

A. Factors

There is no universal consensus about what is determinative in "piercing the corporate veil" cases. In fact, courts have identified numerous factors that may be relevant in a specific fact pattern. Given this bewildering variety, it may be helpful to condense specific examples into broad categories. It might even be possible to conclude that the cases often boil down to two issues (aside from outright fraud): the extent of equity capital at stake and the degree of obedience to corporate formalities. Consider the following delineation of factors stated in *Laya v. Erin Homes, Inc.,* 352 S.E.2d 93, 98–99 (W. Va. 1986) and how all or most could be so classified:

(1) commingling of funds and other assets of the corporation with those of the individual shareholders;

(2) diversion of the corporation's funds or assets to non-corporate uses (to the personal uses of the corporation's shareholders);

(3) failure to maintain the corporate formalities necessary for the issuance of or subscription to the corporation's stock, such as formal approval of the stock issued by the board of directors;

(4) an individual shareholder representing to persons outside the corporation that he or she is personally liable for the debts or other obligations of the corporation;

(5) failure to maintain corporate minutes or adequate corporate records;

(6) identical equitable ownership in two entities;

(7) identity of the directors and officers of two entities who are responsible for supervision and management (a partnership or sole proprietorship and a corporation owned and managed by the same parties);

(8) failure to adequately capitalize a corporation for the reasonable risks of the corporate undertaking;

(9) absence of separately held corporate assets;

(10) use of a corporation as a mere shell or conduit to operate a single venture or some particular aspect of the business of an individual or another corporation;

(11) sole ownership of all the stock by one individual or members of a single family;

(12) use of the same office or business location by the corporation and its individual shareholder(s);

(13) employment of the same employees or attorney by the corporation and its shareholder(s);

(14) concealment or misrepresentation of the identity of the ownership, management or financial interests in the corporation, and concealment of personal business activities of the shareholders (sole shareholders do not reveal the association with a corporation, which makes loans to them without adequate security);

(15) disregard of legal formalities and failure to maintain proper arm's-length relationships among related entities;

(16) use of a corporate entity as a conduit to procure labor, services or merchandise for another person or entity;

(17) diversion of corporate assets from the corporation by or to a stockholder or other person or entity to the detriment of creditors, or the manipulation of assets and liabilities between entities to concentrate the assets in one and the liabilities in another;

(18) contracting by the corporation with another person with the intent to avoid the risk of nonperformance by use of the corporate entity; or the use of a corporation as a subterfuge for illegal transactions;

(19) the formation and use of the corporation to assume the existing liabilities of another person or entity.

As illustrated in the lead cases, justices differ on how flexible the corporate form should be and, consequently, may apply the above factors differently. In both *Baatz* and *Walkovszky*, the majority and dissenting justices were presented with the same facts, but reached opposing conclusions about the appropriateness of the shareholders' conduct. Do you find the majority opinion or dissenting opinion in each case more compelling?

B. Empirical Data

Two empirical studies illuminate the contours of veil piercing litigation and results. In a review of 690 federal district court cases from 2000–06, Professors Boyd and Hoffman classified factors set forth in complaints seeking to pierce veils and tested their relation to success on the merits (whether by judgment favoring piercing or settlement after motions involving piercing were resolved and the claim still alive).[4] They classified the following type and frequency of assertion (akin but not identical to the foregoing list of factors): alter ego (53%), fraud (35%), dominion (34%), informalities (33%), undercapitalization (23%), instrumentality (21%), façade, shell or dummy (12%), intertwining (12%), unity of interest (10%) and sham (9%). They found that complaints alleging more substantive grounds, such as undercapitalization, than rhetorical grounds, such as façade, shell or dummy, were more likely to result in plaintiff success. Can you hypothesize why?

Concerning who gets sued, in the Boyd-Hoffman study, 85% of cases involved corporations, 13% LLCs and the remaining other forms. In about 70% of both corporation and LLC cases, the persons sued were individuals; the defendants were another corporation or other entity in 10% of the LLC cases and 15% of the corporation cases; and the rest sued both individuals and entities. Most targets were relatively small enterprises, 55% employing ten or fewer people, 26% 11–50, 6% 51–100, 7% 501–1000, and 4% more than that. Concerning large enterprises, employing more than 1,000 people, the 4% figure means about 50 complaints filed in federal district court over a 6-year period asserted veil piercing claims against sizable corporations, and some of those were public companies employing more than 30,000 people.

In the Boyd-Hoffman study, of 550 motions raising veil piercing issues, about 50% enabled plaintiffs to proceed without ending the case, 20% ended the case for the plaintiff on the merits (though not necessarily on the veil piercing claim) and 15% ended the case for the defendant on the merits (the rest were still pending when the parties settled). Ignoring the latter, this suggests considerable success or value in veil piercing cases, yielding positive plaintiff results in nearly 80% of the cases; notably, however, only about 6% (37 of the 690 cases) resulted in judicially-enforced veil piercing judgments on the merits.

In an earlier study of 1,583 cases before 1985, Professor Thompson likewise found that most veil piercing cases were filed against smaller, closely-held corporations, rather than large public corporations.[5] Among the few veil piercing cases against public corporations in his study, the public corporation's veil was not pierced in any of them. On the other hand, in the overall population of cases, the veil was pierced in about 40% of them. Some of these included cases where a subsidiary corporation's veil was pierced to hold liable a parent corporation or a sibling corporation. The Thompson study also found that the number of individual shareholders seemed to make a difference: close corporations with one shareholder were pierced in almost 50% of the cases, followed by about 46% in two or three shareholder corporations, and about 35% in corporations with more than three shareholders.

---

4. Christina L. Boyd & David A. Hoffman, *Disputing Limited Liability*, 104 Nw. U.L. Rev. 853 (2010).

5. Robert B. Thompson, *Piercing the Corporate Veil: An Empirical Study*, 76 Cornell L. Rev. 1036 (1991).

C. Tort Claimant

Both *Baatz* and *Walkovszky* involved situations where the corporation's obligations resulted from a tort claim. In contrast to a contract claimant who has deliberately entered into a relationship with the corporation, the typical tort claimant has involuntarily become the corporation's creditor. Thus, one might expect courts to be more sympathetic towards the plaintiffs in tort cases in their attempts to hold shareholders personally liable.

However, both the Boyd-Hoffman and Thompson studies provide evidence to the contrary. In his survey, Professor Thompson found that courts were less inclined to pierce the veil in tort cases (30.97%), than in contract cases (41.98%).[6] This was true although more than two-thirds of the tort cases involved corporate defendants. "This combination of a corporate deep pocket and a nonvoluntary claimant suggests that the plaintiff would have a greater chance of success." The study results, however, concluded otherwise.

The Boyd-Hoffman study likewise provided evidence showing that voluntary, contract creditors are more likely to prevail than involuntary creditors (whether in tort or based on other non-contractual relationships). The authors also found that contract claims are more often the basis for veil piercing assertions than tort claims are, with about half the cases in the study portrayed as contract claimants and about 30% tort claimants. On the other hand, they emphasize difficulty in neatly distinguishing many complaints as asserting contract or tort claims, as many assert both and exact avenues parties pursue change as litigation proceeds and theories are tested against facts.

Section III
Contract-Based Claims and Other Considerations

The following case continues our exploration of the piercing the corporate veil doctrine, adopting an explicit analytical framework that the previous cases seemed to hint at. It organizes its analysis under two prongs: (1) Were the identities of the shareholder and the corporation so inseparable that their separate legal existences should cease? (2) Would some inequitable result occur unless the corporation's veil is pierced? The case also provides the backdrop for a discussion of these factors: undercapitalization, corporate formalities, the contract claimant, intra-enterprise liability and "reverse veil piercing," and equity and fraud.

---

6. *Id.* at 1058, 1068–70.

Sea-Land Services, Inc. v. Pepper Source

United States Court of Appeals, Seventh Circuit
941 F.2d 519 (1991)

BAUER, CHIEF JUDGE:

This spicy case finds its origin in several shipments of Jamaican sweet peppers. Appellee Sea-Land Services, Inc. ("Sea-Land"), an ocean carrier, shipped the peppers on behalf of The Pepper Source ("PS"), one of the appellants here. PS then stiffed Sea-Land on the freight bill, which was rather substantial. Sea-Land filed a federal diversity action for the money it was owed. On December 2, 1987, the district court entered a default judgment in favor of Sea-Land and against PS in the amount of $86,767.70. But PS was nowhere to be found; it had been "dissolved" in mid-1987 for failure to pay the annual state franchise tax. Worse yet for Sea-Land, even had it not been dissolved, PS apparently had no assets. With the well empty, Sea-Land could not recover its judgment against PS. Hence the instant lawsuit.

In June 1988, Sea-Land brought this action against Gerald J. Marchese and five business entities he owns: PS, Caribe Crown, Inc., Jamar Corp., Salescaster Distributors, Inc., and Marchese Fegan Associates. Marchese also was named individually. Sea-Land sought by this suit to pierce PS's corporate veil and render Marchese personally liable for the judgment owed to Sea-Land, and then "reverse pierce" Marchese's other corporations so that they, too, would be on the hook for the $87,000. Thus, Sea-Land alleged in its complaint that all of these corporations "are alter egos of each other and hide behind the veils of alleged separate corporate existence for the purpose of defrauding plaintiff and other creditors." Not only are the corporations alter egos of each other, alleged Sea-Land, but also they are alter egos of Marchese, who should be held individually liable for the judgment because he created and manipulated these corporations and their assets for his own personal uses. (Hot on the heels of the filing of Sea-Land's complaint, PS took the necessary steps to be reinstated as a corporation in Illinois.)

In early 1989, Sea-Land filed an amended complaint adding Tie-Net International, Inc., as a defendant. Unlike the other corporate defendants, Tie-Net is not owned solely by Marchese: he holds half of the stock, and an individual named George Andre owns the other half. Sea-Land alleged that, despite this shared ownership, Tie-Net is but another alter ego of Marchese and the other corporate defendants, and thus it also should be held liable for the judgment against PS....

In an order dated June 22, 1990, the court granted Sea-Land's motion [for summary judgment]. The court discussed and applied the test for corporate veil-piercing explicated in *Van Dorn Co. v. Future Chemical & Oil Corp.*, 753 F.2d 565 (7th Cir. 1985). Analyzing Illinois law, we held in *Van Dorn* that:

> a corporate entity will be disregarded and the veil of limited liability pierced when two requirements are met:

> [F]irst, there must be such unity of interest and ownership that the separate personalities of the corporation and the individual [or other corporation]

no longer exist; and second, circumstances must be such that adherence to the fiction of separate corporate existence would sanction a fraud or promote injustice.

… As for determining whether a corporation is so controlled by another to justify disregarding their separate identities, the Illinois cases, as we summarized them in *Van Dorn*, focus on four factors: "(1) the failure to maintain adequate corporate records or to comply with corporate formalities, (2) the commingling of funds or assets, (3) undercapitalization, and (4) one corporation treating the assets of another corporation as its own." 753 F.2d at 570.

Following the lead of the parties, the district court in the instant case laid the template of *Van Dorn* over the facts of this case. The court concluded that both halves and all features of the test had been satisfied, and, therefore, entered judgment in favor of Sea-Land and against PS, Caribe Crown, Jamar, Salescaster, Tie-Net, and Marchese individually. These defendants were held jointly liable for Sea-Land's $87,000 judgment, as well as for post-judgment interest under Illinois law. From that judgment Marchese and the other defendants brought a timely appeal....

The first and most striking feature that emerges from our examination of the record is that these corporate defendants are, indeed, little but Marchese's playthings. Marchese is the sole shareholder of PS, Caribe Crown, Jamar, and Salescaster. He is one of the two shareholders of Tie-Net. Except for Tie-Net, none of the corporations ever held a single corporate meeting. (At the handful of Tie-Net meetings held by Marchese and Andre, no minutes were taken.) During his deposition, Marchese did not remember any of these corporations ever passing articles of incorporation, bylaws, or other agreements. As for physical facilities, Marchese runs all of these corporations (including Tie-Net) out of the same, single office, with the same phone line, the same expense accounts, and the like. And how he does "run" the expense accounts! When he fancies to, Marchese "borrows" substantial sums of money from these corporations—interest free, of course. The corporations also "borrow" money from each other when need be, which left at least PS completely out of capital when the Sea-Land bills came due. What's more, Marchese has used the bank accounts of these corporations to pay all kinds of personal expenses, including alimony and child support payments to his ex-wife, education expenses for his children, maintenance of his personal automobiles, health care for his pet—the list goes on and on. Marchese did not even have a personal bank account! (With "corporate" accounts like these, who needs one?)

And Tie-Net is just as much a part of this as the other corporations. On appeal, Marchese makes much of the fact that he shares ownership of Tie-Net, and that Sea-Land has not been able to find an example of funds flowing from PS to Tie-Net to the detriment of Sea-Land and PS's other creditors. So what? The record reveals that, in all material senses, Marchese treated Tie-Net like his other corporations: he "borrowed" over $30,000 from Tie-Net; money and "loans" flowed freely between Tie-Net and the other corporations; and Marchese charged up various personal expenses (including $460 for a picture of himself with President Bush) on Tie-Net's credit card.

Marchese was not deterred by the fact that he did not hold all of the stock of Tie-Net; why should his creditors be?[7]

In sum, we agree with the district court that [there] can be no doubt that the "shared control/unity of interest and ownership" part of the *Van Dorn* test is met in this case: corporate records and formalities have not been maintained; funds and assets have been commingled with abandon; PS, the offending corporation, and perhaps others have been undercapitalized; and corporate assets have been moved and tapped and "borrowed" without regard to their source. Indeed, Marchese basically punted this part of the inquiry before the district court by coming forward with little or no evidence in response to Sea-Land's extensively supported argument on these points. That fact alone was enough to do him in; opponents to summary judgment motions cannot simply rest on their laurels, but must come forward with specific facts showing that there is a genuine issue for trial. Regarding the elements that make up the first half of the *Van Dorn* test, Marchese and the other defendants have not done so. Thus, Sea Land is entitled to judgment on these points.

The second part of the *Van Dorn* test is more problematic, however. "Unity of interest and ownership" is not enough; Sea-Land also must show that honoring the separate corporate existences of the defendants "would sanction a fraud or promote injustice." *Van Dorn*, 753 F.2d at 570. This last phrase truly is disjunctive:

> Although an intent to defraud creditors would surely play a part if established, the Illinois test does not require proof of such intent. Once the first element of the test is established, *either* the sanctioning of a fraud (intentional wrongdoing) or the promotion of injustice, will satisfy the second element.

Id. (emphasis in original). Seizing on this, Sea-Land has abandoned the language in its two complaints that make repeated references to "fraud" by Marchese, and has chosen not to attempt to *prove* that PS and Marchese intended to defraud it—which would be quite difficult on summary judgment. Instead, Sea-Land has argued that honoring the defendants' separate identities would "promote injustice."

But what, exactly, does "promote injustice" mean, and how does one establish it on summary judgment? These are the critical, troublesome questions in this case. To start with, as the above passage from *Van Dorn* makes clear, "promote injustice" means something less than an affirmative showing of fraud—but how much less? In its one-sentence treatment of this point, the district court held that it was enough that "Sea-Land would be denied a judicially-imposed recovery." Sea-Land defends this reasoning on appeal, arguing that "permitting the appellants to hide behind the shield of limited liability would clearly serve as an injustice against appellee" because

---

7. [2] We note that the record evidence in this case, if true, establishes that for years Marchese flagrantly has disregarded the tax code concerning the treatment of corporate funds. Yet, when we inquired at oral argument whether Marchese currently is under investigation by the IRS, his counsel informed us that to his knowledge he is not. Marchese also stated in his deposition that he never has been audited by the IRS. If these statements are true, and the IRS has so far shown absolutely no interest in Marchese's financial shenanigans with his "corporations," how and why that has occurred may be the biggest puzzles in this litigation.

it would "impermissibly deny appellee satisfaction." But that cannot be what is meant by "promote injustice." The prospect of an unsatisfied judgment looms in every veil-piercing action; why else would a plaintiff bring such an action? Thus, if an unsatisfied judgment is enough for the "promote injustice" feature of the test, then *every* plaintiff will pass on that score, and *Van Dorn* collapses into a one-step "unity of interest and ownership" test. ...

Federal district courts sitting in Illinois also have on occasion discussed what kind of "injustice" suffices under the second half of the *Van Dorn* test. *In re Conticommodity Services, Inc., Securities Litigation*, 733 F. Supp. 1555 (N.D. Ill. 1990), involved a complex, multidistrict litigation that ultimately had little to do with veil-piercing. At one point in its opinion, however, the district court considered whether a trial was necessary on the claim that a parent corporation should be pierced to satisfy a liability of one of its subsidiaries. The court concluded that the issue should go to trial, because "it may be an injustice" to allow the parent to avoid the sub's liabilities when the parent closed down the sub and left it with insufficient funds to satisfy its liabilities, and those liabilities were caused in part by a practice of the sub mandated by the parent. *Id.* at 1565. In *Boatmen's Nat'l Bank of St. Louis v. Smith*, 706 F. Supp. 30 (N.D. Ill. 1989), the court granted a judgment creditor's request to "reverse pierce" the veil of a corporation whose sole shareholder, director, and president was liable for the judgment. ...

Finally, *Van Dorn* itself is somewhat instructive. In that case, we affirmed the district court's decision to pierce the corporate veil of one corporation ("Future") to get at the assets held by another ("Sovereign of Illinois") for the benefit of a creditor who had shipped Future some packing cans ("Milton"). As to the second half of the test, we stated as follows:

> Eventually Future was stripped of its assets and rendered insolvent to the prejudice of Milton, its only creditor, while Sovereign of Illinois received the benefits of the Milton can shipments. The record supported the trial court's finding that such a result was unjust and warranted piercing the corporate veil between Future and Sovereign of Illinois to hold Sovereign of Illinois liable for the price of the cans.

753 F.2d at 572–73. Further, it is clear from various other passages in the opinion that the district court concluded, and the evidence showed, that Roth, the individual who controlled both Future and Sovereign of Illinois, intentionally manipulated the corporations so that Future assumed the liabilities but held no assets, while other corporations received the assets but not the liabilities. *See, e.g., id.* at 569.

Generalizing from these cases, we see that the courts that properly have pierced corporate veils to avoid "promoting injustice" have found that, unless it did so, some "wrong" beyond a creditor's inability to collect would result: the common sense rules of adverse possession would be undermined; former partners would be permitted to skirt the legal rules concerning monetary obligations; a party would be unjustly enriched; a parent corporation that caused a sub's liabilities and its inability to pay for them would escape those liabilities; or an intentional scheme to squirrel assets into a liability-free corporation while heaping liabilities upon an asset-free corporation

e.g. "shell game"

would be successful. Sea-Land, although it alleged in its complaint the kind of intentional asset- and liability-shifting found in *Van Dorn*, has yet to come forward with evidence akin to the "wrongs" found in these cases. Apparently, it believed, as did the district court, that its unsatisfied judgment was enough. That belief was in error, and the entry of summary judgment premature. We, therefore, reverse the judgment and remand the case to the district court.

On remand, the court should require that Sea-Land produce, if it desires summary judgment, evidence and argument that would establish the kind of additional "wrong" present in the above cases. For example, perhaps Sea-Land could establish that Marchese, like Roth in *Van Dorn*, used these corporate facades to avoid its responsibilities to creditors; or that PS, Marchese, or one of the other corporations will be "unjustly enriched" unless liability is shared by all. Of course, Sea-Land is not required fully to prove intent to defraud, which it probably could not do on summary judgment anyway. But it is required to show the kind of injustice to merit the evocation of the court's essentially equitable power to prevent "injustice." It may well be that, after more of such evidence is adduced, no genuine issue of fact exists to prevent Sea-Land from reaching Marchese's other pet corporations for PS's debt. Or it may be that only a finder of fact will be able to determine whether fraud or "injustice" is involved here. In any event, the record as it currently stands is insufficient to uphold the entry of summary judgment.

Reversed and Remanded with instructions.

Notes and Questions

1. Did the court move too quickly over the questions of Tie-Net and reverse veil piercing? True, holding the companies that Marchese owned 100% of liable for Marchese's debts only punishes Marchese because he is the only shareholder. Yet, to hold Tie-Net liable for Marchese's debts punishes all other shareholders of Tie-Net including George Andre, who did not appear to be a party to the litigation and whose interests were apparently not represented.

The circumstance illustrates one of many ways in which so-called "reverse veil piercing" differs from traditional veil piercing. In traditional veil piercing, a corporation's creditor pierces its veil to hold its shareholder(s) personally liable for their actions and no interests other than that of the shareholder(s) are implicated. In reverse veil piercing, a creditor of a shareholder seeks to go after assets of a corporation that the shareholder owns an interest in — whether or not the corporation has other innocent owners whose interests might be impaired by a judgment adverse to the corporation. For these reasons, while some courts have recognized reverse veil piercing in certain settings, others have rejected the theory.

2. Recall how the plaintiff in *Walkovszky v. Carlton* sought to reach the sibling corporations' assets directly by claims against them or by a personal judgment against the defendant shareholder, which would include access to his shares in those corporations. Compare the approach in *Sea-Land*, where the plaintiff's reverse veil piercing claim would enable direct access to all the assets of the sibling corporations as well

as all of the individual defendant's assets, which would include his shares in those companies.

A. Undercapitalization

Kinney Shoe Corp. v. Polan, 939 F.2d 209 (4th Cir. 1991), and *Radaszewski v. Telecom Corp.*, 981 F.2d 305 (8th Cir. 1992), followed an analytical framework comparable to the court in *Sea-Land*. In *Kinney*, the plaintiff Kinney Shoe Corporation argued that Lincoln Polan should have been held personally liable for the sublease obligation of his wholly-owned corporation. In *Radaszewski*, the plaintiff Konrad Radaszewski was an injured motorcyclist who wanted to reach the assets of Telecom, which was the parent corporation of Contrux, the company whose employee injured Radaszewski.

In determining whether the two prongs of inseparable identities and equity were satisfied, both cases emphasized the role of undercapitalization. As explained in *Radaszewski*:

> Undercapitalizing a subsidiary, which we take to mean creating it and putting it in business without a reasonably sufficient supply of money, has become a sort of proxy under Missouri law for the second [prong]. On the prior appeal, for example, we said that "Missouri courts will disregard the existence of a corporate entity that is operated while undercapitalized."... The reason, we think, is not because undercapitalization, in and of itself, is unlawful (though it may be for some purposes), but rather because the creation of an undercapitalized subsidiary justifies an inference that the parent is either deliberately or recklessly creating a business that will not be able to pay its bills or satisfy judgments against it.... [*Id.* at 308.]

How would you determine what amount is necessary to meet the anticipated financial needs of the corporation, given the type, nature, and size of its business? At what point in time should the corporation be adequately capitalized? Should it be at the time of the initial incorporation, throughout the corporation's business history, or at the time when the corporation incurred the obligation at issue in the case? In *Consumer's Coop. of Walworth County v. Olsen*, 419 N.W.2d 211, 218–19 (Wis. 1988), for example, the court concluded that the critical time was when the corporation was initially formed.

In *Radaszewski*, the court distinguished between undercapitalization in the "accounting sense" and "financial responsibility."

> Here, the District Court held, and we assume, that Contrux was undercapitalized in the accounting sense. Most of the money contributed to its operation by Telecom was in the form of loans, not equity, and, when Contrux first went into business, Telecom did not pay for all of the stock that was issued to it. This is a classic instance of watered stock, of putting a corporation into business without sufficient equity investment. Telecom in effect concedes that Contrux's balance sheet was anemic, and that, from the point of view of generally accepted accounting principles, Contrux was inadequately capitalized. Telecom says, however, that this doesn't matter, because Contrux

had $11,000,000 worth of liability insurance available to pay judgments like the one that Radaszewski hopes to obtain. No one can say, therefore, the argument runs, that Telecom was improperly motivated in setting up Contrux, in the sense of either knowingly or recklessly establishing it without the ability to pay tort judgments.

... Unhappily, Contrux's insurance carrier became insolvent two years after the accident and is now in receivership.... But this insurance, Telecom points out, was sufficient to satisfy federal financial-responsibility requirements.... Contrux, at all times during its operations, was considered financially responsible by the relevant federal agency, the Interstate Commerce Commission. [*Id.* at 308–09.]

Even if the corporation is clearly undercapitalized, is that a sufficient condition for piercing the corporate veil? In *Harris v. Curtis*, [87 Cal. Rptr. 614 (Cal. Ct. App. 1970)], a corporation organized for the purpose of owning and operating motels was underfinanced. The court, noting that being underfinanced was a "condition not uncommon among new small business," held that inadequate capitalization was a factor, but not determinative.

B. Corporate Formalities

In addition to undercapitalization, *Kinney* also emphasized corporate formalities. Citing from *Laya*, the court stated that ... "'[i]ndividuals who wish to enjoy limited personal liability for business activities under a corporate umbrella should be expected to adhere to the relatively simple formalities of creating and maintaining a corporate entity.'" *Laya v. Erin Homes, Inc.*, 352 S.E.2d 93, 100 n.6 (W. Va. 1986) (quoting *Labadie Coal Co. v. Black*, 672 F.2d 92, 96–97 (D.C. Cir. 1982)). This, the court stated, is "'a relatively small price to pay for limited liability.'"

In *Kinney*, the corporation apparently had not followed corporate formalities. What kinds of formalities could the corporation have followed? "While a complete catalogue of dangerous acts is probably impossible to prepare, there appears to be a substantial risk that the separate corporate existence will be ignored when business is commenced without issuance of shares, when shareholders' meetings or directors' meetings are not held, or consents are not signed, when decisions are made by shareholders as if they were partners, when the shareholders do not sharply distinguish between corporate property and personal property, when corporate funds are used to pay personal expenses, when personal funds are used for corporate expenses without proper accounting, or when complete corporate and financial records are not maintained."[8]

Professor Thompson's study[9] also discussed the effects of undercapitalization and corporate formalities. He found that (1) undercapitalization was present in about

---

8. Robert W. Hamilton, *The Corporate Entity*, 49 Tex. L. Rev. 979, 990 (1971).

9. Robert B. Thompson, *Piercing the Corporate Veil: An Empirical Study*, 76 Cornell L. Rev. 1036, 1063 (1991).

19% of the contract cases and in just under 13% of the tort cases in which the courts
pierced the veil; and (2) the lack of corporate formalities was found in 20% of the
contract cases and about 11% of the tort cases in which the courts pierced the veil.
On the other hand, if the courts do find undercapitalization, the courts pierced the
corporate veil over 73% of the time. Absence of formalities led to piercing in about
67% of the cases. Similarly, the Boyd-Hoffman study[10] showed that undercapitalization
was asserted often (in 33% of the cases) and had a much stronger correlation with
success on the merits than flimsier rhetorical assertions, such as characterizing a corporation as a façade, shell or dummy.

C. Contract Claimant

In contrast to the tort claimant who involuntarily becomes a corporate "creditor,"
the contract claimant has deliberately entered into a relationship with the corporation.
The court in *Kinney* considered whether the Kinney Shoe Company, as a contract
claimant, had assumed the risk of the corporation's insolvency.

> In *Laya*, the court also noted that when determining whether to pierce a cor-
> porate veil a third prong may apply in certain cases. The court stated:

> When, under the circumstances, it would be reasonable for that particular
> type of a party [those contract creditors capable of protecting themselves]
> entering into a contract with the corporation, for example, a bank or other
> lending institution, to conduct an investigation of the credit of the corporation
> prior to entering into the contract, such party will be charged with the knowl-
> edge that a reasonable credit investigation would disclose. If such an inves-
> tigation would disclose that the corporation is grossly undercapitalized, based
> upon the nature and the magnitude of the corporate undertaking, such party
> will be deemed to have assumed the risk of the gross undercapitalization and
> will not be permitted to pierce the corporate veil.

939 F.2d 209, 212.

The court in *Kinney* declined to apply an assumption of the risk argument to the
Kinney Co., questioning whether the contract distinction should be extended beyond
the context of the financial institution lender. In contrast, the court in *Brunswick
Corp. v. Waxman*, 459 F. Supp. 1222 (E.D.N.Y. 1978), *aff'd*, 599 F.2d 34, 36 (2d Cir.
1979), was persuaded that the seller of bowling alley equipment was a knowledgeable
bargainer who assumed the risk of selling to a "dummy" corporation.

What if the party entering an agreement with the corporation could have, but
did not, investigate the corporation's financial condition? What if further inquiries
or financial assurances from the corporation are inconsistent with the business customs of the industry or unrealistic given the lack of bargaining power of the contracting party?

---

10. Boyd & Hoffman, *supra*.

D. Intra-Enterprise Liability

In *Sea-Land*, the plaintiff was trying to pierce Pepper Source's corporate veil to reach both the corporation's sibling enterprises, sometimes called intra-enterprise liability, and the individual who owns all the enterprises. Should the courts distinguish between attempts to reach enterprises, such as parent corporations or sibling corporations, and attempts to hold "living, breathing" individuals liable?

Thompson's study[11] found that a significant percentage of piercing the corporate veil cases involve corporate defendants (parents, subsidiaries, siblings). One might reasonably predict that courts would be more willing to hold corporate shareholders liable than individual shareholders. Thompson found, however, that when plaintiffs target individual shareholders, the courts pierced the veil in 43.13% of the cases; when plaintiffs target corporate defendants, courts pierced the veil in 37.21% of the cases. How would you explain this unexpected result?

When a plaintiff tries to reach the assets of a member of the corporate group who is not a shareholder of the original corporation, isn't this a more dramatic extension of the piercing the corporate veil doctrine? The sibling corporation is not the one who injured the plaintiff and also is not the owner of the corporation which has the obligation. Under what circumstances should a member of the corporate group assume this derivative liability? Should the plaintiff be required to pierce the veil to reach the common shareholder before liability can be imposed on other members of the corporate group? Should there be particular links between the original corporation and each sibling that is held liable?

E. Equity and Fraud

As in *Sea-Land*, many courts note an equity prong in their analysis. Some courts, however, do not dwell on it. They presumably reason that satisfying the first prong (requiring proof of inseparable identities) or the plaintiff's proof of an unsatisfied corporate obligation is sufficient evidence of wrongdoing, injustice, misrepresentation, or "constructive" fraud. The court in *Sea-Land* also acknowledged the difficulty of interpreting the appropriate equitable principles. Professor Thompson's study[12] found that courts which observed misrepresentation pierced the veil in approximately 94% of the cases.

Jurisdictions also differ on whether they require *fraud*. In *DeWitt Truck Brokers v. W. Ray Flemming Fruit Co.*, 540 F.2d 681, 684 (4th Cir. 1976), for instance, the court concluded:

> Contrary to the basic contention of the defendant, however, proof of plain fraud is not a necessary element in a finding to disregard the corporate entity. This was made clear in *Anderson v. Abbott*, 321 U.S. 349, 362 (1944), where the Court, after stating that "fraud" has often been found to be a ground for

---

11. Thompson, *Piercing the Corporate Veil, supra* at 1055–56.
12. *Id.* at 1063.

disregarding the principle of limited liability based on the corporate fiction, declared:

> "… The cases of fraud make up part of that exception (which allow the corporate veil to be pierced, citing cases). *But they do not exhaust it.…*"

Texas also has chosen to emphasize fraud in its piercing the corporate veil jurisprudence. In *Castleberry v. Branscum*, 721 S.W.2d 270, 273 (Tex. 1986), the Texas Supreme Court held that a jury could hold shareholders personally liable if plaintiffs could prove "a sham to perpetrate a fraud," which would involve a "flexible fact-specific approach focusing on equity." Either "actual fraud"—defined as "dishonesty of purpose or intent to deceive"—or "constructive fraud" would be acceptable. Constructive fraud was defined expansively as "breach of some legal or equitable duty which, irrespective of moral guilt, the law declares fraudulent because of its tendency to deceive others, to violate confidence, or to injure public interest." [*Id.* (citing Archer v. Griffith, 390 S.W.2d 735, 740 (Tex. 1964))] In addition, the Court rejected the distinction between contract cases, where the parties negotiated the terms of their relationship, and tort cases, where the plaintiffs typically become the corporation's creditors involuntarily.

Concerned that *Castleberry*'s abstract articulation of the piercing the corporate veil doctrine excessively threatened the corporate form, Texas legislators in 1989 enacted Tex. Bus. & Com. Code Ann. § 2.21:

> A. A holder of shares, an owner of any beneficial interest in shares … or any affiliate thereof or of the corporation, or a subscriber for shares shall be under no obligation to the corporation or to its obligees with respect to:
>
> …
>
> (2) any *contractual obligation* of the corporation on the basis that the holder, owner, or subscriber is or was the alter ego of the corporation, or on the basis of actual fraud or constructive fraud, a sham to perpetrate a fraud, or other similar theory, unless the obligee demonstrates that the holder, … did perpetrate an actual fraud on the obligee
>
> (3) any *contractual obligation* of the corporation on the basis of the failure of the corporation to observe any corporate formality, including without limitation: (a) the failure to comply with any requirement of this Act or of the articles of incorporation or bylaws of the corporation; or (b) the failure to observe any requirement prescribed by this Act or by the articles of incorporation or bylaws for acts to be taken by the corporation, its board of directors, or its shareholders.

[Emphasis added.]

If *Castleberry* interpreted piercing the corporate veil doctrine too expansively, does this statute define the scope too narrowly? Which would be the applicable law, *Castleberry* or the statute, if the corporation's obligation arose from a tort claim? *Love v. State of Texas*, 972 S.W.2d 114, 118 (Tex. App. 1998), concluded that the statute should be read literally, and hence the statute is applicable and actual fraud is required only in the context of contractual obligations.

F. Choice of Law

As illustrated by Texas law, state laws may vary in their approach to piercing the corporate veil. In Thompson's study[13] certain states such as California were more inclined, and other states such as Pennsylvania and New York were less inclined, to pierce the corporate veil.

How is the applicable state law determined? If the "internal affairs rule" applies, then the law of the state of incorporation is used. However, it is unclear if piercing the veil cases are "internal affairs." They typically deal with claims of a third-party creditor, although the issue of shareholder liability for a corporate obligation certainly involves the shareholder and corporate relationship. If piercing cases are not considered internal affairs, then the courts would have to choose which conflict of law principle would apply. In tort cases, for instance, the traditional choice-of-law rule is to apply the law of the state in which the tort occurred.

The Texas legislature, apparently anticipating these kinds of conflict of law disputes, expressly provides that its piercing the corporate veil principles would not be applicable to corporations incorporated outside of Texas.[14]

Section IV
Statutory Claims

In addition to contract and tort cases, piercing the corporate veil issues are increasingly triggered in federal and state statutory cases. In tax, workers' compensation, and environmental law cases, for example, the courts are asked whether shareholders should be liable for their corporation's statutory obligations. These statutory cases tend to emphasize the statute's purpose and policy in their determination. The following case is illustrative.

United States v. Bestfoods

United States Supreme Court
524 U.S. 51 (1998)

JUSTICE SOUTER delivered the opinion of the Court.

The United States brought this action for the costs of cleaning up industrial waste generated by a chemical plant. The issue before us, under the Comprehensive Environmental Response, Compensation, and Liability Act of 1980 (CERCLA), 94 Stat. 2767, as amended, 42 U.S.C. § 9601 *et seq.*, is whether a parent corporation that actively participated in, and exercised control over, the operations of a subsidiary may, without more, be held liable as an operator of a polluting facility owned or operated by the subsidiary. We answer no, unless the corporate veil may be pierced. But a cor-

---

13. *Id.* at 1050–53.
14. Tex. Bus. & Com. Code Ann. § 8.02.

porate parent that actively participated in, and exercised control over, the operations of the facility itself may be held directly liable in its own right as an operator of the facility.

I

In 1980, CERCLA was enacted in response to the serious environmental and health risks posed by industrial pollution. If it satisfies certain statutory conditions, the United States may, for instance, use the "Hazardous Substance Superfund" to finance cleanup efforts, which it may then replenish by suits brought under § 107 of the Act against, among others, "any person who at the time of disposal of any hazardous substance owned or operated any facility." So, those actually "responsible for any damage, environmental harm, or injury from chemical poisons [may be tagged with] the cost of their actions." The phrase "owner or operator" is defined only by tautology, however, as "any person owning or operating" a facility, and it is this bit of circularity that prompts our review.

II

In 1957, Ott Chemical Co. (Ott I) began manufacturing chemicals at a plant near Muskegon, Michigan, and its intentional and unintentional dumping of hazardous substances significantly polluted the soil and ground water at the site. In 1965, respondent CPC International Inc. incorporated a wholly owned subsidiary to buy Ott I's assets in exchange for CPC stock. The new company, also dubbed Ott Chemical Co. (Ott II), continued chemical manufacturing at the site, and continued to pollute its surroundings. CPC kept the managers of Ott I, including its founder, president, and principal shareholder, Arnold Ott, on board as officers of Ott II. Arnold Ott and several other Ott II officers and directors were also given positions at CPC, and they performed duties for both corporations.

In 1972, CPC sold Ott II to Story Chemical Company, which operated the Muskegon plant until its bankruptcy in 1977. Shortly thereafter, when respondent Michigan Department of Natural Resources (MDNR) examined the site for environmental damage, it found the land littered with thousands of leaking and even exploding drums of waste, and the soil and water saturated with noxious chemicals. MDNR sought a buyer for the property who would be willing to contribute toward its cleanup, and after extensive negotiations, respondent Aerojet-General Corp. arranged for transfer of the site from the Story bankruptcy trustee in 1977. Aerojet created a wholly owned California subsidiary, Cordova Chemical Company (Cordova/California), to purchase the property, and Cordova/California in turn created a wholly owned Michigan subsidiary, Cordova Chemical Company of Michigan (Cordova/Michigan), which manufactured chemicals at the site until 1986.

By 1981, the federal Environmental Protection Agency had undertaken to see the site cleaned up, and its long-term remedial plan called for expenditures well into the tens of millions of dollars. To recover some of that money, the United States filed this action under § 107 in 1989, naming five defendants as responsible parties: CPC, Aerojet, Cordova/California, Cordova/Michigan, and Arnold Ott. (By that time, Ott I and Ott II were defunct.) ... The trial focused on the issues of whether CPC and

Aerojet, as the parent corporations of Ott II and the Cordova companies, had "owned or operated" the facility within the meaning of § 107(a)(2).

The District Court said that operator liability may attach to a parent corporation both directly, when the parent itself operates the facility, and indirectly, when the corporate veil can be pierced under state law. The court explained that, while CERCLA imposes direct liability in situations in which the corporate veil cannot be pierced under traditional concepts of corporate law, "the statute and its legislative history do not suggest that CERCLA rejects entirely the crucial limits to liability that are inherent to corporate law." ...

The District Court held both CPC and Aerojet liable under § 107(a)(2) as operators. As to CPC, the court found it particularly telling that CPC selected Ott II's board of directors and populated its executive ranks with CPC officials, and that a CPC official, G.R.D. Williams, played a significant role in shaping Ott II's environmental compliance policy.

After a divided panel of the Court of Appeals for the Sixth Circuit reversed in part, that court granted rehearing en banc and vacated the panel decision. This time, 7 judges to 6, the court again reversed the District Court in part. The majority remarked on the possibility that a parent company might be held directly liable as an operator of a facility owned by its subsidiary: "At least conceivably, a parent might independently operate the facility in the stead of its subsidiary; or, as a sort of joint venturer, actually operate the facility alongside its subsidiary." But the court refused to go any further and rejected the District Court's analysis. Applying Michigan veil-piercing law, the Court of Appeals decided that neither CPC nor Aerojet was liable for controlling the actions of its subsidiaries, since the parent and subsidiary corporations maintained separate personalities and the parents did not utilize the subsidiary corporate form to perpetrate fraud or subvert justice.

We granted certiorari, to resolve a conflict among the Circuits over the extent to which parent corporations may be held liable under CERCLA for operating facilities ostensibly under the control of their subsidiaries. We now vacate and remand.

III

It is a general principle of corporate law deeply "ingrained in our economic and legal systems" that a parent corporation (so-called because of control through ownership of another corporation's stock) is not liable for the acts of its subsidiaries. Douglas & Shanks, *Insulation from Liability Through Subsidiary Corporations*, 39 Yale L.J. 193 (1929) (hereinafter Douglas). Thus it is hornbook law that "the exercise of the 'control' which stock ownership gives to the stockholders ... will not create liability beyond the assets of the subsidiary. That 'control' includes the election of directors, the making of by-laws ... and the doing of all other acts incident to the legal status of stockholders. Nor will a duplication of some or all of the directors or executive officers be fatal." Douglas 196 (footnotes omitted). Although this respect for corporate distinctions when the subsidiary is a polluter has been severely criticized in the literature, nothing in CERCLA purports to reject this bedrock principle, and against this venerable common-law backdrop, the congressional silence is audible. The Government has indeed made no claim that a corporate parent is liable as an owner or an operator under § 107 simply because its subsidiary is subject to liability for owning or operating a polluting facility.

But there is an equally fundamental principle of corporate law, applicable to the parent-subsidiary relationship as well as generally, that the corporate veil may be pierced and the shareholder held liable for the corporation's conduct when, the corporate form would otherwise be misused to accomplish certain wrongful purposes, most notably fraud, on the shareholder's behalf. Nothing in CERCLA purports to rewrite this well-settled rule, either. CERCLA is thus like many another congressional enactment in giving no indication "that the entire corpus of state corporation law is to be replaced simply because a plaintiff's cause of action is based upon a federal statute," *Burks v. Lasker*, 441 U.S. 471, 478 (1979), and the failure of the statute to speak to a matter as fundamental as the liability implications of corporate ownership demands application of the rule that "[i]n order to abrogate a common-law principle, the statute must speak directly to the question addressed by the common law," *United States v. Texas*, 507 U.S. 529, 534 (1993). The Court of Appeals was accordingly correct in holding that when (but only when) the corporate veil may be pierced, may a parent corporation be charged with derivative CERCLA liability for its subsidiary's actions.

IV
A

If the act rested liability entirely on ownership of a polluting facility, this opinion might end here; but CERCLA liability may turn on operation as well as ownership, and nothing in the statute's terms bars a parent corporation from direct liability for its own actions in operating a facility owned by its subsidiary. As Justice (then-Professor) Douglas noted almost 70 years ago, derivative liability cases are to be distinguished from those in which "the alleged wrong can seemingly be traced to the parent through the conduit of its own personnel and management" and "the parent is directly a participant in the wrong complained of." The fact that a corporate subsidiary happens to own a polluting facility operated by its parent does nothing, then, to displace the rule that the parent "corporation is [itself] responsible for the wrongs committed by its agents in the course of its business," *Mine Workers v. Coronado Coal Co.*, 259 U.S. 344, 395 (1922), and whereas the rules of veil-piercing limit derivative liability for the actions of another corporation, CERCLA's "operator" provision is concerned primarily with direct liability for one's own actions. It is this direct liability that is properly seen as being at issue here.

Under the plain language of the statute, any person who operates a polluting facility is directly liable for the costs of cleaning up the pollution. This is so regardless of whether that person is the facility's owner, the owner's parent corporation or business partner, or even a saboteur who sneaks into the facility at night to discharge its poisons out of malice. If any such act of operating a corporate subsidiary's facility is done on behalf of a parent corporation, the existence of the parent-subsidiary relationship under state corporate law is simply irrelevant to the issue of direct liability.

This much is easy to say; the difficulty comes in defining actions sufficient to constitute direct parental "operation." Here of course we may again rue the uselessness of CERCLA's definition of a facility's "operator" as "any person ... operating" the facility, which leaves us to do the best we can to give the term its "ordinary or natural meaning." *Bailey v. United States*, 516 U.S. 137, 145 (1995). In a mechanical sense, to "operate" ordinarily means "[t]o control the functioning of; run: operate a sewing machine." American Heritage Dictionary 1268 (3d ed. 1992). And in the organizational sense [more] obviously intended by CERCLA, the word ordinarily means "to conduct the affairs of; manage; *operate a business*." American Heritage Dictionary, *supra*, at 1268. So, under CERCLA, an operator is simply someone who directs the workings of, manages, or conducts the affairs of a facility. To sharpen the definition for purposes of CERCLA's concern with environmental contamination, an operator must manage, direct, or conduct operations specifically related to pollution, that is, operations having to do with the leakage or disposal of hazardous waste, or decisions about compliance with environmental regulations.

B

With this understanding, we are satisfied that the Court of Appeals correctly rejected the District Court's analysis of direct liability. But we also think that the appeals court erred in limiting direct liability under the statute to a parent's sole or joint venture operation, so as to eliminate any possible finding that CPC is liable as an operator on the facts of this case.

1

By emphasizing that "CPC is directly liable under section 107(a)(2) as an operator because CPC actively participated in and exerted significant control over Ott II's business and decision-making," the District Court applied the "actual control" test of whether the parent "actually operated the business of its subsidiary," as several Circuits have employed it.

The well-taken objection to the actual control test, however, is its fusion of direct and indirect liability; the test is administered by asking a question about the relationship between the two corporations (an issue going to indirect liability) instead of a question about the parent's interaction with the subsidiary's facility (the source of any direct liability). If, however, direct liability for the parent's operation of the facility is to be kept distinct from derivative liability for the subsidiary's own operation, the focus of the enquiry must necessarily be different under the two tests. "The question is not whether the parent operates the subsidiary, but rather whether it operates the facility, and that operation is evidenced by participation in the activities of the facility, not the subsidiary. Control of the subsidiary, if extensive enough, gives rise to indirect liability under piercing doctrine, not direct liability under the statutory language." Oswald, *Bifurcation of the Owner and Operator Analysis under CERCLA*, 72 Wash. U. L.Q. 223, 281–82 (1994) (hereinafter Oswald). The District Court was therefore mistaken to rest its analysis on CPC's relationship with Ott II, premising liability on little more than "CPC's 100-percent ownership of Ott II" and "CPC's active participation in, and at times majority control over, Ott II's board of directors." The analysis should instead have rested on the relationship between CPC and the Muskegon facility itself.

In addition to (and perhaps as a reflection of) the erroneous focus on the relationship between CPC and Ott II, even those findings of the District Court that might be taken to speak to the extent of CPC's activity at the facility itself are flawed, for the District Court wrongly assumed that the actions of the joint officers and directors are necessarily attributable to CPC. The District Court emphasized the facts that CPC placed its own high-level officials on Ott II's board of directors and in key management positions at Ott II, and that those individuals made major policy decisions and conducted day-to-day operations at the facility: "Although Ott II corporate officers set the day-to-day operating policies for the company without any need to obtain formal approval from CPC, CPC actively participated in this decision-making because high-ranking CPC officers served in Ott II management positions." (Relying on "CPC's involvement in major decision-making and day-to-day operations through CPC officials who served within Ott II management, including the positions of president and chief executive officer," and on "the conduct of CPC officials with respect to Ott II affairs, particularly Arnold Ott"); ("CPC actively participated in, and at times controlled, the policy-making decisions of its subsidiary thorough its representation on the Ott II board of directors"); ("CPC also actively participated in and exercised control over day-to-day decision-making at Ott II through representation in the highest levels of the subsidiary's management").

In imposing direct liability on these grounds, the District Court failed to recognize that "it is entirely appropriate for directors of a parent corporation to serve as directors of its subsidiary, and that fact alone may not serve to expose the parent corporation to liability for its subsidiary's acts." *American Protein Corp. v. AB Volvo*, 844 F.2d 56, 57 (C.A.2), *cert. denied*, 488 U.S. 852 (1988).

This recognition that the corporate personalities remain distinct has its corollary in the "well established principle [of corporate law] that directors and officers holding positions with a parent and its subsidiary can and do 'change hats' to represent the two corporations separately, despite their common ownership." *Lusk v. Foxmeyer Health Corp.*, 129 F.3d 773, 779 (C.A.5 1997). Since courts generally presume "that the directors are wearing their 'subsidiary hats' and not their 'parent hats' when acting for the subsidiary," P. Blumberg, Law of Corporate Groups: Procedural Problems in the Law of Parent and Subsidiary Corporations § 1.02.1, at 12 (1983), it cannot be enough to establish liability here that dual officers and directors made policy decisions and supervised activities at the facility. The Government would have to show that, despite the general presumption to the contrary, the officers and directors were acting in their capacities as CPC officers and directors, and not as Ott II officers and directors, when they committed those acts. The District Court made no such enquiry here, however, disregarding entirely this time-honored common law rule.

In sum, the District Court's focus on the relationship between parent and subsidiary (rather than parent and facility), combined with its automatic attribution of the actions of dual officers and directors to the corporate parent, erroneously, even if unintentionally, treated CERCLA as though it displaced or fundamentally altered common law standards of limited liability. Indeed, if the evidence of common corporate personnel acting at management and directorial levels were enough to support a finding of a parent corporation's direct operator liability under CERCLA, then the possibility of resort to veil piercing to establish indirect, derivative liability for the subsidiary's violations would be academic. There would in essence be a relaxed, CERCLA-specific rule of derivative liability that would banish traditional standards and expectations from the law of CERCLA liability. But, as we have said, such a rule does not arise from congressional silence, and CERCLA's silence is dispositive.

We accordingly agree with the Court of Appeals that a participation-and-control test looking to the parent's supervision over the subsidiary, especially one that assumes that dual officers always act on behalf of the parent, cannot be used to identify operation of a facility resulting in direct parental liability. Nonetheless, a return to the ordinary meaning of the word "operate" in the organizational sense will indicate why we think that the Sixth Circuit stopped short when it confined its examples of direct parental operation to exclusive or joint ventures, and declined to find at least the possibility of direct operation by CPC in this case.

In our enquiry into the meaning Congress presumably had in mind when it used the verb "to operate," we recognized that the statute obviously meant something more than mere mechanical activation of pumps and valves, and must be read to contemplate "operation" as including the exercise of direction over the facility's activities. The Court of Appeals recognized this by indicating that a parent can be held directly liable when the parent operates the facility in the stead of its subsidiary or alongside the subsidiary in some sort of a joint venture. We anticipated a further possibility above, however, when we observed that a dual officer or director might depart so far from the norms of parental influence exercised through dual officeholding as to serve the parent, even when ostensibly acting on behalf of the subsidiary in operating the facility. Yet another possibility, suggested by the facts of this case, is that an agent of the parent with no hat to wear but the parent's hat might manage or direct activities at the facility.

Identifying such an occurrence calls for line drawing yet again, since the acts of direct operation that give rise to parental liability must necessarily be distinguished from the interference that stems from the normal relationship between parent and subsidiary. Again norms of corporate behavior (undisturbed by any CERCLA provision) are crucial reference points. Just as we may look to such norms in identifying the limits of the presumption that a dual officeholder acts in his ostensible capacity, so here we may refer to them in distinguishing a parental officer's oversight of a subsidiary from such an officer's control over the operation of the subsidiary's facility. "[A]ctivities that involve the facility but which are consistent with the parent's investor status, such as monitoring of the subsidiary's performance, supervision of the subsidiary's finance and capital budget decisions, and articulation of general policies and procedures, should not give rise to direct liability." Oswald 282. The critical question is whether, in degree and detail, actions directed to the facility by an agent of the parent alone are eccentric under accepted norms of parental oversight of a subsidiary's facility.

There is, in fact, some evidence that CPC engaged in just this type and degree of activity at the Muskegon plant. The District Court's opinion speaks of an agent of CPC alone who played a conspicuous part in dealing with the toxic risks emanating from the operation of the plant. G.R.D. Williams worked only for CPC; he was not an employee, officer, or director of Ott II, and thus, his actions were of necessity taken only on behalf of CPC. The District Court found that "CPC became directly involved in environmental and regulatory matters through the work of ... Williams, CPC's governmental and environmental affairs director. Williams ... became heavily involved in environmental issues at Ott II." He "actively participated in and exerted control over a variety of Ott II environmental matters," and he "issued directives regarding Ott II's responses to regulatory inquiries."

We think that these findings are enough to raise an issue of CPC's operation of the facility through Williams's actions, though we would draw no ultimate conclusion from these findings at this point. Not only would we be deciding in the first instance an issue on which the trial and appellate courts did not focus, but the very fact that the District Court did not see the case as we do suggests that there may be still more to be known about Williams's activities. Indeed, even as the factual findings stand, the trial court offered little in the way of concrete detail for its conclusions about Williams's role in Ott II's environmental affairs, and the parties vigorously dispute the extent of Williams's involvement. Prudence thus counsels us to remand, on the theory of direct operation set out here, for reevaluation of Williams's role, and of the role of any other CPC agent who might be said to have had a part in operating the Muskegon facility.[15]

V

The judgment of the Court of Appeals for the Sixth Circuit is vacated, and the case is remanded with instructions to return it to the District Court for further proceedings consistent with this opinion.

A. CERCLA

Bestfoods indicates that the shareholder (the parent corporation) may have liability for the corporate subsidiary's obligations under CERCLA, even though state corporate

---

15. [14] There are some passages in the District Court's opinion that might suggest that, without reference to Williams, some of Ott II's actions in operating the facility were in fact dictated by, and thus taken on behalf of, CPC. ("CPC officials engaged in ... missions to Ott II in which Ott II officials received instructions on how to improve and change"); ("CPC executives who were not Ott II board members also occasionally attended Ott II board meetings"). But nothing in the District Court's findings of fact, as written, even comes close to overcoming the presumption that Ott II officials made their decisions and performed their acts as agents of Ott II. Indeed, the finding that "Ott II corporate officers set the day-to-day operating policies for the company without any need to obtain formal approval from CPC," indicates just the opposite. Still, the Government is, of course, free on remand to point to any additional evidence, not cited by the District Court, that would tend to establish that Ott II's decisionmakers acted on specific orders from CPC.

law would not have pierced the corporate
support CERCLA's statutory intent and

B. Other Statutory Claims

Piercing the corporate veil issues ar
tax, labor, and workers' compensatior
sider each statute's policy in determir
corporation's obligations. For instanc
Coal Co., 81 F.3d 150 (1995), the N
corporate veil may be pierced wher
to maintain separate identities, ar
sanction a fraud, promote injustic
that the shareholders commingle
for personal use, and misrepresei
their companies in legal docume
corporation's remedial and backpay ob...g

Interestingly, Thompson[16] found that courts were less in.. subject areas than in others. Consistent with the tax law principle that corpu. and their shareholders are separate taxable entities, courts pierced the corporate vei in only 31% of the tax law cases. Courts also disfavor piercing arguments in workers' compensation cases, allowing piercing to occur in only 13% of the cases. In these workers' compensation cases, the defendant parent corporations often argue that the parent and subsidiary should be treated as one employing entity. If successful, this self-piercing would block plaintiffs' claims for workers' compensation against both entities.

Other grounds claimants use to reach corporate owners besides traditional veil piercing include the Interstate Land Sales Full Disclosure Act, 15 U.S.C. § 1701. It can be used to reach real estate developers or their backers despite how developers operate through corporate entities, in part because the statute defines "developer" broadly: "any person who, directly or indirectly, sells or leases, or offers to sell or lease, or advertises for sale or lease any lots in a subdivision...." 15 U.S.C. § 1701(5). *See, e.g., Husted v. Amrep Corp.*, 429 F. Supp. 298 (S.D.N.Y. 1977) (allegedly defrauded land buyer permitted to maintain claim against corporation plus its subsidiaries and officers and directors); *Hammar v. Cost Control Marketing & Sales Management of Virginia, Inc.*, 757 F. Supp. 698 (W.D. Va. 1990) (reaching also a commercial bank that funded a development project).

---

16. Robert B. Thompson, *Piercing the Corporate Veil: An Empirical Study*, 76 Cornell L. Rev. 1036, 1060–62 (1991).

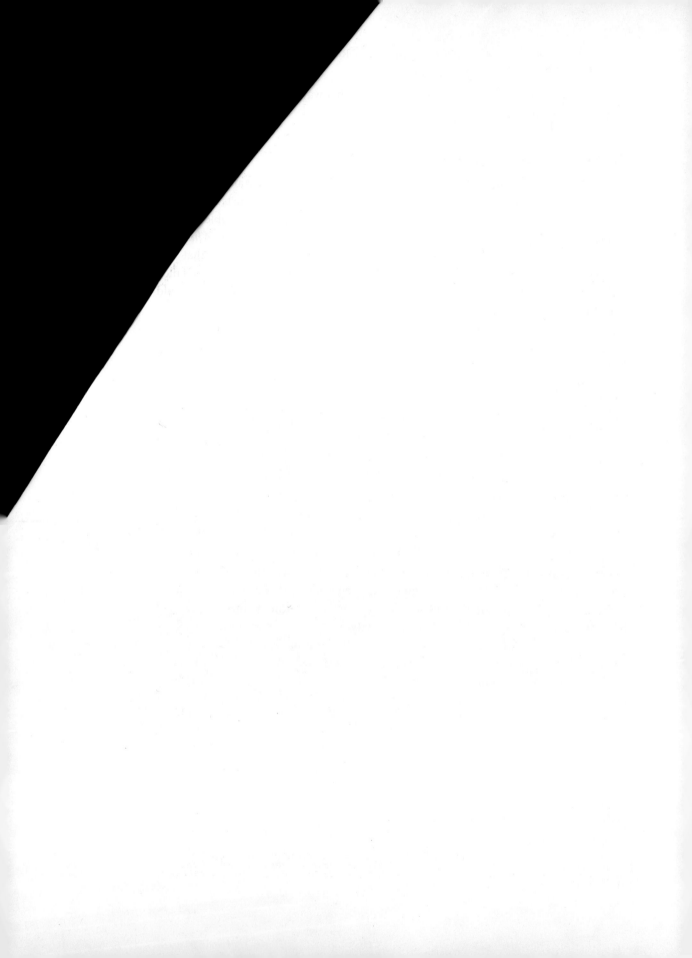

Chapter 9

Dividends and Distributions

Situation

Anderson and Baker, pleased with the company's continued growth and profitability, want to raise their salaries from $40,000 to $110,000 a year. Phillips agrees that salaries should be raised and that at current interest rates it makes sense to take some cash out of the business and borrow from the bank to help finance expansion. But rather than a $70,000 salary increase, Phillips suggests a $40,000 increase plus $90,000 total paid pro rata among the three shareholders as a dividend. After extensive discussion, Anderson and Baker have agreed with Phillips on a compromise salary dividend package: Anderson and Baker's salaries are to be raised to $100,000, and $30,000 total is to be paid to the shareholders as a dividend. You have been asked to look after the legal details.

In a conversation with one of the officers, you are told that all of the surplus of the corporation has been transferred to stated capital. The officer said this was done to "make the balance sheet look better to the bank" and that the transfer was accomplished just prior to a recent bank loan.

Section I
Mechanics of Dividends and Distributions

Corporate lawyers apply the rules governing a corporation's distributions to its shareholders when they advise directors on the legality of paying a dividend or repurchasing shares of the company's stock. The legal rules that apply to corporate distributions are an attempt to accommodate the competing interests of a company's owners and creditors.

To attract and keep investors, a company must provide them with the opportunity to realize a return on their investment. Company owners realize such a return when they receive a part of the company's profits or when they sell their stake in the company and, if the stake has appreciated, capture the increased value. The two routes are not, however, equally attractive. Most owners hope to realize a return on an ongoing basis and not have to wait until they sell their interests in the company. Creditors, on the other hand, are loathe to have company earnings distributed to owners while company debts are outstanding. Such distributions decrease the assets of the company and increase the risk that the creditor will not be paid in full. This reduction of security is particularly problematic for creditors of corporations and limited liability companies; these creditors can look only to the company's assets for satisfaction of their claims. In contrast, creditors of general partnerships can have their claims satisfied from the personal assets of individual owners when company assets are insufficient to pay company liabilities. To provide creditors with some protection, corporation (and limited liability company) statutes restrict distributions of company profits to owners. The focus of this chapter is on the corporate law restrictions. Sophisticated lenders loaning substantial funds also invariably insist upon contractual protections tailored to the borrower and the circumstances.

Lest you be deceived by the apparent simplicity of the preceding description of the desires of investors and creditors, consider the following excerpt from a classic book on the subject, called *Legal Capital*, by Bayless Manning and James Hanks:

> The investor who buys shares of stock in the incorporated enterprise and the investor who lends money to the incorporated enterprise are, as a matter of economics, engaged in the same kind of activity and are motivated by the same basic objectives. They are both making a capital investment; they both expect or hope to get their investment back in the long run, either by liquidating pay-out or by sale of the security; and they both expect and hope to receive income from their investment in the interim before their capital is returned to them in full.
>
> In the stereotypic model transaction, the investor who chose to take a shareholder's position rather than a creditor's position in a particular transaction simply made a calculated economic judgment that was different from the creditor's. The shareholder estimated that he could make more money by relinquishing to creditor investors a "prior" claim for interest and a fixed principal payment on maturity, and by opting for uncertain "dividends" and the residual claim to the assets of the enterprise that would remain after all creditors, with their fixed claims, had been paid off.
>
> The shareholder is willing to admit the "priority" of the creditor's interest claim and claim for principal payment on maturity. That does *not* imply, however, that the shareholder is willing to stand by chronologically until such time as the creditors have been paid in full. The shareholder will usually insist, that if, as he hopes, the enterprise makes money (and perhaps even if it does not), the shareholders will receive some return on (or of) their investment from time to time, regardless of the fact that there are creditor claims outstanding. Such periodic payments to shareholders are characterized as "dividends"; and, in the usual and normal case of the healthy incorporated enterprise, it is assumed that some assets will be regularly distributed out from the corporate treasury to the shareholder investors in dividend form.
>
> Simple as this observation may be, its implications are far-reaching. If it were the case that all creditors had to be paid off before *any* payment could be made to shareholder investors, and if shareholders received nothing until ultimate liquidation of the enterprise when they would divide the residuum left after payment of all creditors—if, in other words, the terms "prior" and "before" were chronological as well as hierarchical—the creditor would not have to worry about assets being drained away into the hands of junior claimants and he would sleep better

at night. But that arrangement would be wholly unacceptable to shareholders. Shareholders insist—and ultimately creditors must concede—that, *during the life* of the creditor's claim, assets may be passed out to an investing group that hierarchically ranks below the creditors. The question becomes unavoidable: How much of the assets in the treasury of the incorporated enterprise may be distributed to shareholders, when, and under what circumstances?

———————

Company owners also have an interest in making sure the company maintains a sufficient asset base for the company to operate profitably and create earnings available for distribution to shareholders. Thus, so long as the company prospers, the competing claims of creditors and shareholders can be satisfied amicably without resorting to legal rules or contracts. The situation changes, however, when the company begins to experience financial constraints, either because of a temporary downturn or because of a general decline. In these situations, the tensions between those with senior and junior claims become more pronounced.

Today's corporation statutes typically deal with dividends and distributions together, although analytically, dividends and distributions are different. In a pure sense, dividends represent a payment to the shareholders of a corporation's profits, whereas distributions are a return to the shareholders of a portion of their capital contributions. As will be seen in the discussions that follow, however, these distinctions between dividends and distributions have become blurred as corporation statutes treat distributions and dividends alike.

Not only do dividends technically differ from distributions, but different types of dividends differ from each other. It will be helpful if we first discuss dividends in cash or other property, then handle stock dividends (and stock splits, which are closely related), and finally turn to repurchase by a corporation of its own shares.

A. Limitations on Distributions

State corporate laws regulating dividends have common elements. One is that the board of directors declares dividends. *See, e.g.,* DGCL 170(a); MBCA 6.40(a). Another is that a dividend may not contravene a restriction on dividends contained in the corporation's charter. *Id.* However, state corporate laws regulating dividend payment use different tests to determine whether a corporation may pay dividends in cash or property to its shareholders. There are numerous potential tests, including the following—all of which are calculated *after giving effect* to the distribution:

1. *earned surplus test*: dividends may be paid only from the company's earned surplus (accumulated retained earnings),

2. *basic balance sheet-based test*: dividends may be paid only if assets exceed liabilities,

3. *balance sheet plus capital test*: dividends may be paid only if assets exceed liabilities plus some minimum amount of stated capital,

4. *insolvency test*: dividends may be paid only if the corporation is able to pay its debts as they come due in the ordinary course of business,

5. *nimble dividends test*: dividends may be paid if the company has current profits, even if it would not meet other tests, such as maintaining a minimum amount of stated capital.

As a thumbnail sketch, prior versions of the MBCA used to adopt test 1; the current MBCA adopts tests 2 and 4 (and both must be met); the DGCL adopts tests 3 and 5 (and permits the dividend if either is met). As noted, loan agreements will typically impose more rigorous and tailored restrictions on dividends (as well as other distributions of assets to shareholders).

The MBCA approach is easier to explain and understand. To start, its restrictions apply not only to dividends but also to every form of distribution of assets to shareholders. It achieves this broad coverage by defining the word "distribution," which includes dividends, as broadly as possible in § 1.40(6):

> "Distribution" means a direct or indirect transfer of money or other property (except its own shares) or incurrence of indebtedness by a corporation to or for the benefit of its shareholders in respect of any of its shares. A distribution may be in the form of a declaration or payment of a dividend; a purchase, redemption, or other acquisition of shares; a distribution of indebtedness; or otherwise.

The MBCA then imposes its two-part limitation on all distributions in § 6.40(c), providing that no distribution may be made unless, after giving it effect, (1) the corporation's assets equal or exceed its liabilities plus (with some exceptions) the dissolution preferences of senior equity securities, and (2) the corporation would be able to meets its debts as they come due in the ordinary course of business. Section 6.40(d) authorizes related determinations to be made on the basis of either (1) financial statements prepared on the basis of accounting practices and principles that are reasonable under the circumstances or (2) a fair valuation or other method that is reasonable under the circumstances.

The DGCL's approach to limitations on distributions to shareholders is more intricate, in part because Delaware continues to use ancient concepts, such as stated capital, that the MBCA has jettisoned. Moreover, the DGCL's approach resembles the approach still taken by quite a few other jurisdictions that have not adopted the MBCA.

Start with DGCL's sections governing the payment of dividends in cash or other property. Section 170 provides as follows:

> (a) The directors of every corporation, subject to any restrictions contained in its certificate of incorporation, may declare and pay dividends upon the shares of its capital stock either: (1) Out of its surplus, as defined in and computed in accordance with §§ 154 and 244 of this title; or (2) In case there shall be no such surplus, out of its net profits for the fiscal year in which the dividend is declared and/or the preceding fiscal year.

So, under Delaware law, dividends may be declared and paid either from the company's surplus (balance sheet-based test) or, in the absence of surplus, out of its net profits for the current and preceding year (nimble dividends test).

What is surplus? Here it might help to remember that the surplus accounts, together with the capital account, make up the shareholders' equity section of the balance sheet. As defined in DGCL § 154, surplus is "the excess … of the net assets of the corporation over the amount … determined to be capital."

Net assets is the amount one gets by subtracting all of the corporation's liabilities from all of its assets. Thus, the value of net assets is the same as the total value of the equity section of the balance sheet. (Shareholders equity is calculated by subtracting liabilities from assets. If Assets = Liabilities + Equity, then Assets – Liabilities = Equity.) Surplus, then, is the amount by which the total equity exceeds the value of the capital account(s). Put differently: surplus = total assets – total liabilities – stated capital.

According to DGCL § 154, stated capital is, at minimum, equal to the aggregate par value of outstanding shares of stock. Capital surplus (paid in capital in excess of par) is the amount shareholders pay for shares in excess of aggregate par value. In contrast, earned surplus (accumulated retained earnings) comes from a corporation's earnings. For example, 100 shares of $1 par value stock issued for $10 a share will yield a minimum capital of $100 (that is, $1 par × 100 shares) and the excess of the purchase price over par value, or $9, can be designated as capital surplus.

If desired, the board may designate as capital a greater portion of the amount paid for stock, and thereby reduce the amount allocated to capital surplus. For instance, in the preceding example, the board could allocate $2 per share to capital and just $8 per share to capital surplus.

Sometimes a lawyer is faced with a corporate client that wants to distribute cash or other property to its shareholders, but has neither earned nor capital surplus. The DGCL gives boards several ways to address this. Section 244(a)(4) permits boards to transfer from stated capital to capital surplus "(ii) some or all of the capital represented by issued shares of its par value capital stock, which capital is in excess of the aggregate par value of such shares; or (iii) some of the capital represented by issued shares of its capital stock without par value." Under § 244(b), such transfers may not, however, be made unless "the assets of the corporation remaining after such reduction shall be sufficient to pay any debts of the corporation for which payment has not been otherwise provided." (Notice how that phrase mimics the insolvency test imposed under MBCA 6.40(c)).

A charter amendment either decreasing the par value of the corporation's shares or changing from par value to no par value stock provides another option for creating capital surplus out of which to make a distribution. If the charter amendment is approved, the board may reduce stated capital as described above. The amount of the reduction becomes capital surplus, out of which the desired distribution may be made.

To amplify, it may be helpful to set out a simple balance sheet and how the various tests apply. Here is a balance sheet as it would appear just after a corporation issues 1,000 shares of $1 par value stock for $10 per share:

Academair, Inc. Balance Sheet
(as of December 31; amounts in dollars)

Assets		Liabilities	
Cash	10,000	None	0
		Owners' Equity	
		Stated Capital	1,000
		Capital Surplus	9,000
		Total Owners' Equity	10,000
Total Assets	10,000	**Total Liabilities and**	10,000
		Owners' Equity	

Assume, for example, that Academair immediately invests its $10,000 cash in an option to purchase an airplane and then one month later sells that option for $15,000 after expenses. Here is how the new balance sheet would look after the sale of the option:

Academair, Inc. Balance Sheet
(as of January 31; amounts in dollars)

Assets		Liabilities	
Cash	15,000	None	0
		Owners' Equity	
		Stated Capital	1,000
		Capital Surplus	9,000
		Earned Surplus	5,000
		Total Owners' Equity	15,000
Total Assets	15,000	**Total Liabilities and**	15,000
		Owners' Equity	

Old-fashioned corporation statutes following the earned surplus rule would permit dividends to be declared and paid only out of earned surplus, a total amount of $5,000.

Under the DGCL, dividends may be paid only out of surplus. Thus, a total of $14,000 would be available, $5,000 from earned surplus and $9,000 from capital surplus. Please note that only earned surplus represents the company's profitability. Dividends paid from capital surplus are actually a return of the shareholders' original capital investment.

Under the MBCA, a maximum dividend of $15,000 would be permitted. There are no liabilities, so the company would satisfy the requirement of being able to pay its debts as they become due. There are no senior securities whose interests must be taken into account. And finally, after a $15,000 dividend, the corporation's assets would not be less than its liabilities.

A number of states also follow Delaware's "nimble dividends" provision. Section 170 allows dividends to be declared and paid either out of surplus or profits of the current fiscal year and/or the prior fiscal year. The nimble dividends provision can be useful to a corporation that has had losses in previous years, which losses have prevented it from having any earned surplus even though the corporation currently is generating profits. To see how that works, it will be helpful to look at another balance sheet of Academair, Inc. This one shows the result of a $50,000 loss, with a $40,000 loan taken out to raise cash to cover the loss, in the month following the last balance sheet shown below.

Academair, Inc. Balance Sheet
(as of February 28; amounts in dollars)

Assets		Liabilities	
Cash	5,000	Note Payable	40,000
		Owners' Equity	
		Stated Capital	1,000
		Capital Surplus	9,000
		Earned Surplus	(45,000)
		Total Owners' Equity	(35,000)
Total Assets	$ 5,000	**Total Liabilities and Owners' Equity**	5,000

Notice that the $50,000 loss has wiped out the corporation's $5,000 earned surplus and has created a $45,000 deficit in earned surplus. (Deficits are shown on financial statements in parentheses.) The corporation could continue having losses, and therefore amassing deficits in earned surplus, for some time. It could then begin generating profits, but it could take some years of profits before the earned surplus deficits are eliminated.

Unless the statute under which this corporation is incorporated has a nimble dividends provision, it will not be able to pay dividends until those deficits are eliminated completely. Under the DGCL, the company potentially may begin paying dividends when it again has profits. If, for example, in the following year, the company earned a $3,000 profit, the earned surplus would be ($42,000). In a nimble dividends jurisdiction, the company would be able to pay dividends in an amount up to $3,000. The introduction of the nimble dividends approach reflects not only the continuing tension between protecting creditors and unduly restricting a going enterprise, but also a way to ease that tension. After all, a financially troubled corporation, whose creditors face risk of nonpayment, may be able to improve its financial position only by attracting additional shareholder capital. Potential investors may only be willing to buy shares if there is at least some basis to forecast a near-term distribution of dividends. One way to do that is to permit the corporation to make distributions from profits even if capital is impaired.

Although corporation statutes typically do not state explicitly how dividends are to be spread among shareholders, dividends must be paid to the various classes of shareholders (*e.g.*, preferred and common) as specified in the charter and, within classes of shareholders, pro rata on a share-for-share basis. An attempt by the directors to favor one shareholder over another in the payment of dividends, in a way not sanctioned by the charter, would be considered an illegal dividend or an unauthorized distribution of corporate assets.

Under MBCA § 8.33(a), a representative statutory provision, directors who vote for or assent to an unauthorized distribution of corporate assets, including a dividend that is not allowed under the statute, are liable to the corporation for the amount of the distribution or dividend in excess of the amount that could have been distributed lawfully. A director held liable for an unlawful distribution is entitled to contribution from other directors who could also be held liable for the unlawful distribution. Liable directors are entitled to recoup the pro-rata portion of the unlawful distribution from each shareholder who accepted it knowing it was unlawful. MBCA § 8.30(e) affords directors some protection if they have relied on opinions, reports or financial statements prepared by legal counsel, public accountants or experts.

In all corporation statutes, the decision to declare dividends is within the board's discretion. Shareholders' legal right to receive dividends arises only when dividends are declared. Although shareholders may have every expectation that dividends will be paid annually in agreed amounts, they do not have a statutory right to have dividends paid.

If a corporation has preferred stock, however, its charter typically contains provisions designed to force the declaration and payment of dividends by making the alternative unpalatable. For example, at a minimum, preferred dividends in a set amount usually are made cumulative, and the charter typically provides that no dividends may be declared on the common stock until all accumulated dividends on the preferred stock have been paid.

It is not uncommon for charters to go further and to provide that if dividends are not paid on preferred stock for four consecutive quarters, the preferred shareholders rather than the common shareholders will have the right to elect some or all of the directors. Once dividends are declared and announced to the shareholders, they become liabilities of the corporation. At that point, shareholders can sue to collect dividends if the corporation does not pay them voluntarily.

The following passage evaluates the general effectiveness of legal capital provisions.

Bayless Manning & James J. Hanks, Legal Capital
91–97, 176–77, 183 (3d ed. 1990)[9]

First, the legal capital machinery makes only the most marginal effort to protect groups or classes of shareholders from each other despite their often conflicting interests. As for creditors, the system makes no attempt to ward off three of their main worries—erosion of the corporation's cash flow out of which debt will be repaid, incurrence by the corporation of additional debt liabilities and creation of secured or senior debt claims.

All the system ever purports to do is to assure that shareholders have put something into the corporate pot and that they will not redistribute corporate assets to themselves without first protecting the corporate creditors.... It is a safe generalization, however, that the statutory legal capital machinery provides little or no significant protection to creditors of corporations.... Some of the reasons are: ...

2. To the extent that the purpose of the legal capital scheme is to protect creditors from transactions that benefit shareholders but prejudice creditors, it is at least odd that the statutes should hand over all the control switches and levers to the shareholders and those whom the shareholders elect, the board of directors.... [I]n no case do the statutes provide for participation by the creditors, consultation with the creditors, or even notice to the creditors.

3. A corporation's "legal capital" is a wholly arbitrary number, unrelated in any way to any economic facts that are relevant to a creditor.... 5.... For purposes of the statute, cash and other quick assets are treated exactly the same as assets that would take years to liquidate for purposes of paying debts....

7. ...

Statutes that provide for nimble dividends admit overtly that companies with heavily-impaired legal capital may still make payments to shareholders....

Where dividend payments may be made to shareholders and charged to capital surplus, the statute offers a direct invitation to the lawyer architect to design a capital structure using low par stock and creating large capital surplus accounts—an invitation that is usually accepted.

Many of the statutes permit payments to shareholders to be charged against reduction surplus,[10] a form of surplus that is usually easy for the board to generate....

8. It may be, though it would be difficult to prove, that the legal capital system ... can operate as a trap. Many lawyers are not sufficiently familiar with the arcana of legal capital to recognize a related problem when it does arise and warn their clients accordingly.

The best argument suggesting that the system has some protective consequence for creditors is the argument historical, cultural, and psychological. For nearly 150 years, it has been thought important that an enterprise have something called its "capital" and the concept has acquired its own independent aura of respectability, whatever its actual significance to real creditors in real business situations.... Deep in the consciousness of the American businessman, lawyer, accountant and banker is the general principle that distributions to shareholders are not supposed to be made "out of" capital. Everybody knows that ways are available to design around statutory restrictions; but the restrictions themselves are a reflection of that general principle....

[Second], statutory provisions may have a degree of actual operating impact upon corporations of the medium-size range. Those in control of the incorporated small enterprise typically manage its, and their, economic lives with little or no awareness of or regard for the niceties of procedure spelled out in legal capital provisions. Large public enterprises on the other hand, can draw on lawyers and other professionals who see to it that wide flexibility of corporate financial action and decisions is maintained while scrupulously observing the statutory mandates.

But it may also be that the managers of a medium-sized incorporated enterprise may be sufficiently conscious of statutory and regulatory requirements to be affected in their behavior, and yet not served with sufficient continuity or professionality of advice to enable them to control their own destinies in the legal capital thicket. And perhaps the medium-sized corporation is the one that offers the greatest problem for the creditor; there he has not the close personal contact that grounds his extension of credit to the incorporated barbershop nor has he the institutional protections that back up a credit to General Motors....

In 1975 California struck out into new territory in the financial provisions of its new General Corporation Law as they substantially reconstructed the traditional edifice.... Distributions to shareholders may be made to the extent that retained earnings are available *or* certain ratios of certain assets to certain liabilities (and current assets to current liabilities) are met.... [The MBCA soon followed suit, as described above.]

---

10. Reduction surplus is created when an amount is transferred from stated capital to surplus. [Eds.]

As the preceding comments indicate, the effectiveness of legal capital provisions and their relevancy to modern business practices are subject to question. In fact, as Manning and Hanks point out, creditors often look to contract for protection rather than state statutory law. A simple sample of the sort of structure and language follows:

The corporation shall not make any distribution of assets to shareholders, whether by dividend, repurchase of stock or otherwise, unless, after giving it effect, all of the following are true:

(a) total assets are at least x times total liabilities;

(b) net cash flow is at least y times annual interest expense;

(c) current assets are least z times greater than current liabilities;

in each case, as determined in accordance with [generally accepted accounting principles and as modified in accordance with generally recognized valuation techniques]....

B. Repurchase of Shares

Corporations have the right to repurchase previously issued shares of their own stock. Under both the Delaware General Corporation Law and the Model Business Corporation Act, the provisions controlling the payment of dividends also apply to a corporation's redemption (repurchase) of its own shares. DGCL § 160 (a) gives a corporation broad powers to deal in its own stock, but, with limited exceptions, prohibits the corporation from purchasing or redeeming "its own shares of capital stock for cash or other property when the capital of the corporation is impaired or when such purchase or redemption would cause any impairment of the capital of the corporation...." Thus, a corporation may repurchase its shares only out of surplus. As the MBCA considers both dividends and redemptions to be a form of distribution, § 6.40 applies equally to both.

If the repurchased stock is not retired or canceled, but is held by the corporation to be reissued later, it is often referred to as treasury stock. Here is a standard definition: "Treasury shares" means shares of a corporation which have been issued, have been subsequently acquired by and belong to a corporation, and have not been canceled or restored to the status of authorized but unissued shares. Treasury shares shall be deemed to be "issued" shares, but not "outstanding" shares.

Remember that treasury shares having a par value may be sold for whatever consideration the board sets, regardless of their par value, because when these shares initially were issued, an amount equal to their par value was placed in stated capital, and that amount remains in stated capital so long as the shares retain their status as "issued" shares. A corporation's board of directors may, however, cancel the issuance of treasury shares and, thus, restore them to the status of authorized but unissued shares at any time it wishes. In this situation, the amount in stated capital may be reduced. If the shares are reissued, all the capitalization rules apply just as they would if the shares never had been issued. The MBCA has eliminated the concepts of par value and treasury shares (except for permitting par value shares if a corporation decides to have them). Under the MBCA, shares that would otherwise become treasury shares are designated as authorized but unissued shares.

Consider the following further discussion of share repurchases by Robert W. Hamilton & Richard A Booth, in *Business Basics for Law Students* (4th ed. 2006), pp. 335–337:

> Superficially, a purchase of shares by the corporation may not be thought of as involving a distribution at all. It appears to be the purchase of an asset rather than the making of a distribution. That analysis, however, confuses transactions in which the corporation repurchases its own shares and transactions in which it purchases shares issued by another corporation. The former is a distribution. The latter an investment.
>
> When a corporation buys back its own stock shares, it does not receive anything of value in the hands of the corporation. The remaining shareholders continue to own 100 per cent of the corporate assets (now reduced by the amount of the payment used to reacquire the shares). A corporation cannot treat shares in itself that it has purchased as an asset any more than it can treat its authorized but unissued shares as an asset. One cannot own 10 percent of oneself and have one's total worth be 110 percent of the value of one's assets. Shares that another corporation issues are entirely different. Shares of Corporation B have value based on the assets that Corporation B owns. If shares of Corporation B are purchased by Corporation A, they are an asset in the hands of Corporation A.
>
> The fact that a repurchase of shares constitutes a distribution can be most easily appreciated by considering a proportionate repurchase of stock in a closely held corporation. Assume that three persons each own 100 shares of stock in a corporation. The shareholders decide that each of them will sell 10 shares back to the corporation for $100 per share, or a total of $1,000 each. When the transaction is completed, each shareholder continues to own one-third of the corporation (now represented by 90 shares rather than 100 shares), the corporation has $3,000 less, and the shareholders each have $1,000 in cash. Clearly there has been a distribution, even though the transaction was cast in the form of a repurchase of stock rather than a dividend.
>
> Under many state statutes, the 300 shares reacquired by the corporation in the previous example are called treasury shares and may be held by the corporation in a sort of twilight zone until they are either retired permanently or resold to someone else in the future. Treasury shares are not an asset, even though they may be sold at some later time. After all, exactly the same thing can be said of every share of authorized but unissued stock....
>
> A repurchase of shares by the corporation is a distribution even if the corporation purchases only shares owned by one shareholder rather than proportionately from each shareholder. Such a transaction is merely a disproportionate distribution. The corporation has made a distribution to a single shareholder equal to the purchase price it paid for the shares. This

transaction is not all bad from the standpoint of the other shareholders, however, since it simultaneously increases their percentage interest in the corporation....

C. Stock Dividends and Stock Splits

Stock dividends are dividends payable to a corporation's shareholders in the corporation's own stock rather than in cash or other property. Stock splits have much in common with stock dividends, in that both stock splits and stock dividends have the same effect of getting a greater number of a corporation's shares into the hands of its shareholders without their paying for the shares. In many states, however, the mechanisms involved are entirely different, as are certain of the consequences. An important consideration that should be noted at the outset is that neither a stock dividend nor a stock split changes the proportion of a shareholder's equity participation in the corporation. Each simply changes the number of shares representing that participation.

Since stock dividends and stock splits do not increase shareholders' interests in the corporation, all that either accomplishes is to cut up the corporate pie into smaller pieces. Take, for example, a corporation that has three shareholders, each owning 100 shares and having a one third interest in the corporation. If the corporation does a two-for-one stock split, each shareholder will now own 200 shares, but will still have the same one third interest in the company. Now, however, each share represents exactly half the ownership percentage that a share in the corporation used to represent. As a result, each new share will be worth exactly half of what an old share was worth. With that in mind, one might question whether there is any good reason for a corporation to pay a stock dividend or to do a stock split.

There are three primary reasons corporations issue stock dividends or do stock splits. Perhaps the most common reason is to force down the price of stock in a publicly held corporation that has risen to "too high" a level in the trading markets. Stock is traded in 100-share lots, and there is an extra commission payable for trading in odd lots. For that reason and for others relating more to tradition than logic, the markets favor shares that trade at particular levels. Assume, for example, that the preferred range is from $15 to $40 per a share for seasoned companies. In this case, if the price of a stock approaches $100, a corporation may want to do a 200% stock dividend or split the stock three for one in order to drive the stock's price down to about $30 per share, with the hope that its rise from there will be easier than if the price were left at $100.

Sometimes corporate managers issue small stock dividends, not exceeding a few percent, to communicate to shareholders that the company is prospering and would be in a position to distribute cash dividends but for the management decision to reinvest profits in the business.

Finally, a stock split or a stock dividend may occur as a necessary financial expedient when a corporation is planning to sell its shares to the public for the first time. In the typical closely held corporation, usually there are no more than a few thousand shares outstanding. An initial public offering might involve the sale of 500,000 new shares representing a 25% interest in the corporation. In that case, the corporation will need to do a stock split or stock dividend to cause the shares currently outstanding to be increased to 1,500,000, so that after the public offering that number of shares will represent a 75% interest in the corporation.

Notice that if the corporation in that example has par value stock, a stock split of the magnitude required probably would cause the stock after the split to have a par value at some fraction of a cent. That would look unusual, and the corporation would wish to avoid it. Doing so would be easy. Since the corporation will file a charter amendment to effect the stock split, it can in the same amendment change to no par value stock or change the par value of the stock to some acceptable amount, such as ten cents or one cent. The only requirement in the latter cases would be to transfer from surplus to stated capital whatever amount is necessary to have stated capital equal to at least par value times the number of shares outstanding.

DGCL § 173 contains typical provisions on stock dividends and stock splits:

> ... If the dividend is to be paid in shares of the corporation's theretofore unissued capital stock the board of directors shall, by resolution, direct that there be designated as capital in respect of such shares an amount which is not less than the aggregate par value of par value shares being declared as a dividend and, in the case of shares without par value being declared as a dividend, such amount as shall be determined by the board of directors....

The requirement that an amount equal to aggregate par value be allocated to stated capital is necessary if the amount of stated capital, at a minimum, is at all times to be equal to the aggregate par value of a corporation's outstanding stock, which is what is at the heart of stated capital. DGCL § 154. For stock without par value, the board must determine the amount of surplus to transfer to stated capital. DGCL §§ 154, 173.

The DGCL addresses stock splits in the last sentence of § 173. It provides: "No such designation as capital shall be necessary if shares are being distributed by a corporation pursuant to a split-up or division of its stock rather than as payment of a dividend declared payable in stock of the corporation." Section 1.40 (6) of the Model Act exempts transfers by a corporation of its own shares from the definition of "distribution." Therefore, the restrictions of § 6.40 do not apply either to stock splits or to stock dividends.

Neither the DGCL nor the MBCA specifies any distinct statutory procedures necessary to declare a stock split. Since a stock split is accomplished by an ordinary charter amendment, the regular authorization for a charter amendment is all the authority needed. *See* DGCL 252; MBCA 10.03. The amendment to effect a stock split would first, if need be, increase the number of authorized shares. Using one dollar par value stock being split two for one as an example, the amendment would accomplish the split with language like the following: "Upon the effectiveness of this amendment, each issued share of common stock, par value $1, is split into two shares of common stock, par value $.50." Stated capital remains the same because aggregate par value of all the shares outstanding is exactly the same before and after the split.

D. Calculations, Accounting, and Judgment

Jurisdictions with legal capital requirements limit a corporation's ability to declare and pay dividends or make distributions, including the repurchase of its shares. The DGCL requires the availability of earnings or surplus for dividend payment or distributions. Surplus can come about in three ways. Capital surplus is basically the amount of the difference between the price at which a corporation issues stock and the stock's par value. Reduction surplus is created when an amount is transferred from stated capital to surplus. Revaluation surplus comes from the unrealized appreciation in the company's fixed assets. Over the years, one of the main questions relating to these limitations is whether a corporation may consider unrealized appreciation in its assets in calculating surplus for dividend or distribution purposes. May, for example, a corporation that owns a $10 million piece of land, which it purchased for $1 million, treat for dividend purposes the $9 million increase in value the same way it would treat a $9 million profit on the sale of a piece of land?

If asked that question, an accountant will think you are crazy — to accountants it is almost a sacred idea that assets are to be valued at their cost. But one might notice that judges have not necessarily listened to accountants in deciding corporation law questions (perhaps because cases are pleaded by lawyers rather than accountants) and corporation statutes do not incorporate accounting theory wholesale. Corporation statutes do not, for example, require that corporations follow generally accepted accounting principles.

In the case below, the Delaware Supreme Court addresses the issue of including unrealized appreciation in the calculation of surplus in connection with a company's repurchase of its own stock.

Klang v. Smith's Food & Drug Centers

Delaware Supreme Court
702 A.2d 150 (1997)

VEASEY, CHIEF JUSTICE.

... Plaintiff in this purported class action alleges that a corporation's repurchase of shares violated the statutory prohibition against the impairment of capital.... No corporation may repurchase or redeem its own shares except out of "surplus," as statutorily defined, or except as expressly authorized by provisions of the statute not relevant here. Balance sheets are not, however, conclusive indicators of surplus or a lack thereof. Corporations may revalue assets to show surplus, but perfection in that process is not required. Directors have reasonable latitude to depart from the balance sheet to calculate surplus, so long as they evaluate assets and liabilities in good faith, on the basis of acceptable data, by methods that they reasonably believe reflect present values, and arrive at a determination of the surplus that is not so far off the mark as to constitute actual or constructive fraud....

Smith's Food & Drug Centers, Inc. ("SFD") is a Delaware corporation that owns and operates a chain of supermarkets in the Southwestern United States.... Plaintiff and the class he purports to represent are holders of common stock in SFD. On January 29, 1996, SFD entered into an agreement with The Yucaipa Companies ("Yucaipa"), a California partnership also active in the supermarket industry. Under the agreement, the following would take place:

(1) Smitty's Supermarkets, Inc. ("Smitty's"), a wholly-owned subsidiary of Yucaipa that operated a supermarket chain in Arizona, was to merge into Cactus Acquisition, Inc. ("Cactus"), a subsidiary of SFD, in exchange for which SFD would deliver to Yucaipa slightly over 3 million newly-issued shares of SFD common stock;

(2) SFD was to undertake a recapitalization, in the course of which SFD would assume a sizable amount of new debt, retire old debt, and offer to repurchase up to fifty percent of its outstanding shares (other than those issued to Yucaipa) for $36 per share; and

(3) SFD was to repurchase 3 million shares of preferred stock from [SFD's majority stockholders].

SFD hired the investment firm of Houlihan Lokey Howard & Zukin ("Houlihan") to examine the transactions and render a solvency opinion. Houlihan eventually issued a report to the SFD Board replete with assurances that the transactions would not endanger SFD's solvency, and would not impair SFD's capital in violation of 8 Del. C. §160. On May 17, 1996, in reliance on the Houlihan opinion, SFD's Board determined that there existed sufficient surplus to consummate the transactions, and enacted a resolution proclaiming as much. On May 23, 1996, SFD's stockholders voted to approve the transactions, which closed on that day. The self-tender offer was over-subscribed, so SFD repurchased fully fifty percent of its shares at the offering price of $36 per share.... Larry F. Klang filed a purported class action in the Court of Chancery ... contend[ing] that the stock repurchases violated 8 Del. C. §160 by impairing SFD's capital.

A corporation may not repurchase its shares if, in so doing, it would cause an impairment of capital, unless expressly authorized by Section 160.[17] A repurchase impairs capital if the funds used in the repurchase exceed the amount of the corporation's "surplus," defined by 8 Del. C. §154 to mean the excess of net assets over the par value of the corporation's issued stock.

[P]laintiff's position breaks down into two analytically distinct arguments. First, he contends that SFD's balance sheets constitute conclusive evidence of capital impairment. He argues that the negative net worth that appeared on SFD's books following the repurchase compels us to find a violation of Section 160. Second, he suggests that even allowing the Board to "go behind the balance sheet" to calculate surplus does not save the transactions from violating Section 160. In connection with this claim, he attacks the SFD Board's off-balance-sheet method of calculating surplus on the theory that it does not adequately take into account all of SFD's assets and li-

17. [4] The provisions of Section 160 permitting a corporation to purchase its shares out of capital under certain circumstances are not implicated in this case.

abilities. Moreover, he argues that the May 17, 1996 resolution of the SFD Board conclusively refutes the Board's claim that revaluing the corporation's assets gives rise to the required surplus. We hold that each of these claims is without merit.

SFD's balance sheets do not establish a violation of 8 Del. C. § 160. In an April 25, 1996 proxy statement, the SFD Board released a *pro forma* balance sheet showing that the merger and self-tender offer would result in a deficit to surplus on SFD's books of more than $100 million. A balance sheet the SFD Board issued shortly after the transactions confirmed this result. Plaintiff asks us to adopt an interpretation of 8 Del. C. § 160 whereby balance-sheet net worth is controlling for purposes of determining compliance with the statute. Defendants do not dispute that SFD's books showed a negative net worth in the wake of its transactions with Yucaipa, but argue that corporations should have the presumptive right to revalue assets and liabilities to comply with Section 160.

Plaintiff advances an erroneous interpretation of Section 160. We understand that the books of a corporation do not necessarily reflect the current values of its assets and liabilities. Among other factors, unrealized appreciation or depreciation can render book numbers inaccurate. It is unrealistic to hold that a corporation is bound by its balance sheets for purposes of determining compliance with Section 160. Accordingly, we adhere to the principles of *Morris v. Standard Gas & Electric Co.*, [31 Del. Ch. 20, 63 A.2d 577 (1949)], allowing corporations to revalue properly its assets and liabilities to show a surplus and thus conform to the statute.

It is helpful to recall the purpose behind Section 160. The General Assembly enacted the statute to prevent boards from draining corporations of assets to the detriment of creditors and the long-term health of the corporation. That a corporation has not yet realized or reflected on its balance sheet the appreciation of assets is irrelevant to this concern. Regardless of what a balance sheet that has not been updated may show, an actual, though unrealized, appreciation reflects real economic value that the corporation may borrow against or that creditors may claim or levy upon. Allowing corporations to revalue assets and liabilities to reflect current realities complies with the statute and serves well the policies behind this statute.

The SFD Board appropriately revalued corporate assets to comply with 8 Del. C. § 160. Plaintiff contends that SFD's repurchase of shares violated Section 160 even without regard to the corporation's balance sheets. Plaintiff claims that the SFD Board was not entitled to rely on the solvency opinion of Houlihan, which showed that the transactions would not impair SFD's capital given a revaluation of corporate assets. The argument is that the methods that underlay the solvency opinion were inappropriate as a matter of law because they failed to take into account all of SFD's assets and liabilities. In addition, plaintiff suggests that the SFD Board's resolution of May 17, 1996 itself shows that the transactions impaired SFD's capital, and that therefore we must find a violation of 8 Del. C. § 160. We disagree, and hold that the SFD Board revalued the corporate assets under appropriate methods. Therefore the self-tender offer complied with Section 160, notwithstanding errors that took place in the drafting of the resolution.

On May 17, 1996, Houlihan released its solvency opinion to the SFD Board, expressing its judgment that the merger and self-tender offer would not impair SFD's capital. Houlihan reached this conclusion by comparing SFD's "Total Invested Capital" of $1.8 billion—a figure Houlihan arrived at by valuing SFD's assets under the "market multiple" approach—with SFD's long-term debt of $1.46 billion. This comparison yielded an approximation of SFD's "concluded equity value" equal to [$340] million, a figure clearly in excess of the outstanding par value of SFD's stock. Thus, Houlihan concluded, the transactions would not violate 8 Del. C. § 160.

Plaintiff contends that Houlihan's analysis relied on inappropriate methods to mask a violation of Section 160. Noting that 8 Del. C. § 154 defines "net assets" as "the amount by which total assets exceeds total liabilities," plaintiff argues that Houlihan's analysis is erroneous as a matter of law because of its failure to calculate "total assets" and "total liabilities" as separate variables. In a related argument, plaintiff claims that the analysis failed to take into account all of SFD's liabilities, *i.e.*, that Houlihan neglected to consider current liabilities in its comparison of SFD's "Total Invested Capital" and long-term debt. Plaintiff contends that the SFD Board's resolution proves that adding current liabilities into the mix shows a violation of Section 160. The resolution declared the value of SFD's assets to be $1.8 billion, and stated that its "total liabilities" would not exceed $1.46 billion after the transactions with Yucaipa. As noted, the $1.46 billion figure described only the value of SFD's long-term debt. Adding in SFD's $372 million in current liabilities, plaintiff argues, shows that the transactions impaired SFD's capital.

We believe that plaintiff reads too much into Section 154. The statute simply defines "net assets" in the course of defining "surplus." It does not mandate a "facts and figures balancing of assets and liabilities" to determine by what amount, if any, total assets exceeds total liabilities. [*See Farland v. Wills*, Del. Ch., 1 Del. J. Corp. L. 467, 475 (1975).] The statute is merely definitional. It does not require any particular method of calculating surplus, but simply prescribes factors that any such calculation must include. Although courts may not determine compliance with Section 160 except by methods that fully take into account the assets and liabilities of the corporation, Houlihan's methods were not erroneous as a matter of law simply because they used Total Invested Capital and long-term debt as analytical categories rather than "total assets" and "total liabilities."

We are satisfied that the Houlihan opinion adequately took into account all of SFD's assets and liabilities. Plaintiff points out that the $1.46 billion figure that approximated SFD's long-term debt failed to include $372 million in current liabilities, and argues that including the latter in the calculations dissipates the surplus. In fact, plaintiff has misunderstood Houlihan's methods. The record shows that Houlihan's calculation of SFD's Total Invested Capital is already net of current liabilities. Thus, subtracting long-term debt from Total Invested Capital does, in fact, yield an accurate measure of a corporation's net assets.

The record contains, in the form of the Houlihan opinion, substantial evidence that the transactions complied with Section 160. Plaintiff has provided no reason to distrust Houlihan's analysis. In cases alleging impairment of capital under Section 160, the trial court may defer to the board's measurement of surplus unless a plaintiff can show that the directors "failed to fulfill their duty to evaluate the assets on the basis of acceptable data and by standards which they are entitled to believe reasonably reflect present values." [*Morris*, 63 A.2d at 582.] In the absence of bad faith or fraud on the part of the board, courts will not "substitute [our] concepts of wisdom for that of the directors." [*Id*. at 583.] Here, plaintiff does not argue that the SFD Board acted in bad faith. Nor has he met his burden of showing that the methods and data that underlay the board's analysis are unreliable or that its determination of surplus is so far off the mark as to constitute actual or constructive fraud. Therefore, we defer to the board's determination of surplus, and hold that SFD's self-tender offer did not violate 8 Del. C. § 160.

On a final note, we hold that the SFD Board's resolution of May 17, 1996 has no bearing on whether the transactions conformed to Section 160. The record shows that the SFD Board committed a serious error in drafting the resolution: the resolution states that, following the transactions, SFD's "total liabilities" would be no more than $1.46 billion. In fact, that figure reflects only the value of SFD's long-term debt. Although the SFD Board was guilty of sloppy work, and did not follow good corporate practices, it does not follow that Section 160 was violated. The statute requires only that there exist a surplus after a repurchase, not that the board memorialize the surplus in a resolution. The statute carves out a class of transactions that directors have no authority to execute, but does not, in fact, require any affirmative act on the part of the board. The SFD repurchase would be valid in the absence of any board resolution. A mistake in documenting the surplus will not negate the substance of the action, which complies with the statutory scheme....

———————

The Model Act approach differs significantly from that of Delaware in several important ways. Under MBCA § 6.40(c), a dividend may be declared and paid so long as the corporation is not insolvent or rendered insolvent by the payment of the dividend. A dividend is permitted if, after the dividend is paid the company would be able to pay its current obligations as they come due and its total assets would equal or exceed the sum of its total liabilities and the liquidation rights of priority claimants. Directors may base their determination that a dividend is permissible either on financial statements based on reasonable accounting practices or on a fair valuation.

According to the Official Comment for § 6.40(c):

> ... [T]he statute authorizes departures from historical cost accounting and sanctions the use of appraisal and current value methods to determine the amount available for distribution. No particular method of valuation is prescribed in the statute, since different methods may have validity depending upon the circumstances, including the type of enterprise and the purpose for which the determination is made. For example, it is inappropriate in most cases to apply a "quick-sale liquidation" method to value an enterprise, particularly with respect to the payment of normal dividends. On the other hand, a "quick-sale liquidation valuation" method might be appropriate in certain circumstances for an enterprise in the course of reducing its asset or business base by a material degree. In most cases, a fair valuation method or a going-concern basis would be appropriate if it is believed that the enterprise will continue as a going concern.

Ordinarily a corporation should not selectively revalue assets. It should consider the value of all its material assets, whether or not reflected in the financial statements (*e.g.* a valuable executory contract). Likewise, all of a corporation's material obligations should be considered and revalued to the extent appropriate and possible. In any event, section 6.40 (d) calls for the application under section 6.40 (c)(2) of a method of determining the aggregate amount of assets and liabilities that is reasonable in the circumstances.

E. Judicial Review of Dividend Policy

Corporation statutes provide that a corporation's board of directors may declare dividends when certain conditions are met. Those statutes never require directors to declare dividends, and for good reason. The directors may determine that retaining company earnings, or using them in another way, may present opportunities for company growth that will be lost if dividends are declared. Courts almost always defer to the good faith business judgments of directors concerning dividend decisions and policy. *Cf. Nixon v. Blackwell, supra.* Plaintiff shareholders face a heavy burden when challenging such good faith business judgments.

The Maine Supreme Court, for example, wrote in *Gay v. Gay's Supermarkets, Inc.*, 343 A.2d 577 (Me. 1975), that to justify judicial intervention, the plaintiff must show: "that the decision not to declare a dividend amounted to fraud, bad faith or an abuse of discretion on the part of the [directors]." Further, the court indicated, "If there are plausible business reasons supportive of the decision of the board of directors, and such reasons can be given credence, a Court will not interfere with a corporate board's right to make that decision." *Id.*

Kamin v. American Express Company

New York Supreme Court
383 N.Y.S.2d 807 (1976)

GREENFIELD, JUSTICE.

In this stockholders' derivative action, the individual defendants, who are the directors of the American Express Company, move for an order dismissing the complaint for failure to state a cause of action pursuant to CPLR 3211(a)(7), and alternatively, for summary judgment pursuant to CPLR 3211(c).

The complaint is brought derivatively by two minority stockholders of the American Express Company, asking for a declaration that a certain dividend in kind is a waste of corporate assets, directing the defendants not to proceed with the distribution, or, in the alternative, for monetary damages. The motion to dismiss the complaint requires the Court to presuppose the truth of the allegations. It is the defendants' contention that, conceding everything in the complaint, no viable cause of action is made out.

... [T]he complaint alleges that in 1972, American Express acquired for investment 1,954,418 shares of common stock of Donaldson, Lufken and Jenrette, Inc. (hereafter DLJ), a publicly traded corporation, at a cost of $29.9 million. It is further alleged that the current market value of those shares is approximately $4.0 million. On July 28, 1975, it is alleged, the Board of Directors of American Express declared a special dividend to all stockholders of record pursuant to which the shares of DLJ would be distributed in kind. Plaintiffs contend further that if American Express were to sell the DLJ shares on the market, it would sustain a capital loss of $25 million, which could be offset against taxable capital gains on other investments. Such a sale, they allege, would result in tax savings to the company of approximately $8 million, which would not be available in the case of the distribution of DLJ shares to stockholders. It is alleged that on October 8, 1975 and October 16, 1975, plaintiffs demanded that the directors rescind the previously declared dividend in DLJ shares and take steps to preserve the capital loss which would result from selling the shares. This demand was rejected by the Board of Directors on October 17, 1975.

It is apparent that all the previously-mentioned allegations of the complaint go to the question of the exercise by the Board of Directors of business judgment in deciding how to deal with the DLJ shares. The crucial allegation which must be scrutinized to determine the legal sufficiency of the complaint is paragraph 19, which alleges:

> "19. All of the defendant Directors engaged in or acquiesced in or negligently permitted the declaration and payment of the Dividend in violation of the fiduciary duty owed by them to Amex to care for and preserve Amex's assets in the same manner as a man of average prudence would care for his own property."

Plaintiffs never moved for temporary injunctive relief, and did nothing to bar the actual distribution of the DLJ shares. The dividend was in fact paid on October 31, 1975. Accordingly, that portion of the complaint seeking a direction not to distribute the shares is deemed to be moot, and the Court will deal only with the request for declaratory judgment or for damages.

Examination of the complaint reveals that there is no claim of fraud or self-dealing, and no contention that there was any bad faith or oppressive conduct. The law is quite clear as to what is necessary to ground a claim for actionable wrongdoing.

> "In actions by stockholders, which assail the acts of their directors or trustees, courts will not interfere unless the powers have been illegally or unconscientiously executed; or unless it be made to appear that the acts were fraudulent or collusive, and destructive of the rights of the stockholders. Mere errors of judgment are not sufficient as grounds for equity interference, for the powers of those entrusted with corporate management are largely discretionary."
> *Leslie v. Lorillard*, 110 N. Y. 519, 532, 18 N. E. 363, 367 (N.Y.C.A. 1888).

More specifically, the question of whether or not a dividend is to be declared or a distribution of some kind should be made is exclusively a matter of business judgment for the Board of Directors.

> … Courts will not interfere with such discretion unless it be first made to appear that the directors have acted or are about to act in bad faith and for a dishonest purpose. It is for the directors to say, acting in good faith of course, when and to what extent dividends shall be declared.... The statute

confers upon the directors this power, and the minority stockholders are not in a position to question this right, so long as the directors are acting in good faith ... *Liebman v. Auto Strop Co.*, 241 N.Y. 427, 433–4, 150 N.E. 505, 506 (N.Y.C.A. 1926).

Thus, a complaint must be dismissed if all that is presented is a decision to pay dividends rather than pursuing some other course of conduct. A complaint which alleges merely that some course of action other than that pursued by the Board of Directors would have been more advantageous gives rise to no cognizable cause of action. Courts have more than enough to do in adjudicating legal rights and devising remedies for wrongs. The directors' room rather than the courtroom is the appropriate forum for thrashing out purely business questions which will have an impact on profits, market prices, competitive situations, or tax advantages. As stated by Cardozo, J., when sitting at Special Term, the substitution of someone else's business judgment for that of the directors "is no business for any court to follow." *Holmes v. St. Joseph Lead Co.*, 84 Misc. 278, 283, 147 N.Y.S. 104, 107 (N.Y. Sup. 1914) quoting from *Gamble v. Queens County Water Co.*, 123 N.Y. 91, 99, 25 N.E. 201, 208 (N.Y. Sup. 1890).

> "Questions of policy of management, expediency of contracts or action, adequacy of consideration, lawful appropriation of corporate funds to advance corporate interests, are left solely to their honest and unselfish decision, for their powers therein are without limitation and free from restraint, and the exercise of them for the common and general interests of the corporation may not be questioned, although the results show that what they did was unwise or inexpedient." *Pollitz v. Wabash Railroad Co.*, 207 N.Y. 113, 124, 100 N.E. 721, 724 (N.Y.C.A. 1912).

Section 720(a)(1)(A) of the Business Corporation Law permits an action against directors for "the neglect of, or failure to perform, or other violation of his duties in the management and disposition of corporate assets committed to his charge." This does not mean that a director is chargeable with ordinary negligence for having made an improper decision, or having acted imprudently. The "neglect" referred to in the statute is neglect of duties (i.e., malfeasance or nonfeasance) and not misjudgment. To allege that a director "negligently permitted the declaration and payment" of a dividend without alleging fraud, dishonesty or nonfeasance, is to state merely that a decision was taken with which one disagrees.

Nor does this appear to a be a case in which a potentially valid cause of action is inartfully stated. The defendants have moved alternatively for summary judgment and have submitted affidavits under CPLR 3211(c), and plaintiffs likewise have submitted papers enlarging upon the allegations of the complaint. The affidavits of the defendants and the exhibits annexed thereto demonstrate that the objections raised by the plaintiffs to the proposed dividend action were carefully considered and unanimously rejected by the Board at a special meeting called precisely for that purpose at the plaintiffs' request. The minutes of the special meeting indicate that the defendants were fully aware that a sale rather than a distribution of the DLJ shares might result in the realization of a substantial income tax saving. Nevertheless, they concluded that there were countervailing considerations primarily with respect to the adverse effect such a sale, realizing a loss of $25 million, would have on the net income figures in the American Express financial statement. Such a reduction of net income would have a serious effect on the market value of the publicly traded American Express stock. This was not a situation in which the defendant directors totally overlooked facts called to their attention. They gave them consideration, and attempted to view the total picture in arriving at their decision.

While plaintiffs contend that according to their accounting consultants the loss on the DLJ stock would still have to be charged against current earnings even if the stock were distributed, the defendants' accounting experts assert that the loss would be a charge against earnings only in the event of a sale, whereas in the event of distribution of the stock as a dividend, the proper accounting treatment would be to charge the loss only against surplus. While the chief accountant for the SEC raised some question as to the appropriate accounting treatment of this transaction, there was no basis for any action to be taken by the SEC with respect to the American Express financial statement.

The only hint of self-interest which is raised, not in the complaint but in the papers on the motion, is that four of the twenty directors were officers and employees of American Express and members of its Executive Incentive Compensation Plan. Hence, it is suggested, by virtue of the action taken earnings may have been overstated and their compensation affected thereby. Such a claim is highly speculative and standing alone can hardly be regarded as sufficient to support an inference of self-dealing. There is no claim or showing that the four company directors dominated and controlled the sixteen outside members of the Board. Certainly, every action taken by the Board has some impact on earnings and may therefore affect the compensation of those whose earnings are keyed to profits. That does not disqualify the inside directors, nor does it put every policy adopted by the Board in question.

All directors have an obligation, using sound business judgment, to maximize income for the benefit of all persons having a stake in the welfare of the corporate entity. What we have here as revealed both by the complaint and by the affidavits and exhibits, is that a disagreement exists between two minority stockholders and a unanimous Board of Directors as to the best way to handle a loss already incurred on an investment. The directors are entitled to exercise their honest business judgment on the information before them, and to act within their corporate powers.

That they may be mistaken, that other courses of action might have differing consequences, or that their action might benefit some shareholders more than others presents no basis for the superimposition of judicial judgment, so long as it appears that the directors have been acting in good faith. The question of to what extent a dividend shall be declared and the manner in which it shall be paid is ordinarily subject only to the qualification that the dividend be paid out of surplus (Business Corporation Law Section 510, subd. b). The Court will not interfere unless a clear case is made out of fraud, oppression, arbitrary action, or breach of trust....

Notes

Kamin v. American Express is an exquisite example of the application of the fundamental corporate law doctrines to which we turn next: the business judgment rule and the duty of care.

Chapter 10

Duty of Care

Situation

Biologistics, Inc. has continued to be successful. It has been in existence three years, and even with greatly increased expenses, its profits have increased incrementally. Its research and development activities have been proceeding satisfactorily, although no patentable process has yet been perfected. The research and development work has been expensive, however, and to raise funds for these activities the corporation has taken another bank loan in the amount of $100,000 and has sold a total of $200,000 of stock to four local investors who have done business with Phillips' investment banking firm. Each new shareholder was given 2.5% of the total outstanding common stock for $50,000. Anderson, Baker, and Phillips now each owns 30% of the common stock.

At the time of the stock sale, the board's composition changed. It now consists of Anderson, Baker, Phillips, Sara Martinez, who is a vice president of the corporation's local bank, and Jason Welsh, who is one of the new shareholders. In the year Welsh has been a director, there have been several board meetings, but he has been unable to attend any of them.

Notwithstanding its success, a problem recently developed that could have serious financial consequences for the corporation. Disturbing amounts of chemical pollution have been discovered recently in wells supplying some of the community's water. Newspaper reporters have focused on Biologistics, Inc. as a possible source of this pollution. The company's employees deny improperly disposing of any chemical wastes or otherwise contaminating the water, and Anderson and Baker say they are quite confident that these denials are sincere. Nevertheless, they cannot be sure.

A special directors' meeting is called for next Monday. The directors anticipate discussing and deciding what to do about the media's inquiries and the possibility that Biologistics somehow contributed to the chemical pollution. Baker has heard of a detection and filtering system for its chemical byproducts that is reportedly very effective but also very expensive. Another alternative is to close the existing facility and relocate to another community.

Meanwhile, the three new shareholders other than Welsh meet with Phillips. They are concerned about the possibility that Biologistics, Inc. is responsible for the pollution and, if so, that a suit against the corporation could bankrupt it. They obliquely raised with Phillips the possibility of suing the directors for mismanagement if this comes to pass.

The directors would like your advice prior to the Monday meeting. In particular, they are concerned about their possible liabilities and want to know ways to diminish their risk of liabilities, and they wonder whether they can make whatever decisions they like.

Section I
Introduction

The corporation's directors and officers are subject to two traditional fiduciary duties: the duty of care, discussed in this chapter, and the duty of loyalty, discussed in the next chapter. Other chapters on shareholder derivative litigation and changes in corporate control continue to explore how these fiduciary duties are construed in particular contexts.

These fiduciary duties impose on key corporate decision makers the primary corporate law parameters within which they manage corporate affairs. While courts acknowledge that directors and officers need discretion to pursue the entrepreneurial and profit-making activities of the corporation, they also recognize that directors and officers must meet certain standards of diligence, accountability, and propriety to serve the corporation and its shareholders properly.

This chapter explores how corporate law has crafted these standards of conduct — beginning with an orientation to the general standard of care, followed by a discussion of the business judgment rule and the requirements of informed decision making. As the materials on the duty of care unfold, consider how the law tries to balance managerial discretion with the protection of various corporate interests including non-shareholder constituencies. These materials further illustrate the rich interplay among courts, legislators, and corporate management — who collectively shape the practices and risks of corporate decision making.

Section II
General Standard of Care and Obligation to Monitor

Francis v. United Jersey Bank

New Jersey Supreme Court
432 A.2d 814 (1981)

POLLOCK, J:

The primary issue on this appeal is whether a corporate director is personally liable in negligence for the failure to prevent the misappropriation of trust funds by other directors who were also officers and shareholders of the corporation.

Plaintiffs are trustees in bankruptcy of Pritchard & Baird Intermediaries Corp. (Pritchard & Baird), a reinsurance broker or intermediary. Defendant Lillian P. Overcash is the daughter of Lillian G. Pritchard and the executrix of her estate. At the time of her death, Mrs. Pritchard was a director and the largest single shareholder of Pritchard & Baird. Because Mrs. Pritchard died after the institution of suit but before trial, her executrix was substituted as a defendant. United Jersey Bank is joined as the administrator of the estate of Charles Pritchard, Sr., who had been president, director and majority shareholder of Pritchard & Baird.

This litigation focuses on payments made by Pritchard & Baird to Charles Pritchard, Jr. and William Pritchard, who were sons of Mr. and Mrs. Charles Pritchard, Sr., as well as officers, directors and shareholders of the corporation. Claims against Charles, Jr. and William are being pursued in bankruptcy proceedings against them.

... [T]he initial question is whether Mrs. Pritchard was negligent in not noticing and trying to prevent the misappropriation of funds held by the corporation in an implied trust. A further question is whether her negligence was the proximate cause of the plaintiffs' losses. Both lower courts found that she was liable in negligence for the losses caused by the wrongdoing of Charles, Jr. and William. We affirm.

I

The matrix for our decision is the customs and practices of the reinsurance industry and the role of Pritchard & Baird as a reinsurance broker. Reinsurance involves a contract under which one insurer agrees to indemnify another for loss sustained under the latter's policy of insurance. Insurance companies that insure against losses arising out of fire or other casualty seek at times to minimize their exposure by sharing risks with other insurance companies. Thus, when the face amount of a policy is comparatively large, the company may enlist one or more insurers to participate in that risk. Similarly, an insurance company's loss potential and overall exposure may be reduced by reinsuring a part of an entire class of policies (e.g., 25% of all of its fire insurance policies). The selling insurance company is known as a ceding company. The entity that assumes the obligation is designated as the reinsurer.

The reinsurance broker arranges the contract between the ceding company and the reinsurer.... In most instances, the ceding company and the reinsurer do not communicate with each other, but rely upon the reinsurance broker....

The reinsurance business was described by an expert at trial as having "a magic aura around it of dignity and quality and integrity." A telephone call which might be confirmed by a handwritten memorandum is sufficient to create a reinsurance obligation....

... When incorporated under the laws of the State of New York in 1959, Pritchard & Baird had five directors: Charles Pritchard, Sr., his wife Lillian Pritchard, their son Charles Pritchard, Jr., George Baird and his wife Marjorie. William Pritchard, another son, became director in 1960.... The corporation issued 200 shares of common stock. Charles Pritchard, Sr. acquired 120 shares, his sons Charles Pritchard, Jr., 15 and William, 15; Mr. and Mrs. Baird owned the remaining 50. In June 1964, Baird and his wife resigned as directors and sold their stock to the corporation. From that time on the corporation operated as a close family corporation with Mr. and Mrs. Pritchard and their two sons as the only directors. After the death of Charles, Sr. in 1973, only the remaining three directors continued to operate as the board. Lillian Pritchard inherited 72 of her husband's 120 shares in Pritchard & Baird, thereby becoming the largest shareholder in the corporation with 48% of the stock.

The corporate minute books reflect only perfunctory activities by the directors, related almost exclusively to the election of officers and adoption of banking resolutions and a retirement plan. None of the minutes for any of the meetings contain a discussion of the loans to Charles, Jr. and William or of the financial condition of the corporation. Moreover, upon instructions of Charles, Jr. that financial statements were not to be circulated to anyone else, the company's statements for the fiscal years beginning February 1, 1970, were delivered only to him.

Charles Pritchard, Sr. was the chief executive and controlled the business in the years following Baird's withdrawal. Beginning in 1966, he gradually relinquished control over the operations of the corporation. In 1968, Charles, Jr. became president and William became executive vice president. Charles, Sr. apparently became ill in 1971 and during the last year and a half of his life was not involved in the affairs of the business. He continued, however, to serve as a director until his death on December 10, 1973. Notwithstanding the presence of Charles, Sr. on the board until his death in 1973, Charles, Jr. dominated the management of the corporation and the board from 1968 until the bankruptcy in 1975.

Contrary to the industry custom of segregating funds, Pritchard & Baird commingled the funds of reinsurers and ceding companies with its own funds. All monies (including commissions, premiums and loss monies) were deposited in a single account. Charles, Sr. began the practice of withdrawing funds from the commingled account in transactions identified on the corporate books as "loans." As long as Charles, Sr. controlled the corporation, the "loans" correlated with corporate profits and were repaid at the end of each year. Starting in 1970, however, Charles, Jr. and William begin to siphon ever-increasing sums from the corporation under the guise of loans. As of January 31, 1970, the "loans" to Charles, Jr. were $230,932 and to William were $207,329. At least by January 31, 1973, the annual increase in the loans exceeded annual corporate revenues. By October 1975, the year of bankruptcy, the "shareholders' loans" had metastasized to a total of $12,333,514.47.

The trial court rejected the characterization of the payments as "loans." 162 N.J. Super. at 365, 392 A.2d 1233. No corporate resolution authorized the "loans," and no note or other instrument evidenced the debt. Charles, Jr. and William paid no interest on the amounts received. The "loans" were not repaid or reduced from one year to the next; rather, they increased annually....

The "loans" were reflected on financial statements that were prepared annually as of January 31, the end of the corporate fiscal year. Although an outside certified public accountant prepared the 1970 financial statement, the corporation prepared only internal financial statements from 1971–1975. In all instances, the statements were simple documents, consisting of three or four 8½ × 11 inch sheets.

The statements of financial condition from 1970 forward demonstrated:

	W.C. Deficit	Shareholder Loans	Net Income
1970	389,022	509,941	807,229
1971	unavailable	unavailable	unavailable
1972	1,684,289	1,825,911	1,546,263
1973	3,506,460	3,700,542	1,736,349
1974	6,939,007	7,080,629	876,182
1975	10,176,419	10,298,039	551,598

Those financial statements showed working capital deficits increasing annually in tandem with the amounts that Charles, Jr. and William withdrew as "shareholders' loans." In the last complete year of business (January 31, 1974, to January 31, 1975), "shareholders' loans" and the correlative working capital deficit increased by approximately $3,200,000....

The pattern that emerges from these figures is the substantial increase in the monies appropriated by Charles Pritchard, Jr. and William Pritchard after their father's withdrawal from the business and the sharp decline in the profitability of the operation after his death. This led ultimately to the filing in December, 1975, of an involuntary petition in bankruptcy and the appointments of the plaintiffs as trustees in bankruptcy of Pritchard & Baird.

Mrs. Pritchard was not active in the business of Pritchard & Baird and knew virtually nothing of its corporate affairs. She briefly visited the corporate offices in Morristown on only one occasion, and she never read or obtained the annual financial statements. She was unfamiliar with the rudiments of reinsurance and made no effort to assure that the policies and practices of the corporation, particularly pertaining to the withdrawal of funds, complied with industry custom or relevant law. Although her husband had warned her that Charles, Jr. would "take the shirt off my back," Mrs. Pritchard did not pay any attention to her duties as a director or to the affairs of the corporation. 162 N.J. Super. at 370, 392 A.2d 1233.

After her husband died in December 1973, Mrs. Pritchard became incapacitated and was bedridden for a six-month period. She became listless at this time and started to drink rather heavily. Her physical condition deteriorated, and in 1978 she died. The trial court rejected testimony seeking to exonerate her because she "was old, was grief-stricken at the loss of her husband, sometimes consumed too much alcohol and was psychologically overborne by her sons." 162 N.J. Super. at 371, 392 A.2d 1233. That court found that she was competent to act and that the reason Mrs. Pritchard never knew what her sons "were doing was because she never made the slightest effort to discharge any of her responsibilities as a director of Pritchard & Baird." 162 N.J. Super. at 372, 392 A.2d 1233....

III

Individual liability of a corporate director for acts of the corporation is a prickly problem. Generally directors are accorded broad immunity and are not insurers of corporate activities. The problem is particularly nettlesome when a third party asserts that a director, because of nonfeasance, is liable for losses caused by acts of insiders, who in this case were officers, directors and shareholders. Determination of the liability of Mrs. Pritchard requires findings that she had a duty to the clients of Pritchard & Baird, that she breached that duty and that her breach was a proximate cause of their losses.

The New Jersey Business Corporation Act, which took effect on January 1, 1969, was a comprehensive revision of the statutes relating to business corporations. One section, N.J.S.A. 14A:6–14, concerning a director's general obligation makes it incumbent upon directors to discharge their duties in good faith and with that degree of diligence, care and skill which ordinarily prudent men would exercise under similar circumstances in like positions.

This provision was based primarily on section 43 of the Model Business Corporation Act and is derived also from section 717 of the New York Business Corporation Law (L.1961, c.855, effective September 1, 1963)....

... In addition to requiring that directors act honestly and in good faith, the New York courts recognized that the nature and extent of reasonable care depended upon the type of corporation, its size and financial resources. Thus, a bank director was held to stricter accountability than the director of an ordinary business....

As a general rule, a director should acquire at least a rudimentary understanding of the business of the corporation. Accordingly, a director should become familiar with the fundamentals of the business in which the corporation is engaged. *Campbell*, 62 N.J. Eq. at 416, 50 A. 120. Because directors are bound to exercise ordinary care, they cannot set up as a defense lack of the knowledge needed to exercise the requisite degree of care. If one "feels that he has not had sufficient business experience to qualify him to perform the duties of a director, he should either acquire the knowledge by inquiry, or refuse to act." *Ibid.*

Directors are under a continuing obligation to keep informed about the activities of the corporation. Otherwise, they may not be able to participate in the overall management of corporate affairs.... Directors may not shut their eyes to corporate misconduct and then claim that because they did not see the misconduct, they did not have a duty to look. The sentinel asleep at his post contributes nothing to the enterprise he is charged to protect.

Directorial management does not require a detailed inspection of day-to-day activities, but rather a general monitoring of corporate affairs and policies. Accordingly, a director is well advised to attend board meetings regularly. Indeed, a director who is absent from a board meeting is presumed to concur in action taken on a corporate matter, unless he files a "dissent with the secretary of the corporation within a reasonable time after learning of such action." N.J.S.A. 14A:6–13 (Supp. 1981–1982).

Regular attendance does not mean that directors must attend every meeting, but that directors should attend meetings as a matter of practice. A director of a publicly held corporation might be expected to attend regular monthly meetings, but a director of a small, family corporation might be asked to attend only an annual meeting. The point is that one of the responsibilities of a director is to attend meetings of the board of which he or she is a member....

While directors are not required to audit corporate books, they should maintain familiarity with the financial status of the corporation by a regular review of financial statements. In some circumstances, directors may be charged with assuring that book-keeping methods conform to industry custom and usage. The extent of review, as well as the nature and frequency of financial statements, depends not only on the customs of the industry, but also on the nature of the corporation and the business in which it is engaged. Financial statements of some small corporations may be prepared internally and only on an annual basis; in a large publicly held corporation, the statements may be produced monthly or at some other regular interval. Adequate financial review normally would be more informal in a private corporation than in a publicly held corporation.

... Sometimes the duty of a director may require more than consulting with outside counsel. A director may have a duty to take reasonable means to prevent illegal conduct by co-directors; in any appropriate case, this may include threat of suit.

A director is not an ornament, but an essential component of corporate governance. Consequently, a director cannot protect himself behind a paper shield bearing the motto, "dummy director." The New Jersey Business Corporation Act, in imposing a standard of ordinary care on all directors, confirms that dummy, figurehead and accommodation directors are anachronisms with no place in New Jersey law.... Thus, all directors are responsible for managing the business and affairs of the corporation.

The factors that impel expanded responsibility in the large, publicly held corporation may not be present in a small, close corporation. Nonetheless, a close corporation may, because of the nature of its business, be affected with a public interest. For example, the stock of a bank may be closely held, but because of the nature of banking the directors would be subject to greater liability than those of another close corporation. Even in a small corporation, a director is held to the standard of that degree of care that an ordinarily prudent director would use under the circumstances.

A director's duty of care does not exist in the abstract, but must be considered in relation to specific obligees. In general, the relationship of a corporate director to the corporation and its stockholders is that of a fiduciary. Shareholders have a right to expect that directors will exercise reasonable supervision and control over the policies and practices of a corporation. The institutional integrity of a corporation depends upon the proper discharge by directors of those duties.

While directors may owe a fiduciary duty to creditors also, that obligation generally has not been recognized in the absence of insolvency. With certain corporations, however, directors are seemed to owe a duty to creditors and other third parties even when the corporation is solvent. Although depositors of a bank are considered in some respects to be creditors, courts have recognized that directors may owe them a fiduciary duty. Directors of nonbanking corporations may owe a similar duty when the corporation holds funds of others in trust....

As a reinsurance broker, Pritchard & Baird received annually as a fiduciary millions of dollars of clients' money which it was under a duty to segregate. To this extent, it resembled a bank rather than a small family business. Accordingly, Mrs. Pritchard's relationship to the clientele of Pritchard & Baird was akin to that of a director of a bank to its depositors....

As a director of a substantial reinsurance brokerage corporation, she should have known that it received annually millions of dollars of loss and premium funds which it held in trust for ceding and reinsurance companies. Mrs. Pritchard should have obtained and read the annual statements of financial condition of Pritchard & Baird. Although she had a right to rely upon financial statements prepared in accordance with N.J.S.A. 14A:6–14, such reliance would not excuse her conduct. The reason is that those statements disclosed on their face the misappropriation of trust funds.

From those statements, she should have realized that, as of January 31, 1970, her sons were withdrawing substantial trust funds under the guise of "Shareholders' Loans." The financial statements for each fiscal year commencing with that of January 31, 1970, disclosed that the working capital deficits and the "loans" were escalating in tandem. Detecting a misappropriation of funds would not have required special expertise or extraordinary diligence; a cursory reading of the financial statements would have revealed the pillage. Thus, if Mrs. Pritchard had read the financial statements, she would have known that her sons were converting trust funds. When financial statements demonstrate that insiders are bleeding a corporation to death, a director should notice and try to stanch the flow of blood.

In summary, Mrs. Pritchard was charged with the obligation of basic knowledge and supervision of the business of Pritchard & Baird. Under the circumstances, this obligation included reading and understanding financial statements, and making reasonable attempts at detection and prevention of the illegal conduct of other officers and directors. She had a duty to protect the clients of Pritchard & Baird against policies and practices that would result in the misappropriation of money they had entrusted to the corporation. She breached that duty.

IV

Nonetheless, the negligence of Mrs. Pritchard does not result in liability unless it is a proximate cause of the loss. Analysis of proximate cause requires an initial determination of cause-in-fact. Causation-in-fact calls for a finding that the defendant's act or omission was a necessary antecedent of the loss, *i.e.*, that if the defendant had observed his or her duty of care, the loss would not have occurred. Further, the plaintiff has the burden of establishing the amount of the loss or damages caused by the negligence of the defendant. Thus, the plaintiff must establish not only a breach of duty, "but in addition that the performance by the director of his duty would have avoided loss, and the amount of the resulting loss." [1 G. Hornstein, Corporation Law and Practice, §446 at 566 (1959).]

Cases involving nonfeasance present a much more difficult causation question than those in which the director has committed an affirmative act of negligence leading to the loss. Analysis in cases of negligent omissions calls for determination of the reasonable steps a director should have taken and whether that course of action would have averted the loss....

In this case, the scope of Mrs. Pritchard's duties was determined by the precarious financial condition of Pritchard & Baird, its fiduciary relationship to its clients and the implied trust in which it held their funds. Thus viewed, the scope of her duties encompassed all reasonable action to stop the continuing conversion. Her duties extended beyond mere objection and resignation to reasonable attempts to prevent the misappropriation of the trust funds.

A leading case discussing causation where the director's liability is predicated upon a negligent failure to act is *Barnes v. Andrews*, 298 F. 614 (S.D.N.Y. 1924). In that case the court exonerated a figurehead director who served for eight months on a board that held one meeting after his election, a meeting he was forced to miss because of the death of his mother. Writing for the court, Judge Learned Hand distinguished a director who fails to prevent general mismanagement from one such as Mrs. Pritchard who failed to stop an illegal "loan":

> When the corporate funds have been illegally lent, it is a fair inference that a protest would have stopped the loan, and that the director's neglect caused the loss. But when a business fails from general mismanagement, business incapacity, or bad judgment, how is it possible to say that a single director could have made the company successful, or how much in dollars he could have saved? [*Id.* at 616–17.]

Pointing out the absence of proof of proximate cause between defendant's negligence and the company's insolvency, Judge Hand also wrote:

> The plaintiff must, however, go further than to show that [the director] should have been more active in his duties. This cause of action rests upon a tort, as much though it be a tort of omission as though it had rested upon a positive act. The plaintiff must accept the burden of showing that the performance of the defendant's duties would have avoided loss, and what loss it would have avoided. [*Id.* at 616.]

... In assessing whether Mrs. Pritchard's conduct was a legal or proximate cause of the conversion, "(l)egal responsibility must be limited to those causes which are so closely connected with the result and of such significance that the law is justified in imposing liability." [W. Prosser, Law of Torts, § 41 at 237 (4th ed. 1971).] Such a judicial determination involves not only considerations of causation-in-fact and matters of policy, but also common sense and logic. The act or the failure to act must be a substantial factor in producing the harm.

Within Pritchard & Baird, several factors contributed to the loss of the funds: commingling of corporate and client monies, conversion of funds by Charles, Jr. and William and dereliction of her duties by Mrs. Pritchard. The wrongdoing of her sons, although the immediate cause of the loss, should not excuse Mrs. Pritchard from her negligence which also was a substantial factor contributing to the loss. Her sons knew that she, the only other director, was not reviewing their conduct; they spawned their fraud in the backwater of her neglect. Her neglect of duty contributed to the climate of corruption; her failure to act contributed to the continuation of that corruption. Consequently, her conduct was a substantial factor contributing to the loss.

Analysis of proximate cause is especially difficult in a corporate context where the allegation is that nonfeasance of a director is a proximate cause of damage to a third party. Where a case involves nonfeasance, no one can say "with absolute certainty what would have occurred if the defendant had acted otherwise." Prosser, *supra*, §41 at 242. Nonetheless, where it is reasonable to conclude that the failure to act would produce a particular result and that result has followed, causation may be inferred. *Ibid.* We conclude that even if Mrs. Pritchard's mere objection had not stopped the depredations of her sons, her consultation with an attorney and the threat of suit would have deterred them. That conclusion flows as a matter of common sense and logic from the record. Whether in other situations a director has a duty to do more than protest and resign is best left to case-by-case determinations. In this case, we are satisfied that there was a duty to do more than object and resign. Consequently, we find that Mrs. Pritchard's negligence was a proximate cause of the misappropriations. [Affirmed.]

Notes and Questions

1. Most challenges to internal corporate conduct and decision making are brought by shareholders not, as in *Francis*, bankruptcy trustees or creditors. Common talk speaks of shareholders as "owners" of a corporation and how this warrants legal protection from managerial misconduct. Many observe that shareholders are the residual claimants on a corporation's assets, standing last in line after obligations a corporation owes to lenders and other creditors (liabilities). Such talk leads one to surmise that, when shareholder claims are worthless, because a corporation's liabilities exceed its assets, the next most junior creditors take the position of the shareholders, last in line, maybe even then constituting a corporation's "owners."

2. It becomes tempting to reconsider to whom corporate managers owe duties when a corporation's assets are less than its liabilities or slightly earlier when, as one court termed it, a corporation is "in the vicinity of insolvency." *Credit Lyonnais Bank v. Pathe Comm. Corp.*, 18 J. Corp. L. 145 (Del. Ch. 1993). The Delaware Supreme Court has qualified that stance. *North American Catholic Educational Programming Foundation, Inc. v. Gheewalla*, 930 A.2d 92 (Del. 2007). It said there is no legally recognized "vicinity of insolvency" that affects corporate law fiduciary duties. Actual insolvency is required.

In the case of insolvency, creditors do gain standing to bring claims against directors for breach of fiduciary duty on behalf of the corporation ("derivative actions"). Besides that, directors of insolvent corporations do not owe creditors any particular duties but rather continue owing general corporate law fiduciary duties to their corporation for the benefit of all the residual claimants, which for an insolvent firm includes creditors. *See also Quadrant Structured Products Co. v. Vertin*, 115 A.3d 535 (Del. Ch. 2015).

2. Later in this chapter we continue exploring to whom directors owe fiduciary duties. Indeed, this question sheds light on the very purpose of a corporation.

A. General Standard

In determining whether directors and officers have met their duty of care, it is helpful to distinguish between two aspects of the duty. First, in carrying out their general responsibilities, directors are subject to a general standard of conduct. As illustrated in *Francis*, this standard is often described in negligence terms: What must ordinarily prudent directors do? Have the directors excessively neglected their obligations?

Once directors actually make conscious business decisions, however, courts refer to the business judgment rule to evaluate the directors' decision-making process. This more frequent application of the duty of care will be explored in later cases in this chapter.

B. ALI and MBCA Approaches

Consider the language of MBCA § 8.30(a) in its articulation of a general standard of care and MBCA § 8.31 regarding the standards of liability for directors. The DGCL and many other corporate statutes avoid codifying such duties and standards, preferring to allow them to continue evolving through common law adjudication as they have for centuries. Despite the value of such case-by-case development, the temptation to synthesize fiduciary obligation as black letter law is strong. Consider the following formulation by the American Law Institute, ALI § 4.01(a):

> (a) A director or officer has a duty to the corporation to perform the director's or officer's functions in good faith, in a manner that he or she reasonably believes to be in the best interests of the corporation, and with the care that an ordinarily prudent person would reasonably be expected to exercise in a like position and under similar circumstances....

The meaning of the key terms is not easily discernible and there is little case law to assist us. Do the following Comments to Model Act § 8.30 clarify the meanings?

> (1) The phrase "reasonably believes" is both subjective and objective in character. Its first level of analysis is geared to what the particular director, acting in good faith, actually believes — not what objective analysis would lead another director (in a like position and acting in similar circumstances) to conclude. The second level of analysis is focused specifically on "reasonably." While a director has wide discretion in marshalling the evidence and reaching conclusions, whether a director's belief is reasonable (*i.e.*, could — not would — a reasonable person in a like position and acting in similar circumstances have arrived at that belief) ultimately involves an overview that is objective in character.

> (2) The phrase "best interests of the corporation" is key to an explication of a director's duties. The term "corporation" is a surrogate for the business en-

terprise as well as a frame of reference encompassing the shareholder body. In determining the corporation's "best interests," the director has wide discretion in deciding how to weigh near-term opportunities versus long-term benefits as well as in making judgments where the interests of various groups within the shareholder body or having other cognizable interests in the enterprise may differ.

C. Oversight Responsibilities

The *Francis* case concludes that a director that does nothing does not do enough, but what specifically must directors and officers do to satisfy their basic standard of care? Corporate statutes do not define directors' and officers' functions with specificity. The provisions in corporate certificates of incorporation, bylaws, and directors' and shareholders' resolutions are typically vague.

Professional handbooks and manuals speak of supporting and overseeing the formulation of business strategy and goals; evaluating senior management, setting related compensation, and planning for succession; developing and overseeing compliance and internal control programs; supervising financial auditors and promoting the accuracy and reliability of financial reporting; and evaluating the effectiveness of the board itself and its various committees. *See* AMERICAN BAR ASSOCIATION, CORPORATE DIRECTOR'S GUIDEBOOK (6th ed. 2012).

Directors are expected to promote the corporate interest and protect shareholders. It is understood that the interests of other stakeholders can also be cognizable. Examples of other constituencies include employees, lenders, suppliers, customers, local communities, and even the environment. As a matter of corporate law, however, directors are not usually directly responsible to any such constituencies, but rather to shareholders.

Directors are expected to act in the best interests of the corporation and all shareholders, even when elected by a given class or group of shareholders or through or at the request of another constituency, such as a labor union, lender, or other party. It is widely understood that many decisions require a balancing between their short-term and long-run consequences and directors enjoy considerable discretion over determining the appropriate time horizon, as a matter of both law and practice.

Effective directors know that they must invest some effort to become informed about the business of companies on whose boards they serve. They learn about the company's industry; its specific business structure; as well its competitors, personnel, products, and customers; they understand the company's strengths, challenges, its source of profits, and its overall financial position. They maintain sufficient knowledge to enable having intelligent discussions with fellow directors about the company and with senior officers about how management is performing.

Given these guidelines, how would you have advised Mrs. Pritchard?

The court in *Francis* held that Mrs. Pritchard breached her general standard of care, but there are surprisingly few cases that have reached the same conclusion. The ALI cites fewer than ten cases that have found "negligent liability," as indicated in ALI Reporter's Note 17 to § 4.01(a). Why? The court also appeared to place on the plaintiff the burden of showing that Mrs. Pritchard breached her general standard of care and that the breach was the proximate cause of the corporation's losses. ALI § 4.01(d) expressly agrees with this allocation of the burden. Exactly what must the plaintiff prove?

Section III
Duty to Monitor

In re Caremark International Inc. Deriv. Litig.

Delaware Court of Chancery
698 A.2d 959 (1996)

ALLEN, CHANCELLOR.

Pending is a motion ... to approve as fair and reasonable a proposed settlement of a consolidated derivative action on behalf of Caremark International, Inc. ("Caremark"). The suit involves claims that the members of Caremark's board of directors (the "Board") breached their fiduciary duty of care to Caremark in connection with alleged violations by Caremark employees of federal and state laws and regulations applicable to health care providers. As a result of the alleged violations, Caremark was subject to an extensive four year investigation by the United States Department of Health and Human Services and the Department of Justice. In 1994 Caremark was charged in an indictment with multiple felonies. It thereafter entered into a number of agreements with the Department of Justice and others. Those agreements included a plea agreement in which Caremark pleaded guilty to a single felony of mail fraud and agreed to pay civil and criminal fines. Subsequently, Caremark agreed to make reimbursements to various private and public parties. In all, the payments that Caremark has been required to make total approximately $250 million.

This suit was filed in 1994, purporting to seek on behalf of the company recovery of these losses from the individual defendants who constitute the board of directors of Caremark. The parties now propose that it be settled and, after notice to Caremark shareholders, a hearing on the fairness of the proposal was held on August 16, 1996....

The ultimate issue then is whether the proposed settlement appears to be fair to the corporation and its absent shareholders. In this effort the court does not determine contested facts, but evaluates the claims and defenses on the discovery record to achieve a sense of the relative strengths of the parties' positions....

Legally, evaluation of the central claim made entails consideration of the legal standard governing a board of directors' obligation to supervise or monitor corporate performance. For the reasons set forth below I conclude, in light of the discovery record, that there is a very low probability that it would be determined that the directors of Caremark breached any duty to appropriately monitor and supervise the enterprise....

I. BACKGROUND

Caremark, a Delaware corporation with its headquarters in Northbrook, Illinois, was created in November 1992 when it was spun-off from Baxter International, Inc. ("Baxter") and became a publicly held company listed on the New York Stock Exchange. The business practices that created the problem pre-dated the spin-off. During the relevant period Caremark was involved in two main health care business segments, providing patient care and managed care services. As part of its patient care business, which accounted for the majority of Caremark's revenues, Caremark provided alternative site health care services, including infusion therapy, growth hormone therapy, HIV/AIDS-related treatments and hemophilia therapy. Caremark's managed care services included prescription drug programs and the operation of multi-specialty group practices.

A. Events Prior to the Government Investigation

A substantial part of the revenues generated by Caremark's businesses is derived from third party payments, insurers, and Medicare and Medicaid reimbursement programs. The latter source of payments are subject to the terms of the Anti-Referral Payments Law ("ARPL") which prohibits health care providers from paying any form of remuneration to induce the referral of Medicare or Medicaid patients. From its inception, Caremark entered into a variety of agreements with hospitals, physicians, and health care providers for advice and services, as well as distribution agreements with drug manufacturers, as had its predecessor prior to 1992. Specifically, Caremark did have a practice of entering into contracts for services (e.g., consultation agreements and research grants) with physicians at least some of whom prescribed or recommended services or products that Caremark provided to Medicare recipients and other patients. Such contracts were not prohibited by the ARPL but they obviously raised a possibility of unlawful "kickbacks."

As early as 1989, Caremark's predecessor issued an internal "Guide to Contractual Relationships" ("Guide") to govern its employees in entering into contracts with physicians and hospitals. The Guide tended to be reviewed annually by lawyers and updated. Each version of the Guide stated as Caremark's and its predecessor's policy that no payments would be made in exchange for or to induce patient referrals. But what one might deem a prohibited quid pro quo was not always clear. Due to a scarcity of court decisions interpreting the ARPL, however, Caremark repeatedly publicly stated that there was uncertainty concerning Caremark's interpretation of the law.

To clarify the scope of the ARPL, the United States Department of Health and Human Services ("HHS") issued "safe harbor" regulations in July 1991 stating conditions under which financial relationships between health care service providers and patient referral sources, such as physicians, would not violate the ARPL. Caremark contends that the narrowly drawn regulations gave limited guidance as to the legality of many of the agreements used by Caremark that did not fall within the safe-harbor. Caremark's predecessor, however, amended many of its standard forms of agreement with health care providers and revised the Guide in an apparent attempt to comply with the new regulations.

B. Government Investigation and Related Litigation

In August 1991, the HHS Office of the Inspector General ("OIG") initiated an investigation of Caremark's predecessor. Caremark's predecessor was served with a subpoena requiring the production of documents, including contracts between Caremark's predecessor and physicians (Quality Service Agreements ("QSAs")). Under the QSAs, Caremark's predecessor appears to have paid physicians fees for monitoring patients under Caremark's predecessor's care, including Medicare and Medicaid recipients. Sometimes apparently those monitoring patients were referring physicians, which raised ARPL concerns.

In March 1992, the Department of Justice ("DOJ") joined the OIG investigation and separate investigations were commenced by several additional federal and state agencies.

C. Caremark's Response to the Investigation

During the relevant period, Caremark had approximately 7,000 employees and ninety branch operations. It had a decentralized management structure. By May 1991, however, Caremark asserts that it had begun making attempts to centralize its management structure in order to increase supervision over its branch operations.

The first action taken by management, as a result of the initiation of the OIG investigation, was an announcement that as of October 1, 1991, Caremark's predecessor would no longer pay management fees to physicians for services to Medicare and Medicaid patients. Despite this decision, Caremark asserts that its management, pursuant to advice, did not believe that such payments were illegal under the existing laws and regulations.

During this period, Caremark's Board took several additional steps consistent with an effort to assure compliance with company policies concerning the ARPL and the contractual forms in the Guide. In April 1992, Caremark published a fourth revised version of its Guide apparently designed to assure that its agreements either complied with the ARPL and regulations or excluded Medicare and Medicaid patients altogether. In addition, in September 1992, Caremark instituted a policy requiring its regional officers, Zone Presidents, to approve each contractual relationship entered into by Caremark with a physician.

Although there is evidence that inside and outside counsel had advised Caremark's directors that their contracts were in accord with the law, Caremark recognized that some uncertainty respecting the correct interpretation of the law existed. In its 1992 annual report, Caremark disclosed the ongoing government investigations, acknowledged that if penalties were imposed on the company they could have a material adverse effect on Caremark's business, and stated that no assurance could be given that its interpretation of the ARPL would prevail if challenged.

Throughout the period of the government investigations, Caremark had an internal audit plan designed to assure compliance with business and ethics policies. In addition, Caremark employed Price Waterhouse as its outside auditor. On February 8, 1993, the [Audit &] Ethics Committee of Caremark's Board received and reviewed an outside auditors report by Price Waterhouse which concluded that there were no material weaknesses in Caremark's control structure. Despite the positive findings of Price Waterhouse, however, on April 20, 1993, the Audit & Ethics Committee adopted a new internal audit charter requiring a comprehensive review of compliance policies and the compilation of an employee ethics handbook concerning such policies.

The Board appears to have been informed about this project and other efforts to assure compliance with the law. For example, Caremark's management reported to the Board that Caremark's sales force was receiving an ongoing education re- garding the ARPL and the proper use of Caremark's form contracts which had been approved by in-house counsel. On July 27, 1993, the new ethics manual, expressly prohibiting payments in exchange for referrals and requiring employees to report all illegal conduct to a toll free confidential ethics hotline, was approved and allegedly disseminated. The record suggests that Caremark continued these policies in sub- sequent years, causing employees to be given revised versions of the ethics manual and requiring them to participate in training sessions concerning compliance with the law.

During 1993, Caremark took several additional steps which appear to have been aimed at increasing management supervision. These steps included new policies re- quiring local branch managers to secure home office approval for all disbursements under agreements with health care providers and to certify compliance with the ethics program. In addition, the chief financial officer was appointed to serve as Caremark's compliance officer. In 1994, a fifth revised Guide was published....

II. LEGAL PRINCIPLES

A. Principles Governing Settlements of Derivative Claims

As noted at the outset of this opinion, this Court is now required to exercise an informed judgment whether the proposed settlement is fair and reasonable in the light of all relevant factors. *Polk v. Good*, Del. Supr., 507 A-2d 531 (1986). On an ap- plication of this kind, this Court attempts to protect the best interests of the corpo- ration and its absent shareholders all of whom will be barred from future litigation on these claims if the settlement is approved. The parties proposing the settlement bear the burden of persuading the court that it is in fact fair and reasonable. *Fins v. Pearlman*, Del. Supr., 424 A.2d 305 (1980).

B. Directors' Duties to Monitor Corporate Operations

The complaint charges the director defendants with breach of their duty of attention or care in connection with the ongoing operation of the corporation's business. The claim is that the directors allowed a situation to develop and continue which exposed the corporation to enormous legal liability and that in so doing they violated a duty to be active monitors of corporate performance. The complaint thus does not charge either director self-dealing or the more difficult loyalty-type problems arising from cases of suspect director motivation, such as entrenchment or sale of control contexts. The theory here advanced is possibly the most difficult theory in corporation law upon which a plaintiff might hope to win a judgment....

1. *Potential liability for directoral decisions*: Director liability for a breach of the duty to exercise appropriate attention may, in theory, arise in two distinct contexts. First, such liability may be said to follow from a board decision that results in a loss because that decision was ill advised or "negligent." Second, liability to the corporation for a loss may be said to arise from an unconsidered failure of the board to act in circumstances in which due attention would, arguably, have prevented the loss.

2. *Liability for failure to monitor*: The second class of cases in which director liability for inattention is theoretically possible entail circumstances in which a loss eventuates not from a decision but, from unconsidered inaction. Most of the decisions that a corporation, acting through its human agents, makes are, of course, not the subject of director attention. Legally, the board itself will be required only to authorize the most significant corporate acts or transactions: mergers, changes in capital structure, fundamental changes in business, appointment and compensation of the CEO, etc. As the facts of this case graphically demonstrate, ordinary business decisions that are made by officers and employees deeper in the interior of the organization can, however, vitally affect the welfare of the corporation and its ability to achieve its various strategic and financial goals.... Financial and organizational disasters such as these raise the question, what is the board's responsibility with respect to the organization and monitoring of the enterprise to assure that the corporation functions within the law to achieve its purposes?

Modernly this question has been given special importance by an increasing tendency, especially under federal law, to employ the criminal law to assure corporate compliance with external legal requirements, including environmental, financial, employee and product safety as well as assorted other health and safety regulations. In 1991, pursuant to the Sentencing Reform Act of 1984, the United States Sentencing Commission adopted Organizational Sentencing Guidelines which impact importantly on the prospective effect these criminal sanctions might have on business corporations. The Guidelines set forth a uniform sentencing structure for organizations to be sentenced for violation of federal criminal statutes and provide for penalties that equal or often massively exceed those previously imposed on corporations. The Guidelines offer powerful incentives for corporations today to have in place compliance programs to detect violations of law, promptly to report violations to appropriate public officials when discovered, and to take prompt, voluntary remedial efforts.

In 1963, the Delaware Supreme Court in *Graham v. Allis-Chalmers Mfg. Co.*, Del. Supr., 188 A.2d 125 (1963), addressed the question of potential liability of board members for losses experienced by the corporation as a result of the corporation having violated the anti-trust laws of the United States. There was no claim in that case that the directors knew about the behavior of subordinate employees of the corporation that had resulted in the liability. Rather, as in this case, the claim asserted was that the directors ought to have known of it and if they had known they would have been under a duty to bring the corporation into compliance with the law and thus save the corporation from the loss. The Delaware Supreme Court concluded that, under the facts as they appeared, there was no basis to find that the directors had breached a duty to be informed of the ongoing operations of the firm. In notably colorful terms, the court stated that "absent cause for suspicion there is no duty upon the directors to install and operate a corporate system of espionage to ferret out wrongdoing which they have no reason to suspect exists." The Court found that there were no grounds for suspicion in that case and, thus, concluded that the directors were blamelessly unaware of the conduct leading to the corporate liability.

How does one generalize this holding today? Can it be said today that, absent some ground giving rise to suspicion of violation of law, that corporate directors have no duty to assure that a corporate information gathering and reporting system exists which represents a good faith attempt to provide senior management and the Board with information respecting material acts, events or conditions within the corporation, including compliance with applicable statutes and regulations? I certainly do not believe so. I doubt that such a broad generalization of the *Graham* holding would have been accepted by the Supreme Court in 1963. The case can be more narrowly interpreted as standing for the proposition that, absent grounds to suspect deception, neither corporate boards nor senior officers can be charged with wrongdoing simply for assuming the integrity of employees and the honesty of their dealings on the company's behalf.

A broader interpretation of *Grabam v. Allis Chalmers*—that it means that a corporate board has no responsibility to assure that appropriate information and reporting systems are established by management—would not, in any event, be accepted by the Delaware Supreme Court in 1996, in my opinion. In stating the basis for this view, I start with the recognition that in recent years the Delaware Supreme Court has made it clear—especially in its jurisprudence concerning takeovers, from *Smith v. Van Gorkom* through *Paramount Communications v. QVC*—the seriousness with which the corporation law views the role of the corporate board. Secondly, I note the elementary fact that relevant and timely information is an essential predicate for satisfaction of the board's supervisory and monitoring role under Section 141 of the Delaware General Corporation Law. Thirdly, I note the potential impact of the federal organizational sentencing guidelines on any business organization. Any rational person attempting in good faith to meet an organizational governance responsibility would be bound to take into account this development and the enhanced penalties and the opportunities for reduced sanctions that it offers.

In light of these developments, it would, in my opinion, be a mistake to conclude that our Supreme Court's statement in *Graham* concerning "espionage" means that corporate boards may satisfy their obligation to be reasonably informed concerning the corporation, without assuring themselves that information and reporting systems exist in the organization that are reasonably designed to provide to senior management and to the board itself timely, accurate information sufficient to allow management and the board, each within its scope, to reach informed judgments concerning both the corporation's compliance with law and its business performance.

Obviously the level of detail that is appropriate for such an information system is a question of business judgment. And obviously too, no rationally designed information and reporting system will remove the possibility that the corporation will violate laws or regulations, or that senior officers or directors may nevertheless sometimes be misled or otherwise fail reasonably to detect acts material to the corporation's compliance with the law. But it is important that the board exercise a good faith judgment that the corporation's information and reporting system is in concept and design adequate to assure the board that appropriate information will come to its attention in a timely manner as a matter of ordinary operations, so that it may satisfy its responsibility.

Thus, I am of the view that a director's obligation includes a duty to attempt in good faith to assure that a corporate information and reporting system, which the board concludes is adequate, exists, and that failure to do so under some circumstances may, in theory at least, render a director liable for losses caused by noncompliance with applicable legal standards. I now turn to an analysis of the claims asserted with this concept of the directors' duty of care, as a duty satisfied in part by assurance of adequate information flows to the board, in mind.

III. ANALYSIS OF THIRD AMENDED COMPLAINT AND SETTLEMENT

A. The Claims

On balance, after reviewing an extensive record in this case, including numerous documents and three depositions, I conclude that this settlement is fair and reasonable....

In order to show that the Caremark directors breached their duty of care by failing adequately to control Caremark's employees, plaintiffs would have to show either (1) that the directors knew or (2) should have known that violations of law were occurring and, in either event, (3) that the directors took no steps in a good faith effort to prevent or remedy that situation, and (4) that such failure proximately resulted in the losses complained of, although under *Cede & Co. v. Technicolor, Inc.*, Del. Supr., 636 A.2d 956 (1994) this last element may be thought to constitute an affirmative defense.

1. *Knowing violation of statute*: Concerning the possibility that the Caremark directors knew of violations of law, none of the documents submitted for review, nor any of the deposition transcripts appear to provide evidence of it. Certainly the Board understood that the company had entered into a variety of contracts with physicians, researchers, and health care providers and it was understood that some of these contracts were with persons who had prescribed treatments that Caremark participated in providing. The Board was informed that the company's reimbursement for patient care was frequently from government funded sources and that such services were subject to the ARPL. But the Board appears to have been informed by experts that the company's practices, while contestable, were lawful. There is no evidence that reliance on such reports was not reasonable. Thus, this case presents no occasion to apply a principle to the effect that knowingly causing the corporation to violate a criminal statute constitutes a breach of a director's fiduciary duty. *See Roth v. Robertson*, N.Y. Sup. Ct., 118 N.Y.S. 351 (1909); *Miller v. American Tel. & Tel. Co.*, 507 F.2d 759 (3d Cir. 1974). It is not clear that the Board knew the detail found, for example, in the indictments arising from the company's payments. But, of course, the duty to act in good faith to be informed cannot be thought to require directors to possess

detailed information about all aspects of the operation of the enterprise. Such a requirement would simply be inconsistent with the scale and scope of efficient organization size in this technological age.

2. *Failure to monitor*: Since it does appear that the Board was to some extent unaware of the activities that led to liability, I turn to a consideration of the other potential avenue to director liability that the pleadings take: director inattention or "negligence." Generally where a claim of directorial liability for corporate loss is predicated upon ignorance of liability creating activities within the corporation, as in *Graham* or in this case, in my opinion only a sustained or systematic failure of the board to exercise oversight—such as an utter failure to attempt to assure a reasonable information and reporting system [exists]—will establish the lack of good faith that is a necessary condition to liability. Such a test of liability—lack of good faith as evidenced by sustained or systematic failure of a director to exercise reasonable oversight—is quite high. But, a demanding test of liability in the oversight context is probably beneficial to corporate shareholders as a class, as it is in the board decision context, since it makes board service by qualified persons more likely, while continuing to act as a stimulus to good faith performance of duty by such directors.

Here the record supplies essentially no evidence that the director defendants were guilty of a sustained failure to exercise their oversight function. To the contrary, insofar as I am able to tell on this record, the corporation's information systems appear to have represented a good faith attempt to be informed of relevant facts. If the directors did not know the specifics of the activities that lead to the indictments, they cannot be faulted.

The liability that eventuated in this instance was huge. But the fact that it resulted from a violation of criminal law alone does not create a breach of fiduciary duty by directors. The record at this stage does not support the conclusion that the defendants either lacked good faith in the exercise of their monitoring responsibilities or conscientiously permitted a known violation of law by the corporation to occur. The claims asserted against them must be viewed at this stage as extremely weak.

Notes and Questions

1. The *Caremark* opinion seems to stress duty of care as the doctrinal foundation of director obligations to inquire and to monitor. The Delaware Supreme Court later affirmed the standard articulated in *Caremark* when also discussing how notions of good faith may relate to the duty of care in the inquiry and monitoring contexts. *Stone v. Ritter*, 911 A.2d 362 (Del. 2006). The latter case is presented in ensuing materials addressing the notion of good faith.

2. The *Caremark* opinion notes the "potential impact" of the Federal Organizational Sentencing Guidelines, referring to federal law addressing criminal penalties against corporations and other organizations. Organizations can commit crimes, as individuals can. Leading crimes that organizations are known to commit include fraud, environmental waste discharge and violations of tax, antitrust and food and drug laws.

Though organizations cannot be imprisoned, they may be fined, given probation, directed to pay restitution, issue public notices of conviction and suffer penalties under various forfeiture statutes.

The Guidelines, promulgated by the US Sentencing Commission and first effective in 1991, provide prosecutorial and judicial guidance to advance two fundamental goals of sentencing organizations for criminal violations: just punishment and deterrence. The Commission recognizes that crimes committed by organizations are directed by individual human beings within them; it may not advance those two goals to impose criminal penalties on organizations despite best efforts to promote compliance. Accordingly, the Guidelines direct mitigation of the potential range of fines and other penalties, sometimes as much as 95%, for organizations that can show they had in place an effective compliance program designed to promote compliance and deter violations.

3. The era of Enron and Sarbanes-Oxley brought renewed intensity to corporate criminal law, just as it did to corporate governance. Sarbanes-Oxley, enacted in 2002, defined new crimes for wrongful financial statement certification, enhanced penalties for other business crimes and directed the Sentencing Commission to assure optimal approaches to corporate criminal liability. President George W. Bush formed the President's Corporate Fraud Task Force within the Department of Justice to fortify this area of law enforcement. The government's rationale was outlined in a series of Justice Department memos "getting tough" on corporate malfeasance, a 2003 version of which stressed "vigorous enforcement" of law against "corporate wrongdoers." *See* Memorandum from Eric Holder, Deputy Attorney General, U.S. Dept. of Justice, to Heads of Department Components and United States Attorneys, *Bringing Criminal Charges Against Corporations* (June 16, 1999).

A perceived risk arose that criminal indictment of whole business organizations may lead, unintentionally and undesirably, to their collapse. To reduce that risk, prosecutors began in the early 2000s increasingly to use deferred prosecution agreements (DPAs), in which firms opt for cooperative settlement. In DPAs, prosecutors agree with target corporations to defer or refrain from prosecution in exchange for the target's admitting allegations, paying fines and committing to various undertakings. Corporate undertakings include reforms such as detailed public disclosure of the matter, enhanced internal compliance programs and top-level governance changes. Terms provide that prosecution is deferred. However, if the government determines that the target breached, it can prosecute. At such a time, given the admissions, conviction is potentially certain.

4. ALI § 4.01(a)(1) addresses the duty to inquire:

> The duty [of care] includes the obligation to make, or cause to be made, an inquiry when, but only when, the circumstances would alert a reasonable director or officer to the need therefor. The extent of such inquiry shall be such as the director or officer reasonably believes to be necessary.

5. Compare MBCA § 8.30(c)–(e) regarding directors' reliance on others, with ALI § 4.02 which provides:

In performing his or her duties and functions, a director or officer who acts in good faith, and reasonably believes that reliance is warranted, is entitled to rely on information, opinions, reports, statements (including financial statements and other financial data), decisions, judgments, and performance (including decisions, judgments, and performance within the scope of § 4.01(b)) prepared, presented, made, or performed by:

(a) One or more directors, officers, or employees of the corporation, or of a business organization under joint control or common control with the corporation, who the director or officer reasonably believes merit confidence; or

(b) Legal counsel, public accountants, engineers, or other persons who the director or officer reasonably believes merit confidence.

ALI § 4.03 also provides that directors may rely on a "duly authorized committee of the board upon which the director does not serve ..." In addition, ALI § 4.01(b) authorizes directors to delegate functions to "committees of the board or to directors, officers, employees, experts, or other persons...."

Thus, both the MBCA and the ALI allow directors to rely on a wide range of information from a wide variety of persons when the directors reasonably believe that such reliance "merits confidence" and, as described in MBCA § 8.30(c) and (d), when directors do "not have knowledge that makes reliance unwarranted."

While directors may rely on others, such reliance does not automatically substitute for their own conduct. As the Introductory Comment *c* to ALI § 4.01 states:

The weight courts should afford to information, opinions, reports, statements, decisions, judgments, or performance on which a director or officer is "entitled to rely" ... will vary with the circumstances. Considerations affecting the weight will include the importance of the issue on which advice is sought, the nature of the advice, the complexity of the issue, the background and experience of the director or officer in the area about which advice is being given, and the precision with which the advice is followed.

Consider finally DGCL 141(e):

§ 141. Board of directors ... (e) A member of the board of directors, or a member of any committee designated by the board of directors, shall, in the performance of such member's duties, be fully protected in relying in good faith upon the records of the corporation and upon such information, opinions, reports or statements presented to the corporation by any of the corporation's officers or employees, or committees of the board of directors, or by any other person as to matters the member reasonably believes are within such other person's professional or expert competence and who has been selected with reasonable care by or on behalf of the corporation.

6. While reliance on others is often necessary, authorizing such reliance poses risks that directors or officers will turn blind eyes toward issues requiring attention. For publicly-held corporations, the Sarbanes-Oxley Act of 2002 imposes specific certification requirements on chief executive officers and chief financial officers. These ex-

ecutives must certify in periodic reports filed with the Securities and Exchange Commission that, among other things, they designed internal controls to promote reliable financial reporting, that they disclosed discovered control deficiencies or weaknesses to their outside auditors and board audit committee, as well as any fraud involving employees with significant internal control roles. The Act also requires companies to include in annual disclosures an internal control report expressing management's responsibility for establishing and maintaining adequate internal controls for financial reporting and assessing their effectiveness. Outside auditors must sign off on the assessment. The Act requires compliance programs, document retention policies and internal investigation procedures.

Section IV
Business Judgment Rule

In carrying out their responsibilities, directors make a variety of decisions — ranging from selection of corporate officers, approval of major transactions, and approval of the general business strategy and policies of the corporation. Recognizing that directors need broad discretion in how and what decisions they make, the courts crafted an alternative analysis to the general standard of care. Thus, once directors make conscious corporate decisions, thereby exercising their business judgment, their conduct is generally subject to the "business judgment rule."

A. The Classic Rule

The following excerpt explores the business judgment rule and the consequences of its application. The author is Ralph Winter, who was featured in this book's earlier discussion of the "race" debate over whether states, such as Delaware, are racing to the top or bottom in the competition for corporate charters (Winter took the "race to the top" position). The excerpt includes only parts of Judge Winter's useful discussion of the standard of care in corporate law and some classic rationales behind the business judgment rule.

Joy v. North
United States Court of Appeals, Second Circuit
692 F.2d 880 (1982)

WINTER, CIRCUIT JUDGE:

... While it is often stated that corporate directors and officers will be liable for negligence in carrying out their corporate duties, all seem agreed that such a statement is misleading. Whereas an automobile driver who makes a mistake in judgment as to speed or distance injuring a pedestrian will likely be called upon to respond in damages, a corporate officer who makes a mistake in judgment as to economic conditions, consumer tastes or production line efficiency will rarely, if ever, be found liable for damages suffered by the corporation. Whatever the terminology, the fact is that liability is rarely imposed upon corporate directors or officers simply for bad judgment and this reluctance to impose liability for unsuccessful business decisions has been doctrinally labelled the business judgment rule. Although the rule has suffered under academic criticism, it is not without rational basis.

First, shareholders to a very real degree voluntarily undertake the risk of bad business judgment. Investors need not buy stock, for investment markets offer an array of opportunities less vulnerable to mistakes in judgment by corporate officers. Nor need investors buy stock in particular corporations. In the exercise of what is genuinely a free choice, the quality of a firm's management is often decisive and information is available from professional advisors. Since shareholders can and do select among investments partly on the basis of management, the business judgment rule merely recognizes a certain voluntariness in undertaking the risk of bad business decisions.

Second, courts recognize that after-the-fact litigation is a most imperfect device to evaluate corporate business decisions. The circumstances surrounding a corporate decision are not easily reconstructed in a courtroom years later, since business imperatives often call for quick decisions, inevitably based on less than perfect information. The entrepreneur's function is to encounter risks and to confront uncertainty, and a reasoned decision at the time made may seem a wild hunch viewed years later against a background of perfect knowledge.

Third, because potential profit often corresponds to the potential risk, it is very much in the interest of shareholders that the law not create incentives for overly cautious corporate decisions. Some opportunities offer great profits at the risk of very substantial losses, while the alternatives offer less risk of loss but also less potential profit. Shareholders can reduce the volatility of risk by diversifying their holdings. In the case of the diversified shareholder, the seemingly more risky alternatives may well be the best choice since great losses in some stocks will over time be offset by even greater gains in others. Given mutual funds and similar forms of diversified investment, courts need not bend over backwards to give special protection to shareholders who refuse to reduce the volatility of risk by not diversifying. A rule which penalizes the choice of seemingly riskier alternatives thus may not be in the interest of shareholders generally.

Whatever its merit, however, the business judgment rule extends only as far as the reasons which justify its existence. Thus, it does not apply in cases, *e.g.*, in which the corporate decision lacks a business purpose [or] is so egregious as to amount to a no-win decision.

Notes and Questions

1. Judge Winter, in *Joy*, describes the historic judicial tendency to defer to management discretion in corporate decision-making. So long as directors do not behave egregiously, the consequence of this classic business judgment rule is to substantially lower the possibility that directors will be found liable for a breach of their duty of care.

Courts have varied in their description of the standard of conduct required under this classic rule. Behavior which is not "grossly negligent" or "reckless," or decisions with "any rational business purpose," for instance, have satisfied the business judgment rule. How does this standard differ from the reasonableness and negligence standards described under the general standard of care?

2. The Introductory Note to ALI § 4.01 further explains:

> The basic policy underpinning of the business judgment rule is that corporate law should encourage, and afford broad protection to, informed business judgments (whether subsequent events prove the judgments right or wrong) in order to stimulate risk taking, innovation, and other creative entrepreneurial activities. Shareholders accept the risk that an informed business decision—honestly undertaken and rationally believed to be in the best interests of the corporation—may not be vindicated by subsequent success. The special protection afforded business judgments is also based on a desire to limit litigation and judicial intrusiveness with respect to private-sector business decision making.

B. Applicability and Exceptions

The business judgment rule applies only when directors have made "conscious" decisions. Prolonged inattention and the failure to monitor business activities, as in the *Francis* case, would clearly not be included. In contrast, decisions formally made at directors' meetings, as in *Kamin v. American Express*, clearly would be included. What if the directors considered, but deliberately decided not to take any action?

Even if directors make a conscious decision, the business judgment rule may not be applicable. The courts have recognized at least two exceptions. Directors and officers who are "interested" in the corporate decision may be subject to a different standard of conduct, described in the chapter on the duty of loyalty. In addition, if the directors' decision itself constitutes illegal conduct, directors will not be protected by the business judgment rule. This exception was explored in *Miller v. American Telephone & Telegraph Co.*, 507 F.2d 759, 761–63 (3d Cir. 1974):

> The suit centered upon the failure of AT&T to collect an outstanding debt of some $1.5 million owed to the company by the Democratic National Committee ("DNC") for communications services provided by AT&T during the 1968 Democratic national convention....
>
> ... The failure to collect was alleged to have involved a breach of the defendant directors' duty to exercise diligence in handling the affairs of the corporation, to have resulted in affording a preference to the DNC in collection procedures in violation of § 202(a) of the Communications Act of 1934, 47 U.S.C. § 202(a) (1970), and to have amounted to AT&T's making a "contribution" to the DNC, in violation of a federal prohibition on corporate campaign spending....
>
> Had plaintiffs' complaint alleged only failure to pursue a corporate claim, application of the sound business judgment rule would support the district court's ruling that a shareholder could not attack the directors' decision. Where, however, the decision not to collect a debt owed the corporation is

itself alleged to have been an illegal act, different rules apply. When New York law regarding such acts by directors is considered in conjunction with the underlying purposes of the particular statute involved here, we are convinced that the business judgment rule cannot insulate the defendant directors from liability if they did in fact breach 18 U.S.C. §610, as plaintiffs have charged.

Roth v. Robertson, 118 N.Y.S. 351 (Sup. Ct. 1909), illustrates the proposition that even though committed to benefit the corporation, illegal acts may amount to a breach of fiduciary duty in New York. In *Roth*, the managing director of an amusement park company had allegedly used corporate funds to purchase the silence of persons who threatened to complain about unlawful Sunday operation of the park. Recovery from the defendant director was sustained on the ground that the money was an illegal payment....

... In [*Abrams v. Allen*, 74 N.E.2d 305 (1947),] the court held that a cause of action was stated by an allegation in a derivative complaint that the directors of Remington Rand, Inc., had relocated corporate plants and curtailed production solely for the purpose of intimidating and punishing employees for their involvement in a labor dispute....

The alleged violation of the federal prohibition against corporate political contributions not only involves the corporation in criminal activity but similarly contravenes a policy of Congress clearly enunciated in 18 U.S.C. §610. That statute and its predecessor reflect congressional efforts: (1) to destroy the influence of corporations over elections through financial contributions and (2) to check the practice of using corporate funds to benefit political parties without the consent of the stockholders.

Note that the federal law at issue in *Miller v. AT&T* remains in effect to prohibit corporations from making direct contributions to political campaigns in federal elections. The statute is unaffected by the ruling in *Citizens United v. Federal Election Regulatory Commission*, 558 U.S. 310 (2010), which struck down as a violation of the First Amendment a federal campaign finance law that prohibited corporations from broadcasting election-related communications within a month or two of primary or general elections.

Contemporary cases continue to invoke the principle stated in *Miller* that the business judgment rule does not apply to knowing violations of law. *See, e.g., Bal Harbour Club, Inc. v. Ava Dev, Inc.*, 316 F.3d 1192 (11th Cir. 2003) (denying business judgment rule deference to corporate decision to file bankruptcy petition when doing so may have amounted to an abuse of judicial process); *In re Abbott Labs. Deriv. Shareholders Litig.*, 325 F.3d 795 (7th Cir. 2003) (applying Illinois and Delaware law) (in case raising, in part, duty to inquire issues appearing in *Caremark*, saying that knowing violations of federal Food and Drug Administration regulations were not protected by the business judgment rule); *Wieboldt Stores, Inc. v. Schottenstein*, 94 B.R. 488 (N.D. Ill. 1988) (applying Illinois law) (decision to make distribution to shareholders in violation of applicable state statutes held outside protection of business judgment rule).

C. Perspectives on the Business Judgment Rule

The business judgment rule was judicially created. As indicated in the Comment to MBCA § 8.31(a), Note on the Business Judgment Rule:

> Section 8.31 does not codify the business judgment rule as a whole. The section recognizes the common law doctrine and provides guidance as to its application in dealing with director liability claims. Because the elements of the business judgment rule and the circumstances for its application are continuing to be developed by the courts, it would not be desirable to freeze the concept in a statute.

ALI § 4.01(c), however, does discuss the doctrine.

> (c) A director or officer who makes a business judgment in good faith fulfills the duty under this Section if the director or officer:
>
> (1) is not interested in the subject of the business judgment;
>
> (2) is informed with respect to the subject of the business judgment to the extent the director or officer reasonably believes to be appropriate under the circumstances; and
>
> (3) rationally believes that the business judgment is in the best interests of the corporation.

As Comment a to § 4.01(c) explains:

> Confusion with respect to the business judgment rule has been created by the numerous varying formulations of the rule and the fact that courts have often stated the rule incompletely or with elliptical shorthand references. The relatively precise formulation of the business judgment rule set forth in § 4.01(c) avoids confusion and helps cover the myriad factual contexts in which business judgment issues arise.

It is not clear, however, if most judges would agree that the business judgment rule can be so precisely articulated. In *Citron v. Fairchild Camera & Instrument Corp.*, 569 A.2d 53, 64 (Del. 1989), the court explained:

> The business judgment rule is an extension of the fundamental principle "that the business and affairs of a corporation are managed by and under the direction of its board. *See* 8 Del. C. § 141(a)." *Pogostin v. Rice*, Del. Supr., 480 A.2d 619, 624 (1984). The rule operates as both a procedural guide for litigants and a substantive rule of law. As a rule of evidence, it creates "a presumption that in making a business decision, the directors of a corporation acted on an informed basis [*i.e.*, with due care], in good faith and in the honest belief that the action taken was in the best interest of the company." *Aronson v. Lewis*, Del. Supr., 473 A.2d 805, 812 (1984). The presumption initially attaches to a director-approved transaction within a board's conferred or apparent authority in the absence of any evidence of "fraud, bad faith, or self-dealing in the usual sense of personal profit or betterment." *Grobow v. Perot*, Del. Supr., 539 A.2d 180, 187 (1988). *See* Allaun v. Consolidated Oil

Co., Del. Ch., 147 A. 257, 261 (1929). The burden falls upon the proponent of a claim to rebut the presumption by introducing evidence either of director self-interest, if not self-dealing, or that the directors either lacked good faith or failed to exercise due care. *Smith v. Van Gorkom*, Del. Supr., 488 A.2d 858, 872 (1985). If the proponent fails to meet her burden of establishing facts rebutting the presumption, the business judgment rule, as a substantive rule, will attach to protect the directors and the decisions they make. . . .

Some in the academic community are concerned that neither the codifications nor the body of case law accurately reflect the true meaning of the business judgment rule. Consider the following observations, for instance, from Douglas M. Branson, *Corporate Governance*, 334–37 (1993):

> The business judgment rule operates as a rule of judicial economy, as a presumption, or as a safe harbor. The business judgment rule, however, is not the rule of conduct, which remains the duty of care. To be sure, the business judgment rule informs conduct, especially in before-the-fact preventive law contexts in which lawyers and others may structure the decision-making process with an eye toward coming within the presumption of safe harbor. But the business judgment rule is not the legal standard itself. . . .

> In the litigation context, among other things, the rule is a filtering device, a device for achievement of judicial economy. In the latter respect, the rule may aid a court in disposing of corporate litigation short of trial, say, by means of ruling on a dispositive motion before trial, based upon the business judgment rule. But should the defendant directors lose that motion, they are not doomed to perdition. Those directors may then fall back and defend on substantive duty of care grounds, by means of further motions or at trial, because the ultimate legal standard is not the business judgment rule but the duty of care.

> . . . Even after losing a first round on business judgment rule turf, directors may fall back to another duty of care argument, that whatever had occurred had not damaged the corporation, another substantive requirement of a duty of care cause of action.

D. Officers and the Business Judgment Rule

Officers generally are understood to owe their corporations the same duties directors do, *see Gantler v. Stephens*, 965 A.2d 695 (Del. 2009), although there are far more cases developing legal standards applicable to directors than to officers. Cases announcing that officers are subject to the same duties as directors, including the duty of care, do not always clarify whether the business judgment rule is equally applicable. Most courts and other authorities addressing the question directly indicate that the business judgment rule applies to officer decisions just as it does to director decisions. *E.g.*, MBCA §8.42 cmt.; *Rosenfield v. Metals Selling Corp.*, 643 A.2d 1253, 1261 n.16 (Conn. 1994); *Potter v. Pohlad*, 560 N.W.2d 389, 391–92 & n.1 (Minn. Ct. App.

1997); *Selcke v. Bove*, 629 N.E.2d 747, 750 (Ill. App. Ct. 1994); *Para-Med. Leasing, Inc. v. Hangen*, 739 P.2d 717, 722 (Wash. App. 1987); *T.S.G. Water Res., Inc. v. D'Alba & Donovan CPA*, 366 F. Supp. 2d 1212, 1226 (S.D. Ga. 2004) (applying Georgia law); *In re Fleet/Norstar Secs. Litig.*, 935 F. Supp. 99, 115 (D.R.I. 1996) (applying Rhode Island law); *FDIC v. Stahl*, 854 F. Supp. 1565, 1570 n.8 (S.D. Fla. 1994), *partially reversed on other grounds by* 89 F.3d 1510 (11th Cir. 1996) (applying Florida law).

Section V
Informed Decision-Making

The following case prompted courts and corporate directors to rethink what the duty of care and the business judgment rules mean. Note the timing of the facts and opinion. The facts occurred in 1980, when the traditional advisory model of the corporate board remained dominant. The opinion was published in 1985, when that model was under attack and the monitoring model, dominant today for publicly-traded companies such as the one featured, had arisen as a strong rival. The case was both a consequence and a cause of the shift in corporate governance, and its statement of informed decision-making continues to define boardroom practice. In evaluating the conflicting positions of the parties, see if you can frame the dispute as one effectively pitting cases such as *Francis v. United Jersey Bank* on one hand against *Kamin v. American Express* on the other.

Smith v. Van Gorkom
Delaware Supreme Court
488 A.2d 858 (1985)

HORSEY, JUSTICE:

This appeal from the Court of Chancery involves a class action brought by shareholders of the defendant Trans Union Corporation ... against the defendant members of the Board of Directors....

I

The nature of this case requires a detailed factual statement. The following facts are essentially uncontradicted ...:

Trans Union was a publicly-traded, diversified holding company, the principal earnings of which were generated by its railcar leasing business. During the period here involved, the Company had a cash flow of hundreds of millions of dollars annually. However, the Company had difficulty in generating sufficient taxable income to [enable profiting from certain federal income tax benefits called] investment tax credits (ITCs)....

On August 27, 1980, Van Gorkom met with Senior Management of Trans Union.... Various alternatives were suggested and discussed preliminarily, including the sale of Trans Union to a company with a large amount of taxable income.

Donald Romans, Chief Financial Officer of Trans Union, stated that his department had done a "very brief bit of work on the possibility of a leveraged buy-out." ... The work consisted of a "preliminary study" of the cash which could be generated by the Company if it participated in a leveraged buy-out. As Romans stated, this analysis "was [a] very first and rough cut at seeing whether a cash flow would support what might be considered a high price for this type of transaction."

On September 5, at another Senior Management meeting which Van Gorkom attended, Romans again brought up the idea of a leveraged buy-out as a "possible strategic alternative" to the Company's acquisition program. Romans and Bruce S. Chelberg, President and Chief Operating Officer of Trans Union, had been working on the matter in preparation for the meeting. According to Romans: They did not "come up" with a price for the Company. They merely "ran the numbers" at $50 a share and at $60 a share with the "rough form" of their cash figures at the time. Their "figures indicated that $50 would be very easy to do but $60 would be very difficult to do under those figures." This work did not purport to establish a fair price for either the Company or 100% of the stock. It was intended to determine the cash flow needed to service the debt that would "probably" be incurred in a leveraged buy-out, based on "rough calculations" without "any benefit of experts to identify what the limits were to that, and so forth." These computations were not considered extensive and no conclusion was reached.

At this meeting, Van Gorkom stated that he would be willing to take $55 per share for his own 75,000 shares. He vetoed the suggestion of a leveraged buy-out by Management, however, as involving a potential conflict of interest for Management. Van Gorkom, a certified public accountant and lawyer, had been an officer of Trans Union for 24 years, its Chief Executive Officer for more than 17 years, and Chairman of its Board for 2 years. It is noteworthy in this connection that he was then approaching 65 years of age and mandatory retirement....

Van Gorkom decided to meet with Jay A. Pritzker, a well-known corporate takeover specialist and a social acquaintance. However, rather than approaching Pritzker simply to determine his interest in acquiring Trans Union, Van Gorkom assembled a proposed per share price for sale of the Company and a financing structure by which to accomplish the sale. Van Gorkom did so without consulting either his Board or any members of Senior Management except one: Carl Peterson, Trans Union's Controller. Telling Peterson that he wanted no other person on his staff to know what he was doing, but without telling him why, Van Gorkom directed Peterson to calculate the feasibility of a leveraged buy-out at an assumed price per share of $55. Apart from the Company's historic stock market price,[5] and Van Gorkom's long association with Trans Union, the record is devoid of any competent evidence that $55 represented the per share intrinsic value of the Company.

5. [5] The common stock of Trans Union was traded on the New York Stock Exchange. Over the five year period from 1975 through 1979, Trans Union's stock had traded within a range of a high of $39½ and a low of $24¼. Its high and low range for 1980 through September 19 (the last trading day before announcement of the merger) was $38¼–$29½.

Having thus chosen the $55 figure, based solely on the availability of a leveraged buy-out, Van Gorkom multiplied the price per share by the number of shares outstanding to reach a total value of the Company of $690 million. Van Gorkom told Peterson to use this $690 million figure and to assume a $200 million equity contribution by the buyer. Based on these assumptions, Van Gorkom directed Peterson to determine whether the debt portion of the purchase price could be paid off in five years or less if financed by Trans Union's cash flow as projected in the Five Year Forecast, and by the sale of certain weaker divisions identified in a study done for Trans Union by the Boston Consulting Group ("BCG study"). Peterson reported that, of the purchase price, approximately $50–80 million would remain outstanding after five years. Van Gorkom was disappointed, but decided to meet with Pritzker nevertheless.

Van Gorkom arranged a meeting with Pritzker at the latter's home on Saturday, September 13, 1980. Van Gorkom prefaced his presentation by stating to Pritzker: "Now as far as you are concerned, I can, I think, show how you can pay a substantial premium over the present stock price and pay off most of the loan in the first five years.... If you could pay $55 for this Company, here is a way in which I think it can be financed."

Van Gorkom then reviewed with Pritzker his calculations based upon his proposed price of $55 per share. Although Pritzker mentioned $50 as a more attractive figure, no other price was mentioned. However, Van Gorkom stated that to be sure that $55 was the best price obtainable, Trans Union should be free to accept any better offer. Pritzker demurred, stating that his organization would serve as a "stalking horse" for an "auction contest" only if Trans Union would permit Pritzker to buy 1,750,000 shares of Trans Union stock at market price which Pritzker could then sell to any higher bidder....

On Monday, September 15, Pritzker advised Van Gorkom that he was interested in the $55 cash-out merger proposal and requested more information on Trans Union.... Van Gorkom was "astounded that events were moving with such amazing rapidity."

On Thursday, September 18, Van Gorkom met again with Pritzker. At that time, Van Gorkom knew that Pritzker intended to make a cash-out merger offer at Van Gorkom's proposed $55 per share. Pritzker instructed his attorney, a merger and acquisition specialist, to begin drafting merger documents. There was no further discussion of the $55 price. However, the number of shares of Trans Union's treasury stock to be offered to Pritzker was negotiated down to one million shares; the price was set at $38–75 cents above the per share price at the close of the market on September 19. At this point, Pritzker insisted that the Trans Union Board act on his merger proposal within the next three days, stating to Van Gorkom: "We have to have a decision by no later than Sunday [evening, September 21] before the opening of the English stock exchange on Monday morning." Pritzker's lawyer was then instructed to draft the merger documents, to be reviewed by Van Gorkom's lawyer, "sometimes with discussion and sometimes not, in the haste to get it finished."

On Friday, September 19, Van Gorkom, Chelberg, and Pritzker consulted with Trans Union's lead bank regarding the financing of Pritzker's purchase of Trans Union.

The bank indicated that it could form a syndicate of banks that would finance the transaction.... [That same day,] Van Gorkom called a special meeting of the Trans Union Board for noon the following day. He also called a meeting of the Company's Senior Management to convene at 11:00 a.m., prior to the meeting of the Board....

Of those present at the Senior Management meeting on September 20, only Chelberg and Peterson had prior knowledge of Pritzker's offer. Van Gorkom disclosed the offer and described its terms, but he furnished no copies of the proposed Merger Agreement. Romans announced that his department had done a second study which showed that, for a leveraged buy-out, the price range for Trans Union stock was between $55 and $65 per share. Van Gorkom neither saw the study nor asked Romans to make it available for the Board meeting.

Senior Management's reaction to the Pritzker proposal was completely negative. No member of Management, except Chelberg and Peterson, supported the proposal.... Nevertheless, Van Gorkom proceeded to the Board meeting as scheduled without further delay ...

Van Gorkom began the Special Meeting of the Board with a twenty-minute oral presentation. Copies of the proposed Merger Agreement were delivered too late for study before or during the meeting.[6] He reviewed the Company's ITC and depreciation problems and the efforts theretofore made to solve them. He discussed his initial meeting with Pritzker and his motivation in arranging that meeting. Van Gorkom did not disclose to the Board, however, the methodology by which he alone had arrived at the $55 figure, or the fact that he first proposed the $55 price in his negotiations with Pritzker.

Van Gorkom outlined the terms of the Pritzker offer as follows: Pritzker would pay $55 in cash for all outstanding shares of Trans Union stock upon completion of which Trans Union would be merged into New T Company, a subsidiary wholly-owned by Pritzker and formed to implement the merger; for a period of 90 days, Trans Union could receive, but could not actively solicit, competing offers; the offer had to be acted on by the next evening, Sunday, September 21; Trans Union could only furnish to competing bidders published information, and not proprietary information; the offer was subject to Pritzker obtaining the necessary financing by October 10, 1980; if the financing contingency were met or waived by Pritzker, Trans Union was required to sell to Pritzker one million newly-issued shares of Trans Union at $38 per share.

Van Gorkom took the position that putting Trans Union "up for auction" through a 90-day market test would validate a decision by the Board that $55 was a fair price. He told the Board that the "free market will have an opportunity to judge whether $55 is a fair price." Van Gorkom framed the decision before the Board not as whether

---

6. [7] The record is not clear as to the terms of the Merger Agreement. The Agreement, as originally presented to the Board on September 20, was never produced by defendants despite demands by the plaintiffs. Nor is it clear that the directors were given an opportunity to study the Merger Agreement before voting on it....

$55 per share was the highest price that could be obtained, but as whether the $55 price was a fair price that the stockholders should be given the opportunity to accept or reject....

The Board meeting of September 20 lasted about two hours. Based solely upon Van Gorkom's oral presentation, Chelberg's supporting representations, Romans' oral statement, [limited] legal advice, and their knowledge of the market history of the Company's stock,[7] the directors approved the proposed Merger Agreement. However, the Board later claimed to have attached two conditions to its acceptance: (1) that Trans Union reserved the right to accept any better offer that was made during the market test period; and (2) that Trans Union could share its proprietary information with any other potential bidders. While the Board now claims to have reserved the right to accept any better offer received after the announcement of the Pritzker agreement (even though the minutes of the meeting do not reflect this), it is undisputed that the Board did not reserve the right to actively solicit alternate offers.

The Merger Agreement was executed by Van Gorkom during the evening of September 20 at a formal social event that he hosted for the opening of the Chicago Lyric Opera. Neither he nor any other director read the agreement prior to its signing and delivery to Pritzker....

On Monday, September 22, the Company issued a press release announcing that Trans Union had entered into a "definitive" Merger Agreement with an affiliate of the Marmon Group, Inc., a Pritzker holding company. Within 10 days of the public announcement, dissent among Senior Management over the merger had become widespread. Faced with threatened resignations of key officers, Van Gorkom met with Pritzker who agreed to several modifications of the Agreement. Pritzker was willing to do so provided that Van Gorkom could persuade the dissidents to remain on the Company payroll for at least six months after consummation of the merger.

Van Gorkom reconvened the Board on October 8 and secured the directors' approval of the proposed amendments—sight unseen. The Board also authorized the employment of Salomon Brothers, its investment banker, to solicit other offers for Trans Union during the proposed "market test" period....

Salomon Brothers' efforts over a three-month period from October 21 to January 21 produced only one serious suitor for Trans Union—General Electric Credit Corporation ("GE Credit"), a subsidiary of the General Electric Company. However, GE Credit was unwilling to make an offer for Trans Union unless Trans Union first rescinded its Merger Agreement with Pritzker. When Pritzker refused, GE Credit terminated further discussions with Trans Union in early January. In the meantime, in

---

7. [9] The Trial Court stated the premium relationship of the $55 price to the market history of the Company's stock as follows:

> ... the merger price offered to the stockholders of Trans Union represented a premium of 62% over the average of the high and low prices at which Trans Union stock had traded in 1980, a premium of 48% over the last closing price, and a premium of 39% over the highest price at which the stock of Trans Union had traded any time during the prior six years.

early December, the investment firm of Kohlberg, Kravis, Roberts & Co. ("KKR"), the only other concern to make a firm offer for Trans Union, withdrew its offer....

On February 10, the stockholders of Trans Union approved the Pritzker merger proposal. Of the outstanding shares, 69.9% were voted in favor of the merger; 7.25% were voted against the merger; and 22.85% were not voted.

II

We turn to the issue of the application of the business judgment rule to the September 20 meeting of the Board....

Under Delaware law, the business judgment rule is the offspring of the fundamental principle, codified in 8 Del. C. § 141(a), that the business and affairs of a Delaware corporation are managed by or under its board of directors. In carrying out their managerial roles, directors are charged with an unyielding fiduciary duty to the corporation and its shareholders. The business judgment rule exists to protect and promote the full and free exercise of the managerial power granted to Delaware directors. The rule itself "is a presumption that in making a business decision, the directors of a corporation acted on an informed basis, in good faith and in the honest belief that the action taken was in the best interests of the company." [*Aronson v. Lewis*, 473 A.2d 805, 812 (Del. 1984)]. Thus, the party attacking a board decision as uninformed must rebut the presumption that its business judgment was an informed one. *Id.*

The determination of whether a business judgment is an informed one turns on whether the directors have informed themselves "prior to making a business decision, of all material information reasonably available to them." *Id.*

... A director's duty to inform himself in preparation for a decision derives from the fiduciary capacity in which he serves the corporation and its stockholders. Since a director is vested with the responsibility for the management of the affairs of the corporation, he must execute that duty with the recognition that he acts on behalf of others. Such obligation does not tolerate faithlessness or self-dealing. But fulfillment of the fiduciary function requires more than the mere absence of bad faith or fraud. Representation of the financial interests of others imposes on a director an affirmative duty to protect those interests and to proceed with a critical eye in assessing information of the type and under the circumstances present here.

Thus, a director's duty to exercise an informed business judgment is in the nature of a duty of care, as distinguished from a duty of loyalty. Here, there were no allegations of fraud, bad faith, or self-dealing, or proof thereof. Hence, it is presumed that the directors reached their business judgment in good faith, and considerations of motive are irrelevant to the issue before us.

The standard of care applicable to a director's duty of care has also been recently restated by this Court. In *Aronson, supra,* we stated:

> While the Delaware cases use a variety of terms to describe the applicable standard of care, our analysis satisfies us that under the business judgment rule director liability is predicated upon concepts of gross negligence.

473 A.2d at 812.

We again confirm that view. We think the concept of gross negligence is also the proper standard for determining whether a business judgment reached by a board of directors was an informed one....

III

The defendants argue that the determination of whether their decision to accept $55 per share for Trans Union represented an informed business judgment requires consideration, not only of that which they knew and learned on September 20, but also of that which they subsequently learned and did over the following four-month period before the shareholders met to vote on the proposal in February, 1981....

... [T]he question of whether the directors reached an informed business judgment in agreeing to sell the Company, pursuant to the terms of the September 20 Agreement presents, in reality, two questions: (A) whether the directors reached an informed business judgment on September 20, 1980; and (B) if they did not, whether the directors' actions taken subsequent to September 20 were adequate to cure any infirmity in their action taken on September 20. We first consider the directors' September 20 action in terms of their reaching an informed business judgment....

On the record before us, we must conclude that the Board of Directors did not reach an informed business judgment on September 20, 1980 in voting to "sell" the Company for $55 per share pursuant to the Pritzker cash-out merger proposal....

The directors (1) did not adequately inform themselves as to Van Gorkom's role in forcing the "sale" of the Company and in establishing the per share purchase price; (2) were uninformed as to the intrinsic value of the Company; and (3) given these circumstances, at a minimum, were grossly negligent in approving the "sale" of the Company upon two hours' consideration, without prior notice, and without the exigency of a crisis or emergency.

As has been noted, the Board based its September 20 decision to approve the cash-out merger primarily on Van Gorkom's representations. None of the directors, other than Van Gorkom and Chelberg, had any prior knowledge that the purpose of the meeting was to propose a cash-out merger of Trans Union. No members of Senior Management were present, other than Chelberg, Romans and Peterson; and the latter two had only learned of the proposed sale an hour earlier....

Without any documents before them concerning the proposed transaction, the members of the Board were required to rely entirely upon Van Gorkom's 20-minute oral presentation of the proposal. No written summary of the terms of the merger was presented; the directors were given no documentation to support the adequacy of $55 price per share for sale of the Company; and the Board had before it nothing more than Van Gorkom's statement of his understanding of the substance of an agreement which he admittedly had never read, nor which any member of the Board had ever seen.

[Board Reliance on Reports]

Under 8 Del. C. § 141(e), "directors are fully protected in relying in good faith on reports made by officers." The term "report" has been liberally construed to include reports of informal personal investigations by corporate officers, *Cheff v. Mathes*, Del. Supr., 199 A.2d 548, 556 (1964). However, there is no evidence that any "report," as defined under § 141(e), concerning the Pritzker proposal, was presented to the Board on September 20. Van Gorkom's oral presentation of his understanding of the terms of the proposed Merger Agreement, which he had not seen, and Romans' brief oral statement of his preliminary study regarding the feasibility of a leveraged buy-out of Trans Union do not qualify as § 141(e) "reports" for these reasons: The former lacked substance because Van Gorkom was basically uninformed as to the essential provisions of the very document about which he was talking. Romans' statement was irrelevant to the issues before the Board since it did not purport to be a valuation study.

At a minimum for a report to enjoy the status conferred by § 141(e), it must be pertinent to the subject matter upon which a board is called to act, and otherwise be entitled to good faith, not blind, reliance. Considering all of the surrounding circumstances — hastily calling the meeting without prior notice of its subject matter, the proposed sale of the Company without any prior consideration of the issue or necessity therefor, the urgent time constraints imposed by Pritzker, and the total absence of any documentation whatsoever — the directors were duty bound to make reasonable inquiry of Van Gorkom and Romans, and if they had done so, the inadequacy of that upon which they now claim to have relied would have been apparent.

[Besides the foregoing rejected assertions of reliance on such reports, the directors point to] the following factors to sustain the Trial Court's finding that the Board's decision was an informed one: (1) the magnitude of the premium or spread between the $55 Pritzker offering price and Trans Union's current market price of $38 per share; (2) the amendment of the Agreement as submitted on September 20 to permit the Board to accept any better offer during the "market test" period; [and] (3) the collective experience and expertise of the Board's "inside" and "outside" directors....

[Premium Price]

A substantial premium may provide one reason to recommend a merger, but in the absence of other sound valuation information, the fact of a premium alone does not provide an adequate basis upon which to assess the fairness of an offering price....

The record is clear that before September 20, Van Gorkom and other members of Trans Union's Board knew that the market had consistently undervalued the worth of Trans Union's stock, despite steady increases in the Company's operating income in the seven years preceding the merger. The Board related this occurrence in large part to Trans Union's inability to use its ITCs as previously noted. Van Gorkom testified that he did not believe the market price accurately reflected Trans Union's true worth; and several of the directors testified that, as a general rule, most chief executives think that the market undervalues their companies' stock. Yet, on September 20, Trans Union's Board apparently believed that the market stock price accurately reflected the value of the Company for the purpose of determining the adequacy of the premium for its sale....

The parties do not dispute that a publicly-traded stock price is solely a measure of the value of a minority position and, thus, market price represents only the value of a single share. Nevertheless, on September 20, the Board assessed the adequacy of the premium over market, offered by Pritzker, solely by comparing it with Trans Union's current and historical stock price.

Indeed, as of September 20, the Board had no other information on which to base a determination of the intrinsic value of Trans Union as a going concern. As of September 20, the Board had made no evaluation of the Company designed to value the entire enterprise, nor had the Board ever previously considered selling the Company or consenting to a buy-out merger. Thus, the adequacy of a premium is indeterminate unless it is assessed in terms of other competent and sound valuation information that reflects the value of the particular business.

Despite the foregoing facts and circumstances, there was no call by the Board, either on September 20 or thereafter, for any valuation study or documentation of the $55 price per share as a measure of the fair value of the Company in a cash-out context. . . .

We do not imply that an outside valuation study is essential to support an informed business judgment; nor do we state that fairness opinions by independent investment bankers are required as a matter of law. Often insiders familiar with the business of a going concern are in a better position than are outsiders to gather relevant information; and under appropriate circumstances, such directors may be fully protected in relying in good faith upon the valuation reports of their management. . . .

Here, the record establishes that the Board did not request its Chief Financial Officer, Romans, to make any valuation study or review of the proposal to determine the adequacy of $55 per share for sale of the Company. On the record before us: The Board rested on Romans' elicited response that the $55 figure was within a "fair price range" within the context of a leveraged buy-out. No director sought any further information from Romans. No director asked him why he put $55 at the bottom of his range. No director asked Romans for any details as to his study, the reason why it had been undertaken or its depth. No director asked to see the study; and no director asked Romans whether Trans Union's finance department could do a fairness study within the remaining 36-hour period available under the Pritzker offer.

Had the Board, or any member, made an inquiry of Romans, he presumably would have responded as he testified: that his calculations were rough and preliminary; and, that the study was not designed to determine the fair value of the Company, but rather to assess the feasibility of a leveraged buy-out financed by the Company's projected cash flow, making certain assumptions as to the purchaser's borrowing needs. Romans would have presumably also informed the Board of his view, and the widespread view of Senior Management, that the timing of the offer was wrong and the offer inadequate.

The record also establishes that the Board accepted without scrutiny Van Gorkom's representation as to the fairness of the $55 price per share for sale of the Company — a subject that the Board had never previously considered. The Board thereby failed to discover that Van Gorkom had suggested the $55 price to Pritzker and, most crucially, that Van Gorkom had arrived at the $55 figure based on calculations designed solely to determine the feasibility of a leveraged buy-out. No questions were raised either as to the tax implications of a cash-out merger or how the price for the one million share option granted Pritzker was calculated....

[Market Test]

This brings us to the post-September 20 "market test" upon which the defendants ultimately rely to confirm the reasonableness of their September 20 decision to accept the Pritzker proposal. In this connection, the directors present a two-part argument: (a) that by making a "market test" of Pritzker's $55 per share offer a condition of their September 20 decision to accept his offer, they cannot be found to have acted impulsively or in an uninformed manner on September 20; and (b) that the adequacy of the $17 premium for sale of the Company was conclusively established over the following 90 to 120 days by the most reliable evidence available—the marketplace. Thus, the defendants impliedly contend that the "market test" eliminated the need for the Board to perform any other form of fairness test either on September 20, or thereafter.

Again, the facts of record do not support the defendants' argument. There is no evidence: (a) that the Merger Agreement was effectively amended to give the Board freedom to put Trans Union up for auction sale to the highest bidder; or (b) that a public auction was in fact permitted to occur....

Van Gorkom states that the Agreement as submitted incorporated the ingredients for a market test by authorizing Trans Union to receive competing offers over the next 90-day period. However, he concedes that the Agreement barred Trans Union from actively soliciting such offers and from furnishing to interested parties any information about the Company other than that already in the public domain. Whether the original Agreement of September 20 went so far as to authorize Trans Union to receive competitive proposals is arguable. The defendants' unexplained failure to produce and identify the original Merger Agreement permits the logical inference that the instrument would not support their assertions in this regard....

[Director Experience and Sophistication]

The directors' unfounded reliance on both the premium and the market test as the basis for accepting the Pritzker proposal undermines the defendants' remaining contention that the Board's collective experience and sophistication was a sufficient basis for finding that it reached its September 20 decision with informed, reasonable deliberation.[8] ...

---

8. [21] Trans Union's five "inside" directors had backgrounds in law and accounting, 116 years of collective employment by the Company and 68 years of combined experience on its Board. Trans Union's five "outside" directors included four chief executives of major corporations and an economist who was a former dean of a major school of business and chancellor of a university. The "outside" directors had 78 years of combined experience as chief executive officers of major corporations and 50 years of cumulative experience as directors of Trans Union. Thus, defendants argue that the Board was eminently qualified to reach an informed judgment on the proposed "sale" of Trans Union notwith-

[Subsequent Review and Approval]

We now examine the Board's post-September 20 conduct for the purpose of determining first, whether it was informed and not grossly negligent; and second, if informed, whether it was sufficient to legally rectify and cure the Board's derelictions of September 20....

[We find that] the primary purpose of the October 8 Board meeting was to amend the Merger Agreement, in a manner agreeable to Pritzker, to permit Trans Union to conduct a "market test." Van Gorkom understood that the proposed amendments were intended to give the Company an unfettered "right to openly solicit offers down through January 31." Van Gorkom presumably so represented the amendments to Trans Union's Board members on October 8. In a brief session, the directors approved Van Gorkom's oral presentation of the substance of the proposed amendments, the terms of which were not reduced to writing until October 10. But rather than waiting to review the amendments, the Board again approved them sight unseen and adjourned, giving Van Gorkom authority to execute the papers when he received them.... [On] October 10, Pritzker delivered to Trans Union the proposed amendments to the September 20 Merger Agreement. Van Gorkom promptly proceeded to countersign all the instruments on behalf of Trans Union without reviewing the instruments to determine if they were consistent with the authority previously granted him by the Board....

In our view, the record compels the conclusion that the directors' conduct on October 8 exhibited the same deficiencies as did their conduct on September 20....

The defendants characterize the Board's Minutes of the January 26 meeting as a "review" of the "entire sequence of events" from Van Gorkom's initiation of the negotiations on September 13 forward. The defendants also rely on the testimony of several of the Board members at trial as confirming the Minutes. On the basis of this evidence, the defendants argue that whatever information the Board lacked to make a deliberate and informed judgment on September 20, or on October 8, was fully divulged to the entire Board on January 26. Hence, the argument goes, the Board's vote on January 26 to again "approve" the Pritzker merger must be found to have been an informed and deliberate judgment.

On the basis of this evidence, the defendants assert: (1) that the Trial Court was legally correct in widening the time frame for determining whether the defendants' approval of the Pritzker merger represented an informed business judgment to include the entire four-month period during which the Board considered the matter from September 20 through January 26; and (2) that, given this extensive evidence of the Board's further review and deliberations on January 26, this Court must affirm the Trial Court's conclusion that the Board's action was not reckless or improvident.

---

standing their lack of any advance notice of the proposal, the shortness of their deliberation, and their determination not to consult with their investment banker or to obtain a fairness opinion.

We cannot agree. We find the Trial Court to have erred, both as a matter of fact and as a matter of law, in relying on the action on January 26 to bring the defendants' conduct within the protection of the business judgment rule....

Reversed and Remanded for proceedings consistent herewith.

McNEILLY, JUSTICE, dissenting:

The majority opinion reads like an advocate's closing address to a hostile jury. And I say that not lightly. Throughout the opinion great emphasis is directed only to the negative, with nothing more than lip service granted the positive aspects of this case....

The majority has spoken and has effectively said that Trans Union's Directors have been the victims of a "fast shuffle" by Van Gorkom and Pritzker. That is the beginning of the majority's comedy of errors. The first and most important error made is the majority's assessment of the directors' knowledge of the affairs of Trans Union and their combined ability to act in this situation under the protection of the business judgment rule.

... At the time the merger was proposed the inside five directors had collectively been employed by the Company for 116 years and had 68 years of combined experience as directors.... The five "outside" directors had 78 years of combined experience as chief executive officers, and 53 years cumulative service as Trans Union directors.

The inside directors wear their badge of expertise in the corporate affairs of Trans Union on their sleeves. But what about the outsiders? Dr. Wallis is or was an economist and math statistician, a professor of economics at Yale University, dean of the graduate school of business at the University of Chicago, and Chancellor of the University of Rochester. Dr. Wallis had been on the Board of Trans Union since 1962. He also was on the Board of Bausch & Lomb, Kodak, Metropolitan Life Insurance Company, Standard Oil and others.

William B. Johnson is a University of Pennsylvania law graduate, President of Railway Express until 1966, Chairman and Chief Executive of I.C. Industries Holding Company, and member of Trans Union's Board since 1968.

Joseph Lanterman, a Certified Public Accountant, is or was President and Chief Executive of American Steel, on the Board of International Harvester, Peoples Energy, Illinois Bell Telephone, Harris Bank and Trust Company, Kemper Insurance Company and a director of Trans Union for four years.

Graham Morgan is a chemist, was Chairman and Chief Executive Officer of U.S. Gypsum, and in the 17 and 18 years prior to the Trans Union transaction had been involved in 31 or 32 corporate takeovers.

Robert Reneker attended University of Chicago and Harvard Business Schools. He was President and Chief Executive of Swift and Company, director of Trans Union since 1971, and member of the Boards of seven other corporations including U.S. Gypsum and the Chicago Tribune.

Directors of this caliber are not ordinarily taken in by a "fast shuffle"....

I have no quarrel with the majority's analysis of the business judgment rule. It is the application of that rule to these facts which is wrong. An overview of the entire record, rather than the limited view of bits and pieces which the majority has exploded like popcorn, convinces me that the directors made an informed business judgment which was buttressed by their test of the market.

Notes and Questions

1. By making the pivotal issue whether or not the directors' decision was "informed," the court in *Smith v. Van Gorkom* stressed that the duty of care analysis focuses on the process by which corporate decisions are made, rather than on the substance and merits of the decision itself. Courts traditionally are hesitant to second-guess management's actual decisions. However, the court's detailed analysis in *Van Gorkom*, for instance, of the price reveals how difficult it is to separate the process from the substance of the decision. In addition, the selection of one decision-making process over another can be considered a substantive decision itself.

2. The parties in *Van Gorkom* ultimately settled, with the plaintiffs receiving $23.5 million. Of this amount, it was reported that the directors and their insurance carrier paid about $10 million, with the remainder being paid by Jay Pritzker and The Marmon Group, the company that Pritzker used to make the acquisition. In 2006, after Jay Pritzker passed away, The Marmon Group, which owned Trans-Union as well as a diverse group of other industrial businesses, was sold to Warren Buffett's Berkshire Hathaway.

3. *Van Gorkom* was widely perceived to elevate the traditional standard of director obligation. In response, insurance companies revised their policies and increased premiums in anticipation of increased litigation against directors—heightening directors' and officers' concerns about the availability of affordable liability insurance. Many directors, becoming increasingly concerned about the increased liability risks and the lack of insurance, considered resigning from their directors' positions. The president of the National Association of Corporate Directors indicated that *Van Gorkom* "created perilous times for corporate directors."

4. In response to *Van Gorkom*, the Delaware General Assembly amended the Delaware General Corporation Law to allow corporations to adopt charter provisions eliminating or limiting the personal liability of directors for breaches of the duty of care. DGCL 102(b)(7). Other states followed suit. Such statutes are considered later in this chapter.

5. Corporate lawyers responded to *Van Gorkom* by developing careful procedures to provide the required information to client boards facing consequential decisions such as mergers. Firms now prepare binders of information and associated slide presentations that report upon the background of transactions, how they were negotiated, valuation questions, and other related matters, and contain supporting documents such as the fairness opinions of bankers and legal opinions of corporate compliance attorneys. Called "board books," critics and cynics say these binders merely "paper

the deal," while proponents stress that putting such data in front of directors often stimulates precisely the kinds of discussions and give-and-take that effective boards engage in to reach the best decisions.

6. Comments to MBCA § 8.30(b) provide:

> The phrase "becoming informed," in the context of the decision-making function, refers to the process of gaining sufficient familiarity with the background facts and circumstances in order to make an informed judgment. Unless the circumstances would permit a reasonable director to conclude that he or she is already sufficiently informed, the standard of care requires every director to take steps to become informed about the background facts and circumstances before taking action on the matter at hand. The process typically involves review of written materials provided before or at the meeting and attention to/participation in the deliberations leading up to a vote. It can involve consideration of information and data generated by persons other than legal counsel, public accountants, etc., retained by the corporation, ... for example, review of industry studies or research articles prepared by unrelated parties could be very useful. It can also involve direct communications, outside of the boardroom, with members of management or other directors. There is no one way for "becoming informed," and both the method and measure—"how to" and "how much"—are matters of reasonable judgment for the director to exercise.

Review the Comment to MBCA § 8.30(b):

> The phrase "devoting attention," in the context of the oversight function, refers to concern with the corporation's information and reporting systems and not to proactive inquiry searching for system inadequacies or noncompliance. While directors typically give attention to future plans and trends as well as current activities, they should not be expected to anticipate the problems which the corporation may face except in those circumstances where something has occurred to make it obvious to the board that the corporation should be addressing a particular problem. The standard of care associated with the oversight function involves gaining assurances from management and advisers that systems believed appropriate have been established coupled with ongoing monitoring of the systems in place, such as those concerned with legal compliance or internal controls—followed up with a proactive response when alerted to the need for inquiry.

Section VI
Corporate Objective and Social Responsibility

When exercising their business judgment, directors and officers often are confronted with myriad factors. Their determination of "corporate interest" and which factors to give relevance or priority to in particular factual circumstances may be complicated.

Fundamental underlying issues in this determination are: (1) the corporation's purpose and (2) to whom corporate directors owe their fiduciary duties.

A. Judicial Guidance

Shlensky v. Wrigley

Illinois Appellate Court

237 N.E.2d 776 (1968)

SULLIVAN, JUSTICE:

This is an appeal from a dismissal of plaintiff's amended complaint on motion of the defendants. The action was a stockholders' derivative suit against the directors for negligence and mismanagement.... Plaintiff sought damages and an order that defendants cause the installation of lights in Wrigley Field and the scheduling of night baseball games.

Plaintiff is a minority stockholder of defendant corporation, Chicago National League Ball Club (Inc.), a Delaware corporation with its principal place of business in Chicago, Illinois. Defendant corporation owns and operates the major league professional baseball team known as the Chicago Cubs. The corporation also engages in the operation of Wrigley Field, the Cubs' home park, the concessionaire sales during Cubs' home games, television and radio broadcasts of Cubs' home games, the leasing of the field for football games and other events and receives its share, as visiting team, of admission moneys from games played in other National League stadia. The individual defendants are directors of the Cubs and have served for varying periods of years. Defendant Philip K. Wrigley is also president of the corporation and owner of approximately 80% of the stock therein.

Plaintiff alleges that since night baseball was first played in 1935 nineteen of the twenty major league teams have scheduled night games. In 1966, out of a total of 1620 games in the major leagues, 932 were played at night. Plaintiff alleges that every member of the major leagues, other than the Cubs, scheduled substantially all of its home games in 1966 at night, exclusive of opening days, Saturdays, Sundays, holidays and days prohibited by league rules. Allegedly this has been done for the specific purpose of maximizing attendance and thereby maximizing revenue and income.

The Cubs, in the years 1961–65, sustained operating losses from ... direct baseball operations. Plaintiff attributes those losses to inadequate attendance at Cubs' home games. He concludes that if the directors continue to refuse to install lights at Wrigley Field and schedule night baseball games, the Cubs will continue to sustain comparable losses and its financial condition will continue to deteriorate.

Plaintiff alleges that, except for the year 1963, attendance at Cubs' home games has been substantially below that at their road games, many of which were played at night.

Plaintiff compares attendance at Cubs' games with that of the Chicago White Sox, an American League club, whose weekday games were generally played at night. The weekend attendance figures for the two teams was similar; however, the White Sox week-night games drew many more patrons than did the Cubs' weekday games.

Plaintiff alleges that the funds for the installation of lights can be readily obtained through financing and the cost of installation would be far more than offset and recaptured by increased revenues and incomes resulting from the increased attendance.

Plaintiff further alleges that defendant Wrigley has refused to install lights, not because of interest in the welfare of the corporation but because of his personal opinions "that baseball is a 'daytime sport' and that the installation of lights and night baseball games will have a deteriorating effect upon the surrounding neighborhood." It is alleged that he has admitted that he is not interested in whether the Cubs would benefit financially from such action because of his concern for the neighborhood, and that he would be willing for the team to play night games if a new stadium were built in Chicago.

Plaintiff alleges that the other defendant directors, with full knowledge of the foregoing matters, have acquiesced in the policy laid down by Wrigley and have permitted him to dominate the board of directors in matters involving the installation of lights and scheduling of night games, even though they knew he was not motivated by a good faith concern as to the best interests of defendant corporation, but solely by his personal views set forth above. It is charged that the directors are acting for a reason or reasons contrary and wholly unrelated to the business interests of the corporation; that such arbitrary and capricious acts constitute mismanagement and waste of corporate assets, and that the directors have been negligent in failing to exercise reasonable care and prudence in the management of the corporate affairs.

The question on appeal is whether plaintiff's amended complaint states a cause of action.... [We] are not satisfied that the motives assigned to Philip K. Wrigley, and through him to the other directors, are contrary to the best interests of the corporation and the stockholders. For example, it appears to us that the effect on the surrounding neighborhood might well be considered by a director who was considering the patrons who would or would not attend the games if the park were in a poor neighborhood. Furthermore, the long run interest of the corporation in its property value at Wrigley Field might demand all efforts to keep the neighborhood from deteriorating. By these thoughts we do not mean to say that we have decided that the decision of the directors was a correct one. That is beyond our jurisdiction and ability. We are merely saying that the decision is one properly before directors and the motives alleged in the amended complaint showed no fraud, illegality or conflict of interest in their making of that decision....

We feel that plaintiff's amended complaint was also defective in failing to allege damage to the corporation.... There is no allegation that the night games played by the other nineteen teams enhanced their financial position or that the profits, if any, of those teams were directly related to the number of night games scheduled. There is an allegation that the installation of lights and scheduling of night games in Wrigley Field would have resulted in large amounts of additional revenues and incomes from increased attendance and related sources of income. Further, the cost of installation of lights, funds for which are allegedly readily available by financing, would be more than offset and recaptured by increased revenues. However, no allegation is made that there will be a net benefit to the corporation from such action, considering all increased costs.

Plaintiff claims that the losses of defendant corporation are due to poor attendance at home games. However, it appears from the amended complaint, taken as a whole, that factors other than attendance affect the net earnings or losses. For example, in 1962, attendance at home and road games decreased appreciably as compared with 1961, and yet the loss from direct baseball operation and of the whole corporation was considerably less.

The record shows that plaintiff did not feel he could allege that the increased revenues would be sufficient to cure the corporate deficit. The only cost plaintiff was at all concerned with was that of installation of lights. No mention was made of operation and maintenance of the lights or other possible increases in operating costs of night games and we cannot speculate as to what other factors might influence the increase or decrease of profits if the Cubs were to play night home games....

Finally, we do not agree with plaintiff's contention that failure to follow the example of the other major league clubs in scheduling night games constituted negligence. Plaintiff made no allegation that these teams' night schedules were profitable or that the purpose for which night baseball had been undertaken was fulfilled. Furthermore, it cannot be said that directors, even those of corporations that are losing money, must follow the lead of the other corporations in the field. Directors are elected for their business capabilities and judgment and the courts cannot require them to forego their judgment because of the decisions of directors of other companies. Courts may not decide these questions in the absence of a clear showing of dereliction of duty on the part of the specific directors and mere failure to 'follow the crowd' is not such a dereliction.

For the foregoing reasons the order of dismissal entered by the trial court is affirmed.

Notes and Questions

1. How did the court in *Shlensky* interpret the corporation's purpose? Did the case impose limits on directors' consideration of the needs and interests of non-shareholder groups—such as employees, communities in which the corporation is located, and customers? How, if at all, should directors and officers incorporate other corporate constituencies into their decision making?

2. *Dodge v. Ford Motor Co.*, 170 N.W. 668 (Mich. 1919), is a classic case. Confronted with an adamant Henry Ford, the court addressed whether there were limits to directors' discretion in determining the corporation's purpose:

> "My ambition," said Mr. Ford, "is to employ still more men, to spread the benefits of this industrial system to the greatest possible number, to help them build up their lives and their homes. To do this we are putting the greatest share of our profits back in the business."

… The record, and especially the testimony of Mr. Ford, convinces that he has to some extent the attitude towards shareholders of one who has dispensed and distributed to them large gains and that they should be content to take what he chooses to give. His testimony creates the impression, also, that he thinks the Ford Motor Company has made too much money, has had too large profits, and that although large profits might be still earned, a sharing of them with the public, by reducing the price of the output of the company, ought to be undertaken....

[But, a] business corporation is organized and carried on primarily for the profit of the stockholders. The powers of the directors are to be employed for that end. The discretion of directors is to be exercised in the choice of means to attain that end and does not extend to a change in the end itself, to the reduction of profits or to the nondistribution of profits among stockholders in order to devote them to other purposes.

B. Other Constituencies Statutes

Many states have statutes that authorize directors to consider the interests of groups other than shareholders in at least some decision making contexts. These statutes were originally drafted in the 1980s and 1990s during the heyday of "hostile takeovers" — efforts to wrest corporate control from incumbent directors by way of acquisition of a majority of stock or election of a majority of directors. Despite the passing of that heyday (which we will examine later in this book), the statutes remain on the books and contain broad language that is not limited to the hostile takeover context. An example appears in the Pennsylvania corporations statute, Pa. Cons. Stat. Ann. 1715, which reads:

(a) General rule. — In discharging the duties of their respective positions, the board of directors, committees of the board and individual directors of a business corporation may, in considering the best interests of the corporation, consider to the extent they deem appropriate:

(1) The effects of any action upon any or all groups affected by such action, including shareholders, employees, suppliers, customers and creditors of the corporation, and upon communities in which offices or other establishments of the corporation are located.

(2) The short-term and long-term interests of the corporation, including benefits that may accrue to the corporation from its long-term plans and the possibility that these interests may be best served by the continued independence of the corporation.

(3) The resources, intent and conduct (past, stated and potential) of any person seeking to acquire control of the corporation.

(4) All other pertinent factors.

(b) Consideration of interests and factors. — The board of directors, committees of the board and individual directors shall not be required, in considering the best interests of the corporation or the effects of any action, to regard any corporate interest or the interests of any particular group affected by such action as a dominant or controlling interest or factor. The consideration of interests and factors in the manner described in this subsection and in subsection (a) shall not constitute a violation of section 1712 (relating to standard of care and justifiable reliance).

Such "other constituencies" statutes remain controversial. Some argue that they merely codify case law, which always allowed directors to consider whatever and whomever they wanted. For example, the Delaware Supreme Court indicated that directors may consider other constituencies in their decision making so long as there is "some rationally related benefit accruing to the stockholders." *See Revlon, Inc. v. MacAndrews & Forbes Holdings, Inc.*, 506 A.2d 173, 176 (Del. 1986) (excerpted later in this book). Others claim that such laws are unwise departures from traditional corporate law principles. They believe that the interests of shareholders should be the boards' primary, if not exclusive, consideration and that considering the interests of non-shareholders weakens directors' fidelity to the shareholders.

Note that the statutes permit but generally do not require directors to consider non-shareholder constituencies. The statutes grant, or clarify that directors command, discretion and flexibility in determining what is in the corporation's best interest. To illustrate, if directors are considering whether to close a plant, there are numerous factors they may consider. If they decide to take into account the interests of non-shareholders, such as employees, shareholders may object because their interests were not the directors' exclusive concern. The other constituencies statutes, however, expressly allow directors to consider the interests of non-shareholders, so the objecting shareholders would have no basis for a lawsuit on these grounds. On the other hand, if the directors decide not to consider the interests of non-shareholders, they also need not worry about being sued by those groups. The statutes, after all, do not give non-shareholder groups any enforceable rights.

C. ALI Principles

§ 2.01. The Objective and Conduct of the Corporation

(a) ... [A] corporation should have as its objective the conduct of business activities with a view to enhancing corporate profit and shareholder gain.

(b) Even if corporate profit and shareholder gain are not thereby enhanced, the corporation, in the conduct of its business:

(1) Is obliged, to the same extent as a natural person, to act within the boundaries set by law;

(2) May take into account ethical considerations that are reasonably regarded as appropriate to the responsible conduct of business; and

(3) May devote a reasonable amount of resources to public welfare, humanitarian, educational, and philanthropic purposes.

[Comment to § 2.01]

> *f. The economic objective.* In very general terms, Subsection (a) [to § 2.01]
> may be thought of as a broad injunction to enhance economic returns, while
> Subsection (b) [to § 2.01] makes clear that certain kinds of conduct must or
> may be pursued whether or not they enhance such returns (that is, even if
> the conduct either yields no economic return or entails a net economic loss).
> In most cases, however, the kinds of conduct described in Subsection (b)
> could be pursued even under the principle embodied in Subsection (a). Such
> conduct will usually be consistent with economic self-interest, because the
> principle embodied in Subsection (a)—that the objective of the corporation
> is to conduct business activities with a view to enhancing corporate profit
> and shareholder gain—does not mean that the objective of the corporation
> must be to realize corporate profit and shareholder gain in the short run. In-
> deed, the contrary is true: long-run profitability and shareholder gain are at
> the core of the economic objective. Activity that entails a short-run cost to
> achieve an appropriately greater long-run profit is therefore not a departure
> from the economic objective. An orientation toward lawful, ethical, and
> public-spirited activity will normally fall within this description. The modern
> corporation by its nature creates interdependencies with a variety of groups
> with whom the corporation has a legitimate concern, such as employees, cus-
> tomers, suppliers, and members of the communities in which the corporation
> operates. The long-term profitability of the corporation generally depends
> on meeting the fair expectations of such groups. Short-term profits may prop-
> erly be subordinated to recognition that responsible maintenance of these
> interdependencies is likely to contribute to long-term corporate profit and
> shareholder gain. The corporation's business may be conducted accordingly.
>
> For comparable reasons, the economic objective does not imply that the cor-
> poration must extract the last penny of profit out of every transaction in
> which it is involved. Similarly, under normal circumstances the economic
> objective is met by focusing on the business in which the corporation is ac-
> tually engaged.
>
> *h. Ethical considerations.* Section 2.01(b)(2) provides that a corporation may
> take into account ethical considerations that are reasonably regarded as ap-
> propriate to the responsible conduct of business. It is sometimes argued
> that because adherence to ethical principles typically involves long-run fi-
> nancial benefits, the concept of a long run dissolves any apparent tension
> between financial and ethical considerations. Certainly, a long-run profit
> motive may often explain conduct that appears to be based on ethical
> grounds.... Furthermore, when ethical considerations enter into corporate
> decisions, they are usually mixed with, rather than opposed to, long-run
> profit considerations. Nevertheless, observation suggests that corporate de-
> cisions are not infrequently made on the basis of ethical considerations even
> when doing so would not enhance corporate profit or shareholder gain.

Such behavior is not only appropriate, but desirable. Corporate officials are not less morally obliged than any other citizens to take ethical considerations into account, and it would be unwise social policy to preclude them from doing so.

D. Corporate Code

Most corporations do not expressly articulate their corporate objective or the factors they consider relevant in their decision making. However, many corporations include in documents such as their "Code of Conduct" an expression of their position on these issues. How would the following Code shape directors' decision making?

Johnson & Johnson's Credo

We believe our first responsibility is to the doctors, nurses and patients, to mothers and fathers and all others who use our products and services. In meeting their needs everything we do must be of high quality. We must constantly strive to reduce our costs in order to maintain reasonable prices. Customers' orders must be serviced promptly and accurately. Our suppliers and distributors must have an opportunity to make a fair profit.

We are responsible to our employees, the men and women who work with us throughout the world. Everyone must be considered as an individual. We must respect their dignity and recognize their merit. They must have a sense of security in their jobs. Compensation must be fair and adequate, and working conditions clean, orderly and safe. We must be mindful of ways to help our employees fulfill their family responsibilities. Employees must feel free to make suggestions and complaints. There must be equal opportunity for employment, development and advancement for those qualified. We must provide competent management, and their actions must be just and ethical.

We are responsible to the communities in which we live and work and to the world community as well. We must be good citizens—support good works and charities and bear our fair share of taxes. We must encourage civic improvements and better health and education. We must maintain in good order the property we are privileged to use, protecting the environment and natural resources.

Our final responsibility is to our stockholders. Business must make a sound profit. We must experiment with new ideas. Research must be carried on, innovative programs developed and mistakes paid for. New equipment must be purchased, new facilities provided and new products launched. Reserves must be created to provide for adverse times. When we operate according to these principles, the stockholders should realize a fair return.

E. Ethics Codes

For publicly held corporations, the Sarbanes-Oxley Act of 2002 directed the Securities and Exchange Commission to promulgate rules requiring annual and quarterly report disclosure concerning whether the company has adopted a code of ethics for senior financial officers and, if not, why not. Changes to ethics codes must be disclosed promptly in current reports.

Section VII
Corporate Governance Reforms

For publicly held corporations, the Sarbanes-Oxley Act of 2002 enacted a variety of corporate governance reforms (including concerning internal control, noted above in Section III, D and Ethics Codes, noted above in Section VI, E). The Act does not require boards of directors to form audit committees, but provides that absent committee formation, the entire board is deemed to constitute an audit committee. Given the Act's particular constraints on audit committee composition and obligation, most boards establish a committee. Stock exchanges are required to prohibit listing securities of companies not complying with the following audit committee rules.

First, the committee must be directly responsible for appointing, paying and supervising outside auditors. Second, all committee members must be independent and not collect fees from the company (other than director compensation). Third, committees must establish procedures to promote employee reporting of misconduct and protect reporting employees (whistle-blowers). Fourth, committees must be empowered to retain independent counsel and other advisors. Fifth, the company must provide sufficient funding, as the committee determines, to pay outside auditors and committee advisors.

The SEC must adopt rules requiring quarterly and annual disclosure of whether at least one audit committee member is a "financial expert" and, if not, why not. The SEC defines the term financial expert, considering a person's education and experience and probable knowledge of generally accepted accounting principles (GAAP), financial statements, audit committee functions, internal accounting controls, and preparing or auditing financial statements.

Section VIII
Legislative Responses to Liability

A. Types of Statutes

In response to what directors and many others perceived as excessive liability risks created by *Van Gorkom*, state legislatures quickly moved to ameliorate the crisis. They enacted laws that, in one way or another, decreased directors' liability risks. At least three types of exculpation statutes emerged.

First, as illustrated by DGCL § 102(b)(7), some statutes allow corporations to include charter provisions limiting or eliminating their directors' liability:

> In addition to the matters required to be set forth in the certificate of incorporation by subsection (a) of this section the certificate of incorporation may also contain any or all of the following matters—
>
> A provision eliminating or limiting the personal liability of a director to the corporation or its stockholders for monetary damages for breach of fiduciary duty as a director, provided that such provision shall not eliminate or limit the liability of a director (i) for any breach of the director's duty of loyalty to the corporation or its shareholders, (ii) for acts or omissions not in good faith or which involve intentional misconduct or a knowing violation of law, (iii) under section 174 of this Title [regarding unlawful payment of dividends, etc.], or (iv) for any transaction from which the director derived an improper personal benefit ...

Second, as illustrated by Virginia Code Ann. § 13.1-690(A), some laws alter the standards of fiduciary duties imposed on all corporate directors, typically lowering the standard of conduct:

> A director shall discharge his duties as a director, including his duties as a member of a committee, in accordance with his good faith business judgment of the best interests of the corporation ...

Finally, another alternative is offered by the ALI § 7.19, allowing shareholders to limit the amount of directors' liability:

> Except as otherwise provided by statute, if a failure by a director or an officer to meet the standard of conduct specified in Part IV (Duty of Care and the Business Judgment Rule) did not either:
>
> (1) Involve a knowing and culpable violation of law by the director or officer;
>
> (2) Show a conscious disregard for the duty of the director or officer to the corporation under circumstances in which the director or officer was aware that the conduct or omission created an unjustified risk of serious injury to the corporation; or
>
> (3) Constitute a sustained and unexcused pattern of inattention that amounted to an abduction of the defendant's duty to the corporation; and the director or officer, or an associate, did not receive a benefit that was improper under Part V (Duty of Fair Dealing),
>
> then a provision in a certificate of incorporation that limits damages against an officer or a director for such failure to an amount not less than such person's annual compensation from the corporation should be given effect, if the provision is adopted by a vote of disinterested shareholders after disclosure concerning the provision, may be repealed by the shareholders at any annual

meeting without prior action by the board, and does not reduce liability with respect to pending actions or losses incurred prior to its adoption.

These laws may vary in the scope of their coverage. For example, some limit the protected group to directors, rather than extending their application to officers. Others limit the possible plaintiffs to the corporation and shareholders filing derivative suits, and exclude the creditor or other potential plaintiffs. Some laws may require the corporation to affirmatively adopt the directors' protections, while others automatically benefit the directors. All attempt to focus on the specifics of *Van Gorkom* by covering hapless violations of the duty of care but not more serious lapses, such as violations of the duty of loyalty or failures to act in good faith. The litigation upshot of many exculpatory provisions, especially those in Delaware, is that plaintiffs challenging director action must assert non-exculpated claims (problems of good faith or loyalty rather than lapses of care).

B. Scope of Statutes

Arnold v. Society for Savings Bancorp

Delaware Supreme Court
650 A.2d 1270 (1994)

VEASEY, CHIEF JUSTICE:

In this appeal from a judgment of the Court of Chancery in favor of defendants we consider the contention of plaintiff below-appellant Robert H. Arnold ("plaintiff") that the trial court erred in granting defendants' summary judgment motion and denying his own. This suit arose out of a merger (the "Merger") of BBC Connecticut Holding Corporation ("BBC"), a wholly-owned Connecticut subsidiary of Bank of Boston Corporation ("BoB"), a Massachusetts corporation, into Society for Savings ("Society"), a wholly-owned Connecticut subsidiary of Society for Savings Bancorp, Incorporated ("Bancorp"), a Delaware corporation. In accordance with the Merger, Bancorp ultimately merged with BoB. Plaintiff was at all relevant times a Bancorp stockholder. Plaintiff named as defendants Bancorp, BoB, BBC, and twelve of fourteen members of Bancorp's board of directors (collectively "defendants").

Plaintiff's central claim is that the trial court erred in holding that certain alleged omissions and misrepresentations in the Merger proxy statement were immaterial and need not have been disclosed. Plaintiff also claims that the Court of Chancery erroneously held that the duties enunciated in [*Revlon Inc. v. MacAndrews & Forbes Holdings, Inc.*, 506 A.2d 173 (Del. 1986)] and its progeny were not implicated. Also at issue on this appeal is whether or not the individual defendants can be held liable if a disclosure violation is found in view of the exemption from liability provision in Bancorp's certificate of incorporation, adopted pursuant to 8 Del. C. §102(b)(7) ("Section 102(b)(7)"). For the reasons set forth below, we hold that the Court of Chancery erred in failing to find that plaintiff's claim that the partial disclosures in the Merger proxy statement made it materially misleading with respect to one particular fact. In all other respects we find that the trial court committed no reversible error.

We further hold that, in all events, the limitation provision in Bancorp's certificate of incorporation shields the individual defendants from personal liability for the disclosure violation found to exist in this case....

VI. *Section 102(b)(7) Protection*

Plaintiff argues that the exemption from liability in Bancorp's certificate of incorporation, adopted pursuant to Section 102(b)(7), does not extend to disclosure claims, and that, even if the provision so extended, the individual defendants' conduct here falls within two exceptions. Plaintiff further contends that his claims against Connell for disclosure violations in his capacity as an officer (rather than a director) would still survive.... The Court of Chancery did not reach the Section 102(b)(7) issue. In view of our finding that there was a disclosure violation, we are required to reach these questions. We hold that Section 102(b)(7), as adopted by Bancorp, shields the individual defendants from liability....

A. *Application of Section 102(b)(7) to Disclosure Claims*

Article XIII of Bancorp's certificate of incorporation, ... parallels the language in Section 102(b)(7).... Plaintiff claims that the legislative history of Section 102(b)(7) supports his argument that the shield is not applicable here. Plaintiff's argument, however, bypasses a logical step in statutory analysis. A court should not resort to legislative history in interpreting a statute where statutory language provides unambiguously an answer to the question at hand....

In the instant case, plaintiff's claim that Section 102(b)(7) does not extend to disclosure violations must be rejected as contrary to the express, unambiguous language of that provision. Section 102(b)(7) provides protection "for breach of fiduciary duty." Given that the fiduciary disclosure requirements were well-established when Section 102(b)(7) was enacted and were nonetheless not excepted expressly from coverage, there is no reason to go beyond the text of the statute. Thus, claims alleging disclosure violations that do not otherwise fall within any exception are protected by Section 102(b)(7) and any certificate of incorporation provision (such as Article XIII) adopted pursuant thereto. In any event, nothing in the legislative history of the adoption of Section 102(b)(7) is inconsistent with the result we reach herein.

B. *Applicability of the Exceptions to Section 102(b)(7)*

Plaintiff argues that the individual defendants' conduct implicates the duty of loyalty and the proscription against knowing, intentional violations of law. He argues that the individual defendants' conduct falls within the exceptions in Section 102(b)(7)(i) & (ii) because they: (i) "improperly interfer[ed] with the voting process by knowingly or deliberately failing to make proper disclosure"; (ii) acted in bad faith and recklessly; and (iii) improperly granted no-shop and lock-up clauses as part of the Merger. Plaintiff also contends that Connell and Stang were interested directors who violated their duty of loyalty and that Connell's actions in his role as an officer fall outside Section 102(b)(7)'s protection.

The individual defendants counter that plaintiff's claims are essentially conclusory for there is no affirmative proof that they knowingly or deliberately failed to disclose facts they knew were material. That is, they argue that they balanced in good faith which facts to disclose against those to withhold as immaterial. Next, they assert that case law does not support plaintiff's claim relating to the no-shop and lock-up clauses under the facts of this case. Finally, the individual defendants contend that the claim relating to Connell's conduct as an officer is barred pursuant to Supreme Court Rule 8 because it was not raised in the Court of Chancery. On the merits, they assert that plaintiff has failed to segregate any of Connell's actions as an officer that fall within the exceptions to Section 102(b)(7).

Plaintiff's claims are not supported by the record or Delaware law. The individual defendants did not violate the duty of loyalty under the facts of this case. Plaintiff's intentional violation argument is unsupported by the record. As to plaintiff's third claim, though the granting of no-shop and lock-up rights can under certain circumstances implicate the duty of loyalty, without any additional, supportive factual basis for his claim, sufficient at least to create a genuine issue of material fact, plaintiff's reliance on [*Mills Acquisition Co. v. MacMillan, Inc.*, 559 A.2d 1261 (Del. 1988), and *Unocal Corp. v. Mesa Petroleum Co.*, 493 A.2d 946 (Del. 1985)] is unpersuasive. Even assuming that plaintiff's final argument is not procedurally barred, it lacks merit because plaintiff has failed to highlight any specific actions Connell undertook as an officer (as distinct from actions as a director) that fall within the two pertinent exceptions to Section 102(b)(7).

Malpiede v. Towson

Delaware Supreme Court
780 A.2d 1075 (2001)

VEASEY, CHIEF JUSTICE:

[Frederick's of Hollywood, half owned by founder's trusts and half publicly, agreed to a merger with Knightsbridge Capital for $6.14 per Frederick share. The agreement limited Frederick's board from soliciting competing bids, subject to contrary requirements of its fiduciary duties. Two months after signing, a third party, Milton Partners, offered $7 per share (all cash, with no financing conditions). Knightsbridge promptly agreed to buy all the trusts' shares for $6.90, giving it functional blocking power over other bids. A week later another bidder, Veritas Capital, offered $7.75 per share. After a month of communications or discussions among Frederick's board and all bidders, Knightsbridge increased its offer to $7.75, and bought some shares on the open market for $8.21 each. Finally, Veritas increased its bid to $9. Frederick's board rejected the $9 bid, going forward with the Knightsbridge merger at $7.75.]

[A shareholder class action resulted that alleged breach of the duties of care and loyalty. The shareholders further alleged that those duties had to be evaluated under the standard applicable to sales of control first set forth in *Revlon, Inc. v. MacAndrews & Forbes Holdings, Inc.*, 506 A.2d 173 (Del. 1986), excerpted later in this book. The trial court granted the board's motion to dismiss the complaint, finding that it did not state a duty of loyalty claim and that Frederick's charter precluded money damages against the directors for breaches of the duty of care. The Supreme Court of Delaware affirmed. The following contains the court's explanation for its decision as to the duty of care claim.]

The primary due care issue is whether the board was grossly negligent, and therefore breached its duty of due care, in failing to implement a routine defensive strategy that could enable the board to negotiate for a higher bid or otherwise create a tactical advantage to enhance stockholder value.... Construing the amended complaint most favorably to the plaintiffs, it can be read to allege that the board was grossly negligent in immediately accepting the Knightsbridge offer and agreeing to various restrictions on further negotiations without first determining whether Veritas would issue a counteroffer. Although the board had conducted a search for a buyer over one year, plaintiffs seem to contend that the board was imprudently hasty in agreeing to a restrictive merger agreement on the day it was proposed—particularly where other bidders had recently expressed interest. Although the board's haste, in itself, might not constitute a breach of the board's duty of care because the board had already conducted a lengthy sale process, the plaintiffs argue that the board's decision to accept allegedly extreme contractual restrictions impacted its ability to obtain a higher sale price. Recognizing that, at the end of the day, plaintiffs would have an uphill battle in overcoming the presumption of the business judgment rule, we must give plaintiffs the benefit of the doubt at this pleading stage to determine if they have stated a due care claim. Because of our ultimate decision, however, we need not finally decide this question in this case.

We assume, therefore, without deciding, that a claim for relief based on gross negligence during the board's auction process is stated by the inferences most favorable to plaintiffs that flow from these allegations. The issue then becomes whether the amended complaint may be dismissed upon a Rule 12(b)(6) motion by reason of the existence and the legal effect of the exculpatory provision of ... Frederick's certificate of incorporation, adopted pursuant to 8 Del. C. § 102(b)(7). [It provided as follows:

> A director of this Corporation shall not be personally liable to the Corporation or its shareholders for monetary damages for breach of fiduciary duty as a director, except for liability (i) for any breach of the director's duty of loyalty to the Corporation or its shareholders, (ii) for acts or omissions not in good faith or which involve intentional misconduct or a knowing violation of law (iii) under Section 174 of the Delaware General Corporation Law, or (iv) for any transaction for which the director derived an improper personal benefit.]

That provision would exempt directors from personal liability in damages with certain exceptions (e.g., breach of the duty of loyalty) that are not applicable here....

We now address plaintiffs' argument that the trial court committed error, based on certain language in [*Emerald Partners v. Berlin*, 726 A.2d 1215 (Del. 1999),] by barring their due care claims. Plaintiffs' arguments on this point are based on an erroneous premise, and our decision here is not inconsistent with *Emerald Partners*.

In *Emerald Partners*, we made two important points about the raising of Section 102(b)(7) charter provisions. First we said: "The shield from liability provided by a certificate of incorporation provision adopted pursuant to 8 Del. C. § 102(b)(7) is in the nature of an affirmative defense." Second, we said:

Where the factual basis for a claim solely implicates a violation of the duty of care, this court has indicated that the protections of such a charter provision may properly be invoked and applied.

Based on this language in *Emerald Partners*, plaintiffs make two arguments. First, they argue that the Court of Chancery in this case should not have dismissed their due care claims because these claims are intertwined with, and thus indistinguishable from, the duty of loyalty and bad faith claims. Second, plaintiffs contend that the Court of Chancery incorrectly assigned to them the burden of going forward with proof.

Plaintiffs here, while not conceding that the Section 102(b)(7) charter provision may be considered on this Rule 12(b)(6) motion nevertheless, in effect, conceded in oral argument in the Court of Chancery and similarly in oral argument in this Court that if a complaint unambiguously and solely asserted only a due care claim, the complaint is dismissible once the corporation's Section 102(b)(7) provision is invoked. This concession is in line with our holding in *Emerald Partners* quoted above.

Plaintiffs contended vigorously, however, that the Section 102(b)(7) charter provision does not apply to bar their claims in this case because the amended complaint alleges breaches of the duty of loyalty and other claims that are not barred by the charter provision. As a result, plaintiffs maintain, this case cannot be boiled down solely to a due care case. They argue, in effect, that their complaint is sufficiently well-pleaded that—as a matter of law—the due care claims are so inextricably intertwined with loyalty and bad faith claims that Section 102(b)(7) is not a bar to recovery of damages against the directors.

We disagree. It is the plaintiffs who have a burden to set forth "a short and plain statement of the claim showing that the pleader is entitled to relief." The plaintiffs are entitled to all reasonable inferences flowing from their pleadings, but if those inferences do not support a valid legal claim, the complaint should be dismissed without the need for the defendants to file an answer and without proceeding with discovery. Here we have assumed, without deciding, that the amended complaint on its face states a due care claim. Because we have determined that the complaint fails properly to invoke loyalty and bad faith claims, we are left with only a due care claim. Defendants had the obligation to raise the bar of Section 102(b)(7) as a defense, and they did. As plaintiffs conceded in oral argument before this Court, if there is only an unambiguous, residual due care claim and nothing else—as a matter of law—then Section 102(b)(7) would bar the claim. Accordingly, the Court of Chancery did not err in dismissing the plaintiffs [sic] due care claim in this case.

Plaintiffs also assert that the trial court in the case before us incorrectly placed on plaintiffs a pleading burden to negate the elements of the 102(b)(7) charter provision. Plaintiffs argue that this ruling is inconsistent with the statement in *Emerald Partners* that "the shield from liability provided by a certificate of incorporation provision adopted pursuant to 8 Del. C. § 102(b)(7) is in the nature of an affirmative defense.... Defendants seeking exculpation under such a provision will normally bear the burden of establishing each of its elements."

The procedural posture here is quite different from that in *Emerald Partners*. There the Court stated that it was incorrect for the trial court to grant summary judgment on the record in that case because the defendants had the burden at trial of demonstrating good faith if they were invoking the statutory exculpation provision. In this case, we focus not on trial burdens, but only on pleading issues. A plaintiff must allege well-pleaded facts stating a claim on which relief may be granted. Had plaintiff alleged such well-pleaded facts supporting a breach of loyalty or bad faith claim, the Section 102(b)(7) charter provision would have been unavailing as to such claims, and this case would have gone forward.

But we have held that the amended complaint here does not allege a loyalty violation or other violation falling within the exceptions to the Section 102(b)(7) exculpation provision. Likewise, we have held that, even if the plaintiffs had stated a claim for gross negligence, such a well-pleaded claim is unavailing because defendants have brought forth the Section 102(b)(7) charter provision that bars such claims. This is the end of the case.

And rightly so, as a matter of the public policy of this State. Section 102(b)(7) was adopted by the Delaware General Assembly in 1986 following a directors and officers insurance [sic] liability crisis and the 1985 Delaware Supreme Court decision in *Smith v. Van Gorkom* [488 A.2d 858 (Del. 1985)]. The purpose of this statute was to permit stockholders to adopt a provision in the certificate of incorporation to free directors of personal liability in damages for due care violations, but not duty of loyalty violations, bad faith claims and certain other conduct. Such a charter provision, when adopted, would not affect injunctive proceedings based on gross negligence. Once the statute was adopted, stockholders usually approved charter amendments containing these provisions because it freed up directors to take business risks without worrying about negligence lawsuits.

Our jurisprudence since the adoption of the statute has consistently stood for the proposition that a Section 102(b)(7) charter provision bars a claim that is found to state only a due care violation. Because we have assumed that the amended complaint here does state a due care claim, the exculpation afforded by the statute must affirmatively be raised by the defendant directors. The directors have done so in this case, and the Court of Chancery properly applied the Frederick's charter provision to dismiss the plaintiffs' due care claim....

In re Cornerstone Therapeutics Inc.

Supreme Court of Delaware
115 A.3d 1173 (2015)

STRINE, CHIEF JUSTICE:

These appeals were scheduled for argument on the same day because they turn on a single legal question: in an action for damages against corporate fiduciaries, where the plaintiff challenges an interested transaction that is presumptively subject to entire fairness review, must the plaintiff plead a non-exculpated claim against the disinterested, independent directors to survive a motion to dismiss by those directors?

We answer … in the affirmative. A plaintiff seeking only monetary damages must plead non-exculpated claims against a director who is protected by an exculpatory charter provision to survive a motion to dismiss, regardless of the underlying standard of review for the board's conduct—be it *Revlon, Unocal,* the entire fairness standard, or the business judgment rule. [Ed.: *Revlon* and *Unocal,* cases excerpted later in this book, articulate special standards for takeovers. The entire fairness standard is the standard that governs duty of loyalty cases, as explored in the next chapter.]

The Court of Chancery in both of these cases denied the defendants' motions to dismiss because it read the precedent of this Court to require doing so, regardless of the exculpatory provision in each company's certificate of incorporation. Under the Court of Chancery's analysis, even if the plaintiffs could not plead a non-exculpated claim against any particular director, as long as the underlying transaction was subject to the entire fairness standard of review, and the plaintiffs were therefore able to state non-exculpated claims against the interested parties and their affiliates, all of the directors were required to remain defendants until the end of litigation. The Court of Chancery was reluctant to embrace that result but felt that it was the reading most faithful to our precedent.

In this decision, we hold that even if a plaintiff has pled facts that, if true, would require the transaction to be subject to the entire fairness standard of review, and the interested parties to face a claim for breach of their duty of loyalty, the independent directors do not automatically have to remain defendants. When the independent directors are protected by an exculpatory charter provision and the plaintiffs are unable to plead a non-exculpated claim against them, those directors are entitled to have the claims against them dismissed, in keeping with this Court's opinion in *Malpiede v. Townson* [excerpted above].... Accordingly, we remand both of these cases to allow the Court of Chancery to determine if the plaintiffs have sufficiently pled non-exculpated claims against the independent directors.

II. BACKGROUND

These appeals both involve damages actions by stockholder plaintiffs arising out of mergers in which the controlling stockholder, who had representatives on the board of directors, acquired the remainder of the shares that it did not own in a Delaware public corporation. Both mergers were negotiated by special committees of independent directors, were ultimately approved by a majority of the minority stockholders, and were at substantial premiums to the pre-announcement market price. Nonetheless, the plaintiffs filed suit...., contending that the directors had breached their fiduciary duty by approving transactions that were unfair to the minority stockholders.

In both appeals, it is undisputed that the companies did not follow the process established in *Kahn v. M & F Worldwide Corporation* as a safe harbor to invoke the business judgment rule in the context of a self-interested transaction. Thus, the entire fairness standard presumptively applied.... In both cases, the defendant directors were insulated from liability for monetary damages for breaches of the fiduciary duty of care by an exculpatory charter provision adopted in accordance with 8 Del. C. § 102(b)(7). Despite that provision, the plaintiffs in each case not only sued the controlling stockholders and their affiliated directors, but also sued the independent directors who had negotiated and approved the mergers.

In the first of these cases to be decided, [*Cornerstone*], the independent director defendants moved to dismiss on the grounds that the plaintiffs had failed to plead any non-exculpated claim against them. The independent directors argued that although the entire fairness standard applied to the Court of Chancery's review of the underlying transaction, and thus the controlling stockholder and its affiliated directors were at risk of being found liable for breaches of the duty of loyalty, the plaintiffs still bore the burden to plead non-exculpated claims against the independent directors.

The independent directors noted that this Court held in *Malpiede v. Townson* that, in the analogous context of review under the *Revlon* standard, plaintiffs seeking damages must plead non-exculpated claims against each individual director or risk dismissal. The independent directors also pointed out that in a number of cases, including several affirmed by this Court, the Court of Chancery dismissed claims against independent directors when the plaintiffs failed to plead non-exculpated claims for breaches of fiduciary duty, notwithstanding the applicability of entire fairness review to the transaction.

In response, the plaintiffs argued that the Court of Chancery could not grant the independent directors' motion to dismiss, regardless of whether they had sufficiently pled non-exculpated claims. Under their reading of language in two of the four decisions issued by this Court in the extensive *Emerald Partners* litigation [noted in the *Malpiede* case, excerpted above], the plaintiffs contended that they could defeat the independent directors' motions to dismiss solely by establishing that the underlying transaction was subject to the entire fairness standard.

In the first of the two relevant *Emerald Partners* decisions ("*Emerald I*"), this Court determined that the plaintiffs had sufficiently pled duty of loyalty claims against the disinterested directors that were "intertwined" with their duty of care claims. In the second of the two decisions ("*Emerald II*"), this Court stated that "when entire fairness is the applicable standard of judicial review, a determination that the director defendants are exculpated from paying monetary damages can be made only *after the basis* for their liability has been decided," on a fully-developed factual record.

The *Cornerstone* plaintiffs argued that this language in *Emerald II* should be read broadly to require the court to deny independent directors' motions to dismiss whenever the applicable standard of review is entire fairness. Although the Court of Chancery suggested that it believed that the defendants' view of the law was the preferable one, it nonetheless concluded that it was bound to deny the motion because its reading of the *Emerald II* decision was the one advocated by the plaintiffs.

In *In re Zhongpin Stockholders Litigation*, the independent director defendants also argued that the claims against them should be dismissed because the plaintiffs had failed to plead any non-exculpated claims. The Court of Chancery in *Zhongpin* deferred to *Cornerstone's* interpretation of precedent and held that the claims against the independent directors survived their motion to dismiss "regardless of whether the Complaint state[d] a non-exculpated claim" because the transaction was subject to entire fairness review.

In each case, the Court of Chancery did not analyze the plaintiffs' duty of loyalty claims against the independent directors because it determined that it was required to deny their motions to dismiss regardless of whether such claims had been sufficiently pled. But, recognizing the important and uncertain issue of corporate law at stake, the Court of Chancery in each case recommended certification of an interlocutory appeal to this Court to determine whether its reading of precedent was correct.

III. ANALYSIS

In answering the legal question raised by these appeals, we acknowledge that the body of law relevant to these disputes presents a debate between two competing but colorable views of the law. These cases thus exemplify a benefit of careful employment of the interlocutory appeal process: to enable this Court to clarify precedent that could arguably be read in two different ways before litigants incur avoidable costs.

We now resolve the question presented by these cases by determining that plaintiffs must plead a non-exculpated claim for breach of fiduciary duty against an independent director protected by an exculpatory charter provision, or that director will be entitled to be dismissed from the suit. That rule applies regardless of the underlying standard of review for the transaction. When a director is protected by an exculpatory charter provision, a plaintiff can survive a motion to dismiss by that director defendant by pleading facts supporting a rational inference that the director harbored self-interest adverse to the stockholders' interests, acted to advance the self-interest of an interested party from whom they could not be presumed to act independently, or acted in bad faith. But the mere fact that a plaintiff is able to plead facts supporting the application of the entire fairness standard to the transaction, and can thus state a duty of loyalty claim against the interested fiduciaries, does not relieve the plaintiff of the responsibility to plead a non-exculpated claim against each director who moves for dismissal. . . .

In *Malpiede*, this Court analyzed the effect of a Section 102(b)(7) provision on a due care claim against directors who approved a transaction which the plaintiffs argued should be subject to review under the *Revlon* standard. This Court noted that although "plaintiffs are entitled to all reasonable inferences flowing from their pleadings, ... if those inferences do not support a valid legal claim, the complaint should be dismissed." Because a director will only be liable for monetary damages if she has breached a non-exculpated duty, a plaintiff who pleads only a due care claim against that director has not set forth any grounds for relief. In such a case, "*as a matter of law* [ ] then Section 102(b)(7) would bar the claim." [*Malpiede*, excerpted above.]

Nevertheless, the plaintiffs in each of these cases contend that their exculpated claims against the independent directors cannot be dismissed solely because the transaction at issue is subject to entire fairness review. The plaintiffs argue that they should be entitled to an automatic inference that a director facilitating an interested transaction is disloyal because the possibility of conflicted loyalties is heightened in controller transactions, and the facts that give rise to a duty of loyalty breach may be unknowable at the pleading stage. But there are several problems with such an inference: to require independent directors to remain defendants solely because the plaintiffs stated a non-exculpated claim against the controller and its affiliates would be inconsistent with Delaware law and would also increase costs for disinterested directors, corporations, and stockholders, without providing a corresponding benefit.

First, this Court and the Court of Chancery have emphasized that each director has a right to be considered individually when the directors face claims for damages in a suit challenging board action. And under Delaware corporate law, that individualized consideration does not start with the assumption that each director was disloyal; rather, "independent directors are presumed to be motivated to do their duty with fidelity." *In re MFW S'holders Litig.*, 67 A.3d 496, 528 (Del. Ch. 2013) ... *aff'd sub nom., Kahn v. M & F Worldwide Corp.*, 88 A.3d 635 (Del.2014).... Thus, in *Aronson v. Lewis* [473 A.2d 805 (Del. 1984)], this Court emphasized that the mere fact that a director serves on the board of a corporation with a controlling stockholder does not automatically make that director not independent....

Adopting the plaintiffs' approach would not only be inconsistent with these basic tenets of Delaware law, it would likely create more harm than benefit for minority stockholders in practice. Our common law of corporations has rightly emphasized the need for independent directors to be willing to say no to interested transactions proposed by controlling stockholders. For that reason, our law has long inquired into the practical negotiating power given to independent directors in conflicted transactions. *E.g., Kahn v. Tremont Corp.*, 694 A.2d 422, 429 (Del.1997). Although it is wise for our law to focus on whether the independent directors can say no, it does not follow that it is prudent to create an invariable rule that any independent director who says yes to an interested transaction subject to entire fairness review must remain as a defendant until the end of the litigation, regardless of the absence of any evidence suggesting that the director acted for an improper motive.

For more than a generation, our law has recognized that the negotiating efforts of independent directors can help to secure transactions with controlling stockholders that are favorable to the minority. *Weinberger v. UOP, Inc.*, 457 A.2d 701, 709 n. 7 (Del.1983) ... Indeed, [there is empirical research providing] evidence that interested transactions subject to special committee approval are often priced on terms that are attractive to minority stockholders. We decline to adopt an approach that would create incentives for independent directors to avoid serving as special committee members, or to reject transactions solely because their role in negotiating on behalf of the stockholders would cause them to remain as defendants until the end of any litigation challenging the transaction.

As is well understood, the fear that directors who faced personal liability for potentially value-maximizing business decisions might be dissuaded from making such decisions is why Section 102(b)(7) was adopted in the first place. As this Court explained in *Malpiede*, "Section 102(b)(7) was adopted by the Delaware General Assembly in 1986 following a directors and officers insurance liability crisis and the 1985 Delaware Supreme Court decision in *Smith v. Van Gorkom*." Because of that "crisis," the General Assembly feared that directors would not be willing to make decisions that would benefit stockholders if they faced personal liability for making them. The purpose of Section 102(b)(7) was to "free up directors to take business risks without worrying about negligence lawsuits." *Id.* Establishing a rule that all directors must remain as parties in litigation involving a transaction with a controlling stockholder would thus reduce the benefits that the General Assembly anticipated in adopting Section 102(b)(7)....

WLR Foods, Inc. v. Tyson Foods, Inc.

United States Court of Appeals, Fourth Circuit

65 F.3d 1172 (1995)

MURNAGHAN, CIRCUIT JUDGE:

The instant case arose from an attempt by Tyson Foods, Inc. ("Tyson"), a nationwide poultry producer, to acquire WLR Foods, Inc. ("WLR"), a chicken and turkey producer. In early 1994, Tyson engaged in extensive discussions with certain members of WLR's Board of Directors ("the WLR Board") in an attempt to arrange a merger between Tyson and WLR. The WLR Board, resistant to the idea of being acquired by Tyson, adopted various defensive measures to protect WLR against the takeover. Tyson eventually presented a tender offer directly to the stockholders of WLR, but withdrew the offer several months later, claiming that, due to actions taken by the WLR Board, Tyson's offering price was no longer reflective of the value of WLR's stock. Tyson now challenges several rulings of the district court, which found that the defensive tactics adopted by the WLR Board were a valid legal means by which to respond to the threatened takeover of WLR by Tyson....

III. *The Business Judgment Statute*

In its next assignment of error, Tyson challenges the district court's finding that the Virginia Business Judgment Statute, Va. Code Ann. § 13.1-690 ("§ 690"), allows an inquiry only into the processes employed by corporate directors in making their decisions regarding a takeover, and not into the substance of those decisions. Pursuant to that interpretation, the district court denied Tyson access during discovery to the substantive content of the materials used by the WLR Board in responding to Tyson's takeover attempt.

... [Section 690, also excerpted earlier in this Section, states that "A director shall discharge his duties as a director ... in accordance with his good faith business judgment of the best interests of the corporation."]

... The district court held that under the standard articulated in § 690, only the good faith business judgment of the directors was at issue in Tyson's claims, and the rationality *vel non* of the decision ultimately reached by the WLR Board was not relevant. The district court thus permitted Tyson to inquire into the procedures followed by the WLR directors during their investigation of Tyson's offer that indicated whether or not they were considering the offer in good faith, but did not allow Tyson access to the actual substantive information that was used by the directors in making their decision regarding the offer.

We find that the district court did not abuse its discretion in limiting discovery in the instant case. First, it is clear from the language of §690 that the actions of a director are to be judged by his or her good faith in performing corporate duties, and not by the substantive merit of the director's decisions themselves. Tyson concedes that good faith is the relevant standard under §690. However, according to Tyson, although §690 itself does not focus on whether a director's decision is substantively correct, knowledge of the substantive content of the information that was available to the director is necessary in order to determine whether the decision was made in good faith. Tyson claims that a litigant cannot prove a director's lack of good faith without having access to all of the information on which the director relied.

In essence, Tyson hopes to prove lack of good faith in the instant case by showing that, based upon the substantive information received by the WLR Board, the Board should have reached a different result. However, that argument imports an aspect into the Virginia standard of director conduct that is not part of Virginia law. It reduces, and nearly eliminates, the ability to rely, in good faith, on experts. Whether a different person would have come to a different conclusion given the information that a director had before him is simply irrelevant to the determination of whether a director in Virginia has acted in good faith in fulfilling his corporate duties.

In fact, it is precisely such a comparison between a director and the hypothetical reasonable person that the Virginia legislature explicitly chose to reject when it enacted §690.... The business judgment rule contained in the Model Act, like §690, is based upon a director's good faith. By referring to an "ordinarily prudent person" and the director's "reasonabl[e] belie[f]" concerning the corporation's best interests, however, the Model Act makes clear that one of the ways in which a litigant may prove that a director did not exercise good faith is by showing that a director's decision is irrational, *i.e.*, that the decision does not comport with what a reasonable person would do under similar circumstances.

Section 690, however, contains no reference to the "reasonable person." In fact, the Virginia legislature expressly chose to reject the Model Act standard:

[Section 690], especially subsection A, is significantly different from the Model Act's treatment of the same subject in §8.30.... The term "reasonable" is intentionally not used in the standard. It thereby eliminates comparison of the conduct in question with the idealized standard and removes the question of how great a deviation from this idealized standard is acceptable.

Virginia Corporation Law with Commentaries and Rules 197–98 (1992 ed.) (Joint Bar Committee Commentary); *see also* [Daniel T. Murphy, "The New Virginia Stock Corporation Act: A Primer," 20 *U. Rich. L. Rev.* 67, 108 (1985)] (Under §690, "[t]he trier of fact need only find good faith and determine whether the conduct in question was a product of the director's own business judgment of what is in the best interest of the corporation. The director's conduct or decision is not to be analyzed in the context of whether a reasonable man would have acted similarly."); *id.* ("The statute ... may ... protect the utterly inept, but well-meaning, good faith director."). Directors' actions in Virginia are not to be judged for their reasonableness, and we, like the district court, reject Tyson's attempt to inject such a standard into Virginia law.

Chapter 11

Duty of Loyalty

Situation

Concern about the possibility of a lawsuit against Biologistics, Inc. dissipated a few weeks ago after investigators for the state health department traced the local water contamination to another business in the same general area. At a board meeting shortly after these developments were announced, Baker reported that the corporation needed to contract with a machine tool company for the manufacture of approximately $50,000 worth of equipment for the research and development operations. She brought the matter up for board approval because the expenditure would put the project well over budget. She recommended that Olivetti Tool, Inc. be given the contract because, though their equipment is expensive, Olivetti's reputation is good. After some discussion of the budget and of Olivetti, the board unanimously approved the contract.

Anderson called you this morning and said he had just learned that Welsh is a part owner and a director of Olivetti. Anderson has no reason to doubt their contract with Olivetti is fair—though he is not sure—but he is very agitated that Welsh did not disclose his interest in Olivetti at the board meeting at which the contract was approved. He wants to know what you think should be done, and he also suggested that you call Welsh and discuss the matter with him. You did so, and Welsh said he has been bothered about his silence, but did not think he had to say anything about his interest in Olivetti because he had nothing to do with Baker's recommending the contract or the negotiations in connection with it. He said he is not an expert in such matters, but that the contract price seemed high to him. He felt, however, that he might violate a duty to Olivetti if he said anything to the Biologistics board.

Section I
Introduction

In addition to the duty of care, directors and officers assume a duty of loyalty to the corporation. As stated in the *Corporate Director's Guidebook* (2d ed. 1994): "The duty of loyalty requires directors to exercise their powers in the interests of the corporation and not in the directors' own interest or in the interest of another person (including a family member) or organization. Simply put, directors should not use their corporate position to make a personal profit or gain or for other personal advantage."

While the duty of loyalty can be "simply put," its meaning and requirements continue to challenge courts and legislators. As the cases in this chapter illustrate, corporate law struggles with many core questions. In order for the duty to be implicated, a conflict between the director's individual pecuniary interests and the corporation's interest must exist. Courts have identified this conflict when directors and officers enter into transactions with their corporations, *i.e.*, they are on both sides of a deal, or when two corporations with common directors enter into transactions, but in what other circumstances should the duty apply? Assuming the duty is implicated, what does the basic common law test of fairness require? What is the role of the safe harbor statutes?

Section II
Common Law Test

Lewis v. S. L. & E., Inc.

United States Court of Appeals, Second Circuit
629 F.2d 764 (1980)

KEARSE, CIRCUIT JUDGE:

This case arises out of an intra-family dispute over the management of two closely-held affiliated corporations. Plaintiff Donald E. Lewis ("Donald"), a shareholder of S.L. & E., Inc. ("SLE"), appeals from judgments entered against him in the United States District Court for the Western District of New York, Harold P. Burke, Judge, after a bench trial of his derivative claim against directors of SLE, and of a claim asserted against him by the other corporation, Lewis General Tires, Inc. ("LGT"), which intervened in the suit. The defendants Alan E. Lewis ("Alan"), Leon E. Lewis, Jr. ("Leon, Jr."), and Richard E. Lewis ("Richard"), are the brothers of Donald; they were, at pertinent times herein, directors of SLE and officers, directors and shareholders of LGT. Donald charged that his brothers had wasted the assets of SLE by causing SLE to lease business premises to LGT from 1966 to 1972 at an unreasonably low rental. LGT was permitted to intervene in the action, and filed a complaint seeking specific performance of an agreement by Donald to sell his SLE stock to LGT in 1972. The district court held that Donald had failed to prove waste by the defendant directors, and entered judgment in their favor. The court also awarded attorneys' fees to the defendant directors and to SLE, and granted LGT specific performance of Donald's agreement to sell his SLE stock.

On appeal, Donald argues that the district court improperly allocated to him the burden of proving his claims of waste, and that since defendants failed to prove that the transactions in question were fair and reasonable, he was entitled to judgment. Donald also argues that the awards of attorneys' fees were improper. We agree with each of these contentions, and therefore reverse and remand.

I

For many years Leon Lewis, Sr., the father of Donald and the defendant directors, was the principal shareholder of SLE and LGT. LGT, formed in 1933, operated a tire dealership in Rochester, New York. SLE, formed in 1943, owned the land and complex of buildings at 260 East Avenue in Rochester. This property was SLE's only significant asset. Prior to 1956 LGT occupied SLE's premises without benefit of a lease; the rent paid was initially $200 per month, and had increased over the years to $800 per month by 1956, when additional parcels were added. On February 28, 1956, SLE granted LGT a 10-year lease on the newly expanded property ("the Property"), for a rent of $1,200 per month, or $14,400 per year. Under the terms of the lease, SLE was responsible for payment of real estate taxes on the Property, while all other current expenses were to be borne by the tenant, LGT.[1]

In 1962, Leon Lewis, Sr., transferred his SLE stock, 90 shares in all, to his six children (defendants Richard, Alan and Leon, Jr., plaintiff Donald, and two daughters, Margaret and Carol), giving 15 shares to each.[2] At that time Richard, Alan and Leon, Jr., were already shareholders, officers and directors of LGT. Contemporaneously with their receipt of SLE stock, all six of the children entered into a "shareholders' agreement" with LGT, under which each child who was not a shareholder of LGT on June 1, 1972 would be required to sell his or her SLE shares to LGT, within 30 days of that date, at a price equal to the book value of the SLE stock as of June 1, 1972.

LGT's lease on the SLE property expired on February 28, 1966. At that time the directors of SLE were Richard, Alan, Leon, Jr., Leon, Sr., and Henry Etsberger; these five were also the directors of LGT. In 1966 Alan owned 44% of LGT, Richard owned 30%, Leon, Jr., owned 19%, and Leon, Sr., owned 7%. From 1967 to 1972 Richard owned 61% of LGT and Leon, Jr., owned the remaining 39%. When the lease expired in 1966, no new lease was entered into. LGT nonetheless continued to occupy the property and to pay SLE at the old rate, $14,400 per year. According to the defendants' testimony at trial, there was never any thought or discussion among the SLE directors of entering into a new lease or of increasing the rent. Richard testified: "We never gave consideration to a new lease." From all that appears, the defendant directors viewed SLE as existing purely for the benefit of LGT. Richard testified, for example, that although real estate taxes rose sharply during the period 1966–1971, from approximately $7,800 to more than $11,000, to be paid by SLE out of its constant $14,400 rental income, raising the rent was never mentioned. He testified that SLE was "only a shell to protect the operating company (LGT)." When this suit was commenced there had not been a formal meeting of either the shareholders or the directors of SLE since 1962. Richard, Alan and Leon, Jr., had largely ignored SLE's separate corporate existence and disregarded the fact that SLE had shareholders who were not shareholders of LGT and who therefore could not profit from actions that used SLE solely for the benefit of LGT.

Neither Donald nor his sisters ever owned LGT stock. As the June 1972 date approached for the required sale of their SLE stock to LGT, Donald apparently came

---

1. [1] It appears that SLE was also responsible for payments due on a mortgage on the Property. In addition, LGT charged SLE for the costs of certain capital improvements, such as the major structural repairs to the principal building's facade, carried out in 1969.

2. [2] SLE had 150 shares outstanding, and each child thus received a ten percent interest. At the same time LGT purchased the remaining 60 outstanding shares from the elder Lewis's business partner, Henry Etsberger.

to believe that SLE's book value was lower than it should have been. He sought SLE financial information from Richard, who had been president of SLE since 1967. Richard refused to provide information. Donald therefore refused to sell his SLE shares in 1972,[3] and commenced this shareholders' derivative action in the district court in August 1973, basing jurisdiction on diversity of citizenship. The sole claim raised in the complaint was that the defendant directors had wasted the assets of SLE by "grossly undercharging" LGT for the latter's occupancy and use of the Property. Although the complaint charged such mismanagement for the period 1962 to 1973, plaintiff subsequently limited this claim to the period between February 28, 1966, the date on which the lease expired, and June 1, 1972, the date contractually set for valuation of the SLE shares which plaintiff had agreed to sell to LGT. LGT intervened and demanded specific performance of Donald's agreement to sell his SLE stock. Donald did not contest his ultimate obligation to sell, but took the position that since the book value of the shares would be increased if he prevailed on his derivative claim, specific performance should be granted only after adjudication of that claim.

There ensued an eight-day bench trial, at which plaintiff sought to prove, by the testimony of several expert witnesses, that the fair rental value of the Property was greater than the $14,400 per year that SLE had been paid by LGT. Defendants sought to show that the rental paid was reasonable, by offering evidence concerning the financial straits of LGT, the cost to LGT of operating the Property, the general economic decline of the East Avenue neighborhood, and rentals paid on two other properties in that neighborhood. LGT presented expert testimony that the value of plaintiff's stock as of June 1972, assuming a successful defense of the derivative claims, was $15,650.

... On this basis, the court held that Donald had failed to establish the rental value of the Property during the period at issue, and that defendants were therefore entitled to judgment on the derivative claims. Implicit in the district court's ruling, granting judgment for defendants upon plaintiff's failure to prove waste, was a determination that plaintiff bore the burden of proof on that issue....

II

Turning first to the question of burden of proof, we conclude that the district court erred in placing upon plaintiff the burden of proving waste. Because the directors of SLE were also officers, directors and/or shareholders of LGT, the burden was on the defendant directors to demonstrate that the transactions between SLE and LGT were fair and reasonable....

Under normal circumstances the directors of a corporation may determine, in the exercise of their business judgment, what contracts the corporation will enter into and what consideration is adequate, without review of the merits of their decisions by the courts. The business judgment rule places a heavy burden on shareholders who would attack corporate transactions. But the business judgment rule presupposes

---

3. [6] Donald's sisters Carol and Margaret sold their SLE shares to LGT in 1972 and 1973 respectively. Alan, who had sold his LGT stock in 1967, sold his SLE stock to LGT in 1972.

that the directors have no conflict of interest. When a shareholder attacks a transaction in which the directors have an interest other than as directors of the corporation, the directors may not escape review of the merits of the transaction. At common law such a transaction was voidable unless shown by its proponent to be fair, and reasonable to the corporation. [New York Business Corporation Law (BCL)] § 713, in both its current and its prior versions, carries forward this common law principle, and provides special rules for scrutiny of a transaction between the corporation and an entity in which its directors are directors or officers or have a substantial financial interest.

The current version of § 713, which became effective on September 1, 1971, and governs at least so much of the dealing between SLE and LGT as occurred after that date, expressly provides that a contract between a corporation and an entity in which its directors are interested may be set aside unless the proponent of the contract "shall establish affirmatively that the contract or transaction was fair and reasonable as to the corporation at the time it was approved by the board...." § 713(b). Thus when the transaction is challenged in a derivative action against the interested directors, they have the burden of proving that the transaction was fair and reasonable to the corporation.

The same was true under the predecessor to § 713(b), former § 713(a)(3), which was in effect prior to September 1, 1971. Section 713(a)(3) was not explicit as to the burden of proof, but simply stated that a transaction with interested directors would not be voidable "If the contract or transaction is fair and reasonable as to the corporation at the time it is approved by the board...." The consensus among the commentators was that § 713(a)(3) carried forward the common law rule, which placed the burden of proof as to fairness on the interested directors. We agree with this construction.

During the entire period 1966–1972, Richard, Alan and Leon, Jr., were directors of both SLE and LGT; there were no SLE directors who were not also directors of LGT. Richard, Alan and Leon, Jr., were all shareholders of LGT in 1966, and from 1967 to 1972 Richard and Leon, Jr., were the sole shareholders of LGT. Under BCL § 713, therefore, Richard, Alan and Leon, Jr., had the burden of proving that $14,400 was a fair and reasonable annual rent for the SLE property for the period February 28, 1966 through June 1, 1972.

Our review of the record convinces us that defendants failed to carry their burden. At trial, there was no direct testimony as to what would have been a fair rental during the relevant period, *i.e.*, 1966 to 1972, and the evidence that was introduced fell far short of establishing that $14,400 was a fair annual rental value for those years.

Quite clearly Richard, Alan and Leon, Jr., had made no effort to determine contemporaneously what rental would be fair during the years 1966–1972. Their view was that the rent should simply cover expenses and that SLE existed for the benefit of LGT. During this period no appraisals were made; no attempts were made to sell or rent the Property; no thought whatever was given to whether $14,400 was a fair and reasonable rent even when real estate taxes had risen to consume nearly all of that amount.

Defendants offered instead evidence of rents paid on other properties. Among their best evidence was the expert testimony of Harvey Rosenbloom, a real estate appraiser. Rosenbloom testified that two other East Avenue buildings, which the district court found to be comparable to the 260 East Avenue premises, were leased at lower per-square-foot rentals than was paid by LGT to SLE. However, as to one of these properties, Rosenbloom testified only to rent paid in 1973 and 1974, and did not consider the 1966–1972 period. As to the other property, Rosenbloom described a fifteen year lease that was entered into in 1961. This testimony, while perhaps not wholly irrelevant to the issues in this suit, fell far short of demonstrating what rental the Property could have fetched in 1966, or in any other of the relevant years. Indeed, Rosenbloom himself testified that rental value could well be different for each year of the period. Thus, rentals that Rosenbloom testified were agreed to in 1961 or 1973 might well have been unfair in 1966 or 1967. This evidence thus could not support a finding that defendants acted fairly in maintaining an annual rental of $14,400 during the years from 1966 to 1972.

Defendants also produced considerable evidence that over the relevant period, the East End neighborhood had been on an economic decline; that businesses had been leaving the area; that urban renewal projects and increased crime had depressed property values there; and that the area had, in general, become a less desirable place to do business. There was also evidence of specific developments that had an adverse effect on the Property: for example, the street running along one side of the Property was made a one-way street, thus limiting customers' access to LGT's premises. The district court credited all of this testimony, and it is fair to say that defendants proved that there was a general downward trend in the value of the Property. However, as noted above, defendants did not establish what was a fair rental value for the Property in 1966. Absent such a point of reference, a general downward trend in value is of no assistance in determining whether the rental actually paid was fair and reasonable during the ensuing years.

Moreover, working in reverse, some of defendants' own evidence as to the value of the Property at the end of the relevant period suggested that $14,400 was less than a fair rental in 1966, and that the figure of $38,099, estimated by plaintiff's expert, was perhaps not far off the mark. First, there was a variety of evidence suggesting that in 1972 the Property was worth more than $200,000. An appraisal by defense witness Harold Grunert in 1972 set the fair market value of the Property as of June 30, 1972, at $220,000. In 1972 Leon, Jr., had offered personally to buy the Property for $200,000, an offer which Richard had rejected. And in 1971, Richard had informed Donald that evaluations by another appraiser, Harold Galloway, had set the value of the Property at $200,000 and $236,000. Second, defendants' expert witness Rosenbloom, asked what he would consider a fair rent for the property, given Grunert's 1972 valuation of $220,000, stated that ten percent of the value would be inadequate and that fifteen to seventeen percent would be closer to adequate. Fifteen percent of $220,000 would have yielded a rent of $33,000 on the basis of the 1972 valuation. Grunert's own expert testimony was entirely consistent with this. While he had made no estimate as to the fair rental value of the property for 1966–1972, he opined that a fair rental as of June 30, 1972, would be $20–21,000 with the tenant paying all expenses including real estate taxes. According to Richard, SLE's real estate taxes in 1972 were about $12,000. Thus Grunert's testimony, too, suggests about $33,000 as the fair rental value in 1972. Finally, consistent with their view of the general downward economic trend, Richard and Alan conceded that, whatever the Property was worth in 1972, it was worth more in 1966. Thus the evidence presented by defendants, far from carrying their burden of showing that $14,400 was a fair and reasonable annual rental in 1966–1972, suggested that the fair rental value of the Property throughout that period exceeded $33,000 per year.

The defendants argued, however, that LGT could not have afforded to pay SLE rent higher than $14,400. They produced evidence designed to show that LGT had made little profit; that this low profitability was due to the expenses of maintenance and upkeep of the 260 East Avenue property; and that LGT therefore would not have been able to pay a higher rent to SLE. The district court credited this evidence, finding that LGT had "experienced a number of years of very severe losses," that during the period from 1962–1973, LGT's overall profit was only $53,876, and that payment of rent at the rate of $39,099 per year during this period could have led to the "demise" of LGT. These findings have only a distorted relationship to this lawsuit.

The period in issue here is 1966–1972. The only "severe" losses shown, totaling nearly $83,000, occurred in 1963 and 1973. Their inclusion in the computation of what LGT could afford to pay in 1966–1972 was patently unfair. In fact LGT's only unprofitable year during the period in issue was 1969 when its loss was small: $1,168. LGT's after-tax profits in 1966–1972 in fact totaled $102,963, or an average of $14,709 per year. Thus, even on paper, LGT could have "afforded" to double its rent payments to SLE during the period in question.

Moreover, the proposition that LGT could not afford to pay as rent more than what its own books showed as profits ignores the fact that LGT was owned and managed by members of the Lewis family, some of whom were also employees of that corporation. It is entirely possible that these family members granted to themselves unusually high salaries or other perquisites, thus reducing LGT's paper profits....

Finally, even if we were to assume that LGT's financial records provided a fair basis for evaluating the SLE-LGT transactions, defendants would not have carried their burden of proof. Defendants did not demonstrate that SLE could not have found some other tenant, stronger financially than LGT, which would have been willing and able to pay a higher rental. Even given the general downward trend of the East Avenue neighborhood, it is entirely possible that at least during the early years of the 1966–1972 period, such a tenant might have been secured. No effort was made during that period to rent to anyone other than LGT.

We conclude, therefore, that defendants failed to prove that the rental paid by LGT to SLE for the years 1966–1972 was fair and reasonable. Thus, Donald is not required to sell his SLE shares to LGT without such upward adjustment in the June 1, 1972, book value of SLE as may be necessary to reflect the amount by which the fair rental value of the Property exceeded $14,400 in any of the years 1966–1972.

III

... We remand to the district court (a) for the entry of judgment in favor of SLE against Richard, Alan and Leon, Jr., jointly and severally, in such amount as the district court shall determine to be equal to the amounts by which the annual fair rental value of the Property exceeded $14,400 in the period February 28, 1966–June 1, 1972, (b) for an accounting as to the value of Donald's SLE shares as of June 1, 1972, in light of such judgment, (c) for an order, following such accounting, of specific performance of the shareholders' agreement, and (d) for such other proceedings as are not inconsistent with this opinion.

Notes and Questions

1. What governance advice would you offer to boards of companies such as SLE? Are there procedures you might design for having transactions with interested directors, like Richard, approved? What if such transactions were approved by fully informed, disinterested directors — that is, directors not otherwise involved in the transaction, who know of the interests of directors like Richard, and still concluded that the transaction was in the best interest of the corporation? What about having fully informed, disinterested shareholders approve such interested transactions? These procedures are considered further in the materials that follow.

2. What is "fairness"? Fairness is an abstract concept and what constitutes fairness to the corporation depends on the facts of the particular case and the court's determination of what is relevant.

What factors did the court in *Lewis* use to determine if the fairness test was satisfied? Did it consider both the corporate decision-making process (procedural fairness) and the merits and terms of the transaction itself (substantive fairness)? How did the court's analysis differ from that used in the duty of care cases? Would the defendants' conduct in the *Lewis* case satisfy the business judgment rule test?

3. Comment to ALI § 5.02(a)(2)(A) offers this explanation of the fairness standard:

> The test of fairness is an objective test, and the director or senior executive must show that the transaction is in the "range of reasonableness" within which conflict-of-interest transactions may be sustained ... In determining fairness, the court may take into account the process by which the transaction was shaped and approved (such as whether there was undue pressure on the corporate decisionmaker who approved the transaction) and any relevant objective indicators of fairness of price (such as comparable transactions between parties dealing at arm's length).
>
> In an additional sense as well, "fairness" and the "best interests of the corporation" may need to be considered in the full business context of a transaction, particularly when it is not in the interest of the corporation to forgo a transaction with a director or senior executive. For example, a particular parcel of property or contract right held by a director or senior executive may have a special strategic value to the corporation that would warrant pay-

ing a price above general market, that is, a price higher than anyone who would not place such strategic value on the property would pay. If the corporation would be warranted in paying that price to a third party dealing at arm's length it would also be warranted in paying that price to the director or senior executive. In mandating fairness, the law does not command the board to ignore the aggregate effects on the corporation of a transaction, and to focus in an isolated fashion only on the fair value of a single component of the total transaction. Fairness will only be judged as of the time a transaction is entered into....

In determining whether to enter into a transaction, the corporate decision-maker who approves the transaction should consider not only whether the transaction will be fair to the corporation as measured by comparison with an arm's-length transaction with an unrelated third party, but whether the transaction affirmatively will be in the corporation's best interest, as in a transaction with an unrelated party. For example, the purchase of a parcel of property by the corporation from a director may be at a fair price, but the corporate decisionmaker should also determine that it is beneficial to the corporation to acquire the property for its business.

... One other issue that is of particular relevance in duty of fair dealing cases is how the transaction is initiated. If a transaction is initiated on behalf of the corporation by disinterested persons, that circumstance may under the facts of a particular case assist in supporting the fairness of the transaction to the corporation.

4. The classic duty of loyalty case deals with a director or officer that enters into a transaction with his or her corporation. There are other circumstances, however, when directors may not be so directly linked, but may still have a pecuniary interest in a corporate decision. What should be the scope of the duty of loyalty?

MBCA §§ 8.60–8.61, for instance, have attempted to answer this difficult question. It posits that only "director's conflicting interest transactions" are subject to its duty of loyalty provisions and offer definitions on each key term (*e.g.*, § 8.60(1) (defining "conflicting interest"), § 8.60(2) (defining "director's conflicting interest transaction"), and § 8.60(3) (defining "related person")). A review of § 8.60 and the Official Comments, however, results in a definitional and situational maze that does not appear to offer a particularly simple or clear answer.

The ALI Introductory Note to Part V. Duty of Fair Dealing, begins by revisiting the term "duty of loyalty."

Courts have traditionally analyzed the obligation of a director or officer who acts with a pecuniary interest in a matter in terms of a "duty of loyalty" to the corporation. However, courts have also used the term "duty of loyalty" in non-pecuniary contexts where a director or officer may be viewed as having conflicting interests. For clarity of analysis, ... [the ALI] avoids the use of the term "duty of loyalty," when dealing with the obligations of a person who acts with a pecuniary interest in a matter, and instead uses the term "duty of fair dealing."

In doing so, ... [the ALI] does not address nonpecuniary conflict-of-interest situations which might be dealt with by the courts in appropriate cases.

It is not the purpose of ... [the ALI] to set forth the duty of fair dealing as a final, complete, and unchanging concept, but rather to recognize that it is a concept that will continue to evolve as new problems and circumstances stimulate and challenge our system of corporate governance.

Rather than developing a single set of principles, the ALI offers different governing principles for varied "duty of fair dealing" fact patterns (*e.g.*, § 5.02 (directors' transactions with the corporation), § 5.03 (directors' compensation arrangements), and § 5.07 (transactions between corporations with common directors)).

Section III
Safe Harbor Statutes

At early common law, many courts held that transactions between a corporation and its directors were *void*. The duty of loyalty prohibited them. But this strict rule prevented corporations from entering into a wide range of advantageous deals. Later courts thus relaxed that stance to render such transactions *voidable*, meaning they were not automatically disallowed, but could be challenged or sustained based upon a judicial assessment of their fairness to the corporation. The burden of proving fairness was on the directors and the business judgment rule did not apply.

This contemporary common law approach is illustrated by *Lewis v. S. L. & E., Inc.*, holding that directors breached their duty of loyalty by effecting interested transactions that were not fair to the corporation. (Chapter 12 explores the notion of entire fairness in Delaware corporation case law.) Notably, the *Lewis* shareholder also asserted that the transactions amounted to *waste* of corporate assets, an independent, though difficult, ground for shareholders to challenge board action.

Due to perceived rigidity even of this more relaxed common law standard, state legislatures (Delaware in 1967 and most others since 1970) adopted so-called interested director transaction statutes (many of which also address interested officers). These were intended in part to embrace the contemporary common law standard of judicial review for fairness and reject the early common law's rigid stance that held these transactions void.

The statutes also authorize internal corporate procedures to approve interested transactions to protect them from judicial rebuke, typically by disinterested and fully-informed director or shareholder approval. The statutes vary in their exact language and, given varying state case law at the time of adoption, the result can be varying judicial approaches to the particular language and interpretations of them.

In general, however, there seem to be three interpretive stances on the consequences of using the director or shareholder approval routes to interested transactions:

(1) shifting the burden of proof and standard of review from directors proving fairness to shareholders subject to the business judgment rule, probably the majority position;

(2) shifting only the burden of proof, from directors proving fairness to shareholders proving unfairness; or

(3) merely codifying the contemporary common law standard but effecting no other change, so that directors still have the burden of proving fairness, seemingly a minority position.

Courts generally hold that interested-director transaction statutes are additional, alternative, means of handling interested transactions. That is, if no authorized approval procedure is followed, the contemporary common law test of fairness, with the burden of proof on directors, applies. There is also agreement that directors have the burden of proving that statutory requirements were met (for example, that the approving directors or shareholders were disinterested and fully informed).

Under the majority position, if directors can demonstrate that the statutory requirements were met, then the transaction enjoys a safe harbor from judicial review as to the claim concerning the interested person's conflict of interest. That does not, however, extinguish other claims shareholders may be able to assert to challenge the transaction. Such alternative grounds include gross negligence, other duty of loyalty breaches that the interested person may have committed plus waste, fraud or lack of board authority. The following principal and note cases explore these matters.

Marciano v. Nakash

Delaware Supreme Court
535 A.2d 400 (1987)

WALSH, JUSTICE:

This is an appeal from a decision of the Court of Chancery which validated a claim in liquidation of Gasoline, Ltd. ("Gasoline"), a Delaware corporation, placed in custodial status pursuant to 8 Del. C. § 226 by reason of a deadlock among its board of directors. Fifty percent of Gasoline is owned by Ari, Joe, and Ralph Nakash (the "Nakashes") and fifty percent by Georges, Maurice, Armand and Paul Marciano (the "Marcianos"). The Vice Chancellor ruled that $2.5 million in loans made by the Nakashes faction to Gasoline were valid and enforceable debts of the corporation, notwithstanding their origin in self-dealing transactions....

I

... The liquidation proceeding marked the end of a joint venture launched in 1984 by the Marcianos and the Nakashes to market designer jeans and sportswear. Through a solely owned corporation called Guess? Inc. ("Guess"), the California based Marcianos had been engaged in the design and distribution of stylized jeans for several years. In 1983 they decided to form a separate division to market copies of Guess creations in a broader retail market. In order to secure financing and broaden market exposure the Marcianos entered into negotiations with the New York based Nakash brothers, the owners of Jordache Enterprises, Inc. a leading manufacturer of jeans. Ultimately, it was agreed that the Nakashes would receive fifty percent of the stock of Guess for a consideration of $4.7 million. As a result, the three Nakash brothers joined three of the Marcianos on the Guess board of directors.

Similarly, when Gasoline was formed, stock ownership and board composition was shared equally by the two families. Although corporate control and direction were equally divided, from an operational standpoint Gasoline functioned in New York under the Nakashes' operational guidance while the parent, Guess, continued under the primary attention of the Marcianos. Differences between the two factions quickly surfaced with resulting deadlocks at the director level of both Guess and Gasoline....

... Prior to March, 1986, Gasoline had secured the necessary financing to support its inventory purchases from the Israel Discount Bank in New York. The bank advanced funds at one percent above prime rate secured by Gasoline's accounts receivable and the Nakashes' personal guarantee. Although requested to do so, the Marcianos were unwilling to participate in loan guarantees because of their dissatisfaction with the Nakashes' management. In response, the Nakashes withdrew their guarantees causing the Israel Discount Bank to terminate its outstanding loan of $1.6 million.

Without consulting the Marcianos, the Nakashes advanced approximately $2.3 million of their personal funds to Gasoline to enable the corporation to pay outstanding bills and acquire inventory. In June, 1986, the Nakashes arranged for U.F. Factors, an entity owned by them, to assume their personal loans and become Gasoline's lender. U.F. Factors charged interest at one percent over prime to which the Nakashes added one percent for their personal guarantees of the U.F. Factors loan. As of April 24, 1987, Gasoline's debt to U.F. Factors amounted to $2,575,000 of which $25,000 represented the Nakashes' guarantee fee. Another Nakash entity, Jordache Enterprises, also sought payment from Gasoline of two percent of the company's gross sales, or $30,000 for warehousing and invoicing services.

... At the time of the court-ordered sale of assets, the Nakashes and their entities were general creditors of Gasoline. If allowed in full the Nakashes' claim will exhaust Gasoline's assets, leaving nothing for its shareholders.

The parties agree that the loans made by the Nakashes to Gasoline were interested transactions. The Nakashes as officers of Gasoline executed the various documents which supported the loans and at the same time guaranteed those loans extended through their wholly owned entities. It is also not disputed that, given the control deadlock, the questioned transactions did not receive majority approval of Gasoline's directors or shareholders. The Marcianos argue that the loan transaction is voidable at the option of the corporation notwithstanding its fairness or the good faith of its participants. A review of this contention, rejected by the Court of Chancery, requires analysis of the concept of director self-dealing under Delaware law.

II

It is a long-established principle of Delaware corporate law that the fiduciary relationship between directors and the corporation imposes fundamental limitations on the extent to which a director may benefit from dealings with the corporation he serves. Thus, the "voting [for] and taking" of compensation may be deemed "constructively fraudulent" in the absence of shareholder ratification, or statutory or bylaw authorization. *Cahall v. Lofland*, Del. Ch., 114 A. 224, 232 (1921). Perhaps the strongest condemnation of interested director conduct appears in *Potter v. Sanitary Co. of America*, Del. Ch., 194 A. 87 (1937), a decision which the Marcianos advance as definitive of the rule of **per se voidability**. In *Potter* the Court of Chancery characterized transactions between corporations having common directors and officers "constructively fraudulent," absent shareholder ratification.

Support can also be found for the per se rule of voidability in this Court's decision in *Kerbs v. California Eastern Airways Inc.*, Del. Supr., 90 A.2d 652 (1952). The *Kerbs* court, in considering the validity of a profit sharing plan, ruled that the self-interest of the directors who voted on the plan caused the transaction to be voidable. The court concluded that the profit sharing plan was voidable based on the common law rule that the vote of an interested director will not be counted in determining whether the challenged action received the affirmative vote of a majority of the board of directors.

The principle of per se voidability for interested transactions, which is sometimes characterized as the common law rule, was significantly ameliorated by the 1967 enactment of Section 144 of the Delaware General Corporation Law.[4] The Marcianos argue that section 144(a) provides the only basis for immunizing self-interested transactions and since none of the statute's component tests are satisfied the stricture of the common law per se rule applies. The Vice Chancellor agreed that the disputed loans did not withstand a section 144(a) analysis but ruled that the common law

---

4. [2] Section 144 of Title 8 Del. C. provides:

(a) No contract or transaction between a corporation and 1 or more of its directors or officers, or between a corporation and any other corporation, partnership, association, or other organization in which 1 or more of its directors or officers, are directors or officers, or have a financial interest, shall be void or voidable solely for this reason, or solely because the director or officer is present at or participates in the meeting of the board or committee which authorizes the contract or transaction, or solely because his or their votes are counted for such purpose, if:

(1) The material facts as to the directors/officers' relationship or interest and as to the contract or transaction are disclosed or are known to the board of directors or the committee, and the board or committee in good faith authorizes the contract or transaction by the affirmative votes of a majority of the disinterested directors, even though the disinterested directors be less than a quorum; or

(2) The material facts as to the directors'/officers' relationship or interest and as to the contract or transaction are disclosed or are known to the shareholders entitled to vote thereon, and the contract or transaction is specifically approved in good faith by vote of the shareholders; or

(3) The contract or transaction is fair as to the corporation as of the time it is authorized, approved or ratified, by the board of directors, a committee or the shareholders.

(b) Common or interested directors may be counted in determining the presence of a quorum at a meeting of the board of directors or of a committee which authorizes the contract or transaction.

rule did not invalidate transactions determined to be intrinsically fair. We agree that section 144(a) does not provide the only validation standard for interested transactions.

It overstates the common law rule to conclude that relationship, alone, is the controlling factor in interested transactions. Although the application of the per se voidability rule in early Delaware cases resulted in the invalidation of interested transactions, the result was not dictated simply by a tainted relationship. Thus in *Potter*, the Court, while adopting the rule of voidability, emphasized that interested transactions should be subject to close scrutiny. Where the undisputed evidence tended to show that the transaction would advance the personal interests of the directors at the expense of stockholders, the stockholders, upon discovery, are entitled to disavow the transaction. *Potter*, 194 A. at 91. Further, the court examined the motives of the defendant directors and the effect the transaction had on the corporation and its shareholders. *Id.*

In other Delaware cases, decided before the enactment of section 144, interested director transactions were deemed voidable only after an examination of the fairness of a particular transaction *vis-à-vis* the nonparticipating shareholders and a determination of whether the disputed conduct received the approval of a noninterested majority of directors or shareholders. The latter test is now crystallized in the ratification criteria of section 144(a), although the non-quorum restriction of *Kerbs* has been superseded by the language of subparagraph (b) of section 144.

 The Marcianos view compliance with section 144 as the sole basis for avoiding the per se rule of voidability. The Court of Chancery rejected this contention and we agree that it is not consonant with Delaware corporate law. This Court in *Fliegler v. Lawrence*, Del. Supr., 361 A.2d 218 (1976), a post-section 144 decision, refused to view section 144 as either completely preemptive of the common law duty of director fidelity or as constituting a grant of broad immunity. As we stated in *Fliegler*: "It merely removes an 'interested director' cloud when its terms are met and provides against invalidation of an agreement 'solely' because such a director or officer is involved." *Id.* at 222. In *Fliegler* this Court applied a two-tiered analysis: application of section 144 coupled with an intrinsic fairness test.

If section 144 validation of interested director transactions is not deemed exclusive, as *Fliegler* clearly holds, the continued viability of the intrinsic fairness test is mandated not only by fact situations, such as here present, where shareholder deadlock prevents ratification but also where shareholder control by interested directors precludes independent review. Indeed, if an independent committee of the board, contemplated by section 144(a)(1) is unavailable, the sole forum for demonstrating intrinsic fairness may be a judicial one. In such situations the intrinsic fairness test furnishes the substantive standard against which the evidential burden of the interested directors is applied. It is this burden which was addressed by this Court in *Weinberger v. UOP, Inc.*, Del. Supr., 457 A.2d 701 (1983):

> When directors of a Delaware corporation are on both sides of a transaction, they are required to demonstrate their utmost good faith and the most scrupulous inherent fairness of the bargain.

...

> The requirement of fairness is unflinching in its demand that where one stands on both sides of a transaction, he has the burden of establishing its entire fairness, sufficient to pass the test of careful scrutiny by the courts.

Id. at 710.

This case illustrates the limitation inherent in viewing section 144 as the touchstone for testing interested director transactions. Because of the shareholder deadlock, even if the Nakashes had attempted to invoke section 144, it was realistically unavailable. The ratification process contemplated by section 144 presupposes the functioning of corporate constituencies capable of providing assents. Just as the statute cannot "sanction unfairness" neither can it invalidate fairness if, upon judicial review, the transaction withstands close scrutiny of its intrinsic elements.[5]

III

On the issue of intrinsic fairness, the Court of Chancery concluded that the "U.F. Factors loans compared favorably with the terms available from unrelated lenders" and that the need for external financing had been clearly demonstrated. The Marcianos attack this ruling as factually and legally erroneous. Since the Vice Chancellor's factual findings were arrived at after an evidentiary hearing we are not free to reject them unless they are without record support or not the product of a logical deductive process. We find this standard to have been fully satisfied here.

Apart from the initial investment of $300,000 contributed equally by the Marcianos and the Nakashes, Gasoline's financial needs had been met through external borrowings. It is unnecessary to lay blame for the impasse which resulted in the Marcianos refusal to supply additional equity funding. It suffices to note that throughout 1985 and 1986, Gasoline was able to function only through cash advances from, and loans obtained by, the Nakashes, first through the Israel Discount Bank and later through U.F. Factors. During this period the evidence reflects the continued threat of bank overdrafts and inability to pay for purchases, particularly imported finished goods.

A finding of fairness is particularly appropriate in this case because the evidence indicates that the loans were made by the Nakashes with the *bona fide* intention of assisting Gasoline's efforts to remain in business. Directors who advance funds to a corporation in such circumstances do not forfeit their claims as creditors merely because of relationship....

---

5. [3] Although in this case none of the curative steps afforded under section 144(a) were available because of the director-shareholder deadlock, a non-disclosing director seeking to remove the cloud of interestedness would appear to have the same burden under section 144(a)(3), as under prior case law, of proving the intrinsic fairness of a questioned transaction which had been approved or ratified by the directors or shareholders. Folk, *The Delaware General Corp. Law: A Commentary and Analysis*, 86 (1972). On the other hand, approval by fully-informed disinterested directors under section 144(a)(1), or disinterested stockholders under section 144(a)(2), permits invocation of the business judgment rule and limits judicial review to issues of gift or waste with the burden of proof upon the party attacking the transaction.

We hold, therefore, that the Court of Chancery properly applied the intrinsic fairness test in determining the validity of the interested director transactions and its finding of full fairness is clearly supported by the record....

Notes and Questions

1. In *Marciano*, the court found that directors' and shareholders' approvals were not possible as a practical matter given the fifty-fifty split and disagreements. Absent following such routes as authorized by DGCL § 144(a)(1) or (2), the court explained that litigation should proceed in the traditional common law manner, as in *Lewis v. S.L. & E*, with the burden of proving fairness on the interested defendants. Given that, what do you make of the language of DGCL § 144(a)(3)? It speaks in terms of abstract fairness to the corporation but fails to address the burden of proof, which, as *Lewis* and *Marciano* suggests, is a pivotal issue in interested director transaction cases.

2. Concerning routes authorized by DGCL § 144(a)(1) or (2), the following case clearly holds what *Marciano* stated in dicta. The effect was to convert the case from what would have been a duty of loyalty claim evaluated under the entire fairness standard, with the burden on the interested directors, into a duty of care case evaluated under the business judgment rule, with the burden of overcoming that formidable barrier on the plaintiff shareholders.

Benihana of Tokyo, Inc. v. Benihana, Inc.

Delaware Supreme Court
906 A.2d 114 (2006)

BERGER, JUSTICE:

In this appeal, we consider whether Benihana, Inc. was authorized to issue $20 million in preferred stock and whether Benihana's board of directors acted properly in approving the transaction. We conclude that the Court of Chancery's factual findings are supported by the record and that it correctly applied settled law in holding that the stock issuance was lawful and that the directors did not breach their fiduciary duties. Accordingly, we affirm.

Factual and Procedural Background. Rocky Aoki founded Benihana of Tokyo, Inc. (BOT), and its subsidiary, Benihana, which own and operate Benihana restaurants in the United States and other countries. Aoki owned 100% of BOT until 1998, when he pled guilty to insider trading charges. In order to avoid licensing problems created by his status as a convicted felon, Aoki transferred his stock to the Benihana Protective Trust. The trustees of the Trust were Aoki's three children (Kana Aoki Nootenboom, Kyle Aoki and Kevin Aoki) and Darwin Dornbush (who was then the family's attorney, a Benihana director, and, effectively, the company's general counsel).

Benihana, a Delaware corporation, has two classes of common stock. There are approximately 6 million shares of Class A common stock outstanding. Each share has 1/10 vote and the holders of Class A common are entitled to elect 25% of the directors. There are approximately 3 million shares of Common stock outstanding. Each share of Common has one vote and the holders of Common stock are entitled to elect the remaining 75% of Benihana's directors. Before the transaction at issue, BOT owned 50.9% of the Common stock and 2% of the Class A stock. The nine member board of directors is classified and the directors serve three-year terms.[6]

In 2003, shortly after Aoki married Keiko Aoki, conflicts arose between Aoki and his children. In August, the children were upset to learn that Aoki had changed his will to give Keiko control over BOT. Joel Schwartz, Benihana's president and chief executive officer, also was concerned about this change in control. He discussed the situation with Dornbush, and they briefly considered various options, including the issuance of sufficient Class A stock to trigger a provision in the certificate of incorporation that would allow the Common and Class A to vote together for 75% of the directors.

The Aoki family's turmoil came at a time when Benihana also was facing challenges. Many of its restaurants were old and outmoded. Benihana hired WD Partners to evaluate its facilities and to plan and design appropriate renovations. The resulting Construction and Renovation Plan anticipated that the project would take at least five years and cost $56 million or more. . . . [T]he company retained Morgan Joseph & Co. to develop other financing options.

On January 9, 2004, after evaluating Benihana's financial situation and needs, Fred Joseph, of Morgan Joseph, met with Schwartz, Dornbush and John E. Abdo, the board's executive committee. Joseph expressed concern that Benihana would not have sufficient available capital to complete the Construction and Renovation Plan and pursue appropriate acquisitions. Benihana was conservatively leveraged, and Joseph discussed various financing alternatives, including bank debt, high yield debt, convertible debt or preferred stock, equity and sale/leaseback options.

The full board met with Joseph on January 29, 2004. He reviewed all the financing alternatives that he had discussed with the executive committee, and recommended that Benihana issue convertible preferred stock. Joseph explained that the preferred stock would provide the funds needed for the Construction and Renovation Plan and also put the company in a better negotiating position if it sought additional financing from Wachovia [then a large commercial bank].

Joseph gave the directors a board book, marked "Confidential," containing an analysis of the proposed stock issuance (the Transaction). The book included, among others, the following anticipated terms: (i) issuance of $20,000,000 of preferred stock, convertible into Common stock; (ii) dividend of 6% +/– 0.5%; (iii) conversion premium of 20% +/– 2.5%; (iv) buyer's approval required for material corporate transactions; and (v) one to two board seats to the buyer. At trial, Joseph testified that the terms had been chosen by looking at comparable stock issuances and analyzing the Morgan Joseph proposal under a theoretical model.

---

6. [1] The directors at the time of the challenged transaction were: Dornbush, John E. Abdo, Norman Becker, Max Pine, Yoshihiro Sano, Joel Schwartz, Robert B. Sturges, Takanori Yoshimoto, and Kevin Aoki.

The board met again on February 17, 2004, to review the terms of the Transaction. The directors discussed Benihana's preferences and Joseph predicted what a buyer likely would expect or require....

Shortly after the February meeting, Abdo contacted Joseph and told him that BFC Financial Corporation was interested in buying the new convertible stock.[7] In [April 2004], Joseph sent BFC a private placement memorandum. Abdo [representing BFC] negotiated with Joseph for several weeks. They agreed to the Transaction on the following basic terms: (i) $20 million issuance in two tranches of $10 million each, with the second tranche to be issued one to three years after the first; (ii) BFC obtained one seat on the board, and one additional seat if Benihana failed to pay dividends for two consecutive quarters; (iii) BFC obtained preemptive rights on any new voting securities; (iv) 5% dividend; (v) 15% conversion premium; (vi) BFC had the right to force Benihana to redeem the preferred stock in full after ten years; and (vii) the stock would have immediate "as if converted" voting rights. Joseph testified that he was satisfied with the negotiations, as he had obtained what he wanted with respect to the most important points.

On April 22, 2004, Abdo sent a memorandum to Dornbush, Schwartz and Joseph, listing the agreed terms of the Transaction. He did not send the memorandum to any other members of the Benihana board. Schwartz did tell Becker, Sturges, Sano, and possibly Pine that BFC was the potential buyer. At its next meeting, held on May 6, 2004, the entire board was officially informed of BFC's involvement in the Transaction. Abdo made a presentation on behalf of BFC and then left the meeting. Joseph distributed an updated board book, which explained that Abdo had approached Morgan Joseph on behalf of BFC, and included the negotiated terms. The trial court found that the board was not informed that Abdo had negotiated the deal on behalf of BFC. But the board did know that Abdo was a principal of BFC. After discussion, the board reviewed and approved the Transaction, subject to the receipt of a fairness opinion.

On May 18, 2004, after he learned that Morgan Joseph was providing a fairness opinion, Schwartz publicly announced the stock issuance. Two days later, Aoki's counsel sent a letter asking the board to abandon the Transaction and pursue other, more favorable, financing alternatives. The letter expressed concern about the directors' conflicts, the dilutive effect of the stock issuance, and its "questionable legality." Schwartz gave copies of the letter to the directors at the May 20 board meeting, and Dornbush advised that he did not believe that Aoki's concerns had merit. Joseph and another Morgan Joseph representative then joined the meeting by telephone and opined that the Transaction was fair from a financial point of view. The board then approved the Transaction.

During the following two weeks, Benihana received three alternative financing proposals. Schwartz asked Becker, Pine and Sturges to act as an independent com-

---

7. [5] BFC, a publicly traded Florida corporation, is a holding company for several investments. Abdo is a director and vice chairman. He owns 30% of BFC's stock.

mittee and review the first offer. The committee decided that the offer was inferior and not worth pursuing. Morgan Joseph agreed with that assessment. Schwartz referred the next two proposals to Morgan Joseph, with the same result.

On June 8, 2004, Benihana and BFC executed the Stock Purchase Agreement. On June 11, 2004, the board met and approved resolutions ratifying the execution of the Stock Purchase Agreement and authorizing the stock issuance. Schwartz then reported on the three alternative proposals that had been rejected by the ad hoc committee and Morgan Joseph. On July 2, 2004, BOT filed this action against all of Benihana's directors, except Kevin Aoki, alleging breaches of fiduciary duties; and against BFC, alleging that it aided and abetted the fiduciary violations. Three months later, as the parties were filing their pre-trial briefs, the board again reviewed the Transaction. After considering the allegations in the amended complaint, the board voted once more to approve it....

Discussion

Before addressing the directors' conduct and motivation, we must decide whether Benihana's certificate of incorporation authorized the board to issue preferred stock with preemptive rights. Article 4, ¶ 2 of the certificate provides that, "[n]o stockholder shall have any preemptive right to subscribe to or purchase any issue of stock ... of the corporation...." Article 4(b) authorizes the board to issue:

> Preferred Stock of any series and to state in the resolution or resolutions providing for the issuance of shares of any series the voting powers, if any, designations, preferences and relative, participating, optional or other special rights, and the qualifications, limitations or restrictions of such series to the full extent now or hereafter permitted by the law of the State of Delaware....

BOT contends that Article 4, ¶ 2 clearly and unambiguously prohibits preemptive rights. BOT acknowledges that Article 4(b) gives the board so-called "blank check" authority to designate the rights and preferences of Benihana's preferred stock. Reading the two provisions together, BOT argues that they give the board blank check authority to designate rights and preferences as to all enumerated matters except preemptive rights.

The trial court reviewed the history of 8 Del. C. § 102, and decided that the boilerplate language in Article 4, ¶ 2 merely confirms that no stockholder has preemptive rights under common law. As a result, the seemingly absolute language in ¶ 2 has no bearing on the availability of contractually created preemptive rights. The trial court explained:

> Before the 1967 amendments, § 102(b)(3) provided that a certificate of incorporation may contain provisions "limiting or denying to the stockholders the preemptive rights to subscribe to any or all additional issues of stock of the corporation." As a result, a common law rule developed that shareholders possess preemptive rights unless the certificate of incorporation provided otherwise. In 1967 the Delaware Legislature reversed this presumption. Section 102(b)(3) was amended to provide in relevant part: "No stockholder shall have any preemptive right ... unless, and except to the extent that, such right is expressly granted to him in the certificate of incorporation."

Thereafter, companies began including boilerplate language in their charters to clarify that no shareholder possessed preemptive rights under common law.

The blank check provision in Benihana's Certificate of Incorporation suggests that the certificate was never intended to limit Benihana's ability to issue preemptive rights by contract to purchasers of preferred stock. Therefore, I do not read Article 4 of the charter as doing anything more than confirming that the common law presumption does not apply and that the Certificate of Incorporation itself does not grant any preemptive rights.

It is settled law that certificates of incorporation are contracts, subject to the general rules of contract and statutory construction. Thus, if the charter language is clear and unambiguous, it must be given its plain meaning. If there is ambiguity, however, the language must be construed in a manner that will harmonize the apparent conflicts and give effect to the intent of the drafters. The Court of Chancery properly applied these principles, and we agree with its conclusion that the Benihana certificate does not prohibit the issuance of preferred stock with preemptive rights.

Even if the Benihana board had the power to issue the disputed stock, BOT maintains that the trial court erred in finding that it acted properly in approving the Transaction. Specifically, BOT argues that the Court of Chancery erred: (1) by applying 8 Del. C. § 144(a)(1), because the board did not know all material facts before it approved the Transaction; (2) by applying the business judgment rule, because Abdo breached his fiduciary duties; and (3) by finding that the board's primary purpose in approving the Transaction was not to dilute BOT's voting power.

A. Section 144(a)(1) Approval

Section 144 of the Delaware General Corporation Law provides a safe harbor for interested transactions, like this one, if "[t]he material facts as to the director's ... relationship or interest and as to the contract or transaction are disclosed or are known to the board of directors ... and the board ... in good faith authorizes the contract or transaction by the affirmative votes of a majority of the disinterested directors...." After approval by disinterested directors, courts review the interested transaction under the business judgment rule, which "is a presumption that in making a business decision, the directors of a corporation acted on an informed basis, in good faith and in the honest belief that the action taken was in the best interest of the company." [*Aronson v. Lewis*, 473 A.2d 805, 812 (Del.1984).]

BOT argues that § 144(a)(1) is inapplicable because, when they approved the Transaction, the disinterested directors did not know that Abdo had negotiated the terms for BFC. Abdo's role as negotiator is material, according to BOT, because Abdo had been given the confidential term sheet prepared by Joseph and knew which of those terms Benihana was prepared to give up during negotiations. We agree that the board needed to know about Abdo's involvement in order to make an informed decision. The record clearly establishes, however, that the board possessed that material information when it approved the Transaction on May 6, 2004 and May 20, 2004.

Shortly before the May 6 meeting, Schwartz told Becker, Sturges and Sano that BFC was the proposed buyer. Then, at the meeting, Abdo made the presentation on behalf of BFC. Joseph's board book also explained that Abdo had made the initial contact that precipitated the negotiations. The board members knew that Abdo is a director, vice-chairman, and one of two people who control BFC. Thus, although no one ever said, "Abdo negotiated this deal for BFC," the directors understood that he was BFC's representative in the Transaction. As Pine testified, "whoever actually did the negotiating, [Abdo] as a principal would have to agree to it. So whether he sat in the room and negotiated it or he sat somewhere else and was brought the results of someone else's negotiation, he was the ultimate decision-maker." Accordingly, we conclude that the disinterested directors possessed all the material information on Abdo's interest in the Transaction, and their approval at the May 6 and May 20 board meetings satisfies § 144(a)(1).[8]

B. Abdo's Alleged Fiduciary Violation

BOT next argues that the Court of Chancery should have reviewed the Transaction under an entire fairness standard because Abdo breached his duty of loyalty when he used Benihana's confidential information to negotiate on behalf of BFC. This argument starts with a flawed premise. The record does not support BOT's contention that Abdo used any confidential information against Benihana. Even without Joseph's comments at the February 17 board meeting, Abdo knew the terms a buyer could expect to obtain in a deal like this. Moreover, as the trial court found, "the negotiations involved give and take on a number of points" and Benihana "ended up where [it] wanted to be" for the most important terms. Abdo did not set the terms of the deal; he did not deceive the board; and he did not dominate or control the other directors' approval of the Transaction. In short, the record does not support the claim that Abdo breached his duty of loyalty.

C. Dilution of BOT's Voting Power

Finally, BOT argues that the board's primary purpose in approving the Transaction was to dilute BOT's voting control. BOT points out that Schwartz was concerned about BOT's control in 2003 and even discussed with Dornbush the possibility of issuing a huge number of Class A shares. Then, despite the availability of other financing options, the board decided on a stock issuance, and agreed to give BFC "as if converted" voting rights. According to BOT, the trial court overlooked this powerful evidence of the board's improper purpose.

It is settled law that, "corporate action ... may not be taken for the sole or primary purpose of entrenchment." [*Williams v. Geier*, 671 A.2d 1368, 1381 n.28 (Del. 1996).] Here, however, the trial court found that "the primary purpose of the ... Transaction was to provide what the directors subjectively believed to be the best financing vehicle available for securing the necessary funds to pursue the agreed upon Construction

---

8. [16] The Court of Chancery also decided that the Benihana directors' ratifying votes on June 11 provide independent grounds to uphold their decision under § 144.... Assuming that the board's initial decision was not an informed one, we question how a vote taken after the June 8 closing could ratify the earlier approval. *See Smith v. Van Gorkom*, 488 A.2d 858, 885–888 (Del.1985). We need not reach this question, however, as we find that the board was adequately informed of all material facts before voting at the May 6 and May 20 meetings.

and Renovation Plan for the Benihana restaurants." That factual determination has ample record support, especially in light of the trial court's credibility determinations....

Notes

1. Mr. Aoki undoubtedly would have been better off had the Benihana charter *granted*, rather than *denied*, preemptive rights.

2. The theory of director entrenchment is considered more fully later in this book in connection with transactions involving corporate control.

Section IV
Good Faith

Traditionally, corporate fiduciary duties are classified as the duty of care and the duty of loyalty. As Chapter 10 explored, the duty of care generally is presumed discharged under the business judgment rule. As the previous section of this Chapter 11 indicated, the duty of loyalty may be satisfied by appropriate use of safe harbor statutes.

From time to time, courts have considered how the notion of good faith operates in the contexts traditionally governed by the duties of care and loyalty. Occasionally, this can lead to the impression that the notion of good faith is a separate fiduciary duty of corporate directors and officers. But it is probably more plausible to understand the notion of good faith as an element of one or both those doctrines, not as an independent duty.

At stake in such classifications are matters such as the tools that have developed under the respective duties of care and loyalty, including the burden of proof, applicability of exculpation provisions such as DGCL § 102(b)(7) for the duty of care (but not the duty of loyalty) and whether safe harbor statutes such as DGCL § 144 may be invoked (typically used to address duty of loyalty matters, but not matters of duty of care). The following pair of opinions by the Delaware Supreme Court, written by different Justices but within six months of one another, may illuminate these stakes and related doctrinal choices.

In re The Walt Disney Company

Delaware Supreme Court
906 A.2d 27 (2006)

JACOBS, JUSTICE:

In August 1995, Michael Ovitz ("Ovitz") and The Walt Disney Company ("Disney" or the "Company") entered into an employment agreement under which Ovitz would serve as President of Disney for five years. In December 1996, only fourteen months after he commenced employment, Ovitz was terminated without cause, resulting in a severance payout to Ovitz valued at approximately $130 million.

In January 1997, several Disney shareholders brought derivative actions in the Court of Chancery, on behalf of Disney, against Ovitz and the directors of Disney who served at the time of the events complained of (the "Disney defendants"). The plaintiffs claimed that the $130 million severance payout was the product of ... breaches of fiduciary duty by the Disney defendants, and a waste of assets. After the disposition of several pretrial motions and an appeal to this Court, the case was tried before the Chancellor over 37 days between October 20, 2004 and January 19, 2005. In August 2005, the Chancellor handed down a well-crafted 174 page Opinion and Order, determining that "the director defendants did not breach their fiduciary duties or commit waste." [We affirm.]

I. THE FACTS

[Michael Eisner, Disney's Board Chair and Chief Executive Officer, identified Ovitz as the prime candidate for President and Chief Operating Officer, and potential successor to Eisner. Ovitz] was the leading partner and one of the founders of Creative Artists Agency ("CAA"), the premier talent agency whose business model had reshaped the entire industry. By 1995, CAA had 550 employees and a roster of about 1400 of Hollywood's top actors, directors, writers, and musicians. That roster generated about $150 million in annual revenues and an annual income of over $20 million for Ovitz, who was regarded as one of the most powerful figures in Hollywood.

Eisner and Ovitz had enjoyed a social and professional relationship that spanned nearly 25 years. Although in the past the two men had casually discussed possibly working together, in 1995, when Ovitz began negotiations to leave CAA and join Music Corporation of America ("MCA"), Eisner became seriously interested in recruiting Ovitz to join Disney. Eisner shared that desire with Disney's board members on an individual basis.

A. *Negotiation of The Ovitz Employment Agreement.* Eisner and Irwin Russell, who was a Disney director and chairman of the compensation committee, first approached Ovitz about joining Disney. Their initial negotiations were unproductive, however, because at that time MCA had made Ovitz an offer that Disney could not match. The MCA-Ovitz negotiations eventually fell apart, and Ovitz returned to CAA in mid-1995. [Negotiations later resumed.] ...

... Ovitz owned 55% of CAA and earned approximately $20 to $25 million a year from that company. From the beginning Ovitz made it clear that he would not give up his 55% interest in CAA without "downside protection." Considerable negotiation then ensued over downside protection issues. During the summer of 1995, the parties agreed to a draft version of Ovitz's employment agreement (the "OEA") modeled after Eisner's.... [The draft agreement contemplated a 5-year term yielding Ovitz millions of Disney stock options vesting at various times with a guaranteed value of at least $50 million. It also provided that if Ovitz's employment ended before the term absent cause, he would be entitled to a so-called "non-fault termination" (NFT) payment measured as remaining salary, $7.5 million in annual "bonuses," vesting of most stock options and an additional $10 million payment in lieu of other options.]

As the basic terms of the OEA were crystallizing, Russell prepared and gave Ovitz and Eisner a "case study" to explain those terms.... Russell acknowledged ... that Ovitz was an "exceptional corporate executive" and "highly successful and unique entrepreneur" who merited "downside protection and upside opportunity." Both would be required to enable Ovitz to adjust to the reduced cash compensation he would receive from a public company, in contrast to the greater cash distributions and other perquisites more typically available from a privately held business. But, Russell did caution that Ovitz's salary would be at the top level for any corporate officer and significantly above that of the Disney CEO. Moreover, the stock options granted under the OEA would exceed the standards applied within Disney and corporate America and would "raise very strong criticism." ...

To assist in evaluating the financial terms of the OEA, Russell recruited Graef Crystal, an executive compensation consultant, and Raymond Watson, a member of Disney's compensation committee and a past Disney board chairman who had helped structure ... Eisner's compensation package.... On August 10, Russell, Watson and Crystal met. They discussed and generated a set of values using different and various inputs and assumptions, accounting for different numbers of options, vesting periods, and potential proceeds of option exercises at various times and prices.... Two days later, Crystal faxed to Russell a memorandum concluding that the OEA would provide Ovitz with approximately $23.6 million per year for the first five years, or $23.9 million a year over seven years if Ovitz exercised a two year renewal option. Those sums, Crystal opined, would approximate Ovitz's current annual compensation at CAA....

On September 26, 1995, the Disney compensation committee (which consisted of [four directors, including Russell and Watson]) met for one hour to consider, among other agenda items, the proposed terms of the OEA. A term sheet was distributed at the meeting, although a draft of the OEA was not.... The committee voted unanimously to approve the OEA terms, subject to "reasonable further negotiations within the framework of the terms and conditions" described in the OEA.

Immediately after the compensation committee meeting, the Disney board met in executive session. The board was told about the reporting structure to which Ovitz had agreed, but [some] initial negative reaction of [two other senior Disney officers] to the hiring was not recounted. Eisner led the discussion relating to Ovitz, and Watson then explained his analysis, and both Watson and Russell responded to questions from the board. After further deliberation, the board voted unanimously to elect Ovitz as President.

[After two more compensation committee meetings, that included amendments to Disney's stock option plans, those plans and related agreements] provided that in the event of a non-fault termination ("NFT"), Ovitz's options would be exercisable until the later of September 30, 2002 or twenty-four months after termination, but in no event later than October 16, 2005.... [T]he committee unanimously approved the terms of the OEA and the award of Ovitz's options.... [The Disney board never did.]

B. *Ovitz's Performance As President of Disney.* Ovitz's tenure as President ... began on October 1, 1995, the date that the OEA was executed. When Ovitz took office, the initial reaction was optimistic, and Ovitz did make some positive contributions while serving as President of the Company. By the fall of 1996, however, it had become clear that Ovitz was "a poor fit with his fellow executives." ... Although the plaintiffs attempted to show that Ovitz acted improperly (*i.e.*, with gross negligence or malfeasance) while in office, the Chancellor found that the trial record did not support those accusations....

C. *Ovitz's Termination At Disney.* After [various] discussions between [Sandy] Litvack [Disney's general counsel] and Ovitz, Eisner and Ovitz met several times. During those meetings they discussed Ovitz's future.... [They concluded that Ovitz should be terminated. Ovitz refused to leave Disney voluntarily.]

During this period Eisner was also working with Litvack to explore whether they could terminate Ovitz under the OEA for cause. If so, Disney would not owe Ovitz the NFT payment. From the very beginning, Litvack advised Eisner that he did not believe there was cause to terminate Ovitz under the OEA. Litvack's advice never changed....

Eisner testified that after Litvack notified Eisner that he did not believe cause existed, Eisner "checked with almost anybody that [he] could find that had a legal degree, and there was just no light in that possibility. It was a total dead end from day one." ...

Litvack ... believed that it would be inappropriate, unethical and a bad idea to attempt to coerce Ovitz (by threatening a for-cause termination) into negotiating for a smaller NFT package than the OEA provided. The reason was that when pressed by Ovitz's attorneys, Disney would have to admit that in fact there was no cause, which could subject Disney to a wrongful termination lawsuit. Litvack believed that attempting to avoid legitimate contractual obligations would harm Disney's reputation as an honest business partner and would affect its future business dealings.

The Disney board next met on November 25.... An executive session took place after the board meeting, from which Ovitz was excluded. At that session, Eisner informed the directors who were present that he intended to fire Ovitz by year's end....

After returning from [a] trip, Ovitz met with Eisner on December 3, to discuss his termination. Ovitz asked for several concessions, all of which Eisner ultimately rejected. Eisner told Ovitz that all he would receive was what he had contracted for in the OEA....

Ovitz's termination was memorialized in a letter, dated December 12, 1996, that Litvack signed on Eisner's instruction. The board was not shown the letter, nor did it meet to approve its terms.... Although the board did not meet to vote on the termination, the Chancellor found that most, if not all, of the Disney directors trusted Eisner's and Litvack's conclusion that there was no cause to terminate Ovitz, and that Ovitz should be terminated without cause even though that involved making the costly NFT payment. [Disney thereafter paid Ovitz the nearly $130 million and a month later shareholders filed this lawsuit.]

[II. CLAIMS]

... A. *Claims Arising From The Approval Of The OEA And Ovitz's Election As President.*... [T]he appellants' core argument in the trial court was that the Disney defendants' approval of the OEA and election of Ovitz as President were not entitled to business judgment rule protection, because those actions were either grossly negligent or not performed in good faith. [After trial, the] Court of Chancery rejected these arguments, and held that the appellants had failed to prove that the Disney defendants had breached any fiduciary duty....

1. The Due Care Determinations.... (a) [Due Care and Bad Faith.] [The first] argument is best understood against the backdrop of the presumptions that cloak director action being reviewed under the business judgment standard. Our law presumes that "in making a business decision the directors of a corporation acted on an informed basis, in good faith, and in the honest belief that the action taken was in the best interests of the company." Those presumptions can be rebutted if the plaintiff shows that the directors breached their fiduciary duty of care or of loyalty or acted in bad faith. If that is shown, the burden then shifts to the director defendants to demonstrate that the challenged act or transaction was entirely fair to the corporation and its shareholders....

The appellants' first claim is that the Chancellor erroneously (i) failed to make a "threshold determination" of gross negligence, and (ii) "conflated" the appellants' burden to rebut the business judgment presumptions, with an analysis of whether the directors' conduct fell within the 8 Del. C. § 102(b)(7) provision that precludes exculpation of directors from monetary liability "for acts or omissions not in good faith." The argument runs as follows: *Emerald Partners v. Berlin*, 787 A.2d 85, 93 (Del. 2001), required the Chancellor first to determine whether the business judgment rule presumptions were rebutted based upon a showing that the board violated its duty of care, *i.e.*, acted with gross negligence. If gross negligence were established, the burden would shift to the directors to establish that the OEA was entirely fair. Only if the directors failed to meet that burden could the trial court then address the directors' Section 102(b)(7) exculpation defense, including the statutory exception for acts not in good faith.

This argument lacks merit. To make the argument the appellants must ignore the distinction between (i) a determination of bad faith for the threshold purpose of rebutting the business judgment rule presumptions, and (ii) a bad faith determination for purposes of evaluating the availability of charter-authorized exculpation from monetary damage liability after liability has been established. Our law clearly permits a judicial assessment of director good faith for that former purpose. Nothing in *Emerald Partners* requires the Court of Chancery to consider only evidence of lack of due care (*i.e.* gross negligence) in determining whether the business judgment rule presumptions have been rebutted....

(b) [Full Board Approval.] The appellants next challenge the Court of Chancery's determination that the full Disney board was not required to consider and approve the OEA, because the Company's governing instruments allocated that decision to the compensation committee. This challenge also cannot survive scrutiny.

As the Chancellor found, under the Company's governing documents the board of directors was responsible for selecting the corporation's officers, but under the compensation committee charter, the committee was responsible for establishing and approving the salaries, together with benefits and stock options, of the Company's CEO and President. The compensation committee also had the charter-imposed duty to "approve employment contracts, or contracts at will" for "all corporate officers who are members of the Board of Directors regardless of salary." That is exactly what occurred here. The full board ultimately selected Ovitz as President and the compensation committee considered and ultimately approved the OEA, which embodied the terms of Ovitz's employment, including his compensation.

The Delaware General Corporation Law (DGCL) expressly empowers a board of directors to appoint committees and to delegate to them a broad range of responsibilities, [DGCL § 141(c)] which may include setting executive compensation. Nothing in the DGCL mandates that the entire board must make those decisions. At Disney, the responsibility to consider and approve executive compensation was allocated to the compensation committee, as distinguished from the full board. The Chancellor's ruling—that executive compensation was to be fixed by the compensation committee—is legally correct....

(c) [Individual Directors or Board as Whole.] In the Court of Chancery the appellants argued that the board had failed to exercise due care, using a director-by-director, rather than a collective analysis. In this Court, however, the appellants argue that the Chancellor erred in following that very approach. An about-face, the appellants now claim that in determining whether the board breached its duty of care, the Chancellor was legally required to evaluate the actions of the ... board collectively.

... The argument ... fails because nowhere do appellants identify how this supposed error caused them any prejudice. The Chancellor viewed the conduct of each director individually, and found that no director had breached his or her fiduciary duty of care (as members of the full board) in electing Ovitz as President or (as members of the compensation committee) in determining Ovitz's compensation. If, as appellants now argue, a due care analysis of the board's conduct must be made collectively, it is incumbent upon them to show how such a collective analysis would yield a different result. The appellants' failure to do that dooms their argument on this basis as well.

(d) [Compensation Committee.] The appellants next challenge the Chancellor's determination that although the compensation committee's decision-making process fell far short of corporate governance "best practices," the committee members breached no duty of care in considering and approving the NFT terms of the OEA.... [T]he overall thrust of [this] claim is that the compensation committee approved the OEA with NFT provisions that could potentially result in an enormous payout, without informing themselves of what the full magnitude of that payout could be....

... [A] helpful approach is to compare what actually happened here to what would have occurred had the committee followed a "best practices" (or "best case") scenario, from a process standpoint. In a "best case" scenario, all committee members would have received [and evaluated extensive analytical information concerning the assumptions underlying the compensation arrangements and a range of possible costs to Disney of a non-fault termination compensation clause]. Had that scenario been followed, there would be no dispute (and no basis for litigation) over what information was furnished to the committee members or when it was furnished. Regrettably, the committee's informational and decisionmaking process used here was not so tidy. That is one reason why the Chancellor found that although the committee's process did not fall below the level required for a proper exercise of due care, it did fall short of what best practices would have counseled.

The Disney compensation committee met twice: on September 26 and October 16, 1995. The minutes of the September 26 meeting reflect that the committee approved the terms of the OEA (at that time embodied in the form of a letter agreement), except for the option grants, which were not approved until October 16.... At the September 26 meeting, the compensation committee considered a "term sheet" which, in summarizing the material terms of the OEA, relevantly disclosed that in the event of a non-fault termination, Ovitz would receive: (i) the present value of his salary ($1 million per year) for the balance of the contract term, (ii) the present value of his annual bonus payments (computed at $7.5 million) for the balance of the contract term, (iii) a $10 million termination fee, and (iv) the acceleration of [stock option rights].

Thus, the compensation committee knew that in the event of an NFT, Ovitz's severance payment alone could be in the range of $40 million cash, plus the value of the accelerated options. Because the actual payout to Ovitz was approximately $130 million, of which roughly $38.5 million was cash, the value of the options at the time of the NFT payout would have been about $91.5 million. Thus, the issue may be framed as whether the compensation committee members knew, at the time they approved the OEA, that the value of the option component of the severance package could reach the $92 million order of magnitude if they terminated Ovitz without cause after one year. The evidentiary record shows that the committee members were so informed.

On this question the documentation is far less than what best practices would have dictated. There is no exhibit to the minutes that discloses, in a single document, the estimated value of the accelerated options in the event of an NFT termination after one year. The information imparted to the committee members on that subject is, however, supported by other evidence, most notably the trial testimony of various witnesses about spreadsheets that were prepared for the compensation committee meetings. [Nevertheless, the committee had some information about the magnitude of an NFT payout from similar payouts previously made to other executives and an understanding of what Ovitz would be giving up in terms of other employment opportunities in order to accept the offer to work at Disney.]

... If measured in terms of the documentation that would have been generated if "best practices" had been followed, that record leaves much to be desired.... But, the Chancellor also found that despite its imperfections, the evidentiary record was sufficient to support the conclusion that the compensation committee had adequately informed itself of the potential magnitude of the entire severance package, including the options, that Ovitz would receive in the event of an early NFT....

2. The Good Faith Determinations. The Court of Chancery held that the business judgment rule presumptions protected the [director] decisions..., not only because they had acted with due care but also because they had not acted in bad faith. That latter ruling, the appellants claim, was reversible error because the Chancellor formulated and then applied an incorrect definition of bad faith. In its Opinion the Court of Chancery defined bad faith as follows:

... the concept of intentional dereliction of duty, a conscious disregard for one's responsibilities, is an appropriate (although not the only) standard for determining whether fiduciaries have acted in good faith. Deliberate indifference and inaction in the face of a duty to act is, in my mind, conduct that is clearly disloyal to the corporation. It is the epitome of faithless conduct.

The appellants contend that definition is erroneous for two reasons. First they claim that the trial court had adopted a different definition in its 2003 decision denying the motion to dismiss the complaint.... Their argument runs as follows: under the Chancellor's 2003 definition of bad faith, the directors must have "consciously and intentionally disregarded their responsibilities, adopting a 'we don't care about the risks' attitude concerning a material corporate decision." Under the 2003 formulation, appellants say, "directors violate their duty of good faith if they are making material decisions without adequate information and without adequate deliberation[,]" but under the 2005 post-trial definition, bad faith requires proof of a subjective bad motive or intent. This definitional change, it is claimed, was procedurally prejudicial because appellants relied on the 2003 definition in presenting their evidence of bad faith at the trial. Without any intervening change in the law, the Court of Chancery could not unilaterally alter its definition and then hold the appellants to a higher, more stringent standard.

Second, the appellants claim that the Chancellor's post-trial definition of bad faith is erroneous substantively. They argue that the 2003 formulation was (and is) the correct definition, because it is "logically tied to board decision-making under the duty of care." The post-trial formulation, on the other hand, "wrongly incorporated substantive elements regarding the rationality of the decisions under review rather than being constrained, as in a due care analysis, to strictly procedural criteria." We conclude that both arguments must fail.[9]

The appellants' first argument—that there is a real, significant difference between the Chancellor's pre-trial and post-trial definitions of bad faith—is plainly wrong. We perceive no substantive difference between the Court of Chancery's 2003 definition of bad faith—a "conscious[ ] and intentional[ ] disregard[ ] [of] responsibilities, adopting a 'we don't care about the risks' attitude ..."—and its 2005 post-trial definition—an "intentional dereliction of duty, a conscious disregard for one's responsibilities." Both formulations express the same concept, although in slightly different language.

The most telling evidence that there is no substantive difference between the two formulations is that the appellants are forced to contrive a difference. Appellants assert that under the 2003 formulation, "directors violate their duty of good faith if they are making material decisions without adequate information and without adequate deliberation." For that ipse dixit they cite no legal authority. That comes as no

9. [95] The appellants also assert that the Chancellor erred by imposing upon them the burden of proving that the Disney directors acted in bad faith. That argument fails because our decisions clearly hold that for purposes of rebutting the business judgment presumptions, the plaintiffs have the burden of proving bad faith. *Emerald Partners*, 787 A.2d at 91; [*Brehm v. Eisner*, 746 A.2d 244, 264 (Del. 2000)].

surprise because their verbal effort to collapse the duty to act in good faith into the duty to act with due care, is not unlike putting a rabbit into the proverbial hat and then blaming the trial judge for making the insertion.

The appellants cite only the Chancellor's 2003 pre-trial Opinion. But nowhere on the cited page does the Court suggest, let alone rule, that making material decisions without adequate information and without adequate deliberation, without more, constitutes bad faith. To the contrary, immediately after identifying the good faith standard, the Court states that "[k]nowing or deliberate indifference by a director to his or her duty to act faithfully and with appropriate care is conduct that, in my opinion, that may not have been taken honestly and in good faith to advance the best interests of the company."

The appellants essentially concede that their proof of bad faith is insufficient to satisfy the standard articulated by the Court of Chancery. That is why they ask this Court to treat a failure to exercise due care as a failure to act in good faith. Unfortunately for appellants, that "rule," even if it were accepted, would not help their case. If we were to conflate these two duties and declare that a breach of the duty to be properly informed violates the duty to act in good faith, the outcome would be no different, because, as the Chancellor and we now have held, the appellants failed to establish any breach of the duty of care. To say it differently, even if the Chancellor's definition of bad faith were erroneous, the error would not be reversible because the appellants cannot satisfy the very test they urge us to adopt.

For that reason, our analysis of the appellants' bad faith claim could end at this point. In other circumstances it would. This case, however, is one in which the duty to act in good faith has played a prominent role, yet to date is not a well-developed area of our corporate fiduciary law. Although the good faith concept has recently been the subject of considerable scholarly writing, which includes articles focused on this specific case, the duty to act in good faith is, up to this point relatively uncharted. Because of the increased recognition of the importance of good faith, some conceptual guidance to the corporate community may be helpful. For that reason we proceed to address the merits of the appellants' second argument.

The precise question is whether the Chancellor's articulated standard for bad faith corporate fiduciary conduct — intentional dereliction of duty, a conscious disregard for one's responsibilities — is legally correct. In approaching that question, we note that the Chancellor characterized that definition as "an appropriate (although not the only) standard for determining whether fiduciaries have acted in good faith." That observation is accurate and helpful, because as a matter of simple logic, at least three different categories of fiduciary behavior are candidates for the "bad faith" pejorative label.

The first category involves so-called "subjective bad faith," that is, fiduciary conduct motivated by an actual intent to do harm. That such conduct constitutes classic, quintessential bad faith is a proposition so well accepted in the liturgy of fiduciary law that it borders on axiomatic. We need not dwell further on this category, because no such conduct is claimed to have occurred, or did occur, in this case.

The second category of conduct, which is at the opposite end of the spectrum, involves lack of due care—that is, fiduciary action taken solely by reason of gross negligence and without any malevolent intent. In this case, appellants assert claims of gross negligence to establish breaches not only of director due care but also of the directors' duty to act in good faith. Although the Chancellor found, and we agree, that the appellants failed to establish gross negligence, to afford guidance we address the issue of whether gross negligence (including a failure to inform one's self of available material facts), without more, can also constitute bad faith. The answer is clearly no.

From a broad philosophical standpoint, that question is more complex than would appear, if only because (as the Chancellor and others have observed) "issues of good faith are (to a certain degree) inseparably and necessarily intertwined with the duties of care and loyalty…." But, in the pragmatic, conduct-regulating legal realm which calls for more precise conceptual line drawing, the answer is that grossly negligent conduct, without more, does not and cannot constitute a breach of the fiduciary duty to act in good faith. The conduct that is the subject of due care may overlap with the conduct that comes within the rubric of good faith in a psychological sense, but from a legal standpoint those duties are and must remain quite distinct. Both our legislative history and our common law jurisprudence distinguish sharply between the duties to exercise due care and to act in good faith, and highly significant consequences flow from that distinction.

The Delaware General Assembly has addressed the distinction between bad faith and a failure to exercise due care (*i.e.*, gross negligence) in two separate contexts. The first is Section 102(b)(7) of the DGCL, which authorizes Delaware corporations, by a provision in the certificate of incorporation, to exculpate their directors from monetary damage liability for a breach of the duty of care. That exculpatory provision affords significant protection to directors of Delaware corporations. The statute carves out several exceptions, however, including most relevantly, "for acts or omissions not in good faith…." Thus, a corporation can exculpate its directors from monetary liability for a breach of the duty of care, but not for conduct that is not in good faith. To adopt a definition of bad faith that would cause a violation of the duty of care automatically to become an act or omission "not in good faith," would eviscerate the protections accorded to directors by the General Assembly's adoption of Section 102(b)(7).

A second legislative recognition of the distinction between fiduciary conduct that is grossly negligent and conduct that is not in good faith, is Delaware's indemnification statute, found at 8 Del. C. § 145. To oversimplify,[10] subsections (a) and (b) of that statute permit a corporation to indemnify (*inter alia*) any person who is or was a director, officer, employee or agent of the corporation against expenses (including attorneys' fees), judgments, fines and amounts paid in settlement of specified actions, suits or proceedings, where (among other things): (i) that person is, was, or is threatened to be made a party to that action, suit or proceeding, and (ii) that person "acted in good faith and in a manner the person reasonably believed to be in or not opposed

---

10. [The law of indemnification of directors and officers, and this Delaware statute, are treated more fully in Chapter 15.—Eds.]

to the best interests of the corporation...." Thus, under Delaware statutory law a director or officer of a corporation can be indemnified for liability (and litigation expenses) incurred by reason of a violation of the duty of care, but not for a violation of the duty to act in good faith.

Section 145, like Section 102(b)(7), evidences the intent of the Delaware General Assembly to afford significant protections to directors (and, in the case of Section 145, other fiduciaries) of Delaware corporations. To adopt a definition that conflates the duty of care with the duty to act in good faith by making a violation of the former an automatic violation of the latter, would nullify those legislative protections and defeat the General Assembly's intent. There is no basis in policy, precedent or common sense that would justify dismantling the distinction between gross negligence and bad faith.

That leaves the third category of fiduciary conduct, which falls in between the first two categories of (1) conduct motivated by subjective bad intent and (2) conduct resulting from gross negligence. This third category is what the Chancellor's definition of bad faith — intentional dereliction of duty, a conscious disregard for one's responsibilities — is intended to capture. The question is whether such misconduct is properly treated as a non-exculpable, non-indemnifiable violation of the fiduciary duty to act in good faith. In our view it must be, for at least two reasons.

First, the universe of fiduciary misconduct is not limited to either disloyalty in the classic sense (*i.e.*, preferring the adverse self-interest of the fiduciary or of a related person to the interest of the corporation) or gross negligence. Cases have arisen where corporate directors have no conflicting self-interest in a decision, yet engage in misconduct that is more culpable than simple inattention or failure to be informed of all facts material to the decision. To protect the interests of the corporation and its shareholders, fiduciary conduct of this kind, which does not involve disloyalty (as traditionally defined) but is qualitatively more culpable than gross negligence, should be proscribed. A vehicle is needed to address such violations doctrinally, and that doctrinal vehicle is the duty to act in good faith....

Second, the legislature has also recognized this intermediate category of fiduciary misconduct, which ranks between conduct involving subjective bad faith and gross negligence. Section 102(b)(7)(ii) of the DGCL expressly denies money damage exculpation for "acts or omissions not in good faith or which involve intentional misconduct or a knowing violation of law." By its very terms that provision distinguishes between "intentional misconduct" and a "knowing violation of law" (both examples of subjective bad faith) on the one hand, and "acts ... not in good faith," on the other. Because the statute exculpates directors only for conduct amounting to gross negligence, the statutory denial of exculpation for "acts ... not in good faith" must encompass the intermediate category of misconduct captured by the Chancellor's definition of bad faith.

For these reasons, we uphold the Court of Chancery's definition as a legally appropriate, although not the exclusive, definition of fiduciary bad faith. We need go no further. To engage in an effort to craft (in the Court's words) "a definitive and categorical definition of the universe of acts that would constitute bad faith" would be unwise and is unnecessary to dispose of the issues presented on this appeal. [Under this definition, we sustain the Chancellor's finding that the Disney directors acted in good faith when approving the OEA and electing Ovitz as President.]

B. *Claims Arising From The Payment Of The NFT Severance Payout To Ovitz.* The appellants advance three alternative claims ... that even if the OEA approval was legally valid, the NFT severance payout to Ovitz pursuant to the OEA was not. [We reject each of them.]

1. [Action By New Board Required?] The Chancellor determined that although the board as constituted upon Ovitz's termination (the "new board") had the authority to terminate Ovitz, neither that board nor the compensation committee was required to act, because Eisner also had, and properly exercised, that authority. The new board, the Chancellor found, was not required to terminate Ovitz under the company's internal documents. Without such a duty to act, the new board's failure to vote on the termination could not give rise to a breach of the duty of care or the duty to act in good faith. ...

Article Tenth of the Company's certificate of incorporation in effect at the termination plainly states that:

> The officers of the Corporation shall be chosen in such a manner, shall hold their offices for such terms and shall carry out such duties as are determined solely by the Board of Directors, subject to the right of the Board of Directors to remove any officer or officers at any time with or without cause.

Article IV of Disney's bylaws provided that the Board Chairman/CEO "shall, subject to the provisions of the Bylaws and the control of the Board of Directors, have general and active management, direction, and supervision over the business of the Corporation and over its officers...."

The issue is whether the Chancellor's interpretation of these instruments, as giving the board and the Chairman/CEO concurrent power to terminate a lesser officer, is legally permissible. In two hypothetical cases there would be a clear answer. If the certificate of incorporation vested the power of removal exclusively in the board, then absent an express delegation of authority from the board, the presiding officer would not have a concurrent removal power. If, on the other hand, the governing instruments expressly placed the power of removal in both the board and specified officers, then there would be concurrent removal power. This case does not fall within either hypothetical fact pattern, because Disney's governing instruments do not vest the removal power exclusively in the board, nor do they expressly give the Board Chairman/CEO a concurrent power to remove officers. Read together, the governing instruments do not yield a single, indisputably clear answer, and could reasonably be interpreted either way. For that reason, with respect to this specific issue, the governing instruments are ambiguous.

Here, the extrinsic evidence clearly supports the conclusion that the board and Eisner understood that Eisner, as Board Chairman/CEO had concurrent power with the board to terminate Ovitz as President. In that regard, the Chancellor credited the testimony of new board members that Eisner, as Chairman and CEO, was empowered to terminate Ovitz without board approval or intervention; and ... many Company officers were terminated [in a related period] and the board never once took action in connection with their terminations. Because Eisner possessed, and exercised, the power to terminate Ovitz unilaterally, we find that the Chancellor correctly concluded that the new board was not required to act in connection with that termination, and, therefore, the board did not violate any fiduciary duty to act with due care or in good faith....

2. [Cause Determination.] It is undisputed that Litvack and Eisner (based on Litvack's advice) both concluded that if Ovitz was to be terminated, it could only be without cause, because no basis existed to terminate Ovitz for cause. The appellants argued in the Court of Chancery that the business judgment presumptions do not protect that conclusion, because by permitting Ovitz to be terminated without cause, Litvack and Eisner acted in bad faith and without exercising due care. Rejecting that claim, the Chancellor determined independently, as a matter of fact and law, that (1) Ovitz had not engaged in any conduct as President that constituted gross negligence or malfeasance — the standard for an NFT under the OEA; and (2) in arriving at that same conclusion in 1996, Litvack and Eisner did not breach their fiduciary duty of care or their duty to act in good faith. [We agree with the Chancellor.]

3. [Director Reliance.] The appellants' third claim of error challenges the Chancellor's conclusion that the remaining new board members could rely upon Litvack's and Eisner's advice that Ovitz could be terminated only without cause. The short answer to that challenge is that, for the reasons previously discussed, the advice the remaining directors received and relied upon was accurate. Moreover, the directors' reliance on that advice was found to be in good faith. Although formal board action was not necessary, the remaining directors all supported the decision to terminate Ovitz based on the information given by Eisner and Litvack. The Chancellor found credible the directors' testimony that they believed that Disney would be better off without Ovitz, and the appellants offer no basis to overturn that finding....

[III. WASTE]

The appellants' final claim is that even if the approval of the OEA was protected by the business judgment rule presumptions, the payment of the severance amount to Ovitz constituted waste.... To recover on a claim of corporate waste, the plaintiffs must shoulder the burden of proving that the exchange was "so one sided that no business person of ordinary, sound judgment could conclude that the corporation has received adequate consideration." [*Brehm v. Eisner*, 746 A.2d 244, 263 (Del. 2000)]. A claim of waste will arise only in the rare, "unconscionable case where directors irrationally squander or give away corporate assets." *Id.* This onerous standard for waste is a corollary of the proposition that where business judgment presumptions are applicable, the board's decision will be upheld unless it cannot be "attributed to any rational business purpose." *Sinclair Oil Corp. v. Levien*, 280 A.2d 717, 720 (Del. 1971); *see also Unocal Corp. v. Mesa Petroleum Co.*, 946, 954 (Del. 1985).

The claim that the payment of the NFT amount to Ovitz, without more, constituted waste is meritless on its face, because at the time the NFT amounts were paid, Disney was contractually obligated to pay them. The payment of a contractually obligated amount cannot constitute waste, unless the contractual obligation is itself wasteful. Accordingly, the proper focus of a waste analysis must be whether the amounts required to be paid in the event of an NFT were wasteful ex ante.

Appellants claim that the NFT provisions of the OEA were wasteful because they incentivized Ovitz to perform poorly in order to obtain payment of the NFT provisions. The Chancellor found that the record did not support that contention:

> [T]erminating Ovitz and paying the NFT did not constitute waste because he could not be terminated for cause and because many of the defendants gave credible testimony that the Company would be better off without Ovitz, meaning that would be impossible for me to conclude that the termination and receipt of NFT benefits result in "an exchange that is so one sided that no business person of ordinary, sound judgment could conclude that the corporation has received adequate consideration," or a situation where the defendants have "irrationally squandered or given away corporate assets." In other words, defendants did not commit waste.

That ruling is erroneous, the appellants argue, because the NFT provisions of the OEA were wasteful in their very design. Specifically, the OEA gave Ovitz every incentive to leave the Company before serving out the full term of his contract. The appellants urge that although the OEA may have induced Ovitz to join Disney as President, no contractual safeguards were in place to retain him in that position. In essence, appellants claim that the NFT provisions of the OEA created an irrational incentive for Ovitz to get himself fired.

That claim does not come close to satisfying the high hurdle required to establish waste. The approval of the NFT provisions in the OEA had a rational business purpose: to induce Ovitz to leave [his employment elsewhere], at what would otherwise be a considerable cost to him, in order to join Disney. The Chancellor found that the evidence does not support any notion that the OEA irrationally incentivized Ovitz to get himself fired. Ovitz had no control over whether or not he would be fired, either with or without cause. To suggest that at the time he entered into the OEA Ovitz would engineer an early departure at the cost of his extraordinary reputation in the entertainment industry and his historical friendship with Eisner, is not only fanciful but also without proof in the record....

Notes

As the foregoing opinion suggests, the talk of good faith (and bad faith) in the various *Disney* opinions led many lawyers and scholars to speculate concerning whether Delaware corporate law should be conceived as including a separate fiduciary duty (apart from the duties of care and loyalty) denominated as a duty of good faith. This speculation should be further informed by the following Delaware Supreme Court opinion, *Stone v. Ritter*, issued about six months after the foregoing opinion in the *Disney* litigation. On *Disney*'s articulation of the concept of good faith, see Joseph K Leahy, *A Decade After Disney: A Primer on Good and Bad Faith*, 83 U. Cin. L. Rev. 859 (2015).

Stone v. Ritter

Delaware Supreme Court
911 A.2d 362 (2006)

HOLLAND, JUSTICE:

This is an appeal from a final judgment of the Court of Chancery dismissing a ... complaint against fifteen present and former directors of AmSouth Bancorporation ("AmSouth"), a Delaware corporation. The plaintiffs-appellants, William and Sandra Stone, are AmSouth shareholders ... The Court of Chancery characterized the allegations in the ... complaint as a "classic *Caremark* claim," a claim that [takes] its name from *In re Caremark Int'l Deriv. Litig.* [698 A.2d 959 (Del. Ch. 1996)]. In *Caremark*, the Court of Chancery recognized that: "[g]enerally where a claim of directorial liability for corporate loss is predicated upon ignorance of liability creating activities within the corporation ... only a sustained or systematic failure of the board to exercise oversight — such as an utter failure to attempt to assure a reasonable information and reporting system exists — will establish the lack of good faith that is a necessary condition to liability."

In this appeal, the plaintiffs acknowledge that the directors neither "knew [n]or should have known that violations of law were occurring," *i.e.*, that there were no "red flags" before the directors. Nevertheless, the plaintiffs argue that the Court of Chancery erred by dismissing the ... complaint which alleged that "the defendants had utterly failed to implement any sort of statutorily required monitoring, reporting or information controls that would have enabled them to learn of problems requiring their attention." ...

Consistent with our opinion in [the *Disney* case excerpted above, 906 A.2d 27 (Del. 2006)], we hold that *Caremark* articulates the necessary conditions for assessing director oversight liability. We also conclude that the *Caremark* standard was properly applied to evaluate the ... complaint in this case. Accordingly, the judgment of the Court of Chancery must be affirmed.

FACTS

... AmSouth, is a Delaware corporation with its principal executive offices in Birmingham, Alabama. During the relevant period, AmSouth's wholly-owned subsidiary, AmSouth Bank, operated about 600 commercial banking branches in six states throughout the southeastern United States and employed more than 11,600 people.

In 2004, AmSouth and AmSouth Bank paid $40 million in fines and $10 million in civil penalties to resolve government and regulatory investigations pertaining principally to the failure by bank employees to file "Suspicious Activity Reports" ("SARs"), as required by the federal Bank Secrecy Act ("BSA") and various anti-money-laundering ("AML") regulations. Those investigations were conducted by the United States Attorney's Office for the Southern District of Mississippi ("USAO"), the Federal Reserve, FinCEN and the Alabama Banking Department. No fines or penalties were imposed on AmSouth's directors, and no other regulatory action was taken against them.

[The government argued that at least one company employee suspected a banking customer of engaging in illegal activities yet the company failed to file required SARs based on that suspicion.]

On October 12, 2004, the Federal Reserve and the Alabama Banking Department concurrently issued a Cease and Desist Order against AmSouth, requiring it, for the first time, to improve its BSA/AML program. That Cease and Desist Order required AmSouth to (among other things) engage an independent consultant "to conduct a comprehensive review of the Bank's AML Compliance program and make recommendations, as appropriate, for new policies and procedures to be implemented by the Bank." KPMG Forensic Services ("KPMG") performed the role of independent consultant and issued its report on December 10, 2004 (the "KPMG Report").

Also on October 12, 2004, FinCEN and the Federal Reserve jointly assessed a $10 million civil penalty against AmSouth for operating an inadequate anti-money-laundering program and for failing to file SARs. In connection with that assessment, FinCEN issued a written Assessment of Civil Money Penalty (the "Assessment"), which included detailed "determinations" regarding AmSouth's BSA compliance procedures. FinCEN found that "AmSouth violated the suspicious activity reporting requirements of the Bank Secrecy Act," and that "[s]ince April 24, 2002, AmSouth has been in violation of the anti-money-laundering program requirements of the Bank Secrecy Act." Among FinCEN's specific determinations were its conclusions that "AmSouth's [AML compliance] program lacked adequate board and management oversight," and that "reporting to management for the purposes of monitoring and oversight of compliance activities was materially deficient." AmSouth neither admitted nor denied FinCEN's determinations in this or any other forum.

LEGAL STANDARDS

It is a fundamental principle of the Delaware General Corporation Law that "[t]he business and affairs of every corporation organized under this chapter shall be managed by or under the direction of a board of directors...." [DGCL § 141.] ... [D]irectors' potential personal liability depends upon whether or not their conduct can be exculpated by the section 102(b)(7) provision contained in the AmSouth certificate of incorporation. Such a provision can exculpate directors from monetary liability for a breach of the duty of care, but not for conduct that is not in good faith or a breach of the duty of loyalty. The standard for assessing a director's potential personal liability for failing to act in good faith in discharging his or her oversight responsibilities has evolved beginning with our decision in *Graham v. Allis-Chalmers Manufacturing Company* [188 A.2d 125 (Del. 1963)] through the Court of Chancery's *Caremark* decision to our most recent decision in *Disney*. A brief discussion of that evolution will help illuminate the standard that we adopt in this case.

Graham and Caremark. Graham was a [case] brought against the directors of Allis-Chalmers for failure to prevent violations of federal anti-trust laws by Allis-Chalmers employees. There was no claim that the Allis-Chalmers directors knew of the employees' conduct that resulted in the corporation's liability. Rather, the plaintiffs claimed that the Allis-Chalmers directors should have known of the illegal conduct by the corporation's employees. In *Graham*, this Court held that "absent cause for suspicion there is no duty upon the directors to install and operate a corporate system of espionage to ferret out wrongdoing which they have no reason to suspect exists."

In *Caremark*, the Court of Chancery reassessed the applicability of our holding in *Graham*, when called upon to approve a settlement of a ... lawsuit brought against the directors of Caremark International, Inc. The plaintiffs claimed that the Caremark directors should have known that certain officers and employees of Caremark were involved in violations of the federal Anti-Referral Payments Law.... The plaintiffs claimed that the *Caremark* directors breached their fiduciary duty for having "allowed a situation to develop and continue which exposed the corporation to enormous legal liability and that in so doing they violated a duty to be active monitors of corporate performance."

In evaluating whether to approve the proposed settlement agreement in *Caremark* the Court of Chancery narrowly construed our holding in *Graham* "as standing for the proposition that, absent grounds to suspect deception, neither corporate boards nor senior officers can be charged with wrongdoing simply for assuming the integrity of employees and the honesty of their dealings on the company's behalf." The *Caremark* Court opined it would be a "mistake" to interpret this Court's decision in *Graham* to mean that:

> corporate boards may satisfy their obligation to be reasonably informed concerning the corporation, without assuring themselves that information and reporting systems exist in the organization that are reasonably designed to provide to senior management and to the board itself timely, accurate information sufficient to allow management and the board, each within its scope, to reach informed judgments concerning both the corporation's compliance with law and its business performance.

To the contrary, the *Caremark* Court stated, "it is important that the board exercise a good faith judgment that the corporation's information and reporting system is in concept and design adequate to assure the board that appropriate information will come to its attention in a timely manner as a matter of ordinary operations, so that it may satisfy its responsibility." The *Caremark* Court recognized, however, that "the duty to act in good faith to be informed cannot be thought to require directors to possess detailed information about all aspects of the operation of the enterprise." The Court of Chancery then formulated the following standard for assessing the liability of directors where the directors are unaware of employee misconduct that results in the corporation being held liable:

> Generally where a claim of directorial liability for corporate loss is predicated upon ignorance of liability creating activities within the corporation, as in *Graham* or in this case, ... only a sustained or systematic failure of the board to exercise oversight—such as an utter failure to attempt to assure a reasonable information and reporting system exists—will establish the lack of good faith that is a necessary condition to liability.

Caremark Standard Approved. [T]he *Caremark* standard for so-called "oversight" liability draws heavily upon the concept of director failure to act in good faith. That is consistent with the definition(s) of bad faith recently approved by this Court in its recent *Disney* decision, where we held that a failure to act in good faith requires conduct that is qualitatively different from, and more culpable than, the conduct giving rise to a violation of the fiduciary duty of care (*i.e.*, gross negligence). In *Disney*, we identified the following examples of conduct that would establish a failure to act in good faith:

> A failure to act in good faith may be shown, for instance, where the fiduciary intentionally acts with a purpose other than that of advancing the best interests of the corporation, where the fiduciary acts with the intent to violate applicable positive law, or where the fiduciary intentionally fails to act in the face of a known duty to act, demonstrating a conscious disregard for his duties. There may be other examples of bad faith yet to be proven or alleged, but these three are the most salient.

The third of these examples describes, and is fully consistent with, the lack of good faith conduct that the *Caremark* court held was a "necessary condition" for director oversight liability, *i.e.*, "a sustained or systematic failure of the board to exercise oversight   such as an utter failure to attempt to assure a reasonable information and reporting system exists ." Indeed, our opinion in *Disney* cited *Caremark* with approval for that proposition. Accordingly, the Court of Chancery applied the correct standard....

It is important, in this context, to clarify a doctrinal issue that is critical to understanding fiduciary liability under *Caremark* as we construe that case. The phraseology used in *Caremark* and that we employ here — describing the lack of good faith as a "necessary condition to liability" — is deliberate. The purpose of that formulation is to communicate that a failure to act in good faith is not conduct that results, *ipso facto*, in the direct imposition of fiduciary liability. The failure to act in good faith may result in liability because the requirement to act in good faith "is a subsidiary element[,]" *i.e.*, a condition, "of the fundamental duty of loyalty." It follows that because a showing of bad faith conduct, in the sense described in *Disney* and *Caremark* is essential to establish director oversight liability, the fiduciary duty violated by that conduct is the duty of loyalty.

This view of a failure to act in good faith results in two additional doctrinal consequences. First, although good faith may be described colloquially as part of a "triad" of fiduciary duties that includes the duties of care and loyalty, the obligation to act in good faith does not establish an independent fiduciary duty that stands on the same footing as the duties of care and loyalty. Only the latter two duties, where violated, may directly result in liability, whereas a failure to act in good faith may do so, but indirectly. The second doctrinal consequence is that the fiduciary duty of loyalty is not limited to cases involving a financial or other cognizable fiduciary conflict of interest. It also encompasses cases where the fiduciary fails to act in good faith....

We hold that *Caremark* articulates the necessary conditions predicate for director oversight liability: (a) the directors utterly failed to implement any reporting or information system or controls; or (b) having implemented such a system or controls, consciously failed to monitor or oversee its operations thus disabling themselves from being informed of risks or problems requiring their attention. In either case, imposition of liability requires a showing that the directors knew that they were not discharging their fiduciary obligations. Where directors fail to act in the face of a known duty to act, thereby demonstrating a conscious disregard for their responsibilities, they breach their duty of loyalty by failing to discharge that fiduciary obligation in good faith.

Chancery Court Decision. The plaintiffs contend that … AmSouth's directors breached their oversight duty … as a result of their "utter failure" to act in good faith to put into place policies and procedures to ensure compliance with BSA and AML obligations. The Court of Chancery found that the plaintiffs did not plead the existence of "red flags"—facts showing that the board ever was aware that AmSouth's internal controls were inadequate, that these inadequacies would result in illegal activity, and that the board chose to do nothing about problems it allegedly knew existed." …

Reasonable Reporting System Existed. The KPMG Report evaluated the various components of AmSouth's longstanding BSA/AML compliance program. The KPMG Report reflects that AmSouth's Board dedicated considerable resources to the BSA/AML compliance program and put into place numerous procedures and systems to attempt to ensure compliance. According to KPMG, the program's various components exhibited between a low and high degree of compliance with applicable laws and regulations. [The Court reviewed the KPMG Report's findings in detail before concluding with the following paragraph.]

The KPMG Report shows that AmSouth's Board at various times enacted written policies and procedures designed to ensure compliance with the BSA and AML regulations. For example, the Board adopted an amended bank-wide "BSA/AML Policy" on July 17, 2003—four months before AmSouth became aware that it was the target of a government investigation. That policy was produced to plaintiffs in response to their demand to inspect AmSouth's books and records pursuant to [DGCL] section 220 and is included in plaintiffs' appendix. Among other things, the July 17, 2003, BSA/AML Policy directs all AmSouth employees to immediately report suspicious transactions or activity to the BSA/AML Compliance Department or Corporate Security.

Complaint Properly Dismissed…. For the plaintiffs'… complaint to withstand a motion to dismiss, "only a sustained or systematic failure of the board to exercise oversight—such as an utter failure to attempt to assure a reasonable information and reporting system exists—will establish the lack of good faith that is a necessary condition to liability." As the *Caremark* decision noted:

> Such a test of liability—a lack of good faith as evidenced by sustained or systematic failure of a director to exercise reasonable oversight—is quite high. But, a demanding test of liability in the oversight context is probably beneficial to corporate shareholders as a class, as it is in the board decision context, since it makes board service by qualified persons more likely, while continuing to act as a stimulus to good faith performance of duty by such directors.

The KPMG Report … refutes the assertion that the directors "never took the necessary steps … to ensure that a reasonable BSA compliance and reporting system existed." KPMG's findings reflect that the Board received and approved relevant policies and procedures, delegated to certain employees and departments the responsibility for filing SARs and monitoring compliance, and exercised oversight by relying on periodic reports from them. Although there ultimately may have been failures by employees to report deficiencies to the Board, there is no basis for an oversight claim seeking to hold the directors personally liable for such failures by the employees.

With the benefit of hindsight, the plaintiffs' complaint seeks to equate a bad outcome with bad faith. The lacuna in the plaintiffs' argument is a failure to recognize that the directors' good faith exercise of oversight responsibility may not invariably prevent employees from violating criminal laws, or from causing the corporation to incur significant financial liability, or both, as occurred in *Graham*, *Caremark* and this very case. In the absence of red flags, good faith in the context of oversight must be measured by the directors' actions "to assure a reasonable information and reporting system exists" and not by second-guessing after the occurrence of employee conduct that results in an unintended adverse outcome. Accordingly, we hold that the Court of Chancery properly applied *Caremark* and dismissed the plaintiffs'… complaint.… [Affirmed.]

Notes and Questions

1. In one way, *Stone v. Ritter* helpfully clarified the law. It abrogated *Disney*'s dicta suggesting that good faith is an affirmative fiduciary duty, the breach of which amounts to a potentially culpable violation. Rather, good faith is an element of other principles in corporate fiduciary law. Good faith is part of the duty of care (and the business judgment rule's presumption of good faith) and is relevant to exculpation under DGCL § 102(b)(7) (no exculpation for acts not taken in good faith). What doctrinal benefits and problems follow from the two alternatives stated in *Disney* and in *Stone*?

2. In another way, *Stone v. Ritter* confused the law. *Caremark* held that director oversight is entailed by the duty of *care*, and is to be evaluated in terms of good faith efforts to maintain related internal reporting systems. *Stone v. Ritter* states that good faith is an element of the duty of *loyalty*—which it may well be. It then ratifies *Caremark*, but in a way that suggests that directors who fail to implement the requisite systems may violate the duty of loyalty rather than the duty of care. If so, what doctrinal adjustments would seem necessary?

Section V
Compensation Agreements

Directors and officers can negotiate a range of compensation packages for themselves, including cash salaries and bonuses, stock option plans, profit sharing arrangements, and retirement and termination plans. Yet as described in ALI § 5.03 Comment *c*, one can distinguish these compensation agreements from other self-interested transactions in the following ways:

First, unlike most other self-interested transactions, which may be foregone because the corporation usually can deal on the market rather than with the director or senior executive, compensation arrangements with directors and senior executives are necessary in all cases. Second, such arrangements are sufficiently recurring and well publicized in public corporations that there is a greater opportunity for comparison of compensation arrangements and a corresponding deterrent to overreaching. Third, institutionalized procedures for disinterested decisionmaking that are now widely practiced by large public corporations may make it less likely that corporations will be disadvantaged by unfair compensation arrangements with senior executives....

With these distinctions in mind, ALI § 5.03 provides the following review standard:

(a) *General Rule.* A director or senior executive who receives compensation from the corporation for services in that capacity fulfills the duty of fair dealing with respect to the compensation if either:

    (1) The compensation is fair to the corporation when approved;

    (2) The compensation is authorized in advance by disinterested directors or, in the case of a senior executive who is not a director, authorized in advance by a disinterested superior, in a manner that satisfies the standards of the business judgment rule;

    (3) The compensation is ratified by disinterested directors who satisfy the requirements of the business judgment rule, provided (i) a corporate decisionmaker who was not interested in receipt of the compensation acted for the corporation in determining the compensation and satisfied the requirements of the business judgment rule; (ii) the interested director or senior executive did not act unreasonably in failing to seek advance authorization of the compensation by disinterested directors or a disinterested superior; and (iii) the failure to obtain advance authorization of the compensation by disinterested directors or a disinterested superior did not adversely affect the interests of the corporation in a significant way; or

    (4) The compensation is authorized in advance or ratified by disinterested shareholders, and does not constitute a waste of corporate assets at the time of the shareholder action.

[As the accompanying Comment explains,] § 5.03 provides that compensation transactions will be subjected to the less intense judicial scrutiny provided by a business judgment review if authorized in advance by disinterested directors, or, in the case of a senior executive who is not a director, by a disinterested superior, or ratified by disinterested directors under § 5.03(a)(3). Section 5.03 does not accord the same standard of review to a situation in which a senior executive receives compensation without such advance authorization or ratification, and in such event the senior executive will have the burden of proving fairness.

Also in *Cohen v. Ayers*, 596 F.2d 733, 739–40 (7th Cir. 1979), the court contrasts the standard of review for compensation agreements in general with self-interested compensation agreements.

> Ordinarily, employee compensation and other corporate payments are not a waste or gift of assets as long as fair consideration is returned to the corporation. The question of the adequacy of consideration is committed to the sound business judgment of the corporation's directors. Thus, a plaintiff attacking a corporate payment has the heavy burden of demonstrating that no reasonable [business person] could find that adequate consideration had been supplied for the payment. However, where the directors have a personal interest in the application of the corporate payments, such as where they are fixing their own compensation, the business judgment rule no longer applies and the burden shifts to the directors to demonstrate affirmatively that the transactions were engaged in with good faith and were fair, *i.e.*, that adequate consideration had been supplied. This alteration in the burden and quantum of proof may only be avoided in two circumstances: after full disclosure the payments must have been ratified either by action of disinterested directors or by vote of the shareholders. If the payments are thus ratified, then the business judgment rule is again applicable and the plaintiff can succeed only by meeting the burden applicable to challenges of any corporate transaction. Thus, although shareholders or disinterested directors cannot ratify waste, the existence of such ratification makes proof of waste more difficult.

In re Tyson Foods, Inc. [I]

Delaware Court of Chancery
919 A.2d 563 (2007)

CHANDLER, CHANCELLOR:

Before me is a motion to dismiss a lengthy and complex complaint that includes almost a decade's worth of challenged transactions. Plaintiffs level charges, more or less indiscriminately, at eighteen individual defendants, one partnership, and the company itself as a nominal defendant....

An SEC investigation regarding the proper classification of executive perquisites aroused the suspicions of plaintiff Eric Meyer, a New Jersey resident and Tyson shareholder. He made a written demand for documents to the company pursuant to 8 Del. C. §220 on August 26, 2004. After almost a year of wrangling over precisely which papers were and were not to be produced, Tyson handed over an agreed upon set of documents on July 21, 2005. Meyer then filed his initial lawsuit on September 12, 2005. [The complaint was consolidated with that of another plaintiff's complaint on January 11, 2006.]

Tyson Foods, Inc., a Delaware corporation with its principal office in Springdale, Arkansas, provides more protein products to the world than any other firm. Founded in the 1930s, the Tyson family has at all times kept the company under its power and direction. Tyson's share ownership structure ensures this: as of October 2, 2004, Tyson had 250,560,172 shares of Class A common stock and 101,625,548 shares of Class B common stock outstanding. Each Class A shareholder may cast one vote per share on all matters subject to the shareholder franchise, while Class B shareholders may cast ten votes for each one of their Class B shares.

The Tyson Limited Partnership ("TLP"), a limited partnership organized in Delaware, owns 99.9% of the Class B stock, thus controlling over 80% of the company's voting power. In turn, Don Tyson controls 99% of TLP, either directly or indirectly through the Randal W. Tyson Testamentary Trust. Tyson Limited Partnership is also a defendant in this matter.

Defendant Don Tyson has served as a director since 1952, and as Senior Chairman of the Board from 1995 to 2001. He has retired from that position, but remains employed as a consultant to the Tyson firm. He maintains his position as the managing general partner of TLP.

Defendant John Tyson, son of Don Tyson, joined the board in 1984 and was elevated to Chairman in 1998. In April 2000, he became Tyson's Chief Executive Officer. Like his father, he is a general partner of TLP.

... Defendant Lloyd V. Hackley came to the board in 1992. Hackley beneficially owns at least 13,510 shares of Tyson Class A common stock and serves as Chairman of the Governance Committee.

... Defendant David A. Jones joined the board in 2000, beneficially owns 2,492 shares of Tyson Class A stock, and served on the Compensation and Audit Committees. He resigned from the Tyson board in 2005, shortly after this action was filed.

... Defendant Jo Ann R. Smith joined the Tyson board in 2001 and remains a director. She is president of Smith Associates, an agricultural marketing business. Chairperson of the Compensation Committee and a member of the Audit and Governance Committees, she is also the beneficial owner of 6,932 shares of Tyson Class A common stock.

... Defendant Neely E. Cassady participated in the board's Audit and Compensation Committees from 1994 to 2000 and was a member of the Special Committee from 1997 to 2000. He started on the board in 1974 and left in 2000.

Defendant Fred Vorsanger held a board position from 1977 until 2000. During his tenure he served on the Audit, Compensation, and Special Committees.

Tyson elected defendant Shelby D. Massey to the board in 1985, where he remained until 2002. He served as Senior Vice Chairman from 1985 until 1988. He was a member of the Compensation Committee (approximately 1994 to 2002), Special Committee (1997 to 2002) and Governance Committee (2002).

... Defendant Barbara Allen served on the board between 2000 and 2002. She was selected at various times to participate on the Compensation and Audit Committees as well as the Compensation Subcommittee.

[The court's similar summary descriptions of numerous other directors are omitted. — Eds.]

II. FACTUAL BACKGROUND

... In 2001, Tyson adopted a Stock Incentive Plan granting the board permission to award Class A shares, stock options, or other incentives to employees, officers, and directors of the company. Tyson gave the Compensation Committee and Compensation Subcommittee complete discretion as to when and to whom they would distribute these awards, but instructed that they were to consult with and receive recommendations from Tyson's Chairman and Chief Executive Officer. Plaintiffs allege that, at all relevant times, the Plan required that the price of the option be no lower than the fair market value of the company's stock on the day of the grant.[11]

Plaintiffs allege that the Compensation Committee, at the behest of several Defendant board members, "spring-loaded" these options. Days before Tyson would issue press releases that were very likely to drive stock prices higher, the Compensation Committee would award options to key employees.[12] Around 2.8 million shares of Tyson stock bounced from the corporate vaults to various defendants in this manner. Plaintiffs specifically identify four instances of allegedly well-timed option grants.

The Compensation Committee (then Massey, Vorsanger, and Cassady) granted John Tyson, former-CEO Wayne Britt, and then-COO Greg Lee options on 150,000 shares, 125,000 shares and 80,000 Class A shares, respectively, at $15 per share on September 28, 1999. The next day, Tyson informed the market that Smithfield Foods, Inc. had agreed to acquire Tyson's Pork Group. The announcement propelled the price upwards to $16.53 per share in less than six days, and to $17.50 per share by December 1, 1999.[13]

Once again, the Compensation Committee (then Massey, Hackley, and Allen) granted options on 200,000 Class A shares to John Tyson, 100,000 to Lee, and 50,000

---

11. [15] Tyson's 2004 Proxy Statement, however, suggests a more complex and nuanced Stock Incentive Plan. The Proxy states:

The Plan provides for the grant of incentive stock options and nonqualified options....
The exercise price of an option shall be set forth in the applicable Stock Incentive agreement. The exercise price of an *incentive stock option* may not be less than the fair market value of the Class A Common Stock on the date of the grant (nor less than 100% of the fair market value if the participant owns more than 10% of the stock of the Company or any subsidiary).... *Nonqualified stock options* may be made exercisable at a price equal to, less than or more than the fair market value of the Class A Common Stock on the date that the option is granted.

The authority of the Compensation Committee to set a strike price depends upon whether the grant of options in question concerns "incentive" or "nonqualified" stock options.

12. [16] A compensation committee that "spring loads" options grants them to executives before the release of material information reasonably expected to drive the shares of such options higher. (An opposite effect, "bullet dodging," is achieved by granting options to employees after the release of materially damaging information.)

13. [17] Plaintiffs and defendants both agree that Tyson subsequently cancelled the grants to John Tyson and Lee, rendering moot any claim with respect to those grants. It remains unclear whether the grant to Britt was also cancelled.

to then-CFO Steven Hankins at $11.50 per share on March 29, 2001. A day later, Tyson publicly cancelled its $3.2 billion deal to acquire IBP, Inc. By the close of that day, the stock price had shot up to $13.47.

The Compensation Committee (then Hackley, Allen, and Massey) granted options on 200,000 Class A shares to John Tyson, 60,000 to Lee, and 15,000 to Hankins sometime in October 2001. Within two weeks, Tyson publicly announced its 2001 fourth-quarter earnings would be more than double those expected by analysts, catapulting the stock price to $11.90 by the end of November.

The Compensation Committee (then Smith, Jones, and Hackley) granted stock options to a number of executives and directors, including 500,000 to John Tyson, 280,000 to Bond, and 160,000 to Lee, at $13.33 per share on September 19, 2003. On September 23, 2003, Tyson publicly announced that earnings were to exceed Wall Street's expectations, propelling the price to $14.25....

VI. ANALYSIS

... Plaintiffs concede that the sole authority to grant these options rested in the Compensation Committee, but argue that the entire board may be challenged because the Committee was required to consider the recommendations of the Chairman and Chief Executive Officer, each of whom were recipients of options themselves. This argument is inconsistent with Delaware law.

A committee of independent directors enjoys the presumption that its actions are prima facie protected by the business judgment rule. Accordingly, [p]laintiffs' complaint should properly target only the members of the compensation committee at the time the options were approved: Vorsanger, Massey, Cassady, Allen, Hackley, Jones and Smith.[14]

As plaintiffs' allegations against these directors are insufficient to suggest a lack of independence, plaintiffs must demonstrate that the grant of the 2003 options could not be within the bounds of the Compensation Committee's business judgment. A severe test faces those seeking to overcome this presumption: "[W]here a director is independent and disinterested, there can be no liability for corporate loss, unless the facts are such that no person could possibly authorize such a transaction if he or she were attempting in good faith to meet their duty."[15]

Whether a board of directors may in good faith grant spring-loaded options is a somewhat more difficult question than that posed by options backdating, a practice

---

14. [72] Although Count III is dismissed except with regard to these seven defendants, none of whom are alleged to have received any financial benefit through the grant of spring-loaded options, the other defendant directors may yet be affected indirectly. Not all acts of disloyalty or bad faith will directly benefit the malefactor, and a director may be held personally liable for a breach of the duty of loyalty in the absence of a personal financial gain. Where the beneficiary of disloyalty is not directly liable for losses, that beneficiary might still be found to retain "money or property of another against the fundamental principles of justice or equity and good conscience," and thus to be unjustly enriched. *Schock v. Nash*, 732 A.2d 217, 232–233 (Del. 1999).

15. [73] *Gagliardi v. TriFoods Int'l, Inc.*, 683 A.2d 1049, 1052–1053 (Del.Ch. 1996).

that has attracted much journalistic, prosecutorial, and judicial thinking of late.[16] At their heart, all backdated options involve a fundamental, incontrovertible lie: directors who approve an option dissemble as to the date on which the grant was actually made. Allegations of springloading implicate a much more subtle deception.[17]

Granting spring-loaded options, without explicit authorization from shareholders, clearly involves an indirect deception. A director's duty of loyalty includes the duty to deal fairly and honestly with the shareholders for whom he is a fiduciary.[18] It is inconsistent with such a duty for a board of directors to ask for shareholder approval of an incentive stock option plan and then later to distribute shares to managers in such a way as to undermine the very objectives approved by shareholders. This remains true even if the board complies with the strict letter of a shareholder-approved plan as it relates to strike prices or issue dates.

The question before the Court is not, as plaintiffs suggest, whether spring-loading constitutes a form of insider trading as it would be understood under federal securities law. The relevant issue is whether a director acts in bad faith by authorizing options with a market-value strike price, as he is required to do by a shareholder-approved incentive option plan, at a time when he knows those shares are actually worth more than the exercise price. A director who intentionally uses inside knowledge not available to shareholders in order to enrich employees while avoiding shareholder-imposed requirements cannot, in my opinion, be said to be acting loyally and in good faith as a fiduciary.

---

16. [74] In a paradigmatic backdating scenario, a company issues stock options to an executive on one date while providing false documentation to show that the options were actually issued earlier, thus granting the executive an "in the money" option. Of the many reasons proposed for director's willingness to backdate options, favorable tax treatment, fairness among successively-hired employees, or shareholder-approved rules requiring at-market options are often mentioned. *See* David I. Walker, *Some Observations on the Stock Options Backdating Scandal of 2006* 1–6 (Boston Univ. Sch. of Law Working Paper Series, Law And Economics, Paper No. 06-31, 2006), *available at* http://ssrn.com/abstract=929702. Although similar to spring-loading, the backdating of options always involves a factual misrepresentation to shareholders. Issuance of options in conjunction with such deception, and against the background of a shareholder-approved stock-incentive program, amounts to a disloyal act taken in bad faith. *See Ryan v. Gifford*, 918 A.2d 341, at 357–58 (Del. 2007).

17. [75] The touchstone of disloyalty or bad faith in a spring-loaded option remains deception, not simply the fact that they are (in every real sense) "in the money" at the time of issue. A board of directors might, in an exercise of good faith business judgment, determine that in the money options are an appropriate form of executive compensation. Recipients of options are generally unable to benefit financially from them until a vesting period has elapsed, and thus an option's value to an executive or employee is of less immediate value than an equivalent grant of cash. A company with a volatile share price, or one that expects that its most explosive growth is behind it, might wish to issue options with an exercise price below current market value in order to encourage a manager to work hard in the future while at the same time providing compensation with a greater present market value. One can imagine circumstances in which such a decision, were it made honestly and disclosed in good faith, would be within the rational exercise of business judgment. But the facts alleged in this case are different.

18. [76] *In re Walt Disney S'holder Derivative Litig.*, 907 A.2d 693, 755 (Del.Ch. 2005) ("To act in good faith, a director must act at all times with an *honesty of purpose* and in the best interests and welfare of the corporation." (emphasis added)).

This conclusion, however, rests upon at least two premises, each of which should be (and, in this case, has been) alleged by a plaintiff in order to show that a spring-loaded option issued by a disinterested and independent board is nevertheless beyond the bounds of business judgment. First, a plaintiff must allege that options were issued according to a shareholder-approved employee compensation plan.[19] Second, a plaintiff must allege that the directors that approved spring-loaded (or bullet-dodging) options (a) possessed material non-public information soon to be released that would impact the company's share price, and (b) issued those options with the intent to circumvent otherwise valid shareholder-approved restrictions upon the exercise price of the options. Such allegations would satisfy a plaintiff's requirement to show adequately at the pleading stage that a director acted disloyally and in bad faith and is therefore unable to claim the protection of the business judgment rule. Of course, it is conceivable that a director might show that shareholders have expressly empowered the board of directors (or relevant committee) to use backdating, spring-loading, or bullet-dodging as part of employee compensation, and that such actions would not otherwise violate applicable law. But defendants make no such assertion here.

Plaintiffs have alleged adequately that the Compensation Committee violated a fiduciary duty by acting disloyally and in bad faith with regard to the grant of options. I therefore deny defendants' motion to dismiss Count III as to the seven members of the committee who are implicated in such conduct....

In re Tyson Foods, Inc. [II]

Delaware Court of Chancery
2007 Del. Ch. LEXIS 120 (Aug. 15, 2007)

Before me is the outside director defendants' Motion for Judgment on the Pleadings concerning plaintiffs' allegations that defendants "spring-loaded" stock options granted to key Tyson directors and executives. In an Opinion dated February 6, 2007, [the opinion excerpted above] I refused to dismiss Count III of plaintiffs' consolidated complaint, holding that the authorization of spring-loaded stock options may, in certain limited circumstances, constitute a breach of a director's fiduciary duties....

Judicial restraint suggests that a court should limit itself to the case or controversy placed before it and, to the extent practicable, not engage in speculation about phantasmal parties or issues that might one day appear.[20] For this reason, the Opinion ranged very little outside the boundaries of the allegations provided by plaintiffs and, to a lesser degree, challenges raised by defendants. Neither party seriously contested

---

19. [78] Shareholder approved employee compensation plans are common partially as a result of I.R.C. § 162(m), the section of the tax code that allows a business to deduct employee compensation above $1 million only if it qualifies as performance-based compensation. Performance-based compensation plans must be approved by a majority vote of shareholders. *See* I.R.C. § 162(m)(4)(C)(ii).

20. [3] Justice Holmes aptly described both the responsibility and the limited authority of a common law judge: "I recognize without hesitation that judges do and must legislate, but they can do so only interstitially; they are confined from molar to molecular motions." *S. Pac. Co. v. Jensen*, 244 U.S. 205, 221 (1917) (Holmes, J., dissenting).

the fact that the options were required to be granted at the market price on the grant date and, although I noted that plaintiffs' allegations and supporting documents were not entirely in accord, I made no assumptions based solely on a few uncited lines scattered throughout multiple proxy statements. Both parties have now directly addressed the issue. With the allegations before the Court more clearly delineated, the holding of the February 6, 2007 Opinion regarding spring-loading can now be considered with greater clarity.

I. STATEMENT OF FACTS

Plaintiffs challenge three separate grants of options issued between 2001 and 2003. Each grant was awarded by the Compensation Committee according to the 2000 Stock Incentive Plan approved by shareholders in 2001. The parties disagree, however, as to whether these were grants of incentive or non-qualified stock options....

On a motion for judgment on the pleadings.... the Court is required to take the well-pled facts alleged in the complaint as admitted and to view the allegations and reasonable inferences drawn from them in the light most favorable to the non-moving party. There are a few exceptions to this general rule, however. The Court may take judicial notice of a corporation's public filings, and the Court may rely upon documents integral to or incorporated by reference in the consolidated complaint....

Although plaintiffs maintain that Tyson's proxy statements do not affirmatively describe the challenged option grants as non-qualified stock options, I find it impossible to reasonably infer that they could be anything else. The Plan defines an Incentive Stock Option as one "contemplated by the provisions of the [Internal Revenue] Code Section 422 or any successor thereto," while non-qualified options are essentially defined as any option that is not an incentive option. The proxy statements do not refer to the status of the options under the Plan, but they explicitly state that the options do not qualify as incentive options under the Code. Given that an option cannot qualify as an incentive stock option under the Plan without first qualifying under the Code, the only reasonable inference is that these were not incentive stock options and, thus, were non-qualified.

Tyson's publicly-filed statements and the shareholder-approved Plan on which plaintiffs rely thus contradict the allegation in the consolidated complaint that "the Plan requires that the price be no lower than the fair market value of the Company's stock on the day of the grant." This conclusion materially alters the appropriate analysis with respect to Count III of the consolidated complaint. The question facing the Court on February 6, 2007, was whether a grant of spring-loaded options could be within the bounds of the Compensation Committee's business judgment in the face of a shareholder-approved agreement explicitly requiring a market value strike-price. Absent such an agreement, the nature of defendants' alleged deception changes significantly.

Based on the allegations now before the Court, the following circumstances may be reasonably inferred from the consolidated complaint. On three separate occasions between 2001 and 2003, defendants suspected that Tyson's share price would climb once the market learned what the board already knew. Armed with this knowledge, members of the Compensation Committee granted non-qualified stock options to select Tyson employees, ensuring that these options would shortly be in the money. When the option grants were later revealed to shareholders, however, defendants did not straightforwardly describe such strike-price prestidigitation. Rather, they provided minimal assurances to investors that these options rested within the limits of the shareholder-approved plan. The crux of defendants' argument is that a scheme that relies upon bare formalism concealed by a poverty of communication somehow sits within the scope of reasonable, good faith business judgment. At this juncture, and based solely on the pleadings and the public documents, I cannot agree.

II. ANALYSIS

Delaware law sets forth few bright-line rules guiding the relationship between shareholders and directors. Nor does the law require corporations to adopt complex sets of articles and bylaws that govern the method by which corporate decisions will be made. Instead, shareholders are protected by the assurance that directors will stand as fiduciaries, exercising business judgment in good faith, solely for the benefit of shareholders.

Case law from the Supreme Court, as well as this Court, is replete with language describing the nature of this relationship. The affairs of Delaware corporations are managed by their board of directors, who owe to shareholders duties of unremitting loyalty. This means that their actions must be taken in the good faith belief that they are in the best interests of the corporation and its stockholders, especially where conflicts with the individual interests of directors are concerned. The question whether a corporation should pursue a lawsuit against an errant director belongs to the board, and will not be taken from disinterested directors, or those who retain their independence from those who might not have shareholder interests firmly at heart. When those same directors communicate with shareholders, they also must do so with complete candor.

Loyalty. Good faith. Independence. Candor. These are words pregnant with obligation. The Supreme Court did not adorn them with half-hearted adjectives. Directors should not take a seat at the board table prepared to offer only conditional loyalty, tolerable good faith, reasonable disinterest or formalistic candor. It is against these standards, and in this spirit, that the alleged actions of spring-loading or backdating should be judged.

Defendants invoke an utterly different vision of Delaware law. Defendants' argument suggests a relationship between director and shareholder that falls beneath any reasonable conception of the fiduciary and into the merely contractual. The 2000 Tyson Stock Incentive Plan clearly stated that non-qualified stock options could be granted at any particular price. All SEC disclosures revealed the stated strike price to be the market price on the day of the grant. A preternaturally-attentive shareholder might have focused in upon the grant dates, matched them to Tyson press releases, and inferred from the relationship between them that the directors intended to issue what amounted to in the money options. All of this is purely to the letter of the agreement (runs defendants' reasoning), and no court should infer from this anything inconsistent with a duty of loyalty.

When directors seek shareholder consent to a stock incentive plan, or any other quasi-contractual arrangement, they do not do so in the manner of a devil in a dime-store novel, hoping to set a trap with a particular pattern of words. Had the 2000 Tyson Stock Incentive Plan never been put to a shareholder vote, the nature of a spring-loading scheme would constitute material information that the Tyson board of directors was obligated to disclose to investors when they revealed the grant. By agreeing to the Plan, shareholders did not implicitly forfeit their right to the same degree of candor from their fiduciaries.

Defendants protest that deceptive or deficient proxy disclosures cannot form the basis of a derivative claim challenging the grant of these options, asserting that "Tyson's later proxy disclosures concerning the challenged option grants are temporally and analytically distinct from the option grants themselves." At this stage, however, I am bound to give plaintiffs the benefit of every reasonable inference, not to give defendants the benefit of every doubt. Where a board of directors intentionally conceals the nature of its earlier actions, it is reasonable for a court to infer that the act concealed was itself one of disloyalty that could not have arisen from a good faith business judgment. The gravamen of Count III lies in the charge that defendants intentionally and deceptively channeled corporate profits to chosen executives (including members of Don Tyson's family). Proxy statements that display an uncanny parsimony with the truth are not "analytically distinct" from a series of improbably fortuitous stock option grants, but rather raise an inference that directors engaged in later dissembling to hide earlier subterfuge. The Court may further infer that grants of spring-loaded stock options were both inherently unfair to shareholders and that the long-term nature of the deceit involved suggests a scheme inherently beyond the bounds of business judgment.[21]

In retrospect, the test applied in the February 6, 2007 Opinion was, although appropriate to the allegations before the Court at the time, couched in too limited a manner. Certainly the elements listed describe a claim sufficient to show that spring-loading would be beyond the bounds of business judgment. Given the additional information now presented by the parties, however, I am not convinced that allegations of an implicit violation of a shareholder-approved stock incentive plan are absolutely necessary for the Court to infer that the decision to spring-load options lies beyond the bounds of business judgment. Instead, I find that where I may reasonably infer

---

21. [18] This is not to say that failure to fully disclose the nature of a transaction in a proxy statement will always lead a court to question the equity of the underlying transaction. For obvious reasons, a company may wish to be less than entirely detailed about trade secrets or other confidential information. Executive compensation, however, is not a realm in which less than forthright disclosure somehow provides a company with an advantage with respect to competitors. Sophism and guile on this subject does not serve shareholder interests. When directors speak out about their own compensation, or that of company managers, shareholders have a right to the full, unvarnished truth.

that a board of directors later concealed the true nature of a grant of stock options, I may further conclude that those options were not granted consistent with a fiduciary's duty of utmost loyalty....

Ryan v. Gifford

Delaware Court of Chancery
918 A.2d 341 (2007)

Chandler, Chancellor:

On March 18, 2006, *The Wall Street Journal* sparked controversy throughout the investment community by publishing a one-page article, based on an academic's statistical analysis of option grants, which revealed an arguably questionable compensation practice. Commonly known as backdating, this practice involves a company issuing stock options to an executive on one date while providing fraudulent documentation asserting that the options were actually issued earlier. These options may provide a windfall for executives because the falsely dated stock option grants often coincide with market lows. Such timing reduces the strike prices and inflates the value of stock options, thereby increasing management compensation. This practice allegedly violates any stock option plan that requires strike prices to be no less than the fair market value on the date on which the option is granted by the board. Further, this practice runs afoul of many state and federal common and statutory laws that prohibit dissemination of false and misleading information.

After the article appeared in the *Journal*, Merrill Lynch issued a report demonstrating that officers of numerous companies, including Maxim Integrated Products, Inc., had benefited from so many fortuitously timed stock option grants that backdating seemed the only logical explanation. The report engendered this action.

Plaintiff Walter E. Ryan alleges that defendants breached their duties of due care and loyalty by approving or accepting backdated options that violated the clear letter of the shareholder-approved Stock Option Plan and Stock Incentive Plan ("option plans"). Individual defendants move to stay this action in favor of earlier filed federal actions in California ("federal actions"). In the alternative, they move to dismiss this action on its merits....

I. FACTS

Maxim Integrated Products, Inc. is a technology leader in design, development, and manufacture of linear and mixed-signal integrated circuits used in microprocessor-based electronic equipment. From 1998 to mid-2002 Maxim's board of directors and compensation committee granted stock options for the purchase of millions of shares of Maxim's common stock to John F. Gifford, founder, chairman of the board, and chief executive officer, pursuant to shareholder-approved stock option plans filed with the Securities and Exchange Commission. Under the terms of these plans, Maxim contracted and represented that the exercise price of all stock options granted would be no less than the fair market value of the company's common stock, measured by the publicly traded closing price for Maxim stock on the date of the grant. Additionally, the plan identified the board or a committee designated by the board as administrators of its terms.

Ryan is a shareholder of Maxim.... He filed this derivative action on June 2, 2006, against Gifford; James Bergman, B. Kipling Hagopian, and A.R. Frank Wazzan, members of the board and compensation committee at all relevant times; Eric Karros, member of the board from 2000 to 2002, and M.D. Sampels, member of the board from 2001–2002. Ryan alleges that nine specific grants were backdated between 1998 and 2002, as these grants seem too fortuitously timed to be explained as simple coincidence. All nine grants were dated on unusually low (if not the lowest) trading days of the years in question, or on days immediately before sharp increases in the market price of the company.

As practices surrounding the timing of options grants for public companies began facing increased scrutiny in early 2006, Merrill Lynch conducted an analysis of the timing of stock option grants from 1997 to 2002 for the semiconductor and semiconductor equipment companies that comprise the Philadelphia Semiconductor Index. Merrill Lynch measured the aggressiveness of timing of option grants by examining the extent to which stock price performance subsequent to options pricing events diverges from stock price performance over a longer period of time. "Specifically, it looked at annualized stock price returns for the twenty day period subsequent to options pricing in comparison to stock price returns for the calendar year in which the options were granted." In theory, companies should not generate systematic excess return in comparison to other investors as a result of the timing of options pricing events. "[I]f the timing of options grants is an arm's length process, and companies have [not] systematically taken advantage of their ability to backdate options..., there shouldn't be any difference between the two measures." Merrill Lynch failed to take a position on whether Maxim actually backdated; however, it noted that if backdating did not occur, management of Maxim was remarkably effective at timing options pricing events.

With regard to Maxim, Merrill Lynch found that the twenty-day return on option grants to management averaged 14% over the five-year period, an annualized return of 243%, or almost ten times higher than the 29% annualized market returns in the same period....

II. CONTENTIONS

Plaintiff contends that all defendants breached their fiduciary duties to Maxim and its shareholders. The shareholder-approved 1983 Stock Option Plan and 1999 Stock Incentive Plan bound the board of directors to set the exercise price according to the terms of the plans. The 1999 plan allowed the board to designate a committee to approve the plans. The designated compensation committee, consisting of Bergman, Hagopian, and Wazzan, approved option grants after 1999. Plaintiff alleges that from 1998 to 2002, the board actively allowed Maxim to backdate at least nine option grants issued to Gifford, in violation of shareholder-approved plans, and to purposefully mislead shareholders regarding its actions. As a result of the active violations of the plan and the active deceit, plaintiff contends that Maxim received lower payments upon exercise of the options than would have been received had they not been back-dated. Further, Maxim suffers adverse effects from tax and accounting rules. The options priced below the stock's fair market value on the date of the grant allegedly bring the recipient an instant paper gain. At the time, such compensation had to be treated as a cost to the company, thereby reducing reported earnings and resulting in overstated profits. This likely necessitates revision of the company's financial statements and tax reporting. Moreover, Gifford, the recipient of the backdated options, is allegedly unjustly enriched due to receipt of compensation in clear violation of the shareholder-approved plans.

… Defendants … seek dismissal under numerous theories [including that] plaintiff fails to state a claim for breach of fiduciary duty because plaintiff fails to rebut the business judgment rule.…

Defendants assert that plaintiff fails to state a claim for breach of fiduciary duty. This defense, stripped to its essence, states that in order to survive a motion to dismiss on a fiduciary duty claim, the complaint must rebut the business judgment rule. That is, plaintiff must raise a reason to doubt that the directors were disinterested or independent. Where the complaint does not rebut the business judgment rule, plaintiff must allege waste. Plaintiff here, argue the defendants, fails to do either. Further, there is no evidence that the defendants acted intentionally, in bad faith, or for personal gain. Therefore, so the argument goes, plaintiff fails to plead facts sufficient to rebut the business judgment rule and cannot maintain an action for breach of fiduciary duties.

Plaintiff responds that … the directors' purposeful failure to honor an unambiguous provision of a shareholder approved stock option plan—also rebuts the business judgment rule for the purpose of a motion to dismiss for failure to state a claim upon which relief can be granted.

…. [T]he complaint here alleges bad faith and, therefore, a breach of the duty of loyalty sufficient to rebut the business judgment rule and survive a motion to dismiss. The business affairs of a corporation are to be managed by or under the direction of its board of directors. In an effort to encourage the full exercise of managerial powers, Delaware law protects the managers of a corporation through the business judgment rule. This rule "is a presumption that in making a business decision the directors of a corporation acted on an informed basis, in good faith and in the honest belief that the action taken was in the best interest of the company." [*Aronson v. Lewis*, 473 A.2d at 812.] Nevertheless, a showing that the board breached either its fiduciary duty of due care or its fiduciary duty of loyalty in connection with a challenged transaction may rebut this presumption. Such a breach may be shown where the board acts intentionally, in bad faith, or for personal gain. [*Malpiede v. Townson*, 780 A.2d 1075, 1093–97 (Del. 2001).]

In *Stone v. Ritter*, the Supreme Court of Delaware held that acts taken in bad faith breach the duty of loyalty. [911 A.2d 362, 370 (Del. 2006).] Bad faith, the Court stated, may be shown where "the fiduciary intentionally acts with a purpose other than that of advancing the best interests of the corporation, where the fiduciary acts with the intent to violate applicable positive law, or where the fiduciary intentionally fails to act in the face of known duty to act, demonstrating a conscious disregard for his duties." [*Id.* at 369.] Additionally, other examples of bad faith might exist. [*Id.*] These examples include any action that demonstrates a faithlessness or lack of true devotion to the interests of the corporation and its shareholders.

Based on the allegations of the complaint, and all reasonable inferences drawn therefrom, I am convinced that the intentional violation of a shareholder approved stock option plan, coupled with fraudulent disclosures regarding the directors' purported compliance with that plan, constitute conduct that is disloyal to the corporation and is therefore an act in bad faith. Plaintiffs allege the following conduct: Maxim's directors affirmatively represented to Maxim's shareholders that the exercise price of any option grant would be no less than 100% of the fair value of the shares, measured by the market price of the shares on the date the option is granted. Maxim shareholders, possessing an absolute right to rely on those assurances when determining whether to approve the plans, in fact relied upon those representations and approved the plans. Thereafter, Maxim's directors are alleged to have deliberately attempted to circumvent their duty to price the shares at no less than market value on the option grant dates by surreptitiously changing the dates on which the options were granted. To make matters worse, the directors allegedly failed to disclose this conduct to their shareholders, instead making false representations regarding the option dates in many of their public disclosures.

I am unable to fathom a situation where the deliberate violation of a shareholder approved stock option plan and false disclosures, obviously intended to mislead shareholders into thinking that the directors complied honestly with the shareholder-approved option plan, is anything but an act of bad faith. It certainly cannot be said to amount to faithful and devoted conduct of a loyal fiduciary. Well-pleaded allegations of such conduct are sufficient, in my opinion, to rebut the business judgment rule and to survive a motion to dismiss....

Note on Executive Compensation[22]

Executive compensation has long engendered considerable public policy interest. As the Delaware Supreme Court's opinion *In re The Walt Disney Co.* may suggest, courts generally give boards of directors essentially carte blanche to determine the form, amount and timing of executive compensation and determination of associated conditions. *See, e.g., Rogers v. Hill*, 289 U.S. 582 (1933). Such determinations are clearly within the statutory authority and duty that boards of directors have to manage a corporation's business and affairs. At least as early as the 1990s, however, the amount of compensation large public corporations paid to their senior executives reached very large multiples of the average workers' pay and did not always appear related to the corporation's performance.

---

22. Adapted from by Linda O. Smiddy & Lawrence A. Cunningham, Soderquist On Corporate Law And Practice (3d ed. 2007 & Supp.). Copyright © 2007, 2008, 2009, 2010, 1011 by Practising Law Institute. Reprinted with permission. All rights reserved.

As a result, federal securities regulations were expanded to require considerable disclosure of executive compensation, as to amount, comparison with peer companies, and basis for determination. *See* Item 402 of Securities and Exchange Commission, Regulation S-K (calling for a section entitled "Compensation Discussion and Analysis" or CD&A in corporate filings with the SEC and a Compensation Committee Report). Often, resulting decisions were reposed in board compensation committees, whose members were otherwise independent of the corporation. In addition, large institutional shareholders often sought to exert more direct influence on executive compensation decisions, including by making proposals to give them a formal vote of approval on certain compensation matters (popularly known as say-on-pay proposals).

Public interest in the subject escalated during the financial crisis that gripped national and global economies beginning in 2007. Amid deteriorating financial conditions of many large corporations, especially but not exclusively financial institutions, the US government provided extensive and unorthodox financial support for many. As a condition to this support, corporate recipients were required to impose limits on the form and amount of compensation they could pay to senior executive officers. In some cases, corporations were required to submit executive compensation proposals outside stated limits to a non-binding vote of their shareholders. Federal legislators explored more comprehensive ways to respond, including by endorsing versions of say-on-pay proposals.

Section 951 of the Dodd-Frank Wall Street Reform and Consumer Protection Act of 2010 ("Dodd-Frank Act"), 15 U.S.C. § 78n-1, requires that public companies permit shareholders to cast advisory votes on executive compensation at least once every three years. The Dodd-Frank Act stated it did not "create or imply any change to the fiduciary duties" or "create or imply any additional fiduciary duties." It nevertheless prompted lawsuits for breach of fiduciary duty following any negative say-on-pay vote.

Courts routinely dismissed the cases at the pleading stages, with courts deferring to board decisions to ignore a shareholder advisory vote, whether the claims alleged breach of fiduciary duty or waste and whether brought as derivative actions (on behalf of the corporation) or as direct actions. *E.g., Gordon v. Goodyear*, 2012 U.S. Dist. LEXIS 97623 (N.D. Ill. July 13, 2012); *Noble v. AAR Corp.*, 2013 U.S. Dist. LEXIS 48075 (N.D. Ill. April 3, 2013).

Pursuant to the Dodd-Frank Act, the SEC adopted rules requiring public companies to disclose the ratio of the highest-paid executives to the median, rank-and-file compensation.

Section VI
Corporate Opportunity Doctrine

Preceding materials focused on transactions between the corporation and its fiduciaries and the conflicts of interest that may arise. The corporate opportunity doctrine, while a part of the duty of loyalty, focuses on a different problem. Directors and officers sometimes pursue economic opportunities on their own behalf. For instance, they buy property, start a new company, or offer consulting services in their individual capacities. In response, the corporation may argue that the opportunities really belong to it and that the directors or officers violated their duty of loyalty by taking the opportunities.

In principle, the corporate opportunity doctrine can apply to any opportunity that the corporation and the fiduciaries both claim as theirs. A survey of cases, however, reveals that most of the contested opportunities deal with opportunities that put the fiduciaries in competition with the corporation. In most cases, the competition is apparent and direct. The classic example of direct competition involves fiduciaries' starting a business that offers the same services or products to the same general market as the corporation. In addition, corporate opportunity cases are much more common in small, closely held corporations than in large, publicly held corporations.

The following materials explore various judicial approaches to this problem. As you study it, consider how the courts have balanced the competing interests of the corporation and its fiduciaries.

Broz v. Cellular Information Systems, Inc.

Delaware Supreme Court
673 A.2d 148 (1996)

VEASEY, CHIEF JUSTICE:

In this appeal, we consider the application of the doctrine of corporate opportunity. The Court of Chancery decided that the defendant, a corporate director, breached his fiduciary duty by not formally presenting to the corporation an opportunity which had come to the director individually and independent of the director's relationship with the corporation. Here the opportunity was not one in which the corporation in its current mode had an interest or which it had the financial ability to acquire, but, under the unique circumstances here, that mode was subject to change by virtue of the impending acquisition of the corporation by another entity.

We conclude that, although a corporate director may be shielded from liability by offering to the corporation an opportunity which has come to the director independently and individually, the failure of the director to present the opportunity does not necessarily result in the improper usurpation of a corporate opportunity. We further conclude that, if the corporation is a target or potential target of an acquisition by another company which has an interest and ability to entertain the opportunity, the director of the target company does not have a fiduciary duty to present the opportunity to the target company. Accordingly, the judgment of the Court of Chancery is [reversed].

I. *The Contentions of the Parties ...*

Robert F. Broz ("Broz") is the President and sole stockholder of RFB Cellular, Inc. ("RFBC"), a Delaware corporation engaged in the business of providing cellular telephone service in the Midwestern United States. At the time of the conduct at issue in this appeal, Broz was also a member of the board of directors of plaintiff ... Cellular Information Systems, Inc. ("CIS"). CIS is a publicly held Delaware corporation and a competitor of RFBC.

The conduct before the Court involves the purchase by Broz of a cellular telephone service license for the benefit of RFBC.[24] The license in question, known as the Michigan-2 Rural Service Area Cellular License ("Michigan-2"), is issued by the Federal Communications Commission ("FCC") and entitles its holder to provide cellular telephone service to a portion of northern Michigan. CIS brought an action against Broz and RFBC for equitable relief, contending that the purchase of this license by Broz constituted a usurpation of a corporate opportunity properly belonging to CIS, irrespective of whether or not CIS was interested in the Michigan-2 opportunity at the time it was offered to Broz.

The principal basis for the contention of CIS is that PriCellular, Inc. ("PriCellular"), another cellular communications company which was contemporaneously engaged in an acquisition of CIS, was interested in the Michigan-2 opportunity. CIS contends that, in determining whether the Michigan-2 opportunity rightfully belonged to CIS, Broz was required to consider the interests of PriCellular insofar as those interests would come into alignment with those of CIS as a result of PriCellular's acquisition plans....

II. *Facts*

Broz has been the President and sole stockholder of RFBC since 1992. RFBC owns and operates an FCC license area, known as the Michigan-4 Rural Service Area Cellular License ("Michigan-4"). The license entitles RFBC to provide cellular telephone service to a portion of rural Michigan. Although Broz' efforts have been devoted primarily to the business operations of RFBC, he also served as an outside director of CIS at the time of the events at issue in this case. CIS was at all times fully aware of Broz' relationship with RFBC and the obligations incumbent upon him by virtue of that relationship.

In April of 1994, Mackinac Cellular Corp. ("Mackinac") [pronounced *mak-in-aw*] sought to divest itself of Michigan-2, the license area immediately adjacent to Michigan-4. To this end, Mackinac contacted Daniels & Associates ("Daniels") and arranged for the brokerage firm to seek potential purchasers for Michigan-2. In compiling a list of prospects, Daniels included RFBC as a likely candidate. In May of 1994, David Rhodes, a representative of Daniels, contacted Broz and broached the subject of RFBC's possible acquisition of Michigan-2. Broz later signed a confidentiality agreement at the request of Mackinac, and received the offering materials pertaining to Michigan-2.

---

24. [1] The Court recognizes that the actual purchase of the ... license [at issue] was consummated by RFBC as a corporate entity, rather than by Broz acting as an individual for his own benefit. Broz is, however, the sole party in interest in RFBC and all actions taken by RFBC, including the acquisition of [the license], are accomplished at the behest of Broz. Therefore, insofar as the purchase of [the license] is concerned, the Court will not distinguish between the actions of Broz and those of RFBC in analyzing Broz' alleged breach of fiduciary duty.

Michigan-2 was not, however, offered to CIS. Apparently, Daniels did not consider CIS to be a viable purchaser for Michigan-2 in light of CIS' recent financial difficulties. The record shows that, at the time Michigan-2 was offered to Broz, CIS had recently emerged from lengthy and contentious Chapter 11 proceedings. Pursuant to the Chapter 11 Plan of Reorganization, CIS entered into a loan agreement that substantially impaired the company's ability to undertake new acquisitions or to incur new debt. In fact, CIS would have been unable to purchase Michigan-2 without the approval of its creditors.

The CIS reorganization resulted from the failure of CIS' rather ambitious plans for expansion. From 1989 onward, CIS had embarked on a series of cellular license acquisitions. In 1992, however, CIS' financing failed, necessitating the liquidation of the company's holdings and reduction of the company's total indebtedness. During the period from early 1992 until the time of CIS' emergence from bankruptcy in 1994, CIS divested itself of some fifteen separate cellular license systems. CIS contracted to sell four additional license areas on May 27, 1994, leaving CIS with only five remaining license areas, all of which were outside of the Midwest.

On June 13, 1994, following a meeting of the CIS board, Broz spoke with CIS' Chief Executive Officer, Richard Treibick ("Treibick"), concerning his interest in acquiring Michigan-2. Treibick communicated to Broz that CIS was not interested in Michigan-2. Treibick further stated that he had been made aware of the Michigan-2 opportunity prior to the conversation with Broz, and that any offer to acquire Michigan-2 was rejected. After the commencement of the PriCellular tender offer [described below], in August of 1994, Broz contacted another CIS director, Peter Schiff ("Schiff"), to discuss the possible acquisition of Michigan-2 by RFBC. Schiff, like Treibick, indicated that CIS had neither the wherewithal nor the inclination to purchase Michigan-2. In late September of 1994, Broz also contacted Stanley Bloch ("Bloch"), a director and counsel for CIS, to request that Bloch represent RFBC in its dealings with Mackinac. Bloch agreed to represent RFBC, and, like Schiff and Treibick, expressed his belief that CIS was not at all interested in the transaction. Ultimately, all the CIS directors testified at trial that, had Broz inquired at that time, they each would have expressed the opinion that CIS was not interested in Michigan-2.[25]

On June 28, 1994, following various overtures from PriCellular concerning an acquisition of CIS, six CIS directors entered into agreements with PriCellular to sell their shares in CIS at a price of $2.00 per share. These agreements were contingent upon, *inter alia*, the consummation of a PriCellular tender offer for all CIS shares at the same price. Pursuant to their agreements with PriCellular, the CIS directors also entered into a "standstill" agreement which prevented the directors from engaging in any transaction outside the regular course of CIS' business or incurring any new li-

---

25. [5] We assume *arguendo* that informal contacts and individual opinions of board members are not a substitute for a formal process of presenting an opportunity to a board of directors. Nevertheless, in our view such a formal process was not necessary under the circumstances of this case in order for Broz to avoid liability. These contacts with individual board members do, however, tend to show that Broz was not acting surreptitiously or in bad faith.

abilities until the close of the PriCellular tender offer. On August 2, 1994, PriCellular commenced a tender offer for all outstanding shares of CIS at $2.00 per share. The PriCellular tender offer mirrored the standstill agreements entered into by the CIS directors.

PriCellular's tender offer was originally scheduled to close on September 16, 1994. At the time the tender offer was launched, however, the source of the $106,000,000 in financing required to consummate the transaction was still in doubt. PriCellular originally planned to structure the transaction around bank loans. When this financing fell through, PriCellular resorted to a junk bond offering. PriCellular's financing difficulties generated a great deal of concern among the CIS insiders whether the tender offer was, in fact, viable. Financing difficulties ultimately caused PriCellular to delay the closing date of the tender offer from September 16, 1994 until October 14, 1994 and then again until November 9, 1994.

On August 6, September 6 and September 21, 1994, Broz submitted written offers to Mackinac for the purchase of Michigan-2. During this time period, PriCellular also began negotiations with Mackinac to arrange an option for the purchase of Michigan-2. PriCellular's interest in Michigan-2 was fully disclosed to CIS' chief executive, Treibick, who did not express any interest in Michigan-2, and was actually incredulous that PriCellular would want to acquire the license. Nevertheless, CIS was fully aware that PriCellular and Broz were bidding for Michigan-2 and did not interpose CIS in this bidding war.

In late September of 1994, PriCellular reached agreement with Mackinac on an option to purchase Michigan-2. The exercise price of the option agreement was set at $6.7 million, with the option remaining in force until December 15, 1994. Pursuant to the agreement, the right to exercise the option was not transferrable to any party other than a subsidiary of PriCellular. Therefore, it could not have been transferred to CIS. The agreement further provided that Mackinac was free to sell Michigan-2 to any party who was willing to exceed the exercise price of the Mackinac-PriCellular option contract by at least $500,000. On November 14, 1994, Broz agreed to pay Mackinac $7.2 million for the Michigan-2 license, thereby meeting the terms of the option agreement. An asset purchase agreement was thereafter executed by Mackinac and RFBC.

Nine days later, on November 23, 1994, PriCellular completed its financing and closed its tender offer for CIS. Prior to that point, PriCellular owned no equity interest in CIS. Subsequent to the consummation of the PriCellular tender offer for CIS, members of the CIS board of directors, including Broz, were discharged and replaced with a slate of PriCellular nominees. On March 2, 1995, this action was commenced by CIS in the Court of Chancery....

IV. *Application of the Corporate Opportunity Doctrine*

The doctrine of corporate opportunity represents but one species of the broad fiduciary duties assumed by a corporate director or officer. A corporate fiduciary agrees to place the interests of the corporation before his or her own in appropriate circumstances. In light of the diverse and often competing obligations faced by directors and officers, however, the corporate opportunity doctrine arose as a means of defining the parameters of fiduciary duty in instances of potential conflict. The classic statement of the doctrine is derived from the venerable case of *Guth v. Loft, Inc.* [5 A.2d 503 (Del. 1939)]. In *Guth*, this Court held that:

> if there is presented to a corporate officer or director a business opportunity which the corporation is financially able to undertake, is, from its nature, in the line of the corporation's business and is of practical advantage to it, is one in which the corporation has an interest or a reasonable expectancy, and, by embracing the opportunity, the self-interest of the officer or director will be brought into conflict with that of the corporation, the law will not permit him to seize the opportunity for himself.

Guth, 5 A.2d at 510–11.

The corporate opportunity doctrine, as delineated by *Guth* and its progeny, holds that a corporate officer or director may not take a business opportunity for his own if: (1) the corporation is financially able to exploit the opportunity; (2) the opportunity is within the corporation's line of business; (3) the corporation has an interest or expectancy in the opportunity; and (4) by taking the opportunity for his own, the corporate fiduciary will thereby be placed in a position inimicable to his duties to the corporation. The Court in *Guth* also derived a corollary which states that a director or officer *may* take a corporate opportunity if: (1) the opportunity is presented to the director or officer in his individual and not his corporate capacity; (2) the opportunity is not essential to the corporation; (3) the corporation holds no interest or expectancy in the opportunity; and (4) the director or officer has not wrongfully employed the resources of the corporation in pursuing or exploiting the opportunity. *Guth*, 5 A.2d at 509.

Thus, the contours of this doctrine are well established. It is important to note, however, that the tests enunciated in *Guth* and subsequent cases provide guidelines to be considered by a reviewing court in balancing the equities of an individual case. No one factor is dispositive and all factors must be taken into account insofar as they are applicable. Cases involving a claim of usurpation of a corporate opportunity range over a multitude of factual settings. Hard and fast rules are not easily crafted to deal with such an array of complex situations. As this Court noted in *Johnston v. Greene*, Del. Supr., 121 A.2d 919 (1956), the determination of "[w]hether or not a director has appropriated for himself something that in fairness should belong to the corporation is 'a factual question to be decided by reasonable inference from objective facts.'" *Id.* at 923 (*quoting Guth*, 5 A.2d at 513). In the instant case, we find that the facts do not support the conclusion that Broz misappropriated a corporate opportunity.

We note at the outset that Broz became aware of the Michigan-2 opportunity in his individual and not his corporate capacity. As the Court of Chancery found, "Broz did not misuse proprietary information that came to him in a corporate capacity nor did he otherwise use any power he might have over the governance of the corporation to advance his own interests." 663 A.2d at 1185. This fact is not the subject of serious dispute. In fact, it is clear from the record that Mackinac did not consider CIS a viable candidate for the acquisition of Michigan-2. Accordingly, Mackinac did not offer the property to CIS. In this factual posture, many of the fundamental concerns undergirding the law of corporate opportunity are not present (*e.g.*, misappropriation of the corporation's proprietary information). The burden imposed upon Broz to show adherence to his fiduciary duties to CIS is thus lessened to some extent. Nevertheless, this fact is not dispositive. The determination of whether a particular fiduciary has usurped a corporate opportunity necessitates a careful examination of the circumstances, giving due credence to the factors enunciated in *Guth* and subsequent cases.

We turn now to an analysis of the factors relied on by the trial court. First, we find that CIS was not financially capable of exploiting the Michigan-2 opportunity. Although the Court of Chancery concluded otherwise, we hold that this finding was not supported by the evidence. *Levitt*, 287 A.2d at 673. The record shows that CIS was in a precarious financial position at the time Mackinac presented the Michigan-2 opportunity to Broz. Having recently emerged from lengthy and contentious bankruptcy proceedings, CIS was not in a position to commit capital to the acquisition of new assets. Further, the loan agreement entered into by CIS and its creditors severely limited the discretion of CIS as to the acquisition of new assets and substantially restricted the ability of CIS to incur new debt.

The Court of Chancery based its contrary finding on the fact that PriCellular had purchased an option to acquire CIS' bank debt. Thus, the court reasoned, PriCellular was in a position to exercise that option and then waive any unfavorable restrictions that would stand in the way of a CIS acquisition of Michigan-2. The trial court, however, disregarded the fact that PriCellular's own financial situation was not particularly stable....

Second, while it may be said with some certainty that the Michigan-2 opportunity was within CIS' line of business, it is not equally clear that CIS had a cognizable interest or expectancy in the license.[26] Under the third factor laid down by this Court in *Guth*, for an opportunity to be deemed to belong to the fiduciary's corporation, the corporation must have an interest or expectancy in that opportunity. As this Court stated in *Johnston*, 121 A.2d at 924, "[f]or the corporation to have an actual or expectant interest in any specific property, there must be some tie between that property and the nature of the corporate business." Despite the fact that the nature

---

26. [7] The language in the *Guth* opinion relating to "line of business" is less than clear:
> Where a corporation is engaged in a certain business, and an opportunity is presented to it embracing an activity as to which it has fundamental knowledge, practical experience and *ability to pursue*, which, logically and naturally, is adaptable to its business *having regard for its financial position*, and *is consonant with its reasonable needs and aspirations for expansion*, it may properly be said that the opportunity is within the corporation's line of business.

Guth, 5 A.2d at 514 (emphasis supplied). This formulation of the definition of the term "line of business" suggests that the business strategy and financial well-being of the corporation are also relevant to a determination of whether the opportunity is within the corporation's line of business. Since we find that these considerations are decisive under the other factors enunciated by the Court in *Guth*, we do not reach the question of whether they are here relevant to a determination of the corporation's line of business.

of the Michigan-2 opportunity was historically close to the core operations of CIS, changes were in process. At the time the opportunity was presented, CIS was actively engaged in the process of divesting its cellular license holdings. CIS' articulated business plan did not involve any new acquisitions. Further, as indicated by the testimony of the entire CIS board, the Michigan-2 license would not have been of interest to CIS even absent CIS' financial difficulties and CIS' then current desire to liquidate its cellular license holdings. Thus, CIS had no interest or expectancy in the Michigan-2 opportunity....

Finally, the corporate opportunity doctrine is implicated only in cases where the fiduciary's seizure of an opportunity results in a conflict between the fiduciary's duties to the corporation and the self-interest of the director as actualized by the exploitation of the opportunity. In the instant case, Broz' interest in acquiring and profiting from Michigan-2 created no duties that were inimicable to his obligations to CIS. Broz, at all times relevant to the instant appeal, was the sole party in interest in RFBC, a competitor of CIS. CIS was fully aware of Broz' potentially conflicting duties. Broz, however, comported himself in a manner that was wholly in accord with his obligations to CIS. Broz took care not to usurp any opportunity which CIS was willing and able to pursue. Broz sought only to compete with an outside entity, PriCellular, for acquisition of an opportunity which both sought to possess. Broz was not obligated to refrain from competition with PriCellular. Therefore, the totality of the circumstances indicates that Broz did not usurp an opportunity that properly belonged to CIS.

A. *Presentation to the Board*

... The teaching of *Guth* and its progeny is that the director or officer must analyze the situation *ex ante* to determine whether the opportunity is one rightfully belonging to the corporation. If the director or officer believes, based on one of the factors articulated above, that the corporation is not entitled to the opportunity, then he may take it for himself. Of course, presenting the opportunity to the board creates a kind of "safe harbor" for the director, which removes the specter of a *post hoc* judicial determination that the director or officer has improperly usurped a corporate opportunity. Thus, presentation avoids the possibility that an error in the fiduciary's assessment of the situation will create future liability for breach of fiduciary duty. It is not the law of Delaware that presentation to the board is a necessary prerequisite to a finding that a corporate opportunity has not been usurped....

B. *Alignment of Interests Between CIS and PriCellular*

... Broz was under no duty to consider the interests of PriCellular when he chose to purchase Michigan-2. As stated in *Guth*, a director's right to "appropriate [an] ... opportunity depends on the circumstances existing at the time it presented itself to him without regard to subsequent events." *Guth*, 5 A.2d at 513. At the time Broz purchased Michigan-2, PriCellular had not yet acquired CIS. Any plans to do so would still have been wholly speculative. Accordingly, Broz was not required to consider the contingent and uncertain plans of PriCellular in reaching his determination of how to proceed.

Whether or not the CIS board would, at some time, have chosen to acquire Michigan-2 in order to make CIS a more attractive acquisition target for PriCellular or to enhance the synergy of any combined enterprise, is speculative. The trial court found this to be a plausible scenario and therefore found that, pursuant to the factors laid down in *Guth*, CIS had a valid interest or expectancy in the license. This speculative finding cuts against the statements made by CIS' Chief Executive and the entire CIS board of directors and ignores the fact that CIS still lacked the wherewithal to acquire Michigan-2, even if one takes into account the possible availability of PriCellular's financing. Thus, the fact of PriCellular's plans to acquire CIS is immaterial and does not change the analysis.

In reaching our conclusion on this point, we note that certainty and predictability are values to be promoted in our corporation law. *See Williams v. Geier*, Del. Supr., 671 A.2d 1368, 1385 n. 36 (1996). Broz, as an active participant in the cellular telephone industry, was entitled to proceed in his own economic interest in the absence of any countervailing duty. The right of a director or officer to engage in business affairs outside of his or her fiduciary capacity would be illusory if these individuals were required to consider every potential, future occurrence in determining whether a particular business strategy would implicate fiduciary duty concerns. In order for a director to engage meaningfully in business unrelated to his or her corporate role, the director must be allowed to make decisions based on the situation as it exists at the time a given opportunity is presented. Absent such a rule, the corporate fiduciary would be constrained to refrain from exploiting any opportunity for fear of liability based on the occurrence of subsequent events. This state of affairs would unduly restrict officers and directors and would be antithetical to certainty in corporation law.

V. *Conclusion*

The corporate opportunity doctrine represents a judicially crafted effort to harmonize the competing demands placed on corporate fiduciaries in a modern business environment. The doctrine seeks to reduce the possibility of conflict between a director's duties to the corporation and interests unrelated to that role. In the instant case, Broz adhered to his obligations to CIS. We hold that the Court of Chancery erred as a matter of law in concluding that Broz had a duty formally to present the Michigan-2 opportunity to the CIS board. We also hold that the trial court erred in its application of the corporate opportunity doctrine under the unusual facts of this case, where CIS had no interest or financial ability to acquire the opportunity, but the impending acquisition of CIS by PriCellular would or could have caused a change in those circumstances....

Notes and Questions

1. Corporate opportunity cases often pose conflicting interests. The corporation relies on fiduciaries to fulfill their duties in good faith. It does not want to have to monitor the fiduciaries' honesty and fair dealing. The corporation provides them with access to information, contacts and experiences so that the fiduciaries can perform effectively. It does not want the fiduciaries to use this information and experience to pursue interests that may conflict with or impair corporate interests.

On the other hand, there is social value and individual interest in free competition. Society gains when individuals pursue opportunities that lead to the creation of new businesses and jobs. In addition, if directors' and officers' freedom of enterprise is too restricted by overly rigid corporate law rules, competent individuals will be discouraged from serving as corporate fiduciaries.

2. *Guth v. Loft, Inc.* remains the most cited case in the corporate opportunity area. As indicated in *Broz* footnote 11, the line of business test articulated in *Guth* may be interpreted in various ways. If interpreted narrowly, it would only preclude fiduciaries from pursuing opportunities that would put them in direct competition with the corporation. If interpreted expansively, it could preclude fiduciaries from any opportunities to which the corporation could possibly adapt. Under this more expansive interpretation, corporations would be entitled to a broad range of opportunities and directors and officers would likely be found liable unless the opportunity was completely unrelated to the corporation's activities.

3. Courts have used a range of approaches to resolving these disputes, several of which were noted in *Broz*. Three frequent inquiries follow:

(a) Does the corporation have a protectable *expectancy* to the opportunity? Under the circumstances, would the corporation and the fiduciary reasonably expect that the opportunity belongs to the corporation? Courts interpret "expectancy" differently. Some may require that the corporation have an express contractual right to the opportunity, such as an option to buy. Others may define expectancy more broadly, allowing the corporation to claim opportunities for which it has no contract, but for which it had some prior interest and dealings. How was "expectancy" interpreted in *Broz*?

(b) Is it "*fair*" to the corporation for the fiduciary to take the opportunity? For instance, a fairness analysis may include the following:

Factors dealing with the relationship between the opportunity and the corporation:

- Whether the opportunity was of special value to the corporation;
- Whether the corporation was actively negotiating for the opportunity; and
- Whether the corporation was in a financial position to pursue the opportunity.

Factors dealing with the relationship between the opportunity and the fiduciaries:

- Whether the fiduciaries received the opportunity because of their corporate positions;
- Whether the fiduciaries were delegated to pursue the opportunity on behalf of the corporation;
- Whether the fiduciaries used the corporate resources in identifying or developing the opportunity; and
- Whether the fiduciaries intended to resell the opportunity to the corporation.

Factors dealing with the relationship between the corporation and the fiduciaries:

- Whether the fiduciaries' dealings with the corporation were fair;
- Whether the fiduciaries carried out their corporate duties in good faith;
- Whether the fiduciaries harmed the corporation by unfair bargaining; and

- Whether the fiduciaries would be put in an adverse and hostile position to the corporation.

This equity-oriented case-by-case approach allows courts to consider whatever is deemed relevant, but may offer no predictable guidelines on which fiduciaries can base their future conduct.

(c) Did the corporation have the actual *capacity* to develop the opportunity? If it does not, then perhaps it would serve broader efficiency and entrepreneurial objectives for fiduciaries to be allowed to pursue the opportunity. Consider, however, how an emphasis on corporate incapacity might shape fiduciaries' conduct.

In determining the corporation's capabilities, courts may consider various corporate capacities. Does the corporation have the legal capacity to pursue the opportunity, or does the corporation's purposes, contractual obligations, or statutory limitations prohibit it from doing so? Are there organizational obstacles, such as the lack of facilities or personnel, to pursuing the opportunity? Or what if the party offering the opportunity is not inclined or refuses to deal with the corporation? Courts have emphasized whether the corporation has the necessary financial resources. In *Broz*, for instance, the court concluded that CIS was not financially capable of pursuing the opportunity. Was it justified in doing so?

4. Section 122(17) of the Delaware General Corporation Law (adopted in 2000) authorizes corporations to include provisions in certificates of incorporation, or resolutions of boards of directors, renouncing, in advance, the corporation's interest or expectancy in specified business opportunities or classes of business opportunities.

* * * * *

The following case describes the ALI's approach. As you read the case, consider the advantages and disadvantages of the approach. In what ways has the model incorporated some of the factors in the notes above and in the *Broz* case? How would the ALI framework have operated when applied to the *Broz* facts? How does *Broz* (and *Guth v. Loft*) apply to the *Harris* facts?

Northeast Harbor Golf Club, Inc. v. Harris

Maine Supreme Judicial Court
661 A.2d 1146 (1995)

ROBERTS, JUSTICE:

Northeast Harbor Golf Club, Inc., appeals from a judgment entered in the Superior Court (Hancock County, *Atwood, J.*) following a nonjury trial. The Club maintains that the trial court erred in finding that Nancy Harris did not breach her fiduciary duty as president of the Club by purchasing and developing property abutting the golf course. Because we today adopt principles different from those applied by the trial court in determining that Harris's activities did not constitute a breach of the corporate opportunity doctrine, we vacate the judgment.

I. *The Facts*

Nancy Harris was the president of the Northeast Harbor Golf Club, a Maine corporation, from 1971 until she was asked to resign in 1990. The Club also had a board of directors that was responsible for making or approving significant policy decisions. The Club's only major asset was a golf course in Mount Desert. During Harris's tenure as president, the board occasionally discussed the possibility of developing some of the Club's real estate in order to raise money. Although Harris was generally in favor of tasteful development, the board always "shied away" from that type of activity.

In 1979, Robert Suminsby informed Harris that he was the listing broker for the Gilpin property, which comprised three noncontiguous parcels located among the fairways of the golf course. The property included an unused right-of-way on which the Club's parking lot and clubhouse were located. It was also encumbered by an easement in favor of the Club allowing foot traffic from the green of one hole to the next tee. Suminsby testified that he contacted Harris because she was the president of the Club and he believed that the Club would be interested in buying the property in order to prevent development.

Harris immediately agreed to purchase the Gilpin property in her own name for the asking price of $45,000. She did not disclose her plans to purchase the property to the Club's board prior to the purchase. She informed the board at its annual August meeting that she had purchased the property, that she intended to hold it in her own name, and that the Club would be "protected." The board took no action in response to the Harris purchase. She testified that at the time of the purchase she had no plans to develop the property and that no such plans took shape until 1988.

In 1984, while playing golf with the postmaster of Northeast Harbor, Harris learned that a parcel of land owned by the heirs of the Smallidge family might be available for purchase. The Smallidge parcel was surrounded on three sides by the golf course and on the fourth side by a house lot. It had no access to the road. With the ultimate goal of acquiring the property, Harris instructed her lawyer to locate the Smallidge heirs. Harris testified that she told a number of individual board members about her attempt to acquire the Smallidge parcel. At a board meeting in August 1985, Harris formally disclosed to the board that she had purchased the Smallidge property.[27] The minutes of that meeting show that she told the board she had no present plans to develop the Smallidge parcel. Harris testified that at the time of the purchase of the Smallidge property she nonetheless thought it might be nice to have some houses there. Again, the board took no formal action as a result of Harris's purchase. Harris acquired the Smallidge property from ten heirs, paying a total of $60,000. In 1990, Harris paid $275,000 for the lot and building separating the Smallidge parcel from the road in order to gain access to the otherwise landlocked parcel.

The trial court expressly found that the Club would have been unable to purchase either the Gilpin or Smallidge properties for itself, relying on testimony that the Club

---

27. [1] In fact, it appears that Harris did not take title to the property until October 26, 1985. She had only signed a purchase and sale agreement at the time of the August board meeting.

continually experienced financial difficulties, operated annually at a deficit, and depended on contributions from the directors to pay its bills. On the other hand, there was evidence that the Club had occasionally engaged in successful fund-raising, including a two-year period shortly after the Gilpin purchase during which the Club raised $115,000. The Club had $90,000 in a capital investment fund at the time of the Smallidge purchase.

In 1987 or 1988, Harris divided the real estate into 41 small lots, 14 on the Smallidge property and 27 on the Gilpin property. Apparently as part of her estate plan, Harris conveyed noncontiguous lots among the 41 to her children and retained others for herself. In 1991, Harris and her children exchanged deeds to reassemble the small lots into larger parcels. At the time the Club filed this suit, the property was divided into 11 lots, some owned by Harris and others by her children who are also defendants in this case. Harris estimated the value of all the real estate at the time of the trial to be $1,550,000.

In 1988, Harris, who was still president of the Club, and her children began the process of obtaining approval for a five-lot subdivision known as Bushwood on the lower Gilpin property. Even when the board learned of the proposed subdivision, a majority failed to take any action. A group of directors formed a separate organization in order to oppose the subdivision on the basis that it violated the local zoning ordinance. After Harris's resignation as president, the Club also sought unsuccessfully to challenge the subdivision.... Plans of Harris and her family for development of the other parcels are unclear, but the local zoning ordinance would permit construction of up to 11 houses on the land as currently divided.

After Harris's plans to develop Bushwood became apparent, the board grew increasingly divided concerning the propriety of development near the golf course. At least two directors, Henri Agnese and Nick Ludington, testified that they trusted Harris to act in the best interests of the Club and that they had no problem with the development plans for Bushwood. Other directors disagreed.

In particular, John Schafer, a Washington, D.C., lawyer and long-time member of the board, took issue with Harris's conduct. He testified that he had relied on Harris's representations at the time she acquired the properties that she would not develop them. According to Schafer, matters came to a head in August 1990 when a number of directors concluded that Harris's development plans irreconcilably conflicted with the Club's interests. As a result, Schafer and two other directors asked Harris to resign as president. In April 1991, after a substantial change in the board's membership, the board authorized the instant lawsuit against Harris for the breach of her fiduciary duty to act in the best interests of the corporation. The board simultaneously resolved that the proposed housing development was contrary to the best interests of the corporation.

The Club filed a complaint against Harris, her sons John and Shepard, and her daughter-in-law Melissa Harris. As amended, the complaint alleged that during her term as president Harris breached her fiduciary duty by purchasing the lots without providing notice and an opportunity for the Club to purchase the property and by subdividing the lots for future development. The Club sought an injunction to prevent development and also sought to impose a constructive trust on the property in question for the benefit of the Club.

The trial court found that Harris had not usurped a corporate opportunity because the acquisition of real estate was not in the Club's line of business. Moreover, it found that the corporation lacked the financial ability to purchase the real estate at issue. Finally, the court placed great emphasis on Harris's good faith. It noted her long and dedicated history of service to the Club, her personal oversight of the Club's growth, and her frequent financial contributions to the Club. The court found that her development activities were "generally ... compatible with the corporation's business." This appeal followed.

II. *The Corporate Opportunity Doctrine*

Corporate officers and directors bear a duty of loyalty to the corporations they serve. As Justice Cardozo explained the fiduciary duty in *Meinhard v. Salmon*, 249 N.Y. 458, 164 N.E. 545, 546 (1928):

> A trustee is held to something stricter than the morals of the marketplace. Not honesty alone, but the punctilio of an honor the most sensitive, is then the standard of behavior. As to this there has developed a tradition that is unbending and inveterate.

Maine has embraced this "unbending and inveterate" tradition. Corporate fiduciaries in Maine must discharge their duties in good faith with a view toward furthering the interests of the corporation. They must disclose and not withhold relevant information concerning any potential conflict of interest with the corporation, and they must refrain from using their position, influence, or knowledge of the affairs of the corporation to gain personal advantage.

Despite the general acceptance of the proposition that corporate fiduciaries owe a duty of loyalty to their corporations, there has been much confusion about the specific extent of that duty when, as here, it is contended that a fiduciary takes for herself a corporate opportunity. This case requires us for the first time to define the scope of the corporate opportunity doctrine in Maine.

Various courts have embraced different versions of the corporate opportunity doctrine. The test applied by the trial court and embraced by Harris is generally known as the "line of business" test. The seminal case applying the line of business test is *Guth v. Loft, Inc.*, 5 A.2d 503 (Del. 1939). In *Guth*, the Delaware Supreme Court adopted an intensely factual test stated in general terms as follows:

> [I]f there is presented to a corporate officer or director a business opportunity which the corporation is financially able to undertake, is, from its nature, in the line of the corporation's business and is of practical advantage to it, is one in which the corporation has an interest or a reasonable expectancy, and, by embracing the opportunity, the self-interest of the officer or director will be brought into conflict with that of his corporation, the law will not permit him to seize the opportunity for himself.

Id. at 511. The "real issue" under this test is whether the opportunity "was so closely associated with the existing business activities as to bring the transaction within that class of cases where the acquisition of the property would throw the corporate officer purchasing it into competition with his company." *Id.* at 513. The Delaware court described that inquiry as "a factual question to be decided by reasonable inferences from objective facts." *Id.*

The line of business test suffers from some significant weaknesses. First, the question whether a particular activity is within a corporation's line of business is conceptually difficult to answer. The facts of the instant case demonstrate that difficulty. The Club is in the business of running a golf course. It is not in the business of developing real estate. In the traditional sense, therefore, the trial court correctly observed that the opportunity in this case was not a corporate opportunity within the meaning of the *Guth* test. Nevertheless, the record would support a finding that the Club had made the policy judgment that development of surrounding real estate was detrimental to the best interests of the Club. The acquisition of land adjacent to the golf course for the purpose of preventing future development would have enhanced the ability of the Club to implement that policy. The record also shows that the Club had occasionally considered reversing that policy and expanding its operations to include the development of surrounding real estate. Harris's activities effectively foreclosed the Club from pursuing that option with respect to prime locations adjacent to the golf course.

Second, the *Guth* test includes as an element the financial ability of the corporation to take advantage of the opportunity. The court in this case relied on the Club's supposed financial incapacity as a basis for excusing Harris's conduct. Often, the injection of financial ability into the equation will unduly favor the inside director or executive who has command of the facts relating to the finances of the corporation. Reliance on financial ability will also act as a disincentive to corporate executives to solve corporate financing and other problems. In addition, the Club could have prevented development without spending $275,000 to acquire the property Harris needed to obtain access to the road.

The Massachusetts Supreme Judicial Court adopted a different test in *Durfee v. Durfee & Canning, Inc.*, 323 Mass. 187, 80 N.E.2d 522 (1948). The *Durfee* test has since come to be known as the "fairness test." According to *Durfee*, the

> true basis of governing doctrine rests on the unfairness in the particular circumstances of a director, whose relation to the corporation is fiduciary, taking advantage of an opportunity [for her personal profit] when the interest of the corporation justly call[s] for protection. This calls for application of ethical standards of what is fair and equitable … in particular sets of facts.

Id. at 529 (*quoting Ballantine on Corporations* 204–05 (rev. ed. 1946)). As with the *Guth* test, the *Durfee* test calls for a broad-ranging, intensely factual inquiry. The *Durfee* test suffers even more than the *Guth* test from a lack of principled content. It provides little or no practical guidance to the corporate officer or director seeking to measure her obligations.

The Minnesota Supreme Court elected "to combine the 'line of business' test with the 'fairness' test." *Miller v. Miller*, 301 Minn. 207, 222 N.W.2d 71, 81 (1974). It engaged in a two-step analysis, first determining whether a particular opportunity was within the corporation's line of business, then scrutinizing "the equitable considerations existing prior to, at the time of, and following the officer's acquisition." *Id.* The *Miller* court hoped by adopting this approach "to ameliorate the often-expressed criticism that the [corporate opportunity] doctrine is vague and subjects today's corporate management to the danger of unpredictable liability." *Id.* In fact, the test adopted in *Miller* merely piles the uncertainty and vagueness of the fairness test on top of the weaknesses in the line of business test.

Despite the weaknesses of each of these approaches to the corporate opportunity doctrine, they nonetheless rest on a single fundamental policy. At bottom, the corporate opportunity doctrine recognizes that a corporate fiduciary should not serve both corporate and personal interests at the same time. As we observed in *Camden Land Co. v. Lewis*, 101 Me. 78, 97, 63 A. 523, 531 (1905), corporate fiduciaries "owe their whole duty to the corporation, and they are not to be permitted to act when duty conflicts with interest. They cannot serve themselves and the corporation at the same time." The various formulations of the test are merely attempts to moderate the potentially harsh consequences of strict adherence to that policy. It is important to preserve some ability for corporate fiduciaries to pursue personal business interests that present no real threat to their duty of loyalty.

III. *The American Law Institute Approach*

In an attempt to protect the duty of loyalty while at the same time providing long-needed clarity and guidance for corporate decisionmakers, the American Law Institute has offered the most recently developed version of the corporate opportunity doctrine. *Principles of Corporate Governance* § 5.05 (May 13, 1992), provides as follows:

§ 5.05 Taking of Corporate Opportunities by Directors or Senior Executives

(a) *General Rule.* A director [§ 1.13] or senior executive [§ 1.33] may not take advantage of a corporate opportunity unless:

    (1) The director or senior executive first offers the corporate opportunity to the corporation and makes disclosure concerning the conflict of interest [§ 1.14(a)] and the corporate opportunity [§ 1.14(b)];

    (2) The corporate opportunity is rejected by the corporation; and

    (3) Either:

        (A) The rejection of the opportunity is fair to the corporation;

        (B) The opportunity is rejected in advance, following such disclosure, by disinterested directors [§ 1.15], or, in the case of a senior executive who is not a director, by a disinterested superior, in a manner that satisfies the standards of the business judgment rule [§ 4.01(c)]; or

        (C) The rejection is authorized in advance or ratified, following such disclosure, by disinterested shareholders [§ 1.16], and the rejection is not equivalent to a waste of corporate assets [§ 1.42].

(b) *Definition of a Corporate Opportunity.* For purposes of this Section, a corporate opportunity means:

    (1) Any opportunity to engage in a business activity of which a director or senior executive becomes aware, either:

        (A) In connection with the performance of functions as a director or senior executive, or under circumstances that should reasonably lead the director or senior executive to believe that the person offering the opportunity expects it to be offered to the corporation; or

        (B) Through the use of corporate information or property, if the resulting opportunity is one that the director or senior executive should reasonably be expected to believe would be of interest to the corporation; or

    (2) Any opportunity to engage in a business activity of which a senior executive becomes aware and knows is closely related to a business in which the corporation is engaged or expects to engage.

(c) *Burden of Proof.* A party who challenges the taking of a corporate opportunity has the burden of proof, except that if such party establishes that the requirements of Subsection (a)(3)(B) or (C) are not met, the director or the senior executive has the burden of proving that the rejection and the taking of the opportunity were fair to the corporation.

(d) *Ratification of Defective Disclosure.* A good faith but defective disclosure of the facts concerning the corporate opportunity may be cured if at any time (but no later than a reasonable time after suit is filed challenging the taking of the corporate opportunity) the original rejection of the corporate opportunity is ratified, following the required disclosure, by the board, the shareholders, or the corporate decision-maker who initially approved the rejection of the corporate opportunity, or such decision-maker's successor. . . .

The central feature of the ALI test is the strict requirement of full disclosure prior to taking advantage of any corporate opportunity. *Id.*, § 5.05(a)(1). "If the opportunity is not offered to the corporation, the director or senior executive will not have satisfied § 5.05(a)." *Id.*, cmt. to § 5.05(a). The corporation must then formally reject the opportunity. *Id.*, § 505(a)(2). The ALI test is discussed at length and ultimately applied by the Oregon Supreme Court in *Klinicki v. Lundgren*, 298 Or. 662, 695 P.2d 906 (1985). As *Klinicki* describes the test, "full disclosure to the appropriate corporate body is … an absolute condition precedent to the validity of any forthcoming rejection as well as to the availability to the director or principal senior executive of the defense of fairness." *Id.* at 920. A "good faith but defective disclosure" by the corporate officer may be ratified after the fact only by an affirmative vote of the disinterested directors or shareholders. *Principles of Corporate Governance* § 5.05(d).

The ALI test defines "corporate opportunity" broadly. It includes opportunities "closely related to a business in which the corporation is engaged." *Id.*, § 5.05(b). It also encompasses any opportunities that accrue to the fiduciary as a result of her position within the corporation. *Id.* This concept is most clearly illustrated by the testimony of Suminsby, the listing broker for the Gilpin property, which, if believed by the factfinder, would support a finding that the Gilpin property was offered to Harris specifically in her capacity as president of the Club. If the factfinder reached that conclusion, then at least the opportunity to acquire the Gilpin property would be a corporate opportunity. The state of the record concerning the Smallidge purchase precludes us from intimating any opinion whether that too would be a corporate opportunity.

Under the ALI standard, once the Club shows that the opportunity is a corporate opportunity, it must show either that Harris did not offer the opportunity to the Club or that the Club did not reject it properly. If the Club shows that the board did not reject the opportunity by a vote of the disinterested directors after full disclosure, then Harris may defend her actions on the basis that the taking of the opportunity was fair to the corporation. *Id.*, § 5.05(c). If Harris failed to offer the opportunity at all, however, then she may not defend on the basis that the failure to offer the opportunity was fair. *Id.*, cmt. to § 5.05(c).

The *Klinicki* court viewed the ALI test as an opportunity to bring some clarity to a murky area of the law. *Klinicki*, 695 P.2d at 915. We agree, and today we follow the ALI test. The disclosure-oriented approach provides a clear procedure whereby a corporate officer may insulate herself through prompt and complete disclosure from the possibility of a legal challenge. The requirement of disclosure recognizes the paramount importance of the corporate fiduciary's duty of loyalty. At the same time it protects the fiduciary's ability pursuant to the proper procedure to pursue her own business ventures free from the possibility of a lawsuit....

IV. *Conclusion*

The question remains how our adoption of the rule affects the result in the instant case. The trial court made a number of factual findings based on an extensive record. The court made those findings, however, in the light of legal principles that are different from the principles that we today announce. Similarly, the parties did not have the opportunity to develop the record in this case with knowledge of the applicable legal standard. In these circumstances, fairness requires that we remand the case for further proceedings. Those further proceedings may include, at the trial court's discretion, the taking of further evidence....

Notes and Questions

1. The Superior Court held for the Club on remand. The Maine Supreme Court on appeal concluded that the Gilpin and Smallridge lots were "corporate opportunities" and that Harris breached her fiduciary duty by not offering the properties to the Club. However, the court also held that the Club's action was barred by the statute of limitations.

2. If the ALI approach applied to the *Broz* facts, could that opinion have ended immediately after the paragraph that begins, "We note at the outset that Broz became aware of the Michigan-2 opportunity in his individual and not his corporate capacity"? The Delaware court, despite stressing that fact, concluded that it "is not dispositive." Under the ALI approach, would such a fact be dispositive?

3. It appears that the trial court in *Harris* followed the Delaware approach of *Guth* (and *Broz*). Which of the relevant factors are highly contestable and which are less so? One fact that seems incontestable is that Ms. Harris did not offer any of the opportunities to the corporation.

Chapter 12

Duties of Controlling Shareholders

Situation

a. Welsh's conflict of interest problem has been handled, but it and the possible shareholder suit for mismanagement may have left some ill feelings behind. In any case, some dissension has developed between Anderson and Baker on the one side and the other shareholders on the other. Given increasing corporate profits, Anderson and Baker want to raise their salaries again. At current revenue levels, reasonable salary increases would still leave enough profits to continue the expansion of the business, especially since bank interest rates are currently attractive and further borrowings are contemplated in any case to fuel the expansion.

Phillips and Welsh agree that it makes sense to take some cash out of the business and to borrow from the bank to help finance expansion. But rather than salary increases for Anderson and Baker, they propose instead a dividend distribution to all the shareholders paid pro rata. In that way, they say, all the shareholders can share in the corporation's success.

At a board meeting held a few days ago, Anderson and Baker wanted their salary increase approved and Phillips and Welsh pushed for their alternative suggestion. The deciding vote could have been cast by Martinez, the only disinterested director. Martinez, however, asked that the vote be put off until she could think about what she should do. She told Anderson and Baker that she realized they hold enough stock to replace her as a director if they wish, but said she hoped they would not do so until she had a chance to make her decision. She also suggested that Anderson and Baker seek your advice.

Anderson and Baker agreed to put off the vote and have spoken to you about this situation and have asked your advice. They believe the corporation's successes have come almost entirely from their efforts and that, while Phillips' investment was necessary in the beginning, he has already done very well on his investment. Also, they believe stock was sold too cheaply to Welsh and the other shareholders who purchased when he did, and they are not anxious to share current profits with them. Anderson and Baker do not want to remove Martinez from the board, but are certain she would vote their way when she realized they would remove her if need be.

b. Meanwhile, Biologistics' work has caught the attention of Daytron Corporation, a large publicly held conglomerate. Representatives of Daytron have discreetly and confidentially approached Anderson and Baker about selling their stock in Biologistics. Daytron appears willing to offer a generous premium for their controlling interest.

While Daytron is vague about what it would do if it obtained controlling interest, it suggests that a merger between Daytron and Biologistics is an attractive possibility.

Anderson and Baker seek your advice about these various possibilities.

———————

While shareholders ordinarily do not assume fiduciary duties, courts in certain circumstances have developed duties owed by controlling shareholders to the corporation and minority shareholders. The materials in this chapter explore these duties in three contexts: in the operation of the corporation, in the sale of control, and in merger transactions.

Section I
Operation of Corporations
Sinclair Oil Corp. v. Levien
Delaware Supreme Court
280 A.2d 717 (1971)

Wolcott, Chief Justice:

This is an appeal by the defendant, Sinclair Oil Corporation (hereafter Sinclair), from an order of the Court of Chancery, 261 A.2d 911 in a derivative action requiring Sinclair to account for damages sustained by its subsidiary, Sinclair Venezuelan Oil Company (hereafter Sinven), organized by Sinclair for the purpose of operating in Venezuela, as a result of dividends paid by Sinven, the denial to Sinven of industrial development, and a breach of contract between Sinclair's wholly-owned subsidiary, Sinclair International Oil Company, and Sinven.

Sinclair, operating primarily as a holding company, is in the business of exploring for oil and of producing and marketing crude oil and oil products. At all times relevant to this litigation, it owned about 97% of Sinven's stock. The plaintiff owns about 3000 of 120,000 publicly held shares of Sinven. Sinven, incorporated in 1922, has been engaged in petroleum operations primarily in Venezuela and since 1959 has operated exclusively in Venezuela.

Sinclair nominates all members of Sinven's board of directors. The Chancellor found as a fact that the directors were not independent of Sinclair. Almost without exception, they were officers, directors, or employees of corporations in the Sinclair complex. By reason of Sinclair's domination, it is clear that Sinclair owed Sinven a fiduciary duty. Sinclair concedes this.

The Chancellor held that because of Sinclair's fiduciary duty and its control over Sinven, its relationship with Sinven must meet the test of intrinsic fairness. The standard of intrinsic fairness involves both a high degree of fairness and a shift in the burden of proof. Under this standard the burden is on Sinclair to prove, subject to careful judicial scrutiny, that its transactions with Sinven were objectively fair.

Sinclair argues that the transactions between it and Sinven should be tested, not by the test of intrinsic fairness with the accompanying shift of the burden of proof, but by the business judgment rule under which a court will not interfere with the judgment of a board of directors unless there is a showing of gross and palpable overreaching....

We think, however, that Sinclair's argument in this respect is misconceived. When the situation involves a parent and a subsidiary, with the parent controlling the transaction and fixing the terms, the test of intrinsic fairness, with its resulting shifting of the burden of proof, is applied. The basic situation for the application of the rule is the one in which the parent has received a benefit to the exclusion and at the expense of the subsidiary.

Recently, this court dealt with the question of fairness in parent-subsidiary dealings in *Getty Oil Co. v. Skelly Oil Co.*, [267 A.2d 883 (Del. 1970)]. In that case, both parent and subsidiary were in the business of refining and marketing crude oil and crude oil products. The Oil Import Board ruled that the subsidiary, because it was controlled by the parent, was no longer entitled to a separate allocation of imported crude oil. The subsidiary then contended that it had a right to share the quota of crude oil allotted to the parent. We ruled that the business judgment standard should be applied to determine this contention. Although the subsidiary suffered a loss through the administration of the oil import quotas, the parent gained nothing. The parent's quota was derived solely from its own past use. The past use of the subsidiary did not cause an increase in the parent's quota. Nor did the parent usurp a quota of the subsidiary. Since the parent received nothing from the subsidiary to the exclusion of the minority stockholders of the subsidiary, there was no self-dealing. Therefore, the business judgment standard was properly applied.

A parent does indeed owe a fiduciary duty to its subsidiary when there are parent-subsidiary dealings. However, this alone will not evoke the intrinsic fairness standard. This standard will be applied only when the fiduciary duty is accompanied by self-dealing—the situation when a parent is on both sides of a transaction with its subsidiary. Self-dealing occurs when the parent, by virtue of its domination of the subsidiary, causes the subsidiary to act in such a way that the parent receives something from the subsidiary to the exclusion of, and detriment to, the minority stockholders of the subsidiary.

We turn now to the facts. The plaintiff argues that, from 1960 through 1966, Sinclair caused Sinven to pay out such excessive dividends that the industrial development of Sinven was effectively prevented, and it became in reality a corporation in dissolution.

From 1960 through 1966, Sinven paid out $108,000,000 in dividends ($38,000,000 in excess of Sinven's earnings during the same period). The Chancellor held that Sinclair caused these dividends to be paid during a period when it had a need for large amounts of cash. Although the dividends paid exceeded earnings, the plaintiff concedes that the payments were made in compliance with 8 Del. C. § 170, authorizing payment of dividends out of surplus or net profits. However, the plaintiff attacks these dividends on the ground that they resulted from an improper motive — Sinclair's need for cash. The Chancellor, applying the intrinsic fairness standard, held that Sinclair did not sustain its burden of proving that these dividends were intrinsically fair to the minority stockholders of Sinven.

Since it is admitted that the dividends were paid in strict compliance with 8 Del. C. § 170, the alleged excessiveness of the payments alone would not state a cause of action. Nevertheless, compliance with the applicable statute may not, under all circumstances, justify all dividend payments. If a plaintiff can meet his burden of proving that a dividend cannot be grounded on any reasonable business objective, then the courts can and will interfere with the board's decision to pay the dividend.

Sinclair contends that it is improper to apply the intrinsic fairness standard to dividend payments even when the board which voted for the dividends is completely dominated....

We do not accept the argument that the intrinsic fairness test can never be applied to a dividend declaration by a dominated board, although a dividend declaration by a dominated board will not inevitably demand the application of the intrinsic fairness standard. If such a dividend is in essence self-dealing by the parent, then the intrinsic fairness standard is the proper standard. For example, suppose a parent dominates a subsidiary and its board of directors. The subsidiary has outstanding two classes of stock, X and Y. Class X is owned by the parent and Class Y is owned by minority stockholders of the subsidiary. If the subsidiary, at the direction of the parent, declares a dividend on its Class X stock only, this might well be self-dealing by the parent. It would be receiving something from the subsidiary to the exclusion of and detrimental to its minority stockholders. This self-dealing, coupled with the parent's fiduciary duty, would make intrinsic fairness the proper standard by which to evaluate the dividend payments.

Consequently it must be determined whether the dividend payments by Sinven were, in essence, self-dealing by Sinclair. The dividends resulted in great sums of money being transferred from Sinven to Sinclair. However, a proportionate share of this money was received by the minority shareholders of Sinven. Sinclair received nothing from Sinven to the exclusion of its minority stockholders. As such, these dividends were not self-dealing. We hold therefore that the Chancellor erred in applying the intrinsic fairness test as to these dividend payments. The business judgment standard should have been applied.

We conclude that the facts demonstrate that the dividend payments complied with the business judgment standard and with 8 Del. C. § 170. The motives for causing the declaration of dividends are immaterial unless the plaintiff can show that the dividend payments resulted from improper motives and amounted to waste. The plaintiff contends only that the dividend payments drained Sinven of cash to such an extent that it was prevented from expanding.

The plaintiff proved no business opportunities which came to Sinven independently and which Sinclair either took to itself or denied to Sinven. As a matter of fact, with two minor exceptions which resulted in losses, all of Sinven's operations have been conducted in Venezuela, and Sinclair had a policy of exploiting its oil properties located in different countries by subsidiaries located in the particular countries.

From 1960 to 1966 Sinclair purchased or developed oil fields in Alaska, Canada, Paraguay, and other places around the world. The plaintiff contends that these were all opportunities which could have been taken by Sinven. The Chancellor concluded that Sinclair had not proved that its denial of expansion opportunities to Sinven was intrinsically fair. He based this conclusion on the following findings of fact. Sinclair made no real effort to expand Sinven. The excessive dividends paid by Sinven resulted in so great a cash drain as to effectively deny to Sinven any ability to expand. During this same period Sinclair actively pursued a company-wide policy of developing through its subsidiaries new sources of revenue, but Sinven was not permitted to participate and was confined in its activities to Venezuela.

However, the plaintiff could point to no opportunities which came to Sinven. Therefore, Sinclair usurped no business opportunity belonging to Sinven. Since Sinclair received nothing from Sinven to the exclusion of and detriment to Sinven's minority stockholders, there was no self-dealing. Therefore, business judgment is the proper standard by which to evaluate Sinclair's expansion policies.

Since there is no proof of self-dealing on the part of Sinclair, it follows that the expansion policy of Sinclair and the methods used to achieve the desired result must, as far as Sinclair's treatment of Sinven is concerned, be tested by the standards of the business judgment rule. Accordingly, Sinclair's decision, absent fraud or gross overreaching, to achieve expansion through the medium of its subsidiaries, other than Sinven, must be upheld.

Even if Sinclair was wrong in developing these opportunities as it did, the question arises, with which subsidiaries should these opportunities have been shared? No evidence indicates a unique need or ability of Sinven to develop these opportunities. The decision of which subsidiaries would be used to implement Sinclair's expansion policy was one of business judgment with which a court will not interfere absent a showing of gross and palpable overreaching. No such showing has been made here.

Next, Sinclair argues that the Chancellor committed error when he held it liable to Sinven for breach of contract.

In 1961 Sinclair created Sinclair International Oil Company (hereafter International), a wholly owned subsidiary used for the purpose of coordinating all of Sinclair's foreign operations. All crude purchases by Sinclair were made thereafter through International.

On September 28, 1961, Sinclair caused Sinven to contract with International whereby Sinven agreed to sell all of its crude oil and refined products to International at specified prices. The contract provided for minimum and maximum quantities and prices. The plaintiff contends that Sinclair caused this contract to be breached in two respects. Although the contract called for payment on receipt, International's payments lagged as much as 30 days after receipt. Also, the contract required International to purchase at least a fixed minimum amount of crude and refined products from Sinven. International did not comply with this requirement.

Clearly, Sinclair's act of contracting with its dominated subsidiary was self-dealing. Under the contract Sinclair received the products produced by Sinven, and of course the minority shareholders of Sinven were not able to share in the receipt of these products. If the contract was breached, then Sinclair received these products to the detriment of Sinven's minority shareholders. We agree with the Chancellor's finding that the contract was breached by Sinclair, both as to the time of payments and the amounts purchased.

Although a parent need not bind itself by a contract with its dominated subsidiary, Sinclair chose to operate in this manner. As Sinclair has received the benefits of this contract, so must it comply with the contractual duties.

Under the intrinsic fairness standard, Sinclair must prove that its causing Sinven not to enforce the contract was intrinsically fair to the minority shareholders of Sinven. Sinclair has failed to meet this burden. Late payments were clearly breaches for which Sinven should have sought and received adequate damages. As to the quantities purchased, Sinclair argues that it purchased all the products produced by Sinven. This, however, does not satisfy the standard of intrinsic fairness. Sinclair has failed to prove that Sinven could not possibly have produced or someway have obtained the contract minimums. As such, Sinclair must account on this claim....

Notes and Questions

1. How do the duties of controlling shareholders differ from those of directors and officers? For example, *Sinclair* indicates that a "fairness" review does not automatically occur in transactions between the corporation and a controlling shareholder as it ordinarily does when the corporation transacts with an interested director or officer. Why the difference?

2. In considering differences between corporate officials and corporate shareholders, recall that corporate officials are fiduciaries by virtue of their positions and law-imposed duties; corporate shareholders are beneficiaries of those duties and generally are free to do as they please.

3. Recall also how the general duties of care and loyalty of corporate officers and directors are modulated by statute. For example, authorized charter exculpation concerning the duty of care applies to directors (as in DGCL § 102(b)(7)) and, in some states, officers. Similarly, interested transaction statutes typically apply to directors and officers (as in DGCL § 144), but such statutes do not address transactions involving controlling shareholders.

4. There is little mechanical guidance on what constitutes "control" for characterizing a shareholder as a controlling shareholder. True, majority voting control would invariably qualify but share ownership at lower levels may too, depending on the circumstances. The circumstances include the size of the interest owned by other shareholders and other positions in the corporation that a shareholder may hold, such as chairman of the board and CEO. The following table showing the "scatter-plot" result is adapted from *In re Crimson Exploration Inc. Stockholder Litig.*, 2014 WL 5449419 (Del. Ch. 2014):

Case[1]	_%_	_Control?_
1. O'Reilly v. Transworld Healthcare, Inc.	49	Yes
2. In re W. Nat'l Corp. S'holder Litig.	46	No
3. Superior Vision Servs., Inc. v. ReliaStar Life Ins.	44	No
4. Kahn v. Lynch	43	Yes
5. In re Primedia, Inc. Deriv. Litig.	40	Yes
6. In re Sea-Land Corp. S'holder Litig.	39	No
7. In re Cysive, Inc. S'holder Litig.	35	Yes
8. In re PNB Hldg. Co. S'holder Litig.	33	No
9. In re Mortons Rest. Gp., Inc. S'holder Litig.	27	No

The court continued:

> As this table makes clear, the cases do not reveal any sort of linear, sliding-scale approach whereby a larger share percentage makes it substantially more likely that the court will find the stockholder was a controlling stockholder. Instead, the scatter-plot nature of the holdings highlights the importance and fact-intensive nature of the actual control factor.... In the seminal case of *Kahn v. Lynch*, Alcatel owned 43.3 percent of Lynch Communications. In finding that Alcatel acted as a controller, the Delaware Supreme Court noted the following factors: (a) Alcatel designated five of the eleven members of the board; (b) the record was replete with instances of Alcatel making its will known to the board and then prevailing in its wishes; (c) certain non-Alcatel board members testified that the Alcatel representative terrified them; and (d) Alcatel dominated the merger discussions and threatened a hostile takeover if the board did not comply....

> At the other end of the spectrum [is] *Cysive*.... *Cysive* involved Nelson Carbonell, the company's founder, CEO, chairman, and a 35% stockholder, who also employed his brother and brother-in-law in high-ranking positions at the company. If his stock holdings were combined with the holdings of his close family member managers and the group's options to purchase shares, Carbonell could command as much 40% of the common stock. This combination of stockholdings and embedded managerial oversight allowed Carbonell "as a practical matter ... to control the corporation." ...

A few weeks after the *Crimson* opinion appeared, a different Delaware Vice Chancellor in another case found a CEO holding 17.3% to be a controlling shareholder.

---

1. The citations are as follows:
   1: 745 A.2d 902 (Del. Ch.1999).
   2: 2000 WL 710192 (Del. Ch. May 22, 2000).
   3: 2006 WL 2521426 (Del. Ch. Aug. 25, 2006).
   4: 638 A.2d 1110 (Del. 2002)
   5: 910 A.2d 248 (Del. Ch.2006).
   6: 1987 WL 11283 (Del. Ch. May 22, 1987).
   7: 836 A.2d 531 (Del. Ch.2003).
   8: 2006 WL 2403999 (Del. Ch. Aug. 18, 2006).
   9: 74 A.3d 656 (Del. Ch.2013).

The opinion emphasized, as do most others concerning non-majority controlling shareholders, whether the shareholder exerted control over the particular transaction being challenged. *See Zhongpin Inc. Stockholder Litig.*, 2014 WL 46735457 (Del. Ch. 2014).

Section II
Sale of Control

Shares constituting a controlling interest in voting power usually can be sold at a premium because of the added benefits to the buyer that flow from the ability to control the corporation. At the same time, a shareholder in general may sell his or her interest for whatever price may be obtained. Some courts have found, however, that in making such a sale a controlling shareholder has a fiduciary obligation to protect the corporation and the other shareholders.

Perlman v. Feldmann

United States Court of Appeals, Second Circuit
219 F.2d 173 (1955)

CLARK, CHIEF JUDGE:

This is a derivative action brought by minority stockholders of Newport Steel Corporation to compel accounting for, and restitution of, allegedly illegal gains which accrued to defendants as a result of the sale in August, 1950, of their controlling interest in the corporation. The principal defendant, C. Russell Feldmann, who represented and acted for the others, members of his family,[1] was at that time not only the dominant stockholder, but also the chairman of the board of directors and the president of the corporation. Newport, an Indiana corporation, operated mills for the production of steel sheets for sale to manufacturers of steel products, first at Newport, Kentucky, and later also at other places in Kentucky and Ohio. The buyers, a syndicate organized as Wilport Company, a Delaware corporation, consisted of end-users of steel who were interested in securing a source of supply in a market becoming ever tighter in the Korean War. Plaintiffs contend that the consideration paid for the stock included compensation for the sale of a corporate asset, a power held in trust for the corporation by Feldmann as its fiduciary. This power was the ability to control the allocation of the corporate product in a time of short supply, through control of the board of directors; and it was effectively transferred in this sale by having Feldmann procure the resignation of his own board and the election of Wilport's nominees immediately upon consummation of the sale.

---

1. [1] The stock was not held personally by Feldmann in his own name, but was held by the members of his family and by personal corporations. The aggregate of stock thus had amounted to 33% of the outstanding Newport stock and gave working control to the holder. The actual sale included 55,552 additional shares held by friends and associates of Feldmann, so that a total of 37% of the Newport stock was transferred.

The present action represents the consolidation of three pending stockholders' actions in which yet another stockholder has been permitted to intervene. Jurisdiction below was based upon the diverse citizenship of the parties. Plaintiffs argue here, as they did in the court below, that in the situation here disclosed the vendors must account to the non-participating minority stockholders for that share of their profit which is attributable to the sale of the corporate power. Judge Hincks denied the validity of the premise, holding that the rights involved in the sale were only those normally incident to the possession of a controlling block of shares, with which a dominant stockholder, in the absence of fraud or foreseeable looting, was entitled to deal according to his own best interests. Furthermore, he held that plaintiffs had failed to satisfy their burden of proving that the sales price was not a fair price for the stock *per se*. Plaintiffs appeal from these rulings of law which resulted in the dismissal of their complaint.

The essential facts found by the trial judge are not in dispute. Newport was a relative newcomer in the steel industry with predominantly old installations which were in the process of being supplemented by more modern facilities. Except in times of extreme shortage Newport was not in a position to compete profitably with other steel mills for customers not in its immediate geographical area. Wilport, the purchasing syndicate, consisted of geographically remote end-users of steel who were interested in buying more steel from Newport than they had been able to obtain during recent periods of tight supply. The price of $20 per share was found by Judge Hincks to be a fair one for a control block of stock, although the over-the-counter market price had not exceeded $12 and the book value per share was $17.03. But this finding was limited by Judge Hincks' statement that "what value the block would have had if shorn of its appurtenant power to control distribution of the corporate product, the evidence does not show." It was also conditioned by his earlier ruling that the burden was on plaintiffs to prove a lesser value for the stock.

Both as director and as dominant stockholder, Feldmann stood in a fiduciary relationship to the corporation and to the minority stockholders as beneficiaries thereof. Although there is no Indiana case directly in point, the most closely analogous one emphasizes the close scrutiny to which Indiana subjects the conduct of fiduciaries when personal benefit may stand in the way of fulfillment of trust obligations. In *Schemmel v. Hill*, 169 N.E. 678, 682, 683, [(Ind. Ap. Ct. 1930)] McMahan, J., said: "... In a transaction between a director and his corporation, where he acts for himself and his principal at the same time in a matter connected with the relation between them, it is presumed, where he is thus [potentially] on both sides of the contract, that self-interest will overcome his fidelity to his principal, to his own benefit and to his principal's hurt." And the judge added: "Absolute and most scrupulous good faith is the very essence of a director's obligation to his corporation. The first principal duty arising from his official relation is to act in all things of trust wholly for the benefit of his corporation."

In Indiana, then, as elsewhere, the responsibility of the fiduciary is not limited to a proper regard for the tangible balance sheet assets of the corporation, but includes the dedication of his uncorrupted business judgment for the sole benefit of the corporation, in any dealings which may adversely affect it. Although the Indiana case is particularly relevant to Feldmann as a director, the same rule should apply to his fiduciary duties as majority stockholder, for in that capacity he chooses and controls the directors, and thus is held to have assumed their liability. This, therefore, is the standard to which Feldmann was by law required to conform in his activities here under scrutiny.

It is true, as defendants have been at pains to point out, that this is not the ordinary case of breach of fiduciary duty. We have here no fraud, no misuse of confidential information, no outright looting of a helpless corporation. But on the other hand, we do not find compliance with that high standard which we have just stated and which we and other courts have come to expect and demand of corporate fiduciaries. In the often-quoted words of Judge Cardozo: "Many forms of conduct permissible in a workaday world for those acting at arm's length, are forbidden to those bound by fiduciary ties. A trustee is held to something stricter than the morals of the market place. Not honesty alone, but the punctilio of an honor the most sensitive, is then the standard of behavior. As to this there has developed a tradition that is unbending and inveterate. Uncompromising rigidity has been the attitude of courts of equity when petitioned to undermine the rule of undivided loyalty by the 'disintegrating erosion' of particular exceptions." *Meinhard v. Salmon*, 164 N.E. 545, 546. The actions of defendants in siphoning off for personal gain corporate advantages to be derived from a favorable market situation do not betoken the necessary undivided loyalty owed by the fiduciary to his principal.

The corporate opportunities of whose misappropriation the minority stockholders complain need not have been an absolute certainty in order to support this action against Feldmann. If there was possibility of corporate gain, they are entitled to recover. In *Young v. Higbee Co.*, 324 U.S. 204, two stockholders appealing the confirmation of a plan of bankruptcy reorganization were held liable for profits received for the sale of their stock pending determination of the validity of the appeal. They were held accountable for the excess of the price of their stock over its normal price, even though there was no indication that the appeal could have succeeded on substantive grounds. And in *Irving Trust Co. v. Deutsch*, 2d Cir., 73 F.2d 121, 124, an accounting was required of corporate directors who bought stock for themselves for corporate use, even though there was an affirmative showing that the corporation did not have the finances itself to acquire the stock. Judge Swan speaking for the court pointed out that "The defendants' argument, contrary to *Wing v. Dillingham* (5th Cir., 239 F. 54), that the equitable rule that fiduciaries should not be permitted to assume a position in which their individual interests might be in conflict with those of the corporation can have no application where the corporation is unable to undertake the venture, is not convincing. If directors are permitted to justify their conduct on such a theory, there will be a temptation to refrain from exerting their strongest efforts on behalf of the corporation since, if it does not meet the obligations, an opportunity of profit will be open to them personally."

This rationale is equally appropriate to a consideration of the benefits which Newport might have derived from the steel shortage. In the past Newport had used and profited by its market leverage by operation of what the industry had come to call the "Feldmann Plan." This consisted of securing interest-free advances from prospective purchasers of steel in return for firm commitments to them from future production. The funds thus acquired were used to finance improvements in existing plants and to acquire new installations. In the summer of 1950 Newport had been negotiating for cold-rolling facilities which it needed for a more fully integrated operation and a more marketable product, and Feldmann plan funds might well have been used toward this end.

Further, as plaintiffs alternatively suggest, Newport might have used the period of short supply to build up patronage in the geographical area in which it could compete profitably even when steel was more abundant. Either of these opportunities was Newport's, to be used to its advantage only. Only if defendants had been able to negate completely any possibility of gain by Newport could they have prevailed. It is true that a trial court finding states: "Whether or not, in August, 1950, Newport's position was such that it could have entered into 'Feldmann Plan' type transactions to procure funds and financing for the further expansion and integration of its steel facilities and whether such expansion would have been desirable for Newport, the evidence does not show." This, however, cannot avail the defendants, who — contrary to the ruling below — had the burden of proof on this issue, since fiduciaries always have the burden of proof in establishing the fairness of their dealings with trust property. . . .

Defendants seek to categorize the corporate opportunities which might have accrued to Newport as too unethical to warrant further consideration. It is true that reputable steel producers were not participating in the gray market brought about by the Korean War and were refraining from advancing their prices, although to do so would not have been illegal. But Feldmann plan transactions were not considered within this self-imposed interdiction; the trial court found that around the time of the Feldmann sale Jones & Laughlin Steel Corporation, Republic Steel Company, and Pittsburgh Steel Corporation were all participating in such arrangements. In any event, it ill becomes the defendants to disparage as unethical the market advantages from which they themselves reaped rich benefits.

We do not mean to suggest that a majority stockholder cannot dispose of his controlling block of stock to outsiders without having to account to his corporation for profits or even never do this with impunity when the buyer is an interested customer, actual or potential, for the corporation's product. But when the sale necessarily results in a sacrifice of this element of corporate good will and consequent unusual profit to the fiduciary who has caused the sacrifice, he should account for his gains. So in a time of market shortage, where a call on a corporation's product commands an unusually large premium, in one form or another, we think it sound law that a fiduciary may not appropriate to himself the value of this premium. Such personal gain at the expense of his coventurers seems particularly reprehensible when made by the trusted president and director of his company. In this case the violation of duty seems to be all the clearer because of this triple role in which Feldmann appears, though we are unwilling to say, and are not to be understood as saying, that we should accept a lesser obligation for any one of his roles alone.

Hence to the extent that the price received by Feldmann and his codefendants included such a bonus, he is accountable to the minority stockholders who sue here. And plaintiffs, as they contend, are entitled to a recovery in their own right, instead of in right of the corporation (as in the usual derivative actions), since neither Wilport nor their successors in interest should share in any judgment which may be rendered. Defendants cannot well object to this form of recovery, since the only alternative, recovery for the corporation as a whole, would subject them to a greater total liability.

The case will therefore be remanded to the district court for a determination of the question expressly left open below, namely, the value of defendants' stock without the appurtenant control over the corporation's output of steel. We reiterate that on this issue, as on all others relating to a breach of fiduciary duty, the burden of proof must rest on the defendants. Judgment should go to these plaintiffs and those whom they represent for any premium value so shown to the extent of their respective stock interests.

The judgment is therefore reversed and the action remanded for further proceedings pursuant to this opinion.

SWAN, CIRCUIT JUDGE (dissenting):

With the general principles enunciated in the majority opinion as to the duties of fiduciaries I am, of course, in thorough accord. But, as Mr. Justice Frankfurter stated in *Securities and Exchange Comm. v. Chenery Corp.*, 318 U.S. 80, 85, "to say that a man is a fiduciary only begins analysis; it gives direction to further inquiry. To whom is he a fiduciary? What obligations does he owe as a fiduciary? In what respect has he failed to discharge these obligations?" My brothers' opinion does not specify precisely what fiduciary duty Feldmann is held to have violated or whether it was a duty imposed upon him as the dominant stockholder or as a director of Newport. Without such specification I think that both the legal profession and the business world will find the decision confusing and will be unable to foretell the extent of its impact upon customary practices in the sale of stock.

The power to control the management of a corporation, that is, to elect directors to manage its affairs, is an inseparable incident to the ownership of a majority of its stock, or sometimes, as in the present instance, to the ownership of enough shares, less than a majority, to control an election. Concededly a majority or dominant shareholder is ordinarily privileged to sell his stock at the best price obtainable from the purchaser. In so doing he acts on his own behalf, not as an agent of the corporation. If he knows or has reason to believe that the purchaser intends to exercise to the detriment of the corporation the power of management acquired by the purchase, such knowledge or reasonable suspicion will terminate the dominant shareholder's privilege to sell and will create a duty not to transfer the power of management to such purchaser. The duty seems to me to resemble the obligation which everyone is under not to assist another to commit a tort rather than the obligation of a fiduciary. But whatever the nature of the duty, a violation of it will subject the violator to liability for damages sustained by the corporation. Judge Hincks found that Feldmann had no reason to think that Wilport would use the power of management it would acquire by the purchase to injure Newport, and that there was no proof that it ever was so used. Feldmann did know, it is true, that the reason Wilport wanted the stock was to put in a board of directors who would be likely to permit Wilport's members to purchase more of Newport's steel than they might otherwise be able to get. But there is nothing illegal in a dominant shareholder purchasing from his own corporation at the same prices it offers to other customers. That is what the members of Wilport did, and there is no proof that Newport suffered any detriment therefrom.

My brothers say that "the consideration paid for the stock included compensation for the sale of a corporate asset," which they describe as "the ability to control the allocation of the corporate product in a time of short supply, through control of the board of directors; and it was effectively transferred in this sale by having Feldmann procure the resignation of his own board and the election of Wilport's nominees immediately upon consummation of the sale." The implications of this are not clear to me. If it means that when market conditions are such as to induce users of a corporation's product to wish to buy a controlling block of stock in order to be able to purchase part of the corporation's output at the same mill list prices as are offered to other customers, the dominant stockholder is under a fiduciary duty not to sell his stock, I cannot agree. For reasons already stated, in my opinion Feldmann was not proved to be under any fiduciary duty as a stockholder not to sell the stock he controlled.

Feldmann was also a director of Newport. Perhaps the quoted statement means that as a director he violated his fiduciary duty in voting to elect Wilport's nominees to fill the vacancies created by the resignations of the former directors of Newport. As a director Feldmann was under a fiduciary duty to use an honest judgment in acting on the corporation's behalf. A director is privileged to resign, but so long as he remains a director he must be faithful to his fiduciary duties and must not make a personal gain from performing them. Consequently, if the price paid for Feldmann's stock included a payment for voting to elect the new directors, he must account to the corporation for such payment, even though he honestly believed that the men he voted to elect were well qualified to serve as directors. He can not take pay for performing his fiduciary duty. There is no suggestion that he did do so, unless the price paid for his stock was more than its value. So it seems to me that decision must turn on whether finding 120 and conclusion 5 of the district judge are supportable on the evidence. They are set out in the margin.[2]

Judge Hincks went into the matter of valuation of the stock with his customary care and thoroughness. He made no error of law in applying the principles relating to valuation of stock. Concededly a controlling block of stock has greater sale value than a small lot. While the spread between $10 per share for small lots and $20 per

2. [1] "120. The 398,927 shares of Newport stock sold to Wilport as of August 31, 1950, had a fair value as a control block of $20 per share. What value the block would have had if shorn of its appurtenant power to control distribution of the corporate product, the evidence does not show."

"5. Even if Feldmann's conduct in cooperating to accomplish a transfer of control to Wilport immediately upon the sale constituted a breach of a fiduciary duty to Newport, no part of the moneys received by the defendants in connection with the sale constituted profits for which they were accountable to Newport."

share for the controlling block seems rather extraordinarily wide, the $20 valuation was supported by the expert testimony of Dr. Badger, whom the district judge said he could not find to be wrong. I see no justification for upsetting the valuation as clearly erroneous. Nor can I agree with my brothers that the $20 valuation "was limited" by the last sentence in finding 120. The controlling block could not by any possibility be shorn of its appurtenant power to elect directors and through them to control distribution of the corporate product. It is this "appurtenant power" which gives a controlling block its value as such block. What evidence could be adduced to show the value of the block "if shorn" of such appurtenant power, I cannot conceive, for it cannot be shorn of it....

The final conclusion of my brothers is that the plaintiffs are entitled to recover in their own right instead of in the right of the corporation. This appears to be completely inconsistent with the theory advanced at the outset of the opinion, namely, that the price of the stock "included compensation for the sale of a corporate asset." If a corporate asset was sold, surely the corporation should recover the compensation received for it by the defendants. Moreover, if the plaintiffs were suing in their own right, Newport was not a proper party....

Notes and Questions

1. Though *Perlman* is a landmark case and helps to frame the issue concerning any duty majority shareholders may owe minority shareholders when selling control block shares, prevailing law generally follows the opposite stance. That is, absent extraordinary circumstances of the sort *Perlman* presented, majority shareholders may sell control block shares and retain the entire premium for doing so. The rationale for this general stance appears in the following analysis from *Zetlin v. Hanson Holdings, Inc.*, 397 N.E.2d 387–89 (N.Y. 1979).

> Plaintiff Zetlin owned approximately 2% of the outstanding shares of Gable Industries, Inc., with defendants Hanson Holdings, Inc., and Sylvestri together with members of the Sylvestri family, owning 44.4% of Gable's shares. The defendants sold their interests to Flintkote Co. for a premium price of $15 per share, at a time when Gable was selling on the open market for $7.38 per share. It is undisputed that the 44.4% acquired by Flintkote represented effective control of Gable.
>
> Recognizing that those who invest the capital necessary to acquire a dominant position in the ownership of a corporation have the right of controlling that corporation, it has long been settled law that, absent looting of corporate assets, conversion of a corporate opportunity, fraud or other acts of bad faith, a controlling stockholder is free to sell, and a purchaser is free to buy, that controlling interest at a premium price....
>
> Certainly, minority shareholders are entitled to protection against such abuse by controlling shareholders. They are not entitled, however, to inhibit the legitimate interests of the other stockholders. It is for this reason that control shares usually command a premium price. The premium is the added amount

an investor is willing to pay for the privilege of directly influencing the corporation's affairs.

In this action plaintiff Zetlin contends that minority stockholders are entitled to an opportunity to share equally in any premium paid for a controlling interest in the corporation. This rule would profoundly affect the manner in which controlling stock interests are now transferred. It would require, essentially, that a controlling interest be transferred only by means of an offer to all stockholders, *i.e.*, a tender offer. This would be contrary to existing law and if so radical a change is to be effected it would best be done by the Legislature....

2. Section 5.16 of the ALI principles of Corporate Governance elaborates:

A controlling shareholder has the same right to dispose of voting equity securities as any other shareholder, including the right to dispose of those securities for a price that is not made proportionally available to other shareholders, but the controlling shareholder does not satisfy the duty of fair dealing to the other shareholders if:

(a) The controlling shareholder does not make disclosure concerning the transaction to other shareholders with whom the controlling shareholder deals in connection with the transaction; or

(b) It is apparent from the circumstances that the purchaser is likely to violate the duty of fair dealing ... in such a way as to obtain a significant financial benefit for the purchaser or an associate.

3. As ALI § 5.16 Comment *c* explains:

Debate over whether a controlling shareholder should be allowed to sell a controlling interest in a corporation at a premium without sharing that premium with other shareholders largely has focused on the explanation for the premium. If the premium is paid for the opportunity to exploit minority shareholders, the sale should be discouraged by requiring the premium to be shared. If the premium reflects only what otherwise would have been the corporation's share of the efficiency gains that will result from the transfer of control, requiring the premium to be shared will not discourage the transfer of control, because even with a sharing requirement the sale will still make the controlling shareholder better off. If, alternatively, the premium reflects a differential in value between controlling and minority shares that is not the result of exploiting minority shareholders — for example, because control allows a controlling shareholder the opportunity to direct the fortunes of the corporation, rather than rely exclusively on independent management whose interests may diverge from those of shareholders — the argument is that there then is no reason to discourage beneficial transfers of control by a sharing requirement. There is empirical evidence that at least in publicly held corporations, premiums are generally not paid to obtain control of a corporation in order to exploit noncontrolling shareholders.

Section III
Cash Out Mergers

A controlling shareholder's interests conflict with the interests of other shareholders when the controlling shareholder attempts to acquire the other shareholders' shares. This can be accomplished in a variety of ways, but a good example is through a cash-out merger: a transaction where the controlling shareholder consolidates ownership by paying cash to the other shareholders in exchange for their stock. This fact pattern cries out for scrutiny.

In a fashion reminiscent of the law's approach toward the interested director transactions that raise duty of loyalty concerns, there are both judicial routes and corporate governance routes to mediating conflicting shareholder interests. The judicial approach is the entire fairness test with the burden of proving fairness on the controlling stockholder (seen in *Weinberger v. UOP*); the governance approach involves vesting the power to negotiate and approve the transaction in an independent board committee and conditioning the transaction's approval on the favorable vote of a majority of the non-controlled shares (referenced in *Weinberger* and acted upon in the ensuing case, *Kahn v. M&F Worldwide*).

Weinberger v. UOP, Inc.

Delaware Supreme Court
457 A.2d 701 (1983)

Moore, Justice:

This post-trial appeal was reheard *en banc* from a decision of the Court of Chancery. It was brought by the class action plaintiff below, a former shareholder of UOP, Inc., who challenged the elimination of UOP's minority shareholders by a cash-out merger between UOP and its majority owner, The Signal Companies, Inc. Originally, the defendants in this action were Signal, UOP, certain officers and directors of those companies, and UOP's investment banker.... The present Chancellor held that the terms of the merger were fair to the plaintiff and the other minority shareholders of UOP. Accordingly, he entered judgment in favor of the defendants....

I

... Signal is a diversified, technically based company operating through various subsidiaries. Its stock is publicly traded on the New York, Philadelphia and Pacific Stock Exchanges. UOP, formerly known as Universal Oil Products Company, was a diversified industrial company engaged in various lines of business, including petroleum and petro-chemical services and related products, construction, fabricated metal products, transportation equipment products, chemicals and plastics, and other products and services including land development, lumber products and waste disposal. Its stock was publicly held and listed on the New York Stock Exchange.

In 1974 Signal sold one of its wholly-owned subsidiaries for $420,000,000 in cash. While looking to invest this cash surplus, Signal became interested in UOP as a possible acquisition. Friendly negotiations ensued, and Signal proposed to acquire a controlling interest in UOP at a price of $19 per share. UOP's representatives sought $25 per share. In the arm's length bargaining that followed, an understanding was reached whereby Signal agreed to purchase from UOP 1,500,000 shares of UOP's authorized but unissued stock at $21 per share.

This purchase was contingent upon Signal making a successful cash tender offer for 4,300,000 publicly held shares of UOP, also at a price of $21 per share. This combined method of acquisition permitted Signal to acquire 5,800,000 shares of stock, representing 50.5% of UOP's outstanding shares. The UOP board of directors advised the company's shareholders that it had no objection to Signal's tender offer at that price. Immediately before the announcement of the tender offer, UOP's common stock had been trading on the New York Stock Exchange at a fraction under $14 per share.

The negotiations between Signal and UOP occurred during April 1975, and the resulting tender offer was greatly oversubscribed. However, Signal limited its total purchase of the tendered shares so that, when coupled with the stock bought from UOP, it had achieved its goal of becoming a 50.5% shareholder of UOP.

Although UOP's board consisted of thirteen directors, Signal nominated and elected only six. Of these, five were either directors or employees of Signal. The sixth, a partner in the banking firm of Lazard Freres & Co., had been one of Signal's representatives in the negotiations and bargaining with UOP concerning the tender offer and purchase price of the UOP shares.

However, the president and chief executive officer of UOP retired during 1975, and Signal caused him to be replaced by James V. Crawford, a long-time employee and senior executive vice president of one of Signal's wholly-owned subsidiaries. Crawford succeeded his predecessor on UOP's board of directors and also was made a director of Signal.

By the end of 1977 Signal basically was unsuccessful in finding other suitable investment candidates for its excess cash, and by February 1978 considered that it had no other realistic acquisitions available to it on a friendly basis. Once again its attention turned to UOP.

The trial court found that at the instigation of certain Signal management personnel, including William W. Walkup, its board chairman, and Forrest N. Shumway, its president, a feasibility study was made concerning the possible acquisition of the balance of UOP's outstanding shares. This study was performed by two Signal officers, Charles S. Arledge, vice president (director of planning), and Andrew J. Chitiea, senior vice president (chief financial officer). Messrs. Walkup, Shumway, Arledge and Chitiea were all directors of UOP in addition to their membership on the Signal board.

Arledge and Chitiea concluded that it would be a good investment for Signal to acquire the remaining 49.5% of UOP shares at any price up to $24 each. Their report was discussed between Walkup and Shumway who, along with Arledge, Chitiea and Brewster L. Arms, internal counsel for Signal, constituted Signal's senior management. In particular, they talked about the proper price to be paid if the acquisition was pursued, purportedly keeping in mind that as UOP's majority shareholder, Signal owed a fiduciary responsibility to both its own stockholders as well as to UOP's minority. It was ultimately agreed that a meeting of Signal's executive committee would be called to propose that Signal acquire the remaining outstanding stock of UOP through a cash-out merger in the range of $20 to $21 per share.

The executive committee meeting was set for February 28, 1978. As a courtesy, UOP's president, Crawford, was invited to attend, although he was not a member of Signal's executive committee. On his arrival, and prior to the meeting, Crawford was asked to meet privately with Walkup and Shumway. He was then told of Signal's plan to acquire full ownership of UOP and was asked for his reaction to the proposed price range of $20 to $21 per share. Crawford said he thought such a price would be "generous," and that it was certainly one which should be submitted to UOP's minority shareholders for their ultimate consideration. He stated, however, that Signal's 100% ownership could cause internal problems at UOP. He believed that employees would have to be given some assurance of their future place in a fully-owned Signal subsidiary. Otherwise, he feared the departure of essential personnel. Also, many of UOP's key employees had stock option incentive programs which would be wiped out by a merger. Crawford therefore urged that some adjustment would have to be made, such as providing a comparable incentive in Signal's shares, if after the merger he was to maintain his quality of personnel and efficiency at UOP.

Thus, Crawford voiced no objection to the $20 to $21 price range, nor did he suggest that Signal should consider paying more than $21 per share for the minority interests. Later, at the executive committee meeting the same factors were discussed, with Crawford repeating the position he earlier took with Walkup and Shumway. Also considered was the 1975 tender offer and the fact that it had been greatly oversubscribed at $21 per share. For many reasons, Signal's management concluded that the acquisition of UOP's minority shares provided the solution to a number of its business problems.

Thus, it was the consensus that a price of $20 to $21 per share would be fair to both Signal and the minority shareholders of UOP. Signal's executive committee authorized its management "to negotiate" with UOP "for a cash acquisition of the minority ownership in UOP, Inc., with the intention of presenting a proposal to [Signal's] board of directors ... on March 6, 1978." Immediately after this February 28, 1978 meeting, Signal issued a press release stating:

> The Signal Companies, Inc. and UOP, Inc. are conducting negotiations for the acquisition for cash by Signal of the 49.5 per cent of UOP which it does not presently own, announced Forrest N. Shumway, president and chief executive officer of Signal, and James v. Crawford, UOP president.
>
> Price and other terms of the proposed transaction have not yet been finalized and would be subject to approval of the boards of directors of Signal and UOP, scheduled to meet early next week, the stockholders of UOP and certain federal agencies.

The announcement also referred to the fact that the closing price of UOP's common stock on that day was $14.50 per share.

Two days later, on March 2, 1978, Signal issued a second press release stating that its management would recommend a price in the range of $20 to $21 per share for UOP's 49.5% minority interest. This announcement referred to Signal's earlier statement that "negotiations" were being conducted for the acquisition of the minority shares.

Between Tuesday, February 28, 1978 and Monday, March 6, 1978, a total of four business days, Crawford spoke by telephone with all of UOP's non-Signal, *i.e.*, outside, directors. Also during that period, Crawford retained Lehman Brothers to render a fairness opinion as to the price offered the minority for its stock. He gave two reasons for this choice. First, the time schedule between the announcement and the board meetings was short (by then only three business days) and since Lehman Brothers had been acting as UOP's investment banker for many years, Crawford felt that it would be in the best position to respond on such brief notice. Second, James W. Glanville, a long time director of UOP and a partner in Lehman Brothers, had acted as a financial advisor to UOP for many years. Crawford believed that Glanville's familiarity with UOP, as a member of its board, would also be of assistance in enabling Lehman Brothers to render a fairness opinion within the existing time constraints.

Crawford telephoned Glanville, who gave his assurance that Lehman Brothers had no conflicts that would prevent it from accepting the task. Glanville's immediate personal reaction was that a price of $20 to $21 would certainly be fair, since it represented almost a 50% premium over UOP's market price. Glanville sought a $250,000 fee for Lehman Brothers' services, but Crawford thought this too much. After further discussions Glanville finally agreed that Lehman Brothers would render its fairness opinion for $150,000.

During this period Crawford also had several telephone contacts with Signal officials. In only one of them, however, was the price of the shares discussed. In a conversation with Walkup, Crawford advised that as a result of his communications with UOP's non-Signal directors, it was his feeling that the price would have to be the top of the proposed range, or $21 per share, if the approval of UOP's outside directors was to be obtained. But again, he did not seek any price higher than $21.

Glanville assembled a three-man Lehman Brothers team to do the work on the fairness opinion. These persons examined relevant documents and information concerning UOP, including its annual reports and its Securities and Exchange Commission filings from 1973 through 1976, as well as its audited financial statements for 1977, its interim reports to shareholders, and its recent and historical market prices and trading volumes. In addition, on Friday, March 3, 1978, two members of the Lehman Brothers team flew to UOP's headquarters in Des Plaines, Illinois, to perform a "due diligence" visit, during the course of which they interviewed Crawford as well as UOP's general counsel, its chief financial officer, and other key executives and personnel.

As a result, the Lehman Brothers team concluded that "the price of either $20 or $21 would be a fair price for the remaining shares of UOP." They telephoned this impression to Glanville, who was spending the weekend in Vermont.

On Monday morning, March 6, 1978, Glanville and the senior member of the Lehman Brothers team flew to Des Plaines to attend the scheduled UOP directors meeting. Glanville looked over the assembled information during the flight. The two had with them the draft of a "fairness opinion letter" in which the price had been left blank. Either during or immediately prior to the directors' meeting, the two-page "fairness opinion letter" was typed in final form and the price of $21 per share was inserted.

On March 6, 1978, both the Signal and UOP boards were convened to consider the proposed merger. Telephone communications were maintained between the two meetings. Walkup, Signal's board chairman, and also a UOP director, attended UOP's meeting with Crawford in order to present Signal's position and answer any questions that UOP's non-Signal directors might have. Arledge and Chitiea, along with Signal's other designees on UOP's board, participated by conference telephone. All of UOP's outside directors attended the meeting either in person or by conference telephone.

First, Signal's board unanimously adopted a resolution authorizing Signal to propose to UOP a cash merger of $21 per share as outlined in a certain merger agreement and other supporting documents. This proposal required that the merger be approved by a majority of UOP's outstanding minority shares voting at the stockholders meeting at which the merger would be considered, and that the minority shares voting in favor of the merger, when coupled with Signal's 50.5% interest would have to comprise at least two-thirds of all UOP shares. Otherwise the proposed merger would be deemed disapproved.

UOP's board then considered the proposal. Copies of the agreement were delivered to the directors in attendance, and other copies had been forwarded earlier to the directors participating by telephone. They also had before them UOP financial data for 1974–1977, UOP's most recent financial statements, market price information, and budget projections for 1978. In addition they had Lehman Brothers' hurriedly prepared fairness opinion letter finding the price of $21 to be fair. Glanville, the Lehman Brothers partner, and UOP director, commented on the information that had gone into preparation of the letter.

Signal also suggests that the Arledge-Chitiea feasibility study, indicating that a price of up to $24 per share would be a "good investment" for Signal, was discussed at the UOP directors' meeting. The Chancellor made no such finding, and our independent review of the record, detailed *infra*, satisfies us by a preponderance of the evidence that there was no discussion of this document at UOP's board meeting. Furthermore, it is clear beyond peradventure that nothing in that report was ever disclosed to UOP's minority shareholders prior to their approval of the merger.

After consideration of Signal's proposal, Walkup and Crawford left the meeting to permit a free and uninhibited exchange between UOP's non-Signal directors. Upon their return a resolution to accept Signal's offer was then proposed and adopted. While Signal's men on UOP's board participated in various aspects of the meeting, they abstained from voting. However, the minutes show that each of them "if voting would have voted yes."

On March 7, 1978, UOP sent a letter to its shareholders advising them of the action taken by UOP's board with respect to Signal's offer. This document pointed out, among other things, that on February 28, 1978 "both companies had announced negotiations were being conducted."

Despite the swift board action of the two companies, the merger was not submitted to UOP's shareholders until their annual meeting on May 26, 1978. In the notice of that meeting and proxy statement sent to shareholders in May, UOP's management and board urged that the merger be approved. The proxy statement also advised:

> The price was determined after *discussions* between James V. Crawford, a director of Signal and Chief Executive Officer of UOP, and officers of Signal which took place during meetings on February 28, 1978, and in the course of several subsequent telephone conversations. (Emphasis added.)

In the original draft of the proxy statement the word "negotiations" had been used rather than "discussions." However, when the Securities and Exchange Commission sought details of the "negotiations" as part of its review of these materials, the term was deleted and the word "discussions" was substituted. The proxy statement indicated that the vote of UOP's board in approving the merger had been unanimous. It also advised the shareholders that Lehman Brothers had given its opinion that the merger price of $21 per share was fair to UOP's minority. However, it did not disclose the hurried method by which this conclusion was reached.

As of the record date of UOP's annual meeting, there were 11,488,302 shares of UOP common stock outstanding, 5,688,302 of which were owned by the minority. At the meeting only 56%, or 3,208,652, of the minority shares were voted. Of these, 2,953,812, or 51.9% of the total minority, voted for the merger, and 254,840 voted against it. When Signal's stock was added to the minority shares voting in favor, a total of 76.2% of UOP's outstanding shares approved the merger while only 2.2% opposed it.

By its terms the merger became effective on May 26, 1978, and each share of UOP's stock held by the minority was automatically converted into a right to receive $21 cash.

II

A

A primary issue mandating reversal is the preparation by two UOP directors, Arledge and Chitiea, of their feasibility study for the exclusive use and benefit of Signal. This document was of obvious significance to both Signal and UOP. Using UOP data, it described the advantages to Signal of ousting the minority at a price range of $21–$24 per share. Mr. Arledge, one of the authors, outlined the benefits to Signal [including that it provides "an outstanding investment opportunity for Signal"].

Having written those words, solely for the use of Signal, it is clear from the record that neither Arledge nor Chitiea shared this report with their fellow directors of UOP. We are satisfied that no one else did either. This conduct hardly meets the fiduciary standards applicable to such a transaction....

The Arledge-Chitiea report speaks for itself in supporting the Chancellor's finding that a price of up to $24 was a "good investment" for Signal. It shows that a return on the investment at $21 would be 15.7% versus 15.5% at $24 per share. This was a difference of only two-tenths of one percent, while it meant over $17,000,000 to the minority. Under such circumstances, paying UOP's minority shareholders $24 would have had relatively little long-term effect on Signal, and the Chancellor's findings concerning the benefit to Signal, even at a price of $24, were obviously correct.

Certainly, this was a matter of material significance to UOP and its shareholders. Since the study was prepared by two UOP directors, using UOP information for the exclusive benefit of Signal, and nothing whatever was done to disclose it to the outside UOP directors or the minority shareholders, a question of breach of fiduciary duty arises. This problem occurs because there were common Signal-UOP directors participating, at least to some extent, in the UOP board's decision-making processes without full disclosure of the conflicts they faced.[4]

B

... Signal designated directors on UOP's board still owed UOP and its shareholders an uncompromising duty of loyalty. The classic language of *Guth v. Loft, Inc.*, Del. Supr., 5 A.2d 503, 510 (1939), requires no embellishment:

> A public policy, existing through the years, and derived from a profound knowledge of human characteristics and motives, has established a rule that demands of a corporate officer or director, peremptorily and inexorably, the most scrupulous observance of his duty, not only affirmatively to protect the interests of the corporation committed to his charge, but also to refrain from doing anything that would work injury to the corporation, or to deprive it of profit or advantage which his skill and ability might properly bring to it, or to enable it to make in the reasonable and lawful exercise of its powers. The rule that requires an undivided and unselfish loyalty to the corporation demands that there shall be no conflict between duty and self-interest.

Given the absence of any attempt to structure this transaction on an arm's-length basis, Signal cannot escape the effects of the conflicts it faced, particularly when its designees on UOP's board did not totally abstain from participation in the matter. There is no "safe harbor" for such divided loyalties in Delaware. When directors of a Delaware corporation are on both sides of a transaction, they are required to demonstrate their utmost good faith and the most scrupulous inherent fairness of the bargain. The requirement of fairness is unflinching in its demand that where one stands on both sides of a transaction, he has the burden of establishing its entire fairness, sufficient to pass the test of careful scrutiny by the courts....

---

4. [7] Although perfection is not possible, or expected, the result here could have been entirely different if UOP had appointed an independent negotiating committee of its outside directors to deal with Signal at arm's length. Since fairness in this context can be equated to conduct by a theoretical, wholly independent, board of directors acting upon the matter before them, it is unfortunate that this course apparently was neither considered nor pursued. Particularly in a parent-subsidiary context, a showing that the action taken was as though each of the contending parties had in fact exerted its bargaining power against the other at arm's length is strong evidence that the transaction meets the test of fairness.

There is no dilution of this obligation where one holds dual or multiple director-ships, as in a parent-subsidiary context. Thus, individuals who act in a dual capacity as directors of two corporations, one of whom is parent and the other subsidiary, owe the same duty of good management to both corporations, and in the absence of an independent negotiating structure, or the directors' total abstention from any participation in the matter, this duty is to be exercised in light of what is best for both companies. The record demonstrates that Signal has not met this obligation.

C

The concept of fairness has two basic aspects: fair dealing and fair price. The former embraces questions of when the transaction was timed, how it was initiated, struc-tured, negotiated, disclosed to the directors, and how the approvals of the directors and the stockholders were obtained. The latter aspect of fairness relates to the eco-nomic and financial considerations of the proposed merger, including all relevant factors: assets, market value, earnings, future prospects, and any other elements that affect the intrinsic or inherent value of a company's stock. However, the test for fairness is not a bifurcated one as between fair dealing and price. All aspects of the issue must be examined as a whole since the question is one of entire fairness. However, in a non-fraudulent transaction we recognize that price may be the pre-ponderant consideration outweighing other features of the merger. Here, we address the two basic aspects of fairness separately because we find reversible error as to both.

D

Part of fair dealing is the obvious duty of candor required by *Lynch I, supra*. More-over, one possessing superior knowledge may not mislead any stockholder by use of corporate information to which the latter is not privy.... With the well-established Delaware law on the subject, and the Court of Chancery's findings of fact here, it is inevitable that the obvious conflicts posed by Arledge and Chitiea's preparation of their "feasibility study," derived from UOP information, for the sole use and benefit of Signal, cannot pass muster.

The Arledge-Chitiea report is but one aspect of the element of fair dealing. How did this merger evolve? It is clear that it was entirely initiated by Signal. The serious time constraints under which the principals acted were all set by Signal. It had not found a suitable outlet for its excess cash and considered UOP a desirable investment, particularly since it was now in a position to acquire the whole company for itself. For whatever reasons, and they were only Signal's, the entire transaction was presented to and approved by UOP's board within four business days. Standing alone, this is not necessarily indicative of any lack of fairness by a majority shareholder. It was what occurred, or more properly, what did not occur, during this brief period that makes the time constraints imposed by Signal relevant to the issue of fairness.

The structure of the transaction, again, was Signal's doing. So far as negotiations were concerned, it is clear that they were modest at best. Crawford, Signal's man at UOP, never really talked price with Signal, except to accede to its management's state-ments on the subject, and to convey to Signal the UOP outside directors' view that as between the $20–$21 range under consideration, it would have to be $21. The latter is not a surprising outcome, but hardly arm's length negotiations. Only the protection of benefits for UOP's key employees and the issue of Lehman Brothers' fee approached any concept of bargaining.

As we have noted, the matter of disclosure to the UOP directors was wholly flawed by the conflicts of interest raised by the Arledge-Chitiea report. All of those conflicts were resolved by Signal in its own favor without divulging any aspect of them to UOP.

This cannot but undermine a conclusion that this merger meets any reasonable test of fairness. The outside UOP directors lacked one material piece of information generated by two of their colleagues, but shared only with Signal. True, the UOP board had the Lehman Brothers' fairness opinion, but that firm has been blamed by the plaintiff for the hurried task it performed, when more properly the responsibility for this lies with Signal. There was no disclosure of the circumstances surrounding the rather cursory preparation of the Lehman Brothers' fairness opinion. Instead, the impression was given UOP's minority that a careful study had been made, when in fact speed was the hallmark, and Mr. Glanville, Lehman's partner in charge of the matter, and also a UOP director, having spent the weekend in Vermont, brought a draft of the "fairness opinion letter" to the UOP directors' meeting on March 6, 1978 with the price left blank. We can only conclude from the record that the rush imposed on Lehman Brothers by Signal's timetable contributed to the difficulties under which this investment banking firm attempted to perform its responsibilities. Yet, none of this was disclosed to UOP's minority.

Finally, the minority stockholders were denied the critical information that Signal considered a price of $24 to be a good investment. Since this would have meant over $17,000,000 more to the minority, we cannot conclude that the shareholder vote was an informed one. Under the circumstances, an approval by a majority of the minority was meaningless.

Given these particulars and the Delaware law on the subject, the record does not establish that this transaction satisfies any reasonable concept of fair dealing, and the Chancellor's findings in that regard must be reversed.

E

Turning to the matter of price, plaintiff also challenges its fairness. His evidence was that on the date the merger was approved the stock was worth at least $26 per share. In support, he offered the testimony of a chartered investment analyst who used two basic approaches to valuation: a comparative analysis of the premium paid over market in ten other tender offer-merger combinations, and a discounted cash flow analysis.

In this breach of fiduciary duty case, the Chancellor perceived that the approach to valuation was the same as that in an appraisal proceeding. Consistent with precedent, he rejected plaintiff's method of proof and accepted defendants' evidence of value as being in accord with practice under prior case law. This means that the so-called "Delaware block" or weighted average method was employed wherein the elements of value, *i.e.*, assets, market price, earnings, etc., were assigned a particular weight and the resulting amounts added to determine the value per share. This procedure has been in use for decades. However, to the extent it excludes other generally accepted techniques used in the financial community and the courts, it is now clearly outmoded. It is time we recognize this in appraisal and other stock valuation proceedings and bring our law current on the subject.

... Accordingly, the standard "Delaware block" or weighted average method of valuation, formerly employed in appraisal and other stock valuation cases, shall no longer exclusively control such proceedings. We believe that a more liberal approach must include proof of value by any techniques or methods which are generally considered acceptable in the financial community and otherwise admissible in court, subject only to our interpretation of 8 Del. C. §262(h), *infra*. This will obviate the very structured and mechanistic procedure that has heretofore governed such matters....

Although the Chancellor received the plaintiff's evidence, his opinion indicates that the use of it was precluded because of past Delaware practice. While we do not suggest a monetary result one way or the other, we do think the plaintiff's evidence should be part of the factual mix and weighed as such. Until the $21 price is measured on remand by the valuation standards mandated by Delaware law, there can be no finding at the present stage of these proceedings that the price is fair. Given the lack of any candid disclosure of the material facts surrounding establishment of the $21 price, the majority of the minority vote, approving the merger, is meaningless....

Kahn v. M&F Worldwide

Delaware Supreme Court
88 A.3d 365 (Del. 2014)

HOLLAND, JUSTICE.

This [case] arises from a 2011 acquisition by MacAndrews & Forbes Holdings, Inc. ("M&F" or "MacAndrews & Forbes")—a 43% stockholder in M&F Worldwide Corp. ("MFW")—of the remaining common stock of MFW (the "Merger"). From the outset, M&F's proposal to take MFW private was made contingent upon two stockholder-protective procedural conditions. First, M&F required the Merger to be negotiated and approved by a special committee of independent MFW directors (the "Special Committee"). Second, M&F required that the Merger be approved by a majority of stockholders unaffiliated with M&F. The Merger closed in December 2011, after it was approved by a vote of 65.4% of MFW's minority stockholders.... [The initial proposal offered $24 cash per share; the final merger price was $25 cash per share. The Court of Chancery granted defendants' pre-trial motion for summary judgment. This Court affirms.]

[Facts]

... MFW was 43.4% owned by MacAndrews & Forbes, which in turn is entirely owned by Ronald O. Perelman. MFW had four business segments [being: a printer of blank checks, a provider of financial technology, Scantron Corporation, maker of testing equipment, and a licorice flavorings manufacturer]. The MFW board had thirteen members. They were: Ronald Perelman [and four other senior executives of MFW or its business units along with eight other persons not so employed].

In May 2011, Perelman began to explore the possibility of taking MFW private. At that time, MFW's stock price traded in the $20 to $24 per share range. MacAndrews & Forbes engaged a bank, Moelis & Company, to advise it. After preparing valuations based on projections that had been supplied to lenders by MFW in April and May 2011, Moelis valued MFW at between $10 and $32 a share.

On June 10, 2011, MFW's shares closed on the New York Stock Exchange at $16.96. The next business day, June 13, 2011, Schwartz [one of the MFW directors who was an executive of both M&F and MFW] sent a letter proposal ("Proposal") to the MFW board to buy the remaining MFW shares for $24 in cash. The Proposal stated, in relevant part:

> The proposed transaction would be subject to the approval of the Board of Directors of the Company [*i.e.*, MFW] and the negotiation and execution of mutually acceptable definitive transaction documents. It is our expectation that the Board of Directors will appoint a special committee of independent directors to consider our proposal and make a recommendation to the Board of Directors. *We will not move forward with the transaction unless it is approved by such a special committee. In addition, the transaction will be subject to a non-waivable condition requiring the approval of a majority of the shares of the Company not owned by M&F or its affiliates....*
>
> In considering this proposal, you should know that in our capacity as a stockholder of the Company we are interested only in acquiring the shares of the Company not already owned by us and that in such capacity we have no interest in selling any of the shares owned by us in the Company nor would we expect, in our capacity as a stockholder, to vote in favor of any alternative sale, merger or similar transaction involving the Company. If the special committee does not recommend or the public stockholders of the Company do not approve the proposed transaction, such determination would not adversely affect our future relationship with the Company and we would intend to remain as a long-term stockholder....
>
> In connection with this proposal, we have engaged Moelis & Company as our financial advisor and Skadden, Arps, Slate, Meagher & Flom LLP as our legal advisor, and we encourage the special committee to retain its own legal and financial advisors to assist it in its review.

... The MFW board met the following day to consider the Proposal. At the meeting, Schwartz presented the offer on behalf of MacAndrews & Forbes. Subsequently, Schwartz and [four other] directors present who were also directors of MacAndrews & Forbes [or executives of its affiliates] recused themselves from the meeting ...

The independent directors then invited counsel from Willkie Farr & Gallagher — a law firm that had recently represented a Special Committee of MFW's independent directors in a potential acquisition of a subsidiary of MacAndrews & Forbes — to join the meeting. The independent directors decided to form the Special Committee, and resolved further that:

> [T]he Special Committee is empowered to: (i) make such investigation of the Proposal as the Special Committee deems appropriate; (ii) evaluate the terms of the Proposal; (iii) negotiate with [M&F] and its representatives any element of the Proposal; (iv) negotiate the terms of any definitive agreement with respect to the Proposal (it being understood that the execution thereof shall be subject to the approval of the Board); (v) report to the Board its recommendations and conclusions with respect to the Proposal, including a determination and *recommendation as to whether the Proposal is fair and in the best interests of the stockholders of the Company other than [M&F]* and its affiliates and should be approved by the Board; and (vi) determine to elect not to pursue the Proposal....

> [T]he Board shall not approve the Proposal without a prior favorable recommendation of the Special Committee....

> [T]he Special Committee [is] empowered to retain and employ legal counsel, a financial advisor, and such other agents as the Special Committee shall deem necessary or desirable in connection with these matters....

The Special Committee consisted of [four directors not otherwise employed by M&F or its other affiliates.]

[Standard of Review]

Where a transaction involving self-dealing by a controlling stockholder is challenged, the applicable standard of judicial review is "entire fairness," with the defendants having the burden of persuasion. In other words, the defendants bear the ultimate burden of proving that the transaction with the controlling stockholder was entirely fair to the minority stockholders. In *Kahn v. Lynch Communication Systems, Inc.*, [638 A.2d 1110 (1994)], however, this Court held that in "entire fairness" cases, the defendants may shift the burden of persuasion to the plaintiff if either (1) they show that the transaction was approved by a well-functioning committee of independent directors; **or** (2) they show that the transaction was approved by an informed vote of a majority of the minority stockholders.

This appeal presents a question of first impression: what should be the standard of review for a merger between a controlling stockholder and its subsidiary, where the merger is conditioned *ab initio* upon the approval of **both** an independent, adequately-empowered Special Committee that fulfills its duty of care, and the uncoerced, informed vote of a majority of the minority stockholders. The question has never been put directly to this Court.

Almost two decades ago, in *Kahn v. Lynch*, we held that the approval by *either* a Special Committee *or* the majority of the noncontrolling stockholders of a merger with a buying controlling stockholder would shift the burden of proof under the entire fairness standard from the defendant to the plaintiff. *Lynch* did not involve a merger conditioned by the controlling stockholder on both procedural protections. The Appellants submit, nonetheless, that statements in *Lynch* and its progeny could be (and were) read to suggest that even if both procedural protections were used, the standard of review would remain entire fairness. However, in *Lynch* ... the controller did not give up its voting power by agreeing to a non-waivable majority-of-the-minority condition. That is the vital distinction between those cases and this one. The question is what the legal consequence of that distinction should be in these circumstances. ...

We hold that business judgment is the standard of review that should govern mergers between a controlling stockholder and its corporate subsidiary, where the merger is conditioned *ab initio* upon both the approval of an independent, adequately-empowered Special Committee that fulfills its duty of care; and the uncoerced, informed vote of a majority of the minority stockholders. We so conclude for several reasons.

First, entire fairness is the highest standard of review in corporate law. It is applied in the controller merger context as a substitute for the dual statutory protections of disinterested board and stockholder approval, because both protections are potentially undermined by the influence of the controller. However, as this case establishes, that undermining influence does not exist in every controlled merger setting, regardless of the circumstances. The simultaneous deployment of the procedural protections employed here create a countervailing, offsetting influence of equal—if not greater—force. That is, where the controller irrevocably and publicly disables itself from using its control to dictate the outcome of the negotiations and the shareholder vote, the controlled merger then acquires the shareholder-protective characteristics of third-party, arm's-length mergers, which are reviewed under the business judgment standard.

Second, the dual procedural protection merger structure optimally protects the minority stockholders in controller buyouts. As the Court of Chancery explained:

> [W]hen these two protections are established up-front, a potent tool to extract good value for the minority is established. From inception, the controlling stockholder knows that it cannot bypass the special committee's ability to say no. And, the controlling stockholder knows it cannot dangle a majority-of-the-minority vote before the special committee late in the process as a deal-closer rather than having to make a price move.

Third, and as the Court of Chancery reasoned, applying the business judgment standard to the dual protection merger structure:

> ... is consistent with the central tradition of Delaware law, which defers to the informed decisions of impartial directors, especially when those decisions have been approved by the disinterested stockholders on full information and without coercion. ...

Fourth, the underlying purposes of the dual protection merger structure utilized here and the entire fairness standard of review both converge and are fulfilled at the same critical point: **price.** Following *Weinberger v. UOP, Inc.*, this Court has consistently held that, although entire fairness review comprises the dual components of fair dealing and fair price, in a non-fraudulent transaction "price may be the preponderant consideration outweighing other features of the merger." The dual protection merger structure requires two price-related pretrial determinations: first, that a fair price was achieved by an empowered, independent committee that acted with care; and, second, that a fully-informed, uncoerced majority of the minority stockholders voted in favor of the price that was recommended by the independent committee....

This approach is consistent with *Weinberger, Lynch* and their progeny. A controller that employs and/or establishes only one of these dual procedural protections would continue to receive burden-shifting within the entire fairness standard of review framework. Stated differently, unless *both* procedural protections for the minority stockholders are established *prior to trial,* the ultimate judicial scrutiny of controller buyouts will continue to be the entire fairness standard of review....

[Application]

To reiterate, in this case, the controlling stockholder conditioned its offer upon the MFW Board agreeing, *ab initio,* to both procedural protections, *i.e.,* approval by a Special Committee and by a majority of the minority stockholders. For the combination of an effective committee process and majority-of-the-minority vote to qualify (jointly) for business judgment review, each of these protections must be effective singly to warrant a burden shift....

[T]he special committee must "function in a manner which indicates that the controlling stockholder did not dictate the terms of the transaction and that the committee exercised real bargaining power 'at an arms-length.'" ... As we have previously noted, deciding whether an independent committee was effective in negotiating a price is a process so fact-intensive and inextricably intertwined with the merits of an entire fairness review (fair dealing and fair price) that a pretrial determination of burden shifting is often impossible. Here, however, the Defendants have successfully established a record of independent committee effectiveness and process that warranted a grant of summary judgment entitling them to a burden shift prior to trial.

[A. The Effectiveness of the Special Committee]

[*Committee Member Independence*]

The Appellants do not challenge the independence of the Special Committee's Chairman.... They claim, however, that the three other Special Committee members ... were beholden to Perelman because of their prior business and/or social dealings with Perelman or Perelman-related entities.

The Appellants first challenge the independence of [Carl] Webb. They urged that Webb and Perelman shared a "longstanding and lucrative business partnership" between 1983 and 2002 which included acquisitions of thrifts and financial institutions, and which led to a 2002 asset sale to Citibank in which Webb made "a significant amount of money." The Court of Chancery concluded, however, that the fact of Webb having engaged in business dealings with Perelman nine years earlier did not raise a triable fact issue regarding his ability to evaluate the Merger impartially. We agree.

Second, the Appellants argued that there were triable issues of fact regarding [Viet] Dinh's independence. The Appellants demonstrated that between 2009 and 2011, Dinh's law firm, Bancroft PLLC, advised M&F and Scientific Games (in which M&F owned a 37.6% stake), during which time the Bancroft firm earned $200,000 in fees.... The Court of Chancery found that the Appellants failed to proffer any evidence to show that compensation received by Dinh's law firm was material to Dinh, in the sense that it would have influenced his decisionmaking with respect to the M&F proposal. The only evidence of record, the Court of Chancery concluded, was that these fees were "*de minimis*" and that the Appellants had offered no contrary evidence that would create a genuine issue of material fact.

The Court of Chancery also found that the relationship between Dinh, a Georgetown University Law Center professor, and M&F's Barry Schwartz, who sits on the Georgetown Board of Visitors, did not create a triable issue of fact as to Dinh's independence. No record evidence suggested that Schwartz could exert influence on Dinh's position at Georgetown based on his recommendation regarding the Merger. Indeed, Dinh had earned tenure as a professor at Georgetown before he ever knew Schwartz....

The Appellants also contend that [Martha] Byorum performed advisory work for Scientific Games in 2007 and 2008 as a senior managing director of Stephens Cori Capital Advisors ("Stephens Cori"). The Court of Chancery found, however, that the Appellants had adduced no evidence tending to establish that the $100,000 fee Stephens Cori received for that work was material to either Stephens Cori or to Byorum personally. Stephens Cori's engagement for Scientific Games, which occurred years before the Merger was announced and the Special Committee was convened, was fully disclosed to the Special Committee, which concluded that "it was not material, and it would not represent a conflict." We uphold the Court of Chancery's findings relating to Byorum as well.

To evaluate the parties' competing positions on the issue of director independence, the Court of Chancery applied well-established Delaware legal principles. To show that a director is not independent, a plaintiff must demonstrate that the director is "beholden" to the controlling party "or so under [the controller's] influence that [the director's] discretion would be sterilized." ... Bare allegations that directors are friendly with, travel in the same social circles as, or have past business relationships with the proponent of a transaction or the person they are investigating are not enough to rebut the presumption of independence....

Despite receiving the chance for extensive discovery, the plaintiffs have done nothing ... to compare the actual economic circumstances of the directors they challenge to the ties the plaintiffs contend affect their impartiality. In other words, the plaintiffs have ignored a key teaching of our Supreme Court, requiring a showing that a specific director's independence is compromised by factors material to her. As to each of the specific directors the plaintiffs challenge, the plaintiffs fail to proffer any real evidence of their economic circumstances....

[*Committee Power*]

It is undisputed that the Special Committee was empowered to hire its own legal and financial advisors, and it retained Willkie Farr & Gallagher LLP as its legal advisor. After interviewing four potential financial advisors, the Special Committee engaged Evercore Partners ("Evercore"). The qualifications and independence of Evercore and Willkie Farr & Gallagher LLP are not contested.

Among the powers given the Special Committee in the board resolution was the authority to "report to the Board its recommendations and conclusions with respect to the [Merger], including a determination and recommendation as to whether the Proposal is fair and in the best interests of the stockholders...." [Its power included] "clear authority to say no definitively to [M&F]" and to "make that decision stick." MacAndrews & Forbes promised that it would not proceed with any going private proposal that did not have the support of the Special Committee....

... [Even] though the Special Committee had the authority to negotiate and "say no," it did not have the authority, as a practical matter, to sell MFW to other buyers. MacAndrews & Forbes stated in its announcement that it was not interested in selling its 43% stake. Moreover, under Delaware law, MacAndrews & Forbes had no duty to sell its block, which was large enough, again as a practical matter, to preclude any other buyer from succeeding unless MacAndrews & Forbes decided to become a seller. Absent such a decision, it was unlikely that any potentially interested party would incur the costs and risks of exploring a purchase of MFW.

... The undisputed record shows that the Special Committee, with the help of its financial advisor, did consider whether there were other buyers who might be interested in purchasing MFW, and whether there were other strategic options, such as asset divestitures, that might generate more value for minority stockholders than a sale of their stock to MacAndrews & Forbes.

[*Committee Process/Care*]

The Special Committee insisted from the outset that MacAndrews (including any "dual" employees who worked for both MFW and MacAndrews) be screened off from the Special Committee's process, to ensure that the process replicated arm's-length negotiations with a third party. In order to carefully evaluate M&F's offer, the Special Committee held a total of eight meetings during the summer of 2011.

From the outset of their work, the Special Committee and Evercore had projections that had been prepared by MFW's business segments in April and May 2011. Early in the process, Evercore and the Special Committee asked MFW management to produce new projections that reflected management's most up-to-date, and presumably most accurate, thinking. Consistent with the Special Committee's determination to conduct its analysis free of any MacAndrews influence, MacAndrews—including "dual" MFW/MacAndrews executives who normally vetted MFW projections—were excluded from the process of preparing the updated financial projections. [Each of MFW's segments updated its respective projections]. Evercore then constructed a valuation model based upon all of these updated projections.

The updated projections, which formed the basis for Evercore's valuation analyses, reflected MFW's deteriorating results, especially in [the] check-printing business. Those projections forecast EBITDA for MFW of $491 million in 2015, as opposed to $535 million under the original projections.

On August 10, Evercore produced a range of valuations for MFW, based on the updated projections, of $15 to $45 per share. Evercore valued MFW using a variety of accepted methods, including a discounted cash flow ("DCF") model. Those valuations generated a range of fair value of $22 to $38 per share, and a premiums paid analysis resulted in a value range of $22 to $45. MacAndrews & Forbes's $24 offer fell within the range of values produced by each of Evercore's valuation techniques.

Although the $24 Proposal fell within the range of Evercore's fair values, the Special Committee directed Evercore to conduct additional analyses and explore strategic alternatives that might generate more value for MFW's stockholders than might a sale to MacAndrews. The Special Committee also investigated the possibility of other buyers, *e.g.,* private equity buyers, that might be interested in purchasing MFW. In addition, the Special Committee considered whether other strategic options, such as asset divestitures, could achieve superior value for MFW's stockholders....

... Based on the undisputed record, the Court of Chancery held that, "there is no triable issue of fact regarding whether the [S]pecial [C]ommittee fulfilled its duty of care." In the context of a controlling stockholder merger, a pretrial determination that the *price* was negotiated by an empowered independent committee that acted with care would shift the burden of persuasion to the plaintiffs under the entire fairness standard of review.

[B. The "Majority of Minority" Vote]

We now consider the second procedural protection invoked by M&F—the majority-of-the-minority stockholder vote. Consistent with the second condition imposed by M&F at the outset, the Merger was then put before MFW's stockholders for a vote. On November 18, 2011, the stockholders were provided with a proxy statement, which contained the history of the Special Committee's work and recommended that they vote in favor of the transaction at a price of $25 per share.

The proxy statement disclosed, among other things, that the Special Committee had countered M&F's initial $24 per share offer at $30 per share, but only was able to achieve a final offer of $25 per share. The proxy statement disclosed that the MFW business divisions had discussed with Evercore whether the initial projections Evercore received reflected management's latest thinking. It also disclosed that the updated projections were lower. The proxy statement also included the [numerous] separate price ranges for the value of MFW's stock that Evercore had generated with its different valuation analyses.

Knowing the proxy statement's disclosures of the background of the Special Committee's work, of Evercore's valuation ranges, and of the analyses supporting Evercore's *fairness opinion,* MFW's stockholders—representing more than 65% of the minority shares—approved the Merger. In the controlling stockholder merger context, it is settled Delaware law that an uncoerced, informed majority-of-the-minority vote, without any other procedural protection, is itself sufficient to shift the burden of persuasion to the plaintiff under the entire fairness standard of review. The Court of Chancery found that "the plaintiffs themselves do not dispute that the majority-of-the-minority vote was fully informed and uncoerced, because they fail to allege any failure of disclosure or any act of coercion."

[Conclusion]

Based on a highly extensive record, the Court of Chancery concluded that the procedural protections upon which the Merger was conditioned—approval by an independent and empowered Special Committee and by a uncoerced informed majority of MFW's minority stockholders—had *both* been undisputedly established *prior to trial.* We agree and conclude the Defendants' motion for summary judgment was properly granted on all of those issues....

We have determined that the business judgment rule standard of review applies to this controlling stockholder buyout. Under that standard, the claims against the Defendants must be dismissed unless no rational person could have believed that the merger was favorable to MFW's minority stockholders. In this case, it cannot be credibly argued (let alone concluded) that no rational person would find the Merger favorable to MFW's minority stockholders.

Notes and Questions

1. The shareholder vote in *Kahn* was not technically a majority of the minority since the controlling shareholder owned less than a majority of shares (about 43%). It is nevertheless customary to speak of such votes of non-controlling shareholders as "majority of the minority votes."

2. *Kahn* creates something of a safe harbor for controlling shareholders prepared to propose cash out mergers conditioned at the outset on approval by a disinterested, fully informed committee of the board plus approval by a fully informed majority of the minority. The opinion creates strong incentives to do so by reducing associated legal risk. It does not eliminate legal risk, of course, because the controlling shareholder still has the burden of proving several elements, such as the committee's effectiveness and that the shareholders were fully informed. Still, *Kahn* provides an enticing way for controlling shareholders to mitigate legal risk. The New York Court of Appeals expressly adopted *Kahn's* approach on similar facts, *In re Kenneth Cole Productions, Inc.* ___ N.E.3d ___ (May 2016).

While taking such steps may reduce legal risk, the procedures entail other kinds of risk, such as business risk. A controlling shareholder must weigh the risk that the special committee will frustrate a desired transaction by guarding minority interests overzealously. Likewise, a controlling shareholder must gauge the likelihood that other shareholders will appreciate the offer's appeal. After all, predicting the outcome of a shareholder vote is often difficult. It may be particularly challenging when the vote is over a merger because merger announcements, like any other extraordinary corporate event, often prompt old shareholders to sell and new shareholders to buy.

Section IV
Short Form Mergers and Appraisal Remedy

So-called short-form mergers are exempt from the heightened juridical scrutiny normally applicable to cash out mergers by controlling shareholders. Short-form mergers are deals in which the parent corporation already owns 90% or more of the subsidiary's stock at the time of the merger. The ensuing case, *Glassman v. Unocal Exploration Corp.*, illustrates a short-form merger. As an introduction, consider a final point made in *Weinberger v. UOP* concerning the nature of the remedy that the plaintiff sought.

> On remand the plaintiff will be permitted to test the fairness of the $21 price by the standards we herein establish, in conformity with the principle applicable to an appraisal—that fair value be determined by taking "into account all relevant factors" [*see* 8 Del. C. §262(h)....]

> While a plaintiff's monetary remedy ordinarily should be confined to the more liberalized appraisal proceeding herein established, we do not intend any limitation on the historic powers of the Chancellor to grant such other relief as the facts of a particular case may dictate. The appraisal remedy we approve may not be adequate in certain cases, particularly where fraud, misrepresentation, self-dealing, deliberate waste of corporate assets, or gross and palpable overreaching are involved. Under such circumstances, the Chancellor's powers are complete to fashion any form of equitable and monetary relief as may be appropriate.... Since it is apparent that this long completed transaction is too involved to undo, and in view of the Chancellor's discretion, the award, if any, should be in the form of monetary damages based upon entire fairness standards, *i.e.*, fair dealing and fair price.

> [Accordingly,] the provisions of 8 Del. C. §262, as herein construed, respecting the scope of an appraisal and the means for perfecting the same, shall govern the financial remedy available to minority shareholders in a cash-out merger. Thus, we return to the well established principles of *Stauffer v. Standard Brands, Inc.*, Del. Supr., 187 A.2d 78 (1962) and *David J. Greene & Co. v. Schenley Industries, Inc.*, Del. Ch., 281 A.2d 30 (1971), mandating a stockholder's recourse to the basic remedy of an appraisal....

The appraisal remedy referred to in *Weinberger* is a statutory right granted to shareholders concerning designated corporate transactions, such as cash out mergers, who object to the price offered. In short, they are entitled to petition a court to appraise the fair value of their shares and have the corporation pay that appraised value.

Appraisal proceedings, which were historically relatively infrequent, have in recent decades become more common, in part due to the more flexible and sophisticated approach to valuation developed under *Weinberger*. Still, shareholders must weigh several factors carefully in deciding whether to accept what is offered in a merger or seek an appraisal. A brief summary of the procedure under DGCL 262 will illuminate.

If the transaction is a merger to which statutory appraisal rights apply (a topic taken up in chapter 13), the notice of the related shareholders' meeting must say so and include a copy of the statute. Shareholders exercise their appraisal rights by delivering a written demand on the company before the scheduled vote occurs and must not vote for the transaction and must continue to hold their shares through its effective time.

Within ten days after the effective date, the surviving company must notify all such shareholders thereof and, within 120 days after the effective date, any such shareholder may commence an appraisal proceeding by filing a petition in the Delaware Court of Chancery seeking a determination of the value of the shares.

In doing so, the Court considers all factors relevant to fair value, as *Weinberger* directs, and may award interest. The appraisal amount may be higher or lower than the consideration offered in the transaction. The appraisal proceeding does not entail litigation about issues other than fair value, such as breach of fiduciary duties or violations of statutes. The Court also allocates the costs of the proceedings, including attorneys' fees, and may decide that such costs should be charged pro rata against the value of all shares entitled to an appraisal.

So shareholders considering whether to dissent or accept the consideration offered must proceed with care. Specifically, the process can take time and expense, and the related interest may be less than what other investments could yield. The outcome is uncertain, so shareholders may end up receiving less than they were offered in the transaction. The appraisal proceeding is most appealing to address manifestly low offers.

Glassman v. Unocal Exploration Corp.

Delaware Supreme Court
777 A.2d 242 (2001)

BERGER, JUSTICE:

In this appeal, we consider the fiduciary duties owed by a parent corporation to the subsidiary's minority stockholders in the context of a "short-form" merger. Specifically, we take this opportunity to reconcile a fiduciary's seemingly absolute duty to establish the entire fairness of any self-dealing transaction with the less demanding requirements of the short-form merger statute. The statute authorizes the elimination of minority stockholders by a summary process that does not involve the "fair dealing" component of entire fairness. Indeed, the statute does not contemplate any "dealing" at all. Thus, a parent corporation cannot satisfy the entire fairness standard if it follows the terms of the short-form merger statute without more.

Unocal Corporation addressed this dilemma by establishing a special negotiating committee and engaging in a process that it believed would pass muster under traditional entire fairness review. We find that such steps were unnecessary. By enacting a statute that authorizes the elimination of the minority without notice, vote, or other traditional indicia of procedural fairness, the General Assembly effectively circumscribed the parent corporation's obligations to the minority in a short-form merger. The parent corporation does not have to establish entire fairness, and, absent fraud or illegality, the only recourse for a minority stockholder who is dissatisfied with the merger consideration is appraisal.

I. Factual and Procedural Background

Unocal Corporation is an earth resources company primarily engaged in the exploration for and production of crude oil and natural gas. At the time of the merger at issue, Unocal owned approximately 96% of the stock of Unocal Exploration Corporation ("UXC"), an oil and gas company operating in and around the Gulf of Mexico. In 1991, low natural gas prices caused a drop in both companies' revenues and earnings. Unocal investigated areas of possible cost savings and decided that, by eliminating the UXC minority, it would reduce taxes and overhead expenses.

In December 1991 the boards of Unocal and UXC appointed special committees to consider a possible merger. The UXC committee consisted of three directors who, although also directors of Unocal, were not officers or employees of the parent company. The UXC committee retained financial and legal advisors and met four times before agreeing to a merger exchange ratio of .54 shares of Unocal stock for each share of UXC. Unocal and UXC announced the merger on February 24, 1992, and it was effected, pursuant to 8 Del. C. §253, on May 2, 1992. The Notice of Merger and Prospectus stated the terms of the merger and advised the former UXC stockholders of their appraisal rights.

Plaintiffs filed this class action, on behalf of UXC's minority stockholders, on the day the merger was announced. They asserted, among other claims, that Unocal and its directors breached their fiduciary duties of entire fairness and full disclosure. The Court of Chancery conducted a two day trial and held that: (i) the Prospectus did not contain any material misstatements or omissions; (ii) the entire fairness standard does not control in a short-form merger; and (iii) plaintiffs' exclusive remedy in this case was appraisal. The decision of the Court of Chancery is affirmed.

II. Discussion

The short-form merger statute, as enacted in 1937, authorized a parent corporation to merge with its wholly-owned subsidiary by filing and recording a certificate evidencing the parent's ownership and its merger resolution. In 1957, the statute was expanded to include parent/subsidiary mergers where the parent company owns at least 90% of the stock of the subsidiary. The 1957 amendment also made it possible, for the first time and only in a short-form merger, to pay the minority cash for their shares, thereby eliminating their ownership interest in the company. In its current form, which has not changed significantly since 1957, 8 Del. C. §253 provides in relevant part:

(a) In any case in which at least 90 percent of the outstanding shares of each class of the stock of a corporation ... is owned by another corporation[ ] ..., the corporation having such stock ownership may ... merge the other corporation ... into itself ... by executing, acknowledging and filing, in accordance with § 103 of this title, a certificate of such ownership and merger setting forth a copy of the resolution of its board of directors to so merge and the date of the adoption; provided, however, that in case the parent corporation shall not own all the outstanding stock of ... the subsidiary corporation[ ], ... the resolution ... shall state the terms and conditions of the merger, including the securities, cash, property or rights to be issued, paid delivered or granted by the surviving corporation upon surrender of each share of the subsidiary corporation....

(d) In the event that all of the stock of a subsidiary Delaware corporation ... is not owned by the parent corporation immediately prior to the merger, the stockholders of the subsidiary Delaware corporation party to the merger shall have appraisal rights as set forth in Section 262 of this Title.

This Court first reviewed § 253 in *Coyne v. Park & Tilford Distillers Corporation.*[5] There, minority stockholders of the merged-out subsidiary argued that the statute could not mean what it says because Delaware law "never has permitted, and does not now permit, the payment of cash for whole shares surrendered in a merger and the consequent expulsion of a stockholder from the enterprise in which he has invested." The *Coyne* court held that § 253 plainly does permit such a result and that the statute is constitutional.

The next question presented to this Court was whether any equitable relief is available to minority stockholders who object to a short-form merger. In *Stauffer v. Standard Brands Incorporated,*[6] minority stockholders sued to set aside the contested merger or, in the alternative, for damages. They alleged that the merger consideration was so grossly inadequate as to constitute constructive fraud and that Standard Brands breached its fiduciary duty to the minority by failing to set a fair price for their stock. The Court of Chancery held that appraisal was the stockholders' exclusive remedy, and dismissed the complaint. This Court affirmed, but explained that appraisal would not be the exclusive remedy in a short-form merger tainted by fraud or illegality:

[T]he exception [to appraisal's exclusivity] ... refers generally to all mergers, and is nothing but a reaffirmation of the ever-present power of equity to deal with illegality or fraud. But it has no bearing here. No illegality or overreaching is shown. The dispute reduces to nothing but a difference of opinion as to value. Indeed it is difficult to imagine a case under the short merger statute in which there could be such actual fraud as would entitle a minority to set aside the merger. This is so because the very purpose of the statute is to provide the parent corporation with a means of eliminating the minority shareholder's interest in the enterprise. Thereafter the former stockholder has only a monetary claim.

5. [1] Del. Supr., 154 A.2d 893 (1959).
6. [3] Del. Supr., 187 A.2d 78 (1962).

The *Stauffer* doctrine's viability rose and fell over the next four decades. Its holding on the exclusivity of appraisal took on added significance in 1967, when the long-form merger statute — § 251 — was amended to allow cash-out mergers. In *David J. Greene & Co. v. Schenley Industries, Inc.*,[7] the Court of Chancery applied *Stauffer* to a long-form cash-out merger. *Schenley* recognized that the corporate fiduciaries had to establish entire fairness, but concluded that fair value was the plaintiff's only real concern and that appraisal was an adequate remedy. The court explained:

> While a court of equity should stand ready to prevent corporate fraud and any overreaching by fiduciaries of the rights of stockholders, by the same token this Court should not impede the consummation of an orderly merger under the Delaware statutes, an efficient and fair method having been furnished which permits a judicially protected withdrawal from a merger by a disgruntled stockholder.

In 1977, this Court started retreating from *Stauffer* (and *Schenley*). *Singer v. Magnavox Co.*[8] held that a controlling stockholder breaches its fiduciary duty if it effects a cash-out merger under § 251 for the sole purpose of eliminating the minority stockholders. The *Singer* court distinguished *Stauffer* as being a case where the only complaint was about the value of the converted shares. Nonetheless, the Court cautioned:

> [T]he fiduciary obligation of the majority to the minority stockholders remains and proof of a purpose, other than such freeze-out, without more, will not necessarily discharge it. In such case the Court will scrutinize the circumstances for compliance with the *Sterling* [*v. Mayflower Hotel Corp.*, Del. Supr., 93 A.2d 107 (1952)] rule of "entire fairness" and, if it finds a violation thereof, will grant such relief as equity may require. Any statement in Stauffer inconsistent herewith is held inapplicable to a § 251 merger.

Singer's business purpose test was extended to short-form mergers two years later in *Roland International Corporation v. Najjar*.[9] The *Roland* majority wrote:

> The short form permitted by § 253 does simplify the steps necessary to effect a merger, and does give a parent corporation some certainty as to result and control as to timing. But we find nothing magic about a 90% ownership of outstanding shares which would eliminate the fiduciary duty owed by the majority to the minority....
>
> As to *Stauffer*, we agree that the purpose of § 253 is to provide the parent with a means of eliminating minority shareholders in the subsidiary but, as we observed in *Singer*, we did "not read the decision [*Stauffer*] as approving a merger accomplished solely to freeze-out the minority without a valid business purpose." We held that any statement in *Stauffer* inconsistent with the principles restated in *Singer* was inapplicable to a § 251 merger. Here we hold that the principles announced in *Singer* with respect to a § 251 merger apply

---

7. [5] Del. Ch., 281 A.2d 30 (1971).
8. [7] Del. Supr., 380 A.2d 969 (1977).
9. [9] Del. Supr., 407 A.2d 1032 (1979).

to a § 253 merger. It follows that any statement in *Stauffer* inconsistent with that holding is overruled.[10]

After *Roland*, there was not much of *Stauffer* that safely could be considered good law. But that changed in 1983, in *Weinberger v. UOP, Inc.*,[11] when the Court dropped the business purpose test, made appraisal a more adequate remedy, and said that it was "return[ing] to the well established principles of *Stauffer* ... and *Schenley* ... mandating a stockholder's recourse to the basic remedy of an appraisal." *Weinberger* focused on two subjects—the "unflinching" duty of entire fairness owed by self-dealing fiduciaries, and the "more liberalized appraisal" it established.

With respect to entire fairness, the [*Weinberger*] Court explained that the concept includes fair dealing (how the transaction was timed, initiated, structured, negotiated, disclosed and approved) and fair price (all elements of value); and that the test for fairness is not bifurcated. On the subject of appraisal, the Court made several important statements: (i) courts may consider "proof of value by any techniques or methods which are generally considered acceptable in the financial community and otherwise admissible in court...." (ii) fair value must be based on "all relevant factors," which include not only "elements of future value ... which are known or susceptible of proof as of the date of the merger" but also, when the court finds it appropriate, "damages, resulting from the taking, which the stockholders sustain as a class;" and (iii) "a plaintiff's monetary remedy ordinarily should be confined to the more liberalized appraisal proceeding herein established...."

By referencing both *Stauffer* and *Schenley*, one might have thought that the *Weinberger* court intended appraisal to be the exclusive remedy "ordinarily" in non-fraudulent mergers where "price ... [is] the preponderant consideration outweighing other features of the merger." In *Rabkin v. Philip A. Hunt Chemical Corp.*,[12] however, the Court dispelled that view. The *Rabkin* plaintiffs claimed that the majority stockholder breached its fiduciary duty of fair dealing by waiting until a one year commitment to pay $25 per share had expired before effecting a cash-out merger at $20 per share. The Court of Chancery dismissed the complaint, reasoning that, under *Weinberger*, plaintiffs could obtain full relief for the alleged unfair dealing in an appraisal proceeding. This Court reversed, holding that the trial court read *Weinberger* too narrowly and that appraisal is the exclusive remedy only if stockholders' complaints are limited to "judgmental factors of valuation."

Rabkin, through its interpretation of *Weinberger*, effectively eliminated appraisal as the exclusive remedy for any claim alleging breach of the duty of entire fairness. But *Rabkin* involved a long-form merger, and the Court did not discuss, in that case or any others, how its refinement of *Weinberger* impacted short-form mergers. Two of this Court's more recent decisions that arguably touch on the subject are *Bershad*

---

10. [10] [In *Roland*,] Justice Quillen dissented, saying that the majority created "an unnecessary damage forum" for a plaintiff whose complaint demonstrated that appraisal would have been an adequate remedy.

11. [11] Del. Supr., 457 A.2d 701 (1983).

12. [18] Del. Supr., 498 A.2d 1099 (1985).

v. Curtiss-Wright Corp.[13] and *Kahn v. Lynch Communication Systems, Inc.*,[14] both long-form merger cases. In *Bershad*, the Court included § 253 when it identified statutory merger provisions from which fairness issues flow:

> In parent-subsidiary merger transactions the issues are those of fairness-fair price and fair dealing. These flow from the statutory provisions permitting mergers, 8 Del. C. §§ 251–253 (1983), and those designed to ensure fair value by an appraisal, 8 Del. C. § 262 (1983) ...

and in *Lynch*, the Court described entire fairness as the "exclusive" standard of review in a cash-out, parent/subsidiary merger.

Mindful of this history, we must decide whether a minority stockholder may challenge a short-form merger by seeking equitable relief through an entire fairness claim. Under settled principles, a parent corporation and its directors undertaking a short-form merger are self-dealing fiduciaries who should be required to establish entire fairness, including fair dealing and fair price. The problem is that § 253 authorizes a summary procedure that is inconsistent with any reasonable notion of fair dealing. In a short-form merger, there is no agreement of merger negotiated by two companies; there is only a unilateral act—a decision by the parent company that its 90% owned subsidiary shall no longer exist as a separate entity. The minority stockholders receive no advance notice of the merger; their directors do not consider or approve it; and there is no vote. Those who object are given the right to obtain fair value for their shares through appraisal.

The equitable claim plainly conflicts with the statute. If a corporate fiduciary follows the truncated process authorized by § 253, it will not be able to establish the fair dealing prong of entire fairness. If, instead, the corporate fiduciary sets up negotiating committees, hires independent financial and legal experts, etc., then it will have lost the very benefit provided by the statute—a simple, fast and inexpensive process for accomplishing a merger. We resolve this conflict by giving effect the intent of the General Assembly. In order to serve its purpose, § 253 must be construed to obviate the requirement to establish entire fairness.

Thus, we again return to *Stauffer*, and hold that, absent fraud or illegality, appraisal is the exclusive remedy available to a minority stockholder who objects to a short-form merger. In doing so, we also reaffirm *Weinberger's* statements about the scope of appraisal. The determination of fair value must be based on all relevant factors, including damages and elements of future value, where appropriate. So, for example, if the merger was timed to take advantage of a depressed market, or a low point in the company's cyclical earnings, or to precede an anticipated positive development, the appraised value may be adjusted to account for those factors. We recognize that these are the types of issues frequently raised in entire fairness claims, and we have held that claims for unfair dealing cannot be litigated in an appraisal. But our prior holdings simply explained that equitable claims may not be engrafted onto a statutory

---

13. [20] Del. Supr., 535 A.2d 840 (1987).
14. [21] Del. Supr., 638 A.2d 1110 (1994).

appraisal proceeding; stockholders may not receive rescissionary relief in an appraisal. Those decisions should not be read to restrict the elements of value that properly may be considered in an appraisal.

Although fiduciaries are not required to establish entire fairness in a short-form merger, the duty of full disclosure remains, in the context of this request for stockholder action. Where the only choice for the minority stockholders is whether to accept the merger consideration or seek appraisal, they must be given all the factual information that is material to that decision. The Court of Chancery carefully considered plaintiffs' disclosure claims and applied settled law in rejecting them. We affirm this aspect of the appeal on the basis of the trial court's decision.

Notes

1. The last paragraph of the court's opinion in *Glassman*, stressing the duty of full disclosure, was the basis for allowing a minority shareholder to challenge the fairness of a short-form merger in *Berger v. Pubco Corp.* 976 A.2d 132 (Del. 2009).

2. The Delaware courts have clearly waxed and waned in their propensity to decide that the appraisal remedy should be exclusive. The variability may be influenced by the relative confidence judges have from time to time in the capacity of the appraisal proceeding to produce fair results.

Chapter 13

Changes in Control

Situation

a. Daytron Corporation, a large publicly held conglomerate, has become increasingly serious about acquiring Biologistics. Daytron's Chair of the Board and Chief Executive Officer, Lauren Lipinsky, has tracked Biologistics' success and believes that Baker's DNA research will yield commercially valuable results sometime in the next few years. Daytron approaches Biologistic's director about a possible corporate combination. Daytron indicates a willingness to pay Baker and Anderson generous salaries but wants total ownership of Biologistics. Anderson's and Baker's initial reaction is to reject Daytron's overture; they are not ready to cash out their investment. Phillips and the other directors, however, are eager to negotiate further. The directors ask you to identify the preliminary issues.

b. Anticipating that Biologistics' directors will reject its overture, Daytron's directors are considering their options. One possibility is for Daytron to acquire control of Biologistics by purchasing individual shareholders' stock directly. Biologistics' directors ask you how they can defend the corporation against this possibility.

Section I
Introduction

This chapter explores two types of corporate acquisitions. In the first, corporate management decides to have the corporation merge into, consolidate with, or sell its assets to another corporation. In these corporate combinations, the acquiring corporation negotiates directly with the target corporation.

In the second type of acquisition, a tender offer, the acquiring corporation purchases directly from the shareholders of the target corporation a controlling interest in the company's stock. Chapter 18 explores what tender offers are, and the applicable federal and state regulations. This chapter discusses the fiduciary duties of directors and officers of target corporations who oppose a tender offer.

Both types of acquisitions typically involve a proposed change in who controls the target corporation. As described in the ALI Part VI Introductory Note, these transactions pose unique issues:

> First, a transaction in control or tender offer is typically the most complex
> business transaction in which a corporation will engage. Shareholders thus

have a need for management's expertise to be employed on their behalf in the evaluation and negotiation of transactions in control. When this face is presented, such transactions may resemble the business decisions that are protected under the business judgment rule....

Second, a transaction in control or tender offer represents a potential conflict of interest for officers who are also directors. If they approve a proposed transaction, the approval may have been influenced by benefits formally or informally promised to be given to them after the transaction is consummated. If they reject a proposed transaction, the rejection may reflect their preference for retaining their positions. Furthermore, even non-officer directors are put in the difficult position of having to evaluate their past and future stewardship of the corporation. When this face is presented, a transaction in control or tender offer may tend to resemble an interested transaction, review of which is controlled by ... [a] more rigorous fairness standard.

Finally, transactions in control and tender offers are mechanisms through which market review of the effectiveness of management's delegated discretion can operate. Under this analysis, if management has not performed effectively, that failure will likely be reflected in the price of the corporation's securities. By purchasing those securities through such a transaction, an acquiror may displace existing management and, in effect, bet its investment on its ability to enhance shareholder value—for example, through improvement of the corporation's economic performance or creation of synergistic benefits through combining the corporation's business with the acquiror's business, or through achievement of a profit through sale of portions of the corporation's business. The existence of this market test is one of the justifications for the breadth of protection accorded the exercise of management discretion under the business judgment rule, in that there is reduced need for judicial review when effective market mechanisms are operative.

Section II
Negotiated Changes In Control

A. Corporate Combinations

There are many alternative structures to facilitate combining one or more corporations (or other business enterprises) into a single corporation or corporate group. It is useful to think about these in terms of what the selling and buying corporations transfer in the exchange.

On the seller's side, the transaction may involve transfer by the selling corporation to the buyer of some or all the selling corporation's assets and liabilities (called an asset transaction) or transfer by the selling corporation's shareholders to the buyer of some or all the selling shareholders' stock (called a stock transaction). On the buyer's side, the transaction may involve transfer by the buyer to the selling corporation or its shareholders of cash (called a cash transaction) or shares of the buying corporation (called a stock transaction). From the four alternatives focusing on what each side transfers, it is possible to characterize these basic forms of business combination as a cash-for-assets transaction, a stock-for-assets transaction, a cash-for-stock transaction or a stock-for-stock transaction.

Some of these transactions, moreover, can be consummated using a statutory procedure called merger, in which the corporations effectively marry one another. The statutory merger is especially common when two corporations exchange stock for stock and is also common when one corporation pays cash to acquire stock in another. It is not used when the buyer pays cash or stock (or other consideration) to acquire the selling corporation's assets and assume its liabilities. In addition, a transaction involving transfer of the selling shareholders' stock may be arranged using a tender offer, a process in which the buyer offers the selling shareholders the chance to tender their shares to it in exchange for offered consideration (cash, buyer stock or other consideration).

As the foregoing description of alternatives should suggest, each poses a series of business and legal issues to evaluate what form is optimal for particular participants. On the business side, a buyer's decision to fund an acquisition using cash or stock depends on factors like whether it has enough cash given its liquidity needs or whether it is willing to risk diluting the ownership interest of existing shareholders when using stock. A seller's decision to transfer assets and liabilities or transfer share ownership interests may depend on whether the goal is to relinquish interest in only a portion of its existing business, hiving off designated assets and liabilities for sale in an asset transaction, or exit entirely, transferring shares.

As a legal matter, these alternative ways to consummate a business combination may pose significant consequences from tax laws and securities regulations. For example, certain transactions, such as asset transfers in exchange for cash, may yield immediate obligations to pay taxes, whereas others, such as stock transfers in exchange for stock, may entitle participants to defer tax consequences until further events occur. Similarly, a public corporation paying stock for assets or another company's stock must comply with rigorous securities regulations, including registering the stock, whereas paying in cash entails less securities law oversight.

Mixed issues of business and law can also factor into the choice of business combination structure. Chief among these are whether third parties are required to approve or consent to the transaction. For example, many contracts, including loan agreements, leases and intellectual property licenses, contain provisions requiring the other party's consent to one party's right to enter into designated business combinations. Often these consent provisions are stricter in the case of an asset transaction than a stock transaction and may have different provisions governing transactions funded in cash or stock. Similarly, regulatory authorities may have the right to approve or consent to certain transactions and not others.

In addition to these legal and business factors, two corporate law factors can be important: whether shareholders of the constituent corporations are entitled to vote to approve a transaction and whether any shareholders dissenting from it are entitled to appraisal rights, statutorily-authorized judicial proceedings to assess the fair value of interests exchanged in a business combination. State corporation law statutes prescribe whether shareholders have voting rights and/or appraisal rights. For corporations with stock listed on a stock exchange, the stock exchange may impose additional rules governing shareholder voting.

Traditional statutory prescriptions on shareholder voting and appraisal rights, including Delaware's, vary according to the form of business combination being used, embracing formal distinctions reflected in the foregoing description of these forms. However, modern statutory approaches, including the Model Act, authorize voting and appraisal rights according to substantive attributes of the combination that focus on whether a shareholder's interests require the protection afforded by voting and appraisal rights. As illustrated by the following cases, this can be important because many of the forms lead to identical substantive results but involve distinct formal procedures.

Consider, for example, a standard form of statutory merger, in which two constituent corporations marry into a single surviving one. In doing so, all the assets and liabilities of each corporation are transferred so that they become, by operation of law, the assets and liabilities of the surviving corporation. Shareholders of the constituent corporations emerge as shareholders of the surviving corporation. Typically, the surviving corporation is one of the constituent corporations so that its pre-merger shareholders continue to be shareholders of the surviving corporation, by owning their pre-merger shares, and the shareholders of the other corporation receive newly-issued shares in the surviving corporation. Traditional statutes, including Delaware's, generally require both shareholder bodies to vote on such a standard statutory merger and offer both appraisal rights.

Voting and appraisal rights can differ if a transaction is designed not as a merger but as the purchase and sale of assets and liabilities. As noted, in such asset transactions, the buying corporation agrees to buy all or substantially all the selling corporation's assets and to assume all or some of its liabilities. The buying corporation can pay for the acquisition using cash or newly-issued shares or other consideration. Upon closing of the purchase and sale, that consideration is distributed to the selling corporation's shareholders and the selling corporation thereafter dissolves. The resulting corporate structure is identical to that resulting from a statutory merger. But, under Delaware law, although the selling corporation's shareholders have voting rights, they do not have appraisal rights. Under the Model Act, the selling corporation's shareholders have voting and appraisal rights identical to those they would have in a statutory merger.

B. De Facto Mergers

The previous section should suggest that laws governing shareholder voting and appraisal rights, when they depend heavily on the form of a transaction rather than its substance, can create anomalous results. For example, why should appraisal rights be available in a merger but not an asset transaction when the deals have otherwise identical results for shareholders? Such seemingly anomalous results lead to flirtation with the so-called de facto merger doctrine. Under it, substance matters more than form and, if a transaction produces the effects of a statutory merger, then the same voting and appraisal rights are required. Despite this flirtation, seen in the following *Farris v. Glen Alden Corp.* case, in most jurisdictions as a matter of corporate law, the doctrine has been abandoned or was never recognized, as the ensuing *Hariton v. ARCO Electronics, Inc.* case attests. On the other hand, as suggested by this section's final case, *Knapp v. Northern American Rockwell Corp.*, the de facto merger doctrine remains viable to protect the rights of creditors, if not shareholders. You might consider why this should be so.

Farris v. Glen Alden Corp.

Pennsylvania Supreme Court
143 A.2d 25 (1958)

COHEN, JUSTICE:

We are required to determine on this appeal whether, as a result of a "Reorganization Agreement" executed by the officers of Glen Alden Corporation and List Industries Corporation, and approved by the shareholders of the former company, the rights and remedies of a dissenting shareholder accrue to the plaintiff.

Glen Alden is a Pennsylvania corporation engaged principally in the mining of anthracite coal and lately in the manufacture of air conditioning units and fire-fighting equipment. In recent years the company's operating revenue has declined substantially, and in fact, its coal operations have resulted in tax loss carryovers of approximately $14,000,000. In October 1957, List, a Delaware holding company owning interests in motion picture theaters, textile companies and real estate, and to a lesser extent, in oil and gas operations, warehouses and aluminum piston manufacturing, purchased through a wholly owned subsidiary 38.5% of Glen Alden's outstanding stock.[2] This acquisition enabled List to place three of its directors on the Glen Alden board.

On March 20, 1958, the two corporations entered into a "reorganization agreement," subject to stockholder approval, which contemplated the following actions:

1. Glen Alden is to acquire all of the assets of List, excepting a small amount of cash reserved for the payment of List's expenses in connection with the transaction. These assets include over $8,000,000 in cash held chiefly in the treasuries of List's wholly owned subsidiaries.

2. In consideration of the transfer, Glen Alden is to issue 3,621,703 shares of stock to List. List in turn is to distribute the stock to its shareholders at a ratio of five shares of Glen Alden stock for each six shares of List stock. In order to accomplish the necessary distribution, Glen Alden is to increase the authorized number of its shares of capital stock from 2,500,000 shares to 7,500,000 shares without according preemptive rights to the present shareholders upon the issuance of any such shares.

---

2. [1] Of the purchase price of $8,719,109, $5,000,000 was borrowed.

3. Further, Glen Alden is to assume all of List's liabilities including a $5,000,000 note incurred by List in order to purchase Glen Alden stock in 1957, outstanding stock options, incentive stock options plans, and pension obligations.

4. Glen Alden is to change its corporate name from Glen Alden Corporation to List Alden Corporation.

5. The present directors of both corporations are to become directors of List Alden.

6. List is to be dissolved and List Alden is to then carry on the operations of both former corporations.

Two days after the agreement was executed notice of the annual meeting of Glen Alden to be held on April 11, 1958, was mailed to the shareholders together with a proxy statement analyzing the reorganization agreement and recommending its approval as well as approval of certain amendments to Glen Alden's articles of incorporation and bylaws necessary to implement the agreement. At this meeting the holders of a majority of the outstanding shares, (not including those owned by List), voted in favor of a resolution approving the reorganization agreement.

On the day of the shareholders' meeting, plaintiff, a shareholder of Glen Alden, filed a complaint in equity against the corporation and its officers seeking to enjoin them temporarily until final hearing, and perpetually thereafter, from executing and carrying out the agreement.

The gravamen of the complaint was that the notice of the annual shareholders' meeting did not conform to the requirements of the Business Corporation Law, 15 P.S. § 2852-1 *et seq.*, in three respects: (1) It did not give notice to the shareholders that the true intent and purpose of the meeting was to effect a merger or consolidation of Glen Alden and List; (2) It failed to give notice to the shareholders of their right to dissent to the plan of merger or consolidation and claim fair value for their shares, and (3) It did not contain copies of the text of certain sections of the Business Corporation Law as required.[3]

By reason of these omissions, plaintiff contended that the approval of the reorganization agreement by the shareholders at the annual meeting was invalid and unless the carrying out of the plan were enjoined, he would suffer irreparable loss by being deprived of substantial property rights.[4]

The defendants answered admitting the material allegations of fact in the complaint but denying that they gave rise to a cause of action because the transaction complained of was a purchase of corporate assets as to which shareholders had no

---

3. [3] The proxy statement included the following declaration: "Appraisal Rights."
"In the opinion of counsel, the shareholders of neither Glen Alden nor List Industries will have any rights of appraisal or similar rights of dissenters with respect to any matter to be acted upon at their respective meetings."
4. [4] The complaint also set forth that the exchange of shares of Glen Alden's stock for those of List would constitute a violation of the pre-emptive rights of Glen Alden shareholders as established by the law of Pennsylvania at the time of Glen Alden's incorporation in 1917. The defendants answered that under both statute and prior common law no pre-emptive rights existed with respect to stock issued in exchange for property.

rights of dissent or appraisal. For these reasons the defendants then moved for judgment on the pleadings.[5]

The court below concluded that the reorganization agreement entered into between the two corporations was a plan for a *de facto* merger, and that therefore the failure of the notice of the annual meeting to conform to the pertinent requirements of the merger provisions of the Business Corporation Law rendered the notice defective and all proceedings in furtherance of the agreement void. Wherefore, the court entered a final decree denying defendants' motion for judgment on the pleadings, entering judgment upon plaintiff's complaint and granting the injunctive relief therein sought. This appeal followed.

When use of the corporate form of business organization first became widespread, it was relatively easy for courts to define a "merger" or a "sale of assets" and to label a particular transaction as one or the other. But prompted by the desire to avoid the impact of adverse, and to obtain the benefits of favorable, government regulations, particularly federal tax laws, new accounting and legal techniques were developed by lawyers and accountants which interwove the elements characteristic of each, thereby creating hybrid forms of corporate amalgamation. Thus, it is no longer helpful to consider an individual transaction in the abstract and solely by reference to the various elements therein [to] determine whether it is a "merger" or a "sale." Instead, to determine properly the nature of a corporate transaction, we must refer not only to all the provisions of the agreement, but also to the consequences of the transaction and to the purposes of the provisions of the corporation law said to be applicable. We shall apply this principle to the instant case.

Section 908, subd. A of the Pennsylvania Business Corporation Law provides: "If any shareholder of a domestic corporation which becomes a party to a plan of merger or consolidation shall object to such plan of merger or consolidation … such shareholder shall be entitled to … [the fair value of his shares upon surrender of the share certificate or certificates representing his shares]." Act of May 5, 1933, P.L. 364, *as amended*, 15 P.S. § 2852-908, subd. A.

… [W]hen a corporation combines with another so as to lose its essential nature and alter the original fundamental relationships of the shareholders among themselves and to the corporation, a shareholder who does not wish to continue his membership therein may treat his membership in the original corporation as terminated and have the value of his shares paid to him....

Does the combination outlined in the present "reorganization" agreement so fundamentally change the corporate character of Glen Alden and the interest of the plaintiff as a shareholder therein, that to refuse him the rights and remedies of a dissenting shareholder would in reality force him to give up his stock in one corporation and

---

5. [5] Counsel for the defendants concedes that if the corporation is required to pay the dissenting shareholders the appraised fair value of their shares, the resultant drain of cash would prevent Glen Alden from carrying out the agreement. On the other hand, plaintiff contends that if the shareholders had been told of their rights as dissenters, rather than specifically advised that they had no such rights, the resolution approving the reorganization agreement would have been defeated.

against his will accept shares in another? If so, the combination is a merger within the meaning of section 908, subd. A of the corporation law....

If the reorganization agreement were consummated plaintiff would find that the "List Alden" resulting from the amalgamation would be quite a different corporation than the "Glen Alden" in which he is now a shareholder. Instead of continuing primarily as a coal mining company, Glen Alden would be transformed, after amendment of its articles of incorporation, into a diversified holding company whose interests would range from motion picture theaters to textile companies, Plaintiff would find himself a member of a company with assets of $169,000,000 and a long-term debt of $38,000,000 in lieu of a company one-half that size and with but one-seventh the long-term debt.

While the administration of the operations and properties of Glen Alden as well as List would be in the hands of management common to both companies, since all executives of List would be retained in List Alden, the control of Glen Alden would pass to the directors of List; for List would hold eleven of the seventeen directorships on the new board of directors.

As an aftermath of the transaction plaintiff's proportionate interest in Glen Alden would have been reduced to only two-fifths of what it presently is because of the issuance of an additional 3,621,703 shares to List which would not be subject to pre-emptive rights. In fact, ownership of Glen Alden would pass to the stockholders of List who would hold 76.5% of the outstanding shares as compared with but 23.5% retained by the present Glen Alden shareholders.

Perhaps the most important consequence to the plaintiff, if he were denied the right to have his shares redeemed at their fair value, would be the serious financial loss suffered upon consummation of the agreement. While the present book value of his stock is $38 a share after combination it would be worth only $21 a share. In contrast, the shareholders of List who presently hold stock with a total book value of $33,000,000 or $7.50 a share, would receive stock with a book value of $76,000,000 or $21 a share.

Under these circumstances it may well be said that if the proposed combination is allowed to take place without right of dissent, plaintiff would have his stock in Glen Alden taken away from him and the stock of a new company thrust upon him in its place. He would be projected against his will into a new enterprise under terms not of his own choosing. It was to protect dissident shareholders against just such a result that ... the legislature ... in section 908, subd. A, granted the right of dissent. And it is to accord that protection to the plaintiff that we conclude that the combination proposed in the case at hand is a merger within the intendment of section 908, subd. A.

Nevertheless, defendants contend that the 1957 amendments to sections 311 and 908 of the corporation law preclude us from reaching this result and require the entry of judgment in their favor. Subsection F of section 311 dealing with the voluntary transfer of corporate assets provides: "The shareholders of a business corporation which acquires by sale, lease or exchange all or substantially all of the property of another corporation by the issuance of stock, securities or otherwise shall not be entitled to the rights and remedies of dissenting shareholders...."

And the amendment to section 908 reads as follows: "The right of dissenting shareholders ... shall not apply to the purchase by a corporation of assets whether or not the consideration therefor be money or property, real or personal, including shares or bonds or other evidences of indebtedness of such corporation. The shareholders of such corporation shall have no right to dissent from any such purchase." ...

... [W]e will not blind our eyes to the realities of the transaction. Despite the designation of the parties and the form employed, Glen Alden does not in fact acquire List, rather, List acquires Glen Alden, ... and under section 311, subd. D the right of dissent would remain with the shareholders of Glen Alden.

We hold that the combination contemplated by the reorganization agreement, although consummated by contract rather than in accordance with the statutory procedure, is a merger within the protective purview of [the Pennsylvania statute]. The shareholders of Glen Alden should have been notified accordingly and advised of their statutory rights of dissent and appraisal. The failure of the corporate officers to take these steps renders the stockholder approval of the agreement at the 1958 shareholders' meeting invalid. The lower court did not err in enjoining the officers and directors of Glen Alden from carrying out this agreement....

Notes and Questions

1. Following this decision, the Pennsylvania legislature acted explicitly to abolish the de facto merger doctrine, amending Pa. Cons. Stat. Ann. §3111(F), 1908(B).

2. Suppose you concur in the judgment of *Farris v. Glen Alden* but either oppose the de facto merger doctrine or decide such a case after the Pennsylvania legislature abolished the doctrine. What other legal theory could you rely upon to concur in the judgment? Remember that List held 38.5% of Glen Alden's stock at the time it orchestrated the asset sale.

Hariton v. Arco Electronics, Inc.

Delaware Supreme Court
188 A.2d 123 (1963)

SOUTHERLAND, CHIEF JUSTICE:

This case involves a sale of assets under §271 of the corporation law, 8 Del. C. It presents for decision the question presented, but not decided, in *Heilbrunn v. Sun Chemical Corporation*, Del., 150 A.2d 755. It may be stated as follows:

A sale of assets is effected under §271 in consideration of shares of stock of the purchasing corporation. The agreement of sale embodies also a plan to dissolve the selling corporation and distribute the shares so received to the stockholders of the seller, so as to accomplish the same result as would be accomplished by a merger of the seller into the purchaser. Is the sale legal?

The facts are these:

The defendant Arco and Loral Electronics Corporation, a New York corporation, are both engaged, in somewhat different forms, in the electronic equipment business.

In the summer of 1961 they negotiated for an amalgamation of the companies. As of October 27, 1961, they entered into a "Reorganization Agreement and Plan." The provisions of this Plan pertinent here are in substance as follows:

1. Arco agrees to sell all its assets to Loral in consideration (*inter alia*) of the issuance to it of 283,000 shares of Loral.

2. Arco agrees to call a stockholders meeting for the purpose of approving the Plan and the voluntary dissolution.

3. Arco agrees to distribute to its stockholders all the Loral shares received by it as a part of the complete liquidation of Arco.

At the Arco meeting all the stockholders voting (about 80%) approved the Plan. It was thereafter consummated.

Plaintiff, a stockholder who did not vote at the meeting, sued to enjoin the consummation of the Plan on the grounds (1) that it was illegal, and (2) that it was unfair. The second ground was abandoned. Affidavits and documentary evidence were filed, and defendant moved for summary judgment and dismissal of the complaint. The Vice Chancellor granted the motion and plaintiff appeals.

The question before us we have stated above. Plaintiff's argument that the sale is illegal runs as follows:

The several steps taken here accomplish the same result as a merger of Arco into Loral. In a "true" sale of assets, the stockholder of the seller retains the right to elect whether the selling company shall continue as a holding company. Moreover, the stockholder of the selling company is forced to accept an investment in a new enterprise without the right of appraisal granted under the merger statute. § 271 cannot therefore be legally combined with a dissolution proceeding under § 275 and a consequent distribution of the purchaser's stock. Such a proceeding is a misuse of the power granted under § 271, and a *de facto* merger results.

The foregoing is a brief summary of plaintiff's contention.

Plaintiff's contention that this sale has achieved the same result as a merger is plainly correct. The same contention was made to us in *Heilbrunn v. Sun Chemical Corporation*, Del., 150 A.2d 755. Accepting it as correct, we noted that this result is made possible by the overlapping scope of the merger statute and section 271, mentioned in *Sterling v. Mayflower Hotel Corporation*, 93 A.2d 107. We also adverted to the increased use, in connection with corporate reorganization plans, of § 271 instead of the merger statute....

We now hold that the reorganization here accomplished through § 271 and a mandatory plan of dissolution and distribution is legal. This is so because the sale-of-assets statute and the merger statute are independent of each other. They are, so to speak, of equal dignity, and the framers of a reorganization plan may resort to either type of corporate mechanics to achieve the desired end. This is not an anomalous result in our corporation law. As the Vice Chancellor pointed out, the elimination of accrued dividends, though forbidden under a charter amendment may be accomplished by a merger....

Notes and Questions

1. The statutory law of appraisal rights in many states, including Delaware, is a detailed labyrinth of rules that first grant rights, then deny those rights, and then restore some of those rights, depending on stated formal attributes of a transaction. For instance, DGCL 262(b) grants appraisal rights to shares of Delaware corporations constituent to mergers, whether such corporation is the surviving or disappearing corporation. But then DGCL 262(b)(1)(i)–(ii) denies appraisal rights where shares eliminated are publicly traded—the so-called "market exception" to appraisal rights—and DGCL 262(b)(1) (last clause) denies appraisal rights for shares of surviving corporations where right to vote is denied under DGCL 251(f). Yet then DGCL 262(b)(2) restores otherwise denied appraisal rights even for publicly-traded shares unless holders are paid entirely in one or more of the following: shares of the surviving corporation (private or public); shares of any other public corporation; or cash for fractional shares. Finally, DGCL 262(c) allows for private ordering: to grant appraisal rights in situations where the statute does not mandate them.

2. The MBCA simplifies the law determining when appraisal rights apply. Indeed, as explained by the Official Comment to MBCA 11.01, de facto merger problems are unlikely to arise since the MBCA's procedural requirements for authorization and consequences of various types of transactions are largely standardized. For example, appraisal rights are granted not only in mergers but also in share exchanges, in sales of all or substantially all the corporate assets, and in amendments to articles of incorporation that significantly affect rights of shareholders.

Knapp v. North American Rockwell Corp.

United States Court of Appeals, Third Circuit
506 F.2d 361 (1974)

ADAMS, CIRCUIT JUDGE:

The principal question here is whether it was error to grant summary judgment on the ground that one injured by a defective machine may not recover from the corporation that purchased substantially all the assets of the manufacturer of the machine because the transaction was a sale of assets rather than a merger or consolidation.

Stanley Knapp, Jr., an employee of Mrs. Smith's Pie Co., was injured on October 6, 1969, when, in the course of his employment, his hand was caught in a machine known as a "Packomatic." The machine had been designed and manufactured by Textile Machine Works (TMW) and had been sold to Mrs. Smith's Pie Co. in 1966 or 1967.

On April 5, 1968, TMW entered into an agreement with North American Rockwell whereby TMW exchanged substantially all its assets for stock in Rockwell. TMW retained only its corporate seal, its articles of incorporation, its minute books and other corporate records, and $500,000 in cash intended to cover TMW's expenses in connection with the transfer. TMW also had the right, prior to closing the transaction with Rockwell, to dispose of land held by TMW or its subsidiary. Among the assets acquired by Rockwell was the right to use the name "Textile Machine Works." TMW was to change its name on the closing date, then to distribute the Rockwell stock to its shareholders and to dissolve TMW "as soon as practicable after the last of such distributions."

The accord reached by Rockwell and TMW also stipulated that Rockwell would assume specified obligations and liabilities of TMW, but among the liabilities not assumed were: "(a) liabilities against which TMW is insured or otherwise indemnified to the extent of such insurance or indemnification unless the insurer or indemnitor agrees in writing to insure and indemnify (Rockwell) to the same extent as it was so insuring and indemnifying TMW."

Closing took place pursuant to the agreement on August 29, 1968. Plaintiff sustained his injuries on October 6, 1969. TMW was dissolved on February 20, 1970, almost 18 months after the bulk of its assets had been exchanged for Rockwell stock.

Plaintiff filed this suit against Rockwell in the district court on March 22, 1971. He alleged that his injuries resulted from the negligence of TMW in designing and manufacturing the machine and that Rockwell, as TMW's successor, is liable for such injuries. Rockwell joined plaintiff's employer, Mrs. Smith's Pie Co., as a third-party defendant.

Rockwell moved for summary judgment in the district court on June 19, 1973. On September 6, 1973, the district court granted the motion, ruling that Rockwell had neither merged nor consolidated with TMW, that Rockwell was not a continuation of TMW, and that Rockwell had not assumed TMW's liability to Knapp. Therefore, the court concluded, Rockwell was not responsible for the obligations of TMW. On October 11, 1973, Knapp filed a motion for rehearing and reconsideration by the district court, which was denied on November 26, 1973. Knapp appealed to this Court on December 11, 1973.

Both parties agree that this case is controlled by the following principle of law:

> The general rule is that "a mere sale of corporate property by one company to another does not make the purchaser liable for the liabilities of the seller not assumed by it."... There are, however, certain exceptions to this rule. Liability for obligations of a selling corporation may be imposed on the purchasing corporation when (1) the purchaser expressly or impliedly agrees to assume such obligations; (2) the transaction amounts to a consolidation or merger of the selling corporation with or into the purchasing corporation; (3) the purchasing corporation is merely a continuation of the selling corporation; or (4) the transaction is entered into fraudulently to escape liability for such obligations.

Shane v. Hobam, Inc., 332 F. Supp. 526, 527–528 (E.D. Pa. 1971) (decided under New York law).

In light of this language, Knapp contends that the transaction in question "amounts to a consolidation or merger of (TMW) with or into the purchasing corporation (Rockwell)" or, alternatively, that Rockwell is a "continuation" of TMW. Although the TMW corporation technically continued to exist until its dissolution approximately 18 months after the consummation of the transaction with Rockwell, TMW was, Knapp argues, a mere shell during that period. It had none of its former assets, no active operations, and was required by the contract with Rockwell to dissolve itself "as soon as practicable." Knapp urges in effect that the transaction between TMW and Rockwell should be considered a *de facto* merger.

Rockwell asserts, in defense of the district court's grant of summary judgment, that a merger, a consolidation and a continuation all require that the corporation being merged, consolidated or continued cease to exist. TMW, Rockwell claims, did not go out of existence at the time of the exchange with Rockwell, but continued its corporate life for 18 months thereafter. Further, Rockwell argues, TMW until its dissolution possessed assets of substantial value, in the form of Rockwell stock.

… No prior cases decided under Pennsylvania law have addressed the problem presently before this Court. However, when courts from other jurisdictions have considered similar questions, they have ascertained the existence *vel non* of a merger, a consolidation or a continuation on the basis of whether, immediately after the transaction, the selling corporation continued to exist as a corporate entity and whether, after the transaction, the selling corporation possessed substantial assets with which to satisfy the demands of its creditors....

Denying Knapp the right to sue Rockwell because of the barren continuation of TMW after the exchange with Rockwell would allow a formality to defeat Knapp's recovery. Although TMW technically existed as an independent corporation, it had no substance. The parties clearly contemplated that TMW would terminate its existence as a part of the transaction. TMW had, in exchange for Rockwell stock, disposed of all the assets it originally held, exclusive of the cash necessary to consummate the transaction. It could not undertake any active operations. Nor was TMW permitted under the agreement to divest itself of the Rockwell stock, so that it might become an effective investment vehicle for its shareholders. Most significantly, TMW was required by the contract with Rockwell to dissolve "as soon as practicable."

On the other hand, Rockwell acquired all the assets of TMW, exclusive of certain real estate that Rockwell did not want, and assumed practically all of TMW's liabilities. Further, Rockwell required that TMW use its "best efforts," prior to the consummation of the transaction, to preserve TMW's business organization intact for Rockwell, to make available to Rockwell TMW's existing officers and employees, and to maintain TMW's relationship with its customers and suppliers. After the exchange, Rockwell continued TMW's former business operations.

If we are to follow the philosophy of the Pennsylvania courts that questions of an injured party's right to seek recovery are to be resolved by an analysis of public policy considerations rather than by a mere procrustean application of formalities, we must, in considering whether the TMW-Rockwell exchange was a merger, evaluate the public policy implications of that determination.

In resolving where the burden of a loss should be imposed, the Pennsylvania Supreme Court has considered which of the two parties is better able to spread the loss. In *Ayala v. Philadelphia Board of Education*, [305 A.2d 877 (Pa. 1973)] a student who had been injured by a shredding machine during an upholstery class sued the Board of Education. The Court, in abolishing the doctrine of immunity in suits against local government, observed that the Board was in a better position than the student to have avoided the injury, and that "The city is a far better loss-distributing agency than the innocent and injured victim." The Court, quoting the Supreme Court of Illinois, decried the injustice of imposing upon an injured party the entire burden of his injuries, rather than distributing the responsibility throughout the community "where it could be borne without hardship upon any individual."

The Pennsylvania courts have also noted the importance of insurance in performing the loss-spreading function. In *Falco v. Pados*, [282 A.2d 351 (Pa. 1970)] the Court concluded that public interest mandated the abolition of parental immunity from liability for a parent's negligent injury to his child because, in the presence of widespread liability insurance coverage, the doctrine of parental immunity unjustly confined the burden of the loss to the injured party alone. "In a time of almost universal liability insurance, such unexpected hardship or ruin is needlessly inflicted by the immunity doctrine."

Interpreting all the allegations in the light most favorable to Knapp, as we must on a motion for summary judgment, neither Knapp nor Rockwell was ever in a position to prevent the occurrence of the injury, inasmuch as neither manufactured the defective device. As between these two parties, however, Rockwell is better able to spread the burden of the loss. Prior to the exchange with Rockwell, TMW had procured insurance that would have indemnified TMW had it been held liable to Knapp for his injuries. Rockwell could have protected itself from sustaining the brunt of the loss by securing from TMW an assignment of TMW's insurance. There is no indication in the record that such an assignment would have placed a burden on either Rockwell or TMW since TMW had already purchased the insurance protection, and the insurance was of no continuing benefit to TMW after its liability to suit was terminated by Pennsylvania statute. Rockwell has adduced no explanation, either in its brief or at oral argument, why it agreed in the contract not to take an assignment of TMW's prepaid insurance. Rockwell therefore should not be permitted to impose the weight of the loss upon a user of an allegedly defective product by delaying the formal dissolution of TMW....

C. Additional Exceptions and Alternatives

Comprehensive treatment of business combinations requires exploration of materials generally considered beyond the scope of a basic course in corporations or business associations. At many law schools, specialized courses are offered that cover these advanced matters (including courses on mergers, corporate finance and/or accounting). Even in a basic corporations or business associations course, however, students can benefit from noting a few additional exceptions to standard requirements, alternatives to basic business combinations and an assortment of miscellaneous issues.

1. Many state corporation law statutes provide exceptions to the usual requirements of shareholder approval and appraisal rights in the context of business combinations. The first concerns short-form mergers of the sort illustrated by *Glassman v. Unocal Exploration Corp.*, 777 A.2d 242 (Del. 2001) (reprinted in Chapter 12). If the surviving corporation already owns at least 90% of the other corporation, no shareholder vote

of either side is required. Second, under many corporation law statutes, including Delaware and the Model Act, if the surviving corporation does not issue stock in the merger that increases its outstanding shares by more than 20%, no shareholder vote of its shareholders is required.

In addition, many statutes dispense with shareholder appraisal rights for public company shareholders receiving either cash or other publicly traded shares in a merger. The rationale for this so-called "market out" exception is that a liquid and reliable public trading market for shares furnishes a superior valuation tool than those available in a judicial appraisal proceeding. Many statutes providing for these exceptions contain detailed specifications concerning their application, requiring corporate lawyers to engage intensively with statutory text to determine whether voting or appraisal rights exist. Section 262(b) of the Delaware General Corporation Law provides an example.

Moreover, state statutory voting and appraisal statutes contain detailed and widely varying provisions concerning what shareholders must do to exercise these rights. For example, some statutes provide that shareholders intending to exercise appraisal rights must vote against the proposed transaction, and must give advance notice of their intention to vote no and exercise appraisal rights. Model Business Corporation Act § 13.21. The statutes also provide procedural rules governing the proceeding, including how it is initiated, what reports and evidence are admitted, and how its expenses are allocated. The ultimate issue in appraisal cases, the fair value of shares being exchanged, can be highly contentious and raise a range of complex valuation issues. *E.g., Advanced Communication Design, Inc. v. Follett*, 615 N.W.2d (Minn. 2000); *Cavalier Oil Corp. v. Harnett*, 564 A.2d 1137 (Del. 1989).

2. An important variation on the standard alternative forms of business combination is the so-called triangular merger, referring to the presence of three corporate parties to the merger. It involves using a subsidiary corporation of one of the constituents to the merger to effectuate it. Doing so can enable avoiding voting or appraisal rights that would otherwise be available to a surviving corporation's shareholders.

In form, the would-be surviving corporation uses or creates a subsidiary corporation that it controls as the parent. It has that subsidiary corporation enter into the merger agreement with the other corporation and become the surviving corporation in the merger. All statutory merger rules described earlier apply, but voting and appraisal rights associated with the surviving corporation are exercised by the parent, owning 100% of that corporation. The Model Act polices triangular mergers by giving the parent corporation's shareholders voting and appraisal rights if it is issuing stock that increases its outstanding shares by more than 20%. Delaware law makes no such provision. The triangular arrangement can be used to effectuate other business combination structures as well.

3. Yet another form of business combination is recognized under the Model Act (but not under Delaware statutory law). It is called a share exchange. The buying corporation issues shares to the selling corporation in exchange for the latter's shares. Afterwards, the buying corporation owns the selling corporation as a subsidiary. The buying corporation's shareholders have voting rights only if it is issuing stock that

increases its outstanding shares by more than 20%; they do not have appraisal rights. The selling corporation's shareholders have both voting and appraisal rights, subject only to the market out exception.

4. Beyond these statutory business combinations and associated voting and appraisal rights, the tender offer is a direct non-statutory means by which a bidder may acquire control of another corporation. Unlike other business combination forms, all of which require board approval on both sides, the tender offer is made directly to the target corporation's shareholders whether or not the target's board approves. Indeed, the so-called hostile tender offer is designed precisely to take a bid directly to shareholders despite objections or resistance from their corporation's board. Target holders do not vote at a shareholder meeting or get or need appraisal rights; they simply "vote" in the market by deciding to accept or reject the offer on its terms. The following section begins to probe associated corporate law issues that tender offers pose, especially as to target board responses to them. Chapter 18 returns to tender offers to probe securities law issues they pose.

Section III
Protecting Control

Chapter 18 describes federal and state securities regulations governing bids for corporate control, whether by tender offer or proxy contest. The following materials explore how fiduciary duties and standards are adapted during such bids. In particular, incumbent management may oppose an unsolicited bid, and the directors may strategize specifically to block its successful culmination. Given shareholders' franchise rights and rights to sell their shares without interference, when is the board justified in implementing these defensive tactics?

A. Traditional Approach and Tactics

Cheff v. Mathes

Delaware Supreme Court
199 A.2d 548 (1964)

CAREY, JUSTICE:

This is an appeal from the decision of the Vice-Chancellor in a derivative suit holding certain directors of Holland Furnace Company liable for loss allegedly resulting from improper use of corporate funds to purchase shares of the company....

Holland Furnace Company, a corporation of the State of Delaware, manufactures warm air furnaces, air conditioning equipment, and other home heating equipment. At the time of the relevant transactions, the board of directors was composed of the seven individual defendants. Mr. Cheff had been Holland's Chief Executive Officer since 1933, received an annual salary of $77,400, and personally owned 6,000 shares of the company. He was also a director. Mrs. Cheff, the wife of Mr. Cheff, was a daughter of the founder of Holland and had served as a director since 1922. She personally owned 5,804 shares of Holland and owned 47.9 percent of Hazelbank United Interest, Inc. Hazelbank is an investment vehicle for Mrs. Cheff and members of the Cheff-Landwehr family group, which owned 164,950 shares of the 883,585 outstanding shares of Holland. As a director, Mrs. Cheff received a compensation of $200.00 for each monthly board meeting, whether or not she attended the meeting....

Prior to the events in question, Holland employed approximately 8500 persons and maintained 400 branch sales offices located in 43 states. The volume of sales had declined from over $41,000,000 in 1948 to less than $32,000,000 in 1956. Defendants contend that the decline in earnings is attributable to the artificial post-war demand generated in the 1946–1948 period. In order to stabilize the condition of the company, the sales department apparently was reorganized and certain unprofitable branch offices were closed. By 1957 this reorganization had been completed and the management was convinced that the changes were manifesting beneficial results. The practice of the company was to directly employ the retail salesman, and the management considered that practice—unique in the furnace business—to be a vital factor in the company's success.

During the first five months of 1957, the monthly trading volume of Holland's stock on the New York Stock Exchange ranged between 10,300 shares to 24,200 shares. In the last week of June 1957, however, the trading increased to 37,800 shares, with a corresponding increase in the market price. In June of 1957, Mr. Cheff met with Mr. Arnold H. Maremont, who was President of Maremont Automotive Products, Inc. and Chairman of the boards of Motor Products Corporation and Allied Paper Corporation. Mr. Cheff testified, on deposition, that Maremont generally inquired about the feasibility of merger between Motor Products and Holland. Mr. Cheff testified that, in view of the difference in sales practices between the two companies, he informed Mr. Maremont that a merger did not seem feasible. In reply, Mr. Maremont stated that, in the light of Mr. Cheff's decision, he had no further interest in Holland nor did he wish to buy any of the stock of Holland.

None of the members of the board apparently connected the interest of Mr. Maremont with the increased activity of Holland stock. However, Mr. Trenkamp [Holland director and general counsel,] and Mr. Staal, the Treasurer of Holland, unsuccessfully made an informal investigation in order to ascertain the identity of the purchaser or purchasers. The mystery was resolved, however, when Maremont called Ames [another Holland director and a financial advisor] in July of 1957 to inform the latter that Maremont then owned 55,000 shares of Holland stock. At this juncture, no requests for change in corporate policy were made, and Maremont made no demand to be made a member of the board of Holland.

Ames reported the above information to the board at its July 30, 1957 meeting. Because of the position now occupied by Maremont, the board elected to investigate the financial and business history of Maremont and corporations controlled by him. Apart from the documentary evidence produced by this investigation, which will be considered *infra*, Staal testified, on deposition, that "leading bank officials" had indicated that Maremont "had been a participant, or had attempted to be, in the liquidation of a number of companies." Staal specifically mentioned only one individual giving such advice, the Vice President of the First National Bank of Chicago. Mr. Cheff testified, at trial, of Maremont's alleged participation in liquidation activities. Mr. Cheff testified that: "Throughout the whole of the Kalamazoo-Battle Creek area, and Detroit too, where I spent considerable time, he is well known and not highly regarded by any stretch." This information was communicated to the board.

On August 23, 1957, at the request of Maremont, a meeting was held between Mr. Maremont and Cheff. At this meeting, Cheff was informed that Motor Products then owned approximately 100,000 shares of Holland stock. Maremont then made a demand that he be named to the board of directors, but Cheff refused to consider it. Since considerable controversy has been generated by Maremont's alleged threat to liquidate the company or substantially alter the sales force of Holland, we believe it desirable to set forth the testimony of Cheff on this point: "Now we have 8500 men, direct employees, so the problem is entirely different. He indicated immediately that he had no interest in that type of distribution, that he didn't think it was modern, that he felt furnaces could be sold as he sold mufflers, through half a dozen salesmen in a wholesale way."

Testimony was introduced by the defendants tending to show that substantial unrest was present among the employees of Holland as a result of the threat of Maremont to seek control of Holland. Thus, Mr. Cheff testified that the field organization was considering leaving in large numbers because of a fear of the consequences of a Maremont acquisition; he further testified that approximately "25 of our key men" were lost as the result of the unrest engendered by the Maremont proposal. Staal, corroborating Cheff's version, stated that a number of branch managers approached him for reassurances that Maremont was not going to be allowed to successfully gain control. Moreover, at approximately this time, the company was furnished with a Dun and Bradstreet report, which indicated the practice of Maremont to achieve quick profits by sales or liquidations of companies acquired by him. The defendants were also supplied with an income statement of Motor Products, Inc., showing a loss of $336,121.00 for the period in 1957.

On August 30, 1957, the board was informed by Cheff of Maremont's demand to be placed upon the board and of Maremont's belief that the retail sales organization of Holland was obsolete. The board was also informed of the results of the investigation by Cheff and Staal. Predicated upon this information, the board authorized the purchase of company stock on the market with corporate funds....

Subsequent to this meeting, substantial numbers of shares were purchased and, in addition, Mrs. Cheff made alternate personal purchases of Holland stock. As a result of purchases by Maremont, Holland and Mrs. Cheff, the market price rose.... On September 4th, Maremont proposed to sell his current holdings of Holland to the corporation for $14.00 a share. However, because of delay in responding to this offer, Maremont withdrew the offer. At this time, Mrs. Cheff was obviously quite concerned over the prospect of a Maremont acquisition, and had stated her willingness to expend her personal resources to prevent it.

On September 30, 1957, Motor Products Corporation, by letter to Mrs. Bowles [a Hazelbank director], made a buy-sell offer to Hazelbank. At the Hazelbank meeting of October 3, 1957, Mrs. Bowles presented the letter to the board. The board took no action, but referred the proposal to its finance committee. Although Mrs. Bowles and Mrs. Putnam [another Hazelbank director] were opposed to any acquisition of Holland stock by Hazelbank, Mr. Landwehr [a Hazelbank and Holland director] conceded that a majority of the board were in favor of the purchase. Despite this fact, the finance committee elected to refer the offer to the Holland board on the grounds that it was the primary concern of Holland.

Thereafter, Mr. Trenkamp arranged for a meeting with Maremont, which occurred on October 14–15, 1957, in Chicago. Prior to this meeting, Trenkamp was aware of the intentions of Hazelbank and Mrs. Cheff to purchase all or portions of the stock then owned by Motor Products if Holland did not so act. As a result of the meeting, there was a tentative agreement on the part of Motor Products to sell its 155,000 shares at $14.40 per share. On October 23, 1957, at a special meeting of the Holland board, the purchase was considered. All directors, except Spatta, were present. The dangers allegedly posed by Maremont were again reviewed by the board. Trenkamp and Mrs. Cheff agree that the latter informed the board that either she or Hazelbank would purchase part or all of the block of Holland stock owned by Motor Products if the Holland board did not so act. The board was also informed that in order for the corporation to finance the purchase, substantial sums would have to be borrowed from commercial lending institutions. A resolution authorizing the purchase of 155,000 shares from Motor Products was adopted by the board. The price paid was in excess of the market price prevailing at the time, and the book value of the stock was approximately $20.00 as compared to approximately $14.00 for the net quick asset value. The transaction was subsequently consummated. The stock option plan mentioned in the minutes has never been implemented. In 1959, Holland stock reached a high of $15.25 a share.

On February 6, 1958, plaintiffs, owners of 60 shares of Holland stock, filed a derivative suit in the court below naming all of the individual directors of Holland, Holland itself and Motor Products Corporation as defendants. The complaint alleged that all of the purchases of stock by Holland in 1957 were for the purpose of insuring the perpetuation of control by the incumbent directors. The complaint requested that the transaction between Motor Products and Holland be rescinded and, secondly, that the individual defendants account to Holland for the alleged damages....

Under the provisions of 8 Del. C. § 160, a corporation is granted statutory power to purchase and sell shares of its own stock. Such a right, as embodied in the statute, has long been recognized in this State. The charge here is not one of violation of statute, but the allegation is that the true motives behind such purchases were improperly centered upon perpetuation of control. In an analogous field, courts have sustained the use of proxy funds to inform stockholders of management's views upon the policy questions inherent in an election to a board of directors, but have not sanctioned the use of corporate funds to advance the selfish desires of directors to perpetuate themselves in office. Similarly, if the actions of the board were motivated by a sincere belief that the buying out of the dissident stockholder was necessary to maintain what the board believed to be proper business practices, the board will not be held liable for such decision, even though hindsight indicates the decision was not the wisest course. *See Kors v. Carey*, Del. Ch., 158 A.2d 136. On the other hand, if the board has acted solely or primarily because of the desire to perpetuate themselves in office, the use of corporate funds for such purposes is improper. *See Bennett v. Propp*, Del., 187 A.2d 405.

Our first problem is the allocation of the burden of proof to show the presence or lack of good faith on the part of the board in authorizing the purchase of shares. Initially, the decision of the board of directors in authorizing a purchase was presumed to be in good faith and could be overturned only by a conclusive showing by plaintiffs of fraud or other misconduct. In *Kors [v. Carey,]* the court merely indicated that the directors are presumed to act in good faith and the burden of proof to show to the contrary falls upon the plaintiff. However, in *Bennett v. Propp, supra,* we stated:

> "We must bear in mind the inherent danger in the purchase of shares with corporate funds to remove a threat to corporate policy when a threat to control is involved. The directors are of necessity confronted with a conflict of interest, and an objective decision is difficult.... Hence, in our opinion, the burden should be on the directors to justify such a purchase as one primarily in the corporate interest." (187 A.2d 409, at page 409).

... To say that the burden of proof is upon the defendants is not to indicate, however, that the directors have the same "self-dealing interest" as is present, for example, when a director sells property to the corporation. The only clear pecuniary interest shown on the record was held by Mr. Cheff, as an executive of the corporation, and Trenkamp, as its attorney. The mere fact that some of the other directors were substantial shareholders does not create a personal pecuniary interest in the decisions made by the board of directors, since all shareholders would presumably share the benefit flowing to the substantial shareholder. Accordingly, these directors other than Trenkamp and Cheff, while called upon to justify their actions, will not be held to the same standard of proof required of those directors having personal and pecuniary interest in the transaction....

Plaintiffs urge that the sale price was unfair in view of the fact that the price was in excess of that prevailing on the open market. However, as conceded by all parties, a substantial block of stock will normally sell at a higher price than that prevailing on the open market, the increment being attributable to a "control premium." Plaintiffs argue that it is inappropriate to require the defendant corporation to pay a control premium, since control is meaningless to an acquisition by a corporation of its own shares. However, it is elementary that a holder of a substantial number of shares would expect to receive the control premium as part of his selling price, and if the corporation desired to obtain the stock, it is unreasonable to expect that the corporation could avoid paying what any other purchaser would be required to pay for the stock. In any event, the financial expert produced by defendant at trial indicated that the price paid was fair and there was no rebuttal. Ames, the financial man on the board, was strongly of the opinion that the purchase was a good deal for the corporation. The Vice Chancellor made no finding as to the fairness of the price other than to indicate the obvious fact that the market price was increasing as a result of open market purchases by Maremont, Mrs. Cheff and Holland.

The question then presented is whether or not defendants satisfied the burden of proof of showing reasonable grounds to believe a danger to corporate policy and effectiveness existed by the presence of the Maremont stock ownership. It is important to remember that the directors satisfy their burden by showing good faith and reasonable investigation; the directors will not be penalized for an honest mistake of judgment, if the judgment appeared reasonable at the time the decision was made.

In holding that employee unrest could as well be attributed to a condition of Holland's business affairs as to the possibility of Maremont's intrusion, the Vice Chancellor must have had in mind one or both of two matters: (1) the pending proceedings before the Federal Trade Commission concerning certain sales practices of Holland; (2) the decrease in sales and profits during the preceding several years. Any other possible reason would be pure speculation. In the first place, the adverse decision of the F.T.C. was not announced until *after* the complained-of transaction. Secondly, the evidence clearly shows that the downward trend of sales and profits had reversed itself, presumably because of the reorganization which had then been completed. Thirdly, everyone who testified on the point said that the unrest was due to the possible threat presented by Maremont's purchases of stock. There was, in fact, no *testimony* whatever of any connection between the unrest and either the F.T.C. proceedings or the business picture.

The Vice Chancellor found that there was no substantial evidence of a liquidation posed by Maremont. This holding overlooks an important contention. The fear of the defendants, according to their testimony, was not limited to the possibility of liquidation; it included the alternate possibility of a material change in Holland's sales policies, which the board considered vital to its future success. The *unrebutted* testimony before the court indicated: (1) Maremont had deceived Cheff as to his original intentions, since his open market purchases were contemporaneous with his disclaimer of interest in Holland; (2) Maremont had given Cheff some reason to believe that he intended to eliminate the retail sales force of Holland; (3) Maremont demanded a place on the board; (4) Maremont substantially increased his purchases after having been refused a place on the board; (5) the directors had good reason to believe that unrest among key employees had been engendered by the Maremont threat; (6) the board had received advice from Dun and Bradstreet indicating the past liquidation or quick sale activities of Motor Products; (7) the board had received professional advice from the firm of [Merrill Lynch], who recommended that the purchase from Motor Products be carried out; (8) the board had received competent advice that the corporation was over-capitalized; (9) Staal and Cheff had made informal personal investigations from contacts in the business and financial community and had reported to the board of the alleged poor reputation of Maremont. The board was within its rights in relying upon that investigation, since 8 Del. C. § 141(f) allows the directors to reasonably rely upon a report provided by corporate officers.

Accordingly, we are of the opinion that the evidence presented in the court below leads inevitably to the conclusion that the board of directors, based upon direct investigation, receipt of professional advice, and personal observations of the contradictory action of Maremont and his explanation of corporate purpose, believed, with justification, that there was a reasonable threat to the continued existence of Holland, or at least existence in its present form, by the plan of Maremont to continue building up his stock holdings. We find no evidence in the record sufficient to justify a contrary conclusion. The opinion of the Vice Chancellor that employee unrest may have been engendered by other factors or that the board had no grounds to suspect Maremont is not supported in any manner by the evidence. . . .

Accordingly, the judgment of the court below is reversed and remanded with instruction to enter judgment for the defendants.

Notes and Questions

1. *Cheff v. Mathes* remains a foundational doctrinal statement of corporate law's evaluation of directors' responses to unwanted threats to corporate control. However, the particular device the directors in that case adopted, the repurchase of corporate shares from the bidder at a premium, is now anachronistic. Federal tax law imposes punishing excise taxes on bidder gains generated by such repurchases, which attracted the negative sobriquet, greenmail, when participants came to regard it as unsavory — a sort of threat to assert control that could be bought off at a premium. *See* I.R.C. § 5881.

2. In 1968, U.S. federal securities laws were amended by the Williams Act to regulate stock acquisitions and tender offers for public companies. One provision requires purchasers of 5% or more of the voting stock of a public company to make a public filing with the Securities and Exchange Commission disclosing the purchase and the acquirer's related intentions. Such filings, called "Schedule 13Ds" after the relevant section of the regulations, remove what would otherwise be much of the mystery surrounding unusual pricing activity on public stock markets. Section 13D and related matters are discussed in Chapter 16.

Note on Takeover Tactics

Bidders and targets alike command a variety of devices to gain the upper hand in contests for corporate control. As a matter of practice, bidders and their advisors in planning a bid for control (whether by tender offer or proxy contest) examine the target's governing state corporation law, charter, by-laws and contracts to identify provisions that exist or could quickly be adopted to defend against an unwanted overture. They design the terms of their bid and their overall strategy by anticipating target invocation of those provisions. Likewise, as a matter of practice, targets receiving unwanted bids, and their advisors, examine them with a view towards deploying or adopting provisions that would be effective defenses.

In this milieu, one may speak of bidder devices or tactics and defensive devices or tactics. Although too numerous to catalogue completely, the following are some examples of the wide variety of bidder and defensive tools that have appeared in this field over the past few decades. Note that, as with many specialized fields, participants often develop colloquial expressions to describe these tools. As examples, the entire collection of target defensive provisions, devices and tactics are collectively referred to as *shark repellants* in the United States and *poison pills* in Europe (in the United States, the colloquial term *poison pill* is reserved to designate one particular tool, as noted below).

On the offensive, bidder, side, it can be common for a bidder to begin a takeover process by communicating its interest and intention to the target's board of directors. This communication is sometimes colloquially called a *bear hug*, as it may purport to propose a friendly business combination while containing explicit or veiled hints that defensive responses will lead the bidder to the *hostile* approach of going directly to the target's shareholders.

A takeover offer may be made for cash, securities or other consideration. It may seek all or only a majority of the target's shares. Some takeover bids contemplate acquiring a majority of the target shares in a first step, followed by a subsequent merger of the target corporation with the bidder. The procedure is called a *two-step*, and the parts called the *front-end* and *back-end* respectively. In cases where the front-end consideration is clearly superior to the proposed back-end consideration, the two-step earned the sobriquet *hostile two-tiered offer*, and generated considerable policy concerns and legal restrictions, as ensuing materials suggest.

When a bidder identifies defensive provisions in a target's charter or by-laws that it could find difficult to overcome, a common strategy is to accompany or precede a tender offer by proposing a special meeting of the target's shareholders to amend these. This is done by requesting a special meeting and then conducting a *proxy solicitation* of target shareholders seeking to dismantle some or all defensive provisions a target corporation may have in place. Indeed, as an alternative to the tender offer, which seeks to result in ownership control, some takeover efforts seek control through board incumbency, and use a *proxy contest* to oust incumbent directors in favor of the bidder's own director nominees.

On the defensive side, as the foregoing point suggests, it is not uncommon for corporate charters or by-laws to anticipate bidder efforts to call special shareholder meetings and pursue proxy contests to amend defensive provisions. Examples of such defensive provisions are charter or by-law limitations on a shareholders' power to call special meetings or amend those documents by mere majority vote following standard procedures, instead requiring a *super-majority vote* (such as 2/3) or specifying additional procedural requirements. Some corporate bylaws require notice of an intention to propose a slate of directors in a proxy contest to be given well in advance of the related shareholders' meeting and call for the disclosure of considerable background information about the proposed directors.

Some corporations make seizing corporate control through a proxy contest to elect bidder directors harder by charter provisions prescribing that directors are elected in classes to multiple-year terms, rather than all being elected annually. Such *staggered boards* mean that a proxy contest proponent cannot gain incumbent control in a single year but needs at least a second year or third to acquire a majority of or all seats.

Among standard devices many corporations commonly have in place, the most ubiquitous is a charter provision that authorizes a class of securities, usually preferred stock, that the board is authorized to issue on such terms as it chooses, without additional shareholder approval. A target board can issue such so-called *black check preferred* for nearly any purpose to defend against an unwanted bidder. Examples are using it to acquire other businesses the bidder would not want or selling it to friendly third parties on terms that decrease the probable percentage of shares interested in tendering to the unwanted bidder.

Another common defensive device is a so-called *shareholder rights plan*, usually providing that upon announcement of a tender offer the target board does not approve, all existing shareholders other than the bidder have the right to receive newly-issued shares in the corporation at a very low price. This device, so formidable that it is dubbed a *poison pill* in the United States, significantly dilutes the bidder's existing ownership interest and adds such cost to its effort, that hostile tender offers invariably are conditioned on removal of the device.

Other contractual terms that can impede takeover interest include so-called *change of control provisions*. These provisions trigger certain payments or other action upon the occurrence of stated events denominated as changes in control, such as a third party successfully waging a tender offer in which it acquires a majority of the target's shares. Among contracts containing such provisions are employment agreements with senior executives or other employees. These produce large payouts upon a change of control, devices dubbed *golden parachutes* when used to refer to high-payout arrangements with senior executives and *silver parachutes* to refer to more broad-based and lower-payout arrangements with other employees.

A relatively common target board response to an unwanted takeover attempt is a search to identify an alternative business partner with which to form a desired business combination. Such a friendly alternative business partner is called a *white knight* when a full-blown combination is pursued or a *white squire* when it acquires a significant ownership position in the target, sufficient to discourage bidder interest. In such friendly alternative transactions, it is also possible for a target corporation to sell or give the white knight or squire the right to buy prized assets, perhaps those of particular interest to the bidder, referred to as *crown jewels*. When target boards grant parties options on crown jewels, the vernacular refers to them as *lock-up options*. That term is also used to describe a target board's action to grant white knights or squires an option to buy additional shares in the target corporation, diluting the bidder and increasing its acquisition costs. In addition, agreements between targets and friendly suitors may restrict the target board's rights to solicit yet other suitors (a *no-shop* provision) or to entertain such proposals (a *no-talk* provision). They also may provide that, if the target terminates the agreement for any reason or designated reasons, it must pay the suitor a termination fee (a *break-up fee* or *topping fee*).

Many of the foregoing tools and devices, plus others, appear in the following series of cases, which are primarily addressed to the corporation law duties of target directors in the takeover context. In reading the cases and thinking about their specific and general contexts, consider how participants seem involved in an endless process of invention, bidders devising new ways to seek corporate control met by defenders devising new ways to retain it, ad infinitum.

B. Enhanced Scrutiny

The *Unocal* and *Revlon* cases that follow build on *Cheff* to define what remains the basic doctrinal structure of the law applicable to directors in the control context.

Unocal Corp. v. Mesa Petroleum Co.

Delaware Supreme Court

493 A.2d 946 (1985)

MOORE, JUSTICE:

We confront an issue of first impression in Delaware—the validity of a corporation's self-tender for its own shares which excludes from participation a stockholder making a hostile tender offer for the company's stock.

The Court of Chancery granted a preliminary injunction to the plaintiffs, Mesa Petroleum Co., Mesa Asset Co., Mesa Partners II, and Mesa Eastern, Inc. (collectively "Mesa"),[7] enjoining an exchange offer of the defendant, Unocal Corporation (Unocal) for its own stock. The trial court concluded that a selective exchange offer, excluding Mesa, was legally impermissible....

I

The factual background of this matter bears a significant relationship to its ultimate outcome.

On April 8, 1985, Mesa, the owner of approximately 13% of Unocal's stock, commenced a two-tier "front loaded" cash tender offer for 64 million shares, or approximately 37%, of Unocal's outstanding stock at a price of $54 per share. The "back-end" was designed to eliminate the remaining publicly held shares by an exchange of securities purportedly worth $54 per share. However, pursuant to an order entered by the United States District Court for the Central District of California on April 26, 1985, Mesa issued a supplemental proxy statement to Unocal's stockholders disclosing that the securities offered in the second-step merger would be highly subordinated, and that Unocal's capitalization would differ significantly from its present structure. Unocal has rather aptly termed such securities "junk bonds."

Unocal's board consists of eight independent outside directors and six insiders. It met on April 13, 1985, to consider the Mesa tender offer. Thirteen directors were present, and the meeting lasted nine and one-half hours. The directors were given

---

7. [1] T. Boone Pickens, Jr., is President and Chairman of the Board of Mesa Petroleum and President of Mesa Asset and controls the related Mesa entities.

no agenda or written materials prior to the session. However, detailed presentations were made by legal counsel regarding the board's obligations under both Delaware corporate law and the federal securities laws. The board then received a presentation from Peter Sachs on behalf of Goldman Sachs & Co. (Goldman Sachs) and Dillon, Read & Co. (Dillon Read) discussing the bases for their opinions that the Mesa proposal was wholly inadequate. Mr. Sachs opined that the minimum cash value that could be expected from a sale or orderly liquidation for 100% of Unocal's stock was in excess of $60 per share. In making his presentation, Mr. Sachs showed slides outlining the valuation techniques used by the financial advisors, and others, depicting recent business combinations in the oil and gas industry. The Court of Chancery found that the Sachs presentation was designed to apprise the directors of the scope of the analyses performed rather than the facts and numbers used in reaching the conclusion that Mesa's tender offer price was inadequate.

Mr. Sachs also presented various defensive strategies available to the board if it concluded that Mesa's two-step tender offer was inadequate and should be opposed. One of the devices outlined was a self-tender by Unocal for its own stock with a reasonable price range of $70 to $75 per share. The cost of such a proposal would cause the company to incur $6.1–6.5 billion of additional debt, and a presentation was made informing the board of Unocal's ability to handle it. The directors were told that the primary effect of this obligation would be to reduce exploratory drilling, but that the company would nonetheless remain a viable entity.

The eight outside directors, comprising a clear majority of the thirteen members present, then met separately with Unocal's financial advisors and attorneys. Thereafter, they unanimously agreed to advise the board that it should reject Mesa's tender offer as inadequate, and that Unocal should pursue a self-tender to provide the stockholders with a fairly priced alternative to the Mesa proposal. The board then reconvened and unanimously adopted a resolution rejecting as grossly inadequate Mesa's tender offer. Despite the nine and one-half hour length of the meeting, no formal decision was made on the proposed defensive self-tender.

On April 15, the board met again with four of the directors present by telephone and one member still absent. This session lasted two hours. Unocal's Vice President of Finance and its Assistant General Counsel made a detailed presentation of the proposed terms of the exchange offer. A price range between $70 and $80 per share was considered, and ultimately the directors agreed upon $72. The board was also advised about the debt securities that would be issued, and the necessity of placing restrictive covenants upon certain corporate activities until the obligations were paid. The board's decisions were made in reliance on the advice of its investment bankers, including the terms and conditions upon which the securities were to be issued. Based upon this advice, and the board's own deliberations, the directors unanimously approved the exchange offer. Their resolution provided that if Mesa acquired 64 million shares of Unocal stock through its own offer (the Mesa Purchase Condition), Unocal would buy the remaining 49% outstanding for an exchange of debt securities having an aggregate par value of $72 per share. The board resolution also stated that the offer would be subject to other conditions that had been described to the board at the meeting, or which were deemed necessary by Unocal's officers, including the exclusion of Mesa from the proposal (the Mesa exclusion)....

Unocal's exchange offer was commenced on April 17, 1985, and Mesa promptly challenged it by filing this suit in the Court of Chancery. On April 22, the Unocal board met again and was advised by Goldman Sachs and Dillon Read to [alter the Mesa Purchase Condition so it would be met if Mesa acquired about 20% of the stock]. This recommendation was in response to a perceived concern of the shareholders that, if shares were tendered to Unocal, no shares would be purchased by either offeror. The directors were also advised that they should tender their own Unocal stock into the exchange offer as a mark of their confidence in it.

Another focus of the board was the Mesa exclusion. Legal counsel advised that under Delaware law Mesa could only be excluded for what the directors reasonably believed to be a valid corporate purpose. The directors' discussion centered on the objective of adequately compensating shareholders at the "back-end" of Mesa's proposal, which the latter would finance with "junk bonds". To include Mesa would defeat that goal, because under the proration aspect of the exchange offer (49%) every Mesa share accepted by Unocal would displace one held by another stockholder. Further, if Mesa were permitted to tender to Unocal, the latter would in effect be financing Mesa's own inadequate proposal....

On April 29, 1985, the Vice Chancellor temporarily restrained Unocal from proceeding with the exchange offer unless it included Mesa....

II

The issues we address involve these fundamental questions: Did the Unocal board have the power and duty to oppose a takeover threat it reasonably perceived to be harmful to the corporate enterprise, and if so, is its action here entitled to the protection of the business judgment rule?

Mesa contends that the discriminatory exchange offer violates the fiduciary duties Unocal owes it. Mesa argues that because of the Mesa exclusion the business judgment rule is inapplicable, because the directors by tendering their own shares will derive a financial benefit that is not available to all Unocal stockholders. Thus, it is Mesa's ultimate contention that Unocal cannot establish that the exchange offer is fair to all shareholders, and argues that the Court of Chancery was correct in concluding that Unocal was unable to meet this burden.

Unocal answers that it does not owe a duty of "fairness" to Mesa, given the facts here. Specifically, Unocal contends that its board of directors reasonably and in good faith concluded that Mesa's $54 two-tier tender offer was coercive and inadequate, and that Mesa sought selective treatment for itself. Furthermore, Unocal argues that the board's approval of the exchange offer was made in good faith, on an informed basis, and in the exercise of due care. Under these circumstances, Unocal contends that its directors properly employed this device to protect the company and its stockholders from Mesa's harmful tactics.

III

We begin with the basic issue of the power of a board of directors of a Delaware corporation to adopt a defensive measure of this type. Absent such authority, all other questions are moot. Neither issues of fairness nor business judgment are pertinent without the basic underpinning of a board's legal power to act.

The board has a large reservoir of authority upon which to draw. Its duties and responsibilities proceed from the inherent powers conferred by 8 Del. C. § 141(a), respecting management of the corporation's "business and affairs." Additionally, the powers here being exercised derive from 8 Del. C. § 160(a), conferring broad authority upon a corporation to deal in its own stock. From this it is now well established that in the acquisition of its shares a Delaware corporation may deal selectively with its stockholders, provided the directors have not acted out of a sole or primary purpose to entrench themselves in office.

Finally, the board's power to act derives from its fundamental duty and obligation to protect the corporate enterprise, which includes stockholders, from harm reasonably perceived, irrespective of its source. Thus, we are satisfied that in the broad context of corporate governance, including issues of fundamental corporate change, a board of directors is not a passive instrumentality.

Given the foregoing principles, we turn to the standards by which director action is to be measured. In *Pogostin v. Rice*, Del. Supr., 480 A.2d 619 (1984), we held that the business judgment rule, including the standards by which director conduct is judged, is applicable in the context of a takeover. *Id.* at 627. The business judgment rule is a "presumption that in making a business decision the directors of a corporation acted on an informed basis, in good faith and in the honest belief that the action taken was in the best interests of the company." *Aronson v. Lewis*, Del. Supr., 473 A.2d 805, 812 (1984). A hallmark of the business judgment rule is that a court will not substitute its judgment for that of the board if the latter's decision can be "attributed to any rational business purpose." *Sinclair Oil Corp. v. Levien*, Del. Supr., 280 A.2d 717, 720 (1971).

When a board addresses a pending takeover bid it has an obligation to determine whether the offer is in the best interests of the corporation and its shareholders. In that respect a board's duty is no different from any other responsibility it shoulders, and its decisions should be no less entitled to the respect they otherwise would be accorded in the realm of business judgment.... There are, however, certain caveats to a proper exercise of this function. Because of the omnipresent specter that a board may be acting primarily in its own interests, rather than those of the corporation and its shareholders, there is an enhanced duty which calls for judicial examination at the threshold before the protections of the business judgment rule may be conferred.

This Court has long recognized that:

> We must bear in mind the inherent danger in the purchase of shares with corporate funds to remove a threat to corporate policy when a threat to control is involved. The directors are of necessity confronted with a conflict of interest, and an objective decision is difficult.

Bennett v. Propp, Del. Supr., 187 A.2d 405, 409 (1962). In the face of this inherent conflict directors must show that they had reasonable grounds for believing that a danger to corporate policy and effectiveness existed because of another person's stock ownership. *Cheff v. Mathes*, 199 A.2d at 554–55. However, they satisfy that burden "by showing good faith and reasonable investigation...." *Id.* at 555. Furthermore, such proof is materially enhanced, as here, by the approval of a board comprised of a majority of outside independent directors who have acted in accordance with the foregoing standards....

IV

A

In the board's exercise of corporate power to forestall a takeover bid our analysis begins with the basic principle that corporate directors have a fiduciary duty to act in the best interests of the corporation's stockholders. As we have noted, their duty of care extends to protecting the corporation and its owners from perceived harm whether a threat originates from third parties or other shareholders. But such powers are not absolute. A corporation does not have unbridled discretion to defeat any perceived threat by any Draconian means available.

The restriction placed upon a selective stock repurchase is that the directors may not have acted solely or primarily out of a desire to perpetuate themselves in office. Of course, to this is added the further caveat that inequitable action may not be taken under the guise of law. The standard of proof established in *Cheff v. Mathes* ... is designed to ensure that a defensive measure to thwart or impede a takeover is indeed motivated by a good faith concern for the welfare of the corporation and its stockholders, which in all circumstances must be free of any fraud or other misconduct. However, this does not end the inquiry.

B

A further aspect is the element of balance. If a defensive measure is to come within the ambit of the business judgment rule, it must be reasonable in relation to the threat posed. This entails an analysis by the directors of the nature of the takeover bid and its effect on the corporate enterprise. Examples of such concerns may include: inadequacy of the price offered, nature and timing of the offer, questions of illegality, the impact on "constituencies" other than shareholders (*i.e.*, creditors, customers, employees, and perhaps even the community generally), the risk of nonconsummation, and the quality of securities being offered in the exchange. While not a controlling factor, it also seems to us that a board may reasonably consider the basic stockholder interests at stake, including those of short term speculators, whose actions may have fueled the coercive aspect of the offer at the expense of the long term investor. Here, the threat posed was viewed by the Unocal board as a grossly inadequate two-tier coercive tender offer coupled with the threat of greenmail.

Specifically, the Unocal directors had concluded that the value of Unocal was substantially above the $54 per share offered in cash at the front end. Furthermore, they determined that the subordinated securities to be exchanged in Mesa's announced squeeze out of the remaining shareholders in the "back-end" merger were "junk bonds" worth far less than $54. It is now well recognized that such offers are a classic coercive measure designed to stampede shareholders into tendering at the first tier, even if the price is inadequate, out of fear of what they will receive at the back end of the transaction. Wholly beyond the coercive aspect of an inadequate two-tier tender offer, the threat was posed by a corporate raider with a national reputation as a "greenmailer."

In adopting the selective exchange offer, the board stated that its objective was either to defeat the inadequate Mesa offer or, should the offer still succeed, provide the 49% of its stockholders, who would otherwise be forced to accept "junk bonds," with $72 worth of senior debt. We find that both purposes are valid.

However, such efforts would have been thwarted by Mesa's participation in the exchange offer. First, if Mesa could tender its shares, Unocal would effectively be subsidizing the former's continuing effort to buy Unocal stock at $54 per share. Second, Mesa could not, by definition, fit within the class of shareholders being protected from its own coercive and inadequate tender offer.

Thus, we are satisfied that the selective exchange offer is reasonably related to the threats posed. [T]he board's decision to offer what it determined to be the fair value of the corporation to the 49% of its shareholders, who would otherwise be forced to accept highly subordinated "junk bonds," is reasonable and consistent with the directors' duty to ensure that the minority stockholders receive equal value for their shares.

V

Mesa contends that it is unlawful, and the trial court agreed, for a corporation to discriminate in this fashion against one shareholder. It argues correctly that no case has ever sanctioned a device that precludes a raider from sharing in a benefit available to all other stockholders. However, as we have noted earlier, the principle of selective stock repurchases by a Delaware corporation is neither unknown nor unauthorized. The only difference is that heretofore the approved transaction was the payment of "greenmail" to a raider or dissident posing a threat to the corporate enterprise. All other stockholders were denied such favored treatment, and given Mesa's past history of greenmail, its claims here are rather ironic.

However, our corporate law is not static. It must grow and develop in response to, indeed in anticipation of, evolving concepts and needs. Merely because the General Corporation Law is silent as to a specific matter does not mean that it is prohibited. In the days when *Cheff, Bennett, Martin* and *Kors* were decided, the tender offer, while not an unknown device, was virtually unused, and little was known of such methods as two-tier "front-end" loaded offers with their coercive effects. Then, the favored attack of a raider was stock acquisition followed by a proxy contest. Various defensive tactics, which provided no benefit whatever to the raider, evolved. Thus, the use of corporate funds by management to counter a proxy battle was approved. Litigation, supported by corporate funds, aimed at the raider has long been a popular device.

More recently, as the sophistication of both raiders and targets has developed, a host of other defensive measures to counter such ever mounting threats has evolved and received judicial sanction. These include defensive charter amendments and other devices bearing some rather exotic, but apt, names: Crown Jewel, White Knight, Pac Man, and Golden Parachute. Each has highly selective features, the object of which is to deter or defeat the raider.

Thus, while the exchange offer is a form of selective treatment, given the nature of the threat posed here the response is neither unlawful nor unreasonable. If the board of directors is disinterested, has acted in good faith and with due care, its decision in the absence of an abuse of discretion will be upheld as a proper exercise of business judgment....

VI

In conclusion, there was directorial power to oppose the Mesa tender offer, and to undertake a selective stock exchange made in good faith and upon a reasonable investigation pursuant to a clear duty to protect the corporate enterprise. Further, the selective stock repurchase plan chosen by Unocal is reasonable in relation to the threat that the board rationally and reasonably believed was posed by Mesa's inadequate and coercive two-tier tender offer. Under those circumstances the board's action is entitled to be measured by the standards of the business judgment rule. Thus, unless it is shown by a preponderance of the evidence that the directors' decisions were primarily based on perpetuating themselves in office, or some other breach of fiduciary duty such as fraud, overreaching, lack of good faith, or being uninformed, a Court will not substitute its judgment for that of the board.

... If the stockholders are displeased with the action of their elected representatives, the powers of corporate democracy are at their disposal to turn the board out....

... The decision of the Court of Chancery is therefore REVERSED, and the preliminary injunction is VACATED.

———————

1. The selective self tender offer used by the target board in *Unocal* was subsequently outlawed by federal securities regulation under the so-called all-holders rule that requires tender offers to be open to all holders of a designated class of securities. 17 C.F.R. § 240.14d-10.

2. The two-step merger proposal made by the bidder in *Unocal* was subsequently made more complicated by numerous state corporation law statutes, including DGCL § 203, which restrict an acquirer's right to complete a second-step merger following a tender offer without prior approval of the target's board of directors or, in some cases, its disinterested shareholders. A similar private device was designed by the target in the *Revlon* case, just ahead.

3. *Unocal* and *Revlon* (below) enhanced the duty of care and business judgment rule standard of review in tender offer contests. In the alternative, a few courts have concluded that incumbent management's defensive tactics are more properly analyzed under the duty of loyalty. In *Norlin Corp. v. Rooney, Pace, Inc.*, 744 F.2d 255 (2d Cir. 1984), Piezo Electric Products, Inc., in conjunction with Rooney, Pace, Inc., attempted to take over Norlin Corporation, a company that operated in New York. In response

to this unwanted overture, the Norlin directors issued shares to Andean Enterprises, Inc., a wholly owned subsidiary, and to an Employee Stock Option Plan and Trust ("ESOP"). As a result of these stock transfers, Norlin directors controlled the votes of 49% of the corporation's outstanding stock.

In determining the appropriate standard for review, the court explained:

> [T]he business judgment rule governs only where the directors are not shown to have a self-interest in the transaction at issue. Once self-dealing or bad faith is demonstrated, the duty of loyalty supersedes the duty of care, and the burden shifts to the directors to "prove that the transaction was fair and reasonable to the corporation." [*Treadway Co. v. Care Corp.*, 638 F.2d 357, 382 (2d Cir. 1980).]

In this case, the evidence adduced was more than adequate to constitute a *prima facie* showing of self-interest on the board's part. All of the stock transferred to Andean and the ESOP was to be voted by the directors; indeed, members of the board were appointed trustees of the ESOP. The precipitous timing of the share issuances, and the fact that the ESOP was created the very same day that stock was issued to it, give rise to a strong inference that the purpose of the transaction was not to benefit the employees but rather to solidify management's control of the company. This is buttressed by the fact that the board offered its shareholders no rationale for the transfers other than its determination to oppose, at all costs, the threat to the company that Piezo's acquisitions ostensibly represented. Where, as here, directors amass voting control of close to a majority of a corporation's shares in their own hands by complex, convoluted and deliberate maneuvers, it strains credulity to suggest that the retention of control over corporate affairs played no part in their plans.

We reject the view, propounded by Norlin, that once it concludes that an actual or anticipated takeover attempt is not in the best interests of the company, a board of directors may take any action necessary to forestall acquisitive moves. The business judgment rule does indeed require the board to analyze carefully any perceived threat to the corporation, and to act appropriately when it decides that the interests of the company and its shareholders might be jeopardized. As we have explained, however, the duty of loyalty requires the board to demonstrate that any actions it does take are fair and reasonable. We conclude that Norlin has failed to make that showing.

Revlon, Inc. v. MacAndrews & Forbes Holdings, Inc.

Delaware Supreme Court
506 A.2d 173 (1986)

MOORE, JUSTICE:

In this battle for corporate control of Revlon, Inc. (Revlon), the Court of Chancery enjoined certain transactions designed to thwart the efforts of Pantry Pride, Inc. (Pantry Pride) to acquire Revlon. The defendants are Revlon, its board of directors, and Forstmann Little & Co. and the latter's affiliated limited partnership (collectively,

Forstmann). The injunction barred consummation of an option granted Forstmann to purchase certain Revlon assets (the lock-up option), a promise by Revlon to deal exclusively with Forstmann in the face of a takeover (the no-shop provision), and the payment of a $25 million cancellation fee to Forstmann if the transaction was aborted. The Court of Chancery found that the Revlon directors had breached their duty of care by entering into the foregoing transactions and effectively ending an active auction for the company. The trial court ruled that such arrangements are not illegal *per se* under Delaware law, but that their use under the circumstances here was impermissible. We agree. Thus, we granted this expedited interlocutory appeal to consider for the first time the validity of such defensive measures in the face of an active bidding contest for corporate control. Additionally, we address for the first time the extent to which a corporation may consider the impact of a takeover threat on constituencies other than shareholders.

In our view, lock ups and related agreements are permitted under Delaware law where their adoption is untainted by director interest or other breaches of fiduciary duty. The actions taken by the Revlon directors, however, did not meet this standard. Moreover, while concern for various corporate constituencies is proper when addressing a takeover threat, that principle is limited by the requirement that there be some rationally related benefit accruing to the stockholders. We find no such benefit here.

Thus, under all the circumstances we must agree with the Court of Chancery that the enjoined Revlon defensive measures were inconsistent with the directors' duties to the stockholders. Accordingly, we affirm....

I

The somewhat complex maneuvers of the parties necessitate a rather detailed examination of the facts. The prelude to this controversy began in June 1985, when Ronald O. Perelman, chairman of the board and chief executive officer of Pantry Pride, met with his counterpart at Revlon, Michel C. Bergerac, to discuss a friendly acquisition of Revlon by Pantry Pride. Perelman suggested a price in the range of $40–50 per share, but the meeting ended with Bergerac dismissing those figures as considerably below Revlon's intrinsic value. All subsequent Pantry Pride overtures were rebuffed, perhaps in part based on Mr. Bergerac's strong personal antipathy to Mr. Perelman.

Thus, on August 14, Pantry Pride's board authorized Perelman to acquire Revlon, either through negotiation in the $42–$43 per share range, or by making a hostile tender offer at $45. Perelman then met with Bergerac and outlined Pantry Pride's alternate approaches. Bergerac remained adamantly opposed to such schemes and conditioned any further discussions of the matter on Pantry Pride executing a standstill agreement prohibiting it from acquiring Revlon without the latter's prior approval.

On August 19, the Revlon board met specially to consider the impending threat of a hostile bid by Pantry Pride. At the meeting, Lazard Freres, Revlon's investment banker, advised the directors that $45 per share was a grossly inadequate price for the company. Felix Rohatyn and William Loomis of Lazard Freres explained to the board that Pantry Pride's financial strategy for acquiring Revlon would be through "junk bond" financing followed by a break-up of Revlon and the disposition of its assets.

With proper timing, according to the experts, such transactions could produce a return to Pantry Pride of $60 to $70 per share, while a sale of the company as a whole would be in the "mid 50" dollar range. Martin Lipton, special counsel for Revlon, recommended ... that it adopt a Note Purchase Rights Plan. Under this plan, each Revlon shareholder would receive as a dividend one Note Purchase Right (the Rights) for each share of common stock, with the Rights entitling the holder to exchange one common share for a $65 principal Revlon note at 12% interest with a one-year maturity. The Rights would become effective whenever anyone acquired beneficial ownership of 20% or more of Revlon's shares, unless the purchaser acquired all the company's stock for cash at $65 or more per share. In addition, the Rights would not be available to the acquiror, and prior to the 20% triggering event the Revlon board could redeem the rights for 10 cents each. Both proposals were unanimously adopted.

Pantry Pride made its first hostile move on August 23 with a cash tender offer for any and all shares of Revlon at $47.50 per common share and $26.67 per preferred share, subject to (1) Pantry Pride's obtaining financing for the purchase, and (2) the Rights being redeemed, rescinded or voided.

The Revlon board met again on August 26. The directors advised the stockholders to reject the offer. Further defensive measures also were planned. On August 29, Revlon commenced its own offer for up to 10 million shares, exchanging for each share of common stock tendered one Senior Subordinated Note (the Notes) of $47.50 principal at 11.75% interest, due 1995, and [preferred stock worth another $10 for a total face value of $57.50]. Revlon stockholders tendered 87 percent of the outstanding shares (approximately 33 million), and the company accepted the full 10 million shares on a pro rata basis. The new Notes contained covenants which limited Revlon's ability to incur additional debt, sell assets, or pay dividends unless otherwise approved by the "independent" (non-management) members of the board.

At this point, both the Rights and the Note covenants stymied Pantry Pride's attempted takeover. The next move came on September 16, when Pantry Pride announced a new tender offer at $42 per share, conditioned upon receiving at least 90% of the outstanding stock. Pantry Pride also indicated that it would consider buying less than 90%, and at an increased price, if Revlon removed the impeding Rights. While this offer was lower on its face than the earlier $47.50 proposal, Revlon's investment banker, Lazard Freres, described the two bids as essentially equal in view of the completed exchange offer.

The Revlon board held a regularly scheduled meeting on September 24. The directors rejected the latest Pantry Pride offer and authorized management to negotiate with other parties interested in acquiring Revlon. Pantry Pride remained determined in its efforts and continued to make cash bids for the company, offering $50 per share on September 27, and raising its bid to $53 on October 1, and then to $56.25 on October 7.

In the meantime, Revlon's negotiations with Forstmann and the investment group Adler & Shaykin had produced results. The Revlon directors met on October 3 to consider Pantry Pride's $53 bid and to examine possible alternatives to the offer. Both

Forstmann and Adler & Shaykin made certain proposals to the board. As a result, the directors unanimously agreed to a leveraged buyout by Forstmann. The terms of this accord were as follows: each stockholder would get $56 cash per share; management would purchase stock in the new company by the exercise of their Revlon "golden parachutes"; Forstmann would assume Revlon's $475 million debt incurred by the issuance of the Notes; and Revlon would redeem the Rights and waive the Notes covenants for Forstmann or in connection with any other offer superior to Forstmann's.... Part of Forstmann's plan was to sell Revlon's Norcliff Thayer and Reheis divisions to American Home Products for $335 million. Before the merger, Revlon was to sell its cosmetics and fragrance division to Adler & Shaykin for $905 million. These transactions would facilitate the purchase by Forstmann or any other acquiror of Revlon.

When the merger, and thus the waiver of the Notes covenants, was announced, the market value of these securities began to fall. The Notes, which originally traded near [face value, lost 87% of their value] by October 8. One director later reported (at the October 12 meeting) a "deluge" of telephone calls from irate noteholders, and on October 10 the Wall Street Journal reported threats of litigation by these creditors.

Pantry Pride countered with a new proposal on October 7, raising its $53 offer to $56.25, subject to nullification of the Rights, a waiver of the Notes covenants, and the election of three Pantry Pride directors to the Revlon board. On October 9, representatives of Pantry Pride, Forstmann and Revlon conferred in an attempt to negotiate the fate of Revlon, but could not reach agreement....

[P]rivately armed with Revlon data, Forstmann met on October 11 with Revlon's special counsel and investment banker. On October 12, Forstmann made a new $57.25 per share offer, based on several conditions. The principal demand was a lock-up option to purchase Revlon's Vision Care and National Health Laboratories divisions for $525 million, some $100–$175 million below the value ascribed to them by Lazard Freres, if another acquiror got 40% of Revlon's shares. Revlon also was required to accept a no-shop provision. The Rights and Notes covenants had to be removed as in the October 3 agreement. There would be a $25 million cancellation fee to be placed in escrow, and released to Forstmann if the new agreement terminated or if another acquiror got more than 19.9% of Revlon's stock. Finally, there would be no participation by Revlon management in the merger. In return, Forstmann agreed to support the par value of the Notes, which had faltered in the market, by an exchange of new notes. Forstmann also demanded immediate acceptance of its offer, or it would be withdrawn. The board unanimously approved Forstmann's proposal....

Pantry Pride, which had initially sought injunctive relief from the Rights plan on August 22, filed an amended complaint on October 14 challenging the lock-up, the cancellation fee, and the exercise of the Rights and the Notes covenants. Pantry Pride also sought a temporary restraining order to prevent Revlon from placing any assets in escrow or transferring them to Forstmann. Moreover, on October 22, Pantry Pride again raised its bid, with a cash offer of $58 per share conditioned upon nullification of the Rights, waiver of the covenants, and an injunction of the Forstmann lock-up.

On October 15, the Court of Chancery prohibited the further transfer of assets, and eight days later enjoined the lock-up, no-shop, and cancellation fee provisions of the agreement. The trial court concluded that the Revlon directors had breached their duty of loyalty by making concessions to Forstmann, out of concern for their liability to the noteholders, rather than maximizing the sale price of the company for the stockholders' benefit.

II

To obtain a preliminary injunction, a plaintiff must demonstrate both a reasonable probability of success on the merits and some irreparable harm which will occur absent the injunction. Additionally, the Court shall balance the conveniences of and possible injuries to the parties.

A

We turn first to Pantry Pride's probability of success on the merits. The ultimate responsibility for managing the business and affairs of a corporation falls on its board of directors. 8 Del. C. § 141(a). In discharging this function the directors owe fiduciary duties of care and loyalty to the corporation and its shareholders. These principles apply with equal force when a board approves a corporate merger pursuant to 8 Del. C. § 251(b) and of course they are the bedrock of our law regarding corporate takeover issues. While the business judgment rule may be applicable to the actions of corporate directors responding to takeover threats, the principles upon which it is founded — care, loyalty and independence — must first be satisfied.

If the business judgment rule applies, there is a "presumption that in making a business decision the directors of a corporation acted on an informed basis, in good faith and in the honest belief that the action taken was in the best interests of the company." *Aronson v. Lewis*, 473 A.2d at 812. However, when a board implements anti-takeover measures there arises "the omnipresent specter that a board may be acting primarily in its own interests, rather than those of the corporation and its shareholders ..." *Unocal Corp. v. Mesa Petroleum Co.*, 493 A.2d at 954. This potential for conflict places upon the directors the burden of proving that they had reasonable grounds for believing there was a danger to corporate policy and effectiveness, a burden satisfied by a showing of good faith and reasonable investigation. In addition, the directors must analyze the nature of the takeover and its effect on the corporation in order to ensure balance — that the responsive action taken is reasonable in relation to the threat posed....

B

The first relevant defensive measure adopted by the Revlon board was the Rights Plan, which would be considered a "poison pill" in the current language of corporate takeovers — a plan by which shareholders receive the right to be bought out by the corporation at a substantial premium on the occurrence of a stated triggering event. *See generally Moran v. Household International, Inc.*, Del. Supr., 500 A.2d 1346 (1985). By 8 Del. C. §§ 141 and 122(13), the board clearly had the power to adopt the measure. Thus, the focus becomes one of reasonableness and purpose.

The Revlon board approved the Rights Plan in the face of an impending hostile takeover bid by Pantry Pride at $45 per share, a price which Revlon reasonably concluded was grossly inadequate. Lazard Freres had so advised the directors, and had also informed them that Pantry Pride was a small, highly leveraged company bent on a "bust-up" takeover by using "junk bond" financing to buy Revlon cheaply, sell the acquired assets to pay the debts incurred, and retain the profit for itself. In adopting the Plan, the board protected the shareholders from a hostile takeover at a price below the company's intrinsic value, while retaining sufficient flexibility to address any proposal deemed to be in the stockholders' best interests.

To that extent the board acted in good faith and upon reasonable investigation. Under the circumstances it cannot be said that the Rights Plan as employed was unreasonable, considering the threat posed. Indeed, the Plan was a factor in causing Pantry Pride to raise its bids from a low of $42 to an eventual high of $58. At the time of its adoption the Rights Plan afforded a measure of protection consistent with the directors' fiduciary duty in facing a takeover threat perceived as detrimental to corporate interests. Far from being a "show-stopper," as the plaintiffs had contended in *Moran*, the measure spurred the bidding to new heights, a proper result of its implementation.

C

The second defensive measure adopted by Revlon to thwart a Pantry Pride takeover was the company's own exchange offer for 10 million of its shares. The directors' general broad powers to manage the business and affairs of the corporation are augmented by the specific authority conferred under 8 Del. C. § 160(a), permitting the company to deal in its own stock. However, when exercising that power in an effort to forestall a hostile takeover, the board's actions are strictly held to the fiduciary standards outlined in *Unocal*. These standards require the directors to determine the best interests of the corporation and its stockholders, and impose an enhanced duty to abjure any action that is motivated by considerations other than a good faith concern for such interests.

The Revlon directors concluded that Pantry Pride's $47.50 offer was grossly inadequate. In that regard the board acted in good faith, and on an informed basis, with reasonable grounds to believe that there existed a harmful threat to the corporate enterprise. The adoption of a defensive measure, reasonable in relation to the threat posed, was proper and fully accorded with the powers, duties, and responsibilities conferred upon directors under our law....

D

However, when Pantry Pride increased its offer to $50 per share, and then to $53, it became apparent to all that the break-up of the company was inevitable. The Revlon board's authorization permitting management to negotiate a merger or buyout with a third party was a recognition that the company was for sale. The duty of the board had thus changed from the preservation of Revlon as a corporate entity to the maximization of the company's value at a sale for the stockholders' benefit. This significantly altered the board's responsibilities under the *Unocal* standards. It no longer faced threats to corporate policy and effectiveness, or to the stockholders' interests, from a grossly inadequate bid. The whole question of defensive measures became moot. The directors' role changed from defenders of the corporate bastion to auctioneers charged with getting the best price for the stockholders at a sale of the company.

III

This brings us to the lock-up with Forstmann and its emphasis on shoring up the sagging market value of the Notes in the face of threatened litigation by their holders. Such a focus was inconsistent with the changed concept of the directors' responsibilities at this stage of the developments. The impending waiver of the Notes covenants had caused the value of the Notes to fall, and the board was aware of the noteholders' ire as well as their subsequent threats of suit. The directors thus made support of the Notes an integral part of the company's dealings with Forstmann, even though their primary responsibility at this stage was to the equity owners.

The original threat posed by Pantry Pride—the break-up of the company—had become a reality which even the directors embraced. Selective dealing to fend off a hostile but determined bidder was no longer a proper objective. Instead, obtaining the highest price for the benefit of the stockholders should have been the central theme guiding director action. Thus, the Revlon board could not make the requisite showing of good faith by preferring the noteholders and ignoring its duty of loyalty to the shareholders. The rights of the former already were fixed by contract. The noteholders required no further protection, and when the Revlon board entered into an auction-ending lock-up agreement with Forstmann on the basis of impermissible considerations at the expense of the shareholders, the directors breached their primary duty of loyalty.

The Revlon board argued that it acted in good faith in protecting the noteholders because *Unocal* permits consideration of other corporate constituencies. Although such considerations may be permissible, there are fundamental limitations upon that prerogative. A board may have regard for various constituencies in discharging its responsibilities, provided there are rationally related benefits accruing to the stockholders. *Unocal*, 493 A.2d at 955. However, such concern for non-stockholder interests is inappropriate when an auction among active bidders is in progress, and the object no longer is to protect or maintain the corporate enterprise but to sell it to the highest bidder.

Revlon also contended that ... it had contractual and good faith obligations to consider the noteholders. However, any such duties are limited to the principle that one may not interfere with contractual relationships by improper actions. Here, the rights of the noteholders were fixed by agreement, and there is nothing of substance to suggest that any of those terms were violated. The Notes covenants specifically contemplated a waiver to permit sale of the company at a fair price. The Notes were accepted by the holders on that basis, including the risk of an adverse market effect stemming from a waiver. Thus, nothing remained for Revlon to legitimately protect, and no rationally related benefit thereby accrued to the stockholders. Under such circumstances we must conclude that the merger agreement with Forstmann was unreasonable in relation to the threat posed.

A lock-up is not *per se* illegal under Delaware law.... Such options can entice other bidders to enter a contest for control of the corporation, creating an auction for the company and maximizing shareholder profit. Current economic conditions in the takeover market are such that a "white knight" like Forstmann might only enter the bidding for the target company if it receives some form of compensation to cover the risks and costs involved. However, while those lock-ups which draw bidders into the battle benefit shareholders, similar measures which end an active auction and foreclose further bidding operate to the shareholders' detriment....

The Forstmann option had a similar destructive effect on the auction process. Forstmann had already been drawn into the contest on a preferred basis, so the result of the lock-up was not to foster bidding, but to destroy it. The board's stated reasons for approving the transactions were: (1) better financing, (2) noteholder protection, and (3) higher price. As the Court of Chancery found, and we agree, any distinctions between the rival bidders' methods of financing the proposal were nominal at best, and such a consideration has little or no significance in a cash offer for any and all shares. The principal object, contrary to the board's duty of care, appears to have been protection of the noteholders over the shareholders' interests.

While Forstmann's $57.25 offer was objectively higher than Pantry Pride's $56.25 bid, the margin of superiority is less when the Forstmann price is adjusted for the time value of money. In reality, the Revlon board ended the auction in return for very little actual improvement in the final bid. The principal benefit went to the directors, who avoided personal liability to a class of creditors to whom the board owed no further duty under the circumstances. Thus, when a board ends an intense bidding contest on an insubstantial basis, and where a significant by-product of that action is to protect the directors against a perceived threat of personal liability for consequences stemming from the adoption of previous defensive measures, the action cannot withstand the enhanced scrutiny which *Unocal* requires of director conduct.

In addition to the lock-up option, the Court of Chancery enjoined the no-shop provision as part of the attempt to foreclose further bidding by Pantry Pride. The no-shop provision, like the lock-up option, while not *per se* illegal, is impermissible under the *Unocal* standards when a board's primary duty becomes that of an auctioneer responsible for selling the company to the highest bidder. The agreement to negotiate only with Forstmann ended rather than intensified the board's involvement in the bidding contest.

It is ironic that the parties even considered a no-shop agreement when Revlon had dealt preferentially, and almost exclusively, with Forstmann throughout the contest. After the directors authorized management to negotiate with other parties, Forstmann was given every negotiating advantage that Pantry Pride had been denied: cooperation from management, access to financial data, and the exclusive opportunity to present merger proposals directly to the board of directors. Favoritism for a white knight to the total exclusion of a hostile bidder might be justifiable when the latter's offer adversely affects shareholder interests, but when bidders make relatively similar offers, or dissolution of the company becomes inevitable, the directors cannot fulfill their enhanced *Unocal* duties by playing favorites with the contending factions....

Affirmed.

C. Refinements of Enhanced Scrutiny

Subsequent cases clarified *Unocal* and *Revlon*'s meaning and applicability. For one, they examine what circumstances lead to the application of the *Unocal* standard compared to the *Revlon* standard. The following cases explore and refine the enhanced scrutiny applied to transactions involving control.

Paramount Communications, Inc. v. Time Inc.

Delaware Supreme Court
571 A.2d 1140 (1989)

Horsey, Justice:

Paramount Communications, Inc. ("Paramount") and two other groups of plaintiffs ("Shareholder Plaintiffs"), shareholders of Time Incorporated ("Time"), a Delaware corporation, separately filed suits in the Delaware Court of Chancery seeking a preliminary injunction to halt Time's tender offer for 51% of Warner Communication, Inc.'s ("Warner") outstanding shares at $70 cash per share. The court below ... denied plaintiffs' motion.... [We affirm.]

The principal ground for reversal, asserted by all plaintiffs, is that Paramount's June 7, 1989 uninvited all-cash, all-shares, "fully negotiable" (though conditional) tender offer for Time triggered duties under *Unocal Corp. v. Mesa Petroleum Co.*, Del. Supr., 493 A.2d 946 (1985), and that Time's board of directors, in responding to Paramount's offer, breached those duties. As a consequence, plaintiffs argue that in our review of the Time board's decision of June 16, 1989 to enter into a revised merger agreement with Warner, Time is not entitled to the benefit and protection of the business judgment rule.

Shareholder Plaintiffs also assert a claim based on *Revlon v. MacAndrews & Forbes Holdings, Inc.*, Del. Supr., 506 A.2d 173 (1986). They argue that the original Time-Warner merger agreement of March 4, 1989 resulted in a change of control which effectively put Time up for sale, thereby triggering *Revlon* duties. Those plaintiffs argue that Time's board breached its *Revlon* duties by failing, in the face of the change of control, to maximize shareholder value in the immediate term.

Applying our standard of review, we affirm the Chancellor's ultimate finding and conclusion under *Unocal*. We find that Paramount's tender offer was reasonably perceived by Time's board to pose a threat to Time and that the Time board's "response" to that threat was, under the circumstances, reasonable and proportionate. Applying

Unocal, we reject the argument that the only corporate threat posed by an all-shares, all-cash tender offer is the possibility of inadequate value.

We also find that Time's board did not by entering into its initial merger agreement with Warner come under a *Revlon* duty either to auction the company or to maximize short-term shareholder value, notwithstanding the unequal share exchange. Therefore, the Time board's original plan of merger with Warner was subject only to a business judgment rule analysis. *See Smith v. Van Gorkom*, Del. Supr., 488 A.2d 858, 873–74 (1985).

I

Time is a Delaware corporation with its principal offices in New York City. Time's traditional business is publication of magazines and books; however, Time also provides pay television programming through its Home Box Office, Inc. and Cinemax subsidiaries. In addition, Time owns and operates cable television franchises through its subsidiary, American Television and Communication Corporation. During the relevant time period, Time's board consisted of sixteen directors. Twelve of the directors were "outside," nonemployee directors. Four of the directors were also officers of the company....

As early as 1983 and 1984, Time's executive board began considering expanding Time's operations into the entertainment industry. In 1987, Time established a special committee of executives to consider and propose corporate strategies for the 1990s. The consensus of the committee was that Time should move ahead in the area of ownership and creation of video programming.... Some of Time's outside directors had opposed this move as a threat to the editorial integrity and journalistic focus of Time.[8]

In late spring of 1987, a meeting took place between Steve Ross, CEO of Warner Brothers, and [Nicholas J. Nicholas, Jr., president and chief operating officer] of Time. Ross and Nicholas discussed the possibility of a joint venture between the two companies through the creation of a jointly-owned cable company....

On August 11, 1987, Gerald M. Levin, Time's vice chairman and chief strategist, wrote J. Richard Munro [Time's chair and CEO] a confidential memorandum in which he strongly recommended a strategic consolidation with Warner....

... On July 21, 1988, Time's board met, with all outside directors present. The meeting's purpose was to consider Time's expansion into the entertainment industry on a global scale. Management presented the board with a profile of various entertainment companies in addition to Warner, including Disney, 20th Century Fox, Universal, and Paramount.

---

8. [4] The primary concern of Time's outside directors was the preservation of the "Time Culture." They believed that Time had become recognized in this country as an institution built upon a foundation of journalistic integrity. Time's management made a studious effort to refrain from involvement in Time's editorial policy. Several of Time's outside directors feared that a merger with an entertainment company would divert Time's focus from news journalism and threaten the Time Culture.

Without any definitive decision on choice of a company, the board approved in principle a strategic plan for Time's expansion. The board gave management the "go-ahead" to continue discussions with Warner concerning the possibility of a merger....

The board's consensus was that a merger of Time and Warner was feasible, but only if Time controlled the board of the resulting corporation and thereby preserved a management committed to Time's journalistic integrity. To accomplish this goal, the board stressed the importance of carefully defining in advance the corporate governance provisions that would control the resulting entity. Some board members expressed concern over whether such a business combination would place Time "*in play*." The board discussed the wisdom of adopting further defensive measures to lessen such a possibility....

From the outset, Time's board favored an all-cash or cash and securities acquisition of Warner as the basis for consolidation. Bruce Wasserstein, Time's financial advisor, also favored an outright purchase of Warner. However, Steve Ross, Warner's CEO, was adamant that a business combination was only practicable on a stock-for-stock basis. Warner insisted on a stock swap in order to preserve its shareholders' equity in the resulting corporation. Time's officers, on the other hand, made it abundantly clear that Time would be the acquiring corporation and that Time would control the resulting board. Time refused to permit itself to be cast as the "acquired" company.

Eventually Time acquiesced in Warner's insistence on a stock-for-stock deal, but talks broke down over corporate governance issues. Time wanted Ross' position as a co-CEO to be temporary and wanted Ross to retire in five years. Ross, however, refused to set a time for his retirement and viewed Time's proposal as indicating a lack of confidence in his leadership. Warner considered it vital that their executives and creative staff not perceive Warner as selling out to Time. Time's request of a guarantee that Time would dominate the CEO succession was objected to as inconsistent with the concept of a Time-Warner merger "of equals." Negotiations ended when the parties reached an impasse. Time's board refused to compromise on its position on corporate governance. Time, and particularly its outside directors, viewed the corporate governance provisions as critical for preserving the "Time Culture" through a pro-Time management at the top....

Warner and Time resumed negotiations in January 1989. The catalyst for the resumption of talks was a private dinner between Steve Ross and Time outside director, Michael Dingman. Dingman was able to convince Ross that the transitional nature of the proposed co-CEO arrangement did not reflect a lack of confidence in Ross. Ross agreed that this course was best for the company and a meeting between Ross and Munro resulted. Ross agreed to retire in five years and let Nicholas succeed him. Negotiations resumed and many of the details of the original stock-for-stock exchange agreement remained intact. In addition, Time's senior management agreed to long-term contracts.

Time insider directors Levin and Nicholas met with Warner's financial advisors to decide upon a stock exchange ratio. Time's board had recognized the potential need to pay a premium in the stock ratio in exchange for dictating the governing arrangement of the new Time-Warner.... Warner's financial advisors informed its board that any exchange rate over. 400 was a fair deal and any exchange rate over. 450 was "one hell of a deal." The parties ultimately agreed upon an exchange rate favoring Warner of. 465. On that basis, Warner stockholders would have owned approximately 62% of the common stock of Time-Warner.

On March 3, 1989, Time's board, with all but one director in attendance, met and unanimously approved the stock-for-stock merger with Warner. Warner's board likewise approved the merger. The agreement called for Warner to be merged into a wholly-owned Time subsidiary with Warner becoming the surviving corporation. The common stock of Warner would then be converted into common stock of Time at the agreed upon ratio. Thereafter, the name of Time would be changed to Time-Warner, Inc....

At its March 3, 1989 meeting, Time's board adopted several defensive tactics. Time entered an automatic share exchange agreement with Warner. Time would receive 17,292,747 shares of Warner's outstanding common stock (9.4%) and Warner would receive 7,080,016 shares of Time's outstanding common stock (11.1%). Either party could trigger the exchange. Time sought out and paid for "confidence" letters from various banks with which it did business. In these letters, the banks promised not to finance any third-party attempt to acquire Time. Time argues these agreements served only to preserve the confidential relationship between itself and the banks. The Chancellor found these agreements to be inconsequential and futile attempts to "dry up" money for a hostile takeover. Time also agreed to a "no-shop" clause, preventing Time from considering any other consolidation proposal, thus relinquishing its power to consider other proposals, regardless of their merits. Time did so at Warner's insistence. Warner did not want to be left "on the auction block" for an unfriendly suitor, if Time were to withdraw from the deal.

Time's board simultaneously established a special committee of outside directors, Finkelstein, Kearns, and Opel, to oversee the merger. The committee's assignment was to resolve any impediments that might arise in the course of working out the details of the merger and its consummation.

... On May 24, 1989, Time sent out extensive proxy statements to the stockholders regarding the approval vote on the merger. In the meantime, with the merger proceeding without impediment, the special committee had concluded, shortly after its creation, that it was not necessary either to retain independent consultants, legal or financial, or even to meet. Time's board was unanimously in favor of the proposed merger with Warner; and, by the end of May, the Time-Warner merger appeared to be an accomplished fact.

On June 7, 1989, these wishful assumptions were shattered by Paramount's surprising announcement of its all-cash offer to purchase all outstanding shares of Time for $175 per share. The following day, June 8, the trading price of Time's stock rose from $126 to $170 per share.... On June 8, 1989, Time formally responded to Paramount's offer. Time's chairman and CEO, J. Richard Munro, sent an aggressively worded letter to Paramount's CEO, Martin Davis. Munro's letter attacked Davis' personal integrity and called Paramount's offer "smoke and mirrors." Time's nonmanagement directors were not shown the letter before it was sent. However, at a board meeting that same day, all members endorsed management's response as well as the letter's content.

Over the following eight days, Time's board met three times to discuss Paramount's $175 offer. The board viewed Paramount's offer as inadequate and concluded that its proposed merger with Warner was the better course of action. Therefore, the board declined to open any negotiations with Paramount and held steady its course toward a merger with Warner.

In June, Time's board of directors met several times. During the course of their June meetings, Time's outside directors met frequently without management, officers or directors being present. At the request of the outside directors, corporate counsel was present during the board meetings and, from time to time, the management directors were asked to leave the board sessions. During the course of these meetings, Time's financial advisors informed the board that, on an auction basis, Time's per share value was materially higher than Warner's $175 per share offer. After this advice, the board concluded that Paramount's $175 offer was inadequate.

At these June meetings, certain Time directors expressed their concern that Time stockholders would not comprehend the long-term benefits of the Warner merger. Large quantities of Time shares were held by institutional investors. The board feared that even though there appeared to be wide support for the Warner transaction, Paramount's cash premium would be a tempting prospect to these investors. In mid-June, Time sought permission from the New York Stock Exchange to alter its rules and allow the Time-Warner merger to proceed without stockholder approval. Time did so at Warner's insistence. The New York Stock Exchange rejected Time's request on June 15; and on that day, the value of Time stock reached $182 per share.

The following day, June 16, Time's board met to take up Paramount's offer. The board's prevailing belief was that Paramount's bid posed a threat to Time's control of its own destiny and retention of the "Time Culture." Even after Time's financial advisors made another presentation of Paramount and its business attributes, Time's board maintained its position that a combination with Warner offered greater potential for Time. Warner provided Time a much desired production capability and an established international marketing chain. Time's advisors suggested various options, including defensive measures. The board considered and rejected the idea of purchasing Paramount in a "Pac Man" defense. The board considered other defenses, including a recapitalization, the acquisition of another company, and a material change in the present capitalization structure or dividend policy. The board determined to retain its same advisors even in light of the changed circumstances. The board rescinded its agreement to pay its advisors a bonus based on the consummation of the Time-Warner merger and agreed to pay a flat fee for any advice rendered. Finally, Time's board formally rejected Paramount's offer.

At the same meeting, Time's board decided to recast its consolidation with Warner into an outright cash and securities acquisition of Warner by Time; and Time so informed Warner. Time accordingly restructured its proposal to acquire Warner as follows: Time would make an immediate all-cash offer for 51% of Warner's outstanding stock at $70 per share. The remaining 49% would be purchased at some later date for a mixture of cash and securities worth $70 per share. To provide the funds required for its outright acquisition of Warner, Time would assume 7–10 billion dollars worth of debt, thus eliminating one of the principal transaction-related benefits of the original merger agreement. Nine billion dollars of the total purchase price would be allocated to the purchase of Warner's goodwill.

Warner agreed but insisted on certain terms. Warner sought a control premium and guarantees that the governance provisions found in the original merger agreement would remain intact. Warner further sought agreements that Time would not employ its poison pill against Warner and that, unless enjoined, Time would be legally bound to complete the transaction. Time's board agreed to these last measures only at the insistence of Warner. For its part, Time was assured of its ability to extend its efforts into production areas and international markets, all the while maintaining the Time identity and culture..,,

On June 23, 1989, Paramount raised its all-cash offer to buy Time's outstanding stock to $200 per share. Paramount still professed that all aspects of the offer were negotiable. Time's board met on June 26, 1989 and formally rejected Paramount's $200 per share second offer. The board reiterated its belief that, despite the $25 increase, the offer was still inadequate. The Time board maintained that the Warner transaction offered a greater long-term value for the stockholders and, unlike Paramount's offer, did not pose a threat to Time's survival and its "culture." Paramount then filed this action in the Court of Chancery.

II

The Shareholder Plaintiffs first assert a *Revlon* claim. They contend that the March 4 Time-Warner agreement effectively put Time up for sale, triggering *Revlon* duties, requiring Time's board to enhance short-term shareholder value and to treat all other interested acquirors on an equal basis. The Shareholder Plaintiffs base this argument on two facts: (i) the ultimate Time-Warner exchange ratio of.465 favoring Warner, resulting in Warner shareholders' receipt of 62% of the combined company; and (ii) the subjective intent of Time's directors as evidenced in their statements that the market might perceive the Time-Warner merger as putting Time up "for sale" and their adoption of various defensive measures.

The Shareholder Plaintiffs further contend that Time's directors, in structuring the original merger transaction to be "takeover-proof," triggered *Revlon* duties by foreclosing their shareholders from any prospect of obtaining a control premium. In short, plaintiffs argue that Time's board's decision to merge with Warner imposed a fiduciary duty to maximize immediate share value and not erect unreasonable barriers to further bids. Therefore, they argue, the Chancellor erred in finding: that Paramount's bid for Time did not place Time "for sale"; that Time's transaction with Warner did not result in any transfer of control; and that the combined Time-Warner was not so large as to preclude the possibility of the stockholders of Time-Warner receiving a future control premium.

Paramount asserts only a *Unocal* claim in which the shareholder plaintiffs join. Paramount contends that the Chancellor, in applying the first part of the *Unocal* test, erred in finding that Time's board had reasonable grounds to believe that Paramount posed both a legally cognizable threat to Time shareholders and a danger to Time's corporate policy and effectiveness. Paramount also contests the court's finding that Time's board made a reasonable and objective investigation of Paramount's offer so as to be informed before rejecting it. Paramount further claims that the court erred in applying *Unocal's* second part in finding Time's response to be "reasonable." Paramount points primarily to the preclusive effect of the revised agreement which denied Time shareholders the opportunity both to vote on the agreement and to respond to Paramount's tender offer. Paramount argues that the underlying motivation of Time's board in adopting these defensive measures was management's desire to perpetuate itself in office....

A

We first take up plaintiffs' principal *Revlon* argument, summarized above. In rejecting this argument, the Chancellor found the original Time-Warner merger agreement not to constitute a "change of control" and concluded that the transaction did not trigger *Revlon* duties. The Chancellor's conclusion is premised on a finding that "[b]efore the merger agreement was signed, control of the corporation existed in a fluid aggregation of unaffiliated shareholders representing a voting majority — in other words, in the market." The Chancellor's findings of fact are supported by the record and his conclusion is correct as a matter of law. However, we premise our rejection of plaintiffs' *Revlon* claim on different grounds, namely, the absence of any substantial evidence to conclude that Time's board, in negotiating with Warner, made the dissolution or break-up of the corporate entity inevitable, as was the case in *Revlon*.

Under Delaware law there are, generally speaking and without excluding other possibilities, two circumstances which may implicate *Revlon* duties. The first, and clearer one, is when a corporation initiates an active bidding process seeking to sell itself or to effect a business reorganization involving a clear break-up of the company. However, *Revlon* duties may also be triggered where, in response to a bidder's offer, a target abandons its long-term strategy and seeks an alternative transaction involving the breakup of the company.[9] Thus, in *Revlon*, when the board responded to Pantry Pride's offer by contemplating a "bust-up" sale of assets in a leveraged acquisition, we imposed upon the board a duty to maximize immediate shareholder value and an obligation to auction the company fairly. If, however, the board's reaction to a hostile tender offer is found to constitute only a defensive response and not an abandonment of the corporation's continued existence, *Revlon* duties are not triggered, though *Unocal* duties attach.

The plaintiffs insist that even though the original Time-Warner agreement may not have worked "an objective change of control," the transaction made a "sale" of Time inevitable. Plaintiffs rely on the subjective intent of Time's board of directors

---

9. [13] As we stated in *Revlon*, in both such cases, "[t]he duty of the board [has] changed from the preservation of ... [the] corporate entity to the maximization of the company's value at a sale for the stockholder's benefit.... [The board] no longer face[s] threats to corporate policy and effectiveness, or to the stockholders' interests, from a grossly inadequate bid." *Revlon v. MacAndrews & Forbes Holdings, Inc.*, Del. Supr., 506 A.2d 173, 182 (1986).

and principally upon certain board members' expressions of concern that the Warner transaction *might* be viewed as effectively putting Time up for sale. Plaintiffs argue that the use of a lock-up agreement, a no-shop clause, and so-called "dry-up" agreements prevented shareholders from obtaining a control premium in the immediate future and thus violated *Revlon*.

We agree with the Chancellor that such evidence is entirely insufficient to invoke *Revlon* duties; and we decline to extend *Revlon*'s application to corporate transactions simply because they might be construed as putting a corporation either "in play" or "up for sale." The adoption of structural safety devices alone does not trigger *Revlon*. Rather, as the Chancellor stated, such devices are properly subject to a *Unocal* analysis.

Finally, we do not find in Time's recasting of its merger agreement with Warner from a share exchange to a share purchase a basis to conclude that Time had either abandoned its strategic plan or made a sale of Time inevitable. The Chancellor found that although the merged Time-Warner company would be large (with a value approaching approximately $30 billion), recent takeover cases have proven that acquisition of the combined company might nonetheless be possible. The legal consequence is that *Unocal* alone applies to determine whether the business judgment rule attaches to the revised agreement. . . .

B

We turn now to plaintiffs' *Unocal* claim. We begin by noting, as did the Chancellor, that our decision does not require us to pass on the wisdom of the board's decision to enter into the original Time-Warner agreement. That is not a court's task. Our task is simply to review the record to determine whether there is sufficient evidence to support the Chancellor's conclusion that the initial Time-Warner agreement was the product of a proper exercise of business judgment.

We have purposely detailed the evidence of the Time board's deliberative approach, beginning in 1983–84, to expand itself. Time's decision in 1988 to combine with Warner was made only after what could be fairly characterized as an exhaustive appraisal of Time's future as a corporation. . . . We find ample evidence in the record to support the Chancellor's conclusion that the Time board's decision to expand the business of the company through its March 3 merger with Warner was entitled to the protection of the business judgment rule.

The Chancellor reached a different conclusion in addressing the Time-Warner transaction as revised three months later. He found that the revised agreement was defense-motivated and designed to avoid the potentially disruptive effect that Paramount's offer would have had on consummation of the proposed merger were it put to a shareholder vote. Thus, the court declined to apply the traditional business judgment rule to the revised transaction and instead analyzed the Time board's June 16 decision under *Unocal*. The court ruled that *Unocal* applied to all director actions taken, following receipt of Paramount's hostile tender offer, that were reasonably determined to be defensive. Clearly that was a correct ruling and no party disputes that ruling.

In *Unocal*, we held that before the business judgment rule is applied to a board's adoption of a defensive measure, the burden will lie with the board to prove (a) reasonable grounds for believing that a danger to corporate policy and effectiveness existed; and (b) that the defensive measure adopted was reasonable in relation to the threat posed. *Unocal*, 493 A.2d 946. Directors satisfy the first part of the *Unocal* test by demonstrating good faith and reasonable investigation. We have repeatedly stated that the refusal to entertain an offer may comport with a valid exercise of a board's business judgment....

The usefulness of *Unocal* as an analytical tool is precisely its flexibility in the face of a variety of fact scenarios. *Unocal* is not intended as an abstract standard; neither is it a structured and mechanistic procedure of appraisal. Thus, we have said that directors may consider, when evaluating the threat posed by a takeover bid, the "inadequacy of the price offered, nature and timing of the offer, questions of illegality, the impact on 'constituencies' other than shareholders ... the risk of nonconsummation, and the quality of securities being offered in the exchange." 493 A.2d at 955. The open-ended analysis mandated by *Unocal* is not intended to lead to a simple mathematical exercise: that is, of comparing the discounted value of Time-Warner's expected trading price at some future date with Paramount's offer and determining which is the higher. Indeed, in our view, precepts underlying the business judgment rule militate against a court's engaging in the process of attempting to appraise and evaluate the relative merits of a long-term versus a short-term investment goal for shareholders. To engage in such an exercise is a distortion of the *Unocal* process and, in particular, the application of the second part of *Unocal*'s test, discussed below.

In this case, the Time board reasonably determined that inadequate value was not the only legally cognizable threat that Paramount's all-cash, all-shares offer could present. Time's board concluded that Paramount's eleventh hour offer posed other threats. One concern was that Time shareholders might elect to tender into Paramount's cash offer in ignorance or a mistaken belief of the strategic benefit which a business combination with Warner might produce. Moreover, Time viewed the conditions attached to Paramount's offer as introducing a degree of uncertainty that skewed a comparative analysis. Further, the timing of Paramount's offer to follow issuance of Time's proxy notice was viewed as arguably designed to upset, if not confuse, the Time stockholders' vote. Given this record evidence, we cannot conclude that the Time board's decision of June 6 that Paramount's offer posed a threat to corporate policy and effectiveness was lacking in good faith or dominated by motives of either entrenchment or self-interest.

Paramount also contends that the Time board had not duly investigated Paramount's offer. Therefore, Paramount argues, Time was unable to make an informed decision that the offer posed a threat to Time's corporate policy. Although the Chancellor did not address this issue directly, his findings of fact do detail Time's exploration of the available entertainment companies, including Paramount, before determining that Warner provided the best strategic "fit." In addition, the court found that Time's board rejected Paramount's offer because Paramount did not serve Time's objectives or meet Time's needs. Thus, the record does, in our judgment, demonstrate that Time's board was adequately informed of the potential benefits of a transaction with Paramount. We agree with the Chancellor that the Time board's lengthy pre-June investigation of potential merger candidates, including Paramount, mooted any obligation on Time's part to halt its merger process with Warner to reconsider Paramount. Time's board was under no obligation to negotiate with Paramount. Time's failure to negotiate cannot be fairly found to have been uninformed. The evidence supporting this finding is materially enhanced by the fact that twelve of Time's sixteen board members were outside independent directors.

We turn to the second part of the *Unocal* analysis. The obvious requisite to determining the reasonableness of a defensive action is a clear identification of the nature of the threat. As the Chancellor correctly noted, this "requires an evaluation of the importance of the corporate objective threatened; alternative methods of protecting that objective; impacts of the 'defensive' action, and other relevant factors." It is not until both parts of the *Unocal* inquiry have been satisfied that the business judgment rule attaches to defensive actions of a board of directors. As applied to the facts of this case, the question is whether the record evidence supports the Court of Chancery's conclusion that the restructuring of the Time-Warner transaction, including the adoption of several preclusive defensive measures, was a *reasonable response* in relation to a perceived threat.

Paramount argues that, assuming its tender offer posed a threat, Time's response was unreasonable in precluding Time's shareholders from accepting the tender offer or receiving a control premium in the immediately foreseeable future. Once again, the contention stems, we believe, from a fundamental misunderstanding of where the power of corporate governance lies. Delaware law confers the management of the corporate enterprise to the stockholders' duly elected board representatives. 8 Del. C. § 141(a). The fiduciary duty to manage a corporate enterprise includes the selection of a time frame for achievement of corporate goals. That duty may not be delegated to the stockholders. Directors are not obliged to abandon a deliberately conceived corporate plan for a short-term shareholder profit unless there is clearly no basis to sustain the corporate strategy....

Paramount Communications, Inc. v. QVC Network, Inc.

Delaware Supreme Court
637 A.2d 34 (1993)

VEASEY, CHIEF JUSTICE:

In this appeal we review an order of the Court of Chancery dated November 24, 1993, ... preliminarily enjoining certain defensive measures designed to facilitate a so-called strategic alliance between Viacom Inc. ("Viacom") and Paramount Communications Inc. ("Paramount") approved by the board of directors of Paramount (the "Paramount Board" or the "Paramount directors") and to thwart an unsolicited, more valuable, tender offer by QVC Network Inc. ("QVC"). In affirming, we hold that the sale of control in this case, which is at the heart of the proposed strategic alliance, implicates enhanced judicial scrutiny of the conduct of the Paramount Board under *Unocal Corp. v. Mesa Petroleum Co.*, Del. Supr., 493 A.2d 946 (1985), and *Revlon, Inc. v. MacAndrews & Forbes Holdings, Inc.*, Del. Supr., 506 A.2d 173 (1986). We further hold that the conduct of the Paramount Board was not reasonable as to process or result.

QVC and certain stockholders of Paramount commenced separate actions (later consolidated) in the Court of Chancery seeking preliminary and permanent injunctive relief against Paramount, certain members of the Paramount Board, and Viacom. This action arises out of a proposed acquisition of Paramount by Viacom through a tender offer followed by a second-step merger (the "Paramount-Viacom transaction"), and a competing unsolicited tender offer by QVC. The Court of Chancery granted a preliminary injunction.

The Court of Chancery found that the Paramount directors violated their fiduciary duties by favoring the Paramount-Viacom transaction over the more valuable unsolicited offer of QVC. The Court of Chancery preliminarily enjoined Paramount and the individual defendants (the "Paramount defendants") from amending or modifying Paramount's stockholder rights agreement (the "Rights Agreement"), including the redemption of the Rights, or taking other action to facilitate the consummation of the pending tender offer by Viacom or any proposed second-step merger, including the Merger Agreement between Paramount and Viacom dated September 12, 1993 (the "Original Merger Agreement"), as amended on October 24, 1993 (the "Amended Merger Agreement"). Viacom and the Paramount defendants were enjoined from taking any action to exercise any provision of the Stock Option Agreement between Paramount and Viacom dated September 12, 1993 (the "Stock Option Agreement"), as amended on October 24, 1993. The Court of Chancery did not grant preliminary injunctive relief as to the termination fee provided for the benefit of Viacom in Section 8.05 of the Original Merger Agreement and the Amended Merger Agreement (the "Termination Fee").

Under the circumstances of this case, the pending sale of control implicated in the Paramount-Viacom transaction required the Paramount Board to act on an informed basis to secure the best value reasonably available to the stockholders. Since we agree with the Court of Chancery that the Paramount directors violated their fiduciary duties, we have AFFIRMED the entry of the order of the Vice Chancellor granting the preliminary injunction and have REMANDED these proceedings to the Court of Chancery for proceedings consistent herewith....

I. *Facts*

... Paramount is a Delaware corporation with its principal offices in New York City. Approximately 118 million shares of Paramount's common stock are outstanding and traded on the New York Stock Exchange. The majority of Paramount's stock is publicly held by numerous unaffiliated investors. Paramount owns and operates a diverse group of entertainment businesses, including motion picture and television studios, book publishers, professional sports teams, and amusement parks.

There are 15 persons serving on the Paramount Board. Four directors are officer-employees of Paramount: Martin S. Davis ("Davis"), Paramount's Chairman and

Chief Executive Officer since 1983; Donald Oresman ("Oresman"), Executive Vice-President, Chief Administrative Officer, and General Counsel; Stanley R. Jaffe, President and Chief Operating Officer; and Ronald L. Nelson, Executive Vice President and Chief Financial Officer. Paramount's 11 outside directors are distinguished and experienced business persons who are present or former senior executives of public corporations or financial institutions.

Viacom is a Delaware corporation with its headquarters in Massachusetts. Viacom is controlled by Sumner M. Redstone ("Redstone"), its Chairman and Chief Executive Officer, who owns indirectly approximately 85.2 percent of Viacom's voting Class A stock and approximately 69.2 percent of Viacom's nonvoting Class B stock through National Amusements, Inc. ("NAI"), an entity 91.7 percent owned by Redstone. Viacom has a wide range of entertainment operations, including a number of well-known cable television channels such as MTV, Nickelodeon, Showtime, and The Movie Channel. Viacom's equity co-investors in the Paramount-Viacom transaction include NYNEX Corporation and Blockbuster Entertainment Corporation.

QVC is a Delaware corporation with its headquarters in West Chester, Pennsylvania. QVC has several large stockholders, including Liberty Media Corporation, Comcast Corporation, Advance Publications, Inc., and Cox Enterprises Inc. Barry Diller ("Diller"), the Chairman and Chief Executive Officer of QVC, is also a substantial stockholder. QVC sells a variety of merchandise through a televised shopping channel. QVC has several equity co-investors in its proposed combination with Paramount including BellSouth Corporation and Comcast Corporation.

Beginning in the late 1980s, Paramount investigated the possibility of acquiring or merging with other companies in the entertainment, media, or communications industry. Paramount considered such transactions to be desirable, and perhaps necessary, in order to keep pace with competitors in the rapidly evolving field of entertainment and communications. Consistent with its goal of strategic expansion, Paramount made a tender offer for Time Inc. in 1989, but was ultimately unsuccessful. *See Paramount Communications, Inc. v. Time Inc.*, Del. Supr., 571 A.2d 1140 (1990) (*"Time-Warner"*).

Although Paramount had considered a possible combination of Paramount and Viacom as early as 1990, ... [a]fter several more meetings between Redstone and Davis, serious negotiations began taking place in early July.

It was tentatively agreed that Davis would be the chief executive officer and Redstone would be the controlling stockholder of the combined company, but the parties could not reach agreement on the merger price and the terms of a stock option to be granted to Viacom. With respect to price, Viacom offered a package of cash and stock (primarily Viacom Class B nonvoting stock) with a market value of approximately $61 per share, but Paramount wanted at least $70 per share.

... After a short hiatus, the parties negotiated in earnest in early September, and performed due diligence with the assistance of their financial advisors, Lazard Freres & Co. ("Lazard") for Paramount and Smith Barney for Viacom. On September 9, 1993, the Paramount Board was informed about the status of the negotiations and was provided information by Lazard, including an analysis of the proposed transaction.

On September 12, 1993, the Paramount Board met again and unanimously approved the Original Merger Agreement whereby Paramount would merge with and into Viacom. The terms of the merger provided that each share of Paramount common stock would be converted into 0.10 shares of Viacom Class A voting stock, 0.90 shares of Viacom Class B nonvoting stock, and $9.10 in cash. In addition, the Paramount Board agreed to amend its "poison pill" Rights Agreement to exempt the proposed merger with Viacom. The Original Merger Agreement also contained several provisions designed to make it more difficult for a potential competing bid to succeed. We focus, as did the Court of Chancery, on three of these defensive provisions: a "no-shop" provision (the "No-Shop Provision"), the Termination Fee, and the Stock Option Agreement.

First, under the No-Shop Provision, the Paramount Board agreed that Paramount would not solicit, encourage, discuss, negotiate, or endorse any competing transaction unless: (a) a third party "makes an unsolicited written, bona fide proposal, which is not subject to any material contingencies relating to financing"; and (b) the Paramount Board determines that discussions or negotiations with the third party are necessary for the Paramount Board to comply with its fiduciary duties.

Second, under the Termination Fee provision, Viacom would receive a $100 million termination fee if: (a) Paramount terminated the Original Merger Agreement because of a competing transaction; (b) Paramount's stockholders did not approve the merger; or (c) the Paramount Board recommended a competing transaction.

The third and most significant deterrent device was the Stock Option Agreement, which granted to Viacom an option to purchase approximately 19.9 percent (23,699,000 shares) of Paramount's outstanding common stock at $69.14 per share if any of the triggering events for the Termination Fee occurred. In addition to the customary terms that are normally associated with a stock option, the Stock Option Agreement contained two provisions that were both unusual and highly beneficial to Viacom: (a) Viacom was permitted to pay for the shares with a senior subordinated note of questionable marketability instead of cash, thereby avoiding the need to raise the $1.6 billion purchase price (the "Note Feature"); and (b) Viacom could elect to require Paramount to pay Viacom in cash a sum equal to the difference between the purchase price and the market price of Paramount's stock (the "Put Feature"). Because the Stock Option Agreement was not "capped" to limit its maximum dollar value, it had the potential to reach (and in this case did reach) unreasonable levels.

After the execution of the Original Merger Agreement and the Stock Option Agreement on September 12, 1993, Paramount and Viacom announced their proposed merger. In a number of public statements, the parties indicated that the pending transaction was a virtual certainty. Redstone described it as a "marriage" that would "never be torn asunder" and stated that only a "nuclear attack" could break the deal. Redstone also called Diller and John Malone of Tele-Communications Inc., a major stockholder of QVC, to dissuade them from making a competing bid.

Despite these attempts to discourage a competing bid, Diller sent a letter to Davis on September 20, 1993, proposing a merger in which QVC would acquire Paramount for approximately $80 per share, consisting of 0.893 shares of QVC common stock and $30 in cash. QVC also expressed its eagerness to meet with Paramount to negotiate the details of a transaction. When the Paramount Board met on September 27, it was advised by Davis that the Original Merger Agreement prohibited Paramount from having discussions with QVC (or anyone else) unless certain conditions were satisfied. In particular, QVC had to supply evidence that its proposal was not subject to financing contingencies. The Paramount Board was also provided information from Lazard describing QVC and its proposal.

On October 5, 1993, QVC provided Paramount with evidence of QVC's financing. The Paramount Board then held another meeting on October 11, and decided to authorize management to meet with QVC. Davis also informed the Paramount Board that Booz-Allen & Hamilton ("Booz-Allen"), a management consulting firm, had been retained to assess, *inter alia*, the incremental earnings potential from a Paramount-Viacom merger and a Paramount-QVC merger. Discussions proceeded slowly, however, due to a delay in Paramount signing a confidentiality agreement. In response to Paramount's request for information, QVC provided two binders of documents to Paramount on October 20.

On October 21, 1993, QVC filed this action and publicly announced an $80 cash tender offer for 51 percent of Paramount's outstanding shares (the "QVC tender offer"). Each remaining share of Paramount common stock would be converted into 1.42857 shares of QVC common stock in a second-step merger. The tender offer was conditioned on, among other things, the invalidation of the Stock Option Agreement, which was worth over $200 million by that point. QVC contends that it had to commence a tender offer because of the slow pace of the merger discussions and the need to begin seeking clearance under federal antitrust laws.

Confronted by QVC's hostile bid, which on its face offered over $10 per share more than the consideration provided by the Original Merger Agreement, Viacom realized that it would need to raise its bid in order to remain competitive. Within hours after QVC's tender offer was announced, Viacom entered into discussions with Paramount concerning a revised transaction. These discussions led to serious negotiations concerning a comprehensive amendment to the original Paramount-Viacom transaction. In effect, the opportunity for a "new deal" with Viacom was at hand for the Paramount Board. With the QVC hostile bid offering greater value to the Paramount stockholders, the Paramount Board had considerable leverage with Viacom.

At a special meeting on October 24, 1993, the Paramount Board approved the Amended Merger Agreement and an amendment to the Stock Option Agreement. The Amended Merger Agreement was, however, essentially the same as the Original Merger Agreement, except that it included a few new provisions. One provision related to an $80 per share cash tender offer by Viacom for 51 percent of Paramount's stock, and another changed the merger consideration so that each share of Paramount would be converted into 0.20408 shares of Viacom Class A voting stock, 1.08317 shares of Viacom Class B nonvoting stock, and 0.20408 shares of a new series of Viacom convertible preferred stock. The Amended Merger Agreement also added a provision giving Paramount the right not to amend its Rights Agreement to exempt Viacom if the Paramount Board determined that such an amendment would be inconsistent with its fiduciary duties because another offer constituted a "better alternative." Finally, the Paramount Board was given the power to terminate the Amended Merger Agreement if it withdrew its recommendation of the Viacom transaction or recommended a competing transaction.

Although the Amended Merger Agreement offered more consideration to the Paramount stockholders and somewhat more flexibility to the Paramount Board than did the Original Merger Agreement, the defensive measures designed to make a competing bid more difficult were not removed or modified. In particular, there is no evidence in the record that Paramount sought to use its newly-acquired leverage to eliminate or modify the No-Shop Provision, the Termination Fee, or the Stock Option Agreement when the subject of amending the Original Merger Agreement was on the table.

Viacom's tender offer commenced on October 25, 1993, and QVC's tender offer was formally launched on October 27, 1993. Diller sent a letter to the Paramount Board on October 28 requesting an opportunity to negotiate with Paramount, and Oresman responded the following day by agreeing to meet. The meeting, held on November 1, was not very fruitful, however, after QVC's proposed guidelines for a "fair bidding process" were rejected by Paramount on the ground that "auction procedures" were inappropriate and contrary to Paramount's contractual obligations to Viacom.

On November 6, 1993, Viacom unilaterally raised its tender offer price to $85 per share in cash and offered a comparable increase in the value of the securities being proposed in the second-step merger. At a telephonic meeting held later that day, the Paramount Board agreed to recommend Viacom's higher bid to Paramount's stockholders.

QVC responded to Viacom's higher bid on November 12 by increasing its tender offer to $90 per share and by increasing the securities for its second-step merger by a similar amount. In response to QVC's latest offer, the Paramount Board scheduled a meeting for November 15, 1993. Prior to the meeting, Oresman sent the members of the Paramount Board a document summarizing the "conditions and uncertainties" of QVC's offer. One director testified that this document gave him a very negative impression of the QVC bid.

At its meeting on November 15, 1993, the Paramount Board determined that the new QVC offer was not in the best interests of the stockholders. The purported basis for this conclusion was that QVC's bid was excessively conditional. The Paramount Board did not communicate with QVC regarding the status of the conditions because it believed that the No-Shop Provision prevented such communication in the absence of firm financing. Several Paramount directors also testified that they believed the Viacom transaction would be more advantageous to Paramount's future business prospects than a QVC transaction. Although a number of materials were distributed to the Paramount Board describing the Viacom and QVC transactions, the only quantitative analysis of the consideration to be received by the stockholders under each proposal was based on then-current market prices of the securities involved, not on the anticipated value of such securities at the time when the stockholders would receive them.[10]

The preliminary injunction hearing in this case took place on November 16, 1993. On November 19, Diller wrote to the Paramount Board to inform it that QVC had obtained financing commitments for its tender offer and that there was no antitrust obstacle to the offer. On November 24, 1993, the Court of Chancery issued its decision granting a preliminary injunction in favor of QVC and the plaintiff stockholders. This appeal followed.

II. *Applicable Principles of Established Delaware Law*

The General Corporation Law of the State of Delaware (the "General Corporation Law") and the decisions of this Court have repeatedly recognized the fundamental principle that the management of the business and affairs of a Delaware corporation is entrusted to its directors, who are the duly elected and authorized representatives of the stockholders. Under normal circumstances, neither the courts nor the stockholders should interfere with the managerial decisions of the directors. The business judgment rule embodies the deference to which such decisions are entitled.

Nevertheless, there are rare situations which mandate that a court take a more direct and active role in overseeing the decisions made and actions taken by directors. In these situations, a court subjects the directors' conduct to enhanced scrutiny to ensure that it is reasonable. The case at bar implicates two such circumstances: (1) the approval of a transaction resulting in a sale of control, and (2) the adoption of defensive measures in response to a threat to corporate control.

A. *The Significance of a Sale or Change of Control*

When a majority of a corporation's voting shares are acquired by a single person or entity, or by a cohesive group acting together, there is a significant diminution in the voting power of those who thereby become minority stockholders. Under the statutory framework of the General Corporation Law, many of the most fundamental corporate changes can be implemented only if they are approved by a majority vote of the stockholders. Such actions include elections of directors, amendments to the certificate of incorporation, mergers, consolidations, sales of all or substantially all of the assets of the corporation, and dissolution. Because of the overriding importance of voting rights, this Court and the Court of Chancery have consistently acted to protect stockholders from unwarranted interference with such rights.

In the absence of devices protecting the minority stockholders, stockholder votes are likely to become mere formalities where there is a majority stockholder. For example, minority stockholders can be deprived of a continuing equity interest in their corporation by means of a cash-out merger. Absent effective protective provisions, minority stockholders must rely for protection solely on the fiduciary duties owed

---

10. [8] The market prices of Viacom's and QVC's stock were poor measures of their actual values because such prices constantly fluctuated depending upon which company was perceived to be the more likely to acquire Paramount.

to them by the directors and the majority stockholder, since the minority stockholders have lost the power to influence corporate direction through the ballot. The acquisition of majority status and the consequent privilege of exerting the powers of majority ownership come at a price. That price is usually a control premium which recognizes not only the value of a control block of shares, but also compensates the minority stockholders for their resulting loss of voting power.

In the case before us, the public stockholders (in the aggregate) currently own a majority of Paramount's voting stock. Control of the corporation is not vested in a single person, entity, or group, but vested in the fluid aggregation of unaffiliated stockholders. In the event the Paramount-Viacom transaction is consummated, the public stockholders will receive cash and a minority equity voting position in the surviving corporation. Following such consummation, there will be a controlling stockholder who will have the voting power to: (a) elect directors; (b) cause a break-up of the corporation; (c) merge it with another company; (d) cash-out the public stockholders; (e) amend the certificate of incorporation; (f) sell all or substantially all of the corporate assets; or (g) otherwise alter materially the nature of the corporation and the public stockholders' interests. Irrespective of the present Paramount Board's vision of a long-term strategic alliance with Viacom, the proposed sale of control would provide the new controlling stockholder with the power to alter that vision.

Because of the intended sale of control, the Paramount-Viacom transaction has economic consequences of considerable significance to the Paramount stockholders. Once control has shifted, the current Paramount stockholders will have no leverage in the future to demand another control premium. As a result, the Paramount stockholders are entitled to receive, and should receive, a control premium and/or protective devices of significant value. There being no such protective provisions in the Viacom-Paramount transaction, the Paramount directors had an obligation to take the maximum advantage of the current opportunity to realize for the stockholders the best value reasonably available.

B. *The Obligations of Directors in a Sale or Change of Control Transaction*

The consequences of a sale of control impose special obligations on the directors of a corporation.[11] In particular, they have the obligation of acting reasonably to seek the transaction offering the best value reasonably available to the stockholders. The courts will apply enhanced scrutiny to ensure that the directors have acted reasonably. The obligations of the directors and the enhanced scrutiny of the courts are well-

---

11. [13] We express no opinion on any scenario except the actual facts before the Court, and our precise holding herein. Unsolicited tender offers in other contexts may be governed by different precedent. For example, where a potential sale of control by a corporation is not the consequence of a board's action, this Court has recognized the prerogative of a board of directors to resist a third party's unsolicited acquisition proposal or offer. The decision of a board to resist such an acquisition, like all decisions of a properly-functioning board, must be informed, *Unocal*, 493 A.2d at 954–55, and the circumstances of each particular case will determine the steps that a board must take to inform itself, and what other action, if any, is required as a matter of fiduciary duty.

established by the decisions of this Court. The directors' fiduciary duties in a sale of control context are those which generally attach....

In the sale of control context, the directors must focus on one primary objective—to secure the transaction offering the best value reasonably available for the stockholders—and they must exercise their fiduciary duties to further that end. The decisions of this Court have consistently emphasized this goal....

In pursuing this objective, the directors must be especially diligent. In particular, this Court has stressed the importance of the board being adequately informed in negotiating a sale of control: "The need for adequate information is central to the enlightened evaluation of a transaction that a board must make." [*Barkan v. Amsted Indus., Inc.*, Del. Supr., 567 A.2d at 1279, at 1287 (1989).] This requirement is consistent with the general principle that "directors have a duty to inform themselves, prior to making a business decision, of all material information reasonably available to them." [*Aronson v. Lewis*, Del. Supr., 473 A.2d 805, at 812 (1984).] Moreover, the role of outside, independent directors becomes particularly important because of the magnitude of a sale of control transaction and the possibility, in certain cases, that management may not necessarily be impartial

Barkan teaches some of the methods by which a board can fulfill its obligation to seek the best value reasonably available to the stockholders. 567 A.2d at 1286–87. These methods are designed to determine the existence and viability of possible alternatives. They include conducting an auction, canvassing the market, etc. Delaware law recognizes that there is "no single blueprint" that directors must follow. *Id.* [*See also Mills Acquisition Co. v. Macmillan*, Del. Supr. 559 A.2d 1261, at 1282 n.29 (1989).] ...

C. *Enhanced Judicial Scrutiny of a Sale or Change of Control Transaction*

... The key features of an enhanced scrutiny test are: (a) a judicial determination regarding the adequacy of the decisionmaking process employed by the directors, including the information on which the directors based their decision; and (b) a judicial examination of the reasonableness of the directors' action in light of the circumstances then existing. The directors have the burden of proving that they were adequately informed and acted reasonably.

Although an enhanced scrutiny test involves a review of the reasonableness of the substantive merits of a board's actions, a court should not ignore the complexity of the directors' task in a sale of control. There are many business and financial considerations implicated in investigating and selecting the best value reasonably available. The board of directors is the corporate decisionmaking body best equipped to make these judgments. Accordingly, a court applying enhanced judicial scrutiny should be deciding whether the directors made *a reasonable* decision, not *a perfect* decision. If a board selected one of several reasonable alternatives, a court should not second-guess that choice even though it might have decided otherwise or subsequent events may have cast doubt on the board's determination. Thus, courts will not substitute their business judgment for that of the directors, but will determine if the directors' decision was, on balance, within a range of reasonableness.

D. Revlon *and* Time-Warner *Distinguished*

The Paramount defendants and Viacom assert that the fiduciary obligations and the enhanced judicial scrutiny discussed above are not implicated in this case in the absence of a "break-up" of the corporation, and that the order granting the preliminary injunction should be reversed. This argument is based on their erroneous interpretation of our decisions in *Revlon* and *Time-Warner*.

In *Revlon*, we reviewed the actions of the board of directors of Revlon, Inc. ("Revlon"), which had rebuffed the overtures of Pantry Pride, Inc. and had instead entered into an agreement with Forstmann Little & Co. ("Forstmann") providing for the acquisition of 100 percent of Revlon's outstanding stock by Forstmann and the subsequent break-up of Revlon. Based on the facts and circumstances present in *Revlon*, we held that "[t]he directors' role changed from defenders of the corporate bastion to auctioneers charged with getting the best price for the stockholders at a sale of the company." 506 A.2d at 182. We further held that "when a board ends an intense bidding contest on an insubstantial basis, ... [that] action cannot withstand the enhanced scrutiny which *Unocal* requires of director conduct." *Id.* at 184.

It is true that one of the circumstances bearing on these holdings was the fact that "the break-up of the company ... had become a reality which even the directors embraced." *Id.* at 182. It does not follow, however, that a "break-up" must be present and "inevitable" before directors are subject to enhanced judicial scrutiny and are required to pursue a transaction that is calculated to produce the best value reasonably available to the stockholders. In fact, we stated in *Revlon* that "when bidders make relatively similar offers, or dissolution of the company becomes inevitable, the directors cannot fulfill their enhanced *Unocal* duties by playing favorites with the contending factions." *Id.* at 184 (emphasis added). *Revlon* thus does not hold that an inevitable dissolution or "break-up" is necessary.

The decisions of this Court following *Revlon* reinforced the applicability of enhanced scrutiny and the directors' obligation to seek the best value reasonably available for the stockholders where there is a pending sale of control, regardless of whether or not there is to be a break-up of the corporation. In *Macmillan*, this Court held:

> We stated in *Revlon*, and again here, that *in a sale of corporate control* the responsibility of the directors is to get the highest value reasonably attainable for the shareholders.

... Although *Macmillan* and *Barkan* are clear in holding that a change of control imposes on directors the obligation to obtain the best value reasonably available to the stockholders, the Paramount defendants have interpreted our decision in *Time-Warner* as requiring a corporate break-up in order for that obligation to apply. The facts in *Time-Warner*, however, were quite different from the facts of this case, and refute Paramount's position here. In *Time-Warner*, the Chancellor held that there was no change of control in the original stock-for-stock merger between Time and Warner because Time would be owned by a fluid aggregation of unaffiliated stockholders both before and after the merger....

In our affirmance of the Court of Chancery's well-reasoned decision, this Court held that "The Chancellor's findings of fact are supported by the record and *his conclusion is correct as a matter of law*." 571 A.2d at 1150 (emphasis added). Nevertheless, the Paramount defendants here have argued that a break-up is a requirement and have focused on the following language in our *Time-Warner* decision:

> However, we premise our rejection of plaintiffs' *Revlon* claim on different grounds, namely, the absence of any substantial evidence to conclude that Time's board, in negotiating with Warner, made the dissolution or break-up of the corporate entity inevitable, as was the case in *Revlon*.
>
> Under Delaware law there are, generally speaking and *without excluding other possibilities*, two circumstances which may implicate *Revlon* duties. The first, and clearer one, is when a corporation *initiates an active bidding process seeking to sell itself* or to effect a business reorganization involving a clear break-up of the company. However, *Revlon* duties may also be triggered where, in response to a bidder's offer, a target abandons its long-term strategy and seeks an alternative transaction involving the breakup of the company.

Id. at 1150 (emphasis added) (citation and footnote omitted).

The Paramount defendants have misread the holding of *Time-Warner*. Contrary to their argument, our decision in *Time-Warner* expressly states that the two general scenarios discussed in the above-quoted paragraph are not the *only* instances where "*Revlon* duties" may be implicated. The Paramount defendants' argument totally ignores the phrase "without excluding other possibilities." Moreover, the instant case is clearly within the first general scenario set forth in *Time-Warner*. The Paramount Board, albeit unintentionally, had "initiate[d] an active bidding process seeking to sell itself" by agreeing to sell control of the corporation to Viacom in circumstances where another potential acquiror (QVC) was equally interested in being a bidder.

The Paramount defendants' position that *both* a change of control *and* a break-up are *required* must be rejected. Such a holding would unduly restrict the application of *Revlon*, is inconsistent with this Court's decisions in *Barkan* and *Macmillan*, and has no basis in policy. There are few events that have a more significant impact on the stockholders than a sale of control or a corporate break-up. Each event represents a fundamental (and perhaps irrevocable) change in the nature of the corporate enterprise from a practical standpoint. It is the significance of *each* of these events that justifies: (a) focusing on the directors' obligation to seek the best value reasonably available to the stockholders; and (b) requiring a close scrutiny of board action which could be contrary to the stockholders' interests.

Accordingly, when a corporation undertakes a transaction which will cause: (a) a change in corporate control; *or* (b) a break-up of the corporate entity, the directors' obligation is to seek the best value reasonably available to the stockholders. This obligation arises because the effect of the Viacom-Paramount transaction, if consummated, is to shift control of Paramount from the public stockholders to a controlling stockholder, Viacom. Neither *Time-Warner* nor any other decision of this Court holds that a "break-up" of the company is essential to give rise to this obligation where there is a sale of control.

III. *Breach of Fiduciary Duties by Paramount Board*

We now turn to duties of the Paramount Board under the facts of this case and our conclusions as to the breaches of those duties which warrant injunctive relief.

A. *The Specific Obligations of the Paramount Board*

... Having decided to sell control of the corporation, the Paramount directors were required to evaluate critically whether or not all material aspects of the Paramount-Viacom transaction (separately and in the aggregate) were reasonable and in the best interests of the Paramount stockholders in light of current circumstances, including: the change of control premium, the Stock Option Agreement, the Termination Fee, the coercive nature of both the Viacom and QVC tender offers, the No-Shop Provision, and the proposed disparate use of the Rights Agreement as to the Viacom and QVC tender offers, respectively.

These obligations necessarily implicated various issues, including the questions of whether or not those provisions and other aspects of the Paramount-Viacom transaction (separately and in the aggregate): (a) adversely affected the value provided to the Paramount stockholders; (b) inhibited or encouraged alternative bids; (c) were enforceable contractual obligations in light of the directors' fiduciary duties; and (d) in the end would advance or retard the Paramount directors' obligation to secure for the Paramount stockholders the best value reasonably available under the circumstances.

The Paramount defendants contend that they were precluded by certain contractual provisions, including the No-Shop Provision, from negotiating with QVC or seeking alternatives. Such provisions, whether or not they are presumptively valid in the abstract, may not validly define or limit the directors' fiduciary duties under Delaware law or prevent the Paramount directors from carrying out their fiduciary duties under Delaware law. To the extent such provisions are inconsistent with those duties, they are invalid and unenforceable.

Since the Paramount directors had already decided to sell control, they had an obligation to continue their search for the best value reasonably available to the stockholders. This continuing obligation included the responsibility, at the October 24 board meeting and thereafter, to evaluate critically both the QVC tender offers and the Paramount-Viacom transaction to determine if: (a) the QVC tender offer was, or would continue to be, conditional; (b) the QVC tender offer could be improved; (c) the Viacom tender offer or other aspects of the Paramount-Viacom transaction could be improved; (d) each of the respective offers would be reasonably likely to come to closure, and under what circumstances; (e) other material information was reasonably available for consideration by the Paramount directors; (f) there were viable and realistic alternative courses of action; and (g) the timing constraints could be managed so the directors could consider these matters carefully and deliberately.

B. *The Breaches of Fiduciary Duty by the Paramount Board*

The Paramount directors made the decision on September 12, 1993, that, in their judgment, a strategic merger with Viacom on the economic terms of the Original Merger Agreement was in the best interests of Paramount and its stockholders. Those terms provided a modest change of control premium to the stockholders. The directors also decided at that time that it was appropriate to agree to certain defensive measures (the Stock Option Agreement, the Termination Fee, and the No-Shop Provision) insisted upon by Viacom as part of that economic transaction. Those defensive measures, coupled with the sale of control and subsequent disparate treatment of competing bidders, implicated the judicial scrutiny of *Unocal, Revlon, Macmillan,* and their progeny. We conclude that the Paramount directors' process was not reasonable, and the result achieved for the stockholders was not reasonable under the circumstances.

When entering into the Original Merger Agreement, and thereafter, the Paramount Board clearly gave insufficient attention to the potential consequences of the defensive measures demanded by Viacom. The Stock Option Agreement had a number of unusual and potentially "draconian" provisions, including the Note Feature and the Put Feature. Furthermore, the Termination Fee, whether or not unreasonable by itself, clearly made Paramount less attractive to other bidders, when coupled with the Stock Option Agreement. Finally, the No-Shop Provision inhibited the Paramount Board's ability to negotiate with other potential bidders, particularly QVC which had already expressed an interest in Paramount.

Throughout the applicable time period, and especially from the first QVC merger proposal on September 20 through the Paramount Board meeting on November 15, QVC's interest in Paramount provided the *opportunity* for the Paramount Board to seek significantly higher value for the Paramount stockholders than that being offered by Viacom. QVC persistently demonstrated its intention to meet and exceed the Viacom offers, and frequently expressed its willingness to negotiate possible further increases.

The Paramount directors had the opportunity in the October 23–24 time frame, when the Original Merger Agreement was renegotiated, to take appropriate action to modify the improper defensive measures as well as to improve the economic terms of the Paramount-Viacom transaction. Under the circumstances existing at that time, it should have been clear to the Paramount Board that the Stock Option Agreement, coupled with the Termination Fee and the No-Shop Clause, were impeding the realization of the best value reasonably available to the Paramount stockholders. Nevertheless, the Paramount Board made no effort to eliminate or modify these counterproductive devices, and instead continued to cling to its vision of a strategic alliance with Viacom. Moreover, based on advice from the Paramount management, the Paramount directors considered the QVC offer to be "conditional" and asserted that they were precluded by the No-Shop Provision from seeking more information from, or negotiating with, QVC.

By November 12, 1993, the value of the revised QVC offer on its face exceeded that of the Viacom offer by over $1 billion at then current values. This significant disparity of value cannot be justified on the basis of the directors' vision of future strategy, primarily because the change of control would supplant the authority of the current Paramount Board to continue to hold and implement their strategic vision in any meaningful way. Moreover, their uninformed process had deprived their strategic vision of much of its credibility.

When the Paramount directors met on November 15 to consider QVC's increased tender offer, they remained prisoners of their own misconceptions and missed opportunities to eliminate the restrictions they had imposed on themselves. Yet, it was not "too late" to reconsider negotiating with QVC. The circumstances existing on November 15 made it clear that the defensive measures, taken as a whole, were problematic: (a) the No-Shop Provision could not define or limit their fiduciary duties; (b) the Stock Option Agreement had become "draconian"; and (c) the Termination Fee, in context with all the circumstances, was similarly deterring the realization of possibly higher bids. Nevertheless, the Paramount directors remained paralyzed by their uninformed belief that the QVC offer was "illusory." This final opportunity to negotiate on the stockholders' behalf and to fulfill their obligation to seek the best value reasonably available was thereby squandered.

IV. *Viacom's Claim of Vested Contract Rights*

Viacom argues that it had certain "vested" contract rights with respect to the No-Shop Provision and the Stock Option Agreement. In effect, Viacom's argument is that the Paramount directors could enter into an agreement in violation of their fiduciary duties and then render Paramount, and ultimately its stockholders, liable for failing to carry out an agreement in violation of those duties. Viacom's protestations about vested rights are without merit. This Court has found that those defensive measures were improperly designed to deter potential bidders, and that such measures do not meet the reasonableness test to which they must be subjected. They are consequently invalid and unenforceable under the facts of this case.

The No-Shop Provision could not validly define or limit the fiduciary duties of the Paramount directors. To the extent that a contract, or a provision thereof, purports to require a board to act or not act in such a fashion as to limit the exercise of fiduciary duties, it is invalid and unenforceable.... Despite the arguments of Paramount and Viacom to the contrary, the Paramount directors could not contract away their fiduciary obligations. Since the No-Shop Provision was invalid, Viacom never had any vested contract rights in the provision.

As discussed previously, the Stock Option Agreement contained several "draconian" aspects, including the Note Feature and the Put Feature. While we have held that lock-up options are not *per se* illegal, no options with similar features have ever been upheld by this Court. Under the circumstances of this case, the Stock Option Agreement clearly is invalid. Accordingly, Viacom never had any vested contract rights in that Agreement.

Viacom, a sophisticated party with experienced legal and financial advisors, knew of (and in fact demanded) the unreasonable features of the Stock Option Agreement. It cannot be now heard to argue that it obtained vested contract rights by negotiating and obtaining contractual provisions from a board acting in violation of its fiduciary duties. As the Nebraska Supreme Court said in rejecting a similar argument in *ConA-*

gra, Inc. v. Cargill, Inc., 222 Neb. 136, 382 N.W.2d 576, 587–88 (1986), "To so hold, it would seem, would be to get the shareholders coming and going." Likewise, we reject Viacom's arguments and hold that its fate must rise or fall, and in this instance fall, with the determination that the actions of the Paramount Board were invalid....

---

1. What is the principal distinction between the two Paramount cases that leads to the application of *Unocal* in *Time-Warner* but *Revlon* in *QVC*? Will it always be easy to determine whether control is being sold in a business combination? What are the principal doctrinal consequences of each classification? Consider the phrase — used dozens of times in the full *QVC* opinion — "best value reasonably available for the stockholders." To what extent is that standard identical to or different from *Revlon*'s notions about the board being an auctioneer with the mission of maximizing immediate cash to shareholders?

2. In *Williams v. Geier*, 671 A.2d 1368, 1377–78 (Del. 1996), the directors of Cincinnati Miacron, Inc., in consultation with outside financial and legal counsel, devised a recapitalization plan to be effected through an amendment to the certificate of incorporation. Under the plan, which shareholders approved, all stockholders owning common stock on the effective date of the plan, would be entitled to ten votes per share. Upon the issuance of new shares, or the sale or other transfer of ownership of existing shares, the voting rights of each share would revert to a single vote per share until the new shareholder held the share for three years. This "tenure voting plan" was in response to a number of corporate objectives, including maximization of the long-term value for shareholders and reduction of the corporation's exposure to corporate raiders.

Josephine Williams, a minority shareholder, challenged the recapitalization as an impermissible attempt at management entrenchment which disproportionately disfavored minority shareholders. In considering the applicable standard of review, Chief Justice Veasey stated:

> A *Unocal* analysis should be used only when a board unilaterally (*i.e.*, without stockholder approval) adopts defensive measures in reaction to a perceived threat. *Unocal*, 493 A.2d at 954–55. *Unocal* is a landmark innovation of the dynamic takeover era of the 1980s. It has stood the test of time, and was recently explicated by this Court in *Unitrin, Inc. v. American General Corp.*, Del. Supr., 651 A.2d 1361 (1995). Yet, it is inapplicable here because there was no unilateral board action....
>
> The instant case does not involve either unilateral director action in the face of a claimed threat or an act of disenfranchisement. Rather, the instant case implicates the traditional review of disinterested and independent director action in recommending, and the vote of the stockholders in approving, the Amendment and the resulting Recapitalization....
>
> The Board's action in recommending the Recapitalization to the stockholders pursuant to Section 242(b)(1) is protected by the presumption of the business judgment rule unless that presumption is rebutted....

3. Unitrin, Inc. was the target of an unsolicited tender offer by American General Corporation in *Unitrin, Inc. v. American Gen. Corp.*, 651 A.2d 1361, 1387–88 (Del. 1995). Unitrin's board responded to American General's unwanted bid with a poison pill and a stock repurchase plan. After determining that *Unocal* provided the proper standard of review of these defensive actions, the court recognized that the ultimate question was the amount of judicial deference to be given to directors under *Unocal*. In response, Justice Holland stated:

> An examination of the cases applying *Unocal* reveals a direct correlation between findings of proportionality or disproportionality and the judicial determination of whether a defensive response was draconian because it was either coercive or preclusive in character. In *Time*, for example, this Court concluded that the Time board's defensive response was reasonable and proportionate since it was not aimed at "cramming down" on its shareholders a management-sponsored alternative, *i.e.*, was not coercive, and because it did not preclude Paramount from making an offer for the combined Time-Warner company, *i.e.*, was not preclusive....
>
> More than a century before *Unocal* was decided, Justice Holmes observed that the common law must be developed through its application and "cannot be dealt with as if it contained only the axioms and corollaries of a book of mathematics." Oliver Wendell Holmes, Jr., The Common Law 1 (1881). As common law applications of *Unocal's* proportionality standard have evolved, at least two characteristics of draconian defensive measures taken by a board of directors in responding to a threat have been brought into focus through enhanced judicial scrutiny. In the modern takeover lexicon, it is now clear that since *Unocal*, this Court has consistently recognized that defensive measures which are either preclusive or coercive are included within the common law definition of draconian.
>
> If a defensive measure is not draconian, however, because it is not either coercive or preclusive, the *Unocal* proportionality test requires the focus of enhanced judicial scrutiny to shift to "the range of reasonableness." *Paramount Communications, Inc. v. QVC Network, Inc.*, Del. Supr., 637 A.2d 34, 45–46 (1994). Proper and proportionate defensive responses are intended and permitted to thwart perceived threats. When a corporation is not for sale, the board of directors is the defender of the metaphorical medieval corporate bastion and the protector of the corporation's shareholders. The fact that a defensive action must not be coercive or preclusive does not prevent a board from responding defensively before a bidder is at the corporate bastion's gate.[12]

---

12. This Court's choice of the term "draconian" in *Unocal* was a recognition that the law affords boards of directors substantial latitude in defending the perimeter of the corporate bastion against perceived threats. Thus, continuing with the medieval metaphor, if a board reasonably perceives that a threat is on the horizon, it has broad authority to respond with a panoply of individual or combined defensive precautions, *e.g.*, staffing the barbican, raising the drawbridge, and lowering the portcullis. Stated more directly, depending upon the circumstances, the board may respond to a reasonably per-

Do tests like "draconian" responses that are "coercive or preclusive in character" and "range of reasonableness" inform us about the amount of judicial deference to be given to directors?

Lyondell Chemical Co. v. Ryan

Delaware Supreme Court

970 A.2d 235 (2009)

BERGER, JUSTICE (FOR THE COURT EN BANC):

[I. FACTS]

... Before the merger at issue, Lyondell Chemical Company ("Lyondell") was the third largest independent, publicly traded chemical company in North America. Dan Smith ("Smith") was Lyondell's Chairman and CEO. Lyondell's other ten directors were independent and many were, or had been, CEOs of other large, publicly traded companies. Basell AF ("Basell") is a privately held Luxembourg company owned by Leonard Blavatnik ("Blavatnik") through his ownership of Access Industries. Basell is in the business of polyolefin technology, production and marketing.

In April 2006, Blavatnik told Smith that Basell was interested in acquiring Lyondell. A few months later, Basell sent a letter to Lyondell's board offering $26.50–$28.50 per share. Lyondell determined that the price was inadequate and that it was not interested in selling. During the next year, Lyondell prospered and no potential acquirors expressed interest in the company. In May 2007, an Access affiliate filed a Schedule 13D with the Securities and Exchange Commission disclosing its right to acquire an 8.3% block of Lyondell stock owned by Occidental Petroleum Corporation.[13] The Schedule 13D also disclosed Blavatnik's interest in possible transactions with Lyondell.

In response to the Schedule 13D, the Lyondell board immediately convened a special meeting. The board recognized that the 13D signaled to the market that the company was "in play,"[14] but the directors decided to take a "wait and see" approach. A few days later, Apollo Management, L.P. contacted Smith to suggest a management-led LBO, but Smith rejected that proposal. In late June 2007, Basell announced that it had entered into a $9.6 billion merger agreement with Huntsman Corporation ("Huntsman"), a specialty chemical company. Basell apparently reconsidered, however, after Hexion Specialty Chemicals, Inc. made a topping bid for Huntsman. Faced with competition for Huntsman, Blavatnik returned his attention to Lyondell.

On July 9, 2007, Blavatnik met with Smith to discuss an all-cash deal at $40 per share. Smith responded that $40 was too low, and Blavatnik raised his offer to $44–$45 per share. Smith told Blavatnik that he would present the proposal to the board,

---

ceived threat by adopting individually or sometimes in combination: advance notice by-laws, super-majority voting provisions, shareholder rights plans, repurchase programs, etc.

13. [Schedule 13D and related federal securities laws and regulations are summarized in Chapter 16.—Eds.]

14. [1] On the day that the 13D was made public, Lyondell's stock went from $33 to $37 per share.

but that he thought the board would reject it. Smith advised Blavatnik to give Lyondell his best offer, since Lyondell really was not on the market. The meeting ended at that point, but Blavatnik asked Smith to call him later in the day. When Smith called, Blavatnik offered to pay $48 per share. Under Blavatnik's proposal, Basell would require no financing contingency, but Lyondell would have to agree to a $400 million break-up fee and sign a merger agreement by July 16, 2007.

Smith called a special meeting of the Lyondell board on July 10, 2007 to review and consider Basell's offer. The meeting lasted slightly less than one hour, during which time the board reviewed valuation material that had been prepared by Lyondell management for presentation at the regular board meeting, which was scheduled for the following day. The board also discussed the Basell offer, the status of the Huntsman merger, and the likelihood that another party might be interested in Lyondell. The board instructed Smith to obtain a written offer from Basell and more details about Basell's financing.

Blavatnik agreed to the board's request, but also made an additional demand. Basell had until July 11 to make a higher bid for Huntsman, so Blavatnik asked Smith to find out whether the Lyondell board would provide a firm indication of interest in his proposal by the end of that day. The Lyondell board met on July 11, again for less than one hour, to consider the Basell proposal and how it compared to the benefits of remaining independent. The board decided that it was interested, authorized the retention of Deutsche Bank Securities, Inc. ("Deutsche Bank") as its financial advisor, and instructed Smith to negotiate with Blavatnik.

Basell then announced that it would not raise its offer for Huntsman, and Huntsman terminated the Basell merger agreement. From July 12–July 15 the parties negotiated the terms of a Lyondell merger agreement; Basell conducted due diligence; Deutsche Bank prepared a "fairness" opinion; and Lyondell conducted its regularly scheduled board meeting. The Lyondell board discussed the Basell proposal again on July 12, and later instructed Smith to try to negotiate better terms. Specifically, the board wanted a higher price, a go-shop provision,[15] and a reduced break-up fee. As the trial court noted, Blavatnik was "incredulous." He had offered his best price, which was a substantial premium, and the deal had to be concluded on his schedule. As a sign of good faith, however, Blavatnik agreed to reduce the break-up fee from $400 million to $385 million.

On July 16, 2007, the board met to consider the Basell merger agreement. Lyondell's management, as well as its financial and legal advisers, presented reports analyzing the merits of the deal. The advisors explained that, notwithstanding the no-shop provision in the merger agreement, Lyondell would be able to consider any superior proposals that might be made because of the "fiduciary out" provision. In addition, Deutsche Bank reviewed valuation models derived from "bullish" and more conservative financial projections. Several of those valuations yielded a range that did not

---

15. [2] A "go-shop" provision allows the seller to seek other buyers for a specified period after the agreement is signed.

even reach $48 per share, and Deutsche Bank opined that the proposed merger price was fair. Indeed, the bank's managing director described the merger price as "an absolute home run." Deutsche Bank also identified other possible acquirors and explained why it believed no other entity would top Basell's offer. After considering the presentations, the Lyondell board voted to approve the merger and recommend it to the stockholders. At a special stockholders' meeting held on November 20, 2007, the merger was approved by more than 99% of the voted shares....

[II. LEGAL ANALYSIS]

The class action complaint challenging this $13 billion cash merger alleges that the Lyondell directors breached their "fiduciary duties of care, loyalty and candor ... and ... put their personal interests ahead of the interests of the Lyondell shareholders." Specifically, the complaint alleges that: 1) the merger price was grossly insufficient; 2) the directors were motivated to approve the merger for their own self-interest;[16] 3) the process by which the merger was negotiated was flawed; 4) the directors agreed to unreasonable deal protection provisions; and 5) the preliminary proxy statement omitted numerous material facts. The trial court rejected all claims except those directed at the process which the directors sold the company and the deal protection provisions in the merger agreement.

The remaining claims are but two aspects of a single claim, under *Revlon v. MacAndrews & Forbes Holdings, Inc.*, [506 A.2d 173, 182 (Del. 1986)], that the directors failed to obtain the best available price in selling the company. As the trial court correctly noted, *Revlon* did not create any new fiduciary duties. It simply held that the "board must perform its fiduciary duties in the service of a specific objective: maximizing the sale price of the enterprise." [*Malpiede v. Townson*, 780 A.2d 1075, 1083 (Del. 2000)]. The trial court reviewed the record, and found that [the plaintiffs] might be able to prevail at trial on a claim that the Lyondell directors breached their duty of care. But Lyondell's charter includes an exculpatory provision, pursuant to 8 Del. C. § 102(b)(7), protecting the directors from personal liability for breaches of the duty of care. Thus, this case turns on whether any arguable shortcomings on the part of the Lyondell directors also implicate their duty of loyalty, a breach of which is not exculpated. Because the trial court determined that the board was independent and was not motivated by self-interest or ill will, the sole issue is whether the directors are entitled to summary judgment on the claim that they breached their duty of loyalty by failing to act in good faith.

This Court examined "good faith"[17] in two recent decisions. In *In re Walt Disney Co. Deriv Litig.* [906 A.2d 27 (Del. 2006)], the Court discussed the range of conduct

---

16. [5] The directors' alleged financial interest is the fact that they would receive cash for their stock options.

17. [8] Our corporate decisions tend to use the terms "bad faith" and "failure to act in good faith" interchangeably, although in a different context we noted that, "[t]he two concepts [of] bad faith and conduct not in good faith are not necessarily identical." *25 Massachusetts Avenue Property LLC v. Liberty Property Limited Partnership*, Del. Supr., No. 188, 2008, Order at p. 5, (November 25, 2008). For purposes of this appeal, we draw no distinction between the terms.

that might be characterized as bad faith, and concluded that bad faith encompasses not only an intent to harm but also intentional dereliction of duty:

> [A]t least three different categories of fiduciary behavior are candidates for the "bad faith" pejorative label. The first category involves so-called "subjective bad faith," that is, fiduciary conduct motivated by an actual intent to do harm.... [S]uch conduct constitutes classic, quintessential bad faith....
>
> The second category of conduct, which is at the opposite end of the spectrum, involves lack of due care—that is, fiduciary action taken solely by reason of gross negligence and without any malevolent intent.... [W]e address the issue of whether gross negligence (including failure to inform one's self of available material facts), without more, can also constitute bad faith. The answer is clearly no....
>
> That leaves the third category of fiduciary conduct, which falls in between the first two categories.... This third category is what the Chancellor's definition of bad faith—intentional dereliction of duty, a conscious disregard for one's responsibilities—is intended to capture. The question is whether such misconduct is properly treated as a non-exculpable, nonindemnifiable violation of the fiduciary duty to act in good faith. In our view, it must be....

The *Disney* decision expressly disavowed any attempt to provide a comprehensive or exclusive definition of "bad faith."

A few months later, in *Stone v. Ritter*, [911 A.2d 362 (Del. 2006)], this Court addressed the concept of bad faith in the context of an "oversight" claim. We adopted the standard articulated ten years earlier, in *In re Caremark Int'l Deriv. Litig.*, [698 A.2d 959, 971 (Del. Ch. 1996)]:

> [W]here a claim of directorial liability for corporate loss is predicated upon ignorance of liability creating activities within the corporation ... only a sustained or systematic failure of the board to exercise oversight—such as an utter failure to attempt to assure a reasonable information and reporting system exists—will establish the lack of good faith that is a necessary condition to liability.

The *Stone* Court explained that the *Caremark* standard is fully consistent with the *Disney* definition of bad faith. *Stone* also clarified any possible ambiguity about the directors' mental state, holding that "imposition of liability requires a showing that the directors knew that they were not discharging their fiduciary obligations."

The Court of Chancery recognized these legal principles, but it denied summary judgment in order to obtain a more complete record before deciding whether the directors had acted in bad faith. Under other circumstances, deferring a decision to expand the record would be appropriate. Here, however, the trial court reviewed the existing record under a mistaken view of the applicable law. Three factors contributed to that mistake. First, the trial court imposed *Revlon* duties on the Lyondell directors before they either had decided to sell, or before the sale had become inevitable. Second, the court read *Revlon* and its progeny as creating a set of requirements that must be satisfied during the sale process. Third, the trial court equated an arguably imperfect attempt to carry out *Revlon* duties with a knowing disregard of one's duties that constitutes bad faith.

… The Court of Chancery identified several undisputed facts that would support the entry of judgment in favor of the Lyondell directors: the directors were "active, sophisticated, and generally aware of the value of the Company and the conditions of the markets in which the Company operated." They had reason to believe that no other bidders would emerge, given the price Basell had offered and the limited universe of companies that might be interested in acquiring Lyondell's unique assets. Smith negotiated the price up from $40 to $48 per share—a price that Deutsche Bank opined was fair. Finally, no other acquiror expressed interest during the four months between the merger announcement and the stockholder vote.

Other facts, however, led the trial court to "question the adequacy of the Board's knowledge and efforts…." After the Schedule 13D was filed in May, the directors apparently took no action to prepare for a possible acquisition proposal. The merger was negotiated and finalized in less than one week, during which time the directors met for a total of only seven hours to consider the matter. The directors did not seriously press Blavatnik for a better price, nor did they conduct even a limited market check. Moreover, although the deal protections were not unusual or preclusive, the trial court was troubled by "the Board's decision to grant considerable protection to a deal that may not have been adequately vetted under *Revlon*."

The trial court found the directors' failure to act during the two months after the filing of the Basell Schedule 13D critical to its analysis of their good faith. The court pointedly referred to the directors' "two months of slothful indifference despite knowing that the Company was in play," and the fact that they "languidly awaited overtures from potential suitors…." In the end, the trial court found that it was this "failing" that warranted denial of their motion for summary judgment….

The problem with the trial court's analysis is that *Revlon* duties do not arise simply because a company is "in play." [*Paramount Communications, Inc. v. Time, Inc.*, 571 A.2d 1140, 1151 (Del. 1989)]. The duty to seek the best available price applies only when a company embarks on a transaction—on its own initiative or in response to an unsolicited offer—that will result in a change of control. Basell's Schedule 13D did put the Lyondell directors, and the market in general, on notice that Basell was interested in acquiring Lyondell. The directors responded by promptly holding a special meeting to consider whether Lyondell should take any action. The directors decided that they would neither put the company up for sale nor institute defensive measures to fend off a possible hostile offer. Instead, they decided to take a "wait and see" approach. That decision was an entirely appropriate exercise of the directors' business judgment. The time for action under *Revlon* did not begin until July 10, 2007, when the directors began negotiating the sale of Lyondell.

The Court of Chancery focused on the directors' two months of inaction, when it should have focused on the one week during which they considered Basell's offer. During that one week, the directors met several times; their CEO tried to negotiate better terms; they evaluated Lyondell's value, the price offered and the likelihood of obtaining a better price; and then the directors approved the merger. The trial court acknowledged that the directors' conduct during those seven days might not demonstrate anything more than lack of due care. But the court remained skeptical about the directors' good faith—at least on the present record. That lingering concern was based on the trial court's synthesis of the *Revlon* line of cases, which led it to the erroneous conclusion that directors must follow one of several courses of action to satisfy their *Revlon* duties.

There is only one *Revlon* duty—to "[get] the best price for the stockholders at a sale of the company." [*Revlon, supra.*] No court can tell directors exactly how to accomplish that goal, because they will be facing a unique combination of circumstances, many of which will be outside their control. As we noted in *Barkan v. Amsted Industries, Inc.*, "there is no single blueprint that a board must follow to fulfill its duties." [567 A.2d 1279, 1286 (Del. 1989)]. That said, our courts have highlighted both the positive and negative aspects of various boards' conduct under *Revlon*.[18] The trial court drew several principles from those cases: directors must "engage actively in the sale process," and they must confirm that they have obtained the best available price either by conducting an auction, by conducting a market check, or by demonstrating "an impeccable knowledge of the market."

The Lyondell directors did not conduct an auction or a market check, and they did not satisfy the trial court that they had the "impeccable" market knowledge that the court believed was necessary to excuse their failure to pursue one of the first two alternatives. As a result, the Court of Chancery was unable to conclude that the directors had met their burden under *Revlon*. In evaluating the totality of the circumstances, even on this limited record, we would be inclined to hold otherwise. But we would not question the trial court's decision to seek additional evidence if the issue were whether the directors had exercised due care. Where, as here, the issue is whether the directors failed to act in good faith, the analysis is very different, and the existing record mandates the entry of judgment in favor of the directors.

As discussed above, bad faith will be found if a "fiduciary intentionally fails to act in the face of a known duty to act, demonstrating a conscious disregard for his duties." [*Disney, supra*]. The trial court decided that the *Revlon* sale process must follow one of three courses, and that the Lyondell directors did not discharge that "known set of [*Revlon*] 'duties.'" But, as noted, there are no legally prescribed steps that directors must follow to satisfy their *Revlon* duties. Thus, the directors' failure to take any specific steps during the sale process could not have demonstrated a conscious disregard of their duties. More importantly, there is a vast difference between an inad-

---

18. [28] *See, e.g.: Barkan v. Amsted Industries, Inc.*, 567 A.2d at 1287 (Directors need not conduct a market check if they have reliable basis for belief that price offered is best possible.); *Paramount Communications, Inc. v. QVC Network, Inc.*, 637 A.2d 34, 49 (Del. 1994) (No-shop provision impermissibly interfered with directors' ability to negotiate with another known bidder); *In re Netsmart Technologies, Inc., Shareholders Litig.*, 924 A.2d 171, 199 (Del. Ch. 2007) (Plaintiff likely to succeed on claim based on board's failure to consider strategic buyers).

equate or flawed effort to carry out fiduciary duties and a conscious disregard for those duties.

Directors' decisions must be reasonable, not perfect. [*Paramount Communications, Inc. v. QVC Network, Inc.*, 637 A.2d at 45.] "In the transactional context, [an] extreme set of facts [is] required to sustain a disloyalty claim premised on the notion that disinterested directors were intentionally disregarding their duties." [*In re Lear Corp. S'holder Litig.*, 2008 WL 4053221 at *11 (Del. Ch.)] The trial court denied summary judgment because the Lyondell directors' "unexplained inaction" prevented the court from determining that they had acted in good faith. But, if the directors failed to do all that they should have under the circumstances, they breached their duty of care. Only if they knowingly and completely failed to undertake their responsibilities would they breach their duty of loyalty. The trial court approached the record from the wrong perspective. Instead of questioning whether disinterested, independent directors did everything that they (arguably) should have done to obtain the best sale price, the inquiry should have been whether those directors utterly failed to attempt to obtain the best sale price. [*See Stone, supra.*]

Viewing the record in this manner leads to only one possible conclusion. The Lyondell directors met several times to consider Basell's premium offer. They were generally aware of the value of their company and they knew the chemical company market. The directors solicited and followed the advice of their financial and legal advisors. They attempted to negotiate a higher offer even though all the evidence indicates that Basell had offered a "blowout" price.[19] Finally, they approved the merger agreement, because "it was simply too good not to pass along [to the stockholders] for their consideration." We assume, as we must on summary judgment, that the Lyondell directors did absolutely nothing to prepare for Basell's offer, and that they did not even consider conducting a market check before agreeing to the merger. Even so, this record clearly establishes that the Lyondell directors did not breach their duty of loyalty by failing to act in good faith. In concluding otherwise, the Court of Chancery reversibly erred....

Notes and Questions

1. In *C&J Energy Services, Inc. v. City of Miami General Employees' & Sanitation Employees' Retirement Trust*, 107 A.3d 1049 (Del. 2014), Chief Justice Strine for the Delaware Supreme Court held that boards are not per se required "to conduct a presigning active solicitation process" in order to satisfy the *Revlon* standard. Specifically: "*Revlon* does not require a board to set aside its own view of what is best for the corporation's stockholders and run an auction whenever the board approves a change of control transaction." Nor does *Revlon* require directors to have "impeccable knowledge" to justify omitting a market check. *Revlon* permits a board "to pursue the transaction it reasonably views as most valuable to stockholders, so long as the transaction

---

19. [37] The trial court disparages the Lyondell directors' characterization of $48 per share as a "blowout" premium. But the record evidence—including testimony from Basell directors who voted against the merger because they believed the price was too high—supports such a description.

is subject to an effective market check under circumstances in which any bidder interested in paying more has a reasonable opportunity to do so."

2. In *Corwin v. KKR Financial Holdings LLC*, 125 A.3d 304 (Del. 2015), the Delaware Supreme Court, in an opinion written by Chief Justice Strine, held that an uncoerced, fully informed vote of disinterested stockholders in favor of a challenged transaction provides an independent basis to invoke the business judgment rule. The case involved a stock-for-stock merger between KKR & Co. (KKR) and KKR Financial Holdings LLC (Financial). Plaintiffs argued that KKR was a controlling stockholder of Financial because, even though KKR owned less than 1 percent of Financial, KKR managed it through an affiliate under a contract containing a hefty termination fee.

The Chancery Court rejected the controlling shareholder assertion thus finding that the entire fairness standard did not apply. The Court of Chancery also held that *Revlon* did not apply because "the transaction was approved by an independent board majority and by a fully informed, uncoerced stockholder vote." Affirming on all counts, the Delaware Supreme Court elaborated concerning *Revlon*:

> [T]he Chancellor was correct in finding that the voluntary judgment of the disinterested stockholders to approve the merger invoked the business judgment rule standard of review and that the plaintiffs' complaint should be dismissed. For sound policy reasons, Delaware corporate law has long been reluctant to second-guess the judgment of a disinterested stockholder majority that determines that a transaction with a party other than a controlling stockholder is in their best interests.…
>
> First, *Unocal* and *Revlon* are primarily designed to give stockholders and the Court of Chancery the tool of injunctive relief to address important M&A decisions in real time, before closing. They were not tools designed with post-closing money damages claims in mind, the standards they articulate do not match the gross negligence standard for director due care liability under *Van Gorkom*, and with the prevalence of exculpatory charter provisions, due care liability is rarely even available.…
>
> Second and most important, the doctrine applies only to fully informed, uncoerced stockholder votes, and if troubling facts regarding director behavior were not disclosed that would have been material to a voting stockholder, then the business judgment rule is not invoked.…
>
> Finally, when a transaction is not subject to the entire fairness standard, the long-standing policy of our law has been to avoid the uncertainties and costs of judicial second-guessing when the disinterested stockholders have had the free and informed chance to decide on the economic merits of a transaction for themselves. There are sound reasons for this policy. When the real parties in interest—the disinterested equity owners—can easily protect themselves at the ballot box by simply voting no, the utility of a litigation-intrusive standard of review promises more costs to stockholders in the form of litigation rents and inhibitions on risk-taking than it promises in terms of benefits to them.

D. Deal Protection

Negotiated agreements for corporate control transactions often include provisions designed to protect the transaction against upset by competing bidders. This may be necessary to give a bidder some assurance that it will close the transaction, not serve as a stalking horse for competing bidders. After all, a bidder invests substantial time and resources lining up a control transaction. Those efforts set a value for the target firm that other bidders can then use to free ride on the bidder's investment.

Deal protection measures include covenants that the target's board will use "best efforts" to obtain shareholder approval or at least to recommend that shareholders approve. They extend to contractual limits on a board's right to talk with third parties about a business combination ("no-talk" provisions) or actively to solicit competing bids ("no-shop" provisions). They can also include a broader range of "lock-up" devices, such as voting agreements among large shareholders or board commitments to proceed to a shareholder vote.

The challenge is to design measures providing bidder assurance while permitting target directors to discharge their fiduciary duties. Customarily, deal protection covenants are accompanied by specific contractual provisions (called "fiduciary outs") expressly authorizing boards to take actions the covenants otherwise prohibit, including terminating the agreement. The following two cases examine resulting issues.

Ace Limited v. Capital Re Corp.

Delaware Court of Chancery

747 A.2d 95 (2000)

STRINE, VICE CHANCELLOR:

Plaintiff ACE Limited ("ACE") has filed a motion requesting a temporary restraining order ("TRO") against defendant Capital Re Corporation ("Capital Re"). ACE requests that I issue an order that restrains Capital Re from taking any action to terminate the June 10, 1999 Agreement and Plan of Merger between and among ACE, Capital Re, and CapRe Acquisition Corporation (the "Merger Agreement"). Capital Re's board of directors wishes to terminate the Merger Agreement and accept an all cash, all shares bid [from XL Capital] that it believes is financially superior to the Merger Agreement. ACE contends that Capital Re cannot, under the Merger Agreement's no-talk and termination provisions, validly terminate the Merger Agreement.

Because Capital Re's argument that termination is permitted by the Merger Agreement is the more plausible one; because ACE's contrary construction, if correct, suggests that the Merger Agreement's "no-talk" provision is likely invalid; and because the risk of harm to Capital Re stockholders outweighs the need to protect ACE from irreparable injury, I deny ACE's motion.

Capital Re, a Delaware corporation, is a specialty reinsurance corporation in the business of municipal and non-municipal guaranty reinsurance, mortgage guaranty reinsurance, title reinsurance, and trade credit reinsurance. ACE is a Cayman Islands holding company that, through subsidiaries, engages in the insurance and reinsurance industries internationally.

According to ACE, Capital Re was in a capital crunch earlier this year. Although Capital Re does not admit that this was the reason, it says that for more than a year it has been exploring a possible business combination or capital infusion. During this exploration, Capital Re engaged ACE in discussions about strategic options. As a result of those discussions, ACE provided Capital Re with a cash infusion of $75 million in February 1999 in exchange for newly issued Capital Re shares, which ultimately amounted to 12.3% of the company's outstanding common shares.

This infusion was apparently insufficient to calm the markets because in March of 1999 Moody's Investors Service, Inc. downgraded Capital Re's financial rating from AAA to AA2. ACE contends that a further downgrading would have seriously affected Capital Re's earnings and that Capital Re therefore contacted ACE in May of 1999 to discuss solutions, including a possible business combination with ACE.

Negotiations following this contact bore fruit in the form of the binding Merger Agreement between ACE and Capital Re, which was publicly announced on June 11, 1999. The terms of the Merger Agreement provide for Capital Re stockholders to receive .6 of a share of ACE stock for each share of Capital Re they hold. On June 10, 1999, the value of .6 of a share of ACE was over $17.00.

At the time the Capital Re board executed the Merger Agreement, it knew that ACE, which owns 12.3% of Capital Re's stock, had stockholder voting agreements with stockholders holding another 33.5% of Capital Re's shares. According to ACE, "representatives of Capital Re significantly participated in the negotiation of, and in obtaining, the shareholder agreements" and Capital Re encouraged the 33.5% holders to sign the agreements. These agreements obligated the 33.5% holders to support the merger if the Capital Re board of directors did not terminate the Merger Agreement in accordance with its provisions. Put simply, ACE would control nearly 46% of the vote going into the merger vote and therefore needed very few of the remaining votes to prevail. Thus the Capital Re board knew when it executed the Merger Agreement that unless it terminated the Merger Agreement, ACE would have, as a virtual certainty, the votes to consummate the merger even if a materially more valuable transaction became available.

Although ACE and Capital Re both agree that the merger, if effectuated, will not result in a "change of control" of Capital Re ... the merger is obviously a transaction of great significance for Capital Re's stockholders and for ACE. The parties therefore bargained over the circumstances in which the Capital Re board could consider another party's acquisition or merger proposal and/or terminate the Merger Agreement.

For its part, ACE says it wanted the "strongest, legally binding commitment from Capital Re, consistent with the Capital Re board's fiduciary duties." This was natural given the investment ACE had made in Capital Re and the significant resources and organizational energy necessary to consummate the merger. Most of all, ACE viewed the merger as a unique strategic opportunity enabling it to expand into a specialized reinsurance market that is, in ACE's view, quite difficult to enter from scratch.

On the other hand, the Capital Re board knew that the "fiduciary out" in the Merger Agreement was crucial if it was to protect its stockholders' rights. Because ACE had contracts in hand guaranteeing it success in a merger vote unless the Capital Re [board] terminated the Merger Agreement, the board's decision whether to terminate was determinative. Capital Re suggests that the stockholder agreements with the 33.5% holders were tied to this termination provision purposely, so that if there was a proposal that the Capital Re board deemed "superior," the 33.5% holders would also be free to consider it. Because the merger would be consummated even if circumstances had greatly changed and even if a much more valuable offer was available unless the board could validly terminate the agreement, Capital Re claims that the board was careful to negotiate sufficient flexibility for itself to terminate the Merger Agreement if necessary to protect the Capital Re stockholders.

The negotiations on this issue resulted in two important sections of the contract. The first, §6.3 (the "no talk"), generally operates to prohibit Capital Re and "its officers, directors, agents, representatives, advisors or other intermediaries" from "soliciting, initiating, encouraging, ... or taking any action knowingly to facilitate the submission of any inquiries, proposals, or offers ... from any person." Of most importance on this motion, §6.3 also restricts Capital Re from participating in discussions or negotiations with or even providing information to a third party in connection with an "unsolicited bona fide Transaction Proposal," unless the following conditions are met:

- Capital Re's board concludes "in good faith ... based on the advice of its outside financial advisors, that such Transaction Proposal is reasonably likely to be or to result in a Superior Proposal";
- Capital Re's board concludes "in good faith ... based on the written advice of its outside legal counsel, that participating in such negotiations or discussions or furnishing such information is required in order to prevent the Board of Directors of the Company from breaching its fiduciary duties to its stockholders under the [Delaware General Corporation Law]";
- the competing offeror enters into a confidentiality agreement no less favorable to Capital Re than its confidentiality agreement with ACE, a copy of which must be provided to ACE; and
- the company's directors provide ACE with contemporaneous notice of their intent to negotiate or furnish information with the competing offeror....

ACE argues that Capital Re has violated the plain language of the Merger Agreement. Its major claim is that Capital Re was forbidden to engage in discussions with XL Capital unless it received written legal advice from outside counsel opining that the board's fiduciary duties mandated such discussions. Because the board did not receive such advice, its decision to enter negotiations with XL Capital and to start a bidding war between ACE and XL Capital is, in ACE's view, a clear breach of contract....

Although perhaps not so clear as to preclude another interpretation, §6.3 of the Agreement is on its face better read as leaving the ultimate "good faith" judgment about whether the board's fiduciary duties required it to enter discussions with XL Capital to the board itself. Though the board must "base" its judgment on the "written advice" of outside counsel, the language of the contract does not preclude the board from concluding, even if its outside counsel equivocates (as lawyers sometimes tend to do) as to whether such negotiations are [mandated by fiduciary duty].

Here, the Capital Re board had good economic reason to believe that consummation of the merger in the face of the XL Capital offer was adverse to the interests of the Capital Re stockholders. The board knew that if it did not explore the XL Capital offer, the Capital Re stockholders—including the 33.5% holders—would be forced into the merger even though the merger's value had plummeted since June 10, 1999 and even though the XL Capital offer was more valuable. Given these circumstances, it seems likely that in the end a fact-finder will conclude that the board had a good faith basis for determining that it must talk with XL Capital and not simply let the Capital Re stockholders ride the merger barrel over the financial falls. Furthermore, even if the contract is read as ACE wishes, [Capital Re's in-house counsel's] written legal advice, when taken as a totality, coupled with his oral advice, and viewed in light of the necessarily hurried deliberative process undertaken by the Capital Re board on October 6, 1999, might well be found to be a sufficient basis for a good faith decision by the board....

Restatement (Second) of Contracts § 193 explicitly provides that a "promise by a fiduciary to violate his [or her] fiduciary duty or a promise that tends to induce such a violation is unenforceable on public policy grounds." ... If § 6.3 of the Merger Agreement in fact required the Capital Re board to eschew even discussing another offer unless it received an opinion of counsel stating that such discussions were required, and if ACE demanded such a provision, it is likely that § 6.3 will ultimately be found invalid. It is one thing for a board of directors to agree not to play footsie with other potential bidders or to stir up an auction. That type of restriction is perfectly understandable, if not necessary, if good faith business transactions are to be encouraged. It is quite another thing for a board of directors to enter into a merger agreement that precludes the board from considering any other offers unless a lawyer is willing to sign an opinion indicating that his client board is "required" to consider that offer in the less than precise corporate law context of a merger agreement that does not implicate *Revlon* but may preclude other transactions in a manner that raises eyebrows under *Unocal*. Such a contractual commitment is particularly suspect when a failure to consider other offers guarantees the consummation of the original transaction, however more valuable an alternative transaction may be and however less valuable the original transaction may have become since the merger agreement was signed.

In one sense, such a provision seems innocuous. I mean, can't the board find someone willing to give the opinion? What is wrong with a contract that simply limits a board from discussing another offer unless the board's lawyers are prepared to opine that such discussions are required?

But in another sense, the provision is much more pernicious in that it involves an abdication by the board of its duty to determine what its own fiduciary obligations require at precisely that time in the life of the company when the board's own judgment is most important. In the typical case, one must remember, the target board is defending the original deal in the face of an arguably more valuable transaction. In that context, does it make sense for the board to be able to hide behind their lawyers?

More fundamentally, one would think that there would be limited circumstances in which a board could prudently place itself in the position of not being able to entertain and consider a superior proposal to a transaction dependent on a stockholder vote. The circumstances in this case would not seem to be of that nature, because the board's inability to consider another offer in effect precludes the stockholders (including the 33.5% holders) from accepting another offer. For the superior proposal "out" in §§ 6.3 and 8.3 of the Merger Agreement to mean anything, the board must be free to explore such a proposal in good faith. A ban on considering such a proposal, even one with an exception where legal counsel opines in writing that such consideration is "required," comes close to self-disablement by the board. Our case law takes a rather dim view of restrictions that tend to produce such a result.

Indeed, ACE admits that it pushed Capital Re to the outer limits of propriety, but it claims to have stopped short of pushing Capital Re beyond that limit. But as I read ACE's view of what § 6.3 means in the context of this Merger Agreement, ACE comes close to saying that § 6.3 provides no "out" at all. According to ACE, it is now clear, per *QVC*, that a board need not obtain the highest value reasonably available unless it decides to engage in a change of control transaction. The ACE-Capital Re merger is not a change of control. Therefore, this syllogism goes, there is no circumstance in which the Capital Re board must consider another higher offer to fulfill its fiduciary duties. Thus Capital Re could not get its outside counsel to issue such an opinion, and the board's contrary judgment of its duties could not have been in good faith. *QVC*, *Q.E.D.*....

In this necessarily hurried posture, it is impossible to examine in depth the appropriate doctrinal prism through which to evaluate the "no-talk" provision in the Merger Agreement. In the wake of *QVC*, parties have tended to imbed provisions in stock-for-stock mergers that are intentionally designed to prevent another bidder, through a tender offer or rival stock-for-stock bid, from preventing the consummation of a transaction. When corporate boards assent to provisions in merger agreements that have the primary purpose of acting as a defensive barrier to other transactions not sought out by the board, some of the policy concerns that animate the *Unocal* standard of review might be implicated. In this case, for example, if § 6.3 is read as precluding board consideration of alternative offers — no matter how much more favorable — in this non-change of control context, the Capital Re board's approval of the Merger Agreement is as formidable a barrier to another offer as a non-redeemable poison pill. Absent an escape clause, the Merger Agreement guarantees the success of the merger vote and precludes any other alternative, no matter how much more lucrative to the Capital Re stockholders and no matter whether the Capital Re board itself prefers the other alternative. As a practical matter, it might therefore be possible to construct a plausible argument that a no-escape merger agreement that locks up the necessary votes constitutes an unreasonable preclusive and coercive defensive obstacle within the meaning of *Unocal*.

But *Unocal* to one side, one can state with much more doctrinal certainty that the Capital Re board was still required to exercise its bedrock duties of care and loyalty when it entered the Merger Agreement. If the board mistakenly entered into a merger agreement believing erroneously that it had negotiated an effective out giving it the ability to consider more favorable offers, its mistake might well be found to be a breach of its duty of care. In this context where the board is making a critical decision affecting stockholder ownership and voting rights, it is especially important that the board negotiate with care and retain sufficient flexibility to ensure that the stockholders are not unfairly coerced into accepting a less than optimal exchange for their shares....

Examined under either doctrinal rubric, §6.3 as construed by ACE is of quite dubious validity. As a sophisticated party who bargained for, nay demanded, §6.3 of the Merger Agreement, ACE was on notice of its possible invalidity. This factor therefore cuts against its claim that its contract rights should take precedence over the interests of the Capital Re stockholders who could be harmed by enforcement of §6.3.

Omnicare, Inc. v. NCS Healthcare, Inc.

Delaware Supreme Court
818 A.2d 914 (2003)

HOLLAND, JUSTICE:

[I. FACTS]

... Beginning in late 1999, changes in the timing and level of reimbursements by government and third-party providers adversely affected market conditions in the health care industry. As a result, NCS [a Delaware corporation] began to experience greater difficulty in collecting accounts receivables, which led to a precipitous decline in the market value of its stock. NCS common shares that traded above $20 in January 1999 were worth as little as $5 at the end of that year. By early 2001, NCS was in default on approximately $350 million in debt, including $206 million in senior bank debt and $102 million of its 5 3/4% Convertible Subordinated Debentures (the "Notes"). After these defaults, NCS common stock traded in a range of $0.09 to $0.50 per share until days before the announcement of the transaction at issue in this case.

NCS began to explore strategic alternatives that might address the problems it was confronting. As part of this effort, in February 2000, NCS retained UBS Warburg, L.L.C. to identify potential acquirers and possible equity investors. UBS Warburg contacted over fifty different entities to solicit their interest in a variety of transactions with NCS. UBS Warburg had marginal success in its efforts. By October 2000, NCS had only received one non-binding indication of interest valued at $190 million, substantially less than the face value of NCS's senior debt. This proposal was reduced by 20% after the offeror conducted its due diligence review.

In December 2000, NCS terminated its relationship with UBS Warburg and retained Brown, Gibbons, Lang & Company as its exclusive financial advisor. During this period, NCS's financial condition continued to deteriorate. In April 2001, NCS received a formal notice of default and acceleration from the trustee for holders of the Notes. As NCS's financial condition worsened, the Noteholders formed a committee to represent their financial interests (the "Ad Hoc Committee"). At about that time, NCS began discussions with various investor groups regarding a restructuring in a "prepackaged" bankruptcy. NCS did not receive any proposal that it believed provided adequate consideration for its stakeholders. At that time, full recovery for NCS's creditors was a remote prospect, and any recovery for NCS stockholders seemed impossible.

In the summer of 2001, NCS invited Omnicare, Inc. to begin discussions with Brown Gibbons regarding a possible transaction. On July 20, Joel Gemunder, Omnicare's President and CEO, sent Shaw[, an NCS director and its president and CEO,] a written proposal to acquire NCS in a bankruptcy sale under Section 363 of the Bankruptcy Code. This proposal was for $225 million subject to satisfactory completion of due diligence. NCS asked Omnicare to execute a confidentiality agreement so that more detailed discussions could take place.

In August 2001, Omnicare increased its bid to $270 million, but still proposed to structure the deal as an asset sale in bankruptcy. Even at $270 million, Omnicare's proposal was substantially lower than the face value of NCS's outstanding debt. It would have provided only a small recovery for Omnicare's Noteholders and no recovery for its stockholders. In October 2001, NCS sent Glen Pollack of Brown Gibbons to meet with Omnicare's financial advisor, Merrill Lynch, to discuss Omnicare's interest in NCS. Omnicare responded that it was not interested in any transaction other than an asset sale in bankruptcy.

There was no further contact between Omnicare and NCS between November 2001 and January 2002. Instead, Omnicare began secret discussions with Judy K. Mencher, a representative of the Ad Hoc Committee. In these discussions, Omnicare continued to pursue a transaction structured as a sale of assets in bankruptcy. In February 2002, the Ad Hoc Committee notified the NCS board that Omnicare had proposed an asset sale in bankruptcy for $313,750,000.

In January 2002, Genesis [a Pennsylvania corporation] was contacted by members of the Ad Hoc Committee concerning a possible transaction with NCS. Genesis executed NCS's standard confidentiality agreement and began a due diligence review. Genesis had recently emerged from bankruptcy because, like NCS, it was suffering from dwindling government reimbursements.

Genesis previously lost a bidding war to Omnicare in a different transaction. This led to bitter feelings between the principals of both companies. More importantly, this bitter experience for Genesis led to its insistence on exclusivity agreements and lock-ups in any potential transaction with NCS.

NCS's operating performance was improving by early 2002. As NCS's performance improved, the NCS directors began to believe that it might be possible for NCS to enter into a transaction that would provide some recovery for NCS stockholders' equity. In March 2002, NCS decided to form an independent committee of board members who were neither NCS employees nor major NCS stockholders (the "Independent Committee"). The NCS board thought this was necessary because, due to NCS's precarious financial condition, it felt that fiduciary duties were owed to the enterprise as a whole rather than solely to NCS stockholders....

The Independent Committee met for the first time on May 14, 2002. At that meeting Pollack suggested that NCS seek a "stalking-horse merger partner" to obtain the highest possible value in any transaction. The Independent Committee agreed with the suggestion.

Two days later, on May 16, 2002, Scott Berlin of Brown Gibbons, Glen Pollack and Boake Sells met with George Hager, CFO of Genesis, and Michael Walker, who was Genesis's CEO. At that meeting, Genesis made it clear that if it were going to engage in any negotiations with NCS, it would not do so as a "stalking horse."...

In June 2002, Genesis proposed a transaction that would take place outside the bankruptcy context. Although it did not provide full recovery for NCS's Noteholders, it provided the possibility that NCS stockholders would be able to recover something for their investment. As discussions continued, the terms proposed by Genesis continued to improve. On June 25, the economic terms of the Genesis proposal included repayment of the NCS senior debt in full, full assumption of trade credit obligations, an exchange offer or direct purchase of the NCS Notes ... and $20 million in value for the NCS common stock. Structurally, the Genesis proposal continued to include consents from a significant majority of the Noteholders as well as support agreements from stockholders owning a majority of the NCS voting power.

NCS's financial advisors and legal counsel met again with Genesis and its legal counsel on June 26, 2002, to discuss a number of transaction-related issues. At this meeting, Pollack asked Genesis to increase its offer to NCS stockholders. Genesis agreed to consider this request. Thereafter, Pollack and Hager had further conversations. Genesis agreed to offer a total of $24 million in consideration for the NCS common stock, or an additional $4 million, in the form of Genesis common stock.

At the June 26 meeting, Genesis's representatives demanded that, before any further negotiations take place, NCS agree to enter into an exclusivity agreement with it.... On June 27, 2002, Genesis's legal counsel delivered a draft form of exclusivity agreement for review and consideration by NCS's legal counsel.

The Independent Committee met on July 3, 2002, to consider the proposed exclusivity agreement. Pollack presented a summary of the terms of a possible Genesis merger....

After NCS executed the exclusivity agreement, Genesis provided NCS with a draft merger agreement, a draft Noteholders' support agreement, and draft voting agreements for Outcalt [NCS's board chairman] and Shaw [the NCS director and its president and CEO], who together held a majority of the voting power of the NCS common stock. Genesis and NCS negotiated the terms of the merger agreement over the next three weeks....

By late July 2002, Omnicare came to believe that NCS was negotiating a transaction, possibly with Genesis or another of Omnicare's competitors, that would potentially present a competitive threat to Omnicare. Omnicare also came to believe, in light of a run-up in the price of NCS common stock, that whatever transaction NCS was negotiating probably included a payment for its stock. Thus, the Omnicare board of directors met on the morning of July 26 and, on the recommendation of its management, authorized a proposal to acquire NCS that did not involve a sale of assets in bankruptcy.

On the afternoon of July 26, 2002, Omnicare faxed to NCS a letter outlining a proposed acquisition. The letter suggested a transaction in which Omnicare would retire NCS's senior and subordinated debt at par plus accrued interest, and pay the NCS stockholders $3 cash for their shares. Omnicare's proposal, however, was expressly conditioned on negotiating a merger agreement, obtaining certain third party consents, and completing its due diligence.

Mencher saw the July 26 Omnicare letter and realized that, while its economic terms were attractive, the "due diligence" condition substantially undercut its strength. In an effort to get a better proposal from Omnicare, Mencher telephoned Gemunder and told him that Omnicare was unlikely to succeed in its bid unless it dropped the "due diligence outs." She explained this was the only way a bid at the last minute would be able to succeed. Gemunder considered Mencher's warning "very real," and followed up with his advisors. They, however, insisted that he retain the due diligence condition "to protect [him] from doing something foolish." Taking this advice to heart, Gemunder decided not to drop the due diligence condition.

Late in the afternoon of July 26, 2002, NCS representatives received voicemail messages from Omnicare asking to discuss the letter. The exclusivity agreement prevented NCS from returning those calls. In relevant part, that agreement precluded NCS from "engaging or participating in any discussions or negotiations with respect to a Competing Transaction or a proposal for one." The July 26 letter from Omnicare met the definition of a "Competing Transaction."

Despite the exclusivity agreement, the Independent Committee met to consider a response to Omnicare. It concluded that discussions with Omnicare about its July 26 letter presented an unacceptable risk that Genesis would abandon merger discussions. The Independent Committee believed that, given Omnicare's past bankruptcy proposals and unwillingness to consider a merger, as well as its decision to negotiate exclusively with the Ad Hoc Committee, the risk of losing the Genesis proposal was too substantial. Nevertheless, the Independent Committee instructed Pollack to use Omnicare's letter to negotiate for improved terms with Genesis.

Genesis responded to the NCS request to improve its offer as a result of the Omnicare fax the next day. On July 27, Genesis proposed substantially improved terms. First, it proposed to retire the Notes in accordance with the terms of the indenture, thus eliminating the need for Noteholders to consent to the transaction. This change involved paying all accrued interest plus a small redemption premium. Second, Genesis increased the exchange ratio for NCS common stock to one-tenth of a Genesis common share for each NCS common share, an 80% increase. Third, it agreed to lower the proposed termination fee in the merger agreement from $10 million to $6 million. In return for these concessions, Genesis stipulated that the transaction had to be approved by midnight the next day, July 28, or else Genesis would terminate discussions and withdraw its offer.

The Independent Committee and the NCS board both scheduled meetings for July 28. The committee met first. Although that meeting lasted less than an hour, the Court of Chancery determined the minutes reflect that the directors were fully informed of all material facts relating to the proposed transaction. After concluding that Genesis was sincere in establishing the midnight deadline, the committee voted unanimously to recommend the transaction to the full board.

The full board met thereafter. After receiving similar reports and advice from its legal and financial advisors, the board concluded that "balancing the potential loss of the Genesis deal against the uncertainty of Omnicare's letter, results in the conclusion that the only reasonable alternative for the Board of Directors is to approve the Genesis transaction." ... The board was advised by its legal counsel that "under the terms of the merger agreement and because NCS shareholders representing in excess of 50% of the outstanding voting power would be required by Genesis to enter into stockholder voting agreements contemporaneously with the signing of the merger agreement, and would agree to vote their shares in favor of the merger agreement, shareholder approval of the merger would be assured even if the NCS Board were to withdraw or change its recommendation. These facts would prevent NCS from engaging in any alternative or superior transaction in the future....

After listening to a summary of the merger terms, the board then resolved that the merger agreement and the transactions contemplated thereby were advisable and fair and in the best interests of all the NCS stakeholders. The NCS board further resolved to recommend the transactions to the stockholders for their approval and adoption. A definitive merger agreement between NCS and Genesis and the stockholder voting agreements were executed later that day. The Court of Chancery held that it was not a per se breach of fiduciary duty that the NCS board never read the NCS/Genesis merger agreement word for word.

Among other things, the NCS/Genesis merger agreement provided ... NCS would submit the merger agreement to NCS stockholders regardless of whether the NCS board continued to recommend the merger [and] NCS would not enter into discussions with third parties concerning an alternative acquisition of NCS, or provide non-public information to such parties, unless (1) the third party provided an unsolicited, bona fide written proposal documenting the terms of the acquisition; (2) the NCS board believed in good faith that the proposal was or was likely to result in an acquisition on terms superior to those contemplated by the NCS/Genesis merger agreement; and (3) before providing non-public information to that third party, the third party would execute a confidentiality agreement at least as restrictive as the one in place between NCS and Genesis....

Outcalt and Shaw, in their capacity as NCS stockholders, entered into voting agreements with Genesis. NCS was also required to be a party to the voting agreements by Genesis. Those agreements provided, among other things, that ... [n]either Outcalt nor Shaw would transfer their shares prior to the stockholder vote on the merger agreement [and] Outcalt and Shaw agreed to vote all of their shares in favor of the merger agreement....

On July 29, 2002, hours after the NCS/Genesis transaction was executed, Omnicare faxed a letter to NCS restating its conditional proposal and attaching a draft merger agreement. Later that morning, Omnicare issued a press release publicly disclosing the proposal.

On August 1, 2002, Omnicare filed a lawsuit attempting to enjoin the NCS/Genesis merger, and announced that it intended to launch a tender offer for NCS's shares at a price of $3.50 per share. On August 8, 2002, Omnicare began its tender offer. By letter dated that same day, Omnicare expressed a desire to discuss the terms of the offer with NCS. Omnicare's letter continued to condition its proposal on satisfactory completion of a due diligence investigation of NCS.

On August 8, 2002, and again on August 19, 2002, the NCS Independent Committee and full board of directors met separately to consider the Omnicare tender offer in light of the Genesis merger agreement. NCS's outside legal counsel and NCS's financial advisor attended both meetings. The board was unable to determine that Omnicare's expressions of interest were likely to lead to a "Superior Proposal," as the term was defined in the NCS/Genesis merger agreement. On September 10, 2002, NCS requested and received a waiver from Genesis allowing NCS to enter into discussions with Omnicare without first having to determine that Omnicare's proposal was a "Superior Proposal."

On October 6, 2002, Omnicare irrevocably committed itself to a transaction with NCS. Pursuant to the terms of its proposal, Omnicare agreed to acquire all the outstanding NCS Class A and Class B shares at a price of $3.50 per share in cash. As a result of this irrevocable offer, on October 21, 2002, the NCS board withdrew its recommendation that the stockholders vote in favor of the NCS/Genesis merger agreement. NCS's financial advisor withdrew its fairness opinion of the NCS/Genesis merger agreement as well.

The Genesis merger agreement permits the NCS directors to furnish non-public information to, or enter into discussions with, "any Person in connection with an unsolicited bona fide written Acquisition Proposal by such person" that the board deems likely to constitute a "Superior Proposal." That provision has absolutely no effect on the Genesis merger agreement. Even if the NCS board "changes, withdraws or modifies" its recommendation, as it did, it must still submit the merger to a stockholder vote....

[II. LEGAL ANALYSIS]

The Delaware corporation statute provides that the board's management decision to enter into and recommend a merger transaction can become final only when ownership action is taken by a vote of the stockholders. Thus, the Delaware corporation law expressly provides for a balance of power between boards and stockholders which makes merger transactions a shared enterprise and ownership decision. Consequently, a board of directors' decision to adopt defensive devices to protect a merger agreement may implicate the stockholders' right to effectively vote contrary to the initial recommendation of the board in favor of the transaction....

[I]n applying enhanced judicial scrutiny to defensive devices designed to protect a merger agreement, a court must first determine that those measures are not preclusive or coercive before its focus shifts to the "range of reasonableness" in making a proportionality determination. If the ... court determines that the defensive devices protecting a merger are not preclusive or coercive, the proportionality paradigm of *Unocal* is applicable....

Unocal requires that any defensive devices must be proportionate to the perceived threat to the corporation and its stockholders if the merger transaction is not consummated. Defensive devices taken to protect a merger agreement executed by a board of directors are intended to give that agreement an advantage over any subsequent transactions that materialize before the merger is approved by the stockholders and consummated. This is analogous to the favored treatment that a board of directors may properly give to encourage an initial bidder when it discharges its fiduciary duties under *Revlon*....

[T]he NCS directors' decision to adopt defensive devices to completely "lock up" the Genesis merger mandated "special scrutiny" under the two-part test set forth in *Unocal*.... The second stage of the *Unocal* test requires the NCS directors to demonstrate that their defensive response was "reasonable in relation to the threat posed." This inquiry involves a two-step analysis. The NCS directors must first establish that the merger deal protection devices adopted in response to the threat were not "coercive" or "preclusive," and then demonstrate that their response was within a "range of reasonable responses" to the threat perceived.... [*Unitrin Inc. v. Am. Gen. Corp.*, 651 A.2d 1361 (Del. 1995).]. If defensive measures are either preclusive or coercive they are draconian and impermissible. In this case, the deal protection devices of the NCS board were both preclusive and coercive....

Although the minority stockholders were not forced to vote for the Genesis merger, they were required to accept it because it was a fait accompli. The record reflects that the defensive devices employed by the NCS board are preclusive and coercive in the sense that they accomplished a fait accompli. In this case, despite the fact that the NCS board has withdrawn its recommendation for the Genesis transaction and recommended its rejection by the stockholders, the deal protection devices approved by the NCS board operated in concert to have a preclusive and coercive effect. Those tripartite defensive measures — the Section 251(c) provision, the voting agreements, and the absence of an effective fiduciary out clause — made it "mathematically impossible" and "realistically unattainable" for the Omnicare transaction or any other proposal to succeed, no matter how superior the proposal.

The defensive measures that protected the merger transaction are unenforceable not only because they are preclusive and coercive but, alternatively, they are unenforceable because they are invalid as they operate in this case. Given the ... voting agreements, the provision in the merger agreement requiring the board to submit the transaction for a stockholder vote and the omission of a fiduciary out clause in the merger agreement completely prevented the board from discharging its fiduciary responsibilities to the minority stockholders when Omnicare presented its superior transaction....

The NCS board was required to contract for an effective fiduciary out clause to exercise its continuing fiduciary responsibilities to the minority stockholders. The issues in this appeal do not involve the general validity of either stockholder voting agreements or the authority of directors to insert a Section 251(c) provision in a merger agreement. In this case, the NCS board combined those two otherwise valid actions and caused them to operate in concert as an absolute lock up, in the absence of an effective fiduciary out clause in the Genesis merger agreement.

In the context of this preclusive and coercive lock up case, the protection of Genesis' contractual expectations must yield to the supervening responsibility of the directors to discharge their fiduciary duties on a continuing basis. The merger agreement and voting agreements, as they were combined to operate in concert in this case, are inconsistent with the NCS directors' fiduciary duties. To that extent, we hold that they are invalid and unenforceable.

VEASEY, CHIEF JUSTICE, with whom STEELE, JUSTICE, joins dissenting:

The beauty of the Delaware corporation law, and the reason it has worked so well for stockholders, directors and officers, is that the framework is based on an enabling statute with the Court of Chancery and the Supreme Court applying principles of fiduciary duty in a common law mode on a case-by-case basis. Fiduciary duty cases are inherently fact-intensive and, therefore, unique. This case is unique in two important respects. First, the peculiar facts presented render this case an unlikely candidate for substantial repetition. Second, this is a rare 3–2 split decision of the Supreme Court.

In the present case, we are faced with a merger agreement and controlling stockholders' commitment that assured stockholder approval of the merger before the emergence of a subsequent transaction offering greater value to the stockholders. This does not adequately summarize the unique facts before us, however....

The process by which this merger agreement came about involved a joint decision by the controlling stockholders and the board of directors to secure what appeared to be the only value-enhancing transaction available for a company on the brink of bankruptcy. The Majority adopts a new rule of law that imposes a prohibition on the NCS board's ability to act in concert with controlling stockholders to lock up this merger. The Majority reaches this conclusion by analyzing the challenged deal protection measures as isolated board actions. The Majority concludes that the board owed a duty to the NCS minority stockholders to refrain from acceding to the Genesis demand for an irrevocable lock-up notwithstanding the compelling circumstances confronting the board and the board's disinterested, informed, good faith exercise of its business judgment.

Because we believe this Court must respect the reasoned judgment of the board of directors and give effect to the wishes of the controlling stockholders, we respectfully disagree with the Majority's reasoning that results in a holding that the confluence of board and stockholder action constitutes a breach of fiduciary duty. The essential fact that must always be remembered is that this agreement and the voting commitments of Outcalt and Shaw concluded a lengthy search and intense negotiation process in the context of insolvency and creditor pressure where no other viable bid had emerged. Accordingly, we endorse the Vice Chancellor's well-reasoned analysis that the NCS board's action before the hostile bid emerged was within the bounds of its fiduciary duties under these facts.

We share with the Majority and the independent NCS board of directors the motivation to serve carefully and in good faith the best interests of the corporate enterprise and, thereby, the stockholders of NCS. It is now known, of course, after the case is over, that the stockholders of NCS will receive substantially more by tendering their shares into the topping bid of Omnicare than they would have received in the Genesis merger, as a result of the post-agreement Omnicare bid and the injunctive relief ordered by the Majority of this Court. Our jurisprudence cannot, however, be seen as turning on such ex post felicitous results. Rather, the NCS board's good faith decision must be subject to a real-time review of the board action before the NCS-Genesis merger agreement was entered into.

The Majority has adopted the Vice Chancellor's findings and has assumed arguendo that the NCS board fulfilled its duties of care, loyalty, and good faith by entering into the Genesis merger agreement. Indeed, this conclusion is indisputable on this record. The problem is that the Majority has removed from their proper context the contractual merger protection provisions. The lock-ups here cannot be reviewed in a vacuum. A court should review the entire bidding process to determine whether the independent board's actions permitted the directors to inform themselves of their available options and whether they acted in good faith.

Going into negotiations with Genesis, the NCS directors knew that, up until that time, NCS had found only one potential bidder, Omnicare. Omnicare had refused to buy NCS except at a fire sale price through an asset sale in bankruptcy. Omnicare's best proposal at that stage would not have paid off all creditors and would have provided nothing for stockholders. The Noteholders, represented by the Ad Hoc Committee, were willing to oblige Omnicare and force NCS into bankruptcy if Omnicare would pay in full the NCS debt. Through the NCS board's efforts, Genesis expressed interest that became increasingly attractive. Negotiations with Genesis led to an offer paying creditors off and conferring on NCS stockholders $24 million — an amount infinitely superior to the prior Omnicare proposals.

But there was, understandably, a sine qua non. In exchange for offering the NCS stockholders a return on their equity and creditor payment, Genesis demanded certainty that the merger would close. If the NCS board would not have acceded to the Section 251(c) provision, if Outcalt and Shaw had not agreed to the voting agreements and if NCS had insisted on a fiduciary out, there would have been no Genesis deal! Thus, the only value-enhancing transaction available would have disappeared. NCS knew that Omnicare had spoiled a Genesis acquisition in the past, and it is not disputed by the Majority that the NCS directors made a reasoned decision to accept as real the Genesis threat to walk away....

A lock-up permits a target board and a bidder to "exchange certainties." Certainty itself has value. The acquirer may pay a higher price for the target if the acquirer is assured consummation of the transaction. The target company also benefits from the certainty of completing a transaction with a bidder because losing an acquirer creates the perception that a target is damaged goods, thus reducing its value. . . .

The Majority invalidates the NCS board's action by announcing a new rule that represents an extension of our jurisprudence. That new rule can be narrowly stated as follows: A merger agreement entered into after a market search, before any prospect of a topping bid has emerged, which locks up stockholder approval and does not contain a "fiduciary out" provision, is per se invalid when a later significant topping bid emerges. As we have noted, this bright-line, per se rule would apply regardless of (1) the circumstances leading up to the agreement and (2) the fact that stockholders who control voting power had irrevocably committed themselves, as stockholders, to vote for the merger. Narrowly stated, this new rule is a judicially-created "third rail" that now becomes one of the given "rules of the game," to be taken into account by the negotiators and drafters of merger agreements. In our view, this new rule is an unwise extension of existing precedent. . . .

Outcalt and Shaw were fully informed stockholders. As the NCS controlling stockholders, they made an informed choice to commit their voting power to the merger. The minority stockholders were deemed to know that when controlling stockholders have 65% of the vote they can approve a merger without the need for the minority votes. Moreover, to the extent a minority stockholder may have felt "coerced" to vote for the merger, which was already a fait accompli, it was a meaningless coercion — or no coercion at all — because the controlling votes, those of Outcalt and Shaw, were already "cast." . . . Therefore, there was no meaningful minority stockholder voting decision to coerce. . . .

It is regrettable that the Court is split in this important case. One hopes that the Majority rule announced here — though clearly erroneous in our view — will be interpreted narrowly and will be seen as *sui generis*. By deterring bidders from engaging in negotiations like those present here and requiring that there must always be a fiduciary out, the universe of potential bidders who could reasonably be expected to benefit stockholders could shrink or disappear. Nevertheless, if the holding is confined to these unique facts, negotiators may be able to navigate around this new hazard. . . .

Steele, Justice, dissenting:

. . . Here the board of directors acted selflessly pursuant to a careful, fair process and determined in good faith that the benefits to the stockholders and corporation flowing from a merger agreement containing reasonable deal protection provisions outweigh any speculative benefits that might result from entertaining a putative higher offer. A court asked to examine the decision-making process of the board should decline to interfere with the consummation and execution of an otherwise valid contract. . . .

The contract terms that NCS' board agreed to included no insidious, camouflaged side deals for the directors or the majority stockholders nor transparent provisions for entrenchment or control premiums. At the time the NCS board and the majority stockholders agreed to a voting lockup, the terms were the best reasonably available for all the stockholders, balanced against a genuine risk of no deal at all. The cost benefit analysis entered into by an independent committee of the board, approved by the full board and independently agreed to by the majority stockholders cannot be second guessed by courts with no business expertise that would qualify them to substitute their judgment for that of a careful, selfless board or for majority stockholders who had the most significant economic stake in the outcome....

Delaware corporate citizens now face the prospect that in every circumstance, boards must obtain the highest price, even if that requires breaching a contract entered into at a time when no one could have reasonably foreseen a truly "Superior Proposal." The majority's proscriptive rule limits the scope of a board's cost benefit analysis by taking the bargaining chip of foregoing a fiduciary out "off the table" in all circumstances. For that new principle to arise from the context of this case, when Omnicare, after striving to buy NCS on the cheap by buying off its creditors, slinked back into the fray, reversed its historic antagonistic strategy and offered a conditional "Superior Proposal" seems entirely counterintuitive....

Lockup provisions attempt to assure parties that have lost business opportunities and incurred substantial costs that their deal will close. I am concerned that the majority decision will remove the certainty that adds value to any rational business plan. Perhaps transactions that include "force-the-vote" and voting agreement provisions that make approval a foregone conclusion will be the only deals invalidated prospectively. Even so, therein lays the problem. Instead of thoughtful, retrospective, restrained flexibility focused on the circumstances existing at the time of the decision, have we now moved to a bright line regulatory alternative?

For the majority to articulate and adopt an inflexible rule where a board has discharged both its fiduciary duty of loyalty and care in good faith seems a most unfortunate turn. Does the majority mean to signal a mandatory, bright line, *per se* efficient breach analysis *ex post* to all challenged merger agreements? Knowing the majority's general, genuine concern to do equity, I trust not. If so, our courts and the structure of our law that we have strived so hard to develop and perfect will prevent a board, responsible under Delaware law to make precisely the kind of decision made here, in good faith, free of self interest, after exercising scrupulous due care from honoring its contract obligations....

Notes and Questions

1. For a retrospective on *Omnicare* and its implications written by one of the dissenting justices, see E. Norman Veasey, *Ten Years After* Omnicare: *The Evolving Market for Deal Protection Devices*, 38 J. Corp. L. 891 (2013).

2. Should *Omnicare* be read to mean that boards must always preserve some fiduciary out? Or should *Omnicare* be limited to cases where there are pre-commitments of shareholder voting?

3. Consider a board's power to irrevocably commit to submitting a merger agreement to a shareholder vote despite no longer supporting it (known colloquially as a "force the vote" provision). Both the Delaware General Corporations Law and Model Act were amended in the period following *Omnicare* to provide some statutory protection for this strategy.

Del. Gen. Corp. Law was amended in 2003 to provide the following section:

§ 146. Submission of matters for stockholder vote.

A corporation may agree to submit a matter to a vote of its stockholders whether or not the board of directors determines at any time subsequent to approving such matter that such matter is no longer advisable and recommends that the stockholders reject or vote against the matter.

The Model Act was amended in 2008 to provide the following section:

§ 8.26. Submission of Matters for Shareholder Vote.

A corporation may agree to submit a matter to a vote of its shareholders even if, after approving the matter, the board of directors determines it no longer recommends the matter.

The Official Comment to Model Act § 8.26 explains:

Section 8.26 is intended to clarify that a corporation can enter into an agreement, such as a merger agreement, containing a force the vote provision. Section 8.26 is broader than some analogous state corporation law provisions and applies to several different provisions of the Model Act that require the directors to approve a matter before recommending that the shareholders vote to approve it. Under section 8.26, directors can agree to submit a matter to the shareholders for approval even if they later determine that they no longer recommend it. This provision is not intended to relieve the board of directors of its duty to consider carefully the proposed transaction and the interests of the shareholders.

Chapter 14

Derivative Litigation and Dispute Resolution

Situation

One of the minority shareholders, Herbert Li, called Phillips this morning to inform him that he intends to initiate a shareholder derivative suit. He claims that Biologistics' directors have repeatedly mismanaged the corporation's operations, thereby breaching their fiduciary duties. He argues, in particular, that they improperly handled the chemical pollution accusations which resulted in the loss of goodwill among employees and the community; that they improperly approved the equipment purchase from Olivetti because the terms were unnecessarily costly; and that they have compensated Anderson and Baker excessively while denying dividends to the shareholders. In addition, Li is especially angered by Anderson's and Baker's opposition to Daytron's interest in acquiring the company.

The directors are aghast. They seek your advice and want to know the following:

1. Can Li proceed with the litigation without the corporation's support?

2. Can the directors terminate the litigation if they think that is the appropriate thing to do?

3. Are there alternative ways to resolve the dispute?

Section I
Derivative Actions

Shareholders who are dissatisfied with management decisions have a number of options. One is the shareholder derivative suit. For example, shareholders, technically on behalf of the corporation, may initiate a lawsuit against the directors for an alleged breach of their fiduciary duties to the corporation. As the materials in this chapter reveal, however, the derivative action raises a number of complex policy and legal issues.

Corporate law vests plenary power in boards of directors. Power extends to decisions about legal matters, including whether and when the corporation should file or settle lawsuits. Judges have long recognized, however, that control over litigation involving directors may pose inherent conflicts. Courts created an exception to the usual allocation of power over some such litigation to shareholders, rather than directors, in a form of legal action called the derivative suit. Doing so entails balancing contending considerations. There are circumstances in which granting shareholders power to sue is vital, such as when directors are charged with violating their fiduciary duties to the corporation; yet many disagreements boil down to business judgments warranting traditional deference to director decisions. Courts developed a rich body of doctrine to define and administer derivative litigation.

The Federal Rules of Civil Procedure address derivative actions in Rule 23.1:

> In a derivative action brought by one or more shareholders or members to enforce a right of a corporation or of an unincorporated association, the corporation or association having failed to enforce a right which may properly be asserted by it, the complaint shall be verified and shall allege (1) that the plaintiff was a shareholder or member at the time of the transaction of which the plaintiff complains or that the plaintiff's share or membership thereafter devolved on the plaintiff by operation of law, and (2) that the action is not a collusive one to confer jurisdiction on a court of the United States which it would not otherwise have. The complaint shall also allege with particularity the efforts, if any, made by the plaintiff to obtain the action the plaintiff desires from the directors or comparable authority and, if necessary, from the shareholders or members, and the reasons for the plaintiff's failure to obtain the action or for not making the effort. The derivative action may not be maintained if it appears that the plaintiff does not fairly and adequately represent the interests of the shareholders or members similarly situated in enforcing the right of the corporation or association. The action shall not be dismissed or compromised without the approval of the court, and notice of the proposed dismissal or compromise shall be given to shareholders or members in such manner as the court directs.

Substantially similar provisions appear in the rules of civil procedure in the various states. Highlights of the Delaware version, Delaware Court of Chancery Rule 23.1:

> (a) In a derivative action brought by one or more shareholders or members to enforce a right of a corporation or of an unincorporated association, the corporation or association having failed to enforce a right which may properly be asserted by it, the complaint shall allege that the plaintiff was a shareholder or member at the time of the transaction of which the plaintiff complains or that the plaintiff's share or membership thereafter devolved on the plaintiff by operation of law. The complaint shall also allege with particularity the efforts, if any, made by the plaintiff to obtain the action the plaintiff desires from the directors or comparable authority and the reasons for the plaintiff's failure to obtain the action or for not making the effort.

> (b) Each person seeking to serve as a representative plaintiff on behalf of a corporation or unincorporated association pursuant to this Rule shall file with the Register in Chancery an affidavit stating that the person has not received, been promised or offered and will not accept any form of com-

pensation, directly or indirectly, for prosecuting or serving as a representative party in the derivative action in which the person or entity is a named party except (i) such fees, costs or other payments as the Court expressly approves to be paid to or on behalf of such person, or (ii) reimbursement, paid by such person's attorneys, of actual and reasonable out-of-pocket expenditures incurred directly in connection with the prosecution of the action....

(c) The action shall not be dismissed or compromised without the approval of the Court....

Besides the greater procedural complexity of derivative litigation, other important differences exist (as explained in ALI § 7.01 Comment *d*):

First, a derivative action distributes the recovery more broadly and evenly than a direct action. Because the recovery in a derivative action goes to the corporation, creditors and others having a stake in the corporation benefit financially from a derivative action and not from a direct one. Similarly, although all shareholders share equally, if indirectly, in the corporate recovery that follows a successful derivative action, the injured shareholders other than the plaintiff will share in the recovery from a direct action only if the action is a class action brought on behalf of all these shareholders.

Second, once finally concluded, a derivative action will have a preclusive effect that spares the corporation and the defendants from being exposed to a multiplicity of suits.

Third, a successful plaintiff is entitled to an award of attorneys' fees in a derivative action directly from the corporation, but in a direct action the plaintiff must generally look to the fund, if any, created by the action.

Finally, characterizing the suit as derivative may entitle the board to take over the action or to seek dismissal of the action.... Thus, in some circumstances the characterization of the action will determine the available defenses.

In practice, the most important result of characterizing an action as direct or derivative is the tendency for derivative actions to be more complex procedurally and to impose restrictions on plaintiffs. For these reasons, the plaintiff usually wishes to characterize the action as direct, while the defendant prefers to characterize it as derivative. Courts are generally more prepared to permit the plaintiff to characterize the action as direct when the plaintiff is seeking only injunctive or prospective relief. In such situations, the policy considerations favoring a derivative action are less persuasive, because typically the requested relief will not involve significant financial damages against corporate officials, the period during which the corporation is exposed to multiple lawsuits will be relatively brief, and the relief will benefit all shareholders proportionately.

Section II
Distinguishing Derivative Suits

A threshold issue in shareholder litigation is whether a particular action is personal or derivative. Personal direct actions are those brought by shareholders to enforce their own rights or to remedy their own injuries. Derivative actions are brought by shareholders, in the name of their corporation, to enforce a right of the corporation or to remedy a wrong inflicted on the corporation. Each type of lawsuit has distinctive procedural requirements, yet it is sometimes difficult to distinguish between the two types of suits.

A number of cases have considered the following claims to be direct actions: (a) a claim to dividends, (b) the right to inspect corporate books and records, (c) the right to vote, (d) a claim that a transaction will improperly dilute the shareholder's proportionate interest in the corporation or violate preemptive rights, (e) claims that corporate officials sought to "entrench" themselves or manipulate the corporate machinery so as to frustrate plaintiff's attempt to secure representation or obtain control, (f) a claim that proposed corporate action should be enjoined as *ultra vires*, fraudulent, or designed to harm a specific shareholder illegitimately, (g) a claim that minority shareholders have been oppressed, and (h) claims that a proposed corporate control transaction, recapitalization, redemption, or similar defensive transaction unfairly affects the plaintiff shareholder.

Tooley v. Donaldson, Lufkin, & Jenrette, Inc.

Delaware Supreme Court
845 A.2d 1031 (2004)

Veasey, Chief Justice:

Plaintiff-stockholders brought a purported class action in the Court of Chancery, alleging that the members of the board of directors of their corporation breached their fiduciary duties by agreeing to a 22-day delay in closing a proposed merger. Plaintiffs contend that the delay harmed them due to the lost time-value of the cash paid for their shares. The Court of Chancery granted the defendants' motion to dismiss on the sole ground that the claims were, "at most," claims of the corporation being asserted derivatively. They were, thus, held not to be direct claims of the stockholders, individually. Thereupon, the Court held that the plaintiffs lost their standing to bring this action when they tendered their shares in connection with the merger.

Although the trial court's legal analysis of whether the complaint alleges a direct or derivative claim reflects some concepts in our prior jurisprudence, we believe those concepts are not helpful and should be regarded as erroneous. We set forth in this Opinion the law to be applied henceforth in determining whether a stockholder's claim is derivative or direct. That issue must turn solely on the following questions: (1) who suffered the alleged harm (the corporation or the suing stockholders, individually); and (2) who would receive the benefit of any recovery or other remedy (the corporation or the stockholders, individually)?

To the extent we have concluded that the trial court's analysis of the direct vs. derivative dichotomy should be regarded as erroneous, we view the error as harmless in this case because the complaint does not set forth any claim upon which relief can be granted. In its opinion, the Court of Chancery properly found on the facts pleaded that the plaintiffs have no separate contractual right to the alleged lost time-value of money arising out of extensions in the closing of a tender offer. . . .

Patrick Tooley and Kevin Lewis are former minority stockholders of Donaldson, Lufkin & Jenrette, Inc. (DLJ), a Delaware corporation engaged in investment banking. [Credit Suisse agreed to acquire DLJ stock owned by a significant DLJ shareholder and then merge DLJ into a Credit Suisse subsidiary. The merger agreement contemplated a time frame for completing the transaction that Credit Suisse and/or DLJ could extend. Plaintiffs complained that DLJ's board extended the deadline, for 22 days, in violation of its fiduciary duties.] They claim[ed] damages representing the time-value of money lost through the delay . . .

The ruling before us on appeal is that the plaintiffs' claim is derivative, purportedly brought on behalf of DLJ. The Court of Chancery, relying upon our confusing jurisprudence on the direct/derivative dichotomy, based its dismissal on the following ground: "Because this delay affected all DLJ shareholders equally, plaintiffs' injury was not a special injury, and this action is, thus, a derivative action, at most."

Plaintiffs argue that they have suffered a "special injury" because they had an alleged contractual right to receive the merger consideration of $90 per share without suffering the 22-day delay arising out of the extensions under the merger agreement. But the trial court's opinion convincingly demonstrates that plaintiffs had no such contractual right. . . .

That conclusion could have ended the case because it portended a definitive ruling that plaintiffs have no claim whatsoever on the facts alleged. But the defendants chose to argue, and the trial court chose to decide, the standing issue, which is predicated on an assertion that this claim is a derivative one asserted on behalf of the corporation, DLJ.

The Court of Chancery correctly noted that "[t]he Court will independently examine the nature of the wrong alleged and any potential relief to make its own determination of the suit's classification. . . . Plaintiffs' classification of the suit is not binding." The trial court's analysis was hindered, however, because it focused on the confusing concept of "special injury" as the test for determining whether a claim is derivative or direct. . . .

In our view, the concept of "special injury" that appears in some Supreme Court and Court of Chancery cases is not helpful to a proper analytical distinction between direct and derivative actions. We now disapprove the use of the concept of "special injury" as a tool in that analysis.

The analysis must be based solely on the following questions: Who suffered the alleged harm—the corporation or the suing stockholder individually—and who would receive the benefit of the recovery or other remedy? This simple analysis is well imbedded in our jurisprudence, but some cases have complicated it by injection of the amorphous and confusing concept of "special injury." ...

The derivative suit has been generally described as "one of the most interesting and ingenious of accountability mechanisms for large formal organizations." *Kramer v. Western Pacific Industries, Inc.*, 546 A.2d at 351 (quoting R. Clark, Corporate Law 639–40 (1986)). It enables a stockholder to bring suit on behalf of the corporation for harm done to the corporation. Because a derivative suit is being brought on behalf of the corporation, the recovery, if any, must go to the corporation. A stockholder who is directly injured, however, does retain the right to bring an individual action for injuries affecting his or her legal rights as a stockholder. Such a claim is distinct from an injury caused to the corporation alone. In such individual suits, the recovery or other relief flows directly to the stockholders, not to the corporation.

Determining whether an action is derivative or direct is sometimes difficult and has many legal consequences, some of which may have an expensive impact on the parties to the action. For example, if an action is derivative, the plaintiffs are then required to comply with the requirements of Court of Chancery Rule 23.1, that the stockholder: (a) retain ownership of the shares throughout the litigation; (b) make presuit demand on the board; and (c) obtain court approval of any settlement. Further, the recovery, if any, flows only to the corporation. The decision whether a suit is direct or derivative may be outcome-determinative. Therefore, it is necessary that a standard to distinguish such actions be clear, simple and consistently articulated and applied by our courts.

In *Elster v. American Airlines, Inc.*, 100 A.2d 219, 222 (Del. Ch. 1953), the stockholder sought to enjoin the grant and exercise of stock options because they would result in a dilution of her stock personally. In *Elster*, the alleged injury was found to be derivative, not direct, because it was essentially a claim of mismanagement of corporate assets. Then came the complication in the analysis: The Court held that where the alleged injury is to both the corporation and to the stockholder, the stockholder must allege a "special injury" to maintain a direct action. The Court did not define "special injury," however. By implication, decisions in later cases have interpreted *Elster* to mean that a "special injury" is alleged where the wrong is inflicted upon the stockholder alone or where the stockholder complains of a wrong affecting a particular right. Examples would be preemptive rights as a stockholder, rights involving control of the corporation or a wrong affecting the stockholder, qua individual holder, and not the corporation.

In *Bokat v. Getty Oil Co.*, 262 A.2d 246 (Del. 1970), a stockholder of a subsidiary brought suit against the director of the parent corporation for causing the subsidiary to invest its resources wastefully, resulting in a loss to the subsidiary. The claim in *Bokat* was essentially for mismanagement of corporate assets. Therefore, the Court held that any recovery must be sought on behalf of the corporation, and the claim was, thus, found to be derivative.

In describing how a court may distinguish direct and derivative actions, the *Bokat* Court stated that a suit must be maintained derivatively if the injury falls equally upon all stockholders. Experience has shown this concept to be confusing and inaccurate. It is confusing because it appears to have been intended to address the fact that an injury to the corporation tends to diminish each share of stock equally because corporate assets or their value are diminished. In that sense, the indirect injury to the stockholders arising out of the harm to the corporation comes about solely by virtue of their stockholdings. It does not arise out of any independent or direct harm to the stockholders, individually. That concept is also inaccurate because a direct, individual claim of stockholders that does not depend on harm to the corporation can also fall on all stockholders equally, without the claim thereby becoming a derivative claim.

In *Lipton v. News International, PLC.*, 514 A.2d 1075, 1078 (Del. 1986), this Court applied the "special injury" test. There, a stockholder began acquiring shares in the defendant corporation presumably to gain control of the corporation. In response, the defendant corporation agreed to an exchange of its shares with a friendly buyer. Due to the exchange and a supermajority voting requirement on certain stockholder actions, the management of the defendant corporation acquired a veto power over any change in management.

The *Lipton* Court concluded that the critical analytical issue in distinguishing direct and derivative actions is whether a "special injury" has been alleged. There, the Court found a "special injury" because the board's manipulation worked an injury upon the plaintiff-stockholder unlike the injury suffered by other stockholders. That was because the plaintiff-stockholder was actively seeking to gain control of the defendant corporation. Therefore, the Court found that the claim was direct. Ironically, the Court could have reached the same correct result by simply concluding that the manipulation directly and individually harmed the stockholders, without injuring the corporation.

In *Kramer v. Western Pacific Industries, Inc.*, 546 A.2d 348, 352 (Del. 1988), this Court found to be derivative a stockholder's challenge to corporate transactions that occurred six months immediately preceding a buy-out merger. The stockholders challenged the decision by the board of directors to grant stock options and golden parachutes to management. The stockholders argued that the claim was direct because their share of the proceeds from the buy-out sale was reduced by the resources used to pay for the options and golden parachutes. Once again, our analysis was that to bring a direct action, the stockholder must allege something other than an injury resulting from a wrong to the corporation. We interpreted *Elster* to require the court to determine the nature of the action based on the "nature of the wrong alleged" and the relief that could result. That was, and is, the correct test. The claim in *Kramer* was essentially for mismanagement of corporate assets. Therefore, we found the claims to be derivative. That was the correct outcome.

In *Grimes v. Donald*, 673 A.2d 1207, 1213 (Del. 1996), we sought to distinguish between direct and derivative actions in the context of employment agreements granted to certain officers that allegedly caused the board to abdicate its authority. Relying on the *Elster* and *Kramer* precedents that the court must look to the nature of the wrong and to whom the relief will go, we concluded that the plaintiff was not seeking to recover any damages for injury to the corporation. Rather, the plaintiff was seeking a declaration of the invalidity of the agreements on the ground that the board had abdicated its responsibility to the stockholders. Thus, based on the relief requested, we affirmed the judgment of the Court of Chancery that the plaintiff was entitled to pursue a direct action.

Grimes was followed by *Parnes v. Bally Entertainment Corp.*, which held, among other things, that the injury to the stockholders must be "independent of any injury to the corporation." 722 A.2d 1243, 1245 (Del. 1999). [N]either *Grimes* nor *Parnes* applies the purported "special injury" test.

Thus, two confusing propositions have encumbered our case law governing the direct/derivative distinction. The "special injury" concept, applied in cases such as *Lipton*, can be confusing in identifying the nature of the action. The same is true of the proposition that stems from *Bokat*—that an action cannot be direct if all stockholders are equally affected or unless the stockholder's injury is separate and distinct from that suffered by other stockholders. The proper analysis has been and should remain that stated in *Grimes*; *Kramer* and *Parnes*. That is, a court should look to the nature of the wrong and to whom the relief should go. The stockholder's claimed direct injury must be independent of any alleged injury to the corporation. The stockholder must demonstrate that the duty breached was owed to the stockholder and that he or she can prevail without showing an injury to the corporation.

In this case it cannot be concluded that the complaint alleges a derivative claim. There is no derivative claim asserting injury to the corporate entity. There is no relief that would go the corporation. Accordingly, there is no basis to hold that the complaint states a derivative claim.

But, it does not necessarily follow that the complaint states a direct, individual claim. While the complaint purports to set forth a direct claim, in reality, it states no claim at all. The trial court analyzed the complaint and correctly concluded that it does not claim that the plaintiffs have any rights that have been injured. Their rights have not yet ripened. The contractual claim is nonexistent until it is ripe, and that claim will not be ripe until the terms of the merger are fulfilled, including the extensions of the closing at issue here. Therefore, there is no direct claim stated in the complaint before us.

Accordingly, the complaint was properly dismissed....

Notes and Questions

1. Look back over the cases you have read in this casebook. Make a list of at least five that were derivative shareholder actions and five more properly characterized as direct.

2. Can you also make a list of five cases that defy tidy classification under the framework stated in *Tooley*? How robust or successful is the *Tooley* opinion's analytical scheme? Is it better than probing issues like "special injury"?

Section III
The Demand Requirement

Under both federal and most state laws, as illustrated by Fed. R. Civ. P. 23.1, shareholders in a derivative action are required to ask the directors to pursue the lawsuit on the corporation's behalf, unless the plaintiff shareholders can demonstrate a sufficient reason for their failure to make such a "demand." As explored in the following materials, courts will often excuse demand if it would be "futile."

The materials in this section and the section on special litigation committees also revisit the business judgment rule in the context of shareholder derivative litigation. Consider, for example, that corporate directors may make a number of decisions in this context, including whether the corporation should (1) pursue the litigation initiated by the shareholders, (2) seek a dismissal of the derivative suit, or (3) address and, if appropriate, internally remedy the allegations raised by the shareholders.

Aronson v. Lewis
Delaware Supreme Court
473 A.2d 805 (1984)

Moore, Justice:

… [W]hen is a stockholder's demand upon a board of directors, to redress an alleged wrong to the corporation, excused as futile prior to the filing of a derivative suit? We granted this interlocutory appeal to the defendants, Meyers Parking System, Inc. (Meyers), a Delaware corporation, and its directors, to review the Court of Chancery's denial of their motion to dismiss this action, pursuant to Chancery Rule 23.1, for the plaintiff's failure to make such a demand or otherwise demonstrate its futility. The Vice Chancellor ruled that plaintiff's allegations raised a "reasonable inference" that the directors' action was unprotected by the business judgment rule. Thus, the board could not have impartially considered and acted upon the demand.

We cannot agree with this formulation of the concept of demand futility. In our view demand can only be excused where facts are alleged with particularity which create a reasonable doubt that the directors' action was entitled to the protections of the business judgment rule. Because the plaintiff failed to make a demand, and to allege facts with particularity indicating that such demand would be futile, we reverse the Court of Chancery and remand with instructions that plaintiff be granted leave to amend the complaint.

I

The issues of demand futility rest upon the allegations of the complaint. The plaintiff, Harry Lewis, is a stockholder of Meyers. The defendants are Meyers and its ten directors, some of whom are also company officers.

In 1979, Prudential Building Maintenance Corp. (Prudential) spun off its shares of Meyers to Prudential's stockholders. Prior thereto Meyers was a wholly owned subsidiary of Prudential. Meyers provides parking lot facilities and related services throughout the country. Its stock is actively traded over-the-counter.

This suit challenges certain transactions between Meyers and one of its directors, Leo Fink, who owns 47% of its outstanding stock. Plaintiff claims that these transactions were approved only because Fink personally selected each director and officer of Meyers.

Prior to January 1, 1981, Fink had an employment agreement with Prudential which provided that upon retirement he was to become a consultant to that company for ten years. This provision became operable when Fink retired in April 1980. Thereafter, Meyers agreed with Prudential to share Fink's consulting services and reimburse Prudential for 25% of the fees paid Fink. Under this arrangement Meyers paid Prudential $48,332 in 1980 and $45,832 in 1981.

On January 1, 1981, the defendants approved an employment agreement between Meyers and Fink for a five year term with provision for automatic renewal each year thereafter, indefinitely. Meyers agreed to pay Fink $150,000 per year, plus a bonus of 5% of its pre-tax profits over $2,400,000. Fink could terminate the contract at any time, but Meyers could do so only upon six months' notice. At termination, Fink was to become a consultant to Meyers and be paid $150,000 per year for the first three years, $125,000 for the next three years, and $100,000 thereafter for life. Death benefits were also included. Fink agreed to devote his best efforts and substantially his entire business time to advancing Meyers' interests. The agreement also provided that Fink's compensation was not to be affected by any inability to perform services on Meyers' behalf. Fink was 75 years old when his employment agreement with Meyers was approved by the directors. There is no claim that he was, or is, in poor health.

Additionally, the Meyers board approved and made interest-free loans to Fink totaling $225,000. These loans were unpaid and outstanding as of August 1982 when the complaint was filed. At oral argument defendants' counsel represented that these loans had been repaid in full.

The complaint charges that these transactions had "no valid business purpose," and were a "waste of corporate assets" because the amounts to be paid are "grossly excessive," that Fink performs "no or little services," and because of his "advanced age" cannot be "expected to perform any such services." The plaintiff also charges that the existence of the Prudential consulting agreement with Fink prevents him from providing his "best efforts" on Meyers' behalf. Finally, it is alleged that the loans to Fink were in reality "additional compensation" without any "consideration" or "benefit" to Meyers.

The complaint alleged that no demand had been made on the Meyers board because:

[Paragraph] 13.... such attempt would be futile for the following reasons:

(a) All of the directors in office are named as defendants herein and they have participated in, expressly approved and/or acquiesced in, and are personally liable for, the wrongs complained of herein.

(b) Defendant Fink, having selected each director, controls and dominates every member of the Board and every officer of Meyers.

(c) Institution of this action by present directors would require the defendant-directors to sue themselves, thereby placing the conduct of this action in hostile hands and preventing its effective prosecution.

The relief sought included the cancellation of the Meyers-Fink employment contract and an accounting by the directors, including Fink, for all damage sustained by Meyers and for all profits derived by the directors and Fink....

III

The defendants make two arguments, one policy-oriented and the other, factual. First, they assert that the demand requirement embraces the policy that directors, rather than stockholders, manage the affairs of the corporation. They contend that this fundamental principle requires the strict construction and enforcement of Chancery Rule 23.1. Second, the defendants point to four of plaintiff's basic allegations and argue that they lack the factual particularity necessary to excuse demand. Concerning the allegation that Fink dominated and controlled the Meyers board, the defendants point to the absence of any facts explaining how he "selected each director." With respect to Fink's 47% stock interest, the defendants say that absent other facts this is insufficient to indicate domination and control. Regarding the claim of hostility to the plaintiff's suit, because defendants would have to sue themselves, the latter assert that this bootstrap argument ignores the possibility that the directors have other alternatives, such as cancelling the challenged agreement. As for the allegation that directorial approval of the agreement excused demand, the defendants reply that such a claim is insufficient, because it would obviate the demand requirement in almost every case. The effect would be to subvert the managerial power of a board of directors. Finally, as to the provision guaranteeing Fink's compensation, even if he is unable to perform any services, the defendants contend that the trial court read this out of context. Based upon the foregoing, the defendants conclude that the plaintiff's allegations fall far short of the factual particularity required by Rule 23.1.

IV
A

A cardinal precept of the General Corporation Law of the State of Delaware is that directors, rather than shareholders, manage the business and affairs of the corporation. 8 Del. C. § 141(a).... The existence and exercise of this power carries with it certain fundamental fiduciary obligations to the corporation and its shareholders. Moreover, a stockholder is not powerless to challenge director action which results in harm to the corporation. The machinery of corporate democracy and the derivative suit are potent tools to redress the conduct of a torpid or unfaithful management. The derivative action developed in equity to enable shareholders to sue in the corporation's name where those in control of the company refused to assert a claim belonging to it. The nature of the action is two-fold. First, it is the equivalent of a suit by the shareholders to compel the corporation to sue. Second, it is a suit by the corporation, asserted by the shareholders on its behalf, against those liable to it.

By its very nature the derivative action impinges on the managerial freedom of directors. Hence, the demand requirement of Chancery Rule 23.1 exists at the threshold, first to insure that a stockholder exhausts his intracorporate remedies, and then to provide a safeguard against strike suits. Thus, by promoting this form of alternate dispute resolution, rather than immediate recourse to litigation, the demand requirement is a recognition of the fundamental precept that directors manage the business and affairs of corporations.

In our view the entire question of demand futility is inextricably bound to issues of business judgment and the standards of that doctrine's applicability. The business judgment rule is an acknowledgment of the managerial prerogatives of Delaware directors under Section 141(a). It is a presumption that in making a business decision the directors of a corporation acted on an informed basis, in good faith and in the honest belief that the action taken was in the best interests of the company. Absent an abuse of discretion, that judgment will be respected by the courts. The burden is on the party challenging the decision to establish facts rebutting the presumption.

The function of the business judgment rule is of paramount significance in the context of a derivative action. It comes into play in several ways—in addressing a demand, in the determination of demand futility, in efforts by independent disinterested directors to dismiss the action as inimical to the corporation's best interests, and generally, as a defense to the merits of the suit. However, in each of these circumstances there are certain common principles governing the application and operation of the rule.

First, its protections can only be claimed by disinterested directors whose conduct otherwise meets the tests of business judgment. From the standpoint of interest, this means that directors can neither appear on both sides of a transaction nor expect to derive any personal financial benefit from it in the sense of self-dealing, as opposed to a benefit which devolves upon the corporation or all stockholders generally. Thus, if such director interest is present, and the transaction is not approved by a majority consisting of the disinterested directors, then the business judgment rule has no application whatever in determining demand futility.

Second, to invoke the rule's protection directors have a duty to inform themselves, prior to making a business decision, of all material information reasonably available to them. Having become so informed, they must then act with requisite care in the discharge of their duties. While the Delaware cases use a variety of terms to describe the applicable standard of care, our analysis satisfies us that under the business judgment rule director liability is predicated upon concepts of gross negligence.

However, it should be noted that the business judgment rule operates only in the context of director action. Technically speaking, it has no role where directors have either abdicated their functions, or absent a conscious decision, failed to act. But it also follows that under applicable principles, a conscious decision to refrain from acting may nonetheless be a valid exercise of business judgment and enjoy the protections of the rule....

Delaware courts have addressed the issue of demand futility on several earlier occasions. The rule emerging from these decisions is that where officers and directors are under an influence which sterilizes their discretion, they cannot be considered proper persons to conduct litigation on behalf of the corporation. Thus, demand would be futile.

However, those cases cannot be taken to mean that any board approval of a challenged transaction automatically connotes "hostile interest" and "guilty participation" by directors, or some other form of sterilizing influence upon them. Were that so, the demand requirements of our law would be meaningless, leaving the clear mandate of Chancery Rule 23.1 devoid of its purpose and substance.

The trial court correctly recognized that demand futility is inextricably bound to issues of business judgment, but stated the test to be based on allegations of fact, which, if true, "show that there is a reasonable inference" the business judgment rule is not applicable for purposes of a pre-suit demand.

The problem with this formulation is the concept of reasonable inferences to be drawn against a board of directors based on allegations in a complaint. As is clear from this case, and the conclusory allegations upon which the Vice Chancellor relied, demand futility becomes virtually automatic under such a test. Bearing in mind the presumptions with which director action is cloaked, we believe that the matter must be approached in a more balanced way.

Our view is that in determining demand futility the Court of Chancery in the proper exercise of its discretion must decide whether, under the particularized facts alleged, a reasonable doubt is created that: (1) the directors are disinterested and independent [or] (2) the challenged transaction was otherwise the product of a valid exercise of business judgment. Hence, the Court of Chancery must make two inquiries, one into the independence and disinterestedness of the directors and the other into the substantive nature of the challenged transaction and the board's approval thereof. As to the latter inquiry the court does not assume that the transaction is a wrong to the corporation requiring corrective steps by the board. Rather, the alleged wrong is substantively reviewed against the factual background alleged in the complaint. As to the former inquiry, directorial independence and disinterestedness, the court reviews the factual allegations to decide whether they raise a reasonable doubt, as a threshold matter, that the protections of the business judgment rule are available to the board. Certainly, if this is an "interested" director transaction, such that the business judgment rule is inapplicable to the board majority approving the transaction, then the inquiry ceases. In that event futility of demand has been established by any objective or subjective standard.[1] This includes situations involving self-dealing directors.

---

1. [8] We recognize that drawing the line at a majority of the board may be an arguably arbitrary dividing point. Critics will charge that we are ignoring the structural bias common to corporate boards throughout America, as well as the other unseen socialization processes cutting against independent discussion and decisionmaking in the boardroom. The difficulty with structural bias in a demand [futility] case is simply one of establishing it in the complaint for purposes of Rule 23.1. We are satisfied that discretionary review by the Court of Chancery of complaints alleging specific facts pointing to bias on a particular board will be sufficient for determining demand futility.

However, the mere threat of personal liability for approving a questioned transaction, standing alone, is insufficient to challenge either the independence or disinterestedness of directors, although in rare cases a transaction may be so egregious on its face that board approval cannot meet the test of business judgment, and a substantial likelihood of director liability therefore exists. In sum the entire review is factual in nature. The Court of Chancery in the exercise of its sound discretion must be satisfied that a plaintiff has alleged facts with particularity which, taken as true, support a reasonable doubt that the challenged transaction was the product of a valid exercise of business judgment. Only in that context is demand excused.

B

Having outlined the legal framework within which these issues are to be determined, we consider plaintiff's claims of futility here: Fink's domination and control of the directors, board approval of the Fink-Meyers employment agreement, and board hostility to the plaintiff's derivative action due to the directors' status as defendants.

Plaintiff's claim that Fink dominates and controls the Meyers' board is based on: (1) Fink's 47% ownership of Meyers' outstanding stock, and (2) that he "personally selected" each Meyers director. Plaintiff also alleges that mere approval of the employment agreement illustrates Fink's domination and control of the board. In addition, plaintiff argued on appeal that 47% stock ownership, though less than a majority, constituted control given the large number of shares outstanding, 1,245,745.

Such contentions do not support any claim under Delaware law that these directors lack independence. In *Kaplan v. Centex Corp.*, Del. Ch., 284 A.2d 119 (1971), the Court of Chancery stated that "[s]tock ownership alone, at least when it amounts to less than a majority, is not sufficient proof of domination or control." *Id.* at 123. Moreover, in the demand context even proof of majority ownership of a company does not strip the directors of the presumptions of independence, and that their acts have been taken in good faith and in the best interests of the corporation. There must be coupled with the allegation of control such facts as would demonstrate that through personal or other relationships the directors are beholden to the controlling person. To date the principal decisions dealing with the issue of control or domination arose only after a full trial on the merits. Thus, they are distinguishable in the demand context unless similar particularized facts are alleged to meet the test of Chancery Rule 23.1.

The requirement of director independence inheres in the conception and rationale of the business judgment rule. The presumption of propriety that flows from an exercise of business judgment is based in part on this unyielding precept. Independence means that a director's decision is based on the corporate merits of the subject before the board rather than extraneous considerations or influences. While directors may confer, debate, and resolve their differences through compromise, or by reasonable reliance upon the expertise of their colleagues and other qualified persons, the end result, nonetheless, must be that each director has brought his or her own informed business judgment to bear with specificity upon the corporate merits of the issues without regard for or succumbing to influences which convert an otherwise valid business decision into a faithless act.

Thus, it is not enough to charge that a director was nominated by or elected at the behest of those controlling the outcome of a corporate election. That is the usual way a person becomes a corporate director. It is the care, attention and sense of individual responsibility to the performance of one's duties, not the method of election, that generally touches on independence.

We conclude that in the demand-futile [sic] context a plaintiff charging domination and control of one or more directors must allege particularized facts manifesting "a direction of corporate conduct in such a way as to comport with the wishes or interests of the corporation (or persons) doing the controlling." *Kaplan*, 284 A.2d at 123. The shorthand shibboleth of "dominated and controlled directors" is insufficient. In recognizing that *Kaplan* was decided after trial and full discovery, we stress that the plaintiff need only allege specific facts; he need not plead evidence....

Here, plaintiff has not alleged any facts sufficient to support a claim of control. The personal-selection-of-directors allegation stands alone, unsupported. At best it is a conclusion devoid of factual support. The causal link between Fink's control and approval of the employment agreement is alluded to, but nowhere specified. The director's approval, alone, does not establish control, even in the face of Fink's 47% stock ownership. The claim that Fink is unlikely to perform any services under the agreement, because of his age, and his conflicting consultant work with Prudential, adds nothing to the control claim. Therefore, we cannot conclude that the complaint factually particularizes any circumstances of control and domination to overcome the presumption of board independence, and thus render the demand futile.

C

Turning to the board's approval of the Meyers-Fink employment agreement, plaintiff's argument is simple: all of the Meyers directors are named defendants, because they approved the wasteful agreement; if plaintiff prevails on the merits all the directors will be jointly and severally liable; therefore, the directors' interest in avoiding personal liability automatically and absolutely disqualifies them from passing on a shareholder's demand.

Such allegations are conclusory at best. In Delaware mere directorial approval of a transaction, absent particularized facts supporting a breach of fiduciary duty claim, or otherwise establishing the lack of independence or disinterestedness of a majority of the directors, is insufficient to excuse demand. Here, plaintiff's suit is premised on the notion that the Meyers-Fink employment agreement was a waste of corporate assets. So, the argument goes, by approving such waste the directors now face potential personal liability, thereby rendering futile any demand on them to bring suit. Unfortunately, plaintiff's claim falls in its initial premise. The complaint does not allege particularized facts indicating that the agreement is a waste of corporate assets. Indeed, the complaint as now drafted may not even state a cause of action, given the directors' broad corporate power to fix the compensation of officers.

In essence, the plaintiff alleged a lack of consideration flowing from Fink to Meyers, since the employment agreement provided that compensation was not contingent on Fink's ability to perform any services. The bare assertion that Fink performed "little or no services" was plaintiff's conclusion based solely on Fink's age and the *existence* of the Fink-Prudential employment agreement. As for Meyers' loans to Fink, beyond the bare allegation that they were made, the complaint does not allege facts indicating the wastefulness of such arrangements. Again, the mere existence of such loans, given the broad corporate powers conferred by Delaware law, does not even state a claim....

D

Plaintiff's final argument is the incantation that demand is excused because the directors otherwise would have to sue themselves, thereby placing the conduct of the litigation in hostile hands and preventing its effective prosecution. This bootstrap argument has been made to and dismissed by other courts. Its acceptance would effectively abrogate Rule 23.1 and weaken the managerial power of directors. Unless facts are alleged with particularity to overcome the presumptions of independence and a proper exercise of business judgment, in which case the directors could not be expected to sue themselves, a bare claim of this sort raises no legally cognizable issue under Delaware corporate law.

V

In sum, we conclude that the plaintiff has failed to allege facts with particularity indicating that the Meyers directors were tainted by interest, lacked independence, or took action contrary to Meyers' best interests in order to create a reasonable doubt as to the applicability of the business judgment rule. Only in the presence of such a reasonable doubt may a demand be deemed futile. Hence, we reverse the Court of Chancery's denial of the motion to dismiss, and remand with instructions that plaintiff be granted leave to amend his complaint to bring it into compliance with Rule 23.1 based on the principles we have announced today.

Notes and Questions

1. On remand, the court held that demand was excused because the plaintiff's amended complaint alleged sufficient facts to create a reasonable doubt regarding the board's independence. *Lewis v. Aronson*, Del. Ch. C.A. No. 6919, Hartnett, V.C. (May 1, 1985).

2. The Supreme Court of Delaware elaborated on the pleading requirements of *Aronson* in *Delaware County Employees Retirement Fund v. Sanchez*, 124 A.3d 1017 (2015), as follows:

> Determining whether a plaintiff has pled facts supporting an inference that a director cannot act independently of an interested director for purposes of demand excusal under *Aronson* can be difficult. And this case illustrates that. But in that determination, it is important that the trial court consider all the particularized facts pled by the plaintiffs about the relationships between the director and the interested party in their totality and not in isolation from each other, and draw all reasonable inferences from the totality of those facts in favor of the plaintiffs. In this case, the plaintiffs pled not only that the director had a close friendship of over half a century with the interested party,

but that consistent with that deep friendship, the director's primary employment (and that of his brother) was as an executive of a company over which
the interested party had substantial influence. These, and other facts of a
similar nature, when taken together, support an inference that the director
could not act independently of the interested party. Because of that, the
plaintiffs pled facts supporting an inference that a majority of the board who
approved the interested transaction they challenged could not consider a demand impartially.

3. MBCA § 7.42 and ALI § 7.03 offer an alternative approach to Delaware law.
Rather than assessing whether demand would be futile in certain circumstances, they
provide that shareholders should always make a written demand upon the board of
directors ("universal demand"). Under ALI § 7.03(b), demand should be excused
"only if the plaintiff makes a specific showing that irreparable injury to the corporation
would otherwise result."

As explained in Model Act § 7.42 Official Comment:

Section 7.42 requires a written demand on the corporation in all cases. The
demand must be made at least 90 days before commencement of suit unless
irreparable injury to the corporation would result. This approach has been
adopted for two reasons. First, even though no director may be independent,
the demand will give the board of directors the opportunity to reexamine
the act complained of in the light of a potential lawsuit and take corrective
action. Secondly, the provision eliminates the time and expense of the litigants
and the court involved in litigating the question whether demand is required.
It is believed that requiring a demand in all cases does not impose an onerous
burden since a relatively short waiting period of 90 days is provided and this
period may be shortened if irreparable injury to the corporation would result
by waiting for the expiration of the 90 day period. Moreover, the cases in
which demand is excused are relatively rare. Many plaintiffs' counsel as a
matter of practice make a demand in all cases rather than litigate the issue
whether demand is excused.

4. You also may want to consider New York's articulation of demand futility in
Marx v. Akers, 666 N.E.2d 1034, 1039–40 (N.Y. 1996):

Although instructive, neither the universal demand requirement nor the
Delaware approach to demand futility is adopted here. Since New York's demand requirement is codified in Business Corporation Law § 626(c), a universal
demand may only be adopted by the Legislature. Delaware's approach, which
resembles New York law in some respects, incorporates a "reasonable doubt"
standard which has provoked criticism as confusing and overly subjective....

[Under New York law,] conclusory allegations of wrongdoing against each
member of the board are not sufficient to excuse demand ... [Various courts]
have misinterpreted [*Barr v. Wackman*, 329 N.E.2d 180 (1975),] as excusing
demand whenever a majority of the board members who approved the transaction are named as defendants.... The problem with such an approach is

that it permits plaintiffs to frame their complaint in such a way as to automatically excuse demand, thereby allowing the exception to swallow the rule.

We thus deem it necessary to offer the following elaboration of *Barr*'s demand/futility standard. (1) Demand is excused because of futility when a complaint alleges with particularity that a majority of the board of directors is interested in the challenged transaction. Director interest may either be self-interest in the transaction at issue or a loss of independence because a director with no direct interest in a transaction is "controlled" by a self-interested director. (2) Demand is excused because of futility when a complaint alleges with particularity that the board of directors did not fully inform themselves about the challenged transaction to the extent reasonably appropriate under the circumstances. (3) Demand is excused because of futility when a complaint alleges with particularity that the challenged transaction was so egregious on its face that it could not have been the product of sound business judgment of the directors.

Section IV
Special Litigation Committees

The special litigation committee has become a formidable obstacle to shareholders who wish to pursue derivative suits. When some impropriety is alleged against the officers or directors, the board of directors often appoints a special litigation committee. This committee typically consists of directors whose conduct is not in question, and they are asked to determine whether the corporation should bring suit. Boards also frequently appoint such committees after a shareholders' derivative action has been filed. In those situations, the committee's task is to decide whether the corporation should seek a dismissal of the suit.

The following cases illustrate alternative ways to conduct judicial review of directors' authority to terminate derivative suits. The first principal case presents New York's approach and the second principal case presents Delaware law. Several note cases afterward present variations on these two principal alternatives. Consider whether, and if so how, these courts have modified the business judgment rule. Also consider which approach is superior and, in doing so, consider whether the suitable approach may vary with states, such that what is optimal for Delaware differs from what is optimal for New York, for instance.

Auerbach v. Bennett
New York Court of Appeals
393 N.E.2d 994 (1979)

JONES, JUDGE:

In the summer of 1975 the management of General Telephone & Electronics Corporation, in response to reports that numerous other multinational companies had made questionable payments to public officials or political parties in foreign countries, directed that an internal preliminary investigation be made to ascertain whether that corporation had engaged in similar transactions. On the basis of the report of this survey, received in October, 1975, management brought the issue to the attention of the corporation's board of directors. At a meeting held on November 6 of that year the board referred the matter to the board's audit committee. The audit committee retained as its special counsel the Washington, D.C., law firm of Wilmer, Cutler & Pickering which had not previously acted as counsel to the corporation. With the assistance of such special counsel and Arthur Andersen & Co., the corporation's outside auditors, the audit committee engaged in an investigation into the corporation's worldwide operations, focusing on whether, in the period January 1, 1971 to December 31, 1975, corporate funds had been (1) paid directly or indirectly to any political party or person or to any officer, employee, shareholder or director of any governmental or private customer, or (2) used to reimburse any officer of the corporation or other person for such payments.

On March 4, 1976 the audit committee released its report which was filed with the Securities and Exchange Commission and disclosed to the corporation's shareholders in a proxy statement prior to the annual meeting of shareholders held in April, 1976. The audit committee reported that it had found evidence that in the period from 1971 to 1975 the corporation or its subsidiaries had made payments abroad and in the United States constituting bribes and kickbacks in amounts perhaps totaling more than 11 million dollars and that some of the individual defendant directors had been personally involved in certain of the transactions.

Almost immediately Auerbach, a shareholder in the corporation, instituted the present shareholders' derivative action on behalf of the corporation against the corporation's directors, Arthur Andersen & Co. and the corporation. The complaint alleged that in connection with the transactions reported by the audit committee defendants, present and former members of the corporation's board of directors and Arthur Andersen & Co., are liable to the corporation for breach of their duties to the corporation and should be made to account for payments made in those transactions.

On April 21, 1976 the board of directors of the corporation adopted a resolution creating a special litigation committee "for the purpose of establishing a point of contact between the Board of Directors and the Corporation's General Counsel concerning the position to be taken by the Corporation in certain litigation involving shareholder derivative claims on behalf of the Corporation against certain of its directors and officers" and authorizing that committee "to take such steps from time to time as it deems necessary to pursue its objectives including the retention of special outside counsel." The special committee comprised three disinterested directors who had joined the board after the challenged transactions had occurred. The board subsequently additionally vested in the committee "all of the authority of the Board of Directors to determine, on behalf of the Board, the position that the Corporation shall take with respect to the derivative claims alleged on its behalf" in the present and similar shareholder derivative actions.

The special litigation committee reported under date of November 22, 1976. It found that defendant Arthur Andersen & Co. had conducted its examination of the corporation's affairs in accordance with generally accepted auditing standards and in good faith and concluded that no proper interest of the corporation or its shareholders would be served by the continued assertion of a claim against it. The committee also concluded that none of the individual defendants had violated the [applicable] standard of care, that none had profited personally or gained in any way, that the claims asserted in the present action are without merit, that if the action were allowed to proceed the time and talents of the corporation's senior management would be wasted on lengthy pretrial and trial proceedings, that litigation costs would be inordinately high in view of the unlikelihood of success, and that the continuing publicity could be damaging to the corporation's business. The committee determined that it would not be in the best interests of the corporation for the present derivative action to proceed, and, exercising the authority delegated to it, directed the corporation's general counsel to take that position in the present litigation as well as in pending comparable shareholders' derivative actions.

On December 17, 1976 the corporation and the four individual defendants who had been served moved for an order ... dismissing the complaint or in the alternative for an order ... for summary judgment. On January 7, 1977 Arthur Andersen & Co. made a similar motion. On May 13, 1977 Supreme Court, Special Term, granted the motions of all defendants and dismissed the complaint on the merits. [The Appellate Division reversed that decision.] ...

As all parties and both courts below recognize, the disposition of this case on the merits turns on the proper application of the business judgment doctrine, in particular to the decision of a specially appointed committee of disinterested directors acting on behalf of the board to terminate a shareholders' derivative action. That doctrine bars judicial inquiry into actions of corporate directors taken in good faith and in the exercise of honest judgment in the lawful and legitimate furtherance of corporate purposes. "Questions of policy of management, expediency of contracts or action, adequacy of consideration, lawful appropriation of corporate funds to advance corporate interests, are left solely to their honest and unselfish decision, for their powers therein are without limitation and free from restraint, and the exercise of them for the common and general interests of the corporation may not be questioned, although the results show that what they did was unwise or inexpedient." (*Pollitz v. Wabash R.R. Co.*, 100 N.E. 721, 724 [(N.Y. 1912)].)

In this instance our inquiry, to the limited extent to which it may be pursued, has a two-tiered aspect. The complaint initially asserted liability on the part of defendants based on the payments made to foreign governmental customers and privately owned customers, some unspecified portions of which were allegedly passed on to officials of the customers, *i.e.*, the focus was on first-tier bribes and kickbacks. Then subsequent to the service of the complaint there came the report of a special litigation committee, particularly appointed by the corporation's board of directors to consider the merits of the present and similar shareholders' derivative actions, and its determination that it would not be in the best interests of the corporation to press claims against defendants based on their possible first-tier liability. The motions for summary judgment were predicated principally on the report and determination of the special litigation committee and on the contention that this second-tier corporate action insulated the first-tier transactions from judicial inquiry and was itself subject to the shelter of the business judgment doctrine. The disposition at Special Term was predicated on this analysis; its decision focused on the actions of the special litigation committee, and the motions for summary judgment were granted on the ground that the business judgment doctrine precluded the courts from going back of the decision of the special litigation committee on behalf of the corporation not to pursue the claims alleged in the complaint. Similarly the reversal at the Appellate Division was based on that court's perception of the proper application of the business judgment rule to the actions and determination of the special litigation committee. We proceed on the same analysis, concluding, however, on the record before us, at variance with the Appellate Division, that the determination of the special litigation committee forecloses further judicial inquiry in this case.

It appears to us that the business judgment doctrine, at least in part, is grounded in the prudent recognition that courts are ill equipped and infrequently called on to evaluate what are and must be essentially business judgments. The authority and responsibilities vested in corporate directors both by statute and decisional law proceed on the assumption that inescapably there can be no available objective standard by which the correctness of every corporate decision may be measured, by the courts or otherwise. Even if that were not the case, by definition the responsibility for business judgments must rest with the corporate directors; their individual capabilities and experience peculiarly qualify them for the discharge of that responsibility. Thus, absent evidence of bad faith or fraud (of which there is none here) the courts must and properly should respect their determinations.

Derivative claims against corporate directors belong to the corporation itself. As with other questions of corporate policy and management, the decision whether and to what extent to explore and prosecute such claims lies within the judgment and control of the corporation's board of directors. Necessarily such decision must be predicated on the weighing and balancing of a variety of disparate considerations to reach a considered conclusion as to what course of action or inaction is best calculated to protect and advance the interests of the corporation. This is the essence of the responsibility and role of the board of directors, and courts may not intrude to interfere.

In the present case we confront a special instance of the application of the business judgment rule and inquire whether it applies in its full vigor to shield from judicial scrutiny the decision of a three-person minority committee of the board acting on behalf of the full board not to prosecute a shareholder's derivative action. The record in this case reveals that the board is a 15-member board, and that the derivative suit was brought against four of the directors. Nothing suggests that any of the other directors participated in any of the challenged first-tier transactions. Indeed the report of the audit committee on which the complaint is based specifically found that no other directors had any prior knowledge of or were in any way involved in any of these transactions. Other directors had, however, been members of the board in the period during which the transactions occurred. Each of the three director members of the special litigation committee joined the board thereafter.

The business judgment rule does not foreclose inquiry by the courts into the disinterested independence of those members of the board chosen by it to make the corporate decision on its behalf here the members of the special litigation committee. Indeed the rule shields the deliberations and conclusions of the chosen representatives of the board only if they possess a disinterested independence and do not stand in a dual relation which prevents an unprejudicial exercise of judgment.

We examine then the proof submitted by defendants. It is not disputed that the members of the special litigation committee were not members of the corporation's board of directors at the time of the first-tier transactions in question. Howard Blauvelt, chairman of the board of Continental Oil Company, had been elected to the corporation's board of directors on October 9, 1975. Dr. John T. Dunlop, Lamont University professor at the Graduate School of Business Administration of Harvard University had been elected to the board on April 21, 1976. James R. Barker, chairman of the board and chief executive officer of Moore McCormack Resources, Inc., was added as the third member of the committee when he was elected to the board on July 19, 1976. None of the three had had any prior affiliation with the corporation. Notwithstanding the vigorous and imaginative hypothesizing and innuendo of counsel there is nothing in this record to raise a triable issue of fact as to the independence and disinterested status of these three directors.

The contention ... that any committee authorized by the board of which defendant directors were members must be held to be legally infirm and may not be delegated power to terminate a derivative action must be rejected. In the very nature of the corporate organization it was only the existing board of directors which had authority on behalf of the corporation to direct the investigation and to assure the cooperation of corporate employees, and it is only that same board by its own action or as here pursuant to authority duly delegated by it which had authority to decide whether to prosecute the claims against defendant directors. The board in this instance, with slight adaptation, followed prudent practice in observing the general policy that when individual members of a board of directors prove to have personal interests which may conflict with the interests of the corporation, such interested directors must be excluded while the remaining members of the board proceed to consideration and action. Courts have consistently held that the business judgment rule applies where some directors are charged with wrongdoing, so long as the remaining directors making the decision are disinterested and independent.

To ... disqualify the entire board would be to render the corporation powerless to make an effective business judgment with respect to prosecution of the derivative action. The possible risk of hesitancy on the part of the members of any committee, even if composed of outside, independent, disinterested directors, to investigate the activities of fellow members of the board where personal liability is at stake is an inherent, inescapable, given aspect of the corporation's predicament. To assign responsibility of the dimension here involved to individuals wholly separate and apart from the board of directors would, except in the most extraordinary circumstances, itself be an act of default and breach of the nondelegable fiduciary duty owed by the members of the board to the corporation and to its shareholders, employees and creditors. For the courts to preside over such determinations would similarly work an ouster of the board's fundamental responsibility and authority for corporate management.

We turn then to the action of the special litigation committee itself which comprised two components. First, there was the selection of procedures appropriate to the pursuit of its charge, and second, there was the ultimate substantive decision, predicated on the procedures chosen and the data produced thereby, not to pursue the claims advanced in the shareholders' derivative actions. The latter, substantive decision falls squarely within the embrace of the business judgment doctrine, involving as it did the weighing and balancing of legal, ethical, commercial, promotional, public relations, fiscal and other factors familiar to the resolution of many if not most corporate problems. To this extent the conclusion reached by the special litigation committee is outside the scope of our review. Thus, the courts cannot inquire as to which factors were considered by that committee or the relative weight accorded them in reaching that substantive decision "the reasons for the payments, the advantages or disadvantages accruing to the corporation by reason of the transactions, the extent of the participation or profit by the respondent directors and the loss, if any, of public confidence in the corporation which might be incurred" [*Auerbach v. Bennett*, 408 N.Y.S.2d 83, 107 (N.Y. App. Div. 1978)]. Inquiry into such matters would go to the very core of the business judgment made by the committee. To permit judicial probing of such issues would be to emasculate the business judgment doctrine as applied to the actions and determinations of the special litigation committee. Its substantive evaluation of the problems posed and its judgment in their resolution are beyond our reach.

As to the other component of the committee's activities, however, the situation is different, and here we agree with the Appellate Division. As to the methodologies and procedures best suited to the conduct of an investigation of facts and the determination of legal liability, the courts are well equipped by long and continuing experience and practice to make determinations. In fact they are better qualified in this regard than are corporate directors in general. Nor do the determinations to be made in the adoption of procedures partake of the nuances or special perceptions or comprehensions of business judgment or corporate activities or interests. The question is solely how appropriately to set about to gather the pertinent data.

While the court may properly inquire as to the adequacy and appropriateness of the committee's investigative procedures and methodologies, it may not under the guise of consideration of such factors trespass in the domain of business judgment. At the same time those responsible for the procedures by which the business judgment is reached may reasonably be required to show that they have pursued their chosen investigative methods in good faith. What evidentiary proof may be required to this end will, of course, depend on the nature of the particular investigation, and the proper reach of disclosure at the instance of the shareholders will in turn relate inversely to the showing made by the corporate representatives themselves. The latter may be expected to show that the areas and subjects to be examined are reasonably complete and that there has been a good-faith pursuit of inquiry into such areas and subjects. What has been uncovered and the relative weight accorded in evaluating and balancing the several factors and considerations are beyond the scope of judicial concern. Proof, however, that the investigation has been so restricted in scope, so shallow in execution, or otherwise so [pro] forma or halfhearted as to constitute a pretext or sham, consistent with the principles underlying the application of the business judgment doctrine, would raise questions of good faith or conceivably fraud which would never be shielded by that doctrine.

In addition to the issue of the disinterested independence of the special litigation committee, addressed above, the disposition of the present appeal turns, then, on whether on defendants' motions for summary judgment predicated on the investigation and determination of the special litigation committee, [the plaintiff has] by tender of evidentiary proof in admissible form has shown facts sufficient to require a trial of any material issue of fact as to the adequacy or appropriateness of the [modus] operandi of that committee or has demonstrated acceptable excuse for failure to make such tender. We conclude that the requisite showing has not been made on this record....

On the submissions made by defendants in support of their motions, we do not find either insufficiency or infirmity as to the procedures and methodologies chosen and pursued by the special litigation committee. That committee promptly engaged eminent special counsel to guide its deliberations and to advise it. The committee reviewed the prior work of the audit committee, testing its completeness, accuracy and thoroughness by interviewing representatives of Wilmer, Cutler & Pickering, reviewing transcripts of the testimony of 10 corporate officers and employees before the Securities and Exchange Commission, and studying documents collected by and work papers of the Washington law firm. Individual interviews were conducted with the directors found to have participated in any way in the questioned payments, and with representatives of Arthur Andersen & Co. Questionnaires were sent to and answered by each of the corporation's nonmanagement directors. At the conclusion of its investigation the special litigation committee sought and obtained pertinent legal advice from its special counsel. The selection of appropriate investigative methods must always turn on the nature and characteristics of the particular subject being investigated, but we find nothing in this record that requires a trial of any material issue of fact concerning the sufficiency or appropriateness of the procedures chosen by this special litigation committee. Nor is there anything in this record to raise a triable issue of fact as to the good-faith pursuit of its examination by that committee....

Notes and Questions

1. On whom did the *Auerbach v. Bennett* put the burden of proof?

2. The *Auerbach* approach manifests familiar corporate law orthodoxy. Recall, for instance, analogous approaches to interested director transactions, controlling shareholder cash out mergers, and even sales of control.

Zapata Corp. v. Maldonado

Delaware Supreme Court
430 A.2d 779 (1981)

QUILLEN, JUSTICE:

This is an interlocutory appeal from an order entered on April 9, 1980, by the Court of Chancery denying appellant-defendant Zapata Corporation's (Zapata) alternative motions to dismiss the complaint or for summary judgment.…

In June, 1975, William Maldonado, a stockholder of Zapata, instituted a derivative action in the Court of Chancery on behalf of Zapata against ten officers and/or directors of Zapata, alleging, essentially, breaches of fiduciary duty. Maldonado did not first demand that the board bring this action, stating instead such demand's futility because all directors were named as defendants and allegedly participated in the acts specified. In June, 1977, Maldonado commenced an action in the United States District Court for the Southern District of New York against the same defendants, save one, alleging federal [securities] law violations as well as the same common law claims made previously in the Court of Chancery.

By June, 1979, four of the defendant-directors were no longer on the board, and the remaining directors appointed two new outside directors to the board. The board then created an "Independent Investigation Committee" (Committee), composed solely of the two new directors, to investigate Maldonado's actions, as well as a similar derivative action then pending in Texas, and to determine whether the corporation should continue any or all of the litigation. The Committee's determination was stated to be "final, … not … subject to review by the Board of Directors and … in all respects … binding upon the Corporation."

Following an investigation, the Committee concluded, in September, 1979, that each action should "be dismissed forthwith as their continued maintenance is inimical to the Company's best interests.…"

As the Vice Chancellor noted, "it is the law of the State of incorporation which determines whether the directors have this power of dismissal …" We limit our review in this interlocutory appeal to whether the Committee has the power to cause the present action to be dismissed.

We begin with an examination of the carefully considered opinion of the Vice Chancellor which states, in part, that the "business judgment" rule does not confer power "to a corporate board of directors to terminate a derivative suit." His conclusion is particularly pertinent because several federal courts, applying Delaware law, have held that the business judgment rule enables boards (or their committees) to terminate derivative suits, decisions now in conflict with the holding below.

As the term is most commonly used, and given the disposition below, we can understand the Vice Chancellor's comment that "the business judgment rule is irrelevant to the question of whether the Committee has the authority to compel the dismissal of this suit." Corporations, existing because of legislative grace, possess authority as granted by the legislature. Directors of Delaware corporations derive their managerial decision making power, which encompasses decisions whether to initiate, or refrain from entering, litigation, from 8 Del. C. § 141 (a). This statute is the fount of directorial powers. The "business judgment" rule is a judicial creation that presumes propriety, under certain circumstances, in a board's decision. Viewed defensively, it does not create authority. In this sense the "business judgment" rule is not relevant in corporate decision making until after a decision is made. It is generally used as a defense to an attack on the decision's soundness. The board's managerial decision making power, however, comes from § 141(a). The judicial creation and legislative grant are related because the "business judgment" rule evolved to give recognition and deference to directors' business expertise when exercising their managerial power under § 141(a).

In the case before us, although the corporation's decision to move to dismiss or for summary judgment was, literally, a decision resulting from an exercise of the directors' (as delegated to the Committee) business judgment, the question of "business judgment," in a defensive sense, would not become relevant until and unless the decision to seek termination of the derivative lawsuit was attacked as improper. This question was not reached by the Vice Chancellor because he determined that the stockholder had an individual right to maintain this derivative action.

Thus, the focus in this case is on the power to speak for the corporation as to whether the lawsuit should be continued or terminated. As we see it, this issue in the current appellate posture of this case has three aspects: the conclusions of the Court below concerning the continuing right of a stockholder to maintain a derivative action; the corporate power under Delaware law of an authorized board committee to cause dismissal of litigation instituted for the benefit of the corporation; and the role of the Court of Chancery in resolving conflicts between the stockholder and the committee.

Accordingly, we turn first to the Court of Chancery's conclusions concerning the right of a plaintiff stockholder in a derivative action. We find that its determination that a stockholder, once demand is made and refused, possesses an independent, individual right to continue a derivative suit for breaches of fiduciary duty over objection by the corporation as an absolute rule, is erroneous....

Consistent with the purpose of requiring a demand, a board decision to cause a derivative suit to be dismissed as detrimental to the company, after demand has been made and refused, will be respected unless it was wrongful.[3] ...

The question to be decided becomes: When, if at all, should an authorized board committee be permitted to cause litigation, properly initiated by a derivative stockholder in his own right, to be dismissed? As noted above, a board has the power to choose not to pursue litigation when demand is made upon it, so long as the decision

---

3. [10] In other words, when stockholders, after making demand and having their suit rejected, attack the board's decision as improper, the board's decision falls under the "business judgment" rule and will be respected if the requirements of the rule are met. That situation should be distinguished from the instant case, where demand was not made, and the power of the board to seek a dismissal, due to disqualification, presents a threshold issue.... We recognize that the two contexts can overlap in practice.

is not wrongful. If the board determines that a suit would be detrimental to the company, the board's determination prevails. Even when demand is excusable, circumstances may arise when continuation of the litigation would not be in the corporation's best interests. Our inquiry is whether, under such circumstances, there is a permissible procedure under § 141(a) by which a corporation can rid itself of detrimental litigation. If there is not, a single stockholder in an extreme case might control the destiny of the entire corporation.... But, when examining the means, including the committee mechanism examined in this case, potentials for abuse must be recognized. This takes us to the second and third aspects of the issue on appeal....

At the risk of stating the obvious, the problem is relatively simple. If, on the one hand, corporations can consistently wrest bona fide derivative actions away from well-meaning derivative plaintiffs through the use of the committee mechanism, the derivative suit will lose much, if not all, of its generally-recognized effectiveness as an intra-corporate means of policing boards of directors. If, on the other hand, corporations are unable to rid themselves of meritless or harmful litigation and strike suits, the derivative action, created to benefit the corporation, will produce the opposite, unintended result. It thus appears desirable to us to find a balancing point where bona fide stock holder power to bring corporate causes of action cannot be unfairly trampled on by the board of directors, but the corporation can rid itself of detrimental litigation.

As we noted, the question has been treated by other courts as one of the "business judgment" of the board committee. If a "committee, composed of independent and disinterested directors, conducted a proper review of the matters before it, considered a variety of factors and reached, in good faith, a business judgment that [the] action was not in the best interest of [the corporation]," the action must be dismissed. *See, e.g., Maldonado v. Flynn, supra,* 485 F. Supp. at 282, 286. The issues become solely independence, good faith, and reasonable investigation. The ultimate conclusion of the committee, under that view, is not subject to judicial review.

We are not satisfied, however, that acceptance of the "business judgment" rationale at this stage of derivative litigation is a proper balancing point. While we admit an analogy with a normal case respecting board judgment, it seems to us that there is sufficient risk in the realities of a situation like the one presented in this case to justify caution beyond adherence to the theory of business judgment.

The context here is a suit against directors where demand on the board is excused. We think some tribute must be paid to the fact that the lawsuit was properly initiated. It is not a board refusal case. Moreover, this complaint was filed in June of 1975 and, while the parties undoubtedly would take differing views on the degree of litigation activity, we have to be concerned about the creation of an "Independent Investigation Committee" four years later, after the election of two new outside directors. Situations could develop where such motions could be filed after years of vigorous litigation for reasons unconnected with the merits of the lawsuit.

Moreover, notwithstanding our conviction that Delaware law entrusts the corporate power to a properly authorized committee, we must be mindful that directors are passing judgment on fellow directors in the same corporation and fellow directors, in this instance, who designated them to serve both as directors and committee members. The question naturally arises whether a "there but for the grace of God go I" empathy might not play a role. And the further question arises whether inquiry as to independence, good faith and reasonable investigation is sufficient safeguard against abuse, perhaps subconscious abuse....

Whether the Court of Chancery will be persuaded by the exercise of a committee power resulting in a summary motion for dismissal of a derivative action, where a demand has not been initially made, should rest, in our judgment, in the independent discretion of the Court of Chancery. We thus steer a middle course between those cases which yield to the independent business judgment of a board committee and this case as determined below which would yield to unbridled plaintiff stockholder control. In pursuit of the course, we recognize that "(t)he final substantive judgment whether a particular lawsuit should be maintained requires a balance of many factors ethical, commercial, promotional, public relations, employee relations, fiscal as well as legal." *Maldonado v. Flynn, supra*, 485 F. Supp. at 285. But we are content that such factors are not "beyond the judicial reach" of the Court of Chancery which regularly and competently deals with fiduciary relationships, disposition of trust property, approval of settlements and scores of similar problems. We recognize the danger of judicial overreaching but the alternatives seem to us to be outweighed by the fresh view of a judicial outsider. Moreover, if we failed to balance all the interests involved, we would in the name of practicality and judicial economy foreclose a judicial decision on the merits. At this point, we are not convinced that is necessary or desirable.

After an objective and thorough investigation of a derivative suit, an independent committee may cause its corporation to file a pretrial motion to dismiss in the Court of Chancery. The basis of the motion is the best interests of the corporation, as determined by the committee. The motion should include a thorough written record of the investigation and its findings and recommendations. Under appropriate Court supervision, akin to proceedings on summary judgment, each side should have an opportunity to make a record on the motion. As to the limited issues presented by the motion noted below, the moving party should be prepared to meet the normal burden under Rule 56 that there is no genuine issue as to any material fact and that the moving party is entitled to dismiss as a matter of law. The Court should apply a two-step test to the motion.

First, the Court should inquire into the independence and good faith of the committee and the bases supporting its conclusions. Limited discovery may be ordered to facilitate such inquiries. The corporation should have the burden of proving independence, good faith and a reasonable investigation, rather than presuming independence, good faith and reasonableness. If the Court determines either that the committee is not independent or has not shown reasonable bases for its conclusions, or, if the Court is not satisfied for other reasons relating to the process, including but not limited to the good faith of the committee, the Court shall deny the corporation's motion. If, however, the Court is satisfied under Rule 56 standards that the committee was independent and showed reasonable bases for good faith findings and recommendations, the Court may proceed, in its discretion, to the next step.

The second step provides, we believe, the essential key in striking the balance between legitimate corporate claims as expressed in a derivative stockholder suit and a corporation's best interests as expressed by an independent investigating committee. The Court should determine, applying its own independent business judgment, whether the motion should be granted. This means, of course, that instances could arise where a committee can establish its independence and sound bases for its good faith decisions and still have the corporation's motion denied. The second step is intended to thwart instances where corporate actions meet the criteria of step one, but the result does not appear to satisfy its spirit, or where corporate actions would simply prematurely terminate a stockholder grievance deserving of further consideration in the corporation's interest. The Court of Chancery of course must carefully consider and weigh how compelling the corporate interest in dismissal is when faced with a non-frivolous lawsuit. The Court of Chancery should, when appropriate, give special consideration to matters of law and public policy in addition to the corporation's best interests.

If the Court's independent business judgment is satisfied, the Court may proceed to grant the motion, subject, of course, to any equitable terms or conditions the Court finds necessary or desirable.

Notes and Questions

1. Which do you consider to be the better approach, *Auerbach* or *Zapata*? The *Zapata* approach obviously is in tension with all the traditional rationales of the business judgment rule. Are those rationales less compelling in the case of SLC judgments to dismiss derivative cases? The *Zapata* court addressed the judicial competency rationale by pointing out that the Delaware Court of Chancery "regularly and competently deals with fiduciary relationships, disposition of trust property, approval of settlements and scores of similar problems." Are such tasks uniquely relevant to evaluating derivative suits as compared to the broad range of business judgments directors make? Is it possible that some judges, because of the type of docket they are accustomed to, might be better at reviewing business judgments such as this than other judges? Might *Zapata* be the best standard in Delaware but not necessarily for other states? While courts in other states ultimately choose either the *Auerbach* test or the *Zapata* approach, many lean toward one or the other while adapting or modifying them, as the examples in ensuing notes highlight.

2. In *Alford v. Shaw*, 358 S.E.2d 323 (N.C. 1987), for example, the court compared the *Auerbach* and *Zapata* approaches, and ultimately offered a slightly different take:

> The sole issue raised by this appeal is whether a special litigation committee's decision to terminate plaintiff minority shareholders' derivative action against defendant corporate directors is binding upon the courts....
>
> The recent trend among courts which have been faced with the choice of applying an *Auerbach*-type rule of judicial deference or a *Zapata*-type rule of

judicial scrutiny has been to require judicial inquiry on the merits of the special litigation committee's report....

... We interpret the trend away from *Auerbach* among other jurisdictions as an indication of growing concern about the deficiencies inherent in a rule giving great deference to the decisions of a corporate committee whose institutional symbiosis with the corporation necessarily affects its ability to render a decision that fairly considers the interest of plaintiffs forced to bring suit on behalf of the corporation. Such concerns are legitimate ones and, upon further reflection, we find that they must be resolved not by slavish adherence to the business judgment rule, but by careful interpretation of the provisions of our own Business Corporation Act. We conclude from our analysis of the pertinent statutes that a modified *Zapata* rule, requiring judicial scrutiny of the merits of the litigation committee's recommendation, is most consistent with the intent of our legislature and is therefore the appropriate rule to be applied in our courts....

Although the recommendation of the special litigation committee is not binding on the court, in making this determination the court may choose to rely on such recommendation. To rely blindly on the report of a corporation-appointed committee which assembled such materials on behalf of the corporation is to abdicate the judicial duty to consider the interests of shareholders imposed by the statute. This abdication is particularly inappropriate in a case such as this one, where shareholders allege serious breaches of fiduciary duties owed to them by the directors controlling the corporation.

... The *Zapata* Court limited its two-step judicial inquiry to cases in which demand upon the corporation was futile and therefore excused. However, we find no justification for such limitation in our statutes.... Thus, court approval is required for disposition of all derivative suits, even where the directors are not charged with fraud or self-dealing, or where the plaintiff and the board agree to discontinue, dismiss, compromise, or settle the lawsuit.

... When N.C.G.S. §§ 55–55 and 55-30(b)(3) are read in pari materia, they indicate that when a stockholder in a derivative action seeks to establish self-dealing on the part of a majority of the board, the burden should be upon those directors to establish that the transactions complained of were just and reasonable to the corporation when entered into or approved. The fact that a special litigation committee appointed by those directors charged with self-dealing recommends that the action should not proceed, while carrying weight, is not binding upon the trial court. Rather, the court must make a fair assessment of the report of the special committee, along with all the other facts and circumstances in the case, in order to determine whether the defendants will be able to show that the transaction complained of was just and reasonable to the corporation. If this appears evident from the materials before the court, then in a proper case summary judgment may be allowed in favor of the defendants.

3. *In re PSE&G Shareholder Litigation*, 801 A.2d 295 (N.J. 2002), a derivative action arising out of alleged "reckless management" of a company's nuclear power plants that resulted in substantial fines imposed by the Nuclear Regulatory Commission. Based upon elaborate investigative reports commissioned from an outside law firm, the SLC recommended that the lawsuits be dismissed. The trial court agreed, granting summary judgment for the defendants, and the New Jersey Supreme Court affirmed. It used the approach taken by the North Carolina Supreme Court in *Alford v. Shaw* of applying a single standard of review to both demand-made and demand-excused cases. The court articulated that standard as follows:

> [W]e shall apply a modified business judgment rule that imposes an initial burden on a corporation to demonstrate that in deciding to reject or terminate a shareholder's suit the members of the board (1) were independent and disinterested, (2) acted in good faith and with due care in their investigation of the shareholder's allegations, and ... (3) the board's decision was reasonable.... [S]hareholders in these circumstances must be permitted access to corporate documents and other discovery [relating to steps the directors took to become informed and the reasonableness of the directors' decision].

801 A.2d at 312. The court noted distinctions between its test for determining demand-futility and its standard for evaluating a board's decision under the modified business judgment rule: (1) plaintiffs have the burden of demonstrating demand-futility, whereas defendants have the burden of satisfying the elements of the modified business judgment rule and (2) defendants' motions to dismiss for failure to make a demand are decided on the pleadings, whereas plaintiffs are entitled to limited discovery before the court rules on whether the corporation properly decided to reject or terminate the litigation.

4. In *Cuker v. Mikalauskas*, 692 A.2d 1042 (Pa. 1997), the Pennsylvania Supreme Court adopted the ALI approach:

> The issue is whether the business judgment rule permits the [board of directors of a Pennsylvania corporation] to terminate derivative lawsuits brought by minority shareholders. The business judgment rule insulates an officer or director of a corporation from liability for a business decision made in good faith if he is not interested in the subject of the business judgment, is informed with respect to the subject of the business judgment to the extent he reasonably believes to be appropriate under the circumstances, and rationally believes that the business judgment is in the best interests of the corporation. 1 ALI, *Principles of Corporate Governance: Analysis and Recommendations*, (1994) ("*ALI Principles*") § 4.01(c)....

> ... [I]f a court makes a preliminary determination that a business decision was made under proper circumstances, however that concept is currently defined, then the business judgment rule prohibits the court from going further and examining the merits of the underlying business decision.

> Decisions regarding litigation by or on behalf of a corporation, including shareholder derivative actions, are business decisions as much as any other financial decisions. As such, they are within the province of the board of di-

rectors.... Such business decisions of a board of directors are, unless taken in violation of a common law or statutory duty, within the scope of the business judgment rule. It follows that the court of common pleas erred when it held that the business judgment rule is not the law of Pennsylvania....

... [T]he practical effect of this holding needs elaboration. Assuming that an independent board of directors may terminate shareholder derivative actions, what is needed is a procedural mechanism for implementation and judicial review of the board's decision. Without considering the merits of the action, a court should determine the validity of the board's decision to terminate the litigation; if that decision was made in accordance with the appropriate standards, then the court should dismiss the derivative action prior to litigation on the merits.

The business judgment rule should insulate officers and directors from judicial intervention in the absence of fraud or self-dealing, if challenged decisions were within the scope of the directors' authority, if they exercised reasonable diligence, and if they honestly and rationally believed their decisions were in the best interests of the company. It is obvious that a court must examine the circumstances surrounding the decisions in order to determine if the conditions warrant application of the business judgment rule. If they do, the court will never proceed to an examination of the merits of the challenged decisions, for that is precisely what the business judgment rule prohibits. In order to make the business judgment rule meaningful, the preliminary examination should be limited and precise so as to minimize judicial involvement when application of the business judgment rule is warranted.

To achieve these goals, a court might stay the derivative action while it determines the propriety of the board's decision. The court might order limited discovery or an evidentiary hearing to resolve issues respecting the board's decision. Factors bearing on the board's decision will include whether the board or its special litigation committee was disinterested, whether it was assisted by counsel, whether it prepared a written report, whether it was independent, whether it conducted an adequate investigation, and whether it rationally believed its decision was in the best interests of the corporation (i.e., acted in good faith). If all of these criteria are satisfied, the business judgment rule applies and the court should dismiss the action.

These considerations and procedures are all encompassed in Part VII, chapter 1 of the *ALI Principles* (relating to the derivative action), which provides a comprehensive mechanism to address shareholder derivative actions. A number of its provisions are implicated in the action at bar. Sections 7.02 (standing), 7.03 (the demand rule), 7.04 (procedure in derivative action), 7.05 (board authority in derivative action), 7.06 (judicial stay of derivative action), 7.07, 7.08, and 7.09 (dismissal of derivative action), 7.10 (standard of judicial review), and 7.13 (judicial procedures) are specifically applicable to this case. These sections set forth guidance which is consistent with Pennsylvania law and precedent, which furthers the policies inherent in the business judgment rule, and which provides an appropriate degree of specificity to guide the trial court in controlling the proceedings in this litigation.

We specifically adopt §§ 7.02–7.10, and § 7.13 of the ALI Principles. In doing so we have weighed many considerations. First, the opinion of the trial court, the questions certified to the Superior Court, and the inability of litigants here to obtain a definitive ruling from the lower courts all demonstrate the need for specific guidance from this court on how such litigation should be managed; the ALI principles provide such guidance in specific terms which will simplify this litigation. Second, we have often found ALI guidance helpful in the past, most frequently in adopting or citing sections of various Restatements; the scholarship reflected in work of the American Law Institute has been consistently reliable and useful. Third, the principles set forth by the ALI are generally consistent with Pennsylvania precedent. Fourth, although the *ALI Principles* incorporate much of the law of New York and Delaware, other states with extensive corporate jurisprudence, the ALI Principles better serve the needs of Pennsylvania. Although New York law parallels Pennsylvania law in many respects, it does not set forth any procedures to govern the review of corporate decisions relating to derivative litigation, and this omission would fail to satisfy the needs evident in this case. Delaware law permits a court in some cases ("demand excused" cases) to apply its own business judgment in the review process when deciding to honor the directors' decision to terminate derivative litigation. [*see Zapata.*] In our view, this is a defect which could eviscerate the business judgment rule and contradict a long line of Pennsylvania precedents. Delaware law also fails to provide a procedural framework for judicial review of corporate decisions under the business judgment rule.

5. ALI § 7.10 develops a dual standard of review regarding a corporate board's motion to dismiss a derivative suit which varies with the nature of the allegations. If the "gravamen of the actions allege only a violation of the duty of care," it is subject to a business judgment rule standard of review. But if more serious violations are alleged, such duty of loyalty violations or knowing violations of law, the court will consider whether the SLC "was adequately informed under the circumstances and reasonably determined that dismissal was in the best interests of the corporation, based on grounds that the court deems to warrant reliance." See § 7.10 and Comment *c*, pp. 134–35.

Schoon v. Smith

Supreme Court of Delaware
953 A.2d 196 (2008)

RIDGELY, JUSTICE (FOR THE COURT EN BANC):

Appellant Richard W. Schoon is a director, but not a stockholder, of Troy Corporation.... He filed a derivative action in the Court of Chancery on behalf of Troy, alleging breaches of fiduciary duties by his fellow directors. Schoon argued below that his role as a fiduciary to the corporation should permit him to have the same standing a stockholder has to bring a derivative action. The Court of Chancery dismissed his complaint....

Troy Corporation is a privately held Delaware corporation whose capital structure consists of three series of common stock. Series A shares are entitled to elect four of the five Troy directors. Daryl Smith, the CEO and Chairman of Troy, owns a majority of the Series A shares, which he voted to elect himself and three others to the board of directors. Series B stockholders have the right to elect the final member of the board. Another privately held Delaware Corporation, Steel, owns a majority of Series B shares, which it voted to elect Schoon, who owns no stock in Troy, to the Troy board of directors. Series C shares have no voting rights.

Schoon alleges that shortly after he became a director of Troy, he discovered that the other three board members were "beholden to Smith," which enabled Smith to dominate and control the board. Schoon alleges that Smith has taken actions on several occasions that were designed to entrench himself in power and, in turn, thwart potential value-maximizing transactions for the benefit of Troy and its stockholders....

Schoon argues that as a matter of equity and public policy, a director should be entitled to assert a derivative claim on behalf of the corporation for the same reasons that stockholders are permitted to do so. He urges that equipping directors with standing to sue derivatively is consistent with the fiduciary duties of directors and "promotes the core Delaware public policy of protecting against misconduct by faithless fiduciaries."...

The traditional concept of standing confers upon the corporation the right to bring a cause of action for its own injury. The equitable standing of a stockholder to bring a derivative action on behalf of a corporation has long been grounded upon the interests of justice.... To prevent "a failure of justice," courts of equity granted equitable standing to stockholders to sue on behalf of the corporation ... Today, the result of this judicially-created doctrine is known as the stockholder derivative action....

We begin with the bedrock statutory principle that "[t]he business and affairs of every corporation ... shall be managed by or under the direction of a board of directors...." [DGCL 141(a).] In discharging their management function, directors owe fiduciary duties of care and loyalty to the corporation and its shareholders.... Since *Guth* [*v. Loft*], we have repeatedly emphasized the important role of independent directors.[1] *Aronson v. Lewis* explains why director independence inheres in the rationale for the business judgment rule [excerpted above]....

---

1. [38] *See, e.g.,*.... *Unocal Corp. v. Mesa Petro. Co.*, 493 A.2d 946, 957 (Del. 1985) ("If the board of directors is disinterested, has acted in good faith and with due care, its decision in the absence of an abuse of discretion will be upheld as a proper exercise of business judgment."); ... *Weinberger v. UOP, Inc.*, 457 A.2d 701, 709 n. 7 (Del. 1983) ("Although perfection is not possible, or expected, the result here could have been entirely different if UOP had appointed an independent negotiating committee of its outside directors to deal with Signal at arm's length.")....

To cite one example of how independent directors may cleanse conflict of interest transactions, Section 144(a) of the DGCL provides a safe harbor for interested transactions if they are approved by disinterested directors. 8 *Del. C.* § 144(a)(1); *Benihana of Tokyo, Inc. v. Benihana, Inc.*, 906 A.2d 114, 120 (Del. 2006) ("After approval by disinterested directors, courts review the interested transaction under the business judgment rule....").

Notwithstanding these considerations, Schoon advances a practical argument for his standing to sue. He contends that to protect the interests of the corporation and the stockholders, a director should be permitted to sue derivatively because the director is in a better position to know and to make his allegations against the board without waiting for a stockholder to do so. This proposed efficiency overlooks the reason why the equitable standing doctrine was adopted, which (to reiterate) is to prevent a complete failure of justice on behalf of the corporation.

No such complete failure is presented in this case. Here, the stockholder who elected Schoon (Steel) is not only aligned with him, but also is actively litigating other matters involving Troy before the Court of Chancery. We take judicial notice that Steel has already begun using the "tools at hand"[2] to obtain books and records information from Troy. Given the well-established duties of a director and the ability and the right of Steel, as a stockholder, to bring a derivative action if Steel deems it necessary, we perceive no new exigencies that require an extension of equitable standing to Schoon, as a director.

In arguing that a grant of standing to directors will further the policy of protecting against misconduct by fiduciaries, Schoon urges us to adopt the 1994 proposal of the American Law Institute ("ALI") that relates to director standing.

Section 7.02(c) of the ALI Principles provides: "A director of a corporation has standing to commence and maintain a derivative action unless the court finds that the director is unable to represent fairly and adequately the interests of the shareholders." The commentary to this provision recognizes that this is a "special right" because "most directors will already have standing to sue as shareholders." The ALI Principles also acknowledge that normally a director will bring his or her concerns regarding illegal or fraudulent conduct to the board and that the preference is for the entire board to provide "a collegial response" to a director's concerns regarding potential misconduct.

The ALI Principles justify the creation of director derivative standing only for those occasions "when the board is dominated by a controlling shareholder, in which the board will fail to act even when clear evidence of misbehavior or illegality has been presented to it...." The ALI Principles further reason that procedural requirements for maintaining a shareholder derivative suit, such as contemporaneous ownership and continuing ownership, do not apply to directors because "the director's fiduciary obligation entitles the director to seek to rectify wrongs to the corporation that do not directly injure the director."

To date, there is little, if any, case law adopting, or legal commentary approving, this particular ALI proposal. Except for the Supreme Court of Pennsylvania's blanket adoption of §§ 7.02–7.10 and § 7.13,[3] no other state supreme court has expressly adopted the ALI Principles relating to standing. Apart from one pre-ALI Proposal reference of an intermediate appellate court to director standing, Schoon cites no

2. [48] *See, e.g., Seinfeld v. Verizon Commc'ns, Inc.,* 909 A.2d 117, 121 (Del. 2006).
3. [56] *Cuker v. Mikalauskas,* 547 Pa. 600, 692 A.2d 1042, 1049 (1997).

case permitting a director, who does not own stock, to sue derivatively. We recognize, as did the ALI, that New York provides by statute that a director can sue other directors on behalf of the corporation derivatively.[4] We regard the New York statute as confirming the prerogative of a legislature to confer standing upon a director by statute. To date, the Delaware General Assembly has not chosen to do so.

Given the absence of statutory authority for his standing to sue as a director, Schoon's argument must succeed or fail on the merits of extending the doctrine of equitable standing judicially. We have explained the rationale for this equitable doctrine and decline to enlarge it by embracing a policy that will divert the doctrine from its original purpose: to prevent a complete failure of justice. Schoon has not shown that a complete failure of justice will occur unless he is granted standing to sue as a director. A stockholder derivative action would fully and adequately redress any injuries to Troy resulting from a breach of fiduciary duty by its board. Accordingly, we decline to extend equitable standing to Schoon to sue derivatively in his capacity as a director.

Notes and Questions

1. Should directors have standing to bring derivative actions against fellow directors? The *Schoon* court, after probing the deep equitable and historical origins of the derivative action, declared that the purpose of derivative suits is to "prevent an otherwise complete failure of justice." So long as a corporation's shareholders have a viable derivative claim, there is no need to permit directors to maintain such a claim—the shareholders can sue to prevent a "complete failure of justice."

2. The Delaware Supreme Court might recognize director standing, however, if shareholders are unable to bring the case. Suppose, for instance, that all shareholders who held stock at the time of the alleged wrong subsequently sold their stock, making it impossible to satisfy the standing requirement set forth in Delaware Court of Chancery Rule 23.1.

Section V
Alternative Dispute Resolution

The complexity and expense of litigation, including shareholder derivative suits, prompts many to consider alternative ways to resolve disputes, eschewing traditional litigation in favor of procedures like mediation and binding arbitration. It is increasingly common for business enterprises, especially limited liability companies, to include provisions in their contracts stipulating that disputes arising under them be resolved using these alternative dispute resolution (ADR) procedures.

Although mediation and arbitration have some things in common, they are also distinctive in important ways. For example, arbitration usually involves two sides

---

4. [58] N.Y. BUS. CORP. LAW §§ 719, 720 (McKinney 2007)....

submitting contending arguments to a panel of experts whose decision, they agree beforehand, is deemed binding on them. Mediation usually involves an expert encouraging two contending sides to appreciate weaknesses in their stance and strengths in the other with a view toward reaching a negotiated settlement. In both, procedures are truncated considerably compared to traditional judicial dispute resolution. There is less discovery (fewer documents produced or depositions taken), juries are not involved, proceedings are more private, costs are lower and results may be more focused (judges writing opinions address the case before them but also the law more broadly) and accurate (judges tend to be generalists).

Corporations may find these alternative approaches appealing to resolve a wide variety of disputes, including those with shareholders, but also with employees, customers, suppliers, lenders and others. Formal expressions of public policy generally support ADR, including in such federal statutes as the Federal Arbitration Act, and the numerous state statutes, court rules and case law cited in the following case. In evaluating alternatives to judicial dispute resolution, and contractual stipulations making them exclusive, binding and non-appealable, consider how attractive they are in various sorts of disputes, such as direct compared to derivative actions, disputes involving close contrasted with public corporations and corporations as opposed to LLCs.

State of Delaware
Delaware Rapid Arbitration Act (2015)

The recently enacted Delaware Rapid Arbitration Act (DRAA) seeks to address an unmet need of sophisticated businesses to have disputes resolved quickly and competently without costly drawn-out legal proceedings. The act employs some of the best practices from private international arbitrations and may be ideal for parties with ongoing commercial relationships seeking quick resolution of business disputes.

Availability The DRAA is available to businesses which specifically contract to resolve disputes under the DRAA and to have such disputes governed by Delaware law. At least one of the businesses must be a Delaware business entity or have its principal place of business in Delaware.

Location Arbitration proceedings may be held anywhere in the world, as agreed to by the parties.

Confidentiality Proceedings under the DRAA are confidential. If an appeal is made to the Supreme Court of Delaware, such appeals likely will be public and will be governed by the rules of the Supreme Court.

Fast Results The arbitrator's final decision must be completed within 120 days of the arbitrator's acceptance of appointment, with the possibility of a one-time 60-day extension if the parties agree. The arbitrator alone determines the scope of the arbitration, avoiding potentially lengthy disputes which can stall arbitrations. The DRAA vests the Court of Chancery with limited jurisdiction to act in specific situations, for example to appoint an arbitrator when the parties cannot agree on one. Unless the parties otherwise provide in their agreement, arbitrators will have broad discretion to grant any appropriate relief, including money damages, injunctions, and specific performance.

Customized Arbitration The DRAA provides maximum flexibility for the parties to agree in advance upon many aspects of arbitration, including the scope of arbitration, the name and number of arbitrators, the location of arbitration proceedings, the extent of evidence to be produced, the scope of relief and the availability of appeal.

Limited Appeal Any appeal from an arbitration under the DRAA is limited to a single direct challenge of the final award to the Delaware Supreme Court, with such challenges governed by the narrow scope of review provided for under the Federal Arbitration Act. The parties may agree to forgo appeals.

ELF Atochem North America, Inc. v. Jaffari

Delaware Supreme Court

727 A.2d 286 (1999)

VEASEY, CHIEF JUSTICE:

[The facts and selected issues appear in Chapter 2 above. The case was a purported derivative suit brought on behalf of a Delaware LLC. The issue addressed below concentrates on the enforceability of an arbitration provision in the governing agreement.]

The Agreement contains an arbitration clause covering all disputes. The clause, Section 13.8, provides that "any controversy or dispute arising out of this Agreement, the interpretation of any of the provisions hereof, or the action or inaction of any Member or Manager hereunder shall be submitted to arbitration in San Francisco, California...." Section 13.8 further provides: "No action ... based upon any claim arising out of or related to this Agreement shall be instituted in any court by any Member except (a) an action to compel arbitration ... or (b) an action to enforce an award obtained in an arbitration proceeding...."

... Elf claims that the Court of Chancery erred in holding that the arbitration and forum selection clauses in the Agreement governed, and thus deprived that court of jurisdiction to adjudicate all of Elf's claims, including its derivative claims made on behalf of Malek LLC.... Elf also argues that the court erred in failing to classify its claim as derivative on behalf of Malek LLC against Jaffari as manager. Therefore, Elf claims that the court of Chancery should have adjudicated the dispute....

Defendants claim that Elf contracted with Malek, Inc. and Jaffari that all disputes that arise out of, under, or in connection with the Agreement must be resolved exclusively in California by arbitration or court proceedings. Defendants allege that the characterization of Elf's claim as direct or derivative is irrelevant, as the Agreement provides that the members would not institute "any" action at law or equity except one to compel arbitration, and that any such action must be brought in California. Defendants also argue that, in reality, Elf's claims are direct, not derivative, claims against its fellow LLC members, Malek, Inc. and Jaffari....

[T]he arbitration provision of the Agreement in this case fosters the Delaware policy favoring alternate dispute resolution mechanisms, including arbitration.

Such mechanisms are an important goal of Delaware legislation,[4] court rules,[5] and jurisprudence.[6]

Elf argues that the Court of Chancery erred in failing to classify its claims against Malek LLC as derivative. Elf contends that, had the court properly characterized its claims as derivative instead of direct, the arbitration ... clause[ ] would not have applied to bar adjudication in Delaware.

... The derivative suit is a corporate concept grafted onto the limited liability company form. The Act expressly allows for a derivative suit, providing that "a member ... may bring an action in the Court of Chancery in the right of a limited liability company to recover a judgment in its favor if managers or members with authority to do so have refused to bring the action or if an effort to cause those managers or members to bring the action is not likely to succeed." Notwithstanding the Agreement to the contrary, Elf argues that [statute] permits the assertion of derivative claims of Malek LLC against Malek LLC's manager, Jaffari.

Although Elf correctly points out that Delaware law allows for derivative suits against management of an LLC, Elf contracted away its right to bring such an action in Delaware and agreed instead to dispute resolution in California. That is, Section 13.8 of the Agreement specifically provides that the parties (*i.e.*, Elf) agree to institute "[n]o action at law or in equity based upon any claim arising out of or related to this Agreement" except an action to compel arbitration or to enforce an arbitration award.[7]

---

4. [32] *See, e.g.*, Chapter 57, Title 10 of the Delaware Code ("Uniform Arbitration Act") ("A written agreement to submit to arbitration any controversy existing at or arising after the effective date of the agreement is valid, enforceable and irrevocable, save upon such grounds as exist at law or in equity for the revocation of any contract...."); Chapter 77, Title 6 of the Delaware Code ("Voluntary Alternative Dispute Resolution Act") (party files certificate with Secretary of State accepting ADR for purposes of "resolv[ing] business disputes without litigation and to permit parties to agree, prior to any disputes arising between them, to utilize alternative dispute resolution...."); Chapter 95, Title 11 of the Delaware Code ("Victim-Offender Mediation") (establishing a Victim-Offender Mediation Committee for purpose of establishing "victim-offender mediation programs to help meet the need for alternatives to the courts for the resolution of certain criminal offenses....") [the opinion cites four additional illustrative Delaware statutory sections].

5. [33] *See, e.g.*, Super. Ct. Civ. R. 16.1 (providing compulsory arbitration in all cases in which monetary damages are $100,000 or less); Super. Ct. Civ. R. 16.2 (providing any civil matter on Superior Court docket is eligible for referral to voluntary mediation); Ch. Ct. R. 174 (providing voluntary mediation in Court of Chancery).

6. [34] *See SBC Interactive, Inc. v. Corporate Media Partners*, Del. Supr., 714 A.2d 758, 761 (1998) (holding that public policy of Delaware favors arbitration and doubt as to arbitrability is to be resolved in favor of arbitration); *Graham v. State Farm Ins. Co.*, Del.Supr., 565 A.2d 908, 911 (1989) (same); *Action Drug Co. v. R. Baylin Co.*, Del.Ch., C.A. No. 9383, Berger, V.C., 1989 WL 69394 (June 19, 1989), Mem.Op. at 3 (same); *Pettinaro Constr. Co., Inc. v. Harry C. Partridge, Jr. & Sons, Inc.*, Del.Ch., 408 A.2d 957, 961–63 (1979) (holding any doubt as to arbitrability is to be resolved in favor of arbitration)....

7. [42].... In its entirety, § 13.8 provides:
   Disputed Matters. Except as otherwise provided in this Agreement, any controversy or dispute arising out of this Agreement, the interpretation of any of the provisions hereof, or the action or inaction of any Member or Manager hereunder shall be submitted to arbitration in San Francisco, California before the American Arbitration Association under the commercial arbitration rules then obtaining of said Association. Any award or decision

Furthermore, under Section 13.7 of the Agreement, each member (*i.e.*, Elf) "consent[ed] to the exclusive jurisdiction of the state and federal courts sitting in California in any action on a claim arising out of, under or in connection with this Agreement or the transactions contemplated by this Agreement."

... [The] Agreement [does] not distinguish between direct and derivative claims. [It] simply state[s] that the members may not initiate any claims outside of California. Elf initiated this action in the Court of Chancery in contravention of its own contractual agreement. As a result, the Court of Chancery correctly held that all claims, whether derivative or direct, arose under, out of or in connection with the Agreement, and thus are covered by the arbitration ... clause[].... The Court of Chancery was correct in holding that Elf's claims bear directly on Jaffari's duties and obligations under the Agreement....

Our conclusion is bolstered by the fact that Delaware recognizes a strong public policy in favor of arbitration. Normally, doubts on the issue of whether a particular issue is arbitrable will be resolved in favor of arbitration.[8] In the case at bar, we do not believe there is any doubt of the parties' intention to agree to arbitrate all disputed matters in California. If we were to hold otherwise, arbitration clauses in existing LLC agreements could be rendered meaningless. By resorting to the alleged "special" jurisdiction of the Court of Chancery, future plaintiffs could avoid their own arbitration agreements simply by couching their claims as derivative. Such a result could adversely affect many arbitration agreements already in existence in Delaware....

Mission Residential, LLC v. Triple Net Properties, LLC

Virginia Supreme Court
654 S.E.2d 888 (2008)

RUSSELL, SENIOR JUSTICE:

... In 2004, Triple Net Properties, LLC (Triple) was a firm engaged in the business of syndicating commercial properties for sale to investors as real estate securities. Mission Residential, LLC (Mission) was a firm with expertise in locating, evaluating, purchasing and managing multi-family apartment properties. The two firms, which were otherwise unrelated, entered into a joint venture for the purpose of identifying, purchasing, managing and selling multi-family properties for investors seeking to avail themselves of the tax advantages offered by Section 1031 of the Internal Revenue Code ... for like-kind exchanges of qualifying properties.

---

obtained from any such arbitration proceeding shall be final and binding on the parties, and judgment upon any award thus obtained may be entered in any court having jurisdiction thereof. No action at law or in equity based upon any claim arising out of or related to this Agreement shall be instituted in any court by any Member except (a) an action to compel arbitration pursuant to this Section 13.8 or (b) an action to enforce an award obtained in an arbitration proceeding in accordance with this Section 13.8.

8. [51] *See SBC Interactive, Inc.*, 714 A.2d at 761. *But see First Options of Chicago, Inc. v. Kaplan*, 514 U.S. 938, 943, (1995) (holding that arbitration award will be enforced only where the parties have agreed to submit to arbitration).

In order to accomplish that purpose, Mission and Triple agreed to form a limited liability company named NNN/Mission Residential Holdings, LLC (Holdings) and executed an "Operating Agreement" for Holdings dated "as of October 1, 2004." The operating agreement provides that Mission and Triple are to be the sole members of Holdings, with equal membership interests, and are to manage Holdings jointly. The sole question presented by this appeal is the effect of Section 13.9 of the operating agreement, which provides in pertinent part:

> *Disputes.* The Members shall in good faith use their best efforts to settle disputes regarding their rights and obligations hereunder. All disputes that the parties have failed to resolve shall be submitted to arbitration. All arbitration to resolve a dispute shall be conducted in accordance with the provisions of this Section 13.9 and to the extent not inconsistent therewith, the Commercial Arbitration Rules of the American Arbitration Association ("AAA")…. The arbitrator's award shall be final, binding and not subject to appeal.

In March 2006, Triple commenced an arbitration proceeding against Mission, asserting a direct claim for breach of contract and also a derivative claim against Mission on behalf of Holdings. The arbitrator ruled that Triple lacked standing to assert the direct claim, but allowed Triple's derivative claim on behalf of Holdings to go forward. In August 2006, Mission brought this action in the circuit court, seeking a declaratory judgment that there was no agreement to arbitrate disputes between Holdings and Mission, requesting an order to stay the arbitration proceeding pursuant to Code s 8.01-581.02(B), and seeking other relief.

Mission asked the arbitrator to defer a ruling on the arbitrability of Triple's derivative claims pending a judicial determination of that issue, but the arbitrator declined to do so, and on August 29, 2006, ruled that the derivative claims were arbitrable. The arbitrator based his ruling on Rule R-7(a) of the Commercial Arbitration Rules of the American Arbitration Association, which was incorporated by reference in Section 13.9 of the operating agreement. Rule R-7(a) makes the arbitrator the sole judge of the issue of arbitrability.

In October 2006, after a review of the pleadings, exhibits and arguments of counsel, the circuit court ruled that the arbitrator had correctly decided the issue of arbitrability. The court entered an order denying the motion to stay arbitration and dismissing Mission's complaint. We awarded Mission an appeal.

The law of contracts governs the question whether there exists a valid and enforceable agreement to arbitrate. Such an agreement must contain the essential elements of a valid contract at common law. The question whether such a contract exists is a pure question of law, to which we apply a de novo standard of review.

"A party cannot be compelled to submit to arbitration unless he has first agreed to arbitrate." *Doyle & Russell, Inc. v. Roanoke Hosp. Ass'n*, 193 S.E.2d 662, 666 (Va. 1973). When the question before the court is whether the parties have agreed to arbitrate, there is no presumption in favor of arbitrability. Rather, the party seeking arbitration has the burden of proving the existence of the agreement. *See First Options of Chicago, Inc. v. Kaplan*, 514 U.S. 938, 945–46 (1995). A presumption in favor of arbitrability arises only after the existence of such an agreement has been proved, and the remaining question is whether the scope of the agreement is broad enough to include the disputed issue. Here, Triple bore the burden of proving that Mission had contracted to arbitrate Mission's disputes with Holdings.

We adhere to the view that the public policy of Virginia favors arbitration. *Delmarva Power, L.L.C. v. NCP of Va., L.L.C.*, 557 S.E.2d 199, 202 (Va. 2002). Nevertheless, that policy does not impair the constitutional right of a party to have access to the courts, including the right to a jury trial if requested, unless that party has, by contract, voluntarily waived those rights.

Triple argues that the operating agreement committed the parties to that agreement, Mission and Triple, to arbitrate all "disputes regarding their rights and obligations hereunder," and that Triple's derivative claim was nothing more than a dispute regarding Mission's duties under the operating agreement. We do not agree. Triple's argument ignores the separate existence of Holdings, which was not a party to the operating agreement.

Like a corporation, a limited liability company is a legal entity entirely separate and distinct from the shareholders or members who compose it. A derivative action is an equitable proceeding in which a member asserts, on behalf of the limited liability company, a claim that belongs to that entity rather than the member. The derivative claims asserted by Triple belonged to Holdings, not to Triple. A party asserting a derivative claim is not the real party in interest, but is "at best the nominal plaintiff." *Ross v. Bernhard*, 396 U.S. 531 (1970). [Though] Mission and Triple might have chosen to employ language that would have committed them to arbitrate their disputes with Holdings, they did not do so. Thus, there was no contractual undertaking by which Mission had agreed to arbitrate any dispute with Holdings. [Reversed and remanded.]

Parfi Holding AB v. Mirror Image Internet, Inc.

Delaware Supreme Court
817 A.2d 149 (2002)

VEASEY, CHIEF JUSTICE (FOR THE COURT EN BANC):

In this appeal, we hold that contracting parties who provide for the arbitration of disputes in their agreements need submit to arbitration only those claims that touch on the legal rights created by their contract. The Court of Chancery dismissed fiduciary duty claims brought by minority stockholders of a Delaware corporation on the ground that the transactions giving rise to the stockholders' causes of action were also the factual basis for contract claims relating to the Underwriting Agreement through which they acquired their interests in the company....

We disagree with this holding because the fiduciary duty claims the minority stockholders asserted are not based on the rights and obligations created by the underlying agreement that required arbitration of claims "arising out of or in connection with" the agreement itself. When contracting parties provide for the arbitration of claims in their agreement, the arbitration provision, no matter how broadly drafted, can reach only the claims within the scope of the contract, and the fiduciary duty claims here are beyond that scope....

Mirror Image Internet, Inc. is a Delaware corporation involved in designing hardware to speed information retrieval and transmission across the Internet. Mirror Image was formed in 1997 as a subsidiary of Mirror AB, a Swedish corporation. As a struggling start-up enterprise, Mirror Image required frequent infusions of capital to stay operational. Mirror AB could not, on its own, meet the financing needs of its subsidiary. By 1999, Mirror AB had to seek outside investors who could provide enough funds so that Mirror Image could meet its short-term obligations and stave off bankruptcy.

... Mirror Image entered into an agreement (the "Underwriting Agreement") with a corporation that is currently known as Xcelera Inc., and Plenteous Corp.... The Underwriting Agreement provided Mirror Image $2 million in capital, $1.75 million of which would be contributed by Xcelera and the balance provided by Plenteous. Once the Agreement closed, Xcelera became the controlling stockholder with a 62% interest in Mirror Image. Plenteous and two other stockholders, Grandsen, Ltd. and Gillberg, who were Mirror AB stockholders, were given the right to participate in the offering. They provided the balance of the $2 million and became minority stockholders in the corporation along with Mirror AB. In addition to setting the price and quantity terms of the stock offering, the Agreement granted Xcelera and Plenteous the right to appoint directors to the Mirror Image board. Mirror AB retained the right to appoint one director. Finally, the parties agreed that any dispute, controversy or claim "arising out of or in connection with this Agreement, or the breach, termination or invalidity thereof, shall be settled by arbitration" in Sweden.

The relationship among the parties deteriorated quickly after the stock offering closed. After gaining control of the corporation, Xcelera initiated a series of transactions that it claims were designed to benefit Mirror Image. The minority stockholders believe Xcelera has [benefited] only itself. [The court's summary of the schemes is omitted. They included assertions that (1) Mirror Image issued new stock to Xcelera that increased its ownership from 62.5% to 91.8% at a price below value without offering minority stockholders a chance to participate, through preemptive rights or otherwise; (2) Xcelera used its control of Mirror Image's board to time the announcement of a strategic business alliance between Hewlett-Packard and Mirror Image in a way that Xcelera profited and (3) Xcelera usurped a corporate opportunity that belonged to Mirror Image. It believed these raised breach of contract claims and breach of fiduciary duty claims.]

Abiding by the terms of the Underwriting Agreement, Parfi submitted its breach of contract claims to arbitration in Sweden. The contract claims Parfi presented at arbitration did not involve a breach of any specific provision of the Underwriting Agreement. Parfi sought to prove that Xcelera led its fellow underwriters to rely on certain assumptions that induced them to enter into the contract.... Parfi did not base any of its arbitration claims on its status as a stockholder of Mirror Image....

... Parfi and Plenteous could not convince the Tribunal that Xcelera entered into the Underwriting Agreement with ... intent to dilute the interests of the other investors.

The Tribunal held that the Agreement was meant to provide a short-term investment in capital, and any long-term plan to secure financing was not a basic assumption upon which the Agreement was based. The Tribunal awarded damages to Plenteous, however, because the arbitrators found that Plenteous' participation in the Agreement was based on Xcelera's assurance that it would seek Plenteous' consent before engaging Mirror Image in any "corporate action." The Tribunal determined that the [new stock offerings] were "corporate actions," and the Tribunal awarded Plenteous damages for any resulting dilution in their interest in Mirror Image.

Parfi [separately] filed an action in the Court of Chancery alleging that Xcelera breached fiduciary duties it owed to Mirror Image stockholders. Parfi alleged various claims of fraud, conspiracy, implied contract and misappropriation of a corporate opportunity against Xcelera and the Xcelera directors who sit on the Mirror Image board. [Among other defenses, Xcelera asserted] failure to submit the fiduciary duty claims to mandatory arbitration as provided in the Underwriting Agreement. The Court of Chancery granted Xcelera's motion for summary judgment and dismissed Parfi's claims, holding that the broad arbitration clause in the Underwriting Agreement required Parfi to submit for arbitration all claims related to the series of transactions that were challenged in Sweden....

When the arbitrability of a claim is disputed, the court is faced with two issues. First, the court must determine whether the arbitration clause is broad or narrow in scope. Second, the court must apply the relevant scope of the provision to the asserted legal claim to determine whether the claim falls within the scope of the contractual provisions that require arbitration. If the court is evaluating a narrow arbitration clause, it will ask if the cause of action pursued in court directly relates to a right in the contract. If the arbitration clause is broad in scope, the court will defer to arbitration on any issues that touch on contract rights or contract performance....

The parties do not dispute that Section 20.2 of the Underwriting Agreement has a broad scope. By agreeing to submit to arbitration "any dispute, controversy, or claim arising out of or in connection with" the Underwriting Agreement, Xcelera, Mirror AB, and Plenteous have signaled an intent to arbitrate all possible claims that touch on the rights set forth in their contract. The issue is whether the arbitrable contract claims are connected to the fiduciary duty claims that are independently grounded on Delaware corporation law.

The Vice Chancellor applied the arbitration clause to the fiduciary duty claims because he read the contract term to require "the resolution of claims related to a common set of underlying facts in a single forum." We disagree with this interpretation of what Mirror AB, Plenteous, and Xcelera intended to provide for in their contract. The issue is whether the fiduciary duty claims implicate any of the rights and obligations provided for in the Underwriting Agreement....

When parties to an agreement decide that they will submit their claims to arbitration, Delaware courts strive to honor the reasonable expectations of the parties and ordinarily resolve any doubt as to arbitrability in favor of arbitration. Nevertheless, arbitration is a mechanism of dispute resolution created by contract. An arbitration clause, no matter how broadly construed, can extend only so far as the series of obligations set forth in the underlying agreement. Thus, arbitration clauses should be applied only to claims that bear on the duties and obligations under the Agreement. The policy that favors alternate dispute resolution mechanisms, such as arbitration, does not trump basic principles of contract interpretation.

When Xcelera, Mirror AB, and Plenteous agreed to the arbitration provision in the Underwriting Agreement they did not commit to bring into arbitration every possible breach of duty that could occur between the parties. The arbitration clause signals only an intent to arbitrate matters that touch on the rights and performance related to the contract. The term "arising out of or in connection with" must be considered in that light. The Court of Chancery should have concentrated on the similarity of the separate rights pursued by plaintiffs under both the contract and the independent fiduciary duties rather than the similarity of the conduct that led to potential claims for both the contract and fiduciary breaches of duty.

Parfi can maintain an action based on the alleged breaches of the independent set of fiduciary duties that Xcelera owes Mirror Image stockholders even though the claims arise from some or all of the same facts that relate to the transactions that provided the basis for its contract claims. Xcelera's fiduciary duties to Mirror Image consist of a set of rights and obligations that are independent of any contract and need be submitted to arbitration only if the claims based on fiduciary duties touch on the obligations created in the Underwriting Agreement. If the Underwriting Agreement does not implicate Xcelera's fiduciary duties, the arbitration clause cannot bar Parfi from seeking the relief every other stockholder is entitled to under Delaware law.

The Underwriting Agreement does not establish rights and obligations extensive enough to encompass the dispute Parfi has brought in the Court of Chancery. The purpose of this Underwriting Agreement, like similar underwriting agreements, was to [reflect the terms of raising capital, designing the shares and setting the underwriter's compensation]. The Agreement set out the typical warranties related to compliance with securities laws and other regulations. . . . Reviewing the provisions of the Agreement, Xcelera cannot point to any contract term that creates a species of obligation upon which Parfi can base a breach of a fiduciary duty claim. . . .

By comparing [a separate] side agreement between the underwriters with the fiduciary duty claim, obvious differences in the scope and the nature of the obligations prove that the side agreement is a collateral matter to the Underwriting Agreement while the unfair dilution claims and the corporate opportunity claims are not. The side agreement was confined to only two parties, Xcelera and Plenteous. Xcelera's fiduciary duties as a controlling stockholder, by contrast, are owed to all Mirror Image stockholders. Plenteous cannot claim a right to consent unless it bargained for such a right. The right to protection against a controlling stockholder, however, applies automatically when a party becomes a Mirror Image stockholder. The consent Plenteous bargained for was confined to "corporate actions" taken by Xcelera through Mirror Image. An unfair dilution claim and corporate opportunity claim would encompass all transactions initiated by Xcelera that prove a breach of Xcelera's fiduciary duty.

Applying the arbitration clause to bar Parfi's action would lead to an absurd outcome: every stockholder except Parfi could bring the unfair dilution claim. The Vice Chancellor acknowledged this result but concluded that Parfi chose its predicament by basing a contract claim on the conduct that could have provided a stronger fiduciary duty claim. We disagree because the mandatory arbitration clause in the Agreement applies only to the rights relating to the initial offering of Mirror Image stock. The parties likely did not intend the provision to act as a bar to litigation over a set of rights and remedies that lay outside the scope of the Agreement itself.

… The right to vindicate breaches of fiduciary duty inflicted by a majority stockholder on the minority is a central doctrine of Delaware law. Absent a clear expression of an intent to arbitrate breach of fiduciary duty claims, Parfi has the right to have the merits of those claims adjudicated by the Court of Chancery….

Professor Seligman describes[9] an alternative process to derivative litigation and the special litigation committee, where the court appoints a "distinterested person" who investigates and determines whether a derivative proceeding is not in the best interests of the corporation. In comparison to a special litigation committee, the disinterested person procedure is more "neutral and should provide a good faith, intellectually honest effort to evaluate the merits of a derivative claim." In smaller companies, Professor Seligman suggests, the disinterested person who also is a lawyer may be viewed as a "bargain" compared to the special litigation committee. Fewer special counsels are necessary and the disinterested person can perform a "role trying to inspire settlements…." In cases involving complex claims and facts, the disinterested person can perform a useful "triage" role, by helping the court and the parties better understand the facts and distinguish between meritorious and nonmeritorious claims.

------

9. Joel Seligman, *The Disinterested Person: An Alternative to Shareholder Derivative Litigation*, Law & Contemp. Prob., 357, 362–65, 376–77 (1992).

Chapter 15

Indemnification and Insurance

Situation

Biologistics' directors now realize that their corporate decision making may lead to personal liabilities. They want to know how the corporation can help protect them, including the possibility of reimbursing them for any expenses and liabilities they may incur for breaches of their duties to the corporation. What strategies would you recommend?

Section I
Introduction

Surveys reveal the most common types of lawsuits against directors and officers. The most likely plaintiff group is shareholders, who allege that directors and officers act improperly in mergers, acquisitions, tender offers, and other major corporate transactions. Much of the material in this casebook explores these types of claims. The second most likely plaintiff group is employees, who make claims involving wrongful termination, employment discrimination, or breach of the employment contract. Finally, the third largest plaintiff class is customers and clients.

Given these risks, the corporation can significantly alter the actual personal liability of directors and officers in at least three ways. First, the corporation can utilize exculpation statutes. Recall, as discussed in Chapter 10, Duty of Care, these state corporate laws take various forms. Some allow the corporation, typically through its articles of incorporation, to diminish or eliminate directors' liability for certain breaches of duty. Others may alter the standards of conduct or impose a cap on the amount of liability that directors may incur personally.

Second, the corporation may advance to or reimburse directors for the expenses and liabilities they incur as a result of their corporate decisionmaking. For instance, directors who are found personally liable for a breach of their duty of care may seek corporate assistance under mandatory, permissive, and court-ordered indemnification statutes. If they are successful, the financial burden will effectively be shifted from the directors to the corporation.

Finally, the corporation can purchase insurance to cover the cost of directors' and officers' liabilities. Insurance policies may provide for repayment to the corporation for its indemnification of directors' liabilities. In addition, the policies may cover directors' liabilities for which they were not indemnified.

Keep in mind, however, there is a difference between what exculpation, permissive indemnification, and insurance statutes allow and what money directors in a specific case actually receive. For instance, these statutes typically authorize, but do not require, a corporation to provide the maximum benefits allowed under the law. Directors can rely only on their particular agreement with the corporation, as documented in a contract or in the corporate articles or bylaws. In negotiating this agreement, the corporation may have lesser standards than the individual directors and officers for what constitutes adequate protection. Because of the expense, a corporation may want to obtain only the minimum amount of insurance coverage for the risks of directors' and officers' liability.

In addition, while corporate agreements may provide for indemnification, receiving payments according to those agreements may be a problem. New management may be resistant to reimbursing disfavored directors and officers. Or the corporation may be experiencing financial problems that make indemnification payments from the corporation's general cash funds scarce or simply unavailable. Thus, directors may need to safeguard against these risks with reserve funds or escrow arrangements.

This chapter explores some of the legal and policy issues raised by indemnification and insurance. Consider whether the legal rules encourage fiduciaries to serve in corporate positions, yet do not prompt improper conduct.

Section II
Indemnification

As MBCA Subchapter E, Indemnification, Introductory Comment 1 explains:

> Indemnification (including advance for expenses) provides financial protection by the corporation for its directors against exposure to expenses and liabilities that may be incurred by them in connection with legal proceedings based on an alleged breach of duty in their service to or on behalf of the corporation. Today, when both the volume and the cost of litigation have increased dramatically, it would be difficult to persuade responsible persons to serve as directors if they were compelled to bear personally the cost of vindicating the propriety of their conduct in every instance in which it might be challenged.

> If permitted too broadly, however, indemnification may violate equally basic tenets of public policy. It is inappropriate to permit management to use corporate funds to avoid the consequences of certain conduct. For example, a director who intentionally inflicts harm on the corporation should not expect to receive assistance from the corporation for legal or other expenses and should be required to satisfy from his personal assets not only any adverse judgment but also expenses incurred in connection with the proceeding. Any other rule would tend to encourage socially undesirable conduct.

A further policy issue is raised in connection with indemnification against liabilities or sanctions imposed under state or federal civil or criminal statutes. A shift of the economic cost of these liabilities from the individual director to the corporation by way of indemnification may in some instances frustrate the public policy of those statutes.

The fundamental issue that must be addressed by an indemnification statute is the establishment of policies consistent with these broad principles: to ensure that indemnification is permitted only where it will further sound corporate policies and to prohibit indemnification where it might protect or encourage wrongful or improper conduct....

A. Mandatory Indemnification

The corporation is required to indemnify directors and officers in certain circumstances. In most states, directors are entitled by statute to be indemnified for expenses if they are "successful on the merits" in their lawsuits. A classic and venerable evaluation of this assertion appears in the following opinion which, though by a federal court, is recognized as a reliable statement of Delaware law.

Waltuch v. Conticommodity Services

United States Court of Appeals, Second Circuit
88 F.3d 87 (1996)

JACOBS, CIRCUIT JUDGE:

Famed silver trader Norton Waltuch spent $2.2 million in unreimbursed legal fees to defend himself against numerous civil lawsuits and an enforcement proceeding brought by the Commodity Futures Trading Commission (CFTC). In this action under Delaware law, Waltuch seeks indemnification of his legal expenses from his former employer. The district court denied any indemnity, and Waltuch appeals.

As vice-president and chief metals trader for Conticommodity Services, Inc., Waltuch traded silver for the firm's clients, as well as for his own account. In late 1979 and early 1980, the silver price spiked upward as the then-billionaire Hunt brothers and several of Waltuch's foreign clients bought huge quantities of silver futures contracts. Just as rapidly, the price fell until (on a day remembered in trading circles as "Silver Thursday") the silver market crashed. Between 1981 and 1985, angry silver speculators filed numerous lawsuits against Waltuch and Conticommodity, alleging fraud, market manipulation, and antitrust violations. All of the suits eventually settled and were dismissed with prejudice, pursuant to settlements in which Conticommodity paid over $35 million to the various suitors. Waltuch himself was dismissed from the suits with no settlement contribution. His unreimbursed legal expenses in these actions total approximately $1.2 million.

Waltuch was also the subject of an enforcement proceeding brought by the CFTC, charging him with fraud and market manipulation. The proceeding was settled, with Waltuch agreeing to a penalty that included a $100,000 fine and a six-month ban on buying or selling futures contracts from any exchange floor. Waltuch spent $1 million in unreimbursed legal fees in the CFTC proceeding. [This branch of the case appears later in this chapter.]

Waltuch brought suit in the United States District Court for the Southern District of New York (Lasker, J.) against Conticommodity and its parent company, Continental Grain Co. (together "Conti"), for indemnification of his unreimbursed expenses....

Waltuch's ... claim is that subsection (c) of § 145 requires Conti to indemnify him because he was "successful on the merits or otherwise" in the private lawsuits. The district court ruled for Conti on this claim.... The court explained that, even though all the suits against Waltuch were dismissed without his making any payment, he was not "successful on the merits or otherwise," because Conti's settlement payments to the plaintiffs were partially on Waltuch's behalf. For the reasons stated below, we reverse this portion of the district court's ruling, and hold that Conti must indemnify Waltuch under § 145(c) for the $1.2 million in unreimbursed legal fees he spent in defending the private lawsuits....

Unlike § 145(a), which grants a discretionary indemnification power, § 145(c) affirmatively *requires* corporations to indemnify its officers and directors for the "successful" defense of certain claims:

> To the extent that a director, officer, employee or agent of a corporation has been successful on the merits or otherwise in defense of any action, suit or proceeding referred to in subsections (a) and (b) of this section, or in defense of any claim, issue or matter therein, he shall be indemnified against expenses (including attorneys' fees) actually and reasonably incurred by him in connection therewith.

Waltuch argues that he was "successful on the merits or otherwise" in the private lawsuits, because they were dismissed with prejudice without any payment or assumption of liability by him. Conti argues that the claims against Waltuch were dismissed only because of Conti's $35 million settlement payments, and that this payment was contributed, in part, "on behalf of Waltuch."

The district court agreed with Conti that "the successful settlements cannot be credited to Waltuch but are attributable solely to Conti's settlement payments. It was not Waltuch who was successful, but Conti who was successful for him." 833 F. Supp. at 311. The district court held that § 145(c) mandates indemnification when the director or officer "is vindicated," but that there was no vindication here:

> Vindication is also ordinarily associated with a dismissal with prejudice without any payment. However, a director or officer is not vindicated when the reason he did not have to make a settlement payment is because someone else assumed that liability. Being bailed out is not the same thing as being vindicated.

Id. We believe that this understanding and application of the "vindication" concept is overly broad and is inconsistent with a proper interpretation of § 145(c).

No Delaware court has applied § 145(c) in the context of indemnification stemming from the settlement of civil litigation. One lower court, however, has applied that subsection to an analogous case in the criminal context, and has illuminated the link between "vindication" and the statutory phrase, "successful on the merits or otherwise." In *Merritt-Chapman & Scott Corp. v. Wolfson*, 321 A.2d 138 (Del. Super. Ct. 1974), the corporation's agents were charged with several counts of criminal conduct. A jury found them guilty on some counts, but deadlocked on the others. The agents entered into a "settlement" with the prosecutor's office by pleading nolo contendere to one of the counts in exchange for the dropping of the rest. The agents claimed entitlement to mandatory indemnification under § 145(c) as to the counts that were dismissed. In opposition, the corporation raised an argument similar to the argument raised by Conti:

> [The corporation] argues that the statute and sound public policy require indemnification only where there has been vindication by a finding or concession of innocence. *It contends that the charges against [the agents] were dropped for practical reasons*, not because of their innocence....
>
> The statute requires indemnification to the extent that the claimant "has been successful on the merits or otherwise." *Success is vindication*. In a criminal action, any result other than conviction must be considered success. *Going behind the result*, as [the corporation] attempts, is neither authorized by subsection (c) nor consistent with the presumption of innocence.

Id. at 141 (emphasis added).

Although the underlying proceeding in *Merritt* was criminal, the court's analysis is instructive here. The agents in *Merritt* rendered consideration—their guilty plea on one count—to achieve the dismissal of the other counts. The court considered these dismissals both "success" and (therefore) "vindication," and refused to "go[] behind the result" or to appraise the reason for the success. In equating "success" with "vindication," the court thus rejected the more expansive view of vindication urged by the corporation. Under *Merritt*'s holding, then, vindication, when used as a synonym for "success" under § 145(c), does not mean moral exoneration. Escape from an adverse judgment or other detriment, for whatever reason, is determinative. According to *Merritt*, the only question a court may ask is what the result was, not why it was.[1]

---

1. [12] Our adoption of *Merritt*'s interpretation of the statutory term "successful" does not necessarily signal our endorsement of the result in that case. The *Merritt* court sliced the case into individual counts, with indemnification pegged to each count independently of the others. We are not faced with a case in which the corporate officer claims to have been "successful" on some parts of the case but was clearly "unsuccessful" on others, and therefore take no position on this feature of the *Merritt* holding.

We also do not mean our discussion of *Merritt* to suggest that the line between success and failure in a criminal case may be drawn in the same way in the civil context. In a criminal case, conviction on a particular count is obvious failure, and dismissal of the charge is obvious success. In a civil suit for damages, however, there is a monetary continuum between complete success (dismissal of the suit without any payment) and complete failure (payment of the full amount of damages requested by the plaintiff). Because Waltuch made no payment in connection with the dismissal of the suits against him, we need not decide whether a defendant's settlement payment automatically renders that defendant "unsuccessful" under § 145(c).

Conti's contention that, because of its $35 million settlement payments, Waltuch's settlement without payment should not really count as settlement without payment, is inconsistent with the rule in *Merritt*. Here, Waltuch was sued, and the suit was dismissed without his having paid a settlement. Under the approach taken in *Merritt*, it is not our business to ask why this result was reached. Once Waltuch achieved his settlement gratis, he achieved success "on the merits or otherwise." And, as we know from *Merritt*, success is sufficient to constitute vindication (at least for the purposes of § 145(c)). Waltuch's settlement thus vindicated him.

The concept of "vindication" pressed by Conti is also inconsistent with the fact that a director or officer who is able to defeat an adversary's claim by asserting a technical defense is entitled to indemnification under § 145(c). In such cases, the indemnitee has been "successful" in the palpable sense that he has won, and the suit has been dismissed, whether or not the victory is deserved in merits terms. If a technical defense is deemed "vindication" under Delaware law, it cannot matter why Waltuch emerged unscathed, or whether Conti "bailed [him] out," or whether his success was deserved. Under § 145(c), mere success is vindication enough.

This conclusion comports with the reality that civil judgments and settlements are ordinarily expressed in terms of cash rather than moral victory. No doubt, it would make sense for Conti to buy the dismissal of the claims against Waltuch along with its own discharge from the case, perhaps to avoid further expense or participation as a non-party, potential cross-claims, or negative publicity. But Waltuch apparently did not accede to that arrangement, and Delaware law cannot allow an indemnifying corporation to escape the mandatory indemnification of subsection (c) by paying a sum in settlement on behalf of an unwilling indemnitee.

We note that two non-Delaware precedents (one from this Court) support our conclusion. In *Wisener v. Air Express Int'l Corp.*, 583 F.2d 579 (2d Cir. 1978), we construed an Illinois indemnification statute that was intentionally enacted as a copy of Delaware's § 145. Our holding in that case is perfectly applicable here:

> It is contended that [the director] was not "successful" in the litigation, since the third-party claims against him never proceeded to trial. The statute, however, refers to success "on the merits or otherwise," which surely is broad enough to cover a termination of claims by agreement without any payment or assumption of liability.

583 F.2d at 583. It is undisputed that the private lawsuits against Conti and Waltuch were dismissed with prejudice, "without any payment of assumption of liability" by Waltuch. Applying the analysis of *Wisener*, Conti must indemnify Waltuch for his expenses in connection with the private lawsuits.

The second case, from the Eastern District of Pennsylvania, is almost on point. In *B & B Investment Club v. Kleinert's, Inc.*, 472 F. Supp. 787 (E.D. Pa. 1979), suit had been brought against a corporation and two of its officers. The corporation settled the suit against it (on unspecified terms). One of the officers (Stephens) settled by paying $35,000, and the other (Brubaker) settled without paying anything. Brubaker claimed indemnification under a Pennsylvania statute that was virtually identical to

§ 145(c), *id.* at 789 n. 3, as the court noted, *id.* at 791 n. 5. The corporation argued that Brubaker was not "successful on the merits or otherwise," because his settlement was achieved only as a result of Stephens's $35,000 payment. The court rejected this argument, explaining that "[Brubaker] is entitled to indemnification because *he* made no monetary payment and the case was dismissed with prejudice *as to him*." *Id.* at 790 (emphasis added). Even though there was evidence that the plaintiffs dismissed their claims against Brubaker only because of Stephens's payment, this payment was irrelevant to the determination of "success":

> That the class plaintiffs at one point in the negotiations sought a cash payment from Brubaker but later settled with him for no monetary consideration does not render Brubaker any less successful than the plaintiff in *Wisener*. Nor is the extent of Brubaker's success affected by Stephens' having paid sufficient consideration to enable Brubaker to negotiate a dismissal with prejudice without making any payment. In short, Brubaker was "successful on the merits or otherwise"....

Id. at 791. The same logic applies to our case. "[T]he extent of [Waltuch's] success" is not lessened by Conti's payments, even if it is true (as it stands to reason) that his success was achieved because Conti was willing to pay. Whatever the impetus for the plaintiffs' dismissal of their claims against Waltuch, he still walked away without liability and without making a payment. This constitutes a success that is untarnished by the process that achieved it.

For all of these reasons, we agree with Waltuch that he is entitled to indemnification under § 145(c) for his expenses pertaining to the private lawsuits.

Notes and Questions

1. Most claims against directors and officers are settled. As a result, a question in many directors' and officers' minds is whether the mandatory indemnification provision applies to settlements. The answer appears to be that a settlement that is with prejudice and results in the dismissal of the case without any payment or assumption of liability may be considered a "success" within the meaning of that provision. Settlements that are without prejudice to a claimant's right to assert further claims against an officer are not "successes" under DGCL § 145(c).

2. While Delaware law allows for mandatory indemnification "to the extent" possible, consider the alternative approach illustrated by MBCA § 8.52 requiring that the director be "wholly" successful. As indicated in § 8.52 Official Comment:

> ... The word "wholly" is added to avoid the argument accepted in *Merritt-Chapman & Scott Corp. v. Wolfson*, 321 A.2d 138 (Del. 1974), that a defendant may be entitled to partial mandatory indemnification if, by plea bargaining or otherwise, he was able to obtain the dismissal of some but not all counts of an indictment. A defendant is "wholly successful" only if the entire proceeding is disposed of on a basis which does not involve a finding of liability.

3. Consistent with Delaware law, MBCA § 8.52 allows for mandatory indemnification if wholly successful "on the merits or otherwise." Section 8.52 Official Comment explains the significance of the word "otherwise":

> ... While this standard may result in an occasional defendant becoming entitled to indemnification because of procedural defenses not related to the merits, *e.g.*, the statute of limitations or disqualification of the plaintiff, it is unreasonable to require a defendant with a valid procedural defense to undergo a possibly prolonged and expensive trial on the merits in order to establish eligibility for mandatory indemnification.

B. Permissive Indemnification

In contrast to the mandatory indemnification situation where the corporation is required by statute to indemnify, permissive indemnification empowers but does not require the corporation to indemnify directors and officers in a wide range of other circumstances. The following opinion, another federal classic seen as a reliable statement of Delaware law, weights fundamental issues concerning permissive indemnification.

Heffernan v. Pacific Dunlop GNB Corp.

United States Court of Appeals, Seventh Circuit
965 F.2d 369 (1992)

Eschbach, Senior Circuit Judge.

Litigation is an occupational hazard for corporate directors, albeit one that may often be shifted to the corporation through indemnification. In this diversity case, we consider whether Delaware law precludes a former director from obtaining indemnification from the corporations he served. For the reasons that follow, we hold that the district court prematurely dismissed this case under Rule 12(b)(6) by concluding that it was one in which the director could prove no set of facts entitling him to indemnification. Accordingly, we reverse and remand for further proceedings.

I

Daniel E. Heffernan is a former director and 6.7% shareholder of GNB Holdings, Inc. (Holdings) and its wholly-owned subsidiary, GNB Inc. (GNB). In October 1987, a third firm, Pacific Dunlop Holdings, Inc. (Pacific) acquired control of Holdings (and in turn, GNB) pursuant to a stock purchase transaction whereby Pacific acquired approximately 60% of Holdings' stock, boosting its total ownership to 92%. Prior to Pacific's stock purchase, Holdings had filed a registration statement with the Securities and Exchange Commission (SEC) in contemplation of an initial public offering of its stock. Holdings later abandoned the public offering, opting instead to structure a private transaction with Pacific. The transaction was pursuant to an agreement (the Stock Purchase Agreement) by and among Pacific, Holdings, certain management shareholders, Heffernan and Allen & Co. (an investment company that owned approximately 20% of Holdings' stock and for which Heffernan was a vice president). Pursuant to the Stock Purchase Agreement, which apparently incorporated the material that Holdings previously had prepared for the SEC, Heffernan sold Pacific his 6.7% interest in Holdings and ceased to be a director.

Litigation subsequently arose out of the Stock Purchase Agreement. In September 1990, Pacific sued Heffernan and Allen & Co. under section 12(2) of the Securities Act of 1933, 15 U.S.C. §771(2), and under Illinois securities law. Pacific sought to rescind its purchase of Heffernan's and Allen & Co.'s shares in Holdings on the ground that the Stock Purchase Agreement was materially misleading in regard to its disclosure of certain liabilities facing Holdings and GNB. At oral argument, the parties indicated that Pacific has sued some of the other parties to the Stock Purchase Agreement as well, although the record leaves unclear specifically whom it sued. Heffernan requested indemnification and an advance on his litigation expenses from Holdings and GNB pursuant to section 145 of the Delaware General Corporation Law and the companies' corporate bylaws. When Holdings refused (and GNB failed to respond to) Heffernan's request, he initiated this action against the two companies seeking to establish his rights to indemnification and advances.

Under Delaware law, "a corporation may indemnify any person who was or is a party to any [suit] by reason of the fact that he is or was a director. . . ." § 145(a). Holdings' and GNB's bylaws make mandatory the provision for permissive indemnification in section 145(a). Holdings' bylaws state that "the Corporation shall, to the fullest extent permitted by the Delaware General Corporation law ... indemnify and hold harmless any person who is or was a party [to] any [suit] by reason of his status as, or the fact that he is or was or has agreed to become, a director [of] the Corporation or of an affiliate, and as to acts performed in the course of the [director's] duty to the Corporation...." GNB's bylaws simply state that "[t]he corporation shall indemnify its officers, directors, employees and agents to the extent permitted by the law of Delaware."

Heffernan does not argue that there is a material difference between the statutory requirement that a director be sued "by reason of the fact that" he was a director and Holdings' bylaw requirement that a director be sued "by reason of his status as, or the fact that" he was a director. And Holdings' brief footnote argument that its bylaw standard is narrower in scope than the statutory one fails in light of its bylaws' stated objective to indemnify directors "to the fullest extent permitted" by Delaware law. Thus, we focus our inquiry on whether Pacific may have sued Heffernan "by reason of the fact that" he was a director of Holdings and GNB.

II

The district court dismissed Heffernan's complaint, holding that he was not entitled to indemnification under the terms of the statute and bylaws because he had been sued for "wrongs he committed as an individual, not as a director." Furthermore, the district court reasoned that because "Heffernan's status as a director is not a necessary element of the section 12(2) claim" he was not sued by reason of the fact that he was a director. On appeal, Heffernan argues that although he was sued over a transaction in which he sold his own stock in Holdings, it does not necessarily follow as a matter of law that he was not sued "by reason of the fact that" he was a director of Holdings and GNB. He asserts that Delaware's "by reason of the fact that" phrase reaches

Pacific's suit against him because the suit involves his status as a director. Conversely, appellees Holdings and GNB contend that Pacific's complaint against Heffernan has nothing whatsoever to do with Heffernan's former status as a director for Holdings and GNB. They argue that Delaware's "by reason of the fact that" requirement means that a director must be sued for a breach of duty to the corporation or for a wrong committed on behalf of the corporation to be entitled to indemnification. Accordingly, Holdings and GNB assert that Heffernan is not entitled to indemnification because the "sale of his stock was a personal transaction which did not involve his duties or status as a director."

Despite a surprising dearth of case law addressing the reach of Delaware's "by reason of the fact that" language, our review of the substance of Pacific's complaint against Heffernan in light of the language and purpose of Delaware'[s] indemnification law convinces us that the district court's view of Pacific's complaint and Delaware's indemnification law is too restrictive. Standing alone, neither the fact that Heffernan sold his own shares in Holdings during the transaction nor the particular statutory provision on which Pacific's suit is based thwarts Heffernan's right to indemnification as a matter of law. Rather, the substance of Pacific's allegations and the nature and context of the transaction giving rise to the complaint indicate that Heffernan may have been sued, at least in part, because he was a director of Holdings and GNB. Furthermore, we find no support in the language and purpose of Delaware's indemnification statute for the defendants' argument that it limits indemnification to suits asserted against a director for breaching a duty of his directorship or for acting wrongfully on behalf of the corporation he serves. Thus, we conclude that Heffernan's complaint was improperly dismissed; it does not appear beyond doubt that Heffernan can prove no set of facts in support of his claim that would entitle him to the advances or indemnification he requests.

III

To determine whether Heffernan was sued "by reason of the fact" that he was a director of Holdings and GNB, we begin by reviewing the allegations in the underlying action's complaint. Here, the underlying complaint is based on Heffernan's sale of his shares in Holdings to Pacific pursuant to the Stock Purchase Agreement. More specifically, Pacific contends that Heffernan violated section 12(2) of the Securities Act by selling those securities pursuant to a misleading prospectus—that is, the Stock Purchase Agreement. Under section 12(2), a person who offers or sells a security through a prospectus or oral communication containing a material misrepresentation or omission may be liable to the purchaser. To avoid liability, the seller must prove that he did not know, and in the exercise of reasonable care could not have known, of the misrepresentation or omission.

In complaining of Heffernan's alleged failure to disclose environmental and other liabilities of Holdings and GNB in the Stock Purchase Agreement, Pacific's complaint repeatedly states that Heffernan's status as a director put him in a position where, in the performance of his duties as a director, he either learned or should have learned of those liabilities. Because Pacific realleges these provisions under both counts of its complaint, its argument that Heffernan's status as a director was not specifically alleged in the complaint is without merit. Moreover, assuming for the moment that Pacific's section 12(2) claim against Heffernan is viable, his status as a director is directly relevant to his defense. As noted earlier, to avoid liability under section 12(2), a defendant must prove that he did not know, and in the exercise of reasonable care could not have known, of the misrepresentation or omission. The defendant's position gives content to the term "reasonable care." For instance, reasonable care for a director requires more than does reasonable care for an individual owning a few shares of stock with no other connection to the corporation. It is accordingly no answer to our inquiry as to whether Heffernan was sued "by reason of the fact that" he was a director to label his participation in Pacific's acquisition of Holdings a "personal" transaction. Despite the fact that Heffernan sold his own shares to Pacific, a nexus exists between Heffernan's status as a director and Pacific's suit.

Moreover, the transaction at the heart of Pacific's complaint is not a purely personal transaction of Heffernan's. Despite Holdings' and GNB's arguments to the contrary, Heffernan was not "trading securities for his own account" in the usual meaning of that phrase. That is, this is not a situation in which Heffernan maintained a personal trading portfolio and encountered litigation over his individual sale of a security in an unrelated company. In such a scenario, "there is no reason why the corporation should be obligated or permitted to bear the executives' [litigation] expenses." Joseph W. Bishop, Jr., *The Law of Corporate Officers and Directors: Indemnification and Insurance* § 2.03 at 4 (1988). Rather, this was a structured sale of control transaction pursuant to one agreement—all of the stock that Pacific acquired in this transaction was pursuant to the Stock Purchase Agreement. We decline to distort the context in which Pacific's complaint arose by accepting Holdings' and GNB's unsupported invitation to carve Pacific's acquisition of Holdings' into various component parts.

Furthermore, neither the specific statutory provision under which a director is sued nor the mere form of the underlying complaint is dispositive of his right to indemnification. The logical extension of the district court's reliance on the "necessary elements" of section 12(2) in denying Heffernan indemnification as a matter of law is that Delaware did not intend for any suit under section 12(2) to fall within its indemnification provisions. Delaware's case-by-case approach to indemnification counsels against such a formalistic gloss. Otherwise, a director could be forced to bear the costs of unfounded, harassing litigation just because the particular cause of action does not specify a breach of a duty to the corporation, regardless of the connection between the suit and the individual's service as a director. As a practical matter, it is unsurprising that Pacific's complaint is not more explicit in its reliance on Heffernan's role as a director of Holdings and GNB. Because Pacific now controls Holdings and GNB, those three corporations' interests are aligned; thus Pacific has the incentive and opportunity to structure its complaint so as to avoid triggering its subsidiaries' duty of indemnification. Nevertheless, artful drafting cannot disguise the fact that the gravamen of Pacific's complaint is that Heffernan, at least in part because he was a director of Holdings and GNB, either knew or should have known that Holdings and GNB may be subject to environmental and other liabilities inadequately reflected in the Stock Purchase Agreement. We recognize that because Heffernan wore three hats—director, shareholder and investment banker—his director status may not be the *only* reason that he was sued by Pacific. But at this stage of this litigation, we cannot, as a matter of law, rule out the fact that it may have been one reason.

IV

Having established that Pacific's complaint is connected to Heffernan's status as a director, we now turn to whether Delaware's "by reason of" requirement necessarily requires more than the nexus present here. Without delineating the precise contours of the "by reason of" phrase, we conclude that it may be broad enough to encompass the litigation that Heffernan has incurred, at least in part, because of his status as a director of Holdings and GNB. Both the language and the purpose of Delaware's indemnification statute support interpreting its scope expansively.

First, Delaware is no neophyte in corporate law matters. Had it desired to limit permissible indemnification solely to those suits in which a director is sued for breaching a duty of his directorship or for certain enumerated causes of action, it would have jettisoned the supple "by reason of the fact that" phrase in favor of more specific language. Had Delaware desired to so limit its indemnification statute, we are confident that it could have found the words. Holdings and GNB have given us no reason to doubt that Delaware's choice of language was anything but purposeful and strategic. We believe that Delaware's "by reason of the fact that" phrase is broad enough to encompass suits against a director in his official capacity as well as suits against a director that arise more tangentially from his role, position or status as a director. Flexibility of language is vexing as well as liberating. In employing its "by reason of" phrase, Delaware is able to cover a myriad of potential factual scenarios that cannot be anticipated *ex ante* by the legislature or by corporate officials in drafting their articles and bylaws. The task of giving content to that flexible phrase, however, falls on the courts when the parties encounter interpretive differences.

Finally, we think that the policy of Delaware's indemnification statute supports permitting Heffernan to proceed to establish his right to advances and indemnification from Holdings and GNB. One of the primary purposes of Delaware's indemnification statute is to encourage capable individuals "to serve as corporate directors, secure in the knowledge that expenses incurred by them in upholding their honesty and integrity as directors will be borne by the corporation they serve." *MCI Telecommunications Corp. v. Wanzer*, 1990 Del. Super. LEXIS 222. Additionally, the statute ought to promote the "desirable end that corporate officials will resist what they consider unjustified suits and claims, secure in the knowledge that their reasonable expenses will be borne by the corporation they have served if they are vindicated." *Id.* Delaware has effectuated these policies by gradually expanding its indemnification provisions to cover the ever-changing contexts in which a director may encounter litigation. The district court's restrictive interpretation of Heffernan's claim diminishes the broad and expansive flavor of Delaware's indemnification provisions.

V

In sum, while a fine line often separates those suits emanating purely from a director's personal transactions and those suits emanating from a director's duties, role or status, we think the district court erred in prematurely concluding that Pacific's suit against Heffernan fell squarely on the personal side. We emphasize that our inquiry in this case has been a narrow one, confined to whether Heffernan's indemnification and advances claim against Holdings and GNB should be allowed to proceed. We express no opinion on the merits of Heffernan's right to advances, or on his ultimate right to indemnification. We hold only that his suit was prematurely dismissed under an unduly restrictive reading of Delaware's indemnification law. Holdings' bylaws have numerous prerequisites that a director must meet before being entitled to indemnification. Those remain to be explored in the district court. In addition, on remand the district court should first consider Heffernan's right to advances, which the Delaware Supreme Court has recently indicated may present a prior and distinct inquiry from a director's ultimate right to indemnification.

Reversed and Remanded.

Notes and Questions

1. MBCA §8.51 offers a complicated set of rules governing permissive indemnification, beginning with a general basis for permissive indemnification, followed by rules on the broadening or narrowing of indemnification. Section 8.51(a)(1) begins with the general basis, emphasizing the director's "good faith" and the "best interests of the corporation" standards. So long as these two standards are met, the director is allowed indemnification even though he or she may not satisfy the general duty of care standard in MBCA §8.30. Official Comment 1 to §8.51.

In addition to this general basis for permissive indemnification, §8.51(a)(2) allows the corporation to broaden indemnification through a provision in its articles of incorporation. The charter may provide indemnification to a director for liability "to any person for any action taken, or any failure to take any action, as a director," subject to exceptional circumstances such as the director's intentionally harming the corporation or improper financial benefit.

2. Permissive indemnification statutes typically include a "good faith" requirement. *In re Landmark Land Co. of Carolina*, 76 F.3d 553, 562–65 (4th Cir. 1996), *cert. denied*, 117 S. Ct. 59 (1996), addressed both the meaning of the requirement and who may determine if the directors acted in "good faith":

> Thus, there are two requirements for permissive indemnification under [Cal. Corp. Code] §317(b): (1) the corporation must authorize the indemnification, and (2) the agent must have acted in good faith and in the best interests of the corporation. It is not clear, however, whether the good faith determination should be made by a court or by the corporation itself.... At first glance, §317(e) suggests that the corporation's finding of good faith settles the matter, and that the court's role is limited to ensuring that the corporation made its finding of good faith by proper procedures.

We do not agree that the court's role is so narrow. Although a corporation has to find that the agent acted in good faith before authorizing indemnification, nothing in § 317(e) restricts a court's authority under § 317(b) to make an independent assessment of the agent's good faith. Section 317(b) allows permissive indemnification where the agent has acted in good faith, not where the corporation finds that the agent has acted in good faith. Reading § 317(b) together with § 317(e), we conclude that the issue of an agent's good faith is a question for the courts to decide....

In the instant case, it is not clear whether the district court — the indemnification court in this case — recognized the proper scope of its "good faith" determination. In finding that the Directors acted in good faith and in the best interest of the [corporation] when they filed the petitions for bankruptcy, the district court offered little explanation on how it reached its finding.... [I]mportantly, the district court did not explain how the Directors could have acted in good faith if the OTS [Office of Thrift Supervision, a federal regulatory authority] charges filed against them were true....

According to the OTS charges, the OTS investigated the Bank on June 4, 1990 and found that the Bank was inadequately capitalized and had demonstrated a pattern of repeated losses. The OTS directed the Bank to infuse sufficient capital to meet the minimum capitalization requirement, but the Bank did not submit an acceptable plan. Because of the Bank's inability to meet the requirement, the OTS forced the Bank directors to sign a Consent Agreement on January 15, 1991, signalling to the Directors that an OTS takeover was imminent. Instead of working with the OTS to correct the Bank's capitalization problem, the Directors filed the bankruptcy petitions to prevent the OTS from exercising control of the Bank's subsidiaries.

We cannot conclude that the Directors' action was taken in good faith. If the OTS charges are accurate, the Director's action to place the [corporation] in bankruptcy was a deliberate attempt to prevent the OTS from exercising control over the Bank's assets, thus hindering the OTS's ability to deal effectively with a failing savings and loan.... [T]he OTS therefore had a statutory duty to force the Bank's management to comply with the capitalization requirement. The Directors acknowledged the OTS's regulatory authority when they signed the Consent Agreement and agreed that the Bank's subsidiaries would not enter into any material transaction without prior approval from the OTS. When the OTS threatened to take control of the Bank, however, the Directors' used the bankruptcy code to stymie the OTS, even though their action breached the Consent Agreement with the OTS and violated their fiduciary duties to the Bank. We cannot condone the Directors' blatant attempt to circumvent the OTS's regulatory authority by holding that they acted in good faith.

Even if the bankruptcy filings benefitted the [corporation], we still could not conclude that the Directors acted in good faith. An agent who has intentionally participated in illegal activity or wrongful conduct against third persons cannot be said to have acted in good faith, even if the conduct benefits the corporation. "For example, corporate executives who participate in a deliberate price-fixing conspiracy with competing firms could not be found to have acted in good faith, even though they may have reasonably believed that a deliberate flouting of the antitrust laws would increase the profits of the corporation." 1 Harold Marsh, Jr. and R. Roy Finkle, *Marsh's California Corporation Law* (3d ed.) § 10.43, at 751. We recognize that the Directors did not break any law by filing the bankruptcy petitions, and that the OTS has not filed criminal charges against the Directors. Nonetheless, we find that a deliberate attempt to undermine the regulatory authority of a government agency cannot constitute good faith conduct, even if such actions benefit the corporation.

The Directors intentionally breached their fiduciary duties to the Bank and their Consent Agreement with the OTS in order to prevent the OTS from exercising the powers granted to it [by law]. The Directors knew the impropriety of their actions, and one of the Directors ... resigned his position when he learned of the scheme. We therefore conclude that the Directors did not act in good faith when they placed the [corporation] in bankruptcy.

C. Non-Exclusivity Statutes

It is not always clear whether the mandatory, permissive, and court-ordered indemnification discussed above exhaust the forms of indemnification available in a particular state. Whether the corporation can indemnify officers and directors further depends on whether the statutes described above are considered nonexclusive.

Waltuch v. Conticommodity Services
United States Court of Appeals, Second Circuit
88 F.3d 87 (1996)

[In this case, in addition to addressing the mandatory indemnification issue explored earlier in this Chapter, the court also addressed the effect of Delaware's non-exclusivity statute on expenses incurred in the CFTC proceeding.]

Waltuch claims that Article Ninth of Conticommodity's articles of incorporation requires Conti to indemnify him for his expenses in both the private and CFTC actions. Conti responds that this claim is barred by subsection (a) of § 145 of Delaware's General Corporation Law, which permits indemnification only if the corporate officer acted "in good faith," something that Waltuch has not established. Waltuch counters that subsection (f) of the same statute permits a corporation to grant indemnification rights outside the limits of subsection (a), and that Conticommodity did so with Article Ninth (which has no stated good-faith limitation). The district court held that, notwithstanding § 145(f), Waltuch could recover under Article Ninth only if Waltuch met the "good faith" requirement of § 145(a). On the factual issue of whether Waltuch had acted "in good faith," the court denied Conti's summary judgment motion and cleared the way for trial. The parties then stipulated that they would forego trial on the issue of Waltuch's "good faith," agree to an entry of final judgment against Waltuch on his claim under Article Ninth and § 145(f), and allow Waltuch to take an immediate appeal of the judgment to this Court. Thus, as to Waltuch's first claim, the only question left is how to interpret §§ 145(a) and 145(f), assuming Waltuch acted with less than "good faith." As we explain ... below, we affirm the district court's judgment as to this claim and hold that § 145(f) does not permit a corporation to bypass the "good faith" requirement of § 145(a)....

Article Ninth, [of Conticommodity's articles of incorporation] on which Waltuch bases his first claim, is categorical and contains no requirement of "good faith":

> The Corporation shall indemnify and hold harmless each of its incumbent or former directors, officers, employees and agents ... against expenses actually and necessarily incurred by him in connection with the defense of any action, suit or proceeding threatened, pending or completed, in which [such a person] is made a party, by reason of ... serving in or having held such position or capacity, except in relation to matters as to which [the person] shall be adjudged in such action, suit or proceeding to be liable for negligence or misconduct in the performance of duty.

Conti argues that § 145(a) of Delaware's General Corporation Law, which does contain a "good faith" requirement, fixes the outer limits of a corporation's power to indemnify; Article Ninth is thus invalid under Delaware law, says Conti, to the extent that it requires indemnification of officers who have acted in bad faith. The affirmative grant of power in § 145(a) is as follows:

> *A corporation shall have power to indemnify* any person who was or is a party or is threatened to be made a party to any threatened, pending or completed action, suit or proceeding, whether civil, criminal, administrative or investigative (other than an action by or in the right of the corporation) by reason of the fact that [the person] is or was a director, officer, employee or agent of the corporation, or is or was serving at the request of the corporation as a director, officer, employee or agent of another corporation, partnership, joint venture, trust or other enterprise, against expenses (including attorneys' fees), judgments, fines and amounts paid in settlement actually and reasonably incurred by [the person] in connection with such action, suit or proceeding *if [the person] acted in good faith and in a manner [the person] reasonably believed to be in or not opposed to the best interests of the corporation*, and, with respect to any criminal action or proceeding, had no reasonable cause to believe [the person's] conduct was unlawful....

In order to escape the "good faith" clause of § 145(a), Waltuch argues that § 145(a) is not an *exclusive* grant of indemnification power, because § 145(f) expressly allows corporations to indemnify officers in a manner broader than that set out in § 145(a). The "nonexclusivity" language of § 145(f) provides:

> The indemnification and advancement of expenses provided by, or granted pursuant to, the other subsections of this section *shall not be deemed exclusive*

of any other rights to which those seeking indemnification or advancement of expenses may be entitled under any bylaw, agreement, vote of stockholders or disinterested directors or otherwise, both as to action in [the person's] official capacity and as to action in another capacity while holding such office.

Waltuch contends that the "nonexclusivity" language in § 145(f) is a separate grant of indemnification power, not limited by the good faith clause that governs the power granted in § 145(a). Conti on the other hand contends that § 145(f) must be limited by "public policies," one of which is that a corporation may indemnify its officers only if they act in "good faith."

In a thorough and scholarly opinion, Judge Lasker agreed with Conti's reading of § 145(f), writing that "it has been generally agreed that there are public policy limits on indemnification under Section 145(f)," although it was "difficult ... to define precisely what limitations on indemnification public policy imposes." 833 F. Supp. at 307, 308. After reviewing cases from Delaware and elsewhere and finding that they provided no authoritative guidance, Judge Lasker surveyed the numerous commentators on this issue and found that they generally agreed with Conti's position. He also found that Waltuch's reading of § 145(f) failed to make sense of the statute as a whole:

> [T]here would be no point to the carefully crafted provisions of Section 145 spelling out the permissible scope of indemnification under Delaware law if subsection (f) allowed indemnification in additional circumstances without regard to these limits. The exception would swallow the rule.

Id. at 309. The fact that § 145(f) was limited by § 145(a) did not make § 145(f) meaningless, wrote Judge Lasker, because § 145(f) "still 'may authorize the adoption of various procedures and presumptions to make the process of indemnification more favorable to the indemnitee without violating the statute.'" *Id.* at 309 (quoting 1 Balotti & Finkelstein § 4.16 at 4-321). As will be evident from the discussion below, we adopt much of Judge Lasker's analysis.

A. *Delaware Cases*

No Delaware court has decided the very issue presented here; but the applicable cases tend to support the proposition that a corporation's grant of indemnification rights cannot be *inconsistent* with the substantive statutory provisions of § 145, notwithstanding § 145(f). We draw this rule of "consistency" primarily from our reading of the Delaware Supreme Court's opinion in *Hibbert v. Hollywood Park, Inc.*, 457 A.2d 339 (Del. 1983). In that case, Hibbert and certain other directors sued the corporation and the remaining directors, and then demanded indemnification for their expenses and fees related to the litigation. The company refused indemnification on the ground that directors were entitled to indemnification only as *defendants* in legal proceedings. The court reversed the trial court and held that Hibbert was entitled to indemnification under the plain terms of a company bylaw that did not draw an express distinction between plaintiff directors and defendant directors. The court then proceeded to test the bylaw for consistency with § 145(a):

> Furthermore, *indemnification here is consistent with current Delaware law.*
> Under 8 Del. C. § 145(a)..., "a corporation may indemnify any person who

was or is a party or is threatened to be made a party to any threatened, pending or completed" derivative or third-party action. By this language, indemnity is *not limited* to only those who stand as a defendant in the main action. The corporation can also grant indemnification rights beyond those provided by statute. 8 Del. C. § 145(f).

Id. at 344 (emphasis added and citations omitted). This passage contains two complementary propositions. Under § 145(f), a corporation may provide indemnification rights that go "beyond" the rights provided by § 145(a) and the other substantive subsections of § 145. At the same time, any such indemnification rights provided by a corporation must be "consistent with" the substantive provisions of § 145, including § 145(a). In *Hibbert*, the corporate bylaw was "consistent with" § 145(a), because this subsection was "not limited to" suits in which directors were defendants. *Hibbert*'s holding may support an inverse corollary that illuminates our case: if § 145(a) had been expressly limited to directors who were named as defendants, the bylaw could not have stood, regardless of § 145(f), because the bylaw would not have been "consistent with" the substantive statutory provision.

A more recent opinion of the Delaware Supreme Court, analyzing a different provision of § 145, also supports the view that the express limits in § 145's substantive provisions are not subordinated to § 145(f). In *Citadel Holding Corp. v. Roven*, 603 A.2d 818, 823 (Del. 1992), a corporation's bylaws provided indemnification "to the full extent permitted by the General Corporation Law of Delaware." The corporation entered into an indemnification agreement with one of its directors, reciting the parties' intent to afford enhanced protection in some unspecified way. The director contended that the agreement was intended to afford mandatory advancement of expenses, and that this feature (when compared with the merely permissive advancement provision of § 145(e)) was the enhancement intended by the parties. The corporation, seeking to avoid advancement of expenses, argued instead that the agreement enhanced the director's protection only in the sense that the precontract indemnification rights were subject to statute, whereas his rights under the contract could not be diminished without his consent.

In rejecting that argument, the court explained that indemnification rights provided by contract could not exceed the "scope" of a corporation's indemnification powers as set out by the statute:

> If the General Assembly were to amend Delaware's director indemnification statute with the effect of curtailing the scope of indemnification a corporation may grant a director, the fact that [the director's] rights were also secured by contract would be of little use to him. Private parties may not circumvent the legislative will simply by agreeing to do so.

Id. Citadel thus confirms the dual propositions stated in *Hibbert*: indemnification rights may be broader than those set out in the statute, but they cannot be inconsistent with the "scope" of the corporation's power to indemnify, as delineated in the statute's substantive provisions....

B. *Statutory Reading*

The "consistency" rule suggested by these Delaware cases is reinforced by our reading of § 145 as a whole. Subsections (a) (indemnification for third-party actions) and (b) (similar indemnification for derivative suits) expressly grant a corporation the power to indemnify directors, officers, and others, if they "acted in good faith and in a manner reasonably believed to be in or not opposed to the best interest of the corporation." These provisions thus limit the scope of the power that they confer. They are permissive in the sense that a corporation may exercise less than its full power to grant the indemnification rights set out in these provisions. By the same token, subsection (f) permits the corporation to grant additional rights: the rights provided in the rest of § 145 "shall not be deemed exclusive of any other rights to which those seeking indemnification may be entitled." But crucially, subsection (f) merely acknowledges that one seeking indemnification may be entitled to "other rights" (of indemnification or otherwise); it does not speak in terms of corporate power, and therefore cannot be read to free a corporation from the "good faith" limit explicitly imposed in subsections (a) and (b)....

When the Legislature intended a subsection of § 145 to augment the powers limited in subsection (a), it set out the additional powers expressly. Thus subsection (g) explicitly allows a corporation to circumvent the "good faith" clause of subsection (a) by purchasing a directors and officers liability insurance policy. Significantly, that subsection is framed as a grant of corporate power:

> A corporation shall have power to purchase and maintain insurance on behalf of any person who is or was a director, officer, employee or agent of the corporation ... against any liability asserted against him and incurred by him in any such capacity, or arising out of his status as such, *whether or not the corporation would have the power to indemnify him against such liability under this section.*

The italicized passage reflects the principle that corporations have the power under § 145 to indemnify in some situations and not in others. Since § 145(f) is neither a grant of corporate power nor a limitation on such power, subsection (g) must be referring to the limitations set out in § 145(a) and the other provisions of § 145 that describe corporate power. If § 145 (through subsection (f) or another part of the statute) gave corporations unlimited power to indemnify directors and officers, then the final clause of subsection (g) would be unnecessary: that is, its grant of "power to purchase and maintain insurance" (exercisable regardless of whether the corporation itself would have the power to indemnify the loss directly) is meaningful only because, in some insurable situations, the corporation simply lacks the power to indemnify its directors and officers directly.

A contemporaneous account from the principal drafter of Delaware's General Corporation Law confirms what an integral reading of § 145 demonstrates: the statute's affirmative grants of power also impose limitations on the corporation's power to indemnify. Specifically, the good faith clause (unchanged since the Law's original enactment in 1967) was included in subsections (a) and (b) as a carefully calculated improvement on the prior indemnification provision and as an explicit limit on a corporation's power to indemnify:

> During the three years of the Revision Committee's study, no subject was more discussed among members of the corporate bar than the subject of indemnification of officers and directors. As far as Delaware law was concerned, the existing statutory provision on the subject had been found inadequate. Numerous by-laws and charter provisions had been adopted clarifying and extending its terms, but *uncertainty existed in many instances as to whether such provisions transgressed the limits* which the courts had indicated they would establish based on public policy....
>
> It was ... apparent that revision was appropriate with respect to *the limitations which must necessarily be placed on the power to indemnify* in order to prevent the statute from undermining the substantive provisions of the criminal law and corporation law....
>
> [There was a] need for a ... provision to protect the corporation law's requirement of loyalty to the corporation.... Ultimately, it was decided that *the power to indemnify should not be granted unless* it appeared that the person seeking indemnification had "acted in good faith and in a manner reasonably believed to be in or not opposed to the best interest of the corporation."

S. Samuel Arsht & Walter K. Stapleton, *Delaware's New General Corporation Law: Substantive Changes*, 23 Bus. Law. 75, 77–78 (1967). This passage supports *Hibbert's* rule of "consistency" and makes clear that a corporation has no power to transgress the indemnification limits set out in the substantive provisions of § 145.

Waltuch argues at length that reading § 145(a) to bar the indemnification of officers who acted in bad faith would render § 145(f) meaningless. This argument misreads § 145(f). That subsection refers to "any other rights to which those seeking indemnification or advancement of expenses may be entitled." Delaware commentators have identified various indemnification rights that are "beyond those provided by statute," *Hibbert*, 457 A.2d at 344, and that are at the same time consistent with the statute:

> [S]ubsection (f) provides general authorization for the adoption of various procedures and presumptions making the process of indemnification more favorable to the indemnitee. For example, indemnification agreements or by-laws could provide for: (i) mandatory indemnification unless prohibited by statute; (ii) mandatory advancement of expenses, which the indemnitee can, in many instances, obtain on demand; (iii) accelerated procedures for the "determination" required by section 145(d) to be made in the "specific case"; (iv) litigation "appeal" rights of the indemnitee in the event of an unfavorable determination, (v) procedures under which a favorable determination will be deemed to have been made under circumstances where the board fails or refuses to act; [and] (vi) reasonable funding mechanisms.

E. Norman Veasey, et al., *Delaware Supports Directors With a Three-Legged Stool of Limited Liability, Indemnification, and Insurance*, 42 Bus. Law. 399, 415 (1987).

Moreover, subsection (f) may reference nonindemnification rights, such as advancement rights or rights to other payments from the corporation that do not qualify as indemnification.

We need not decide in this case the precise scope of those "other rights" adverted to in § 145(f). We simply conclude that § 145(f) is not rendered meaningless or inoperative by the conclusion that a Delaware corporation lacks power to indemnify an officer or director "unless [he or she] 'acted in good faith and in a manner reasonably believed to be in or not opposed to the best interest of the corporation.'" *See* Arsht & Stapleton, 23 Bus. Law. at 78. As a result, we hold that Conti's Article Ninth, which would require indemnification of Waltuch even if he acted in bad faith, is inconsistent with § 145(a) and thus exceeds the scope of a Delaware corporation's power to indemnify. Since Waltuch has agreed to forego his opportunity to prove at trial that he acted in good faith, he is not entitled to indemnification under Article Ninth for the [monies] he spent in connection with the private lawsuits and the CFTC proceeding. We therefore affirm the district court on this issue.

Notes and Questions

1. Note that Waltcuh paid $1 million in settlement of the CFTC proceeding. Presumably all agreed that this meant he was not "successful on the merits or otherwise," under DGCL 145(c) as interpreted in the private investor branch of *Waltcuh* (where he paid nothing in the settlement).

2. Can you give additional examples of "other rights" that might be adverted to in DGCL 145(c)? The materials above make reference to (a) making permissive provisions of the DGCL mandatory, concerning both indemnification and advancement and (b) extending coverage to participation on all sides of litigation (which might extend beyond mere defendants and plaintiffs to encompass counterclaimants, interpleaders, impleaders and others). A further example of an "other right" might cover the expenses reasonably and actually incurred in prosecuting a demand for indemnification or advancement.

3. *PepsiCo, Inc. v. Continental Casualty Co.*, 640 F. Supp. 656, 660 (S.D.N.Y. 1986), offers an alternative view of the meaning of nonexclusivity statutes. Corporate officers and directors there were accused of violating federal securities laws. In the course of the proceedings, including settlement agreements, the corporation indemnified its officers and directors. It then sought reimbursement under an insurance policy covering officer and director liability (discussed further in the next section).

The insurance company argued that the corporation had not complied with Delaware's permissive indemnification statutes. It argued that the corporation had not determined that the defendants acted in "good faith" and in the "best interests of the corporation." In addition, the corporation had not followed the proper process for determining if these standards were met. The corporation responded that its bylaws broadened its ability to indemnify. The bylaws made indemnification of directors and officers "the rule rather than the exception."

The court agreed with the corporation. It indicated that the standards and processes of the Delaware permissive indemnification statutes were "simply 'fall back' provisions which a Delaware corporation may or may not adopt." *Id.* at 661. The corporation's decision to supplant the terms of the statute with its own standards and processes for indemnification was permitted under the statute's nonexclusivity provisions.

Section III
Insurance

Insurance can be preferable to indemnification for certain conduct. For example, longstanding SEC policy opposes indemnification for officers and directors arising from violations of the Securities Act of 1933. The rationale is an interpretation of that Act as intended more to promote managerial diligence through deterrence and prevention than to provide recompense. *See generally* 17 C.F.R. §229.510 (stating SEC policy, including requiring registrants to disclose in registration statements that they have been advised of this policy).

Insurance covering corporate directors and officers (commonly called "D&O insurance") was first marketed in the late 1960s, when state corporate law statutes were amended specifically to authorize corporations to provide it. Such statutes allow corporations to purchase this insurance "whether or not the corporation would have the power to indemnify" against such liabilities under the indemnification provisions. MBCA §8.57. In other words, the corporation may purchase insurance coverage under circumstances where the permissive indemnification statutes would often prohibit indemnification—for instance, to cover the amounts paid in settlement or adverse judgments in derivative actions. Consequently, insurance theoretically can fill the gap between the directors' and officers' total amount of liability and the amount that the corporation indemnified.

Most state corporation law statutes, however, impose limits. As ALI §7.20(b)(2) illustrates:

> A corporation should not be entitled to purchase insurance ... to the extent that the insurance would furnish protection against liability for conduct directly involving a knowing and culpable violation of law or involving a significant pecuniary benefit obtained by an insured person to which the person is not legally entitled.

Similarly, federal securities law cases construing D&O insurance policies recognize a public policy against insuring persons for losses arising from willful or criminal misconduct, as this would dilute the goals of securities law to deter such conduct and to promote diligence among persons subject to those laws. Coverage is pretty much limited to breach of duty, neglect, error, misstatement, misleading statement, omission, or act. Recklessness, residing in the median, is placed sometimes on the insurable and sometimes on the uninsurable side of this line.

Furthermore, D&O insurance policies invariably contain an express coverage exclusion for certain fraudulent acts. A typical policy provides: "The insurer shall not be liable to make any payment for Loss in connection with any Claim made against an Insured ... arising out of, based upon or attributable to the committing in fact of any criminal or deliberate fraudulent act...." Ty R. Sagalow & Michael R. Young, Dealing with the D&O Insurer (in Michael R. Young, ed., Accounting Irregularities and Financial Fraud (2d ed. 2002), at 140, 157). This, therefore, excludes criminal and deliberate fraud, but "provides coverage for fraud that arises out of recklessness." *Id.*

Such statutory, judicial and contractual limitations reflect general principles of insurance law and practice. A basic and ancient principle of insurance law holds that losses must be "fortuitous." This doctrine excludes as uninsurable those losses an insured party causes intentionally. Dean Jerry summarizes:

> It is a fundamental requirement in insurance law that the insurer will not pay for a loss unless the loss is "fortuitous," meaning that the loss must be accidental in some sense [citing *Waller v. Truck Ins. Exch.*, 900 P.2d 619, 626 (Cal. 1995)] ("This concept of fortuity is basic to insurance law"). The public policy underlying the fortuity requirement is so strong that if the insurance policy itself does not expressly require that the loss be accidental courts will imply such a requirement. The fortuity principle is often expressed with reference to certainty: losses that are certain to occur, or which have already occurred, are not fortuitous. In some jurisdictions, the fortuity doctrine is codified [citing N.Y. INS. LAW §1101[a] (2001); CAL. INS. CODE §22 (2001)].

ROBERT H. JERRY, II, UNDERSTANDING INSURANCE LAW (3d ed. 2002), at 450–51.

In each case, on the other hand, a mechanism is needed to determine the class of conduct involved. A typical policy provides that denial of coverage due to designated classes of conduct must be based on a final adjudication. But it is rare for any class action to go through trial to a final judgment, including claims for breach of fiduciary duties or violations of securities laws. Other policy provisions state that the denial must be based on findings of fact reached, for example, by a corporation's directors independent from the issues and persons involved. Insurers cannot always rely upon the objectivity of such a body. For these reasons, as a practical matter, insurance covers a wide range of culpable behavior despite contrary public policy or insurance policy exclusions.

Plaintiffs' lawyers further circumvent these public-policy and insurance-coverage exclusions for intentional misconduct by not pressing fraud claims that they fear will give insurers grounds to deny coverage. When D&O insurance exists, for example, this leads plaintiffs to avoid alleging "actual intent" in order to keep coverage in place. They try to meet the relevant culpability standard, being careful not to proffer evidence of "intent or conscious knowledge."

Apart from the fortuity requirement and associated limitations, the scope of D&O insurance coverage and exclusions varies over time with market conditions. Although authorized by state corporation law in the late 1960s, such policies were relatively rare before the 1980s, and then began to proliferate. The proliferation was slowed somewhat by two cases where directors were held personally liable for staggering sums that their D&O insurance covered. [*Smith v. Van Gorkom*, 488 A.2d 858 (Del. 1985) and *Fox v. Chase Manhattan Corp.*, Del. Ch. Case No. 8192-85 (Dec. 6, 1985)].

The market recovered from these shocks, in part by using more tailored contracts that expanded policy amounts and risks covered while more effectively managing risks. Protections against frivolous litigation provided by Congress in the late 1990s sustained market growth, but a reversal occurred in the early 2000s amid a wave of large insurance settlements and the September 11, 2001 terrorist attacks that shook all insurance markets. Readjustments followed, with premiums increasing, coverage decreasing, and various self-insurance requirements imposed.

Subject to these variations driven by market and regulatory changes, a few generalizations about D&O insurance are possible. The typical D&O liability insurance policy contains two types of coverage: the first covers the corporation for its responsibility to indemnify directors and officers ("Company Reimbursement") and the second covers losses incurred by the directors and officers which the corporation is not permitted or required to indemnify ("Directors and Officers Liability"). The policy contains provisions defining the rights of those insured and the obligations of the insurance company. A description of the coverage, for instance, indicates the limits of the coverage, deductibles for which the corporation and individual directors and officers are responsible, and the policy period.

Chapter 16

Impact of Securities Laws on Corporations

Situation

Biologistics, Inc. has been in existence just over five years, and it has had continuing success. Earnings have increased steadily, with those for the last year reaching almost $600,000. What may be more important, the corporation has just patented a process for manipulating the DNA of plants so as to create increased resistance to certain diseases. Developing efficient production techniques will be expensive, however. Further bank borrowings or sales of securities will be necessary if the process is to be exploited fully.

Phillips has discussed with Anderson and Baker the possibility of selling perhaps 25% of the corporation to a small group of wealthy investors. He believes that his investment banking firm could sell common stock representing that much ownership for $3 million. Alternatively, he has suggested that the corporation do, through his firm, a $3 million public offering of the corporation's common stock. That, of course, would make Biologistics a publicly held rather than a closely held corporation. Anderson and Baker would like your advice about those alternatives.

Many and various corporate transactions have securities law implications. So pervasive, in fact, is the involvement of securities law in corporate transactions that it is impossible to practice corporate law without also practicing securities law, at least to a limited extent. Lawyers handling corporation law matters need to have at least some understanding of the most important features of the federal securities laws — as well as the securities laws of the state or states involved in the lawyer's corporate transactions. The primary federal statutes are the Securities Act of 1933 (called the Securities Act) and the Securities Exchange Act of 1934 (called the Exchange Act), as these have been amended from time to time, including by the Williams Act of 1968 and the Sarbanes-Oxley Act of 2002, among others. This relatively modest chapter highlights basic aspects of these federal statutes, which ensuing chapters explore in greater detail. Note that these subjects, while important to many corporate lawyers, are complex and treated more completely in law school courses on Securities Regulation.

Section I
Securities Act of 1933

Anytime a corporation, or anyone else for that matter, offers or sells securities, the application of federal and state securities laws needs to be considered. At the most basic level, the analysis under federal law can be quite simple. A registration statement must be filed, under the Securities Act of 1933, before a security may be offered, and the registration statement must be effective before a security may be sold, and prospectuses must be prepared and used in prescribed ways in each case, unless an exemption is available. The usual 1933 Act analysis of a particular transaction, then, basically goes like this:

(1) Does the transaction involve a security?

(2) Is the security being offered or sold?

(3) Is a registration exemption available?

The first of these issues is much trickier than it may at first seem. Many commercial schemes that the uninitiated would never dream involve a security—from those relating to warehouse receipts for scotch whiskey to condominium time sharing plans—may, in fact, involve one. Basically, if such a transaction involves the investment of money in a common enterprise, with profits to come solely from the efforts of others, a security (in the form of an "investment contract") exists. Of course, determining what is a "common enterprise," what are "profits" and what "solely" means present many difficulties (for example, "solely" means, among other things, something like "mainly").

Federal courts once struggled with a "What is a security?" question at the other end of the spectrum. The question was whether a "security," for purposes of the federal securities laws, is involved when a corporation is sold by means of a sale of its stock, particularly when the sale has been to one or a very small number of purchasers. That is, whether in this particular context, a corporation's stock is a "security"? In a series of decisions, the circuit courts split on the question. The Supreme Court held that a sale of a business, by means of selling the stock in the corporation that gives structure to the business, is a security for the purposes of federal securities law.

The resolution of the second issue listed above, "Is a security being offered or sold?", is usually quite straightforward—but not always. The question is raised in perhaps its most interesting form in connection with corporate mergers and assets acquisitions where the acquiring corporation pays for the acquisition with its own securities. The tricky thing here is that the shareholders of the acquired corporation, who may ultimately receive the acquiring corporation's securities, personally have no dealings with the acquiring corporation. They may vote to approve or disapprove the merger or asset sale, but this can be viewed simply as a part of the decision-making process within their own corporation. What the questions come down to are these: "When the shareholders are asked to vote, are the acquiring corporation's securities being offered to them?" and, "When the securities come to them, have the securities been sold?" The answer to both questions is "Yes."

The third issue above, "Is a registration exemption available?", is extremely important, because registration is expensive and time consuming. If a privately held company "goes public" by registering and selling its securities to the public, the securities will be sold by securities firms who buy the securities from the issuer at a discount. In relatively small transactions, the discount to the securities firms will be 10%. So, in a $5 million offering, that will mean $500,000 comes off the top. Also, legal and accounting fees, and printing expenses, are likely to total a minimum of another $500,000.

Most publicly held companies can register and sell securities for a lower percentage of the dollar amount involved, so registration is, for them, more practical. It is clear, however, that registration is not an option for a privately owned company that does not want to go public. Therefore, an exemption must be available for every offer and sale of its securities — including the securities issued upon formation of a corporation. Usually an exemption can be found. The company just needs to be represented by counsel who is expert enough in securities law to know exactly how the offering has to be done. What this means for business lawyers is that, to represent privately held companies, they or someone in their firm must understand the relevant portions of the Securities Act very well.

Section II
Securities Exchange Act of 1934[1]

The Securities Exchange Act of 1934 is broader than the Securities Act of 1933. As its name indicates, the Exchange Act regulates securities exchanges. It also regulates securities firms and other securities professionals. In those respects, the Exchange Act is the province of a relatively small number of securities lawyers. But, in addition, the Exchange Act contains provisions that apply broadly to publicly held companies, and others that apply to anyone who engages in securities transactions.

The Exchange Act mandates registration of securities under two distinct circumstances. First, an issuer or securities must register securities under Exchange Act Section 12(b) when the securities are to be traded on a stock exchange. Second, an issuer must register securities under that Act when the issuer meets stated tests with respect to number of shareholders and amount of assets. Under Exchange Act Section 12(g)(1), read along with Exchange Act Rule 12g-1, promulgated by the Securities and Exchange Commission, an issuer must register a class of equity securities when the securities are held by 500 or more shareholders and the issuer's total assets exceed $10 million.

a. *Periodic Reporting.* By registering securities under the Exchange Act, an issuer becomes a "reporting company." That means it is subject to the periodic reporting requirements of Section 13(a). Under Section 13(a) and related SEC rules, reporting

---

1. Adapted from Linda O. Smiddy & Lawrence A. Cunningham, *Soderquist on Corporate Law and Practice* (3d ed. 2009). Copyright © 2007, 2008, 2009 by Practicing Law Institute. All rights reserved.

companies must file a wide variety of reports with the SEC on a continuing basis. The most common of those reports are the Form 10-K annual report, Form 10-Q quarterly report, and Form 8-K current report, which is filed upon the occurrence of specified material events.

b. *Proxy Rules.* Proxy voting by shareholders is a fact of life for most publicly held corporations. State corporation laws require annual meetings, and typically such corporations cannot satisfy quorum requirements unless most shareholders are represented by proxy holders. For that reason, management usually solicits proxies from a corporation's shareholders annually and whenever a special shareholders' meeting is called. In addition to that ordinary use of proxies, those attempting to take over the management of a corporation sometimes solicit proxies from shareholders to gather needed votes.

At the heart of the Exchange Act's regulation of proxy solicitations is Section 14(a), which makes it illegal to violate the SEC's proxy rules with respect to the solicitation of a proxy to vote securities registered under the Exchange Act. Those rules are voluminous and generate much work for a corporation's lawyers and accountants in connection with each meeting of a publicly held corporation's shareholders.

Any security holder may solicit proxies from fellow security holders. In a large corporation, however, preparation and dissemination costs are considerable, making direct solicitation impractical. In light of that, the SEC promulgated Rule 14a-8, which requires management to include in its proxy statement proposals made by security holders, along with supporting statements, when certain conditions are met. Those conditions cover things like timeliness, amount of securities held by the proposer, and the subject of the proposal.

The most important proxy rule, at least in terms of danger of litigation, is Rule 14a-9. It is the SEC's anti-fraud provision in the proxy area, and basically prohibits soliciting a proxy with respect to a security registered under the Exchange Act on the basis of materially false or misleading information.

c. *Tender Offer Rules.* The Exchange Act subjects tender offers for publicly held companies to substantial regulation under legislation passed in 1968, known as the Williams Act. That Act added to the Exchange Act Sections 13(d) and (e) and 14(d), (e) and (f). Section 13(d) is aimed at tender offers only indirectly. It requires a person acquiring more than 5% of a class of equity securities registered under the Exchange Act to disclose in public filings with the SEC that fact and related intentions (along with other information) within ten days after the acquisition (and then periodic updates). Section 13(e) empowers the SEC to regulate repurchases by issuers of their own equity securities.

Section 14(d) is the centerpiece of the Williams Act. It makes it unlawful, unless prescribed filings are made and other procedures complied with, to make a tender offer for a registered equity security if success in the offer would result in ownership of more than 5% of the class. Section 14(d) also contains some substantive regulation of tender offers. For example, it provides that if an offeror raises the offering price, it must pay that higher price to all tendering security holders.

The Williams Act also contains an antifraud provision, Section 14(e), making it unlawful to conduct a tender offer on the basis of materially false or misleading information. Unlike other provisions in the Williams Act, Section 14(e) relates not only to tender offers for specified types of securities (basically those registered under the Exchange Act), but to tender offers for any kind of security.

Section 14(f) is a specialized provision requiring stated disclosures to the SEC and security holders when a majority of a corporation's directorships are to be filled, other than at a meeting of security holders, following an acquisition of securities that is subject to Sections 13(d) or 14(d). The usual trigger of that provision is filling a vacant directorship by sitting directors, generally allowed under state corporation law. It is intended to deal with situations when corporate control is sold and, as a part of the transaction, existing directors agree to resign seriatim, and remaining directors elect replacements chosen by the buyer.

d. *General Anti-Fraud Rule: 10b-5.* Exchange Act Rule 10b-5 is the Commission's most important anti-fraud tool. It renders it unlawful to make any materially untrue or misleading statement in connection with the purchase or sale of any security; "to employ any device, scheme, or artifice to defraud"; or "to engage in any act, practice, or course of business which operates or would operate as a fraud or deceit upon any person." Although by its terms Rule 10b-5 is a criminal provision, courts consistently have implied a private right of action under it.

The most frequent use of Rule 10b-5 has been in insider trading cases, typically those when an officer, director, or other insider buys or sells securities when possessing material, nonpublic information. But the rule also is used in other situations, including: (1) when a corporation issues false or misleading information to the public, or keeps silent when it has a duty to disclose; (2) when an insider selectively discloses material, nonpublic information to another person, who then trades; and (3) when a person mismanages a corporation in ways connected with the purchase or sale of securities.

e. *Section 16 Short-Swing Profit Rules.* Exchange Act Section 16(b) is designed to minimize unfair use of inside information. Under it, profits made by insiders from transactions involving publicly traded stock, when a purchase and a sale are made within less than six months of each other, must be disgorged and paid over to the issuer. Section 16(a) requires beneficial owners of more than 10% of any class of equity security (other than an exempted security) registered under the Exchange Act, and officers and directors of issuers of such securities, to file reports with the SEC and relevant securities exchanges concerning their holdings of all equity securities of such issuers.

Section 16(b) is complicated. It provides that: (i) any profit, (ii) by any person subject to the reporting requirements of Section 16(a), (iii) realized on any purchase and sale, or sale and purchase, (iv) within any period of less than six months, of any nonexempt equity security of an issuer that has an equity security registered under the Exchange Act, "shall inure to and be recoverable by the issuer" (subject to narrow exceptions). An issuer may sue to recover those so-called short-swing profits, or any security holder of the issuer may sue derivatively to recover the profits when after a request the issuer fails to bring suit within sixty days or when it fails diligently to prosecute a claim once filed.

Section III
Sarbanes-Oxley Act of 2002[2]

While the Securities Act of 1933 and the Exchange Act of 1934 (along with the Williams Act of 1968) concentrate on matters traditionally recognized as securities laws, regulating offers, sales, and exchanges of securities, the Sarbanes-Oxley Act of 2002 addresses many matters traditionally recognized as involving corporation law. The Sarbanes-Oxley Act, passed in the wake of numerous sizable corporate debacles proliferating during the economic boom of the late 1990s, sought to correct some of the excesses perceived to contribute to a norm of corporate governance laxity in that era, particularly in the contexts of accounting, auditing and internal control over financial reporting.

Sarbanes-Oxley established requirements concerning the composition and activities of board audit committees. Members of such bodies must otherwise be independent of the corporation and, as a group, be directly responsible for appointing, paying, and supervising outside auditors, among other stated duties. Disclosure is required as to whether at least one audit committee member is a "financial expert" and, if not, why not.

Audit committees are to be the chief point of contact for a corporation's outside auditors. Accordingly, auditors must report a series of specified matters to the audit committee. First, auditors must report to the committee all critical accounting policies and practices that a corporation uses. Second, auditors must report to the audit committee all alternative accounting treatments that they discussed with management, the implication of the choices, and which the auditor prefers. Third, auditors must share with audit committees all material written communications between the auditor and corporate management, including any information concerning unresolved differences of opinion between the auditor and management.

Audit committees must assure that auditors are independent of the corporation, according to criteria the Sarbanes-Oxley Act specifies. First, auditors are not considered independent of their clients if they perform non-audit services for them (other than tax services and providing comfort letters to underwriters in public offerings of securities). Second, no audit firm is independent of a corporation if certain of its senior officers worked at the audit firm and on that corporation's audit within the year before the start of the audit in question. Third, auditors must rotate lead and reviewing partners so that neither role is performed by the same individual for the same company for more than five consecutive years. Fourth, audit committees must pre-approve all

---

2. Adapted from Linda O. Smiddy & Lawrence A. Cunningham, *Soderquist on Corporate Law and Practice* (3d ed. 2009). Copyright © 2007, 2008, 2009 by Practicing Law Institute. All rights reserved.

services, including tax services and comfort letters, performed by outside auditors and disclose them in regular periodic reports.

Sarbanes-Oxley also contains requirements concerning management reports and auditor review of internal controls. Officers must certify in periodic reports that they designed internal controls, disclosed control deficiencies or weaknesses to outside auditors and board audit committees, and disclosed any fraud involving employees with significant internal control roles. Companies must provide annual internal control reports expressing management's responsibility for establishing and maintaining internal controls and assessing their effectiveness. Outside auditors must review and opine upon the assessment.

Concerning these audits of internal control, the auditor's letter includes a description of "the scope of the auditor's testing of [a registrant's] internal control structure and procedure." The letter must present the findings from that testing and an evaluation of whether controls produce record-retention and reporting practices necessary to produce financial statements in accordance with generally accepted accounting principles (GAAP) and meet managerial and board directives. Companies must disclose any significant internal control changes.

The Sarbanes-Oxley Act requires CEOs and chief financial officers (CFOs) to certify in periodic financial statements that the statements "fairly present, in all material respects, the financial condition and results of operations of the company." They must certify that the CEO and CFO designed corporate internal controls to ensure that relevant information flows to those officers and that they evaluated, within the preceding ninety days, the effectiveness of internal controls. These officers also must affirm that they disclosed discovered control deficiencies or weaknesses to their outside auditors and board audit committee, as well as any fraud, material or not, involving employees with significant internal control roles.

Penalty rules impose forfeiture of bonuses on senior officers if their company must restate its financials due to misconduct producing material noncompliance with financial reporting requirements. Those officers must repay bonuses and stock options received for the war after the incorrect report was made, along with any profits generated on the award during that year.

The Sarbanes-Oxley Act imposes criminal penalties. The "knowing" or "corrupt" destruction, alteration, or falsification of records with intent to frustrate federal investigations yields fines and imprisonment of up to twenty years. The Sarbanes-Oxley Act creates offenses for "securities fraud schemes" and for attempts. Violations can result in criminal and civil liability, with maximum fines for individuals of $5 million rand for organizations of $25 million). For individuals, sanctions apply to conspiracies, attempted fraud, and mail and wire fraud. "Knowing" violations of the CEO/CFO certification rules carry penalties of up to ten years imprisonment and $1 million in fines, and "willful" violations yield up to twenty years and $5 million.

The Sarbanes-Oxley Act requires compliance programs, document retention policies, and internal investigation procedures. Annual and quarterly report disclosure must state whether the company has adopted a code of ethics for senior officers and, if not, why not. Changes to ethics codes, including waivers, must be disclosed promptly. Companies may not retaliate against employees for assisting in internal or external investigations of corporate violations of federal securities or antifraud laws. The Sarbanes-Oxley Act expressly grants whistle-blowers private rights of action for retaliation by a public company.

The Sarbanes-Oxley Act prohibits loans to directors and executives. It also forbids officers and directors to trade in securities received by them as employees when the company's pension plan participants are restricted from trading under other applicable federal laws. Violations of this rule result in individual forfeiture of the profits to the company without regard to intent. The Sarbanes-Oxley Act authorizes derivative lawsuits to recover such profits.

Pursuant to the Sarbanes-Oxley Act, the SEC established minimum standards of attorney professional conduct that require attorneys to "report evidence of a material violation of securities law or breach of fiduciary duty or similar violation" to the company's chief legal counsel or chief executive officer (CEO). If those individuals do not respond appropriately, then the lawyer must report up to the audit committee or any other board committee comprised solely of independent directors.

Section IV
Special Position of Securities Lawyers

The environment in which securities lawyers practice is quite different from that of most other lawyers. That difference is probably the result of two distinguishing characteristics of securities law practice. First, it is usually a securities lawyer who decides whether a particular transaction can proceed or, because of legal problems, must be cancelled. As a matter of common practice, for example, it is often true that unless a lawyer attests to the legality of a transaction by the delivery of an opinion, the parties to the transaction will not agree to proceed. Second, a securities lawyer typically does not merely advise clients on how to accomplish a transaction, but rather, he or she usually is an active participant in the transaction.

The first of those characteristics, coupled with the knowledge of the Commission that its own enforcement resources are wholly insufficient to police a significant fraction of securities transactions, has caused the Commission to advocate that a lawyer has a special responsibility to protect the public when working in the securities area. The second of these characteristics, the active involvement by lawyers in securities transactions, sometimes insures that when the legality of a completed transaction is questioned, one or more securities lawyers will find themselves in the middle of the controversy, rather than somewhat comfortably on the sidelines.

There are a number of cases that point up the distinguishing characteristics of securities law practice and the results that can flow from these characteristics. Some of these have been brought by the Commission under Rule 102(e) of its rules of practice, which relates to unethical or improper professional conduct by those appearing before it. In one famous case, *In re Carter*,[3] the Commission announced the test for unethical or improper professional conduct it would apply:

> The Commission is of the view that a lawyer engages in "unethical or improper professional conduct" under the following circumstances: When a lawyer with significant responsibilities in the effectuation of a company's compliance with the disclosure requirements of the federal securities laws becomes aware that his client is engaged in a substantial and continuing failure to satisfy those disclosure requirements, his continued participation violates professional standards unless he takes prompt steps to end the client's noncompliance.

Section 602 of the Sarbanes-Oxley Act of 2002 codifies (with minor changes) the main part of Rule 102(e) as a new section 4C of the Exchange Act. This new section relates to improper or unethical professional conduct, and other related problems, in the context of all federal securities laws. More importantly, section 307 of Sarbanes-Oxley mandates the Commission to pass rules that set minimum standards of professional conduct for securities lawyers representing issuers (which, under that Act's definition, essentially means Exchange Act reporting companies and companies that have filed a Securities Act registration statement). Such rules must meet the specifications of section 307. The Commission issued these rules in a compendium entitled "Standards of Professional Conduct for Attorneys Appearing and Practicing Before the Commission in the Representation of an Issuer." The rules are complex and go beyond the section 307 mandate. Basically, they lay reporting obligations on both in-house and outside counsel in the case of material violations of the securities laws or fiduciary duties, or similar violations.

Rule 3 requires lawyers to report evidence of a material violation by an issuer or by an officer, director, employee, or agent of an issuer. In most cases, the lawyer would report such a violation to the issuer's chief legal officer or to that officer and the chief executive officer. The chief legal officer then has the obligation to cause an inquiry into the allegation and to report back to the lawyer who made the report of a possible violation. If the chief legal officer finds no violation, his or her response to the reporting lawyer must state the basis for the finding. If the chief legal officer finds a violation, he or she must advise the reporting attorney of his or her findings and the action he or she took relating to the violation. As an alternative to causing an inquiry into an allegation from a reporting attorney, the chief legal officer may refer the attorney's report to a qualified legal compliance committee of the board (these committees are discussed below).

If the reporting lawyer receives an appropriate response within a reasonable time, his or her obligations usually are complete. If the reporting lawyer does not receive an appropriate response within a reasonable time, he or she must report the evidence of a material violation to the audit committee, to another committee of independent directors, or to the full board of directors if the board has no committee consisting

---

3. Exchange Act Release No. 17, 597 (Feb. 28, 1981).

only of independent directors. Alternatively, the report may be made to a "qualified legal compliance committee" of independent directors, if the board has established such a committee. (The "qualified legal compliance committee" does not have to be a separate committee, but may be a board committee, such as the audit committee, that meets the Commission's requirements and that is named as such.) If the reporting lawyer does not believe that the issuer has made an appropriate response, then his or her responsibility does not stop at receiving the report mentioned at the beginning of this paragraph. In such a situation, the lawyer must explain the reasons for his or her belief to the chief legal officer and the chief executive officer, and to directors to whom the lawyer may have reported the evidence of a material violation.

Rule 3 provides reporting lawyers with an alternative to reporting evidence of material violations to the chief legal officer or to the chief legal officer and the chief executive officer. A lawyer may bypass these officers and report his or her evidence directly to a qualified legal compliance committee and, in that case, need not receive or access any report from such a committee.

Rules 4 and 5 establish the responsibilities of subordinate lawyers and those who supervise them. Rule 6 details the manner in which the Commission will prosecute violations by lawyers. In this respect, it should be noted that, under Rule 6, lawyers who violate the Standards of Professional Conduct may be sanctioned by the Commission as if they had violated one of the federal securities laws. Rule 7 provides that nothing in the Standards of Professional Conduct creates a private right of action and that the Commission has exclusive authority to enforce compliance.

The Commission once proposed that lawyers be required to make a "noisy withdrawal" when issuers fail to take appropriate actions with respect to a lawyer's report. This withdrawal would include disaffirming to the Commission any past tainted submissions, and essentially equates to informing on the client. The Commission also proposed an alternative to "noisy withdrawal." Under this alternative, the issuer, and not the lawyer, would have the responsibility to report the lawyer's withdrawal or failure to receive an appropriate response to his or his report of evidence of material violation. An issuer typically would make the required disclosure on a Form 8-K current report under the Exchange Act.

Chapter 17

Proxy Regulation

Situation

Before Biologistics, Inc. got very far in its thinking about raising cash through a sale of securities, it found itself presented with another opportunity. Daytron Corporation, a large conglomerate that is incorporated in the same state as Biologistics and whose common stock is traded on a national stock exchange, became interested in acquiring Biologistics. Daytron's officers said they would wish to retain current management and would give them a free hand so long as Biologistics remains successful. Daytron would provide the needed cash for exploitation of the just patented process along with production and marketing assistance.

Daytron and the shareholders of Biologistics, Inc. have now come to an agreement on an exchange of stock. Certain Daytron shareholders are against Daytron's doing further acquisitions, however, and have indicated that they may fight this acquisition by one means or another. Daytron does not have any authorized but unissued shares, so it will have to amend its Articles of Incorporation to increase its number of authorized shares. It will hold a special meeting of its shareholders to approve the amendment and will solicit shareholders' proxies for the meeting. In its proxy materials it will describe Biologistics, Inc. and its business, and because of this has asked that your firm assist in the drafting of the proxy materials.

Anderson and Baker have agreed that you should help Daytron's lawyers with the proxy work. In light of the opposition of some Daytron shareholders to the acquisition, Anderson and Baker want you to discuss with them the chance that Daytron will not be able to proceed with the exchange of stock.

———

Shareholders may vote either in person or by proxy. To do the latter, a shareholder simply appoints someone else as his or her agent for the purpose of voting. State corporation statutes typically say very little about proxy voting, leaving to agency law most of its regulation at the state level. This is probably all the law that is needed in the typical close corporation, where a shareholder is likely to be personally involved in the corporation, or at least is likely to know whoever solicits his or her proxy. What is missing in state law, however, is regulation to protect shareholders of publicly held corporations from being asked to give their proxies, to persons they do not know, for purposes that are not fully explained.

The Securities Exchange Act of 1934 has filled this gap in state proxy law. The federal proxy regulation scheme is found in § 14 of the Exchange Act and the rules of the Securities and Exchange Commission. The thrust of the regulation is disclosure. That is, with minor exceptions neither Congress nor the SEC has attempted to regulate who may solicit proxies or under what circumstances proxies may be solicited. In the main, the regulation simply requires full and detailed disclosure of prescribed information anytime proxies are solicited in respect of securities (other than exempted securities) that are registered under the Exchange Act. This is covered in § 14(a) and its rules. Much of the litigation under § 14 has involved Rule 14a-9, which prohibits false or misleading statements, or material omissions, in connection with proxy solicitations.

The cases that follow deal with some of the more interesting questions relating to proxy solicitations.

Section I
General

Mills v. Electric Auto-Lite Co.

United States Supreme Court
396 U.S. 375 (1970)

Mr. Justice Harlan delivered the opinion of the Court.

This case requires us to consider a basic aspect of the implied private right of action for violation of § 14(a) of the Securities Exchange Act of 1934, recognized by this Court in *J.I. Case Co. v. Borak*, 377 U.S. 426 (1964). As in *Borak* the asserted wrong is that a corporate merger was accomplished through the use of a proxy statement that was materially false or misleading. The question with which we deal is what causal relationship must be shown between such a statement and the merger to establish a cause of action based on the violation of the Act.

I

Petitioners were shareholders of the Electric Auto-Lite Company until 1963, when it was merged into Mergenthaler Linotype Company. They brought suit on the day before the shareholders' meeting at which the vote was to take place on the merger, against Auto-Lite, Mergenthaler, and a third company, American Manufacturing Company, Inc. The complaint sought an injunction against the voting by Auto-Lite's management of all proxies obtained by means of an allegedly misleading proxy solicitation; however, it did not seek a temporary restraining order, and the voting went ahead as scheduled the following day. Several months later petitioners filed an amended complaint, seeking to have the merger set aside and to obtain such other relief as might be proper.

In Count II of the amended complaint, which is the only count before us, petitioners predicated jurisdiction on § 27 of the 1934 Act. They alleged that the proxy statement sent out by the Auto-Lite management to solicit shareholders' votes in favor of the merger was misleading, in violation of § 14(a) of the Act and SEC Rule 14a-9 thereunder. Petitioners recited that before the merger Mergenthaler owned over 50% of the outstanding shares of Auto-Lite common stock, and had been in control of

Auto-Lite for two years. American Manufacturing in turn owned about one-third of the outstanding shares of Mergenthaler, and for two years had been in voting control of Mergenthaler and, through it, of Auto-Lite. Petitioners charged that in light of these circumstances the proxy statement was misleading in that it told Auto-Lite shareholders that their board of directors recommended approval of the merger without also informing them that all 11 of Auto-Lite's directors were nominees of Mergenthaler and were under the "control and domination of Mergenthaler." Petitioners asserted the right to complain of this alleged violation both derivatively on behalf of Auto-Lite and as representatives of the class of all its minority shareholders.

On petitioners' motion for summary judgment with respect to Count II, the District Court for the Northern District of Illinois ruled as a matter of law that the claimed defect in the proxy statement was, in light of the circumstances in which the statement was made, a material omission. The District Court concluded, from its reading of the *Borak* opinion, that it had to hold a hearing on the issue whether there was "a causal connection between the finding that there has been a violation of the disclosure requirements of § 14(a) and the alleged injury to the plaintiffs" before it could consider what remedies would be appropriate.

After holding such a hearing, the court found that under the terms of the merger agreement, an affirmative vote of two-thirds of the Auto-Lite shares was required for approval of the merger, and that the respondent companies owned and controlled about 54% of the outstanding shares. Therefore, to obtain authorization of the merger, respondents had to secure the approval of a substantial number of the minority shareholders. At the stockholders' meeting, approximately 950,000 shares, out of 1,160,000 shares outstanding, were voted in favor of the merger. This included 317,000 votes obtained by proxy from the minority shareholders, votes that were "necessary and indispensable to the approval of the merger." The District Court concluded that a causal relationship had thus been shown, and it granted an interlocutory judgment in favor of petitioners on the issue of liability, referring the case to a master for consideration of appropriate relief.

The District Court made the certification required by 28 U.S.C. § 1292(b), and respondents took an interlocutory appeal to the Court of Appeals for the Seventh Circuit. That court affirmed the District Court's conclusion that the proxy statement was materially deficient, but reversed on the question of causation. The court acknowledged that, if an injunction had been sought a sufficient time before the stockholders' meeting, "corrective measures would have been appropriate." 403 F.2d 429, 435 (1968). However, since this suit was brought too late for preventive action, the courts had to determine "whether the misleading statement and omission caused the submission of sufficient proxies," as a prerequisite to a determination of liability under the Act. If the respondents could show, "by a preponderance of probabilities, that the merger would have received a sufficient vote even if the proxy statement had not been misleading in the respect found," petitioners would be entitled to no relief of any kind. *Id.*, at 436.

The Court of Appeals acknowledged that this test corresponds to the common-law fraud test of whether the injured party relied on the misrepresentation. However, rightly concluding that "[r]eliance by thousands of individuals, as here, can scarcely be inquired into" (*id.*, at 436, n. 10), the court ruled that the issue was to be determined by proof of the fairness of the terms of the merger. If respondents could show that the merger had merit and was fair to the minority shareholders, the trial court would be justified in concluding that a sufficient number of shareholders would have approved the merger had there been no deficiency in the proxy statement. In that case respondents would be entitled to a judgment in their favor.

Claiming that the Court of Appeals has construed this Court's decision in *Borak* in a manner that frustrates the statute's policy of enforcement through private litigation, the petitioners then sought review in this Court. We granted certiorari, believing that resolution of this basic issue should be made at this stage of the litigation and not postponed until after a trial under the Court of Appeals' decision.

II

As we stressed in *Borak*, § 14(a) stemmed from a congressional belief that "[f]air corporate suffrage is an important right that should attach to every equity security bought on a public exchange." H.R. Rep. No. 1383, 73d Cong., 2d Sess., 13. The provision was intended to promote "the free exercise of the voting rights of stockholders" by ensuring that proxies would be solicited with "explanation to the stockholder of the real nature of the questions for which authority to cast his vote is sought." *Id.*, at 14; S. Rep. No. 792, 73d Cong., 2d Sess., 12. The decision below, by permitting all liability to be foreclosed on the basis of a finding that the merger was fair, would allow the stockholders to be bypassed, at least where the only legal challenge to the merger is a suit for retrospective relief after the meeting has been held. A judicial appraisal of the merger's merits could be substituted for the actual and informed vote of the stockholders.

The result would be to insulate from private redress an entire category of proxy violations—those relating to matters other than the terms of the merger. Even outrageous misrepresentations in a proxy solicitation, if they did not relate to the terms of the transaction, would give rise to no cause of action under § 14(a). Particularly if carried over to enforcement actions by the Securities and Exchange Commission itself, such a result would subvert the congressional purpose of ensuring full and fair disclosure to shareholders.

Further, recognition of the fairness of the merger as a complete defense would confront small shareholders with an additional obstacle to making a successful challenge to a proposal recommended through a defective proxy statement. The risk that they would be unable to rebut the corporation's evidence of the fairness of the proposal, and thus to establish their cause of action, would be bound to discourage such shareholders from the private enforcement of the proxy rules that "provides a necessary supplement to Commission action." *J.I. Case Co. v. Borak*, 377 U.S., at 432.[1]

---

1. [5] The Court of Appeals' ruling that "causation" may be negated by proof of the fairness of the merger also rests on a dubious behavioral assumption. There is no justification for presuming that the shareholders of every corporation are willing to accept any and every fair merger offer put before them; yet such a presumption is implicit in the opinion of the Court of Appeals. That court gave no indication of what evidence petitioners might adduce, once respondents had established that the merger proposal

Such a frustration of the congressional policy is not required by anything in the wording of the statute or in our opinion in the *Borak* case. Section 14(a) declares it "unlawful" to solicit proxies in contravention of Commission rules, and SEC Rule 14a-9 prohibits solicitations "containing any statement which ... is false or misleading with respect to any material fact, or which omits to state any material fact necessary in order to make the statements therein not false or misleading...." Use of a solicitation that is materially misleading is itself a violation of law, as the Court of Appeals recognized in stating that injunctive relief would be available to remedy such a defect if sought prior to the stockholders' meeting. In *Borak*, which came to this Court on a dismissal of the complaint, the Court limited its inquiry to whether a violation of § 14(a) gives rise to "a federal cause of action for rescission or damages," 377 U.S., at 428. Referring to the argument made by petitioners there "that the merger can be dissolved only if it was fraudulent or non-beneficial, issues upon which the proxy material would not bear," the Court stated: "But the causal relationship of the proxy material and the merger are questions of fact to be resolved at trial, not here. We therefore do not discuss this point further." *Id.*, at 431. In the present case there has been a hearing specifically directed to the causation problem. The question before the Court is whether the facts found on the basis of that hearing are sufficient in law to establish petitioners' cause of action, and we conclude that they are.

Where the misstatement or omission in a proxy statement has been shown to be "material," as it was found to be here, that determination itself indubitably embodies a conclusion that the defect was of such a character that it might have been considered important by a reasonable shareholder who was in the process of deciding how to vote. This requirement that the defect have a significant *propensity* to affect the voting process is found in the express terms of Rule 14a-9, and it adequately serves the purpose of ensuring that a cause of action cannot be established by proof of a defect so trivial, or so unrelated to the transaction for which approval is sought, that correction of the defect or imposition of liability would not further the interests protected by § 14(a).

There is no need to supplement this requirement, as did the Court of Appeals, with a requirement of proof of whether the defect actually had a decisive effect on the voting. Where there has been a finding of materiality, a shareholder has made a sufficient showing of causal relationship between the violation and the injury for which he seeks redress if, as here, he proves that the proxy solicitation itself, rather than the particular defect in the solicitation materials, was an essential link in the accomplishment of the transaction. This objective test will avoid the impracticalities of determining how many votes were affected, and, by resolving doubts in favor of those the statute is designed to protect, will effectuate the congressional policy of en-

---

was equitable, in order to show that the shareholders would nevertheless have rejected it if the solicitation had not been misleading. Proof of actual reliance by thousands of individuals would, as the court acknowledged, not be feasible; and reliance on the *nondisclosure* of a fact is a particularly difficult matter to define or prove. In practice, therefore, the objective fairness of the proposal would seemingly be determinative of liability. But, in view of the many other factors that might lead shareholders to prefer their current position to that of owners of a larger, combined enterprise, it is pure conjecture to assume that the fairness of the proposal will always be determinative of their vote.

suring that the shareholders are able to make an informal choice when they are consulted on corporate transactions.[2]

III

Our conclusion that petitioners have established their case by showing that proxies necessary to approval of the merger were obtained by means of a materially misleading solicitation implies nothing about the form of relief to which they may be entitled. We held in *Borak* that upon finding a violation the courts were "to be alert to provide such remedies as are necessary to make effective the congressional purpose," noting specifically that such remedies are not to be limited to prospective relief. 377 U.S., at 433, 434. In devising retrospective relief for violation of the proxy rules, the federal courts should consider the same factors that would govern the relief granted for any similar illegality or fraud. One important factor may be the fairness of the terms of the merger. Possible forms of relief will include setting aside the merger or granting other equitable relief, but, as the Court of Appeals below noted, nothing in the statutory policy "requires the court to unscramble a corporate transaction merely because a violation occurred." 403 F.2d, at 436. In selecting a remedy the lower courts should exercise "'the sound discretion which guides the determinations of courts of equity,'" keeping in mind the role of equity as "the instrument for nice adjustment and reconciliation between the public interest and private needs as well as between competing private claims." *Hecht Co. v. Bowles*, 321 U.S. 321, 329–330 (1944), quoting from *Meredith v. Winter Haven*, 320 U.S. 228, 235 (1943).

We do not read § 29(b) of the Act, which declares contracts made in violation of the Act or a rule thereunder "void ... as regards the rights of" the violator and knowing successors in interest, as requiring that the merger be set aside simply because the merger agreement is a "void" contract. This language establishes that the guilty party is precluded from enforcing the contract against an unwilling innocent party, but it does not compel the conclusion that the contract is a nullity, creating no enforceable rights even in a party innocent of the violation. The lower federal courts have read § 29(b), which has counterparts in the Holding Company Act, the Investment Company Act, and the Investment Advisers Act, as rendering the contract merely voidable at the option of the innocent party. This interpretation is eminently sensible. The interests of the victim are sufficiently protected by giving him the right to rescind; to regard the contract as void where he has not invoked that right would only create the possibility of hardships to him or others without necessarily advancing the statutory policy of disclosure.

The United States, as *amicus curiae*, points out that as representatives of the minority shareholders, petitioners are not parties to the merger agreement and thus do not enjoy a statutory right under § 29(b) to set it aside. Furthermore, while they do have a derivative right to invoke Auto-Lite's status as a party to the agreement, a de-

---

2. [7] We need not decide in this case whether causation could be shown where the management controls a sufficient number of shares to approve the transaction without any votes from the minority. Even in that situation, if the management finds it necessary for legal or practical reasons to solicit proxies from minority shareholders, at least one court has held that the proxy solicitation might be sufficiently related to the merger to satisfy the causation requirement....

termination of what relief should be granted in Auto-Lite's name must hinge on whether setting aside the merger would be in the best interests of the shareholders as a whole. In short, in the context of a suit such as this one, § 29(b) leaves the matter of relief where it would be under *Borak* without specific statutory language — the merger should be set aside only if a court of equity concludes, from all the circumstances, that it would be equitable to do so.

Monetary relief will, of course, also be a possibility. Where the defect in the proxy solicitation relates to the specific terms of the merger, the district court might appropriately order an accounting to ensure that the shareholders receive the value that was represented as coming to them. On the other hand, where, as here, the misleading aspect of the solicitation did not relate to terms of the merger, monetary relief might be afforded to the shareholders only if the merger resulted in a reduction of the earnings or earnings potential of their holdings. In short, damages should be recoverable only to the extent that they can be shown. If commingling of the assets and operations of the merged companies makes it impossible to establish direct injury from the merger, relief might be predicated on a determination of the fairness of the terms of the merger at the time it was approved. These questions, of course, are for decision in the first instance by the District Court on remand, and our singling out of some of the possibilities is not intended to exclude others....

For the foregoing reasons we conclude that the judgment of Court of Appeals should be vacated and case remanded to that court for further proceedings consistent with this opinion.

TSC Industries, Inc. v. Northway, Inc.

United States Supreme Court
426 U.S. 438 (1976)

JUSTICE MARSHALL delivered the opinion of the Court.

[A corporation proposed a merger with another corporation that owned 34% of its stock. The proxy statement disclosed the existence of the 34% shareholder and stated that no other shareholder owned more than 10% of its stock. It also disclosed that the 34% shareholder nominated five of the corporation's ten directors. The proxy statement did not state that the 34% ownership position rendered that shareholder a controlling shareholder or parent of the corporation. Nor did it disclose the facts that the corporation's board chair and chair of its executive committee were both also senior officers of the 34% shareholder.]

The proxy rules promulgated by the Securities and Exchange Commission under the Securities Exchange Act of 1934 bar the use of proxy statements that are false or misleading with respect to the presentation or omission of material facts. We are called upon to consider the definition of a material fact under those rules, and the appropriateness of resolving the question of materiality by summary judgment in this case....

The question of materiality, it is universally agreed, is an objective one, involving the significance of an omitted or misrepresented fact to a reasonable investor. Variations in the formulation of a general test of materiality occur in the articulation of just how significant a fact must be or, put another way, how certain it must be that the fact would affect a reasonable investor's judgment.

The Court of Appeals in this case concluded that material facts include "all facts which a reasonable shareholder *might* consider important." 512 F.2d, at 330 (emphasis added). This formulation of the test of materiality has been explicitly rejected by at least two courts as setting too low a threshold for the imposition of liability under Rule 14a-9. *Gerstle v. Gamble-Skogmo, Inc.*, 478 F.2d 1281, 1301–1302 (CA2 1973); *Smallwood v. Pearl Brewing Co.*, 489 F.2d 579, 603–604 (CA5 1974). In these cases, panels of the Second and Fifth Circuits opted for the conventional tort test of materiality—whether a reasonable man *would* attach importance to the fact misrepresented or omitted in determining his course of action. *Gerstle* v. *Gamble-Skogmo, supra*, at 1302, also approved the following standard, which had been formulated with reference to statements issued in a contested election: "whether, taking a properly realistic view, there is a substantial likelihood that the misstatement or omission may have led a stockholder to grant a proxy to the solicitor or to withhold one from the other side, whereas in the absence of this he would have taken a contrary course." *General Time Corp. v. Talley Industries, Inc.*, 403 F.2d 159, 162 (CA2 1968), *cert. denied*, 393 U.S. 1026 (1969).

In arriving at its broad definition of a material fact as one that a reasonable shareholder *might* consider important, the Court of Appeals in this case relied heavily upon language of this Court in *Mills v. Electric Auto-Lite Co.*, [396 U.S. 375 (1970)]. That reliance was misplaced. The *Mills* Court did characterize a determination of materiality as at least "embod[ying] a conclusion that the defect was of such a character that it might have been considered important by a reasonable shareholder who was in the process of deciding how to vote." 396 U.S., at 384. But if any language in *Mills* is to be read as suggesting a general notion of materiality, it can only be the opinion's subsequent reference to materiality as a "requirement that the defect have a significant *propensity* to affect the voting process." *Ibid.* (emphasis in original). For it was that requirement that the Court said "adequately serves the purpose of ensuring that a cause of action cannot be established by proof of a defect so trivial, or so unrelated to the transaction for which approval is sought, that correction of the defect or imposition of liability would not further the interests protected by § 14(a)." *Ibid.* Even this language must be read, however, with appreciation that the Court specifically declined to consider the materiality of the omissions in *Mills*. The references to materiality were simply preliminary to our consideration of the sole question in the case—whether proof of the materiality of an omission from a proxy statement must be supplemented by a showing that the defect actually caused the outcome of the vote. It is clear, then, that *Mills* did not intend to foreclose further inquiry into the meaning of materiality under Rule 14a-9....

In formulating a standard of materiality under Rule 14a-9, we are guided, of course, by the recognition in *Borak* and *Mills* of the Rule's broad remedial purpose. That purpose is not merely to ensure by judicial means that the transaction, when judged by its real terms, is fair and otherwise adequate, but to ensure disclosures by corporate management in order to enable the shareholders to make an informed choice. As an abstract proposition, the most desirable role for a court in a suit of this sort, coming after the consummation of the proposed transaction, would perhaps be to determine whether in fact the proposal would have been favored by the shareholders and consummated in the absence of any misstatement or omission. But as we recognized in *Mills, supra,* at 382 n. 5, such matters are not subject to determination with certainty. Doubts as to the critical nature of information misstated or omitted will be commonplace. And particularly in view of the prophylactic purpose of the Rule and the fact that the content of the proxy statement is within management's control, it is appropriate that these doubts be resolved in favor of those the statute is designed to protect.

We are aware, however, that the disclosure policy embodied in the proxy regulations is not without limit. Some information is of such dubious significance that insistence on its disclosure may accomplish more harm than good. The potential liability for a Rule 14a-9 violation can be great indeed, and if the standard of materiality is unnecessarily low, not only may the corporation and its management be subjected to liability for insignificant omissions or misstatements, but also management's fear of exposing itself to substantial liability may cause it simply to bury the shareholders in an avalanche of trivial information—a result that is hardly conducive to informed decisionmaking. Precisely these dangers are presented, we think, by the definition of a material fact adopted by the Court of Appeals in this case—a fact which a reasonable shareholder *might* consider important. We agree with Judge Friendly, speaking for the Court of Appeals in *Gerstle,* that the "might" formulation is "too suggestive of mere possibility, however unlikely." 478 F.2d, at 1302.

The general standard of materiality that we think best comports with the policies of Rule 14a-9 is as follows: An omitted fact is material if there is a substantial likelihood that a reasonable shareholder would consider it important in deciding how to vote. This standard is fully consistent with *Mills'* general description of materiality as a requirement that "the defect have a significant *propensity* to affect the voting process." It does not require proof of a substantial likelihood that disclosure of the omitted fact would have caused the reasonable investor to change his vote. What the standard does contemplate is a showing of a substantial likelihood that, under all the circumstances, the omitted fact would have assumed actual significance in the deliberations of the reasonable shareholder. Put another way, there must be a substantial likelihood that the disclosure of the omitted fact would have been viewed by the reasonable investor as having significantly altered the "total mix" of information made available....

The issue of materiality may be characterized as a mixed question of law and fact, involving as it does the application of a legal standard to a particular set of facts. In considering whether summary judgment on the issue is appropriate, we must bear in mind that the underlying objective facts, which will often be free from dispute, are merely the starting point for the ultimate determination of materiality. The determination requires delicate assessments of the inferences a "reasonable shareholder" would draw from a given set of facts and the significance of those inferences to him, and these assessments are peculiarly ones for the trier of fact. Only if the established omissions are "so obviously important to an investor, that reasonable minds cannot differ on the question of materiality" is the ultimate issue of materiality appropriately resolved "as a matter of law" by summary judgment....

Virginia Bankshares, Inc. v. Sandberg

United States Supreme Court

501 U.S. 1083 (1991)

JUSTICE SOUTER delivered the opinion of the Court.

... The questions before us are whether a statement couched in conclusory or qualitative terms purporting to explain directors' reasons for recommending certain corporate action can be materially misleading within the meaning of Rule 14a-9, and whether causation of damages compensable under § 14(a) can be shown by a member of a class of minority shareholders whose votes are not required by law or corporate bylaw to authorize the corporate action subject to the proxy solicitation. We hold that knowingly false statements of reasons may be actionable even though conclusory in form, but that respondents have failed to demonstrate the equitable basis required to extend the § 14(a) private action to such shareholders when any indication of congressional intent to do so is lacking.

I

In December 1986, First American Bankshares, Inc. (FABI), a bank holding company, began a "freeze-out" merger, in which the First American Bank of Virginia (Bank) eventually merged into Virginia Bankshares, Inc., (VBI), a wholly owned subsidiary of FABI. VBI owned 85% of the Bank's shares, the remaining 15% being in the hands of some 2,000 minority shareholders. FABI hired the investment banking firm of Keefe, Bruyette & Woods (KBW) to give an opinion on the appropriate price for shares of the minority holders, who would lose their interests in the Bank as a result of the merger. Based on market quotations and unverified information from FABI, KBW gave the Bank's executive committee an opinion that $42 a share would be a fair price for the minority stock. The executive committee approved the merger proposal at that price, and the full board followed suit.

Although Virginia law required only that such a merger proposal be submitted to a vote at a shareholders' meeting, and that the meeting be preceded by circulation of a statement of information to the shareholders, the directors nevertheless solicited proxies for voting on the proposal at the annual meeting set for April 21, 1987. In their solicitation, the directors urged the proposal's adoption and stated they had approved the plan because of its opportunity for the minority shareholders to achieve a "high" value, which they elsewhere described as a "fair" price, for their stock.

Although most minority shareholders gave the proxies requested, respondent Sandberg did not, and after approval of the merger she sought damages in the United States District Court for the Eastern District of Virginia from VBI, FABI, and the directors of the Bank. She pleaded two counts, one for soliciting proxies in violation of § 14(a) and Rule 14a-9, and the other for breaching fiduciary duties owed to the minority shareholders under state law. Under the first count, Sandberg alleged, among other things, that the directors had not believed that the price offered was high or that the terms of the merger were fair, but had recommended the merger only because they believed they had no alternative if they wished to remain on the board. At trial, Sandberg invoked language from this Court's opinion in *Mills v. Electric Auto-Lite Co.*, 396 U.S. 375, 385 (1970), to obtain an instruction that the jury could find for her without a showing of her own reliance on the alleged misstatements, so long as they were material and the proxy solicitation was an "essential link" in the merger process.

The jury's verdicts were for Sandberg on both counts, after finding violations of Rule 14a-9 by all defendants and a breach of fiduciary duties by the Bank's directors. The jury awarded Sandberg $18 a share, having found that she would have received $60 if her stock had been valued adequately.

While Sandberg's case was pending, a separate action on similar allegations was brought against petitioners in the United States District Court for the District of Columbia by several other minority shareholders including respondent Weinstein, who, like Sandberg, had withheld his proxy. This case was transferred to the Eastern District of Virginia. After Sandberg's action had been tried, the Weinstein respondents successfully pleaded collateral estoppel to get summary judgment on liability.

On appeal, the United States Court of Appeals for the Fourth Circuit affirmed the judgments, holding that certain statements in the proxy solicitation were materially misleading for purposes of the Rule, and that respondents could maintain their action even though their votes had not been needed to effectuate the merger....

II

The Court of Appeals affirmed petitioners' liability for two statements found to have been materially misleading in violation of § 14(a) of the Act, one of which was that "The Plan of Merger has been approved by the Board of Directors because it provides an opportunity for the Bank's public shareholders to achieve a high value for their shares." Petitioners argue that statements of opinion or belief incorporating indefinite and unverifiable expressions cannot be actionable as misstatements of material fact within the meaning of Rule 14a-9, and that such a declaration of opinion or belief should never be actionable when placed in a proxy solicitation incorporating statements of fact sufficient to enable readers to draw their own, independent conclusions.

A

We consider first the actionability *per se* of statements of reasons, opinion or belief. Because such a statement by definition purports to express what is consciously on the speaker's mind, we interpret the jury verdict as finding that the directors' statements of belief and opinion were made with knowledge that the directors did not hold the beliefs or opinions expressed, and we confine our discussion to statements so made. That such statements may be materially significant raises no serious question.... Shareholders know that directors usually have knowledge and expertness far exceeding the normal investor's resources, and the directors' perceived superiority is magnified even further by the common knowledge that state law customarily obliges them to exercise their judgment in the shareholders' interest. Naturally, then, the share owner faced with a proxy request will think it important to know the directors' beliefs about the course they recommend, and their specific reasons for urging the stockholders to embrace it.

B

1

But, assuming materiality, the question remains whether statements of reasons, opinions, or beliefs are statements "with respect to ... material fact[s]" so as to fall within the strictures of the Rule....

Such statements are factual in two senses: as statements that the directors do act for the reasons given or hold the belief stated and as statements about the subject matter of the reason or belief expressed.... Reasons for directors' recommendations or statements of belief are ... characteristically matters of corporate record subject to documentation, to be supported or attacked by evidence of historical fact outside a plaintiff's control. Such evidence would include not only corporate minutes and other statements of the directors themselves, but circumstantial evidence bearing on the facts that would reasonably underlie the reasons claimed and the honesty of any statement that those reasons are the basis for a recommendation or other action, a point that becomes especially clear when the reasons or beliefs go to valuations in dollars and cents.

It is no answer to argue, as petitioners do, that the quoted statement on which liability was predicated did not express a reason in dollars and cents, but focused instead on the "indefinite and unverifiable" term, "high" value, much like the similar claim that the merger's terms were "fair" to shareholders. The objection ignores the fact that such conclusory terms in a commercial context are reasonably understood to rest on a factual basis that justifies them as accurate, the absence of which renders them misleading....

2

Under § 14(a), then, a plaintiff is permitted to prove a specific statement of reason knowingly false or misleadingly incomplete, even when stated in conclusory terms. In reaching this conclusion we have considered statements of reasons of the sort exemplified here, which misstate the speaker's reasons and also mislead about the stated subject matter (*e.g.*, the value of the shares). A statement of belief may be open to objection only in the former respect, however, solely as a misstatement of the psychological fact of the speaker's belief in what he says. In this case, for example, the Court of Appeals alluded to just such limited falsity in observing that "the jury was certainly justified in believing that the directors did not believe a merger at $42 per share was in the minority stockholders' interest but, rather, that they voted as they did for other reasons, *e.g.*, retaining their seats on the board."

The question arises, then, whether disbelief, or undisclosed belief or motivation, standing alone, should be a sufficient basis to sustain an action under § 14(a), absent proof by the sort of objective evidence described above that the statement also expressly or impliedly asserted something false or misleading about its subject matter. We think that proof of mere disbelief or belief undisclosed should not suffice for liability under § 14(a), and if nothing more had been required or proven in this case we would reverse for that reason....

[T]o recognize liability on mere disbelief or undisclosed motive without any demonstration that the proxy statement was false or misleading about its subject would authorize § 14(a) litigation confined solely to what one skeptical court spoke of as the "impurities" of a director's "unclean heart." *Stedman v. Storer*, 308 F. Supp. 881, 887 (SDNY 1969) (dealing with § 10(b)).... While it is true that the liability, if recognized, would rest on an actual, not hypothetical, psychological fact, the temptation to rest an otherwise nonexistent § 14(a) action on psychological enquiry alone would threaten ... strike suits and attrition by discovery.... We therefore hold disbelief or undisclosed motivation, standing alone, insufficient to satisfy the element of fact that must be established under § 14(a).

C

Petitioners' fall-back position assumes the same relationship between a conclusory judgment and its underlying facts that we described in Part II-B-1, *supra*. [P]etitioners argue that even if conclusory statements of reason or belief can be actionable under § 14(a), we should confine liability to instances where the proxy material fails to disclose the offending statement's factual basis. There would be no justification for holding the shareholders entitled to judicial relief, that is, when they were given evidence that a stated reason for a proxy recommendation was misleading, and an opportunity to draw that conclusion themselves.

The answer to this argument rests on the difference between a merely misleading statement and one that is materially so. While a misleading statement will not always lose its deceptive edge simply by joinder with others that are true, the true statements may discredit the other one so obviously that the risk of real deception drops to nil. Since liability under § 14(a) must rest not only on deceptiveness but materiality as well (*i.e.*, it has to be significant enough to be important to a reasonable investor deciding how to vote), petitioners are on perfectly firm ground insofar as they argue that publishing accurate facts in a proxy statement can render a misleading proposition too unimportant to ground liability.

But not every mixture with the true will neutralize the deceptive. If it would take a financial analyst to spot the tension between the one and the other, whatever is misleading will remain materially so, and liability should follow. The point of a proxy statement, after all, should be to inform, not to challenge the reader's critical wits. Only when the inconsistency would exhaust the misleading conclusion's capacity to influence the reasonable shareholder would a § 14(a) action fail on the element of materiality.

Suffice it to say that the evidence invoked by petitioners in the instant case fell short of compelling the jury to find the facial materiality of the misleading statement neutralized....

III

The second issue before us, left open in *Mills v. Electric Auto-Lite Co.*, is whether causation of damages compensable through the implied private right of action under § 14(a) can be demonstrated by a member of a class of minority shareholders whose votes are not required by law or corporate bylaw to authorize the transaction giving rise to the claim....

Although a majority stockholder in *Mills* controlled just over half the corporation's shares, a two-thirds vote was needed to approve the merger proposal.... In [*Mills*], the Court found the solicitation essential, as contrasted with one addressed to a class of minority shareholders without votes required by law or by-law to authorize the action proposed, and left it for another day to decide whether such a minority shareholder could demonstrate causation.

In this case, respondents address *Mills'* open question by proffering two theories that the proxy solicitation addressed to them was an "essential link" under the *Mills* causation test. They argue, first, that a link existed and was essential simply because VBI and FABI would have been unwilling to proceed with the merger without the approval manifested by the minority shareholders' proxies, which would not have been obtained without the solicitation's express misstatements and misleading omissions. On this reasoning, the causal connection would depend on a desire to avoid bad shareholder or public relations, and the essential character of the causal link would stem not from the enforceable terms of the parties' corporate relationship, but from one party's apprehension of the ill will of the other.

In the alternative, respondents argue that the proxy statement was an essential link between the directors' proposal and the merger because it was the means to satisfy a state statutory requirement of minority shareholder approval, as a condition for saving the merger from voidability resulting from a conflict of interest on the part of one of the Bank's directors, Jack Beddow, who voted in favor of the merger while also serving as a director of FABI. Under the terms of Va. Code § 13.1-691(A) (1989), minority approval after disclosure of the material facts about the transaction and the director's interest was one of three avenues to insulate the merger from later attack for conflict, the two others being ratification by the Bank's directors after like disclosure, and proof that the merger was fair to the corporation. On this theory, causation would depend on the use of the proxy statement for the purpose of obtaining votes sufficient to bar a minority shareholder from commencing proceedings to declare the merger void.

Although respondents have proffered each of these theories as establishing a chain of causal connection in which the proxy statement is claimed to have been an "essential link," neither theory presents the proxy solicitation as essential in the sense of *Mills'* causal sequence, in which the solicitation links a directors' proposal with the votes legally required to authorize the action proposed. As a consequence, each theory would, if adopted, extend the scope of [*J.I. Case Co. v. Borak*, 377 U.S. 426 (1964),] actions beyond the ambit of *Mills*, and expand the class of plaintiffs entitled to bring *Borak* actions to include shareholders whose initial authorization of the transaction prompting the proxy solicitation is unnecessary.

Assessing the legitimacy of any such extension or expansion calls for the application of some fundamental principles governing recognition of a right of action implied by a federal statute, the first of which was not, in fact, the considered focus of the *Borak* opinion. The rule that has emerged in the years since *Borak* and *Mills* came down is that recognition of any private right of action for violating a federal statute must ultimately rest on congressional intent to provide a private remedy, *Touche Ross & Co. v. Redington*, 442 U.S. 560, 575 (1979). From this the corollary follows that the breadth of the right once recognized should not, as a general matter, grow beyond the scope congressionally intended.

This rule and corollary present respondents with a serious obstacle, for we can find no manifestation of intent to recognize a cause of action (or class of plaintiffs) as broad as respondents' theory of causation would entail....

Looking to the Act's text and legislative history ... reveals little that would help toward understanding the intended scope of any private right....

The congressional silence that is thus a serious obstacle to the expansion of cognizable *Borak* causation is not, however, a necessarily insurmountable barrier. This is not the first effort in recent years to expand the scope of an action originally inferred from the Act without "conclusive guidance" from Congress, *see Blue Chip Stamps v. Manor Drug Stores*, 421 U.S. [729, 737 (1975)], and we may look to that earlier case for the proper response to such a plea for expansion. There, we accepted the proposition that where a legal structure of private statutory rights has developed without clear indications of congressional intent, the contours of that structure need not be frozen absolutely when the result would be demonstrably inequitable to a class of would-be plaintiffs with claims comparable to those previously recognized. Faced in that case with such a claim for equality in rounding out the scope of an implied private statutory right of action, we looked to policy reasons for deciding where the outer limits of the right should lie. We may do no less here, in the face of respondents' pleas for a private remedy to place them on the same footing as shareholders with votes necessary for initial corporate action.

A

Blue Chip Stamps set an example worth recalling as a preface to specific policy analysis of the consequences of recognizing respondents' first theory, that a desire to avoid minority shareholders' ill will should suffice to justify recognizing the requisite causality of a proxy statement needed to garner that minority support. It will be recalled that in *Blue Chip Stamps* we raised concerns about the practical consequences of allowing recovery, under § 10(b) of the Act and Rule 10b-5, on evidence of what a merely hypothetical buyer or seller might have done on a set of facts that never occurred, and foresaw that any such expanded liability would turn on "hazy" issues inviting self-serving testimony, strike suits, and protracted discovery, with little chance of reasonable resolution by pretrial process. These were good reasons to deny recognition to such claims in the absence of any apparent contrary congressional intent.

The same threats of speculative claims and procedural intractability are inherent in respondents' theory of causation linked through the directors' desire for a cosmetic vote. Causation would turn on inferences about what the corporate directors would have thought and done without the minority shareholder approval unneeded to authorize action. A subsequently dissatisfied minority shareholder would have virtual license to allege that managerial timidity would have doomed corporate action but for the ostensible approval induced by a misleading statement, and opposing claims of hypothetical diffidence and hypothetical boldness on the part of directors would probably provide enough depositions in the usual case to preclude any judicial resolution short of the credibility judgments that can only come after trial. Reliable evidence would seldom exist. Directors would understand the prudence of making a few statements about plans to proceed even without minority endorsement, and discovery would be a quest for recollections of oral conversations at odds with the official pronouncements, in hopes of finding support for *ex post facto* guesses about how much heat the directors would have stood in the absence of minority approval. The issues would be hazy, their litigation protracted, and their resolution unreliable. Given a choice, we would reject any theory of causation that raised such prospects, and we reject this one.

B

The theory of causal necessity derived from the requirements of Virginia law dealing with postmerger ratification seeks to identify the essential character of the proxy solicitation from its function in obtaining the minority approval that would preclude a minority suit attacking the merger. Since the link is said to be a step in the process of barring a class of shareholders from resort to a state remedy otherwise available, this theory of causation rests upon the proposition of policy that § 14(a) should provide a federal remedy whenever a false or misleading proxy statement results in the loss under state law of a shareholder plaintiff's state remedy for the enforcement of a state right. Respondents agree with the suggestions of counsel for the SEC and FDIC that causation be recognized, for example, when a minority shareholder has been induced by a misleading proxy statement to forfeit a state-law right to an appraisal remedy by voting to approve a transaction, or when such a shareholder has been deterred from obtaining an order enjoining a damaging transaction by a proxy solicitation that misrepresents the facts on which an injunction could properly have been issued. Respondents claim that in this case a predicate for recognizing just such a causal link exists in Va. Code § 13.1-691(A)(2)(1989), which sets the conditions under which the merger may be insulated from suit by a minority shareholder seeking to void it on account of Beddow's conflict.

This case does not, however, require us to decide whether § 14(a) provides a cause of action for lost state remedies, since there is no indication in the law or facts before us that the proxy solicitation resulted in any such loss. The contrary appears to be the case. Assuming the soundness of respondents' characterization of the proxy statement as materially misleading, the very terms of the Virginia statute indicate that a favorable minority vote induced by the solicitation would not suffice to render the merger invulnerable to later attack on the ground of the conflict. The statute bars a shareholder from seeking to avoid a transaction tainted by a director's conflict if, *inter alia*, the minority shareholders ratified the transaction following disclosure of the material facts of the transaction and the conflict. Assuming that the material facts about the merger and Beddow's interests were not accurately disclosed, the minority votes were inadequate to ratify the merger under state law, and there was no loss of state remedy to connect the proxy solicitation with harm to minority shareholders irredressable under state law. Nor is there a claim here that the statement misled respondents into entertaining a false belief that they had no chance to upset the merger, until the time for bringing suit had run out....

Section II
Shareholders' Proposals

Rule 14a-8, relating to proposals of shareholders, is an anomaly in the federal proxy regulation scheme in that it essentially has nothing to do with disclosure by proxy solicitors. Rather, it sets up an elaborate mechanism by which a shareholder may, if certain conditions are met, have a proposal of shareholders' action included in the proxy statement management sends to shareholders. If a shareholder's proposal is included in the proxy statement, management will also have to provide a means by which all shareholders can instruct the proxyholder how to vote on the proposal. If management opposes a shareholder's proposal, and it usually does, the shareholder must be given the opportunity to include a supporting statement in management's proxy materials.

The cases that follow represent the two forms of shareholder activism typically seen. The first involves a struggle by a shareholder to secure from the corporation rights intended to benefit shareholders in a traditional sense. The second presents a situation where a shareholder uses the shareholder proposal mechanism to work toward greater corporate social responsibility.

American Federation of State, County & Municipal Employees v. American International Group, Inc.

United States Court of Appeals, Second Circuit
462 F.3d 121 (2006)

WESLEY, CIRCUIT JUSTICE:

This case raises the question of whether a shareholder proposal requiring a company to include certain shareholder-nominated candidates for the board of directors on the corporate ballot can be excluded from the corporate proxy materials on the basis that the proposal "relates to an election" under Securities Exchange Act Rule 14a-8(i)(8) ("election exclusion" or "Rule 14a-8(i)(8)"). Complicating this question is not only the ambiguity of Rule 14a-8(i)(8) itself but also the fact that the Securities Exchange Commission (the "SEC" or "Commission") has ascribed two different interpretations to the Rule's language.

The SEC's first interpretation was published in 1976, the same year that it last revised the election exclusion. The Division of Corporation Finance (the "Division"), the group within the SEC that handles investor disclosure matters and issues no-action letters,[3] continued to apply this interpretation consistently for fifteen years until 1990, when it began applying a different interpretation, although at first in an ad hoc and inconsistent manner. The result of this gradual interpretive shift is the SEC's second interpretation, as set forth in its amicus brief to this Court.

We believe that an agency's interpretation of an ambiguous regulation made at the time the regulation was implemented or revised should control unless that agency has offered sufficient reasons for its changed interpretation. Accordingly, we hold that a shareholder proposal that seeks to amend the corporate bylaws to establish a procedure by which shareholder-nominated candidates may be included on the corporate ballot does not relate to an election within the meaning of the Rule and therefore cannot be excluded from corporate proxy materials under that regulation.

Background. The American Federation of State, County & Municipal Employees ("AFSCME") is one of the country's largest public service employee unions. Through its pension plan, AFSCME holds 26,965 shares of voting common stock of American International Group ("AIG" or "Company"), a multi-national corporation operating in the insurance and financial services sectors. On December 1, 2004, AFSCME submitted to AIG for inclusion in the Company's 2005 proxy statement a shareholder proposal that, if adopted by a majority of AIG shareholders at the Company's 2005 annual meeting, would amend the AIG bylaws to require the Company, under certain circumstances, to publish the names of shareholder-nominated candidates for director positions together with any candidates nominated by AIG's board of directors ("Proposal"). AIG sought the input of the Division regarding whether AIG could exclude the Proposal from its proxy statement under the election exclusion on the basis that it "relates to an election." The Division issued a no-action letter in which it indicated that it would not recommend an enforcement action against AIG should the Company exclude the Proposal from its proxy statement....

Armed with the no-action letter, AIG then proceeded to exclude the Proposal from the Company's proxy statement. In response, AFSCME brought suit in the United States District Court for the Southern District of New York (Stanton, J.) seeking a court order compelling AIG to include the Proposal in its next proxy statement. [T]he district court entered final judgment denying plaintiff's claims for declaratory and injunctive relief and dismissing plaintiff's complaint.

Discussion. Rule 14a-8(i)(8), also known as "the town meeting rule," regulates what are referred to as "shareholders proposals," that is, "recommendation[s] or requirement[s]

---

3. [1] Elaborating upon the nature of the no-action process, the Court has stated:
   The no-action process works as follows: Whenever a corporation decides to exclude a shareholder proposal from its proxy materials, it "shall file" a letter with the Division explaining the legal basis for its decision. *See* Rule 14a-8(d)(3). If the Division staff agrees that the proposal is excludable, it may issue a no-action letter, stating that, based on the facts presented by the corporation, the staff will not recommend that the SEC sue the corporation for violating Rule 14a-8.... The no-action letter, however, is an informal response, and does not amount to an official statement of the SEC's views.... No-action letters are deemed interpretive because they do not impose or fix legal relationship upon any of the parties.
   N.Y. City Employees' Ret. Sys. v. SEC, 45 F.3d 7, 12 (2d Cir. 1995).

that the company and/or its board of directors take [some] action, which [the submitting shareholder(s)] intend to present at a meeting of the company's shareholders." If a shareholder seeking to submit a proposal meets certain eligibility and procedural requirements, the corporation is required to include the proposal in its proxy statement and identify the proposal in its form of proxy, unless the corporation can prove to the SEC that a given proposal may be excluded based on one of thirteen grounds enumerated in the regulations. One of these grounds, Rule 14a-8(i)(8), provides that a corporation may exclude a shareholder proposal "[i]f the proposal relates to an election for membership on the company's board of directors or analogous governing body."

We must determine whether, under Rule 14a-8(i)(8), a shareholder proposal "relates to an election" if it seeks to amend the corporate bylaws to establish a procedure by which certain shareholders are entitled to include in the corporate proxy materials their nominees for the board of directors ("proxy access bylaw proposal"). "In interpreting an administrative regulation, as in interpreting a statute, we must begin by examining the language of the provision at issue." *Resnik v. Swartz*, 303 F.3d 147, 151–52 (2d Cir.2002) (citing *New York Currency Research Corp. v. CFTC*, 180 F.3d 83, 92 (2d Cir.1999)).

The relevant language here — "relates to an election" — is not particularly helpful. AFSCME reads the election exclusion as creating an obvious distinction between proposals addressing a particular seat in a particular election (which AFSCME concedes are excludable) and those, like AFSCME's proposal, that simply set the background rules governing elections generally (which AFSCME claims are not excludable). AFSCME's distinction rests on Rule 14a-8(i)(8)'s use of the article "an," which AFSCME claims "necessarily implies that the phrase 'relates to an election' is intended to relate to proposals that address *particular elections*, instead of simply 'elections' generally." It is at least plausible that the words "an election" were intended to narrow the scope of the election exclusion, confining its application to proposals relating to "a particular election *and not* elections generally." It is, however, also plausible that the phrase was intended to create a comparatively broader exclusion, one covering "a particular election *or* elections generally" since any proposal that relates to elections in general will necessarily relate to an election in particular. The language of Rule 14a8(i)(8) provides no reason to adopt one interpretation over the other.

When the language of a regulation is ambiguous, we typically look for guidance in any interpretation made by the agency that promulgated the regulation in question. We are aware of two statements published by the SEC that offer informal interpretations of Rule 14a-8(i)(8). The first is a statement appearing in the amicus brief that the SEC filed in this case at our request. The second interpretation is contained in a statement the SEC published in 1976, the last time the SEC revised the election exclusion. Neither of these interpretations has the force of law. But, while agency interpretations that lack the force of law do not warrant deference when they interpret ambiguous *statutes*, they do normally warrant deference when they interpret ambiguous *regulations*.

In its amicus brief, the SEC interprets Rule 14a-8(i)(8) as permitting the exclusion of shareholder proposals that "would result in contested elections." The SEC explains that "[f]or purposes of Rule 14a-8, a proposal would result in a contested election if it is a means either to campaign for or against a director nominee or to require a company to include shareholder-nominated candidates in the company's proxy materials." Under this interpretation, a proxy access bylaw proposal like AFSCME's would be excludable under Rule 14a-8(i)(8) because it "is a means to require AIG to include shareholder-nominated candidates in the company's proxy materials." However, that interpretation is plainly at odds with the interpretation the SEC made in 1976.

In that year, the SEC amended Rule 14a-8(i)(8) in an effort to clarify the purpose of the existing election exclusion. The SEC explained that "with respect to corporate elections, [ ] Rule 14a-8 is not the proper means for conducting campaigns or effecting reforms in elections of that nature [i.e., "corporate, political or other elections to office"], *since other proxy rules, including Rule 14a-11, are applicable thereto.*" ... ("1976 Statement"). The district court opinion quoted the 1976 Statement but omitted the italicized language and concluded that shareholder proposals were not intended to be used to accomplish any type of election reform. *Am. Fed'n of State, County & Mun. Employees Pension Plan*, 361 F. Supp. 2d at 346–47.

Clearly, however, that cannot be what the 1976 Statement means. Indeed, when the SEC finally adopted the revision of Rule 14a-8(i)(8) four months after publication of the 1976 Statement, it explained that it was rejecting a previous proposed rule (which would have authorized the exclusion of proposals that "relate[ ] to a corporate, political or other election to office") in favor of the current version (which authorizes the exclusion of proposals that simply "relate[ ] to an election") so as to avoid creating "the erroneous belief that the Commission intended to expand the scope of the existing exclusion to cover proposals dealing with matters previously held not excludable by the Commission, such as cumulative voting rights, general qualifications for directors, and political contributions by the issuer." Adoption of Amendments Relating to Proposals by Security Holders, Exchange Act Release No. 34-129999, 41 Fed. Reg. 52,994, 52,998 (Nov. 22, 1976) ("1976 Adoption"). And yet, all three of these shareholder proposal topics—cumulative voting rights, general qualifications for directors, and political contributions—fit comfortably within the category "election reform."

In its amicus brief, the SEC places a slightly different gloss on the 1976 Statement than did the district court. The SEC reads the 1976 Statement as implying that the purpose of Rule 14a-8(i)(8) is to authorize the exclusion of proposals that seek to effect, not election reform in general, but only certain types of election reform, namely those to which "other proxy rules, including Rule 14a-11," are generally applicable. In 1976, Rule 14a-11 was essentially the equivalent of current Rule 14a-12, which requires certain disclosures where a solicitation is made "for the purpose of opposing" a solicitation by any other person "with respect to the election or removal of directors." The SEC reasons that, based on the 1976 Statement, "a proposal may be excluded pursuant to Rule 14a-8(i)(8) if it would result in an immediate election contest (e.g., by making a director nomination for a particular meeting) or would set up a process for shareholders to conduct an election contest in the future by requiring the company to include shareholder director nominees in the company's proxy materials for subsequent meetings."

We agree with the SEC that, based on the 1976 Statement, shareholder proposals can be excluded under the election exclusion if they would result in an immediate election contest. We understand the phrase "since other proxy rules, including Rule 14a-11, are applicable thereto" in the 1976 Statement to mean that under Rule 14a-8(i)(8), companies can exclude shareholder proposals dealing with those election-related matters that, if addressed in a proxy solicitation — the alternative to a shareholder proposal — would trigger Rule 14a-12, or the former Rule 14a-11. A proxy solicitation nominating a candidate for a specific election would be made "for the purpose of opposing" the company's proxy solicitation and therefore would clearly trigger Rule 14a-12. Accordingly, based on the 1976 Statement, a shareholder proposal seeking to contest management's nominees would be excludable under Rule 14a-8(i)(8).

By contrast, a proxy solicitation seeking to add a proxy access amendment to the corporate bylaws does not involve opposing solicitations dealing with "the election or removal of directors," and therefore Rule 14a-12, or, equivalently, the former Rule 14a-11, would not apply to a proposal seeking to accomplish the same end. Thus, we cannot agree with the second half of the SEC's interpretation of the 1976 Statement: that a proposal may be excluded under Rule 14a8(i)(8) if it would simply establish a process for shareholders to wage a future election contest.

The 1976 Statement clearly reflects the view that the election exclusion is limited to shareholder proposals used to oppose solicitations dealing with an identified board seat in an upcoming election and rejects the somewhat broader interpretation that the election exclusion applies to shareholder proposals that would institute procedures making such election contests more likely. The SEC suggested as much when, four months after its 1976 Statement, it explained that the scope of the election exclusion does not cover shareholder proposals dealing with matters such as cumulative voting and general director requirements, both of which have the potential to increase the likelihood of election contests. *See* 1976 Adoption, 41 Fed. Reg. at 52,998.

That the 1976 statement adopted this narrower view of the election exclusion finds further support in the fact that it was also the view that the Division adopted for roughly sixteen years following publication of the SEC's 1976 Statement. It was not until 1990 that the Division first signaled a change of course by deeming excludable proposals that *might* result in contested elections, even if the proposal only purports to alter general procedures for nominating and electing directors.

Because the interpretation of Rule 14a-8(i)(8) that the SEC advances in its amicus brief — that the election exclusion applies to proxy access bylaw proposals — conflicts with the 1976 Statement, it does not merit the usual deference we would reserve for an agency's interpretation of its own regulations. The SEC has not provided, nor to our knowledge has it or the Division ever provided, reasons for its changed position regarding the excludability of proxy access bylaw proposals. Although the SEC has substantial discretion to adopt new interpretations of its own regulations in light of, for example, changes in the capital markets or even simply because of a shift in the

Commission's regulatory approach, it nevertheless has a "duty to explain its departure from prior norms."

In its amicus submission, the SEC fails to so much as acknowledge a changed position, let alone offer a reasoned analysis of the change. The amicus brief is curiously silent on any Division action prior to 1990 and characterizes the intermittent post-1990 no-action letters which continued to apply the pre-1990 position as mere "mistake[s]." While we by no means wish to imply that the Commission or the Division cannot correct analytical errors following a refinement of their thinking, we have a difficult time accepting the SEC's characterization of a policy that the Division consistently applied for sixteen years as nothing more than a "mistake." Although we are willing to afford the Commission considerable latitude in explaining departures from prior interpretations, its reasoned analysis must consist of something more than *mea culpas.*

Accordingly, we deem it appropriate to defer to the 1976 Statement, which represents the SEC's interpretation of the election exclusion the last time the Rule was substantively revised. We therefore interpret the election exclusion as applying to shareholder proposals that relate to a particular election and not to proposals that, like AFSCME's, would establish the procedural rules governing elections generally....

Roosevelt v. E.I. Du Pont De Nemours & Co.

United States Court of Appeals, District of Columbia Circuit

958 F.2d 416 (1992)

RUTH BADER GINSBURG, CIRCUIT JUDGE.

Amelia Roosevelt appeals the district court's judgment that E.I. Du Pont de Nemours & Co. ("Du Pont") could omit her shareholder proposal from its proxy materials for the 1992 annual meeting. The district court concluded that Roosevelt's proposal "deals with a matter relating to the conduct of [Du Pont's] ordinary business operations," and is therefore excludable under Securities and Exchange Commission ("SEC") Rule 14a-8(c)(7). [The SEC later revised the Rule's nomenclature, so that former Rule 14a-8(c)(7) became Rule 14a-8(i)(7).—Eds.] ...

I. *Background*

Prior to Du Pont's 1991 annual shareholder meeting, Friends of the Earth Oceanic Society ("Friends of the Earth") submitted a proposal, on behalf of Roosevelt, regarding: (1) the timing of Du Pont's phase out of the production of chlorofluorocarbons ("CFCs") and halons; and (2) the presentation to shareholders of a report detailing (a) research and development efforts to find environmentally sound substitutes, and (b) marketing plans to sell those substitutes. Du Pont opposed inclusion of the proposal in its proxy materials; as required by SEC rule, the company notified the SEC staff of its intention to omit the proposal and its reasons for believing the omission proper. Friends of the Earth filed with the staff a countersubmission on Roosevelt's behalf urging that the proposal was not excludable.

The SEC staff issued a "no-action letter"; citing the Rule 14a-8(c)(7) exception for matters "relating to the conduct of the [company's] ordinary business operations," the staff stated that it would not recommend Commission enforcement action against Du Pont if the company excluded the proposal. Roosevelt did not seek Commission review of the staff's disposition.... [Instead it sued]....

III. *Roosevelt's Proposals and the Rule 14a-8(c)(7) Exception for "Ordinary Business Operations"*

... In reviewing [the district court's] ruling, we emphasize that Roosevelt's disagreement with Du Pont's current policy is not about whether to eliminate CFC production or even whether to do so at once. The former is an end to which Du Pont is committed, and immediate cessation, before environmentally safe alternatives are available, is not what Roosevelt proposes.

Roosevelt differs with Du Pont on a less fundamental matter — the rapidity with which the near-term phase out should occur. Roosevelt seeks a target no later than 1995 ("surpassing [Du Pont's] global competitors which have set a 1995 target date"). In contrast, when this litigation began, Du Pont had set a target of "as soon as possible, but at least by the year 2000."

In recent months and days, the "at least by" year has moved ever closer to Roosevelt's target. Prior to oral argument, Roosevelt informed the court that Du Pont had issued a press release reiterating its "as soon as possible" policy, but "advancing the end point to year-end 1994 for Halons and 1996 for CFCs." Following oral argument, Du Pont informed the court that, "in response to an announcement issued by the White House today regarding an accelerated phaseout of CFCs and Halons," the company "will accelerate its CFC end date to no later than December 31, 1995 in developed countries." Du Pont Statement on Accelerated CFC Phaseout, Feb. 12, 1992.

Although the regulation necessary to give effect to the President's announcement has not yet been adopted, Du Pont immediately reported that it "supports the Administration's position," and that it will phase out CFC production by December 31, 1995. We accept that public statement as the company's current timetable. While the SEC staff and the district court considered Roosevelt's proposal with the company's year-2000 end point in view, we think it proper to take account of the current reality: Roosevelt's proposal would have Du Pont surpass its global competitors' target of 1995; Du Pont projects completion of the phase out "as soon as possible," but no later than year-end 1995.

Roosevelt has confirmed that the first, or phase-out portion of her proposal is the "core issue" and that, if necessary, she would withdraw the second, or report-to-shareholders portion, so that the first portion could be included in Du Pont's 1992 proxy materials. We therefore consider separately the two portions of Roosevelt's proposal.

Because both parts of Roosevelt's proposal must be measured against the Rule 14a-8(c)(7) "ordinary business operations" exception, we set out here the Commission's general understanding of that phrase. When the Commission adopted the current version of the "ordinary business operations" exception, it announced its intention to interpret the phrase both "more restrictively" and "more flexibly than in the past."

Adoption of Amendments Relating to Proposals by Security Holders, Exchange Act Release No. 12,999, 41 FR 52,994, 52,998 (1976) ("*1976 Rule 14a-8 Amendments*"). Specifically, the Commission explained:

> [T]he term "ordinary business operations" has been deemed on occasion to include certain matters which have significant policy, economic or other implications inherent in them. For instance, a proposal that a utility company not construct a proposed nuclear power plant has in the past been considered excludable under [the predecessor of (c)(7)]. In retrospect, however, it seems apparent that the economic and safety considerations attendant to nuclear power plants are of such magnitude that a determination whether to construct one is not an "ordinary" business matter. Accordingly, proposals of that nature, as well as others that have major implications, will in the future be considered beyond the realm of an issuer's ordinary business operations....

Id. The Commission contrasted with matters of such moment as a decision not to build a nuclear power plant, "matters ... mundane in nature [that] do not involve any substantial policy ... considerations." *1976 Rule 14a-8 Amendments*, 41 Fed. Reg. at 52,998. Proposals of that genre, the Commission said, may be safely omitted from proxy materials.

In its brief as amicus curiae, the SEC stated that it regarded the first portion of Roosevelt's proposal, on the timing of the CFC phase out, as not excludable under Rule 14a-8(c)(7), but the second part, on research and development programs and marketing plans, as fitting within the "ordinary business operations" exception. The Commission noted that "[its] staff, in contrast, viewed the timing of the phase-out as an ordinary business matter." We agree with the Commission on the second part of Roosevelt's proposal but not on the first.

A. The Phase Out Target Date

It is not debated in this case that CFCs contribute intolerably to depletion of the ozone layer and that their manufacture has caused a grave environmental hazard. However, Roosevelt's proposal, we emphasize again, relates not to *whether* CFC production should be phased out, but *when* the phase out should be completed.

Timing questions no doubt reflect "significant policy" when large differences are at stake. That would be the case, for example, if Du Pont projected a phase-out period extending into the new century. On the other hand, were Roosevelt seeking to move up Du Pont's target date by barely a season, the matter would appear much more of an "ordinary" than an extraordinary business judgment. In evaluating the Commission's classification of the timing question here as extraordinary, *i.e.*, one involving "fundamental business strategy" or "long-term goals," we are mindful that the SEC conceived of a five-year interval, not an interval now cut to one year.

We are furthermore mindful that we sit in this case as a court of review and owe respect to the findings made by the district court. The trial judge concluded from the record that "Du Pont's 'as soon as possible' policy," contrary to Roosevelt's argument, "does not lack definition." The judge found the policy genuine based on evidence that Du Pont had already spent more than $240 million developing alternatives to CFCs and had just announced the shutdown of the facility that had been the largest CFC plant in the world. Du Pont, the district court also observed, continues to work "toward a global policy of phasing out CFCs" and "with CFC consumers to phase out their use of CFCs."

Stressing the undisputed need for the responsible development of safe substitutes, and the acknowledged irresponsibility of suddenly cutting off all CFC production, the trial judge highlighted the essential difference between this case and the nuclear power plant in the Commission's *1976 Rule 14a-8 Amendments* example. Phasing out CFC production is not a go/no go matter. The phase out takes work "day-to-day ... with equipment manufacturers to help develop the technology needed for alternative compounds." It takes careful planning "in sensitive areas, such as the storage of perishable food and medical products (like vaccines and transfusable blood)," and expertise "in technical fields, such as the sterilization of temperature-sensitive surgical instruments."

We recognize that "ordinary business operations" ordinarily do not attract the interest of both the executive and legislative branches of the federal government. But government regulation of the CFC phase out, even the President's headline-attracting decision to accelerate the schedule initially set by Congress, does not automatically elevate shareholder proposals on timing to the status of "significant policy." What the President and Congress have said about CFCs is not the subject of our closest look. Instead, Rule 14a-8(c)(7) requires us to home in on Roosevelt's proposal, to determine whether her request dominantly implicates ordinary business matters. The gap between her proposal and the company's schedule is now one year, not five. The steps to be taken to accomplish the phase out are complex; as the district court found, the company, having agreed on the essential policy, must carry it out safely, using "business and technical skills" day-to-day that are not meant for "shareholder debate and participation."

In sum, the parties agree that CFC production must be phased out, that substitutes must be developed, and that both should be achieved sooner rather than later. Du Pont has undertaken to eliminate the products in question by year-end 1995, and has pledged to do so sooner if "possible." The trial judge has found Du Pont's "as soon as possible" pledge credible. In these circumstances, we conclude that what is at stake is the "implementation of a policy," "the timing for an agreed-upon action," *see* Brief of the Securities and Exchange Commission, Amicus Curiae, at 31, and we therefore hold the target date for the phase out a matter excludable under Rule 14a-8(c)(7).

B. The Report to Shareholders

The second part of Roosevelt's proposal solicits a report from management within six months detailing research and development efforts on environmentally safe substitutes and a marketing plan to sell those substitutes. This portion of the proposal, the SEC concluded in agreement with its staff, "requires detailed information about the company's day-to-day business operations [and] is subject to exclusion pursuant to [Rule 14a-8(c)(7)]." Roosevelt concedes that the report is not central to her proposal, and we find no cause to place the matter outside the "ordinary business operations" exception.

For a time, the Commission staff "ha[d] taken the position that proposals requesting issuers to prepare reports on specific aspects of their business or to form [study committees] would not be excludable under Rule 14a-8(c)(7)." *Amendments to Rule 14a-8 Under the Securities Exchange Act of 1934 Relating to Proposals by Security Holders*, Exchange Act Rel. No. 20,091, 48 FR 38,218, 38,221 (Aug. 23, 1983). The Commission has changed that position. Pointing out that the staff's interpretation "raise[d] form over substance," the Commission instructed the staff to "consider whether the subject matter of the [requested] report or [study] committee involves a matter of ordinary business: where it does, the proposal [is] excludable under Rule 14a-8(c)(7)." *Id.*

We need not linger over the report issue. The staff's no-action letters in this respect are unremarkable and entirely in keeping with current practice. *See, e.g.*, Carolina Power & Light Co., SEC No-Action Letter (available Mar. 8, 1990) (shareholder proposal requesting preparation of a report on specific aspects of company's nuclear operations, covering, *inter alia*, safety, regulatory compliance, emissions problems, hazardous waste disposal and related cost information, may be omitted as relating to ordinary business operations).

Just as the Commission has clarified that requests for special reports or committee studies are not automatically includable in proxy materials, we caution that such requests are not inevitably excludable. But Roosevelt has not shown that the detailed research and development or marketing information she seeks implicates significant policy issues, and not merely implementation arrangements. She does not, for example, suggest that Du Pont is developing or planning to market hazardous substitutes. *Cf. Lovenheim v. Iroquois Brands, Ltd.*, 618 F. Supp. 554, 556, 561 (D.D.C. 1985) (in light of "ethical and social significance" of proposal, court granted preliminary injunction barring corporation from excluding from its proxy materials shareholder proposal that requested formation of committee to study, and submission of report to shareholders about, whether company's supplier produced pate de foie gras in a manner involving undue pain or suffering to animals and whether distribution should be discontinued until a more humane method is developed).

In agreement with the district judge, the Commission, and the staff, we hold that the second part of Roosevelt's proposal falls within the "ordinary business operations" exception.

Conclusion

... Roosevelt's proposal ... may be excluded by Du Pont because, in both of its parts, the proposal falls within the exception furnished by Rule 14a-8(c)(7) for matters relating to "ordinary business operations."....

Section III
Proxy Contests

The shareholder proposal mechanism of Rule 14a-8, while providing shareholders a means of being heard by management, does not serve as a tool for wresting control from management. If this is desired, a shareholder or shareholder group must solicit proxies for use at a shareholders' meeting. Since management will do so also, what will develop is a proxy contest.

Proxy contests in publicly held corporations go in and out of fashion. They were popular in the 1950s, then were eclipsed by tender offers as the preferred way to take over a corporation, and now have reemerged to a limited extent as an alternative to the tender offer. Economics is one of the most important reasons for a reemergence. Proxy contests are expensive. For a publicly held corporation of any size, millions of dollars will need to be spent to have any real chance of success. But, if the alternative is a cash tender offer for at least majority ownership, a proxy contest will be several times cheaper. Also, shareholders who win proxy contests can typically have the corporation reimburse them for their expenses.

What one obtains through a tender offer is, of course, quite different from what can be gained as the result of a proxy contest. In the tender offer it is stock ownership and in the proxy contest voting control, sometimes control over only one question (for example, as illustrated in the following case, whether the corporation should merge with another), but more often over the choosing of directors at a particular meeting (as was the situation in the second case below). However, because boards essentially are self-perpetuating — except when a proxy contest is won by insurgents — winning one election typically will lead to long-term management control (except in the case of a staggered board, where obtaining control is more difficult).

Kennecott Copper Corp. v. Curtiss-Wright Corp.

United States Court of Appeals, Second Circuit
584 F.2d 1195 (1978)

Van Graafeiland, Circuit Judge:

Curtiss-Wright Corporation has appealed from a judgment of the United States District Court for the Southern District of New York entered in the midst of a proxy fight between Curtiss-Wright and Kennecott Copper Corporation. At issue was the election of directors to the board of Kennecott, in which Curtiss-Wright had become a minority shareholder. The judgment, dated May 1, 1978, permanently enjoined Curtiss-Wright from further solicitation of Kennecott proxies and from voting the shares and proxies it then held at the May 2, 1978, annual meeting of Kennecott. On May 2, 1978, prior to the meeting, this Court granted a stay of the district court's judgment and an expedited appeal. For reasons that follow, we have concluded that the judgment must, in substantial part, be reversed.

In 1968, Kennecott, the largest producer of copper in the United States, sought to diversify by acquiring Peabody Coal Company. This acquisition was attacked by the Federal Trade Commission on antitrust grounds, and in 1977, following the Commission's order to divest, Peabody was sold. As consideration, Kennecott received $809 million in cash and some five per cent subordinated income notes due in 2007, which were in the face amount of $400 million but were carried on Kennecott's balance sheet at a value of $171 million. A number of shareholders urged the company to distribute the proceeds of the sale, either by making a cash tender offer for outstanding shares or by declaring an extraordinary cash dividend. Indeed, one shareholder commenced a shareholders' suit, the underlying purpose of which was to force such a distribution. Instead of acceding to these requests, Kennecott, in January 1978, purchased the Carborundum Company for $567 million in cash.

In November 1977, Curtiss-Wright, a diversified manufacturing company, decided to acquire an interest in Kennecott. By March 13, 1978, ... it had acquired 9.9 per cent of the outstanding Kennecott shares at a cost of approximately $77 million. On March 15, officials of Curtiss-Wright met with Kennecott officials to determine whether they could work together, and Curtiss-Wright suggested the nomination of a joint slate of candidates for Kennecott's board which would give Curtiss-Wright's nominees a minority position on the board. When these overtures were rejected, Curtiss-Wright, on March 23, 1978, announced its own slate and a campaign platform which, in effect, took up the cause of the shareholders who had sought distribution of the Peabody proceeds. In essence, Curtiss-Wright proposed that Kennecott try to sell Carborundum at or above the $567 million which Kennecott had paid for it and use the proceeds and other Kennecott funds to make either a tender offer for half the outstanding Kennecott shares at $40 per share, or a $20 per share cash distribution.

Kennecott did not wait for the battle lines thus to be drawn; it struck first. On [March 21, 1978,] Kennecott commenced the instant action in the District Court for the Southern District of New York.

Kennecott's original complaint alleged both securities and antitrust law violations arising out of Curtiss-Wright's acquisition of Kennecott stock. On April 5, 1978, Curtiss-Wright counterclaimed, alleging improper proxy solicitation by Kennecott. On April 17, 1978, the district court permitted Kennecott to amend its complaint to allege improper proxy solicitation by Curtiss-Wright. Each party sought injunctive relief. The trial commenced on April 24 and was completed on April 27.

The district court held that ... Curtiss-Wright's proxy solicitations had violated section 14(a) of the Securities Exchange Act of 1934 and Rule 14a-9(a) of the Commission, but Kennecott's solicitations had not.... The court enjoined Curtiss-Wright from voting its shares and proxies, while permitting Kennecott's annual meeting to go forward....

Rule 14a-9(a) Disclosures

Rule 14a-9(a) prohibits solicitation by a proxy statement that is false or misleading with respect to a material fact or which omits to state a material fact needed to make other statements therein not false or misleading. This rule, a typical securities regulation, was enacted to implement a "philosophy of full disclosure." *Santa Fe Industries, Inc. v. Green*, 430 U.S. 462 (1977). If full and fair disclosure is made, the wisdom and fairness of the program for which support is solicited are of tangential concern.

Curtiss-Wright's program, which followed upon its investment of $77 million in Kennecott, was not created in a vacuum. Although its officers were not privy to the inner workings of Kennecott, they studied the annual reports of Kennecott and its competitors and publications of the financial and copper industries. Curtiss-Wright's executive vice-president analyzed Kennecott's balance sheet, made a number of suggestions as to how it could be improved, and prepared a pro forma balance sheet showing the effect of Curtiss-Wright's proposals. However, Curtiss-Wright's consideration of the effect of its proposed plan was limited in nature, and it said so. Its April 4 proxy statement contained the following caveat:

> Curtiss-Wright has not made a detailed study of the consequences to Kennecott of the program described above. It and the nominees believe, however, that the program would not result in Kennecott's inability to continue its metals operations or to finance them. This belief is based upon the following: In the approximately nine years during which Kennecott owned Peabody it contributed approximately $532 million to Peabody's capital. Peabody thus represented a very substantial cash drain on Kennecott during the period it operated Peabody. Despite this Kennecott was able to continue its metals operations and to finance them.

> The sale of Peabody produced $809 million in cash plus $400 million in subordinated income notes which are now valued by Kennecott at $171 million. The Peabody sale thus yielded approximately $980 million in present value of assets, of which $567 million was invested in Carborundum. The program of the nominees, described above, envisages the sale of Carborundum for about the same price and a distribution equivalent to approximately $20 per share, or $663 million in the aggregate. This would leave the Kennecott metal operations with approximately $317 million more in assets than were available to them at the time Kennecott owned Peabody, and without the need for continued cash contributions to Peabody.

Despite this clear and unequivocal statement by Curtiss-Wright that it had not made a "detailed study of the consequences to Kennecott of the program," the district judge held that its "proxy materials misled shareholders to believe that the feasibility of the plan had been thoroughly studied." He based this holding on a belief that Curtiss-Wright's disclaimer of a "detailed study" did not fully disclose that it had not conducted a thorough investigation. In making a Rule 14a-9(a) violation out of this semantic differentiation between "detailed study" and "thorough investigation," the district court erred.

Rare indeed is the proxy statement whose language could not be improved upon by a judicial craftsman sitting in the serenity of his chambers. This is particularly so where the statement is prepared in the "hurly-burly" of a contested election. "[N]ot every corporate counsel is a Benjamin Cardozo...," *Ash v. LFE Corp.*, 525 F.2d 215, 221 (3d Cir. 1975), and nit-picking should not become the name of the game.

Assuming for the argument that the words "thorough investigation" would have been more descriptive than "detailed study," the latter term conveyed a sufficiently accurate picture so as not to mislead. Fair accuracy, not perfection, is the appropriate standard....

Because of the stay granted by this Court, Kennecott's annual meeting went on as scheduled; and this Court has been informed that management's slate was elected by a narrow margin. There is a strong likelihood, however, that the election results were influenced by the criticism of Curtiss-Wright contained in the district court's election-eve decision. Equity demands, therefore, that the proceedings of the 1978 annual meeting be voided in whole or in part so as to permit a new election of directors.

Because there must be another election in any event, we need not dwell upon Curtiss-Wright's allegations of improper solicitation by Kennecott. However, several of Curtiss-Wright's charges of wrongdoing merit comment. The first of these charges concerns alleged misstatements regarding Kennecott's inability to survive if Curtiss-Wright's plan was adopted. In a letter to its shareholders dated March 31, 1978, Kennecott stated:

> At the time of the Peabody divestiture your Board of Directors considered in depth what to do with the proceeds of the divestiture. To assist the Board it retained a major national investment banking firm to evaluate Kennecott's financial situation and opportunities.

> Among the alternatives considered was the possibility of a substantial direct distribution or the reacquisition of Kennecott shares. The Board concluded that this alternative would not be consistent with the maintenance of Kennecott as a viable company.

"Viable" in this context must mean capable of existing as an economic unit or able to generate enough income to pay expenses. That this was the meaning that Kennecott intended is shown by its statement in its April 17 mailing that "the Board and Management believe no other cause of action [save diversification] was possible if the Company were to survive."

The district court held that, inasmuch as the Kennecott board and its financial consultant, Morgan Stanley & Co., had investigated and rejected a plan of cash distribution of the Peabody proceeds, the March 31 material did not misstate facts in this regard. We disagree. There is nothing in the board minutes or the report of Kennecott's investment banking firm indicating that a conclusion concerning non-viability was reached. Moreover, Kennecott's board chairman conceded at the trial that the board did not examine the question whether the use of the Peabody proceeds for any other purpose except diversification was possible if the company was to survive. A conclusion reached by a company's board of directors that the company will not survive a proposed change is obviously a material matter. It should not be misstated.

Curtiss-Wright also contends that Kennecott misstated facts concerning the calling of certain loans. On March 31, 1978, just after the proxy contest had begun, Kennecott negotiated a new $450 million line of credit with a consortium of banks, against which it borrowed $234 million. This agreement contains several negative covenants, some of which would be breached if Curtiss-Wright's program were adopted. The agreement also provides that, if such a breach occurs, any bank holding forty per cent or more of the notes outstanding "may" terminate the bank's commitments and declare the entire principal to be due and payable.

On April 12, 1978, Kennecott advised its shareholders that adoption of the Curtiss-Wright program would result in a default under the loan agreement and would "trigger" the repayment of the $234 million. In its April 17 mailing Kennecott said that the sale of Carborundum and the distribution of the proceeds would result in a default and that "current borrowings would have to be repaid." The record discloses that Kennecott had attempted unsuccessfully to induce the major lending banks to sign a letter stating that, if requested to waive the covenants in question, they would refuse and, if Curtiss-Wright's program were carried out, they would require immediate repayment of their loaned funds. The shareholders were never notified that this conference took place.

The district court ignored Curtiss-Wright's argument that the above quoted words in Kennecott's proxy solicitations were misleading, holding only that the record supported Kennecott's statements that the Curtiss-Wright plan would breach certain negative covenants in the credit agreement. The question, however, was not whether the covenants would be breached, but whether the banks "would" require repayment of the loans. It seems to us that Kennecott was less than forthright in its disclosures on this point.

Curtiss-Wright's final complaint regarding Kennecott's proxy materials involves an alleged misstatement of figures. Curtiss-Wright's program envisioned the distribution to Kennecott shareholders of $663 million of the $980 million derived from the sale of Peabody, which, Curtiss-Wright stated, would leave an unused balance of $317 million. In Kennecott's mailing of April 12, 1978, it stated that Curtiss-Wright was ignoring the fact that $235 million of the Peabody proceeds had been used to reduce indebtedness. The mailing then continued:

> This simply means that even if all of the opposition group's other premises are assumed to be correct and constant, then without this $235,000,000, in order for Kennecott to repurchase one-half of its outstanding stock with the resources assumed by the opposition group's soliciting material, the purchase price would have to be reduced by more than $14.17 per share—from the promised $40.00 to less than $25.83 per share.

What Kennecott was saying, in a somewhat convoluted fashion, was that, inasmuch as $235 million had been used to reduce indebtedness, the company would not end up with a balance of $317 million unless it paid no more than $25.83 per share for redeemed stock. We would not endorse this poor, or perhaps clever, choice of language as a Rule 14a-9(a) model. However, we think that Curtiss-Wright's characterization of it as "false and misleading" puts the matter too strongly.

Curtiss-Wright does not contend that Kennecott should have been unconditionally enjoined from voting its proxies at the 1978 annual meeting because of its alleged wrongful statements. Indeed, such a contention would be inconsistent with Curtiss-Wright's argument that the district judge erred in granting such drastic relief against it. The appropriate remedy, says Curtiss-Wright, would have been to adjourn the annual meeting and permit resolicitation, because then the shareholders who opted for the wrongdoing party would not have been disenfranchised. This, in effect, is the remedy we now provide by ordering a new election.

The district court will make the necessary orders to see that a new election is promptly scheduled, that further solicitation of proxies by both parties is permitted, and that proxy materials used in the solicitation comply with SEC rules and the decision of this Court.

Chapter 18

Tender Offers

Situation

Daytron completed the purchase of Biologistics, Inc. with minimal shareholder opposition. Shortly thereafter, Daytron decides to attempt an acquisition of Harvest Electronics Corporation, a publicly held corporation headquartered in your state. Daytron's management believes that Harvest can only be acquired by means of a tender offer directed at its shareholders. It also believes that Harvest's management will fight the acquisition, among other things by filing a lawsuit in the local federal district court. Because of the expected litigation, Daytron has retained your firm as local counsel and wants you to be prepared to help defend its tender offer.

A tender offer is a form of acquisition in which the acquiring corporation goes directly to the shareholders of the target corporation and asks them to "tender" their shares in exchange for whatever the acquiring corporation is willing to offer. Typically it offers cash or some security, usually its own common stock. Sometimes tender offers are "friendly," in that they have the blessing of the target corporation's management. More often they are not. In a "hostile" tender offer, management of the target typically engages in various defenses in an attempt to fight off the acquisition.

Tender offers in which the acquiring corporation offers some security in exchange for the target's stock always have been regulated to some extent by the Securities Act of 1933. Under the Securities Act, the security to be offered has to be registered, unless an exemption is available. Since an exemption in this circumstance is a rarity, the target corporation's shareholders are almost always provided with the full disclosures that accompany registration.

Cash tender offers have been a different story. Until 1968 they were unregulated by the securities laws. In that year Congress, concerned about various abuses, passed legislation known as the Williams Act. That Act added §§ 13(d) and (e), and 14(d), (e) and (f), to the Securities Exchange Act of 1934. The bulk of this regulation, which covers both cash and non-cash tender offers, takes three forms: (1) disclosure requirements, (2) mandated tender offer provisions, and (3) an anti-fraud provision. But before examining Williams Act issues, it is important to look at the question of just what a tender offer is.

Section I
What Is a Tender Offer?

The Williams Act does not define "tender offer," and the Securities and Exchange Commission has never defined it by rule. The next case provides a good introduction to judicial interpretations of the term.

Hanson Trust PLC v. SCM Corp.

United States Court of Appeals, Second Circuit
774 F.2d 47 (1985)

Mansfield, Circuit Judge:

Hanson Trust PLC, HSCM Industries, Inc., and Hanson Holdings Netherlands B.V. (hereinafter sometimes referred to collectively as "Hanson") appeal from an order of the Southern District of New York ... granting SCM Corporation's motion for a preliminary injunction restraining them, their officers, agents, employees and any persons acting in concert with them, from acquiring any shares of SCM and from exercising any voting rights with respect to 3.1 million SCM shares acquired by them on September 11, 1985. The injunction was granted on the ground that Hanson's September 11 acquisition of the SCM stock through five private and one open market purchases amounted to a "tender offer" for more than 5% of SCM's outstanding shares, which violated §§ 14(d)(1) and (6) of the Williams Act, and rules promulgated by the Securities and Exchange Commission (SEC) thereunder. We reverse.

The setting is the familiar one of a fast-moving bidding contest for control of a large public corporation: first, a cash tender offer of $60 per share by Hanson, an outsider, addressed to SCM stockholders; next, a counterproposal by an "insider" group consisting of certain SCM managers and their "White Knight," Merrill Lynch Capital Markets (Merrill), for a "leveraged buyout" at a higher price ($70 per share); then an increase by Hanson of its cash offer to $72 per share, followed by a revised SCM-Merrill leveraged buyout offer of $74 per share with a "crown jewel" irrevocable lock-up option to Merrill designed to discourage Hanson from seeking control by providing that if any other party (in this case Hanson) should acquire more than one-third of SCM's outstanding shares (66?% being needed under N.Y.Bus.L. § 903(a)(2) to effectuate a merger) Merrill would have the right to buy SCM's two most profitable businesses (consumer foods and pigments) at prices characterized by some as "bargain basement." The final act in this scenario was the decision of Hanson, having been deterred by the SCM-Merrill option (colloquially described in the market as a "poison pill"), to terminate its cash tender offer and then to make private purchases, amounting to 25% of SCM's outstanding shares, leading SCM to seek and obtain the preliminary injunction from which this appeal is taken....

Since ... the material relevant facts in the present case are not in dispute, this appeal turns on whether the district court erred as a matter of law in holding that when Hanson terminated its offer and immediately thereafter made private purchases of a substantial share of the target company's outstanding stock, the purchases became a "tender offer" within the meaning of § 14(d) of the Williams Act. Absent any express definition of "tender offer" in the Act, the answer requires a brief review of the background and purposes of § 14(d)....

The typical tender offer, as described in the Congressional debates, hearings and reports on the Williams Act, consisted of a general, publicized bid by an individual or group to buy shares of a publicly-owned company, the shares of which were traded on a national securities exchange, at a price substantially above the current market price. The offer was usually accompanied by newspaper and other publicity, a time limit for tender of shares in response to it, and a provision fixing a quantity limit on the total number of shares of the target company that would be purchased.

... The average shareholder, pressured by the fact that the tender offer would be available for only a short time and restricted to a limit number of shares, was forced "with severely limited information, [to] decide what course of action he should take." H.R. Rep. No. 1711, 90th Cong., 2d Sess. 2 (1968)....

The purpose of the Williams Act was, accordingly, to protect the shareholders from that dilemma by insuring "that public shareholders who are confronted by a cash tender offer for their stock will not be required to respond without adequate information." *Piper v. Chris-Craft Industries*, 430 U.S. 1, 35 (1977)....

Although § 14(d)(1) clearly applies to "classic" tender offers of the type described above, courts soon recognized that in the case of privately negotiated transactions or solicitations for private purchases of stock many of the conditions leading to the enactment of § 14(d) for the most part do not exist. The number and percentage of stockholders are usually far less than those involved in public offers. The solicitation involves less publicity than a public tender offer or none. The solicitees, who are frequently directors, officers or substantial stockholders of the target, are more apt to be sophisticated, inquiring or knowledgeable concerning the target's business, the solicitor's objectives, and the impact of the solicitation on the target's business prospects. In short, the solicitee in the private transaction is less likely to be pressured, confused, or ill-informed regarding the businesses and decisions at stake than solicitees who are the subjects of a public tender offer.

These differences between public and private securities transactions have led most courts to rule that private transactions or open market purchases do not qualify as a "tender offer" requiring the purchaser to meet the pre-filing strictures of § 14(d). The borderline between public solicitations and privately negotiated stock purchases is not bright and it is frequently difficult to determine whether transactions falling close to the line or in a type of "no man's land" are "tender offers" or private deals. This has led some to advocate a broader interpretation of the term "tender offer" than that followed by us in *Kennecott Copper Corp. v. Curtiss-Wright Corp.*, and to adopt the eight-factor "test" of what is a tender offer, which was recommended by the SEC and applied by the district court in *Wellman v. Dickinson*, 475 F. Supp. 783, 823–24 (S.D.N.Y. 1979), and by the Ninth Circuit in *SEC v. Carter Hawley Hale Stores, Inc.*, [760 F.2d 945 (9th Cir. 1985)]. The eight factors are:

(1) active and widespread solicitation of public shareholders for the shares of an issuer;

(2) solicitation made for a substantial percentage of the issuer's stock;

(3) offer to purchase made at a premium over the prevailing market price;

(4) terms of the offer are firm rather than negotiable;

(5) offer contingent on the tender of a fixed number of shares, often subject to a fixed maximum number to be purchased;

(6) offer open only for a limited period of time;

(7) offeree subjected to pressure to sell his stock; ...

(8) public announcements of a purchasing program concerning the target company precede or accompany rapid accumulation of large amounts of the target company's securities.

Although many of the above-listed factors are relevant for purposes of determining whether a given solicitation amounts to a tender offer, the elevation of such a list to a mandatory "litmus test" appears to be both unwise and unnecessary. As even the advocates of the proposed test recognize, in any given case a solicitation may constitute a tender offer even though some of the eight factors are absent or, when many factors are present, the solicitation may nevertheless not amount to a tender offer because the missing factors outweigh those present.

We prefer to be guided by the principle followed by the Supreme Court in deciding what transactions fall within the private offering exemption provided by § 4(1) of the Securities Act of 1933, and by ourselves in *Kennecott Copper* in determining whether the Williams Act applies to private transactions. That principle is simply to look to the statutory purpose. In *SEC v. Ralston Purina Co.*, 346 U.S. 119 (1953), the Court stated, "the applicability of § 4(1) should turn on whether the particular class of persons affected need the protection of the Act. An offering to those who are shown to be able to fend for themselves is a transaction 'not involving any public offering.'" Similarly, since the purpose of § 14(d) is to protect the ill-informed solicitee, the question of whether a solicitation constitutes a "tender offer" within the meaning of § 14(d) turns on whether, viewing the transaction in the light of the totality of circumstances, there appears to be a likelihood that unless the pre-acquisition filing strictures of that statute are followed there will be a substantial risk that solicitees will lack information needed to make a carefully considered appraisal of the proposal put before them.

Applying this standard, we are persuaded on the undisputed facts that Hanson's September 11 negotiation of five private purchases and one open market purchase of SCM shares, totalling 25% of SCM's outstanding stock, did not under the circumstances constitute a "tender offer" within the meaning of the Williams Act. Putting aside for the moment the events preceding the purchases, there can be little doubt that the privately negotiated purchases would not, standing alone, qualify as a tender offer, for the following reasons:

(1) In a market of 22,800 SCM shareholders the number of SCM sellers here involved, six in all, was minuscule compared with the numbers involved in public solicitations of the type against which the Act was directed.

(2) At least five of the sellers were highly sophisticated professionals, knowledgeable in the market place and well aware of the essential facts needed to exercise their professional skills and to appraise Hanson's offer, including its financial condition as well as that of SCM, the likelihood that the purchases might block the SCM-Merrill bid, and the risk that if Hanson acquired more than 33⅓% of SCM's stock the SCM-Merrill lockup of the "crown jewel" might be triggered....

(3) The sellers were not "pressured" to sell their shares by any conduct that the Williams Act was designed to alleviate, but by the forces of the market place....

(4) There was no active or widespread advance publicity or public solicitation, which is one of the earmarks of a conventional tender offer....

(5) The price received by the six sellers, $73.50 per share, unlike that appearing in most tender offers, can scarcely be dignified with the label "premium." The stock market price on September 11 ranged from $72.50 to $73.50 per share....

(6) Unlike most tender offers, the purchases were not made contingent upon Hanson's acquiring a fixed minimum number or percentage of SCM's outstanding shares....

(7) Unlike most tender offers, there was no general time limit within which Hanson would make purchases of SCM stock....

There remains the question whether Hanson's private purchases take on a different hue, requiring them to be treated as a "*de facto*" continuation of its earlier tender offer, when considered in the context of Hanson's earlier acknowledged tender offer, the competing offer of SCM-Merrill and Hanson's termination of its tender offer. After reviewing all of the undisputed facts we conclude that the district court erred in so holding.

In the first place, we find no record support for the contention by SCM that Hanson's September 11 termination of its outstanding tender offer was false, fraudulent or ineffective. Hanson's termination notice was clear, unequivocal and straightforward. Directions were given, and presumably are being followed, to return all of the tendered shares to the SCM shareholders who tendered them. Hanson also filed with the SEC a statement pursuant to § 14(d)(1) of the Williams Act terminating its tender offer. As a result, at the time when Hanson made its September 11 private purchases of SCM stock it owned no SCM stock other than those shares revealed in its § 14(d) pre-acquisition report filed with the SEC on August 26, 1985....

Nor does the record support SCM's contention that Hanson had decided, before terminating its tender offer, to engage in each purchases.... Absent evidence or a finding that Hanson had decided to seek control of SCM through purchases of its stock, no duty of disclosure existed under the federal securities laws.

Second, Hanson had expressly reserved the right in its August 26, 1985, pre-acquisition tender offer filing papers, whether or not tendered shares were purchased, "*thereafter* ... to purchase additional Shares in the open market, in privately negotiated transactions, through another tender offer or otherwise." (Emphasis added). Thus,

The Williams Act also contains an antifraud provision, §14(e), that makes it unlawful to make a tender offer on the basis of materially false or misleading information. Unlike other provisions in the Williams Act, that section relates not only to tender offers for specified types of securities (basically those registered under the Exchange Act), but to tender offers for any kind of security.

Section 14(f) is a specialized provision that calls for certain disclosures to the Commission and to security holders when a majority of a corporation's directorships are to be filled, otherwise than at a meeting of security holders, following an acquisition of securities that is subject to the requirements of §13(d) or 14(d). The usual trigger of that provision is the filling of vacant directorships by sitting directors, which generally is allowed under state corporation law. That provision is intended to deal with the situation in which control of the corporation is sold and, as a part of the transaction, it is agreed that the existing directors will resign seriatim and that the remaining directors will elect new directors who are chosen by the entity acquiring control.

The following cases touch on many of the important Williams Act issues that have arisen in litigation.

Piper v. Chris-Craft Industries, Inc.

United States Supreme Court
430 U.S. 1 (1977)

MR. CHIEF JUSTICE BURGER delivered the opinion of the Court.

We granted certiorari in these cases to consider, among other issues, whether an unsuccessful tender offeror in a contest for control of a corporation has an implied cause of action for damages under §14(e) of the Securities Exchange Act of 1934, as amended by the Williams Act of 1968..., based on alleged antifraud violations by the successful competitor, its investment adviser, and individuals comprising the management of the target corporation.

I
Background

The factual background of this complex contest for control, including the protracted litigation culminating in the case now before us, is essential to a full understanding of the contending parties' claims.

The three petitions present questions of first impression, arising out of a "sophisticated and hard fought contest" for control of Piper Aircraft Corporation, a Pennsylvania-based manufacturer of light aircraft. Piper's management consisted principally of members of the Piper family, who owned 31% of Piper's outstanding stock. Chris-Craft Industries, Inc., a diversified manufacturer of recreational products, attempted to secure voting control of Piper through cash and exchange tender offers for Piper common stock. Chris-Craft's takeover attempt failed, and Bangor Punta Corporation, with the support of the Piper family, obtained control of Piper in September 1969. Chris-Craft brought suit under §14(e) of the Securities Exchange Act of 1934..., alleging that Bangor Punta achieved control of the target corporation as a result of violations of the federal securities laws by the Piper family, Bangor Punta, and Bangor Punta's underwriter, First Boston Corporation, who together had successfully repelled Chris-Craft's takeover attempt.

The struggle for control of Piper began in December 1968. At that time, Chris-Craft began making cash purchases of Piper common stock. By January 22, 1969, Chris-Craft had acquired 203,700 shares, or approximately 13% of Piper's 1,644,790 outstanding shares. On the next day, following unsuccessful preliminary overtures to Piper by Chris-Craft's president, Herbert Siegel, Chris-Craft publicly announced a cash tender offer for up to 300,000 Piper shares at $65 per share, which was approximately $12 above the then current market price. Responding promptly to Chris-Craft's bid, Piper's management met on the same day with the company's investment banker, First Boston, and other advisers. On January 24, the Piper family decided to oppose Chris-Craft's tender offer. As part of its resistance to Chris-Craft's takeover campaign, Piper management sent several letters to the company's stockholders between January 25–27, arguing against acceptance of Chris-Craft's offer. On January 27, a letter to shareholders from W.T. Piper, Jr., president of the company, stated that the Piper Board "has carefully studied this offer and is convinced that it is inadequate and not in the best interests of Piper's shareholders."

In addition to communicating with shareholders, Piper entered into an agreement with Grumman Aircraft Corporation on January 29, whereby Grumman agreed to purchase 300,000 authorized but unissued Piper shares at $65 per share. The agreement increased the amount of stock necessary for Chris-Craft to secure control and thus rendered Piper less vulnerable to Chris-Craft's attack. A Piper press release and letter to shareholders announced the Grumman transaction but failed to state either that Grumman had a "put" or option to sell the shares back to Piper at cost, plus interest, or that Piper was required to maintain the proceeds of the transaction in a separate fund free from liens.

Despite Piper's opposition, Chris-Craft succeeded in acquiring 304,606 shares by the time its cash tender offer expired on February 3. To obtain the additional 17% of Piper stock needed for control, Chris-Craft decided to make an exchange offer of Chris-Craft securities for Piper stock. Although Chris-Craft filed a registration statement and preliminary prospectus with the SEC in late February 1969, the exchange offer did not go into effect until May 15, 1969.

In the meantime, Chris-Craft made cash purchases of Piper stock on the open market until Mr. Siegel, the company's president, was expressly warned by SEC officials that such purchases, when made during the pendency of an exchange offer, violated SEC Rule 10b-6. At Mr. Siegel's direction, Chris-Craft immediately complied with the SEC's directive and canceled all outstanding orders for purchases of Piper stock.

While Chris-Craft's exchange offer was in registration, Piper in March 1969 terminated the agreement with Grumman and entered into negotiations with Bangor Punta. Bangor had initially been contacted by First Boston about the possibility of a Piper takeover in the wake of Chris-Craft's initial cash tender offer in January. With Grumman out of the picture, the Piper family agreed on May 8, 1969, to exchange their 31% stockholdings in Piper for Bangor Punta securities. Bangor also agreed to use its best efforts to achieve control of Piper by means of an exchange offer of Bangor securities for Piper common stock. A press release issued the same day announced the terms of the agreement, including a provision that the forthcoming exchange offer would involve Bangor securities to be valued, in the judgment of First Boston, "at not less than $80 per Piper share."

While awaiting the effective date of its exchange offer, Bangor in mid-May 1969 purchased 120,200 shares of Piper stock in privately negotiated, off-exchange transactions from three large institutional investors. All three purchases were made after the SEC's issuance of a release on May 5 announcing proposed Rule 10b-13, a provision which, upon becoming effective in November 1969, would expressly prohibit a tender offeror from making purchases of the target company's stock during the pendency of an exchange offer. The SEC release stated that the proposed rule was "in effect, a codification of existing interpretations under Rule 10b-6," the provision invoked by SEC officials against Mr. Siegel of Chris-Craft a month earlier. Bangor officials, although aware of the release at the time of the three off-exchange purchases, made no attempt to secure an exemption for the transactions from the SEC, as provided by Rule 10b-6(f). The Commission, however, took no action concerning these purchases as it had with respect to Chris-Craft's open market transactions.

With these three block purchases, amounting to 7% of Piper stock, Bangor Punta in mid-May took the lead in the takeover contest. The contest then centered upon the competing exchange offers. Chris-Craft's first exchange offer, which began in mid-May 1969, failed to produce tenders of the specified minimum number of Piper shares (80,000). Meanwhile, Bangor Punta's exchange offer, which had been announced on May 8, became effective on July 18. The registration materials which Bangor filed with the SEC in connection with the exchange offer included financial statements, reviewed by First Boston, representing that one of Bangor's subsidiaries, the Bangor and Aroostock Railroad (BAR), had a value of $18.4 million. This valuation was based upon a 1965 appraisal by investment bankers after a proposed sale of the BAR failed to materialize. The financial statements did not indicate that Bangor was considering the sale of BAR or that an offer to purchase the railroad for $5 million had been received.

In the final phase of the see-saw of competing offers, Chris-Craft modified the terms of its previously unsuccessful exchange offer to make it more attractive. The revised offer succeeded in attracting 112,089 additional Piper shares, while Bangor's exchange offer, which terminated on July 29, resulted in the tendering of 110,802 shares. By August 4, 1969, at the conclusion of both offers, Bangor Punta owned a total of 44.5%, while Chris-Craft owned 40.6% of Piper stock. The remainder of Piper stock, 14.9%, remained in the hands of the public.

After completion of their respective exchange offers, both companies renewed market purchases of Piper stock, but Chris-Craft, after purchasing 29,200 shares for cash in mid-August, withdrew from competition. Bangor Punta continued making cash purchases until September 5, by which time it had acquired a majority interest in Piper. The final tally in the nine-month takeover battle showed that Bangor Punta held over 50% and Chris-Craft held 42% of Piper stock.

II

Before either side had achieved control, the contest moved from the marketplace to the courts. Then began more than seven years of complex litigation growing out of the contest for control of Piper Aircraft.

[Chris-Craft first filed suit, seeking damages and injunctive relicf, in May 1969. Over the next six years the District Court and the Court of Appeals issued several opinions with respect to various aspects of the litigation. Ultimately the Court of Appeals held that Chris-Craft had standing to sue under § 14(e), that Piper had violated § 14(e) and that Chris-Craft was entitled to damages, the amount of which to be set by the District Court. The District Court then set damages at $1,673,988, measured by comparing the value of Chris-Craft's Piper stock prior and subsequent to Bangor's achieving control. The District Court also granted an award of prejudgment interest.]

Court of Appeals Opinion on Relief
April 11, 1975

In the final phase of the litigation, the Court of Appeals reversed on the damages issue and calculated Chris-Craft's damages without further remand to the District Court. The Court of Appeals fixed damages as the difference between what Chris-Craft had actually paid for Piper shares and the price at which the large minority block could have been sold at the earliest point after Bangor Punta gained control. Application of this formula produced damages in the amount of $36.98 per Piper share held by Chris-Craft, or a total of $25,793,365. The court instructed the District Court to recompute prejudgment interest based on the revised damage award. This new computation increased Chris-Craft's prejudgment interest from $600,000 to approximately $10 million.

It is this judgment which is now under review.

III
The Williams Act

...

Besides requiring disclosure and providing specific benefits for tendering shareholders, the Williams Act ... contains a broad antifraud prohibition, which is the basis of Chris-Craft's claim. Section 14(e) of the Act provides:

> It shall be unlawful for any person to make any untrue statement of a material fact or omit to state any material fact necessary in order to make the statements made, in the light of the circumstances under which they are made, not misleading, or to engage in any fraudulent, deceptive, or manipulative acts or practices, in connection with any tender offer or request or invitation for tenders, or any solicitation of security holders in opposition to or in favor of any such offer, request, or invitation.

This provision was expressly directed at the conduct of a broad range of persons, including those engaged in making or opposing tender offers or otherwise seeking to influence the decision of investors or the outcome of the tender offer.

The threshold issue in these cases is whether tender offerors such as Chris-Craft, whose activities are regulated by the Williams Act, have a cause of action for damages against other regulated parties under the statute on a claim that antifraud violations by other parties have frustrated the bidder's efforts to obtain control of the target corporation. Without reading such a cause of action into the Act, none of the other issues need be reached.

IV

Our analysis begins, of course, with the statute itself. Section 14(e), like § 10(b), makes no provision whatever for a private cause of action, such as those explicitly provided in other sections of the 1933 and 1934 Acts. This Court has nonetheless held that in some circumstances a private cause of action can be implied with respect to the 1934 Act's antifraud provisions, even though the relevant provisions are silent as to remedies. *J.I. Case Co. v. Borak*, 377 U.S. 426 (1964) (§ 14(a)); *Superintendent of Insurance v. Bankers Life & Cas. Co.*, 404 U.S. 6, 13 n. 9 (1971) (§ 10(b)).

The reasoning of these holdings is that, where congressional purposes are likely to be undermined absent private enforcement, private remedies may be implied in favor of the particular class intended to be protected by the statute. For example, in *J.I. Case Co. v. Borak, supra*, recognizing an implied right of action in favor of a shareholder complaining of a misleading proxy solicitation, the Court concluded as to such a shareholder's right:

> While [§ 14(a)] makes no specific reference to a private right of action, among its chief purposes is "*the protection of investors*," which certainly implies the availability of judicial relief *where necessary to achieve that result.* 377 U.S., at 432. (Emphasis supplied.)

Indeed, the Court in *Borak* carefully noted that because of practical limitations upon the SEC's enforcement capabilities, "[p]rivate enforcement of the proxy rules provides *a necessary supplement to Commission action.*" *Ibid.* (Emphasis added.) ...

Against this background we must consider whether § 14(e), which is entirely silent as to private remedies, permits this Court to read into the statute a damages remedy for unsuccessful tender offerors. To resolve that question we turn to the legislative history to discern the congressional purpose underlying the specific statutory prohibition in § 14(e). Once we identify the legislative purpose, we must then determine whether the creation by judicial interpretation of the implied cause of action asserted by Chris-Craft is necessary to effectuate Congress' goals.

...

The legislative history thus shows that Congress was intent upon regulating takeover bidders, theretofore operating covertly, in order to protect the shareholders of target companies. That tender offerors were not the intended beneficiaries of the bill was graphically illustrated by the statements of Senator Kuchel, co-sponsor of the legislation, in support of requiring takeover bidders, whom he described as "corporate raiders" and "takeover pirates," to disclose their activities.

Today there are those individuals in our financial community who seek to reduce our proudest businesses into nothing but corporate shells. They seize control of the corporation with unknown assets, sell or trade away the best assets, and later split up the remains among themselves. The tragedy of such collusion is that the corporation can be financially raped without management *or shareholders* having any knowledge of the acquisitions.... The corporate raider may thus act under a cloak of secrecy while obtaining the shares needed to put him on the road to a successful capture of the company. 113 Cong. Rec. 857-858 (Jan. 18, 1967) (remarks of Sen. Kuchel). (Emphasis supplied.)...

Moreover, the Senate Subcommittee heard the testimony of Professor Hayes, speaking on behalf of himself and his co-author of a comprehensive study on takeover attempts, who stated:

> The two major protagonists — the bidder and the defending management — *do not need any additional protection*, in our opinion. They have the resources and the arsenal of moves and countermoves which can adequately protect their interests. Rather, *the investor* — who is the subject of these entreaties of both major protagonists — *is the one who needs a more effective champion....* Senate Hearings, at 57. (Emphasis supplied.)

... In this Court, however, Chris-Craft and the SEC contend that Congress clearly intended to protect tender offerors as part of a "pervasive scheme of federal regulation of tender offers." In support of their reading of the legislative history, they emphasize, first, that in enacting the legislation Congress was intent upon establishing a policy of even-handedness in takeover regulation. Congress was particularly anxious, Chris-Craft argues "to avoid tipping the balance of regulation...."

Congress was indeed committed to a policy of neutrality in contests for control, but its policy of even-handedness does not go either to the purpose of the legislation or to whether a private cause of action is implicit in the statute. Neutrality is, rather, but one characteristic of legislation directed toward a different purpose — the protection of investors. Indeed, the statements concerning the need for Congress to maintain a neutral posture in takeover attempts are contained in the section of the Senate Report entitled, "Protection of Investors." Taken in their totality, these statements confirm that what Congress had in mind was the protection of shareholders, the "pawn[s] in a form of industrial warfare."...

Accordingly, the congressional policy of "even-handedness" is nonprobative of the quite disparate proposition that the Williams Act was intended to confer rights for money damages upon an injured takeover bidder.

Besides the policy of even-handedness, Chris-Craft emphasizes that the matter of implied private causes of action was raised in written submissions to the Senate Subcommittee. Specifically, Chris-Craft points to the written statements of Professors Israels and Painter, who made reference to *J. I. Case v. Borak, supra.* Chris-Craft contends, therefore, that Congress was aware that private actions were implicit in § 14(e).

But this conclusion places more freight on the passing reference to *Borak* than can reasonably be carried. Even accepting the value of written statements received without comment by the committee and without cross-examination, the statements do not refer to implied private actions by *offeror-bidders*. For example, Professor Israels' statement on this subject reads:

> [A] private litigant could seek similar relief before or after the significant fact *such as the acceptance of his tender of securities.* Senate Report, at 67. (Emphasis supplied.)

Similarly, Professor Painter in his written submission referred to "injured investors." *Id.*, at 140. Neither Israels nor Painter discussed or even alluded to remedies potentially available to takeover bidders.

More important, these statements referred to a case in which the remedy was afforded to shareholders—the *direct* and *intended* beneficiaries of the legislation. In *Borak*, the Court emphasized that § 14(a), the proxy provision, was adopted expressly for "the protection of investors," 377 U.S., at 432, the very class of persons there seeking relief. The Court found no difficulty in identifying the legislative objective and concluding that remedies should be available if necessary "to make effective the congressional purpose." *Id.*, at 433. *Borak* did not involve, and the statements in the legislative history relied upon by Chris-Craft do not implicate, the interests of parties such as offeror-bidders who are outside the scope of the concerns articulated in the evolution of this legislation ...

Finally, Chris-Craft emphasizes what it perceives as the Commission's express concern with the plight of takeover bidders faced with "unfair tactics by entrenched management." The SEC Chairman did indeed speak in the Subcommittee Hearings of the need to "regulate improper practices by management and others opposing a tender offer...." Senate Hearings, at 184. But in so doing, he was not pleading the cause of takeover bidders; on the contrary, he testified that imposing disclosure duties upon management would "make it much easier for *stockholders* to evaluate the offer on its merits." *Ibid.* (Emphasis supplied.)

In short, by extending the statute's coverage to solicitations in opposition to tender offers, Congress was seeking to broaden the scope of protection afforded to shareholders confronted with competing claims....

The legislative history thus shows that the sole purpose of the Williams Act was the protection of investors who are confronted with a tender offer. As we stated in *Rondeau v. Mosinee Paper Corp.*, 422 U.S., at 58: "The purpose of the Williams Act is to insure that public shareholders who are confronted by a cash tender offer for their stock will not be required to respond without adequate information...." We find no hint in the legislative history, on which respondent so heavily relies, that Congress contemplated a private cause of action for damages by one of several contending offerors against a successful bidder or by a losing contender against the target corporation....

Our conclusion as to the legislative history is confirmed by the analysis in *Cort v. Ash*, 422 U.S. 66 (1975). There, the Court identified four factors as "relevant" in determining whether a private remedy is implicit in a statute not expressly providing one. The first is whether the plaintiff is "'one of the class for whose *especial* benefit the statute was enacted....'" As previously indicated, examination of the statute and its genesis shows that Chris-Craft is not an intended beneficiary of the Williams Act, and surely is not one "for whose *especial* benefit the statute was enacted." ...

Second, in *Cort v. Ash* we inquired whether there was "any indication of legislative intent, explicit or implicit, either to create such a remedy or to deny one." Although the historical materials are barren of any express intent to deny a damages remedy to tender offerors as a class, there is, as we have noted, no indication that Congress intended to create a damages remedy in favor of the loser in a contest for control....

Third, *Cort v. Ash* tells us that we must ascertain whether it is "consistent with the underlying purposes of the legislative scheme to imply such a remedy for the plaintiff." We conclude that it is not. As a disclosure mechanism aimed especially at protecting shareholders of target corporations, the Williams Act cannot consistently be interpreted as conferring a monetary remedy upon regulated parties, particularly where the award would not redound to the direct benefit of the protected class....

Fourth, under the *Cort v. Ash* analysis, we must decide whether "the cause of action [is] one traditionally relegated to state law...." Despite the pervasiveness of federal securities regulation, the Court of Appeals concluded in these cases that Chris-Craft's complaint would give rise to a cause of action under common-law principles of interference with a prospective commercial advantage. Although Congress is, of course, free to create a remedial scheme in favor of contestants in tender offers, we conclude, as we did in *Cort v. Ash*, that "it is entirely appropriate in this instance to relegate [the offeror-bidder] and others in [that] situation to whatever remedy is created by state law," at least to the extent that the offeror seeks damages for having been wrongfully denied a "fair opportunity" to compete for control of another corporation....

We therefore conclude that Chris-Craft, as a defeated tender offeror, has no implied cause of action for damages under § 14(e).

Schreiber v. Burlington Northern, Inc.

United States Supreme Court
472 U.S. 1 (1985)

CHIEF JUSTICE BURGER delivered the opinion of the Court.

We granted certiorari to resolve a conflict in the Circuits over whether misrepresentation or nondisclosure is a necessary element of a violation of § 14(e) of the Securities Exchange Act of 1934.

I

On December 21, 1982, Burlington Northern, Inc., made a hostile tender offer for El Paso Gas Co. Through a wholly owned subsidiary, Burlington proposed to purchase 25.1 million El Paso shares at $24 per share. Burlington reserved the right to terminate the offer if any of several specified events occurred. El Paso management initially opposed the takeover, but its shareholders responded favorably, fully subscribing the offer by the December 30, 1982 deadline.

Burlington did not accept those tendered shares; instead, after negotiations with El Paso management, Burlington announced on January 10, 1983, the terms of a new and friendly takeover agreement. Pursuant to the new agreement, Burlington undertook, *inter alia*, to (1) rescind the December tender offer, (2) purchase 4,166,667 shares from El Paso at $24 per share, (3) substitute a new tender offer for only 21 million shares at $24 per share, (4) provide procedural protections against a squeeze-out merger[2] of the remaining El Paso shareholders, and (5) recognize "golden parachute"[3] contracts between El Paso and four of its senior officers. By February 8, more than 40 million shares were tendered in response to Burlington's January offer, and the takeover was completed.

The rescission of the first tender offer caused a diminished payment to those shareholders who had tendered during the first offer. The January offer was greatly oversubscribed and consequently those shareholders who retendered were subject to substantial proration. Petitioner Barbara Schreiber filed suit on behalf of herself and similarly situated shareholders, alleging that Burlington, El Paso, and members of El Paso's board violated §14(e)'s prohibition of "fraudulent, deceptive or manipulative acts or practices ... in connection with any tender offer." She claimed that Burlington's withdrawal of the December tender offer coupled with the substitution of the January tender offer was a "manipulative" distortion of the market for El Paso stock. Schreiber also alleged that Burlington violated §14(e) by failing ... to disclose the "golden parachutes" offered to four of El Paso's managers. She claims that this January nondisclosure was a deceptive act forbidden by §14(e).

---

2. [1] A "squeeze-out" merger occurs when Corporation A, which holds a controlling interest in Corporation B, uses its control to merge B into itself or into a wholly owned subsidiary. The minority shareholders in Corporation B are, in effect, forced to sell their stock. The procedural protection provided in the agreement between El Paso and Burlington required the approval of non-Burlington members of El Paso's board of directors before a squeeze-out merger could proceed. Burlington eventually purchased all the remaining shares of El Paso for $12 cash and one quarter share of Burlington preferred stock per share. The parties dispute whether this consideration was equal to that paid to those tendering during the January tender offer.

3. [2] Petitioner alleged in her complaint that respondent Burlington failed to disclose that four officers of El Paso had entered into "golden parachute" agreements with El Paso for "extended employment benefits in the event El Paso should be taken over, which benefits would give them millions of dollars of extra compensation." The term "golden parachute" refers generally to agreements between a corporation and its top officers which guarantee those officers continued employment, payment of a lump sum, or other benefits in the event of a change of corporate ownership. As described in the Schedule 14D-9 filed by El Paso with the Commission on January 12, 1983, El Paso entered into "employment agreements" with two of its officers for a period of not less than five years, and with two other officers for a period of three years. The Schedule 14D-9 also disclosed that El Paso's Deferred Compensation Plan had been amended "to provide that for the purposes of such Plan a participant shall be deemed to have retired at the instance of the Company if his duties as a director, officer or employee of the Company have been diminished or curtailed by the Company in any material respect."

The District Court dismissed the suit for failure to state a claim....

The Court of Appeals for the Third Circuit affirmed....

II

A

We are asked in this case to interpret § 14(e) of the Securities Exchange Act. The starting point is the language of the statute. Section 14(e) provides:

> It shall be unlawful for any person to make any untrue statement of a material fact or omit to state any material fact necessary in order to make the statements made, in the light of the circumstances under which they are made, not misleading, or to engage in any fraudulent, deceptive or manipulative acts or practices, in connection with any tender offer or request or invitation for tenders, or any solicitation of security holders in opposition to or in favor of any such offer, request, or invitation....

Petitioner relies on a construction of the phrase, "fraudulent, deceptive or manipulative acts or practices." Petitioner reads the phrase "fraudulent, deceptive or manipulative acts or practices" to include acts which, although fully disclosed, "artificially" affect the price of the takeover target's stock. Petitioner's interpretation relies on the belief that § 14(e) is directed at purposes broader than providing full and true information to investors.

Petitioner's reading of the term "manipulative" conflicts with the normal meaning of the term. We have held in the context of an alleged violation of § 10(b) of the Securities Exchange Act:

> Use of the word "manipulative" is especially significant. It is and was virtually a term of art when used in connection with the securities markets. It connotes intentional or willful conduct *designed to deceive or defraud* investors by controlling or artificially affecting the price of securities. *Ernst & Ernst v. Hochfelder*, 425 U.S. 185, 199 (1976) (emphasis added).

Other cases interpreting the term reflect its use as a general term comprising a range of misleading practices.... The meaning the Court has given the term "manipulative" is consistent with the use of the term at common law, and with its traditional dictionary definition....

B

Our conclusion that "manipulative" acts under § 14(e) require misrepresentation or nondisclosure is buttressed by the purpose and legislative history of the provision....

It is clear that Congress relied primarily on disclosure to implement the purpose of the Williams Act. Senator Williams, the Bill's Senate sponsor, stated in the debate:

> Today, the public shareholder in deciding whether to accept or reject a tender offer possesses limited information. No matter what he does, he acts without adequate knowledge to enable him to decide rationally what is the best course of action. This is precisely the dilemma which our securities laws are designed to prevent. 113 Cong. Rec. 24664 (1967) (remarks of Sen. Williams).

The expressed legislative intent was to preserve a neutral setting in which the contenders could fully present their arguments....

While legislative history specifically concerning § 14(e) is sparse, the House and Senate Reports discuss the role of § 14(e). Describing § 14(e) as regulating "fraudulent transactions," and stating the thrust of the section:

> This provision would affirm the fact that persons engaged in making or opposing tender offers or otherwise seeking to influence the decision of investors or the outcome of the tender offer are under an obligation to make *full disclosure* of material information to those with whom they deal. H.R. Rep. No. 1711, 90th Cong., 2d Sess., 11 (1968) (emphasis added); S.R. Rep. No. 550, 90th Cong., 1st Sess., 11 (1967) (emphasis added).

Nowhere in the legislative history is there the slightest suggestion that § 14(e) serves any purpose other than disclosure, or that the term "manipulative" should be read as an invitation to the courts to oversee the substantive fairness of tender offers; the quality of any offer is a matter for the marketplace.

To adopt the reading of the term "manipulative" urged by petitioner would not only be unwarranted in light of the legislative purpose but would be at odds with it. Inviting judges to read the term "manipulative" with their own sense of what constitutes "unfair" or "artificial" conduct would inject uncertainty into the tender offer process. An essential piece of information—whether the court would deem the fully disclosed actions of one side or the other to be "manipulative"—would not be available until after the tender offer had closed. This uncertainty would directly contradict the expressed Congressional desire to give investors full information.

Congress' consistent emphasis on disclosure persuades us that it intended takeover contests to be addressed to shareholders. In pursuit of this goal, Congress, consistent with the core mechanism of the Securities Exchange Act, created sweeping disclosure requirements and narrow substantive safeguards. The same Congress that placed such emphasis on shareholder choice would not at the same time have required judges to oversee tender offers for substantive fairness. It is even less likely that a Congress implementing that intention would express it only through the use of a single word placed in the middle of a provision otherwise devoted to disclosure.

C

We hold that the term "manipulative" as used in § 14(e) requires misrepresentation or nondisclosure. It connotes "conduct designed to deceive or defraud investors by controlling or artificially affecting the price of securities." *Ernst & Ernst v. Hochfelder*, 425 U.S. at 199. Without misrepresentation or nondisclosure, § 14(e) has not been violated.

Applying that definition to this case, we hold that the actions of respondents were not manipulative. The amended complaint fails to allege that the cancellation of the first tender offer was accompanied by any misrepresentation, nondisclosure or deception. The District Court correctly found, "All activity of the defendants that could have conceivably affected the price of El Paso shares was done openly."

Petitioner also alleges that El Paso management and Burlington entered into certain undisclosed and deceptive agreements during the making of the second tender offer. The substance of the allegations is that, in return for certain undisclosed benefits, El Paso managers agreed to support the second tender offer. But both courts noted that petitioner's complaint seeks redress only for injuries related to the cancellation of the first tender offer. Because the deceptive and misleading acts alleged by the petitioner all occurred with reference to the making of the second tender offer — when the injuries suffered by petitioner had already been sustained — these acts bear no possible causal relationship to petitioner's alleged injuries....

Section III
State Regulation

Shortly after passage of the Williams Act, state legislatures began adopting their own takeover statutes. Finally, more than two-thirds of the states passed such a statute in one form or the other. While the Williams Act is generally viewed as neutral on takeovers, the state statutes tended to be protective of "local" target corporation management. The reasons for that seem clear enough. First, managements of in-state corporations have substantial political power in state legislatures, while those of outside corporations have very little. Second, legislatures properly fear that industry is less likely to be responsive to local needs, and also is more likely to be moved out of state, if decisionmaking power is in the hands of distant management.

During the years when most of those state statutes were being passed, there was much controversy about their constitutionality. It was argued that they impermissibly burdened interstate commerce and that they were preempted by the Williams Act. The Supreme Court found the first generation of these statutes to be unconstitutional, *Edgar v. MITE Corp.*, 457 U.S. 624 (1982), but an ensuing second generation passed constitutional muster in the following case, *CTS Corp. v. Dynamics Corp. of America*, 481 U.S. 69 (1987). After the *CTS* decision, a number of states enacted statutes like the one upheld in that case. (You may recall the Delaware Supreme Court discussing the *CTS* case in *VantagePoint Venture Partners v. Examen, Inc.*, concerning the internal affairs doctrine, in Chapter 3.)

CTS Corp. v. Dynamics Corp. of America
United States Supreme Court
481 U.S. 69 (1987)

Justice Powell delivered the opinion of the Court.

This case presents the questions whether the Control Share Acquisitions Chapter of the Indiana Business Corporation Law is pre-empted by the Williams Act or violates the Commerce Clause of the Federal Constitution.

I

A

On March 4, 1986, the Governor of Indiana signed a revised Indiana Business Corporation Law. That law included the Control Share Acquisitions Chapter (Indiana Act or Act). Beginning on August 1, 1987, the Act will apply to any corporation incorporated in Indiana unless the corporation amends its articles of incorporation or bylaws to opt out of the Act. The Act applies only to "issuing public corporations." The term "corporation" includes only businesses incorporated in Indiana. An "issuing public corporation" is defined as:

a corporation that has:

(1) one hundred (100) or more shareholders;

(2) its principal place of business, its principal office, or substantial assets within Indiana; and

(3) either:

(A) more than ten percent (10%) of its shareholders resident in Indiana;

(B) more than ten percent (10%) of its shares owned by Indiana residents; or

(C) ten thousand (10,000) shareholders resident in Indiana.

The Act focuses on the acquisition of "control shares" in an issuing public corporation. Under the Act, an entity acquires "control shares" whenever it acquires shares that, but for the operation of the Act, would bring its voting power in the corporation to or above any of three thresholds: 20%, 33?%, or 50%. An entity that acquires control shares does not necessarily acquire voting rights. Rather, it gains those rights only "to the extent granted by resolution approved by the shareholders of the issuing public corporation." Section 9 requires a majority vote of all disinterested shareholders holding each class of stock for passage of such a resolution. The practical effect of this requirement is to condition acquisition of control of a corporation on approval of a majority of the pre-existing disinterested shareholders.

The shareholders decide whether to confer rights on the control shares at the next regularly scheduled meeting of the shareholders, or at a specially scheduled meeting. The acquiror can require management of the corporation to hold such a special meeting within 50 days if it files an "acquiring person statement," requests the meeting, and agrees to pay the expenses of the meeting. If the shareholders do not vote to restore voting rights to the shares, the corporation may redeem the control shares from the acquiror at fair market value, but it is not required to do so. Similarly, if the acquiror does not file an acquiring person statement with the corporation, the corporation may, if its bylaws or articles of incorporation so provide, redeem the shares at any time after 60 days after the acquiror's last acquisition.

B

On March 10, 1986, appellee Dynamics Corporation of America (Dynamics) owned 9.6% of the common stock of appellant CTS Corporation, an Indiana corporation. On that day, six days after the Act went into effect, Dynamics announced a tender offer for another million shares in CTS; purchase of those shares would have brought Dynamics' ownership interest in CTS to 27.5%. Also on March 10, Dynamics filed suit in the United States District Court for the Northern District of Illinois, alleging that CTS had violated the federal securities laws in a number of respects no longer relevant to these proceedings....

[Dynamics then amended its complaint to challenge the constitutionality of the Indiana Act. The district court ultimately found the Act to be unconstitutional under both the Supremacy and Commerce Clauses of the federal constitution, and the Seventh Circuit affirmed.]

II

The first question in this cause is whether the Williams Act pre-empts the Indiana Act....

. . .

B

The Indiana Act differs in major respects from the Illinois statute that the Court considered in *Edgar v. MITE Corp.*, 457 U.S. 624 (1982)....

C

As the plurality opinion in *MITE* did not represent the views of a majority of the Court, we are not bound by its reasoning. We need not question that reasoning, however, because we believe the Indiana Act passes muster even under the broad interpretation of the Williams Act articulated by Justice White in *MITE*.... [T]he overriding concern of the *MITE* plurality was that the Illinois statute considered in that case operated to favor management against offerors, to the detriment of shareholders. By contrast, the statute now before the Court protects the independent shareholder against both of the contending parties....

The Indiana Act operates on the assumption, implicit in the Williams Act, that independent shareholders faced with tender offers often are at a disadvantage. By allowing such shareholders to vote as a group, the Act protects them from the coercive aspects of some tender offers. If, for example, shareholders believe that a successful tender offer will be followed by a purchase of nontendering shares at a depressed price, individual shareholders may tender their shares—even if they doubt the tender offer is in the corporation's best interest—to protect themselves from being forced to sell their shares at a depressed price.... In such a situation under the Indiana Act, the shareholders as a group, acting in the corporation's best interest, could reject the offer, although individual shareholders might be inclined to accept it. The desire of the Indiana Legislature to protect shareholders of Indiana corporations from this type of coercive offer does not conflict with the Williams Act. Rather, it furthers the federal policy of investor protection.

In implementing its goal, the Indiana Act avoids the problems the plurality discussed in *MITE*. Unlike the *MITE* statute, the Indiana Act does not give either management or the offeror an advantage in communicating with the shareholders about the impending offer. The Act also does not impose an indefinite delay on tender offers. Nothing in the Act prohibits an offeror from consummating an offer on the 20th business day, the earliest day permitted under applicable federal regulations. Nor does the Act allow the state government to interpose its views of fairness between willing buyers and sellers of shares of the target company. Rather, the Act allows *shareholders* to evaluate the fairness of the offer collectively.

D

The Court of Appeals based its finding of pre-emption on its view that the practical effect of the Indiana Act is to delay consummation of tender offers until 50 days after the commencement of the offer....

The Act does not impose an absolute 50-day delay on tender offers, nor does it preclude an offeror from purchasing shares as soon as federal law permits. If the offeror fears an adverse shareholder vote under the Act, it can make a conditional tender offer, offering to accept shares on the condition that the shares receive voting rights within a certain period of time....

Even assuming that the Indiana Act imposes some additional delay, nothing in *MITE* suggested that *any* delay imposed by state regulation, however short, would create a conflict with the Williams Act. The plurality argued only that the offeror should "be free to go forward without *unreasonable* delay." (emphasis added.) In that case, the Court was confronted with the potential for indefinite delay and presented with no persuasive reason why some deadline could not be established. By contrast, the Indiana Act provides that full voting rights will be vested—if this eventually is to occur—within 50 days after commencement of the offer. This period is within the 60-day maximum period Congress established for tender offers in [the Williams Act]. We cannot say that a delay within that congressionally determined period is unreasonable.

... Accordingly, we hold that the Williams Act does not pre-empt the Indiana Act.

III

As an alternative basis for its decision, the Court of Appeals held that the Act violates the Commerce Clause of the Federal Constitution....

A

The principal objects of dormant Commerce Clause scrutiny are statutes that discriminate against interstate commerce. The Indiana Act is not such a statute. It has the same effects on tender offers whether or not the offeror is a domiciliary or resident of Indiana....

Because nothing in the Indiana Act imposes a greater burden on out-of-state of-ferors than it does on similarly situated Indiana offerors, we reject the contention that the Act discriminates against interstate commerce.

B

This Court's recent Commerce Clause cases also have invalidated statutes that ad-versely may affect interstate commerce by subjecting activities to inconsistent regu-lations. The Indiana Act poses no such problem. So long as each State regulates voting rights only in the corporations it has created, each corporation will be subject to the law of only one State. No principle of corporation law and practice is more firmly established than a State's authority to regulate domestic corporations, including the authority to define the voting rights of shareholders. Accordingly, we conclude that the Indiana Act does not create an impermissible risk of inconsistent regulation by different States.

C

The Court of Appeals did not find the Act unconstitutional for either of these threshold reasons. Rather, its decision rested on its view of the Act's potential to hinder tender offers. We think the Court of Appeals failed to appreciate the significance for Commerce Clause analysis of the fact that state regulation of corporate governance is regulation of entities whose very existence and attributes are a product of state law. As Chief Justice Marshall explained:

> A corporation is an artificial being, invisible, intangible, and existing only in contemplation of law. Being the mere creature of law, it possesses only those properties which the charter of its creation confers upon it, either ex-pressly, or as incidental to its very existence. These are such as are supposed best calculated to effect the object for which it was created. *Trustees of Dart-mouth College v. Woodward*, 4 Wheat. 518, 636 (1819).

Every State in this country has enacted laws regulating corporate governance. By prohibiting certain transactions, and regulating others, such laws necessarily affect certain aspects of interstate commerce. This necessarily is true with respect to cor-porations with shareholders in States other than the State of incorporation. Large corporations that are listed on national exchanges, or even regional exchanges, will have shareholders in many States and shares that are traded frequently. The markets that facilitate this national and international participation in ownership of corporations are essential for providing capital not only for new enterprises but also for established companies that need to expand their businesses. This beneficial free market system depends at its core upon the fact that a corporation—except in the rarest situations—is organized under, and governed by, the law of a single jurisdiction, traditionally the corporate law of the State of its incorporation.

These regulatory laws may affect directly a variety of corporate transactions. Mergers are a typical example. In view of the substantial effect that a merger may have on the shareholders' interests in a corporation, many States require supermajority votes to approve mergers. By requiring a greater vote for mergers than is required for other transactions, these laws make it more difficult for corporations to merge. State laws also may provide for "dissenters' rights" under which minority shareholders who disagree with corporate decisions to take particular actions are entitled to sell their shares to the corporation at fair market value. By requiring the corporation to purchase the shares of dissenting shareholders, these laws may inhibit a corporation from engaging in the specified transactions.

It thus is an accepted part of the business landscape in this country for States to create corporations, to prescribe their powers, and to define the rights that are acquired by purchasing their shares. A State has an interest in promoting stable relationships among parties involved in the corporations it charters, as well as in ensuring that investors in such corporations have an effective voice in corporate affairs.

There can be no doubt that the Act reflects these concerns. The primary purpose of the Act is to protect the shareholders of Indiana corporations. It does this by affording shareholders, when a takeover offer is made, an opportunity to decide collectively whether the resulting change in voting control of the corporation, as they perceive it, would be desirable. A change of management may have important effects on the shareholders' interests; it is well within the State's role as overseer of corporate governance to offer this opportunity. The autonomy provided by allowing shareholders collectively to determine whether the takeover is advantageous to their interests may be especially beneficial where a hostile tender offer may coerce shareholders into tendering their shares.

Dynamics argues ... that the State has "'no legitimate interest in protecting the nonresident shareholders.'" Dynamics relies heavily on the statement by the *MITE* Court that "[i]nsofar as the ... law burdens out-of-state transactions, there is nothing to be weighed in the balance to sustain the law." But that comment was made in reference to an Illinois law that applied as well to out-of-state corporations as to in-state corporations. We agree that Indiana has no interest in protecting nonresident shareholders *of nonresident corporations*. But this Act applies only to corporations incorporated in Indiana. We reject the contention that Indiana has no interest in providing for the shareholders of its corporations the voting autonomy granted by the Act. Indiana has a substantial interest in preventing the corporate form from becoming a shield for unfair business dealing. Moreover, unlike the Illinois statute invalidated in *MITE*, the Indiana Act applies only to corporations that have a substantial number of shareholders in Indiana. Thus, every application of the Indiana Act will affect a substantial number of Indiana residents, whom Indiana indisputably has an interest in protecting....

IV

On its face, the Indiana Control Share Acquisitions Chapter evenhandedly determines the voting rights of shares of Indiana corporations. The Act does not conflict with the provisions or purposes of the Williams Act. To the limited extent that the Act affects interstate commerce, this is justified by the State's interests in defining the attributes of shares in its corporations and in protecting shareholders. Congress has never questioned the need for state regulation of these matters. Nor do we think such regulation offends the Constitution. Accordingly, we reverse the judgment of the Court of Appeals....

Chapter 19

Insider Trading and Other Securities Fraud

Situation

Biologistics, Inc. has been a wholly-owned subsidiary of Daytron Corporation for a year, and your firm remains its counsel. Anderson and Baker continue as officers and, three months ago, Baker joined Daytron's Board of Directors.

Anderson and Baker each acquired a substantial number of Daytron shares in exchange for their Biologistics shares. During the last year each has purchased, on the stock exchange, a total of several thousand more Daytron shares. These purchases began shortly after the acquisition and have continued at intervals of a month or two. At the time of the share exchange, Daytron stock was selling at $55 per share. Since the Biologistics acquisition, Daytron stock has been rising in price, and is currently selling at $75 per share.

Daytron has recently sent Anderson and Baker a questionnaire inquiring about purchases of Daytron stock. The questionnaire is worded in such a way as to make them suspect there may be problems with their purchases, and they have asked your advice.

Section I
State Insider Trading Law

The regulation of improper "insider trading" (basically the buying or selling of securities, by those having some duty not to do so, on the basis of information not publicly available) has become in recent decades largely the province of federal law. But not the entire province. State regulation in this area has some continued importance, as indicated in the following case.

Beyond state case law, there are statutes in many states governing insider trading and other acts that can loosely be called securities fraud. Some of these statutes are patterned after Rule 10b-5 under the Securities Exchange Act of 1934, which serves as the basis for much of the federal regulation.

Freeman v. Decio

United States Court of Appeals, Seventh Circuit

584 F.2d 186 (1978)

HARLINGTON WOOD, JR., CIRCUIT JUDGE.

The principal question presented by this case is whether under Indiana law the plaintiff may sustain a derivative action against certain officers and directors of the Skyline Corporation for allegedly trading in the stock of the corporation on the basis of material inside information. The district court granted summary judgment for the defendants on the ground that in light of the defendants' affidavits and documentary evidence, the plaintiff had failed to create a genuine dispute as to whether the defendants' sales of stock were based on material inside information. Alternatively, the court held that the plaintiff had failed to state a cause of action in that Indiana law has never recognized a right in a corporation to recover profits from insider trading and is not likely to follow the lead of the New York Court of Appeals in *Diamond v. Oreamuno*, 24 N.Y.2d 494, 301 N.Y.S.2d 78, 248 N.E.2d 910 (1969), in creating such a cause of action. We affirm....

Plaintiff-appellant Marcia Freeman is a stockholder of the Skyline Corporation, a major producer of mobile homes and recreational vehicles. Skyline is a publicly owned corporation whose stock is traded on the New York Stock Exchange (NYSE). Defendant Arthur J. Decio is the largest shareholder of Skyline, the chairman of its board of directors, and until September 25, 1972, was also the president of the company. Defendant Dale Swikert is a director of Skyline and prior to assuming the presidency from Decio in 1972 was Skyline's executive vice president and chief operating officer. Defendants Samuel P. Mandell and Ira J. Kaufman are outside directors of Skyline.

Throughout the 1960's and into 1972 Skyline experienced continual growth in sales and earnings. At the end of fiscal 1971 the company was able to report to its shareholders that over the previous five years sales had increased at a 40% average compound rate and that net income had grown at a 64% rate. This enormous success was reflected in increases in the price of Skyline stock. By April of 1972 Skyline common had reached a high of $72.00 per share, representing a price/earnings ratio of greater than 50 times earnings. Then, on December 22, 1972, Skyline reported that earnings for the quarter ending November 30, 1972, declined from $4,569,007 to $3,713,545 compared to the comparable period of the preceding year, rather than increasing substantially as they had done in the past. The NYSE immediately suspended trading in the stock. Trading was resumed on December 26 at $34.00 per share, down $13.50 from the preannouncement price. This represented a drop in value of almost 30%.

Plaintiff alleges that the defendants sold Skyline stock on the basis of material inside information during two distinct periods. Firstly, it is alleged that the financial results reported by Skyline for the quarters ending May 31 and August 31, 1972, significantly understated material costs and overstated earnings. It is further alleged that Decio, Kaufman and Mandell made various sales of Skyline stock totalling nearly $10 million during the quarters in question, knowing that earnings were overstated. Secondly, plaintiff asserts that during the quarter ending November 30 and up to December 22, 1972, Decio and Mandell made gifts and sales of Skyline stock totaling nearly $4 million while knowing that reported earnings for the November 30 quarter would decline....

After three years of extensive discovery both sides moved for summary judgment. The district court granted the defendants' Fed. R. Civ. P. 56 motions on the insider trading counts on the ground that Indiana law does not provide for a derivative cause of action on behalf of a corporation to recover profits from insider trading. Alternatively, the court found that, in view of the defendants' affidavits and depositions, the plaintiff had not succeeded in creating a genuine dispute as to whether the defendants' stock sales were made on the basis of material inside information....

I. Diamond v. Oreamuno and Indiana Law

Both parties agree that there is no Indiana precedent directly dealing with the question of whether a corporation may recover the profits of corporate officials who trade in the corporation's securities on the basis of inside information. However, the plaintiff suggests that were the question to be presented to the Indiana courts, they would adopt the holding of the New York Court of Appeals in *Diamond v. Oreamuno*, 24 N.Y.2d 494, 301 N.Y.S.2d 78, 248 N.E.2d 910 (1969). There, building on the Delaware case of *Brophy v. Cities Service Co.*, 31 Del. Ch. 241, 70 A.2d 5 (1949), the court held that the officers and directors of a corporation breached their fiduciary duties owed to the corporation by trading in its stock on the basis of material non-public information acquired by virtue of their official positions and that they should account to the corporation for their profits from those transactions. Since *Diamond* was decided, few courts have had an opportunity to consider the problem there presented. In fact, only one case has been brought to our attention which raised the question of whether *Diamond* would be followed in another jurisdiction. In *Schein v. Chasen*, 478 F.2d 817 (2d Cir. 1973), *vacated and remanded sub nom., Lehman Bros. v. Schein*, 416 U.S. 386 (1974), *on certification to the Fla. Sup. Ct.*, 313 So. 2d 739 (Fla. 1975), the Second Circuit, sitting in diversity, considered whether the Florida courts would permit a *Diamond*-type action to be brought on behalf of a corporation. The majority not only tacitly concluded that Florida would adopt *Diamond*, but that the *Diamond* cause of action should be extended so as to permit recovery of the profits of non-insiders who traded in the corporation's stock on the basis of inside information received as tips from insiders. Judge Kaufman, dissenting, agreed with the policies underlying a *Diamond*-type cause of action, but disagreed with the extension of liability to outsiders. He also failed to understand why the panel was not willing to utilize Florida's certified question statute so as to bring the question of law before the Florida Supreme Court. Granting *certiorari*, the United States Supreme Court agreed with the dissent on this last point and on remand the case was certified to the Florida Supreme Court. That court not only stated that it would not "give the unprecedented expansive reading to *Diamond* sought by appellants" but that, furthermore, it did not "choose to adopt the innovative ruling of the New York Court of Appeals in *Diamond* [itself]." Thus, the question here is whether the Indiana courts are more likely to follow the New York Court of Appeals or to join the Florida Supreme Court in refusing to undertake such a change from existing law.

It appears that from a policy point of view it is widely accepted that insider trading should be deterred because it is unfair to other investors who do not enjoy the benefits of access to inside information. The goal is not one of equality of possession of information — since some traders will always be better "informed" than others by dint of greater expenditures of time and resources, greater experience, or greater analytical abilities — but rather equality of access to information....

[T]he New York Court of Appeals in *Diamond* found the existing remedies for controlling insider trading to be inadequate. Although the court felt that the device of a class action under the federal securities laws held out hope of a more effective remedy in the future, it concluded that "the desirability of creating an effective common-law remedy is manifest." It went on to do so by engineering an innovative extension of the law governing the relation between a corporation and its officers and directors. The court held that corporate officials who deal in their corporation's securities on the basis of non-public information gained by virtue of their inside position commit a breach of their fiduciary duties to the corporation. This holding represents a departure from the traditional common law approach, which was that a corporate insider did not ordinarily violate his fiduciary duty to the corporation by dealing in the corporation's stock, unless the corporation was thereby harmed....

There are a number of difficulties with the *Diamond* court's ruling. Perhaps the thorniest problem was posed by the defendants' objection that whatever the ethical status of insider trading, there is no injury to the corporation which can serve as a basis for recognizing a right of recovery in favor of the latter. The Court of Appeals' response to this argument was two-fold, suggesting first that no harm to the corporation need be shown and second that it might well be inferred that the insiders' activities did in fact cause some harm to the corporation.... Some might see the *Diamond* court's decision as resting on a broad, strict-trust notion of the fiduciary duty owed to the corporation: no director is to receive any profit, beyond what he receives from the corporation, solely because of his position. Although, once accepted, this basis for the *Diamond* rule would obviate the need for finding a potential for injury to the corporation, it is not at all clear that current corporation law contemplates such an extensive notion of fiduciary duty. It is customary to view the *Diamond* result as resting on a characterization of inside information as a corporate asset. The lack of necessity for looking for an injury to the corporation is then justified by the traditional "no inquiry" rule with respect to profits made by trustees from assets belonging to the trust *res*. However, to start from the premise that all inside information should be considered a corporate asset may presuppose an answer to the inquiry at hand. It might be better to ask whether there is any potential loss to the corporation from the use of such information in insider trading before deciding to characterize the inside information as an asset with respect to which the insider owes the corporation a duty of loyalty (as opposed to a duty of care). This approach would be in keeping with the modern view of another area of

Hanson's privately negotiated purchases could hardly have taken the market by surprise. Indeed, professional arbitrageurs and market experts rapidly concluded that it was Hanson which was making the post-termination purchase.

Last, Hanson's prior disclosures of essential facts about itself and SCM in the preacquisition papers it filed on August 26, 1985, with the SEC pursuant to § 14(d)(1), are wholly inconsistent with the district court's characterization of Hanson's later private purchases as "a deliberate attempt to do an 'end run' around the requirements of the Williams Act." On the contrary, the record shows that Hanson had already filed with the SEC and made public substantially the same information as SCM contends that Hanson should have filed before making the cash purchases....

It may well be that Hanson's private acquisition of 25% of SCM's shares after termination of Hanson's tender offer was designed to block the SCM-Merrill leveraged buyout group from acquiring the 66?% of SCM's stock needed to effectuate a merger. It may be speculated that such a blocking move might induce SCM to buy Hanson's 25% at a premium or lead to negotiations between the parties designed to resolve their differences. But we know of no provision in the federal securities laws or elsewhere that prohibits such tactics in "hardball" market battles of the type encountered here....

The order of the district court is reversed, the preliminary injunction against Hanson is vacated, and the case is remanded for further proceedings in accordance with this opinion....

Section II
Williams Act Issues

As indicated above, the Williams Act added to the Exchange Act §§ 13(d) and (e) and 14(d), (e), and (f). Section 13(d) is aimed at tender offers only indirectly. It requires a person who owns more that 5% of a class of equity security registered under the Exchange Act to provide certain information to the issuer and to the Commission within ten days after the acquisition of securities that triggers the reporting requirement. The other Williams Act provision in § 13 is § 13(e). It gives the Commission the power to regulate repurchases by issuers of their own equity securities.

The centerpiece of the Williams Act is § 14(d). Under that provision, it is unlawful, unless certain filings are made, to make a tender offer for an Exchange Act-registered equity security and certain other securities[1] if success in the offer would result in ownership of more than 5% of the class. Section 14(d) also contains a limited amount of substantive regulation of tender offers. For example, it provides that if a tender offeror increases the price offered, it must pay the higher price to security holders who already name tendered at a lower price.

---

1. These are an insurance company's equity securities that would be required to be registered under the Exchange Act save for a registration exemption and equity securities issued by a closed-end investment company registered under the Investment Company Act of 1940.